CHAMBERS *Quick Reference* ENGLISH THESAURUS

Editor
Martin H. Manser

Assistant Editors
Karen Dunnell
Rosalind Fergusson
Jenny Roberts
Gloria Wren

Chambers

CHAMBERS
An imprint of Larousse plc
43–45 Annandale Street, Edinburgh EH7 4AZ

We have made every effort to mark as such all words which we believe to be trademarks. We should also like to make it clear that the presence of a word in the thesaurus, whether marked or unmarked, in no way affects its legal status as a trademark.

ISBN 0-550-18303-5 Paperback

Typeset by Hewer Text Composition Services, Edinburgh
Printed in England by Clays Ltd, St Ives plc

Introduction

A synonym is a word that means something similar to another word, and a thesaurus is a listing of such words. This thesaurus lists about 150,000 synonyms for common English words. *Chambers Quick Reference English Thesaurus* is based on *Chambers Thesaurus*, which itself is drawn from the extensive *Chambers Dictionary* database.

This thesaurus has been compiled to help you find the most appropriate word for a particular occasion. You will be able to include a more exact term in an essay or a report, a livelier phrase in a speech or a simpler expression in a letter. We hope that not only will your skills in using English improve, but also that you will enjoy sampling more of the varied delights of the English language.

Suppose you want to find a synonym for the word *summarize*, either because you have used this word already, or because you want to vary the style of what you are writing or saying. If you look up the entry **summarize**, you will see a list of synonyms arranged according to shades of meaning, and in order from the most common to the least frequently used, or specialized, term: outline, précis, condense, abridge, abbreviate, shorten, sum up, encapsulate, review.

Many entries are divided into numbered sections, indicating that the word has several meanings. After each number comes either a key synonym in small capitals or an example to help you find precisely which meaning you want. For example:

> **arrest** *v* **1** *arrest a criminal*: capture, catch, seize, nick (*infml*), run in, apprehend, detain. **2** STOP, stem, check, restrain, inhibit, halt, interrupt, stall, delay, slow, retard, block, obstruct, impede, hinder.

This means that for the sense shown by the example *arrest a criminal* the synonyms are capture, catch, seize, *etc*, and for the sense shown by the key synonym STOP, other possible synonyms are stem, check, restrain, *etc*.

Note that no one word can be used in the place of another word in every context. So if you are not sure of the meaning or use of one of the words included as a synonym, look up the word in a general dictionary such as *The Chambers Dictionary*.

At the end of many entries, antonyms – words that mean the opposite of another word – are shown after the symbol ≠. For example, at **boring**: interesting, exciting, stimulating, original.

About three hundred special entries are printed with a shaded background. These entries, *eg* at **agricultural**, **animal**, **chemical elements**, **flower**, **photography** and **sport**, are lists of related words which present examples of different flowers, sports, types of agricultural machinery, *etc*.

eg **sport**

> *Sports include*: badminton, fives, lacrosse, squash, table-tennis, ping-pong (*infml*), tennis; American football, baseball, basketball, billiards, boules, bowls, cricket, croquet, football, golf, handball, hockey, netball, pétanque, pitch and putt, polo, pool, putting, rounders, Rugby, snooker, soccer, tenpin bowling, volleyball;...

Abbreviations

adj	adjective	*prep*	preposition
adv	adverb	®	trademark
conj	conjunction	*sl*	slang
infml	informal	*US*	American English
interj	interjection	*v*	verb
fml	formal	≠	antonym(s)
n	noun		

A

abandon *v* **1** DESERT, leave, forsake, jilt, ditch (*sl*), leave in the lurch (*infml*), maroon, strand, leave behind, scrap. **2** *abandon ship*: vacate, evacuate, withdraw from, quit. **3** RENOUNCE, resign, give up, forgo, relinquish, surrender, yield, waive, drop.
≠ **1** support, maintain, keep. **3** continue.

abandoned *adj* **1** DESERTED, unoccupied, derelict, neglected, forsaken, forlorn, desolate. **2** DISSOLUTE, wild, uninhibited, wanton, wicked.
≠ **1** kept, occupied. **2** restrained.

abandonment *n* **1** DESERTION, leaving, forsaking, jilting, neglect, scrapping. **2** RENUNCIATION, resignation, giving up, relinquishment, surrender, sacrifice, waiver, dropping, discontinuation.

abashed *adj* **1** ASHAMED, shamefaced, embarrassed, mortified, humiliated, humbled. **2** CONFUSED, bewildered, nonplussed, confounded, perturbed, discomposed, disconcerted, taken aback, dumbfounded, floored (*infml*), dismayed.
≠ **2** composed, at ease.

abate *v* **1** DECREASE, reduce, lessen, diminish, decline, sink, dwindle, taper off, fall off. **2** MODERATE, ease, relieve, alleviate, mitigate, remit, pacify, quell, subside, let up (*infml*), weaken, wane, slacken, slow, fade.
≠ **1** increase. **2** strengthen.

abbey *n* monastery, priory, friary, seminary, convent, nunnery, cloister.

abbreviate *v* shorten, cut, trim, clip, truncate, curtail, abridge, summarize, précis, abstract, digest, condense, compress, reduce, lessen, shrink, contract.
≠ extend, lengthen, expand, amplify.

abbreviation *n* shortening, clipping, curtailment, abridgement, summarization, summary, synopsis, résumé, précis, abstract, digest, compression, reduction, contraction.
≠ extension, expansion, amplification.

abdicate *v* renounce, give up, relinquish, surrender, cede, yield, forgo, abandon, quit, vacate, retire, resign, step down (*infml*).

abdomen *n* belly, guts, stomach, tummy (*infml*), paunch, midriff.

abdominal *adj* ventral, intestinal, visceral, gastric.

abduct *v* carry off, run away with, run off with (*infml*), make off with, spirit away, seduce, kidnap, snatch, seize, appropriate.

aberration *n* deviation, straying, wandering, divergence, irregularity, nonconformity, anomaly, oddity, peculiarity, eccentricity, quirk, freak, lapse, defect.
≠ conformity.

abhor *v* hate, detest, loathe, abominate, shudder at, recoil from, shrink from, spurn, despise.
≠ love, adore.

abhorrence *n* hate, hatred, aversion, loathing, abomination, horror, repugnance, revulsion, disgust, distaste.
≠ love, adoration.

abhorrent *adj* detestable, loathsome, abominable, execrable, heinous, obnoxious, odious, hated, hateful, horrible, horrid, offensive, repugnant, repellent, repulsive, revolting, nauseating, disgusting, distasteful.
≠ delightful, attractive.

abide *v* **1** BEAR, stand, endure, tolerate, put up with, stomach, accept. **2** REMAIN, last, endure, continue, persist.
abide by 1 *abide by the rules*: obey, observe, follow, comply with, adhere to,

conform to, submit to, go along with, agree to. **2** FULFIL, discharge, carry out, stand by, hold to, keep to.

ability *n* **1** CAPABILITY, capacity, faculty, facility, potentiality, power. **2** SKILL, dexterity, deftness, adeptness, competence, proficiency, qualification, aptitude, talent, gift, endowment, knack, flair, touch, expertise, know-how (*infml*), genius, forte, strength.
≠ **1** inability. **2** incompetence, weakness.

abject *adj* **1** CONTEMPTIBLE, worthless, low, mean, ignoble, dishonourable, deplorable, despicable, vile, sordid, debased, degenerate, submissive, servile, grovelling, slavish. **2** MISERABLE, wretched, forlorn, hopeless, pitiable, pathetic, outcast, degraded.
≠ **1** proud, exalted.

ablaze *adj* **1** BLAZING, flaming, burning, on fire, ignited, lighted, alight, illuminated, luminous, glowing, aglow, radiant, flashing, gleaming, sparkling, brilliant. **2** IMPASSIONED, passionate, fervent, ardent, fiery, enthusiastic, excited, exhilarated, stimulated, aroused, angry, furious, raging, incensed, frenzied.

able *adj* capable, fit, fitted, dexterous, adroit, deft, adept, competent, proficient, qualified, practised, experienced, skilled, accomplished, clever, expert, masterly, skilful, ingenious, talented, gifted, strong, powerful, effective, efficient, adequate.
≠ unable, incapable, incompetent, ineffective.

able-bodied *adj* fit, healthy, sound, strong, robust, hardy, tough, vigorous, powerful, hale, hearty, lusty, sturdy, strapping, stout, stalwart, staunch.
≠ infirm, delicate.

abnormal *adj* odd, strange, singular, peculiar, curious, queer, weird, eccentric, paranormal, unnatural, uncanny, extraordinary, exceptional, unusual, uncommon, unexpected, irregular, anomalous, aberrant, erratic, wayward, deviant, divergent, different.
≠ normal, regular, typical.

abnormality *n* oddity, peculiarity, singularity, eccentricity, strangeness, bizarreness, unnaturalness, unusualness, irregularity, exception, anomaly, deformity, flaw, aberration, deviation, divergence, difference.
≠ normality, regularity.

abolish *v* do away with, annul, nullify, invalidate, quash, repeal, rescind, revoke, cancel, obliterate, blot out, suppress, destroy, eliminate, eradicate, get rid of (*infml*), stamp out, end, put an end to, terminate, subvert, overthrow, overturn.
≠ create, retain, authorize, continue.

abolition *n* annulment, nullification, invalidation, quashing, repeal, abrogation, cancellation, obliteration, suppression, eradication, extinction, end, ending, termination, subversion, overturning, dissolution.
≠ creation, retention, continuance.

abominable *adj* loathsome, detestable, hateful, horrid, horrible, abhorrent, execrable, odious, repugnant, repulsive, repellent, disgusting, revolting, obnoxious, nauseating, foul, vile, heinous, atrocious, appalling, terrible, reprehensible, contemptible, despicable, wretched.
≠ delightful, pleasant, desirable.

abominate *v* hate, loathe, detest, abhor, execrate, despise, condemn.
≠ love, adore.

abomination *n* hate, hatred, aversion, loathing, abhorrence, repugnance, revulsion, disgust, distaste, hostility, offence, outrage, disgrace, anathema, horror, evil, curse, plague, torment, bête noire.
≠ adoration, delight.

abort *v* miscarry, terminate, end, stop, arrest, halt, check, frustrate, thwart, nullify, call off, fail.
≠ continue.

abortion *n* miscarriage, termination, frustration, failure, misadventure.
≠ continuation, success.

abortive *adj* failed, unsuccessful, fruitless, unproductive, barren, sterile, vain, idle, futile, useless, ineffective, unavailing.
≠ successful, fruitful.

abound *v* be plentiful, proliferate, flourish, thrive, swell, increase, superabound, swarm, teem, run riot, overflow.

about *prep* **1** REGARDING, concerning, relating to, referring to, connected with, concerned with, as regards, with regard to, with respect to, with reference to. **2** CLOSE TO, near, nearby, beside, adjacent to. **3** ROUND, around, surrounding, encircling, encompassing, throughout, all over.
adv **1** *about twenty*: around, approximately, roughly, in the region of, more or less, almost, nearly, approaching, nearing. **2** *run about*: to and fro, here and there, from place to place.
about to on the point of, on the verge of, all but, ready to, intending to, preparing to.

above *prep* over, higher than, on top of, superior to, in excess of, exceeding, surpassing, beyond, before, prior to.
≠ below, under.
adv overhead, aloft, on high, earlier.
≠ below, underneath.
adj above-mentioned, above-stated, foregoing, preceding, previous, earlier, prior.

above-board *adj* honest, legitimate, straight, on the level, fair, fair and square, square, true, open, frank, candid, guileless, straightforward, forthright, truthful, veracious, trustworthy, honourable, reputable, upright.
≠ dishonest, shady (*infml*), underhand.

abrasion *n* graze, scratch, scratching, scraping, scrape, scouring, grating, grinding, abrading, chafing, chafe, friction, rubbing, erosion, wearing away, wearing down.

abrasive *adj* scratching, scraping, grating, rough, harsh, chafing, frictional, galling, irritating, annoying, sharp, biting, caustic, hurtful, nasty, unpleasant.
≠ smooth, pleasant.

abreast *adj* acquainted, informed, knowledgeable, in the picture, au courant, up to date, in touch, au fait, conversant, familiar.
≠ unaware, out of touch.

abridge *v* shorten, cut (down), prune, curtail, abbreviate, contract, reduce, decrease, lessen, summarize, précis, abstract, digest, condense, compress, concentrate.
≠ expand, amplify, pad out.

abridgement *n* **1** SHORTENING, cutting, reduction, decrease, diminishing, concentration, contraction, restriction, limitation. **2** SUMMARY, synopsis, résumé, outline, précis, abstract, digest, epitome.
≠ **1** expansion, padding.

abroad *adv* **1** OVERSEAS, in foreign parts, out of the country, far and wide, widely, extensively. **2** AT LARGE, around, about, circulating, current.
≠ **1** at home.

abrupt *adj* **1** *abrupt departure*: sudden, unexpected, unforeseen, surprising, quick, rapid, swift, hasty, hurried, precipitate. **2** SHEER, precipitous, steep, sharp. **3** BRUSQUE, curt, terse, short, brisk, snappy, gruff, rude, uncivil, impolite, blunt, direct.
≠ **1** gradual, slow, leisurely. **3** expansive, ceremonious, polite.

abscond *v* run away, run off, make off, decamp, flee, fly, escape, bolt, quit, clear out (*infml*), disappear, take French leave.

absence *n* **1** NON-ATTENDANCE, non-appearance, truancy, absenteeism, non-existence. **2** LACK, need, want, deficiency, dearth, scarcity, unavailability, default, omission, vacancy.
≠ **1** presence, attendance, appearance. **2** existence.

absent *adj* **1** MISSING, not present, away, out, unavailable, gone, lacking, truant. **2** INATTENTIVE, daydreaming, dreamy, faraway, elsewhere, absent-minded, vacant, vague, distracted, preoccupied, unaware, oblivious, unheeding.
≠ **1** present. **2** alert, aware.

absent-minded *adj* forgetful, scatterbrained, absent, abstracted,

withdrawn, faraway, distracted, preoccupied, absorbed, engrossed, pensive, musing, dreaming, dreamy, inattentive, unaware, oblivious, unconscious, heedless, unheeding, unthinking, impractical.
≠ attentive, practical, matter-of-fact.

absolute *adj* **1** UTTER, total, complete, entire, full, thorough, exhaustive, supreme, consummate, definitive, conclusive, final, categorical, definite, unequivocal, unquestionable, decided, decisive, positive, sure, certain, genuine, pure, perfect, sheer, unmixed, unqualified, downright, out-and-out, outright. **2** OMNIPOTENT, totalitarian, autocratic, tyrannical, despotic, dictatorial, sovereign, unlimited, unrestricted.

absolutely *adv* utterly, totally, dead, completely, entirely, fully, wholly, thoroughly, exhaustively, perfectly, supremely, unconditionally, conclusively, finally, categorically, definitely, positively, unequivocally, unambiguously, unquestionably, decidedly, decisively, surely, certainly, infallibly, genuinely, truly, purely, exactly, precisely.

absorb *v* **1** TAKE IN, ingest, drink in, imbibe, suck up, soak up, consume, devour, engulf, digest, assimilate, understand, receive, hold, retain. **2** ENGROSS, involve, fascinate, enthral, monopolize, preoccupy, occupy, fill (up).
≠ **1** exude.

absorbing *adj* interesting, amusing, entertaining, diverting, engrossing, preoccupying, intriguing, fascinating, captivating, enthralling, spellbinding, gripping, riveting, compulsive, unputdownable (*infml*).
≠ boring, off-putting.

abstain *v* refrain, decline, refuse, reject, resist, forbear, shun, avoid, keep from, stop, cease, desist, give up, renounce, forgo, go without, deny oneself.
≠ indulge.

abstemious *adj* abstinent, self-denying, self-disciplined, disciplined, sober, temperate, moderate, sparing, frugal, austere, ascetic, restrained.
≠ intemperate, gluttonous, luxurious.

abstinence *n* abstaining, abstention, abstemiousness, self-denial, non-indulgence, avoidance, forbearance, refraining, refusal, restraint, self-restraint, self-control, self-discipline, sobriety, teetotalism, temperance, moderation, frugality, asceticism.
≠ indulgence, self-indulgence.

abstract *adj* non-concrete, conceptual, intellectual, hypothetical, theoretical, unpractical, unrealistic, general, generalized, indefinite, metaphysical, philosophical, academic, complex, abstruse, deep, profound, subtle.
≠ concrete, real, actual.
n synopsis, outline, summary, recapitulation, résumé, précis, epitome, digest, abridgement, compression.
v **1** SUMMARIZE, outline, précis, digest, condense, compress, abridge, abbreviate, shorten. **2** EXTRACT, remove, withdraw, isolate, detach, dissociate, separate.
≠ **1** expand. **2** insert.

abstraction *n* **1** IDEA, notion, concept, thought, conception, theory, hypothesis, theorem, formula, generalization, generality. **2** INATTENTION, dream, dreaminess, absent-mindedness, distraction, pensiveness, preoccupation, absorption. **3** EXTRACTION, withdrawal, isolation, separation.

absurd *adj* ridiculous, ludicrous, preposterous, fantastic, incongruous, illogical, paradoxical, implausible, untenable, unreasonable, irrational, nonsensical, meaningless, senseless, foolish, silly, stupid, idiotic, crazy, daft (*infml*), farcical, comical, funny, humorous, laughable, risible, derisory.
≠ logical, rational, sensible.

abundant *adj* plentiful, in plenty, full, filled, well-supplied, ample, generous, bountiful, rich, copious, profuse, lavish, exuberant, teeming, overflowing.
≠ scarce, sparse.

abuse *v* **1** MISUSE, misapply, exploit, take advantage of, oppress, wrong, ill-

treat, maltreat, hurt, injure, molest, damage, spoil, harm. **2** INSULT, swear at, defame, libel, slander, smear, disparage, malign, revile, scold, upbraid.
≠ **1** cherish, care for. **2** compliment, praise.
n **1** MISUSE, misapplication, exploitation, imposition, oppression, wrong, ill-treatment, maltreatment, hurt, injury, molestation, damage, spoiling, harm. **2** INSULTS, swearing, cursing, offence, defamation, libel, slander, disparagement, reproach, scolding, upbraiding, tirade.
≠ **1** care, attention. **2** compliment, praise.

abusive *adj* insulting, offensive, rude, scathing, hurtful, injurious, cruel, destructive, defamatory, libellous, slanderous, derogatory, disparaging, pejorative, vilifying, maligning, reviling, censorious, reproachful, scolding, upbraiding.
≠ complimentary, polite.

abyss *n* gulf, chasm, crevasse, fissure, gorge, canyon, crater, pit, depth, void.

academic *adj* **1** SCHOLARLY, erudite, learned, well-read, studious, bookish, scholastic, pedagogical, educational, instructional, literary, highbrow. **2** THEORETICAL, hypothetical, conjectural, speculative, notional, abstract, impractical.
n professor, don, master, fellow, lecturer, tutor, student, scholar, man of letters, pedant.

accelerate *v* quicken, speed, speed up, pick up speed, step up, expedite, hurry, hasten, precipitate, stimulate, facilitate, advance, further, promote, forward.
≠ decelerate, slow down, delay.

accent *n* pronunciation, enunciation, articulation, brogue, twang (*infml*), tone, pitch, intonation, inflection, accentuation, stress, emphasis, intensity, force, cadence, rhythm, beat, pulse, pulsation.

accentuate *v* accent, stress, emphasize, underline, highlight, intensify, strengthen, deepen.
≠ play down, weaken.

accept *v* **1** *accept a gift*: take, receive, obtain, acquire, gain, secure. **2** ACKNOWLEDGE, recognize, admit, allow, approve, agree to, consent to, take on, adopt. **3** TOLERATE, put up with, stand, bear, abide, face up to, yield to.
≠ **1** refuse, turn down. **2** reject.

acceptable *adj* satisfactory, tolerable, moderate, passable, adequate, all right, OK (*infml*), so-so (*infml*), unexceptionable, admissible, suitable, conventional, correct, desirable, pleasant, gratifying, welcome.
≠ unacceptable, unsatisfactory, unwelcome.

acceptance *n* **1** TAKING, accepting, receipt, obtaining, getting, acquiring, gaining, securing. **2** ACKNOWLEDGEMENT, recognition, admission, concession, affirmation, concurrence, agreement, assent, consent, permission, ratification, approval, stamp of approval, OK (*infml*), adoption, undertaking, belief, credence.
≠ **1** refusal. **2** rejection, dissent.

accepted *adj* authorized, approved, ratified, sanctioned, agreed, acknowledged, recognized, admitted, confirmed, acceptable, correct, conventional, orthodox, traditional, customary, time-honoured, established, received, universal, regular, standard, normal, usual, common.
≠ unconventional, unorthodox, controversial.

access *n* admission, admittance, entry, entering, entrance, gateway, door, key, approach, passage, road, path, course.
≠ exit, outlet.

accessible *adj* **1** REACHABLE, get-at-able (*infml*), attainable, achievable, possible, obtainable, available, on hand, ready, handy, convenient, near, nearby. **2** FRIENDLY, affable, approachable, sociable, informal.
≠ **1** inaccessible, remote. **2** unapproachable.

accessory *n* **1** EXTRA, supplement, addition, appendage, attachment, extension, component, fitting, accompaniment, decoration, adornment, frill, trimming. **2** ACCOMPLICE, partner, associate, colleague, confederate, assistant, helper, help, aid.

accident *n* **1** CHANCE, hazard, fortuity, luck, fortune, fate, serendipity, contingency, fluke. **2** MISFORTUNE, mischance, misadventure, mishap, casualty, blow, calamity, disaster. **3** *road accident*: collision, crash, shunt (*sl*), prang (*sl*), pile-up.

accidental *adj* unintentional, unintended, inadvertent, unplanned, uncalculated, unexpected, unforeseen, unlooked-for, chance, fortuitous, flukey, uncertain, haphazard, random, casual, incidental.
≠ intentional, deliberate, calculated, premeditated.

acclaim *v* praise, commend, extol, exalt, honour, hail, salute, welcome, applaud, clap, cheer, celebrate.
n acclamation, praise, commendation, homage, tribute, eulogy, exaltation, honour, welcome, approbation, approval, applause, ovation, clapping, cheers, cheering, shouting, celebration.
≠ criticism, disapproval.

accommodate *v* **1** LODGE, board, put up, house, shelter. **2** OBLIGE, help, assist, aid, serve, provide, supply, comply, conform. **3** ADAPT, accustom, acclimatize, adjust, modify, fit, harmonize, reconcile, settle, compose.

accommodating *adj* obliging, indulgent, helpful, co-operative, willing, kind, considerate, unselfish, sympathetic, friendly, hospitable.
≠ disobliging, selfish.

accommodation

> *Types of accommodation include*: flat, apartment, bedsit, bedsitter, digs (*infml*), lodgings, hostel, halls of residence, rooms, residence, dwelling, shelter, pad (*infml*), squat (*infml*); bed and breakfast, board, guest house, hotel, youth hostel, villa, timeshare, motel, inn, pension, boarding-house; barracks, billet, married quarters. *see also* **house**; **room**.

accompany *v* **1** ESCORT, attend, convoy, chaperon, usher, conduct, follow. **2** COEXIST, coincide, belong to, go with, complement, supplement.

accomplice *n* assistant, helper, abettor, mate, henchman, conspirator, collaborator, ally, confederate, partner, associate, colleague, participator, accessory.

accomplish *v* achieve, attain, do, perform, carry out, execute, fulfil, discharge, finish, complete, conclude, consummate, realize, effect, bring about, engineer, produce, obtain.

accomplished *adj* skilled, professional, practised, proficient, gifted, talented, skilful, adroit, adept, expert, masterly, consummate, polished, cultivated.
≠ unskilled, inexpert, incapable.

accomplishment *n* **1** *the accomplishment of a task*: achievement, attainment, doing, performance, carrying out, execution, fulfilment, discharge, finishing, completion, conclusion, consummation, perfection, realization, fruition, production. **2** SKILL, art, aptitude, faculty, ability, capability, proficiency, gift, talent, forte. **3** EXPLOIT, feat, deed, stroke, triumph.

accord *v* **1** AGREE, concur, harmonize, match, conform, correspond, suit. **2** GIVE, tender, grant, allow, bestow, endow, confer.
≠ **1** disagree. **2** deny.
n accordance, agreement, assent, unanimity, concert, unity, correspondence, conformity, harmony, sympathy.
≠ conflict, discord, disharmony.

according to in accordance with, in keeping with, obedient to, in conformity with, in line with, consistent with, commensurate with, in proportion to, in relation to, after, in the light of, in the manner of, after the manner of.

accordingly *adv* in accordance, in accord with, correspondingly, so, as a result, consequently, in consequence, therefore, thus, hence, appropriately, properly, suitably.

accost *v* approach, confront, buttonhole, waylay, stop, halt, detain, importune, solicit.

account *n* **1** *an account of what happened*: narrative, story, tale, chronicle, history, memoir, record, statement, report, communiqué, write-up, version, portrayal, sketch, description, presentation, explanation. **2** LEDGER, book, books, register, inventory, statement, invoice, bill, tab, charge, reckoning, computation, tally, score, balance.
account for explain, elucidate, illuminate, clear up, rationalize, justify, vindicate, answer for, put paid to, destroy, kill.

accountable *adj* answerable, responsible, liable, amenable, obliged, bound.

accumulate *v* gather, assemble, collect, amass, aggregate, cumulate, accrue, grow, increase, multiply, build up, pile up, hoard, stockpile, stash (*infml*), store.
≠ disseminate.

accumulation *n* gathering, assembly, collection, growth, increase, build-up, conglomeration, mass, heap, pile, stack, stock, store, reserve, hoard, stockpile.

accuracy *n* correctness, precision, exactness, authenticity, truth, veracity, closeness, faithfulness, fidelity, carefulness.
≠ inaccuracy.

accurate *adj* correct, right, unerring, precise, exact, well-directed, spot-on (*infml*), faultless, perfect, word-perfect, sound, authentic, factual, nice, true, truthful, veracious, just, proper, close, faithful, well-judged, careful, rigorous, scrupulous, meticulous, strict, minute.
≠ inaccurate, wrong, imprecise, inexact.

accusation *n* charge, allegation, imputation, indictment, denunciation, impeachment, recrimination, complaint, incrimination.

accuse *v* charge, indict, impugn, denounce, arraign, impeach, cite, allege, attribute, impute, blame, censure, recriminate, incriminate, criminate, inform against.

accustomed *adj* used, in the habit of, given to, confirmed, seasoned, hardened, inured, disciplined, trained, adapted, acclimatized, acquainted, familiar, wonted, habitual, routine, regular, normal, usual, ordinary, everyday, conventional, customary, traditional, established, fixed, prevailing, general.
≠ unaccustomed, unusual.

ache *v* **1** HURT, be sore, pain, suffer, agonize, throb, pound, twinge, smart, sting. **2** YEARN, long, pine, hanker, desire, crave, hunger, thirst, itch.
n **1** PAIN, hurt, soreness, suffering, anguish, agony, throb, throbbing, pounding, pang, twinge, smarting, stinging. **2** YEARNING, longing, craving, itch.

achieve *v* accomplish, attain, reach, get, obtain, acquire, procure, gain, earn, win, succeed, manage, do, perform, carry out, execute, fulfil, finish, complete, consummate, effect, bring about, realize, produce.
≠ miss, fail.

achievement *n* **1** *the achievement of our aims*: accomplishment, attainment, acquirement, performance, execution, fulfilment, completion, success, realization, fruition. **2** ACT, deed, exploit, feat, effort.

acid *adj* sour, bitter, tart, vinegary, sharp, pungent, acerbic, caustic, corrosive, stinging, biting, mordant, cutting, incisive, trenchant, harsh, hurtful.

> *Types of acid include*: acetic, acrylic, amino, aqua fortis, aqua regia, ascorbic, benzoic, boric, carbolic, chloric, citric, DNA (deoxyribonucleic acid), fatty, folic, formic, hydrochloric, hydrocyanic, lactic, malic, nitric, nitrohydrochloric, nitrous, palmitic, pectic, phenol, phosphoric, prussic, RNA (ribonucleic acid), salicylic, spirits of salt, stearic, sulphuric, tannic, tartaric, uric. *see also* **amino acid**.

acknowledge *v* **1** *acknowledge an*

error: admit, confess, own up to, declare, recognize, accept, grant, allow, concede. **2** GREET, address, notice, recognize. **3** *acknowledge a letter*: answer, reply to, respond to, confirm.
≠ **1** deny. **2** ignore.

acknowledged *adj* recognized, accepted, approved, accredited, declared, professed, attested, avowed, confirmed.

acknowledgement *n* **1** ADMISSION, confession, declaration, profession, recognition, acceptance. **2** GREETING, salutation, notice, recognition. **3** ANSWER, reply, response, reaction, affirmation. **4** GRATITUDE, thanks, appreciation, tribute.

acquaint *v* accustom, familiarize, tell, notify, advise, inform, brief, enlighten, divulge, disclose, reveal, announce.

acquaintance *n* **1** AWARENESS, knowledge, understanding, experience, familiarity, intimacy, relationship, association, fellowship, companionship. **2** FRIEND, companion, colleague, associate, contact.

acquire *v* buy, purchase, procure, appropriate, obtain, get, cop (*sl*), receive, collect, pick up, gather, net, gain, secure, earn, win, achieve, attain, realize.
≠ relinquish, forfeit.

acquisition *n* purchase, buy (*infml*), procurement, appropriation, gain, securing, achievement, attainment, accession, takeover, property, possession.

acquit *v* absolve, clear, reprieve, let off, exonerate, exculpate, excuse, vindicate, free, liberate, deliver, relieve, release, dismiss, discharge, settle, satisfy, repay.
≠ convict.

acquittal *n* absolution, clearance, reprieve, exoneration, exculpation, excusing, vindication, freeing, liberation, deliverance, relief, release, dismissal, discharge.
≠ conviction.

acrid *adj* pungent, sharp, stinging, acid, burning, caustic, acerbic, biting, cutting, incisive, trenchant, sarcastic, sardonic, bitter, acrimonious, virulent, harsh, vitriolic, nasty, malicious, venomous.

acrimonious *adj* bitter, biting, cutting, trenchant, sharp, virulent, severe, spiteful, censorious, abusive, ill-tempered.
≠ peaceable, kindly.

acrimony *n* bitterness, rancour, resentment, ill-will, petulance, gall, ill temper, irascibility, trenchancy, sarcasm, astringency, acerbity, harshness, virulence.

act *n* **1** DEED, action, undertaking, enterprise, operation, manoeuvre, move, step, doing, execution, accomplishment, achievement, exploit, feat, stroke. **2** *put on an act*: pretence, make-believe, sham, fake, feigning, dissimulation, affectation, show, front. **3** LAW, statute, ordinance, edict, decree, resolution, measure, bill. **4** TURN, item, routine, sketch, performance, gig (*sl*).
v **1** BEHAVE, conduct, exert, make, work, function, operate, do, execute, carry out. **2** PRETEND, feign, put on, assume, simulate, mimic, imitate, impersonate, portray, represent, mime, play, perform, enact.
act on 1 *act on orders*: carry out, fulfil, comply with, conform to, obey, follow, heed, take. **2** AFFECT, influence, alter, modify, change, transform.

acting *adj* temporary, provisional, interim, stopgap, supply, stand-by, substitute, reserve.
n theatre, stagecraft, artistry, performing, performance, play-acting, melodrama, dramatics, theatricals, portrayal, characterization, impersonation, imitating.

action *n* **1** ACT, move, deed, exploit, feat, accomplishment, achievement, performance, effort, endeavour, enterprise, undertaking, proceeding, process, activity, liveliness, spirit, energy, vigour, power, force, exercise, exertion, work, functioning, operation, mechanism, movement, motion. **2** *killed in action*: warfare, battle, conflict, combat, fight, fray, engagement, skirmish, clash. **3** LITIGATION, lawsuit, suit, case, prosecution.

activate *v* start, initiate, trigger, set off, fire, switch on, set in motion, mobilize, propel, move, stir, rouse, arouse, stimulate, motivate, prompt, animate, energize, impel, excite, galvanize.
≠ deactivate, stop, arrest.

active *adj* **1** BUSY, occupied, on the go (*infml*), industrious, diligent, hard-working, forceful, spirited, vital, forward, enterprising, enthusiastic, devoted, engaged, involved, committed, militant, activist. **2** AGILE, nimble, sprightly, light-footed, quick, alert, animated, lively, energetic, vigorous. **3** IN OPERATION, functioning, working, running.
≠ **1** passive. **2** inert, dormant. **3** inactive.

activity *n* **1** LIVELINESS, life, activeness, action, motion, movement, commotion, bustle, hustle, industry, labour, exertion, exercise. **2** OCCUPATION, job, work, act, deed, project, scheme, task, venture, enterprise, endeavour, undertaking, pursuit, hobby, pastime, interest.

actor *n* actress, play-actor, comedian, tragedian, ham, player, performer, artist, impersonator, mime.

actual *adj* **1** REAL, existent, substantial, tangible, material, physical, concrete, positive, definite, absolute, certain, unquestionable, indisputable, confirmed, verified, factual, truthful, true, genuine, legitimate, bona fide, authentic, realistic. **2** CURRENT, present, present-day, prevailing, live, living.
≠ **1** theoretical, apparent, imaginary.

actually *adv* in fact, as a matter of fact, as it happens, in truth, in reality, really, truly, indeed, absolutely.

acumen *n* astuteness, shrewdness, sharpness, keenness, quickness, penetration, insight, intuition, discrimination, discernment, judgement, perception, sense, wit, wisdom, intelligence, cleverness, ingenuity.

acute *adj* **1** SEVERE, intense, extreme, violent, dangerous, serious, grave, urgent, crucial, vital, decisive, sharp, cutting, poignant, distressing. **2** *an acute mind*: sharp, keen, incisive, penetrating, astute, shrewd, judicious, discerning, observant, perceptive.
≠ **1** mild, slight.

adamant *adj* hard, resolute, determined, set, firm, insistent, rigid, stiff, inflexible, unbending, unrelenting, intransigent, unyielding, stubborn, uncompromising, tough, fixed, immovable, unshakable.
≠ hesitant, flexible, yielding.

adapt *v* alter, change, qualify, modify, adjust, convert, remodel, customize, fit, tailor, fashion, shape, harmonize, match, suit, conform, comply, prepare, familiarize, acclimatize.

adaptable *adj* alterable, changeable, variable, modifiable, adjustable, convertible, conformable, versatile, plastic, malleable, flexible, compliant, amenable, easy-going.
≠ inflexible, refractory.

adaptation *n* alteration, change, shift, transformation, modification, adjustment, accommodation, conversion, remodelling, reworking, reshaping, refitting, revision, variation, version.

add *v* append, annex, affix, attach, tack on, join, combine, supplement, augment.
≠ take away, remove.
add up 1 ADD, sum up, tot up, total, tally, count (up), reckon, compute. **2** AMOUNT, come to, constitute, include. **3** *it doesn't add up*: be consistent, hang together, fit, be plausible, be reasonable, make sense, mean, signify, indicate.
≠ **1** subtract.

addict *n* **1** ENTHUSIAST, fan, buff (*infml*), fiend, freak, devotee, follower, adherent. **2** DRUG-ADDICT, user (*infml*), dope-fiend, junkie (*infml*), tripper (*sl*), mainliner (*sl*).

addicted *adj* dependent, hooked, obsessed, absorbed, devoted, dedicated, fond, inclined, disposed, accustomed.

addiction *n* dependence, craving, habit, monkey (*sl*), obsession.

addition *n* **1** ADDING, annexation, accession, extension, enlargement,

increasing, increase, gain. **2** ADJUNCT, supplement, additive, addendum, appendix, appendage, accessory, attachment, extra, increment. **3** SUMMING-UP, totting-up, totalling, counting, reckoning, inclusion.
≠ **1** removal. **3** subtraction.
in addition additionally, too, also, as well, besides, moreover, further, furthermore, over and above.

additional *adj* added, extra, supplementary, spare, more, further, increased, other, new, fresh.

address *n* **1** RESIDENCE, dwelling, abode, house, home, lodging, direction, inscription, whereabouts, location, situation, place. **2** SPEECH, talk, lecture, sermon, discourse, dissertation.
v lecture, speak to, talk to, greet, salute, hail, invoke, accost, approach, buttonhole.

adept *adj* skilled, accomplished, expert, masterly, experienced, versed, practised, polished, proficient, able, adroit, deft, nimble.

adequate *adj* enough, sufficient, commensurate, requisite, suitable, fit, able, competent, capable, serviceable, acceptable, satisfactory, passable, tolerable, fair, respectable, presentable.
≠ inadequate, insufficient.

adhere *v* **1** STICK, glue, paste, cement, fix, fasten, attach, join, link, combine, coalesce, cohere, hold, cling, cleave to. **2** *adhere to the agreement*: observe, follow, abide by, comply with, fulfil, obey, keep, heed, respect, stand by.

adherent *n* supporter, upholder, advocate, partisan, follower, disciple, satellite, henchman, hanger-on, votary, devotee, admirer, fan, enthusiast, freak, nut.

adhesion *n* adherence, adhesiveness, bond, attachment, grip, cohesion.

adhesive *adj* sticky, tacky, self-adhesive, gummed, gummy, gluey, adherent, adhering, sticking, clinging, holding, attaching, cohesive.
n glue, gum, paste, cement.

adjacent *adj* adjoining, abutting, touching, contiguous, bordering, alongside, beside, juxtaposed, next-door, neighbouring, next, closest, nearest, close, near.
≠ remote, distant.

adjoin *v* abut, touch, meet, border, verge, neighbour, interconnect, link, connect, join, combine, unite, couple, attach, annex, add.

adjourn *v* interrupt, suspend, discontinue, break off, delay, stay, defer, postpone, put off, recess, retire.
≠ assemble, convene.

adjournment *n* interruption, suspension, discontinuation, break, pause, recess, delay, stay, deferment, deferral, postponement, putting off, dissolution.

adjudicate *v* judge, arbitrate, umpire, referee, settle, determine, decide, pronounce.

adjust *v* **1** MODIFY, change, adapt, alter, convert, dispose, shape, remodel, fit, accommodate, suit, measure, rectify, regulate, balance, temper, tune, fine-tune, fix, set, arrange, compose, settle, square. **2** ACCUSTOM, habituate, acclimatize, reconcile, harmonize, conform.
≠ **1** disarrange, upset.

adjustment *n* **1** MODIFICATION, change, adaptation, alteration, conversion, remodelling, shaping, fitting, accommodation, rectification, regulation, tuning, fixing, setting, arranging, arrangement, ordering, settlement. **2** HABITUATION, orientation, acclimatization, naturalization, reconciliation, harmonization, conforming.

ad-lib *v* improvise, extemporize, make up, invent.
adj impromptu, improvised, extempore, extemporaneous, off-the-cuff, unprepared, unpremeditated, unrehearsed, spontaneous, made up.
≠ prepared.
adv impromptu, extempore, extemporaneously, off the cuff, off the top of one's head, spontaneously, impulsively.

administer *v* **1** *administer an organization*: govern, rule, lead, head, preside over, officiate, manage, run, organize, direct, conduct, control, regulate, superintend, supervise, oversee. **2** GIVE, provide, supply, distribute, dole out, dispense, measure out, mete out, execute, impose, apply.

administration *n* **1** ADMINISTERING, governing, ruling, leadership, management, execution, running, organization, direction, control, superintendence, supervision, overseeing. **2** GOVERNING BODY, regime, government, ministry, leadership, directorship, management, executive, term of office.

administrative *adj* governmental, legislative, authoritative, directorial, managerial, management, executive, organizational, regulatory, supervisory.

admirable *adj* praiseworthy, commendable, laudable, creditable, deserving, worthy, respected, fine, excellent, superior, wonderful, exquisite, choice, rare, valuable.
≠ contemptible, despicable, deplorable.

admiration *n* esteem, regard, respect, reverence, veneration, worship, idolism, adoration, affection, approval, praise, appreciation, pleasure, delight, wonder, astonishment, amazement, surprise.
≠ contempt.

admire *v* esteem, respect, revere, venerate, worship, idolize, adore, approve, praise, laud, applaud, appreciate, value.
≠ despise, censure.

admirer *n* follower, disciple, adherent, supporter, fan, enthusiast, devotee, worshipper, idolizer, suitor, boyfriend, girlfriend, sweetheart, lover.
≠ critic, opponent.

admissible *adj* acceptable, tolerable, tolerated, passable, allowable, permissible, allowed, permitted, lawful, legitimate, justifiable.
≠ inadmissible, illegitimate.

admission *n* confession, granting, acknowledgement, recognition, acceptance, allowance, concession, affirmation, declaration, profession, disclosure, divulgence, revelation, exposé.
≠ denial.

admit *v* **1** CONFESS, own (up), grant, acknowledge, recognize, accept, allow, concede, agree, affirm, declare, profess, disclose, divulge, reveal. **2** LET IN, allow to enter, give access, accept, receive, take in, introduce, initiate.
≠ **1** deny. **2** shut out, exclude.

admittance *n* admitting, admission, letting in, access, entrance, entry, acceptance, reception, introduction, initiation.
≠ exclusion.

adolescence *n* teens, puberty, youth, minority, boyhood, girlhood, development, immaturity, youthfulness, boyishness, girlishness.

adolescent *adj* teenage, young, youthful, juvenile, puerile, boyish, girlish, immature, growing, developing.
n teenager, youth, juvenile, minor.

adopt *v* take on, accept, assume, take up, appropriate, embrace, follow, choose, select, take in, foster, support, maintain, back, endorse, ratify, approve.
≠ repudiate, disown.

adorable *adj* lovable, dear, darling, precious, appealing, sweet, winsome, charming, enchanting, captivating, winning, delightful, pleasing, attractive, fetching.
≠ hateful, abominable.

adore *v* love, cherish, dote on, admire, esteem, honour, revere, venerate, worship, idolize, exalt, glorify.
≠ hate, abhor.

adorn *v* decorate, deck, bedeck, ornament, crown, trim, garnish, gild, enhance, embellish, doll up, enrich, grace.

adult *adj* grown-up, of age, full-grown, fully grown, developed, mature, ripe, ripened.
≠ immature.

adulterate *v* contaminate, pollute, taint, corrupt, defile, debase, dilute, water down, weaken, devalue, deteriorate.
≠ purify.

advance *v* **1** PROCEED, go forward, move on, go ahead, progress, prosper, flourish, thrive, improve. **2** ACCELERATE, speed, hasten, send forward. **3** FURTHER, promote, upgrade, foster, support, assist, benefit, facilitate, increase, grow. **4** *advance an idea*: present, submit, suggest, allege, cite, bring forward, offer, provide, supply, furnish. **5** *advance a sum of money*: lend, loan, pay beforehand, pay, give.
≠ **1** retreat. **2** retard. **3** impede.
n **1** PROGRESS, forward movement, onward movement, headway, step, advancement, furtherance, breakthrough, development, growth, increase, improvement, amelioration. **2** DEPOSIT, down payment, prepayment, credit, loan.
≠ **1** retreat, recession.
in advance beforehand, previously, early, earlier, sooner, ahead, in front, in the lead, in the forefront.
≠ later, behind.

advanced *adj* leading, foremost, ahead, forward, precocious, progressive, forward-looking, avant-garde, ultra-modern, sophisticated, complex, higher.
≠ backward, retarded, elementary.

advancement *n* furtherance, promotion, preferment, betterment, improvement, development, growth, rise, gain, advance, progress, headway.
≠ demotion, retardation.

advantage *n* **1** ASSET, blessing, benefit, good, welfare, interest, service, help, aid, assistance, use, avail, convenience, usefulness, utility, profit, gain, start. **2** LEAD, edge, upper hand, superiority, precedence, pre-eminence, sway.
≠ **1** disadvantage, drawback, hindrance.

advantageous *adj* beneficial, favourable, opportune, convenient, helpful, useful, worthwhile, valuable, profitable, gainful, remunerative, rewarding.
≠ disadvantageous, adverse, damaging.

adventure *n* exploit, venture, undertaking, enterprise, risk, hazard, chance, speculation, experience, incident, occurrence.

adventurous *adj* daring, intrepid, bold, audacious, headstrong, impetuous, reckless, rash, risky, venturesome, enterprising.
≠ cautious, chary, prudent.

adverse *adj* hostile, antagonistic, opposing, opposite, counter, contrary, conflicting, counter-productive, negative, disadvantageous, unfavourable, inauspicious, unfortunate, unlucky, inopportune, detrimental, harmful, noxious, injurious, hurtful, unfriendly, uncongenial.
≠ advantageous, favourable.

adversity *n* misfortune, ill fortune, bad luck, ill luck, reverse, hardship, hard times, misery, wretchedness, affliction, suffering, distress, sorrow, woe, trouble, trial, tribulation, calamity, disaster, catastrophe.
≠ prosperity.

advertise *v* publicize, promote, push, plug (*infml*), praise, hype (*sl*), trumpet, blazon, herald, announce, declare, proclaim, broadcast, publish, display, make known, inform, notify.

advertisement *n* advert (*infml*), ad (*infml*), commercial, publicity, promotion, plug (*infml*), hype (*sl*), display, blurb, announcement, notice, poster, bill, placard, leaflet, handbill, circular, handout, propaganda.

advice *n* **1** WARNING, caution, do's and don'ts, injunction, instruction, counsel, help, guidance, direction, suggestion, recommendation, opinion, view. **2** NOTIFICATION, notice, memorandum, communication, information, intelligence.

advisable *adj* suggested, recommended, sensible, wise, prudent, judicious, sound, profitable, beneficial, desirable, suitable, appropriate, apt, fitting, fit, proper, correct.
≠ inadvisable, foolish.

advise *v* **1** COUNSEL, guide, warn, forewarn, caution, instruct, teach, tutor, suggest, recommend, commend, urge. **2** NOTIFY, inform, tell, acquaint, make known, report.

adviser *n* counsellor, consultant, authority, guide, teacher, tutor, instructor, coach, helper, aide, right-hand man, mentor, confidant(e), counsel, lawyer.

advocate *v* defend, champion, campaign for, press for, argue for, plead for, justify, urge, encourage, advise, recommend, propose, promote, endorse, support, uphold, patronize, adopt, subscribe to, favour, countenance.
≠ impugn, disparage, deprecate.
n defender, supporter, upholder, champion, campaigner, pleader, vindicator, proponent, promoter, speaker, spokesperson.
≠ opponent, critic.

affable *adj* friendly, amiable, approachable, open, expansive, genial, good-humoured, good-natured, mild, benevolent, kindly, gracious, obliging, courteous, amicable, congenial, cordial, warm, sociable, pleasant, agreeable.
≠ unfriendly, reserved, reticent, cool.

affair *n* **1** BUSINESS, transaction, operation, proceeding, undertaking, activity, project, responsibility, interest, concern, matter, question, issue, subject, topic, circumstance, happening, occurrence, incident, episode, event. **2** *have an affair*: relationship, liaison, intrigue, love affair, romance, amour.

affect *v* **1** CONCERN, regard, involve, relate to, apply to, bear upon, impinge upon, act on, change, transform, alter, modify, influence, sway, prevail over, attack, strike, impress, interest, stir, move, touch, upset, disturb, perturb, trouble, overcome. **2** ADOPT, assume, put on, feign, simulate, imitate, fake, counterfeit, sham, pretend, profess, aspire to.

affectation *n* airs, pretentiousness, mannerism, pose, act, show, appearance, façade, pretence, sham, simulation, imitation, artificiality, insincerity.
≠ artlessness, ingenuousness.

affected *adj* assumed, put-on, feigned, simulated, artificial, fake, counterfeit, sham, phoney (*infml*), contrived, studied, precious, mannered, pretentious, pompous, stiff, unnatural, insincere.
≠ genuine, natural.

affection *n* fondness, attachment, devotion, love, tenderness, care, warmth, feeling, kindness, friendliness, goodwill, favour, liking, partiality, inclination, penchant, passion, desire.
≠ dislike, antipathy.

affectionate *adj* fond, attached, devoted, doting, loving, tender, caring, warm, warm-hearted, kind, friendly, amiable, cordial.
≠ cold, undemonstrative.

affirm *v* confirm, corroborate, endorse, ratify, certify, witness, testify, swear, maintain, state, assert, declare, pronounce.
≠ refute, deny.

affirmative *adj* agreeing, concurring, approving, assenting, positive, confirming, corroborative, emphatic.
≠ negative, dissenting.

afflict *v* strike, visit, trouble, burden, oppress, distress, grieve, pain, hurt, wound, harm, try, harass, beset, plague, torment, torture.
≠ comfort, solace.

affliction *n* distress, grief, sorrow, misery, depression, suffering, pain, torment, disease, illness, sickness, plague, curse, cross, ordeal, trial, tribulation, trouble, hardship, adversity, misfortune, calamity, disaster.
≠ comfort, consolation, solace, blessing.

affluence *n* wealthiness, wealth, riches, fortune, substance, property, prosperity, opulence, abundance, profusion, plenty.
≠ poverty.

affluent *adj* wealthy, rich, moneyed, loaded (*sl*), flush (*infml*), well-off, prosperous, well-to-do, opulent, comfortable.
≠ poor, impoverished.

afford *v* **1** HAVE ENOUGH FOR, spare,

allow, manage, sustain, bear. **2** PROVIDE, supply, furnish, give, grant, offer, impart, produce, yield, generate.

affront *v* offend, insult, abuse, snub, slight, provoke, displease, irritate, annoy, anger, vex, incense, outrage.
≠ compliment, appease.
n offence, insult, slur, rudeness, discourtesy, disrespect, indignity, snub, slight, wrong, injury, abuse, provocation, vexation, outrage.
≠ compliment.

afraid *adj* frightened, scared, alarmed, terrified, fearful, timorous, daunted, intimidated, faint-hearted, cowardly, reluctant, apprehensive, anxious, nervous, timid, distrustful, suspicious.
≠ unafraid, brave, bold, confident.

after *prep* following, subsequent to, in consequence of, as a result of, behind, below.
≠ before.

again *adv* once more, once again, another time, over again, afresh, anew, encore.

against *prep* **1** *against the wall*: abutting, adjacent to, close up to, touching, in contact with, on. **2** OPPOSITE TO, facing, fronting, in the face of, confronting, opposing, versus, opposed to, in opposition to, hostile to, resisting, in defiance of, in contrast to.
≠ **2** for, pro.

age *n* **1** ERA, epoch, day, days, generation, date, time, period, duration, span, years, aeon. **2** OLD AGE, maturity, elderliness, seniority, dotage, senility, decline.
≠ **2** youth.
v grow old, mature, ripen, mellow, season, decline, deteriorate, degenerate.

agency *n* **1** *recruitment agency*: bureau, office, department, organization, business, work. **2** MEANS, medium, instrumentality, power, force, influence, effect, intervention, action, activity, operation, mechanism, workings.

agent *n* **1** SUBSTITUTE, deputy, delegate, envoy, emissary, representative, rep (*infml*), broker, middleman, go-between, intermediary, negotiator, mover, doer, performer, operator, operative, functionary, worker. **2** INSTRUMENT, vehicle, channel, means, agency, cause, force.

aggravate *v* **1** *aggravate a problem*: exacerbate, worsen, inflame, increase, intensify, heighten, magnify, exaggerate. **2** (*infml*) ANNOY, irritate, vex, irk, exasperate, incense, provoke, tease, pester, harass.
≠ **1** improve, alleviate. **2** appease, mollify.

aggregate *n* total, sum, amount, whole, totality, entirety, generality, combination, collection, accumulation.
adj cumulative, accumulated, collected, combined, united, added, total, complete, composite, mixed, collective.
≠ individual, particular.

aggression *n* **1** ANTAGONISM, provocation, offence, injury, attack, offensive, assault, onslaught, raid, incursion, invasion, intrusion. **2** AGGRESSIVENESS, militancy, belligerence, combativeness, hostility.
≠ **1** peace, resistance. **2** passivity, gentleness.

aggressive *adj* argumentative, quarrelsome, contentious, belligerent, hostile, offensive, provocative, intrusive, invasive, bold, assertive, pushy, go-ahead, forceful, vigorous, zealous, ruthless, destructive.
≠ peaceable, friendly, submissive, timid.

aggrieved *adj* wronged, offended, hurt, injured, insulted, maltreated, ill-used, resentful, pained, distressed, saddened, unhappy, upset, annoyed.
≠ pleased.

aghast *adj* shocked, appalled, horrified, horror-struck, thunderstruck, stunned, stupefied, amazed, astonished, astounded, startled, confounded, dismayed.

agile *adj* active, lively, nimble, spry, sprightly, mobile, flexible, limber, lithe, fleet, quick, swift, brisk, prompt,

sharp, acute, alert, quick-witted, clever, adroit, deft.
≠ clumsy, stiff.

agitate *v* **1** ROUSE, arouse, stir up, excite, stimulate, incite, inflame, ferment, work up, worry, trouble, upset, alarm, disturb, unsettle, disquiet, discompose, fluster, ruffle, flurry, unnerve, confuse, distract, disconcert. **2** SHAKE, rattle, rock, stir, beat, churn, toss, convulse.
≠ **1** calm, tranquillize.

agitator *n* troublemaker, rabble-rouser, revolutionary, stirrer (*sl*), inciter, instigator.

agony *n* anguish, torment, torture, pain, spasm, throes, suffering, affliction, tribulation, distress, woe, misery, wretchedness.

agree *v* **1** CONCUR, see eye to eye, get on, settle, accord, match, suit, fit, tally, correspond, conform. **2** CONSENT, allow, permit, assent, accede, grant, admit, concede, yield, comply.
≠ **1** disagree, differ, conflict. **2** refuse.

agreeable *adj* pleasant, congenial, likable, attractive, delightful, enjoyable, gratifying, satisfying, palatable, acceptable, proper, appropriate, suitable, fitting, in accord, consistent.
≠ disagreeable, nasty, distasteful.

agreement *n* **1** SETTLEMENT, compact, covenant, treaty, pact, contract, deal, bargain, arrangement, understanding. **2** *be in agreement*: concurrence, accord, concord, unanimity, union, harmony, sympathy, affinity, compatibility, similarity, correspondence, consistency, conformity, compliance, adherence, acceptance.
≠ **2** disagreement.

agricultural *adj* agronomic, agrarian, farming, farmed, cultivated, rural, pastoral, bucolic.

Types of agricultural implement and machinery include: axe, chainsaw, clover broadcaster, fertilizer distributor, field sprinkler, fork, hayfork, pitchfork, hoe, potato planter, rake, hayrake, reaping hook, saw, scythe, shovel, sickle, spade, wheelbarrow, whetstone; all-terrain vehicle (ATV), baler, bale wrapper, cultivator, drill, corn drill, seed drill, fertilizer spreader, fork-lift truck, front end loader, harrow, combination seed-harrow, disc harrow, harvester, combine harvester, hedgecutter, irrigator, milking machine, mower, flail mower, muckspreader, potato planter, plough, reversible plough, wheel plough, power lift, rotary hoe, Rotovator®, scarifier, slurry tanker, sprayer, tedder, tractor, trailer.

agriculture *n* agronomics, farming, husbandry, cultivation, culture, tillage.

ahead *adv* forward, onward, leading, at the head, in front, in the lead, winning, at an advantage, advanced, superior, to the fore, in the forefront, in advance, before, earlier on.

aid *v* help, assist, succour, rally round, relieve, support, subsidize, sustain, second, serve, oblige, accommodate, favour, promote, boost, encourage, expedite, facilitate, ease.
≠ hinder, impede, obstruct.
n help, assistance, prop, support, relief, benefit, subsidy, donation, contribution, funding, grant, sponsorship, patronage, favour, encouragement, service.
≠ hindrance, impediment, obstruction.

ailing *adj* unwell, ill, sick, poorly, indisposed, out of sorts (*infml*), under the weather (*infml*), off-colour, suffering, languishing, sickly, diseased, invalid, infirm, unsound, frail, weak, feeble, failing.
≠ healthy, thriving, flourishing.

ailment *n* illness, sickness, complaint, malady, disease, infection, disorder, affliction, infirmity, disability, weakness.

aim *v* **1** POINT, direct, take aim, level, train, sight, zero in on (*infml*), target. **2** *aim to achieve*: aspire, want, wish, seek, resolve, purpose, intend, propose, mean, plan, design, strive, try, attempt, endeavour.
n aspiration, ambition, hope, dream, desire, wish, plan, design, scheme, purpose, motive, end, intention, object,

objective, target, mark, goal, direction, course.

aimless *adj* pointless, purposeless, unmotivated, irresolute, directionless, rambling, undirected, unguided, stray, chance, random, haphazard, erratic, unpredictable, wayward.
≠ purposeful, positive, determined.

air *n* **1** ATMOSPHERE, oxygen, sky, heavens, breath, puff, waft, draught, breeze, wind, blast. **2** APPEARANCE, look, aspect, aura, bearing, demeanour, manner, character, effect, impression, feeling.
v **1** *air a room*: ventilate, aerate, freshen. **2** *air an opinion*: utter, voice, express, give vent to, make known, communicate, tell, declare, reveal, disclose, divulge, expose, make public, broadcast, publish, circulate, disseminate, exhibit, display, parade, publicize.

aircraft

> *Types of aircraft include*: aeroplane, plane, jet, jumbo, Concorde, airbus, helicopter, monoplane, two-seater, air-ambulance, freighter, sea-plane, glider, hang-glider, microlight, hot-air balloon; fighter, spitfire, bomber, kite (*infml*), jump-jet, dive-bomber, chopper (*sl*), spy plane, delta-wing, swing-wing, troop-carrier, airship, turbojet, VTOL (vertical take-off and landing), warplane, zeppelin.

airless *adj* unventilated, stuffy, musty, stale, suffocating, stifling, sultry, muggy, close, heavy, oppressive.
≠ airy, fresh.

airy *adj* **1** ROOMY, spacious, open, well-ventilated, draughty, breezy, blowy, windy, gusty. **2** CHEERFUL, happy, light-hearted, high-spirited, lively, nonchalant, offhand.
≠ **1** airless, stuffy, close, heavy, oppressive.

aisle *n* gangway, corridor, passage, passageway, alleyway, walkway, path, lane.

alarm *v* frighten, scare, startle, put the wind up (*infml*), terrify, panic, unnerve, daunt, dismay, distress, agitate.
≠ reassure, calm, soothe.
n **1** FRIGHT, scare, fear, terror, panic, horror, shock, consternation, dismay, distress, anxiety, nervousness, apprehension, trepidation, uneasiness. **2** DANGER SIGNAL, alert, warning, distress signal, siren, bell, alarm-bell.
≠ **1** calmness, composure.

alarming *adj* frightening, scary, startling, terrifying, unnerving, daunting, ominous, threatening, dismaying, disturbing, distressing, shocking, dreadful.
≠ reassuring.

alcohol *n* drink, booze (*sl*), liquor, spirits, hard stuff (*sl*), intoxicant.

alcoholic *adj* intoxicating, brewed, fermented, distilled, strong, hard.
n drunk, drunkard, inebriate, hard drinker, dipsomaniac, wino (*sl*), alkie (*sl*).

alcove *n* niche, nook, recess, bay, corner, cubby-hole, compartment, cubicle, booth, carrel.

alert *adj* attentive, wide-awake, watchful, vigilant, on the lookout, sharp-eyed, observant, perceptive, sharp-witted, on the ball (*infml*), active, lively, spirited, quick, brisk, agile, nimble, ready, prepared, careful, heedful, circumspect, wary.
≠ slow, listless, unprepared.
v warn, forewarn, notify, inform, tip off, signal, alarm.

algae and lichen

> *Types of algae and lichen include*: anabaena, badderlocks, bladderwrack, bull kelp, carrageen, Ceylon moss, chlorella, conferva, desmid, diatom, dinaflagellate, dulse, euglena, fucoid, fucus, gulfweed, Irish moss, kelp, laminaria, laver, lecanora, nostoc, nullipore, oak moss, oarweed, peacock's tail, redware, reindeer moss, rock tripe, rockweed, sargassum, sea lace, sea lettuce, sea tangle, seaware, sea wrack, Spanish moss, spirogyra, stonewort, wrack.

alias *n* pseudonym, false name, assumed name, nom de guerre, nom de plume, pen name, stage name, nickname, sobriquet.

prep also known as, also called, otherwise, formerly.

alibi *n* defence, justification, story, explanation, excuse, pretext, reason.

alien *adj* strange, unfamiliar, outlandish, incongruous, foreign, exotic, extraterrestial, extraneous, remote, estranged, separated, opposed, contrary, conflicting, antagonistic, incompatible.
≠ akin.
n foreigner, immigrant, newcomer, stranger, outsider.
≠ native.

alight[1] *v* descend, get down, dismount, get off, disembark, land, touch down, come down, come to rest, settle, light, perch.
≠ ascend, board.

alight[2] *adj* lighted, lit, ignited, on fire, burning, blazing, ablaze, flaming, fiery, lit up, illuminated, bright, radiant, shining, brilliant.
≠ dark.

align *v* **1** STRAIGHTEN, range, line up, make parallel, even (up), adjust, regulate, regularize, order, co-ordinate. **2** ALLY, side, sympathize, associate, affiliate, join, co-operate, agree.

alike *adj* similar, resembling, comparable, akin, analogous, corresponding, equivalent, equal, the same, identical, duplicate, parallel, even, uniform.
≠ dissimilar, unlike, different.
adv similarly, analogously, correspondingly, equally, in common.

alive *adj* **1** LIVING, having life, live, animate, breathing, existent, in existence, real. **2** LIVELY, animated, spirited, awake, alert, active, brisk, energetic, vigorous, zestful, vivacious, vibrant, vital.
≠ **1** dead, extinct. **2** lifeless, apathetic.

all *adj* **1** EACH, every, each and every, every single, every one of, the whole of, every bit of. **2** COMPLETE, entire, full, total, utter, outright, perfect, greatest.
≠ **1** no, none.
n everything, sum, total, aggregate, total amount, whole amount, whole, entirety, utmost, comprehensiveness, universality.
≠ nothing, none.
adv completely, entirely, wholly, fully, totally, utterly, altogether, wholesale.

all right *adj* **1** SATISFACTORY, passable, unobjectionable, acceptable, allowable, adequate, fair, average, OK (*infml*). **2** *are you all right?*: well, healthy, unhurt, uninjured, unharmed, unimpaired, whole, sound, safe, secure.
≠ **1** unacceptable, inadequate.
adv satisfactorily, well enough, passably, unobjectionably, acceptably, suitably, appropriately, adequately, reasonably, OK (*infml*).
≠ unsatisfactorily, unacceptably.

allay *v* alleviate, relieve, soothe, ease, smooth, calm, tranquillize, quiet, quell, pacify, mollify, soften, blunt, lessen, reduce, diminish, check, moderate.
≠ exacerbate, intensify.

allegation *n* accusation, charge, claim, profession, assertion, affirmation, declaration, statement, testimony, plea.

allege *v* assert, affirm, declare, state, attest, maintain, insist, hold, contend, claim, profess, plead.

alleged *adj* supposed, reputed, putative, inferred, so-called, professed, declared, stated, claimed, described, designated, doubtful, dubious, suspect, suspicious.

allegiance *n* loyalty, fidelity, faithfulness, constancy, duty, obligation, obedience, devotion, support, adherence, friendship.
≠ disloyalty, enmity.

allergic *adj* sensitive, hypersensitive, susceptible, affected, incompatible, averse, disinclined, opposed, hostile, antagonistic.
≠ tolerant.

alleviate *v* relieve, soothe, ease, palliate, mitigate, soften, cushion, dull, deaden, allay, abate, lessen, reduce, diminish, check, moderate, temper, subdue.
≠ aggravate.

alliance *n* confederation, federation, association, affiliation, coalition, league, bloc, cartel, conglomerate,

consortium, syndicate, guild, union, partnership, marriage, agreement, compact, bond, pact, treaty, combination, connection.
≠ separation, divorce, estrangement, enmity, hostility.

allocate *v* assign, designate, budget, allow, earmark, set aside, allot, apportion, share out, distribute, dispense, mete.

allocation *n* allotment, lot, apportionment, measure, share, portion, stint, ration, quota, budget, allowance, grant.

allot *v* divide, ration, apportion, share out, distribute, dispense, mete, dole out, allocate, assign, designate, budget, allow, grant, earmark, set aside.

allotment *n* division, partition, allocation, apportionment, measure, percentage, lot, portion, share, stint, ration, quota, allowance, grant.

all-out *adj* complete, full, total, undivided, comprehensive, exhaustive, thorough, intensive, thoroughgoing, wholesale, vigorous, powerful, full-scale, no-holds-barred, maximum, utmost, unlimited, unrestrained, resolute, determined.
≠ perfunctory, half-hearted.

allow *v* **1** PERMIT, let, enable, authorize, sanction, approve, tolerate, put up with, endure, suffer. **2** ADMIT, confess, own, acknowledge, concede, grant. **3** *allow two hours for the journey*: allot, allocate, assign, apportion, afford, give, provide.
≠ **1** forbid, prevent. **2** deny.
allow for take into account, make provision for, make allowances for, provide for, foresee, plan for, arrange for, bear in mind, keep in mind, consider, include.
≠ discount.

allowance *n* **1** ALLOTMENT, lot, amount, allocation, portion, share, ration, quota. **2** REBATE, reduction, deduction, discount, concession, subsidy, weighting. **3** PAYMENT, remittance, pocket money, grant, maintenance, stipend, pension, annuity.

alloy *n* blend, compound, composite, amalgam, combination, mixture, fusion, coalescence.

allure *v* lure, entice, seduce, lead on, tempt, coax, cajole, persuade, win over, disarm, charm, enchant, attract, interest, fascinate, captivate, entrance, beguile.
≠ repel.
n lure, enticement, seduction, temptation, appeal, attraction, magnetism, fascination, glamour, captivation, charm, enchantment.

allusion *n* mention, reference, citation, quotation, remark, observation, suggestion, hint, intimation, implication, insinuation.

ally *n* confederate, associate, leaguer, consort, partner, sidekick, colleague, co-worker, collaborator, helper, helpmate, accomplice, accessory, friend.
≠ antagonist, enemy.
v confederate, affiliate, league, associate, collaborate, join forces, band together, team up, fraternize, side, join, connect, link, marry, unite, unify, amalgamate, combine.
≠ estrange, separate.

almighty *adj* **1** OMNIPOTENT, all-powerful, supreme, absolute, great, invincible. **2** ENORMOUS, severe, intense, overwhelming, overpowering, terrible, awful, desperate.
≠ **1** impotent, weak.

almost *adv* nearly, well-nigh, practically, virtually, just about, as good as, all but, close to, not far from, approaching, nearing, not quite, about, approximately.

alone *adj* only, sole, single, unique, solitary, separate, detached, unconnected, isolated, apart, by oneself, by itself, on one's own, lonely, lonesome, deserted, abandoned, forsaken, forlorn, desolate, unaccompanied, unescorted, unattended, solo, single-handed, unaided, unassisted, mere.
≠ together, accompanied, escorted.

aloof *adj* distant, remote, offish, standoffish, haughty, supercilious, unapproachable, inaccessible, detached,

forbidding, cool, chilly, cold, unsympathetic, unresponsive, indifferent, uninterested, reserved, unforthcoming, unfriendly, unsociable, formal.
≠ sociable, friendly, concerned.

aloud *adv* out loud, audibly, intelligibly, clearly, plainly, distinctly, loudly, resoundingly, sonorously, noisily, vociferously.
≠ silently.

alphabets and writing systems

Alphabets and writing systems include: Byzantine, Chalcidian alphabet, cuneiform, Cyrillic, devanagari, estrangelo, finger-alphabet, futhark, Glagol, Glossic, Greek, Gurmukhi, hieroglyphs, hiragana, ideograph, initial teaching alphabet (i.t.a.), International Phonetic Alphabet (IPA), kana, kanji, katakana, Kufic, linear A, linear B, logograph, nagari, naskhi, ogam, pictograph, romaji, Roman, runic, syllabary.

also *adv* too, as well, and, plus, along with, including, as well as, additionally, in addition, besides, further, furthermore, moreover.

alter *v* change, vary, diversify, modify, qualify, shift, transpose, adjust, adapt, convert, turn, transmute, transform, reform, reshape, remodel, recast, revise, amend, emend.
≠ fix.

alteration *n* change, variation, variance, difference, diversification, shift, transposition, modification, adjustment, adaptation, conversion, transformation, transfiguration, metamorphosis, reformation, reshaping, remodelling, revision, amendment.
≠ fixity.

alternate *v* interchange, reciprocate, rotate, take turns, follow one another, replace each other, substitute, change, alter, vary, oscillate, fluctuate, intersperse.
adj alternating, every other, every second, interchanging, reciprocal, rotating, alternative.

alternative *n* option, choice, selection, preference, other, recourse, substitute, back-up.
adj substitute, second, another, other, different, unorthodox, unconventional, fringe, alternate.

altitude *n* height, elevation, loftiness, tallness, stature.
≠ depth.

altogether *adv* totally, completely, entirely, wholly, fully, utterly, absolutely, quite, perfectly, thoroughly, in all, all told, in toto, all in all, as a whole, on the whole, generally, in general.

altruistic *adj* unselfish, self-sacrificing, disinterested, public-spirited, philanthropic, charitable, humanitarian, benevolent, generous, considerate, humane.
≠ selfish.

always *adv* every time, consistently, invariably, without exception, unfailingly, regularly, repeatedly, continually, constantly, perpetually, unceasingly, eternally, endlessly, evermore, forever, ever.
≠ never.

amalgamate *v* merge, blend, mingle, commingle, intermix, homogenize, incorporate, alloy, integrate, compound, fuse, coalesce, synthesize, combine, unite, unify, ally.
≠ separate.

amateur *n* non-professional, layman, ham (*infml*), dilettante, dabbler, enthusiast, fancier, buff (*infml*).
≠ professional.
adj non-professional, lay, unpaid, unqualified, untrained, amateurish, inexpert, unprofessional.
≠ professional.

amaze *v* surprise, startle, astonish, astound, stun, stupefy, daze, stagger, floor (*infml*), dumbfound, flabbergast (*infml*), shock, dismay, disconcert, confound, bewilder.

amazement *n* surprise, astonishment, shock, dismay, confusion, perplexity, bewilderment, admiration, wonderment, wonder, marvel.

ambassador *n* emissary, envoy,

legate, diplomat, consul, plenipotentiary, deputy, representative, agent, minister, apostle.

ambiguity *n* double meaning, double entendre, equivocality, equivocation, enigma, puzzle, confusion, obscurity, unclearness, vagueness, woolliness, dubiousness, doubt, doubtfulness, uncertainty.
≠ clarity.

ambiguous *adj* double-meaning, equivocal, multivocal, double-edged, back-handed, cryptic, enigmatic, puzzling, confusing, obscure, unclear, vague, indefinite, woolly, confused, dubious, doubtful, uncertain, inconclusive, indeterminate.
≠ clear, definite.

ambition *n* **1** ASPIRATION, aim, goal, target, objective, intent, purpose, design, object, ideal, dream, hope, wish, desire, yearning, longing, hankering, craving, hunger. **2** *a woman of ambition*: enterprise, drive, push, thrust, striving, eagerness, commitment, zeal.
≠ **2** apathy, diffidence.

ambitious *adj* **1** ASPIRING, hopeful, desirous, intent, purposeful, pushy, bold, assertive, go-ahead, enterprising, driving, energetic, enthusiastic, eager, keen, striving, industrious, zealous. **2** FORMIDABLE, hard, difficult, arduous, strenuous, demanding, challenging, exacting, impressive, grandiose, elaborate.
≠ **1** lazy, unassuming. **2** modest, uninspiring.

ambivalent *adj* contradictory, conflicting, clashing, warring, opposed, inconsistent, mixed, confused, fluctuating, vacillating, wavering, hesitant, irresolute, undecided, unresolved, unsettled, uncertain, unsure, doubtful, debatable, inconclusive.

amble *v* walk, saunter, toddle (*infml*), stroll, promenade, wander, drift, meander, ramble.
≠ stride, march.

ambush *n* waylaying, surprise attack, trap, snare, cover, hiding-place.
v lie in wait, waylay, surprise, trap, ensnare.

amenable *adj* accommodating, flexible, open, agreeable, persuadable, compliant, tractable, submissive, responsive, susceptible, liable, responsible.
≠ intractable.

amend *v* revise, correct, rectify, emend, fix, repair, mend, remedy, redress, reform, change, alter, adjust, modify, qualify, enhance, improve, ameliorate, better.
≠ impair, worsen.

amendment *n* revision, correction, corrigendum, rectification, emendation, repair, remedy, reform, change, alteration, adjustment, modification, qualification, clarification, addendum, addition, adjunct, improvement.
≠ impairment, deterioration.

amends *n* atonement, expiation, requital, satisfaction, recompense, compensation, indemnification, indemnity, reparation, redress, restoration, restitution.

amiable *adj* affable, friendly, approachable, genial, cheerful, good-tempered, good-natured, kind, obliging, charming, engaging, likable, pleasant, agreeable, congenial, companionable, sociable.
≠ unfriendly, curt, hostile.

amid *prep* amidst, midst, in the midst of, in the thick of, among, amongst, in the middle of, surrounded by.

amino acid

> *Amino acids include*: alanine, arginine, asparagine, aspartic acid, cysteine, glutamic acid, glutamine, glycine, histidine, isoleucine, leucine, lysine, methionine, phenylalanine, proline, serine, threonine, trytophan, tyrosine, valine.

amnesty *n* pardon, forgiveness, absolution, mercy, lenience, indulgence, reprieve, remission, dispensation, immunity, oblivion.

among *prep* amongst, between, in the middle of, surrounded by, amid, amidst, midst, in the midst of, in the thick of, with, together with.

amount *n* quantity, number, sum, total, sum total, whole, entirety, aggregate, lot, quota, supply, volume, mass, bulk, measure, magnitude, extent, expanse.
amount to add up to, total, aggregate, come to, make, equal, mean, be tantamount to, be equivalent to, approximate to, become, grow.

amphibians

> *Amphibians include*: frog, bullfrog, tree frog, toad, horned toad, midwife toad, natterjack, newt, eft, salamander, conger eel, axolotl.

ample *adj* large, big, extensive, expansive, broad, wide, full, voluminous, roomy, spacious, commodious, great, considerable, substantial, handsome, generous, bountiful, munificent, liberal, lavish, copious, abundant, plentiful, plenty, unrestricted, profuse, rich.
≠ insufficient, inadequate, meagre.

amplify *v* enlarge, magnify, expand, dilate, fill out, bulk out, add to, supplement, augment, increase, extend, lengthen, widen, broaden, develop, elaborate, enhance, boost, intensify, strengthen, deepen, heighten, raise.
≠ reduce, decrease, abridge.

amputate *v* cut off, remove, sever, dissever, separate, dock, lop, curtail, truncate.

amuse *v* entertain, divert, regale, make laugh, tickle (*infml*), crease (*infml*), slay (*infml*), cheer (up), gladden, enliven, please, charm, delight, enthral, engross, absorb, interest, occupy, recreate, relax.
≠ bore, displease.

amusement *n* entertainment, diversion, distraction, fun, enjoyment, pleasure, delight, merriment, mirth, hilarity, laughter, joke, prank, game, sport, recreation, hobby, pastime, interest.
≠ boredom, monotony.

amusing *adj* funny, humorous, hilarious, comical, laughable, ludicrous, droll, witty, facetious, jocular, jolly, enjoyable, pleasant, charming, delightful, entertaining, interesting.
≠ dull, boring.

anaemic *adj* bloodless, ashen, chalky, livid, pasty, pallid, sallow, whey-faced, pale, wan, colourless, insipid, weak, feeble, ineffectual, enervated, frail, infirm, sickly.
≠ ruddy, sanguine, full-blooded.

anaesthetize *v* desensitize, numb, deaden, dull, drug, dope, stupefy.

analogy *n* comparison, simile, metaphor, likeness, resemblance, similarity, parallel, correspondence, equivalence, relation, correlation, agreement.

analyse *v* break down, separate, divide, take apart, dissect, anatomize, reduce, resolve, sift, investigate, study, examine, scrutinize, review, interpret, test, judge, evaluate, estimate, consider.

analysis *n* breakdown, separation, division, dissection, reduction, resolution, sifting, investigation, enquiry, study, examination, scrutiny, review, exposition, explication, explanation, interpretation, test, judgement, opinion, evaluation, estimation, reasoning.
≠ synthesis.

analytic *adj* analytical, dissecting, detailed, in-depth, searching, critical, questioning, enquiring, inquisitive, investigative, diagnostic, systematic, methodical, logical, rational, interpretative, explanatory, expository, studious.

anarchic *adj* lawless, ungoverned, anarchistic, libertarian, nihilist, revolutionary, rebellious, mutinous, riotous, chaotic, disordered, confused, disorganized.
≠ submissive, orderly.

anarchist *n* revolutionary, rebel, insurgent, libertarian, nihilist, terrorist.

anarchy *n* lawlessness, unrule, misrule, anarchism, revolution, rebellion, insurrection, mutiny, riot, pandemonium, chaos, disorder, confusion.
≠ rule, control, order.

anathema *n* aversion, abhorrence, abomination, object of loathing, bête noire, bugbear, bane, curse, proscription, taboo.

anatomical terms

> *Anatomical terms include*: aural, biceps, bone, cardiac, cartilage, cerebral, dental, diaphragm, dorsal, duodenal, elbow, epidermis, epiglottis, Fallopian tubes, foreskin, funny bone, gastric, genitalia, gingival, gristle, groin, gullet, hamstring, helix, hepatic, hock, intercostal, jugular, lachrymal, ligament, lumbar, mammary, membral, muscle, nasal, neural, ocular, oesophagus, optical, pectoral, pedal, pulmonary, renal, spine, tendon, triceps, umbilicus, uterus, uvula, voice-box, vulva, windpipe, womb. *see also* **bones**; **brain**; **ear**; **eye**; **glands**; **heart**; **mouth**; **tooth**; **vein**.

ancestor *n* forebear, forefather, progenitor, predecessor, forerunner, precursor, antecedent.
≠ descendant.

ancestral *adj* familial, parental, genealogical, lineal, hereditary, genetic.

ancestry *n* ancestors, forebears, forefathers, progenitors, parentage, family, lineage, line, descent, blood, race, stock, roots, pedigree, genealogy, extraction, derivation, origin, heritage, heredity.

anchor *v* moor, berth, tie up, make fast, fasten, attach, affix, fix.

> *Types of anchor include*: car, double fluked, grapnel, kedge, killick, mushroom, navy, sea, stocked, stockless, yachtsman.

ancient *adj* **1** OLD, aged, time-worn, age-old, antique, antediluvian, prehistoric, fossilized, primeval, immemorial. **2** OLD-FASHIONED, out-of-date, antiquated, archaic, obsolete, bygone, early, original.
≠ **1** recent, contemporary. **2** modern, up-to-date.

anecdote *n* story, tale, yarn, sketch, reminiscence.

angel *n* **1** *angel of God*: divine messenger.

> *The nine orders of angels are*: seraph, cherub, throne, domination/dominion, virtue, power, principality, archangel, angel.

2 DARLING, treasure, saint, paragon, ideal.
≠ **1** devil, fiend.

angelic *adj* cherubic, seraphic, celestial, heavenly, divine, holy, pious, saintly, pure, innocent, unworldly, virtuous, lovely, beautiful, adorable.
≠ devilish, fiendish.

anger *n* annoyance, irritation, antagonism, displeasure, irritability, temper, pique, vexation, ire, rage, fury, wrath, exasperation, outrage, indignation, gall, bitterness, rancour, resentment.
≠ forgiveness, forbearance.
v annoy, irritate, aggravate (*infml*), wind up (*infml*), vex, irk, rile, miff (*infml*), needle, nettle, bother, ruffle, provoke, antagonize, offend, affront, gall, madden, enrage, incense, infuriate, exasperate, outrage.
≠ please, appease, calm.

angle *n* **1** CORNER, nook, bend, flexure, hook, crook, elbow, knee, crotch, edge, point. **2** ASPECT, outlook, facet, side, approach, direction, position, standpoint, viewpoint, point of view, slant, perspective.

angry *adj* annoyed, cross, irritated, aggravated (*infml*), displeased, uptight (*infml*), irate, mad (*infml*), enraged, incensed, infuriated, furious, raging, passionate, heated, hot, exasperated, outraged, indignant, bitter, resentful.
≠ content, happy, calm.

animal *n* creature, mammal, beast, brute, barbarian, savage, monster, cur, pig, swine.

> *Animals include*: cat, dog, hamster, gerbil, mouse, rat, rabbit, hare, fox, badger, beaver, mole, otter, weasel, ferret, ermine, mink, hedgehog, squirrel, horse, pig, cow, bull, goat, sheep; monkey, lemur, gibbon, ape, chimpanzee, orang-utan, baboon, gorilla; seal, sea lion, dolphin,

walrus, whale; lion, tiger, cheetah, puma, panther, cougar, jaguar, ocelot, leopard; aardvark, armadillo, wolf, wolverine, hyena, mongoose, skunk, racoon, wombat, platypus, koala, polecat; deer, antelope, gazelle, eland, impala, reindeer, elk, caribou, moose; wallaby, kangaroo, bison, buffalo, gnu, camel, zebra, llama, panda, giant panda, grizzly bear, polar bear, giraffe, hippopotamus, rhinoceros, elephant. *see also* **amphibian**; **bird**; **butterflies and moths**; **cats**; **cattle**; **dog**; **fish**; **horses**; **insects**; **invertebrates**; **mammals**; **marsupials**; **molluscs**; **monkey**; **reptiles**; **rodents**.

adj bestial, brutish, inhuman, savage, wild, instinctive, bodily, physical, carnal, fleshly, sensual.

animate *adj* alive, living, live, breathing, conscious.
≠ inanimate.

animated *adj* lively, spirited, buoyant, vibrant, ebullient, vivacious, alive, vital, quick, brisk, vigorous, energetic, active, passionate, impassioned, vehement, ardent, fervent, glowing, radiant, excited, enthusiastic, eager.
≠ lethargic, sluggish, inert.

animosity *n* ill feeling, ill-will, acrimony, bitterness, rancour, resentment, spite, malice, malignity, malevolence, hate, hatred, loathing, antagonism, hostility, enmity, feud.
≠ goodwill.

annex *v* **1** ADD, append, affix, attach, fasten, adjoin, join, connect, unite, incorporate. **2** ACQUIRE, appropriate, seize, usurp, occupy, conquer, take over.

annexe *n* wing, extension, attachment, addition, supplement, expansion.

annihilate *v* eliminate, eradicate, obliterate, erase, wipe out, liquidate (*infml*), murder, assassinate, exterminate, extinguish, raze, destroy, abolish.

anniversaries

Names of wedding anniversaries include: 1st cotton, 2nd paper, 3rd leather, 4th flowers/fruit, 5th wood, 6th iron/sugar, 7th copper/wool, 8th bronze/pottery, 9th pottery/willow, 10th tin, 11th steel, 12th silk/linen, 13th lace, 14th ivory, 15th crystal, 20th china, 25th silver, 30th pearl, 35th coral, 40th ruby, 45th sapphire, 50th gold, 55th emerald, 60th diamond, 70th platinum.

annotate *v* note, gloss, comment, explain, interpret, elucidate.

annotation *n* note, footnote, gloss, comment, commentary, exegesis, explanation, elucidation.

announce *v* declare, proclaim, report, state, reveal, disclose, divulge, make known, notify, intimate, promulgate, propound, publish, broadcast, advertise, publicize, blazon.
≠ suppress.

announcement *n* declaration, proclamation, report, statement, communiqué, dispatch, bulletin, notification, intimation, revelation, disclosure, divulgence, publication, broadcast, advertisement.

announcer *n* broadcaster, newscaster, newsreader, commentator, compère, master of ceremonies, MC, town crier, herald, messenger.

annoy *v* irritate, rile, aggravate (*infml*), displease, anger, vex, irk, madden, exasperate, tease, provoke, ruffle, trouble, disturb, bother, pester, plague, harass, molest.
≠ please, gratify, comfort.

annoyance *n* **1** NUISANCE, pest, disturbance, bother, trouble, bore, bind (*sl*), pain (*infml*), headache (*infml*), tease, provocation. **2** *express one's annoyance*: irritation, aggravation (*infml*), displeasure, anger, vexation, exasperation, harassment.
≠ **2** pleasure.

annoyed *adj* irritated, cross, displeased, angry, vexed, piqued, exasperated, provoked, harassed.
≠ pleased.

annoying *adj* irritating, aggravating (*infml*), vexatious, irksome, troublesome, bothersome, tiresome, trying, maddening, exasperating,

galling, offensive, teasing, provoking, harassing.
≠ pleasing, welcome.

annul *v* nullify, invalidate, void, rescind, abrogate, suspend, cancel, abolish, quash, repeal, revoke, countermand, negate, retract, recall, reverse.
≠ enact, restore.

anoint *v* **1** OIL, grease, lubricate, embrocate, rub, smear, daub. **2** BLESS, consecrate, sanctify, dedicate.

anomalous *adj* abnormal, atypical, exceptional, irregular, inconsistent, incongruous, deviant, freakish, eccentric, peculiar, odd, unusual, singular, rare.
≠ normal, regular, ordinary.

anomaly *n* abnormality, exception, irregularity, inconsistency, incongruity, aberration, deviation, divergence, departure, freak, misfit, eccentricity, peculiarity, oddity, rarity.

anonymous *adj* unnamed, nameless, unsigned, unacknowledged, unspecified, unidentified, unknown, incognito, faceless, impersonal, nondescript, unexceptional.
≠ named, signed, identifiable, distinctive.

answer *n* **1** REPLY, acknowledgement, response, reaction, rejoinder, retort, riposte, comeback, retaliation, rebuttal, vindication, defence, plea.
2 SOLUTION, explanation.
v **1** REPLY, acknowledge, respond, react, retort, retaliate, refute, solve.
2 *answer one's needs*: fulfil, fill, meet, satisfy, match up to, correspond, correlate, conform, agree, fit, suit, serve, pass.
answer back talk back, retort, riposte, retaliate, contradict, disagree, argue, dispute, rebut.

answerable *adj* liable, responsible, accountable, chargeable, blameworthy, to blame.

antagonism *n* hostility, opposition, rivalry, antipathy, ill feeling, ill-will, animosity, friction, discord, dissension, contention, conflict.
≠ rapport, sympathy, agreement.

antagonist *n* opponent, adversary, enemy, foe, rival, competitor, contestant, contender.
≠ ally, supporter.

antagonistic *adj* conflicting, opposed, adverse, at variance, incompatible, hostile, belligerent, contentious, unfriendly, ill-disposed, averse.
≠ sympathetic, friendly.

antagonize *v* alienate, estrange, disaffect, repel, embitter, offend, insult, provoke, annoy, irritate, anger, incense.
≠ disarm.

anthem *n* hymn, song, chorale, psalm, canticle, chant.

anthology *n* selection, collection, compilation, compendium, digest, treasury, miscellany.

anticipate *v* **1** FORESTALL, pre-empt, intercept, prevent, obviate, preclude.
2 EXPECT, foresee, predict, forecast, look for, await, look forward to, hope for, bank on, count upon.

anticlimax *n* bathos, comedown, let-down, disappointment, fiasco.

antics *n* foolery, tomfoolery, silliness, buffoonery, clowning, frolics, capers, skylarking, playfulness, mischief, tricks, monkey-tricks, pranks, stunts, doings.

antidote *n* remedy, cure, counter-agent, antitoxin, neutralizer, countermeasure, corrective.

antipathy *n* aversion, dislike, hate, hatred, loathing, abhorrence, distaste, disgust, repulsion, antagonism, animosity, ill-will, bad blood, enmity, hostility, opposition, incompatibility.
≠ sympathy, affection, rapport.

antique *adj* antiquarian, ancient, old, veteran, vintage, quaint, antiquated, old-fashioned, outdated, archaic, obsolete.
n antiquity, relic, bygone, period piece, heirloom, curio, museum piece, curiosity, rarity.

antiquity *n* ancient times, time immemorial, distant past, olden days, age, old age, oldness, agedness.
≠ modernity, novelty.

antiseptic *adj* disinfectant, medicated, aseptic, germ-free, clean, pure, unpolluted, uncontaminated, sterile, sterilized, sanitized, sanitary, hygienic. *n* disinfectant, germicide, bactericide, purifier, cleanser.

antisocial *adj* asocial, unacceptable, disruptive, disorderly, rebellious, belligerent, antagonistic, hostile, unfriendly, unsociable, uncommunicative, reserved, retiring, withdrawn, alienated, unapproachable.
≠ sociable, gregarious.

anxiety *n* worry, concern, care, distress, nervousness, apprehension, dread, foreboding, misgiving, uneasiness, restlessness, fretfulness, impatience, suspense, tension, stress.
≠ calm, composure, serenity.

anxious *adj* worried, concerned, nervous, apprehensive, afraid, fearful, uneasy, restless, fretful, impatient, in suspense, on tenterhooks, tense, taut, distressed, disturbed, troubled, tormented, tortured.
≠ calm, composed.

apart *adv* **1** SEPARATELY, independently, individually, singly, alone, on one's own, by oneself, privately, aside, to one side, away, afar, distant, aloof, excluded, isolated, cut off, separated, divorced, separate, distinct. **2** *tear apart*: to pieces, to bits, into parts, in pieces, in bits, piecemeal.
≠ **1** connected. **2** together.

apathetic *adj* uninterested, uninvolved, indifferent, cool, unemotional, emotionless, impassive, unmoved, unconcerned, cold, unfeeling, numb, unresponsive, passive, listless, unambitious.
≠ enthusiastic, involved, concerned, feeling, responsive.

apathy *n* uninterestedness, indifference, coolness, impassivity, unconcern, coldness, insensibility, passivity, listlessness, lethargy, sluggishness, torpor, inertia.
≠ enthusiasm, interest, concern.

ape *v* copy, imitate, echo, mirror, parrot, mimic, take off, caricature, parody, mock, counterfeit, affect.
n monkey, chimpanzee, gibbon, gorilla, baboon, orang-utan.

aplomb *n* composure, calmness, equanimity, poise, balance, coolness, confidence, assurance, self-assurance, audacity.
≠ discomposure.

apocryphal *adj* unauthenticated, unverified, unsubstantiated, unsupported, questionable, spurious, equivocal, doubtful, dubious, fabricated, concocted, fictitious, imaginary, legendary, mythical.
≠ authentic, true.

apologetic *adj* sorry, repentant, penitent, contrite, remorseful, conscience-stricken, regretful, rueful.
≠ unrepentant, impenitent, defiant.

apology *n* acknowledgement, confession, excuse, explanation, justification, vindication, defence, plea.
≠ defiance.

appal *v* horrify, shock, outrage, disgust, dismay, disconcert, daunt, intimidate, unnerve, alarm, scare, frighten, terrify.
≠ reassure, encourage.

appalling *adj* horrifying, horrific, harrowing, shocking, outrageous, atrocious, disgusting, awful, dreadful, frightful, terrible, dire, grim, hideous, ghastly, horrible, horrid, loathsome, daunting, intimidating, unnerving, alarming, frightening, terrifying.
≠ reassuring, encouraging.

apparatus *n* machine, appliance, gadget, device, contraption, equipment, gear, tackle, outfit, tools, implements, utensils, materials, machinery, system, mechanism, means.

apparent *adj* seeming, outward, visible, evident, noticeable, perceptible, plain, clear, distinct, marked, unmistakable, obvious, manifest, patent, open, declared.
≠ hidden, obscure.

apparently *adv* seemingly, ostensibly, outwardly, superficially, plainly, clearly, obviously, manifestly, patently.

apparition *n* ghost, spectre, phantom,

spirit, chimera, vision, manifestation, materialization, presence.

appeal *n* **1** REQUEST, application, petition, suit, solicitation, plea, entreaty, supplication, prayer, invocation. **2** ATTRACTION, allure, interest, fascination, enchantment, charm, attractiveness, winsomeness, beauty, charisma, magnetism.
v **1** *appeal for help*: ask, request, call, apply, address, petition, sue, solicit, plead, beg, beseech, implore, entreat, supplicate, pray, invoke, call upon. **2** ATTRACT, draw, allure, lure, tempt, entice, invite, interest, engage, fascinate, charm, please.

appear *v* **1** ARRIVE, enter, turn up, attend, materialize, develop, show (up), come into sight, come into view, loom, rise, surface, arise, occur, crop up, come to light, come out, emerge, issue, be published. **2** SEEM, look, turn out. **3** *appear in a show*: act, perform, play, take part.
≠ **1** disappear, vanish.

appearance *n* **1** APPEARING, arrival, advent, coming, rise, emergence, début, introduction. **2** LOOK, expression, face, aspect, air, bearing, demeanour, manner, looks, figure, form, semblance, show, front, guise, illusion, impression, image.
≠ **1** disappearance.

appendix *n* addition, appendage, adjunct, addendum, supplement, epilogue, codicil, postscript, rider.

appetite *n* hunger, stomach, relish, zest, taste, propensity, inclination, liking, desire, longing, yearning, craving, eagerness, passion, zeal.
≠ distaste.

appetizing *adj* mouthwatering, tempting, inviting, appealing, palatable, tasty, delicious, scrumptious (*infml*), succulent, piquant, savoury.
≠ disgusting, distasteful.

applaud *v* clap, cheer, acclaim, compliment, congratulate, approve, commend, praise, laud, eulogize, extol.
≠ criticize, censure.

applause *n* ovation, clapping, cheering, cheers, acclaim, acclamation, accolade, congratulation, approval, commendation, praise.
≠ criticism, censure.

appliance *n* machine, device, contrivance, contraption, gadget, tool, implement, instrument, apparatus, mechanism.

applicable *adj* relevant, pertinent, apposite, apt, appropriate, fitting, suited, useful, suitable, fit, proper, valid, legitimate.
≠ inapplicable, inappropriate.

applicant *n* candidate, interviewee, contestant, competitor, aspirant, suitor, petitioner, inquirer.

application *n* **1** REQUEST, appeal, petition, suit, claim, inquiry. **2** RELEVANCE, pertinence, function, purpose, use, value. **3** DILIGENCE, industry, assiduity, effort, commitment, dedication, perseverance, keenness, attentiveness.

apply *v* **1** REQUEST, ask for, requisition, put in for, appeal, petition, solicit, sue, claim, inquire. **2** *apply oneself to a task*: address, buckle down, settle down, commit, devote, dedicate, give, direct, concentrate, study, persevere. **3** USE, exercise, utilize, employ, bring into play, engage, harness, ply, wield, administer, execute, implement, assign, direct, bring to bear, practise, resort to. **4** REFER, relate, be relevant, pertain, fit, suit. **5** *apply ointment*: put on, spread on, lay on, cover with, paint, anoint, smear, rub.

appoint *v* **1** NAME, nominate, elect, install, choose, select, engage, employ, take on, commission, delegate, assign, allot, designate, command, direct, charge, detail. **2** DECIDE, determine, arrange, settle, fix, set, establish, ordain, decree, destine.
≠ **1** reject, dismiss, discharge.

appointment *n* **1** ARRANGEMENT, engagement, date, meeting, rendezvous, interview, consultation. **2** JOB, position, situation, post, office, place. **3** NAMING, nomination, election, choosing, choice, selection, commissioning, delegation.

appraisal *n* valuation, rating, survey, inspection, review, examination, once-over (*infml*), evaluation, assessment, estimate, estimation, judgement, reckoning, opinion, appreciation.

appreciate *v* **1** ENJOY, relish, savour, prize, treasure, value, cherish, admire, respect, regard, esteem, like, welcome, take kindly to. **2** *appreciate in value*: grow, increase, rise, mount, inflate, gain, strengthen, improve, enhance. **3** UNDERSTAND, comprehend, perceive, realize, recognize, acknowledge, sympathize with, know.
≠ **1** despise. **2** depreciate. **3** overlook.

appreciation *n* **1** ENJOYMENT, relish, admiration, respect, regard, esteem, gratitude, gratefulness, thankfulness, indebtedness, obligation, liking, sensitivity, responsiveness, valuation, assessment, estimation, judgement. **2** GROWTH, increase, rise, inflation, gain, improvement, enhancement. **3** UNDERSTANDING, comprehension, perception, awareness, realization, recognition, acknowledgement, sympathy, knowledge.
≠ **1** ingratitude. **2** depreciation.

appreciative *adj* **1** GRATEFUL, thankful, obliged, indebted, pleased. **2** ADMIRING, encouraging, enthusiastic, respectful, sensitive, responsive, perceptive, knowledgeable, conscious, mindful.
≠ **1** ungrateful.

apprehension *n* dread, foreboding, misgiving, qualm, uneasiness, anxiety, worry, concern, disquiet, alarm, fear, doubt, suspicion, mistrust.

apprehensive *adj* nervous, anxious, worried, concerned, uneasy, doubtful, suspicious, mistrustful, distrustful, alarmed, afraid.
≠ assured, confident.

apprentice *n* trainee, probationer, student, pupil, learner, novice, beginner, starter, recruit, newcomer.
≠ expert.

approach *v* **1** ADVANCE, move towards, draw near, near, gain on, catch up, reach, meet. **2** APPLY TO, appeal to, sound out. **3** BEGIN, commence, set about, undertake, introduce, mention. **4** RESEMBLE, be like, compare with, approximate, come close.
n **1** *the approach of winter*: advance, coming, advent, arrival. **2** ACCESS, road, avenue, way, passage, entrance, doorway, threshold. **3** APPLICATION, appeal, overture, proposition, proposal. **4** ATTITUDE, manner, style, technique, procedure, method, means.

appropriate *adj* applicable, relevant, pertinent, to the point, well-chosen, apt, fitting, meet (*fml*), suitable, fit, befitting, becoming, proper, right, correct, spot-on (*infml*), well-timed, timely, seasonable, opportune.
≠ inappropriate, irrelevant, unsuitable.
v **1** SEIZE, take, expropriate, commandeer, requisition, confiscate, impound, assume, usurp. **2** STEAL, pocket, filch, pilfer, purloin, embezzle, misappropriate.

approval *n* **1** ADMIRATION, esteem, regard, respect, good opinion, liking, appreciation, approbation, favour, recommendation, praise, commendation, acclaim, acclamation, honour, applause. **2** AGREEMENT, concurrence, assent, consent, permission, leave, sanction, authorization, licence, mandate, go-ahead, green light (*infml*), blessing, OK (*infml*), certification, ratification, validation, confirmation, support.
≠ **1** disapproval, condemnation.

approve *v* **1** ADMIRE, esteem, regard, like, appreciate, favour, recommend, praise, commend, acclaim, applaud. **2** *approve a proposal*: agree to, assent to, consent to, accede to, allow, permit, pass, sanction, authorize, mandate, bless, countenance, OK (*infml*), ratify, rubber-stamp (*infml*), validate, endorse, support, uphold, second, back, accept, adopt, confirm.
≠ **1** disapprove, condemn.

approximate *adj* estimated, guessed, rough, inexact, loose, close, near, like, similar, relative.
≠ exact.
v approach, border on, verge on, be tantamount to, resemble.

approximately *adv* roughly, around, about, circa, more or less, loosely, approaching, close to, nearly, just about.

apt *adj* **1** RELEVANT, applicable, apposite, appropriate, fitting, suitable, fit, seemly, proper, correct, accurate, spot-on (*infml*), timely, seasonable. **2** CLEVER, gifted, talented, skilful, expert, intelligent, quick, sharp. **3** LIABLE, prone, given, disposed, likely, ready.
≠ **1** inapt. **2** stupid.

aptitude *n* ability, capability, capacity, faculty, gift, talent, flair, facility, proficiency, cleverness, intelligence, quickness, bent, inclination, leaning, disposition, tendency.
≠ inaptitude.

arable crop

> *Types of arable crop include*: alfalfa (*US*), barley, bean, mung bean, soya bean, corn, popcorn, sweetcorn, fodder beet, mangel wurzel, sugar beet, cassava, kale, lucerne, linseed, millet, oats, oilseed rape, pea, potato, sweet potato, yam, rice, rye, sorghum, swede, turnip, wheat.

arbitrary *adj* **1** RANDOM, chance, capricious, inconsistent, discretionary, subjective, instinctive, unreasoned, illogical, irrational, unreasonable. **2** DESPOTIC, tyrannical, dictatorial, autocratic, absolute, imperious, magisterial, domineering, overbearing, high-handed, dogmatic.
≠ **1** reasoned, rational, circumspect.

arbitrate *v* judge, adjudicate, referee, umpire, mediate, settle, decide, determine.

arbitration *n* judgement, adjudication, intervention, mediation, negotiation, settlement, decision, determination.

arbitrator *n* judge, adjudicator, arbiter, referee, umpire, moderator, mediator, negotiator, intermediary, go-between.

arch *n* archway, bridge, span, dome, vault, concave, bend, curve, curvature, bow, arc, semicircle.

> *Types of arch include*: basket handle, convex, corbel, equilateral, four-centre, Gothic, horseshoe, keel, lancet, Norman, ogee, parabolic, round, segmental, shouldered, skew, stilted, tented, trefoil, Tudor.

v bend, curve, bow, arc, vault, camber.

archaic *adj* antiquated, old-fashioned, outmoded, old hat (*infml*), passé, outdated, out-of-date, obsolete, old, ancient, antique, quaint, primitive.
≠ modern, recent.

archetype *n* pattern, model, standard, form, type, prototype, original, precursor, classic, paradigm, ideal.

architect *n* designer, planner, master builder, prime mover, originator, founder, instigator, creator, author, inventor, engineer, maker, constructor, shaper.

architecture and building

> *Architectural and building terms include*: alcove, annexe, architrave, baluster, barge-board, baroque, bas relief, capstone, classical, coping stone, Corinthian, corner-stone, cornice, coving, dado, dogtooth, dome, Doric, drawbridge, dry-stone, duplex, Early English, eaves, Edwardian, elevation, Elizabethan, façade, fascia, festoon, fillet, finial, flamboyant, Flemish bond, fletton, fluting, frieze, frontispiece, gargoyle, gatehouse, Georgian, Gothic, groin, groundplan, half-timbered, Ionic, jamb, lintel, mullion, Norman, pagoda, pantile, parapet, pinnacle, plinth, Queen-Anne, rafters, Regency, reveal, ridge, rococo, Romanesque, roof, rotunda, roughcast, sacristy, scroll, soffit, stucco, terrazzo, Tudor, Tuscan, wainscot, weathering. *see also* **arch**; **roofs**; **towers**; **walls**; **window**.

archives *n* records, annals, chronicles, memorials, papers, documents, deeds, ledgers, registers, roll.

ardent *adj* fervent, fiery, warm, passionate, impassioned, fierce, vehement, intense, spirited, enthusiastic, eager, keen, dedicated, devoted, zealous.
≠ apathetic, unenthusiastic.

arduous *adj* hard, difficult, tough, rigorous, severe, harsh, formidable, strenuous, tiring, taxing, fatiguing, exhausting, backbreaking, punishing, gruelling, uphill, laborious, onerous.
≠ easy.

area *n* locality, neighbourhood, environment, environs, patch, terrain, district, region, zone, sector, department, province, domain, realm, territory, sphere, field, range, scope, compass, size, extent, expanse, width, breadth, stretch, tract, part, portion, section.

argue *v* **1** QUARREL, squabble, bicker, row, wrangle, haggle, remonstrate, join issue, fight, feud, fall out, disagree, dispute, question, debate, discuss.
2 REASON, assert, contend, hold, maintain, claim, plead, exhibit, display, show, manifest, demonstrate, indicate, denote, prove, evidence, suggest, imply.

argument *n* **1** QUARREL, squabble, row, wrangle, controversy, debate, discussion, dispute, disagreement, clash, conflict, fight, feud.
2 REASONING, reason, logic, assertion, contention, claim, demonstration, defence, case, synopsis, summary, theme.

argumentative *adj* quarrelsome, contentious, polemical, opinionated, belligerent, perverse, contrary.
≠ complaisant.

arid *adj* **1** *arid landscape*: dry, parched, waterless, desiccated, torrid, barren, infertile, unproductive, desert, waste. **2** DULL, uninteresting, boring, monotonous, tedious, dry, sterile, dreary, colourless, lifeless, spiritless, uninspired.
≠ **1** fertile. **2** lively.

arise *v* **1** ORIGINATE, begin, start, commence, derive, stem, spring, proceed, flow, emerge, issue, appear, come to light, crop up, occur, happen, result, ensue, follow. **2** RISE, get up, stand up, go up, ascend, climb, mount, lift, soar, tower.

aristocracy *n* upper class, gentry, nobility, peerage, ruling class, gentility, élite.
≠ common people.

aristocrat *n* noble, patrician, nobleman, noblewoman, peer, peeress, lord, lady.
≠ commoner.

aristocratic *adj* upper-class, highborn, well-born, noble, patrician, blue-blooded, titled, lordly, courtly, gentle, thoroughbred, élite.
≠ plebeian, vulgar.

arm[1] *n* limb, upper limb, appendage, bough, branch, projection, extension, offshoot, section, division, detachment, department.

arm[2] *v* provide, supply, furnish, issue, equip, rig, outfit, ammunition, prime, prepare, forearm, gird, steel, brace, reinforce, strengthen, fortify, protect.

armed services

> *Units in the armed services include*: task-force, militia, garrison; *air force*: wing, squadron, flight; *army*: patrol, troop, corps, platoon, squad, battery, company, brigade, battalion, regiment; *marines*: Royal Marines, commandos; *navy*: fleet, flotilla, squadron, convoy. *see also* **rank**.

armoured *adj* armour-plated, steel-plated, iron-clad, reinforced, protected, bullet-proof, bomb-proof.

armoury *n* arsenal, ordnance depot, ammunition dump, magazine, depot, repository, stock, stockpile.

arms *n* **1** WEAPONS, weaponry, firearms, guns, artillery, instruments of war, armaments, ordnance, munitions, ammunition. **2** COAT-OF-ARMS, armorial bearings, insignia, heraldic device, escutcheon, shield, crest, heraldry, blazonry.

army *n* armed force, military, militia, land forces, soldiers, troops, legions, cohorts, multitude, throng, host, horde.

aroma *n* smell, odour, scent, perfume, fragrance, bouquet, savour.

aromatic *adj* perfumed, fragrant, sweet-smelling, balmy, redolent, savoury, spicy, pungent.

around *prep* **1** SURROUNDING, round, encircling, encompassing, enclosing, on

all sides of, on every side of. **2** *around a dozen*: approximately, roughly, about, circa, more or less.
adv **1** EVERYWHERE, all over, in all directions, on all sides, about, here and there, to and fro. **2** CLOSE, close by, near, nearby, at hand.

arouse *v* rouse, startle, wake up, waken, awaken, instigate, summon up, call forth, spark, kindle, inflame, whet, sharpen, quicken, animate, excite, prompt, provoke, stimulate, galvanize, goad, spur, incite, agitate, stir up, whip up.
≠ calm, lull, quieten.

arrange *v* **1** ORDER, tidy, range, array, marshal, dispose, distribute, position, set out, lay out, align, group, class, classify, categorize, sort (out), sift, file, systematize, methodize, regulate, adjust. **2** ORGANIZE, co-ordinate, prepare, fix, plan, project, design, devise, contrive, determine, settle. **3** *arrange music*: adapt, set, score, orchestrate, instrument, harmonize.
≠ **1** untidy, disorganize, muddle.

arrangement *n* **1** ORDER, array, display, disposition, layout, line-up, grouping, classification, structure, system, method, set-up, organization, preparation, planning, plan, scheme, design, schedule. **2** AGREEMENT, settlement, contract, terms, compromise. **3** ADAPTATION, version, interpretation, setting, score, orchestration, instrumentation, harmonization.

array *n* ARRANGEMENT, display, show, exhibition, exposition, assortment, collection, assemblage, muster, order, formation, line-up, parade.
v **1** ARRANGE, order, range, dispose, group, line up, align, draw up, marshal, assemble, muster, parade, display, show, exhibit. **2** CLOTHE, dress, robe, deck, adorn, decorate.

arrest *v* **1** *arrest a criminal*: capture, catch, seize, nick (*infml*), run in, apprehend, detain. **2** STOP, stem, check, restrain, inhibit, halt, interrupt, stall, delay, slow, retard, block, obstruct, impede, hinder.

arrival *n* appearance, entrance, advent, coming, approach, occurrence.
≠ departure.

arrive *v* reach, get to, appear, materialize, turn up, show up (*infml*), roll up (*infml*), enter, come, occur, happen.
≠ depart, leave.

arrogant *adj* haughty, supercilious, disdainful, scornful, contemptuous, superior, condescending, patronizing, high and mighty, lordly, overbearing, high-handed, imperious, self-important, presumptuous, assuming, insolent, proud, conceited, boastful.
≠ humble, unassuming, bashful.

art *n* **1** FINE ART, painting, sculpture, drawing, artwork, craft, artistry, draughtsmanship, craftsmanship. **2** SKILL, knack, technique, method, aptitude, facility, dexterity, finesse, ingenuity, mastery, expertise, profession, trade. **3** ARTFULNESS, cunning, craftiness, slyness, guile, deceit, trickery, astuteness, shrewdness.

Schools of art include: abstract, action painting, Aestheticism, Art Deco, Art Nouveau, Barbizon, Baroque, Bohemian, Byzantine, classical revival, classicism, Conceptual Art, Constructivism, Cubism, Dadaism, Etruscan art, Expressionism, Fauvism, Florentine, folk art, Futurism, Gothic, Hellenistic, Impressionism, junk art, Mannerism, medieval art, Minimal Art, Modernism, the Nabis, Naturalism, Neoclassicism, Neoexpressionism, Neoimpressionism, Neo-Plasticism, Op Art, plastic art, Pop Art, Postimpressionism, Post-Modernism, Purism, quattrocento, Realism, renaissance, Rococo, Romanesque, Romanticism, Suprematism, Surrealism, Symbolism, Venetian, Vorticism. *see also* **painting**; **picture**; **sculpture**.

art and craft

Arts and crafts include: painting, oil painting, watercolour, fresco, portraiture; architecture, drawing, sketching, caricature, illustration; graphics, film, video; sculpture, modelling, woodcarving, woodcraft, marquetry, metalwork, enamelling, cloisonné, engraving, etching, pottery, ceramics, mosaic, jewellery, stained glass, photography, lithography, calligraphy, collage, origami, spinning, weaving, batik, silk-screen printing, needlework, tapestry, embroidery, patchwork, crochet, knitting. *see also* **embroidery**.

tful *adj* cunning, crafty, sly, foxy, wily, tricky, scheming, designing, deceitful, devious, subtle, sharp, shrewd, smart, clever, masterly, ingenious, resourceful, skilful, dexterous.
≠ artless, naïve, ingenuous.

ticle *n* **1** *article in a magazine*: feature, report, story, account, piece, review, commentary, composition, essay, paper. **2** ITEM, thing, object, commodity, unit, part, constituent, piece, portion, division.

ticulate *adj* distinct, well-spoken, clear, lucid, intelligible, comprehensible, understandable, coherent, fluent, vocal, expressive, meaningful.
≠ inarticulate, incoherent.
v say, utter, speak, talk, express, voice, vocalize, verbalize, state, pronounce, enunciate, breathe.

ticulation *n* saying, utterance, speaking, talking, expression, voicing, vocalization, verbalization, pronunciation, enunciation, diction, delivery.

tificial *adj* false, fake, bogus, counterfeit, spurious, phoney (*infml*), pseudo, specious, sham, insincere, assumed, affected, mannered, forced, contrived, made-up, feigned, pretended, simulated, imitation, mock, synthetic, plastic, man-made, manufactured, non-natural, unnatural.
≠ genuine, true, real, natural.

tisan *n* craftsman, craftswoman, artificer, journeyman, expert, skilled worker, mechanic, technician.

tist

Types of artist include: architect, graphic designer, designer, draughtsman, draughtswoman, illustrator, cartoonist, photographer, printer, engraver, goldsmith, silversmith, blacksmith, carpenter, potter, weaver, sculptor, painter; craftsman, craftswoman, master.

artiste *n* performer, entertainer, variety artist, vaudevillian, comic, comedian, comedienne, player, trouper, actor, actress.

artistic *adj* aesthetic, ornamental, decorative, beautiful, exquisite, elegant, stylish, graceful, harmonious, sensitive, tasteful, refined, cultured, cultivated, skilled, talented, creative, imaginative.
≠ inelegant, tasteless.

artistry *n* craftsmanship, workmanship, skill, craft, talent, flair, brilliance, genius, finesse, style, mastery, expertise, proficiency, accomplishment, deftness, touch, sensitivity, creativity.
≠ ineptitude.

as *conj, prep* **1** WHILE, when. **2** SUCH AS, for example, for instance, like, in the manner of. **3** BECAUSE, since, seeing that, considering that, inasmuch as, being.
as for with reference to, as regards, with regard to, on the subject of, in connection with, in relation to, with relation to, with respect to.

ascend *v* rise, take off, lift off, go up, move up, slope upwards, climb, scale, mount, tower, float up, fly up, soar.
≠ descend, go down.

ascent *n* **1** ASCENDING, ascension, climb, climbing, scaling, escalation, rise, rising, mounting. **2** SLOPE, gradient, incline, ramp, hill, elevation.
≠ **1** descent.

ascertain *v* find out, learn, discover, determine, fix, establish, settle, locate, detect, identify, verify, confirm, make certain.

ascribe *v* attribute, credit, accredit, put down, assign, impute, charge, chalk up to.

ashamed *adj* sorry, apologetic, remorseful, contrite, guilty, conscience-stricken, sheepish, embarrassed, blushing, red-faced, mortified, humiliated, abashed, humbled,

crestfallen, distressed, discomposed, confused, reluctant, hesitant, shy, self-conscious, bashful, modest, prudish.
≠ shameless, proud, defiant.

aside *adv* apart, on one side, in reserve, away, out of the way, separately, in isolation, alone, privately, secretly.
n digression, parenthesis, departure, soliloquy, stage whisper, whisper.

ask *v* **1** REQUEST, appeal, petition, sue, plead, beg, entreat, implore, clamour, beseech, pray, supplicate, crave, demand, order, bid, require, seek, solicit, invite, summon. **2** INQUIRE, query, question, interrogate, quiz, press.

asleep *adj* sleeping, napping, snoozing, fast asleep, sound asleep, dormant, resting, inactive, inert, unconscious, numb, dozing.

aspect *n* angle, direction, elevation, side, facet, feature, face, expression, countenance, appearance, look, air, manner, bearing, attitude, condition, situation, position, standpoint, point of view, view, outlook, prospect, scene.

aspiration *n* aim, intent, purpose, endeavour, object, objective, goal, ambition, hope, dream, ideal, wish, desire, yearning, longing, craving, hankering.

aspire *v* aim, intend, purpose, seek, pursue, hope, dream, wish, desire, yearn, long, crave, hanker.

aspiring *adj* would-be, aspirant, striving, endeavouring, ambitious, enterprising, keen, eager, hopeful, optimistic, wishful, longing.

assassin *n* murderer, killer, slayer, cut-throat, executioner, hatchet man (*infml*), gunman, hit-man (*sl*), liquidator (*infml*).

assassinate *v* murder, kill, slay, dispatch, hit (*sl*), eliminate (*infml*), liquidate (*infml*).

assault *n* **1** ATTACK, offensive, onslaught, blitz, strike, raid, invasion, incursion, storm, storming, charge. **2** *charged with assault*: battery, grievous bodily harm, GBH (*infml*), mugging (*sl*), rape, abuse.
v attack, charge, invade, strike, hit, set upon, fall on, beat up (*infml*), mu (*sl*), rape, molest, abuse.

assemble *v* **1** GATHER, congregate, muster, rally, convene, meet, join up, flock, group, collect, accumulate, amass, bring together, round up, marshal, mobilize. **2** CONSTRUCT, build, put together, piece together, compose, make, fabricate, manufacture.
≠ **1** scatter, disperse. **2** dismantle.

assembly *n* **1** GATHERING, rally, meeting, convention, conference, convocation, congress, council, group body, company, congregation, flock, crowd, multitude, throng, collection, assemblage. **2** CONSTRUCTION, building, fabrication, manufacture.

assert *v* affirm, attest, swear, testify t allege, claim, contend, maintain, insis stress, protest, defend, vindicate, uphold, promote, declare, profess, state, pronounce, lay down, advance.
≠ deny, refute.

assertion *n* affirmation, attestation, word, allegation, claim, contention, insistence, vindication, declaration, profession, statement, pronouncemen
≠ denial.

assertive *adj* bold, confident, self-assured, forward, pushy, insistent, emphatic, forceful, firm, decided, strong-willed, dogmatic, opinionated, presumptuous, assuming, overbearin domineering, aggressive.
≠ timid, diffident.

assess *v* gauge, estimate, evaluate, appraise, review, judge, consider, weigh, size up, compute, determine, value, rate, tax, levy, impose, deman

assessment *n* gauging, estimation, estimate, evaluation, appraisal, revie judgement, opinion, consideration, calculation, determination, valuation rating, taxation.

asset *n* strength, resource, virtue, plu (*infml*), benefit, advantage, blessing, boon, help, aid.
≠ liability.

assets *n* estate, property, possession

goods, holdings, securities, money, wealth, capital, funds, reserves, resources, means.

ssign *v* **1** ALLOCATE, apportion, grant, give, dispense, distribute, allot, consign, delegate, name, nominate, designate, appoint, choose, select, determine, set, fix, specify, stipulate. **2** ATTRIBUTE, accredit, ascribe, put down.

ssignment *n* commission, errand, task, project, job, position, post, duty, responsibility, charge, appointment, delegation, designation, nomination, selection, allocation, consignment, grant, distribution.

ssist *v* help, aid, abet, rally round, co-operate, collaborate, back, second, support, reinforce, sustain, relieve, benefit, serve, enable, facilitate, expedite, boost, further, advance.
≠ hinder, thwart.

ssistance *n* help, aid, succour, co-operation, collaboration, backing, support, reinforcement, relief, benefit, service, boost, furtherance.
≠ hindrance, resistance.

ssistant *n* helper, helpmate, aide, right-hand man, auxiliary, ancillary, subordinate, backer, second, supporter, accomplice, accessory, abettor, collaborator, colleague, partner, ally, confederate, associate.

ssociate *v* **1** AFFILIATE, confederate, ally, league, join, amalgamate, combine, unite, link, connect, correlate, relate, couple, pair, yoke. **2** *associate with bad company*: socialize, mingle, mix, fraternize, consort, hang around (*infml*).
n partner, ally, confederate, affiliate, collaborator, co-worker, mate, colleague, peer, compeer, fellow, comrade, companion, friend, sidekick (*infml*), assistant, follower.

ssociation *n* **1** ORGANIZATION, corporation, company, partnership, league, alliance, coalition, confederation, confederacy, federation, affiliation, consortium, cartel, syndicate, union, society, club, fraternity, fellowship, clique, group, band. **2** BOND, tie, connection, correlation, relation, relationship, involvement, intimacy, friendship, companionship, familiarity.

assorted *adj* miscellaneous, mixed, varied, different, differing, heterogeneous, diverse, sundry, various, several, manifold.

assortment *n* miscellany, medley, pot-pourri, jumble, mixture, variety, diversity, collection, selection, choice, arrangement, grouping.

assume *v* **1** PRESUME, surmise, accept, take for granted, expect, understand, deduce, infer, guess, postulate, suppose, think, believe, imagine, fancy. **2** AFFECT, take on, feign, counterfeit, simulate, put on, pretend. **3** *assume command*: undertake, adopt, embrace, seize, arrogate, commandeer, appropriate, usurp, take over.

assumed *adj* false, bogus, counterfeit, fake, phoney (*infml*), sham, affected, feigned, simulated, pretended, made-up, fictitious, hypothetical.
≠ true, real, actual.

assumption *n* presumption, surmise, inference, supposition, guess, conjecture, theory, hypothesis, premise, postulate, idea, notion, belief, fancy.

assurance *n* **1** ASSERTION, declaration, affirmation, guarantee, pledge, promise, vow, word, oath. **2** CONFIDENCE, self-confidence, aplomb, boldness, audacity, courage, nerve, conviction, sureness, certainty.
≠ **2** shyness, doubt, uncertainty.

assure *v* affirm, guarantee, warrant, pledge, promise, vow, swear, tell, convince, persuade, encourage, hearten, reassure, soothe, comfort, boost, strengthen, secure, ensure, confirm.

assured *adj* **1** SURE, certain, indisputable, irrefutable, confirmed, positive, definite, settled, fixed, guaranteed, secure. **2** SELF-ASSURED, confident, self-confident, self-possessed, bold, audacious, assertive.
≠ **1** uncertain. **2** shy.

astonish *v* surprise, startle, amaze, astound, stun, stupefy, daze, stagger, floor (*infml*), dumbfound, flabbergast (*infml*), shock, confound, bewilder.

astonishment *n* surprise, amazement, shock, dismay, consternation, confusion, bewilderment, wonder.

astounding *adj* surprising, startling, amazing, astonishing, stunning, breathtaking, stupefying, overwhelming, staggering, shocking, bewildering.

astray *adv* adrift, off course, lost, amiss, wrong, off the rails (*infml*), awry, off the mark.

astute *adj* shrewd, prudent, sagacious, wise, canny, knowing, intelligent, sharp, penetrating, keen, perceptive, discerning, subtle, clever, crafty, cunning, sly, wily.
≠ stupid, slow.

asylum *n* haven, sanctuary, refuge, shelter, retreat, safety.

asymmetric *adj* unsymmetrical, unbalanced, uneven, crooked, awry, unequal, disproportionate, irregular.
≠ symmetrical.

atheism *n* unbelief, non-belief, disbelief, scepticism, irreligion, ungodliness, godlessness, impiety, infidelity, paganism, heathenism, free-thinking, rationalism.

atheist *n* unbeliever, non-believer, disbeliever, sceptic, infidel, pagan, heathen, free-thinker.

athlete *n* sportsman, sportswoman, runner, gymnast, competitor, contestant, contender.

athletic *adj* fit, energetic, vigorous, active, sporty, muscular, sinewy, brawny, strapping, robust, sturdy, strong, powerful, well-knit, well-proportioned, wiry.
≠ puny.

athletics *n* sports, games, races, track events, field events, exercises, gymnastics.

atmosphere *n* **1** AIR, sky, aerospace, heavens, ether. **2** AMBIENCE, environment, surroundings, aura, feel, feeling, mood, spirit, tone, tenor, character, quality, flavour.

atom *n* molecule, particle, bit, morsel, crumb, grain, spot, speck, mite, shred, scrap, hint, trace, scintilla, jot, iota, whit.

> *Subatomic particles include*: photon, electron, positron, neutrino, anti-neutrino, muon, pion, kaon, proton, anti-proton, neutron, anti-neutron, lambda particle, sigma particle, omega particle, psi particle.

atrocious *adj* shocking, appalling, abominable, dreadful, terrible, horrible, hideous, ghastly, heinous, grievous, savage, vicious, monstrous, fiendish, ruthless.
≠ admirable, fine.

atrocity *n* outrage, abomination, enormity, horror, monstrosity, savagery, barbarity, brutality, cruelty, viciousness, evil, villainy, wickedness, vileness, heinousness, hideousness, atrociousness.

attach *v* **1** *attach a label*: affix, stick, adhere, fasten, fix, secure, tie, bind, weld, join, unite, connect, link, couple, add, annex. **2** ASCRIBE, attribute, impute, assign, put, place, associate, relate to, belong.
≠ **1** detach, unfasten.

attachment *n* **1** ACCESSORY, fitting, fixture, extension, appendage, extra, supplement, addition, adjunct, codicil. **2** FONDNESS, affection, tenderness, love, liking, partiality, loyalty, devotion, friendship, affinity, attraction, bond, tie, link.

attack *n* **1** OFFENSIVE, blitz, bombardment, invasion, incursion, foray, raid, strike, charge, rush, onslaught, assault, battery, aggression, criticism, censure, abuse. **2** SEIZURE, fit, convulsion, paroxysm, spasm, stroke.
v **1** invade, raid, strike, storm, charge, assail, assault, set about, set upon, fall on, lay into, do over (*sl*). **2** CRITICIZE, censure, blame, denounce, revile, malign, abuse.
≠ **1** defend, protect.

attacker *n* assailant, mugger (*sl*), aggressor, invader, raider, critic, detractor, reviler, abuser, persecutor.
≠ defender, supporter.

attain *v* accomplish, achieve, fulfil, complete, effect, realize, earn, reach, touch, arrive at, grasp, get, acquire, obtain, procure, secure, gain, win, net.

attainment *n* accomplishment, achievement, feat, fulfilment, completion, consummation, realization, success, ability, capability, competence, proficiency, skill, art, talent, gift, aptitude, facility, mastery.

attempt *n* try, endeavour, shot (*infml*), go (*infml*), stab (*infml*), bash (*infml*), push, effort, struggle, bid, undertaking, venture, trial, experiment.
v try, endeavour, have a go (*infml*), aspire, seek, strive, undertake, tackle, venture, experiment.

attend *v* **1** *attend a meeting*: be present, go to, frequent, visit. **2** ESCORT, chaperon, accompany, usher, follow, guard, look after, take care of, care for, nurse, tend, minister to, help, serve, wait on. **3** PAY ATTENTION, listen, hear, heed, mind, mark, note, notice, observe.
attend to deal with, see to, take care of, look after, manage, direct, control, oversee, supervise.

attendance *n* presence, appearance, turnout, audience, house, crowd, gate.

attendant *n* aide, helper, assistant, auxiliary, steward, waiter, servant, page, retainer, guide, marshal, usher, escort, companion, follower, guard, custodian.
adj accompanying, attached, associated, related, incidental, resultant, consequent, subsequent.

attention *n* alertness, vigilance, concentration, heed, notice, observation, regard, mindfulness, awareness, recognition, thought, contemplation, consideration, concern, care, treatment, service.
≠ inattention, disregard, carelessness.

attentive *adj* **1** ALERT, awake, vigilant, watchful, observant, concentrating, heedful, mindful, careful, conscientious. **2** CONSIDERATE, thoughtful, kind, obliging, accommodating, polite, courteous, devoted.
≠ **1** inattentive, heedless. **2** inconsiderate.

attitude *n* feeling, disposition, mood, aspect, manner, bearing, pose, posture, stance, position, point of view, opinion, view, outlook, perspective, approach.

attract *v* pull, draw, lure, allure, entice, seduce, tempt, invite, induce, incline, appeal to, interest, engage, fascinate, enchant, charm, bewitch, captivate, excite.
≠ repel, disgust.

attraction *n* pull, draw, magnetism, lure, allure, bait, enticement, inducement, seduction, temptation, invitation, appeal, interest, fascination, enchantment, charm, captivation.
≠ repulsion.

attractive *adj* pretty, fair, fetching, good-looking, handsome, beautiful, gorgeous, stunning, glamorous, lovely, pleasant, pleasing, agreeable, appealing, winsome, winning, enticing, seductive, tempting, inviting, interesting, engaging, fascinating, charming, captivating, magnetic.
≠ unattractive, repellent.

attribute *v* ascribe, accredit, credit, impute, assign, put down, blame, charge, refer, apply.
n property, quality, virtue, point, aspect, facet, feature, trait, characteristic, idiosyncrasy, peculiarity, quirk, note, mark, sign, symbol.

auburn *adj* red, chestnut, tawny, russet, copper, Titian.

audible *adj* clear, distinct, recognizable, perceptible, discernible, detectable, appreciable.
≠ inaudible, silent, unclear.

audience *n* spectators, onlookers, house, auditorium, listeners, viewers, crowd, turnout, gathering, assembly, congregation, fans, devotees, regulars, following, public.

audit *n* examination, inspection, check, verification, investigation, scrutiny, analysis, review, statement, balancing.

augur *v* bode, forebode, herald, presage, portend, prophesy, predict, promise, signify.

auspices *n* aegis, authority, patronage,

sponsorship, backing, support, protection, charge, care, supervision, control, influence, guidance.

auspicious *adj* favourable, propitious, encouraging, cheerful, bright, rosy, promising, hopeful, optimistic, fortunate, lucky, opportune, happy, prosperous.
≠ inauspicious, ominous.

austere *adj* **1** STARK, bleak, plain, simple, unadorned, grim, forbidding. **2** SEVERE, stern, strict, cold, formal, rigid, rigorous, exacting, hard, harsh, spartan, grave, serious, solemn, sober, abstemious, self-denying, restrained, economical, frugal, ascetic, self-disciplined, puritanical, chaste.
≠ **1** ornate, elaborate. **2** genial.

austerity *n* plainness, simplicity, severity, coldness, formality, hardness, harshness, solemnity, abstemiousness, abstinence, economy, asceticism, puritanism.
≠ elaborateness, materialism.

authentic *adj* genuine, true, real, actual, certain, bona fide, legitimate, honest, valid, original, pure, factual, accurate, true-to-life, faithful, reliable, trustworthy.
≠ false, fake, counterfeit, spurious.

authenticate *v* guarantee, warrant, vouch for, attest, authorize, accredit, validate, certify, endorse, confirm, verify, corroborate.

authenticity *n* genuineness, certainty, authoritativeness, validity, truth, veracity, truthfulness, honesty, accuracy, correctness, faithfulness, fidelity, reliability, dependability, trustworthiness.
≠ spuriousness, invalidity.

author *n* **1** WRITER, novelist, dramatist, playwright, composer, pen, penman, penwoman. **2** CREATOR, founder, originator, initiator, parent, prime mover, mover, inventor, designer, architect, planner, maker, producer.

authoritarian *adj* strict, disciplinarian, severe, harsh, rigid, inflexible, unyielding, dogmatic, doctrinaire, absolute, autocratic, dictatorial, despotic, tyrannical, oppressive, domineering, imperious.
≠ liberal.

authoritative *adj* scholarly, learned, official, authorized, legitimate, valid, approved, sanctioned, accepted, definitive, decisive, authentic, factual, true, truthful, accurate, faithful, convincing, sound, reliable, dependable, trustworthy.
≠ unofficial, unreliable.

authority *n* **1** SOVEREIGNTY, supremacy, rule, sway, control, dominion, influence, power, force, government, administration, officialdom. **2** AUTHORIZATION, permission, sanction, permit, warrant, licence, credentials, right, prerogative. **3** *an authority on antiques*: expert, pundit, connoisseur, specialist, professional, master, scholar.

authorize *v* legalize, validate, ratify, confirm, license, entitle, accredit, empower, enable, commission, warrant, permit, allow, consent to, sanction, approve, give the go-ahead.

autocracy *n* absolutism, totalitarianism, dictatorship, despotism, tyranny, authoritarianism, fascism.
≠ democracy.

autocrat *n* absolutist, totalitarian, dictator, despot, tyrant, authoritarian, (little) Hitler (*infml*), fascist.

autocratic *adj* absolute, all-powerful, totalitarian, despotic, tyrannical, authoritarian, dictatorial, domineering overbearing, imperious.
≠ democratic, liberal.

automatic *adj* **1** AUTOMATED, self-activating, mechanical, mechanized, programmed, self-regulating, computerized, push-button, robotic, self-propelling, unmanned. **2** SPONTANEOUS, reflex, involuntary, unwilled, unconscious, unthinking, natural, instinctive, routine, necessary, certain, inevitable, unavoidable, inescapable.

autonomy *n* self-government, self-rule home rule, sovereignty, independence, self-determination, freedom, free will.

≠ subjection, compulsion.

ıxiliary *adj* ancillary, assistant, subsidiary, accessory, secondary, supporting, supportive, helping, assisting, aiding, extra, supplementary, spare, reserve, back-up, emergency, substitute.

ailable *adj* free, vacant, to hand, within reach, at hand, accessible, handy, convenient, on hand, ready, on tap, obtainable.
≠ unavailable.

alanche *n* landslide, landslip, cascade, torrent, deluge, flood, inundation, barrage.

ant-garde *adj* innovative, innovatory, pioneering, experimental, unconventional, far-out (*sl*), way-out (*sl*), progressive, advanced, forward-looking, enterprising, inventive.
≠ conservative.

arice *n* covetousness, rapacity, acquisitiveness, greed, greediness, meanness.
≠ generosity, liberality.

aricious *adj* covetous, grasping, rapacious, acquisitive, greedy, mercenary, mean, miserly.
≠ generous.

enge *v* take revenge for, take vengeance for, punish, requite, repay, retaliate.

erage *n* mean, mid-point, norm, standard, rule, par, medium, run.
≠ extreme, exception.
adj mean, medial, median, middle, intermediate, medium, moderate, satisfactory, fair, mediocre, middling, indifferent, so-so (*infml*), passable, tolerable, undistinguished, run-of-the-mill, ordinary, everyday, common, usual, normal, regular, standard, typical, unexceptional.
≠ extreme, exceptional, remarkable.

erse *adj* reluctant, unwilling, loth, disinclined, ill-disposed, hostile, opposed, antagonistic, unfavourable.
≠ willing, keen, sympathetic.

ersion *n* dislike, hate, hatred, loathing, detestation, abhorrence, abomination, horror, phobia, reluctance, unwillingness, disinclination, distaste, disgust, revulsion, repugnance, repulsion, hostility, opposition, antagonism.
≠ liking, sympathy, desire.

avert *v* turn away, deflect, turn aside, parry, fend off, ward off, stave off, forestall, frustrate, prevent, obviate, avoid, evade.

aviation *n* flying, aircraft industry.

Aviation terms include: aeronautics, aeroplane, aerospace, aileron, aircraft, airfield, air hostess, airline, air miss, airplane (*US*), airport, airship, airspace, air steward, airstrip, air-traffic control, airway, altitude, automatic pilot, biplane, black box, captain, chocks away (*infml*), cockpit, console, control tower, crash-dive, crash-landing, dive, drag, fixed-wing, flap, flight, flight crew, flight deck, flight recorder, fly-by, fly-by-wire, fly-past, fuselage, George (*sl*), glider, ground-control, ground-speed, hangar, helicopter, hop, hot-air balloon, jet, jet engine, jet propulsion, jetstream, joystick, jumbo jet, landing, landing-gear, landing-strip, lift-off, loop-the-loop, Mach number, maiden flight, mid-air collision, monoplane, night-flying, nose dive, overshoot, parachute, pilot, plane, pressurised cabin, prang (*sl*), propeller, rotor blade, rudder, runway, solo flight, sonic boom, sound barrier, spoiler, supersonic, swing-wing, take-off, taxi, test flight, test pilot, thrust, touchdown, undercarriage, undershoot, vapour trail, vertical take-off and landing (VTOL), windsock, wingspan. *see also* **aircraft**.

avid *adj* eager, earnest, keen, enthusiastic, fanatical, devoted, dedicated, zealous, ardent, fervent, intense, passionate, insatiable, ravenous, hungry, thirsty, greedy, grasping, covetous.
≠ indifferent.

avoid *v* evade, elude, sidestep, dodge, shirk, duck (*infml*), escape, get out of, bypass, circumvent, balk, prevent, avert, shun, abstain from, refrain from, steer clear of.

avoidable *adj* escapable, preventable.
≠ inevitable.

avowed *adj* sworn, declared, professed, self-proclaimed, self-confessed, confessed, admitted, acknowledged, open, overt.

awake *v* awaken, waken, wake, wake up, rouse, arouse.
adj wakeful, wide-awake, aroused, alert, vigilant, watchful, observant, attentive, conscious, aware, sensitive, alive.

awakening *n* awaking, wakening, waking, rousing, arousal, stimulation, animating, enlivening, activation, revival, birth.

award *v* give, present, distribute, dispense, bestow, confer, accord, endow, gift, grant, allot, apportion, assign, allow, determine.
n prize, trophy, decoration, medal, presentation, dispensation, bestowal, conferral, endowment, gift, grant, allotment, allowance, adjudication, judgement, decision, order.

aware *adj* conscious, alive to, sensitive, appreciative, sentient, familiar, conversant, acquainted, informed, enlightened, au courant, knowing, knowledgeable, cognizant, mindful, heedful, attentive, observant, sharp, alert, on the ball (*infml*), shrewd, sensible.
≠ unaware, oblivious, insensitive.

awe *n* wonder, veneration, reverence, respect, admiration, amazement, astonishment, fear, terror, dread, apprehension.
≠ contempt.

awe-inspiring *adj* wonderful, sublime, magnificent, stupendous, overwhelming, breathtaking, stupefying, stunning, astonishing, amazing, impressive, imposing, majestic, solemn, moving, awesome, formidable, daunting, intimidating, fearsome.
≠ contemptible, tame.

awful *adj* terrible, dreadful, fearful, frightful, ghastly, unpleasant, nasty, horrible, hideous, ugly, gruesome, dir[e], abysmal, atrocious, horrific, shocking, appalling, alarming, spine-chilling.
≠ wonderful, excellent.

awkward *adj* **1** CLUMSY, gauche, inept, inexpert, unskilful, bungling, ham-fisted, unco-ordinated, ungainly, graceless, ungraceful, inelegant, cumbersome, unwieldy, inconvenient, difficult, fiddly, delicate, troublesome, perplexing. **2** *feeling awkward in their presence*: uncomfortable, ill at ease, embarrassed. **3** OBSTINATE, stubborn, unco-operative, irritable, touchy, prickly, rude, unpleasant.
≠ **1** graceful, elegant, convenient, handy. **2** comfortable, relaxed. **3** amenable, pleasant.

axe *n* hatchet, chopper, cleaver, tomahawk, battle-axe.
v **1** CUT (DOWN), fell, hew, chop, cleave, split. **2** CANCEL, terminate, discontinue, remove, withdraw, eliminate, get rid of, throw out, dismiss, discharge, sack (*infml*), fire (*infml*).

axiom *n* principle, fundamental, trut[h], truism, precept, dictum, byword, maxim, adage, aphorism.

axis *n* centre-line, vertical, horizontal, pivot, hinge.

axle *n* shaft, spindle, rod, pin, pivot.

B

babble *v* **1** CHATTER, gabble, jabber, cackle, prate, mutter, mumble, murmur. **2** *the stream babbled*: burble, gurgle.
n chatter, gabble, clamour, hubbub, gibberish, burble, murmur.

baby *n* babe, infant, suckling, child, tiny, toddler.
adj miniature, small-scale, mini (*infml*), midget, small, little, tiny, minute, diminutive.

babyish *adj* childish, juvenile, puerile, infantile, silly, foolish, soft (*infml*), sissy (*infml*), baby, young, immature, naïve.
≠ mature, precocious.

back *n* rear, stern, end, tail, tail end, hind part, hindquarters, posterior, backside, reverse.
≠ front, face.
v **1** GO BACKWARDS, reverse, recede, regress, backtrack, retreat, retire, withdraw, back away, recoil. **2** SUPPORT, sustain, assist, side with, champion, advocate, encourage, promote, boost, favour, sanction, countenance, endorse, second, countersign, sponsor, finance, subsidize, underwrite.
≠ **1** advance, approach. **2** discourage, weaken.
adj rear, end, tail, posterior, hind, hindmost, reverse.
≠ **1** front.
back down concede, yield, give in, surrender, submit, retreat, withdraw, back-pedal.
back out abandon, give up, chicken out (*infml*), withdraw, pull out (*infml*), resign, recant, go back on, cancel.
back up confirm, corroborate, substantiate, endorse, second, champion, support, reinforce, bolster, assist, aid.
≠ let down.

backbone *n* **1** SPINE, spinal column, vertebrae, vertebral column, mainstay, support, core, foundation, basis, character. **2** COURAGE, mettle, pluck, nerve, grit, determination, resolve, tenacity, steadfastness, toughness, stamina, strength, power.
≠ **2** spinelessness, weakness.

backfire *v* recoil, rebound, ricochet, boomerang, miscarry, fail, flop.

background *n* **1** SETTING, surroundings, environment, context, circumstances. **2** HISTORY, record, credentials, experience, grounding, preparation, education, upbringing, breeding, culture, tradition.

backing *n* support, accompaniment, aid, assistance, helpers, championing, advocacy, encouragement, moral support, favour, sanction, promotion, endorsement, seconding, patronage, sponsorship, finance, funds, grant, subsidy.

backlash *n* reaction, response, repercussion, reprisal, retaliation, recoil, kickback, backfire, boomerang.

backlog *n* accumulation, stock, supply, resources, reserve, reserves, excess.

backsliding *n* lapse, relapse, apostasy, defection, desertion, defaulting.

backward *adj* **1** *a backward step*: retrograde, retrogressive, regressive. **2** SHY, bashful, reluctant, unwilling, hesitant, hesitating, wavering, slow, behind, behindhand, late, immature, underdeveloped, retarded, subnormal, stupid.
≠ **1** forward. **2** precocious.

bacteria *n* germs, bugs (*infml*), viruses, microbes, micro-organisms, bacilli.

bad *adj* **1** UNPLEASANT, disagreeable, nasty, undesirable, unfortunate, distressing, adverse, detrimental, harmful, damaging, injurious, serious, grave, severe, harsh. **2** EVIL, wicked, sinful, criminal, corrupt, immoral, vile.

3 *bad workmanship*: poor, inferior, substandard, imperfect, faulty, defective, deficient, unsatisfactory, useless. **4** ROTTEN, mouldy, decayed, spoilt, putrid, rancid, sour, off, tainted, contaminated. **5** *a bad child*: naughty, mischievous, ill-behaved, disobedient.
≠ **1** good, pleasant, mild, slight. **2** virtuous. **3** skilled. **4** fresh. **5** well-behaved.

badge *n* identification, emblem, device, insignia, sign, mark, token, stamp, brand, trademark, logo.

badly *adv* **1** GREATLY, extremely, exceedingly, intensely, deeply, acutely, bitterly, painfully, seriously, desperately, severely, critically, crucially. **2** WICKEDLY, criminally, immorally, shamefully, unfairly. **3** WRONG, wrongly, incorrectly, improperly, defectively, faultily, imperfectly, inadequately, unsatisfactorily, poorly, incompetently, negligently, carelessly. **4** UNFAVOURABLY, adversely, unfortunately, unsuccessfully.
≠ **3** well.

bad-tempered *adj* irritable, cross, crotchety, crabbed, crabby, snappy, grumpy, querulous, petulant, fractious, stroppy (*infml*).
≠ good-tempered, genial, equable.

baffle *v* puzzle, perplex, mystify, bemuse, bewilder, confuse, confound, bamboozle (*infml*), flummox (*infml*), daze, upset, disconcert, foil, thwart, frustrate, hinder, check, defeat, stump (*infml*).
≠ enlighten, help.

bag *v* **1** CATCH, capture, trap, land, kill, shoot. **2** OBTAIN, acquire, get, gain, corner, take, grab, appropriate, commandeer, reserve.
n container, sack, case, suitcase, grip, carrier, hold-all, handbag, shoulder-bag, satchel, rucksack, haversack, pack.

baggage *n* luggage, suitcases, bags, belongings, things, equipment, gear, paraphernalia, impedimenta (*fml*).

baggy *adj* loose, slack, roomy, ill-fitting, billowing, bulging, floppy, sagging, droopy.
≠ tight, firm.

bail *n* security, surety, pledge, bond, guarantee, warranty.
bail out[1] help, aid, assist, relieve, rescue finance.
bail out[2], **bale out** withdraw, retreat, quit, back out, cop out (*sl*), escape.

bait *n* lure, incentive, inducement, bribe, temptation, enticement, allurement, attraction.
≠ disincentive.
v tease, provoke, goad, irritate, annoy, irk, needle (*infml*), harass, persecute, torment.

balance *v* **1** STEADY, poise, stabilize, level, square, equalize, equate, match, counterbalance, counteract, neutralize, offset, adjust. **2** COMPARE, consider, weigh, estimate.
≠ **1** unbalance, overbalance.
n **1** EQUILIBRIUM, steadiness, stability, evenness, symmetry, equality, parity, equity, equivalence, correspondence. **2** COMPOSURE, self-possession, poise, equanimity. **3** REMAINDER, rest, residue, surplus, difference.
≠ **1** imbalance, instability.

balcony *n* terrace, veranda, gallery, upper circle, gods.

bald *adj* **1** BALD-HEADED, hairless, smooth, uncovered. **2** BARE, naked, unadorned, plain, simple, severe, stark barren, treeless. **3** *a bald statement*: forthright, direct, straight, outright, downright, straightforward.
≠ **1** hairy, hirsute. **2** adorned.

bale *n* bundle, truss, pack, package, parcel.
bale out *see* **bail out**[2].

balk, baulk *v* **1** FLINCH, recoil, shrink jib, boggle, hesitate, refuse, resist, dodge, evade, shirk. **2** THWART, frustrate, foil, forestall, disconcert, baffle, hinder, obstruct, check, stall, bar, prevent, defeat, counteract.

ball[1] *n* sphere, globe, orb, globule, drop, conglomeration, pellet, pill, sho bullet, slug (*infml*).

ball[2] *n* dance, dinner-dance, party, soirée, masquerade, carnival, assembly

ballad *n* poem, song, folk-song, shant carol, ditty.

ballet

Terms used in ballet include: à pointe, arabesque, attitude, ballerina, prima ballerina, ballon, barre, battement, batterie, battu, bourrée, capriole, chassé, choreography, ciseaux, company, corps de ballet, coryphée, divertissement, écarté, élevation, entrechat, fish dive, five positions, fouetté, fouetté en tournant, glissade, jeté, grande jeté, leotard, pas de deux, pas de seul, pirouette, plié, pointes, sur les pointes, ports de bras, principal male dancer, régisseur, répétiteur, ballet shoe, point shoe, splits, stulchak, tutu.

ballot *n* poll, polling, vote, voting, election, referendum, plebiscite.

ban *v* forbid, prohibit, disallow, proscribe, bar, exclude, ostracize, outlaw, banish, suppress, restrict.
≠ allow, permit, authorize.
n prohibition, embargo, veto, boycott, stoppage, restriction, suppression, censorship, outlawry, proscription, condemnation, denunciation, curse, taboo.
≠ permission, dispensation.

banal *adj* trite, commonplace, ordinary, everyday, humdrum, boring, unimaginative, hackneyed, clichéed, stock, stereotyped, corny (*infml*), stale, threadbare, tired, empty.
≠ original, fresh, imaginative.

band[1] *n* strip, belt, ribbon, tape, bandage, binding, tie, ligature, bond, strap, cord, chain.

band[2] *n* **1** TROOP, gang, crew, group, herd, flock, party, body, association, company, society, club, clique. **2** *the band played on*: group, orchestra, ensemble.
v group, gather, join, unite, ally, collaborate, consolidate, amalgamate, merge, affiliate, federate.
≠ disband, disperse.

bandage *n* dressing, plaster, compress, ligature, tourniquet, swathe, swaddle.
v bind, dress, cover, swathe, swaddle.

bandit *n* robber, thief, brigand, marauder, outlaw, highwayman, pirate, buccaneer, hijacker, cowboy, gunman, desperado, gangster.

bandy[1] *v* exchange, swap, trade, barter, interchange, reciprocate, pass, toss, throw.

bandy[2] *adj* bandy-legged, bow-legged, curved, bowed, bent, crooked.

bang *n* **1** BLOW, hit, knock, bump, crash, collision, smack, punch, thump, wallop (*infml*), stroke, whack (*infml*). **2** *a loud bang*: explosion, detonation, pop, boom, clap, peal, clang, clash, thud, thump, slam, noise, report, shot.
v **1** STRIKE, hit, bash, knock, bump, rap, drum, hammer, pound, thump, stamp. **2** EXPLODE, burst, detonate, boom, echo, resound, crash, slam, clatter, clang, peal, thunder.
adv straight, directly, headlong, right, precisely, slap, smack, hard, noisily, suddenly, abruptly.

banish *v* expel, eject, evict, deport, transport, exile, outlaw, ban, bar, debar, exclude, shut out, ostracize, excommunicate, dismiss, oust, dislodge, remove, get rid of, discard, dispel, eliminate, eradicate.
≠ recall, welcome.

banishment *n* expulsion, eviction, deportation, expatriation, transportation, exile, outlawry, ostracism, excommunication.
≠ return, recall, welcome.

bank[1] *n* accumulation, fund, pool, reservoir, depository, repository, treasury, savings, reserve, store, stock, stockpile, hoard, cache.
v deposit, save, keep, store, accumulate, stockpile.
≠ spend.

bank[2] *n* heap, pile, mass, mound, earthwork, ridge, rampart, embankment, side, slope, tilt, edge, shore.
v **1** HEAP, pile, stack, mass, amass, accumulate, mound, drift. **2** SLOPE, incline, pitch, slant, tilt, tip.

bank[3] *n* array, panel, bench, group, tier, rank, line, row, series, succession, sequence, train.

bankrupt *adj* insolvent, in liquidation, ruined, failed, beggared, destitute,

impoverished, broke (*infml*), spent, exhausted, depleted, lacking.
≠ solvent, wealthy.
n insolvent, debtor, pauper.

banner *n* flag, standard, colours, ensign, pennant, streamer.

banquet *n* feast, dinner, meal, repast (*fml*), treat.

banter *n* joking, jesting, pleasantry, badinage, repartee, word play, chaff, chaffing, kidding (*infml*), ribbing (*sl*), derision, mockery, ridicule.

baptism *n* christening, dedication, beginning, initiation, introduction, debut, launch, launching, immersion, sprinkling, purification.

baptize *v* christen, name, call, term, style, title, introduce, initiate, enrol, recruit, immerse, sprinkle, purify, cleanse.

bar *n* **1** PUBLIC HOUSE, pub (*infml*), inn, tavern, saloon, lounge, counter. **2** SLAB, block, lump, chunk, wedge, ingot, nugget. **3** ROD, stick, shaft, pole, stake, stanchion, batten, cross-piece, rail, railing, paling, barricade. **4** OBSTACLE, impediment, hindrance, obstruction, barrier, stop, check, deterrent.
v **1** EXCLUDE, debar, ban, forbid, prohibit, prevent, preclude, hinder, obstruct, restrain. **2** *bar the door*: barricade, lock, bolt, latch, fasten, secure.

barbarian *n* savage, brute, ruffian, hooligan, vandal, lout, oaf, boor, philistine, ignoramus, illiterate.

barbaric *adj* barbarous, primitive, wild, savage, fierce, ferocious, cruel, inhuman, brutal, brutish, uncivilized, uncouth, vulgar, coarse, crude, rude.
≠ humane, civilized, gracious.

barbarity *n* barbarousness, wildness, savagery, ferocity, viciousness, cruelty, inhumanity, brutality, brutishness, rudeness.
≠ civilization, humanity, civility.

barbed *adj* **1** PRICKLY, spiny, thorny, spiked, pronged, hooked, jagged, toothed, pointed. **2** *a barbed remark*: cutting, caustic, acid, hurtful, unkind, nasty, snide, hostile, critical.

bare *adj* **1** NAKED, nude, unclothed, undressed, stripped, denuded, uncovered, exposed. **2** PLAIN, simple, unadorned, unfurnished, empty, barren, bald, stark, basic, essential.
≠ **1** clothed. **2** decorated, detailed.

barely *adv* hardly, scarcely, only just, just, almost.

bargain *n* **1** DEAL, transaction, contract, treaty, pact, pledge, promise, agreement, understanding, arrangement, negotiation. **2** DISCOUNT, reduction, snip, giveaway, special offer.
v negotiate, haggle, deal, trade, traffic barter, buy, sell, transact, contract, covenant, promise, agree.
bargain for expect, anticipate, plan for include, reckon on, look for, foresee, imagine, contemplate, consider.

barge *v* bump, hit, collide, impinge, shove, elbow, push (in), muscle in, butt in, interrupt, gatecrash, intrude, interfere.
n canal-boat, flatboat, narrow-boat, houseboat, lighter.

bark *n* yap, woof, yelp, snap, snarl, growl, bay, howl.
v yap, woof, yelp, snap, snarl, growl, bay, howl.

baroque *adj* elaborate, ornate, rococo florid, flamboyant, exuberant, vigorous, bold, convoluted, overdecorated, overwrought, extravagant, fanciful, fantastic, grotesque.
≠ plain, simple.

barracks *n* garrison, camp, encampment, guardhouse, quarters, billet, lodging, accommodation.

barrage *n* bombardment, shelling, gunfire, cannonade, broadside, volley, salvo, burst, assault, attack, onset, onslaught, deluge, torrent, stream, storm, hail, rain, shower, mass, profusion.

barrel *n* cask, keg, tun, butt, water-butt.

barren *adj* **1** ARID, dry, desert, desolate, waste, empty, flat, dull,

uninteresting, uninspiring, uninformative, uninstructive, unrewarding, unproductive, profitless, unfruitful, fruitless, pointless, useless, boring. **2** INFERTILE, sterile, childless, unprolific, unbearing.
≠ **1** productive, fruitful, useful. **2** fertile.

barricade *n* blockade, obstruction, barrier, fence, stockade, bulwark, rampart, protection.
v block, obstruct, bar, fortify, defend, protect.

barrier *n* **1** WALL, fence, railing, barricade, blockade, boom, rampart, fortification, ditch, frontier, boundary, bar, check. **2** *a barrier to success*: obstacle, hurdle, stumbling-block, impediment, obstruction, hindrance, handicap, limitation, restriction, drawback, difficulty.

bartender *n* barman, barmaid, barkeeper, publican.

barter *v* exchange, swap, trade, traffic, deal, negotiate, bargain, haggle.

base *n* **1** *the base of the statue*: bottom, foot, pedestal, plinth, stand, rest, support, foundation, bed, groundwork. **2** BASIS, fundamental, essential, principal, key, heart, core, essence, root, origin, source. **3** HEADQUARTERS, centre, post, station, camp, settlement, home, starting point.
v establish, found, ground, locate, station, build, construct, derive, depend, hinge.

baseless *adj* groundless, unfounded, unsupported, unsubstantiated, unauthenticated, unconfirmed, unjustified, uncalled-for, gratuitous.
≠ justifiable.

bashful *adj* shy, retiring, backward, reticent, reserved, unforthcoming, hesitant, shrinking, nervous, timid, coy, diffident, modest, inhibited, self-conscious, embarrassed, blushing, abashed, shamefaced, sheepish.
≠ bold, confident, aggressive.

basic *adj* fundamental, elementary, primary, root, underlying, key, central, inherent, intrinsic, essential, indispensable, vital, necessary, important.
≠ inessential, minor, peripheral.

basically *adv* fundamentally, at bottom, at heart, inherently, intrinsically, essentially, principally, primarily.

basics *n* fundamentals, rudiments, principles, essentials, necessaries, practicalities, brass tacks (*infml*), grass roots, bedrock, rock bottom, core, facts.

basin *n* bowl, dish, sink, crater, cavity, hollow, depression, dip.

basis *n* base, bottom, footing, support, foundation, ground, groundwork, fundamental, premise, principle, essential, heart, core, thrust.

bask *v* sunbathe, lie, lounge, relax, laze, wallow, revel, delight in, enjoy, relish, savour.

basket *n* hamper, creel, pannier, punnet, bassinet.

bass *adj* deep, low, low-toned, grave, resonant.

bastion *n* stronghold, citadel, fortress, defence, bulwark, mainstay, support, prop, pillar, rock.

batch *n* lot, consignment, parcel, pack, bunch, set, assortment, collection, assemblage, group, contingent, amount, quantity.

bath *n* wash, scrub, soak, shower, douche, tub, Jacuzzi®.
v bathe, wash, clean, soak, shower.

bathe *v* swim, wet, moisten, immerse, wash, cleanse, rinse, soak, steep, flood, cover, suffuse.
n swim, dip, paddle, wash, rinse, soak.

battalion *n* army, force, brigade, regiment, squadron, company, platoon, division, contingent, legion, horde, multitude, throng, host, mass, herd.

batter *v* beat, pound, pummel, buffet, smash, dash, pelt, lash, thrash, wallop (*infml*), abuse, maltreat, ill-treat, manhandle, maul, assault, hurt, injure, bruise, disfigure, mangle, distress, crush, demolish, destroy, ruin, shatter.

battered *adj* beaten, abused, ill-treated, injured, bruised, weather-beaten, dilapidated, tumbledown, ramshackle, crumbling, damaged, crushed.

battle *n* war, warfare, hostilities, action, conflict, strife, combat, fight, engagement, encounter, attack, fray, skirmish, clash, struggle, contest, campaign, crusade, row, disagreement, dispute, debate, controversy.
v fight, combat, war, feud, contend, struggle, strive, campaign, crusade, agitate, clamour, contest, argue, dispute.

battle-cry *n* war cry, war song, slogan, motto, watchword, catchword.

baulk *see* **balk**.

bay[1] *n* gulf, bight, arm, inlet, cove.

bay[2] *n* recess, alcove, niche, nook, opening, compartment, cubicle, booth, stall, carrel.

bay[3] *v* howl, roar, bellow, bell, bawl, cry, holler (*infml*), bark.

bazaar *n* market, marketplace, mart, exchange, sale, fair, fête, bring-and-buy.

be *v* **1** EXIST, breathe, live, inhabit, reside, dwell. **2** STAY, remain, abide, last, endure, persist, continue, survive, stand, prevail, obtain. **3** HAPPEN, occur, arise, come about, take place, come to pass, befall, develop.

beach *n* sand, sands, shingle, shore, strand, seashore, seaside, water's edge, coast, seaboard.

beacon *n* signal, fire, watch fire, bonfire, light, beam, lighthouse, flare, rocket, sign.

bead *n* drop, droplet, drip, globule, glob (*infml*), blob, dot, bubble, pearl, jewel, pellet.

beaker *n* glass, tumbler, jar, cup, mug, tankard.

beam *n* **1** *a beam of light*: ray, shaft, gleam, glint, glimmer, glow. **2** PLANK, board, timber, rafter, joist, girder, spar, boom, bar, support.
v **1** EMIT, broadcast, transmit, radiate, shine, glare, glitter, glow, glimmer. **2** SMILE, grin.

beans and pulses

Varieties of bean and pulse include: adzuki bean, alfalfa, beansprout, black-eyed pea, broad bean, butter bean, carob bean, chick pea, chilli bean, dal, dwarf runner bean, fava bean, French bean, garbanzo pea, green bean, haricot bean, kidney bean, lentil, lima bean (*US*), locust bean, mange tout, marrowfat pea, mung bean, navy bean (*US*), okra, pea, pinto bean (*US*), red kidney bean, runner bean, scarlet runner (*US*), snap bean, soya bean, split pea, string bean, sugar bean, tonka bean, wax bean (*US*).

bear *v* **1** CARRY, convey, transport, move, take, bring. **2** HOLD, support, shoulder, uphold, sustain, maintain, harbour, cherish. **3** *bear children*: give birth to, breed, propagate, beget, engender, produce, generate, develop, yield, bring forth, give up. **4** TOLERATE, stand, put up with, endure, abide, suffer, permit, allow, admit.
bear on refer to, relate to, affect, concern, involve.
bear out confirm, endorse, support, uphold, prove, demonstrate, corroborate, substantiate, vindicate, justify.
bear up persevere, soldier on, carry on, suffer, endure, survive, withstand.
bear with tolerate, put up with, endure, suffer, forbear, be patient with, make allowances for.

bearable *adj* tolerable, endurable, sufferable, supportable, sustainable, acceptable, manageable.
≠ unbearable, intolerable.

bearded *adj* unshaven, bristly, whiskered, tufted, hairy, hirsute, shaggy, bushy.
≠ beardless, clean-shaven, smooth.

bearer *n* carrier, conveyor, porter, courier, messenger, runner, holder, possessor.

bearing *n* **1** *have no bearing on the matter*: relevance, significance, connection, relation, reference. **2** DEMEANOUR, manner, mien, air, aspect, attitude, behaviour, comportment, poise, deportment, carriage, posture.

bearings *n* orientation, position, situation, location, whereabouts, course, track, way, direction, aim.

beast *n* animal, creature, brute, monster, savage, barbarian, pig, swine, devil, fiend.

beat *v* **1** WHIP, flog, lash, tan (*infml*), cane, strap, thrash, lay into, hit, punch, strike, swipe, knock, bang, wham, bash, pound, hammer, batter, buffet, pelt, bruise. **2** PULSATE, pulse, throb, thump, race, palpitate, flutter, vibrate, quiver, tremble, shake, quake. **3** DEFEAT, trounce, best, worst, hammer (*infml*), slaughter (*sl*), conquer, overcome, overwhelm, vanquish, subdue, surpass, excel, outdo, outstrip, outrun.
n **1** PULSATION, pulse, stroke, throb, thump, palpitation, flutter. **2** RHYTHM, time, tempo, metre, measure, rhyme, stress, accent. **3** *a policeman's beat*: round, rounds, territory, circuit, course, journey, way, path, route.
beat up (*infml*) attack, assault, knock about, knock around, batter, do over (*infml*).

beaten *adj* **1** HAMMERED, stamped, forged, wrought, worked, formed, shaped, fashioned. **2** WHISKED, whipped, mixed, blended, frothy, foamy.

beating *n* **1** CORPORAL PUNISHMENT, chastisement, whipping, flogging, caning, thrashing. **2** DEFEAT, conquest, rout, ruin, downfall.

beautiful *adj* attractive, fair, pretty, lovely, good-looking, handsome, gorgeous, radiant, ravishing, stunning (*infml*), pleasing, appealing, alluring, charming, delightful, fine, exquisite.
≠ ugly, plain, hideous.

beautify *v* embellish, enhance, improve, grace, gild, garnish, decorate, ornament, deck, bedeck, adorn, array, glamorize, titivate (*infml*), tart up (*sl*).
≠ disfigure, spoil.

beauty *n* attractiveness, fairness, prettiness, loveliness, (good) looks, handsomeness, glamour, appeal, allure, charm, grace, elegance, symmetry, excellence.
≠ ugliness, repulsiveness.

because *conj* as, for, since, owing to, on account of, by reason of, thanks to.

beckon *v* summon, motion, gesture, signal, nod, wave, gesticulate, call, invite, attract, pull, draw, lure, allure, entice, tempt, coax.

become *v* **1** *become old-fashioned*: turn, grow, get, change into, develop into. **2** SUIT, befit, flatter, enhance, grace, embellish, ornament, set off, harmonize.

bed *n* **1** divan, couch, bunk, berth, cot, mattress, pallet, sack (*sl*). **2** LAYER, stratum, substratum, matrix, base, bottom, foundation, groundwork, watercourse, channel. **3** *bed of flowers*: garden, border, patch, plot.

bedclothes *n* bedding, bed-linen, covers.

Kinds of bedclothes include: mattress cover, pillow, pillow sham, bolster, pillowcase, pillowslip, sheet, fitted sheet, valanced sheet, valance, blanket, cellular blanket, electric blanket, quilt, patchwork quilt, duvet, quilt cover, duvet cover, eiderdown, bedspread, candlewick bedspread, throwover, counterpane, coverlet, comforter (*US*), bed canopy, sleeping-bag, bedroll.

bedraggled *adj* untidy, unkempt, dishevelled, disordered, scruffy, slovenly, messy, dirty, muddy, muddied, soiled, wet, sodden, drenched.
≠ neat, tidy, clean.

before *adv* ahead, in front, in advance, sooner, earlier, formerly, previously.
≠ after, later.

beforehand *adv* in advance, preliminarily, already, before, previously, earlier, sooner.

befriend *v* help, aid, assist, succour, back, support, stand by, uphold, sustain, comfort, encourage, welcome, favour, benefit, take under one's wing, make friends with, get to know.
≠ neglect, oppose.

beg *v* request, require, desire, crave, beseech, plead, entreat, implore, pray, supplicate, petition, solicit, cadge, scrounge, sponge.

beggar *n* mendicant, supplicant, pauper, down-and-out, tramp, vagrant, cadger, scrounger, sponger.

begin *v* start, commence, set about, embark on, set in motion, activate, originate, initiate, introduce, found, institute, instigate, arise, spring, emerge, appear.
≠ end, finish, cease.

beginner *n* novice, tiro, starter, learner, trainee, apprentice, student, freshman, fresher, recruit, cub, tenderfoot, fledgling.
≠ veteran, old hand, expert.

beginning *n* start, commencement, onset, outset, opening, preface, prelude, introduction, initiation, establishment, inauguration, inception, starting point, birth, dawn, origin, source, fountainhead, root, seed, emergence, rise.
≠ end, finish.

begrudge *v* resent, grudge, mind, object to, envy, covet, stint.
≠ allow.

beguile *v* **1** CHARM, enchant, bewitch, captivate, amuse, entertain, divert, distract, occupy, engross. **2** DECEIVE, fool, hoodwink, dupe, trick, cheat, delude, mislead.

behalf *n* sake, account, good, interest, benefit, advantage, profit, name, authority, side, support.

behave *v* act, react, respond, work, function, run, operate, perform, conduct oneself, acquit oneself, comport oneself (*fml*).

behaviour *n* conduct, comportment (*fml*), manner, manners, actions, doings, dealings, ways, habits, action, reaction, response, functioning, operation, performance.

behead *v* decapitate, execute, guillotine.

behind *prep* **1** FOLLOWING, after, later than, causing, responsible for, instigating, initiating. **2** SUPPORTING, backing, for.
adv after, following, next, subsequently, behindhand, late, overdue, in arrears, in debt.
n rump, rear, posterior (*infml*), buttocks, seat, bottom, backside (*infml*), bum (*sl*), butt (*US infml*), tail (*infml*).

beige *adj* buff, fawn, mushroom, camel, sandy, khaki, coffee, neutral.

being *n* **1** EXISTENCE, actuality, reality, life, animation, essence, substance, nature, soul, spirit. **2** CREATURE, animal, beast, human being, mortal, person, individual, thing, entity.

belated *adj* late, tardy, overdue, delayed, behindhand, unpunctual.
≠ punctual, timely.

belch *v* burp (*infml*), hiccup, emit, discharge, disgorge, spew.
n burp (*infml*), hiccup.

beleaguered *adj* harassed, pestered, badgered, bothered, worried, vexed, plagued, persecuted, surrounded, beset, besieged.

belief *n* **1** CONVICTION, persuasion, credit, trust, reliance, confidence, assurance, certainty, sureness, presumption, expectation, feeling, intuition, impression, notion, theory, view, opinion, judgement.
2 IDEOLOGY, faith, creed, doctrine, dogma, tenet, principle.
≠ **1** disbelief.

believable *adj* credible, imaginable, conceivable, acceptable, plausible, possible, likely, probable, authoritative, reliable, trustworthy.
≠ unbelievable, incredible, unconvincing.

believe *v* accept, wear (*infml*), swallow (*infml*), credit, trust, count on, depend on, rely on, swear by, hold, maintain, postulate, assume, presume, gather, speculate, conjecture, guess, imagine, think, consider, reckon, suppose, deem, judge.
≠ disbelieve, doubt.

believer *n* convert, proselyte, disciple, follower, adherent, devotee, zealot, supporter, upholder.
≠ unbeliever, sceptic.

belittle *v* minimize, play down, dismiss, underrate, undervalue, underestimate, lessen, diminish, detract from, deprecate, decry, disparage, run down, deride, scorn, ridicule.
≠ exaggerate, praise.

belligerent *adj* aggressive, militant, argumentative, quarrelsome, contentious, combative, pugnacious, violent, bullying, antagonistic, warring, warlike, bellicose.
≠ peaceable.

bellow *v* roar, yell, shout, bawl, cry, scream, shriek, howl, clamour.

belong *v* fit, go with, be part of, attach to, link up with, tie up with, be connected with, relate to.

belongings *n* possessions, property, chattels, goods, effects, things, stuff (*infml*), gear (*infml*), paraphernalia.

beloved *adj* loved, adored, cherished, treasured, prized, precious, pet, favourite, dearest, dear, darling, admired, revered.

below *adv* beneath, under, underneath, down, lower, lower down.
≠ above.
prep **1** UNDER, underneath, beneath. **2** INFERIOR TO, lesser than, subordinate to, subject to.
≠ above.

belt *n* **1** SASH, girdle, waistband, girth, strap. **2** STRIP, band, swathe, stretch, tract, area, region, district, zone, layer.

bemused *adj* confused, muddled, bewildered, puzzled, perplexed, dazed, befuddled, stupefied.
≠ clear-headed, clear, lucid.

bench *n* **1** SEAT, form, settle, pew, ledge, counter, table, stall, workbench, worktable. **2** COURT, courtroom, tribunal, judiciary, judicature, judge, magistrate.

bend *v* curve, turn, deflect, swerve, veer, diverge, twist, contort, flex, shape, mould, buckle, bow, incline, lean, stoop, crouch.
≠ straighten.
n curvature, curve, arc, bow, loop, hook, crook, elbow, angle, corner, turn, twist, zigzag.

beneath *adv* below, under, underneath, lower, lower down.
prep **1** UNDER, underneath, below, lower than. **2** UNWORTHY OF, unbefitting.

benefactor *n* philanthropist, patron, sponsor, angel (*infml*), backer, supporter, promoter, donor, contributor, subscriber, provider, helper, friend, well-wisher.
≠ opponent, persecutor.

beneficial *adj* advantageous, favourable, useful, helpful, profitable, rewarding, valuable, improving, edifying, wholesome.
≠ harmful, detrimental, useless.

beneficiary *n* payee, receiver, recipient, inheritor, legatee, heir, heiress, successor.

benefit *n* advantage, good, welfare, interest, favour, help, aid, assistance, service, use, avail, gain, profit, asset, blessing.
≠ disadvantage, harm, damage.
v help, aid, assist, serve, avail, advantage, profit, improve, enhance, better, further, advance, promote.
≠ hinder, harm, undermine.

benevolent *adj* philanthropic, humanitarian, charitable, generous, liberal, munificent, altruistic, benign, humane, kind, kindly, well-disposed, compassionate, caring, considerate.
≠ mean, selfish, malevolent.

benign *adj* **1** BENEVOLENT, good, gracious, gentle, kind, obliging, friendly, amiable, genial, sympathetic. **2** *a benign tumour*: curable, harmless. **3** FAVOURABLE, propitious, beneficial, temperate, mild, warm, refreshing, restorative, wholesome.
≠ **1** hostile. **2** malignant. **3** harmful, unpleasant.

bent *adj* **1** ANGLED, curved, bowed, arched, folded, doubled, twisted, hunched, stooped. **2** (*infml*) DISHONEST, crooked (*infml*), illegal, criminal, corrupt, untrustworthy.
≠ **1** straight, upright. **2** honest.
n tendency, inclination, leaning, preference, ability, capacity, faculty, aptitude, facility, gift, talent, knack,

flair, forte.
bent on determined, resolved, set, fixed, inclined, disposed.

bequeath *v* will, leave, bestow, gift, endow, grant, settle, hand down, pass on, impart, transmit, assign, entrust, commit.

bequest *n* legacy, inheritance, heritage, trust, bestowal, endowment, gift, donation, estate, devisal, settlement.

bereavement *n* loss, deprivation, dispossession, death.

bereft *adj* deprived, robbed, stripped, destitute, devoid, lacking, wanting, minus.

berserk *adj* mad, crazy, demented, insane, deranged, frantic, frenzied, wild, raging, furious, violent, rabid, raving.
≠ sane, calm.

berth *n* **1** BED, bunk, hammock, billet. **2** MOORING, anchorage, quay, wharf, dock, harbour, port.

beside *prep* alongside, abreast of, next to, adjacent, abutting, bordering, neighbouring, next door to, close to, near, overlooking.

besides *adv* also, as well, too, in addition, additionally, further, furthermore, moreover.
prep apart from, other than, in addition to, over and above.

besiege *v* **1** LAY SIEGE TO, blockade, surround, encircle, confine. **2** TROUBLE, bother, importune, assail, beset, beleaguer, harass, pester, badger, nag, hound, plague.

besotted *adj* infatuated, doting, obsessed, smitten, hypnotized, spellbound, intoxicated.
≠ indifferent, disenchanted.

best *adj* optimum, optimal, first, foremost, leading, unequalled, unsurpassed, matchless, incomparable, supreme, greatest, highest, largest, finest, excellent, outstanding, superlative, first-rate, first-class, perfect.
≠ worst.
adv greatly, extremely, exceptionally, excellently, superlatively.
≠ worst.
n finest, cream, prime, élite, top, first, pick, choice, favourite.
≠ worst.

bestow *v* award, present, grant, confer, endow, bequeath, commit, entrust, impart, transmit, allot, apportion, accord, give, donate, lavish.
≠ withhold, deprive.

bet *n* wager, flutter (*infml*), gamble, speculation, risk, venture, stake, ante, bid, pledge.
v wager, gamble, punt, speculate, risk, hazard, chance, venture, lay, stake, bid, pledge.

betray *v* **1** *betray a friend*: inform on, shop (*sl*), sell (out), double-cross, desert, abandon, forsake. **2** DISCLOSE, give away, tell, divulge, expose, reveal, show, manifest.
≠ **1** defend, protect. **2** conceal, hide.

betrayal *n* treachery, treason, sell-out, disloyalty, unfaithfulness, double-dealing, duplicity, deception, trickery, falseness.
≠ loyalty, protection.

betrayer *n* traitor, Judas, informer, grass (*sl*), supergrass (*sl*), double-crosser, deceiver, conspirator, renegade, apostate.
≠ protector, supporter.

better *adj* **1** SUPERIOR, bigger, larger, longer, greater, worthier, finer, surpassing, preferable. **2** IMPROVING, progressing, on the mend, recovering, fitter, healthier, stronger, recovered, restored.
≠ **1** inferior. **2** worse.
v **1** IMPROVE, ameliorate, enhance, raise, further, promote, forward, reform, mend, correct. **2** SURPASS, top, beat, outdo, outstrip, overtake.
≠ **1** worsen, deteriorate.

between *prep* mid, amid, amidst, among, amongst.

beverage *n* drink, draught, liquor, liquid, refreshment.

bevy *n* gathering, band, company, troupe, group, flock, gaggle, pack, bunch, crowd, throng.

beware *v* watch out, look out, mind,

take heed, steer clear of, avoid, shun, guard against.

bewilder *v* confuse, muddle, disconcert, confound, bamboozle (*infml*), baffle, puzzle, perplex, mystify, daze, stupefy, disorient.

bewildered *adj* confused, muddled, uncertain, disoriented, nonplussed, bamboozled (*infml*), baffled, puzzled, perplexed, mystified, bemused, surprised, stunned.
≠ unperturbed, collected.

bewitch *v* charm, enchant, allure, beguile, spellbind, possess, captivate, enrapture, obsess, fascinate, entrance, hypnotize.

beyond *prep* past, further than, apart from, away from, remote from, out of range of, out of reach of, above, over, superior to.

bias *n* slant, angle, distortion, bent, leaning, inclination, tendency, propensity, partiality, favouritism, prejudice, one-sidedness, unfairness, bigotry, intolerance.
≠ impartiality, fairness.

biased *adj* slanted, angled, distorted, warped, twisted, loaded, weighted, influenced, swayed, partial, predisposed, prejudiced, one-sided, unfair, bigoted, blinkered, jaundiced.
≠ impartial, fair.

bicker *v* squabble, row, quarrel, wrangle, argue, scrap, spar, fight, clash, disagree, dispute.
≠ agree.

bicycle *n* cycle, bike (*infml*), two-wheeler, push-bike, racer, mountain-bike, tandem, penny-farthing.

bid *v* **1** ASK, request, desire, instruct, direct, command, enjoin, require, charge, call, summon, invite, solicit. **2** *he bid more than the painting was worth*: offer, proffer, tender, submit, propose.
n **1** OFFER, tender, sum, amount, price, advance, submission, proposal. **2** ATTEMPT, effort, try, go (*infml*), endeavour, venture.

big *adj* **1** LARGE, great, sizable, considerable, substantial, huge, enormous, immense, massive, colossal, gigantic, mammoth, burly, bulky, extensive, spacious, vast, voluminous. **2** IMPORTANT, significant, momentous, serious, main, principal, eminent, prominent, influential. **3** *that's big of you*: generous, magnanimous, gracious, unselfish.
≠ **1** small, little. **2** insignificant, unknown.

bigot *n* chauvinist, sectarian, racist, sexist, dogmatist, fanatic, zealot.
≠ liberal, humanitarian.

bigoted *adj* prejudiced, biased, intolerant, illiberal, narrow-minded, narrow, blinkered, closed, dogmatic, opinionated, obstinate.
≠ tolerant, liberal, broad-minded, enlightened.

bigotry *n* prejudice, discrimination, bias, injustice, unfairness, intolerance, narrow-mindedness, chauvinism, jingoism, sectarianism, racism, racialism, sexism, dogmatism, fanaticism.
≠ tolerance.

bilious *adj* **1** IRRITABLE, choleric, cross, grumpy, crotchety, testy, grouchy, peevish. **2** SICK, queasy, nauseated, sickly, out of sorts (*infml*).

bill *n* **1** INVOICE, statement, account, charges, reckoning, tally, score. **2** CIRCULAR, leaflet, handout, bulletin, handbill, broadsheet, advertisement, notice, poster, placard, playbill, programme. **3** *parliamentary bill*: proposal, measure, legislation.
v invoice, charge, debit.

billet *n* **1** ACCOMMODATION, quarters, barracks, lodging, housing, berth. **2** EMPLOYMENT, post, occupation.

billow *v* swell, expand, bulge, puff out, fill out, balloon, rise, heave, surge, roll, undulate.

bind *v* **1** ATTACH, fasten, secure, clamp, stick, tie, lash, truss, strap, bandage, cover, dress, wrap. **2** OBLIGE, force, compel, constrain, necessitate, restrict, confine, restrain, hamper.

binding *adj* obligatory, compulsory, mandatory, necessary, requisite, permanent, conclusive, irrevocable,

unalterable, indissoluble, unbreakable, strict.
n border, edging, trimming, tape, bandage, covering, wrapping.

biography *n* life story, life, history, autobiography, memoirs, recollections, curriculum vitae, account, record.

biology

Biological terms include: bacteriology, biochemistry, biology, bionics, botany, cybernetics, cytology, Darwinism, neo-Darwinism, ecology, embryology, endocrinology, evolution, Haeckel's law, genetics, Mendelism, Lamarckism, marine biology, natural history, palaeontology, pathology, physiology, systematics, taxonomy, zoology; amino acid, anatomy, animal behaviour, animal kingdom, bacillus, bacteria, biologist, botanist, cell, chromosome, class, coccus, conservation, corpuscle, cultivar, cytoplasm, deoxyribonucleic acid (DNA), diffusion, ecosystem, ectoplasm, embryo, endoplasmic reticulum (ER), enzyme, evolution, excretion, extinction, flora and fauna, food chain, fossil, gene, genetic engineering, genetic fingerprinting, population genetics, germ, Golgi apparatus, hereditary factor, homeostasis, living world, meiosis, membrane, metabolism, micro-organism, microbe, mitosis, molecule, mutation, natural selection, nuclear membrane, nucleus, nutrition, order, organism, osmosis, parasitism, photosynthesis, pollution, protein, protoplasm, reproduction, respiration, reticulum, ribonucleic acid (RNA), ribosome, secretion, survival of the fittest, symbiosis, virus.

bird

Birds include: sparrow, thrush, starling, blackbird, bluetit, chaffinch, greenfinch, bullfinch, dunnock, robin, wagtail, swallow, tit, wren, martin, swift, crow, magpie, dove, pigeon, skylark, nightingale, linnet, warbler, jay, jackdaw, rook, raven, cuckoo, woodpecker, yellowhammer; duck, mallard, eider, teal, swan, goose, heron, stork, flamingo, pelican, kingfisher, moorhen, coot, lapwing, peewit, plover, curlew, snipe, avocet, seagull, guillemot, tern, petrel, crane, bittern, petrel, albatross, gannet, cormorant, auk, puffin, dipper; eagle, owl, hawk, sparrowhawk, falcon, kestrel, osprey, buzzard, vulture, condor; emu, ostrich, kiwi, peacock, penguin; chicken, grouse, partridge, pheasant, quail, turkey; canary, budgerigar, budgie (*infml*), cockatiel, cockatoo, lovebird, parakeet, parrot, macaw, toucan, myna bird, mockingbird, kookaburra, bird of paradise.

birth *n* **1** CHILDBIRTH, parturition, confinement, delivery, nativity. **2** *of noble birth*: ancestry, family, parentage, descent, line, lineage, genealogy, pedigree, blood, stock, race, extraction, background, breeding.
3 BEGINNING, rise, emergence, origin, source, derivation.

birthplace *n* place of origin, native town, native country, fatherland, mother country, roots, provenance, source, fount.

bisect *v* halve, divide, separate, split, intersect, cross, fork, bifurcate.

bit *n* fragment, part, segment, piece, slice, crumb, morsel, scrap, atom, mite, whit, jot, iota, grain, speck.
bit by bit gradually, little by little, step by step, piecemeal.
≠ wholesale.

bitchy *adj* catty, snide, nasty, mean, spiteful, malicious, vindictive, backbiting, venomous, cruel, vicious.
≠ kind.

bite *v* **1** CHEW, masticate, munch, gnaw, nibble, champ, crunch, crush.
2 *the dog bit her hand*: nip, pierce, wound, tear, rend. **3** SMART, sting, tingle. **4** GRIP, hold, seize, pinch, take effect.
n **1** NIP, wound, sting, smarting, pinch. **2** *a bite to eat*: snack, refreshment, mouthful, morsel, taste.
3 PUNGENCY, piquancy, kick (*infml*), punch.

biting *adj* **1** COLD, freezing, bitter, harsh, severe. **2** CUTTING, incisive, piercing, penetrating, raw, stinging, sharp, tart, caustic, scathing, cynical, hurtful.
≠ **1** mild. **2** bland.

bitter *adj* **1** SOUR, tart, sharp, acid, vinegary, unsweetened. **2** RESENTFUL, embittered, jaundiced, cynical, rancorous, acrimonious, acerbic, hostile. **3** INTENSE, severe, harsh, fierce, cruel, savage, merciless, painful, stinging, biting, freezing, raw.
≠ **1** sweet. **2** contented. **3** mild.

bizarre *adj* strange, odd, queer, curious, weird, peculiar, eccentric, way-out (*infml*), outlandish, ludicrous, ridiculous, fantastic, extravagant, grotesque, freakish, abnormal, deviant, unusual, extraordinary.
≠ normal, ordinary.

black *adj* **1** JET-BLACK, coal-black, jet, ebony, sable, inky, sooty, dusky, swarthy. **2** DARK, unlit, moonless, starless, overcast, dingy, gloomy, sombre, funereal. **3** FILTHY, dirty, soiled, grimy, grubby.
≠ **1** white. **2** bright. **3** clean.
v boycott, blacklist, ban, bar, taboo.
black out 1 FAINT, pass out, collapse, flake out (*infml*). **2** DARKEN, eclipse, cover up, conceal, suppress, withhold, censor, gag.

blacken *v* **1** DARKEN, dirty, soil, smudge, cloud. **2** DEFAME, malign, slander, libel, vilify, revile, denigrate, detract, smear, besmirch, sully, stain, tarnish, taint, defile, discredit, dishonour.
≠ **2** praise, enhance.

blackmail *n* extortion, chantage, hush money (*infml*), intimidation, protection, pay-off, ransom.
v extort, bleed, milk, squeeze, hold to ransom, threaten, lean on (*infml*), force, compel, coerce, demand.

blackout *n* **1** *a news blackout*: suppression, censorship, cover-up (*infml*), concealment, secrecy. **2** FAINT, coma, unconsciousness, oblivion. **3** power failure, power cut.

blade *n* edge, knife, dagger, sword, scalpel, razor, vane.

blame *n* censure, criticism, stick (*sl*), reprimand, reproof, reproach, recrimination, condemnation, accusation, charge, rap (*sl*), incrimination, guilt, culpability, fault, responsibility, accountability, liability, onus.
v accuse, charge, tax, reprimand, chide, reprove, upbraid, reprehend, admonish, rebuke, reproach, censure, criticize, find fault with, disapprove, condemn.
≠ exonerate, vindicate.

blameless *adj* innocent, guiltless, clear, faultless, perfect, unblemished, stainless, virtuous, sinless, upright, above reproach, irreproachable, unblamable, unimpeachable.
≠ guilty, blameworthy.

blanch *v* blench, whiten, pale, fade, bleach.
≠ colour, blush, redden.

bland *adv* boring, monotonous, humdrum, tedious, dull, uninspiring, uninteresting, unexciting, nondescript, characterless, flat, insipid, tasteless, weak, mild, smooth, soft, gentle, non-irritant.
≠ lively, stimulating, sharp.

blank *adj* **1** *a blank page*: empty, unfilled, void, clear, bare, unmarked, plain, clean, white. **2** EXPRESSIONLESS, deadpan, poker-faced, impassive, apathetic, glazed, vacant, uncomprehending.
n space, gap, break, void, emptiness, vacancy, vacuity, nothingness, vacuum.

blanket *n* covering, coating, coat, layer, film, carpet, rug, cloak, mantle, cover, sheet, envelope, wrapper, wrapping.
v cover, coat, eclipse, hide, conceal, mask, cloak, surround, muffle, deaden, obscure, cloud.

blare *v* trumpet, clamour, roar, blast, boom, resound, ring, peal, clang, hoot, toot, honk.

blasé *adj* nonchalant, offhand, unimpressed, unmoved, unexcited, jaded, weary, bored, uninterested, uninspired, apathetic, indifferent, cool, unconcerned.
≠ excited, enthusiastic.

blaspheme *v* profane, desecrate, swear, curse, imprecate, damn, execrate, revile, abuse.

blasphemous *adj* profane, impious, sacrilegious, imprecatory, godless, ungodly, irreligious, irreverent.

blasphemy *n* profanity, curse, expletive, imprecation, cursing, swearing, execration, impiety, irreverence, sacrilege, desecration, violation, outrage.

blast *n* **1** EXPLOSION, detonation, bang, crash, clap, crack, volley, burst, outburst, discharge. **2** *a blast of cold air*: draught, gust, gale, squall, storm, tempest. **3** SOUND, blow, blare, roar, boom, peal, hoot, wail, scream, shriek.
v **1** EXPLODE, blow up, burst, shatter, destroy, demolish, ruin, assail, attack. **2** SOUND, blare, roar, boom, peal, hoot, wail, scream, shriek.

blatant *adj* flagrant, brazen, barefaced, arrant, open, overt, undisguised, ostentatious, glaring, conspicuous, obtrusive, prominent, pronounced, obvious, sheer, outright, unmitigated.

blaze *n* fire, flames, conflagration, bonfire, flare-up, explosion, blast, burst, outburst, radiance, brilliance, glare, flash, gleam, glitter, glow, light, flame.
v burn, flame, flare (up), erupt, explode, burst, fire, flash, gleam, glare, beam, shine, glow.

bleach *v* whiten, blanch, decolorize, fade, pale, lighten.

bleak *adj* **1** GLOOMY, sombre, leaden, grim, dreary, dismal, depressing, joyless, cheerless, comfortless, hopeless, discouraging, disheartening. **2** COLD, chilly, raw, weather-beaten, unsheltered, windy, windswept, exposed, open, barren, bare, empty, desolate, gaunt.
≠ **1** bright, cheerful.

bleed *v* **1** HAEMORRHAGE, gush, spurt, flow, run, exude, weep, ooze, seep, trickle. **2** DRAIN, suck dry, exhaust, squeeze, milk, sap, reduce, deplete.

blemish *n* flaw, imperfection, defect, fault, deformity, disfigurement, mark, speck, smudge, blotch, blot, stain, taint, disgrace, dishonour.

> *Kinds of blemish include*: acne, birthmark, blackhead, blister, boil, bump, bunion, callus, carbuncle, chilblain, corn, freckle, mole, naevus, pimple, pockmark, pustule, scab, scar, spot, strawberry mark, verruca, wart, whitehead, zit (*sl*).

v flaw, deface, disfigure, spoil, mar, damage, impair, spot, mark, blot, blotch, stain, sully, taint, tarnish.

blend *v* **1** MERGE, amalgamate, coalesce, compound, synthesize, fuse, unite, combine, mix, mingle. **2** HARMONIZE, complement, fit, match.
≠ **1** separate.
n compound, composite, alloy, amalgam, amalgamation, synthesis, fusion, combination, union, mix, mixture, concoction.

bless *v* **1** ANOINT, sanctify, consecrate, hallow, dedicate, ordain. **2** PRAISE, extol, magnify, glorify, exalt, thank. **3** APPROVE, countenance, favour, grace, bestow, endow, provide.
≠ **1** curse. **2** condemn.

blessed *adj* **1** HOLY, sacred, hallowed, sanctified, revered, adored, divine. **2** HAPPY, contented, glad, joyful, joyous, lucky, fortunate, prosperous, favoured, endowed.
≠ **1** cursed.

blessing *n* **1** CONSECRATION, dedication, benediction, grace, thanksgiving, invocation. **2** BENEFIT, advantage, favour, godsend, windfall, gift, gain, profit, help, service. **3** *give a proposal one's blessing*: approval, concurrence, backing, support, authority, sanction, consent, permission, leave.
≠ **2** curse, blight. **3** condemnation.

blight *n* curse, bane, evil, scourge, affliction, disease, cancer, canker, fungus, mildew, rot, decay, pollution, contamination, corruption, infestation.
≠ blessing, boon.
v spoil, mar, injure, undermine, ruin, wreck, crush, shatter, destroy, annihilate, blast, wither, shrivel, frustrate, disappoint.
≠ bless.

blind *adj* **1** SIGHTLESS, unsighted, unseeing, eyeless, purblind, partially sighted.

Ways of describing sight impairment include: amaurotic, astigmatic, having cataracts, colour-blind, far-sighted, glaucomatous, hemeralopic, hypermetropic, long-sighted, myopic, near-sighted, night-blind, nyctalopic, presbyopic, sand-blind, short-sighted, snow-blind, stone-blind, trachomatous, visually handicapped, visually impaired, blind as a bat (*infml*).

2 IMPETUOUS, impulsive, hasty, rash, reckless, wild, mad, indiscriminate, careless, heedless, mindless, unthinking, unreasoning, irrational. **3** *blind to their needs*: ignorant, oblivious, unaware, unconscious, unobservant, inattentive, neglectful, indifferent, insensitive, thoughtless, inconsiderate. **4** CLOSED, obstructed, hidden, concealed, obscured.
≠ **1** sighted. **2** careful, cautious. **3** aware, sensitive.
n screen, cover, cloak, mask, camouflage, masquerade, front, façade, distraction, smokescreen, cover-up (*infml*).

bliss *n* blissfulness, ecstasy, euphoria, rapture, joy, happiness, gladness, blessedness, paradise, heaven.
≠ misery, hell, damnation.

blissful *adj* ecstatic, euphoric, elated, enraptured, rapturous, delighted, enchanted, joyful, joyous, happy.
≠ miserable, wretched.

blister *n* sore, swelling, cyst, boil, abscess, ulcer, pustule, pimple, carbuncle.

blizzard *n* snowstorm, squall, storm, tempest.

bloated *adj* swollen, puffy, blown up, inflated, distended, dilated, expanded, enlarged, turgid, bombastic.
≠ thin, shrunken, shrivelled.

blob *n* drop, droplet, globule, glob (*infml*), bead, pearl, bubble, dab, spot, gob, lump, mass, ball, pellet, pill.

block *n* **1** *a block of stone*: piece, lump, mass, chunk, hunk, square, cube, brick, bar. **2** OBSTACLE, barrier, bar, jam, blockage, stoppage, resistance, obstruction, impediment, hindrance, let, delay.
v choke, clog, plug, stop up, dam up, close, bar, obstruct, impede, hinder, stonewall, stop, check, arrest, halt, thwart, scotch, deter.

blockade *n* barrier, barricade, siege, obstruction, restriction, stoppage, closure.

blockage *n* blocking, obstruction, stoppage, occlusion, block, clot, jam, log-jam, congestion, hindrance, impediment.

blond, blonde *adj* fair, flaxen, golden, fair-haired, golden-haired, light-coloured, bleached.

blood *n* extraction, birth, descent, lineage, family, kindred, relations, ancestry, descendants, kinship, relationship.

bloodcurdling *adj* horrifying, chilling, spine-chilling, hair-raising, terrifying, frightening, scary, dreadful, fearful, horrible, horrid, horrendous.

bloodshed *n* killing, murder, slaughter, massacre, blood-bath, butchery, carnage, gore, bloodletting.

bloodthirsty *adj* murderous, homicidal, warlike, savage, barbaric, barbarous, brutal, ferocious, vicious, cruel, inhuman, ruthless.

bloody *adj* bleeding, bloodstained, gory, sanguinary, murderous, savage, brutal, ferocious, fierce, cruel.

bloom *n* **1** BLOSSOM, flower, bud. **2** PRIME, heyday, perfection, blush, flush, glow, rosiness, beauty, radiance, lustre, health, vigour, freshness.
v bud, sprout, grow, wax, develop, mature, blossom, flower, blow, open.
≠ fade, wither.

blossom *n* bloom, flower, bud.
v develop, mature, bloom, flower, blow, flourish, thrive, prosper, succeed.
≠ fade, wither.

blot *n* spot, stain, smudge, blotch, smear, mark, speck, blemish, flaw, fault, defect, taint, disgrace.
v spot, mark, stain, smudge, blur,

sully, taint, tarnish, spoil, mar, disfigure, disgrace.
blot out obliterate, cancel, delete, erase, expunge, darken, obscure, shadow, eclipse.

blotch *n* patch, splodge, splotch, splash, smudge, blot, spot, mark, stain, blemish.

blotchy *adj* spotty, spotted, patchy, uneven, smeary, blemished, reddened, inflamed.

blow[1] *v* **1** BREATHE, exhale, pant, puff, waft, fan, flutter, float, flow, stream, rush, whirl, whisk, sweep, fling, buffet, drive, blast. **2** *blow a horn*: play, sound, pipe, trumpet, toot, blare.
n puff, draught, flurry, gust, blast, wind, gale, squall, tempest.
blow over die down, subside, end, finish, cease, pass, vanish, disappear, dissipate, fizzle out, peter out.
blow up 1 EXPLODE, go off, detonate, burst, blast, bomb. **2** LOSE ONE'S TEMPER, blow one's top (*infml*), erupt, hit the roof (*infml*), rage, go mad (*infml*). **3** INFLATE, pump up, swell, fill (out), puff up, bloat, distend, dilate, expand, enlarge, magnify, exaggerate, overstate.

blow[2] *n* **1** *a blow on the head*: concussion, box, cuff, clip, clout, swipe, biff (*infml*), bash, slap, smack, whack (*infml*), wallop (*infml*), belt (*infml*), buffet, bang, clap, knock, rap, stroke, thump, punch. **2** MISFORTUNE, affliction, reverse, setback, comedown, disappointment, upset, jolt, shock, bombshell, calamity, catastrophe, disaster.

blowy *adj* breezy, windy, fresh, blustery, gusty, squally, stormy.

bludgeon *v* **1** BEAT, strike, club, batter, cosh (*sl*), cudgel. **2** FORCE, coerce, bulldoze, badger, hector, harass, browbeat, bully, terrorize, intimidate.

blue *adj* **1** AZURE, sapphire, cobalt, ultramarine, navy, indigo, aquamarine, turquoise, cyan. **2** DEPRESSED, low, down in the dumps (*infml*), dejected, downcast, dispirited, down-hearted, despondent, gloomy, glum, dismal, sad, unhappy, miserable, melancholy, morose, fed up (*infml*). **3** *a blue joke*: obscene, offensive, indecent, improper, coarse, vulgar, lewd, dirty, pornographic, bawdy, smutty, near the bone, near the knuckle, risqué.
≠ **2** cheerful, happy. **3** decent, clean.

blueprint *n* archetype, prototype, model, pattern, design, outline, draft, sketch, pilot, guide, plan, scheme, project.

bluff *v* lie, pretend, feign, sham, fake, deceive, delude, mislead, hoodwink, blind, bamboozle (*infml*), fool.
n lie, idle boast, bravado, humbug, pretence, show, sham, fake, fraud, trick, subterfuge, deceit, deception.

blunder *n* mistake, error, solecism, howler (*infml*), bloomer (*infml*), clanger (*infml*), inaccuracy, slip, boob (*infml*), indiscretion, gaffe, faux pas, slip-up (*infml*), oversight, fault, cock-up (*sl*).
v stumble, flounder, bumble, err, slip up (*infml*), miscalculate, misjudge, bungle, botch, fluff (*infml*), mismanage, cock up (*sl*).

blunt *adj* **1** UNSHARPENED, dull, worn, pointless, rounded, stubbed. **2** FRANK, candid, direct, forthright, unceremonious, explicit, plain-spoken, honest, downright, outspoken, tactless, insensitive, rude, impolite, uncivil, brusque, curt, abrupt.
≠ **1** sharp, pointed. **2** subtle, tactful.
v dull, take the edge off, dampen, soften, deaden, numb, anaesthetize, alleviate, allay, abate, weaken.
≠ sharpen, intensify.

blur *v* smear, smudge, mist, fog, befog, cloud, becloud, blear, dim, darken, obscure, mask, conceal, soften.
n smear, smudge, blotch, haze, mist, fog, cloudiness, fuzziness, indistinctness, muddle, confusion, dimness, obscurity.

blurred *adj* out of focus, fuzzy, unclear, indistinct, vague, ill-defined, faint, hazy, misty, foggy, cloudy, bleary, dim, obscure, confused.
≠ clear, distinct.

blurt out *v* exclaim, cry, gush, spout, utter, tell, reveal, disclose, divulge,

blab (*infml*), let out, leak, let slip, spill the beans (*infml*).
≠ bottle up, hush up.

blush *v* flush, redden, colour, glow.
≠ blanch.
n flush, reddening, rosiness, ruddiness, colour, glow.

blushing *adj* flushed, red, rosy, glowing, confused, embarrassed, ashamed, modest.
≠ pale, white, composed.

bluster *v* boast, brag, crow, talk big (*infml*), swagger, strut, vaunt, show off, rant, roar, storm, bully, hector.
n boasting, crowing, bravado, bluff, swagger.

blustery *adj* windy, gusty, squally, stormy, tempestuous, violent, wild, boisterous.
≠ calm.

board *n* **1** *a wooden board*: sheet, panel, slab, plank, beam, timber, slat. **2** COMMITTEE, council, panel, jury, commission, directorate, directors, trustees, advisers. **3** MEALS, food, provisions, rations.
v get on, embark, mount, enter, catch.

boast *v* brag, crow, swank (*infml*), claim, exaggerate, talk big (*infml*), bluster, trumpet, vaunt, strut, swagger, show off, exhibit, possess.
≠ belittle, deprecate.
n brag, swank (*infml*), claim, vaunt, pride, joy, gem, treasure.

boastful *adj* proud, conceited, vain, swollen-headed, big-headed (*infml*), puffed up, bragging, crowing, swanky (*infml*), cocky, swaggering.
≠ modest, self-effacing, humble.

boats and ships

Types of boat or ship include: canoe, dinghy, lifeboat, rowing-boat, kayak, coracle, skiff, punt, sampan, dhow, gondola, pedalo, catamaran, trimaran, yacht; cabin-cruiser, motor-boat, motor-launch, speedboat, trawler, barge, narrow boat, houseboat, dredger, junk, smack, lugger; hovercraft, hydrofoil; clipper, cutter, ketch, packet, brig, schooner, square-rigger, galleon; ferry, paddle-steamer, tug, freighter, liner, container-ship, tanker; warship, battleship, destroyer, submarine, U-boat, frigate, aircraft-carrier, cruiser, dreadnought, corvette, minesweeper, man-of-war.

bob *v* bounce, hop, skip, spring, jump, leap, twitch, jerk, jolt, shake, quiver, wobble, oscillate, nod, bow, curtsy.
bob up appear, emerge, arrive, show up (*infml*), materialize, rise, surface, pop up, spring up, crop up, arise.

bodily *adj* physical, corporeal, carnal, fleshly, real, actual, tangible, substantial, concrete, material.
≠ spiritual.
adv altogether, en masse, collectively, as a whole, completely, fully, wholly, entirely, totally, in toto.
≠ piecemeal.

body *n* **1** ANATOMY, physique, build, figure, trunk, torso. **2** CORPSE, cadaver, carcase, stiff (*sl*). **3** COMPANY, association, society, corporation, confederation, bloc, cartel, syndicate, congress, collection, group, band, crowd, throng, multitude, mob, mass. **4** CONSISTENCY, density, solidity, firmness, bulk, mass, substance, essence, fullness, richness.

bodyguard *n* guard, protector, minder (*infml*).

bog *n* marsh, swamp, fen, mire, quagmire, quag, slough, morass, quicksands, marshland, swampland, wetlands.
bog down encumber, hinder, impede, overwhelm, deluge, sink, stick, slow down, slow up, delay, retard, halt, stall.

bogus *adj* false, fake, counterfeit, forged, fraudulent, phoney (*infml*), spurious, sham, pseudo, artificial, imitation, dummy.
≠ genuine, true, real, valid.

bohemian *adj* artistic, arty (*infml*), unconventional, unorthodox, nonconformist, alternative, eccentric, offbeat, way-out (*sl*), bizarre, exotic.
≠ bourgeois, conventional, orthodox.
n beatnik, hippie, drop-out, nonconformist.
≠ bourgeois, conformist.

boil[1] *v* **1** SIMMER, stew, seethe, brew, gurgle, bubble, fizz, effervesce, froth, foam, steam. **2** *boil with anger*: erupt, explode, rage, rave, storm, fulminate, fume.
boil down reduce, concentrate, distil, condense, digest, abstract, summarize, abridge.

boil[2] *n* pustule, abscess, gumboil, ulcer, tumour, pimple, carbuncle, blister, inflammation.

boiling *adj* **1** *boiling water*: turbulent, gurgling, bubbling, steaming. **2** HOT, baking, roasting, scorching, blistering. **3** ANGRY, indignant, incensed, infuriated, enraged, furious, fuming, flaming.

boisterous *adj* exuberant, rumbustious (*infml*), rollicking, bouncy, turbulent, tumultuous, loud, noisy, clamorous, rowdy, rough, disorderly, riotous, wild, unrestrained, unruly, obstreperous.
≠ quiet, calm, restrained.

bold *adj* **1** FEARLESS, dauntless, daring, audacious, brave, courageous, valiant, heroic, gallant, intrepid, adventurous, venturesome, enterprising, plucky, spirited, confident, outgoing. **2** EYE-CATCHING, striking, conspicuous, prominent, strong, pronounced, bright, vivid, colourful, loud, flashy, showy, flamboyant. **3** BRAZEN, brash, forward, shameless, unabashed, cheeky (*infml*), impudent, insolent.
≠ **1** cautious, timid, shy. **2** faint, restrained.

bolt *n* bar, rod, shaft, pin, peg, rivet, fastener, latch, catch, lock.
v **1** FASTEN, secure, bar, latch, lock. **2** ABSCOND, escape, flee, fly, run, sprint, rush, dash, hurtle. **3** *bolt one's food*: gulp, wolf, gobble, gorge, devour, cram, stuff.

bomb *n* atom bomb, petrol bomb, shell, bombshell, explosive, charge, grenade, mine, torpedo, rocket, missile, projectile.
v bombard, shell, torpedo, attack, blow up, destroy.

bombard *v* attack, assault, assail, pelt, pound, strafe, blast, bomb, shell, blitz, besiege, hound, harass, pester.

bombardment *n* attack, assault, air-raid, bombing, shelling, blitz, barrage, cannonade, fusillade, salvo, fire, flak.

bombastic *adj* grandiloquent, magniloquent, grandiose, pompous, high-flown, inflated, bloated, windy, wordy, verbose.

bond *n* **1** CONNECTION, relation, link, tie, union, affiliation, attachment, affinity. **2** CONTRACT, covenant, agreement, pledge, promise, word, obligation. **3** FETTER, shackle, manacle, chain, cord, band, binding.
v connect, fasten, bind, unite, fuse, glue, gum, paste, stick, seal.

bondage *n* imprisonment, incarceration, captivity, confinement, restraint, slavery, enslavement, serfdom, servitude, subservience, subjection, subjugation, yoke.
≠ freedom, independence.

bones

> *Human bones include*: clavicle, coccyx, collar-bone, femur, fibula, hip-bone, humerus, ilium, ischium, mandible, maxilla, metacarpal, metatarsal, patella, pelvic girdle, pelvis, pubis, radius, rib, scapula, shoulder-blade, skull, sternum, stirrup-bone, temporal, thigh-bone, tibia, ulna, vertebra.

bonus *n* advantage, benefit, plus (*infml*), extra, perk (*infml*), perquisite, commission, dividend, premium, prize, reward, honorarium, tip, gratuity, gift, hand out.
≠ disadvantage, disincentive.

bony *adj* thin, lean, angular, lanky, gawky, gangling, skinny, scrawny, emaciated, rawboned, gaunt, drawn.
≠ fat, plump.

book *n* volume, tome, publication, work, booklet, tract.

> *Types of book include*: hardback, paperback, bestseller; fiction, novel, story, thriller, romantic novel; children's book, primer, picture-book, annual; reference book, encyclopedia, dictionary, lexicon, thesaurus, concordance, anthology, compendium, omnibus, atlas, guidebook, gazetteer, directory,

anthology, pocket companion, handbook, manual, cookbook, yearbook, almanac, catalogue; notebook, exercise book, textbook, scrapbook, album, sketchbook, diary, jotter, pad, ledger; libretto, manuscript, hymn-book, hymnal, prayer-book, psalter, missal, lectionary. *see also* **literature**.

v reserve, bag (*infml*), engage, charter, procure, order, arrange, organize, schedule, programme.
≠ cancel.

bookbinding

Terms used in bookbinding include: adhesive binding, all edges gilt (aeg), backboard, backbone, back cornering, back lining, binder's board (*US*), binder's brass, binder's die (*US*), binding, blind blocking, blocking, boards, bolts, book block, buckram, case, casebound, casing-in, cloth-lined board, comb-binding, drawn-on, dust cover, embossing, endpaper, flyleaf, fore edge, front board, full bound, gather, half bound, hardback, head, headband, headcap, hinge, jacket, laminating, library binding, limp, lining, Linson®, loose-leaf, mechanical binding, millboard, morocco, notch binding, open-flat, paperback, pasteboard, perfect binding, quarter bound, raised band, ring binding, rounding and backing, saddle-stitch, sewing, shoulder, side-stitch, signature, smashing, soft-cover, spine, spiral binding, square back, stab-stitch, stamping (*US*), strawboard, tail, tailband, thermoplastic binding, thread sewing, unsewn binding, varnishing, whole bound, wire binding, wire stitching, wiro binding, yapp.

boom *v* **1** BANG, crash, roar, thunder, roll, rumble, resound, reverberate, blast, explode. **2** FLOURISH, thrive, prosper, succeed, develop, grow, increase, gain, expand, swell, escalate, intensify, strengthen, explode.
≠ **2** fail, collapse, slump.
n **1** BANG, clap, crash, roar, thunder, rumble, reverberation, blast, explosion, burst. **2** INCREASE, growth, expansion, gain, upsurge, jump, spurt, boost, upturn, improvement, advance, escalation, explosion.
≠ **2** failure, collapse, slump, recession, depression.

boon *n* blessing, advantage, benefit, godsend, windfall, favour, kindness, gift, present, grant, gratuity.
≠ disadvantage, blight.

boorish *adj* uncouth, oafish, loutish, ill-mannered, rude, coarse, crude, vulgar, unrefined, uncivilized, uneducated, ignorant.
≠ polite, refined, cultured.

boost *n* improvement, enhancement, expansion, increase, rise, jump, increment, addition, supplement, booster, lift, hoist, heave, push, thrust, help, advancement, promotion, praise, encouragement, fillip, ego-trip (*sl*).
≠ setback, blow.
v raise, elevate, improve, enhance, develop, enlarge, expand, amplify, increase, augment, heighten, lift, hoist, jack up, heave, push, thrust, help, aid, assist, advance, further, promote, advertise, plug (*infml*), praise, inspire, encourage, foster, support, sustain, bolster, supplement.
≠ hinder, undermine.

boot *n* gumboot, wellington, welly (*infml*), galosh, overshoe, walking-boot, riding-boot, top-boot.

booth *n* kiosk, stall, stand, hut, box, compartment, cubicle, carrel.

booty *n* loot, plunder, pillage, spoils, swag (*sl*), haul, gains, takings, pickings, winnings.

border *n* **1** BOUNDARY, frontier, bound, bounds, confine, confines, limit, demarcation, borderline, margin, fringe, periphery, surround, perimeter, circumference, edge, rim, brim, verge, brink. **2** TRIMMING, frill, valance, skirt, hem, frieze.
border on 1 ADJOIN, abut, touch, impinge, join, connect, communicate with. **2** RESEMBLE, approximate, approach, verge on.

bore[1] *v* drill, mine, pierce, perforate, penetrate, sink, burrow, tunnel, undermine, sap.

bore² *v* tire, weary, fatigue, jade, trouble, bother, worry, irritate, annoy, vex, irk.
≠ interest, excite.
n (*infml*) nuisance, bother, bind (*infml*), drag (*infml*), pain (*infml*), headache (*infml*).
≠ pleasure, delight.

boredom *n* tedium, tediousness, monotony, dullness, apathy, listlessness, weariness, world-weariness.
≠ interest, excitement.

boring *adj* tedious, monotonous, routine, repetitious, uninteresting, unexciting, uneventful, dull, dreary, humdrum, commonplace, trite, unimaginative, uninspired, dry, stale, flat, insipid.
≠ interesting, exciting, stimulating, original.

borrow *v* steal, pilfer, filch, lift, plagiarize, crib, copy, imitate, mimic, echo, take, draw, derive, obtain, adopt, use, scrounge, cadge, sponge, appropriate, usurp.
≠ lend.

bosom *n* **1** BUST, breasts, chest, breast. **2** HEART, core, centre, midst, protection, shelter, sanctuary.

boss *n* employer, governor, master, owner, captain, head, chief, leader, supremo, administrator, executive, director, manager, foreman, gaffer, superintendent, overseer, supervisor.
boss around order around, order about, domineer, tyrannize, bully, bulldoze, browbeat, push around, dominate.

bossy *adj* authoritarian, autocratic, tyrannical, despotic, dictatorial, domineering, overbearing, oppressive, lordly, high-handed, imperious, insistent, assertive, demanding, exacting.
≠ unassertive.

bother *v* disturb, inconvenience, harass, hassle (*infml*), pester, plague, nag, annoy, irritate, irk, molest, trouble, worry, concern, alarm, dismay, distress, upset, vex.
n inconvenience, trouble, problem, difficulty, hassle (*infml*), fuss, bustle, flurry, nuisance, pest, annoyance, irritation, aggravation (*infml*), vexation, worry, strain.

bottle

Types of bottle include: ampulla, calabash, carafe, carboy, decanter, demijohn, flacon, flagon, flask, gourd, jack, phial, pitcher, vial; apothecary bottle, beer bottle, cruet, feeding bottle, hip flask, hot-water bottle, milk bottle, scent bottle, snuff bottle, Thermos® flask, vinegar bottle, wine bottle. *see also* **wine-bottle sizes**.

bottle up hide, conceal, restrain, curb, hold back, suppress, inhibit, restrict, enclose, contain.
≠ unbosom, unburden.

bottle-neck *n* hold-up, traffic jam, snarl-up, congestion, clogging, blockage, obstruction, block, obstacle.

bottom *n* **1** UNDERSIDE, underneath, sole, base, foot, plinth, pedestal, support, foundation, substructure, ground, floor, bed, depths, nadir. **2** RUMP, rear, behind, posterior (*infml*), buttocks, seat, backside (*infml*), bum (*sl*), butt (*US infml*), tail (*infml*).
≠ **1** top.

bottomless *adj* deep, profound, fathomless, unfathomed, unplumbed, immeasurable, measureless, infinite, boundless, limitless, unlimited, inexhaustible.
≠ shallow, limited.

bounce *v* spring, jump, leap, bound, bob, ricochet, rebound, recoil.
n **1** SPRING, bound, springiness, elasticity, give, resilience, rebound, recoil. **2** EBULLIENCE, exuberance, vitality, vivacity, energy, vigour, go (*infml*), zip (*infml*), animation, liveliness.

bound¹ *adj* **1** FASTENED, secured, fixed, tied (up), chained, held, restricted, bandaged. **2** LIABLE, committed, duty-bound, obliged, required, forced, compelled, constrained, destined, fated, doomed, sure, certain.

bound² *v* jump, leap, vault, hurdle, spring, bounce, bob, hop, skip, frisk,

gambol, frolic, caper, prance.
n jump, leap, vault, spring, bounce, bob, hop, skip, gambol, frolic, caper, dance, prance.

boundary *n* border, frontier, barrier, line, borderline, demarcation, bounds, confines, limits, margin, fringe, verge, brink, edge, perimeter, extremity, termination.

boundless *adj* unbounded, limitless, unlimited, unconfined, countless, untold, incalculable, vast, immense, measureless, immeasurable, infinite, endless, unending, interminable, inexhaustible, unflagging, indefatigable.
≠ limited, restricted.

bounds *n* confines, limits, borders, marches, margins, fringes, periphery, circumference, edges, extremities.

bounty *n* **1** GENEROSITY, liberality, munificence, largesse, almsgiving, charity, philanthropy, beneficence, kindness. **2** REWARD, recompense, premium, bonus, gratuity, gift, present, donation, grant, allowance.

bouquet *n* **1** *bouquet of flowers*: bunch, posy, nosegay, spray, corsage, buttonhole, wreath, garland. **2** AROMA, smell, odour, scent, perfume, fragrance.

bourgeois *adj* middle-class, materialistic, conservative, traditional, conformist, conventional, hide-bound, unadventurous, dull, humdrum, banal, commonplace, trite, unoriginal, unimaginative.
≠ bohemian, unconventional, original.

bout *n* **1** FIGHT, battle, engagement, encounter, struggle, set-to, match, contest, competition, round, heat. **2** PERIOD, spell, time, stint, turn, go (*infml*), term, stretch, run, course, session, spree, attack, fit.

bow *v* **1** *bow one's head*: incline, bend, nod, bob, curtsy, genuflect (*fml*), kowtow, salaam, stoop. **2** YIELD, give in, consent, surrender, capitulate, submit, acquiesce, concede, accept, comply, defer. **3** SUBDUE, overpower, conquer, vanquish, crush, subjugate.
n inclination, bending, nod, bob, curtsy, genuflexion (*fml*), kowtow, salaam, obeisance (*fml*), salutation, acknowledgement.
bow out withdraw, pull out, desert, abandon, defect, back out, chicken out (*infml*), retire, resign, quit, stand down, step down, give up.

bowels *n* **1** INTESTINES, viscera, entrails, guts, insides, innards (*infml*). **2** DEPTHS, interior, inside, middle, centre, core, heart.

bowl[1] *n* receptacle, container, vessel, dish, basin, sink.

bowl[2] *v* throw, hurl, fling, pitch, roll, spin, whirl, rotate, revolve.
bowl over surprise, amaze, astound, astonish, stagger, stun, dumbfound, flabbergast (*infml*), floor (*infml*).

box[1] *n* container, receptacle, case, carton, packet, present, chest.

> *Types of box include*: bin, caddy, canister, cartridge, casket, coffer, coffin, crate, locker, pack, package, punnet, sarcophagus, tea chest, tin, trunk; ballot-box, black box, box-file, cardboard box, cigarette box, collection-box, cool-box, dispatch box, hatbox, jewellery box, knife box, matchbox, pencilbox, pillbox, pillar box, postbox, safe, sewing box, shoebox, snuffbox, strongbox, suggestion box, toolbox, trinket box, vesta, writing-slope.

v case, encase, package, pack, wrap.
box in enclose, surround, circumscribe, cordon off, hem in, corner, trap, confine, restrict, imprison, cage, coop up, contain.

box[2] *v* fight, spar, punch, hit, strike, slap, buffet, cuff, clout, sock (*sl*), wallop (*infml*), whack (*infml*).

boxer *n* pugilist, fighter, prizefighter, sparring partner, flyweight, featherweight, lightweight, welterweight, middleweight, heavyweight.

boxing *n* pugilism, prizefighting, fisticuffs, sparring.

boy *n* son, lad, youngster, kid (*infml*), nipper (*infml*), stripling, youth, fellow.

boycott *v* refuse, reject, embargo, black, ban, prohibit, disallow, bar,

exclude, blacklist, outlaw, ostracize, cold-shoulder, ignore, spurn.
≠ encourage, support.

boyfriend *n* young man, man, fellow (*infml*), bloke (*infml*), admirer, date, sweetheart, lover, fiancé.

brace *n* pair, couple, twosome, duo.
v strengthen, reinforce, fortify, bolster, buttress, prop, shore (up), support, steady, tighten, fasten, tie, strap, bind, bandage.

bracing *adj* fresh, crisp, refreshing, reviving, strengthening, fortifying, tonic, rousing, stimulating, exhilarating, invigorating, enlivening, energizing, brisk, energetic, vigorous.
≠ weakening, debilitating.

braid *v* plait, interweave, interlace, intertwine, weave, lace, twine, entwine, ravel, twist, wind.
≠ undo, unravel.

brain *n* **1** grey matter, head, mind, intellect, nous, brains (*infml*), intelligence, wit, reason, sense, common sense, shrewdness, understanding. **2** MASTERMIND, intellectual, highbrow, egghead (*infml*), scholar, expert, boffin, genius, prodigy.
≠ **2** simpleton.

> *Parts of the brain include*: brainstem, cerebellum, cerebral cortex (grey matter), cerebrum, corpus callosum, forebrain, frontal lobe, hindbrain, hypothalamus, medulla oblongata, mesencephalon, midbrain, occipital lobe, optic thalamus, parietal lobe, pineal body, pituitary gland, pons, spinal cord, temporal lobe, thalamus.

brainy (*infml*) *adj* intellectual, intelligent, clever, smart, bright, brilliant.
≠ dull.

brake *n* check, curb, rein, restraint, control, restriction, constraint, drag.
v slow, decelerate, retard, drag, slacken, moderate, check, halt, stop, pull up.
≠ accelerate.

branch *n* **1** BOUGH, limb, sprig, shoot, offshoot, arm, wing, prong. **2** *a different branch of the company*: department, office, part, section, division, subsection, subdivision.
branch out diversify, vary, develop, expand, enlarge, extend, broaden out, increase, multiply, proliferate, ramify.

brand *n* make, brand-name, tradename, trademark, logo, mark, symbol, sign, emblem, label, stamp, hallmark, grade, quality, class, kind, type, sort, line, variety, species.
v mark, stamp, label, type, stigmatize, burn, scar, stain, taint, disgrace, discredit, denounce, censure.

brandish *v* wave, flourish, shake, raise, swing, wield, flash, flaunt, exhibit, display, parade.

brash *adj* **1** BRAZEN, forward, impertinent, impudent, insolent, rude, cocky, assured, bold, audacious. **2** RECKLESS, rash, impetuous, impulsive, hasty, precipitate, foolhardy, incautious, indiscreet.
≠ **1** reserved. **2** cautious.

bravado *n* swagger, boasting, bragging, bluster, bombast, talk, boast, vaunting, showing off, parade, show, pretence.
≠ modesty, restraint.

brave *adj* courageous, plucky, unafraid, fearless, dauntless, undaunted, bold, audacious, daring, intrepid, stalwart, hardy, stoical, resolute, stout-hearted, valiant, gallant, heroic, indomitable.
≠ cowardly, afraid, timid.
v face, confront, defy, challenge, dare, stand up to, face up to, suffer, endure, bear, withstand.
≠ capitulate.

bravery *n* courage, pluck, guts (*infml*), fearlessness, dauntlessness, boldness, audacity, daring, intrepidity, stalwartness, hardiness, fortitude, resolution, stout-heartedness, valiance, valour, gallantry, heroism, indomitability, grit, mettle, spirit.
≠ cowardice, faint-heartedness, timidity.

brawl *n* fight, punch-up (*infml*), scrap, scuffle, dust-up (*infml*), mêlée, free-for-all, fray, affray, broil, fracas, rumpus,

disorder, row, argument, quarrel, squabble, altercation, dispute, clash.
v fight, scrap, scuffle, wrestle, tussle, row, argue, quarrel, squabble, wrangle, dispute.

brawny *adj* muscular, sinewy, athletic, well-built, burly, beefy, hefty, solid, bulky, hulking, massive, strapping, strong, powerful, vigorous, sturdy, robust, hardy, stalwart.
≠ slight, frail.

brazen *adj* blatant, flagrant, brash, brassy, bold, forward, saucy, pert, barefaced, impudent, insolent, defiant, shameless, unashamed, unabashed, immodest.
≠ shy, shamefaced, modest.

breach *n* **1** *a breach of the rules*: violation, contravention, infringement, trespass, disobedience, offence, transgression, lapse, disruption.
2 QUARREL, disagreement, dissension, difference, variance, schism, rift, rupture, split, division, separation, parting, estrangement, alienation, disaffection, dissociation. **3** BREAK, crack, rift, rupture, fissure, cleft, crevice, opening, aperture, gap, space, hole, chasm.

bread *n* loaf, roll, food, provisions, diet, fare, nourishment, nutriment, sustenance, subsistence, necessities.

breadth *n* width, broadness, wideness, latitude, thickness, size, magnitude, measure, scale, range, reach, scope, compass, span, sweep, extent, expanse, spread, comprehensiveness, extensiveness, vastness.

break *v* **1** FRACTURE, crack, snap, split, sever, separate, divide, rend, smash, disintegrate, splinter, shiver, shatter, ruin, destroy, demolish.
2 *break the law*: violate, contravene, infringe, breach, disobey, flout.
3 PAUSE, halt, stop, discontinue, interrupt, suspend, rest. **4** SUBDUE, tame, weaken, enfeeble, impair, undermine, demoralize. **5** *break the news*: tell, inform, impart, divulge, disclose, reveal, announce. **6** *break a record*: exceed, beat, better, excel, surpass, outdo, outstrip.
≠ **1** mend. **2** keep, observe, abide by. **4** strengthen.
n **1** FRACTURE, crack, split, rift, rupture, schism, separation, tear, gash, fissure, cleft, crevice, opening, gap, hole, breach. **2** INTERVAL, intermission, interlude, interruption, pause, halt, lull, let-up (*infml*), respite, rest, breather (*infml*), time out, holiday. **3** OPPORTUNITY, chance, advantage, fortune, luck.
break away separate, split, part company, detach, secede, leave, depart, quit, run away, escape, flee, fly.
break down 1 *the van broke down*: fail, stop, pack up (*infml*), conk out (*sl*), seize up, give way, collapse, crack up (*infml*).
2 ANALYSE, dissect, separate, itemize, detail.
break in 1 INTERRUPT, butt in, interpose, interject, intervene, intrude, encroach, impinge. **2** BURGLE, rob, raid, invade.
break off 1 DETACH, snap off, sever, separate, part, divide, disconnect.
2 PAUSE, interrupt, suspend, discontinue, halt, stop, cease, end, finish, terminate.
break out 1 START, begin, commence, arise, emerge, happen, occur, erupt, flare up, burst out. **2** ESCAPE, abscond, bolt, flee.
break up 1 DISMANTLE, take apart, demolish, destroy, disintegrate, splinter, sever, divide, split, part, separate, divorce. **2** DISBAND, disperse, dissolve, adjourn, suspend, stop, finish, terminate.

breakable *adj* brittle, fragile, delicate, flimsy, insubstantial, frail.
≠ unbreakable, durable, sturdy.

breakdown *n* **1** FAILURE, collapse, disintegration, malfunction, interruption, stoppage. **2** ANALYSIS, dissection, itemization, classification, categorization.

break-in *n* burglary, house-breaking, robbery, raid, invastion, intrusion, trespass.

breakthrough *n* discovery, find, finding, invention, innovation, advance, progress, headway, step, leap, development, improvement.

break-up *n* divorce, separation, parting, split, rift, finish, termination, dissolution, dispersal, disintegration, crumbling.

breakwater *n* groyne, mole, jetty, pier, quay, wharf, dock.

breath *n* **1** AIR, breathing, respiration, inhalation, exhalation, sigh, gasp, pant, gulp. **2** BREEZE, puff, waft, gust. **3** AROMA, smell, odour, whiff. **4** HINT, suggestion, suspicion, undertone, whisper, murmur.

breathe *v* **1** RESPIRE, inhale, exhale, expire, sigh, gasp, pant, puff. **2** SAY, utter, express, voice, articulate, murmur, whisper, impart, tell. **3** INSTIL, imbue, infuse, inject, inspire.

breathless *adj* **1** SHORT-WINDED, out of breath, panting, puffing, puffed (out), exhausted, winded, gasping, wheezing, choking. **2** *breathless anticipation*: expectant, impatient, eager, agog, excited, feverish, anxious.

breathtaking *adj* awe-inspiring, impressive, magnificent, overwhelming, amazing, astonishing, stunning, exciting, thrilling, stirring, moving.

breed *v* **1** REPRODUCE, procreate, multiply, propagate, hatch, bear, bring forth, rear, raise, bring up, educate, train, instruct. **2** PRODUCE, create, originate, arouse, cause, occasion, engender, generate, make, foster, nurture, nourish, cultivate, develop.
n species, strain, variety, family, ilk, sort, kind, type, stamp, stock, race, progeny, line, lineage, pedigree.

breeding *n* **1** REPRODUCTION, procreation, nurture, development, rearing, raising, upbringing, education, training, background, ancestry, lineage, stock. **2** MANNERS, politeness, civility, gentility, urbanity, refinement, culture, polish.
≠ **2** vulgarity.

breeze *n* wind, gust, flurry, waft, puff, breath, draught, air.

breezy *adj* **1** WINDY, blowing, fresh, airy, gusty, blustery, squally. **2** ANIMATED, lively, vivacious, jaunty, buoyant, blithe, debonair, carefree, cheerful, easy-going (*infml*), casual, informal, light, bright, exhilarating.
≠ **1** still. **2** staid, serious.

brevity *n* briefness, shortness, terseness, conciseness, succinctness, pithiness, crispness, incisiveness, abruptness, curtness, impermanence, ephemerality, transience, transitoriness.
≠ verbosity, permanence, longevity.

brew *v* **1** INFUSE, stew, boil, seethe, ferment, prepare, soak, steep, mix, cook. **2** PLOT, scheme, plan, project, devise, contrive, concoct, hatch, excite, foment, build up, gather, develop.
n infusion, drink, beverage, liquor, potion, broth, gruel, stew, mixture, blend, concoction, preparation, fermentation, distillation.

bribe *n* incentive, inducement, allurement, enticement, back-hander (*infml*), kickback, payola, refresher (*infml*), sweetener (*infml*), hush money (*infml*), protection money.
v corrupt, suborn, buy off, reward.

bribery *n* corruption, graft (*sl*), palm-greasing, inducement, lubrication.

bric-à-brac *n* knick-knacks, ornaments, curios, antiques, trinkets, baubles.

bridal *adj* wedding, nuptial, marriage, matrimonial, marital, conjugal.

bridge *n* arch, span, causeway, link, connection, bond, tie.

> *Types of bridge include*: suspension bridge, arch bridge, cantilever bridge, flying bridge, flyover, overpass, footbridge, railway bridge, viaduct, aqueduct, humpback bridge, toll bridge, pontoon bridge, Bailey bridge, rope bridge, drawbridge, swing bridge.

v span, cross, traverse, fill, link, connect, couple, join, unite, bind.

bridle *v* check, curb, restrain, control, govern, master, subdue, moderate, repress, contain.

brief *adj* **1** SHORT, terse, succinct, concise, pithy, crisp, compressed, thumbnail, laconic, abrupt, sharp, brusque, blunt, curt, surly. **2** SHORT-LIVED, momentary, ephemeral, transient, fleeting, passing, transitory,

temporary, limited, cursory, hasty, quick, swift, fast.
≠ **1** long. **2** lengthy.
n **1** ORDERS, instructions, directions, remit, mandate, directive, advice, briefing, data, information.
2 OUTLINE, summary, précis, dossier, case, defence, argument.
v instruct, direct, explain, guide, advise, prepare, prime, inform, fill in (*infml*), gen up (*sl*).

briefing *n* meeting, conference, preparation, priming, filling-in (*infml*), gen (*sl*), low-down (*sl*), information, advice, guidance, directions, instructions, orders.

bright *adj* **1** LUMINOUS, illuminated, radiant, shining, beaming, flashing, gleaming, glistening, glittering, sparkling, twinkling, shimmering, glowing, brilliant, resplendent, glorious, splendid, dazzling, glaring, blazing, intense, vivid. **2** HAPPY, cheerful, glad, joyful, merry, jolly, lively, vivacious. **3** *the future looks bright*: promising, propitious, auspicious, favourable, rosy, optimistic, hopeful, encouraging.
4 CLEVER, brainy (*infml*), smart, intelligent, quick-witted, quick, sharp, acute, keen, astute, perceptive.
5 CLEAR, transparent, translucent, lucid. **6** *a bright day*: fine, sunny, cloudless, unclouded.
≠ **1** dull. **2** sad. **3** depressing. **4** stupid. **5** muddy. **6** dark.

brighten *v* **1** LIGHT UP, illuminate, lighten, clear up. **2** POLISH, burnish, rub up, shine, gleam, glow. **3** CHEER UP, gladden, hearten, encourage, enliven, perk up.
≠ **1** darken. **2** dull, tarnish.

brilliance *n* **1** TALENT, virtuosity, genius, greatness, distinction, excellence, aptitude, cleverness. **2** RADIANCE, brightness, sparkle, dazzle, intensity, vividness, gloss, lustre, sheen, glamour, glory, magnificence, splendour.

brilliant *adj* **1** *a brilliant pianist*: gifted, talented, accomplished, expert, skilful, masterly, exceptional, outstanding, superb, illustrious, famous, celebrated. **2** SPARKLING, glittering, scintillating, dazzling, glaring, blazing, intense, vivid, bright, shining, glossy, showy, glorious, magnificent, splendid. **3** CLEVER, brainy (*infml*), intelligent, quick, astute.
≠ **1** undistinguished. **2** dull. **3** stupid.

brim *n* rim, perimeter, circumference, lip, edge, margin, border, brink, verge, top, limit.

bring *v* **1** CARRY, bear, convey, transport, fetch, take, deliver, escort, accompany, usher, guide, conduct, lead. **2** CAUSE, produce, engender, create, prompt, provoke, force, attract, draw.
bring about cause, occasion, create, produce, generate, effect, accomplish, achieve, fulfil, realize, manage, engineer, manoeuvre, manipulate.
bring in earn, net, gross, produce, yield, fetch, return, accrue, realize.
bring off achieve, accomplish, fulfil, execute, discharge, perform, succeed, win.
bring on cause, occasion, induce, lead to, give rise to, generate, inspire, prompt, provoke, precipitate, expedite, accelerate, advance.
≠ inhibit.
bring out 1 EMPHASIZE, stress, highlight, enhance, draw out.
2 PUBLISH, print, issue, launch, introduce.
bring up 1 REAR, raise, foster, nurture, educate, teach, train, form. **2** *bring up a subject*: introduce, broach, mention, submit, propose. **3** VOMIT, regurgitate, throw up (*infml*).

brink *n* verge, threshold, edge, margin, fringe, border, boundary, limit, extremity, lip, rim, brim, bank.

brisk *adj* **1** ENERGETIC, vigorous, quick, snappy, lively, spirited, active, busy, bustling, agile, nimble, alert.
2 INVIGORATING, exhilarating, stimulating, bracing, refreshing, fresh, crisp.
≠ **1** lazy, sluggish.

bristle *n* hair, whisker, stubble, spine, prickle, barb, thorn.

bristly *adj* hairy, whiskered, bearded, unshaven, stubbly, rough, spiny, prickly, spiky, thorny.
≠ clean-shaven, smooth.

brittle *adj* breakable, fragile, delicate, frail, crisp, crumbly, crumbling, friable, shattery, shivery.
≠ durable, resilient.

broad *adj* **1** WIDE, large, vast, roomy, spacious, capacious, ample, extensive, widespread. **2** WIDE-RANGING, far-reaching, encyclopedic, catholic, eclectic, all-embracing, inclusive, comprehensive, general, sweeping, universal, unlimited.
≠ **1** narrow. **2** restricted.

broadcast *v* air, show, transmit, beam, relay, televise, report, announce, publicize, advertise, publish, circulate, promulgate, disseminate, spread.
n transmission, programme, show.

broaden *v* widen, thicken, swell, spread, enlarge, expand, extend, stretch, increase, augment, develop, open up, branch out, diversify.

broadminded *adj* liberal, tolerant, permissive, enlightened, free-thinking, open-minded, receptive, unbiased, unprejudiced.
≠ narrow-minded, intolerant, biased.

brochure *n* leaflet, booklet, pamphlet, prospectus, broadsheet, handbill, circular, handout, folder.

broke (*infml*) *adj* insolvent, penniless, bankrupt, bust, ruined, impoverished, destitute.
≠ solvent, rich, affluent.

broken *adj* **1** FRACTURED, burst, ruptured, severed, separated, faulty, defective, out of order, shattered, destroyed, demolished. **2** DISJOINTED, disconnected, fragmentary, discontinuous, interrupted, intermittent, spasmodic, erratic, hesitating, stammering, halting, imperfect. **3** *a broken man*: beaten, defeated, crushed, demoralized, down, weak, feeble, exhausted, tamed, subdued, oppressed.
≠ **1** mended. **2** fluent.

broken-down *adj* dilapidated, worn-out, ruined, collapsed, decayed, inoperative, out of order.

broken-hearted *adj* heartbroken, inconsolable, devastated, grief-stricken, desolate, despairing, miserable, wretched, mournful, sorrowful, sad, unhappy, dejected, despondent, crestfallen, disappointed.

brooch *n* badge, pin, clip, clasp.

brood *v* ponder, ruminate, meditate, muse, mull over, go over, rehearse, dwell on, agonize, fret, mope.
n clutch, chicks, hatch, litter, young, offspring, issue, progeny, children, family.

brook *n* stream, rivulet, beck, burn, watercourse, channel.

brother *n* sibling, relation, relative, comrade, friend, mate, partner, colleague, associate, fellow, companion, monk, friar.

brotherhood *n* fraternity, association, society, league, confederation, confederacy, alliance, union, guild, fellowship, community, clique.

browbeat *v* bully, coerce, dragoon, bulldoze, awe, cow, intimidate, threaten, tyrannize, domineer, overbear, oppress, hound.
≠ coax.

brown *adj* mahogany, chocolate, coffee, hazel, bay, chestnut, umber, sepia, tan, tawny, russet, rust, rusty, brunette, dark, dusky, sunburnt, tanned, bronzed, browned, toasted.

browse *v* **1** LEAF THROUGH, flick through, dip into, skim, survey, scan, peruse. **2** GRAZE, pasture, feed, eat, nibble.

bruise *v* discolour, blacken, mark, blemish, pound, pulverize, crush, hurt, injure, insult, offend, grieve.
n contusion, discoloration, black eye, shiner (*sl*), mark, blemish, injury.

brush[1] *n* broom, sweeper, besom.
v **1** CLEAN, sweep, flick, burnish, polish, shine. **2** TOUCH, contact, graze, kiss, stroke, rub, scrape.
brush aside dismiss, pooh-pooh, belittle, disregard, ignore, flout, override.
brush off disregard, ignore, slight, snub,

cold-shoulder, rebuff, dismiss, spurn, reject, repulse, disown, repudiate.
brush up 1 REVISE, relearn, improve, polish up, study, read up, swot (*infml*). **2** REFRESH, freshen up, clean, tidy.

brush[2] *n* scrub, thicket, bushes, shrubs, brushwood, undergrowth, ground cover.

brush[3] *n* confrontation, encounter, clash, conflict, fight, scrap, skirmish, set-to, tussle, dust-up (*infml*), fracas.

brusque *adj* abrupt, sharp, short, terse, curt, gruff, surly, discourteous, impolite, uncivil, blunt, tactless, undiplomatic.
≠ courteous, polite, tactful.

brutal *adj* animal, bestial, beastly, brutish, inhuman, savage, bloodthirsty, vicious, ferocious, cruel, inhumane, remorseless, pitiless, merciless, ruthless, callous, insensitive, unfeeling, heartless, harsh, gruff, rough, coarse, crude, rude, uncivilized, barbarous.
≠ kindly, humane, civilized.

brutality *n* savagery, bloodthirstiness, viciousness, ferocity, cruelty, inhumanity, violence, atrocity, ruthlessness, callousness, roughness, coarseness, barbarism, barbarity.
≠ gentleness, kindness.

brute *n* animal, beast, swine, creature, monster, ogre, devil, fiend, savage, sadist, bully, lout.

bubble *n* blister, vesicle, globule, ball, drop, droplet, bead.
v effervesce, fizz, sparkle, froth, foam, seethe, boil, burble, gurgle.

bubbly *adj* **1** EFFERVESCENT, fizzy, sparkling, carbonated, frothy, foaming, sudsy. **2** LIVELY, bouncy, happy, merry, elated, excited.
≠ **1** flat, still. **2** lethargic.

bucket *n* pail, can, bail, scuttle, vessel.

buckle *n* clasp, clip, catch, fastener.
v **1** *buckle one's belt*: fasten, clasp, catch, hook, hitch, connect, close, secure. **2** BEND, warp, twist, distort, bulge, cave in, fold, wrinkle, crumple, collapse.

bud *n* shoot, sprout, germ, embryo.
v shoot, sprout, burgeon, develop, grow.
≠ wither, waste away.

budding *adj* potential, promising, embryonic, burgeoning, developing, growing, flowering.

budge *v* move, stir, shift, remove, dislodge, push, roll, slide, propel, sway, influence, persuade, convince, change, bend, yield, give (way).

budget *n* finances, funds, resources, means, allowance, allotment, allocation, estimate.
v plan, estimate, alow, allot, allocate, apportion, ration.

buff[1] *adj* yellowish-brown, straw, sandy, fawn, khaki.
v polish, burnish, shine, smooth, rub, brush.

buff[2] (*infml*) *n* expert, connoisseur, enthusiast, fan, admirer, devotee, addict, fiend, freak.

buffer *n* shock-absorber, bumper, fender, pad, cushion, pillow, intermediary, screen, shield.

buffet[1] *n* snack-bar, counter, café, cafeteria.

buffet[2] *v* batter, hit, strike, knock, bang, bump, push, shove, pound, pummel, beat, thump, box, cuff, clout, slap.
n blow, knock, bang, bump, jar, jolt, push, shove, thump, box, cuff, clout, slap, smack.

bug *n* **1** VIRUS, bacterium, germ, microbe, micro-organism, infection, disease. **2** FAULT, defect, flaw, blemish, imperfection, failing, error, gremlin (*infml*).
v (*infml*) annoy, irritate, vex, irk, needle (*infml*), bother, disturb, harass, badger.

build *v* **1** ERECT, raise, construct, fabricate, make, form, constitute, assemble, knock together, develop, enlarge, extend, increase, augment, escalate, intensify. **2** BASE, found, establish, institute, inaugurate, initiate, begin.
≠ **1** destroy, demolish, knock down, lessen.
n physique, figure, body, form, shape,

size, frame, structure.
build up strengthen, reinforce, fortify, extend, expand, develop, amplify, increase, escalate, intensify, heighten, boost, improve, enhance, publicize, advertise, promote, plug (*infml*), hype (*sl*).
≠ weaken, lessen.

building *n* edifice, dwelling, erection, construction, fabrication, structure, architecture.

Types of building include: house, bungalow, cottage, block of flats, cabin, farmhouse, villa, mansion, chateau, castle, palace; church, chapel, cathedral, abbey, monastery, temple, pagoda, mosque, synagogue; shop, store, garage, factory, warehouse, silo, office block, tower block, skyscraper, theatre, cinema, gymnasium, sports hall, restaurant, café, hotel, pub (*infml*), public house, inn, school, college, museum, library, hospital, prison, power station, observatory; barracks, fort, fortress, monument, mausoleum; shed, barn, outhouse, stable, mill, lighthouse, pier, pavilion, boat-house, beach-hut, summerhouse, gazebo, dovecote, windmill. *see also* **house**; **restaurant**; **shops**.

building materials

Types of building material include: aluminium, ashlar, asphalt, bitumen, breeze block, brick, building block, cast iron, cement, chipboard, clay, concrete, reinforced concrete, fixings, flagstone, girder, glass, glass fibre, gravel, granite, grout, gypsum, hardboard, hard core, insulation, foam insulation, loose fill insulation, lagging, lintel, lumber (*US*), marble, mortar, paving stone, paviour, plaster, plasterboard, plastic, plywood, sand, sandstone, shingle, slate, stainless steel, steel, steel beam, stone, tarmac, thatch, tile, floor tile, roof tile, timber, wattle and daub, wood.

build-up *n* **1** ENLARGEMENT, expansion, development, increase, gain, growth, escalation, publicity, promotion, plug (*infml*), hype (*sl*). **2** ACCUMULATION, mass, load, heap, stack, store, stockpile.
≠ **1** reduction, decrease.

bulbs and corms

Plants grown from bulbs and corms include: acidanthera, allium, amaryllis, anemone, bluebell (endymion), chincherinchee, chionodoxa, crocosmia, crocus, autumn crocus (colchicum), cyclamen, daffodil, crown imperial (fritillaria), galtonia, garlic, gladiolus, grape hyacinth (muscari), hyacinth, iris, ixia, jonquil, lily, montbretia, narcissus, nerine, ranunculus, scilla, snowdrop (galanthus), sparaxis, tulip, winter aconite.

bulge *n* **1** SWELLING, bump, lump, hump, distension, protuberance, projection. **2** RISE, increase, surge, upsurge, intensification.
v swell, puff out, bulb, hump, dilate, expand, enlarge, distend, protrude, project.

bulk *n* size, magnitude, dimensions, extent, amplitude, bigness, largeness, immensity, volume, mass, weight, substance, body, preponderance, majority, most.

bulky *adj* substantial, big, large, huge, enormous, immense, mammoth, massive, colossal, hulking, hefty, heavy, weighty, unmanageable, unwieldy, awkward, cumbersome.
≠ insubstantial, small, handy.

bullet *n* shot, pellet, ball, slug (*infml*), missile, projectile.

bulletin *n* report, newsflash, dispatch, communiqué, statement, announcement, notification, communication, message.

bully *n* persecutor, tormentor, browbeater, intimidator, bully-boy, heavy (*sl*), ruffian, tough.
v persecute, torment, terrorize, bulldoze, coerce, browbeat, bullyrag, intimidate, cow, tyrannize, domineer, overbear, oppress, push around.

bump *v* **1** HIT, strike, knock, bang, crash, collide (with). **2** JOLT, jerk, jar, jostle, rattle, shake, bounce.
n **1** BLOW, hit, knock, bang, thump,

thud, smash, crash, collision, impact, jolt, jar, shock. **2** LUMP, swelling, bulge, hump, protuberance.
bump into meet, encounter, run into, chance upon, come across.
bump off (*infml*) kill, murder, assassinate, eliminate (*sl*), liquidate (*sl*), do in (*sl*), top (*sl*).

bumper *adj* plentiful, abundant, large, great, enormous, massive, excellent, exceptional.
≠ small.

bumptious *adj* self-important, pompous, officious, overbearing, pushy, assertive, over-confident, presumptuous, forward, impudent, arrogant, cocky, conceited, swaggering, boastful, full of oneself, egotistic.
≠ humble, modest.

bumpy *adj* jerky, jolting, bouncy, choppy, rough, lumpy, knobbly, knobby, uneven, irregular.
≠ smooth, even.

bunch *n* **1** BUNDLE, sheaf, tuft, clump, cluster, batch, lot, heap, pile, stack, mass, number, quantity, collection, assortment. **2** *bunch of flowers*: bouquet, posy, spray. **3** GANG, band, troop, crew, team, party, gathering, flock, swarm, crowd, mob, multitude.
v group, bundle, cluster, collect, assemble, congregate, gather, flock, herd, crowd, mass, pack, huddle.
≠ disperse, scatter, spread out.

bundle *n* bunch, sheaf, roll, bale, truss, parcel, package, packet, carton, box, bag, pack, batch, consignment, group, set, collection, assortment, quantity, mass, accumulation, pile, stack, heap.
v pack, wrap, bale, truss, bind, tie, fasten.

bungle *v* mismanage, cock up (*sl*), screw up (*sl*), foul up (*infml*), mess up (*infml*), ruin, spoil, mar, botch, fudge, blunder.

buoy *n* float, marker, signal, beacon.
buoy up support, sustain, raise, lift, boost, encourage, cheer, hearten.
≠ depress, discourage.

buoyant *adj* **1** *in buoyant mood*: light-hearted, carefree, bright, cheerful, happy, joyful, lively, animated, bouncy. **2** FLOATABLE, floating, afloat, light, weightless.
≠ **1** depressed, despairing. **2** heavy.

burden *n* cargo, load, weight, dead-weight, encumbrance, millstone, onus, responsibility, obligation, duty, strain, stress, worry, anxiety, care, trouble, trial, affliction, sorrow.
v load, weigh down, encumber, handicap, bother, worry, tax, strain, overload, lie heavy on, oppress, overwhelm.
≠ unburden, relieve.

bureau *n* service, agency, office, branch, department, division, counter, desk.

bureaucracy *n* administration, government, ministry, civil service, the authorities, the system, officialdom, red tape, regulations.

burglar *n* housebreaker, robber, thief, pilferer, trespasser.

burglary *n* housebreaking, break-in, robbery, theft, stealing, trespass.

burial *n* burying, interment, entombment, funeral, obsequies.

burly *adj* big, well-built, hulking, hefty, heavy, stocky, sturdy, brawny, beefy, muscular, athletic, strapping, strong, powerful.
≠ small, puny, thin, slim.

burn *v* **1** FLAME, blaze, flare, flash, glow, flicker, smoulder, smoke, fume, simmer, seethe. **2** IGNITE, light, kindle, incinerate, cremate, consume, corrode. **3** SCALD, scorch, parch, shrivel, singe, char, toast, brand, sear, smart, sting, bite, hurt, tingle.

burning *adj* **1** ABLAZE, aflame, afire, fiery, flaming, blazing, flashing, gleaming, glowing, smouldering, alight, lit, illuminated. **2** HOT, scalding, scorching, searing, piercing, acute, smarting, stinging, prickling, tingling, biting, caustic, pungent. **3** *burning desire*: ardent, fervent, eager, earnest, intense, vehement, passionate, impassioned, frantic, frenzied, consuming. **4** *burning issue*: urgent, pressing, important, significant, crucial, essential, vital.
≠ **2** cold. **3** apathetic. **4** unimportant.

burrow *n* warren, hole, earth, set, den, lair, retreat, shelter, tunnel.
v tunnel, dig, delve, excavate, mine, undermine.

burst *v* puncture, rupture, tear, split, crack, break, fragment, shatter, shiver, disintegrate, explode, blow up, erupt, gush, spout, rush, run.
n **1** PUNCTURE, blow-out (*infml*), rupture, split, crack, break, breach, explosion, blast, bang, eruption. **2** DISCHARGE, gush, spurt, surge, rush, spate, torrent, outpouring, outburst, outbreak, fit.

bury *v* **1** *bury the dead*: inter, entomb, lay to rest, shroud. **2** SINK, submerge, immerse, plant, implant, embed, conceal, hide, cover, enshroud, engulf, enclose, engross, occupy, engage, absorb.
≠ **1** disinter, exhume. **2** uncover.

bush *n* **1** SHRUB, hedge, thicket. **2** SCRUB, brush, scrubland, backwoods, wilds.

business *n* **1** TRADE, commerce, industry, manufacturing, dealings, transactions, bargaining, trading, buying, selling. **2** COMPANY, firm, corporation, establishment, organization, concern, enterprise, venture. **3** JOB, occupation, work, employment, trade, profession, line, calling, career, vocation, duty, task, responsibility. **4** AFFAIR, matter, issue, subject, topic, question, problem, point.

businesslike *adj* professional, efficient, thorough, systematic, methodical, organized, orderly, well-ordered, practical, matter-of-fact, precise, correct, formal, impersonal.
≠ inefficient, disorganized.

businessman, businesswoman *n* entrepreneur, industrialist, trader, merchant, tycoon, magnate, capitalist, financier, employer, executive.

bust *n* **1** SCULPTURE, head, torso, statue. **2** BOSOM, beasts, chest, breast.

bustle *v* dash, rush, scamper, scurry, hurry, hasten, scramble, fuss.
n activity, stir, commotion, tumult, agitation, excitement, fuss, ado, flurry, hurry, haste.

busy *adj* occupied, engaged, tied up (*infml*), employed, working, slaving, stirring, restless, tireless, diligent, industrious, active, lively, energetic, strenuous, tiring, full, crowded, swarming, teeming, bustling, hectic, eventful.
≠ idle, lazy, quiet.
v occupy, engage, employ, engross, absorb, immerse, interest, concern, bother.

busybody *n* meddler, nosey parker (*infml*), intruder, pry, gossip, eavesdropper, snoop, snooper, troublemaker.

butt[1] *n* stub, end, tip, tail, base, foot, shaft, stock, handle, haft.

butt[2] *n* target, mark, object, subject, victim, laughing-stock, dupe.

butt[3] *v, n* hit, bump, knock, buffet, push, shove, ram, thrust, punch, jab, prod, poke.
butt in interrupt, cut in, interpose, intrude, meddle, interfere.

butterflies and moths

Types of butterfly include: red admiral, white admiral, apollo, cabbage white, chalkhill blue, common blue, brimstone, meadow brown, Camberwell beauty, clouded yellow, comma, large copper, small copper, fritillary, Duke of Burgundy fritillary, heath fritillary, gatekeeper, grayling, hairstreak, purple hairstreak, white letter hairstreak, hermit, monarch, orange-tip, painted lady, peacock, purple emperor, ringlet, grizzled skipper, swallowtail, tortoiseshell. *Types of moth include*: brown-tail, buff-tip, burnet, six-spot, carpet, cinnabar, clothes, emperor, garden tiger, gypsy, death's head hawkmoth, privet hawkmoth, Kentish glory, lackey, lappet, leopard, lobster, magpie, oak hook-tip, pale tussock, peach blossom, peppered, puss, red underwing, silkworm, silver-Y, swallowtail, turnip, wax, winter.

buttocks *n* rump, hindquarters, rear, posterior (*infml*), seat, bottom, behind, backside (*infml*), arse (*sl*).

buttonhole *v* accost, waylay, catch, grab, nab, detain, importune.

buttress *n* support, prop, shore, stay, brace, pier, strut, stanchion, mainstay, reinforcement.
v support, prop up, shore up, hold up, brace, strengthen, reinforce, bolster up, sustain.
≠ undermine, weaken.

buy *v* purchase, invest in (*infml*), pay for, procure, acquire, obtain, get.
≠ sell.
n purchase, acquisition, bargain, deal.

buyer *n* purchaser, shopper, consumer, customer, vendee, emptor.
≠ seller, vendor.

by *prep* near, next to, beside, along, over, through, via, past.
adv near, close, handy, at hand, past, beyond, away, aside.

bypass *v* avoid, dodge, sidestep, skirt, circumvent, ignore, neglect, omit.
n ring road, detour, diversion.

by-product *n* consequence, result, side-effect, fallout (*infml*), repercussion, after-effect.

bystander *n* spectator, onlooker, looker-on, watcher, observer, witness, eye-witness, passer-by.

C

cabin *n* **1** BERTH, quarters, compartment, room. **2** HUT, shack, shanty, lodge, chalet, cottage, shed, shelter.

cabinet *n* cupboard, closet, dresser, case, locker.

cable *n* line, rope, cord, chain, wire, flex, lead.

cadge *v* scrounge, sponge, beg, hitch.

café *n* coffee shop, tea shop, tea room, coffee bar, cafeteria, snackbar, bistro, brasserie, restaurant.

cage *v* encage, coop up, shut up, confine, restrain, fence in, imprison, impound, incarcerate, lock up.
≠ release, let out, free.
n aviary, coop, hutch, enclosure, pen, pound, corral.

cajole *v* coax, persuade, wheedle, flatter, sweet-talk (*infml*), butter up (*infml*), tempt, lure, seduce, entice, beguile, mislead, dupe.
≠ bully, force, compel.

cake *v* coat, cover, encrust, dry, harden, solidify, consolidate, coagulate, congeal, thicken.
n **1** *tea and cakes*: gâteau, fancy, madeleine, bun, pie, flan. **2** LUMP, mass, bar, slab, block, loaf.

calamitous *adj* disastrous, catastrophic, ruinous, devastating, deadly, fatal, dire, ghastly, dreadful, tragic, woeful, grievous.
≠ good, fortunate, happy.

calamity disaster, catastrophe, mishap, misadventure, mischance, misfortune, adversity, reverse, trial, tribulation, affliction, distress, tragedy, ruin, downfall.
≠ blessing, godsend.

calculate *v* compute, work out, count, enumerate, reckon, figure, determine, weigh, rate, value, estimate, gauge, judge, consider, plan, intend, aim.

calculating *adj* crafty, cunning, sly, devious, scheming, designing, contriving, sharp, shrewd.
≠ artless, naïve.

calculation *n* sum, computation, answer, result, reckoning, figuring, estimate, forecast, judgement, planning, deliberation.

calibre *n* **1** DIAMETER, bore, gauge, size, measure. **2** *candidates of the right calibre*: talent, gifts, strength, worth, merit, quality, character, ability, capacity, faculty, stature, distinction.

call *v* **1** NAME, christen, baptize, title, entitle, dub, style, term, label, designate. **2** SHOUT, yell, exclaim, cry. **3** SUMMON, invite, bid, convene, assemble. **4** TELEPHONE, phone, ring (up), contact.
n **1** CRY, exclamation, shout, yell, scream. **2** VISIT, ring, summons, invitation. **3** *there's no call for it*: demand, need, occasion, cause, excuse, justification, reason, grounds, right. **4** APPEAL, request, plea, order, command, claim, announcement, signal.
call for 1 DEMAND, require, need, necessitate, involve, entail, occasion, suggest. **2** FETCH, collect, pick up.
call off cancel, drop, abandon, discontinue, break off, withdraw.

calling *n* mission, vocation, career, profession, occupation, job, trade, business, line, work, employment, field, province, pursuit.

callous *adj* heartless, hard-hearted, cold, indifferent, uncaring, unsympathetic, unfeeling, insensitive, hardened, thick-skinned.
≠ kind, caring, sympathetic, sensitive.

calm *adj* **1** COMPOSED, self-possessed, collected, cool, dispassionate, unemotional, impassive, unmoved, placid, sedate, imperturbable,

unflappable, unexcitable, laid back (*sl*), relaxed, unexcited, unruffled, unflustered, unperturbed, undisturbed, untroubled, unapprehensive. **2** *calm waters*: smooth, still, windless, unclouded, mild, tranquil, serene, peaceful, quiet, uneventful, restful.
≠ **1** excitable, worried, anxious. **2** rough, wild, stormy.
v compose, soothe, relax, sedate, tranquillize, hush, quieten, placate, pacify.
≠ excite, worry.
n calmness, stillness, tranquillity, serenity, peacefulness, peace, quiet, hush, repose.
≠ storminess, restlessness.

camera

Types of camera include: automatic, bellows, binocular, box Brownie®, camcorder, camera obscura, cine, cinematographic, compact, daguerreotype, disc, disposable, film, Instamatic®, large-format, miniature, subminiature, panoramic, plate, dry-plate, half-plate, quarter-plate, wet-plate, point-and-press, Polaroid®, press, reflex, folding reflex, single-lens reflex (SLR), twin-lens reflex (TLR), security, sliding box, sound, still, stereo, Super 8®, TV, video. *see also* **photographic equipment**.

camouflage *n* disguise, guise, masquerade, mask, cloak, screen, blind, front, cover, concealment, deception.
v disguise, mask, cloak, veil, screen, cover, conceal, hide, obscure.
≠ uncover, reveal.

campaign *n* crusade, movement, promotion, drive, push, offensive, attack, battle, expedition, operation.
v crusade, promote, push, advocate, fight, battle.

cancel *v* call off, abort, abandon, drop, abolish, annul, quash, rescind, revoke, repeal, countermand, delete, erase, obliterate, eliminate, offset, compensate, redeem, neutralize, nullify.

cancer *n* **1** EVIL, blight, canker, pestilence, sickness, corruption, rot. **2** TUMOUR, growth, malignancy, carcinoma.

candid *adj* frank, open, truthful, honest, sincere, forthright, straightforward, ingenuous, guileless, simple, plain, clear, unequivocal, blunt, outspoken.
≠ guarded, evasive, devious.

candidate *n* applicant, aspirant, contender, contestant, competitor, entrant, runner, possibility, nominee, claimant, pretender, suitor.

candour *n* frankness, openness, truthfulness, honesty, plain-dealing, sincerity, straightforwardness, directness, ingenuousness, guilelessness, naïvety, artlessness, simplicity, plainness, unequivocalness, bluntness, outspokenness.
≠ evasiveness, deviousness.

canonical hours

Names of canonical hours include: compline, lauds, matins, none, prime, sext, terce, vespers.

canopy *n* awning, covering, shade, shelter, sunshade, umbrella.

cantankerous *adj* irritable, irascible, grumpy, grouchy, crusty, crotchety, crabbed, crabby, testy, bad-tempered, ill-humoured, cross, peevish, difficult, perverse, contrary, quarrelsome.
≠ good-natured, easy-going (*infml*).

canvass *v* **1** ELECTIONEER, agitate, campaign, solicit, ask for, seek, poll. **2** EXAMINE, inspect, scrutinize, study, scan, investigate, analyse, sift, discuss, debate.
n poll, survey, examination, scrutiny, investigation, inquiry.

canyon *n* gorge, ravine, gully, valley.

cap *v* exceed, surpass, transcend, better, beat, outdo, outstrip, eclipse, complete, finish, crown, top, cover.
n **1** HAT, skullcap, beret, tam-o'-shanter. **2** LID, top, cover.

capability *n* ability, capacity, faculty, power, potential, means, facility, competence, qualification, skill, proficiency, talent.
≠ inability, incompetence.

capable *adj* able, competent, efficient, qualified, experienced, accomplished, skilful, proficient, gifted, talented,

masterly, clever, intelligent, fitted, suited, apt, liable, disposed.
≠ incapable, incompetent, useless.

capacity *n* **1** VOLUME, space, room, size, dimensions, magnitude, extent, compass, range, scope. **2** CAPABILITY, ability, faculty, power, potential, competence, efficiency, skill, gift, talent, genius, cleverness, intelligence, aptitude, readiness. **3** *in her capacity as president*: role, function, position, office, post, appointment, job.

cape[1] *n* headland, head, promontory, point, ness, peninsula.

cape[2] *n* cloak, shawl, wrap, robe, poncho, coat.

capital *n* funds, finance, principal, money, cash, savings, investment(s), wealth, means, wherewithal, resources, assets, property, stock.

capitalize on *v* profit from, take advantage of, exploit, cash in on.

capitulate *v* surrender, throw in the towel, yield, give in, relent, submit, succumb.
≠ fight on.

capsize *v* overturn, turn over, turn turtle, invert, keel over, upset.

capsule *n* pill, tablet, lozenge, receptacle, shell, sheath, pod, module.

captain *n* commander, master, skipper, pilot, head, chief, leader, boss, officer.

captivate *v* charm, enchant, bewitch, beguile, fascinate, enthral, hypnotize, mesmerize, lure, allure, seduce, win, attract, enamour, infatuate, enrapture, dazzle.
≠ repel, disgust, appal.

captive *n* prisoner, hostage, slave, detainee, internee, convict.
adj imprisoned, caged, confined, restricted, secure, locked up, enchained, enslaved, ensnared.
≠ free.

captivity *n* custody, detention, imprisonment, incarceration, internment, confinement, restraint, bondage, duress, slavery, servitude.
≠ freedom.

capture *v* catch, trap, snare, take, seize, arrest, apprehend, imprison, secure.
n catching, trapping, taking, seizure, arrest, imprisonment.

car *n* automobile, motor car, motor, vehicle.

> *Types of car include*: saloon, hatchback, fastback, estate, sports car, cabriolet, convertible, limousine, limo (*infml*), wheels (*sl*), banger (*infml*), Mini, bubble-car, coupé, station wagon, shooting brake, veteran car, vintage car, Beetle (*infml*), four-wheel drive, jeep, buggy, Land Rover, Range Rover, panda car, patrol car, taxi, cab.

carcase *n* body, corpse, cadaver, remains, relics, skeleton, shell, structure, framework, hulk.

care *n* **1** WORRY, anxiety, stress, strain, pressure, concern, trouble, distress, affliction, tribulation, vexation. **2** CAREFULNESS, caution, prudence, forethought, vigilance, watchfulness, pains, meticulousness, attention, heed, regard, consideration, interest. **3** *in their care*: keeping, custody, guardianship, protection, ward, charge, responsibility, control, supervision.
≠ **2** carelessness, thoughtlessness, inattention, neglect.
v worry, mind, bother.
care for 1 LOOK AFTER, nurse, tend, mind, watch over, protect, minister to, attend. **2** LIKE, be fond of, love, be keen on, enjoy, delight in, want, desire.

career *n* vocation, calling, life-work, occupation, pursuit, profession, trade, job, employment, livelihood.
v rush, dash, tear, hurtle, race, run, gallop, speed, shoot, bolt.

carefree *adj* unworried, untroubled, unconcerned, blithe, breezy, happy-go-lucky, cheery, light-hearted, cheerful, happy, easy-going (*infml*), laid back (*infml*).
≠ worried, anxious, despondent.

careful *adj* **1** CAUTIOUS, prudent, circumspect, judicious, wary, chary, vigilant, watchful, alert, attentive, mindful. **2** METICULOUS, painstaking, conscientious, scrupulous, thorough, detailed, punctilious, particular,

accurate, precise, thoughtful.
≠ **1** careless, inattentive, thoughtless, reckless. **2** careless.

careless *adj* **1** UNTHINKING, thoughtless, inconsiderate, uncaring, unconcerned, heedless, unmindful, forgetful, remiss, negligent, irresponsible, unguarded. **2** *careless work*: inaccurate, messy, untidy, disorderly, sloppy, neglectful, slipshod, slap-dash, hasty, cursory, offhand, casual.
≠ **1** thoughtful, prudent. **2** careful, accurate, meticulous.

caress *v* stroke, pet, fondle, cuddle, hug, embrace, kiss, touch, rub.
n stroke, pat, fondle, cuddle, hug, embrace, kiss.

caretaker *n* janitor, porter, watchman, keeper, custodian, curator, warden, superintendent.

cargo *n* freight, load, pay-load, lading, tonnage, shipment, consignment, contents, goods, merchandise, baggage.

caricature *n* cartoon, parody, lampoon, burlesque, satire, send-up, take-off, imitation, representation, distortion, travesty.
v parody, mock, ridicule, satirize, send up, take off, mimic, distort, exaggerate.

carnage *n* bloodshed, blood-bath, butchery, slaughter, killing, murder, massacre, holocaust.

carnival *n* festival, fiesta, gala, jamboree, fête, fair, holiday, jubilee, celebration, merrymaking, revelry.

carriage *n* **1** COACH, wagon, car, vehicle. **2** DEPORTMENT, posture, bearing, air, manner, mien, demeanour, behaviour, conduct. **3** CARRYING, conveyance, transport, transportation, delivery, postage.

carry *v* **1** BRING, convey, transport, haul, move, transfer, relay, release, conduct, take, fetch. **2** BEAR, shoulder, support, underpin, maintain, uphold, sustain, suffer, stand.
carry on 1 CONTINUE, proceed, last, endure, maintain, keep on, persist, persevere. **2** *carry on a business*: operate, run, manage, administer.
≠ **1** stop, finish.
carry out do, perform, undertake, discharge, conduct, execute, implement, fulfil, accomplish, achieve, realize, bring off.

cart *n* barrow, handcart, wheel-barrow, wagon, truck.
v move, convey, transport, haul, lug (*infml*), hump (*infml*), bear, carry.

carton *n* box, packet, pack, case, container, package, parcel.

cartoon *n* comic strip, animation, sketch, drawing, caricature, parody.

cartridge *n* cassette, canister, cylinder, tube, container, case, capsule, shell, magazine, round, charge.

carve *v* cut, slice, hack, hew, chisel, chip, sculpt, sculpture, shape, form, fashion, mould, etch, engrave, incise, indent.

cascade *n* rush, gush, outpouring, flood, deluge, torrent, avalanche, cataract, waterfall, falls, fountain, shower.
≠ trickle.
v rush, gush, surge, flood, overflow, spill, tumble, fall, descend, shower, pour, plunge, pitch.

case[1] *n* container, receptacle, holder, suitcase, trunk, crate, box, carton, casket, chest, cabinet, showcase, casing, cartridge, shell, capsule, sheath, cover, jacket, wrapper.

case[2] *n* **1** CIRCUMSTANCES, context, state, condition, position, situation, contingency, occurrence, occasion, event, specimen, example, instance, illustration, point. **2** LAWSUIT, suit, trial, proceedings, action, process, cause, argument, dispute.

cash *n* money, hard money, ready money, bank-notes, notes, coins, change, legal tender, currency, hard currency, bullion, funds, resources, wherewithal.
v encash, exchange, realize, liquidate.

cashier *n* clerk, teller, treasurer, bursar, purser, banker, accountant.

cask *n* barrel, tun, hogshead, firkin, vat, tub, butt.

cast *v* **1** THROW, hurl, lob, pitch, fling,

toss, sling, shy, launch, impel, drive, direct, project, shed, emit, diffuse, spread, scatter. **2** MOULD, shape, form, model, found.
n **1** COMPANY, troupe, actors, players, performers, entertainers, characters, dramatis personae.
2 CASTING, mould, shape, form.
cast down depress, discourage, dishearten, deject, sadden, crush, desolate.
≠ cheer up, encourage.

castle *n* stronghold, fortress, citadel, keep, tower, château, palace, mansion, stately home, country house.

> *Parts of a castle include*: approach, bailey, barbican, bartizan, bastion, battlements, brattice, buttress, chapel, corbel, courtyard, crenel, crenellation, curtain wall, ditch, donjon, drawbridge, dungeon, embrasure, enclosure wall, fosse, gatehouse, inner wall, keep, merlon, moat, motte, mound, outer bailey, parapet, portcullis, postern, rampart, scarp, stockade, tower, lookout tower, turret, ward, watchtower.

casual *adj* **1** *a casual meeting*: chance, fortuitous, accidental, unintentional, unpremeditated, unexpected, unforeseen, irregular, random, occasional, incidental, superficial, cursory. **2** NONCHALANT, blasé, lackadaisical, negligent, couldn't-care-less (*infml*), apathetic, indifferent, unconcerned, informal, offhand, relaxed, laid back (*infml*).
≠ **1** deliberate, planned. **2** formal.

casualty *n* injury, loss, death, fatality, victim, sufferer, injured person, wounded, dead person.

cats

> *Breeds of cat include*: Abyssinian, American shorthair, Balinese, Birman, Bombay, British shorthair, British longhair, Burmese, Carthusian, chinchilla, Cornish rex, Cymric, Devon rex, domestic tabby, Egyptian Mau, Exotic shorthair, Foreign Blue, Foreign spotted shorthair, Foreign White, Havana, Himalayan, Japanese Bobtail, Korat, Maine Coon, Manx, Norwegian Forest, Persian, rag-doll, rex, Russian Blue, Scottish Fold, Siamese, silver tabby, Singapura, Somali, Tiffany, Tonkinese, Tortoiseshell, Turkish Angora, Turkish Van.

catalogue *n* list, inventory, roll, register, roster, schedule, record, table, index, directory, gazetteer, brochure, prospectus.
v list, register, record, index, classify, alphabetize, file.

catapult *v* hurl, fling, throw, pitch, toss, sling, launch, propel, shoot, fire.

cataract *n* waterfall, falls, rapids, force, cascade, downpour, torrent, deluge.

catastrophe *n* disaster, calamity, cataclysm, debacle, fiasco, failure, ruin, devastation, tragedy, blow, reverse, mischance, misfortune, adversity, affliction, trouble, upheaval.

catch *v* **1** SEIZE, grab, take, hold, grasp, grip, clutch, capture, trap, entrap, snare, ensnare, hook, net, arrest, apprehend. **2** HEAR, understand, perceive, recognize. **3** SURPRISE, expose, unmask, find (out), discover, detect, discern. **4** *catch a cold*: contract, get, develop, go down with.
≠ **1** drop, release, free. **2** miss.
n **1** FASTENER, clip, hook, clasp, hasp, latch, bolt. **2** DISADVANTAGE, drawback, snag, hitch, obstacle, problem.
catch up gain on, draw level with, overtake.

catching *adj* infectious, contagious, communicable, transmittable.

catchword *n* catch-phrase, slogan, motto, watchword, byword, password.

catchy *adj* memorable, haunting, popular, melodic, tuneful, attractive, captivating.
≠ dull, boring.

categorical *adj* absolute, total, utter, unqualified, unreserved, unconditional, downright, positive, definite, emphatic, unequivocal, clear, explicit, express, direct.
≠ tentative, qualified, vague.

categorize *v* class, classify, group, sort, grade, rank, order, list.

category *n* class, classification, group, grouping, sort, type, section, division, department, chapter, head, heading, grade, rank, order, list.

cater *v* provision, victual, provide, supply, furnish, serve, indulge, pander.

catholic *adj* broad, wide, wide-ranging, universal, global, general, comprehensive, inclusive, all-inclusive, all-embracing, liberal, tolerant, broad-minded.
≠ narrow, limited, narrow-minded.

cattle *n* cows, bulls, oxen, livestock, stock, beasts.

> *Breeds of cattle include*: Aberdeen Angus, Africander, Alderney, Ankole, Ayrshire, Blonde d'Aquitaine, Brahman, Brown Swiss, cattabu, cattalo, Charolais, Chillingham, Devon, dexter, Durham, Friesian, Galloway, Guernsey, Hereford, Highland, Holstein, Jersey, Latvian, Limousin, Longhorn, Luing, Red Poll, Romagnola, Santa Gertrudis, Shetland, Shorthorn, Simmenthaler, Teeswater, Ukrainian, Welsh Black.

cause *n* **1** SOURCE, origin, beginning, root, basis, spring, originator, creator, producer, maker, agent, agency. **2** REASON, motive, grounds, motivation, stimulus, incentive, inducement, impulse. **3** *a worthy cause*: object, purpose, end, ideal, belief, conviction, movement, undertaking, enterprise.
≠ **1** effect, result, consequence.
v begin, give rise to, lead to, result in, occasion, bring about, effect, produce, generate, create, precipitate, motivate, stimulate, provoke, incite, induce, force, compel.
≠ stop, prevent.

caustic *adj* corrosive, acid, burning, stinging, biting, cutting, mordant, trenchant, keen, pungent, bitter, acrimonious, sarcastic, scathing, virulent, severe.
≠ soothing, mild.

caution *n* **1** CARE, carefulness, prudence, vigilance, watchfulness, alertness, heed, discretion, forethought, deliberation, wariness. **2** WARNING, caveat, injunction, admonition, advice, counsel.
≠ **1** carelessness, recklessness.
v warn, admonish, advise, urge.

cautious *adj* careful, prudent, circumspect, judicious, vigilant, watchful, alert, heedful, discreet, tactful, chary, wary, cagey (*infml*), guarded, tentative, softly-softly, unadventurous.
≠ incautious, imprudent, heedless, reckless.

cavalcade *n* procession, parade, march-past, troop, array, retinue, train.

cavalier *n* horseman, equestrian, knight, gentleman, gallant, escort, partner.
adj supercilious, condescending, lordly, haughty, lofty, arrogant, swaggering, insolent, scornful, disdainful, curt, offhand, free-and-easy.

cave *n* cavern, grotto, hole, pothole, hollow, cavity.
cave in collapse, subside, give way, yield, fall, slip.

cavernous *adj* hollow, concave, gaping, yawning, echoing, resonant, deep, sunken.

cavity *n* hole, gap, dent, hollow, crater, pit, well, sinus, ventricle.

cavort *v* caper, frolic, gambol, prance, skip, dance, frisk, sport, romp.

cease *v* stop, desist, refrain, pack in (*sl*), halt, call a halt, break off, discontinue, finish, end, conclude, terminate, fail, die.
≠ begin, start, commence.

ceaseless *adj* endless, unending, never-ending, eternal, everlasting, continuous, non-stop, incessant, interminable, constant, perpetual, continual, persistent, untiring, unremitting.
≠ occasional, irregular.

cede *v* surrender, give up, resign, abdicate, renounce, abandon, yield, relinquish, convey, transfer, hand over, grant, allow, concede.

celebrate *v* commemorate, remember, observe, keep, rejoice, toast, drink to, honour, exalt, glorify, praise, extol, eulogize, commend, bless, solemnize.

celebrated *adj* famous, well-known, famed, renowned, illustrious, glorious, eminent, distinguished, notable, prominent, outstanding, popular, acclaimed, exalted, revered.
≠ unknown, obscure, forgotten.

celebration *n* observance, merrymaking, jollification, revelry, festivity, rave-up (*infml*).

Celebrations include: anniversary, banquet, baptism, bar mitzvah, birthday, centenary, christening, coming-of-age, commemoration, feast, fête, festival, gala, graduation, harvest festival, homecoming, Independence Day, jubilee, marriage, May Day, name-day, party, reception, remembrance, retirement, reunion, saint's day, thanksgiving, tribute, wedding. *see also* **anniversaries**; **party**.

celebrity *n* personage, dignitary, VIP (*infml*), luminary, worthy, personality, name, big name, star, superstar.
≠ nobody, nonentity.

celibacy *n* singleness, bachelorhood, spinsterhood, virginity, chastity, purity, abstinence, continence.

cell *n* dungeon, prison, room, cubicle, chamber, compartment, cavity, unit.

cellar *n* basement, crypt, vault, storeroom, wine cellar.

cement *v* stick, bond, weld, solder, join, unite, bind, combine.
n plaster, mortar, concrete.

cemetery *n* burial-ground, graveyard, churchyard.

censor *v* cut, edit, blue-pencil, bowdlerize, expurgate.

censorious *adj* condemnatory, disapproving, disparaging, fault-finding, carping, cavilling, critical, hypercritical, severe.
≠ complimentary, approving.

censure *n* condemnation, blame, disapproval, criticism, admonishment, admonition, reprehension, reproof, reproach, rebuke, reprimand, telling-off (*infml*).
≠ praise, compliments, approval.
v condemn, denounce, blame, criticize, castigate, admonish, reprehend, reprove, upbraid, reproach, rebuke, reprimand, scold, tell off (*infml*).
≠ praise, compliment, approve.

central *adj* middle, mid, inner, interior, focal, main, chief, key, principal, primary, fundamental, vital, essential, important.
≠ peripheral, minor, secondary.

centre *n* middle, mid-point, bull's-eye, heart, core, nucleus, pivot, hub, focus, crux.
≠ edge, periphery, outskirts.
v focus, concentrate, converge, gravitate, revolve, pivot, hinge.

ceremonial *adj* formal, official, stately, solemn, ritual, ritualistic.
≠ informal, casual.
n ceremony, formality, protocol, solemnity, ritual, rite.

ceremonious *adj* stately, dignified, grand, solemn, ritual, civil, polite, courteous, deferential, courtly, formal, stiff, starchy, exact, precise, punctilious.
≠ unceremonious, informal, relaxed.

ceremony *n* **1** *wedding ceremony*: service, rite, commemoration, observance, celebration, function, parade. **2** ETIQUETTE, protocol, decorum, propriety, formality, form, niceties, ceremonial, ritual, pomp, show.

certain *adj* **1** SURE, positive, assured, confident, convinced, undoubted, indubitable, unquestionable, incontrovertible, undeniable, irrefutable, plain, conclusive, absolute, convincing, true. **2** INEVITABLE, unavoidable, bound, destined, fated. **3** SPECIFIC, special, particular, individual, precise, express, fixed, established, settled, decided, definite. **4** DEPENDABLE, reliable, trustworthy, constant, steady, stable.
≠ **1** uncertain, unsure, hesitant, doubtful. **2** unlikely. **4** unreliable.

certainly *adv* of course, naturally, definitely, for sure, undoubtedly, doubtlessly.

certainty *n* sureness, positiveness, assurance, confidence, conviction, faith, trust, truth, validity, fact, reality, inevitability.
≠ uncertainty, doubt, hesitation.

certificate *n* document, award, diploma, qualification, credentials, testimonial, guarantee, endorsement, warrant, licence, authorization, pass, voucher.

certify *v* declare, attest, aver, assure, guarantee, endorse, corroborate, confirm, vouch, testify, witness, verify, authenticate, validate, authorize, license.

chain *n* **1** FETTER, manacle, restraint, bond, link, coupling, union. **2** *chain of events*: sequence, succession, progression, string, train, series, set.
v tether, fasten, secure, bind, restrain, confine, fetter, shackle, manacle, handcuff, enslave.
≠ release, free.

chairman, chairwoman *n* chairperson, chair, president, convenor, organizer, director, master of ceremonies, MC, toastmaster, speaker.

challenge *v* **1** DARE, defy, throw down the gauntlet, confront, brave, accost, provoke, test, tax, try. **2** DISPUTE, question, query, protest, object to.
n dare, defiance, confrontation, provocation, test, trial, hurdle, obstacle, question, ultimatum.

champion *n* winner, victor, conqueror, hero, guardian, protector, defender, vindicator, patron, backer, supporter, upholder, advocate.
v defend, stand up for, back, support, maintain, uphold, espouse, advocate, promote.

chance *n* **1** ACCIDENT, fortuity, coincidence, fluke (*infml*), luck, fortune, providence, fate, destiny, risk, gamble, speculation, possibility, prospect, probability, likelihood, odds. **2** *a second chance*: opportunity, opening, occasion, time.
≠ **1** certainty.
v **1** RISK, hazard, gamble, wager, stake, try, venture. **2** HAPPEN, occur.
adj fortuitous, casual, accidental, inadvertent, unintentional, unintended, unforeseen, unlooked-for, random, haphazard, incidental.
≠ deliberate, intentional, foreseen, certain.

change *v* alter, modify, convert, reorganize, reform, remodel, restyle, transform, transfigure, metamorphose, mutate, vary, fluctuate, vacillate, shift, displace, swap, exchange, trade, switch, transpose, substitute, replace, alternate, interchange.
n alteration, modification, conversion, transformation, metamorphosis, mutation, variation, fluctuation, shift, exchange, transposition, substitution, interchange, difference, diversion, novelty, innovation, variety, transition, revolution, upheaval.

changeable *adj* variable, mutable, fluid, kaleidoscopic, shifting, mobile, unsettled, uncertain, unpredictable, unreliable, erratic, irregular, inconstant, fickle, capricious, volatile, unstable, unsteady, wavering, vacillating.
≠ constant, reliable.

channel *n* **1** DUCT, conduit, main, groove, furrow, trough, gutter, canal, flume, watercourse, waterway, strait, sound. **2** *channel of communication*: route, course, path, avenue, way, means, medium, approach, passage.
v direct, guide, conduct, convey, send, transmit, force.

chant *n* plainsong, psalm, song, melody, chorus, refrain, slogan, war cry.
v recite, intone, sing, chorus.

chaos *n* disorder, confusion, disorganization, anarchy, lawlessness, tumult, pandemonium, bedlam.
≠ order.

chaotic *adj* disordered, confused, disorganized, topsy-turvy, deranged, anarchic, lawless, riotous, tumultuous, unruly, uncontrolled.
≠ ordered, organized.

chap (*infml*) *n* fellow, bloke (*infml*), guy (*infml*), man, boy, person, individual, character, sort, type.

chapter *n* part, section, division, clause, topic, episode, period, phase, stage.

character *n* **1** PERSONALITY, nature, disposition, temperament, temper, constitution, make-up, individuality, peculiarity, feature, attributes, quality, type, stamp, calibre, reputation, status, position, trait. **2** LETTER, figure, symbol, sign, mark, type, cipher, rune, hieroglyph, ideograph. **3** INDIVIDUAL, person, sort, type, role, part.

characteristic *adj* distinctive, distinguishing, individual, idiosyncratic, peculiar, specific, special, typical, representative, symbolic, symptomatic.
≠ uncharacteristic, untypical.
n peculiarity, idiosyncrasy, mannerism, feature, trait, attribute, property, quality, hallmark, mark, symptom.

characterize *v* typify, mark, stamp, brand, identify, distinguish, indicate, represent, portray.

charge *v* **1** *charge a high price*: ask, demand, levy, exact, debit. **2** ACCUSE, indict, impeach, incriminate, blame. **3** ATTACK, assail, storm, rush.
n **1** PRICE, cost, fee, rate, amount, expense, expenditure, outlay, payment. **2** ACCUSATION, indictment, allegation, imputation. **3** ATTACK, assault, onslaught, sortie, rush. **4** *in your charge*: custody, keeping, care, safekeeping, guardianship, ward, trust, responsibility, duty.

charitable *adj* philanthropic, humanitarian, benevolent, benign, kind, compassionate, sympathetic, understanding, considerate, generous, magnanimous, liberal, tolerant, broad-minded, lenient, forgiving, indulgent, gracious.
≠ uncharitable, inconsiderate, unforgiving.

charity *n* **1** GENEROSITY, bountifulness, alms-giving, beneficence, philanthropy, unselfishness, altruism, benevolence, benignness, kindness, goodness, humanity, compassion, tender-heartedness, love, affection, clemency, indulgence. **2** ALMS, gift, handout, aid, relief, assistance.
≠ **1** selfishness, malice.

charm *v* please, delight, enrapture, captivate, fascinate, beguile, enchant, bewitch, mesmerize, attract, allure, cajole, win, enamour.
≠ repel.
n **1** ATTRACTION, allure, magnetism, appeal, desirability, fascination, enchantment, spell, sorcery, magic. **2** *lucky charm*: trinket, talisman, amulet, fetish, idol.

charming *adj* pleasing, delightful, pleasant, lovely, captivating, enchanting, attractive, fetching, appealing, sweet, winsome, seductive, winning, irresistible.
≠ ugly, unattractive, repulsive.

chart *n* diagram, table, graph, map, plan, blueprint.
v map, map out, sketch, draw, draft, outline, delineate, mark, plot, place.

charter *n* right, privilege, prerogative, authorization, permit, licence, franchise, concession, contract, indenture, deed, bond, document.
v hire, rent, lease, commission, engage, employ, authorize, sanction, license.

chase *v* pursue, follow, hunt, track, drive, expel, rush, hurry.

chasm *n* gap, opening, gulf, abyss, void, hollow, cavity, crater, breach, rift, split, cleft, fissure, crevasse, canyon, gorge, ravine.

chaste *adj* pure, virginal, unsullied, undefiled, immaculate, abstinent, continent, celibate, virtuous, moral, innocent, wholesome, modest, decent, plain, simple, austere.
≠ corrupt, lewd, vulgar, indecorous.

chasten *v* humble, humiliate, tame, subdue, repress, curb, moderate, soften, discipline, punish, correct, chastise, castigate, reprove.

chastise *v* punish, discipline, correct, beat, flog, whip, lash, scourge, smack, spank, castigate, reprove, admonish, scold, upbraid, berate, censure.

hat *n* talk, conversation, natter (*infml*), gossip, chinwag (*infml*), tête-à-tête, heart-to-heart.
v talk, crack, natter (*infml*), gossip, chatter, rabbit (on) (*infml*).

hatter *v, n* prattle, babble, chat, natter (*infml*), gossip, tattle.

hatty *adj* talkative, gossipy, newsy, friendly, informal, colloquial, familiar.
≠ quiet.

heap *adj* **1** INEXPENSIVE, reasonable, dirt-cheap, bargain, reduced, cut-price, knock-down, budget, economy, economical. **2** TAWDRY, tatty, cheapo (*sl*), shoddy, inferior, second-rate, worthless, vulgar, common, poor, paltry, mean, contemptible, despicable, low.
≠ **1** expensive, costly. **2** superior, noble, admirable.

heapen *v* devalue, degrade, lower, demean, depreciate, belittle, disparage, denigrate, downgrade.

heat *v* defraud, swindle, diddle, short-change, do (*infml*), rip off (*sl*), fleece, con (*infml*), double-cross, mislead, deceive, dupe, fool, trick, hoodwink, bamboozle (*infml*), beguile.
n cheater, dodger, fraud, swindler, shark (*infml*), con man (*infml*), extortioner, double-crosser, impostor, charlatan, deceiver, trickster, rogue.

heck *v* **1** EXAMINE, inspect, scrutinize, give the once-over (*infml*), investigate, probe, test, monitor, study, research, compare, cross-check, confirm, verify. **2** *check an impulse*: curb, bridle, restrain, control, limit, repress, inhibit, damp, thwart, hinder, impede, obstruct, bar, retard, delay, stop, arrest, halt.
n **1** EXAMINATION, inspection, scrutiny, once-over (*infml*), check-up, investigation, audit, test, research. **2** CURB, restraint, control, limitation, constraint, inhibition, damper, blow, disappointment, reverse, setback, frustration, hindrance, impediment, obstruction, stoppage.

heek (*infml*) *n* impertinence, impudence, insolence, disrespect, effrontery, brazenness, temerity, audacity, nerve (*infml*), gall.

cheeky (*infml*) *adj* impertinent, impudent, insolent, disrespectful, forward, brazen, pert, saucy (*infml*), audacious.
≠ respectful, polite.

cheer *v* **1** ACCLAIM, hail, clap, applaud. **2** COMFORT, console, brighten, gladden, warm, uplift, elate, exhilarate, encourage, hearten.
≠ **1** boo, jeer. **2** dishearten.
n acclamation, hurrah, bravo, applause, ovation.
cheer up encourage, hearten, take heart, rally, buck up (*infml*), perk up (*infml*).

cheerful *adj* happy, glad, contented, joyful, joyous, blithe, carefree, light-hearted, cheery, good-humoured, sunny, optimistic, enthusiastic, hearty, genial, jovial, jolly, merry, lively, animated, bright, chirpy, breezy, jaunty, buoyant, sparkling.
≠ sad, dejected, depressed.

cheese

Varieties of cheese include: Amsterdam, Bel Paese, Bleu d'Auvergne, Blue Cheshire, Blue Vinny, Boursin, Brie, Caboc, Caerphilly, Camembert, Carré, Cheddar, Cheshire, Churnton, cottage cheese, cream cheese, Crowdie, curd cheese, Danish blue, Derby, Dolcelatte, Dorset Blue, Double Gloucester, Dunlop, Edam, Emmental, Emmentaler, ewe-cheese, Feta, fromage frais, Gloucester, Gorgonzola, Gouda, Gruyère, Huntsman, Jarlsberg, Killarney, Lancashire, Leicester, Limburg(er), Lymeswold, mascarpone, mouse-trap, mozzarella, Neufchâtel, Orkney, Parmesan, Petit Suisse, Pont-l'Eveque, Port Salut, processed cheese, quark, Red Leicester, Red Windsor, ricotta, Roquefort, sage Derby, Saint-Paulin, Stilton, stracchino, vegetarian cheese, Vacherin, Wensleydale.

chemical elements

The chemical elements (with their symbols) are: actinium (Ac), aluminium (Al), americium (Am), antimony (Sb), argon (Ar), arsenic (As), astatine (At), barium (Ba), berkelium (Bk), beryllium (Be), bismuth (Bi), boron (B), bromine (Br), cadmium (Cd), caesium (Cs), calcium (Ca), californium (Cf), carbon (C), cerium (Ce), chlorine (Cl), chromium (Cr), cobalt (Co), copper (Cu), curium (Cm), dysprosium (Dy), einsteinium (Es), erbium (Er), europium (Eu), fermium (Fm), fluorine (F), francium (Fr), gadolinium (Gd), gallium (Ga), germanium (Ge), gold (Au), hafnium (Hf), hahnium (Ha), helium (He), holmium (Ho), hydrogen (H), indium (In), iodine (I), iridium (Ir), iron (Fe), krypton (Kr), lanthanum (La), lawrencium (Lr), lead (Pb), lithium (Li), lutetium (Lu), magnesium (Mg), manganese (Mn), mendelevium (Md), mercury (Hg), molybdenum (Mo), neodymium (Nd), neon (Ne), neptunium (Np), nickel (Ni), niobium (Nb), nitrogen (N), nobelium (No), osmium (Os), oxygen (O), palladium (Pd), phosphorus (P), platinum (Pt), plutonium (Pu), polonium (Po), potassium (K), praseodymium (Pr), promethium (Pm), protactinium (Pa), radium (Ra), radon (Rn), rhenium (Re), rhodium (Rh), rubidium (Rb), ruthenium (Ru), rutherfordium (Rf), samarium (Sm), scandium (Sc), selenium (Se), silicon (Si), silver (Ag), sodium (Na), strontium (Sr), sulphur (S), tantalum (Ta), technetium (Tc), tellurium (Te), terbium (Tb), thallium (Tl), thorium (Th), thulium (Tm), tin (Sn), titanium (Ti), tungsten (W), uranium (U), vanadium (V), xenon (Xe), ytterbium (Yb), yttrium (Y), zinc (Zn), zirconium (Zr).

chemistry

Terms used in chemistry include: analytical chemistry, biochemistry, inorganic chemistry, organic chemistry, physical chemistry; acid, alkali, analysis, atom, atomic number, atomic structure, subatomic particles, base, bond, buffer, catalysis, catalyst, chain reaction, chemical bond, chemical compound, chemical element, chemical equation, chemical reaction, chemist, chlorination, combustion, compound, corrosion, covalent bond, crystal, cycle, decomposition, diffusion, dissociation, distillation, electrochemical cell, electrode, electron, electrolysis, emulsion, fermentation, fixation, formula, free radical, gas, halogen, hydrolysis, immiscible, indicator, inert gas, ion, ionic bond, isomer, isotope, lipid, liquid, litmus paper, litmus test, mass, matter, metallic bond, mixture, mole, molecule, neutron, noble gas, nucleus, oxidation, periodic table, pH, polymer, proton, radioactivity, reaction, reduction, respiration, salt, solids, solution, solvent, substance, suspension, symbol, synthesis, valency, zwitterion. *see also* **acid**; **subatomic particles**; **gas**; **minerals**.

cherish *v* foster, care for, look after, nurse, nurture, nourish, sustain, support, harbour, shelter, entertain, hold dear, value, prize, treasure.

chest *n* trunk, crate, box, case, casket, coffer, strongbox.

chew *v* masticate, gnaw, munch, champ, crunch, grind.

chief *adj* leading, foremost, uppermost, highest, supreme, grand, arch, premier, principal, main, key, central, prime, prevailing, predominant, pre-eminent, outstanding, vital, essential, primary, major.
≠ minor, unimportant.
n ruler, chieftain, lord, master, supremo, head, principal, leader, commander, captain, governor, boss, director, manager, superintendent, superior, ringleader.

chiefly *adv* mainly, mostly, for the most part, predominantly, principally, primarily, essentially, especially, generally, usually.

child *n* youngster, kid (*infml*), nipper (*infml*), brat (*infml*), baby, infant, toddler, tot (*infml*), minor, juvenile, offspring, issue, progeny, descendant.

childhood *n* babyhood, infancy, boyhood, girlhood, schooldays, youth adolescence, minority, immaturity.

childish *adj* babyish, boyish, girlish, infantile, puerile, juvenile, immature, silly, foolish, frivolous.
≠ mature, sensible.

childlike *adj* innocent, naïve, ingenuous, artless, guileless, credulous, trusting, trustful, simple, natural.

chill *v* **1** COOL, refrigerate, freeze, ice. **2** FRIGHTEN, terrify, dismay, dishearten, discourage, depress, dampen.
≠ **1** warm, heat.
n coolness, cold, coldness, frigidity, rawness, bite, nip, crispness.
≠ warmth.

chilly *adj* **1** *chilly weather*: cold, fresh, brisk, crisp, nippy (*infml*), wintry. **2** *a chilly response*: cool, frigid, unsympathetic, unwelcoming, aloof, stony, unfriendly, hostile.
≠ **1** warm. **2** friendly.

chime *v* sound, strike, toll, ring, peal, clang, dong, jingle, tinkle.

china *adj* porcelain, ceramic, pottery, earthenware, terracotta.

Chinese calendar

> *The animals representing the years in which people are born*: rat, buffalo, tiger, rabbit (or hare), dragon, snake, horse, goat (or sheep), monkey, rooster, dog, pig.

chink *n* crack, rift, cleft, fissure, crevice, slot, opening, aperture, gap, space.

chip *n* **1** NOTCH, nick, scratch, dent, flaw. **2** FRAGMENT, scrap, wafer, sliver, flake, shaving, paring.
v chisel, whittle, nick, notch, gash, damage.

chirp *v, n* chirrup, tweet, cheep, peep, twitter, warble, sing, pipe, whistle.

chivalrous *adj* gentlemanly, polite, courteous, gallant, heroic, valiant, brave, courageous, bold, noble, honourable.
≠ ungallant, cowardly.

chivalry *n* gentlemanliness, politeness, courtesy, gallantry, bravery, courage, boldness.

choice *n* option, alternative, selection, variety, pick, preference, say, decision, dilemma, election, discrimination, choosing, opting.
adj best, superior, prime, plum, excellent, fine, exquisite, exclusive, select, hand-picked, special, prize, valuable, precious.
≠ inferior, poor.

choke *v* **1** THROTTLE, strangle, asphyxiate, suffocate, stifle, smother, suppress. **2** OBSTRUCT, constrict, congest, clog, block, dam, bar, close, stop. **3** COUGH, gag, retch.

choose *v* pick, select, single out, designate, predestine, opt for, plump for, vote for, settle on, fix on, adopt, elect, prefer, wish, desire, see fit.

choosy (*infml*) *adj* selective, discriminating, picky (*infml*), fussy, particular, finicky, fastidious, exacting.
≠ undemanding.

chop *v* cut, hack, hew, lop, sever, truncate, cleave, divide, split, slash.
chop up cut (up), slice (up), divide, cube, dice, mince.

choppy *adj* rough, turbulent, tempestuous, stormy, squally, ruffled, wavy, uneven, broken.
≠ calm, still.

chore *n* task, job, errand, duty, burden.

chorus *n* **1** REFRAIN, burden, response, call, shout. **2** CHOIR, choristers, singers, vocalists, ensemble.

christen *v* baptize, name, call, dub, title, style, term, designate, inaugurate, use.

Christmas *n* Xmas, Noel, Yule, Yuletide.

chronic *adj* **1** INCURABLE, deep-seated, recurring, incessant, persistent, inveterate, confirmed, habitual, ingrained, deep-rooted. **2** (*infml*) *a chronic film*: awful, terrible, dreadful, appalling, atrocious.
≠ **1** acute, temporary.

chronological *adj* historical, consecutive, sequential, progressive, ordered.

chubby *adj* plump, podgy, fleshy,

flabby, stout, portly, rotund, round, tubby, paunchy.
≠ slim, skinny.

chuckle *v* laugh, giggle, titter, snigger, chortle, snort, crow.

chunk *n* lump, hunk, mass, wodge (*infml*), wedge, block, slab, piece, portion.

church *n* chapel, house of God, cathedral, minster, abbey, temple.

Parts of a church or cathedral include: aisle, almonry, altar, ambulatory, apse, arcade, arch, belfry, bell screen, bell tower, chancel, chapel, choir, clerestory, cloister, confessional, credence, crossing, crypt, fenestella, font, frontal, gallery, keystone, lectern, narthex, nave, parvis, pew, pinnacle, piscina, porch, portal, predella, presbytery, pulpit, reredos, rood, rood screen, sacristy, sanctuary, sedile, shrine, slype, spire, squint, stall, steeple, stoup, tomb, tower, transept, triforium, vault, vestry.

church service

Names of church services include: baptism, christening, Christingle, communion, Holy Communion, confirmation, dedication, Eucharist, evening service, evensong, funeral, Lord's Supper, marriage, Mass, High Mass, Midnight Mass, Nuptial Mass, Requiem Mass, Holy Matrimony, memorial service, morning prayers, morning service. *see also* **canonical hours**.

cinema *n* **1** films, pictures, movies (*infml*), flicks (*sl*), big screen. **2** picture-house, picture-palace, fleapit (*infml*).

circle *n*

Types of circle include: annulus, ball, band, belt, circuit, circumference, coil, cordon, coronet, crown, curl, cycle, disc, discus, ellipse, girdle, globe, halo, hoop, lap, loop, orb, orbit, oval, perimeter, plate, revolution, ring, rotation, round, saucer, sphere, spiral, turn, tyre, wheel, wreath.

circle of friends: group, band, company, crowd, set, clique, coterie, club, society, fellowship, fraternity.
v **1** RING, loop, encircle, surround, gird, encompass, enclose, hem in, circumscribe, circumnavigate.
2 ROTATE, revolve, pivot, gyrate, whirl, turn, coil, wind.

circuit *n* lap, orbit, revolution, tour, journey, course, route, track, round, beat, district, area, region, circumference, boundary, bounds, limit, range, compass, ambit.

circuitous *adj* roundabout, periphrastic, indirect, oblique, devious, tortuous, winding, meandering, rambling, labyrinthine.
≠ direct, straight.

circular *adj* round, annular, ring-shaped, hoop-shaped, disc-shaped.
n handbill, leaflet, pamphlet, notice, announcement, advertisement, letter.

circulate *v* **1** *circulate information*: spread, diffuse, broadcast, publicize, publish, issue, propagate, pass round, distribute. **2** GO ROUND, rotate, revolve, gyrate, whirl, swirl, flow.

circulation *n* **1** BLOOD-FLOW, flow, motion, rotation, circling. **2** SPREAD, transmission, publication, dissemination, distribution.

circumference *n* circuit, perimeter, rim, edge, outline, boundary, border, bounds, limits, extremity, margin, verge, fringe, periphery.

circumstances *n* details, particulars, facts, items, elements, factors, conditions, state, state of affairs, situation, position, status, lifestyle, means, resources.

cistern *n* tank, reservoir, sink, basin, vat.

citadel *n* fortress, stronghold, bastion, castle, keep, tower, fortification, acropolis.

cite *v* quote, adduce, name, specify, enumerate, mention, refer to, advance, bring up.

citizen *n* city-dweller, townsman, townswoman, inhabitant, denizen, resident, householder, taxpayer, subject.

city *n* metropolis, town, municipality, conurbation.

civic *adj* city, urban, municipal, borough, community, local, public, communal.

civil *adj* **1** POLITE, courteous, well-mannered, well-bred, courtly, refined, civilized, polished, urbane, affable, complaisant, obliging, accommodating. **2** *civil affairs*: domestic, home, national, internal, interior, state, municipal, civic.
≠ **1** uncivil, discourteous, rude. **2** international, military.

civility *n* politeness, courteousness, courtesy, breeding, refinement, urbanity, graciousness, affability, amenity.
≠ discourtesy, rudeness.

civilization *n* progress, advancement, development, education, enlightenment, cultivation, culture, refinement, sophistication, urbanity.
≠ barbarity, primitiveness.

civilize *v* tame, humanize, educate, enlighten, cultivate, refine, polish, sophisticate, improve, perfect.

civilized *adj* advanced, developed, educated, enlightened, cultured, refined, sophisticated, urbane, polite, sociable.
≠ uncivilized, barbarous, primitive.

claim *v* **1** ALLEGE, pretend, profess, state, affirm, assert, maintain, contend, hold, insist. **2** *claim a refund*: ask, request, require, need, demand, exact, take, collect.
n **1** ALLEGATION, pretension, affirmation, assertion, contention, insistence. **2** APPLICATION, petition, request, requirement, demand, call, right, privilege.

clairvoyant *adj* psychic, prophetic, visionary, telepathic, extra-sensory.
n psychic, fortune-teller, prophet, prophetess, visionary, seer, soothsayer, augur, oracle, diviner, telepath.

clammy *adj* damp, moist, sweaty, sweating, sticky, slimy, dank, muggy, heavy, close.

clamp *n* vice, grip, press, brace, bracket, fastener.
v fasten, secure, fix, clinch, grip, brace.

clan *n* tribe, family, house, race, society, brotherhood, fraternity, confraternity, sect, faction, group, band, set, clique, coterie.

clap *v* **1** APPLAUD, acclaim, cheer. **2** SLAP, smack, pat, wallop (*infml*), whack (*infml*), bang.

clarify *v* **1** EXPLAIN, throw light on, illuminate, elucidate, gloss, define, simplify, resolve, clear up. **2** REFINE, purify, filter, clear.
≠ **1** obscure, confuse. **2** cloud.

clarity *n* clearness, transparency, lucidity, simplicity, intelligibility, comprehensibility, explicitness, unambiguousness, obviousness, definition, precision.
≠ obscurity, vagueness, imprecision.

clash *v* **1** CRASH, bang, clank, clang, jangle, clatter, rattle, jar. **2** CONFLICT, disagree, quarrel, wrangle, grapple, fight, feud, war.
n **1** CRASH, bang, jangle, clatter, noise. **2** *a clash with the police*: confrontation, showdown, conflict, disagreement, fight, brush.

clasp *n* **1** FASTENER, buckle, clip, pin, hasp, hook, catch. **2** HOLD, grip, grasp, embrace, hug.
v **1** HOLD, grip, grasp, clutch, embrace, enfold, hug, squeeze, press. **2** FASTEN, connect, attach, grapple, hook, clip, pin.

class *n* **1** CATEGORY, classification, group, set, section, division, department, sphere, grouping, order, league, rank, status, caste, quality, grade, type, genre, sort, kind, species, genus, style. **2** *a French class*: lesson, lecture, seminar, tutorial, course.

Social classes/groups include: aristocracy, nobility, gentry, landed gentry, gentlefolk, élite, nob (*sl*), high society, top drawer (*infml*), upper class, Sloane Ranger (*sl*), ruling class, jet set, middle class, lower class, working class, bourgeoisie, proletariat, hoi-polloi, commoner, serf, plebeian, pleb (*infml*). *see also* **nobility**.

v categorize, classify, group, sort, rank, grade, rate, designate, brand.

classic *adj* typical, characteristic, standard, regular, usual, traditional, time-honoured, established, archetypal, model, exemplary, ideal, best, finest, first-rate, consummate, definitive, masterly, excellent, ageless, immortal, undying, lasting, enduring, abiding.
≠ unrepresentative, second-rate.
n standard, model, prototype, exemplar, masterwork, masterpiece, pièce de résistance.

classical *adj* elegant, refined, pure, traditional, excellent, well-proportioned, symmetrical, harmonious, restrained.
≠ modern, inferior.

classification *n* categorization, taxonomy, sorting, grading, arrangement, systematization, codification, tabulation, cataloguing.

classify *v* categorize, class, group, pigeonhole, sort, grade, rank, arrange, dispose, distribute, systematize, codify, tabulate, file, catalogue.

clause *n* article, item, part, section, subsection, paragraph, heading, chapter, passage, condition, proviso, provision, specification, point.

claw *n* talon, nail, pincer, nipper, gripper.
v scratch, scrabble, scrape, graze, tear, rip, lacerate, maul, mangle.

clean *adj* **1** WASHED, laundered, sterile, aseptic antiseptic, hygienic, sanitary, sterilized, decontaminated, purified, pure, unadulterated, fresh, unpolluted, uncontaminated, immaculate, spotless, unspotted, unstained, unsoiled, unsullied, perfect, faultless, flawless, unblemished. **2** *a clean life*: innocent, guiltless, virtuous, upright, moral, honest, honourable, respectable, decent, chaste. **3** SMOOTH, regular, straight, neat, tidy.
≠ **1** dirty, polluted. **2** dishonourable, indecent. **3** rough.

Ways to clean include: bath, bathe, bleach, brush, buff, cleanse, comb, decontaminate, deodorize, disinfect, distil, dry-clean, dust, filter, floss, flush, freshen, freshen up, fumigate, groom, hoover, launder, mop, muck out, pasteurize, pick, polish, purge, purify, refine, rinse, rub, sandblast, sanitize, scour, scrape, scrub, shampoo, shine, shower, soak, soap, sponge, spring-clean, spruce, spruce up, steep, sterilize, swab, sweep, swill, vacuum, valet, wash, wipe.

cleanser *n* soap, soap powder, detergent, cleaner, solvent, scourer, scouring powder, purifier, disinfectant.

clear *adj* **1** PLAIN, distinct, comprehensible, intelligible, coherent, lucid, explicit, precise, unambiguous, well-defined, apparent, evident, patent, obvious, manifest, conspicuous, unmistakable, unquestionable. **2** SURE, certain, positive, definite, convinced. **3** *clear water*: transparent, limpid, crystalline, glassy, see-through, clean, unclouded, colourless. **4** *a clear day*: cloudless, unclouded, fine, bright, sunny, light, luminous, undimmed. **5** UNOBSTRUCTED, unblocked, open, free, empty, unhindered, unimpeded. **6** AUDIBLE, perceptible, pronounced, distinct, recognizable.
≠ **1** unclear, vague, ambiguous, confusing. **2** unsure, muddled. **3** opaque, cloudy. **4** dull. **5** blocked. **6** inaudible, indistinct.
v **1** UNBLOCK, unclog, decongest, free, rid, extricate, disentangle, loosen. **2** CLEAN, wipe, erase, cleanse, refine, filter, tidy, empty, unload. **3** ACQUIT, exculpate, exonerate, absolve, vindicate, excuse, justify, free, liberate, release, let go.
≠ **1** block. **2** dirty, defile. **3** condemn.
clear up 1 EXPLAIN, clarify, elucidate, unravel, solve, resolve, answer. **2** TIDY, order, sort, rearrange, remove.

clearance *n* **1** AUTHORIZATION, sanction, endorsement, permission, consent, leave, OK (*infml*), go-ahead, green light (*infml*). **2** SPACE, gap, headroom, margin, allowance.

clearing *n* space, gap, opening, glade, dell.

clergy *n* clergymen, churchmen, clerics, the church, the cloth, ministry, priesthood.

clergyman *n* churchman, cleric, ecclesiastic, divine, man of God, minister, priest, reverend, father, vicar, pastor, padre, parson, rector, canon, dean, deacon, chaplain, curate, presbyter, rabbi.

clerical *adj* **1** OFFICE, secretarial, white-collar, official, administrative. **2** ECCLESIASTIC(AL), pastoral, ministerial, priestly, episcopal, canonical, sacerdotal.

clerical vestments

Types of clerical vestment include: alb, amice, biretta, cassock, chasuble, chimere, clerical collar, dog-collar (*infml*), cope, cotta, cowl, dalmatic, ephod, frock, Geneva bands, Geneva gown, habit, hood, maniple, mantle, mitre, mozzetta, pallium, rochet, scapular, scarf, skullcap, soutane, stole, surplice, tallith, tippet, tunicle, wimple, yarmulka.

clever *adj* intelligent, brainy (*infml*), bright, smart, witty, gifted, expert, knowledgeable, adroit, apt, able, capable, quick, quick-witted, sharp, keen, shrewd, knowing, discerning, cunning, ingenious, inventive, resourceful, sensible, rational.
≠ foolish, stupid, senseless, ignorant.

cliché *n* platitude, commonplace, banality, truism, bromide, chestnut, stereotype.

client *n* customer, patron, regular, buyer, shopper, consumer, user, patient, applicant.

cliff *n* bluff, face, rock-face, scar, scarp, escarpment, crag, overhang, precipice.

climate *n* weather, temperature, setting, milieu, environment, ambience, atmosphere, feeling, mood, temper, disposition, tendency, trend.

climax *n* culmination, height, high point, highlight, acme, zenith, peak, summit, top, head.
≠ nadir.

climb *v* ascend, scale, shin up, clamber, mount, rise, soar, top.
climb down retract, eat one's words, back down, retreat.

cling *v* clasp, clutch, grasp, grip, stick, adhere, cleave, fasten, embrace, hug.

clip[1] *v* trim, snip, cut, prune, pare, shear, crop, dock, poll, truncate, curtail, shorten, abbreviate.

clip[2] *v* pin, staple, fasten, attach, fix, hold.

clipping *n* cutting, snippet, quotation, citation, passage, section, excerpt, extract, clip.

clique *n* circle, set, coterie, group, bunch, pack, gang, crowd, faction, clan.

cloak *n* cape, mantle, robe, wrap, coat, cover, shield, mask, front, pretext.
v cover, veil, mask, screen, hide, conceal, obscure, disguise, camouflage.

clocks and watches

Types of clock or watch include: alarm-clock, digital clock, mantel clock, bracket clock, carriage clock, cuckoo-clock, longcase clock, grandfather clock, grandmother clock, speaking clock, Tim (*infml*); wrist-watch, fob-watch, repeating watch, chronograph, pendant watch, ring-watch, stop-watch; chronometer, sundial.

clog *v* block, choke, stop up, bung up, dam, congest, jam, obstruct, impede, hinder, hamper, burden.
≠ unblock.

close[1] *v* **1** SHUT, fasten, secure, lock, bar, obstruct, block, clog, plug, cork, stop up, fill, seal, fuse, join, unite. **2** END, finish, complete, conclude, terminate, wind up, stop, cease.
≠ **1** open, separate. **2** start.
n end, finish, completion, conclusion, culmination, ending, finale, dénouement, termination, cessation, stop, pause.

close[2] *adj* **1** NEAR, nearby, at hand, neighbouring, adjacent, adjoining, impending, imminent. **2** INTIMATE, dear, familiar, attached, devoted, loving. **3** OPPRESSIVE, heavy, muggy, humid, sultry, sweltering, airless, stifling, suffocating, stuffy, unventilated. **4** MISERLY, mean, parsimonious, tight (*infml*), stingy,

niggardly. **5** SECRETIVE, uncommunicative, taciturn, private, secret, confidential. **6** *a close translation*: exact, precise, accurate, strict, literal, faithful. **7** *pay close attention*: fixed, concentrated, intense, keen. **8** DENSE, solid, packed, cramped.
≠ **1** far, distant. **2** cool, unfriendly. **3** fresh, airy. **4** generous. **5** open. **6** rough.

clot *n* lump, mass, thrombus, thrombosis, clotting, coagulation.
v coalesce, curdle, coagulate, congeal, thicken, solidify, set, gel.

cloth *n* **1** FABRIC, material, stuff, textile. **2** RAG, face-cloth, flannel, dish-cloth, floorcloth, duster, towel.

clothe *v* dress, put on, robe, attire, deck, outfit, rig, vest, invest, drape, cover.
≠ undress, strip, disrobe.

clothes *n* clothing, garments, wear, attire, garb, gear (*infml*), togs (*infml*), outfit, get-up (*infml*), dress, costume, wardrobe.

Clothes include: suit, trouser suit, dress suit, catsuit, jumpsuit, tracksuit, shell suit, wet suit; dress, frock, evening-dress, shirtwaister, caftan, kimono, sari; skirt, mini skirt, dirndl, pencil-skirt, pinafore-skirt, divided-skirt, culottes, kilt, sarong; cardigan, jumper, jersey, sweater, polo-neck, turtle-neck, guernsey, pullover, twin-set, shirt, dress-shirt, sweat-shirt, tee-shirt, T-shirt, waistcoat, blouse, smock, tabard, tunic; trousers, jeans, Levis®, denims, slacks, cords, flannels, drainpipes, bell-bottoms, dungarees, leggings, pedal-pushers, breeches, plus-fours, jodhpurs, Bermuda shorts, hot pants, shorts; bra, brassière, body stocking, camisole, liberty bodice, corset, girdle, garter, suspender belt, suspenders, shift, slip, petticoat, teddy, basque, briefs, pants, panties, French knickers, camiknickers, pantihose, tights, stockings; underpants, boxer-shorts, Y-fronts, vest, string vest, singlet; swimsuit, bathing-costume, bikini, swimming costume, swimming trunks, leotard, salopette; nightdress, nightie (*infml*), pyjamas, bed-jacket, bedsocks, dressing-gown, housecoat, negligee; scarf, glove, mitten, muffler, earmuffs, leg-warmers, sock, tie, bow-tie, cravat, stole, shawl, belt, braces, cummerbund, veil, yashmak. *see also* **clerical vestments**; **coat**; **footwear**; **hats**.

cloud *n* vapour, haze, mist, fog, gloom, darkness, obscurity.

Types of cloud include: cirrus, cirrostratus, cirrocumulus, altocumulus, altostratus, cumulus, stratocumulus, nimbostratus, fractostratus, fractocumulus, cumulonimbus, stratus.

v mist, fog, blur, dull, dim, darken, shade, shadow, overshadow, eclipse, veil, shroud, obscure, muddle, confuse, obfuscate.
≠ clear.

cloudy *adj* nebulous, hazy, misty, foggy, blurred, blurry, opaque, milky, muddy, dim, indistinct, obscure, dark, murky, sombre, leaden, lowering, overcast, dull, sunless.
≠ clear, bright, sunny, cloudless.

clown *n* buffoon, comic, comedian, joker, jester, fool, harlequin, pierrot.

club *n* **1** ASSOCIATION, society, company, league, guild, order, union, fraternity, group, set, circle, clique. **2** BAT, stick, mace, bludgeon, truncheon, cosh (*sl*), cudgel.
v hit, strike, beat, bash, clout, clobber (*sl*), bludgeon, cosh (*sl*), batter, pummel.

clue *n* hint, tip, suggestion, idea, notion, lead, tip-off, pointer, sign, indication, evidence, trace, suspicion, inkling, intimation.

clump *n* cluster, bundle, bunch, mass, tuft, thicket.
v tramp, clomp, stamp, stomp, plod, lumber, thump, thud.

clumsy *adj* bungling, ham-fisted, unhandy, unskilful, inept, bumbling, blundering, lumbering, gauche, ungainly, gawky (*infml*), unco-ordinated, awkward, ungraceful, uncouth, rough, crude, ill-made,

shapeless, unwieldy, heavy, bulky, cumbersome.
≠ careful, graceful, elegant.

cluster *n* bunch, clump, batch, group, knot, mass, crowd, gathering, collection, assembly.
v bunch, group, gather, collect, assemble, flock.

clutch *v* hold, clasp, grip, hang on to, grasp, seize, snatch, grab, catch, grapple, embrace.

clutter *n* litter, mess, jumble, untidiness, disorder, disarray, muddle, confusion.
v litter, encumber, fill, cover, strew, scatter.

coach *n* trainer, instructor, tutor, teacher.
v train, drill, instruct, teach, tutor, cram, prepare.

coagulate *v* clot, curdle, congeal, thicken, solidify, gel.
≠ melt.

coalition *n* merger, amalgamation, combination, integration, fusion, alliance, league, bloc, compact, federation, confederation, confederacy, association, affiliation, union.

coarse *adj* **1** ROUGH, unpolished, unfinished, uneven, lumpy, unpurified, unrefined, unprocessed. **2** *coarse humour*: bawdy, ribald, earthy, smutty, vulgar, crude, offensive, foul-mouthed, boorish, loutish, rude, impolite, indelicate, improper, indecent, immodest.
≠ **1** smooth, fine. **2** refined, sophisticated, polite.

coast *n* coastline, seaboard, shore, beach, seaside.
v free-wheel, glide, slide, sail, cruise, drift.

coat *n* **1** FUR, hair, fleece, pelt, hide, skin. **2** LAYER, coating, covering.

> *Types of coat include*: overcoat, greatcoat, car-coat, duffel coat, Afghan, blanket, frock-coat, tail-coat, jacket, bomber jacket, dinner-jacket, donkey-jacket, hacking-jacket, reefer, pea-jacket, shooting-jacket, safari jacket, Eton jacket, matinee jacket, tuxedo, blazer, raincoat, trench-coat, mackintosh, mac (*infml*), Burberry, parka, anorak, cagoul, windcheater, jerkin, blouson, cape, cloak, poncho.

v cover, paint, spread, smear, plaster.

coating *n* covering, layer, dusting, wash, coat, blanket, sheet, membrane, film, glaze, varnish, finish, veneer, lamination, overlay.

coax *v* persuade, cajole, wheedle, sweet-talk (*infml*), soft-soap, flatter, beguile, allure, entice, tempt.

cocky *adj* arrogant, bumptious, self-important, conceited, vain, swollen-headed, egotistical, swaggering, brash, cocksure, self-assured, self-confident, overconfident.
≠ humble, modest, shy.

code *n* **1** ETHICS, rules, regulations, principles, system, custom, convention, etiquette, manners. **2** *written in code*: cipher, secret language.

coerce *v* force, drive, compel, constrain, pressurize, bully, intimidate, browbeat, bludgeon, bulldoze, dragoon, press-gang.

coercion *n* force, duress, compulsion, constraint, pressure, bullying, intimidation, threats, browbeating.

coffer *n* casket, case, box, chest, trunk, strongbox, treasury, repository.

cognition *n* perception, awareness, knowledge, apprehension, discernment, insight, comprehension, understanding, intelligence, reasoning.

cohere *v* **1** STICK, adhere, cling, fuse, unite, bind, combine, coalesce, consolidate. **2** *the argument does not cohere*: agree, square, correspond, harmonize, hold, hang together.
≠ **1** separate.

coherent *adj* articulate, intelligible, comprehensible, meaningful, lucid, consistent, logical, reasoned, rational, sensible, orderly, systematic, organized.
≠ incoherent, unintelligible, meaningless.

coil *v* wind, spiral, convolute, curl, loop, twist, writhe, snake, wreathe, twine, entwine.
n roll, curl, loop, ring, convolution,

spiral, corkscrew, helix, twist.

coin *v* invent, make up, think up, conceive, devise, formulate, originate, create, fabricate, produce, mint, forge. *n* piece, bit, money, cash, change, small change, loose change, silver, copper.

> *Types of coin include*: angel, bezant, bob (*infml*), copper, crown, dandiprat, denarius, dime, doubloon, ducat, farthing, florin, groat, guilder, guinea, half-crown, half guinea, halfpenny, half sovereign, ha'penny, krugerrand, louis d'or, moidore, napoleon, nickel, noble, obol, penny, pound, quid (*infml*), rap, real, sesterce, shilling, sixpence, solidus, sou, sovereign, spade guinea, stater, tanner (*infml*), thaler, threepenny bit.

coincide *v* coexist, synchronize, agree, concur, correspond, square, tally, accord, harmonize, match.

coincidence *n* **1** CHANCE, accident, eventuality, fluke (*infml*), luck, fortuity. **2** COEXISTENCE, conjunction, concurrence, correspondence, correlation.

coincidental *adj* **1** CHANCE, accidental, casual, unintentional, unplanned, flukey (*infml*), lucky, fortuitous. **2** COINCIDENT, coexistent, concurrent, simultaneous, synchronous.
≠ **1** deliberate, planned.

cold *adj* **1** UNHEATED, cool, chilled, chilly, chill, shivery, nippy, parky (*infml*), raw, biting, bitter, wintry, frosty, icy, glacial, freezing, frozen, arctic, polar. **2** UNSYMPATHETIC, unmoved, unfeeling, stony, frigid, unfriendly, distant, aloof, standoffish, reserved, undemonstrative, unresponsive, indifferent, lukewarm.
≠ **1** hot, warm. **2** friendly, responsive.
n coldness, chill, chilliness, coolness, frigidity, iciness.
≠ warmth.

cold-blooded *adj* cruel, inhuman, brutal, savage, barbaric, barbarous, merciless, pitiless, callous, unfeeling, heartless.
≠ compassionate, merciful.

collaborate *v* conspire, collude, work together, co-operate, join forces, team up, participate.

collaboration *n* conspiring, collusion, association, alliance, partnership, teamwork, co-operation.

collaborator *n* co-worker, associate, partner, team-mate, colleague, assistant, accomplice.
≠ traitor, turncoat.

collapse *v* **1** *collapse with exhaustion*: faint, pass out, crumple. **2** FALL, sink, founder, fail, fold (*infml*), fall apart, disintegrate, crumble, subside, cave in. *n* failure, breakdown, flop, debacle, downfall, ruin, disintegration, subsidence, cave-in, faint, exhaustion.

colleague *n* workmate, co-worker, team-mate, partner, collaborator, ally, associate, confederate, confrère, comrade, companion, aide, helper, assistant, auxiliary.

collect *v* gather, assemble, congregate, convene, muster, rally, converge, cluster, aggregate, accumulate, amass, heap, hoard, stockpile, save, acquire, obtain, secure.
≠ disperse, scatter.

collected *adj* composed, self-possessed, placid, serene, calm, unruffled, unperturbed, imperturbable, cool.
≠ anxious, worried, agitated.

collection *n* **1** GATHERING, assembly, convocation, congregation, crowd, group, cluster, accumulation, conglomeration, mass, heap, pile, hoard, stockpile, store. **2** SET, assemblage, assortment, job-lot, anthology, compilation.

collective *adj* united, combined, concerted, co-operative, joint, common, shared, corporate, democratic, composite, aggregate, cumulative.
≠ individual.

collective nouns

> *Collective nouns (by animal) include*: shrewdness of *apes*, cete of *badgers*, sloth of *bears*, swarm of *bees*, obstinacy of *buffaloes*, clowder

of *cats*, drove of *cattle*, brood of *chickens*, bask of *crocodiles*, murder of *crows*, herd of *deer*, pack of *dogs*, school of *dolphins*, dole of *doves*, team of *ducks*, parade of *elephants*, busyness of *ferrets*, charm of *finches*, shoal of *fish*, skulk of *foxes*, army of *frogs*, gaggle/skein of *geese*, tribe of *goats*, husk of *hares*, cast of *hawks*, brood of *hens*, bloat of *hippopotamuses*, string of *horses*, pack of *hounds*, troop of *kangaroos*, kindle of *kittens*, exaltation of *larks*, leap of *leopards*, pride of *lions*, swarm of *locusts*, tittering of *magpies*, troop of *monkeys*, watch of *nightingales*, family of *otters*, parliament of *owls*, pandemonium of *parrots*, covey of *partridges*, muster of *peacocks*, rookery of *penguins*, nye of *pheasants*, litter of *pigs*, school of *porpoises*, bury of *rabbits*, colony of *rats*, unkindness of *ravens*, crash of *rhinoceroses*, building of *rooks*, pod of *seals*, flock of *sheep*, murmuration of *starlings*, ambush of *tigers*, rafter of *turkeys*, turn of *turtles*, descent of *woodpeckers*, gam of *whales*, rout of *wolves*, zeal of *zebras*.

collectors and enthusiasts

Names of collectors and enthusiasts include: zoophile (*animals*), antiquary (*antiques*), tegestollogist (*beer mats*), campanologist (*bell-ringing*), ornithologist (*birds*), bibliophile (*books*), audiophile (*broadcast and recorded sound*), lepidopterist (*butterflies*), cartophilist (*cigarette cards*), numismatist (*coins/medals*), conservationist (*countryside*), environmentalist (*the environment*), xenophile (*foreigners*), gourmet (*good food*), gastronome (*good-living*), discophile (*gramophone records*), chirographist (*hand-writing*), hippophile (*horses*), entomologist (*insects*), phillumenist (*matches/ matchboxes*), monarchist (*the monarchy*), deltiologist (*postcards*), arachnologist (*spiders/arachnids*), philatelist (*stamps*), arctophile (*teddy bears*), etymologist (*words*).

collide *v* crash, bump, smash, clash, conflict, confront, meet.

collision *n* impact, crash, bump, smash, accident, pile-up, clash, conflict, confrontation, opposition.

colloquial *adj* conversational, informal, familiar, everyday, vernacular, idiomatic.
≠ formal.

collude *v* conspire, plot, connive, collaborate, scheme, machinate, intrigue.

colonist *n* colonial, settler, immigrant, emigrant, pioneer.

colonize *v* settle, occupy, people, populate.

colony *n* settlement, outpost, dependency, dominion, possession, territory, province.

colossal *adj* huge, enormous, immense, vast, massive, gigantic, mammoth, monstrous, monumental.
≠ tiny, minute.

colour *n* **1** HUE, shade, tinge, tone, tincture, tint, dye, paint, wash, pigment, pigmentation, coloration, complexion. **2** VIVIDNESS, brilliance, rosiness, ruddiness, glow, liveliness, animation.

The range of colours includes: red, crimson, scarlet, vermilion, cherry, cerise, magenta, maroon, burgundy, ruby, orange, tangerine, apricot, coral, salmon, peach, amber, brown, chestnut, mahogany, bronze, auburn, rust, copper, cinnamon, chocolate, tan, sepia, taupe, beige, fawn, yellow, lemon, canary, ochre, saffron, topaz, gold, chartreuse, green, eau de nil, emerald, jade, bottle, avocado, sage, khaki, turquoise, aquamarine, cobalt, blue, sapphire, gentian, indigo, navy, violet, purple, mauve, plum, lavender, lilac, pink, rose, magnolia, cream, ecru, milky, white, grey, silver, charcoal, ebony, jet, black.

v **1** PAINT, crayon, dye, tint, stain, tinge. **2** BLUSH, flush, redden. **3** *colour one's judgement*: affect, bias, prejudice, distort, pervert, exaggerate, falsify.

colourful *adj* **1** MULTICOLOURED, kaleidoscopic, variegated, parti-coloured, vivid, bright, brilliant, rich,

intense. **2** *a colourful description*: vivid, graphic, picturesque, lively, stimulating, exciting, interesting.
≠ **1** colourless, drab.

colourless *adj* **1** TRANSPARENT, neutral, bleached, washed out, faded, pale, ashen, sickly, anaemic. **2** INSIPID, lacklustre, dull, dreary, drab, plain, characterless, unmemorable, uninteresting, tame.
≠ **1** colourful. **2** bright, exciting.

column *n* **1** PILLAR, post, shaft, upright, support, obelisk. **2** LIST, line, row, rank, file, procession, queue, string.

comb *v* **1** *comb one's hair*: groom, neaten, tidy, untangle. **2** SEARCH, hunt, scour, sweep, sift, screen, rake, rummage, ransack.

combat *n* war, warfare, hostilities, action, battle, fight, skirmish, struggle, conflict, clash, encounter, engagement, contest, bout, duel.
v fight, battle, strive, struggle, contend, contest, oppose, resist, withstand, defy.

combination *n* **1** BLEND, MIX, mixture, composite, amalgam, synthesis, compound. **2** MERGER, amalgamation, unification, alliance, coalition, association, federation, confederation, confederacy, combine, consortium, syndicate, union, integration, fusion, coalescence, connection.

combine *v* merge, amalgamate, unify, blend, mix, integrate, incorporate, synthezise, compound, fuse, bond, bind, join, connect, link, marry, unite, pool, associate, cooperate.
≠ divide, separate, detach.

come *v* advance, move towards, approach, near, draw near, reach, attain, arrive, enter, appear, materialize, happen, occur.
≠ go, depart, leave.
come about happen, occur, come to pass, transpire, result, arise.
come across find, discover, chance upon, happen upon, bump into, meet, encounter, notice.
come along arrive, happen, develop, improve, progress, rally, mend, recover, recuperate.
come apart disintegrate, fall to bits, break, separate, split, tear.
come between separate, part, divide, split up, disunite, estrange, alienate.
come down descend, fall, reduce, decline, deteriorate, worsen, degenerate.
come in enter, appear, show up (*infml*), arrive, finish.
come off happen, occur, take place, succeed.
come on begin, appear, advance, proceed, progress, develop, improve, thrive, succeed.
come out result, end, conclude, terminate.
come out with say, state, affirm, declare, exclaim, disclose, divulge.
come round 1 *come around from the anaesthetic*: recover, wake, awake. **2** YIELD, relent, concede, allow, grant, accede.
come through endure, withstand, survive, prevail, triumph, succeed, accomplish, achieve.
come up rise, arise, happen, occur, crop up.

comeback *n* return, reappearance, resurgence, revival, recovery.

comedian *n* comic, clown, humorist, wit, joker, wag.

comedown *n* anticlimax, let-down, disappointment, deflation, blow, reverse, decline, descent, demotion, humiliation, degradation.

comedy *n* farce, slapstick, clowning, hilarity, drollery, humour, wit, joking, jesting, facetiousness.

comfort *v* ease, soothe, relieve, alleviate, assuage, console, cheer, gladden, reassure, hearten, encourage, invigorate, strengthen, enliven, refresh.
n **1** CONSOLATION, compensation, cheer, reassurance, encouragement, alleviation, relief, help, aid, support. **2** EASE, relaxation, luxury, snugness, cosiness, wellbeing, satisfaction, contentment, enjoyment.
≠ **1** distress. **2** discomfort.

comfortable *adj* **1** SNUG, cosy, comfy (*infml*), relaxing, restful, easy,

convenient, pleasant, agreeable, enjoyable, delightful. **2** AT EASE, relaxed, contented, happy. **3** AFFLUENT, well-off, well-to-do, prosperous.
≠ **1** uncomfortable, unpleasant. **2** uneasy, nervous. **3** poor.

comic *adj* funny, hilarious, side-splitting, comical, droll, humorous, witty, amusing, entertaining, diverting, joking, facetious, light, farcical, ridiculous, ludicrous, absurd, laughable, priceless (*infml*), rich (*infml*).
≠ tragic, serious.
n comedian, gagster (*infml*), joker, jester, clown, buffoon, humorist, wit, wag.

coming *adj* next, forthcoming, impending, imminent, due, approaching, near, future, aspiring, rising, up-and-coming.
n advent, approach, arrival, accession.

command *v* **1** ORDER, bid, charge, enjoin, direct, instruct, require, demand, compel. **2** LEAD, head, rule, reign, govern, control, dominate, manage, supervise.
n **1** COMMANDMENT, decree, edict, precept, mandate, order, bidding, charge, injunction, directive, direction, instruction, requirement. **2** *be in command*: power, authority, leadership, control, domination, dominion, rule, sway, government, management.

commander *n* leader, head, chief, boss, commander-in-chief, general, admiral, captain, commanding officer, officer.

commemorate *v* celebrate, solemnize, remember, memorialize, mark, honour, salute, immortalize, observe, keep.

commemoration *n* celebration, observance, remembrance, tribute, honouring, ceremony.

commence *v* begin, start, embark on, originate, initiate, inaugurate, open, launch.
≠ finish, end, cease.

commend *v* **1** PRAISE, compliment, acclaim, extol, applaud, approve, recommend. **2** COMMIT, entrust, confide, consign, deliver, yield.
≠ **1** criticize, censure.

comment *v* say, mention, interpose, interject, remark, observe, note, annotate, interpret, explain, elucidate, criticize.
n statement, remark, observation, note, annotation, footnote, marginal note, explanation, elucidation, illustration, exposition, commentary, criticism.

commentary *n* narration, voice-over, analysis, description, review, critique, explanation, notes, treatise.

commentator *n* sportscaster, broadcaster, reporter, narrator, commenter, critic, annotator, interpreter.

commerce *n* trade, traffic, business, dealings, relations, dealing, trafficking, exchange, marketing, merchandizing.

commercial *adj* trade, trading, business, sales, profit-making, profitable, sellable, saleable, popular, monetary, financial, mercenary, venal.

commission *n* **1** ASSIGNMENT, mission, errand, task, job, duty, function, appointment, employment, mandate, warrant, authority, charge, trust. **2** COMMITTEE, board, delegation, deputation, representative. **3** *commission on a sale*: percentage, cut (*infml*), rake-off (*infml*), allowance, fee.
v nominate, select, appoint, engage, employ, authorize, empower, delegate, depute, send, order, request, ask for.

commit *v* **1** *commit a crime*: do, perform, execute, enact, perpetrate. **2** ENTRUST, confide, commend, consign, deliver, hand over, give, deposit. **3** BIND, obligate, pledge, engage, involve.
commit oneself decide, undertake, promise, pledge, bind oneself.

commitment *n* undertaking, guarantee, assurance, promise, word, pledge, vow, engagement, involvement, dedication, devotion, adherence, loyalty, tie, obligation, duty, responsibility, liability.

≠ vacillation, wavering.

committee *n* advisory group.

Types of committee include: assembly, board, caucus, commission, congress, council, delegation, deputation, discussion group, group, jury, legation, mission, panel, quango, quorum, steering committee, steering group, sub-committee, synod, task-force, team, think tank (*infml*), working party, workshop.

common *adj* **1** FAMILIAR, customary, habitual, usual, daily, everyday, routine, regular, frequent, widespread, prevalent, general, universal, standard, average, ordinary, plain, simple, workaday, run-of-the-mill, undistinguished, unexceptional, conventional, accepted, popular, commonplace. **2** VULGAR, coarse, unrefined, crude, inferior, low, ill-bred, loutish, plebeian. **3** COMMUNAL, public, shared, mutual, joint, collective.
≠ **1** uncommon, unusual, rare, noteworthy. **2** tasteful, refined.

commonplace *adj* ordinary, everyday, common, humdrum, pedestrian, banal, trite, widespread, frequent, hackneyed, stock, stale, obvious, worn out, boring, uninteresting, threadbare.
≠ memorable, exceptional.

commonsense *adj* commonsensical, matter-of-fact, sensible, level-headed, sane, sound, reasonable, practical, down-to-earth, pragmatic, hard-headed, realistic, shrewd, astute, prudent, judicious.
≠ foolish, unreasonable, unrealistic.

commotion *n* agitation, hurly-burly, turmoil, tumult, excitement, ferment, fuss, bustle, ado, to-do (*infml*), uproar, furore, ballyhoo (*infml*), hullabaloo (*infml*), racket, hubbub, rumpus, fracas, disturbance, bust-up (*infml*), disorder, riot.

communal *adj* public, community, shared, joint, collective, general, common.
≠ private, personal.

commune *n* collective, co-operative, kibbutz, community, fellowship, colony, settlement.
v converse, discourse, communicate, make contact.

communicate *v* **1** ANNOUNCE, declare, proclaim, report, reveal, disclose, divulge, impart, inform, acquaint, intimate, notify, publish, disseminate, spread, diffuse, transmit, convey. **2** TALK, converse, commune, correspond, write, phone, telephone, contact.

communication *n* information, intelligence, intimation, disclosure, contact, connection, transmission, dissemination.

Forms of communication include: broadcasting, radio, wireless, television, TV, cable TV, satellite, video, teletext; newspaper, press, news, newsflash, magazine, journal, advertising, publicity, poster, leaflet, pamphlet, brochure, catalogue; post, dispatch, correspondence, letter, postcard, aerogram, telegram, cable, wire (*infml*), chain letter, junk mail, mailshot; conversation, word, message, dialogue, speech, gossip, grapevine (*infml*); notice, bulletin, announcement, communiqué, circular, memo, note, report; telephone, intercom, answering machine, walkie-talkie, bleeper, tannoy, telex, teleprinter, facsimile, fax, computer, word processor, typewriter, dictaphone, megaphone, loud-hailer; radar, Morse code, semaphore, Braille, sign language. *see also* **telephone**.

communicative *adj* talkative, voluble, expansive, informative, chatty, sociable, friendly, forthcoming, outgoing, extrovert, unreserved, free, open, frank, candid.
≠ quiet, reserved, reticent, secretive.

community *n* district, locality, population, people, populace, public, residents, nation, state, colony, commune, kibbutz, society, association, fellowship, brotherhood, fraternity.

commute *v* **1** REDUCE, decrease, shorten, curtail, lighten, soften,

mitigate, remit, adjust, modify, alter, change, exchange, alternate.
2 *commute by train*: travel, journey.

compact *adj* small, short, brief, terse, succinct, concise, condensed, compressed, close, dense, impenetrable, solid, firm.
≠ large, rambling, diffuse.

companion *n* fellow, comrade, friend, buddy (*infml*), crony (*infml*), intimate, confidant(e), ally, confederate, colleague, associate, partner, mate, consort, escort, chaperon, attendant, aide, assistant, accomplice, follower.

companionship *n* fellowship, comradeship, camaraderie, esprit de corps, support, friendship, company, togetherness, conviviality, sympathy, rapport.

company *n* **1** *a manufacturing company*: firm, business, concern, association, corporation, establishment, house, partnership, syndicate, cartel, consortium. **2** TROUPE, group, band, ensemble, set, circle, crowd, throng, body, troop, crew, party, assembly, gathering, community, society.
3 GUESTS, visitors, callers, society, companionship, fellowship, support, attendance, presence.

comparable *adj* similar, alike, related, akin, cognate, corresponding, analogous, equivalent, tantamount, proportionate, commensurate, parallel, equal.
≠ dissimilar, unlike, unequal.

compare *v* liken, equate, contrast, juxtapose, balance, weigh, correlate, resemble, match, equal, parallel.

comparison *n* juxtaposition, analogy, parallel, correlation, relationship, likeness, resemblance, similarity, comparability, contrast, distinction.

compartment *n* section, division, subdivision, category, pigeonhole, cubbyhole, niche, alcove, bay, area, stall, booth, cubicle, locker, carrel, cell, chamber, berth, carriage.

compassion *n* kindness, tenderness, fellow-feeling, humanity, mercy, pity, sympathy, commiseration, condolence, sorrow, concern, care.
≠ cruelty, indifference.

compassionate *adj* kind-hearted, kindly, tender-hearted, tender, caring, warm-hearted, benevolent, humanitarian, humane, merciful, clement, lenient, pitying, sympathetic, understanding, supportive.
≠ cruel, indifferent.

compatible *adj* harmonious, consistent, congruous, matching, consonant, accordant, suitable, reconcilable, adaptable, conformable, sympathetic, like-minded, well-matched, similar.
≠ incompatible, antagonistic, contradictory.

compel *v* force, make, constrain, oblige, necessitate, drive, urge, impel, coerce, pressurize, hustle, browbeat, bully, strongarm, bulldoze, press-gang, dragoon.

compelling *adj* forceful, coercive, imperative, urgent, pressing, irresistible, overriding, powerful, cogent, persuasive, convincing, conclusive, incontrovertible, irrefutable, gripping, enthralling, spellbinding, mesmeric, compulsive.
≠ weak, unconvincing, boring.

compensate *v* balance, counterbalance, cancel, neutralize, counteract, offset, redress, satisfy, requite, repay, refund, reimburse, indemnify, recompense, reward, remunerate, atone, redeem, make good, restore.

compensation *n* amends, redress, satisfaction, requital, repayment, refund, reimbursement, indemnification, indemnity, damages, reparation, recompense, reward, payment, remuneration, return, restoration, restitution, consolation, comfort.

compete *v* vie, contest, fight, battle, struggle, strive, oppose, challenge, rival, emulate, contend, participate, take part.

competent *adj* capable, able, adept, efficient, trained, qualified, well-qualified, skilled, experienced, proficient, expert, masterly, equal, fit,

suitable, appropriate, satisfactory, adequate, sufficient.
≠ incompetent, incapable, unable, inefficient.

competition *n* **1** CONTEST, championship, tournament, cup, event, race, match, game, quiz. **2** RIVALRY, opposition, challenge, contention, conflict, struggle, strife, competitiveness, combativeness. **3** COMPETITORS, rivals, opponents, challengers, field.

competitive *adj* combative, contentious, antagonistic, aggressive, pushy, ambitious, keen, cut-throat.

competitor *n* contestant, contender, entrant, candidate, challenger, opponent, adversary, antagonist, rival, emulator, competition, opposition.

compile *v* compose, put together, collect, gather, garner, cull, accumulate, amass, assemble, marshal, organize, arrange.

complacent *adj* smug, self-satisfied, gloating, triumphant, proud, self-righteous, unconcerned, serene, self-assured, pleased, gratified, contented, satisfied.
≠ diffident, concerned, discontented.

complain *v* protest, grumble, grouse, gripe, beef, carp, fuss, lament, bemoan, bewail, moan, whine, groan, growl.

complaint *n* **1** PROTEST, objection, grumble, grouse, gripe, beef, moan, grievance, dissatisfaction, annoyance, fault-finding, criticism, censure, accusation, charge. **2** *a chest complaint*: ailment, illness, sickness, disease, malady, malaise, indisposition, affliction, disorder, trouble, upset.

complementary *adj* reciprocal, interdependent, correlative, interrelated, corresponding, matching, twin, fellow, companion.
≠ contradictory, incompatible.

complete *adj* **1** UTTER, total, absolute, downright, out-and-out, thorough, perfect. **2** FINISHED, ended, concluded, over, done, accomplished, achieved. **3** UNABRIDGED, unabbreviated, unedited, unexpurgated, integral, whole, entire, full, undivided, intact.
≠ **1** partial. **2** incomplete. **3** abridged.
v finish, end, close, conclude, wind up, terminate, finalize, settle, clinch, perform, discharge, execute, fulfil, realize, accomplish, achieve, consummate, crown, perfect.

completion *n* finish, end, close, conclusion, termination, finalization, settlement, discharge, fulfilment, realization, accomplishment, achievement, attainment, fruition, culmination, consummation, perfection.

complex *adj* complicated, intricate, elaborate, involved, convoluted, circuitous, tortuous, devious, mixed, varied, diverse, multiple, composite, compound, ramified.
≠ simple, easy.
n **1** NETWORK, structure, system, scheme, organization, establishment, institute, development. **2** FIXATION, obsession, preoccupation, hang-up (*infml*), phobia.

complexion *n* **1** skin, colour, colouring, pigmentation. **2** look, appearance, aspect, light, character, nature, type, kind.

complicate *v* compound, elaborate, involve, muddle, mix up, confuse, tangle, entangle.
≠ simplify.

complicated *adj* complex, intricate, elaborate, involved, convoluted, tortuous, difficult, problematic, puzzling, perplexing.
≠ simple, easy.

complication *n* difficulty, drawback, snag, obstacle, problem, ramification, repercussion, complexity, intricacy, elaboration, convolution, tangle, web, confusion, mixture.

compliment *n* flattery, admiration, favour, approval, congratulations, tribute, honour, accolade, bouquet, commendation, praise, eulogy.
≠ insult, criticism.
v flatter, admire, commend, praise, extol, congratulate, applaud, salute.
≠ insult, condemn.

complimentary *adj* **1** FLATTERING, admiring, favourable, approving,

appreciative, congratulatory, commendatory, eulogistic.
2 *complimentary ticket*: free, gratis, honorary, courtesy.
≠ **1** insulting, unflattering, critical.

comply *v* agree, consent, assent, accede, yield, submit, defer, respect, observe, obey, fall in, conform, follow, perform, discharge, fulfil, satisfy, meet, oblige, accommodate.
≠ defy, disobey.

component *n* part, constituent, ingredient, element, factor, item, unit, piece, bit, spare part.

compose *v* **1** CONSTITUTE, make up, form. **2** CREATE, invent, devise, write, arrange, produce, make, form, fashion, build, construct, frame. **3** CALM, soothe, quiet, still, settle, tranquillize, quell, pacify, control, regulate.

composed *adj* calm, tranquil, serene, relaxed, unworried, unruffled, level-headed, cool, collected, self-possessed, confident, imperturbable, unflappable, placid.
≠ agitated, worried, troubled.

composition *n* **1** MAKING, production, formation, creation, invention, design, formulation, writing, compilation, proportion. **2** CONSTITUTION, make-up, combination, mixture, form, structure, configuration, layout, arrangement, organization, harmony, consonance, balance, symmetry. **3** *a musical composition*: work, opus, piece, study, exercise.

composure *n* calm, tranquillity, serenity, ease, coolness, self-possession, confidence, assurance, self-assurance, aplomb, poise, dignity, imperturbability, placidity, equanimity, dispassion, impassivity.
≠ agitation, nervousness, discomposure.

compound *v* **1** COMBINE, amalgamate, unite, fuse, coalesce, synthesize, alloy, blend, mix, mingle, intermingle. **2** WORSEN, exacerbate, aggravate, complicate, intensify, heighten, magnify, increase, augment.
n alloy, blend, mixture, medley, composite, amalgam, synthesis, fusion, composition, amalgamation, combination.
adj composite, mixed, multiple, complex, complicated, intricate.

comprehend *v* **1** UNDERSTAND, conceive, see, grasp, fathom, penetrate, tumble to (*infml*), realize, appreciate, know, apprehend, perceive, discern, take in, assimilate. **2** INCLUDE, comprise, encompass, embrace, cover.
≠ **1** misunderstand.

comprehensible *adj* understandable, intelligible, coherent, explicit, clear, lucid, plain, simple, straightforward.
≠ incomprehensible, obscure.

comprehension *n* understanding, conception, grasp, realization, appreciation, knowledge, apprehension, perception, discernment, judgement, sense, intelligence.
≠ incomprehension, unawareness.

comprehensive *adj* thorough, exhaustive, full, complete, encyclopedic, compendious, broad, wide, extensive, sweeping, general, blanket, inclusive, all-inclusive, all-embracing, across-the-board.
≠ partial, incomplete, selective.

compress *v* press, squeeze, crush, squash, flatten, jam, wedge, cram, stuff, compact, concentrate, condense, contract, telescope, shorten, abbreviate, summarize.
≠ expand, diffuse.

comprise *v* consist of, include, contain, incorporate, embody, involve, encompass, embrace, cover.

compromise *v* **1** NEGOTIATE, bargain, arbitrate, settle, agree, concede, make concessions, meet halfway, adapt, adjust. **2** *compromise one's principles*: weaken, undermine, expose, endanger, imperil, jeopardize, risk, prejudice. **3** DISHONOUR, discredit, embarrass, involve, implicate.
n bargain, trade-off, settlement, agreement, concession, give and take, co-operation, accommodation, adjustment.
≠ disagreement, intransigence.

compulsive *adj* **1** IRRESISTIBLE, overwhelming, overpowering, uncontrollable, compelling, driving, urgent. **2** *a compulsive gambler*: obsessive, hardened, incorrigible, irredeemable, incurable, hopeless.

compulsory *adj* obligatory, mandatory, imperative, forced, required, requisite, set, stipulated, binding, contractual.
≠ optional, voluntary, discretionary.

computer

Computer terms include: mainframe, microcomputer, minicomputer, PC (personal computer); Applemac®, Internet, World-Wide Web (WWW), motherboard, hardware, CPU (central processing unit), disk drive, joystick, keyboard, lap-top, light pen, microprocessor, modem, monitor, mouse, mouse mat, notebook computer, printer, bubblejet printer, daisywheel printer, dot-matrix printer, ink-jet printer, laser printer, screen, VDU (visual display unit); software, program, Windows®, WordPerfect®, Wordstar®; disk, magnetic disk, floppy disk, hard disk, optical disk, magnetic tape; programming language, BASIC, COBOL, FORTRAN; memory, backing storage, external memory, immediate access memory, internal memory, RAM (Random Access Memory), ROM (Read Only Memory), CD-ROM (Compact Disc Read Only Memory); access, ASCII, backup, bit, boot, buffer, byte, kilobyte, megabyte, character, chip, silicon chip, computer game, computer graphics, computer literate, computer simulation, computer terminal, cursor, data, databank, database, default, desktop publishing (DTP), digitizer, directory, DOS (disk operating system), electronic mail, E-mail, format, function, grammar checker, graphics, hacking, interface, macro, menu, MSDOS (Microsoft® disk operating system), network, peripheral, pixel, scrolling, spellchecker, spreadsheet, template, toggle, toolbar, user-friendly, user interface, video game, virtual reality, virus, window, word-processing, work station, WYSIWYG (what you see is what you get).

con (*infml*) *v* trick, hoax, dupe, deceive, mislead, inveigle, hoodwink, bamboozle (*infml*), cheat, double-cross, swindle, defraud, rip off (*sl*), rook.
n confidence trick, trick, bluff, deception, swindle, fraud.

concave *adj* hollow, hollowed, cupped, scooped, excavated, sunken, depressed.
≠ convex.

conceal *v* hide, obscure, disguise, camouflage, mask, screen, veil, cloak, cover, bury, submerge, smother, suppress, keep dark, keep quiet, hush up (*infml*).
≠ reveal, disclose, uncover.

concede *v* **1** ADMIT, confess, acknowledge, recognize, own, grant, allow, accept. **2** YIELD, give up, surrender, relinquish, forfeit, sacrifice.
≠ **1** deny.

conceit *n* conceitedness, vanity, boastfulness, swagger, egotism, self-love, self-importance, cockiness, self-satisfaction, complacency, pride, arrogance.
≠ modesty, diffidence.

conceited *adj* vain, boastful, swollen-headed, bigheaded (*infml*), egotistical, self-important, cocky, self-satisfied, complacent, smug, proud, arrogant, stuck-up (*infml*), toffee-nosed (*infml*).
≠ modest, self-effacing, diffident, humble.

conceivable *adj* imaginable, credible, believable, thinkable, tenable, possible, likely, probable.
≠ inconceivable, unimaginable.

conceive *v* **1** IMAGINE, envisage, visualize, see, grasp, understand, comprehend, realize, appreciate, believe, think, suppose. **2** INVENT, design, devise, formulate, create, originate, form, produce, develop.

concentrate *v* **1** FOCUS, converge, centre, cluster, crowd, congregate, gather, collect, accumulate. **2** APPLY ONESELF, think, pay attention, attend. **3** CONDENSE, evaporate, reduce, thicken, intensify.
≠ **1** disperse. **3** dilute.

concentrated *adj* **1** *concentrated liquid*: condensed, evaporated, reduced,

thickened, dense, rich, strong, undiluted. **2** INTENSE, intensive, all-out, concerted, hard, deep.
≠ **1** diluted. **2** half-hearted.

concentration *n* **1** CONVERGENCE, centralization, cluster, crowd, grouping, collection, accumulation, agglomeration, conglomeration. **2** ATTENTION, heed, absorption, application, single-mindedness, intensity. **3** COMPRESSION, reduction, consolidation, denseness, thickness.
≠ **1** dispersal. **2** distraction. **3** dilution.

concept *n* idea, notion, plan, theory, hyphothesis, thought, abstraction, conception, conceptualization, visualization, image, picture, impression.

conception *n* **1** CONCEPT, idea, notion, thought. **2** KNOWLEDGE, understanding, appreciation, perception, visualization, image, picture, impression, inkling, clue. **3** INVENTION, design, birth, beginning, origin, outset, initiation, inauguration, formation. **4** *from conception to birth*: impregnation, insemination, fertilization.

concern *v* **1** UPSET, distress, trouble, disturb, bother, worry. **2** RELATE TO, refer to, regard, involve, interest, affect, touch.
n **1** *a cause for concern*: anxiety, worry, unease, disquiet, care, sorrow, distress. **2** REGARD, consideration, attention, heed, thought. **3** *it's not my concern*: duty, responsibility, charge, job, task, field, business, affair, matter, problem, interest, involvement. **4** COMPANY, firm, business, corporation, establishment, enterprise, organization.
≠ **1** joy. **2** indifference.

concerned *adj* **1** ANXIOUS, worried, uneasy, apprehensive, upset, unhappy, distressed, troubled, disturbed, bothered, attentive, caring. **2** CONNECTED, related, involved, implicated, interested, affected.
≠ **1** unconcerned, indifferent, apathetic.

concerning *prep* about, regarding, with regard to, as regards, respecting, with reference to, relating to, in the matter of.

concerted *adj* combined, united, joint, collective, shared, collaborative, co-ordinated, organized, prearranged, planned.
≠ separate, unco-ordinated, disorganized.

concession *n* compromise, adjustment, grant, allowance, exception, privilege, favour, indulgence, permit, admission, acknowledgement.

concise *adj* short, brief, terse, succinct, pithy, compendious, compact, compressed, condensed, abridged, abbreviated, summary, synoptic.
≠ diffuse, wordy.

conclude *v* **1** INFER, deduce, assume, surmise, suppose, reckon, judge. **2** END, close, finish, complete, consummate, cease, terminate, culminate. **3** SETTLE, resolve, decide, establish, determine, clinch.
≠ **2** start, commence.

conclusion *n* **1** INFERENCE, deduction, assumption, opinion, conviction, judgement, verdict, decision, resolution, settlement, result, consequence, outcome, upshot, answer, solution. **2** END, close, finish, completion, consummation, termination, culmination, finale.

conclusive *adj* final, ultimate, definitive, decisive, clear, convincing, definite, undeniable, irrefutable, indisputable, incontrovertible, unarguable, unanswerable, clinching.
≠ inconclusive, questionable.

concoct *v* fabricate, invent, devise, contrive, formulate, plan, plot, hatch, brew, prepare, develop.

concoction *n* brew, potion, preparation, mixture, blend, compound, creation, contrivance.

concrete *adj* real, actual, factual, solid, physical, material, substantial, tangible, touchable, perceptible, visible, firm, definite, specific, explicit.
≠ abstract, vague.

concurrent *adj* simultaneous, synchronous, contemporaneous, coinciding, coincident, concomitant, coexisting, coexistent.

condemn *v* disapprove, reprehend, reprove, upbraid, reproach, castigate, blame, disparage, revile, denounce, censure, slam (*infml*), slate (*infml*), damn, doom, convict.
≠ praise, approve.

condemnation *n* disapproval, reproof, reproach, castigation, blame, disparagement, denunciation, censure, thumbs-down (*infml*), damnation, conviction, sentence, judgement.
≠ praise, approval.

condensation *n* **1** *condensation of liquid*: distillation, liquefaction, precipitation, concentration, evaporation, reduction, consolidation. **2** ABRIDGEMENT, précis, synopsis, digest, contraction, compression, curtailment.

condense *v* **1** *condense a book*: shorten, curtail, abbreviate, abridge, précis, summarize, encapsulate, contract, compress, compact. **2** DISTIL, precipitate, concentrate, evaporate, reduce, thicken, solidify, coagulate.
≠ **1** expand. **2** dilute.

condescend *v* deign, see fit, stoop, bend, lower oneself, patronize, talk down.

condescending *adj* patronizing, disdainful, supercilious, snooty, snobbish, haughty, lofty, superior, lordly, imperious, gracious.
≠ humble.

condition *n* **1** CASE, state, circumstances, position, situation, predicament, plight. **2** REQUIREMENT, obligation, prerequisite, terms, stipulation, proviso, qualification, limitation, restriction, rule. **3** *a heart condition*: disorder, defect, weakness, infirmity, problem, complaint, disease. **4** *out of condition*: fitness, health, state, shape, form, fettle, nick (*sl*).
v indoctrinate, brainwash, influence, mould, educate, train, groom, equip, prepare, prime, accustom, season, temper, adapt, adjust, tune.

conditional *adj* provisional, qualified, limited, restricted, tied, relative, dependent, contingent.
≠ unconditional, absolute.

conditions *n* surroundings, environment, milieu, setting, atmosphere, background, context, circumstances, situation, state.

condom *n* sheath, French letter (*sl*), johnnie (*sl*), rubber (*sl*), protective.

condone *v* forgive, pardon, excuse, overlook, ignore, disregard, tolerate, brook, allow.
≠ condemn, censure.

conducive *adj* leading, tending, contributory, productive, advantageous, beneficial, favourable, helpful, encouraging.
≠ detrimental, adverse, unfavourable.

conduct *n* **1** *good conduct*: behaviour, comportment, actions, ways, manners, bearing, attitude. **2** ADMINISTRATION, management, direction, running, organization, operation, control, supervision, leadership, guidance.
v **1** ADMINISTER, manage, run, organize, orchestrate, chair, control, handle, regulate. **2** ACCOMPANY, escort, usher, lead, guide, direct, pilot, steer. **3** *conduct heat*: convey, carry, bear, transmit. **4** *conduct oneself*: behave, acquit, comport, act.

confer *v* **1** DISCUSS, debate, deliberate, consult, talk, converse. **2** BESTOW, award, present, give, grant, accord, impart, lend.

conference *n* meeting, convention, congress, convocation, symposium, forum, discussion, debate, consultation.

confess *v* admit, confide, own (up), come clean (*infml*), grant, concede, acknowledge, recognize, affirm, assert, profess, declare, disclose, divulge, expose.
≠ deny, conceal.

confession *n* admission, acknowledgement, affirmation, assertion, profession, declaration, disclosure, divulgence, revelation, unburdening.
≠ denial, concealment.

confide *v* confess, admit, reveal, disclose, divulge, whisper, breathe, tell, impart, unburden.
≠ hide, suppress.

confidence *n* certainty, faith, credence, trust, reliance, dependence, assurance, composure, calmness, self-possession, self-confidence, self-reliance, self-assurance, boldness, courage.
≠ distrust, diffidence.

confident *adj* sure, certain, positive, convinced, assured, composed, self-possessed, cool, self-confident, self-reliant, self-assured, unselfconscious, bold, fearless, dauntless, unabashed.
≠ doubtful, diffident.

confidential *adj* secret, top secret, classified, restricted, hush-hush (*infml*), off-the-record, private, personal, intimate, privy.

confine *v* enclose, circumscribe, bound, limit, restrict, cramp, constrain, imprison, incarcerate, intern, cage, shut up, immure, bind, shackle, trammel, restrain, repress, inhibit.
≠ free.

confinement *n* **1** IMPRISONMENT, incarceration, internment, custody, detention, house arrest. **2** CHILDBIRTH, birth, labour, delivery.
≠ **1** freedom, liberty.

confines *n* limits, bounds, border, boundary, frontier, circumference, perimeter, edge.

confirm *v* **1** ENDORSE, back, support, reinforce, strengthen, fortify, validate, authenticate, corroborate, substantiate, verify, prove, evidence. **2** ESTABLISH, fix, settle, clinch, ratify, sanction, approve.
≠ **1** refute, deny.

confirmation *n* ratification, sanction, approval, assent, acceptance, agreement, endorsement, backing, support, validation, authentication, corroboration, substantiation, verification, proof, evidence, testimony.
≠ denial.

confirmed *adj* inveterate, entrenched, dyed-in-the-wool, rooted, established, long-established, long-standing, habitual, chronic, seasoned, hardened, incorrigible, incurable.

confiscate *v* seize, appropriate, expropriate, remove, take away, impound, sequester, commandeer.
≠ return, restore.

conflict *n* **1** DIFFERENCE, variance, discord, contention, disagreement, dissension, dispute, opposition, antagonism, hostility, friction, strife, unrest, confrontation. **2** BATTLE, war, warfare, combat, fight, contest, engagement, skirmish, set-to, fracas, brawl, quarrel, feud, encounter, clash.
≠ **1** agreement, harmony, concord.
v differ, clash, collide, disagree, contradict, oppose, contest, fight, combat, battle, war, strive, struggle, contend.
≠ agree, harmonize.

conform *v* agree, accord, harmonize, match, correspond, tally, square, adapt, adjust, accommodate, comply, obey, follow.
≠ differ, conflict, rebel.

conformity *n* conventionality, orthodoxy, traditionalism, compliance, observance, allegiance, affinity, agreement, consonance, harmony, correspondence, congruity, likeness, similarity, resemblance.
≠ nonconformity, rebellion, difference.

confound *v* **1** CONFUSE, bewilder, baffle, perplex, mystify, bamboozle (*infml*), nonplus, surprise, amaze, astonish, astound, flabbergast (*infml*), dumbfound, stupefy. **2** *confound their plans*: thwart, upset, defeat, overwhelm, overthrow, destroy, demolish, ruin.

confront *v* face, meet, encounter, accost, address, oppose, challenge, defy, brave, beard.
≠ evade.

confrontation *n* encounter, clash, collision, showdown, conflict, disagreement, fight, battle, quarrel, set-to, engagement, contest.

confuse *v* **1** PUZZLE, baffle, perplex, mystify, confound, bewilder, disorient, disconcert, fluster, discompose, upset, embarrass, mortify. **2** MUDDLE, mix up, mistake, jumble, disarrange,

disorder, tangle, entangle, involve, mingle.
≠ **1** enlighten, clarify.

confused *adj* **1** MUDDLED, jumbled, disarranged, disordered, untidy, disorderly, higgledy-piggledy (*infml*), chaotic, disorganized. **2** PUZZLED, baffled, perplexed, flummoxed (*infml*), nonplussed, bewildered, disorientated.
≠ **1** orderly.

confusion *n* **1** DISORDER, disarray, untidiness, mess, clutter, jumble, muddle, mix-up, disorganization, chaos, turmoil, commotion, upheaval. **2** MISUNDERSTANDING, puzzlement, perplexity, mystification, bewilderment.
≠ **1** order. **2** clarity.

congeal *v* clot, curdle, coalesce, coagulate, thicken, stiffen, harden, solidify, set, gel, freeze.
≠ dissolve, melt.

congested *adj* clogged, blocked, jammed, packed, stuffed, crammed, full, crowded, overcrowded, overflowing, teeming.
≠ clear.

congestion *n* clogging, blockage, overcrowding, jam, traffic jam, snarl-up, gridlock, bottle-neck.

conglomeration *n* mass, agglomeration, aggregation, accumulation, collection, assemblage, composite, medley, hotchpotch.

congratulate *v* praise, felicitate, compliment, wish well.
≠ commiserate.

congregate *v* gather, assemble, collect, muster, rally, rendezvous, meet, convene, converge, flock, crowd, throng, mass, accumulate, cluster, clump, conglomerate.
≠ disperse.

congregation *n* assembly, crowd, throng, multitude, host, flock, parishioners, parish, laity, fellowship.

conical *adj* cone-shaped, pyramidal, tapering, tapered, pointed.

conjecture *v* speculate, theorize, hypothesize, guess, estimate, reckon, suppose, surmise, assume, infer, imagine, suspect.
n speculation, theory, hypothesis, notion, guesswork, guess, estimate, supposition, surmise, assumption, presumption, conclusion, inference, extrapolation, projection.

conjure *v* summon, invoke, rouse, raise, bewitch, charm, fascinate, compel.
conjure up evoke, create, produce, excite, awaken, recollect, recall.

connect *v* join, link, unite, couple, combine, fasten, affix, attach, relate, associate, ally.
≠ disconnect, cut off, detach.

connected *adj* joined, linked, united, coupled, combined, related, akin, associated, affiliated, allied.
≠ disconnected, unconnected.

connection *n* junction, coupling, fastening, attachment, bond, tie, link, association, alliance, relation, relationship, interrelation, contact, communication, correlation, correspondence, relevance.
≠ disconnection.

connoisseur *n* authority, specialist, expert, judge, devotee, buff (*infml*), gourmet, epicure.

connotation *n* implication, suggestion, hint, nuance, undertone, overtone, colouring, association.

conquer *v* **1** DEFEAT, beat, overthrow, vanquish, rout, overrun, best, worst, get the better of, overcome, surmount, win, succeed, triumph, prevail, overpower, master, crush, subdue, quell, subjugate, humble. **2** SEIZE, take, annex, occupy, possess, acquire, obtain.
≠ **1** surrender, yield, give in.

conqueror *n* victor, winner, champion, champ (*infml*), hero, vanquisher, master, lord.

conquest *n* victory, triumph, defeat, overthrow, coup, rout, mastery, subjugation, subjection, invasion, occupation, capture, appropriation, annexation, acquisition.

conscience *n* principles, standards, morals, ethics, scruples, qualms.

conscientious *adj* diligent, hard-

working, scrupulous, painstaking, thorough, meticulous, punctilious, particular, careful, attentive, responsible, upright, honest, faithful, dutiful.
≠ careless, irresponsible, unreliable.

conscious *adj* **1** AWAKE, alive, responsive, sentient, sensible, rational, reasoning, alert. **2** AWARE, self-conscious, heedful, mindful, knowing, deliberate, intentional, calculated, premeditated, studied, wilful, voluntary.
≠ **1** unconscious. **2** unaware.

consciousness *n* awareness, sentience, sensibility, knowledge, intuition, realization, recognition.
≠ unconciousness.

consecrate *v* sanctify, hallow, bless, dedicate, devote, ordain, venerate, revere, exalt.

consecutive *adj* sequential, successive, continuous, unbroken, uninterrupted, following, succeeding, running.
≠ discontinuous.

consent *v* agree, concur, accede, assent, approve, permit, allow, grant, admit, concede, acquiesce, yield, comply.
≠ refuse, decline, oppose.
n agreement, concurrence, assent, approval, permission, go-ahead, green light (*infml*), sanction, concession, acquiescence, compliance.
≠ disagreement, refusal, opposition.

consequence *n* **1** RESULT, outcome, issue, end, upshot, effect, side effect, repercussion. **2** *of no consequence*: importance, significance, concern, value, weight, note, eminence, distinction.
≠ **1** cause. **2** unimportance, insignificance.

consequent *adj* resultant, resulting, ensuing, subsequent, following, successive, sequential.

conservation *n* keeping, safe-keeping, custody, saving, economy, husbandry, maintenance, upkeep, preservation, protection, safeguarding, ecology, environmentalism.
≠ destruction.

conservative *adj* Tory, right-wing, hidebound, die-hard, reactionary, establishmentarian, unprogressive, conventional, traditional, moderate, middle-of-the-road, cautious, guarded, sober.
≠ left-wing, radical, innovative.
n Tory, right-winger, die-hard, stick-in-the-mud, reactionary, traditionalist, moderate.
≠ left-winger, radical.

conservatory *n* greenhouse, glasshouse, hothouse.

conserve *v* keep, save, store up, hoard, maintain, preserve, protect, guard, safeguard.
≠ use, waste, squander.

consider *v* **1** PONDER, deliberate, reflect, contemplate, meditate, muse, mull over, chew over, examine, study, weigh, respect, remember, take into account. **2** *consider it an honour*: regard, deem, think, believe, judge, rate, count.

considerable *adj* great, large, big, sizable, substantial, tidy (*infml*), ample, plentiful, abundant, lavish, marked, noticeable, perceptible, appreciable, reasonable, tolerable, respectable, important, significant, noteworthy, distinguished, influential.
≠ small, slight, insignificant, unremarkable.

considerate *adj* kind, thoughtful, caring, attentive, obliging, helpful, charitable, unselfish, altruistic, gracious, sensitive, tactful, discreet.
≠ inconsiderate, thoughtless, selfish.

consideration *n* **1** THOUGHT, deliberation, reflection, contemplation, meditation, examination, analysis, scrutiny, review, attention, notice, regard. **2** KINDNESS, thoughtfulness, care, attention, regard, respect.
≠ **1** disregard. **2** thoughtlessness.

consign *v* entrust, commit, devote, hand over, transfer, deliver, convey, ship, banish, relegate.

consignment *n* cargo, shipment, load, batch, delivery, goods.

consist of comprise, be composed of, contain, include, incorporate, embody, embrace, involve, amount to.

consistency *n* **1** *of the consistency of porridge*: viscosity, thickness, density, firmness. **2** STEADINESS, regularity, evenness, uniformity, sameness, identity, constancy, steadfastness. **3** AGREEMENT, accordance, correspondence, congruity, compatibility, harmony.
≠ **3** inconsistency.

consistent *adj* **1** STEADY, stable, regular, uniform, unchanging, undeviating, constant, persistent, unfailing, dependable. **2** AGREEING, accordant, consonant, congruous, compatible, harmonious, logical.
≠ **1** irregular, erratic. **2** inconsistent.

console *v* comfort, cheer, hearten, encourage, relieve, soothe, calm.
≠ upset, agitate.

consolidate *v* reinforce, strengthen, secure, stabilize, unify, unite, join, combine, amalgamate, fuse, cement, compact, condense, thicken, harden, solidify.

conspicuous *adj* apparent, visible, noticeable, marked, clear, obvious, evident, patent, manifest, prominent, striking, blatant, flagrant, glaring, ostentatious, showy, flashy, garish.
≠ inconspicuous, concealed, hidden.

conspiracy *n* plot, scheme, intrigue, machination, fix (*infml*), frame-up (*infml*), collusion, league, treason.

conspirator *n* conspirer, plotter, schemer, intriguer, traitor.

conspire *v* plot, scheme, intrigue, manoeuvre, connive, collude, hatch, devise.

constancy *n* **1** STABILITY, steadiness, permanence, firmness, regularity, uniformity, resolution, perseverance, tenacity. **2** LOYALTY, faithfulness, fidelity, devotion.
≠ **1** change, irregularity. **2** fickleness.

constant *adj* **1** CONTINUOUS, unbroken, never-ending, non-stop, endless, interminable, ceaseless, incessant, eternal, everlasting, perpetual, continual, unremitting, relentless, persistent, resolute, persevering, unflagging, unwavering, stable, steady, unchanging, unvarying, changeless, immutable, invariable, unalterable, fixed, permanent, firm, even, regular, uniform. **2** *a constant friend*: loyal, faithful, staunch, steadfast, dependable, trustworthy, true, devoted.
≠ **1** variable, irregular, fitful, occasional. **2** disloyal, fickle.

constituent *adj* component, integral, essential, basic, intrinsic, inherent.
n ingredient, element, factor, principle, component, part, bit, section, unit.
≠ whole.

constitute *v* represent, make up, compose, comprise, form, create, establish, set up, found.

constrain *v* **1** FORCE, compel, oblige, necessitate, drive, impel, urge. **2** limit, confine, constrict, restrain, check, curb, bind.

constrained *adj* uneasy, embarrassed, inhibited, reticent, reserved, guarded, stiff, forced, unnatural.
≠ relaxed, free.

constraint *n* **1** FORCE, duress, compulsion, coercion, pressure, necessity, deterrent. **2** RESTRICTION, limitation, hindrance, restraint, check, curb, damper.

constrict *v* squeeze, compress, pinch, cramp, narrow, tighten, contract, shrink, choke, strangle, inhibit, limit, restrict.
≠ expand.

construct *v* build, erect, raise, elevate, make, manufacture, fabricate, assemble, put together, compose, form, shape, fashion, model, design, engineer, create, found, establish, formulate.
≠ demolish, destroy.

construction *n* building, edifice, erection, structure, fabric, form, shape, figure, model, manufacture, fabrication, assembly, composition, constitution, formation, creation.
≠ destruction.

constructive *adj* practical, productive, positive, helpful, useful, valuable, beneficial, advantageous.
≠ destructive, negative, unhelpful.

consult *v* refer to, ask, question, interrogate, confer, discuss, debate, deliberate.

consultant *n* adviser, expert, authority, specialist.

consultation *n* discussion, deliberation, dialogue, conference, meeting, hearing, interview, examination, appointment, session.

consume *v* **1** EAT, drink, swallow, devour, gobble. **2** USE, absorb, spend, expend, deplete, drain, exhaust, use up, dissipate, squander, waste. **3** DESTROY, demolish, annihilate, devastate, ravage.

consumer *n* user, end-user, customer, buyer, purchaser, shopper.

consumption *n* use, utilization, spending, expenditure, depletion, exhaustion, waste.

contact *n* touch, impact, juxtaposition, contiguity, communication, meeting, junction, union, connection, association.
v approach, apply to, reach, get hold of, get in touch with, telephone, phone, ring, call, notify.

contagious *adj* infectious, catching, communicable, transmissible, spreading, epidemic.

contain *v* **1** INCLUDE, comprise, incorporate, embody, involve, embrace, enclose, hold, accommodate, seat.
2 *contain one's feelings*: repress, stifle, restrain, control, check, curb, limit.
≠ **1** exclude.

container *n* receptacle, vessel, holder.

> *Types of container include*: bag, barrel, basin, basket, bath, beaker, bin, bottle, bowl, box, bucket, can, canister, carton, case, cask, casket, cauldron, chest, churn, cistern, crate, crock, cup, cylinder, dish, drum, dustbin, glass, hamper, jar, jug, keg, kettle, locker, mug, pack, packet, pail, pan, pannier, pitcher, pot, punnet, sack, suitcase, tank, tea caddy, tea chest, teapot, tin, trough, trunk, tub, tube, tumbler, tureen, urn, vase, waste bin, waste-paper basket, water-butt, well. *see also* **box**.

contaminate *v* infect, pollute, adulterate, taint, soil, sully, defile, corrupt, deprave, debase, stain, tarnish.
≠ purify.

contemplate *v* **1** MEDITATE, reflect on, ponder, mull over, deliberate, consider, regard, view, survey, observe, study, examine, inspect, scrutinize. **2** EXPECT, foresee, envisage, plan, design, propose, intend, mean.

contemporary *adj* **1** MODERN, current, present, present-day, recent, latest, up-to-date, fashionable, up-to-the-minute, ultra-modern.
2 CONTEMPORANEOUS, coexistent, concurrent, synchronous, simultaneous.
≠ **1** out-of-date, old-fashioned.

contempt *n* scorn, disdain, condescension, derision, ridicule, mockery, disrespect, dishonour, disregard, neglect, dislike, loathing, detestation.
≠ admiration, regard.

contemptible *adj* despicable, shameful, ignominious, low, mean, vile, detestable, loathsome, abject, wretched, pitiful, paltry, worthless.
≠ admirable, honourable.

contemptuous *adj* scornful, disdainful, sneering, supercilious, condescending, arrogant, haughty, high and mighty, cynical, derisive, insulting, disrespectful, insolent.
≠ humble, respectful.

contend *v* **1** MAINTAIN, hold, argue, allege, assert, declare, affirm.
2 COMPETE, vie, contest, dispute, clash, wrestle, grapple, struggle, strive, cope.

content *v* satisfy, humour, indulge, gratify, please, delight, appease, pacify, placate.
≠ displease.
n **1** SUBSTANCE, matter, essence, gist, meaning, significance, text, subject matter, ideas, contents, load, burden.
2 CAPACITY, volume, size, measure.
adj satisfied, fulfilled, contented, untroubled, pleased, happy, willing.
≠ dissatisfied, troubled.

contented *adj* happy, glad, pleased,

cheerful, comfortable, relaxed, content, satisfied.
≠ discontented, unhappy, annoyed.

contentment *n* contentedness, happiness, gladness, pleasure, gratification, comfort, ease, complacency, peace, peacefulness, serenity, equanimity, content, satisfaction, fulfilment.
≠ unhappiness, discontent, dissatisfaction.

contents *n* **1** *the contents of the package*: constituents, parts, elements, ingredients, content, load, items.
2 CHAPTERS, divisions, subjects, topics, themes.

contest *n* competition, game, match, tournament, encounter, fight, battle, set-to, combat, conflict, struggle, dispute, debate, controversy.
v **1** DISPUTE, debate, question, doubt, challenge, oppose, argue against, litigate, deny, refute. **2** COMPETE, vie, contend, strive, fight.
≠ **1** accept.

contestant *n* competitor, contender, player, participant, entrant, candidate, aspirant, rival, opponent.

context *n* background, setting, surroundings, framework, frame of reference, situation, position, circumstances, conditions.

contingent *n* body, company, deputation, delegation, detachment, section, group, set, batch, quota, complement.

continual *adj* constant, perpetual, incessant, interminable, eternal, everlasting, regular, frequent, recurrent, repeated.
≠ occasional, intermittent, temporary.

continuation *n* resumption, maintenance, prolongation, extension, development, furtherance, addition, supplement.
≠ cessation, termination.

continue *v* resume, recommence, carry on, go on, proceed, persevere, stick at, persist, last, endure, survive, remain, abide, stay, rest, pursue, sustain, maintain, lengthen, prolong, extend, project.
≠ discontinue, stop.

continuity *n* flow, progression, succession, sequence, linkage, interrelationship, connection, cohesion.
≠ discontinuity.

continuous *adj* unbroken, uninterrupted, consecutive, non-stop, endless, ceaseless, unending, unceasing, constant, unremitting, prolonged, extended, continued, lasting.
≠ discontinuous, broken, sporadic.

contort *v* twist, distort, warp, wrench, disfigure, deform, misshape, convolute, gnarl, knot, writhe, squirm, wriggle.

contour *n* outline, silhouette, shape, form, figure, curve, relief, profile, character, aspect.

contract *v* **1** SHRINK, lessen, diminish, reduce, shorten, curtail, abbreviate, abridge, condense, compress, constrict, narrow, tighten, tense, shrivel, wrinkle.
2 *contract pneumonia*: catch, get, go down with, develop. **3** PLEDGE, promise, undertake, agree, stipulate, arrange, negotiate, bargain.
≠ **1** expand, enlarge, lengthen.
n bond, commitment, engagement, covenant, treaty, convention, pact, compact, agreement, transaction, deal, bargain, settlement, arrangement, understanding.

contradict *v* deny, disaffirm, confute, challenge, oppose, impugn, dispute, counter, negate, gainsay.
≠ agree, confirm, corroborate.

contradictory *adj* contrary, opposite, paradoxical, conflicting, discrepant, inconsistent, incompatible, antagonistic, irreconcilable, opposed, repugnant.
≠ consistent.

contraption *n* contrivance, device, gadget, apparatus, rig, machine, mechanism.

contrary *adj* **1** OPPOSITE, counter, reverse, conflicting, antagonistic, opposed, adverse, hostile. **2** PERVERSE, awkward, disobliging, difficult, wayward, obstinate, intractable, cantankerous, stroppy (*infml*).
≠ **1** like. **2** obliging.

n opposite, converse, reverse.

contrast *n* difference, dissimilarity, disparity, divergence, distinction, differentiation, comparison, foil, antithesis, opposition.
≠ similarity.
v compare, differentiate, distinguish, discriminate, differ, oppose, clash, conflict.

contravene *v* infringe, violate, break, breach, disobey, defy, flout, transgress.
≠ uphold, observe, obey.

contribute *v* donate, subscribe, chip in (*infml*), add, give, bestow, provide, supply, furnish, help, lead, conduce.
≠ withhold.

contribution *n* donation, subscription, gift, gratuity, handout, grant, offering, input, addition.

contributor *n* **1** DONOR, subscriber, giver, patron, benefactor, sponsor, backer, supporter. **2** WRITER, journalist, reporter, correspondent, freelance.

contrite *adj* sorry, regretful, remorseful, repentant, penitent, conscience-stricken, chastened, humble, ashamed.

contrivance *n* **1** INVENTION, device, contraption, gadget, implement, appliance, machine, mechanism, apparatus, equipment, gear.
2 STRATAGEM, ploy, trick, dodge, ruse, expedient, plan, design, project, scheme, plot, intrigue, machination.

contrived *adj* unnatural, artificial, false, forced, strained, laboured, mannered, elaborate, overdone.
≠ natural, genuine.

control *v* **1** LEAD, govern, rule, command, direct, manage, oversee, supervise, superintend, run, operate.
2 *control the temperature*: regulate, adjust, monitor, verify. **3** *control one's temper*: restrain, check, curb, subdue, repress, hold back, contain.
n **1** POWER, charge, authority, command, mastery, government, rule, direction, management, oversight, supervision, superintendence, discipline, guidance. **2** RESTRAINT, check, curb, repression. **3** INSTRUMENT, dial, switch, button, knob, lever.

controversial *adj* contentious, polemical, disputed, doubtful, questionable, debatable, disputable.

controversy *n* debate, discussion, war of words, polemic, dispute, disagreement, argument, quarrel, squabble, wrangle, strife, contention, dissension.
≠ accord, agreement.

convenience *n* **1** ACCESSIBILITY, availability, handiness, usefulness, use, utility, serviceability, service, benefit, advantage, help, suitability, fitness. **2** *all modern conveniences*: facility, amenity, appliance.
≠ **1** inconvenience.

convenient *adj* nearby, at hand, accessible, available, handy, useful, commodious, beneficial, helpful, labour-saving, adapted, fitted, suited, suitable, fit, appropriate, opportune, timely, well-timed.
≠ inconvenient, awkward.

convention *n* **1** CUSTOM, tradition, practice, usage, protocol, etiquette, formality, matter of form, code. **2** ASSEMBLY, congress, conference, meeting, council, delegates, representatives.

conventional *adj* traditional, orthodox, formal, correct, proper, prevalent, prevailing, accepted, received, expected, unoriginal, ritual, routine, usual, customary, regular, standard, normal, ordinary, straight, stereotyped, hidebound, pedestrian, commonplace, common, run-of-the-mill.
≠ unconventional, unusual, exotic.

converge *v* focus, concentrate, approach, merge, coincide, meet, join, combine, gather.
≠ diverge, disperse.

convergence *n* concentration, approach, merging, confluence, blending, meeting, coincidence, junction, intersection, union.
≠ divergence, separation.

conversation *n* talk, chat, gossip, discussion, discourse, dialogue, exchange, communication.

converse *n* opposite, reverse, contrary, antithesis, obverse.
adj opposite, reverse, counter, contrary, reversed, transposed.

conversion *n* alteration, change, transformation, adaptation, modification, remodelling, reconstruction, reorganization, reformation, regeneration, rebirth.

convert *v* **1** ALTER, change, turn, transform, adapt, modify, remodel, restyle, revise, reorganize. **2** WIN OVER, convince, persuade, reform, proselytize.

convex *adj* rounded, bulging, protuberant.
≠ concave.

convey *v* carry, bear, bring, fetch, move, transport, send, forward, deliver, transfer, conduct, guide, transmit, communicate, impart, tell, relate, reveal.

convict *v* condemn, sentence, imprison.
n criminal, felon, culprit, prisoner.

conviction *n* assurance, confidence, fervour, earnestness, certainty, firmness, persuasion, view, opinion, belief, faith, creed, tenet, principle.

convince *v* assure, persuade, sway, win over, bring round, reassure, satisfy.

convincing *adj* persuasive, cogent, powerful, telling, impressive, credible, plausible, likely, probable, conclusive, incontrovertible.
≠ unconvincing, improbable.

convoluted *adj* twisting, winding, meandering, tortuous, involved, complicated, complex, tangled.
≠ straight, straightforward.

convoy *n* fleet, escort, guard, protection, attendance, train.

convulsion *n* **1** FIT, seizure, paroxysm, spasm, cramp, contraction, tic, tremor. **2** ERUPTION, outburst, furore, disturbance, commotion, tumult, agitation, turbulence, upheaval.

convulsive *adj* jerky, spasmodic, fitful, sporadic, uncontrolled, violent.

cook

Ways of cooking include: bake, barbecue, boil, braise, broil, casserole, coddle, deep-fry, fry, grill, microwave, poach, pot-roast, roast, sauté, scramble, simmer, spit-roast, steam, stew, stir-fry, toast; prepare, heat.

cook up concoct, prepare, brew, invent, fabricate, contrive, devise, plan, plot, scheme.

cool *adj* **1** CHILLY, fresh, breezy, nippy, cold, chilled, iced, refreshing. **2** CALM, unruffled, unexcited, composed, self-possessed, level-headed, unemotional, quiet, relaxed, laid-back (*infml*). **3** *a cool reception*: unfriendly, unwelcoming, cold, frigid, lukewarm, half-hearted, unenthusiastic, apathetic, uninterested, unresponsive, uncommunicative, reserved, distant, aloof, standoffish.
≠ **1** warm, hot. **2** excited, angry. **3** friendly, welcoming.
v **1** CHILL, refrigerate, ice, freeze, fan. **2** MODERATE, lessen, temper, dampen, quiet, abate, calm, allay, assuage.
≠ **1** warm, heat. **2** excite.
n coolness, calmness, collectedness, composure, poise, self-possession, self-discipline, self-control, control, temper.

co-operate *v* collaborate, work together, play ball (*infml*), help, assist, aid, contribute, participate, combine, unite, conspire.

co-operation *n* helpfulness, assistance, participation, collaboration, teamwork, unity, co-ordination, give-and-take.
≠ opposition, rivalry, competition.

co-operative *adj* **1** HELPFUL, supportive, obliging, accommodating, willing. **2** COLLECTIVE, joint, shared, combined, united, concerted, co-ordinated.
≠ **1** unco-operative, rebellious.

co-ordinate *v* organize, arrange, systematize, tabulate, integrate, mesh, synchronize, harmonize, match, correlate, regulate.

cope *v* manage, carry on, survive, get by, make do.
cope with deal with, encounter, contend with, struggle with, grapple with, wrestle with, handle, manage, weather.

copious *adj* abundant, plentiful,

inexhaustible, overflowing, profuse, rich, lavish, bountiful, liberal, full, ample, generous, extensive, great, huge.
≠ scarce, meagre.

copy *n* duplicate, carbon copy, photocopy, Photostat®, Xerox®, facsimile, reproduction, print, tracing, transcript, transcription, replica, model, pattern, archetype, representation, image, likeness, counterfeit, forgery, fake, imitation, borrowing, plagiarism, crib.
≠ original.
v duplicate, photocopy, reproduce, print, trace, transcribe, forge, counterfeit, simulate, imitate, impersonate, mimic, ape, parrot, repeat, echo, mirror, follow, emulate, borrow, plagiarize, crib.

cord *n* string, twine, rope, line, cable, flex, connection, link, bond, tie.

core *n* kernel, nucleus, heart, centre, middle, nub, crux, essence, gist, nitty-gritty (*infml*).
≠ surface, exterior.

corner *n* **1** *round the corner*: angle, joint, crook, bend, turning. **2** NOOK, cranny, niche, recess, cavity, hole, hideout, hide-away, retreat.

corporation *n* council, authorities, association, society, organization, company, firm, combine, conglomerate.

corpse *n* body, stiff (*sl*), carcase, skeleton, remains.

correct *v* **1** *correct an error*: rectify, put right, right, emend, remedy, cure, debug, adjust, regulate, improve, amend. **2** PUNISH, discipline, reprimand, reprove, reform.
adj **1** *the correct answer*: right, accurate, precise, exact, strict, true, truthful, word-perfect, faultless, flawless. **2** PROPER, acceptable, OK (*infml*), standard, regular, just, appropriate, fitting.
≠ **1** incorrect, wrong, inaccurate.

correction *n* rectification, emendation, adjustment, alteration, modification, amendment, improvement.

correspond *v* **1** MATCH, fit, answer, conform, tally, square, agree, concur, coincide, correlate, accord, harmonize, dovetail, complement.
2 COMMUNICATE, write.

correspondence *n* **1** COMMUNICATION, writing, letters, post, mail. **2** CONFORMITY, agreement, concurrence, coincidence, correlation, relation, analogy, comparison, comparability, similarity, resemblance, congruity, equivalence, harmony, match.
≠ **2** divergence, incongruity.

correspondent *n* journalist, reporter, contributor, writer.

corresponding *adj* matching, complementary, reciprocal, interrelated, analogous, equivalent, similar, identical.

corridor *n* aisle, passageway, passage, hallway, hall, lobby.

corroborate *v* confirm, prove, bear out, support, endorse, ratify, substantiate, validate, authenticate, document, underpin, sustain.
≠ contradict.

corrode *v* erode, wear away, eat away, consume, waste, rust, oxidize, tarnish, impair, deteriorate, crumble, disintegrate.

corrosive *adj* corroding, acid, caustic, cutting, abrasive, erosive, wearing, consuming, wasting.

corrugated *adj* ridged, fluted, grooved, channelled, furrowed, wrinkled, crinkled, rumpled, creased.

corrupt *adj* rotten, unscrupulous, unprincipled, unethical, immoral, fraudulent, shady (*infml*), dishonest, bent (*infml*), crooked (*infml*), untrustworthy, depraved, degenerate, dissolute.
≠ ethical, virtuous, upright, honest, trustworthy.
v contaminate, pollute, adulterate, taint, defile, debase, pervert, deprave, lead astray, lure, bribe, suborn.
≠ purify.

corruption *n* unscrupulousness, immorality, impurity, depravity, degeneration, degradation, perversion, distortion, dishonesty, crookedness (*infml*), fraud, shadiness (*infml*),

bribery, extortion, vice, wickedness, iniquity, evil.
≠ honesty, virtue.

cosmetic *adj* superficial, surface.
≠ essential.

cosmetics *n* make-up, grease paint.

Types of cosmetics include: blusher, cleanser, eyebrow pencil, eyelash dye, eyeliner, eye shadow, face cream, face mask, face pack, face powder, false eyelashes, foundation, kohl pencil, lip gloss, lip liner, lipstick, loose powder, mascara, moisturizer, nail polish, nail varnish, Pan-cake®, pressed powder, rouge, toner.

cosmopolitan *adj* worldly, worldly-wise, well-travelled, sophisticated, urbane, international, universal.
≠ insular, parochial, rustic.

cosset *v* coddle, mollycoddle, baby, pamper, indulge, spoil, pet, fondle, cuddle, cherish.

cost *n* **1** EXPENSE, outlay, payment, disbursement, expenditure, charge, price, rate, amount, figure, worth. **2** DETRIMENT, harm, injury, hurt, loss, deprivation, sacrifice, penalty, price.

costly *adj* **1** EXPENSIVE, dear, pricey (*infml*), exorbitant, excessive, lavish, rich, splendid, valuable, precious, priceless. **2** HARMFUL, damaging, disastrous, catastrophic, loss-making.
≠ **1** cheap, inexpensive.

costume *n* outfit, uniform, livery, robes, vestments, dress, clothing, get-up (*infml*), fancy dress.

cosy *adj* snug, comfortable, comfy (*infml*), warm, sheltered, secure, homely, intimate.
≠ uncomfortable, cold.

cottage *n* lodge, chalet, bungalow, hut, cabin, shack.

couch *n* sofa, settee, chesterfield, chaise-longue, ottoman, divan, bed.

council *n* committee, panel, board, cabinet, ministry, parliament, congress, assembly, convention, conference.

counsel *n* **1** ADVICE, suggestion, recommendation, guidance, direction, information, consultation, deliberation, consideration, forethought. **2** *counsel for the defence*: lawyer, advocate, solicitor, attorney, barrister.
v advise, warn, caution, suggest, recommend, advocate, urge, exhort, guide, direct, instruct.

count *v* **1** NUMBER, enumerate, list, include, reckon, calculate, compute, tell, check, add, total, tot up, score. **2** MATTER, signify, qualify. **3** *count yourself lucky*: consider, regard, deem, judge, think, reckon, hold.
n numbering, enumeration, poll, reckoning, calculation, computation, sum, total, tally.
count on depend on, rely on, bank on, reckon on, expect, believe, trust.

counter *adv* against, in opposition, conversely.
adj contrary, opposite, opposing, conflicting, contradictory, contrasting, opposed, against, adverse.
v parry, resist, offset, answer, respond, retaliate, retort, return, meet.

counteract *v* neutralize, counterbalance, offset, countervail, act against, oppose, resist, hinder, check, thwart, frustrate, foil, defeat, undo, negate, annul, invalidate.
≠ support, assist.

counterfeit *v* fake, forge, fabricate, copy, imitate, impersonate, pretend, feign, simulate, sham.
adj fake, false, phoney (*infml*), forged, copied, fraudulent, bogus, pseudo, sham, spurious, imitation, artificial, simulated, feigned, pretended.
≠ genuine, authentic, real.
n fake, forgery, copy, reproduction, imitation, fraud, sham.

counterpart *n* equivalent, opposite number, complement, supplement, match, fellow, mate, twin, duplicate, copy.

countless *adj* innumerable, myriad, numberless, unnumbered, untold, incalculable, infinite, endless, immeasurable, measureless, limitless.
≠ finite, limited.

country *n* **1** STATE, nation, people, kingdom, realm, principality.

2 COUNTRYSIDE, green belt, farmland, provinces, sticks (*infml*), backwoods, wilds. **3** TERRAIN, land, territory, region, area, district.
≠ **2** town, city.
adj rural, provincial, agrarian, agricultural, pastoral, rustic, bucolic, landed.
≠ urban.

countryside *n* landscape, scenery, country, green belt, farmland, outdoors.

county *n* shire, province, region, area, district.

couple *n* pair, brace, twosome, duo.
v pair, match, marry, wed, unite, join, link, connect, fasten, hitch, clasp, buckle, yoke.

coupon *n* voucher, token, slip, check, ticket, certificate.

courage *n* bravery, pluck, guts (*infml*), fearlessness, dauntlessness, heroism, gallantry, valour, boldness, audacity, nerve, daring, resolution, fortitude, spirit, mettle.
≠ cowardice, fear.

courageous *adj* brave, plucky, fearless, dauntless, indomitable, heroic, gallant, valiant, lion-hearted, hardy, bold, audacious, daring, intrepid, resolute.
≠ cowardly, afraid.

course *n* **1** CURRICULUM, syllabus, classes, lessons, lectures, studies. **2** FLOW, movement, advance, progress, development, furtherance, order, sequence, series, succession, progression. **3** DURATION, time, period, term, passage. **4** DIRECTION, way, path, track, road, route, channel, trail, line, circuit, orbit, trajectory, flight path. **5** *course of action*: plan, schedule, programme, policy, procedure, method, mode.

court *n* **1** LAW-COURT, bench, bar, tribunal, trial, session. **2** COURTYARD, yard, quadrangle, square, cloister, forecourt, enclosure. **3** ENTOURAGE, attendants, retinue, suite, train, cortège.

courteous *adj* polite, civil, respectful, well-mannered, well-bred, ladylike, gentlemanly, gracious, obliging, considerate, attentive, gallant, courtly, urbane, debonair, refined, polished.
≠ discourteous, impolite, rude.

courtesy *n* politeness, civility, respect, manners, breeding, graciousness, consideration, attention, gallantry, urbanity.
≠ discourtesy, rudeness.

courtier *n* noble, nobleman, lord, lady, steward, page, attendant, follower, flatterer, sycophant, toady.

courtyard *n* yard, quadrangle, quad (*infml*), area, enclosure, court.

cove *n* bay, bight, inlet, estuary, firth, fiord, creek.

cover *v* **1** HIDE, conceal, obscure, shroud, veil, screen, mask, disguise, camouflage. **2** *covered with mud*: coat, spread, daub, plaster, encase, wrap, envelop, clothe, dress. **3** SHELTER, protect, shield, guard, defend. **4** *cover a topic*: deal with, treat, consider, examine, investigate, encompass, embrace, incorporate, embody, involve, include, contain, comprise.
≠ **1** uncover. **2** strip. **3** expose. **4** exclude.
n **1** COATING, covering, top, lid, cup, veil, screen, mask, front, façade, jacket, wrapper, case, envelope, clothing, dress, bedspread, canopy. **2** SHELTER, refuge, protection, shield, guard, defence, concealment, disguise, camouflage.
cover up (*infml*) conceal, hide, whitewash, dissemble, suppress, hush up, keep dark, repress.
≠ disclose, reveal.

covering *n* layer, coat, coating, blanket, film, veneer, skin, crust, shell, casing, housing, wrapping, clothing, protection, mask, overlay, cover, top, shelter, roof.

cover-up (*infml*) *n* concealment, whitewash, smokescreen, front, façade, pretence, conspiracy, complicity.

covet *v* envy, begrudge, crave, long for, yearn for, hanker for, want, desire, fancy (*infml*), lust after.

coward *n* craven, faint-heart, chicken (*infml*), scaredy-cat, yellow-belly (*sl*),

wimp (*infml*), renegade, deserter.
≠ hero.

cowardice *n* cowardliness, faint-heartedness, timorousness, spinelessness.
≠ courage, valour.

cowardly *adj* faint-hearted, craven, fearful, timorous, scared, unheroic, chicken-hearted, chicken-livered, chicken (*infml*), yellow-bellied (*sl*), yellow (*sl*), spineless, weak, weak-kneed, soft.
≠ brave, courageous, bold.

cower *v* crouch, grovel, skulk, shrink, flinch, cringe, quail, tremble, shake, shiver.

coy *adj* modest, demure, prudish, diffident, shy, bashful, timid, shrinking, backward, retiring, self-effacing, reserved, evasive, arch, flirtatious, coquettish, skittish, kittenish.
≠ bold, forward.

crack *v* **1** SPLIT, burst, fracture, break, snap, shatter, splinter, chip.
2 EXPLODE, burst, pop, crackle, snap, crash, clap, slap, whack (*infml*).
3 *crack a code*: decipher, work out, solve.
n **1** BREAK, fracture, split, rift, gap, crevice, fissure, chink, line, flaw, chip.
2 EXPLOSION, burst, pop, snap, crash, clap, blow, smack, slap, whack (*infml*).
3 JOKE, quip, witticism, gag (*infml*), wisecrack, gibe, dig.
adj (*infml*) first-class, first-rate, top-notch (*infml*), excellent, superior, choice, hand-picked.
crack down on clamp down on, end, stop, put a stop to, crush, suppress, check, repress, act against.
crack up go mad, go to pieces, break down, collapse.

cradle *n* **1** COT, crib, bed. **2** SOURCE, origin, spring, wellspring, fount, fountain-head, birthplace, beginning.
v hold, support, rock, lull, nurse, nurture, tend.

craft *n* **1** SKILL, expertise, mastery, talent, knack, ability, aptitude, dexterity, cleverness, art, handicraft, handiwork. **2** TRADE, business, calling, vocation, job, occupation, work, employment. **3** VESSEL, boat, ship, aircraft, spacecraft, spaceship.

craftsman, craftswoman *n* artisan, technician, master, maker, wright, smith.

craftsmanship *n* artistry, workmanship, technique, dexterity, expertise, mastery.

crafty *adj* sly, cunning, artful, wily, devious, subtle, scheming, calculating, designing, deceitful, fraudulent, sharp, shrewd, astute, canny.
≠ artless, naïve.

cram *v* stuff, jam, ram, force, press, squeeze, crush, compress, pack, crowd, overfill, glut, gorge.

cramp[1] *v* hinder, hamper, obstruct, impede, inhibit, handicap, thwart, frustrate, check, restrict, confine, shackle, tie.

cramp[2] *n* pain, ache, twinge, pang, contraction, convulsion, spasm, crick, stitch, pins and needles, stiffness.

cramped *adj* narrow, tight, uncomfortable, restricted, confined, crowded, packed, squashed, squeezed, overcrowded, jam-packed, congested.
≠ spacious.

crash *n* **1** *car crash*: accident, collision, bump, smash, pile-up, smash-up (*infml*), wreck. **2** BANG, clash, clatter, clang, thud, thump, boom, thunder, racket, din. **3** *stock-market crash*: collapse, failure, ruin, downfall, bankruptcy, depression.
v **1** COLLIDE, hit, knock, bump, bang. **2** BREAK, fracture, smash, dash, shatter, splinter, shiver, fragment, disintegrate. **3** FALL, topple, pitch, plunge, collapse, fail, fold (up), go under, go bust (*infml*).

crate *n* container, box, case, tea-chest, packing-box, packing-case.

crave *v* hunger for, thirst for, long for, yearn for, pine for, hanker after, fancy (*infml*), desire, want, need, require.
≠ dislike.

craving *n* appetite, hunger, thirst, longing, yearning, hankering, lust, desire, urge.
≠ dislike, distaste.

crawl *v* **1** CREEP, inch, edge, slither, wriggle. **2** GROVEL, cringe, toady, fawn, flatter, suck up (*sl*).

craze *n* fad, novelty, fashion, vogue, mode, trend, rage (*infml*), thing (*infml*), obsession, preoccupation, mania, frenzy, passion, infatuation, enthusiasm.

crazy *adj* **1** MAD, insane, lunatic, unbalanced, deranged, demented, crazed, potty (*infml*), barmy (*infml*), daft (*infml*), silly, foolish, idiotic, senseless, unwise, imprudent, nonsensical, absurd, ludicrous, ridiculous, preposterous, outrageous, half-baked, impracticable, irresponsible, wild, berserk. **2** (*infml*) *crazy about golf*: enthusiastic, fanatical, zealous, ardent, passionate, infatuated, enamoured, smitten, mad, wild.
≠ **1** sane, sensible. **2** indifferent.

creak *v* squeak, groan, grate, scrape, rasp, scratch, grind, squeal, screech.

cream *n* **1** PASTE, emulsion, oil, lotion, ointment, salve, cosmetic. **2** BEST, pick, élite, prime.

creamy *adj* **1** cream-coloured, off-white, yellowish-white. **2** milky, buttery, oily, smooth, velvety, rich, thick.

crease *v* fold, pleat, wrinkle, pucker, crumple, rumple, crinkle, crimp, corrugate, ridge.
n fold, line, pleat, tuck, wrinkle, pucker, ruck, crinkle, corrugation, ridge, groove.

create *v* invent, coin, formulate, compose, design, devise, concoct, hatch, originate, initiate, found, establish, set up, institute, cause, occasion, produce, generate, engender, make, form, appoint, install, invest, ordain.
≠ destroy.

creation *n* **1** MAKING, formation, constitution, invention, concoction, origination, foundation, establishment, institution, production, generation, procreation, conception, birth. **2** INVENTION, brainchild, concept, product, handiwork, chef d'oeuvre, achievement.
≠ **1** destruction.

creative *adj* artistic, inventive, original, imaginative, inspired, visionary, talented, gifted, clever, ingenious, resourceful, fertile, productive.
≠ unimaginative.

creator *n* maker, inventor, designer, architect, author, originator, initiator.

creature *n* animal, beast, bird, fish, organism, being, mortal, individual, person, man, woman, body, soul.

credentials *n* diploma, certificate, reference, testimonial, recommendation, accreditation, authorization, warrant, licence, permit, passport, identity card, papers, documents, deed, title.

credibility *n* integrity, reliability, trustworthiness, plausibility, probability.
≠ implausibility.

credible *adj* believable, imaginable, conceivable, thinkable, tenable, plausible, likely, probable, possible, reasonable, persuasive, convincing, sincere, honest, trustworthy, reliable, dependable.
≠ incredible, unbelievable, implausible, unreliable.

credit *n* acknowledgement, recognition, thanks, approval, commendation, praise, acclaim, tribute, glory, fame, prestige, distinction, honour, reputation, esteem, estimation.
≠ discredit, shame.
v believe, swallow (*infml*), accept, subscribe to, trust, rely on.
≠ disbelieve.

creditable *adj* honourable, reputable, respectable, estimable, admirable, commendable, praiseworthy, good, excellent, exemplary, worthy, deserving.
≠ shameful, blameworthy.

credulous *adj* naïve, gullible, wide-eyed, trusting, unsuspecting, uncritical.
≠ sceptical, suspicious.

creed *n* belief, faith, persuasion, credo, catechism, doctrine, principles, tenets, articles, canon, dogma.

creek *n* inlet, estuary, cove, bay, bight.

creep *v* inch, edge, tiptoe, steal, sneak, slink, crawl, slither, worm, wriggle, squirm, grovel, writhe.

creepy *adj* eerie, spooky, sinister, threatening, frightening, scary, terrifying, hair-raising, nightmarish, macabre, gruesome, horrible, unpleasant, disturbing.

crest *n* **1** *the crest of the hill*: ridge, crown, top, peak, summit, pinnacle, apex, head. **2** TUFT, tassel, plume, comb, mane. **3** INSIGNIA, device, symbol, emblem, badge.

crevice *n* crack, fissure, split, rift, cleft, slit, chink, cranny, gap, hole, opening, break.

crew *n* team, party, squad, troop, corps, company, gang, band, bunch, crowd, mob, set, lot.

crime *n* law-breaking, lawlessness, delinquency, offence, felony, misdemeanour, misdeed, wrongdoing, misconduct, transgression, violation, sin, iniquity, vice, villainy, wickedness, atrocity, outrage.

> *Crimes include*: theft, robbery, burglary, larceny, pilfering, mugging, poaching; assault, rape, grievous bodily harm, GBH (*infml*), battery, manslaughter, homicide, murder, assassination; fraud, bribery, corruption, embezzlement, extortion, blackmail; arson, treason, terrorism, hijack, piracy, kidnapping, sabotage, vandalism, hooliganism, drug-smuggling, forgery, counterfeiting, perjury, joy-riding, drink-driving, drunk and disorderly.

criminal *n* law-breaker, felon, delinquent, offender, wrongdoer, miscreant, culprit, convict, prisoner.

> *Types of criminal include*: armed robber, arsonist, assassin, bandit, batterer, bigamist, blackmailer, bootlegger, brigand, buccaneer, burglar, car-thief, cat burglar, counterfeiter, cracksman, crook, dope pusher, drink-driver, drug-smuggler, embezzler, extortionist, fire-raiser, forger, gangster, gunman, highwayman, hijacker, hood (*sl*), hoodlum, housebreaker, jailbird (*infml*), joyrider, kerb-crawler, kidnapper, killer, lag (*sl*), larcenist, mobster (*US*), mugger, murderer, perjurer, pickpocket, pirate, poacher, racketeer, ram-raider, rapist, receiver, robber, rustler, saboteur, safecracker, sexual abuser, shoplifter, smuggler, strangler, swindler, terrorist, thief, thug, trespasser, vandal, war criminal.

adj illegal, unlawful, illicit, lawless, wrong, culpable, indictable, crooked (*infml*), bent (*infml*), dishonest, corrupt, wicked, scandalous, deplorable.
≠ legal, lawful, honest, upright.

cringe *v* shrink, recoil, shy, start, flinch, wince, quail, tremble, quiver, cower, crouch, bend, bow, stoop, grovel, crawl, creep.

cripple *v* lame, paralyse, disable, handicap, injure, maim, mutilate, damage, impair, spoil, ruin, destroy, sabotage, incapacitate, weaken, debilitate.

crippled *adj* lame, paralysed, disabled, handicapped, incapacitated.

crisis *n* emergency, extremity, crunch (*infml*), catastrophe, disaster, calamity, dilemma, quandary, predicament, difficulty, trouble, problem.

crisp *adj* **1** *a crisp biscuit*: crispy, crunchy, brittle, crumbly, firm, hard. **2** BRACING, invigorating, refreshing, fresh, brisk. **3** TERSE, pithy, snappy, brief, short, clear, incisive.
≠ **1** soggy, limp, flabby. **2** muggy. **3** wordy, vague.

criterion *n* standard, norm, touchstone, benchmark, yardstick, measure, gauge, rule, principle, canon, test.

critic *n* reviewer, commentator, analyst, pundit, authority, expert, judge, censor, carper, fault-finder, attacker, knocker (*infml*).

critical *adj* **1** *at the critical moment*: crucial, vital, essential, all-important, momentous, decisive, urgent, pressing, serious, grave, dangerous, perilous. **2** ANALYTICAL, diagnostic, penetrating, probing, discerning,

perceptive. **3** UNCOMPLIMENTARY, derogatory, disparaging, disapproving, censorious, carping, fault-finding, cavilling, nit-picking (*infml*).
≠ **1** unimportant. **3** complimentary, appreciative.

criticism *n* **1** CONDEMNATION, disapproval, disparagement, fault-finding, censure, blame, brickbat, flak (*infml*). **2** REVIEW, critique, assessment, evaluation, appraisal, judgement, analysis, commentary, appreciation.
≠ **1** praise, commendation.

criticize *v* **1** CONDEMN, slate (*infml*), slam (*infml*), knock (*infml*), disparage, carp, find fault, censure, blame.
2 REVIEW, assess, evaluate, appraise, judge, analyse.
≠ **1** praise, commend.

crockery *n* dishes, tableware, china, porcelain, earthenware, stoneware, pottery.

> *Items of crockery include*: cup, saucer, coffee cup, mug, beaker, plate, side plate, dinner plate, bowl, cereal bowl, soup bowl, salad-bowl, sugar bowl, jug, milk-jug, basin, pot, teapot, coffee pot, percolator, cafetière, cakestand, meat dish, butter-dish, tureen, gravy boat, cruet, teaset, dinner service.

crook *n* criminal, thief, robber, swindler, cheat, shark (*infml*), rogue, villain.

crooked *adj* **1** ASKEW, skew-whiff (*infml*), awry, lopsided, asymmetric, irregular, uneven, off-centre, tilted, slanting, bent, angled, hooked, curved, bowed, warped, distorted, misshapen, deformed, twisted, tortuous, winding, zigzag. **2** (*infml*) ILLEGAL, unlawful, illicit, criminal, nefarious, dishonest, deceitful, bent (*infml*), corrupt, fraudulent, shady (*infml*), shifty, underhand, treacherous, unscrupulous, unprincipled, unethical.
≠ **1** straight. **2** honest.

crop *n* growth, yield, produce, fruits, harvest, vintage, gathering. *see also* **arable crop**.
v cut, snip, clip, shear, trim, pare, prune, lop, shorten, curtail.
crop up arise, emerge, appear, arrive, occur, happen.

cross *adj* **1** IRRITABLE, annoyed, angry, vexed, shirty (*infml*), bad-tempered, ill-tempered, crotchety, grumpy, grouchy, irascible, crabby, short, snappy, snappish, surly, sullen, fractious, fretful, impatient.
2 TRANSVERSE, crosswise, oblique, diagonal, intersecting, opposite, reciprocal.
≠ **1** placid, pleasant.
v **1** *cross the river*: go across, traverse, ford, bridge, span.
2 INTERSECT, meet, criss-cross, lace, intertwine. **3** CROSSBREED, interbreed, mongrelize, hybridize, cross-fertilize, cross-pollinate, blend, mix. **4** THWART, frustrate, foil, hinder, impede, obstruct, block, oppose.
n **1** BURDEN, load, affliction, misfortune, trouble, worry, trial, tribulation, grief, misery, woe.
2 CROSSBREED, hybrid, mongrel, blend, mixture, amalgam, combination.

> *Types of cross include*: ankh, Avelian, botoné, Calvary, capital, cardinal, Celtic, Constantinian, Cornish, crosslet, crucifix, encolpion, fleury, fylfot, Geneva, Greek, Jerusalem, Latin, Lorraine, Maltese, moline, papal, patriarchal, potent, quadrate, rood, Russian, saltire, St Andrew's, St Anthony's, St George's, St Peter's, swastika, tau, Y-cross.

crouch *v* squat, kneel, stoop, bend, bow, hunch, duck, cower, cringe.

crowd *n* **1** THRONG, multitude, host, mob, masses, populace, people, public, riff-raff, rabble, horde, swarm, flock, herd, pack, press, crush, squash, assembly, company, group, bunch, lot, set, circle, clique. **2** SPECTATORS, gate, attendance, audience.
v gather, congregate, muster, huddle, mass, throng, swarm, flock, surge, stream, push, shove, elbow, jostle, press, squeeze, bundle, pile, pack, congest, cram, compress.

crowded *adj* full, filled, packed, jammed, jam-packed, congested,

cramped, overcrowded, overpopulated, busy, teeming, swarming, overflowing.
≠ empty, deserted.

crown *n* **1** CORONET, diadem, tiara, circlet, wreath, garland. **2** PRIZE, trophy, reward, honour, laurels. **3** SOVEREIGN, monarch, king, queen, ruler, sovereignty, monarchy, royalty. **4** TOP, tip, apex, crest, summit, pinnacle, peak, acme.
v **1** ENTHRONE, anoint, adorn, festoon, honour, dignify, reward. **2** TOP, cap, complete, fulfil, consummate, perfect.

crucial *adj* urgent, pressing, vital, essential, key, pivotal, central, important, momentous, decisive, critical, trying, testing, searching.
≠ unimportant, trivial.

crude *adj* **1** RAW, unprocessed, unrefined, rough, unfinished, unpolished, natural, primitive. **2** *a crude remark*: VULGAR, coarse, rude, indecent, obscene, gross, dirty, lewd.
≠ **1** refined, finished. **2** polite, decent.

cruel *adj* fierce, ferocious, vicious, savage, barbarous, bloodthirsty, murderous, cold-blooded, sadistic, brutal, inhuman, inhumane, unkind, malevolent, spiteful, callous, heartless, unfeeling, merciless, pitiless, flinty, hard-hearted, stony-hearted, implacable, ruthless, remorseless, relentless, unrelenting, inexorable, grim, hellish, atrocious, bitter, harsh, severe, cutting, painful, excruciating.
≠ kind, compassionate, merciful.

cruelty *n* ferocity, viciousness, savagery, barbarity, bloodthirstiness, murderousness, violence, sadism, brutality, bestiality, inhumanity, spite, venom, callousness, heartlessness, hard-heartedness, mercilessness, ruthlessness, tyranny, harshness, severity.
≠ kindness, compassion, mercy.

crumble *v* fragment, break up, decompose, disintegrate, decay, degenerate, deteriorate, collapse, crush, pound, grind, powder, pulverize.

crumple *v* crush, wrinkle, pucker, crinkle, rumple, crease, fold, collapse.

crunch *v* munch, chomp, champ, masticate, grind, crush.

crusade *n* campaign, drive, push, movement, cause, undertaking, expedition, holy war, jihad.

crush *v* **1** SQUASH, compress, squeeze, press, pulp, break, smash, pound, pulverize, grind, crumble, crumple, wrinkle. **2** *the rebels were crushed*: conquer, vanquish, demolish, devastate, overpower, overwhelm, overcome, quash, quell, subdue, put down, humiliate, shame, abash.

crust *n* surface, exterior, outside, covering, coat, coating, layer, film, skin, rind, shell, scab, incrustation, caking, concretion.

crux *n* nub, heart, core, essence.

cry *v* **1** WEEP, sob, blubber, wail, bawl, whimper, snivel. **2** SHOUT, call, exclaim, roar, bellow, yell, scream, shriek, screech.
n **1** WEEP, sob, blubber, wail, bawl, whimper, snivel. **2** SHOUT, call, plea, exclamation, roar, bellow, yell, scream, shriek.

cryptic *adj* enigmatic, ambiguous, equivocal, puzzling, perplexing, mysterious, strange, bizarre, secret, hidden, veiled, obscure, abstruse, esoteric, dark, occult.
≠ straightforward, clear, obvious.

cuddle *v* hug, embrace, clasp, hold, nurse, nestle, snuggle, pet, fondle, caress.

cuddly *adj* cuddlesome, lovable, huggable, plump, soft, warm, cosy.

cue *n* signal, sign, nod, hint, suggestion, reminder, prompt, incentive, stimulus.

cuff *v* hit, thump, box, clip, knock, biff (*infml*), buffet, slap, smack, strike, clout, clobber (*sl*), belt (*infml*), beat, whack (*infml*).

culminate *v* climax, end (up), terminate, close, conclude, finish, consummate.
≠ start, begin.

culmination *n* climax, height, peak, pinnacle, summit, top, crown, perfection, consummation, finale,

conclusion, completion.
≠ start, beginning.

culprit *n* guilty party, offender, wrongdoer, miscreant, law-breaker, criminal, felon, delinquent.

cult *n* **1** SECT, denomination, school, movement, party, faction. **2** CRAZE, fad, fashion, vogue, trend.

cultivate *v* **1** FARM, till, work, plough, grow, sow, plant, tend, harvest. **2** FOSTER, nurture, cherish, help, aid, support, encourage, promote, further, work on, develop, train, prepare, polish, refine, improve, enrich.
≠ **2** neglect.

cultural *adj* artistic, aesthetic, liberal, civilizing, humanizing, enlightening, educational, edifying, improving, enriching, elevating.

culture *n* **1** CIVILIZATION, society, lifestyle, way of life, customs, mores, the arts. **2** CULTIVATION, taste, education, enlightenment, breeding, gentility, refinement, politeness, urbanity.

cultured *adj* cultivated, civilized, advanced, enlightened, educated, well-read, well-informed, scholarly, highbrow, well-bred, refined, polished, genteel, urbane.
≠ uncultured, uneducated, ignorant.

cumbersome *adj* awkward, inconvenient, bulky, unwieldy, unmanageable, burdensome, onerous, heavy, weighty.
≠ convenient, manageable.

cunning *adj* crafty, sly, artful, wily, tricky, devious, subtle, deceitful, guileful, sharp, shrewd, astute, canny, knowing, deep, imaginative, ingenious, skilful, deft, dexterous.
≠ naïve, ingenuous, gullible.
n craftiness, slyness, artfulness, trickery, deviousness, subtlety, deceitfulness, guile, sharpness, shrewdness, astuteness, ingenuity, cleverness, adroitness.

cup *n* mug, tankard, beaker, goblet, chalice, trophy.

cupboard *n* cabinet, locker, closet, wardrobe.

curb *v* restrain, constrain, restrict, contain, control, check, moderate, bridle, muzzle, suppress, subdue, repress, inhibit, hinder, impede, hamper, retard.
≠ encourage, foster.

curdle *v* coagulate, congeal, clot, thicken, turn, sour, ferment.

cure *v* **1** HEAL, remedy, correct, restore, repair, mend, relieve, ease, alleviate, help. **2** PRESERVE, dry, smoke, salt, pickle, kipper.
n remedy, antidote, panacea, medicine, specific, corrective, restorative, healing, treatment, therapy, alleviation, recovery.

curiosity *n* **1** INQUISITIVENESS, nosiness, prying, snooping, interest. **2** CURIO, objet d'art, antique, bygone, novelty, trinket, knick-knack. **3** ODDITY, rarity, freak, phenomenon, spectacle.

curious *adj* **1** INQUISITIVE, nose, prying, meddlesome, questioning, inquiring, interested. **2** *a curious sight*: ODD, queer, funny (*infml*), strange, peculiar, bizarre, mysterious, puzzling, extraordinary, unusual, rare, unique, novel, exotic, unconventional, unorthodox, quaint.
≠ **1** uninterested, indifferent. **2** ordinary, usual, normal.

curl *v* crimp, frizz, wave, ripple, bend, curve, meander, loop, turn, twistle, wind, wreathe, twine, coil, spiral, corkscrew, scroll.
≠ uncurl.
n wave, kink, swirl, twist, ringlet, coil, spiral, whorl.

curly *adj* wavy, kinky, curling, spiralled, corkscrew, curled, crimped, permed, frizzy, fuzzy.
≠ straight.

currency *n* **1** MONEY, legal tender, coinage, coins, notes, bills. **2** ACCEPTANCE, publicity, popularity, vogue, circulation, prevalence, exposure.

> *Currencies of the world include*: baht (*Thailand*), bolivar (*Venezuela*), cent (*US, Canada, Australia, NZ, S Africa, etc*),

centavo (*Portugal, Brazil, Mexico, etc*), centime (*France, Belgium, Algeria, etc*), cruzeiro (*Brazil*), dinar (*Iraq, Jordan, etc*), dirham (*Morocco*), dollar (*US, Canada, Australia, NZ, etc*), dong (*Vietnam*), drachma (*Greece*), ecu (*EC*), escudo (*Portugal*), fils (*Iraq, Jordan, etc*), guilder (*Netherlands*), franc (*France, Belgium, Switzerland, etc*), karbovanets (*Ukraine*), kopeck (*Russia*), koruna (*Czech Republic, Slovakia*), krona (*Sweden*), króna (*Iceland*), krone (*Denmark, Norway*), kyat (*Myanmar*), lek (*Albania*), leu (*Romania*), lev (*Bulgaria*), lira (*Italy*), mark (*Germany*), pence (*UK*), peseta (*Spain*), peso (*Mexico, Chile, etc*), pfennig (*Germany*), piastre (*Egypt, Syria, etc*), pound (*UK, Egypt, etc*), punt (*Ireland*), rand (*S Africa*), rial (*Iran*), riyal (*Saudi Arabia*), rouble (*Russia*), rupee (*India, Pakistan, etc*), schilling (*Austria*), shekel (*Israel*), shilling (*Kenya, Uganda, etc*), som (*Uzbekistan*), sterling (*UK*), sucre (*Ecuador*), tolar (*Slovenia*), won (*N Korea, S Korea*), yen (*Japan*), yuan (*China*), zaïre (*Zaire*), zloty (*Poland*).

current *adj* present, on-going, existing, contemporary, present-day, modern, fashionable, up-to-date, up-to-the-minute, trendy (*infml*), popular, widespread, prevalent, common, general, prevailing, reigning, accepted.
≠ obsolete, old-fashioned.
n draught, stream, jet, flow, drift, tide, course, trend, tendency, undercurrent, mood, feeling.

curse *n* **1** SWEAR-WORD, oath, expletive, obscenity, profanity, blasphemy. **2** JINX, anathema, bane, evil, plague, scourge, affliction, trouble, torment, ordeal, calamity, disaster.
≠ **2** blessing, advantage.
v **1** SWEAR, blaspheme, damn, condemn, denounce, fulminate. **3** BLIGHT, plague, scourge, afflict, trouble, torment.
≠ **2** bless.

curtail *v* shorten, truncate, cut, trim, abridge, abbreviate, lessen, decrease, reduce, restrict.
≠ lengthen, extend, prolong.

curtain *n* blind, screen, backdrop, hanging, drapery, tapestry.

curve *v* bend, arch, arc, bow, bulge, hook, crook, turn, wind, twist, spiral, coil.
n bend, turn, arc, trajectory, loop, camber, curvature.

curved *adj* bent, arched, bowed, rounded, humped, convex, concave, crooked, twisted, sweeping, sinuous, serpentine.
≠ straight.

cushion *n* pad, buffer, shock absorber, bolster, pillow, headrest, hassock.
v soften, deaden, dampen, absorb, muffle, stifle, suppress, lessen, mitigate, protect, bolster, buttress, support.

custody *n* **1** KEEPING, possession, charge, care, safe-keeping, protection, preservation, custodianship, trusteeship, guardianship, supervision. **2** DETENTION, confinement, imprisonment, incarceration.

custom *n* tradition, usage, use, habit, routine, procedure, practice, policy, way, manner, style, form, convention, etiquette, formality, observance, ritual.

customary *adj* traditional, conventional, accepted, established, habitual, routine, regular, usual, normal, ordinary, everyday, familiar, common, general, popular, fashionable, prevailing.
≠ unusual, rare.

customer *n* client, patron, regular, punter (*infml*), consumer, shopper, buyer, purchaser, prospect.

cut *v* **1** CLIP, trim, crop, shear, mow, shave, pare, chop, hack, hew, slice, carve, divide, part, split, bisect, dock, lop, sever, prune, excise, incise, penetrate, pierce, stab, wound, nick, gash, slit, slash, lacerate, score, engrave, chisel, sculpt. **2** REDUCE, decrease, lower, shorten, curtail, abbreviate, abridge, condense, précis, edit, delete. **3** IGNORE, cold-shoulder, spurn, avoid, snub, slight, rebuff, insult.

n **1** INCISION, wound, nick, gash, slit, slash, rip, laceration. **2** *spending cuts*: REDUCTION, decrease, lowering, cutback, saving, economy.
cut down 1 *cut down a tree*: fell, hew, lop, level, raze. **2** REDUCE, decrease, lower, lessen, diminish.
cut in interrupt, butt in, interject, interpose, intervene, intrude.
cut off 1 SEVER, amputate, separate, isolate, disconnect, block, obstruct, intercept. **2** STOP, end, halt, suspend, discontinue, disown, disinherit.
cut out excise, extract, remove, delete, eliminate, exclude, debar, stop, cease.
cut up chop, dice, mince, dissect, divide, carve, slice, slash.

cutback *n* cut, saving, economy, retrenchment, reduction, decrease, lowering, lessening.

cutlery

Items of cutlery include: knife, butter-knife, carving-knife, fish knife, steak knife, cheese knife, breadknife, vegetable knife, fork, fish fork, carving fork, spoon, dessert-spoon, tablespoon, teaspoon, soup-spoon, caddy spoon, salt spoon, apostle spoon, ladle, salad servers, fish slice, cake server, sugar tongs, chopsticks, canteen of cutlery.

cut-price *adj* reduced, sale, discount, bargain, cheap, low-priced.

cutter

Types of cutter include: axe, billhook, blade, chisel, chopper, clippers, guillotine, hedgetrimmer, knife, flick knife, penknife, pocket knife, Stanley knife®, Swiss army knife, lopper, machete, mower, lawnmower, plane, razor, saw, chainsaw, fretsaw, hacksaw, jigsaw, scalpel, scissors, scythe, secateurs, shears, pinking shears, sickle, Strimmer®, sword. *see also* **cutlery**; **saws**; **weapon**.

cutting *adj* sharp, keen, pointed, trenchant, incisive, penetrating, piercing, wounding, stinging, biting, mordant, caustic, acid, scathing, sarcastic, malicious, bitter, raw, chill.
n clipping, extract, piece.

cycle *n* circle, round, rotation, revolution, series, sequence, phase, period, era, age, epoch, aeon.

cylinder *n* column, barrel, drum, reel, bobbin, spool, spindle.

cynic *n* sceptic, doubter, pessimist, killjoy, spoilsport (*infml*), scoffer, knocker (*infml*).

cynical *adj* sceptical, doubtful, distrustful, pessimistic, negative, scornful, derisive, contemptuous, sneering, scoffing, mocking, sarcastic, sardonic, ironic.

cynicism *n* scepticism, doubt, disbelief, distrust, pessimism, scorn, sarcasm, irony.

D

dab *v* pat, tap, daub, swab, wipe.
n **1** BIT, dollop (*infml*), drop, speck, spot, trace, smear, smudge, fleck. **2** TOUCH, pat, stroke, tap.

dabble *v* **1** TRIFLE, tinker, toy, dally, potter. **2** PADDLE, moisten, wet, sprinkle, splash.

dabbler *n* amateur, dilettante, trifler.
≠ professional, expert.

daft *adj* **1** FOOLISH, crazy, silly, stupid, absurd, dotty (*infml*), idiotic, inane. **2** INSANE, mad, lunatic, simple, crazy, mental. **3** (*infml*) INFATUATED.
≠ **1** sensible. **2** sane.

daily *adj* **1** REGULAR, routine, everyday, customary, common, commonplace, ordinary. **2** EVERYDAY, diurnal (*fml*).

dainty *adj* **1** DELICATE, elegant, exquisite, refined, fine, graceful, neat, charming, delectable. **2** FASTIDIOUS, fussy, particular, scrupulous, nice (*fml*).
≠ **1** gross, clumsy.

dam *n* barrier, barrage, embankment, blockage, obstruction, hindrance.
v block, confine, restrict, check, barricade, staunch, stem, obstruct.

damage *n* harm, injury, hurt, destruction, devastation, loss, suffering, mischief, mutilation, impairment, detriment.
≠ repair.
v harm, injure, hurt, spoil, ruin, impair, mar, wreck, deface, mutilate, weaken, tamper with, play havoc with, incapacitate.
≠ mend, repair, fix.

damn *v* **1** CURSE, swear, blast, imprecate, blaspheme. **2** ABUSE, revile, denounce, criticize, censure, slate (*infml*), execrate, castigate, slam (*infml*). **3** CONDEMN, doom, sentence.
≠ **1** bless.

damnation *n* condemnation, doom, denunciation, perdition, excommunication, anathema.

damp *n* dampness, moisture, clamminess, dankness, humidity, wet, dew, drizzle, fog, mist, vapour.
≠ dryness.
adj moist, wet, clammy, dank, humid, dewy, muggy, drizzly, misty, soggy.
≠ dry, arid.

dampen *v* **1** MOISTEN, wet, spray. **2** DISCOURAGE, dishearten, deter, dash, dull, deaden, restrain, check, depress, dismay, reduce, lessen, moderate, decrease, diminish, muffle, stifle, smother.
≠ **1** dry. **2** encourage.

dance *n* ball, hop (*infml*), knees-up (*infml*), social, shindig (*infml*).

> *Dances include*: waltz, quickstep, foxtrot, tango, polka, one-step, military two-step, valeta, Lancers, rumba, samba, mambo, bossanova, beguine, fandango, flamenco, mazurka, bolero, paso doble, can-can; rock 'n' roll, jive, twist, stomp, bop, jitterbug, mashed potato; black bottom, Charleston, cha-cha, turkey-trot; Circassian circle, Paul Jones, jig, reel, quadrille, Highland fling, morris-dance, clog dance, hoe-down, hokey-cokey, Lambeth Walk, conga, belly-dance; galliard, gavotte, minuet.
> *Types of dancing include*: ballet, tap, ballroom, old-time, disco, folk, country, Irish, Highland, Latin-American, flamenco, clog-dancing, morris dancing, limbo-dancing, break-dancing, robotics. *see also* **ballet**.
> *Dance functions include*: disco, dance, social, tea dance, barn dance, ball, fancy dress ball, charity ball, hunt ball, hop (*infml*), knees-up (*sl*), shindig (*infml*), rave (*infml*), prom (*US*), ceilidh.

danger *n* **1** *in danger of falling*:

insecurity, endangerment, jeopardy, precariousness, liability, vulnerability. **2** *the dangers of smoking*: risk, threat, peril, hazard, menace.
≠ **1** safety, security. **2** safety.

dangerous *adj* unsafe, insecure, risky, threatening, breakneck, hairy (*infml*), hazardous, perilous, precarious, reckless, treacherous, vulnerable, menacing, exposed, alarming, critical, severe, serious, grave, daring, nasty.
≠ safe, secure, harmless.

dangle *v* **1** HANG, droop, swing, sway, flap, trail. **2** TEMPT, entice, flaunt, flourish, lure, tantalize.

dank *adj* damp, moist, clammy, dewy, slimy, soggy.
≠ dry.

dappled *adj* speckled, mottled, spotted, stippled, dotted, flecked, freckled, variegated, bespeckled, piebald, checkered.

dare *v* **1** RISK, venture, brave, hazard, adventure, endanger, stake, gamble. **2** CHALLENGE, goad, provoke, taunt. **3** DEFY, presume.
n challenge, provocation, taunt, gauntlet.

daredevil *n* adventurer, desperado, madcap.
≠ coward.

daring *adj* bold, adventurous, intrepid, fearless, brave, plucky, audacious, dauntless, reckless, rash, impulsive, valiant.
≠ cautious, timid, afraid.
n boldness, fearlessness, courage, bravery, nerve, audacity, guts (*infml*), intrepidity, defiance, pluck, rashness, spirit, grit, gall, prowess.
≠ caution, timidity, cowardice.

dark *adj* **1** *a dark room*: unlit, overcast, black, dim, unilluminated, shadowy, murky, cloudy, dusky, dingy, drab. **2** *a dark manner*: gloomy, grim, cheerless, dismal, bleak, forbidding, sombre, sinister, mournful, ominous, menacing. **3** *dark secrets*: hidden, mysterious, obscure, secret, unintelligible, enigmatic, cryptic, abstruse.
≠ **1** light. **2** bright, cheerful. **3** comprehensible.
n **1** DARKNESS, dimness, night, night-time, nightfall, gloom, dusk, twilight, murkiness. **2** CONCEALMENT, secrecy, obscurity.
≠ **1** light. **2** openness.

darken *v* **1** DIM, obscure, blacken, cloud (over), shadow, overshadow, eclipse. **2** DEPRESS, sadden.
≠ **1** lighten. **2** brighten.

darling *n* beloved, dear, dearest, favourite, sweetheart, love, pet.
adj dear, beloved, adored, cherished, precious, treasured.

dart *v* **1** DASH, bound, sprint, flit, flash, fly, rush, run, race, spring, tear. **2** THROW, hurl, fling, shoot, sling, launch, propel, send.
n bolt, arrow, barb, shaft.

dash *v* **1** RUSH, dart, hurry, race, sprint, run, bolt, tear. **2** FLING, throw, crash, hurl. **3** DISCOURAGE, disappoint, dampen, confound, blight, ruin, destroy, spoil, frustrate, smash, shatter.
n **1** DROP, pinch, touch, flavour, soupçon, suggestion, hint, bit, little. **2** SPRINT, dart, bolt, rush, spurt, race, run.

dashing *adj* **1** LIVELY, vigorous, spirited, gallant, daring, bold, plucky, exuberant. **2** SMART, stylish, elegant, debonair, showy, flamboyant.
≠ **1** lethargic. **2** dowdy.

data *n* information, documents, facts, input, statistics, figures, details, materials.

date *n* **1** TIME, age, period, era, stage, epoch. **2** APPOINTMENT, engagement, assignation, meeting, rendezvous. **3** ESCORT, steady (*infml*), partner, friend.
out-of-date *adj* old-fashioned, unfashionable, outdated, obsolete, dated, outmoded, antiquated, passé.
≠ fashionable, modern.
up-to-date *adj* fashionable, modern, current, contemporary.
≠ old-fashioned, dated.

daunt *v* **1** DISCOURAGE, dishearten, put off, dispirit, deter. **2** INTIMIDATE,

overawe, unnerve, alarm, dismay, frighten, scare.
≠ **1** encourage.

dauntless *adj* fearless, undaunted, resolute, brave, courageous, bold, intrepid, daring, plucky, valiant.
≠ discouraged, disheartened.

dawdle *v* delay, loiter, lag, hang about, dally, trail, potter, dilly-dally (*infml*).
≠ hurry.

dawn *n* **1** SUNRISE, daybreak, morning, daylight. **2** BEGINNING, start, emergence, onset, origin, birth, advent.
≠ **1** dusk. **2** end.
v **1** BREAK, brighten, lighten, gleam, glimmer. **2** BEGIN, appear, emerge, open, develop, originate, rise.

day *n* **1** DAYTIME, daylight. **2** AGE, period, time, date, era, generation, epoch.
≠ **1** night.
day after day regularly, continually, endlessly, persistently, monotonously, perpetually, relentlessly.
day by day gradually, progressively, slowly but surely, steadily.

daydream *n* fantasy, imagining, reverie, castles in the air, pipe dream, vision, musing, wish, dream, figment.
v fantasize, imagine, muse, fancy, dream.

daze *v* **1** STUN, stupefy, shock. **2** DAZZLE, bewilder, blind, confuse, baffle, dumbfound, amaze, surprise, startle, perplex, astonish, flabbergast (*infml*), astound, stagger.
n bewilderment, confusion, stupor, trance, shock, distraction.

dazzle *v* **1** DAZE, blind, confuse, blur. **2** SPARKLE, fascinate, impress, overwhelm, awe, overawe, scintillate, bedazzle, amaze, astonish, bewitch, stupefy.
n sparkle, brilliance, magnificence, splendour, scintillation, glitter, glare.

dead *adj* **1** LIFELESS, deceased, inanimate, defunct, departed, late, gone. **2** UNRESPONSIVE, apathetic, dull, indifferent, insensitive, numb, cold, frigid, lukewarm, torpid. **3** EXHAUSTED, tired, worn out, dead-beat (*infml*). **4** EXACT, absolute, perfect, unqualified, utter, outright, complete, entire, total, downright.
≠ **1** alive. **2** lively. **3** refreshed.

deaden *v* reduce, blunt, muffle, lessen, quieten, suppress, weaken, numb, diminish, stifle, alleviate, anaesthetize, desensitize, smother, check, abate, allay, dampen, hush, mute, paralyse.
≠ heighten.

deadlock *n* standstill, stalemate, impasse, halt.

deadly *adj* **1** *deadly poison*: lethal, fatal, dangerous, venomous, destructive, pernicious, malignant, murderous, mortal. **2** *a deadly lecture*: dull, boring, uninteresting, tedious, monotonous. **3** *deadly aim*: unerring, effective, true.
≠ **1** harmless. **2** exciting.

deaf *adj* **1** HARD OF HEARING, stone-deaf. **2** UNCONCERNED, indifferent, unmoved, oblivious, heedless, unmindful.
≠ **2** aware, conscious.

deafening *adj* piercing, ear-splitting, booming, resounding, thunderous, ringing, roaring.
≠ quiet.

deal *v* **1** APPORTION, distribute, share, dole out, divide, allot, dispense, assign, mete out, give, bestow. **2** TRADE, negotiate, traffic, bargain, treat.
n **1** QUANTITY, amount, extent, degree, portion, share. **2** AGREEMENT, contract, understanding, pact, transaction, bargain, buy. **3** ROUND, hand, distribution.
deal with attend to, concern, see to, manage, handle, cope with, treat, consider, oversee.

dealer *n* trader, merchant, wholesaler, marketer, merchandizer.

dear *adj* **1** LOVED, beloved, treasured, valued, cherished, precious, favourite, esteemed, intimate, close, darling, familiar. **2** EXPENSIVE, high-priced, costly, overpriced, pric(e)y (*infml*).
≠ **1** disliked, hated. **2** cheap.
n beloved, loved one, precious, darling, treasure.

dearly *adv* **1** *he loves her dearly*: fondly, affectionately, lovingly, devotedly, tenderly. **2** *I wish it dearly*: greatly, extremely, profoundly.

dearth *n* scarcity, shortage, insufficiency, inadequacy, deficiency, lack, want, absence, scantiness, sparsity, need, paucity, poverty, famine.
≠ excess, abundance.

death *n* **1** DECEASE, end, finish, loss, demise, departure, fatality, cessation, passing, expiration, dissolution. **2** DESTRUCTION, ruin, undoing, annihilation, downfall, extermination, extinction, obliteration, eradication.
≠ **1** life, birth.

deathly *adj* **1** ASHEN, grim, haggard, pale, pallid, ghastly, wan. **2** FATAL, deadly, mortal, intense.

debase *v* **1** DEGRADE, demean, devalue, disgrace, dishonour, shame, humble, humiliate, lower, reduce, abase, defile. **2** CONTAMINATE, pollute, corrupt, adulterate, taint.
≠ **1** elevate. **2** purify.

debatable *adj* questionable, uncertain, disputable, contestable, controversial, arguable, open to question, doubtful, contentious, undecided, unsettled, problematical, dubious, moot.
≠ unquestionable, certain, incontrovertible.

debate *v* **1** DISPUTE, argue, discuss, contend, wrangle. **2** CONSIDER, deliberate, ponder, reflect, meditate on, mull over, weigh.
n discussion, argument, controversy, disputation, deliberation, consideration, contention, dispute, reflection, polemic.

debauchery *n* depravity, intemperance, overindulgence, dissipation, licentiousness, dissoluteness, excess, decadence, wantonness, lewdness, carousal, orgy, revel, lust, riot.
≠ restraint, temperance.

debilitate *v* weaken, enervate, undermine, sap, incapacitate, wear out, exhaust, impair.
≠ strengthen, invigorate, energize.

debris *n* remains, ruins, rubbish, waste, wreck, wreckage, litter, fragments, rubble, trash, pieces, bits, sweepings, drift.

debt *n* indebtedness, obligation, debit, arrears, due, liability, duty, bill, commitment, claim, score.
≠ credit, asset.

debtor *n* borrower, bankrupt, insolvent, defaulter, mortgagor.
≠ creditor.

debunk *v* expose, deflate, show up, ridicule, mock, explode, lampoon.

debut *n* introduction, launching, beginning, entrance, presentation, inauguration, première, appearance, initiation.

decadent *adj* **1** CORRUPT, debased, debauched, depraved, dissolute, immoral, degenerate, degraded, self-indulgent. **2** DECAYING, declining.
≠ **1** moral.

decay *v* **1** ROT, go bad, putrefy, decompose, spoil, perish, mortify. **2** DECLINE, deteriorate, disintegrate, corrode, crumble, waste away, degenerate, wear away, dwindle, shrivel, wither, sink.
≠ **2** flourish, grow.
n **1** ROT, decomposition, rotting, perishing. **2** DECLINE, deterioration, disintegration, degeneration, collapse, decadence, wasting, failing, withering, fading.

decease *n* death, dying, demise, departure, passing, dissolution.

deceased *adj* dead, departed, former, late, lost, defunct, expired, gone, finished, extinct.
n dead, departed.

deceit *n* deception, pretence, cheating, misrepresentation, fraud, duplicity, trickery, fraudulence, double-dealing, underhandedness, fake, guile, sham, subterfuge, swindle, treachery, hypocrisy, artifice, ruse, cunning, slyness, craftiness, stratagem, wile, imposition, feint, shift, abuse.
≠ honesty, openness, frankness.

deceitful *adj* dishonest, deceptive, deceiving, false, insincere, untrustworthy, double-dealing, fraudulent, two-faced (*infml*),

treacherous, duplicitous, guileful, tricky (*infml*), underhand, sneaky, counterfeit, crafty, hypocritical, designing, illusory, knavish.
≠ honest, open.

deceive *v* mislead, delude, cheat, betray, fool, take in (*infml*), trick, dissemble, hoax, con (*infml*), have on (*infml*), take for a ride (*infml*), double-cross (*infml*), dupe, kid (*infml*), swindle, impose upon, bamboozle (*infml*), two-time (*infml*), lead on, outwit, hoodwink, beguile, ensnare, camouflage, abuse, befool, gull.

decency *n* propriety, courtesy, modesty, decorum, respectability, civility, correctness, fitness, etiquette, helpfulness.
≠ impropriety, discourtesy.

decent *adj* **1** RESPECTABLE, proper, fitting, decorous, chaste, seemly, suitable, modest, appropriate, presentable, pure, fit, becoming, befitting, nice. **2** KIND, obliging, courteous, helpful, generous, polite, gracious. **3** ADEQUATE, acceptable, satisfactory, reasonable, sufficient, tolerable, competent.
≠ **1** indecent. **2** disobliging.

deception *n* deceit, pretence, trick, cheat, fraud, imposture, lie, dissembling, deceptiveness, insincerity, con (*infml*), sham, subterfuge, artifice, hypocrisy, bluff, treachery, hoax, fraudulence, duplicity, ruse, snare, stratagem, leg-pull (*infml*), illusion, wile, guile, craftiness, cunning.
≠ openness, honesty.

deceptive *adj* dishonest, false, fraudulent, misleading, unreliable, illusive, fake, illusory, spurious, mock, fallacious, ambiguous, specious.
≠ genuine, artless, open.

decide *v* choose, determine, resolve, reach a decision, settle, elect, opt, judge, adjudicate, conclude, fix, purpose, decree.

decided *adj* **1** DEFINITE, certain, undeniable, indisputable, absolute, clear-cut, undisputed, unmistakable, unquestionable, positive, unambiguous, categorical, distinct, emphatic. **2** RESOLUTE, decisive, determined, firm, unhesitating, deliberate, forthright.
≠ **1** inconclusive. **2** irresolute.

decipher *v* decode, unscramble, crack, construe, interpret, make out (*infml*), figure out (*infml*), understand, transliterate.
≠ encode.

decision *n* **1** RESULT, conclusion, outcome, verdict, finding, settlement, judgement, arbitration, ruling. **2** DETERMINATION, decisiveness, firmness, resolve, purpose.

decisive *adj* **1** CONCLUSIVE, definite, definitive, absolute, final. **2** DETERMINED, resolute, decided, positive, firm, forceful, forthright, strong-minded. **3** SIGNIFICANT, critical, crucial, influential, momentous, fateful.
≠ **1** inconclusive. **2** indecisive. **3** insignificant.

declaration *n* **1** AFFIRMATION, acknowledgement, assertion, statement, testimony, attestation, disclosure, profession, revelation. **2** ANNOUNCEMENT, notification, pronouncement, proclamation, edict, manifesto, promulgation.

declare *v* **1** AFFIRM, assert, claim, profess, maintain, state, attest, certify, confess, confirm, disclose, reveal, show, aver, swear, testify, witness, validate. **2** ANNOUNCE, proclaim, pronounce, decree, broadcast.

decline *v* **1** REFUSE, reject, deny, forgo, avoid, balk. **2** DIMINISH, decrease, dwindle, lessen, fall, sink, wane. **3** DECAY, deteriorate, worsen, degenerate. **4** DESCEND, sink, slope, dip, slant.
≠ **3** improve. **4** rise.
n **1** DETERIORATION, dwindling, lessening, decay, degeneration, weakening, worsening, failing, downturn, diminution, falling-off, recession, slump, abatement. **2** DESCENT, dip, declivity, declination, hill, slope, incline, divergence, deviation.
≠ **1** improvement. **2** rise.

decode *v* decipher, interpret,

unscramble, translate, transliterate, uncipher.
≠ encode.

decompose *v* disintegrate, rot, decay, putrefy, break down, break up, crumble, spoil, dissolve, separate, fester.

décor *n* decoration, furnishings, colour scheme, ornamentation, scenery.

decorate *v* **1** ORNAMENT, adorn, beautify, embellish, trim, deck, tart up (*sl*), grace, enrich, prettify, trick out. **2** RENOVATE, do up (*infml*), paint, paper, colour, refurbish. **3** HONOUR, crown, cite, garland, bemedal.

decoration *n* **1** ORNAMENT, adornment, ornamentation, trimming, embellishment, beautification, garnish, flourish, enrichment, elaboration, frill, scroll, bauble. **2** AWARD, medal, order, badge, garland, crown, colours, ribbon, laurel, star, emblem.

decorative *adj* ornamental, fancy, adorning, beautifying, embellishing, non-functional, pretty, ornate, enhancing.
≠ plain.

decorum *n* propriety, seemliness, etiquette, good manners, respectability, protocol, behaviour, decency, dignity, deportment, restraint, politeness, modesty, grace, breeding.
≠ impropriety, indecorum, bad manners.

decoy *n* lure, trap, enticement, inducement, ensnarement, pretence, attraction, bait.
v bait, lure, entrap, entice, ensnare, allure, tempt, deceive, attract, seduce, lead, draw.

decrease *v* lessen, lower, diminish, dwindle, decline, fall off, reduce, subside, abate, cut down, contract, drop, ease, shrink, taper, wane, slim, slacken, peter out, curtail.
≠ increase.
n lessening, reduction, decline, falling-off, dwindling, loss, diminution, abatement, cutback, contraction, downturn, ebb, shrinkage, subsidence, step-down.
≠ increase.

decree *n* order, command, law, ordinance, regulation, ruling, statute, act, enactment, edict, proclamation, mandate, precept, interlocution.
v order, command, rule, lay down, dictate, decide, determine, ordain, prescribe, proclaim, pronounce, enact.

decrepit *adj* dilapidated, run-down, rickety, broken-down, worn-out, tumble-down.

dedicate *v* **1** DEVOTE, commit, assign, give over to, pledge, present, offer, sacrifice, surrender. **2** CONSECRATE, bless, sanctify, set apart, hallow. **3** *dedicate a book*: inscribe, address.

dedicated *adj* devoted, committed, enthusiastic, single-minded, whole-hearted, single-hearted, zealous, given over to, purposeful.
≠ uncommitted, apathetic.

dedication *n* **1** COMMITMENT, devotion, single-mindedness, whole-heartedness, allegiance, attachment, adherence, faithfulness, loyalty, self-sacrifice. **2** CONSECRATION, hallowing, presentation. **3** INSCRIPTION, address.
≠ **1** apathy.

deduce *v* derive, infer, gather, conclude, reason, surmise, understand, draw, glean.

deduct *v* subtract, take away, remove, reduce by, decrease by, knock off (*infml*), withdraw.
≠ add.

deduction *n* **1** INFERENCE, reasoning, finding, conclusion, corollary, assumption, result. **2** SUBTRACTION, reduction, decrease, diminution, abatement, withdrawal, discount, allowance.
≠ **2** addition, increase.

deed *n* **1** ACTION, act, achievement, performance, exploit, feat, fact, truth, reality. **2** DOCUMENT, contract, record, title, transaction, indenture (*fml*).

deep *adj* **1** PROFOUND, bottomless, unplumbed, fathomless, yawning, immersed. **2** OBSCURE, mysterious, difficult, recondite, abstruse, esoteric. **3** WISE, perceptive, discerning, profound, learned, astute. **4** INTENSE,

serious, earnest, extreme. **5** LOW, bass, resonant, booming.
≠ **1** shallow, open. **2** clear, plain, open. **3** superficial. **4** light. **5** high.

deepen *v* **1** INTENSIFY, grow, increase, strengthen, reinforce, magnify. **2** HOLLOW, scoop out.

deep-seated *adj* ingrained, entrenched, deep-rooted, fixed, confirmed, deep, settled.
≠ eradicable, temporary.

deface *v* damage, spoil, disfigure, blemish, impair, mutilate, mar, sully, tarnish, vandalize, deform, obliterate, injure, destroy.
≠ repair.

defamation (*fml*) *n* vilification, aspersion (*fml*), slander, libel, disparagement, slur, smear, innuendo, scandal.
≠ commendation, praise.

defamatory (*fml*) *adj* vilifying, slanderous, libellous, denigrating, disparaging, pejorative, insulting, injurious, derogatory.
≠ complimentary, appreciative.

default *n* failure, absence, neglect, non-payment, omission, deficiency, lapse, fault, want, lack, defect.
v fail, evade, defraud, neglect, dodge, swindle, backslide.

defaulter *n* non-payer, offender.

defeat *v* **1** CONQUER, beat, overpower, subdue, overthrow, worst, repel, subjugate, overwhelm, rout, ruin, thump (*infml*), quell, vanquish (*fml*). **2** FRUSTRATE, confound, balk, get the better of, disappoint, foil, thwart, baffle, checkmate.
n **1** CONQUEST, beating, overthrow, rout, subjugation, vanquishment (*fml*). **2** FRUSTRATION, failure, setback, reverse, disappointment, checkmate.

defeatist *n* pessimist, quitter, prophet of doom.
≠ optimist.
adj pessimistic, resigned, fatalistic, despondent, helpless, hopeless, despairing, gloomy.
≠ optimistic.

defect *n* imperfection, fault, flaw, deficiency, failing, mistake, inadequacy blemish, error, bug (*infml*), shortcoming, want, weakness, frailty, lack, spot, absence, taint.
v desert, break faith, rebel, apostatize (*fml*), revolt, renegue.

defective *adj* faulty, imperfect, out of order, flawed, deficient, broken, abnormal.
≠ in order, operative.

defence *n* **1** PROTECTION, resistance, security, fortification, cover, safeguard, shelter, guard, shield, deterrence, barricade, bastion, immunity, bulwark, rampart, buttress. **2** JUSTIFICATION, explanation, excuse, argument, exoneration, plea, vindication, apologia (*fml*), pleading, alibi, case.
≠ **1** attack, assault. **2** accusation.

defenceless *adj* unprotected, undefended, unarmed, unguarded, vulnerable, exposed, helpless, powerless.
≠ protected, guarded.

defend *v* **1** PROTECT, guard, safeguard shelter, fortify, secure, shield, screen, cover, contest. **2** SUPPORT, stand up for, stand by, uphold, endorse, vindicate, champion, argue for, speak up for, justify, plead.
≠ **1** attack. **2** accuse.

defendant *n* accused, offender, prisoner, respondent.

defender *n* **1** PROTECTOR, guard, bodyguard. **2** SUPPORTER, advocate, vindicator, champion, patron, sponsor, counsel.
≠ **1** attacker. **2** accuser.

defensive *adj* **1** PROTECTIVE, defending, safeguarding, wary, opposing, cautious, watchful. **2** SELF-JUSTIFYING, apologetic.

defer[1] *v* delay, postpone, put off, adjourn, hold over, shelve, suspend, procrastinate, prorogue (*fml*), protract, waive.

defer[2] *v* yield, give way, comply, submit, accede, capitulate, respect, bow.

deference *n* **1** SUBMISSION, submissiveness, compliance,

acquiescence, obedience, yielding. **2** RESPECT, regard, honour, esteem, reverence, courtesy, civility, politeness, consideration.
≠ **1** resistance. **2** contempt.

defiance *n* opposition, confrontation, resistance, challenge, disobedience, rebelliousness, contempt, insubordination, disregard, insolence.
≠ compliance, acquiescence, submissiveness.

defiant *adj* challenging, resistant, antagonistic, aggressive, rebellious, insubordinate, disobedient, intransigent, bold, contumacious (*fml*), insolent, obstinate, unco-operative, provocative.
≠ compliant, acquiescent, submissive.

deficiency *n* **1** SHORTAGE, lack, inadequacy, scarcity, insufficiency, dearth, want, scantiness, absence, deficit. **2** IMPERFECTION, shortcoming, weakness, fault, defect, flaw, failing, frailty.
≠ **1** excess, surfeit. **2** perfection.

deficient *adj* **1** INADEQUATE, insufficient, scarce, short, lacking, wanting, meagrè, scanty, skimpy, incomplete. **2** IMPERFECT, impaired, flawed, faulty, defective, unsatisfactory, inferior, weak.
≠ **1** excessive. **2** perfect.

deficit *n* shortage, shortfall, deficiency, loss, arrears, lack, default.
≠ excess.

defile *v* pollute, violate, contaminate, degrade, dishonour, desecrate, debase, soil, stain, sully, tarnish, taint, profane, corrupt, disgrace.

define *v* **1** *define the boundaries*: bound, limit, delimit, demarcate, mark out. **2** *define the meaning*: explain, characterize, describe, interpret, expound, determine, designate, specify, spell out, detail.

definite *adj* **1** CERTAIN, settled, sure, positive, fixed, decided, determined, assured, guaranteed. **2** CLEAR, clear-cut, exact, precise, specific, explicit, particular, obvious, marked.
≠ **1** indefinite. **2** vague.

definitely *adv* positively, surely, unquestionably, absolutely, certainly, categorically, undeniably, clearly, doubtless, unmistakably, plainly, obviously, indeed, easily.

definition *n* **1** DELINEATION, demarcation, delimitation. **2** EXPLANATION, description, interpretation, exposition, clarification, elucidation, determination. **3** DISTINCTNESS, clarity, precision, clearness, focus, contrast, sharpness.

definitive *adj* decisive, conclusive, final, authoritative, standard, correct, ultimate, reliable, exhaustive, perfect, exact, absolute, complete.
≠ interim.

deflate *v* **1** FLATTEN, puncture, collapse, exhaust, squash, empty, contract, void, shrink, squeeze. **2** DEBUNK, humiliate, put down (*infml*), dash, dispirit, humble, mortify, disconcert. **3** DECREASE, devalue, reduce, lessen, lower, diminish, depreciate, depress.
≠ **1** inflate. **2** boost. **3** increase.

deflect *v* deviate, diverge, turn (aside), swerve, veer, sidetrack, twist, avert, wind, glance off, bend, ricochet.

deform *v* distort, contort, disfigure, warp, mar, pervert, ruin, spoil, twist.

deformed *adj* distorted, misshapen, contorted, disfigured, crippled, crooked, bent, twisted, warped, buckled, defaced, mangled, maimed, marred, ruined, mutilated, perverted, corrupted.

deformity *n* distortion, misshapenness, malformation, disfigurement, abnormality, irregularity, misproportion, defect, ugliness, monstrosity, corruption.

defraud *v* cheat, swindle, dupe, fleece, sting (*infml*), rip off (*infml*), do (*infml*), diddle (*infml*), rob, trick, con (*infml*), rook, deceive, delude, embezzle, beguile.

deft *adj* adept, handy, dexterous, nimble, skilful, adroit, agile, expert, nifty, proficient, able, neat, clever.
≠ clumsy, awkward.

defunct *adj* **1** DEAD, deceased, departed, gone, expired, extinct. **2** OBSOLETE, invalid, inoperative, expired.
≠ **1** alive, live. **2** operative.

defy *v* **1** *defy the authorities*: challenge, confront, resist, dare, brave, face, repel, spurn, beard, flout, withstand, disregard, scorn, despise, defeat, provoke, thwart. **2** *her writings defy categorization*: elude, frustrate, baffle, foil.
≠ **1** obey. **2** permit.

degenerate *adj* dissolute, debauched, depraved, degraded, debased, base, low, decadent, corrupt, fallen, immoral, mean, degenerated, perverted, deteriorated.
≠ moral, upright.
v decline, deteriorate, sink, decay, rot, slip, worsen, regress, fall off, lapse, decrease.
≠ improve.

degradation *n* **1** DETERIORATION, degeneration, decline, downgrading, demotion. **2** ABASEMENT, humiliation, mortification, dishonour, disgrace, shame, ignominy, decadence.
≠ **1** virtue. **2** enhancement.

degrade *v* **1** DISHONOUR, disgrace, debase, abase, shame, humiliate, humble, discredit, demean, lower, weaken, impair, deteriorate, cheapen, adulterate, corrupt. **2** DEMOTE, depose, downgrade, deprive, cashier.
≠ **1** exalt. **2** promote.

degree *n* **1** GRADE, class, rank, order, position, standing, status. **2** EXTENT, measure, range, stage, step, level, intensity, standard. **3** LEVEL, limit, unit, mark.

deify *v* exalt, elevate, worship, glorify, idolize, extol, venerate, immortalize, ennoble, idealize.

deign *v* condescend, stoop, lower oneself, consent, demean oneself.

deity *n* god, goddess, divinity, godhead, idol, demigod, demigoddess, power, immortal.

dejected *adj* downcast, despondent, depressed, downhearted, disheartened, down, low, melancholy, disconsolate, sad, miserable, cast down, gloomy, glum, crestfallen, dismal, wretched, doleful, morose, spiritless.
≠ cheerful, high-spirited, happy.

delay *v* **1** OBSTRUCT, hinder, impede, hold up, check, hold back, set back, stop, halt, detain. **2** DEFER, put off, postpone, procrastinate, suspend, shelve, hold over, stall. **3** DAWDLE, linger, lag, loiter, dilly-dally (*infml*), tarry.
≠ **1** accelerate. **2** bring forward. **3** hurry.
n **1** OBSTRUCTION, hindrance, impediment, hold-up, check, setback, stay, stoppage. **2** DEFERMENT, postponement, procrastination, suspension. **3** DAWDLING, lingering, tarrying. **4** INTERRUPTION, lull, interval, wait.
≠ **1** hastening. **3** hurry. **4** continuation.

delegate *n* representative, agent, envoy, messenger, deputy, ambassador, commissioner.
v authorize, appoint, depute, charge, commission, assign, empower, entrust, devolve, consign, designate, nominate, name, hand over.

delegation *n* **1** DEPUTATION, commission, legation, mission, contingent, embassy. **2** AUTHORIZATION, commissioning, assignment.

delete *v* erase, remove, cross out, cancel, rub out, strike (out), obliterate, edit (out), blot out, efface.
≠ add, insert.

deliberate *v* consider, ponder, reflect, think, cogitate, meditate, mull over, debate, discuss, weigh, consult.
adj **1** INTENTIONAL, planned, calculated, prearranged, premeditated, willed, conscious, designed, considered, advised. **2** CAREFUL, unhurried, thoughtful, methodical, cautious, circumspect, studied, prudent, slow, ponderous, measured, heedful.
≠ **1** unintentional, accidental. **2** hasty.

deliberation *n* **1** CONSIDERATION, reflection, thought, calculation, forethought, meditation, rumination, study, debate, discussion, consultation speculation. **2** CARE, carefulness, caution, circumspection, prudence.

delicacy *n* **1** DAINTINESS, fineness, elegance, exquisiteness, lightness, precision. **2** REFINEMENT, sensitivity, subtlety, finesse, discrimination, tact, niceness. **3** TITBIT, dainty, taste, sweetmeat, savoury, relish.
≠ **1** coarseness, roughness. **2** tactlessness.

delicate *adj* **1** FINE, fragile, dainty, exquisite, flimsy, elegant, graceful. **2** FRAIL, weak, ailing, faint. **3** SENSITIVE, scrupulous, discriminating, careful, accurate, precise. **4** SUBTLE, muted, pastel, soft.
≠ **1** coarse, clumsy. **2** healthy.

delicious *adj* **1** ENJOYABLE, pleasant, agreeable, delightful. **2** APPETIZING, palatable, tasty, delectable, scrumptious (*infml*), mouth-watering, succulent, savoury.
≠ **1** unpleasant. **2** unpalatable.

delight *n* bliss, happiness, joy, pleasure, ecstasy, enjoyment, gladness, rapture, transport, gratification, jubilation.
≠ disgust, displeasure.
v please, charm, gratify, enchant, tickle, thrill, ravish.
≠ displease, dismay.
delight in enjoy, relish, like, love, appreciate, revel in, take pride in, glory in, savour.
≠ dislike, hate.

delighted *adj* charmed, elated, happy, pleased, enchanted, captivated, ecstatic, thrilled, overjoyed, jubilant, joyous.
≠ disappointed, dismayed.

delightful *adj* charming, enchanting, captivating, enjoyable, pleasant, thrilling, agreeable, pleasurable, engaging, attractive, pleasing, gratifying, entertaining, fascinating.
≠ nasty, unpleasant.

delinquency *n* crime, offence, wrong-doing, misbehaviour, misconduct, law-breaking, misdemeanour, criminality.

delinquent *n* offender, criminal, wrong-doer, law-breaker, hooligan, culprit, miscreant (*fml*).

delirious *adj* demented, raving, incoherent, beside oneself, deranged, frenzied, light-headed, wild, mad, frantic, insane, crazy, ecstatic.
≠ sane.

deliver *v* **1** *deliver a parcel*: convey, bring, send, give, carry, supply. **2** SURRENDER, hand over, relinquish, yield, transfer, grant, entrust, commit. **3** UTTER, speak, proclaim, pronounce. **4** ADMINISTER, inflict, direct. **5** SET FREE, liberate, release, emancipate.

delivery *n* **1** CONVEYANCE, consignment, dispatch, transmission, transfer, surrender. **2** ARTICULATION, enunciation, speech, utterance, intonation, elocution. **3** CHILDBIRTH, labour, confinement.

delude *v* deceive, mislead, beguile, dupe, take in, trick, hoodwink, hoax, cheat, misinform.

deluge *n* flood, inundation, downpour, torrent, spate, rush.
v flood, inundate, drench, drown, overwhelm, soak, swamp, engulf, submerge.

delusion *n* illusion, hallucination, fancy, misconception, misapprehension, deception, misbelief, fallacy.

demand *v* **1** ASK, request, call for, insist on, solicit, claim, exact, inquire, question, interrogate. **2** NECESSITATE, need, require, involve.
n **1** REQUEST, question, claim, order, inquiry, desire, interrogation. **2** NEED, necessity, call.

demanding *adj* hard, difficult, challenging, exacting, taxing, tough, exhausting, wearing, back-breaking, insistent, pressing, urgent, trying.
≠ easy, undemanding, easy-going.

demean *v* lower, humble, degrade, humiliate, debase, abase, descend, stoop, condescend.
≠ exalt, enhance.

demeanour *n* bearing, manner, deportment, conduct, behaviour, air.

demented *adj* mad, insane, lunatic, out of one's mind, crazy, loony (*sl*), deranged, unbalanced, frenzied.
≠ sane.

demise *n* **1** DEATH, decease, end,

passing, departure, termination, expiration. **2** DOWNFALL, fall, collapse, failure, ruin. **3** TRANSFER, conveyance, inheritance, transmission, alienation.

democracy *n* self-government, commonwealth, autonomy, republic.

democratic *adj* self-governing, representative, egalitarian, autonomous, popular, populist, republican.

demolish *v* **1** DESTROY, dismantle, knock down, pull down, flatten, bulldoze, raze, tear down, level. **2** RUIN, defeat, destroy, annihilate, wreck, overturn, overthrow.
≠ **1** build up.

demolition *n* destruction, dismantling, levelling, razing.

demon *n* **1** DEVIL, fiend, evil spirit, fallen angel, imp. **2** VILLAIN, devil, rogue, monster.

demonstrable *adj* verifiable, provable, arguable, attestable, self-evident, obvious, evident, certain, clear, positive.
≠ unverifiable.

demonstrate *v* **1** SHOW, display, prove, establish, exhibit, substantiate, manifest, testify to, indicate. **2** EXPLAIN, illustrate, describe, teach. **3** PROTEST, march, parade, rally, picket, sit in.

demonstration *n* **1** DISPLAY, exhibition, manifestation, proof, confirmation, affirmation, substantiation, validation, evidence, testimony, expression. **2** EXPLANATION, illustration, description, exposition, presentation, test, trial. **3** PROTEST, march, demo (*infml*), rally, picket, sit-in, parade.

demonstrative *adj* affectionate, expressive, expansive, emotional, open, loving.
≠ reserved, cold, restrained.

demoralize *v* **1** DISCOURAGE, dishearten, dispirit, undermine, depress, deject, crush, lower, disconcert. **2** CORRUPT, deprave, debase.
≠ **1** encourage. **2** improve.

demote *v* downgrade, degrade, relegate, reduce, cashier.
≠ promote, upgrade.

demur *v* disagree, dissent, object, take exception, refuse, protest, dispute, balk, scruple, doubt, hesitate.

demure *adj* modest, reserved, reticent, prim, coy, shy, retiring, prissy, grave, prudish, sober, strait-laced, staid.
≠ wanton, forward.

den *n* lair, hide-out, hole, retreat, study, hide-away, shelter, sanctuary, haunt.

denial *n* **1** CONTRADICTION, negation, dissent, repudiation, disavowal, disclaimer, dismissal, renunciation. **2** REFUSAL, rebuff, rejection, prohibition, veto.

denigrate *v* disparage, run down, slander, revile, defame, malign, vilify, decry, besmirch, impugn, belittle, abuse, assail, criticize.
≠ praise, acclaim.

denomination *n* **1** CLASSIFICATION, category, class, kind, sort. **2** RELIGION, persuasion, sect, belief, faith, creed, communion, school.

denote *v* indicate, stand for, signify, represent, symbolize, mean, express, designate, typify, mark, show, imply.

dénouement *n* climax, culmination, conclusion, outcome, upshot, pay-off (*infml*), finale, resolution, finish, solution, close.

denounce *v* condemn, censure, accuse, revile, decry, attack, inform against, betray, impugn, vilify, fulminate.
≠ acclaim, praise.

dense *adj* **1** COMPACT, thick, compressed, condensed, close, close-knit, heavy, solid, opaque, impenetrable, packed, crowded. **2** STUPID, thick (*infml*), crass, dull, slow, slow-witted.
≠ **1** thin, sparse. **2** quick-witted, clever.

dent *n* hollow, depression, dip, concavity, indentation, crater, dimple, dint, pit.
v depress, gouge, push in, indent.

denude *v* strip, divest, expose,

uncover, bare, deforest.
≠ cover, clothe.

denunciation *n* condemnation, denouncement, censure, accusation, incrimination, invective, criticism.
≠ praise.

deny *v* **1** *deny God's existence*: contradict, oppose, refute, disagree with, disaffirm, disprove. **2** *deny one's parentage*: disown, disclaim, renounce, repudiate, recant. **3** *deny their human rights*: refuse, turn down, forbid, reject, withhold, rebuff, veto.
≠ **1** admit. **3** allow.

depart *v* **1** GO, leave, withdraw, exit, make off, quit, decamp, take one's leave, absent oneself, set off, remove, retreat, migrate, escape, disappear, retire, vanish. **2** DEVIATE, digress, differ, diverge, swerve, veer.
≠ **1** arrive, return. **2** keep to.

departed *adj* dead, deceased, gone, late, expired.

department *n* **1** DIVISION, branch, subdivision, section, sector, office, station, unit, region, district. **2** SPHERE, realm, province, domain, field, area, concern, responsibility, speciality, line.

departure *n* **1** EXIT, going, leave-taking, removal, withdrawal, retirement, exodus. **2** DEVIATION, digression, divergence, variation, innovation, branching (out), difference, change, shift, veering.
≠ **1** arrival, return.

depend on **1** RELY UPON, count on, bank on (*infml*), calculate on, reckon on (*infml*), build upon, trust in, lean on, expect. **2** HINGE ON, rest on, revolve around, be contingent upon, hang on.

dependable *adj* reliable, trustworthy, steady, trusty, responsible, faithful, unfailing, sure, honest, conscientious, certain.
≠ unreliable, fickle.

dependence *n* **1** RELIANCE, confidence, faith, trust, need, expectation. **2** SUBORDINATION, attachment, subservience, helplessness, addiction.
≠ **2** independence.

dependent *adj* **1** RELIANT, helpless, weak, immature, subject, subordinate, vulnerable. **2** CONTINGENT, conditional, determined by, relative.
≠ **1** independent.

depict *v* portray, illustrate, delineate, sketch, outline, draw, picture, paint, trace, describe, characterize, detail.

deplete *v* empty, drain, exhaust, evacuate, use up, expend, run down, reduce, lessen, decrease.

deplorable *adj* **1** GRIEVOUS, lamentable, pitiable, regrettable, unfortunate, wretched, distressing, sad, miserable, heartbreaking, melancholy, disastrous, dire, appalling. **2** REPREHENSIBLE, disgraceful, scandalous, shameful, dishonourable, disreputable.
≠ **1** excellent. **2** commendable.

deplore *v* **1** GRIEVE FOR, lament, mourn, regret, bemoan, rue. **2** CENSURE, condemn, denounce, deprecate.
≠ **2** extol.

deploy *v* dispose, arrange, position, station, use, utilize, distribute.

deport *v* **1** expel, banish, exile, extradite, transport, expatriate, oust, ostracize.

depose *v* demote, dethrone, downgrade, dismiss, unseat, topple, disestablish, displace, oust.

deposit *v* **1** LAY, drop, place, put, settle, dump (*infml*), park, precipitate, sit, locate. **2** SAVE, store, hoard, bank, amass, consign, entrust, lodge, file.
n **1** SEDIMENT, accumulation, dregs, precipitate, lees, silt. **2** SECURITY, stake, down payment, pledge, retainer, instalment, part payment, money.

depot *n* **1** *military depot*: storehouse, store, warehouse, depository, repository, arsenal. **2** *bus depot*: station, garage, terminus.

deprave *v* corrupt, debauch, debase, degrade, pervert, subvert, infect, demoralize, seduce.
≠ improve, reform.

depraved *adj* corrupt, debauched,

degenerate, perverted, debased, dissolute, immoral, base, shameless, licentious, wicked, sinful, vile, evil.
≠ moral, upright.

deprecate (*fml*) *v* deplore, condemn, censure, disapprove of, object to, protest at, reject.
≠ approve, commend.

depreciate *v* **1** DEVALUE, deflate, downgrade, decrease, reduce, lower, drop, fall, lessen, decline, slump. **2** DISPARAGE, belittle, undervalue, underestimate, underrate, slight.
≠ **1** appreciate. **2** overrate.

depreciation *n* **1** DEVALUATION, deflation, depression, slump, fall. **2** DISPARAGEMENT, belittlement, underestimation.

depress *v* **1** DEJECT, sadden, dishearten, discourage, oppress, upset, daunt, burden, overburden. **2** WEAKEN, undermine, sap, tire, drain, exhaust, weary, impair, reduce, lessen, press, lower, level. **3** DEVALUE, bring down, lower.
≠ **1** cheer. **2** fortify. **3** increase, raise.

depressed *adj* **1** DEJECTED, low-spirited, melancholy, dispirited, sad, unhappy, low, down, downcast, disheartened, fed up (*infml*), miserable, moody, cast down, discouraged, glum, downhearted, distressed, despondent, morose, crestfallen, pessimistic. **2** POOR, disadvantaged, deprived, destitute. **3** SUNKEN, recessed, concave, hollow, indented, dented.
≠ **1** cheerful. **2** affluent. **3** convex, protuberant.

depressing *adj* dejecting, dismal, bleak, gloomy, saddening, cheerless, dreary, disheartening, sad, melancholy, sombre, grey, black, daunting, discouraging, heartbreaking, distressing, hopeless.
≠ cheerful, encouraging.

depression *n* **1** DEJECTION, despair, despondency, melancholy, low spirits, sadness, gloominess, doldrums, blues (*infml*), glumness, dumps (*infml*), hopelessness. **2** RECESSION, slump, stagnation, hard times, decline, inactivity. **3** INDENTATION, hollow, dip, concavity, dent, dimple, valley, pit, sink, dint, bowl, cavity, basin, impression, dish, excavation.
≠ **1** cheerfulness. **2** prosperity, boom. **3** convexity, protuberance.

deprive *v* **1** DISPOSSESS, strip, divest, denude, bereave, expropriate, rob. **2** DENY, withhold, refuse.
≠ **1** endow. **2** provide.

deprived *adj* poor, needy, underprivileged, disadvantaged, impoverished, destitute, lacking, bereft.
≠ prosperous.

depth *n* **1** DEEPNESS, profoundness, extent, measure, drop. **2** MIDDLE, midst, abyss, deep, gulf. **3** WISDOM, insight, discernment, penetration. **4** INTENSITY, strength.
≠ **1** shallowness. **2** surface.

deputation *n* commission, delegation, embassy, mission, representatives, legation.

deputise *n* **1** REPRESENT, stand in for, substitute, replace, understudy, double. **2** DELEGATE, commission.

deputy *n* representative, agent, delegate, proxy, substitute, second-in-command, ambassador, commissioner, lieutenant, surrogate, subordinate, assistant, locum.

deranged *adj* disordered, demented, crazy, mad, lunatic, insane, unbalanced, disturbed, confused, frantic, delirious, distraught, berserk.
≠ sane, calm.

derelict *adj* abandoned, neglected, deserted, forsaken, desolate, discarded, dilapidated, ruined.

deride *v* ridicule, mock, scoff, scorn, jeer, sneer, satirize, knock (*infml*), gibe, disparage, insult, belittle, disdain, taunt.
≠ respect, praise.

derision *n* ridicule, mockery, scorn, contempt, scoffing, satire, sneering, disrespect, insult, disparagement, disdain.
≠ respect, praise.

derisive *adj* mocking, scornful, contemptuous, disrespectful, irreverent, jeering, disdainful, taunting.

≠ respectful, flattering.

derivation *n* source, origin, root, beginning, etymology, extraction, foundation, genealogy, ancestry, basis, descent, deduction, inference.

derivative *adj* unoriginal, acquired, copied, borrowed, derived, imitative, obtained, second-hand, secondary, plagiarized, cribbed (*infml*), hackneyed, trite.
n derivation, offshoot, by-product, development, branch, outgrowth, spin-off, product, descendant.

derive *v* **1** GAIN, obtain, get, draw, extract, receive, procure, acquire, borrow. **2** ORIGINATE, arise, spring, flow, emanate, descend, proceed, stem, issue, follow, develop. **3** INFER, deduce, trace, gather, glean.

derogatory *adj* insulting, pejorative, offensive, disparaging, depreciative, critical, defamatory, injurious.
≠ flattering.

descend *v* **1** DROP, go down, fall, plummet, plunge, tumble, swoop, sink, arrive, alight, dismount, dip, slope, subside. **2** DEGENERATE, deteriorate. **3** CONDESCEND, deign, stoop. **4** ORIGINATE, proceed, spring, stem.
≠ **1** ascend, rise.

descendants *n* offspring, children, issue, progeny, successors, lineage, line, seed (*infml*).

descent *n* **1** FALL, drop, plunge, dip, decline, incline, slope. **2** COMEDOWN, debasement, degradation. **3** ANCESTRY, parentage, heredity, family tree, genealogy, lineage, extraction, origin.
≠ **1** ascent, rise.

describe *v* portray, depict, delineate, illustrate, characterize, specify, draw, define, detail, explain, express, tell, narrate, outline, relate, recount, present, report, sketch, mark out, trace.

description *n* **1** PORTRAYAL, representation, characterization, account, delineation, depiction, sketch, presentation, report, outline, explanation, exposition, narration. **2** SORT, type, kind, variety, specification, order.

descriptive *adj* illustrative, explanatory, expressive, detailed, graphic, colourful, pictorial, vivid.

desert[1] *n* wasteland, wilderness, wilds, void.
adj bare, barren, waste, wild, uninhabited, uncultivated, dry, arid, infertile, desolate, sterile, solitary.

desert[2] *v* abandon, forsake, leave, maroon, strand, decamp, defect, give up, renounce, relinquish, jilt, abscond, quit.
≠ stand by, support.

desert[3] *n* **1** DUE, right, reward, deserts, return, retribution, come-uppance (*infml*), payment, recompense, remuneration. **2** WORTH, merit, virtue.

deserted *adj* abandoned, forsaken, empty, derelict, desolate, godforsaken, neglected, underpopulated, stranded, isolated, bereft, vacant, betrayed, lonely, solitary, unoccupied.
≠ populous.

deserter *n* runaway, absconder, escapee, truant, renegade, defector, rat (*infml*), traitor, fugitive, betrayer, apostate, backslider, delinquent.

deserve *v* earn, be worthy of, merit, be entitled to, warrant, justify, win, rate, incur.

deserved *adj* due, earned, merited, justifiable, warranted, right, rightful, well-earned, suitable, proper, fitting, fair, just, appropriate, apt, legitimate, apposite, meet (*fml*).
≠ gratuitous, undeserved.

deserving *adj* worthy, estimable, exemplary, praiseworthy, admirable, commendable, laudable, righteous.
≠ undeserving, unworthy.

design *n* **1** BLUEPRINT, draft, pattern, plan, prototype, sketch, drawing, outline, model, guide. **2** STYLE, shape, form, figure, structure, organization, arrangement, composition, construction, motif. **3** AIM, intention, goal, purpose, plan, end, object, objective, scheme, plot, project, meaning, target, undertaking.
v **1** PLAN, plot, intend, devise, purpose, aim, scheme, shape, project, propose, tailor, mean. **2** SKETCH,

draft, outline, draw (up). **3** INVENT, originate, conceive, create, think up, develop, construct, fashion, form, model, fabricate, make.

designation *n* **1** NAME, title, label, epithet, nickname. **2** INDICATION, specification, description, definition, classification, category. **3** NOMINATION, appointment, selection.

designer *n* deviser, originator, maker, stylist, inventor, creator, contriver, fashioner, architect, author.

designing *adj* artful, crafty, scheming, conspiring, devious, intriguing, plotting, tricky, wily, sly, deceitful, cunning, guileful, underhand, sharp, shrewd.
≠ artless, naïve.

desirable *adj* **1** ADVANTAGEOUS, profitable, worthwhile, advisable, appropriate, expedient, beneficial, preferable, sensible, eligible, good, pleasing. **2** ATTRACTIVE, alluring, sexy (*infml*), seductive, fetching, tempting.
≠ **1** undesirable. **2** unattractive.

desire *v* **1** ASK, request, petition, solicit. **2** WANT, wish for, covet, long for, need, crave, hunger for, yearn for, fancy (*infml*), hanker after.
n **1** WANT, longing, wish, need, yearning, craving, hankering, appetite, aspiration. **2** LUST, passion, concupiscence (*fml*), ardour. **3** REQUEST, petition, appeal, supplication.

desist *v* stop, cease, leave off, refrain, discontinue, end, break off, give up, halt, abstain, suspend, pause, peter out, remit, forbear (*fml*).
≠ continue, resume.

desolate *adj* **1** DESERTED, uninhabited, abandoned, unfrequented, barren, bare, arid, bleak, gloomy, dismal, dreary, lonely, god-forsaken, forsaken, waste, depressing. **2** FORLORN, bereft, depressed, dejected, forsaken, despondent, distressed, melancholy, miserable, lonely, gloomy, disheartened, dismal, downcast, solitary, wretched.
≠ **1** populous. **2** cheerful.
v devastate, lay waste, destroy, despoil, spoil, wreck, denude, depopulate, ruin, waste, ravage, plunder, pillage.

desolation *n* **1** DESTRUCTION, ruin, devastation, ravages. **2** DEJECTION, despair, despondency, gloom, misery, sadness, melancholy, sorrow, unhappiness, anguish, grief, distress, wretchedness. **3** BARRENNESS, bleakness, emptiness, forlornness, loneliness, isolation, solitude, wildness.

despair *v* lose heart, lose hope, give up, give in, collapse, surrender.
≠ hope.
n despondency, gloom, hopelessness, desperation, anguish, inconsolableness, melancholy, misery, wretchedness.
≠ cheerfulness, resilience.

despairing *adj* despondent, distraught, inconsolable, desolate, desperate, heart-broken, suicidal, grief-stricken, hopeless, disheartened, dejected, miserable, wretched, sorrowful, dismayed, downcast.
≠ cheerful, hopeful.

despatch *see* **dispatch**.

desperado *n* bandit, criminal, brigand, gangster, hoodlum (*infml*), outlaw, ruffian, thug, cut-throat, law-breaker.

desperate *adj* **1** HOPELESS, inconsolable, wretched, despondent, abandoned. **2** RECKLESS, rash, impetuous, audacious, daring, dangerous, do-or-die, foolhardy, risky, hazardous, hasty, precipitate, wild, violent, frantic, frenzied, determined. **3** CRITICAL, acute, serious, severe, extreme, urgent.
≠ **1** hopeful. **2** cautious.

desperately *adv* dangerously, critically, gravely, hopelessly, seriously, severely, badly, dreadfully, fearfully, frightfully.

desperation *n* **1** DESPAIR, despondency, anguish, hopelessness, misery, agony, distress, pain, sorrow, trouble, worry, anxiety. **2** RECKLESSNESS, rashness, frenzy, madness, hastiness.

despicable *adj* contemptible, vile,

worthless, detestable, disgusting, mean, wretched, disgraceful, disreputable, shameful, reprobate.
≠ admirable, noble.

despise *v* scorn, deride, look down on, disdain, condemn, spurn, undervalue, slight, revile, deplore, dislike, detest, loathe.
≠ admire.

despite *prep* in spite of, notwithstanding, regardless of, in the face of, undeterred by, against, defying.

despondent *adj* depressed, dejected, disheartened, downcast, down, low, gloomy, glum, discouraged, miserable, melancholy, sad, sorrowful, doleful, despairing, heart-broken, inconsolable, mournful, wretched.
≠ cheerful, heartened, hopeful.

despot *n* autocrat, tyrant, dictator, oppressor, absolutist, boss.

despotic *adj* autocratic, tyrannical, imperious, oppressive, dictatorial, authoritarian, domineering, absolute, overbearing, arbitrary, arrogant.
≠ democratic, egalitarian, liberal, tolerant.

despotism *n* autocracy, totalitarianism, tyranny, dictatorship, absolutism, oppression, repression.
≠ democracy, egalitarianism, liberalism, tolerance.

destination *n* **1** GOAL, aim, objective, object, purpose, target, end, intention, aspiration, design, ambition.
2 JOURNEY'S END, terminus, station, stop.

destined *adj* **1** FATED, doomed, inevitable, predetermined, ordained, certain, foreordained, meant, unavoidable, inescapable, intended, designed, appointed. **2** BOUND, directed, en route, headed, heading, scheduled, assigned, booked.

destiny *n* fate, doom, fortune, karma, lot (*fml*), portion (*fml*), predestiny, kismet.

destitute *adj* **1** LACKING, needy, wanting, devoid of, bereft, innocent of, deprived, deficient, depleted. **2** POOR, penniless, poverty-stricken, impoverished, down and out (*infml*), distressed, bankrupt.
≠ **2** prosperous, rich.

destroy *v* **1** DEMOLISH, ruin, shatter, wreck, devastate, smash, break, crush, overthrow, sabotage, undo, dismantle, thwart, undermine, waste, gut, level, ravage, raze, torpedo, unshape. **2** KILL, annihilate, eliminate, extinguish, eradicate, dispatch, slay (*fml*), nullify.
≠ **1** build up. **2** create.

destruction *n* **1** RUIN, devastation, shattering, crushing, wreckage, demolition, defeat, downfall, overthrow, ruination, desolation, undoing, wastage, havoc, ravagement.
2 ANNIHILATION, extermination, eradication, elimination, extinction, slaughter, massacre, end, liquidation, nullification.
≠ **2** creation.

destructive *adj* **1** *destructive storms*: devastating, damaging, catastrophic, disastrous, deadly, harmful, fatal, disruptive, lethal, ruinous, detrimental, hurtful, malignant, mischievous, nullifying, slaughterous. **2** *destructive criticism*: adverse, hostile, negative, discouraging, disparaging, contrary, undermining, subversive, vicious.
≠ **1** creative. **2** constructive.

desultory *adj* random, erratic, aimless, disorderly, haphazard, irregular, spasmodic, inconsistent, undirected, unco-ordinated, unsystematic, unmethodical, fitful, disconnected, loose, capricious.
≠ systematic, methodical.

detach *v* separate, disconnect, unfasten, disjoin, cut off, disengage, remove, undo, uncouple, sever, dissociate, isolate, loosen, free, unfix, unhitch, segregate, divide, disentangle, estrange.
≠ attach.

detached *adj* **1** SEPARATE, disconnected, dissociated, severed, free, loose, divided, discrete. **2** ALOOF, dispassionate, impersonal, neutral, impartial, independent, disinterested, objective.

≠ 1 connected. 2 involved.

detachment *n* 1 ALOOFNESS, remoteness, coolness, unconcern, indifference, impassivity, disinterestedness, neutrality, impartiality, objectivity, fairness. 2 SEPARATION, disconnection, disunion, disengagement. 3 SQUAD, unit, force, corps, brigade, patrol, task force.

detail *n* particular, item, factor, element, aspect, component, feature, point, specific, ingredient, attribute, count, respect, technicality, complication, intricacy, triviality, fact, thoroughness, elaboration, meticulousness, refinement, nicety. *v* 1 LIST, enumerate, itemize, specify, catalogue, recount, relate. 2 ASSIGN, appoint, charge, delegate, commission.

detailed *adj* comprehensive, exhaustive, full, blow-by-blow (*infml*), thorough, minute, exact, specific, particular, itemized, intricate, elaborate, complex, complicated, meticulous, descriptive.
≠ cursory, general.

detain *v* 1 DELAY, hold (up), hinder, impede, check, retard, slow, stay, stop. 2 CONFINE, arrest, intern, hold, restrain, keep.
≠ 2 release.

detect *v* 1 NOTICE, ascertain, note, observe, perceive, recognize, discern, distinguish, identify, sight, spot, spy. 2 UNCOVER, catch, discover, disclose, expose, find, track down, unmask, reveal.

detective *n* investigator, private eye (*infml*), sleuth (*infml*), sleuth-hound (*infml*).

detention *n* 1 DETAINMENT, custody, confinement, imprisonment, restraint, incarceration, constraint, quarantine. 2 DELAY, hindrance, holding back.
≠ 1 release.

deter *v* discourage, put off, inhibit, intimidate, dissuade, daunt, turn off (*infml*), check, caution, warn, restrain, hinder, frighten, disincline, prevent, prohibit, stop.
≠ encourage.

deteriorate *v* 1 WORSEN, decline, degenerate, depreciate, go downhill (*infml*), fail, fall off, lapse, slide, relapse, slip. 2 DECAY, disintegrate, decompose, weaken, fade.
≠ 1 improve. 2 progress.

determination *n* 1 RESOLUTENESS, tenacity, firmness, will-power, perseverance, persistence, purpose, backbone, guts (*infml*), grit (*infml*), steadfastness, single-mindedness, will, insistence, conviction, dedication, drive, fortitude. 2 DECISION, judgement, settlement, resolution, conclusion.
≠ 1 irresolution.

determine *v* 1 DECIDE, settle, resolve, make up one's mind, choose, conclude, fix on, elect, clinch, finish. 2 DISCOVER, establish, find out, ascertain, identify, check, detect, verify. 3 AFFECT, influence, govern, control, dicture, direct, guide, regulate, ordain.

determined *adj* resolute, firm, purposeful, strong-willed, single-minded, persevering, persistent, strong-minded, steadfast, tenacious, dogged, insistent, intent, fixed, convinced, decided, unflinching.
≠ irresolute, wavering.

deterrent *n* hindrance, impediment, obstacle, repellent, check, bar, discouragement, obstruction, curb, restraint, difficulty.
≠ incentive, encouragement.

detest *v* hate, abhor, loathe, abominate, execrate (*fml*), dislike, recoil from, deplore, despise.
≠ adore, love.

detestable *adj* hateful, loathsome, abhorrent, abominable, repellent, obnoxious, execrable (*fml*), despicable, revolting, repulsive, repugnant, offensive, vile, disgusting, accursed (*fml*), heinous, shocking, sordid.
≠ adorable, admirable.

detour *n* deviation, diversion, indirect route, circuitous route, roundabout route, digression, byroad, byway, bypath, bypass.

detract (from) *v* diminish, subtract from, take away from, reduce, lessen,

lower, devaluate, depreciate, belittle, disparage.
≠ add to, enhance, praise.

detriment *n* damage, harm, hurt, disadvantage, loss, ill, injury, disservice, evil, mischief, prejudice.
≠ advantage, benefit.

detrimental *adj* damaging, harmful, hurtful, adverse, disadvantageous, injurious, prejudicial, mischievous, destructive.
≠ advantageous, favourable, beneficial.

devastate *v* **1** DESTROY, desolate, lay waste, demolish, spoil, despoil, wreck, ruin, ravage, waste, ransack, plunder, level, raze, pillage, sack. **2** DISCONCERT, overwhelm, take aback, confound, shatter (*infml*), floor (*infml*), nonplus, discomfit.

devastating *adj* **1** *devastating storms*: destructive, disastrous. **2** *a devastating argument*: effective, incisive, overwhelming, stunning.

devastation *n* destruction, desolation, havoc, ruin, wreckage, ravages, demolition, annihilation, pillage, plunder, spoliation.

develop *v* **1** ADVANCE, evolve, expand, progress, foster, flourish, mature, prosper, branch out. **2** ELABORATE, amplify, argument, enhance, unfold. **3** ACQUIRE, contract, begin, generate, create, invent. **4** RESULT, come about, grow, ensue, arise, follow, happen.

development *n* **1** GROWTH, evolution, advance, blossoming, elaboration, furtherance, progress, unfolding, expansion, extension, spread, increase, improvement, maturity, promotion, refinement, issue. **2** OCCURRENCE, happening, event, change, outcome, situation, result, phenomenon.

deviate *v* diverge, veer, turn (aside), digress, swerve, vary, differ, depart, stray, yaw, wander, err, go astray, go off the rails (*infml*), drift, part.

deviation *n* divergence, aberration, departure, abnormality, irregularity, variance, variation, digression, eccentricity, anomaly, deflection, alteration, disparity, discrepancy, detour, fluctuation, change, quirk, shift, freak.
≠ conformity, regularity.

device *n* **1** TOOL, implement, appliance, gadget, contrivance, contraption (*infml*), apparatus, utensil, instrument, machine. **2** SCHEME, ruse, strategy, plan, plot, gambit, manoeuvre, wile, trick, dodge (*infml*), machination. **3** EMBLEM, symbol, motif, logo (*infml*), design, insignia, crest, badge, shield.

devil *n* **1** DEMON, Satan, fiend, evil spirit, arch-fiend, Lucifer, imp, Evil One, Prince of Darkness, Adversary, Beelzebub, Mephistopheles, Old Nick (*infml*), Old Harry (*infml*). **2** BRUTE, rogue, monster, ogre.

devious *adj* **1** UNDERHAND, deceitful, dishonest, disingenuous, double-dealing, scheming, tricky (*infml*), insidious, insincere, calculating, cunning, evasive, wily, sly, slippery (*infml*), surreptitious, treacherous, misleading. **2** INDIRECT, circuitous, rambling, roundabout, wandering, winding, tortuous, erratic.
≠ straightforward.

devise *v* invent, contrive, plan, plot, design, conceive, arrange, formulate, imagine, scheme, construct, concoct, forge, frame, project, shape, form.

devoid *adj* lacking, wanting, without, free, bereft, destitute, deficient, deprived, barren, empty, vacant, void.
≠ endowed.

devote *v* dedicate, consecrate, commit, give oneself, set apart, set aside, reserve, apply, allocate, allot, sacrifice, enshrine, assign, appropriate, surrender, pledge.

devoted *adj* dedicated, ardent, committed, loyal, faithful, devout, loving, staunch, steadfast, true, constant, fond, unswerving, tireless, concerned, attentive, caring.
≠ indifferent, disloyal.

devotee *n* enthusiast, fan (*infml*), fanatic, addict, aficionado, follower, supporter, zealot, adherent, admirer, disciple, buff (*infml*), freak (*infml*), merchant (*infml*), fiend (*infml*), hound.

devotion *n* **1** DEDICATION, commitment, consecration, ardour, loyalty, allegiance, adherence, zeal, support, love, passion, fervour, fondness, attachment, adoration, affection, faithfulness, reverence, steadfastness, regard, earnestness. **2** DEVOUTNESS, piety, godliness, faith, holiness, spirituality. **3** PRAYER, worship.
≠ **1** inconstancy. **2** irreverence.

devour *v* **1** EAT, consume, guzzle, gulp, gorge, gobble, bolt, wolf down, swallow, stuff (*infml*), cram, polish off (*infml*), gormandize, feast on, relish, revel in. **2** DESTROY, consume, absorb, engulf, ravage, dispatch.

devout *adj* **1** SINCERE, earnest, devoted, fervent, genuine, staunch, steadfast, ardent, passionate, serious, whole-hearted, constant, faithful, intense, heartfelt, zealous, unswerving, deep, profound. **2** PIOUS, godly, religious, reverent, prayerful, saintly, holy, orthodox.
≠ **1** insincere. **2** irreligious.

dexterous *adj* deft, adroit, agile, able, nimble, proficient, skilful, clever, expert, nifty, nippy, handy, facile, nimble-fingered, neat-handed.
≠ clumsy, inept, awkward.

diabolical *adj* devilish, fiendish, demonic, hellish, damnable, evil, infernal, wicked, vile, dreadful, outrageous, shocking, disastrous, excruciating, atrocious.

diagnose *v* identify, determine, recognize, pinpoint, distinguish, analyse, explain, isolate, interpret, investigate.

diagnosis *n* identification, verdict, explanation, conclusion, answer, interpretation, analysis, opinion, investigation, examination, scrutiny.

diagonal *adj* oblique, slanting, cross, crosswise, sloping, crooked, angled, cornerways.

diagram *n* plan, sketch, chart, drawing, figure, representation, schema, illustration, outline, graph, picture, layout, table.

dial *n* circle, disc, face, clock, control.
v phone, ring, call (up).

dialect *n* idiom, language, regionalism, patois, provincialism, vernacular, argot, jargon, accent, lingo (*infml*), speech, diction.

dialectic *adj* dialectical, logical, rational, argumentative, analytical, rationalistic, logistic, polemical, inductive, deductive.
n dialectics, logic, reasoning, rationale, disputation, analysis, debate, argumentation, contention, discussion, polemics, induction, deduction.

dialogue *n* **1** CONVERSATION, interchange, discourse, communication, talk, exchange, discussion, converse, debate, conference. **2** LINES, script.

diametric *adj* diametrical, opposed, opposite, contrary, counter, contrasting, antithetical.

diary *n* journal, day-book, logbook, chronicle, year-book, appointment book, engagement book.

diatribe *n* tirade, invective, abuse, harangue, attack, onslaught, denunciation, criticism, insult, reviling, upbraiding.
≠ praise, eulogy.

dicey (*infml*) *adj* risky, chancy, unpredictable, tricky, problematic, dangerous, difficult, iffy (*infml*), dubious, hairy (*infml*).
≠ **1** certain.

dictate *v* **1** SAY, speak, utter, announce, pronounce, transmit. **2** COMMAND, order, direct, decree, instruct, rule.
n command, decree, precept, principle, rule, direction, injunction, edict, order, ruling, statute, requirement, ordinance, law, bidding, mandate, ultimatum, word.

dictator *n* despot, autocrat, tyrant, supremo (*infml*), Big Brother (*infml*).

dictatorial *adj* tyrannical, despotic, totalitarian, authoritarian, autocratic, oppressive, imperious, domineering, bossy (*infml*), absolute, repressive, overbearing, arbitrary, dogmatic.
≠ democratic, egalitarian, liberal.

diction *n* speech, articulation, language

elocution, enunciation, intonation, pronunciation, inflection, fluency, delivery, expression, phrasing.

dictionary *n* lexicon, glossary, thesaurus, vocabulary, wordbook, encyclopaedia, concordance.

dictum *n* pronouncement, ruling, maxim, decree, dictate, edict, fiat (*fml*), precept, axiom, command, order, utterance.

didactic *adj* instructive, educational, educative, pedagogic, prescriptive, pedantic, moralizing, moral.

die *v* **1** DECEASE, perish, pass away, expire, depart, breathe one's last, peg out (*infml*), snuff it (*sl*), bite the dust (*infml*), kick the bucket (*sl*). **2** DWINDLE, fade, ebb, sink, wane, wilt, wither, peter out, decline, decay, finish, lapse, end, disappear, vanish, subside. **3** LONG FOR, pine for, yearn, desire.
≠ **1** live.

die-hard *n* reactionary, intransigent, hardliner, blimp (*infml*), ultra-conservative, old fogey (*infml*), stick-in-the-mud (*infml*), rightist, fanatic.

diet *n* **1** FOOD, nutrition, provisions, sustenance, rations, foodstuffs, subsistence. **2** FAST, abstinence, regimen.
v lose weight, slim, fast, reduce, abstain, weight-watch (*infml*).

differ *v* **1** VARY, diverge, deviate, depart from, contradict, contrast. **2** DISAGREE, argue, conflict, oppose, dispute, dissent, be at odds with, clash, quarrel, fall out, debate, contend, take issue.
≠ **1** conform. **2** agree.

difference *n* **1** DISSIMILARITY, unlikeness, discrepancy, divergence, diversity, variation, variety, distinctness, distinction, deviation, differentiation, contrast, disparity, singularity, exception. **2** DISAGREEMENT, clash, dispute, conflict, contention, controversy. **3** REMAINDER, rest.
≠ **1** conformity. **2** agreement.

different *adj* **1** DISSIMILAR, unlike, contrasting, divergent, inconsistent, deviating, at odds, clashing, opposed. **2** VARIED, various, diverse, miscellaneous, assorted, disparate, many, numerous, several, sundry, other. **3** UNUSUAL, unconventional, unique, distinct, distinctive, extraordinary, individual, original, special, strange, separate, peculiar, rare, bizarre, anomalous.
≠ **1** similar. **2** same. **3** conventional.

differentiate *v* distinguish, tell apart, discriminate, contrast, separate, mark off, individualize, particularize.

difficult *adj* **1** HARD, laborious, demanding, arduous, strenuous, tough, wearisome, uphill, formidable. **2** COMPLEX, complicated, intricate, involved, abstruse, obscure, dark, knotty, thorny, problematical, perplexing, abstract, baffling, intractable. **3** UNMANAGEABLE, perverse, troublesome, trying, unco-operative, tiresome, stubborn, obstinate, intractable.
≠ **1** easy. **2** manageable. **3** straightforward.

difficulty *n* **1** HARDSHIP, trouble, labour, arduousness, painfulness, trial, tribulation, awkwardness. **2** PROBLEM, predicament, dilemma, quandary, perplexity, embarrassment, plight, distress, fix (*infml*), mess (*infml*), jam (*infml*), spot (*infml*), hiccup (*infml*), hang-up. **3** OBSTACLE, hindrance, hurdle, impediment, objection, opposition, block, complication, pitfall, protest, stumbling-block.
≠ **1** ease.

diffidence *n* unassertiveness, modesty, shyness, self-consciousness, self-effacement, timidity, insecurity, reserve, bashfulness, humility, inhibition, meekness, self-distrust, self-doubt, hesitancy, reluctance, backwardness.
≠ confidence.

diffident *adj* unassertive, modest, shy, timid, self-conscious, self-effacing, insecure, bashful, abashed, meek, reserved, withdrawn, tentative, shrinking, inhibited, hesitant, reluctant, unsure, shamefaced.
≠ assertive, confident.

diffuse *adj* 1 *diffuse outbreaks of rain*: scattered, unconcentrated, diffused, dispersed, disconnected. 2 *a diffuse prose style*: verbose, imprecise, wordy, rambling, long-winded, waffling (*infml*), vague, discursive.
≠ 1 concentrated. 2 succinct.
v spread, scatter, disperse, distribute, propagate, dispense, disseminate, circulate, dissipate.
≠ concentrate.

dig *v* 1 EXCAVATE, penetrate, burrow, mine, quarry, scoop, tunnel, till, gouge, delve, pierce. 2 POKE, prod. 3 INVESTIGATE, probe, go into, research, search.
n gibe, jeer, sneer, taunt, crack, insinuation, insult, wisecrack.
≠ compliment.
dig up discover, unearth, uncover, disinter, expose, extricate, exhume, find, retrieve, track down.
≠ bury, obscure.

digest *v* 1 ABSORB, assimilate, incorporate, process, dissolve. 2 TAKE IN, absorb, understand, assimilate, grasp, study, consider, contemplate, meditate, ponder. 3 SHORTEN, summarize, condense, compress, reduce.
n summary, abridgement, abstract, précis, synopsis, résumé, reduction, abbreviation, compression, compendium.

dignified *adj* stately, solemn, imposing, majestic, noble, august, lordly, lofty, exalted, formal, distinguished, grave, impressive, reserved, honourable.
≠ undignified, lowly.

dignitary *n* worthy, notable, VIP (*infml*), high-up, personage, bigwig (*infml*).

dignity *n* stateliness, propriety, solemnity, decorum, courtliness, grandeur, loftiness, majesty, honour, eminence, importance, nobility, self-respect, self-esteem, standing, poise, respectability, greatness, status, pride.

digress *v* diverge, deviate, stray, wander, go off at a tangent, drift, depart, ramble.

dilapidated *adj* ramshackle, shabby, broken-down, neglected, tumble-down, uncared-for, rickety, decrepit, crumbling, run-down, worn-out, ruined, decayed, decaying.

dilate *v* distend, enlarge, expand, spread, broaden, widen, increase, extend, stretch, swell.
≠ contract.

dilatory *adj* delaying, procrastinating, slow, tardy, tarrying, sluggish, lingering, lackadaisical, slack.
≠ prompt.

dilemma *n* quandary, conflict, predicament, problem, catch-22 (*infml*), difficulty, puzzle, embarrassment, perplexity, plight.

diligent *adj* assiduous, industrious, hard-working, conscientious, painstaking, busy, attentive, tireless, careful, meticulous, persevering, persistent, studious.
≠ negligent, lazy.

dilute *v* adulterate, water down, thin (out), attenuate, weaken, diffuse, diminish, decrease, lessen, reduce, temper, mitigate.
≠ concentrate.

dim *adj* 1 DARK, dull, dusky, cloudy, shadowy, gloomy, sombre, dingy, lack-lustre, feeble, imperfect. 2 INDISTINCT, blurred, hazy, ill-defined, obscure, misty, unclear, foggy, fuzzy, vague, faint, weak. 3 STUPID, dense, obtuse, thick (*infml*), doltish.
≠ 1 bright. 2 distinct. 3 bright, intelligent.
v darken, dull, obscure, cloud, blur, fade, tarnish, shade.
≠ brighten, illuminate.

dimension(s) *n* extent, measurement, measure, size, scope, magnitude, largeness, capacity, mass, scale, range, bulk, importance, greatness.

diminish *v* 1 DECREASE, lessen, reduce, lower, contract, decline, dwindle, shrink, recede, taper off, wane, weaken, abate, fade, sink, subside, ebb, slacken, cut. 2 BELITTLE, disparage, deprecate, devalue.
≠ 1 increase. 2 exaggerate.

diminutive *adj* undersized, small, tiny, little, miniature, minute, infinitesimal,

wee, petite, midget, mini (*infml*), teeny (*infml*), teeny-weeny (*infml*), Lilliputian, dinky (*infml*), pint-size(d) (*infml*), pocket(-sized), pygmy.
≠ big, large, oversized.

din *n* noise, row, racket, clash, clatter, clamour, pandemonium, uproar, commotion, crash, hullabaloo (*infml*), hubbub, outcry, shout, babble.
≠ quiet, calm.

dine *v* eat, feast, sup, lunch, banquet, feed.

dingy *adj* dark, drab, grimy, murky, faded, dull, dim, shabby, soiled, discoloured, dirty, dreary, gloomy, seedy, sombre, obscure, run-down, colourless, dusky, worn.
≠ bright, clean.

dinner *n* meal, supper, tea (*infml*), banquet, feast, spread, repast (*fml*).

dinosaurs

Dinosaurs include: Ornithischia, Saurischia; Allosaurus, Ankylosaurus, Apatosaurus, Barosaurus, Brachiosaurus, Brontosaurus, Camptosaurus, Coelophysis, Compsognathus, Corythosaurus, Deinonychus, Diplodocus, Heterodontosaurus, Iguanodon, Ophiacodon, Ornithomimus, Pachycephalosaurus, Parasaurolophus, Plateosaurus, Stegosaurus, Styracosaurus, Triceratops, Tyrannosaurus.

dip *v* **1** PLUNGE, immerse, submerge, duck, dunk, bathe, douse, sink. **2** DESCEND, decline, drop, fall, subside, slump, sink, lower.
n **1** HOLLOW, basin, decline, hole, concavity, incline, depression, fall, slope, slump, lowering. **2** BATHE, immersion, plunge, soaking, ducking, swim, drenching, infusion, dive.

diplomacy *n* **1** TACT, tactfulness, finesse, delicacy, discretion, savoir-faire, subtlety, skill, craft. **2** STATECRAFT, statesmanship, politics, negotiation, manoeuvring.

diplomat *n* go-between, mediator, negotiator, ambassador, envoy, conciliator, peacemaker, moderator, politician.

diplomatic *adj* tactful, politic, discreet, judicious, subtle, sensitive, prudent, discreet.
≠ tactless.

dire *adj* **1** DISASTROUS, dreadful, awful, appalling, calamitous, catastrophic. **2** DESPERATE, urgent, grave, drastic, crucial, extreme, alarming, ominous.

direct *v* **1** CONTROL, manage, run, administer, organize, lead, govern, regulate, superintend, supervise. **2** INSTRUCT, command, order, charge. **3** GUIDE, lead, conduct, point. **4** AIM, point, focus, turn.
adj **1** STRAIGHT, undeviating, through, uninterrupted. **2** STRAIGHTFORWARD, outspoken, blunt, frank, unequivocal, sincere, candid, honest, explicit. **3** IMMEDIATE, first-hand, face-to-face, personal.
≠ **1** circuitous. **2** equivocal. **3** indirect.

direction *n* **1** CONTROL, administration, management, government, supervision, guidance, leadership. **2** ROUTE, way, line, road.

directions *n* instructions, guidelines, orders, briefing, guidance, recommendations, indication, plan.

directive *n* command, instruction, order, regulation, ruling, imperative, dictate, decree, charge, mandate, injunction, ordinance, edict, fiat, notice.

directly *adv* **1** IMMEDIATELY, instantly, promptly, right away, speedily, forthwith, instantaneously, quickly, soon, presently, straightaway, straight. **2** FRANKLY, bluntly, candidly, honestly.

director *n* manager, head, boss, chief, controller, executive, principal, governor, leader, organizer, supervisor, administrator, producer, conductor.

dirt *n* **1** EARTH, soil, clay, dust, mud. **2** FILTH, grime, muck, mire, excrement, stain, smudge, slime, tarnish. **3** INDECENCY, impurity, obscenity, pornography.

dirty *adj* **1** FILTHY, grimy, grubby, mucky, soiled, unwashed, foul, messy, muddy, polluted, squalid, dull, miry,

scruffy, shabby, sullied, clouded, dark. **2** INDECENT, obscene, filthy, smutty, sordid, salacious, vulgar, pornographic, corrupt.
≠ **1** clean. **2** decent.
v pollute, soil, stain, foul, mess up, defile, smear, smirch, spoil, smudge, sully, muddy, blacken.
≠ clean, cleanse.

disability *n* handicap, impairment, disablement, disorder, inability, incapacity, infirmity, defect, unfitness, disqualification, affliction, ailment, complaint, weakness.

disable *v* cripple, lame, incapacitate, damage, handicap, impair, debilitate, disqualify, weaken, immobilize, invalidate, paralyse, prostrate.

disabled *adj* handicapped, incapacitated, impaired, infirm, crippled, lame, immobilized, maimed, weak, weakened, paralysed, wrecked.
≠ able, able-bodied.

disadvantage *n* **1** HARM, damage, detriment, hurt, injury, loss, prejudice. **2** DRAWBACK, snag, hindrance, handicap, impediment, inconvenience, flaw, nuisance, weakness, trouble.
≠ **2** advantage, benefit.

disadvantaged *adj* deprived, underprivileged, poor, handicapped, impoverished, struggling.
≠ privileged.

disadvantageous *adj* harmful, detrimental, inopportune, unfavourable, prejudicial, adverse, damaging, hurtful, injurious, inconvenient, ill-timed.
≠ advantageous, auspicious.

disaffected *adj* disloyal, hostile, estranged, alienated, antagonistic, rebellious, dissatisfied, disgruntled, discontented.
≠ loyal.

disaffection *n* disloyalty, hostility, alienation, discontentment, resentment, ill-will, dissatisfaction, animosity, coolness, unfriendliness, antagonism, disharmony, discord, disagreement, aversion, dislike.
≠ loyalty, contentment.

disagree *v* **1** DISSENT, oppose, quarrel, argue, bicker, fall out (*infml*), wrangle, fight, squabble, contend, dispute, contest, object. **2** CONFLICT, clash, diverge, contradict, counter, differ, deviate, depart, run counter to, vary.
≠ **1** agree. **2** correspond.

disagreeable *adj* **1** *disagreeable old man*: bad-tempered, ill-humoured, difficult, peevish, rude, surly, churlish, irritable, contrary, cross, brusque. **2** *a disagreeable taste*: disgusting, offensive, repulsive, repellent, obnoxious, unsavoury, objectionable, nasty.
≠ **1** amiable, pleasant. **2** agreeable.

disagreement *n* **1** DISPUTE, argument, conflict, altercation (*fml*), quarrel, clash, dissent, falling-out, contention, strife, misunderstanding, squabble, tiff (*infml*), wrangle. **2** DIFFERENCE, variance, unlikeness, disparity, discrepancy, deviation, discord, dissimilarity, incompatibility, divergence, diversity, incongruity.
≠ **1** agreement, harmony. **2** similarity.

disappear *v* **1** VANISH, wane, recede, fade, evaporate, dissolve, ebb. **2** GO, depart, withdraw, retire, flee, fly, escape, scarper (*infml*), hide. **3** END, expire, perish, pass.
≠ **1** appear. **3** emerge.

disappearance *n* vanishing, fading, evaporation, departure, loss, going, passing, melting, desertion, flight.
≠ appearance, manifestation.

disappoint *v* fail, dissatisfy, let down, disillusion, dash, dismay, disenchant, sadden, thwart, vex, frustrate, foil, dishearten, disgruntle, disconcert, hamper, hinder, deceive, defeat, delude.
≠ satisfy, please, delight.

disappointed *adj* let down, frustrated, thwarted, disillusioned, dissatisfied, miffed (*infml*), upset, discouraged, disgruntled, disheartened, distressed, down-hearted, saddened, despondent, depressed.
≠ pleased, satisfied.

disappointment *n* **1** FRUSTRATION, dissatisfaction, failure, disenchantment,

disillusionment, displeasure, discouragement, distress, regret. **2** FAILURE, let-down, setback, comedown, blow, misfortune, fiasco, disaster, calamity, washout (*infml*), damp squib (*infml*), swiz (*infml*), swizzle (*infml*).
≠ **1** pleasure, satisfaction, delight. **2** success.

disapproval *n* censure, disapprobation (*fml*), condemnation, criticism, displeasure, reproach, objection, dissatisfaction, denunciation, dislike.
≠ approbation (*fml*), approval.

disapprove of censure, condemn, blame, take exception to, object to, deplore, denounce, disparage, dislike, reject, spurn.
≠ approve of.

disarm *v* **1** DISABLE, unarm, demilitarize, demobilize, deactivate, disband. **2** APPEASE, conciliate, in over, mollify, persuade.
≠ **1** arm.

disarray *n* disorder, confusion, chaos, mess, muddle, shambles (*infml*), disorganization, clutter, untidiness, unruliness, jumble, indiscipline, tangle, upset.
≠ order.

disaster *n* calamity, catastrophe, misfortune, reverse, tragedy, blow, accident, act of God, cataclysm, debacle, mishap, failure, flop (*infml*), fiasco, ruin, stroke, trouble, mischance, ruination.
≠ success, triumph.

disastrous *adj* calamitous, catastrophic, cataclysmic, devastating, ruinous, tragic, unfortunate, dreadful, dire, terrible, destructive, ill-fated, fatal, miserable.
≠ successful, auspicious.

disband *v* disperse, break up, scatter, dismiss, demobilize, part company, separate, dissolve.
≠ assemble, muster.

disbelief *n* unbelief, incredulity, doubt, scepticism, suspicion, distrust, mistrust, rejection.
≠ belief.

disbelieve *v* discount, discredit, repudiate, reject, mistrust, suspect.
≠ believe, trust.

disc *n* **1** CIRCLE, face, plate, ring. **2** RECORD, album, LP, CD. **3** DISK, diskette, hard disk, floppy disk, CD-ROM.

discard *v* reject, abandon, dispose of, get rid of, jettison, dispense with, cast aside, ditch (*infml*), dump (*infml*), drop, scrap, shed, remove, relinquish.
≠ retain, adopt.

discern *v* **1** PERCEIVE, make out, observe, detect, recognize, see, ascertain, notice, determine, discover, descry. **2** DISCRIMINATE, distinguish, differentiate, judge.

discernible *adj* perceptible, noticeable, detectable, appreciable, distinct, observable, recognizable, visible, apparent, clear, obvious, plain, patent, manifest, discoverable.
≠ imperceptible.

discerning *adj* discriminating, perceptive, astute, clear-sighted, sensitive, shrewd, wise, sharp, subtle, sagacious, penetrating, acute, piercing, critical, eagle-eyed.
≠ dull, obtuse.

discharge *v* **1** LIBERATE, free, pardon, release, clear, absolve, exonerate, acquit, relieve, dismiss. **2** EXECUTE, carry out, perform, fulfil, dispense. **3** FIRE, shoot, let off, detonate, explode. **4** EMIT, sack (*infml*), remove, fire (*infml*), expel, oust, eject.
≠ **1** detain. **2** neglect. **4** appoint.
n **1** LIBERATION, release, acquittal, exoneration. **2** EMISSION, secretion, ejection. **3** EXECUTION, accomplishment, fulfilment.
≠ **1** confinement, detention. **2** absorption. **3** neglect.

disciple *n* follower, convert, proselyte, adherent, believer, devotee, supporter, learner, pupil, student.

disciplinarian *n* authoritarian, taskmaster, autocrat, stickler, despot, tyrant.

discipline *n* **1** TRAINING, exercise, drill, practice. **2** PUNISHMENT, chastisement, correction. **3** STRICTNESS, restraint, regulation,

self-control, orderliness.
≠ **3** indiscipline.
v **1** TRAIN, instruct, drill, educate, exercise, break in. **2** CHECK, control, correct, restrain, govern. **3** PUNISH, chastise, chasten, penalize, reprimand, castigate.

disclaim *v* deny, disown, repudiate, abandon, renounce, reject, abjure (*fml*).
≠ accept, confess.

disclose *v* **1** DIVULGE, make known, reveal, tell, confess, let slip, relate, publish, communicate, impart, leak (*infml*). **2** EXPOSE, reveal, uncover, lay bare, unveil, discover.
≠ conceal.

disclosure *n* divulgence, exposure, exposé, revelation, uncovering, publication, leak (*infml*), discovery, admission, acknowledgement, announcement, declaration.

discomfort *n* ache, pain, uneasiness, malaise, trouble, distress, disquiet, hardship, vexation, irritation, annoyance.
≠ comfort, ease.

disconcerting *adj* disturbing, confusing, upsetting, unnerving, alarming, bewildering, off-putting (*infml*), distracting, embarrassing, awkward, baffling, perplexing, dismaying, bothersome.

disconnect *v* cut off, disengage, uncouple, sever, separate, detach, unplug, unhook, part, divide.
≠ attach, connect.

disconnected *adj* confused, incoherent, rambling, unco-ordinated, unintelligible, loose, irrational, disjointed, illogical, jumbled.
≠ coherent, connected.

disconsolate *adj* desolate, dejected, dispirited, sad, melancholy, unhappy, wretched, miserable, gloomy, forlorn, inconsolable, crushed, heavy-hearted, hopeless.
≠ cheerful, joyful.

discontent *n* uneasiness, dissatisfaction, disquiet, restlessness, fretfulness, unrest, impatience, vexation, regret.
≠ content.

discontented *adj* dissatisfied, fed up (*infml*), disgruntled, unhappy, browned off (*infml*), cheesed off (*infml*), disaffected, miserable, exasperated, complaining.
≠ contented, satisfied.

discontinue *v* stop, end, finish, cease, break off, terminate, halt, drop, suspend, abandon, cancel, interrupt.
≠ continue.

discord *n* **1** DISSENSION, disagreement, discordance, clashing, disunity, incompatibility, conflict, difference, dispute, contention, friction, division, opposition, strife, split, wrangling. **2** DISSONANCE, disharmony, cacophony (*fml*), jangle, jarring, harshness.
≠ **1** concord, agreement. **2** harmony.

discordant *adj* **1** DISAGREEING, conflicting, at odds, clashing, contradictory, incongruous, incompatible, inconsistent. **2** DISSONANT, cacophonous (*fml*), grating, jangling, jarring, harsh.
≠ **1** harmonious. **2** harmonious.

discount[1] *v* **1** DISREGARD, ignore, overlook, disbelieve, gloss over. **2** REDUCE, deduct, mark down, knock off (*infml*).

discount[2] *n* reduction, rebate, allowance, cut, concession, deduction, mark-down.

discourage *v* **1** DISHEARTEN, dampen, dispirit, depress, demoralize, dismay, unnerve, deject, disappoint. **2** DETER, dissuade, hinder, put off, restrain, prevent.
≠ **1** hearten. **2** encourage.

discouragement *n* **1** DOWNHEARTEDNESS, despondency, pessimism, dismay, depression, dejection, despair, disappointment. **2** DETERRENT, damper, setback, impediment, obstacle, opposition, hindrance, restraint, rebuff.
≠ **1** encouragement. **2** incentive.

discourse *n* **1** CONVERSATION, dialogue, chat, communication, talk, converse, discussion. **2** SPEECH, address, oration (*fml*), lecture, sermon, essay, treatise, dissertation, homily. *v* converse, talk, discuss, debate, confer, lecture.

discourteous *adj* rude, bad-mannered, ill-mannered, impolite, boorish, disrespectful, ill-bred, uncivil, unceremonious, insolent, offhand, curt, brusque, abrupt.
≠ courteous, polite.

discover *v* **1** FIND, uncover, unearth, dig up, disclose, reveal, light on, locate. **2** ASCERTAIN, determine, realize, notice, recognize, perceive, see, find out, spot, discern, learn, detect. **3** ORIGINATE, invent, pioneer.
≠ **1** miss. **2** conceal, cover (up).

discovery *n* **1** BREAKTHROUGH, find, origination, introduction, innovation, invention, exploration. **2** DISCLOSURE, detection, revelation, location.

discredit *v* **1** DISBELIEVE, distrust, doubt, question, mistrust, challenge. **2** DISPARAGE, dishonour, degrade, defame, disgrace, slander, slur, smear, reproach, vilify.
≠ **1** believe. **2** honour.
n **1** DISBELIEF, distrust, doubt, mistrust, scepticism, suspicion. **2** DISHONOUR, disrepute, censure, aspersion, disgrace, blame, shame, reproach, slur, smear, scandal.
≠ **1** belief. **2** credit.

discreditable *adj* dishonourable, disreputable, disgraceful, reprehensible, scandalous, blameworthy, shameful, infamous, degrading, improper.
≠ creditable.

discreet *adj* tactful, careful, diplomatic, politic, prudent, cautious, delicate, judicious, reserved, wary, sensible.
≠ tactless, indiscreet.

discrepancy *n* difference, disparity, variance, variation, inconsistency, dissimilarity, discordance, divergence, disagreement, conflict, inequality.

discretion *n* **1** TACT, diplomacy, judiciousness, caution, prudence, wisdom, circumspection, discernment, judgement, care, carefulness, consideration, wariness. **2** CHOICE, freedom, preference, will, wish.
≠ **1** indiscretion.

discriminate *v* distinguish, differentiate, discern, tell apart, make a distinction, segregate, separate.
≠ confuse, confound.
discriminate (against) be prejudiced, be biased, victimize.

discriminating *adj* discerning, fastidious, selective, critical, perceptive, particular, tasteful, astute, sensitive, cultivated.

discrimination *n* **1** BIAS, prejudice, intolerance, unfairness, bigotry, favouritism, inequity, racism, sexism. **2** DISCERNMENT, judgement, acumen, perception, acuteness, insight, penetration, subtlety, keenness, refinement, taste.

discursive *adj* rambling, digressing, wandering, long-winded, meandering, wide-ranging, circuitous.
≠ terse.

discuss *v* debate, talk about, confer, argue, consider, deliberate, converse, consult, examine.

discussion *n* debate, conference, argument, conversation, dialogue, exchange, consultation, discourse, deliberation, consideration, analysis, review, examination, scrutiny, seminar, symposium.

disdain *n* scorn, contempt, arrogance, haughtiness, derision, sneering, dislike, snobbishness.
≠ admiration, respect.

disdainful *adj* scornful, contemptuous, derisive, haughty, aloof, arrogant, supercilious, sneering, superior, proud, insolent.
≠ respectful.

disease *n* illness, sickness, ill-health, infirmity, complaint, disorder, ailment, indisposition, malady, condition, affliction, infection, epidemic.
≠ health.

Diseases and disorders include: Addison's disease, AIDS, alopecia, Alzheimer's disease, anaemia, angina, anorexia nervosa, anthrax, arthritis, asbestosis, asthma, athlete's foot, autism, Bell's Palsy, beriberi,

Black Death, botulism, Bright's disease, bronchitis, brucellosis, bubonic plague, bulimia, cancer, cerebral palsy, chickenpox, cholera, cirrhosis, coeliac disease, common cold, consumption, croup, cystic fibrosis, diabetes, diptheria, dropsy, dysentery, eclampsia, emphysema, encephalitis, endometriosis, enteritis, farmer's lung, flu (*infml*), foot-and-mouth disease, gangrene, German measles, gingivitis, glandular fever, glaucoma, gonorrhoea, haemophilia, herpes, hepatitis, Hodgkin's disease, Huntington's chorea, hydrophobia, impetigo, influenza, Lassa fever, Legionnaires' disease, leprosy, leukaemia, lockjaw, malaria, mastoiditis, measles, meningitis, motor neurone disease, multiple sclerosis (MS), mumps, muscular dystrophy, myalgic encephalomyelitis (ME), nephritis, osteomyelitis, osteoporosis, Paget's disease, Parkinson's disease, peritonitis, pneumonia, poliomyelitis, psittacosis, psoriasis, pyorrhoea, rabies, rheumatic fever, rheumatoid arthritis, rickets, ringworm, rubella, scabies, scarlet fever, schistosomiasis, schizophrenia, scurvy, septicaemia, shingles, silicosis, smallpox, syphilis, tapeworm, tetanus, thrombosis, thrush, tinnitus, tuberculosis (TB), typhoid, typhus, vertigo, whooping cough, yellow fever.

diseased *adj* sick, ill, unhealthy, ailing, unsound, contaminated, infected.
≠ healthy.

disembark *v* land, arrive, alight, debark.
≠ embark.

disembodied *adj* bodiless, incorporeal (*fml*), ghostly, phantom, spiritual, immaterial, intangible.

disengage *v* disconnect, detach, loosen, free, extricate, undo, release, liberate, separate, disentangle, untie, withdraw.
≠ connect, engage.

disentangle *v* **1** LOOSE, free, extricate, disconnect, untangle, disengage, detach, unravel, separate, unfold. **2** RESOLVE, clarify, simplify.
≠ **1** entangle.

disfigure *v* deface, blemish, mutilate, scar, mar, deform, distort, damage, spoil.
≠ adorn, embellish.

disgrace *n* shame, ignominy, disrepute, dishonour, disfavour, humiliation, defamation, discredit, scandal, reproach, slur, stain.
≠ honour, esteem.
v shame, dishonour, abase, defame, humiliate, disfavour, stain, discredit, reproach, slur, sully, taint, stigmatize.
≠ honour, respect.

disgraceful *adj* shameful, dishonourable, disreputable, ignominious, scandalous, shocking, unworthy, dreadful, appalling.
≠ honourable, respectable.

disguise *v* **1** CONCEAL, cover, camouflage, mask, hide, dress up, cloak, screen, veil, shroud. **2** FALSIFY, deceive, dissemble, misrepresent, fake, fudge.
≠ **1** reveal, expose.
n concealment, camouflage, cloak, cover, costume, mask, front, façade, masquerade, deception, pretence, travesty, screen, veil.

disgust *v* offend, displease, nauseate, revolt, sicken, repel, outrage, put off.
≠ delight, please.
n revulsion, repulsion, repugnance, distaste, aversion, abhorrence, nausea, loathing, detestation, hatred.

disgusted *adj* repelled, repulsed, revolted, offended, appalled, outraged.
≠ attracted, delighted.

disgusting *adj* repugnant, repellent, revolting, offensive, sickening, nauseating, odious, foul, unappetizing, unpleasant, vile, obscene, abominable, detestable, objectionable, nasty.
≠ delightful, pleasant.

dish *n* plate, bowl, platter, food, recipe.
dish out distribute, give out, hand out, hand round, dole out, allocate, mete out, inflict.
dish up serve, present, ladle, spoon, dispense, scoop.

dishearten *v* discourage, dispirit, dampen, cast down, depress, dismay, dash, disappoint, deject, daunt, crush, deter.
≠ encourage, hearten.

dishevelled *adj* tousled, unkempt, uncombed, untidy, bedraggled, messy, ruffled, slovenly, disordered.
≠ neat, tidy.

dishonest *adj* untruthful, fraudulent, deceitful, false, lying, deceptive, double-dealing, cheating, crooked (*infml*), treacherous, unprincipled, swindling, shady (*infml*), corrupt, disreputable.
≠ honest, trustworthy, scrupulous.

dishonesty *n* deceit, falsehood, falsity, fraudulence, fraud, criminality, insincerity, treachery, cheating, crookedness (*infml*), corruption, unscrupulousness, trickery.
≠ honesty, truthfulness.

dishonour *v* disgrace, shame, humiliate, debase, defile, degrade, defame, discredit, demean, debauch.
≠ honour.
n disgrace, abasement, humiliation, shame, degradation, discredit, disrepute, indignity, ignominy, reproach, slight, slur, scandal, insult, disfavour, outrage, aspersion, abuse, discourtesy.
≠ honour.

disillusioned *adj* disenchanted, disabused, undeceived, disappointed.

disinclined *adj* averse, reluctant, resistant, indisposed, loath, opposed, hesitant.
≠ inclined, willing.

disinfect *v* sterilize, fumigate, sanitize, decontaminate, cleanse, purify, purge, clean.
≠ contaminate, infect.

disinfectant *n* sterilizer, antiseptic, sanitizer.

disintegrate *v* break up, decompose, fall apart, crumble, rot, moulder, separate, splinter.

disinterest *n* disinterestedness, impartiality, neutrality, detachment, unbiasedness, dispassionateness, fairness.

disinterested *adj* unbiased, neutral, impartial, unprejudiced, dispassionate, detached, uninvolved, open-minded, equitable, even-handed, unselfish.
≠ biased, concerned.

disjointed *adj* **1** DISCONNECTED, dislocated, divided, separated, disunited, displaced, broken, fitful, split, disarticulated. **2** INCOHERENT, aimless, confused, disordered, loose, unconnected, bitty, rambling, spasmodic.
≠ **2** coherent.

dislike *n* aversion, hatred, repugnance, hostility, distaste, disinclination, disapproval, disapprobation, displeasure, animosity, antagonism, enmity, detestation, disgust, loathing.
≠ liking, predilection.
v hate, detest, object to, loathe, abhor, abominate, disapprove, shun, despise, scorn.
≠ like, favour.

dislocate *v* disjoint, displace, misplace, disengage, put out (*infml*), disorder, shift, disconnect, disrupt, disunite.

dislodge *v* displace, eject, remove, oust, extricate, shift, move, uproot.

disloyal *adj* treacherous, faithless, false, traitorous, two-faced (*infml*), unfaithful, apostate, unpatriotic.
≠ loyal, trustworthy.

dismal *adj* dreary, gloomy, depressing, bleak, cheerless, dull, drab, low-spirited, melancholy, sad, sombre, lugubrious, forlorn, despondent, dark, sorrowful, long-faced (*infml*), hopeless, discouraging.
≠ cheerful, bright.

dismantle *v* demolish, take apart, disassemble, strip.
≠ assemble, put together.

dismay *v* alarm, daunt, frighten, unnerve, unsettle, scare, put off, dispirit, distress, disconcert, dishearten, discourage, disillusion, depress, horrify, disappoint.
≠ encourage, hearten.
n consternation, alarm, distress, apprehension, agitation, dread, fear, trepidation, fright, horror, terror,

discouragement, disappointment.
≠ boldness, encouragement.

dismember *v* disjoint, amputate, dissect, dislocate, divide, mutilate, sever.
≠ assemble, join.

dismiss *v* **1** *the class was dismissed*: discharge, free, let go, release, send away, remove, drop, discord, banish. **2** *dismiss employees*: sack (*infml*), make redundant, lay off, fire (*infml*), relegate. **3** *dismiss it from your mind*: discount, disregard, reject, repudiate, set aside, shelve, spurn.
≠ **1** retain. **2** appoint. **3** accept.

disobey *v* contravene, infringe, violate, transgress, flout, disregard, defy, ignore, resist, rebel.
≠ obey.

disorder *n* **1** CONFUSION, chaos, muddle, disarray, mess, untidiness, shambles (*infml*), clutter, disorganization, jumble. **2** DISTURBANCE, tumult, riot, confusion, commotion, uproar, fracas, brawl, fight, clamour, quarrel. **3** ILLNESS, complaint, disease, sickness, disability, ailment, malady, affliction.
≠ **1** neatness, order. **2** law and order, peace.
v disturb, mess up, disarrange, mix up, muddle, upset, disorganize, confuse, confound, clutter, jumble, discompose, scatter, unsettle.
≠ arrange, organize.

disorderly *adj* **1** DISORGANIZED, confused, chaotic, irregular, messy, untidy. **2** UNRULY, undisciplined, unmanageable, obstreperous, rowdy, turbulent, rebellious, lawless.
≠ **1** neat, tidy. **2** well-behaved.

disorganize *v* disorder, disrupt, disturb, disarrange, muddle, upset, confuse, discompose, jumble, play havoc with, unsettle, break up, destroy.
≠ organize.

disown *v* repudiate, renounce, disclaim, deny, cast off, disallow, reject, abandon.
≠ accept, acknowledge.

disparaging *adj* derisive, derogatory, mocking, scornful, critical, insulting, snide (*infml*).
≠ flattering, praising.

dispassionate *adj* detached, objective, impartial, neutral, disinterested, impersonal, fair, cool, calm, composed.
≠ biased, emotional.

dispatch, despatch *v* **1** SEND, express, transmit, forward, consign, expedite, accelerate. **2** DISPOSE OF, finish, perform, discharge, conclude. **3** KILL, murder, execute.
≠ **1** receive.
n **1** COMMUNICATION, message, report, bulletin, communiqué, news, letter, account. **2** PROMPTNESS, speed, alacrity, expedition, celerity, haste, rapidity, swiftness.
≠ **2** slowness.

dispense *v* **1** DISTRIBUTE, give out, apportion, allot, allocate, assign, share, mete out. **2** ADMINISTER, apply, implement, enforce, discharge, execute, operate.
dispense with dispose of, get rid of, abolish, discard, omit, disregard, cancel, forgo, ignore, waive.

disperse *v* scatter, dispel, spread, distribute, diffuse, dissolve, break up, dismiss, separate.
≠ gather.

displace *v* **1** DISLODGE, move, shift, misplace, disturb, dislocate. **2** DEPOSE, oust, remove, replace, dismiss, discharge, supplant, eject, evict, succeed, supersede.

display *v* **1** SHOW, present, demonstrate, exhibit. **2** BETRAY, disclose, reveal, show, expose. **3** SHOW OFF, flourish, parade, flaunt.
≠ **1** conceal. **2** disguise.
n show, exhibition, demonstration, presentation, parade, spectacle, revelation.

displease *v* offend, annoy, irritate, anger, upset, put out (*infml*), infuriate, exasperate, incense.
≠ please.

displeasure *n* offence, annoyance, disapproval, irritation, resentment, disfavour, anger, indignation, wrath.
≠ pleasure.

disposal *n* **1** ARRANGEMENT, grouping, order. **2** CONTROL, direction, command. **3** REMOVAL, riddance, discarding, jettisoning.

dispose of **1** DEAL WITH, decide, settle. **2** GET RID OF, discard, scrap, destroy, dump (*infml*), jettison.
≠ **2** keep.

disposed *adj* liable, inclined, predisposed, prone, likely, apt, minded, subject, ready, willing.
≠ disinclined.

disposition *n* character, nature, temperament, inclination, make-up, bent, leaning, predisposition, constitution, habit, spirit, tendency, proneness.

disproportionate *adj* unequal, uneven, incommensurate, excessive, unreasonable.
≠ balanced.

disprove *v* refute, rebut, confute, discredit, invalidate, contradict, expose.
≠ confirm, prove.

dispute *v* argue, debate, question, contend, challenge, discuss, doubt, contest, contradict, deny, quarrel, clash, wrangle, squabble.
≠ agree.
n argument, debate, disagreement, controversy, conflict, contention, quarrel, wrangle, feud, strife, squabble.
≠ agreement, settlement.

disqualify *v* **1** INCAPACITATE, disable, invalidate. **2** DEBAR, preclude, rule out, disentitle, eliminate, prohibit.
≠ **2** qualify, accept.

disquiet *n* anxiety, worry, concern, nervousness, uneasiness, restlessness, alarm, distress, fretfulness, fear, disturbance, trouble.
≠ calm, reassurance.

disregard *v* **1** IGNORE, overlook, discount, neglect, pass over, disobey, make light of, turn a blind eye to (*infml*), brush aside. **2** SLIGHT, snub, despise, disdain, disparage.
≠ **1** heed, pay attention to. **2** respect.
n neglect, negligence, inattention, oversight, indifference, disrespect, contempt, disdain, brush-off (*infml*).
≠ attention, heed.

disrepair *n* dilapidation, deterioration, decay, collapse, ruin, shabbiness.
≠ good repair.

disreputable *adj* **1** DISGRACEFUL, discreditable, dishonourable, unrespectable, notorious, scandalous, shameful, shady, base, contemptible, low, mean, shocking. **2** SCRUFFY, shabby, seedy, unkempt.
≠ **1** respectable. **2** smart.

disrespectful *adj* rude, discourteous, impertinent, impolite, impudent, insolent, uncivil, unmannerly, cheeky, insulting, irreverent, contemptuous.
≠ polite, respectful.

disrupt *v* disturb, disorganize, confuse, interrupt, break up, unsettle, intrude, upset.

dissatisfaction *n* discontent, displeasure, dislike, discomfort, disappointment, frustration, annoyance, irritation, exasperation, regret, resentment.
≠ satisfaction.

dissect *v* **1** DISMEMBER, anatomize. **2** ANALYSE, investigate, scrutinize, examine, inspect, pore over.

dissension *n* disagreement, discord, dissent, dispute, contention, conflict, strife, friction, quarrel.
≠ agreement.

dissent *v* disagree, differ, protest, object, refuse, quibble.
≠ assent.
n disagreement, difference, dissension, discord, resistance, opposition, objection.
≠ agreement, conformity.

disservice *n* disfavour, injury, wrong, bad turn, harm, unkindness, injustice.
≠ favour.

dissident *adj* disagreeing, differing, dissenting, discordant, nonconformist, heterodox (*fml*).
≠ acquiescent, orthodox.
n dissenter, protestor, nonconformist, rebel, agitator, revolutionary, schismatic, recusant.
≠ assenter.

dissimilar *adj* unlike, different, divergent, disparate, unrelated,

incompatible, mismatched, diverse, various, heterogeneous.
≠ similar, like.

dissipate *v* **1** *he dissipated his inheritance*: spend, waste, squander, expend, consume, deplete, fritter away, burn up. **2** *the clouds dissipated*: disperse, vanish, disappear, dispel, diffuse, evaporate, dissolve.
≠ **1** accumulate. **2** appear.

dissociate *v* separate, detach, break off, disunite, disengage, disconnect, cut off, disband, divorce, disrupt, isolate, segregate.
≠ associate, join.

dissolute *adj* dissipated, debauched, degenerate, depraved, wanton, abandoned, corrupt, immoral, licentious, lewd, wild.
≠ restrained, virtuous.

dissolution *n* **1** DISINTEGRATION, decomposition, separation, resolution, division. **2** ENDING, termination, conclusion, finish, discontinuation, divorce, dismissal, dispersal, destruction, overthrow. **3** EVAPORATION, disappearance.

dissolve *v* **1** EVAPORATE, disintegrate, liquefy, melt. **2** DECOMPOSE, disintegrate, disperse, break up, disappear, crumble. **3** END, terminate, separate, sever, divorce.

dissuade *v* deter, discourage, put off, disincline.
≠ persuade.

distance *n* **1** SPACE, interval, gap, extent, range, reach, length, width. **2** ALOOFNESS, reserve, coolness, coldness, remoteness.
≠ **1** closeness. **2** approachability.

distant *adj* **1** FAR, faraway, far-flung, out-of-the-way, remote, outlying, abroad, dispersed. **2** ALOOF, cool, reserved, stand-offish (*infml*), formal, cold, restrained, stiff.
≠ **1** close. **2** approachable.

distaste *n* dislike, aversion, repugnance, disgust, revulsion, loathing, abhorrence.
≠ liking.

distasteful *adj* disagreeable, offensive, unpleasant, objectionable, repulsive, obnoxious, repugnant, unsavoury, loathsome, abhorrent.
≠ pleasing.

distinct *adj* **1** SEPARATE, different, detached, individual, dissimilar. **2** CLEAR, plain, evident, obvious, apparent, marked, definite, noticeable, recognizable.
≠ **2** indistinct, vague.

distinction *n* **1** DIFFERENTIATION, discrimination, discernment, separation, difference, dissimilarity, contrast. **2** CHARACTERISTIC, peculiarity, individuality, feature, quality, mark. **3** RENOWN, fame, celebrity, prominence, eminence, importance, reputation, greatness, honour, prestige, repute, superiority, worth, merit, excellence, quality.
≠ **3** unimportance, obscurity.

distinctive *adj* characteristic, distinguishing, individual, peculiar, different, unique, singular, special, original, extraordinary, idiosyncratic.
≠ ordinary, common.

distinguish *v* **1** DIFFERENTIATE, tell apart, discriminate, determine, categorize, characterize, classify. **2** DISCERN, perceive, identify, ascertain, make out, recognize, see, discriminate.

distinguished *adj* famous, eminent, celebrated, well-known, acclaimed, illustrious, notable, noted, renowned, famed, honoured, outstanding, striking, marked, extraordinary, conspicuous.
≠ insignificant, obscure, unimpressive.

distort *v* **1** DEFORM, contort, bend, misshape, disfigure, twist, warp. **2** FALSIFY, misrepresent, pervert, slant, colour, garble.

distract *v* **1** DIVERT, sidetrack, deflect. **2** CONFUSE, disconcert, bewilder, confound, disturb, perplex, puzzle. **3** AMUSE, occupy, divert, engross.

distraught *adj* agitated, anxious, overwrought, upset, distressed, distracted, beside oneself, worked up, frantic, hysterical, raving, mad, wild, crazy.
≠ calm, untroubled.

distress *n* **1** ANGUISH, grief, misery, sorrow, heartache, affliction, suffering, torment, wretchedness, sadness, worry, anxiety, desolation, pain, agony. **2** ADVERSITY, hardship, poverty, need, privation, destitution, misfortune, trouble, difficulties, trial.
≠ **1** content. **2** comfort, ease.
v upset, afflict, grieve, disturb, trouble, sadden, worry, torment, harass, harrow, pain, agonize, bother.
≠ comfort.

distribute *v* **1** DISPENSE, allocate, dole out, dish out, share, deal, divide, apportion. **2** DELIVER, hand out, spread, issue, circulate, diffuse, disperse, scatter.
≠ **2** collect.

distribution *n* **1** ALLOCATION, apportionment, division, sharing. **2** CIRCULATION, spreading, scattering, delivery, dissemination, supply, dealing, handling. **3** ARRANGEMENT, grouping, classification, organization.
≠ **2** collection.

district *n* region, area, quarter, neighbourhood, locality, sector, precinct, parish, locale, community, vicinity, ward.

distrust *v* mistrust, doubt, disbelieve, suspect, question.
≠ trust.
n mistrust, doubt, disbelief, suspicion, misgiving, wariness, scepticism, question, qualm.
≠ trust.

disturb *v* **1** DISRUPT, interrupt, distract. **2** AGITATE, unsettle, upset, distress, worry, fluster, annoy, bother. **3** DISARRANGE, disorder, confuse, upset.
≠ **2** reassure. **3** order.

disturbance *n* **1** DISRUPTION, agitation, interruption, intrusion, upheaval, upset, confusion, annoyance, bother, trouble, hindrance. **2** DISORDER, uproar, commotion, tumult, turmoil, fracas, fray, brawl, riot.
≠ **1** peace. **2** order.

disuse *n* neglect, desuetude (*fml*), abandonment, discontinuance, decay.
≠ use.

ditch *n* trench, dyke, channel, gully, furrow, moat, drain, level, watercourse.

dither *v* hesitate, shilly-shally (*infml*), waver, vacillate.

dive *v* plunge, plummet, dip, submerge, jump, leap, nose-dive, fall, drop, swoop, descend, pitch.
n **1** PLUNGE, lunge, header, jump, leap, nose-dive, swoop, dash, spring. **2** (*infml*) BAR, club, saloon.

diverge *v* **1** DIVIDE, branch, fork, separate, spread, split. **2** DEVIATE, digress, stray, wander. **3** DIFFER, vary, disagree, dissent, conflict.
≠ **1** converge. **3** agree.

diverse *adj* various, varied, varying, sundry, different, differing, assorted, dissimilar, miscellaneous, discrete, separate, several, distinct.
≠ similar, identical.

diversify *v* vary, change, expand, branch out, spread out, alter, mix, assort.

diversion *n* **1** DEVIATION, detour. **2** AMUSEMENT, entertainment, distraction, pastime, recreation, relaxation, play, game. **3** ALTERATION, change.

diversity *n* variety, dissimilarity, difference, variance, assortment, range, medley.
≠ similarity, likeness.

divert *v* **1** DEFLECT, redirect, reroute, side-track, avert, distract, switch. **2** AMUSE, entertain, occupy, distract, interest.

divide *v* **1** SPLIT, separate, part, cut, break up, detach, bisect, disconnect. **2** DISTRIBUTE, share, allocate, deal out, allot, apportion. **3** DISUNITE, separate, estrange, alienate. **4** CLASSIFY, group, sort, grade, segregate.
≠ **1** join. **2** collect. **3** unite.

divine *adj* **1** GODLIKE, superhuman, supernatural, celestial, heavenly, angelic, spiritual. **2** HOLY, sacred, sanctified, consecrated, transcendent, exalted, glorious, religious, supreme.
≠ **1** human. **2** mundane.

divinity *n* god, goddess, deity,

godliness, holiness, sanctity, godhead, spirit.

division *n* **1** SEPARATION, detaching, parting, cutting, disunion. **2** BREACH, rupture, split, schism, disunion, estrangement, disagreement, feud. **3** DISTRIBUTION, sharing, allotment, apportionment. **4** SECTION, sector, segment, part, department, category, class, compartment, branch.
≠ **1** union. **2** unity. **3** collection. **4** whole.

divorce *n* dissolution, annulment, break-up, split-up, rupture, separation, breach, disunion.
v separate, part, annul, split up, sever, dissolve, divide, dissociate.
≠ marry, unite.

divulge *v* disclose, reveal, communicate, tell, leak (*infml*), impart, confess, betray, uncover, let slip, expose, publish, proclaim.

dizzy *adj* **1** GIDDY, faint, light-headed, woozy (*infml*), shaky, reeling. **2** CONFUSED, bewildered, dazed, muddled.

do *v* **1** PERFORM, carry out, execute, accomplish, achieve, fulfil, implement, complete, undertake, work, put on, present, conclude, end, finish. **2** BEHAVE, act, conduct oneself. **3** FIX, prepare, organize, arrange, deal with, look after, manage, produce, make, create, cause, proceed. **4** SUFFICE, satisfy, serve.
n (*infml*) function, affair, event, gathering, party, occasion.
do away with get rid of, dispose of, exterminate, eliminate, abolish, discontinue, remove, destroy, discard, kill, murder.
do up 1 FASTEN, tie, lace, pack. **2** RENOVATE, restore, decorate, redecorate, modernize, repair.
do without dispense with, abstain from, forgo, give up, relinquish.

docile *adj* tractable, co-operative, manageable, submissive, obedient, amenable, controlled, obliging.
≠ truculent, unco-operative.

dock[1] *n* harbour, wharf, quay, boat-yard, pier, waterfront, marina.
v anchor, moor, drop anchor, land, berth, put in, tie up.

dock[2] *v* crop, clip, cut, shorten, curtail, deduct, reduce, lessen, withhold, decrease, subtract, diminish.

doctor *n* physician, medic (*infml*), medical officer, consultant, clinician.

> *Types of medical doctor include*: general practitioner (GP), family doctor, family practitioner, locum, hospital doctor, houseman, intern, resident, registrar, consultant, medical officer (MO), doc (*infml*), bones (*infml*), quack (*infml*), dentist, veterinary surgeon, vet (*infml*). *see also* **medical specialists**; **surgeon**.

v **1** ALTER, tamper with, falsify, misrepresent, pervert, adulterate, change, disguise, dilute. **2** REPAIR, fix, patch up.

doctrine *n* dogma, creed, belief, tenet, principle, teaching, precept, conviction, opinion, canon.

document *n* paper, certificate, deed, record, report, form, instrument (*infml*).
v **1** RECORD, report, chronicle, list, detail, cite. **2** SUPPORT, prove, corroborate, verify.

dodge *v* avoid, elude, evade, swerve, side-step, shirk, shift.
n trick, ruse, ploy, wile, scheme, stratagem, machination, manoeuvre.

dog *n* hound, cur, mongrel, canine, puppy, pup, bitch, mutt (*infml*), pooch (*infml*).

> *Breeds of dog include*: Afghan hound, alsatian, basset-hound, beagle, Border collie, borzoi, bull-mastiff, bulldog, bull-terrier, cairn terrier, chihuahua, chow, cocker spaniel, collie, corgi, dachshund, Dalmatian, Doberman pinscher, foxhound, fox-terrier, German Shepherd, golden retriever, Great Dane, greyhound, husky, Irish wolfhound, Jack Russell, King Charles spaniel, Labrador, lhasa apso, lurcher, Maltese, Old English sheepdog, Pekingese, pit bull terrier, pointer, poodle, pug, Rottweiler, saluki, sausage-dog (*infml*),

schnauzer, Scottie (*infml*), Scottish-terrier, Sealyham, setter, sheltie, shih tzu, springer spaniel, St Bernard, terrier, whippet, West Highland terrier, Westie (*infml*), wolf-hound, Yorkshire terrier.

v pursue, follow, trail, track, tail, hound, shadow, plague, harry, haunt, trouble, worry.

dogged *adj* determined, resolute, persistent, persevering, intent, tenacious, firm, steadfast, staunch, single-minded, indefatigable, steady, unshakable, stubborn, obstinate, relentless, unyielding.
≠ irresolute, apathetic.

dogma *n* doctrine, creed, belief, precept, principle, article (of faith), credo, tenet, conviction, teaching, opinion.

dogmatic *adj* opinionated, assertive, authoritative, positive, doctrinaire, dictatorial, doctrinal, categorical, emphatic, overbearing, arbitrary.

dole out *v* distribute, allocate, hand out, dish out, apportion, allot, mete out, share, divide, deal, issue, ration, dispense, administer, assign.

domain *n* **1** DOMINION, kingdom, realm, territory, region, empire, lands, province. **2** FIELD, area, speciality, concern, department, sphere, discipline, jurisdiction.

domestic *adj* **1** HOME, family, household, home-loving, stay-at-home, homely, house-trained, tame, pet, private. **2** INTERNAL, indigenous, native.
n servant, maid, charwoman, char, daily help, daily, au pair.

domestic appliances

Types of domestic appliance include: washing machine, washer, washer/drier, tumble-drier, clothes airer, iron, steam iron, steam press, trouser press; dishwasher, vacuum cleaner, upright cleaner, cylinder cleaner, wet-and-dry cleaner, Hoover®, floor polisher, carpet sweeper, carpet shampooer; oven, Aga®, barbecue, cooker, Dutch oven, electric cooker, fan oven, gas stove, kitchen range, microwave oven, stove, hob, hotplate, grill, electric grill, griddle, rotisserie, spit, waffle iron, deep fryer, slow cooker, sandwich maker, toaster; food processor, mixer, blender, liquidizer, ice-cream maker, juicer, juice extractor, food slicer, electric knife, knife sharpener, kettle, tea/coffee maker, percolator, coffee mill, electric tin opener, timer, water filter; refrigerator, fridge (*infml*), icebox, fridge/freezer, freezer, deep-freeze; hostess-trolley, humidifier, ionizer, fire extinguisher. *see also* **kitchen utensils**.

domesticate *v* tame, house-train, break, train, accustom, familiarize.

dominant *adj* **1** AUTHORITATIVE, controlling, governing, ruling, powerful, assertive, influential. **2** PRINCIPAL, main, outstanding, chief, important, predominant, primary, prominent, leading, pre-eminent, prevailing, prevalent, commanding.
≠ **1** submissive. **2** subordinate.

dominate *v* **1** CONTROL, domineer, govern, rule, direct, monopolize, master, lead, overrule, prevail, overbear, tyrannize. **2** OVERSHADOW, eclipse, dwarf.

domineering *adj* overbearing, authoritarian, imperious, autocratic, bossy (*infml*), dictatorial, despotic, masterful, high-handed, oppressive, tyrannical, arrogant.
≠ meek, servile.

dominion *n* **1** POWER, authority, domination, command, control, rule, sway, jurisdiction, government, lordship, mastery, supremacy, sovereignty. **2** DOMAIN, country, territory, province, colony, realm, kingdom, empire.

donate *v* give, contribute, present, bequeath, cough up (*infml*), fork out (*infml*), bestow (*fml*), confer (*fml*), subscribe.
≠ receive.

donation *n* gift, present, offering, grant, gratuity, largess(e), contribution, presentation, subscription, alms, benefaction (*fml*), bequest.

done *adj* 1 FINISHED, over, accomplished, completed, ended, concluded, settled, realized, executed. 2 CONVENTIONAL, acceptable, proper. 3 COOKED, ready.

donor *n* giver, donator, benefactor, contributor, philanthropist, provider, fairy godmother (*infml*).
≠ beneficiary.

doom *n* 1 FATE, fortune, destiny, portion, lot. 2 DESTRUCTION, catastrophe, downfall, ruin, death, death-knell. 3 CONDEMNATION, judgement, sentence, verdict.
v condemn, damn, consign, judge, sentence, destine.

doomed *adj* condemned, damned, fated, ill-fated, ill-omened, cursed, destined, hopeless, luckless, ill-starred.

door *n* opening, entrance, entry, exit, doorway, portal, hatch.

dope (*infml*) *n* 1 NARCOTIC, drugs, marijuana, cannabis, opiate, hallucinogen. 2 FOOL, dolt, idiot, half-wit (*infml*), dimwit (*infml*), dunce, simpleton, clot (*infml*), blockhead. 3 INFORMATION, facts, low-down (*infml*), details.
v drug, sedate, anaesthetize, stupefy, medicate, narcotize, inject, doctor.

dormant *adj* 1 INACTIVE, asleep, sleeping, inert, resting, slumbering, sluggish, torpid, hibernating, fallow, comatose. 2 LATENT, unrealized, potential, undeveloped, undisclosed.
≠ 1 active, awake. 2 realized, developed.

dose *n* measure, dosage, amount, portion, quantity, draught, potion, prescription, shot.
v medicate, administer, prescribe, dispense, treat.

dot *n* point, spot, speck, mark, fleck, circle, pin-point, atom, decimal point, full stop, iota, jot.
v spot, sprinkle, stud, dab, punctuate.

dote on adore, idolize, treasure, admire, indulge.

double *adj* dual, twofold, twice, duplicate, twin, paired, doubled, coupled.
≠ single, half.
v duplicate, enlarge, increase, repeat, multiply, fold, magnify.
n twin, duplicate, copy, clone, replica, doppelgänger, lookalike, spitting image (*infml*), ringer (*infml*), image, counterpart, impersonator.
at the double immediately, at once, quickly, without delay.

double-cross *v* cheat, swindle, defraud, trick, con (*infml*), hoodwink, betray, two-time (*infml*), mislead.

doubt *v* 1 DISTRUST, mistrust, query, question, suspect, fear. 2 BE UNCERTAIN, be dubious, hesitate, vacillate, waver.
≠ 1 believe, trust.
n 1 DISTRUST, suspicion, mistrust, scepticism, reservation, misgiving, incredulity, apprehension, hesitation. 2 UNCERTAINTY, difficulty, confusion, ambiguity, problem, indecision, perplexity, dilemma, quandary.
≠ 1 trust, faith. 2 certainty, belief.

doubtful *adj* 1 *doubtful about his future*: uncertain, unsure, undecided, suspicious, irresolute, wavering, hesitant, vacillating, tentative, sceptical. 2 *writing of doubtful origin*: dubious, questionable, unclear, ambiguous, vague, obscure, debatable.
≠ 1 certain, decided. 2 definite, settled.

doubtless *adv* 1 CERTAINLY, without doubt, undoubtedly, unquestionably, indisputably, no doubt, clearly, surely, of course, truly, precisely.
2 PROBABLY, presumably, most likely, seemingly, supposedly.

dour *adj* 1 GLOOMY, dismal, forbidding, grim, morose, unfriendly, dreary, austere, sour, sullen. 2 HARD, inflexible, unyielding, rigid, severe, rigorous, strict, obstinate.
≠ 1 cheerful, bright. 2 easy-going.

douse, dowse *v* 1 SOAK, saturate, steep, submerge, immerse, immerge, dip, duck, drench, dunk, plunge. 2 EXTINGUISH, put out, blow out, smother, snuff.

dowdy *adj* unfashionable, ill-dressed, frumpish, drab, shabby, tatty (*infml*),

frowsy, tacky (*infml*), dingy, old-fashioned, slovenly.
≠ fashionable, smart.

down *v* **1** KNOCK DOWN, fell, floor, prostrate, throw, topple. **2** SWALLOW, drink, gulp, swig (*infml*), knock back (*infml*).
down and out destitute, impoverished, penniless, derelict, ruined.

downcast *adj* dejected, depressed, despondent, sad, unhappy, miserable, down, low, disheartened, dispirited, blue (*infml*), fed up (*infml*), discouraged, disappointed, crestfallen, dismayed.
≠ cheerful, happy, elated.

downfall *n* fall, ruin, failure, collapse, destruction, disgrace, debacle, undoing, overthrow.

downgrade *v* **1** DEGRADE, demote, lower, humble. **2** DISPARAGE, denigrate, belittle, run down, decry.
≠ **1** upgrade, improve. **2** praise.

downhearted *adj* depressed, dejected, despondent, sad, downcast, discouraged, disheartened, low-spirited, unhappy, gloomy, glum, dismayed.
≠ cheerful, enthusiastic.

downpour *n* cloudburst, deluge, rainstorm, flood, inundation, torrent.

downright *adj, adv* absolute(ly), outright, plain(ly), utter(ly), clear(ly), complete(ly), out-and-out, frank(ly), explicit(ly).

down-trodden *adj* oppressed, subjugated, subservient, exploited, trampled on, abused, tyrannized, victimized, helpless.

downward *adj* descending, declining, downhill, sliding, slipping.
≠ upward.

dowse *see* **douse**.

doze *v* sleep, nod off, drop off, snooze (*infml*), kip (*infml*), zizz (*sl*).
n nap, catnap, siesta, snooze (*infml*), forty winks (*infml*), kip (*infml*), shut-eye (*infml*), zizz (*sl*).

drab *adj* dull, dingy, dreary, dismal, gloomy, flat, grey, lacklustre, cheerless, sombre, shabby.
≠ bright, cheerful.

draft[1] *v* draw (up), outline, sketch, plan, design, formulate, compose.
n outline, sketch, plan, delineation, abstract, rough, blueprint, protocol (*fml*).

draft[2] *n* bill of exchange, cheque, money order, letter of credit, postal order.

drag *v* **1** DRAW, pull, haul, lug, tug, trail, tow. **2** GO SLOWLY, creep, crawl, lag.
n (*infml*) bore, annoyance, nuisance, pain (*infml*), bother.

drain *v* **1** EMPTY, remove, evacuate, draw off, strain, dry, milk, bleed. **2** DISCHARGE, trickle, flow out, leak, ooze. **3** EXHAUST, consume, sap, use up, deplete, drink up, swallow.
≠ **1** fill.
n **1** CHANNEL, conduit, culvert, duct, outlet, trench, ditch, pipe, sewer. **2** DEPLETION, exhaustion, sap, strain.

drama *n* **1** PLAY, acting, theatre, show, spectacle, stage-craft, scene, melodrama. **2** EXCITEMENT, crisis, turmoil.

dramatic *adj* **1** EXCITING, striking, stirring, thrilling, marked, significant, expressive, impressive. **2** HISTRIONIC, exaggerated, melodramatic, flamboyant.

dramatize *v* **1** STAGE, put on, adapt. **2** ACT, play-act, exaggerate, overdo, overstate.

drape *v* cover, wrap, hang, fold, drop, suspend.

drastic *adj* extreme, radical, strong, forceful, severe, harsh, far-reaching, desperate, dire.
≠ moderate, cautious.

draught *n* **1** PUFF, current, influx, flow. **2** DRINK, potion, quantity. **3** PULLING, traction.

draw *v* **1** ATTRACT, allure, entice, bring in, influence, persuade, elicit. **2** PULL, drag, haul, tow, tug. **3** DELINEATE, map out, sketch, portray, trace, pencil, depict, design. **4** TIE, be equal, be even.
≠ **1** repel. **2** push.
n **1** ATTRACTION, enticement, lure,

appeal, bait, interest. **2** TIE, stalemate, dead-heat.

draw out protract, extend, prolong, drag out, spin out, elongate, stretch, lengthen, string out.

≠ shorten.

draw up 1 DRAFT, compose, formulate, prepare, frame, write out. **2** PULL UP, stop, halt, run in.

drawback *n* disadvantage, snag, hitch, obstacle, impediment, hindrance, difficulty, flaw, fault, fly in the ointment (*infml*), catch, stumbling block, nuisance, trouble, defect, handicap, deficiency, imperfection.

≠ advantage, benefit.

drawing *n* sketch, picture, outline, representation, delineation, portrayal, illustration, cartoon, graphic, portrait.

dread *v* fear, shrink from, quail, cringe at, flinch, shy, shudder, tremble.

n fear, apprehension, misgiving, trepidation, dismay, alarm, horror, terror, fright, disquiet, worry, quietly, qualm.

≠ confidence, security.

dreadful *adj* awful, terrible, frightful, horrible, appalling, dire, shocking, ghastly, horrendous, tragic, grievous, hideous, tremendous.

≠ wonderful, comforting.

dream *n* **1** VISION, illusion, reverie, trance, fantasy, daydream, nightmare, hallucination, delusion, imagination. **2** ASPIRATION, wish, hope, ambition, desire, pipe-dream, ideal, goal, design, speculation.

v imagine, envisage, fancy, fantasize, daydream, hallucinate, conceive, visualize, conjure up, muse.

dream up invent, devise, conceive, think up, imagine, concoct, hatch, create, spin, contrive.

dreamer *n* idealist, visionary, fantasizes, romancer, daydreamer, star-gazer, theorizer.

≠ realist, pragmatist.

dreamy *adj* **1** FANTASTIC, unreal, imaginary, shadowy, vague, misty. **2** IMPRACTICAL, fanciful, daydreaming, romantic, visionary, faraway, absent, musing, pensive.

≠ **1** real. **2** practical, down-to-earth.

dreary *adj* **1** *a dreary job*: boring, tedious, uneventful, dull, humdrum, routine, monotonous, wearisome, commonplace, colourless, lifeless. **2** *a dreary landscape*: gloomy, depressing, drab, dismal, bleak, sombre, sad, mournful.

≠ **1** interesting. **2** cheerful.

dregs *n* **1** SEDIMENT, deposit, residue, lees, grounds, scum, dross, trash, waste. **2** OUTCASTS, rabble, riff-raff, scum, down-and-outs.

drench *v* soak, saturate, steep, wet, douse, souse, immerse, inundate, duck, flood, imbue, drown.

dress *n* **1** FROCK, gown, robe. **2** CLOTHES, clothing, garment(s), outfit, costume, garb, get-up (*infml*), gear (*infml*), togs (*infml*).

v **1** CLOTHE, put on, garb, rig, robe, wear, don, decorate, deck, garnish, trim, adorn, fit, drape. **2** ARRANGE, adjust, dispose, prepare, groom, straighten. **3** BANDAGE, tend, treat.

≠ **1** strip, undress.

dress up beautify, adorn, embellish, improve, deck, doll up, tart up (*infml*), gild, disguise.

dribble *v* **1** TRICKLE, drip, leak, run, seep, drop, ooze. **2** DROOL, slaver, slobber, drivel.

drift *v* **1** WANDER, waft, stray, float, freewheel, coast. **2** GATHER, accumulate, pile up, drive.

n **1** ACCUMULATION, mound, pile, bank, mass, heap. **2** TREND, tendency, course, direction, flow, movement, current, rush, sweep. **3** MEANING, intention, implication, gist, tenor, thrust, significance, aim, design, scope.

drill *v* **1** TEACH, train, instruct, coach, practise, school, rehearse, exercise, discipline. **2** BORE, pierce, penetrate, puncture, perforate.

n **1** INSTRUCTION, training, practice, coaching, exercise, repetition, tuition, preparation, discipline. **2** BORER, awl, bit, gimlet.

drink *v* **1** IMBIBE, swallow, sip, drain, down, gulp, swig (*infml*), knock back (*infml*), sup, quaff, absorb, guzzle,

partake of (*fml*), swill. **2** GET DRUNK, booze (*infml*), tipple (*infml*), indulge, carouse, revel, tank up (*infml*).
n **1** BEVERAGE, liquid, refreshment, draught, sip, swallow, swig (*infml*), gulp.

Types of non-alcoholic drink include: tea, Assam, Indian, Earl Grey, China tea, lapsang souchong, green tea, herbal tea, camomile tea, peppermint tea, rosehip tea, lemon tea, tisane, julep, mint-julep; coffee, café au lait, café filtre, café noir, cappuccino, expresso, Irish coffee, Turkish coffee; cocoa, hot chocolate, Horlicks®, Ovaltine®, milk, milk shake, float (*US*); fizzy drink, pop (*infml*), cherryade, Coca Cola®, coke (*infml*), cream soda, ginger beer, lemonade, limeade, Pepsi®, root beer, sarsaparilla, cordial, squash, barley water, Ribena®, fruit juice, mixer, bitter lemon, Canada Dry®, ginger ale, soda water, tonic water, mineral water, Perrier®, seltzer, Vichy water, Lucozade®, Wincarnis®, beef tea.

2 ALCOHOL, spirits, booze (*infml*), liquor, tipple (*infml*), tot, the bottle (*infml*), stiffener (*infml*).

Alcoholic drinks include: ale, beer, cider, lager, shandy, stout, Guinness®; aquavit, Armagnac, bourbon, brandy, Calvados, Cognac, gin, gin-and-tonic, pink gin, sloe gin, rum, grog, rye, vodka, whisky, Scotch and soda, hot toddy; wine, red wine, vin rouge, vin rosé, white wine, vin blanc, champagne, bubbly (*infml*), hock, mead, perry, vino (*infml*), plonk (*infml*); absinthe, advocaat, Benedictine, Chartreuse, black velvet, bloody Mary, Buck's fizz, Campari, cherry brandy, cocktail, Cointreau®, crème de menthe, daiquiri, eggnog, ginger wine, kirsch, Marsala, Martini®, ouzo, Pernod®, piña colada, port, punch, retsina, sake, sangria, schnapps, sherry, snowball, tequila, Tom Collins, vermouth. *see also* **wine**.

drip *v* drop, dribble, trickle, plop, percolate, drizzle, splash, sprinkle, weep.
n **1** DROP, trickle, dribble, leak, bead, tear. **2** (*infml*) WEAKLING, wimp (*infml*), softy (*infml*), bore, wet (*infml*), ninny (*infml*).

drive *v* **1** DIRECT, control, manage, operate, run, handle, motivate. **2** FORCE, compel, impel, coerce, constrain, press, push, urge, dragoon, gpad, guide, oblige. **3** STEER, motor, propel, ride, travel.
n **1** ENERGY, enterprise, ambition, initiative, get-up-and-go (*infml*), vigour, motivation, determination. **2** CAMPAIGN, crusade, appeal, effort, action. **3** EXCURSION, outing, journey, ride, spin, trip, jaunt. **4** URGE, instinct, impulse, need, desire.
drive at imply, allude to, intimate, mean, suggest, hint, get at, intend, refer to, signify, insinuate, indicate.

driving *adj* compelling, forceful, vigorous, dynamic, energetic, forthright, heavy, violent, sweeping.

drizzle *n* mist, mizzle, rain, spray, shower.
v spit, spray, sprinkle, rain, spot, shower.

droop *v* **1** HANG (DOWN), dangle, sag, bend. **2** LANGUISH, decline, flag, falter, slump, lose heart, wilt, wither, drop, faint, fall down, fade, slouch. **3** sink.
≠ **1** straighten. **2** flourish, rise.

drop *n* **1** DROPLET, bead, lear, drip, bubble, globule, trickle. **2** DASH, pinch, spot, sip, trace, dab. **3** FALL, decline, falling-off, lowering, downturn, decrease, reduction, slump, plunge, deterioration. **4** DESCENT, precipice, slope, chasm, abyss.
v **1** FALL, sink, decline, plunge, plummet, tumble, dive, descend, lower, droop, depress, diminish. **2** ABANDON, forsake, desert, give up, relinquish, reject, jilt, leave, renounce, throw over, repudiate, cease, discontinue, quit.
≠ **1** rise.
drop off 1 NOD OFF, doze, snooze (*infml*), have forty winks (*infml*). **2** DECLINE, fall off, decrease, dwindle, lessen, diminish, slacken. **3** DELIVER, set down, leave.
≠ **1** wake up. **2** increase. **3** pick up.
drop out back out, abandon, cry off, withdraw, forsake, leave, quit.

drought *n* dryness, aridity, parchedness, dehydration, desiccation, shortage, want.

drove *n* herd, horde, gathering, crowd, multitude, swarm, throng, flock, company, mob, press.

drown *v* **1** SUBMERGE, immerse, inundate, go under, flood, sink, deluge, engulf, drench. **2** OVERWHELM, overpower, overcome, swamp, wipe out, extinguish.

drowsy *adj* sleepy, tired, lethargic, nodding, dreamy, dozy, somnolent (*fml*).
≠ alert, awake.

drudge *n* toiler, menial, dogsbody (*infml*), hack, servant, slave, factotum, worker, skivvy (*infml*), galley-slave, lackey.
v plod, toil, work, slave, plug away (*infml*), grind (*infml*), labour, beaver (*infml*).
≠ idle, laze.

drudgery *n* labour, donkey-work (*infml*), hack-work, slog (*infml*), grind (*infml*), slavery, sweat, sweated labour, toil, skivvying, chore.

drug *n* medication, medicine, remedy, potion.

> *Types of drug include*: anaesthetic, analgesic, antibiotic, antidepressant, antihistamine, barbiturate, narcotic, opiate, hallucinogenic, sedative, steroid, stimulant, tranquillizer; chloroform, aspirin, codeine, paracetamol, morphine, penicillin, diazepam, Valium®, cortisone, insulin, digitalis, laudanum, quinine, progesterone, oestrogen, cannabis, marijuana, smack, LSD, acid, ecstasy, E (*sl*), heroin, opium, cocaine, crack, dope (*infml*). *see also* **medicine**.

v medicate, sedate, tranquillize, dope (*infml*), anaesthetize, dose, knock out (*infml*), stupefy, deaden, numb.

drum *v* beat, pulsate, tap, throb, thrum, tattoo, reverberate, rap.
drum up obtain, round up, collect, gather, solicit, canvass, petition, attract.

drunk *adj* inebriated, intoxicated, under the influence, drunken, stoned (*sl*), legless (*sl*), paralytic (*infml*), sloshed (*infml*), merry (*infml*), tight (*infml*), tipsy (*infml*), tanked up (*infml*), tiddly (*infml*), plastered (*infml*), loaded (*infml*), lit up (*infml*), sozzled (*infml*), well-oiled (*infml*), canned (*sl*), blotto (*sl*).
≠ sober, temperate, abstinent, teetotal.

drunkard *n* drunk, inebriate, alcoholic, dipsomaniac, boozer (*infml*), wino (*infml*), tippler (*infml*), soak (*infml*), lush (*infml*), sot (*infml*).

dry *adj* **1** ARID, parched, thirsty, dehydrated, desiccated, barren. **2** BORING, dull, dreary, tedious, monotonous. **3** *dry humour*: ironic, cynical, droll, deadpan, sarcastic, cutting.
≠ **1** wet. **2** interesting.
v dehydrate, parch, desiccate, drain, shrivel, wither.
≠ soak.

dual *adj* double, twofold, duplicate, duplex, binary, combined, paired, twin, matched.

dubious *adj* **1** DOUBTFUL, uncertain, undecided, unsure, wavering, unsettled, suspicious, sceptical, hesitant. **2** QUESTIONABLE, debatable, unreliable, ambiguous, suspect, obscure, fishy (*infml*), shady (*infml*).
≠ **1** certain. **2** trustworthy.

duck *v* **1** CROUCH, stoop, bob, bend. **2** AVOID, dodge, evade, shirk, sidestep. **3** DIP, immerse, plunge, dunk, dive, submerge, douse, souse, wet, lower.

due *adj* **1** OWED, owing, payable, unpaid, outstanding, in arrears. **2** RIGHTFUL, fitting, appropriate, proper, merited, deserved, justified, suitable. **3** ADEQUATE, enough, sufficient, ample, plenty of. **4** EXPECTED, scheduled.
≠ **1** paid. **3** inadequate.
adv exactly, direct(ly), precisely, straight, dead (*infml*).

duel *n* affair of honour, combat, contest, fight, clash, competition, rivalry, encounter.

dull *adj* **1** BORING, uninteresting, unexciting, flat, dreary, monotonous, tedious, uneventful, humdrum,

unimaginative, dismal, lifeless, plain, insipid, heavy. **2** DARK, gloomy, drab, murky, indistinct, grey, cloudy, lack-lustre, opaque, dim, overcast. **3** UNINTELLIGENT, dense, dim, dimwitted (*infml*), thick (*infml*), stupid, slow.
≠ **1** interesting, exciting. **2** bright. **3** intelligent, clever.
v **1** BLUNT, alleviate, mitigate, moderate, lessen, relieve, soften. **2** DEADEN, numb, paralyse. **3** DISCOURAGE, dampen, subdue, sadden. **4** DIM, obscure, fade.

dumb *adj* silent, mute, soundless, speechless, tongue-tied, inarticulate, mum (*infml*).

dumbfounded *adj* astonished, amazed, astounded, overwhelmed, speechless, taken aback, thrown (*infml*), startled, overcome, confounded, flabbergasted (*infml*), staggered, confused, bowled over, dumb, floored (*infml*), paralysed.

dummy *n* **1** COPY, duplicate, imitation, counterfeit, substitute. **2** MODEL, lay-figure, mannequin, figure, form. **3** TEAT, pacifier.
adj **1** ARTIFICIAL, fake, imitation, false, bogus, mock, sham, phoney. **2** SIMULATED, practice, trial.

dump *v* **1** DEPOSIT, drop, offload, throw down, let fall, unload, empty out, discharge, park. **2** GET RID OF, scrap, throw away, dispose of, ditch, tip, jettison.
n **1** RUBBISH-TIP, junk-yard, rubbish-heap, tip. **2** HOVEL, slum, shack, shanty, hole (*infml*), joint (*infml*), pigsty, mess.

dungeon *n* cell, prison, jail, gaol, cage, lock-up, keep, oubliette, vault.

dupe *n* victim, sucker (*infml*), fool, gull, mug (*infml*), push-over (*infml*), fall guy (*infml*), pawn, puppet, instrument, stooge (*infml*), simpleton.
v deceive, delude, fool, trick, outwit, con (*infml*), cheat, hoax, swindle, rip off (*infml*), take in, hoodwink, defraud, bamboozle (*infml*).

duplicate *adj* identical, matching, twin, twofold, corresponding, matched.
n copy, replica, reproduction, photocopy, carbon (copy), match, facsimile.
v copy, reproduce, repeat, photocopy, double, clone, echo.

durable *adj* lasting, enduring, long-lasting, abiding, hard-wearing, strong, sturdy, tough, unfading, substantial, sound, reliable, dependable, stable, resistant, persistent, constant, permanent, firm, fixed, fast.
≠ perishable, weak, fragile.

duress *n* constraint, coercion, compulsion, pressure, restraint, threat, force.

dusk *n* twilight, sunset, nightfall, evening, sundown, gloaming, darkness, dark, gloom, shadows, shade.
≠ dawn, brightness.

dust *n* powder, particles, dirt, earth, soil, ground, grit, grime.

dusty *adj* **1** DIRTY, grubby, filthy. **2** POWDERY, granular, crumbly, chalky, sandy.
≠ **1** clean. **2** solid, hard.

dutiful *adj* obedient, respectful, conscientious, devoted, filial, reverential, submissive.

duty *n* **1** OBLIGATION, responsibility, assignment, calling, charge, role, task, job, business, function, work, office, service. **2** OBEDIENCE, respect, loyalty. **3** TAX, toll, tariff, levy, customs, excise.
on duty at work, engaged, busy.

dwarf *n* **1** PERSON OF RESTRICTED GROWTH, midget, pygmy, Tom Thumb, Lilliputian. **2** GNOME, goblin.
adj miniature, small, tiny, pocket, mini (*infml*), diminutive, petite, Lilliputian, baby.
≠ large.
v **1** STUNT, retard, check. **2** OVERSHADOW, tower over, dominate.

dwell *v* live, inhabit, reside, stay, settle, populate, people, lodge, rest, abide (*fml*).

dwindle *v* diminish, decrease, decline, lessen, subside, ebb, fade, weaken, taper off, tail off, shrink, peter out, fall, wane, waste away, die out, wither, shrivel, disappear.
≠ increase, grow.

dye *n* colour, colouring, stain, pigment, tint, tinge.
v colour, tint, stain, pigment, tinge, imbue.

dying *adj* moribund, passing, final, going, mortal, not long for this world, perishing, failing, fading, vanishing.
≠ reviving.

dynamic *adj* forceful, powerful, energetic, vigorous, go-ahead, high-powered, driving, self-starting, spirited, vital, lively, active.
≠ inactive, apathetic.

dynasty *n* house, line, succession, dominion, regime, government, rule, empire, sovereignty.

E

eager *adj* **1** KEEN, enthusiastic, fervent, intent, earnest, zealous. **2** LONGING, yearning.
≠ **1** unenthusiastic, indifferent.

ear *n* **1** ATTENTION, heed, notice, regard. **2** *an ear for language*: perception, sensitivity, discrimination, appreciation, hearing, skill, ability.

Parts of the ear include: anvil (incus), auditory canal, auditory nerve, auricle, cochlea, concha, eardrum, eustachian tube, hammer (malleus), helix, labyrinth, lobe, oval window, pinna, round window, semicircular canal, stirrup (stapes), tragus, tympanum, vestibular nerve, vestibule.

early *adj* **1** *early symptoms*: forward, advanced, premature, untimely, undeveloped. **2** *early theatre*: primitive, ancient, primeval.
adv ahead of time, in good time, beforehand, in advance, prematurely.
≠ late.

earn *v* **1** *earn a good salary*: receive, obtain, make, get, draw, bring in (*infml*), gain, realize, gross, reap. **2** *earn one's reputation*: deserve, merit, warrant, win, rate.
≠ **1** spend, lose.

earnest *adj* **1** RESOLUTE, devoted, ardent, conscientious, intent, keen, fervent, firm, fixed, eager, enthusiastic, steady. **2** SERIOUS, sincere, solemn, grave, heartfelt.
≠ **1** apathetic. **2** frivolous, flippant.

earnings *n* pay, income, salary, wages, profits, gain, proceeds, reward, receipts, return, revenue, remuneration, stipend.
≠ expenditure, outgoings.

earth *n* **1** WORLD, planet, globe, sphere. **2** LAND, ground, soil, clay, loam, sod, humus.

earthenware *n* pottery, ceramics, crockery, pots.

earthly *adj* **1** *our earthly life*: material, physical, human, worldly, mortal, mundane, fleshly, secular, sensual, profane, temporal. **2** *no earthly explanation*: possible, likely, conceivable, slightest.
≠ **1** spiritual, heavenly.

earthy *adj* crude, coarse, vulgar, bawdy, rough, raunchy (*infml*), down-to-earth, ribald, robust.
≠ refined, modest.

ease *n* **1** FACILITY, effortlessness, skilfulness, deftness, dexterity, naturalness, cleverness. **2** COMFORT, contentment, peace, affluence, repose, leisure, relaxation, rest, quiet, happiness.
≠ **1** difficulty. **2** discomfort.
v **1** *ease the pain*: alleviate, moderate, lessen, lighten, relieve, mitigate, abate, relent, allay, assuage, relax, comfort, calm, soothe, facilitate, smooth. **2** *ease it into position*: inch, steer, slide, still.
≠ **1** aggravate, intensify, worsen.

easily *adv* **1** EFFORTLESSLY, comfortably, readily, simply. **2** BY FAR, undoubtedly, indisputably, definitely, certainly, doubtlessly, clearly, far and away, undeniably, simply, surely, probably, well.
≠ **1** laboriously.

easy *adj* **1** EFFORTLESS, simple, uncomplicated, undemanding, straightforward, manageable, cushy (*infml*). **2** RELAXED, carefree, easy-going, comfortable, informal, calm, natural, leisurely.
≠ **1** difficult, demanding, exacting. **2** tense, uneasy.

easy-going *adj* relaxed, tolerant, laid-back (*infml*), amenable, happy-go-lucky (*infml*), carefree, calm, even-tempered, serene.
≠ strict, intolerant, critical.

eat *v* **1** CONSUME, feed, swallow,

devour, chew, scoff (*infml*), munch, dine. **2** CORRODE, erode, wear away, decay, rot, crumble, dissolve.

eatable *adj* edible, palatable, good, wholesome, digestible, comestible (*fml*), harmless.
≠ inedible, unpalatable.

eavesdrop *v* listen in, spy, overhear, snoop (*infml*), tap (*infml*), bug (*infml*), monitor.

eccentric *adj* odd, peculiar, abnormal, unconventional, strange, quirky, weird, way-out (*infml*), queer, outlandish, idiosyncratic, bizarre, freakish, erratic, singular, dotty.
≠ conventional, orthodox, normal.
n nonconformist, oddball (*infml*), oddity, crank (*infml*), freak (*infml*), character (*infml*).

eccentricity *n* UNCONVENTIONALITY, strangeness, peculiarity, nonconformity, abnormality, oddity, weirdness, idiosyncrasy, singularity, quirk, freakishness, aberration, anomaly, capriciousness.
≠ conventionality, ordinariness.

ecclesiastical *adj* church, churchly, religious, clerical, priestly, divine, spiritual.

echo *v* **1** REVERBERATE, resound, repeat, reflect, reiterate, ring. **2** IMITATE, copy, reproduce, mirror, resemble, mimic.
n **1** REVERBERATION, reiteration, repetition, reflection. **2** IMITATION, copy, reproduction, mirror image, image, parallel.

eclipse *v* **1** BLOT OUT, obscure, cloud, veil, darken, dim. **2** OUTDO, overshadow, outshine, surpass, transcend.
n **1** OBSCURATION, overshadowing, darkening, shading, dimming. **2** DECLINE, failure, fall, loss.

economic *adj* **1** COMMERCIAL, business, industrial. **2** FINANCIAL, budgetary, fiscal, monetary. **3** PROFITABLE, profit-making, money-making, productive, cost-effective, viable.

economical *adj* **1** THRIFTY, careful, prudent, saving, sparing, frugal. **2** CHEAP, inexpensive, low-priced, reasonable, cost-effective, modest, efficient.
≠ **1** wasteful. **2** expensive, uneconomical.

economize *v* save, cut back, tighten one's belt (*infml*), cut costs.
≠ waste, squander.

economy *n* thrift, saving, restraint, prudence, frugality, parsimony, providence, husbandry.
≠ extravagance.

ecstasy *n* delight, rapture, bliss, elation, joy, euphoria, frenzy, exaltation, fervour.
≠ misery, torment.

ecstatic *adj* elated, blissful, joyful, rapturous, overjoyed, euphoric, delirious, frenzied, fervent.
≠ downcast.

eddy *n* whirlpool, swirl, vortex, twist.
v swirl, whirl.

edge *n* **1** BORDER, rim, boundary, limit, brim, threshold, brink, fringe, margin, outline, side, verge, line, perimeter, periphery, lip. **2** ADVANTAGE, superiority, force. **3** SHARPNESS, acuteness, keenness, incisiveness, pungency, zest.
v creep, inch, ease, sidle.

edgy *adj* on edge, nervous, tense, anxious, ill at ease, keyed-up, touchy, irritable.
≠ calm.

edible *adj* eatable, palatable, digestible, wholesome, good, harmless.
≠ inedible.

edict *n* command, order, proclamation, law, decree, regulation, pronouncement, ruling, mandate, statute, injunction, manifesto.

edifice *n* building, construction, structure, erection.

edify *v* instruct, improve, enlighten, inform, guide, educate, nurture, teach.

edit *v* correct, emend, revise, rewrite, reorder, rearrange, adapt, check, compile, rephrase, select, polish, annotate, censor.

edition *n* copy, volume, impression, printing, issue, version, number.

educate *v* teach, train, instruct, tutor, coach, school, inform, cultivate, edify, drill, improve, discipline, develop.

educated *adj* learned, taught, schooled, trained, knowledgeable, informed, instructed, lettered, cultured, civilized, tutored, refined, well-bred.
≠ uneducated, uncultured.

education *n* teaching, training, schooling, tuition, tutoring, coaching, guidance, instruction, cultivation, culture, scholarship, improvement, enlightenment, knowledge, nurture, development.

Educational establishments include: kindergarten, nursery school, infant school, primary school, middle school, combined school, secondary school, secondary modern, upper school, high school, grammar school, grant-maintained school, preparatory school, public school, private school, boarding-school, college, sixth-form college, polytechnic, poly, city technical college (CTC), technical college, university, adult-education centre, academy, seminary, finishing school, business school, secretarial college, Sunday school, convent school, summer-school.
Educational terms include: adult education, assisted places scheme, A-level, baccalaureate, board of governors, break time, bursar, campus, catchment area, certificate, classroom, coeducation, common entrance, course, curriculum, degree, diploma, double-first, eleven-plus, enrolment, examination, exercise book, final exam, finals, further education, GCSE (General Certificate of Secondary Education), governor, graduation, half-term, head boy, head girl, head teacher, higher education, homework, intake, invigilator, lecture, literacy, matriculation, matron, mixed-ability teaching, modular course, national curriculum, NVQ (national vocational qualification), numeracy, O-level, opting out, parent governor, PTA (parent teacher association), playground, playtime, prefect, primary education, proctor, professor, pupil, quadrangle, qualification, refresher course, register, report, scholarship, school term, secondary education, special education, statement, streaming, student, student grant, student loan, study, subject, syllabus, teacher, teacher training, test paper, textbook, thesis, timetable, truancy, university entrance, work experience, YTS (Youth Training Scheme).

eerie *adj* weird, strange, uncanny, spooky (*infml*), creepy, frightening, scary, spine-chilling.

effect *n* **1** OUTCOME, result, conclusion, consequence, upshot, aftermath, issue. **2** POWER, force, impact, efficacy, impression, strength. **3** MEANING, significance, import.
v cause, execute, create, achieve, accomplish, perform, produce, make, initiate, fulfil, complete.
in effect in fact, actually, really, in reality, to all intents and purposes, for all practical purposes, essentially, effectively, virtually.
take effect be effective, become operative, come into force, come into operation, be implemented, begin, work.

effective *adj* **1** EFFICIENT, efficacious, productive, adequate, capable, useful. **2** OPERATIVE, in force, functioning, current, active. **3** STRIKING, impressive, forceful, cogent, powerful, persuasive, convincing, telling.
≠ **1** ineffective, powerless.

effects *n* belongings, possessions, property, goods, gear (*infml*), movables, chattels (*fml*), things, trappings.

effeminate *adj* unmanly, womanly, womanish, feminine, sissy (*infml*), delicate.
≠ manly.

effervescent *adj* **1** BUBBLY, sparkling, fizzy, frothy, carbonated, foaming. **2** LIVELY, ebullient, vivacious, animated, buoyant, exhilarated, enthusiastic, exuberant, excited, vital.
≠ **1** flat. **2** dull.

efficiency *n* effectiveness, competence, proficiency, skill, expertise, skilfulness, capability, ability, productivity.
≠ inefficiency, incompetence.

efficient *adj* effective, competent,

proficient, skilful, capable, able, productive, well-organized, businesslike, powerful, well-conducted.
≠ inefficient, incompetent.

effort *n* **1** EXERTION, strain, application, struggle, trouble, energy, toil, striving, pains, travail (*fml*). **2** ATTEMPT, try, go (*infml*), endeavour, shot, stab. **3** ACHIEVEMENT, accomplishment, feat, exploit, production, creation, deed, product, work.

effortless *adj* easy, simple, undemanding, facile, painless, smooth.
≠ difficult.

effrontery *n* audacity, impertinence, insolence, cheek (*infml*), impudence, temerity, boldness, brazenness, cheekiness, gall, nerve, presumption, disrespect, arrogance, brashness.
≠ respect, timidity.

effusive *adj* fulsome, gushing, unrestrained, expansive, ebullient, demonstrative, profuse, overflowing, enthusiastic, exuberant, extravagant, lavish, talkative, voluble.
≠ reserved, restrained.

egotism *n* egoism, egomania, self-centredness, self-importance, conceitedness, self-regard, self-love, self-conceit, narcissism, self-admiration, vanity, bigheadedness (*infml*).
≠ humility.

egotistic *adj* egoistic, egocentric, self-centred, self-important, conceited, vain, swollen-headed (*infml*), bigheaded (*infml*), boasting, bragging.
≠ humble.

ejaculate *v* **1** DISCHARGE, eject, spurt, emit. **2** EXCLAIM, call, blurt (out), cry, shout, yell, utter, scream.

eject *v* **1** EMIT, expel, discharge, spout, spew, evacuate, vomit. **2** OUST, evict, throw out, drive out, turn out, expel, remove, banish, deport, dismiss, exile, kick out, fire (*infml*), sack (*infml*).

elaborate *adj* **1** *elaborate plans*: detailed, careful, thorough, exact, extensive, painstaking, precise, perfected, minute, laboured, studied. **2** *elaborate design*: intricate, complex, complicated, involved, ornamental, ornate, fancy, decorated, ostentatious, showy, fussy.
≠ **2** simple, plain.
v amplify, develop, enlarge, expand, flesh out, polish, improve, refine, devise, explain.
≠ précis, simplify.

elapse *v* pass, lapse, go by, slip away.

elastic *adj* **1** PLIABLE, flexible, stretchable, supple, resilient, yielding, springy, rubbery, pliant, plastic, bouncy, buoyant. **2** ADAPTABLE, accommodating, flexible, tolerant, adjustable.
≠ **1** rigid. **2** inflexible.

elasticity *n* **1** PLIABILITY, flexibility, resilience, stretch, springiness, suppleness, give, plasticity, bounce, buoyancy. **2** ADAPTABILITY, flexibility, tolerance, adjustability.
≠ **1** rigidity. **2** inflexibility.

elated *adj* exhilarated, excited, euphoric, ecstatic, exultant, jubilant, overjoyed, joyful.
≠ despondent, downcast.

elbow *v* jostle, nudge, push, shove, bump, crowd, knock, shoulder.

elder *adj* older, senior, first-born, ancient.
≠ younger.

elderly *adj* aging, aged, old, hoary, senile.
≠ young, youthful.

elect *v* choose, pick, opt for, select, vote for, prefer, adopt, designate, appoint, determine.
adj choice, elite, chosen, designated, designate, picked, prospective, selected, to be, preferred, hand-picked.

election *n* choice, selection, voting, ballot, poll, appointment, determination, decision, preference.

elector *n* selector, voter, constituent.

electric *adj* electrifying, exciting, stimulating, thrilling, charged, dynamic, stirring, tense, rousing.
≠ unexciting, flat.

electrical components

> *Types of electrical components and devices include*: adaptor, ammeter, armature, battery, bayonet fitting,

cable, ceiling rose, circuit breaker, conduit, continuity tester, copper conductor, dimmer switch, dry-cell battery, earthed plug, electrical screwdriver, electricity meter, extension lead, fluorescent tube, fuse, fusebox, fuse carrier, high voltage tester, insulating tape, lampholder, light bulb, multimeter, neon lamp, socket, test lamp, three-core cable, three-pin plug, transducer, transformer, two-pin plug, universal test meter, voltage doubler, wire strippers.

electricity

Electricity and electronics terms include: alternating current (AC), alternator, amp, ampere, amplifier, analogue signal, anode, band-pass filter, battery, bioelectricity, capacitance, capacitor, cathode, cathode-ray tube, cell, commutator, condenser, conductivity, coulomb, digital signal, diode, direct current (DC), Dolby® (system), dynamo, eddy current, electrode, electrolyte, electromagnet, electron tube, farad, Faraday cage, Foucault current, frequency modulation, galvanic, galvanometer, generator, grid system, henry, impedance, induced current, inductance, integrated circuit, isoelectric, isoelectronic, logic gate, loudspeaker, microchip, mutual induction, ohm, optoelectronics, oscillator, oscilloscope, piezoelectricity, polarity, power station, reactance, resistance, resistor, rheostat, semiconductor, siemens, silicon chip, solenoid, solid state circuit, static electricity, step-down transformer, superconductivity, switch, thermionics, thermistor, thyristor, transformer, transistor, triode, truth table, turboalternator, tweeter, valve, volt, voltaic, voltage amplifier, watt, Wheatstone bridge, woofer.

electrify *v* thrill, excite, shock, invigorate, animate, stimulate, stir, rouse, fire, jolt, galvanize, amaze, astonish, astound, stagger.
≠ bore.

elegant *adj* stylish, chic, fashionable, modish, smart, refined, polished, genteel, smooth, tasteful, fine, exquisite, beautiful, graceful, handsome, delicate, neat, artistic.
≠ inelegant, unrefined, unfashionable.

elegy *n* dirge, lament, requiem, plaint.

element *n* factor, component, constituent, ingredient, member, part, piece, fragment, feature, trace.
≠ **1** whole.

elementary *adj* basic, fundamental, rudimentary, principal, primary, clear, easy, introductory, straightforward, uncomplicated, simple.
≠ advanced.

elements *n* basics, fundamentals, foundations, principles, rudiments, essentials.

elevate *v* **1** LIFT, raise, hoist, heighten, intensify, magnify. **2** EXALT, advance, promote, aggrandize, upgrade. **3** UPLIFT, rouse, boost, brighten.
≠ **1** lower. **2** downgrade.

elevated *adj* raised, lofty, exalted, high, grand, noble, dignified, sublime.
≠ base.

elevation *n* **1** RISE, promotion, advancement, preferment, aggrandizement. **2** EXALTATION, loftiness, grandeur, eminence, nobility. **3** HEIGHT, altitude, hill, rise.
≠ **1** demotion. **2** dip.

elicit *v* evoke, draw out, derive, extract, obtain, exact, extort, cause.

eligible *adj* qualified, fit, appropriate, suitable, acceptable, worthy, proper, desirable.
≠ ineligible.

eliminate *v* remove, get rid of, cut out, take out, exclude, delete, dispense with, rub out, omit, reject, disregard, dispose of, drop, do away with, eradicate, expel, extinguish, stamp out, exterminate, knock out, kill, murder.
≠ include, accept.

elite *n* best, elect, aristocracy, upper classes, nobility, gentry, crème de la crème, establishment, high society.
adj choice, best, exclusive, selected, first-class, aristocratic, noble, upper-class.

elocution *n* delivery, articulation, diction, enunciation, pronunciation, oratory, rhetoric, speech, utterance.

elongated *adj* lengthened, extended, prolonged, protracted, stretched, long.

elope *v* run off, run away, decamp, bolt, abscond, do a bunk (*infml*), escape, steal away, leave, disappear.

eloquent *adj* articulate, fluent, well-expressed, glib, expressive, vocal, voluble, persuasive, moving, forceful, graceful, plausible, stirring, vivid.
≠ inarticulate, tongue-tied.

elucidate *v* explain, clarify, clear up, interpret, spell out, illustrate, unfold.
≠ confuse.

elude *v* **1** AVOID, escape, evade, dodge, shirk, duck (*infml*), flee. **2** PUZZLE, frustrate, baffle, confound, thwart, stump, foil.

elusive *adj* **1** INDEFINABLE, intangible, unanalysable, subtle, puzzling, baffling, transient, transitory. **2** EVASIVE, shifty, slippery, tricky.

emaciated *adj* thin, gaunt, lean, haggard, wasted, scrawny, skeletal, pinched, attenuated, meagre, lank.
≠ plump, well-fed.

emanate *v* **1** ORIGINATE, proceed, arise, derive, issue, spring, stem, flow, come, emerge. **2** DISCHARGE, send out, emit, give out, give off, radiate.

emancipate *v* free, liberate, release, set free, enfranchise, deliver, discharge, loose, unchain, unshackle, unfetter.
≠ enslave.

embankment *n* causeway, dam, rampart, levee, earthwork.

embargo *n* restriction, ban, prohibition, restraint, proscription, bar, barrier, interdiction (*fml*), impediment, check, hindrance, blockage, stoppage, seizure.

embark *v* board (ship), go aboard, take ship.
≠ disembark.
embark on begin, start, commence, set about, launch, undertake, enter, initiate, engage.
≠ complete, finish.

embarrass *v* disconcert, mortify, show up, discompose, fluster, humiliate, shame, distress.

embarrassment *n* **1** DISCOMPOSURE, self-consciousness, chagrin, mortification, humiliation, shame, awkwardness, confusion, bashfulness. **2** DIFFICULTY, constraint, predicament, distress, discomfort.

embellish *v* adorn, ornament, decorate, deck, dress up, beautify, gild, garnish, festoon, elaborate, embroider, enrich, exaggerate, enhance, varnish, grace.
≠ simplify, denude.

embellishment *n* adornment, ornament, ornamentation, decoration, elaboration, garnish, trimming, gilding, enrichment, enhancement, embroidery, exaggeration.

embezzle *v* appropriate, misappropriate, steal, pilfer, filch, pinch (*infml*).

embezzlement *n* appropriation, misappropriation, pilfering, fraud, stealing, theft, filching.

embittered *adj* bitter, disaffected, sour, disillusioned.

emblem *n* symbol, sign, token, representation, logo, insignia, device, crest, mark, badge, figure.

embodiment *n* incarnation, personification, exemplification, expression, epitome, example, incorporation, realization, representation, manifestation, concentration.

embody *v* **1** PERSONIFY, exemplify, represent, stand for, symbolize, incorporate, express, manifest. **2** INCLUDE, contain, integrate.

embrace *v* **1** HUG, clasp, cuddle, hold, grasp, squeeze. **2** INCLUDE, encompass, incorporate, contain, comprise, cover, involve. **3** ACCEPT, take up, welcome.
n hug, cuddle, clasp, clinch (*infml*).

embroidery

Types of embroidery stitch include: backstitch, blanket, bullion, chain, chevron, cross, feather, fishbone, French knot, half-cross, herringbone, lazy-daisy, longstitch, long-and-short, moss, Oriental couching, Romanian couching, running, satin, stem, straight, Swiss darning, tent.

embroil *v* involve, implicate, entangle, enmesh, mix up, incriminate.

embryo *n* nucleus, germ, beginning, root.

embryonic *adj* undeveloped, rudimentary, immature, early, germinal, primary.
≠ developed.

emerge *v* **1** ARISE, rise, surface, appear, develop, crop up (*infml*), transpire, turn up, materialize. **2** EMANATE, issue, proceed.
≠ **1** disappear.

emergence *n* appearance, rise, advent, coming, dawn, development, arrival, disclosure, issue.
≠ disappearance.

emergency *n* crisis, danger, difficulty, exigency (*fml*), predicament, plight, pinch, strait, quandary.

emigrate *n* migrate, relocate, move, depart.

eminence *n* distinction, fame, pre-eminence, prominence, renown, reputation, greatness, importance, esteem, note, prestige, rank.

eminent *adj* distinguished, famous, prominent, illustrious, outstanding, notable, pre-eminent, prestigious, celebrated, renowned, noteworthy, conspicuous, esteemed, important, well-known, elevated, respected, great, high-ranking, grand, superior.
≠ unknown, obscure, unimportant.

emissary *n* ambassador, agent, envoy, messenger, delegate, herald, courier, representative, scout, deputy, spy.

emission *n* discharge, issue, ejection, emanation, ejaculation, diffusion, transmission, exhalation, radiation, release, exudation, vent.

emit *v* discharge, issue, eject, emanate, exude, give out, give off, diffuse, radiate, release, shed, vent.
≠ absorb.

emotion *n* feeling, passion, sensation, sentiment, ardour, fervour, warmth, reaction, vehemence, excitement.

emotional *adj* **1** FEELING, passionate, sensitive, responsive, ardent, tender, warm, roused, demonstrative, excitable, enthusiastic, fervent, impassioned, moved, sentimental, zealous, hot-blooded, heated, tempestuous, overcharged, temperamental, fiery. **2** EMOTIVE, moving, poignant, thrilling, touching, stirring, heart-warming, exciting, pathetic.
≠ **1** unemotional, cold, detached, calm.

emphasis *n* stress, weight, significance, importance, priority, underscoring, accent, force, power, prominence, pre-eminence, attention, intensity, strength, urgency, positiveness, insistence, mark, moment.

emphasize *v* stress, accentuate, underline, highlight, accent, feature, dwell on, weight, point up, spotlight, play up, insist on, press home, intensify, strengthen, punctuate.
≠ play down, understate.

emphatic *adj* forceful, positive, insistent, certain, definite, decided, unequivocal, absolute, categorical, earnest, marked, pronounced, significant, strong, striking, vigorous, distinct, energetic, forcible, important, impressive, momentous, powerful, punctuated, telling, vivid, graphic, direct.
≠ tentative, hesitant, understated.

empire *n* **1** SUPREMACY, sovereignty, rule, authority, command, government, jurisdiction, control, power, sway. **2** DOMAIN, dominion, kingdom, realm, commonwealth, territory.

employ *v* **1** ENGAGE, hire, take on, recruit, enlist, commission, retain, fill, occupy, take up. **2** USE, utilize, make use of, apply, bring to bear, ply, exercise.

employee *n* worker, member of staff, job-holder, hand, wage-earner.

employer *n* boss, proprietor, owner, manager, gaffer (*infml*), management, company, firm, business, establishment.

employment *n* 1 JOB, work, occupation, situation, business, calling, profession, line (*infml*), vocation, trade, pursuit, craft. 2 ENLISTMENT, employ, engagement, hire.
≠ 1 unemployment.

empower *v* authorize, warrant, enable, license, sanction, permit, entitle, commission, delegate, qualify.

emptiness *n* 1 VACUUM, vacantness, void, hollowness, hunger, bareness, barrenness, desolation. 2 FUTILITY, meaninglessness, worthlessness, aimlessness, ineffectiveness, unreality.
≠ 1 fullness.

empty *adj* 1 VACANT, void, unoccupied, uninhabited, unfilled, deserted, bare, hollow, desolate, blank, clear. 2 FUTILE, aimless, meaningless, senseless, trivial, vain, worthless, useless, insubstantial, ineffective, insincere. 3 VACUOUS, inane, expressionless, blank, vacant.
≠ 1 full. 2 meaningful.
v drain, exhaust, discharge, clear, evacuate, vacate, pour out, unload, void, gut.
≠ fill.

empty-headed *adj* inane, silly, frivolous, scatter-brained (*infml*), feather-brained (*infml*).

emulate *v* match, copy, mimic, follow, imitate, echo, compete with, contend with, rival, vie with.

enable *v* equip, qualify, empower, authorize, sanction, warrant, allow, permit, prepare, fit, facilitate, license, commission, endue.
≠ prevent, inhibit, forbid.

enact *v* 1 DECREE, ordain, order, authorize, command, legislate, sanction, ratify, pass, establish. 2 ACT (OUT), perform, play, portray, represent, depict.
≠ 1 repeal, rescind.

enamoured *adj* charmed, infatuated, in love with, enchanted, captivated, entranced, smitten, keen, taken, fascinated, fond.

enchant *v* 1 CAPTIVATE, charm, fascinate, enrapture, attract, allure, appeal, delight, thrill. 2 ENTRANCE, enthral, bewitch, spellbind, hypnotize, mesmerize.
≠ 1 repel.

enclose *v* encircle, encompass, surround, fence, hedge, hem in, bound, encase, embrace, envelop, confine, hold, shut in, wrap, pen, cover, circumscribe, incorporate, include, insert, contain, comprehend.

enclosure *n* pen, pound, compound, paddock, fold, stockade, sty, arena, corral, court, ring, cloister.

encompass *v* 1 ENCIRCLE, circle, ring, surround, gird, envelop, circumscribe, hem in, enclose, hold. 2 INCLUDE, cover, embrace, contain, comprise, admit, incorporate, involve, embody, comprehend.

encounter *v* 1 MEET, come across, run into (*infml*), happen on, chance upon, run across, confront, face, experience. 2 FIGHT, clash with, combat, cross swords with (*infml*), engage, grapple with, struggle, strive, contend.
n 1 MEETING, brush, confrontation. 2 CLASH, fight, combat, conflict, contest, battle, set-to (*infml*), dispute, engagement, action, skirmish, run-in, collision.

encourage *v* 1 HEARTEN, exhort, stimulate, spur, reassure, rally, inspire, incite, egg on (*infml*), buoy up, cheer, urge, rouse, comfort, console. 2 PROMOTE, advance, aid, boost, forward, further, foster, support, help, strengthen.
≠ 1 discourage, depress. 2 discourage.

encouragement *n* 1 REASSURANCE, inspiration, cheer, exhortation, incitement, pep talk (*infml*), urging, stimulation, consolation, succour (*fml*). 2 PROMOTION, help, aid, boost, shot in the arm (*infml*), incentive, support, stimulus.
≠ 1 discouragement, disapproval.

encouraging *adj* heartening, promising, hopeful, reassuring, stimulating, uplifting, auspicious, cheering, comforting, bright, rosy, cheerful, satisfactory.
≠ discouraging.

encroach *v* intrude, invade, impinge,

trespass, infringe, usurp, overstep, make inroads, muscle in (*infml*).

encumber *v* burden, overload, weigh down, saddle, oppress, handicap, hamper, hinder, impede, slow down, obstruct, inconvenience, prevent, retard, cramp.

encumbrance *n* burden, cumbrance, load, cross, millstone, albatross, difficulty, handicap, impediment, obstruction, obstacle, inconvenience, hindrance, liability.

end *n* **1** FINISH, conclusion, termination, close, completion, cessation, culmination, dénouement. **2** EXTREMITY, boundary, edge, limit, tip. **3** REMAINDER, tip, butt, left-over, remnant, stub, scrap, fragment. **4** AIM, object, objective, purpose, intention, goal, point, reason, design. **5** RESULT, outcome, consequence, upshot. **6** DEATH, demise, destruction, extermination, downfall, doom, ruin, dissolution.
≠ **1** beginning, start. **6** birth.
v **1** FINISH, close, cease, conclude, stop, terminate, complete, culminate, wind up. **2** DESTROY, annihilate, exterminate, extinguish, ruin, abolish, dissolve.
≠ **1** begin, start.

endanger *v* imperil, hazard, jeopardize, risk, expose, threaten, compromise.
≠ protect.

endearing *adj* lovable, charming, appealing, attractive, winsome, delightful, enchanting.

endeavour *n* attempt, effort, go (*infml*), try, shot (*infml*), stab (*infml*), undertaking, enterprise, aim, venture.
v attempt, try, strive, aim, aspire, undertake, venture, struggle, labour, take pains.

ending *n* end, close, finish, completion, termination, conclusion, culmination, climax, resolution, consummation, dénouement, finale, epilogue.
≠ beginning, start.

endless *adj* **1** INFINITE, boundless, unlimited, measureless. **2** EVERLASTING, ceaseless, perpetual, constant, continual, continuous, undying, eternal, interminable, monotonous.
≠ **1** finite, limited. **2** temporary.

endorse *v* **1** APPROVE, sanction, authorize, support, back, affirm, ratify, confirm, vouch for, advocate, warrant, recommend, subscribe to, sustain, adopt. **2** SIGN, countersign.

endorsement *n* **1** APPROVAL, sanction, authorization, support, backing, affirmation, ratification, confirmation, advocacy, warrant, recommendation, commendation, seal of approval, testimonial, OK (*infml*). **2** SIGNATURE, countersignature.

endow *v* bestow, bequeath, leave, will, give, donate, endue (*fml*), confer, grant, present, award, finance, fund, support, make over, furnish, provide, supply.

endowment *n* **1** BEQUEST, legacy, award, grant, fund, gift, provision, settlement, donation, bestowal, benefaction, dowry, income, revenue. **2** TALENT, attribute, faculty, gift, ability, quality, flair, genius, qualification.

endurance *n* fortitude, patience, staying power, stamina, resignation, stoicism, tenacity, perseverance, resolution, stability, persistence, strength, toleration.

endure *v* **1** *endure hardship*: bear, stand, put up with, tolerate, weather, brave, cope with, face, go through, experience, submit to, suffer, sustain, swallow, undergo, withstand, stick, stomach, allow, permit, support. **2** *a peace that will endure for ever*: last, abide (*fml*), remain, live, survive, stay, persist, hold, prevail.

enemy *n* adversary, opponent, foe (*fml*), rival, antagonist, the opposition, competitor, opposer, other side.
≠ friend, ally.

energetic *adj* lively, vigorous, active, animated, dynamic, spirited, tireless, zestful, brisk, strong, forceful, potent, powerful, strenuous, high-powered.
≠ lethargic, sluggish, inactive, idle.

energy *n* liveliness, vigour, activity,

animation, drive, dynamism, get-up-and-go (*infml*), life, spirit, verve, vivacity, vitality, zest, zeal, ardour, fire, efficiency, force, forcefulness, zip (*infml*), strength, power, intensity, exertion, stamina.
≠ lethargy, inertia, weakness.

enforce *v* impose, administer, implement, apply, execute, discharge, insist on, compel, oblige, urge, carry out, constrain, require, coerce, prosecute, reinforce.

engage *v* **1** PARTICIPATE, take part, embark on, take up, practise, involve. **2** ATTRACT, allure, draw, captivate, charm, catch. **3** OCCUPY, engross, absorb, busy, tie up, grip. **4** EMPLOY, hire, appoint, take on, enlist, enrol, commission, recruit, contract. **5** INTERLOCK, mesh, interconnect, join, interact, attach. **6** FIGHT, battle with, attack, take on, encounter, assail, combat.
≠ **2** repel. **4** dismiss, discharge. **5** disengage.

engaged *adj* **1** *engaged in his work*: occupied, busy, engrossed, immersed, absorbed, preoccupied, involved, employed. **2** *engaged to be married*: promised, betrothed (*fml*), pledged, spoken for, committed. **3** *the phone is engaged*: busy, tied up, unavailable.

engagement *n* **1** APPOINTMENT, meeting, date, arrangement, assignation, fixture, rendezvous. **2** PROMISE, pledge, betrothal (*fml*), commitment, obligation, assurance, vow, troth (*fml*). **3** FIGHT, battle, combat, conflict, action, encounter, confrontation, contest.

engaging *adj* charming, attractive, appealing, captivating, pleasing, delightful, winsome, lovable, likable, pleasant, fetching, fascinating, agreeable.
≠ repulsive, repellant.

engine *n* motor, machine, mechanism, appliance, contraption, apparatus, device, instrument, tool, locomotive, dynamo.

Types of engine include: diesel, donkey, fuel-injection, internal-combustion, jet, petrol, steam, turbine, turbojet, turboprop, V-engine.
Parts of an automotive engine and its ancillaries include: air filter, alternator, camshaft, camshaft cover, carburettor, choke, connecting rod, con-rod (*infml*), cooling fan, crankshaft, crankshaft pulley, cylinder block, cylinder head, drive belt, exhaust manifold, exhaust valve, fan belt, flywheel, fuel and ignition ECU (electronic control unit), fuel injector, gasket, ignition coil, ignition distributor, inlet manifold, inlet valve, oil filter, oil pump, oil seal, petrol pump, piston, piston ring, power-steering pump, push-rod, radiator, rocker arm, rocker cover, rotor arm, spark plug, starter motor, sump, tappet, thermostat, timing belt, timing pulley, turbocharger.

engineer *n* **1** MECHANIC, technician, engine driver. **2** DESIGNER, originator, planner, inventor, deviser, mastermind, architect.
v plan, contrive, devise, manoeuvre, cause, manipulate, control, bring about, mastermind, originate, orchestrate, effect, plot, scheme, manage, create, rig.

engrave *v* **1** INSCRIBE, cut, carve, chisel, etch, chase. **2** *engraved on her mind*: imprint, impress, fix, stamp, lodge, ingrain.

engraving *n* print, impression, inscription, carving, etching, woodcut, plate, block, cutting, chiselling, mark.

engross *v* absorb, occupy, engage, grip, hold, preoccupy, rivet, fascinate, captivate, enthral, arrest, involve, intrigue.
≠ bore.

enhance *v* heighten, intensify, increase, improve, elevate, magnify, swell, exalt, raise, lift, boost, strengthen, reinforce, embellish.
≠ reduce, minimize.

enigma *n* mystery, riddle, puzzle, conundrum, problem, poser (*infml*), brain-teaser.

enigmatic *adj* mysterious, puzzling, cryptic, obscure, strange, perplexing.

≠ simple, straightforward.

enjoy *v* take pleasure in, delight in, appreciate, like, relish, revel in, rejoice in, savour.
≠ dislike, hate.
enjoy oneself have a good time, have fun, make merry.

enjoyable *adj* pleasant, agreeable, delightful, pleasing, gratifying, entertaining, amusing, fun, delicious, good, satisfying.
≠ disagreeable.

enjoyment *n* **1** PLEASURE, delight, amusement, gratification, entertainment, relish, joy, fun, happiness, diversion, indulgence, recreation, zest, satisfaction.
2 POSSESSION, use, advantage, benefit.
≠ **1** displeasure.

enlarge *v* increase, expand, augment, add to, grow, extend, magnify, inflate, swell, wax, stretch, multiply, develop, amplify, blow up, widen, broaden, lengthen, heighten, elaborate.
≠ diminish, shrink.

enlighten *v* instruct, edify, educate, inform, illuminate, teach, counsel, apprise, advise.
≠ confuse.

enlightened *adj* informed, aware, knowledgeable, educated, civilized, cultivated, refined, sophisticated, conversant, wise, reasonable, liberal, open-minded, literate.
≠ ignorant, confused.

enlist *v* engage, enrol, register, sign up, recruit, conscript, employ, volunteer, join (up), gather, muster, secure, obtain, procure, enter.

enmity *n* animosity, hostility, antagonism, discord, strife, feud, antipathy, acrimony, bitterness, hatred, aversion, ill-will, bad blood, rancour, malevolence, malice, venom.
≠ friendship.

enormity *n* atrocity, outrage, iniquity, horror, evil, crime, abomination, monstrosity, wickedness, vileness, depravity, atrociousness, viciousness.

enormous *adj* huge, immense, vast, gigantic, massive, colossal, gross, gargantuan, monstrous, mammoth, jumbo (*infml*), tremendous, prodigious.
≠ small, tiny.

enough *adj* sufficient, adequate, ample, plenty, abundant.
n sufficiency, adequacy, plenty, abundance.
adv sufficiently, adequately, reasonably, tolerably, passably, moderately, fairly, satisfactorily, amply.

enquire *see* **inquire**.

enquiry *see* **inquiry**.

enrage *v* incense, infuriate, anger, madden, provoke, incite, inflame, exasperate, irritate, rile.
≠ calm, placate.

enrich *v* **1** ENDOW, enhance, improve, refine, develop, cultivate, augment.
2 ADORN, ornament, beautify, embellish, decorate, grace.
≠ **1** impoverish.

enrol *v* **1** REGISTER, enlist, sign on, sign up, join up, recruit, engage, admit. **2** RECORD, list, note, inscribe.

enrolment *n* registration, recruitment, enlistment, admission, acceptance.

ensemble *n* **1** WHOLE, total, entirety, sum, aggregate, set, collection.
2 OUTFIT, costume, get-up (*infml*), rig-out (*infml*). **3** GROUP, band, company, troupe, chorus.

ensign *n* banner, standard, flag, colours, pennant, jack, badge.

enslave *v* subjugate, subject, dominate, bind, enchain, yoke.
≠ free, emancipate.

ensue *v* follow, issue, proceed, succeed, result, arise, happen, turn out, befall, flow, derive, stem.
≠ precede.

ensure *v* **1** CERTIFY, guarantee, warrant. **2** PROTECT, guard, safeguard, secure.

entail *v* involve, necessitate, occasion, require, demand, cause, give rise to, lead to, result in.

entangle *v* enmesh, ensnare, embroil, involve, implicate, snare, tangle,

entrap, trap, catch, mix up, knot, ravel, muddle.
≠ disentangle.

enter *v* **1** COME IN, go in, arrive, insert, introduce, board, penetrate. **2** RECORD, log, note, register, take down, inscribe. **3** JOIN, embark upon, enrol, enlist, set about, sign up, participate, commence, start, begin.
≠ **1** depart. **2** delete.

enterprise *n* **1** UNDERTAKING, venture, project, plan, effort, operation, programme, endeavour. **2** INITIATIVE, resourcefulness, drive, adventurousness, boldness, get-up-and-go (*infml*), push, energy, enthusiasm, spirit. **3** BUSINESS, company, firm, establishment, concern.
≠ **2** apathy.

enterprising *adj* venturesome, adventurous, bold, daring, go-ahead, imaginative, resourceful, self-reliant, enthusiastic, energetic, keen, ambitious, aspiring, spirited, active.
≠ unenterprising, lethargic.

entertain *v* **1** AMUSE, divert, please, delight, cheer. **2** RECEIVE, have guests, accommodate, put up, treat. **3** HARBOUR, countenance, contemplate, consider, imagine, conceive.
≠ **1** bore. **3** reject.

entertainer

> *Entertainers include*: acrobat, actor, actress, busker, chat-show host, clown, comedian, comic, conjuror, dancer, disc jockey, DJ (*infml*), escapologist, game-show host, hypnotist, ice-skater, impressionist, jester, juggler, magician, mimic, mind-reader, minstrel, musician, presenter, singer, song-and-dance act, stand-up comic, striptease-artist, stripper (*infml*), trapeze-artist, tight-rope walker, ventriloquist; performer, artiste *see also* **musician**; **singers**.

entertaining *adj* amusing, diverting, fun, delightful, interesting, pleasant, pleasing, humorous, witty.
≠ boring.

entertainment *n* **1** AMUSEMENT, diversion, recreation, enjoyment, play, pastime, fun, sport, distraction, pleasure. **2** SHOW, spectacle, performance, extravaganza.

> *Forms of entertainment include*: cinema, cartoon show, video, radio, television, theatre, pantomime; dance, disco, discothèque, concert, recital, musical, opera, variety show, music hall, revue, karaoke, cabaret, night-club, casino; magic-show, puppet show, Punch-and-Judy show, circus, gymkhana, waxworks, laser-light show, zoo, rodeo, carnival, pageant, fête, festival, firework party, barbecue. *see also* **performance**; **theatrical**.

enthral *v* captivate, entrance, enchant, fascinate, charm, beguile, thrill, intrigue, hypnotize, mesmerize, engross.
≠ bore.

enthusiasm *n* zeal, ardour, fervour, passion, keenness, eagerness, vehemence, warmth, frenzy, excitement, earnestness, relish, spirit, devotion, craze, mania, rage.
≠ apathy.

enthusiast *n* devotee, zealot, admirer, fan (*infml*), supporter, follower, buff (*infml*), freak (*infml*), fanatic, fiend (*infml*), lover.

enthusiastic *adj* keen, ardent, eager, fervent, vehement, passionate, warm, whole-hearted, zealous, vigorous, spirited, earnest, devoted, avid, excited, exuberant.
≠ unenthusiastic, apathetic.

entice *v* tempt, lure, attract, seduce, lead on, draw, coax, persuade, induce, sweet-talk (*infml*).

entire *adj* complete, whole, total, full, intact, perfect.
≠ incomplete, partial.

entirely *adv* completely, wholly, totally, fully, utterly, unreservedly, absolutely, in toto, thoroughly, altogether, perfectly, solely, exclusively, every inch.
≠ partially.

entitle *v* **1** AUTHORIZE, qualify, empower, enable, allow, permit, license, warrant. **2** NAME, call, term, title, style, christen, dub, label, designate.

entity *n* being, existence, thing, body, creature, individual, organism, substance.

entrance[1] *n* **1** ACCESS, admission, admittance, entry, entrée. **2** ARRIVAL, appearance, debut, initiation, introduction, start. **3** OPENING, way in, door, doorway, gate.
≠ **2** departure. **3** exit.

entrance[2] *v* charm, enchant, enrapture, captivate, bewitch, spellbind, fascinate, delight, ravish, transport, hypnotize, mesmerize.
≠ repel.

entrant *n* **1** NOVICE, beginner, newcomer, initiate, convert, probationer. **2** COMPETITOR, candidate, contestant, contender, entry, participant, player.

entreat *v* beg, implore, plead with, beseech, crave, supplicate, pray, invoke, ask, petition, request, appeal to.

entreaty *n* appeal, plea, prayer, petition, supplication, suit, invocation, cry, solicitation, request.

entrench *v* establish, fix, embed, dig in, ensconce, install, lodge, root, ingrain, settle, seat, plant, anchor, set.
≠ dislodge.

entrust *v* trust, commit, confide, consign, authorize, charge, assign, turn over, commend, depute, invest, delegate, deliver.

entry *n* **1** ENTRANCE, appearance, admittance, admission, access, entrée, introduction. **2** OPENING, entrance, door, doorway, access, threshold, way in, passage, gate. **3** RECORD, item, minute, note, memorandum, statement, account. **4** ENTRANT, competitor, contestant, candidate, participant, player.
≠ **2** exit.

enumerate *v* list, name, itemize, cite, detail, specify, count, number, relate, recount, spell out, tell, mention, calculate, quote, recite, reckon.

enunciate *v* **1** ARTICULATE, pronounce, vocalize, voice, express, say, speak, utter, sound. **2** STATE, declare, proclaim, announce, propound.

envelop *v* wrap, enfold, enwrap, encase, cover, swathe, shroud, engulf, enclose, encircle, encompass, surround, cloak, veil, blanket, conceal, obscure, hide.

envelope *n* wrapper, wrapping, cover, case, casing, sheath, covering, shell, skin, jacket, coating.

enviable *adj* desirable, privileged, favoured, blessed, fortunate, lucky, advantageous, sought-after, excellent, fine.
≠ unenviable.

envious *adj* covetous, jealous, resentful, green (with envy), dissatisfied, grudging, jaundiced, green-eyed (*infml*).

environment *n* surroundings, conditions, circumstances, milieu, atmosphere, habitat, situation, element, medium, background, ambience, setting, context, territory, domain.

envisage *v* visualize, imagine, picture, envision, conceive of, preconceive, predict, anticipate, foresee, image, see, contemplate.

envoy *n* agent, representative, ambassador, diplomat, messenger, legate, emissary, minister, delegate, deputy, courier, intermediary.

envy *n* covetousness, jealousy, resentfulness, resentment, dissatisfaction, grudge, ill-will, malice, spite.
v covet, resent, begrudge, grudge, crave.

epidemic *adj* widespread, prevalent, rife, rampant, pandemic, sweeping, wide-ranging, prevailing.
n plague, outbreak, spread, rash, upsurge, wave.

epilogue *n* afterword, postscript, coda, conclusion.
≠ foreword, prologue, preface.

episode *n* **1** INCIDENT, event, occurrence, happening, occasion, circumstance, experience, adventure, matter, business. **2** INSTALMENT, part, chapter, passage, section, scene.

epitome *n* **1** PERSONIFICATION, embodiment, representation, model, archetype, type, essence. **2** SUMMARY, abstract, abridgement, digest.

epoch *n* age, era, period, time, date.

equable *adj* **1** *an equable person*: even-tempered, placid, calm, serene, unexcitable, tranquil, unflappable, composed, level-headed, easy-going. **2** *an equable climate*: uniform, even, consistent, constant, regular, temperate, unvarying, steady, stable, smooth.
≠ **1** excitable. **2** variable.

equal *adj* **1** IDENTICAL, the same, alike, like, equivalent, corresponding, commensurate, comparable. **2** EVEN, uniform, regular, unvarying, balanced, matched. **3** COMPETENT, able, adequate, fit, capable, suitable.
≠ **1** different. **2** unequal. **3** unsuitable.
n peer, counterpart, equivalent, coequal, match, parallel, twin, fellow.
v match, parallel, correspond to, balance, square with, tally with, equalize, equate, rival, level, even.

equality *n* **1** UNIFORMITY, evenness, equivalence, correspondence, balance, parity, par, symmetry, proportion, identity, sameness, likeness. **2** IMPARTIALITY, fairness, justice, egalitarianism.
≠ **2** inequality.

equalize *v* level, even up, match, equal, equate, draw level, balance, square, standardize, compensate, smooth.

equate *v* compare, liken, match, pair, correspond to, correspond with, balance, parallel, equalize, offset, square, agree, tally, juxtapose.

equation *n* equality, correspondence, equivalence, balancing, agreement, parallel, pairing, comparison, match, likeness, juxtaposition.

equilibrium *n* **1** BALANCE, poise, symmetry, evenness, stability. **2** EQUANIMITY, self-possession, composure, calmness, coolness, serenity.
≠ **1** imbalance.

equip *v* provide, fit out, supply, furnish, prepare, arm, fit up, kit out, stock, endow, rig, dress, array, deck out.

equipment *n* apparatus, gear, supplies, tackle, rig-out (*infml*), tools, material, furnishings, baggage, outfit, paraphernalia, stuff, things, accessories, furniture.

equivalence *n* identity, parity, correspondence, agreement, likeness, interchangeability, similarity, substitutability, correlation, parallel, conformity, sameness.
≠ unlikeness, dissimilarity.

equivalent *adj* equal, same, similar, substitutable, corresponding, alike, comparable, interchangeable, even, tantamount, twin.
≠ unlike, different.

equivocal *adj* ambiguous, uncertain, obscure, vague, evasive, oblique, misleading, dubious, confusing, indefinite.
≠ unequivocal, clear.

equivocate *v* prevaricate, evade, dodge, fence, beat about the bush (*infml*), hedge, mislead.

era *n* age, epoch, period, date, day, days, time, aeon, stage, century.

eradicate *v* eliminate, annihilate, get rid of, remove, root out, suppress, destroy, exterminate, extinguish, weed out, stamp out, abolish, erase, obliterate.

erase *v* obliterate, rub out, expunge (*fml*), delete, blot out, cancel, efface, get rid of, remove, eradicate.

erect *adj* upright, straight, vertical, upstanding, standing, raised, rigid, stiff.
v build, construct, put up, establish, set up, elevate, assemble, found, form, institute, initiate, raise, rear, lift, mount, pitch, create.

erode *v* wear away, eat away, wear down, corrode, abrade, consume, grind down, disintegrate, deteriorate, spoil.

erosion *n* wear, corrosion, abrasion, attrition, denudation, disintegration, deterioration, destruction, undermining.

erotic *adj* aphrodisiac, seductive, sexy, sensual, titillating, pornographic, lascivious, stimulating, suggestive, amorous, amatory, venereal, carnal, lustful, voluptuous.

err *v* **1** MAKE A MISTAKE, be wrong, miscalculate, mistake, misjudge, slip up, blunder, misunderstand. **2** DO WRONG, sin, misbehave, go astray, offend, transgress, deviate.

errand *n* commission, charge, mission, assignment, message, task, job, duty.

erratic *adj* changeable, variable, fitful, fluctuating, inconsistent, irregular, unstable, shifting, inconstant, unpredictable, unreliable, aberrant, abnormal, eccentric, desultory, meandering.
≠ steady, consistent, stable.

erroneous *adj* incorrect, wrong, mistaken, false, untrue, inaccurate, inexact, invalid, illogical, unfounded, faulty, flawed.
≠ correct, right.

error *n* mistake, inaccuracy, slip, slip-up, blunder, howler (*infml*), gaffe, faux pas, solecism, lapse, miscalculation, misunderstanding, misconception, misapprehension, misprint, oversight, omission, fallacy, flaw, fault, wrong.

erudite *adj* learned, scholarly, well-educated, knowledgeable, lettered, educated, well-read, literate, academic, cultured, wise, highbrow, profound.
≠ illiterate, ignorant.

erupt *v* break out, explode, belch, discharge, burst, gush, spew, spout, eject, expel, emit, flare up, vomit, break.

eruption *n* **1** OUTBURST, discharge, ejection, emission, explosion, flare-up. **2** RASH, outbreak, inflammation.

escalate *v* increase, intensify, grow, accelerate, rise, step up, heighten, raise, spiral, magnify, enlarge, expand, extend, mount, ascend, climb, amplify.
≠ decrease, diminish.

escapade *n* adventure, exploit, fling, prank, caper, romp, spree, lark (*infml*), antic, stunt, trick.

escape *v* **1** GET AWAY, break free, run away, bolt, abscond, flee, fly, decamp, break loose, break out, do a bunk (*infml*), flit, slip away, shake off, slip. **2** AVOID, evade, elude, dodge, skip, shun. **3** LEAK, seep, flow, drain, gush, issue, discharge, ooze, trickle, pour forth, pass.
n **1** GETAWAY, flight, bolt, flit, break-out, decampment, jail-break. **2** AVOIDANCE, evasion. **3** LEAK, seepage, leakage, outflow, gush, drain, discharge, emission, spurt, outpour, emanation. **4** ESCAPISM, diversion, distraction, recreation, relaxation, pastime, safety-valve.

escapist *n* dreamer, daydreamer, fantasizer, wishful thinker, non-realist, ostrich (*infml*).
≠ realist.

escort *n* **1** COMPANION, chaperon(e), partner, attendant, aide, squire, guide, bodyguard, protector. **2** ENTOURAGE, company, retinue, suite, train, guard, convoy, cortège.
v accompany, partner, chaperon(e), guide, lead, usher, conduct, guard, protect.

esoteric *adj* recondite, obscure, abstruse, cryptic, inscrutable, mysterious, mystic, mystical, occult, hidden, secret, confidential, private, inside.
≠ well-known, familiar.

especially *adv* **1** CHIEFLY, mainly, principally, primarily, pre-eminently, above all. **2** PARTICULARLY, specially, markedly, notably, exceptionally, outstandingly, expressly, supremely, uniquely, unusually, strikingly, very.

essay *n* composition, dissertation, paper, article, assignment, thesis, piece, commentary, critique, discourse, treatise, review, leader, tract.

essence *n* **1** NATURE, being, quintessence, substance, soul, spirit, core, centre, heart, meaning, quality, significance, life, entity, crux, kernel, marrow, pith, character, characteristics, attributes, principle. **2** CONCENTRATE, extract, distillation, spirits.

essential *adj* **1** FUNDAMENTAL, basic, intrinsic, inherent, principal, main, key, characteristic, definitive, typical, constituent. **2** CRUCIAL, indispensable, necessary, vital, requisite, required, needed, important.
≠ **1** incidental. **2** dispensable, inessential.
n necessity, prerequisite, must, requisite, sine qua non (*fml*), requirement, basic, fundamental, necessary, principle.
≠ inessential.

establish *v* **1** SET UP, found, start, form, institute, create, organize, inaugurate, introduce, install, plant, settle, secure, lodge, base. **2** PROVE, substantiate, demonstrate, authenticate, ratify, verify, validate, certify, confirm, affirm.
≠ **1** uproot. **2** refute.

establishment *n* **1** FORMATION, setting up, founding, creation, foundation, installation, institution, inauguration. **2** BUSINESS, company, firm, institute, organization, concern, institution, enterprise. **3** RULING CLASS, the system, the authorities, the powers that be.

estate *n* **1** POSSESSIONS, effects, assets, belongings, holdings, property, goods, lands. **2** AREA, development, land, manor. **3** (*fml*) STATUS, standing, situation, position, class, place, condition, state, rank.

estimate *v* assess, reckon, evaluate, calculate, gauge, guess, value, conjecture, consider, judge, think, number, count, compute, believe.
n reckoning, valuation, judgement, guess, approximation, assessment, estimation, evaluation, computation, opinion.

estimation *n* **1** JUDGEMENT, opinion, belief, consideration, estimate, view, evaluation, assessment, reckoning, conception, calculation, computation. **2** RESPECT, regard, appreciation, esteem, credit.

estranged *adj* divided, separate, alienated, disaffected, antagonized.
≠ reconciled, united.

estuary *n* inlet, mouth, firth, fjord, creek, arm, sea-loch.

eternal *adj* **1** *eternal bliss*: unending, endless, ceaseless, everlasting, never-ending, infinite, limitless, immortal, undying, imperishable. **2** *eternal truths*: unchanging, timeless, enduring, lasting, perennial, abiding. **3** (*infml*) *eternal quarrelling*: constant, continuous, perpetual, incessant, interminable.
≠ **1** ephemeral, temporary. **2** changeable.

eternity *n* **1** EVERLASTINGNESS, endlessness, everlasting, imperishability, infinity, timelessness, perpetuity, immutability, ages, age, aeon. **2** AFTER-LIFE, hereafter, immortality, heaven, paradise, next world, world to come.

ethical *adj* moral, principled, just, right, proper, virtuous, honourable, fair, upright, righteous, seemly, honest, good, correct, commendable, fitting, noble, meet (*fml*).
≠ unethical.

ethics *n* moral values, morality, principles, standards, code, moral philosophy, rules, beliefs, propriety, conscience, equity.

ethnic *adj* racial, native, indigenous, traditional, tribal, folk, cultural, national, aboriginal.

ethos *n* attitude, beliefs, standards, manners, ethics, morality, code, principles, spirit, tenor, rationale, character, disposition.

etiquette *n* code, formalities, standards, correctness, conventions, customs, protocol (*fml*), rules, manners, politeness, courtesy, civility, decorum, ceremony, decency.

euphemism *n* evasion, polite term, substitution, genteelism, politeness, understatement.

euphoria *n* elation, ecstasy, bliss, rapture, high spirits, well-being, high (*infml*), exhilaration, exultation, joy,

intoxication, jubilation, transport, glee, exaltation, enthusiasm, cheerfulness.
≠ depression, despondency.

evacuate *v* **1** LEAVE, depart, withdraw, quit, remove, retire from, clear (out) (*infml*), abandon, desert, forsake, vacate, decamp, relinquish. **2** EMPTY, eject, void, expel, discharge, eliminate, defecate, purge.

evacuation *n* **1** DEPARTURE, withdrawal, retreat, exodus, removal, quitting, desertion, abandonment, clearance, relinquishment, retirement, vacation. **2** EMPTYING, expulsion, ejection, discharge, elimination, defecation, urination.

evade *v* **1** *evade one's duties*: elude, avoid, escape, dodge, shirk, steer clear of, shun, sidestep, duck (*infml*), balk, skive (*infml*), fend off, chicken out (*infml*), cop out (*infml*). **2** *evade a question*: prevaricate, equivocate, fence, fudge, parry, quibble, hedge.
≠ **1** confront, face.

evaluate *v* value, assess, appraise, estimate, reckon, calculate, gauge, judge, rate, size up, weigh, compute, rank.

evaluation *n* valuation, appraisal, assessment, estimation, estimate, judgement, reckoning, calculation, opinion, computation.

evaporate *v* **1** DISAPPEAR, dematerialize, vanish, melt (away), dissolve, disperse, dispel, dissipate, fade. **2** VAPORIZE, dry, dehydrate, exhale.

evasion *n* avoidance, escape, dodge, equivocation, excuse, prevarication, put-off, trickery, subterfuge, shirking.
≠ frankness, directness.

evasive *adj* equivocating, indirect, prevaricating, devious, shifty (*infml*), unforthcoming, slippery (*infml*), misleading, deceitful, deceptive, cagey (*infml*), oblique, secretive, tricky, cunning.
≠ direct, frank.

eve *n* day before, verge, brink, edge, threshold.

even *adj* **1** LEVEL, flat, smooth, horizontal, flush, parallel, plane. **2** STEADY, unvarying, constant, regular, uniform. **3** EQUAL, balanced, matching, same, similar, like, symmetrical, fifty-fifty, level, side by side, neck and neck (*infml*). **4** EVEN-TEMPERED, calm, placid, serene, tranquil, composed, unruffled. **5** EVEN-HANDED, balanced, equitable, fair, impartial.
≠ **1** uneven. **3** unequal.
v smooth, flatten, level, match, regularize, balance, equalize, align, square, stabilize, steady, straighten.

evening *n* nightfall, dusk, eve, eventide, twilight, sunset, sundown.

event *n* **1** HAPPENING, occurrence, incident, occasion, affair, circumstance, episode, eventuality, experience, matter, case, adventure, business, fact, possibility, milestone. **2** CONSEQUENCE, result, outcome, conclusion, end, effect, issue, termination. **3** GAME, match, competition, contest, tournament, engagement.

even-tempered *adj* calm, level-headed, placid, stable, tranquil, serene, composed, cool, steady, peaceful, peaceable.
≠ excitable, erratic.

eventful *adj* busy, exciting, lively, active, full, interesting, remarkable, significant, memorable, momentous, notable, noteworthy, unforgettable.
≠ dull, ordinary.

eventual *adj* final, ultimate, resulting, concluding, ensuing, future, later, subsequent, prospective, projected, planned, impending.

eventually *adv* finally, ultimately, at last, in the end, at length, subsequently, after all, sooner or later.

ever *adv* **1** ALWAYS, evermore, for ever, perpetually, constantly, at all times, continually, endlessly. **2** AT ANY TIME, in any case, in any circumstances, at all, on any account.
≠ **1** never.

everlasting *adj* eternal, undying, never-ending, endless, immortal, infinite, imperishable, constant,

permanent, perpetual, indestructible, timeless.
≠ temporary, transient.

everyday *adj* ordinary, common, commonplace, day-to-day, familiar, run-of-the-mill, regular, plain, routine, usual, workaday, common-or-garden (*infml*), normal, customary, stock, accustomed, conventional, daily, habitual, monotonous, frequent, simple, informal.
≠ unusual, exceptional, special.

everyone *n* everybody, one and all, each one, all and sundry, the whole world.

everywhere *adv* all around, all over, throughout, far and near, far and wide, high and low, ubiquitous, left, right and centre (*infml*).

evict *v* expel, eject, dispossess, put out, turn out, turf out (*infml*), kick out (*infml*), force out, remove, cast out, chuck out (*infml*), oust, dislodge, expropriate.

evidence *n* **1** PROOF, verification, confirmation, affirmation, grounds, substantiation, documentation, data. **2** TESTIMONY, declaration.
3 INDICATION, manifestation, suggestion, sign, mark, hint, demonstration, token.

evident *adj* clear, obvious, manifest, apparent, plain, patent, visible, conspicuous, noticeable, clear-cut, unmistakable, perceptible, distinct, discernible, tangible, incontestable, indisputable, incontrovertible.

evidently *adv* clearly, apparently, plainly, patently, manifestly, obviously, seemingly, undoubtedly, doubtless(ly), indisputably.

evil *adj* **1** WICKED, wrong, sinful, bad, immoral, vicious, vile, malevolent, iniquitous, cruel, base, corrupt, heinous, malicious, malignant, devilish, depraved, mischievous. **2** HARMFUL, pernicious, destructive, deadly, detrimental, hurtful, poisonous.
3 DISASTROUS, ruinous, calamitous, catastrophic, adverse, dire, inauspicious. **4** OFFENSIVE, noxious, foul.

n **1** WICKEDNESS, wrong-doing, wrong, immorality, badness, sin, sinfulness, vice, viciousness, iniquity, depravity, baseness, corruption, malignity, mischief, heinousness.
2 ADVERSITY, affliction, calamity, disaster, misfortune, suffering, sorrow, ruin, catastrophe, blow, curse, distress, hurt, harm, ill, injury, misery, woe.

evoke *v* summon (up), call, elicit, invoke, arouse, stir, raise, stimulate, call forth, call up, conjure up, awaken, provoke, excite, recall.
≠ suppress.

evolution *n* development, growth, progression, progress, expansion, increase, ripening, derivation, descent.

evolve *v* develop, grow, increase, mature, progress, unravel, expand, enlarge, emerge, descend, derive, result, elaborate.

exact *adj* **1** PRECISE, accurate, correct, faithful, literal, flawless, faultless, right, true, veracious, definite, explicit, detailed, specific, strict, unerring, close, factual, identical, express, word-perfect, blow-by-blow (*infml*).
2 CAREFUL, scrupulous, particular, rigorous, methodical, meticulous, orderly, painstaking.
≠ **1** inexact, imprecise.
v extort, extract, claim, insist on, wrest, wring, compel, demand, command, force, impose, require, squeeze, milk (*infml*).

exacting *adj* demanding, difficult, hard, laborious, arduous, rigorous, taxing, tough, harsh, painstaking, severe, strict, unsparing.
≠ easy.

exactly *adv* **1** PRECISELY, accurately, literally, faithfully, correctly, specifically, rigorously, scrupulously, veraciously, verbatim, carefully, faultlessly, unerringly, strictly, to the letter, particularly, methodically, explicitly, expressly, dead (*infml*).
2 ABSOLUTELY, definitely, precisely, indeed, certainly, truly, quite, just, unequivocally.
≠ **1** inaccurately, roughly.

exaggerate *v* overstate, overdo,

magnify, overemphasize, emphasize, embellish, embroider, enlarge, amplify, oversell, pile it on (*infml*).
≠ understate.

examination *n* **1** INSPECTION, enquiry, scrutiny, study, survey, search, analysis, exploration, investigation, probe, appraisal, observation, research, review, scan, once-over (*infml*), perusal, check, check-up, audit, critique. **2** TEST, exam, quiz, questioning, cross-examination, cross-questioning, trial, inquisition, interrogation, viva.

examine *v* **1** INSPECT, investigate, scrutinize, study, survey, analyse, explore, enquire, consider, probe, review, scan, check (out), ponder, pore over, sift, vet, weigh up, appraise, assay, audit, peruse, case (*sl*). **2** TEST, quiz, question, cross-examine, cross-question, interrogate, grill (*infml*), catechize (*fml*).

example *n* instance, case, case in point, illustration, exemplification, sample, specimen, model, pattern, ideal, archetype, prototype, standard, type, lesson, citation.

exasperate *v* infuriate, annoy, anger, incense, irritate, madden, provoke, get on someone's nerves, enrage, irk, rile, rankle, rouse, get to (*infml*), goad, vex.
≠ appease, pacify.

excavate *v* dig (out), dig up, hollow, burrow, tunnel, delve, unearth, mine, quarry, disinter, gouge, scoop, exhume, uncover.

excavation *n* hole, hollow, pit, quarry, mine, dugout, dig, diggings, burrow, cavity, crater, trench, trough, shaft, ditch, cutting.

exceed *v* surpass, outdo, outstrip, beat, better, pass, overtake, top, outshine, eclipse, outreach, outrun, transcend, cap, overdo, overstep.

excel *v* **1** SURPASS, outdo, beat, outclass, outperform, outrank, eclipse, better. **2** BE EXCELLENT, succeed, shine, stand out, predominate.

excellence *n* superiority, pre-eminence, distinction, merit, supremacy, quality, worth, fineness, eminence, goodness, greatness, virtue, perfection, purity.

excellent *adj* superior, first-class, first-rate, prime, superlative, unequalled, outstanding, surpassing, remarkable, distinguished, great, good, exemplary, select, superb, admirable, commendable, top-notch (*infml*), splendid, noteworthy, notable, fine, wonderful, worthy.
≠ inferior, second-rate.

except *prep* excepting, but, apart from, other than, save, omitting, not counting, leaving out, excluding, except for, besides, bar, minus, less.
v leave out, omit, bar, exclude, reject, rule out.

exception *n* oddity, anomaly, deviation, abnormality, irregularity, peculiarity, inconsistency, rarity, special case, quirk.

exceptional *adj* **1** ABNORMAL, unusual, anomalous, strange, odd, irregular, extraordinary, peculiar, special, rare, uncommon.
2 OUTSTANDING, remarkable, phenomenal, prodigious, notable, noteworthy, superior, unequalled, marvellous.
≠ **1** normal. **2** mediocre.

excerpt *n* extract, passage, portion, section, selection, quote, quotation, part, citation, scrap, fragment.

excess *n* **1** SURFEIT, overabundance, glut, plethora, superfluity, superabundance, surplus, overflow, overkill, remainder, left-over.
2 OVERINDULGENCE, dissipation, immoderateness, intemperance, extravagance, unrestraint, debauchery.
≠ **1** deficiency. **2** restraint.
adj extra, surplus, spare, redundant, remaining, residual, left-over, additional, superfluous, supernumerary.
≠ inadequate.

excessive *adj* immoderate, inordinate, extreme, undue, uncalled-for, disproportionate, unnecessary, unneeded, superfluous, unreasonable, exorbitant, extravagant, steep (*infml*).
≠ insufficient.

exchange *v* barter, change, trade, swap, switch, replace, interchange, convert, commute, substitute, reciprocate, bargain, bandy.
n **1** CONVERSATION, discussion, chat. **2** TRADE, commerce, dealing, market, traffic, barter, bargain. **3** INTERCHANGE, swap, switch, replacement, substitution, reciprocity.

excitable *adj* temperamental, volatile, passionate, emotional, highly-strung, fiery, hot-headed, hasty, nervous, hot-tempered, irascible, quick-tempered, sensitive, susceptible.
≠ calm, stable.

excite *v* **1** MOVE, agitate, disturb, upset, touch, stir up, thrill, elate, turn on (*infml*), impress. **2** AROUSE, rouse, animate, awaken, fire, inflame, kindle, motivate, stimulate, engender, inspire, instigate, incite, induce, ignite, galvanize, generate, provoke, sway, quicken, evoke.
≠ **1** calm.

excited *adj* aroused, roused, stimulated, stirred, thrilled, elated, enthusiastic, eager, moved, high (*infml*), worked up, wrought-up, overwrought, restless, frantic, frenzied, wild.
≠ calm, apathetic.

excitement *n* **1** UNREST, ado, action, activity, commotion, fuss, tumult, flurry, furore, adventure. **2** DISCOMPOSURE, agitation, passion, thrill, animation, elation, enthusiasm, restlessness, kicks (*infml*), ferment, fever, eagerness, stimulation.
≠ **1** calm. **2** apathy.

exciting *adj* stimulating, stirring, intoxicating, exhilarating, thrilling, rousing, moving, enthralling, electrifying, nail-biting (*infml*), cliff-hanging (*infml*), striking, sensational, provocative, inspiring, interesting.
≠ dull, unexciting.

exclaim *v* cry (out), declare, blurt (out), call, yell, shout, proclaim, utter.

exclamation *n* cry, call, yell, shout, expletive, interjection, ejaculation, outcry, utterance.

exclude *v* **1** BAN, bar, prohibit, disallow, veto, proscribe, forbid, blacklist. **2** OMIT, leave out, keep out, refuse, reject, ignore, shut out, rule out, ostracize, eliminate. **3** EXPEL, eject, evict, excommunicate.
≠ **1** admit. **2** include.

exclusive *adj* **1** SOLE, single, unique, only, undivided, unshared, whole, total, peculiar. **2** RESTRICTED, limited, closed, private, narrow, restrictive, choice, select, discriminative, cliquey, chic, classy (*infml*), elegant, fashionable, posh (*infml*), snobbish.

excruciating *adj* agonizing, painful, severe, tormenting, unbearable, insufferable, acute, intolerable, intense, sharp, piercing, extreme, atrocious, racking, harrowing, savage, burning, bitter.

excursion *n* outing, trip, jaunt, expedition, day trip, journey, tour, airing, breather, junket (*infml*), ride, drive, walk, ramble.

excuse *v* **1** FORGIVE, pardon, overlook, absolve, acquit, exonerate, tolerate, ignore, indulge. **2** RELEASE, free, discharge, liberate, let off, relieve, spare, exempt. **3** CONDONE, explain, mitigate, justify, vindicate, defend, apologize for.
≠ **1** criticize. **2** punish.
n justification, explanation, grounds, defence, plea, alibi, reason, apology, pretext, pretence, exoneration, evasion, cop-out (*infml*), shift, substitute.

execute *v* **1** PUT TO DEATH, kill, liquidate, hang, electrocute, shoot, guillotine, decapitate, behead. **2** CARRY OUT, perform, do, accomplish, achieve, fulfil, complete, discharge, effect, enact, deliver, enforce, finish, implement, administer, consummate, realize, dispatch, expedite, validate, serve, render, sign.

execution *n* **1** DEATH PENALTY, capital punishment, killing, firing squad.

Means of execution include: beheading, burning, crucifixion, decapitation, electrocution, garrotting, gassing, guillotining, hanging, lethal injection, lynching, shooting, stoning, stringing up (*infml*).

2 ACCOMPLISHMENT, operation, performance, completion, achievement, administration, effect, enactment, implementation, realization, discharge, dispatch, consummation, enforcement. **3** STYLE, technique, rendition, delivery, performance, manner, mode.

executive *n* **1** ADMINISTRATION, management, government, leadership, hierarchy. **2** ADMINISTRATOR, manager, organizer, leader, controller, director, governor, official.
adj administrative, managerial, controlling, supervisory, regulating, decision-making, governing, organizing, directing, directorial, organizational, leading, guiding.

exemplary *adj* **1** MODEL, ideal, perfect, admirable, excellent, faultless, flawless, correct, good, commendable, praiseworthy, worthy, laudable, estimable, honourable. **2** CAUTIONARY, warning.
≠ **1** imperfect, unworthy.

exemplify *v* illustrate, demonstrate, show, instance, represent, typify, manifest, embody, epitomize, exhibit, depict, display.

exempt *v* excuse, release, relieve, let off, free, absolve, discharge, dismiss, liberate, spare.
adj excused, not liable, immune, released, spared, absolved, discharged, excluded, free, liberated, clear.
≠ liable.

exercise *v* **1** USE, utilize, employ, apply, exert, practise, wield, try, discharge. **2** TRAIN, drill, practise, work out (*infml*), keep fit. **3** WORRY, disturb, trouble, upset, burden, distress, vex, annoy, agitate, afflict.
n **1** TRAINING, drill, practice, effort, exertion, task, lesson, work, discipline, activity, physical jerks (*infml*), work-out (*infml*), aerobics, labour. **2** USE, utilization, employment, application, implementation, practice, operation, discharge, assignment, fulfilment, accomplishment.

exert *v* use, utilize, employ, apply, exercise, bring to bear, wield, expend.
exert oneself strive, struggle, strain, make and effort, take pains, toil, labour, work, sweat (*infml*), endeavour, apply oneself.

exertion *n* **1** EFFORT, industry, labour, toil, work, struggle, diligence, assiduousness, perseverance, pains, endeavour, attempt, strain, travail (*fml*), trial. **2** USE, utilization, employment, application, exercise, operation, action.
≠ **1** idleness, rest.

exhaust *v* **1** CONSUME, empty, deplete, drain, sap, spend, waste, squander, dissipate, impoverish, use up, finish, dry, bankrupt. **2** TIRE (OUT), weary, fatigue, tax, strain, weaken, overwork, wear out.
≠ **1** renew. **2** refresh.
n emission, exhalation, discharge, fumes.

exhausted *adj* **1** EMPTY, finished, depleted, spent, used up, drained, dry, worn out, void. **2** TIRED (OUT), dead tired, dead-beat (*infml*), all in (*infml*), done (in) (*infml*), fatigued, weak, washed-out, whacked (*infml*), knackered (*infml*), jaded.
≠ **1** fresh. **2** vigorous.

exhausting *adj* tiring, strenuous, taxing, gruelling, arduous, hard, laborious, backbreaking, draining, severe, testing, punishing, formidable, debilitating.
≠ refreshing.

exhaustion *n* fatigue, tiredness, weariness, debility, feebleness, jet-lag.
≠ freshness, liveliness.

exhaustive *adj* comprehensive, all-embracing, all-inclusive, far-reaching, complete, extensive, encyclopedic, full-scale, thorough, full, in-depth, intensive, detailed, definitive, all-out, sweeping.
≠ incomplete, restricted.

exhibit *v* display, show, present, demonstrate, manifest, expose, parade, reveal, express, disclose, indicate, air, flaunt, offer.
≠ conceal.

n display, exhibition, show, illustration, model.

exhibition *n* display, show, demonstration, exhibit, presentation, manifestation, spectacle, exposition, expo (*infml*), showing, fair, performance, airing, representation, showcase.

exhilarate *v* thrill, excite, elate, animate, enliven, invigorate, vitalize, stimulate.
≠ bore.

exile *n* **1** BANISHMENT, deportation, expatriation, expulsion, ostracism, transportation. **2** EXPATRIATE, refugee, émigré, deportee, outcast.
v banish, expel, deport, expatriate, drive out, ostracize, oust.

exist *v* **1** BE, live, abide, continue, endure, have one's being, breathe, prevail. **2** SUBSIST, survive. **3** BE PRESENT, occur, happen, be available, remain.

existence *n* **1** BEING, life, reality, actuality, continuance, continuation, endurance, survival, breath, subsistence. **2** CREATION, the world. **3** (*fml*) ENTITY, creature, thing.
≠ **1** death, non-existence.

exit *n* **1** DEPARTURE, going, retreat, withdrawal, leave-taking, retirement, farewell, exodus. **2** DOOR, way out, doorway, gate, vent.
≠ **1** entrance, arrival. **2** entrance.
v depart, leave, go, retire, withdraw, take one's leave, retreat, issue.
≠ arrive, enter.

exonerate *v* **1** ABSOLVE, acquit, clear, vindicate, exculpate (*fml*), justify, pardon, discharge. **2** EXEMPT, excuse, spare, let off, release, relieve.
≠ **1** incriminate.

exorbitant *adj* excessive, unreasonable, unwarranted, undue, inordinate, immoderate, extravagant, extortionate, enormous, preposterous.
≠ reasonable, moderate.

exotic *adj* **1** FOREIGN, alien, imported, introduced. **2** UNUSUAL, striking, different, unfamiliar, extraordinary, bizarre, curious, strange, fascinating, colourful, peculiar, outlandish.
≠ **1** native. **2** ordinary.

expand *v* **1** STRETCH, swell, widen, lengthen, thicken, magnify, multiply, inflate, broaden, blow up, open out, fill out, fatten. **2** INCREASE, grow, extend, enlarge, develop, amplify, spread, branch out, diversify, elaborate.
≠ **1** contract.

expanse *n* extent, space, area, breadth, range, stretch, sweep, field, plain, tract.

expansive *adj* **1** FRIENDLY, genial, outgoing, open, affable, sociable, talkative, warm, communicative, effusive. **2** EXTENSIVE, broad, comprehensive, wide-ranging, all-embracing, thorough.
≠ **1** reserved, cold. **2** restricted, narrow.

expect *v* **1** *expect the money soon*: anticipate, await, look forward to, hope for, look for, bank on, bargain for, envisage, predict, forecast, contemplate, project, foresee. **2** *expect you to comply*: require, want, wish, insist on, demand, rely on, count on. **3** *expect you're right*: suppose, surmise, assume, believe, think, presume, imagine, reckon, guess (*infml*), trust.

expectant *adj* **1** AWAITING, anticipating, hopeful, in suspense, ready, apprehensive, anxious, watchful, eager, curious. **2** PREGNANT, expecting (*infml*), with child (*fml*).

expedition *n* **1** JOURNEY, excursion, trip, voyage, tour, exploration, trek, safari, hike, sail, ramble, raid, quest, pilgrimage, mission, crusade. **2** (*fml*) PROMPTNESS, speed, alacrity, haste.

expel *v* **1** DRIVE OUT, eject, evict, banish, throw out, ban, bar, oust, exile, expatriate. **2** DISCHARGE, evacuate, void, cast out.
≠ **1** welcome.

expend *v* **1** SPEND, pay, disburse (*fml*), fork out (*infml*). **2** CONSUME, use (up), dissipate, exhaust, employ.
≠ **1** save. **2** conserve.

expenditure *n* spending, expense, outlay, outgoings, disbursement (*fml*), payment, output.
≠ income.

expense *n* spending, expenditure, disbursement (*fml*), outlay, payment, loss, cost, charge.

expensive *adj* dear, high-priced, costly, exorbitant, extortionate, steep (*infml*), extravagant, lavish.
≠ cheap, inexpensive.

experience *n* **1** KNOWLEDGE, familiarity, know-how, involvement, participation, practice, understanding. **2** INCIDENT, event, episode, happening, encounter, occurrence, adventure.
≠ **1** inexperience.
v undergo, go through, live through, suffer, feel, endure, encounter, face, meet, know, try, perceive, sustain.

experienced *adj* **1** PRACTISED, knowledgeable, familiar, capable, competent, well-versed, expert, accomplished, qualified, skilled, tried, trained, professional. **2** MATURE, seasoned, wise, veteran.
≠ **1** inexperienced, unskilled.

experiment *n* trial, test, investigation, experimentation, research, examination, trial run, venture, trial and error, attempt, procedure, proof.
v try, test, investigate, examine, research, sample, verify.

experimental *adj* trial, test, exploratory, empirical (*fml*), tentative, provisional, speculative, pilot, preliminary, trial-and-error.

expert *n* specialist, connoisseur, authority, professional, pro (*infml*), dab hand (*infml*), maestro, virtuoso.
adj proficient, adept, skilled, skilful, knowledgeable, experienced, able, practised, professional, masterly, specialist, qualified, virtuoso.
≠ amateurish, novice.

expertise *n* expertness, proficiency, skill, skilfulness, know-how, knack (*infml*), knowledge, mastery, dexterity, virtuosity.
≠ inexperience.

expire *v* end, cease, finish, stop, terminate, close, conclude, discontinue, run out, lapse, die, depart, decease, perish.
≠ begin.

explain *v* **1** INTERPRET, clarify, describe, define, make clear, elucidate, simplify, resolve, solve, spell out, translate, unfold, unravel, untangle, illustrate, demonstrate, disclose, expound, teach. **2** JUSTIFY, excuse, account for, rationalize.
≠ **1** obscure, confound.

explanation *n* **1** INTERPRETATION, clarification, definition, elucidation, illustration, demonstration, account, description, exegesis (*fml*). **2** JUSTIFICATION, excuse, warrant, rationalization. **3** ANSWER, meaning, motive, reason, key, sense, significance.

explanatory *adj* descriptive, interpretive, explicative, demonstrative, expository (*fml*), justifying.

explicit *adj* **1** CLEAR, distinct, exact, categorical, absolute, certain, positive, precise, specific, unambiguous, express, definite, declared, detailed, stated. **2** OPEN, direct, frank, outspoken, straightforward, unreserved, plain.
≠ **1** implicit, unspoken, vague.

explode *v* **1** BLOW UP, burst, go off, set off, detonate, discharge, blast, erupt. **2** DISCREDIT, disprove, give the lie to, debunk, invalidate, refute, rebut, repudiate.
≠ **2** prove, confirm.

exploit *n* deed, feat, adventure, achievement, accomplishment, attainment, stunt.
v **1** USE, utilize, capitalize on, profit by, turn to account, take advantage of, cash in on, make capital out of. **2** MISUSE, abuse, oppress, ill-treat, impose on, manipulate, rip off (*infml*), fleece (*infml*).

exploration *n* **1** INVESTIGATION, examination, enquiry, research, scrutiny, study, inspection, analysis, probe. **2** EXPEDITION, survey, reconnaissance, search, trip, tour, voyage, travel, safari.

explore *v* **1** INVESTIGATE, examine, inspect, research, scrutinize, probe, analyse. **2** TRAVEL, tour, search, reconnoitre, prospect, scout, survey.

explosion *n* detonation, blast, burst,

outburst, discharge, eruption, bang, outbreak, clap, crack, fit, report.

explosive *adj* unstable, volatile, sensitive, tense, fraught, charged, touchy, overwrought, dangerous, hazardous, perilous, stormy.
≠ stable, calm.

expose *v* **1** REVEAL, show, exhibit, display, disclose, uncover, bring to light, present, manifest, detect, divulge, unveil, unmask, denounce.
2 ENDANGER, jeopardize, imperil, risk, hazard.
≠ **1** conceal. **2** cover up.

exposed *adj* bare, open, revealed, laid bare, unprotected, vulnerable, exhibited, on display, on show, on view, shown, susceptible.
≠ covered, sheltered.

exposure *n* **1** REVELATION, uncovering, disclosure, exposé, showing, unmasking, unveiling, display, airing, exhibition, presentation, publicity, manifestation, discovery, divulgence. **2** FAMILIARITY, experience, knowledge, contact. **3** JEOPARDY, danger, hazard, risk, vulnerability.

express *v* **1** ARTICULATE, verbalize, utter, voice, say, speak, state, communicate, pronounce, tell, assert, declare, put across, formulate, intimate, testify, convey. **2** SHOW, manifest, exhibit, disclose, divulge, reveal, indicate, denote, depict, embody. **3** SYMBOLIZE, stand for, represent, signify, designate.
adj **1** SPECIFIC, explicit, exact, definite, clear, categorical, precise, distinct, clear-cut, certain, plain, manifest, particular, stated, unambiguous. **2** FAST, speedy, rapid, quick, high-speed, non-stop.
≠ **1** vague.

expression *n* **1** LOOK, air, aspect, countenance, appearance, mien (*fml*).
2 REPRESENTATION, manifestation, demonstration, indication, exhibition, embodiment, show, sign, symbol, style.
3 UTTERANCE, verbalization, communication, articulation, statement, assertion, announcement, declaration, pronouncement, speech.
4 TONE, intonation, delivery, diction, enunciation, modulation, wording.
5 PHRASE, term, turn of phrase, saying, set phrase, idiom.

expressionless *adj* dull, blank, deadpan, impassive, straight-faced, poker-faced (*infml*), inscrutable, empty, vacuous, glassy.
≠ expressive.

expressive *adj* eloquent, meaningful, forceful, telling, revealing, informative, indicative, communicative, demonstrative, emphatic, moving, poignant, lively, striking, suggestive, significant, thoughtful, vivid, sympathetic.

expulsion *n* ejection, eviction, exile, banishment, removal, discharge, exclusion, dismissal.

exquisite *adj* **1** BEAUTIFUL, attractive, dainty, delicate, charming, elegant, delightful, lovely, pleasing. **2** PERFECT, flawless, fine, excellent, choice, precious, rare, outstanding.
3 REFINED, discriminating, meticulous, sensitive, impeccable. **4** INTENSE, keen, sharp, poignant.
≠ **1** ugly. **2** flawed. **3** unrefined.

extend *v* **1** SPREAD, stretch, reach, continue. **2** ENLARGE, increase, expand, develop, amplify, lengthen, widen, elongate, draw out, protract, prolong, spin out, unwind. **3** OFFER, give, grant, hold out, impart, present, bestow, confer.
≠ **2** contract, shorten. **3** withhold.

extension *n* **1** ENLARGEMENT, increase, stretching, broadening, widening, lengthening, expansion, elongation, development, enhancement, protraction, continuation. **2** ADDITION, supplement, appendix, annexe, addendum (*fml*). **3** DELAY, postponement.

extensive *adj* **1** BROAD, comprehensive, far-reaching, large-scale, thorough, widespread, universal, extended, all-inclusive, general, pervasive, prevalent. **2** LARGE, huge, roomy, spacious, vast, voluminous, long, lengthy, wide.

≠ **1** restricted, narrow. **2** small.

extent *n* **1** DIMENSION(S), amount, magnitude, expanse, size, area, bulk, degree, breadth, quantity, spread, stretch, volume, width, measure, duration, term, time. **2** LIMIT, bounds, lengths, range, reach, scope, compass, sphere, play, sweep.

exterior *n* outside, surface, covering, coating, face, façade, shell, skin, finish, externals, appearance.
≠ inside, interior.
adj outer, outside, outermost, surface, external, superficial, surrounding, outward, peripheral, extrinsic.
≠ inside, interior.

exterminate *v* annihilate, eradicate, destroy, eliminate, massacre, abolish, wipe out.

external *adj* outer, surface, outside, exterior, superficial, outward, outermost, apparent, visible, extraneous, extrinsic, extramural, independent.
≠ internal.

extinct *adj* **1** DEFUNCT, dead, gone, obsolete, ended, exterminated, terminated, vanished, lost, abolished. **2** EXTINGUISHED, quenched, inactive, out.
≠ **1** living.

extinction *n* annihilation, extermination, death, eradication, obliteration, destruction, abolition, excision.

extinguish *v* **1** PUT OUT, blow out, snuff out, stifle, smother, douse, quench. **2** ANNIHILATE, exterminate, eliminate, destroy, kill, eradicate, erase, expunge, abolish, remove, end, suppress.

extort *v* extract, wring, exact, coerce, force, milk (*infml*), blackmail, squeeze, bleed (*infml*), bully.

extortionate *adj* exorbitant, excessive, grasping, exacting, immoderate, rapacious, unreasonable, oppressive, blood-sucking (*infml*), rigorous, severe, hard, harsh, inordinate.

extra *adj* **1** ADDITIONAL, added, auxiliary, supplementary, new, more, further, ancillary, fresh, other. **2** EXCESS, spare, superfluous, supernumerary, surplus, unused, unneeded, leftover, reserve, redundant.
≠ **1** integral. **2** essential.
n addition, supplement, extension, accessory, appendage, bonus, complement, adjunct, addendum (*fml*), attachment.
adv especially, exceptionally, extraordinarily, particularly, unusually, remarkably, extremely.

extract *v* **1** REMOVE, take out, draw out, exact, uproot, withdraw. **2** DERIVE, draw, distil, obtain, get, gather, glean, wrest, wring, elicit. **3** CHOOSE, select, cull, abstract, cite, quote.
≠ **1** insert.
n **1** DISTILLATION, essence, juice. **2** EXCERPT, passage, selection, clip, cutting, quotation, abstract, citation.

extraordinary *adj* remarkable, unusual, exceptional, notable, noteworthy, outstanding, unique, special, strange, peculiar, rare, surprising, amazing, wonderful, unprecedented, marvellous, fantastic, significant, particular.
≠ commonplace, ordinary.

extravagance *n* **1** OVERSPENDING, profligacy, squandering, waste. **2** EXCESS, immoderation, recklessness, profusion, outrageousness, folly.
≠ **1** thrift. **2** moderation.

extravagant *adj* **1** PROFLIGATE, prodigal, spendthrift, thriftless, wasteful, reckless. **2** IMMODERATE, flamboyant, preposterous, outrageous, ostentatious, pretentious, lavish, ornate, flashy (*infml*), fanciful, fantastic, wild. **3** OVERPRICED, exorbitant, expensive, excessive, costly.
≠ **1** thrifty. **2** moderate. **3** reasonable.

extreme *adj* **1** INTENSE, great, immoderate, inordinate, utmost, utter, out-and-out, maximum, acute, downright, extraordinary, exceptional, greatest, highest, unreasonable, remarkable. **2** FARTHEST, far-off, faraway, distant, endmost, outermost, remotest, uttermost, final, last, terminal, ultimate. **3** RADICAL,

zealous, extremist, fanatical. **4** DRASTIC, dire, uncompromising, stern, strict, rigid, severe, harsh.
≠ **1** mild. **3** moderate.
n extremity, limit, maximum, ultimate, utmost, excess, top, pinnacle, peak, height, end, climax, depth, edge, termination.

extremity *n* **1** EXTREME, limit, boundary, brink, verge, bound, border, apex, height, tip, top, edge, excess, end, acme, termination, peak, pinnacle, margin, terminal, terminus, ultimate, pole, maximum, minimum, frontier, depth. **2** CRISIS, danger, emergency, plight, hardship.

extricate *v* disentangle, clear, disengage, free, deliver, liberate, release, rescue, relieve, remove, withdraw.
≠ involve.

extroverted *adj* outgoing, friendly, sociable, amicable, amiable, exuberant.
≠ introverted.

exuberant *adj* **1** LIVELY, vivacious, spirited, zestful, high-spirited, effervescent, ebullient, enthusiastic, sparkling, excited, exhilarated, effusive, cheerful, fulsome. **2** PLENTIFUL, lavish, overflowing, plenteous.
≠ **1** apathetic. **2** scarce.

exult *v* rejoice, revel, delight, glory, celebrate, relish, crow, gloat, triumph.

eye *n* **1** APPRECIATION, discrimination, discernment, perception, recognition. **2** VIEWPOINT, opinion, judgement, mind. **3** WATCH, observation, lookout.

> *Parts of the eye include*: anterior chamber, aqueous humour, blind spot, choroid, ciliary body, cone, conjunctiva, cornea, eyelash, fovea, iris, lacrimal duct, lens, lower eyelid, ocular muscle, optic nerve, papilla, pupil, posterior chamber, retina, rod, sclera, suspension ligament, upper eyelid, vitreous humour.

v look at, watch, regard, observe, stare at, gaze at, glance at, view, scrutinize, scan, examine, peruse, study, survey, inspect, contemplate.

eyesight *n* vision, sight, perception, observation, view.

eyesore *n* ugliness, blemish, monstrosity, blot on the landscape, disfigurement, horror, blight, atrocity, mess.

eye-witness *n* witness, observer, spectator, looker-on, onlooker, bystander, viewer, passer-by.

F

fable *n* allegory, parable, story, tale, yarn, myth, legend, fiction, fabrication, invention, lie, untruth, falsehood, tall story, old wives' tale.

fabric *n* **1** CLOTH, material, textile, stuff, web, texture. **2** STRUCTURE, framework, construction, make-up, constitution, organization, infrastructure, foundations.

> *Fabrics include*: alpaca, angora, astrakhan, barathea, bouclé, cashmere, chenille, duffel, felt, flannel, fleece, Harris tweed®, mohair, paisley, serge, sheepskin, Shetland wool, tweed, vicuña, wool, worsted; brocade, buckram, calico, cambric, candlewick, canvas, chambray, cheesecloth, chino, chintz, cord, corduroy, cotton, crepe, denim, drill, jean, flannelette, gaberdine, gingham, jersey, lawn, linen, lisle, madras, moleskin, muslin, needlecord, piqué, poplin, sateen, seersucker, terry towelling, ticking, Viyella®, webbing, winceyette; brocade, grosgrain, damask, Brussels lace, chiffon, georgette, gossamer, voile, organza, organdie, tulle, net, crepe de Chine, silk, taffeta, shantung, velvet, velour; polycotton, polyester, rayon, nylon, Crimplene®, Terylene®, Lurex®, lamé; hessian, horsehair, chamois, kid, leather, leather-cloth, sharkskin, suede.

fabricate *v* **1** FAKE, falsify, forge, invent, make up, trump up, concoct. **2** MAKE, manufacture, construct, assemble, build, erect, form, shape, fashion, create, devise.
≠ **2** demolish, destroy.

fabulous *adj* **1** WONDERFUL, marvellous, fantastic, superb, breathtaking, spectacular, phenomenal, amazing, astounding, unbelievable, incredible, inconceivable. **2** *a fabulous beast*: mythical, legendary, fabled, fantastic, fictitious, invented, imaginary.
≠ **2** real.

face *n* **1** FEATURES, countenance, visage, physiognomy. **2** EXPRESSION, look, appearance, air. **3** *pull a face*: grimace, frown, scowl, pout. **4** EXTERIOR, outside, surface, cover, front, façade, aspect, side.
v **1** BE OPPOSITE, give on to, front, overlook. **2** CONFRONT, face up to, deal with, cope with, tackle, brave, defy, oppose, encounter, meet, experience. **3** COVER, coat, dress, clad, overlay, veneer.
face to face opposite, eye to eye, eyeball to eyeball, in confrontation.
face up to accept, come to terms with, acknowledge, recognize, cope with, deal with, confront, meet head-on, stand up to.

facet *n* surface, plane, side, face, aspect, angle, point, feature, characteristic.

facetious *adj* flippant, frivolous, playful, jocular, jesting, tongue-in-cheek, funny, amusing, humorous, comical, witty.
≠ serious.

facile *adj* easy, simple, simplistic, ready, quick, hasty, glib, fluent, smooth, slick, plausible, shallow, superficial.
≠ complicated, profound.

facilitate *v* ease, help, assist, further, promote, forward, expedite, speed up.

facilities *n* amenities, services, conveniences, resources, prerequisites, equipment, mod cons (*infml*), means, opportunities.

facility *n* ease, effortlessness, readiness, quickness, fluency, proficiency, skill, skilfulness, talent, gift, knack, ability.

fact *n* **1** *facts and figures*: information, datum, detail, particular, specific,

point, item, circumstance, event, incident, occurrence, happening, act, deed, fait accompli. **2** REALITY, actuality, truth.
≠ **2** fiction.
in fact actually, in actual fact, in point of fact, as a matter of fact, in reality, really, indeed.

faction *n* splinter group, ginger group, minority, division, section, contingent, party, camp, set, clique, coterie, cabal, junta, lobby, pressure group.

factor *n* cause, influence, circumstance, contingency, consideration, element, ingredient, component, part, point, aspect, fact, item, detail.

factory *n* works, plant, mill, shop floor, assembly line, manufactory.

factual *adj* true, historical, actual, real, genuine, authentic, correct, accurate, precise, exact, literal, faithful, close, detailed, unbiased, objective.
≠ false, fictitious, imaginary, fictional.

faculties *n* wits, senses, intelligence, reason, powers, capabilities.

faculty *n* ability, capability, capacity, power, facility, knack, gift, talent, skill, aptitude, bent.

fad *n* craze, rage (*infml*), mania, fashion, mode, vogue, trend, whim, fancy, affectation.

fade *v* **1** DISCOLOUR, bleach, blanch, blench, pale, whiten, dim, dull.
2 DECLINE, fall, diminish, dwindle, ebb, wane, disappear, vanish, flag, weaken, droop, wilt, wither, shrivel, perish, die.

fail *v* **1** GO WRONG, miscarry, misfire, flop, miss, flunk (*sl*), fall through, come to grief, collapse, fold (*infml*), go bankrupt, go bust, go under, founder, sink, decline, fall, weaken, dwindle, fade, wane, peter out, cease, die. **2** *fail to pay a bill*: omit, neglect, forget. **3** LET DOWN, disappoint, leave, desert, abandon, forsake.
≠ **1** succeed, prosper.

failing *n* weakness, foible, fault, defect, imperfection, flaw, blemish, drawback, deficiency, shortcoming, failure, lapse, error.
≠ strength, advantage.

failure *n* **1** MISCARRIAGE, flop, wash-out (*infml*), fiasco, disappointment, loss, defeat, downfall, decline, decay, deterioration, ruin, bankruptcy, crash, collapse, breakdown, stoppage.
2 OMISSION, slip-up (*infml*), neglect, negligence, failing, shortcoming, deficiency.
≠ **1** success, prosperity.

faint *adj* **1** SLIGHT, weak, feeble, soft, low, hushed, muffled, subdued, faded, bleached, light, pale, dull, dim, hazy, indistinct, vague. **2** *I feel faint*: dizzy, giddy, woozy (*infml*), light-headed, weak, feeble, exhausted.
≠ **1** strong, clear.
v black out, pass out, swoon, collapse, flake out (*infml*), keel over (*infml*), drop.
n blackout, swoon, collapse, unconsciousness.

fair[1] *adj* **1** JUST, equitable, square, even-handed, dispassionate, impartial, objective, disinterested, unbiased, unprejudiced, right, proper, lawful, legitimate, honest, trustworthy, upright, honourable. **2** FAIR-HAIRED, fair-headed, blond(e), light. **3** *fair weather*: fine, dry, sunny, bright, clear, cloudless, unclouded. **4** AVERAGE, moderate, middling, not bad, all right, OK (*infml*), satisfactory, adequate, acceptable, tolerable, reasonable, passable, mediocre, so-so (*infml*).
≠ **1** unfair. **2** dark. **3** inclement, cloudy. **4** excellent, poor.

fair[2] *n* show, exhibition, exposition, expo (*infml*), market, bazaar, fête, festival, carnival, gala.

faith *n* **1** BELIEF, credit, trust, reliance, dependence, conviction, confidence, assurance. **2** RELIGION, denomination, persuasion, church, creed, dogma. **3** FAITHFULNESS, fidelity, loyalty, allegiance, honour, sincerity, honesty, truthfulness.
≠ **1** mistrust. **3** unfaithfulness, treachery.

faithful *adj* **1** LOYAL, devoted, staunch, steadfast, constant, trusty, reliable, dependable, true. **2** *a faithful*

description: accurate, precise, exact, strict, close, true, truthful.
≠ **1** disloyal, treacherous. **2** inaccurate, vague.

fake *v* forge, fabricate, counterfeit, copy, imitate, simulate, feign, sham, pretend, put on, affect, assume.
n forgery, copy, reproduction, replica, imitation, simulation, sham, hoax, fraud, phoney (*infml*), impostor, charlatan.
adj forged, counterfeit, false, spurious, phoney (*infml*), pseudo, bogus, assumed, affected, sham, artificial, simulated, mock, imitation, reproduction.
≠ genuine.

fall *v* **1** TUMBLE, stumble, trip, topple, keel over, collapse, slump, crash.
2 DESCEND, go down, drop, slope, incline, slide, sink, dive, plunge, plummet, nose-dive, pitch.
3 DECREASE, lessen, decline, diminish, dwindle, fall off, subside.
≠ **2** rise. **3** increase.
n **1** TUMBLE, descent, slope, incline, dive, plunge, decrease, reduction, lessening, drop, decline, dwindling, slump, crash. **2** *the fall of Rome*: defeat, conquest, overthrow, downfall, collapse, surrender, capitulation.
fall apart break, go to pieces, shatter, disintegrate, crumble, decompose, decay, rot.
fall asleep drop off, doze off, nod off (*infml*).
fall back on resort to, have recourse to, use, turn to, look to.
fall behind lag, trail, drop back.
fall in cave in, come down, collapse, give way, subside, sink.
fall in with agree with, assent to, go along with, accept, comply with, co-operate with.
fall off decrease, lessen, drop, slump, decline, deteriorate, worsen, slow, slacken.
fall out quarrel, argue, squabble, bicker, fight, clash, disagree, differ.
≠ agree.
fall through come to nothing, fail, miscarry, founder, collapse.
≠ come off, succeed.

fallacy *n* misconception, delusion, mistake, error, flaw, inconsistency, falsehood.
≠ truth.

fallow *adj* uncultivated, unplanted, unsown, undeveloped, unused, idle, inactive, dormant, resting.

false *adj* **1** wrong, incorrect, mistaken, erroneous, inaccurate, inexact, misleading, faulty, fallacious, invalid.
2 UNREAL, artificial, synthetic, imitation, simulated, mock, fake, counterfeit, forged, feigned, pretended, sham, bogus, assumed, fictitious.
3 *false friends*: disloyal, unfaithful, faithless, lying, deceitful, insincere, hypocritical, two-faced, double-dealing, treacherous, unreliable.
≠ **1** true, right. **2** real, genuine.
3 faithful, reliable.

falsehood *n* untruth, lie, fib, story, fiction, fabrication, perjury, untruthfulness, deceit, deception, dishonesty.
≠ truth, truthfulness.

falsify *v* alter, cook (*infml*), tamper with, doctor, distort, pervert, misrepresent, misstate, forge, counterfeit, fake.

falter *v* totter, stumble, stammer, stutter, hesitate, waver, vacillate, flinch, quail, shake, tremble, flag, fail.

fame *n* renown, celebrity, stardom, prominence, eminence, illustriousness, glory, honour, esteem, reputation, name.

familiar *adj* **1** EVERYDAY, routine, household, common, ordinary, well-known, recognizable. **2** INTIMATE, close, confidential, friendly, informal, free, free-and-easy, relaxed. **3** *familiar with the procedure*: aware, acquainted, abreast, knowledgeable, versed, conversant.
≠ **1** unfamiliar, strange. **2** formal, reserved. **3** unfamiliar, ignorant.

familiarity *n* **1** INTIMACY, liberty, closeness, friendliness, sociability, openness, naturalness, informality.
2 AWARENESS, acquaintance, experience, knowledge, understanding, grasp.

familiarize *v* accustom, acclimatize, school, train, coach, instruct, prime, brief.

family *n* **1** RELATIVES, relations, kin, kindred, kinsmen, people, folk (*infml*), ancestors, forebears, children, offspring, issue, progeny, descendants. **2** CLAN, tribe, race, dynasty, house, pedigree, ancestry, parentage, descent, line, lineage, extraction, blood, stock, birth. **3** CLASS, group, classification.

Members of a family include: ancestor, forebear, forefather, descendant, offspring, heir; husband, wife, spouse, parent, father, dad (*infml*), daddy (*infml*), old man (*infml*), mother, mum (*infml*), mummy (*infml*), mom (*US infml*), grandparent, grandfather, grandmother, granny (*infml*), nanny (*infml*), grandchild, son, daughter, brother, half-brother, sister, half-sister, sibling, uncle, aunt, nephew, niece, cousin, godfather, godmother, godchild, stepfather, stepmother, foster-parent, foster-child.

family tree ancestry, pedigree, genealogy, line, lineage, extraction.

famine *n* starvation, hunger, destitution, want, scarcity, death.
≠ plenty.

famous *adj* well-known, famed, renowned, celebrated, noted, great, distinguished, illustrious, eminent, honoured, acclaimed, glorious, legendary, remarkable, notable, prominent, signal.
≠ unheard-of, unknown, obscure.

fan[1] *v* **1** COOL, ventilate, air, air-condition, air-cool, blow, refresh. **2** INCREASE, provoke, stimulate, rouse, arouse, excite, agitate, stir up, work up, whip up.
n extractor fan, ventilator, air-conditioner, blower, propeller, vane.

fan[2] *n* enthusiast, admirer, supporter, follower, adherent, devotee, lover, buff (*infml*), fiend, freak.

fanatic *n* zealot, devotee, enthusiast, addict, fiend, freak, maniac, visionary, bigot, extremist, militant, activist.

fanatical *adj* overenthusiastic, extreme, passionate, zealous, fervent, burning, mad, wild, frenzied, rabid, obsessive, single-minded, bigoted, visionary.
≠ moderate, unenthusiastic.

fanaticism *n* extremism, monomania, single-mindedness, obsessiveness, madness, infatuation, bigotry, zeal, fervour, enthusiasm, dedication.
≠ moderation.

fanciful *adj* imaginary, mythical, fabulous, fantastic, visionary, romantic, fairy-tale, airy-fairy, vaporous, whimsical, wild, extravagant, curious.
≠ real, ordinary.

fancy *v* **1** LIKE, be attracted to, take a liking to, take to, go for, prefer, favour, desire, wish for, long for, yearn for. **2** THINK, conceive, imagine, dream of, picture, conjecture, believe, suppose, reckon, guess.
≠ **1** dislike.
n **1** DESIRE, craving, hankering, urge, liking, fondness, inclination, preference. **2** NOTION, thought, impression, imagination, dream, fantasy.
≠ **1** dislike, aversion. **2** fact, reality.
adj elaborate, ornate, decorated, ornamented, rococo, baroque, elegant, extravagant, fantastic, fanciful, far-fetched.
≠ plain.

fantastic *adj* **1** WONDERFUL, marvellous, sensational, superb, excellent, first-rate, tremendous, terrific, great, incredible, unbelievable, overwhelming, enormous, extreme. **2** STRANGE, weird, odd, exotic, outlandish, fanciful, fabulous, imaginative, visionary.
≠ **1** ordinary. **2** real.

fantasy *n* dream, daydream, reverie, pipe-dream, nightmare, vision, hallucination, illusion, mirage, apparition, invention, fancy, flight of fancy, delusion, misconception, imagination, unreality.
≠ reality.

far *adv* a long way, a good way, miles (*infml*), much, greatly, considerably, extremely, decidedly, incomparably.

≠ near, close.
adj distant, far-off, faraway, far-flung, outlying, remote, out-of-the-way, godforsaken, removed, far-removed, further, opposite, other.
≠ nearby, close.

farce *n* **1** COMEDY, slapstick, buffoonery, satire, burlesque.
2 TRAVESTY, sham, parody, joke, mockery, ridiculousness, absurdity, nonsense.

fare *n* **1** *pay one's fare*: charge, cost, price, fee, passage. **2** FOOD, eatables (*infml*), provisions, rations, sustenance, meals, diet, menu, board, table.

far-fetched *adj* implausible, improbable, unlikely, dubious, incredible, unbelievable, fantastic, preposterous, crazy, unrealistic.
≠ plausible.

farm *n* ranch, farmstead, grange, homestead, station, land, holding, acreage, acres.

> *Types of farm include*: arable farm, cattle ranch, dairy farm, fish farm, mixed farm, organic farm, pig farm, sheep station, croft, smallholding, estate, plantation.

v cultivate, till, work the land, plant, operate.

farmer *n* agriculturist, crofter, smallholder, husbandman, yeoman.

farming *n* agriculture, cultivation, husbandry, crofting.

far-reaching *adj* broad, extensive, widespread, sweeping, important, significant, momentous.
≠ insignificant.

fascinate *v* absorb, engross, intrigue, delight, charm, captivate, spellbind, enthral, rivet, transfix, hypnotize, mesmerize.
≠ bore, repel.

fascination *n* interest, attraction, lure, magnetism, pull, charm, enchantment, spell, sorcery, magic.
≠ boredom, repulsion.

fashion *n* **1** MANNER, way, method, mode, style, shape, form, pattern, line, cut, look, appearance, type, sort, kind.
2 VOGUE, trend, mode, style, fad, craze, rage (*infml*), latest (*infml*), custom, convention.
v create, form, shape, mould, model, design, fit, tailor, alter, adjust, adapt, suit.

fashionable *adj* chic, smart, elegant, stylish, modish, à la mode, in vogue, trendy (*infml*), in, all the rage (*infml*), popular, prevailing, current, latest, up-to-the-minute, contemporary, modern, up-to-date.
≠ unfashionable.

fast[1] *adj* **1** QUICK, swift, rapid, brisk, accelerated, speedy, nippy (*infml*), hasty, hurried, flying. **2** FASTENED, secure, fixed, immovable, immobile, firm, tight.
≠ **1** slow, unhurried. **2** loose.
adv quickly, swiftly, rapidly, speedily, like a flash, like a shot, hastily, hurriedly, apace, presto.
≠ slowly, gradually.

fast[2] *v* go hungry, diet, starve, abstain.
n fasting, diet, starvation, abstinence.
≠ gluttony, self-indulgence.

fasten *v* fix, attach, clamp, grip, anchor, rivet, nail, seal, close, shut, lock, bolt, secure, tie, bind, chain, link, interlock, connect, join, unite, do up, button, lace, buckle.
≠ unfasten, untie.

fastener

> *Types of fastener include*: button, catch, clasp, clip, collar stud, cotter, cufflink, eyelet, frog, hasp, hinge, hook, hook-and-eye, knot, lace, loop, nail, paperclip, press stud, rivet, screw, shoelace, split pin, staple, stitch, stud, tie, toggle, treasury tag, Velcro®, zip, zipper (*US*).

fat *adj* plump, obese, tubby, stout, corpulent, portly, round, rotund, paunchy, pot-bellied, overweight, heavy, beefy, solid, chubby, podgy, fleshy, flabby, gross.
≠ thin, slim, poor.
n fatness, obesity, overweight, corpulence, paunch, pot (belly), blubber, flab (*infml*).

fatal *adj* deadly, lethal, mortal, killing, incurable, malignant, terminal, final,

destructive, calamitous, catastrophic, disastrous.
≠ harmless.

fatality *n* death, mortality, loss, casualty, deadliness, lethality, disaster.

fate *n* destiny, providence, chance, future, fortune, horoscope, stars, lot, doom, end, outcome, ruin, destruction, death.

fated *adj* destined, predestined, preordained, foreordained, doomed, unavoidable, inevitable, inescapable, certain, sure.
≠ avoidable.

fateful *adj* crucial, critical, decisive, important, momentous, significant, fatal, lethal, disastrous.
≠ unimportant.

father *n* **1** PARENT, begetter, procreator, progenitor, sire (*fml*), papa, dad (*infml*), daddy (*infml*), old man (*infml*), patriarch, elder, forefather, ancestor, forebear, predecessor. **2** FOUNDER, creator, originator, inventor, maker, architect, author, patron, leader, prime mover. **3** PRIEST, padre, abbé, curé.
v beget, procreate, sire, produce.

fathom *v* **1** MEASURE, gauge, plumb, sound, probe, penetrate.
2 UNDERSTAND, comprehend, grasp, see, work out, get to the bottom of, interpret.

fatigue *n* tiredness, weariness, exhaustion, lethargy, listlessness, lassitude, weakness, debility.
≠ energy.
v tire, wear out, weary, exhaust, drain, weaken, debilitate.

fatten *v* feed, nourish, build up, overfeed, cram, stuff, bloat, swell, fill out, spread, expand, thicken.

fatty *adj* fat, greasy, oily.

fault *n* **1** DEFECT, flaw, blemish, imperfection, deficiency, shortcoming, weakness, failing, foible, negligence, omission, oversight. **2** ERROR, mistake, blunder, slip-up (*infml*), slip, lapse, misdeed, offence, wrong, sin. **3** *it's your fault*: responsibility, accountability, liability, culpability.
v find fault with, pick holes in, criticize, knock (*infml*), impugn, censure, blame, call to account.
≠ praise.
at fault (in the) wrong, blameworthy, to blame, responsible, guilty, culpable.

faultless *adj* perfect, flawless, unblemished, spotless, immaculate, unsullied, pure, blameless, exemplary, model, correct, accurate.
≠ faulty, imperfect, flawed.

faulty *adj* imperfect, defective, flawed, blemished, damaged, impaired, out of order, broken, wrong.
≠ faultless.

favour *n* **1** APPROVAL, esteem, support, backing, sympathy, goodwill, patronage, favouritism, preference, partiality. **2** *he did me a favour*: kindness, service, good turn, courtesy.
≠ **1** disapproval.
v **1** PREFER, choose, opt for, like, approve, support, back, advocate, champion. **2** HELP, assist, aid, benefit, promote, encourage, pamper, spoil.
≠ **1** dislike. **2** mistreat.
in favour of for, supporting, on the side of.
≠ against.

favourable *adj* beneficial, advantageous, helpful, fit, suitable, convenient, timely, opportune, good, fair, promising, auspicious, hopeful, positive, encouraging, complimentary, enthusiastic, friendly, amicable, well-disposed, kind, sympathetic, understanding, reassuring.
≠ unfavourable, unhelpful, negative.

favourite *adj* preferred, favoured, pet, best-loved, dearest, beloved, esteemed, chosen.
≠ hated.
n preference, choice, pick, pet, blue-eyed boy, teacher's pet, the apple of one's eye, darling, idol.
≠ bête noire, pet hate.

favouritism *n* nepotism, preferential treatment, preference, partiality, one-sidedness, partisanship, bias, injustice.
≠ impartiality.

fear *n* alarm, fright, terror, horror, panic, agitation, worry, anxiety,

consternation, concern, dismay, distress, uneasiness, qualms, misgivings, apprehension, trepidation, dread, foreboding, awe, phobia, nightmare.
≠ courage, bravery, confidence.
v take fright, shrink from, dread, shudder at, tremble, worry, suspect, anticipate, expect, foresee, respect, venerate.

fearful *adj* **1** FRIGHTENED, afraid, scared, alarmed, nervous, anxious, tense, uneasy, apprehensive, hesitant, nervy, panicky. **2** TERRIBLE, fearsome (*fml*), dreadful, awful, frightful, atrocious, shocking, appalling, monstrous, gruesome, hideous, ghastly, horrible.
≠ **1** brave, courageous, fearless. **2** wonderful, delightful.

feasible *adj* practicable, practical, workable, achievable, attainable, realizable, viable, reasonable, possible, likely.
≠ impossible.

feast *n* **1** BANQUET, dinner, spread, blow-out (*sl*), binge (*infml*), beano (*infml*), junket. **2** FESTIVAL, holiday, gala, fête, celebration, revels.
v gorge, eat one's fill, wine and dine, treat, entertain.

feat *n* exploit, deed, act, accomplishment, achievement, attainment, performance.

feature *n* **1** ASPECT, facet, point, factor, attribute, quality, property, trait, lineament, characteristic, peculiarity, mark, hallmark, speciality, highlight. **2** *a magazine feature*: column, article, report, story, piece, item, comment.
v **1** EMPHASIZE, highlight, spotlight, play up, promote, show, present. **2** APPEAR, figure, participate, act, perform, star.

fee *n* charge, terms, bill, account, pay, remuneration, payment, retainer, subscription, reward, recompense, hire, toll.

feeble *adj* **1** WEAK, faint, exhausted, frail, delicate, puny, sickly, infirm, powerless, helpless. **2** INADEQUATE, lame, poor, thin, flimsy, ineffective, incompetent, indecisive.
≠ **1** strong, powerful.

feed *v* nourish, cater for, provide for, supply, sustain, suckle, nurture, foster, strengthen, fuel, graze, pasture, eat, dine.
n food, fodder, forage, pasture, silage.
feed on eat, consume, devour, live on, exist on.

feel *v* **1** EXPERIENCE, go through, undergo, suffer, endure, enjoy. **2** TOUCH, finger, handle, manipulate, hold, stroke, caress, fondle, paw, fumble, grope. **3** *feel soft*: seem, appear. **4** THINK, believe, consider, reckon, judge. **5** SENSE, perceive, notice, observe, know.
n texture, surface, finish, touch, knack, sense, impression, feeling, quality.
feel for pity, sympathize (with), commiserate (with), be sorry for.
feel like fancy, want, desire.

feeling *n* **1** SENSATION, perception, sense, instinct, hunch, suspicion, inkling, impression, idea, notion, opinion, view, point of view. **2** EMOTION, passion, intensity, warmth, compassion, sympathy, understanding, pity, concern, affection, fondness, sentiment, sentimentality, susceptibility, sensibility, sensitivity, appreciation. **3** AIR, aura, atmosphere, mood, quality.

fell *v* cut down, hew, knock down, strike down, floor, level, flatten, raze, demolish.

fellow *n* **1** PERSON, man, boy, chap (*infml*), bloke (*infml*), guy (*infml*), individual, character. **2** PEER, compeer, equal, partner, associate, colleague, co-worker, companion, comrade, friend, counterpart, match, mate, twin, double.
adj co-, associate, associated, related, like, similar.

fellowship *n* **1** COMPANIONSHIP, camaraderie, communion, familiarity, intimacy. **2** ASSOCIATION, league, guild, society, club, fraternity, brotherhood, sisterhood, order.

female *adj* feminine, she-, girlish, womanly.
≠ male.

Female terms include: girl, lass, maiden, woman, lady, daughter, sister, girlfriend, fiancèe, bride, wife, mother, aunt, niece, grandmother, matriarch, godmother, widow, dowager, dame, madam, mistress, virgin, spinster, old-maid, bird (*sl*), chick (*sl*), lesbian, bitch (*sl*), prostitute, whore, harlot; cow, heifer, bitch, doe, ewe, hen, mare, filly, nanny-goat, sow, tigress, vixen.

feminine *adj* **1** FEMALE, womanly, ladylike, graceful, gentle, tender. **2** EFFEMINATE, unmanly, womanish, girlish, sissy.
≠ **1** masculine. **2** manly.

feminism *n* women's movement, women's lib(eration), female emancipation, women's rights.

fence *n* barrier, railing, paling, wall, hedge, windbreak, guard, defence, barricade, stockade, rampart.
v **1** SURROUND, encircle, bound, hedge, wall, enclose, pen, coop, confine, restrict, separate, protect, guard, defend, fortify. **2** PARRY, dodge, evade, hedge, equivocate, quibble, pussyfoot, stonewall.

fencing

Fencing terms include: appel, attack, balestra, barrage, coquille, disengage, en garde, épée, feint, flèche, foible, foil, forte, hit, lunge, on guard, parry, counter-parry, pink, piste, plastron, remise, reprise, riposte, counter-riposte, sabre, tac-au-tac, thrust, touch, touché, volt.

fend for look after, take care of, shift for, support, maintain, sustain, provide for.

fend off ward off, beat off, parry, deflect, avert, resist, repel, repulse, hold at bay, keep off, shut out.

ferment *v* **1** BUBBLE, effervesce, froth, foam, boil, seethe, smoulder, fester, brew, rise. **2** ROUSE, stir up, excite, work up, agitate, foment, incite, provoke, inflame, heat.
n unrest, agitation, turbulence, stir, excitement, turmoil, disruption, commotion, tumult, hubbub, uproar, furore, frenzy, fever, glow.
≠ calm.

ferocious *adj* vicious, savage, fierce, wild, barbarous, barbaric, brutal, inhuman, cruel, sadistic, murderous, bloodthirsty, violent, merciless, pitiless, ruthless.
≠ gentle, mild, tame.

ferocity *n* viciousness, savagery, fierceness, wildness, barbarity, brutality, inhumanity, cruelty, sadism, bloodthirstiness, violence, ruthlessness.
≠ gentleness, mildness.

ferry *n* ferry-boat, car ferry, ship, boat, vessel.
v transport, ship, convey, carry, take, shuttle, taxi, drive, run, move, shift.

fertile *adj* fruitful, productive, generative, yielding, prolific, teeming, abundant, plentiful, rich, lush, luxuriant, fat.
≠ infertile, barren, sterile, unproductive.

fertilize *v* **1** IMPREGNATE, inseminate, pollinate. **2** *fertilize land*: enrich, feed, dress, compost, manure, dung.

fertilizer *n* dressing, compost, manure, dung.

fervent *adj* ardent, earnest, eager, enthusiastic, whole-hearted, excited, energetic, vigorous, fiery, spirited, intense, vehement, passionate, full-blooded, zealous, devout, impassioned, heartfelt, emotional, warm.
≠ cool, indifferent, apathetic.

fervour *n* ardour, eagerness, enthusiasm, excitement, animation, energy, vigour, spirit, verve, intensity, vehemence, passion, zeal, warmth.
≠ apathy.

fester *v* ulcerate, gather, suppurate, discharge, putrefy, rot, decay, rankle, smoulder.

festival *n* celebration, commemoration, anniversary, jubilee, holiday, feast, gala, fête, carnival, fiesta, party, merrymaking, entertainment, festivities.

festive *adj* celebratory, festal, holiday,

gala, carnival, happy, joyful, merry, hearty, cheery, jolly, jovial, cordial, convivial.
≠ gloomy, sombre, sober.

festivity *n* celebration, jubilation, feasting, banqueting, fun, enjoyment, pleasure, entertainment, sport, amusement, merriment, merrymaking, revelry, jollity, joviality, conviviality.

festoon *v* adorn, deck, bedeck, garland, wreathe, drape, hang, swathe, decorate, garnish.

fetch *v* **1** *fetch a bucket*: get, collect, bring, carry, transport, deliver, escort. **2** SELL FOR, go for, bring in, yield, realize, make, earn.

fetching *adj* attractive, pretty, sweet, cute, charming, enchanting, fascinating, captivating.
≠ repellent.

fête *n* fair, bazaar, sale of work, garden party, gala, carnival, festival.
v entertain, treat, regale, welcome, honour, lionize.

feud *n* vendetta, quarrel, row, argument, disagreement, dispute, conflict, strife, discord, animosity, ill will, bitterness, enmity, hostility, antagonism, rivalry.
≠ agreement, peace.

fever *n* **1** FEVERISHNESS, (high) temperature, delirium. **2** EXCITEMENT, agitation, turmoil, unrest, restlessness, heat, passion, ecstasy.

feverish *adj* **1** DELIRIOUS, hot, burning, flushed. **2** EXCITED, impatient, agitated, restless, nervous, overwrought, frenzied, frantic, hectic, hasty, hurried.
≠ **1** cool. **2** calm.

few *adj* scarce, rare, uncommon, sporadic, infrequent, sparse, thin, scant, scanty, meagre, inconsiderable, inadequate, insufficient, in short supply.
≠ many.
pron not many, hardly any, one or two, a couple, scattering, sprinkling, handful, some.
≠ many.

fibre *n* **1** FILAMENT, strand, thread, nerve, sinew, pile, texture. **2** *moral fibre*: character, calibre, backbone, strength, stamina, toughness, courage, resolution, determination.

fickle *adj* inconstant, disloyal, unfaithful, faithless, treacherous, unreliable, unpredictable, changeable, capricious, mercurial, irresolute, vacillating.
≠ constant, steady, stable.

fiction *n* **1** FANTASY, fancy, imagination, figment, invention, fabrication, concoction, improvisation, story-telling. **2** NOVEL, romance, story, tale, yarn, fable, parable, legend, myth, lie.
≠ **2** non-fiction, fact, truth.

fictional *adj* literary, invented, made-up, imaginary, make-believe, legendary, mythical, mythological, fabulous, non-existent, unreal.
≠ factual, real.

fictitious *adj* false, untrue, invented, made-up, fabricated, apocryphal, imaginary, non-existent, bogus, counterfeit, spurious, assumed, supposed.
≠ true, genuine.

fiddle *v* **1** *fiddling with her necklace*: play, tinker, toy, trifle, tamper, mess around, meddle, interfere, fidget. **2** CHEAT, swindle, diddle, cook the books (*infml*), juggle, manoeuvre, racketeer, graft (*sl*).
n swindle, con (*infml*), rip-off (*sl*), fraud, racket, sharp practice, graft (*sl*).

fiddling *adj* trifling, petty, trivial, insignificant, negligible, paltry.
≠ important, significant.

fidelity *n* **1** FAITHFULNESS, loyalty, allegiance, devotion, constancy, reliability. **2** ACCURACY, exactness, precision, closeness, adherence.
≠ **1** infidelity, inconstancy, treachery. **2** inaccuracy.

fidget *v* squirm, wriggle, shuffle, twitch, jerk, jump, fret, fuss, bustle, fiddle, mess about, play around.

fidgety *adj* restless, impatient, uneasy, nervous, agitated, jittery, jumpy, twitchy, on edge.
≠ still.

field *n* **1** GRASSLAND, meadow, pasture, paddock, playing-field, ground, pitch, green, lawn. **2** RANGE, scope, bounds, limits, confines, territory, area, province, domain, sphere, environment, department, discipline, speciality, line, forte. **3** PARTICIPANTS, entrants, contestants, competitors, contenders, runners, candidates, applicants, opponents, opposition, competition.

fiend *n* **1** EVIL SPIRIT, demon, devil, monster. **2** *a health fiend*: enthusiast, fanatic, addict, devotee, freak (*infml*), nut (*infml*).

fiendish *adj* devilish, diabolical, infernal, wicked, malevolent, cunning, cruel, inhuman, savage, monstrous, unspeakable.

fierce *adj* ferocious, vicious, savage, cruel, brutal, merciless, aggressive, dangerous, murderous, frightening, menacing, threatening, stern, grim, relentless, raging, wild, passionate, intense, strong, powerful.
≠ gentle, kind, calm.

fiery *adj* **1** BURNING, afire, flaming, aflame, blazing, ablaze, red-hot, glowing, aglow, flushed, hot, torrid, sultry. **2** PASSIONATE, inflamed, ardent, fervent, impatient, excitable, impetuous, impulsive, hot-headed, fierce, violent, heated.
≠ **1** cold. **2** impassive.

fight *v* **1** WRESTLE, box, fence, joust, brawl, scrap, scuffle, tussle, skirmish, combat, battle, do battle, war, wage war, clash, cross swords, engage, grapple, struggle, strive, contend. **2** QUARREL, argue, dispute, squabble, bicker, wrangle. **3** OPPOSE, contest, campaign against, resist, withstand, defy, stand up to.
n **1** BOUT, contest, duel, combat, action, battle, war, hostilities, brawl, scrap, scuffle, tussle, struggle, skirmish, set-to, clash, engagement, brush, encounter, conflict, fray, free-for-all, fracas, riot. **2** QUARREL, row, argument, dispute, dissension.
fight back 1 RETALIATE, defend oneself, resist, put up a fight, retort, reply. **2** *fight back the tears*: hold back, restrain, curb, control, repress, bottle up, contain, suppress.
fight off hold off, keep at bay, ward off, stave off, resist, repel, rebuff, beat off, rout, put to flight.

fighter *n* combatant, contestant, contender, disputant, boxer, wrestler, pugilist, prizefighter, soldier, trouper, mercenary, warrior, man-at-arms, swordsman, gladiator.

figurative *adj* metaphorical, symbolic, emblematic, representative, allegorical, parabolic, descriptive, pictorial.
≠ literal.

figure *n* **1** NUMBER, numeral, digit, integer, sum, amount. **2** SHAPE, form, outline, silhouette, body, frame, build, physique. **3** *public figure*: dignitary, celebrity, personality, character, person. **4** DIAGRAM, illustration, picture, drawing, sketch, image, representation, symbol.
v **1** RECKON, guess, estimate, judge, think, believe. **2** FEATURE, appear, crop up.
figure out work out, calculate, compute, reckon, puzzle out, resolve, fathom, understand, see, make out, decipher.

figurehead *n* mouthpiece, front man, name, dummy, puppet.

filament *n* fibre, strand, thread, hair, whisker, wire, string, pile.

file[1] *v* rub (down), sand, abrade, scour, scrape, grate, rasp, hone, whet, shave, plane, smooth, polish.

file[2] *n* folder, dossier, portfolio, binder, case, record, documents, data, information.
v record, register, note, enter, process, store, classify, categorize, pigeonhole, catalogue.

file[3] *n* line, queue, column, row, procession, cortège, train, string, stream, trail.
v march, troop, parade, stream, trail.

fill *v* **1** REPLENISH, stock, supply, furnish, satisfy, pack, crowd, cram, stuff, congest, block, clog, plug, bung, cork, stop, close, seal. **2** PERVADE, imbue, permeate, soak, impregnate. **3** *fill a post*: take up, hold, occupy, discharge, fulfil.

≠ 1 empty, drain.
fill in 1 *fill in a form*: complete, fill out, answer. **2** (*infml*) STAND IN, deputize, understudy, substitute, replace, represent, act for. **3** (*infml*) BRIEF, inform, advise, acquaint, bring up to date.

filling *n* contents, inside, stuffing, padding, wadding, filler.
adj satisfying, nutritious, square, solid, substantial, heavy, large, big, generous, ample.
≠ insubstantial.

film *n* **1** MOTION PICTURE, picture, movie (*infml*), video, feature film, short, documentary. **2** LAYER, covering, dusting, coat, coating, glaze, skin, membrane, tissue, sheet, veil, screen, cloud, mist, haze.
v photograph, shoot, video, videotape.

filter *v* strain, sieve, sift, screen, refine, purify, clarify, percolate, ooze, seep, leak, trickle, dribble.
n strainer, sieve, sifter, colander, mesh, gauze, membrane.

filth *n* **1** DIRT, grime, muck, dung, excrement, faeces, sewage, refuse, rubbish, garbage, trash, slime, sludge, effluent, pollution, contamination, corruption, impurity, uncleanness, foulness, sordidness, squalor.
2 OBSCENITY, pornography, smut, indecency, vulgarity, coarseness.
≠ **1** cleanness, cleanliness, purity.

filthy *adj* **1** DIRTY, soiled, unwashed, grimy, grubby, mucky, muddy, slimy, sooty, unclean, impure, foul, gross, sordid, squalid, vile, low, mean, base, contemptible, despicable. **2** OBSCENE, pornographic, smutty, bawdy, suggestive, indecent, offensive, foul-mouthed, vulgar, coarse, corrupt, depraved.
≠ **1** clean, pure. **2** decent.

final *adj* last, latest, closing, concluding, finishing, end, ultimate, terminal, dying, last-minute, eventual, conclusive, definitive, decisive, definite, incontrovertible.
≠ first, initial.

finale *n* climax, dénouement, culmination, crowning glory, end, conclusion, close, curtain, epilogue.

finalize *v* conclude, finish, complete, round off, resolve, settle, agree, decide, close, clinch, sew up (*infml*), wrap up (*infml*).

finally *adv* lastly, in conclusion, ultimately, eventually, at last, at length, in the end, conclusively, once and for all, for ever, irreversibly, irrevocably, definitely.

finance *n* economics, money management, accounting, banking, investment, stock market, business, commerce, trade, money, funding, sponsorship, subsidy.
v pay for, fund, sponsor, back, support, underwrite, guarantee, subsidize, capitalize, float, set up.

finances *n* accounts, affairs, budget, bank account, income, revenue, liquidity, resources, assets, capital, wealth, money, cash, funds, wherewithal.

financial *adj* monetary, money, pecuniary, economic, fiscal, budgetary, commercial.

financier *n* financialist, banker, stockbroker, money-maker, investor, speculator.

find *v* **1** DISCOVER, locate, track down, trace, retrieve, recover, unearth, uncover, expose, reveal, come across, chance on, stumble on, meet, encounter, detect, recognize, notice, observe, perceive, realize, learn.
2 ATTAIN, achieve, win, reach, gain, obtain, get. **3** *find it difficult*: consider, think, judge, declare.
≠ **1** lose.
find out 1 LEARN, ascertain, discover, detect, note, observe, perceive, realize.
2 UNMASK, expose, show up, uncover, reveal, disclose, catch, suss out (*sl*), rumble (*sl*), tumble to (*infml*).

finding *n* **1** FIND, discovery, breakthrough. **2** DECISION, conclusion, judgement, verdict, pronouncement, decree, recommendation, award.

fine[1] *adj* **1** EXCELLENT, outstanding, exceptional, superior, exquisite, splendid, magnificent, brilliant,

beautiful, handsome, attractive, elegant, lovely, nice, good. **2** THIN, slender, sheer, gauzy, powdery, flimsy, fragile, delicate, dainty.
3 SATISFACTORY, acceptable, all right, OK (*infml*). **4** *fine weather*: bright, sunny, clear, cloudless, dry, fair.
≠ **1** mediocre. **2** thick, coarse.
4 cloudy.

fine[2] *n* penalty, punishment, forfeit, forfeiture, damages.

finger *v* touch, handle, manipulate, feel, stroke, caress, fondle, paw, fiddle with, toy with, play about with, meddle with.

finicky *adj* **1** PARTICULAR, finickety, pernickety, fussy, choosy (*infml*), fastidious, meticulous, scrupulous, critical, hypercritical, nit-picking.
2 FIDDLY, intricate, tricky, difficult, delicate.
≠ **1** easy-going. **2** easy.

finish *v* **1** END, terminate, stop, cease, complete, accomplish, achieve, fulfil, discharge, deal with, do, conclude, close, wind up, settle, round off, culminate, perfect. **2** DESTROY, ruin, exterminate, get rid of, annihilate, defeat, overcome, rout, overthrow.
3 USE (UP), consume, devour, eat, drink, exhaust, drain, empty.
≠ **1** begin, start.
n **1** END, termination, completion, conclusion, close, ending, finale, culmination. **2** SURFACE, appearance, texture, grain, polish, shine, gloss, lustre, smoothness.
≠ **1** beginning, start, commencement.

finite *adj* limited, restricted, bounded, demarcated, terminable, definable, fixed, measurable, calculable, countable, numbered.
≠ infinite.

fire *n* **1** FLAMES, blaze, bonfire, conflagration, inferno, burning, combustion. **2** PASSION, feeling, excitement, enthusiasm, spirit, intensity, heat, radiance, sparkle.
v **1** IGNITE, light, kindle, set fire to, set on fire, set alight. **2** *fire a missile*: shoot, launch, set off, let off, detonate, explode. **3** DISMISS, discharge, sack (*infml*), eject. **4** EXCITE, whet, enliven, galvanize, electrify, stir, arouse, rouse, stimulate, inspire, incite, spark off, trigger off.
on fire burning, alight, ignited, flaming, in flames, aflame, blazing, ablaze, fiery.

fireplace

Types of fireplace include: backboiler, boiler, bonfire, brazier, campfire, electric fire, firebox, forge, furnace, gas fire, grate, hearth, incinerator, kiln, open fire, oven, stove, paraffin stove, wood burning stove.

firework

Types of firework include: banger, Catherine wheel, cracker, Chinese cracker, firecracker, fountain, golden rain, indoor firework, jumping-jack, pinwheel, rocket, roman candle, sky-rocket, sparkler, squib.

firm[1] *adj* **1** *firm ground*: dense, compressed, compact, concentrated, set, solid, hard, unyielding, stiff, rigid, inflexible. **2** FIXED, embedded, fast, tight, secure, fastened, anchored, immovable, motionless, stationary, steady, stable, sturdy, strong.
3 ADAMANT, unshakable, resolute, determined, dogged, unwavering, strict, constant, steadfast, staunch, dependable, true, sure, convinced, definite, settled, committed.
≠ **1** soft, flabby. **2** unsteady.
3 hesitant.

firm[2] *n* company, corporation, business, enterprise, concern, house, establishment, institution, organization, association, partnership, syndicate, conglomerate.

first *adj* **1** INITIAL, opening, introductory, preliminary, elementary, primary, basic, fundamental. **2** ORIGINAL, earliest, earlier, prior, primitive, primeval, oldest, eldest, senior. **3** CHIEF, main, key, cardinal, principal, head, leading, ruling, sovereign, highest, uppermost, paramount, prime, predominant, pre-eminent.
≠ **1** last, final.

adv initially, to begin with, to start with, at the outset, beforehand, originally, in preference, rather, sooner.
first name forename, Christian name, baptismal name, given name.

first-rate *adj* first-class, A1, second-to-none, matchless, peerless, top, top-notch (*infml*), top-flight, leading, supreme, superior, prime, excellent, outstanding, superlative, exceptional, splendid, superb, fine, admirable.
≠ inferior.

fish

Types of fish include: bloater, brisling, cod, coley, Dover sole, haddock, hake, halibut, herring, jellied eel, kipper, mackerel, pilchard, plaice, rainbow trout, salmon, sardine, sole, sprat, trout, tuna, turbot, whitebait; bass, Bombay duck, bream, brill, carp, catfish, chub, conger eel, cuttlefish, dab, dace, dogfish, dory, eel, goldfish, guppy, marlin, minnow, monkfish, mullet, octopus, perch, pike, piranha, roach, shark, skate, snapper, squid, stickleback, stingray, sturgeon, swordfish, tench, whiting; clam, cockle, crab, crayfish, crawfish (*US*), kingprawn, lobster, mussel, oyster, prawn, scallop, shrimp, whelk. *see also* **sharks**.

v angle, trawl, delve, hunt, seek, invite, solicit.
fish out produce, take out, extract, find, come up with, dredge up, haul up.

fishing *n* angling, trawling.

fit[1] *adj* **1** SUITABLE, appropriate, apt, fitting, correct, right, proper, ready, prepared, able, capable, competent, qualified, eligible, worthy. **2** HEALTHY, well, able-bodied, in good form, in good shape, sound, sturdy, strong, robust, hale and hearty.
≠ **1** unsuitable, unworthy. **2** unfit.
v **1** MATCH, correspond, conform, follow, agree, concur, tally, suit, harmonize, go, belong, dovetail, interlock, join, meet, arrange, place, position, accommodate. **2** ALTER, modify, change, adjust, adapt, tailor, shape, fashion.
fit out equip, rig out, kit out, outfit, provide, supply, furnish, prepare, arm.

fit[2] *n* seizure, convulsion, spasm, paroxysm, attack, outbreak, bout, spell, burst, surge, outburst, eruption, explosion.

fitful *adj* sporadic, intermittent, occasional, spasmodic, erratic, irregular, uneven, broken, disturbed.
≠ steady, regular.

fitted *adj* **1** *fitted wardrobe*: built-in, permanent. **2** EQUIPPED, rigged out, provided, furnished, appointed, prepared, armed. **3** SUITED, right, suitable, fit, qualified.

fitting *adj* apt, appropriate, suitable, fit, correct, right, proper, seemly, meet (*fml*), desirable, deserved.
≠ unsuitable, improper.
n connection, attachment, accessory, part, component, piece, unit, fitment.

fittings *n* equipment, furnishings, furniture, fixtures, installations, fitments, accessories, extras.

fix *v* **1** FASTEN, secure, tie, bind, attach, join, connect, link, couple, anchor, pin, nail, rivet, stick, glue, cement, set, harden, solidify, stiffen, stabilize, plant, root, implant, embed, establish, install, place, locate, position. **2** *fix a date*: arrange, set, specify, define, agree on, decide, determine, settle, resolve, finalize. **3** MEND, repair, correct, rectify, adjust, restore.
≠ **1** move, shift. **3** damage.
n (*infml*) dilemma, quandary, predicament, plight, difficulty, hole (*infml*), corner, spot (*infml*), mess, muddle.
fix up arrange, organize, plan, lay on, provide, supply, furnish, equip, settle, sort out, produce, bring about.

fixation *n* preoccupation, obsession, mania, fetish, thing (*infml*), infatuation, compulsion, hang-up (*infml*), complex.

fixed *adj* decided, settled, established, definite, arranged, planned, set, firm, rigid, inflexible, steady, secure, fast, rooted, permanent.
≠ variable.

fizz *v* effervesce, sparkle, bubble, froth, foam, fizzle, hiss, sizzle, sputter, spit.

fizzy *adj* effervescent, sparkling, aerated, carbonated, gassy, bubbly, bubbling, frothy, foaming.

flabbergasted (*infml*) *adj* amazed, confounded, astonished, astounded, staggered, dumbfounded, speechless, stunned, dazed, overcome, overwhelmed, bowled over.

flabby *adj* fleshy, soft, yielding, flaccid, limp, floppy, drooping, hanging, sagging, slack, loose, lax, weak, feeble.
≠ firm, strong.

flag[1] *v* lessen, diminish, decline, fall (off), abate, subside, sink, slump, dwindle, peter out, fade, fail, weaken, slow, falter, tire, weary, wilt, droop, sag, flop, faint, die.
≠ revive.

flag[2]

> *Types of flag include*: banner, bunting, burgee, colours, cornet, gonfalon, jack, oriflamme, pennant, pilot flag, signal flag, standard, streamer, swallow tail.
> *Names of flag include*: Blue Ensign, Blue Peter, Crescent, Hammer and Sickle, Jolly Roger, Old Glory, Olympic Flag, Red Ensign, Rising Sun, Skull and Crossbones, Star-Spangled Banner, Stars and Stripes, Tricolour, Union Jack, White Ensign, Yellow Jack.

v **1** SIGNAL, wave, salute, motion. **2** MARK, indicate, label, tag, note.

flail *v* thresh, thrash, beat, whip.

flair *n* skill, ability, aptitude, faculty, gift, talent, facility, knack, mastery, genius, feel, taste, discernment, acumen, style, elegance, stylishness, panache.
≠ inability, ineptitude.

flake *n* scale, peeling, paring, shaving, sliver, wafer, chip, splinter.
v scale, peel, chip, splinter.

flamboyant *adj* showy, ostentatious, flashy, gaudy, colourful, brilliant, dazzling, striking, extravagant, rich, elaborate, ornate, florid.
≠ modest, restrained.

flame *v* burn, flare, blaze, glare, flash, beam, shine, glow, radiate.
n **1** FIRE, blaze, light, brightness, heat, warmth. **2** PASSION, ardour, fervour, enthusiasm, zeal, intensity, radiance.

flaming *adj* **1** *a flaming torch*: burning, alight, aflame, blazing, fiery, brilliant, scintillating, red-hot, glowing, smouldering. **2** INTENSE, vivid, aroused, impassioned, hot, raging, frenzied.

flammable *adj* inflammable, ignitable, combustible.
≠ non-flammable, incombustible, flameproof, fire-resistant.

flank *n* side, edge, quarter, wing, loin, hip, thigh.
v edge, fringe, skirt, line, border, bound, confine, wall, screen.

flap *v* flutter, vibrate, wave, agitate, shake, wag, swing, swish, thrash, beat.
n **1** FOLD, fly, lapel, tab, lug, tag, tail, skirt, aileron. **2** (*infml*) PANIC, state (*infml*), fuss, commotion, fluster, agitation, flutter, dither, tizzy (*infml*).

flare *v* **1** FLAME, burn, blaze, glare, flash, flicker, burst, explode, erupt. **2** BROADEN, widen, flare out, spread out, splay.
n **1** FLAME, blaze, glare, flash, flicker, burst. **2** BROADENING, widening, splay.
flare up erupt, break out, explode, blow up.

flash *v* **1** BEAM, shine, light up, flare, blaze, glare, gleam, glint, flicker, twinkle, sparkle, glitter, shimmer. **2** *the train flashed past*: streak, fly, dart, race, dash.
n beam, ray, shaft, spark, blaze, flare, burst, streak, gleam, glint, flicker, twinkle, sparkle, shimmer.

flashy *adj* showy, ostentatious, flamboyant, glamorous, bold, loud, garish, gaudy, jazzy, flash, tawdry, cheap, vulgar, tasteless.
≠ plain, tasteful.

flat[1] *adj* **1** LEVEL, plane, even, smooth, uniform, unbroken, horizontal, outstretched, prostrate, prone, recumbent, reclining, low. **2** DULL, boring, monotonous, tedious, uninteresting, unexciting, stale, lifeless, dead, spiritless, lacklustre, vapid,

insipid, weak, watery, empty, pointless.
3 *a flat refusal*: absolute, utter, total, unequivocal, categorical, positive, unconditional, unqualified, point-blank, direct, straight, explicit, plain, final.
4 *a flat tyre*: punctured, burst, deflated, collapsed.
≠ **1** bumpy, vertical. **2** exciting, full. **3** equivocal.
flat out at top speed, at full speed, all out, for all one is worth.

flat[2] *n* apartment, penthouse, maisonnette, tenement, flatlet, rooms, suite, bed-sit(ter).

flatten *v* **1** SMOOTH, iron, press, roll, crush, squash, compress, level, even out. **2** KNOCK DOWN, prostrate, floor, fell, demolish, raze, overwhelm, subdue.

flatter *v* praise, compliment, sweet-talk (*infml*), adulate, fawn, butter up (*infml*), wheedle, humour, play up to, court, curry favour with.
≠ criticize.

flattery *n* adulation, eulogy, sweet talk (*infml*), soft soap (*infml*), flannel (*infml*), blarney, cajolery, fawning, toadyism, sycophancy, ingratiation, servility.
≠ criticism.

flavour *n* **1** TASTE, tang, smack, savour, relish, zest, zing (*infml*), aroma, odour. **2** QUALITY, property, character, style, aspect, feeling, feel, atmosphere. **3** HINT, suggestion, touch, tinge, tone.
v season, spice, ginger up, infuse, imbue.

flavouring *n* seasoning, zest, essence, extract, additive.

flaw *n* defect, imperfection, fault, blemish, spot, mark, speck, crack, crevice, fissure, cleft, split, rift, break, fracture, weakness, shortcoming, failing, fallacy, lapse, slip, error, mistake.

flawed *adj* imperfect, defective, faulty, blemished, marked, damaged, spoilt, marred, cracked, chipped, broken, unsound, fallacious, erroneous.
≠ flawless, perfect.

flawless *adj* perfect, faultless, unblemished, spotless, immaculate, stainless, sound, intact, whole, unbroken, undamaged.
≠ flawed, imperfect.

fleck *v* dot, spot, mark, speckle, dapple, mottle, streak, sprinkle, dust.
n dot, point, spot, mark, speck, speckle, streak.

flee *v* run away, bolt, fly, take flight, take off, make off, cut and run, escape, get away, decamp, abscond, leave, depart, withdraw, retreat, vanish, disappear.
≠ stay.

fleet *n* flotilla, armada, navy, task force, squadron.

fleeting *adj* short, brief, flying, short-lived, momentary, ephemeral, transient, transitory, passing, temporary.
≠ lasting, permanent.

flesh *n* body, tissue, fat, muscle, brawn, skin, meat, pulp, substance, matter, physicality.

flex *v* bend, bow, curve, angle, ply, double up, tighten, contract.
≠ straighten, extend.
n cable, wire, lead, cord.

flexible *adj* **1** BENDABLE, bendy (*infml*), pliable, pliant, plastic, malleable, mouldable, elastic, stretchy, springy, yielding, supple, lithe, limber, double-jointed, mobile. **2** ADAPTABLE, adjustable, amenable, accommodating, variable, open.
≠ **1** inflexible, rigid.

flick *v* hit, strike, rap, tap, touch, dab, flip, jerk, whip, lash.
n rap, tap, touch, dab, flip, jerk, click.
flick through flip through, thumb through, leaf through, glance at, skim, scan.

flicker *v* flash, blink, wink, twinkle, sparkle, glimmer, shimmer, gutter, flutter, vibrate, quiver, waver.
n flash, gleam, glint, twinkle, glimmer, spark, trace, drop, iota, atom, indication.

flight[1] *n* **1** FLYING, aviation, aeronautics, air transport, air travel.

2 JOURNEY, trip, voyage.

flight² *n* fleeing, escape, getaway, breakaway, exit, departure, exodus, retreat.

flimsy *adj* thin, fine, light, slight, insubstantial, ethereal, fragile, delicate, shaky, rickety, makeshift, weak, feeble, meagre, inadequate, shallow, superficial, trivial, poor, unconvincing, implausible.
≠ sturdy.

flinch *v* wince, start, cringe, cower, quail, tremble, shake, quake, shudder, shiver, shrink, recoil, draw back, balk, shy away, duck, shirk, withdraw, retreat, flee.

fling *v* throw, hurl, pitch, lob, toss, chuck (*infml*), cast, sling, catapult, launch, propel, send, let fly, heave, jerk.

flip *v* flick, spin, twirl, twist, turn, toss, throw, cast, pitch, jerk, flap.
n flick, spin, twirl, twist, turn, toss, jerk, flap.

flippant *adj* facetious, light-hearted, frivolous, superficial, offhand, flip, glib, pert, saucy (*infml*), cheeky (*infml*), impudent, impertinent, rude, disrespectful, irreverent.
≠ serious, respectful.

flirt *v* chat up, make up to, lead on, philander, dally.
flirt with consider, entertain, toy with, play with, trifle with, dabble in, try.

flit *v* dart, speed, flash, fly, wing, flutter, whisk, skim, slip, pass, bob, dance.

float *v* **1** GLIDE, sail, swim, bob, drift, waft, hover, hang. **2** LAUNCH, initiate, set up, promote.
≠ **1** sink.

floating *adj* **1** AFLOAT, buoyant, unsinkable, sailing, swimming, bobbing, drifting. **2** VARIABLE, fluctuating, movable, migratory, transitory, wandering, unattached, free, uncommitted.
≠ **1** sinking. **2** fixed.

flock *v* herd, swarm, troop, converge, mass, bunch, cluster, huddle, crowd, throng, group, gather, collect, congregate.
n herd, pack, crowd, throng, multitude, mass, bunch, cluster, group, gathering, assembly, congregation.

flog *v* beat, whip, lash, flagellate, scourge, birch, cane, flay, drub, thrash, whack (*infml*), chastise, punish.

flogging *n* beating, whipping, lashing, flagellation, scourging, birching, caning, flaying, thrashing, hiding.

flood *v* **1** DELUGE, inundate, soak, drench, saturate, fill, overflow, immerse, submerge, engulf, swamp, overwhelm, drown. **2** FLOW, pour, stream, rush, surge, gush.
n deluge, inundation, downpour, torrent, flow, tide, stream, rush, spate, outpouring, overflow, glut, excess, abundance, profusion.
≠ drought, trickle, dearth.

floor *n* **1** FLOORING, ground, base, basis. **2** *on the third floor*: storey, level, stage, landing, deck, tier.
v (*infml*) defeat, overwhelm, beat, stump (*infml*), frustrate, confound, perplex, baffle, puzzle, bewilder, disconcert, throw.

flop *v* **1** DROOP, hang, dangle, sag, drop, fall, topple, tumble, slump, collapse. **2** FAIL, misfire, fall flat, founder, fold.
n failure, non-starter, fiasco, debacle, wash-out (*infml*), disaster.

floppy *adj* droopy, hanging, dangling, sagging, limp, loose, baggy, soft, flabby.
≠ firm.

florid *adj* **1** FLOWERY, ornate, elaborate, fussy, overelaborate, baroque, rococo, flamboyant, grandiloquent. **2** *a florid complexion*: ruddy, red, purple.
≠ **1** plain, simple. **2** pale.

flotsam *n* jetsam, wreckage, debris, rubbish, junk, oddments.

flounder *v* wallow, struggle, grope, fumble, blunder, stagger, stumble, falter.

flourish *v* **1** THRIVE, grow, wax, increase, flower, blossom, bloom, develop, progress, get on, do well, prosper, succeed, boom. **2** BRANDISH, wave, shake, twirl, swing, display,

wield, flaunt, parade, vaunt.
≠ **1** decline, languish, fail.
n display, parade, show, gesture, wave, sweep, fanfare, ornament, decoration, panache, pizzazz (*infml*).

flourishing *adj* thriving, blooming, prosperous, successful, booming.

flout *v* defy, disobey, violate, break, disregard, spurn, reject, scorn, jeer at, scoff at, mock, ridicule.
≠ obey, respect, regard.

flow *v* **1** CIRCULATE, ooze, trickle, ripple, bubble, well, spurt, squirt, gush, spill, run, pour, cascade, rush, stream, teem, flood, overflow, surge, sweep, move, drift, slip, slide, glide, roll, swirl. **2** ORIGINATE, derive, arise, spring, emerge, issue, result, proceed, emanate.
n course, flux, tide, current, drift, outpouring, stream, deluge, cascade, spurt, gush, flood, spate, abundance, plenty.

flower *n* **1** BLOOM, blossom, bud, floret. **2** BEST, cream, pick, choice, élite.

Flowers include: African violet, alyssum, anemone, aster, aubrietia, azalea, begonia, bluebell, busy lizzie (impatiens), calendula, candytuft, carnation, chrysanthemum, cornflower, cowslip, crocus, cyclamen, daffodil, dahlia, daisy, delphinium, forget-me-not, foxglove (digitalis), freesia, fuchsia, gardenia, geranium, gladioli, hollyhock, hyacinth, iris (flag), lily, lily-of-the-valley, lobelia, lupin, marigold, narcissus, nasturtium, nemesia, nicotiana, night-scented stock, orchid, pansy, petunia, pink (dianthus), phlox, poinsettia, polyanthus, poppy, primrose, primula, rose, salvia, snapdragon (antirrhinum), snowdrop, stock, sunflower, sweet pea, sweet william, tulip, verbena, viola, violet, wallflower, zinnia. *see also* **bulbs and corms**; **plant**; **shrubs**; **wild flowers**.
Parts of a flower include: anther, calyx, capitulum, carpel, corolla, corymb, dichasium, filament, gynoecium, monochasium, nectary, ovary, ovule, panicle, pedicel, petal, pistil, raceme, receptacle, sepal, spadix, spike, stalk, stamen, stigma, style, thalamus, torus, umbel.

v bud, burgeon, bloom, blossom, open, come out.

flowery *adj* florid, ornate, elaborate, fancy, baroque, rhetorical.
≠ plain, simple.

fluctuate *v* vary, change, alter, shift, rise and fall, seesaw, ebb and flow, alternate, swing, sway, oscillate, vacillate, waver.

fluent *adj* flowing, smooth, easy, effortless, articulate, eloquent, voluble, glib, ready.
≠ broken, inarticulate, tongue-tied.

fluff *n* down, nap, pile, fuzz, floss, lint, dust.

fluffy *adj* furry, fuzzy, downy, feathery, fleecy, woolly, hairy, shaggy, velvety, silky, soft.

fluid *adj* **1** LIQUID, liquefied, aqueous, watery, running, runny, melted, molten. **2** *a fluid situation*: variable, changeable, unstable, inconstant, shifting, mobile, adjustable, adaptable, flexible, open. **3** *fluid movements*: flowing, smooth, graceful.
≠ **1** solid. **2** stable.
n liquid, solution, liquor, juice, gas, vapour.

flurry *n* **1** BURST, outbreak, spell, spurt, gust, blast, squall. **2** BUSTLE, hurry, fluster, fuss, to-do, commotion, tumult, whirl, disturbance, stir, flap (*infml*).

flush[1] *v* **1** BLUSH, go red, redden, crimson, colour, burn, glow, suffuse. **2** CLEANSE, wash, rinse, hose, swab, clear, empty, evacuate.
adj **1** ABUNDANT, lavish, generous, full, overflowing, rich, wealthy, moneyed, prosperous, well-off, well-heeled, well-to-do. **2** LEVEL, even, smooth, flat, plane, square, true.

flush[2] *v* start, rouse, disturb, drive out, force out, expel, eject, run to earth, discover, uncover.

fluster *v* bother, upset, embarrass, disturb, perturb, agitate, ruffle, discompose, confuse, confound, unnerve, disconcert, rattle (*infml*), put

off, distract.
≠ calm.
n flurry, bustle, commotion, disturbance, turmoil, state (*infml*), agitation, embarrassment, flap (*infml*), dither, tizzy (*infml*).
≠ calm.

fluted *adj* grooved, furrowed, channelled, corrugated, ribbed, ridged.

flutter *v* flap, wave, beat, bat, flicker, vibrate, palpitate, agitate, shake, tremble, quiver, shiver, ruffle, ripple, twitch, toss, waver, fluctuate.
n flapping, beat, flicker, vibration, palpitation, tremble, tremor, quiver, shiver, shudder, twitch.

flux *n* fluctuation, instability, change, alteration, modification, fluidity, flow, movement, motion, transition, development.
≠ stability, rest.

fly *v* **1** TAKE OFF, rise, ascend, mount, soar, glide, float, hover, flit, wing. **2** RACE, sprint, dash, tear, rush, hurry, speed, zoom, shoot, dart, career.
fly at attack, go for, fall upon.

foam *n* froth, lather, suds, head, bubbles, effervescence.
v froth, lather, bubble, effervesce, fizz, boil, seethe.

fob off foist, pass off, palm off (*infml*), get rid of, dump, unload, inflict, impose, deceive, put off.

focus *n* focal point, target, centre, heart, core, nucleus, kernel, crux, hub, axis, linchpin, pivot, hinge.
v converge, meet, join, centre, concentrate, aim, direct, fix, spotlight, home in, zoom in, zero in (*infml*).

fog *n* **1** MIST, haze, cloud, gloom, murkiness, smog, pea-souper. **2** PERPLEXITY, puzzlement, confusion, bewilderment, daze, trance, vagueness, obscurity.
v mist, steam up, cloud, dull, dim, darken, obscure, blur, confuse, muddle.

foggy *adj* misty, hazy, smoggy, cloudy, murky, dark, shadowy, dim, indistinct, obscure.
≠ clear.

foil[1] *v* defeat, outwit, frustrate, thwart, baffle, counter, nullify, stop, check, obstruct, block, circumvent, elude.
≠ abet.

foil[2] *n* setting, background, relief, contrast, complement, balance.

fold *v* **1** BEND, ply, double, overlap, tuck, pleat, crease, crumple, crimp, crinkle. **2** (*infml*) *the business folded*: fail, go bust, shut down, collapse, crash. **3** ENFOLD, embrace, hug, clasp, envelop, wrap (up), enclose, entwine, intertwine.
n bend, turn, layer, ply, overlap, tuck, pleat, crease, knife-edge, line, wrinkle, furrow, corrugation.

folder *n* file, binder, folio, portfolio, envelope, holder.

folk *n* people, society, nation, race, tribe, clan, family, kin, kindred.
adj ethnic, national, traditional, native, indigenous, tribal, ancestral.

follow *v* **1** *night follows day*: come after, succeed, come next, replace, supersede, supplant. **2** CHASE, pursue, go after, hunt, track, trail, shadow, tail, hound, catch. **3** ACCOMPANY, go (along) with, escort, attend. **4** RESULT, ensue, develop, emanate, arise. **5** OBEY, comply with, adhere to, heed, mind, observe, conform to, carry out, practise. **6** GRASP, understand, comprehend, fathom.
≠ **1** precede. **3** abandon, desert. **5** disobey.
follow through continue, pursue, see through, finish, complete, conclude, fulfil, implement.
follow up investigate, check out, continue, pursue, reinforce, consolidate.

follower *n* attendant, retainer, helper, companion, sidekick (*infml*), apostle, disciple, pupil, imitator, emulator, adherent, hanger-on, believer, convert, backer, supporter, admirer, fan, devotee, freak (*infml*), buff (*infml*).
≠ leader, opponent.

following *adj* subsequent, next, succeeding, successive, resulting, ensuing, consequent, later.
≠ previous.
n followers, suite, retinue, entourage,

circle, fans, supporters, support, backing, patronage, clientèle, audience, public.

folly *n* foolishness, stupidity, senselessness, rashness, recklessness, irresponsibility, indiscretion, craziness, madness, lunacy, insanity, idiocy, imbecility, silliness, absurdity, nonsense.
≠ wisdom, prudence, sanity.

fond *adj* affectionate, warm, tender, caring, loving, adoring, devoted, doting, indulgent.
fond of partial to, attached to, enamoured of, keen on, addicted to, hooked on.

fondle *v* caress, stroke, pat, pet, cuddle.

food *n* foodstuffs, comestibles, eatables (*infml*), provisions, stores, rations, eats (*infml*), grub (*sl*), nosh (*sl*), refreshment, sustenance, nourishment, nutrition, nutriment, subsistence, feed, fodder, diet, fare, cooking, cuisine, menu, board, table, larder.

Kinds of food include: soup, broth, minestrone, bouillabaisse, borsch, cockaleekie, consommé, gazpacho, goulash, vichyssoise; chips, French fries, ratatouille, sauerkraut, bubble-and-squeak, nut cutlet, cauliflower cheese, chilladas, hummus, macaroni cheese; pasta, cannelloni, fettuccine, ravioli, spaghetti bolognese, tortellini, lasagne; fish and chips, fishcake, fish-finger, fisherman's pie, kedgeree, gefilte fish, kipper, pickled herring, scampi, calamari, prawn cocktail, caviar; meat, casserole, cassoulet, hotpot, shepherd's pie, cottage pie, chilli con carne, biriyani, chop suey, moussaka, paella, samosa, pizza, ragout, risotto, tandoori, vindaloo, Wiener schnitzel, smorgasbord, stroganoff, Scotch woodcock, welsh rarebit, faggot, haggis, sausage, frankfurter, hot dog, fritter, hamburger, McDonald's®, Big Mac®, Wimpy®, bacon, egg, omelette, quiche, tofu, Quorn®, Yorkshire pudding, toad-in-the-hole; ice cream, charlotte russe, egg custard, fruit salad, fruit cocktail, gateau, millefeuilles, pavlova, profiterole, Sachertorte, soufflé, summer pudding, Bakewell tart, trifle, yogurt, sundae, syllabub, queen of puddings, Christmas pudding, tapioca, rice pudding, roly-poly pudding, spotted dick, zabaglione; doughnut, Chelsea bun, Eccles cake, éclair, flapjack, fruitcake, Danish pastry, Genoa cake, Battenburg cake, Madeira cake, lardy cake, hot-cross-bun, ginger nut, gingerbread, shortbread, ginger snap, macaroon, Garibaldi biscuit; bread, French bread, French toast, pumpernickel, cottage loaf, croissant; gravy, fondue, salad cream, mayonnaise, French dressing; sauces: tartare, Worcestershire, bechamel, white, barbecue, tomato ketchup, hollandaise, Tabasco®, apple, mint, cranberry, horseradish, pesto. *see also* **cheese**; **fish**; **fruit**; **meat**; **nut**; **pasta**; **pastry**; **sugar**; **sweets**; **vegetable**; **vegetable dishes**.

fool *n* blockhead, fat-head, nincompoop (*infml*), ass (*infml*), chump (*infml*), ninny (*infml*), clot (*infml*), dope (*infml*), wally (*sl*), twit (*infml*), nitwit (*infml*), nit (*infml*), dunce, dimwit, simpleton, halfwit, idiot, imbecile, moron, dupe, sucker (*infml*), mug (*infml*), stooge, clown, buffoon, jester.
v deceive, take in, delude, mislead, dupe, gull, hoodwink, put one over on, trick, hoax, con (*infml*), cheat, swindle, diddle (*infml*), string along (*infml*), have on (*infml*), kid (*infml*), tease, joke, jest.
fool about lark about, horse around (*sl*), play about, mess about (*infml*), mess around (*infml*).

foolhardy *adj* rash, reckless, imprudent, ill-advised, irresponsible.
≠ cautious, prudent.

foolish *adj* stupid, senseless, unwise, ill-advised, ill-considered, short-sighted, half-baked, daft (*infml*), crazy, mad, insane, idiotic, moronic, hare-brained, half-witted, simple-minded, simple, unintelligent, inept, inane, silly, absurd, ridiculous, ludicrous, nonsensical.
≠ wise, prudent.

foolproof *adj* idiot-proof, infallible,

fail-safe, sure, certain, sure-fire (*infml*), guaranteed.
≠ unreliable.

footing *n* base, foundation, basis, ground, relations, relationship, terms, conditions, state, standing, status, grade, rank, position, balance, foothold, purchase.

footprint *n* footmark, track, trail, trace, vestige.

footwear

Types of footwear include: shoe, court-shoe, brogue, casual, lace-up (*infml*), slip-on (*infml*), slingback, sandal, espadrille, stiletto heel, platform heel, moccasin, Doc Martens®, slipper, flip-flop (*infml*), boot, bootee, wellington boot, welly (*infml*), galosh, gumboot, football boot, rugby boot, tennis shoe, plimsoll, pump, sneaker, trainer, ballet shoe, clog, sabot, snow-shoe, beetle-crushers (*sl*), brothel-creepers (*sl*).

forage *n* fodder, pasturage, feed, food, foodstuffs.
v rummage, search, cast about, scour, hunt, scavenge, ransack, plunder, raid.

forbid *v* prohibit, disallow, ban, proscribe, interdict, veto, refuse, deny, outlaw, debar, exclude, rule out, preclude, prevent, block, hinder, inhibit.
≠ allow, permit, approve.

forbidden *adj* prohibited, banned, proscribed, taboo, vetoed, outlawed, out of bounds.

forbidding *adj* stern, formidable, awesome, daunting, off-putting, uninviting, menacing, threatening, ominous, sinister, frightening.
≠ approachable, congenial.

force *n* **1** COMPULSION, impulse, influence, coercion, constraint, pressure, duress, violence, aggression. **2** POWER, might, strength, intensity, effort, energy, vigour, drive, dynamism, stress, emphasis. **3** ARMY, troop, body, corps, regiment, squadron, battalion, division, unit, detachment, patrol.
≠ **2** weakness.
v **1** COMPEL, make, oblige, necessitate, urge, coerce, constrain, press, pressurize, lean on (*infml*), press-gang, bulldoze, drive, propel, push, thrust. **2** PRISE, wrench, wrest, extort, exact, wring.

forced *adj* unnatural, stiff, wooden, stilted, laboured, strained, false, artificial, contrived, feigned, affected, insincere.
≠ spontaneous, sincere.

forceful *adj* strong, mighty, powerful, potent, effective, compelling, convincing, persuasive, cogent, telling, weighty, urgent, emphatic, vehement, forcible, dynamic, energetic, vigorous.
≠ weak, feeble.

forebear *n* ancestor, forefather, father, predecessor, forerunner, antecedent.
≠ descendant.

foreboding *n* misgiving, anxiety, worry, apprehension, dread, fear, omen, sign, token, premonition, warning, prediction, prognostication, intuition, feeling.

forecast *v* predict, prophesy, foretell, foresee, anticipate, expect, estimate, calculate.
n prediction, prophecy, expectation, prognosis, outlook, projection, guess, guesstimate (*infml*).

forefront *n* front, front line, firing line, van, vanguard, lead, fore, avant-garde.
≠ rear.

foregoing *adj* preceding, antecedent, above, previous, earlier, former, prior.
≠ following.

foreign *adj* alien, immigrant, imported, international, external, outside, overseas, exotic, faraway, distant, remote, strange, unfamiliar, unknown, uncharacteristic, incongruous, extraneous, borrowed.
≠ native, indigenous.

foreigner *n* alien, immigrant, incomer, stranger, newcomer, visitor.
≠ native.

foremost *adj* first, leading, front, chief, main, principal, primary, cardinal, paramount, central, highest, uppermost, supreme, prime, pre-eminent.

forerunner *n* predecessor, ancestor, antecedent, precursor, harbinger, herald, envoy, sign, token.
≠ successor, follower.

foresee *v* envisage, anticipate, expect, forecast, predict, prophesy, prognosticate, foretell, forebode, divine.

foreshadow *v* prefigure, presage, augur, predict, prophesy, signal, indicate, promise.

foresight *n* anticipation, planning, forethought, far-sightedness, vision, caution, prudence, circumspection, care, readiness, preparedness, provision, precaution.
≠ improvidence.

forestall *v* pre-empt, anticipate, preclude, obviate, avert, head off, ward off, parry, balk, frustrate, thwart, hinder, prevent.

foretaste *n* preview, trailer, sample, specimen, example, whiff, indication, warning, premonition.

foretell *v* prophesy, forecast, predict, prognosticate, augur, presage, signify, foreshadow, forewarn.

forethought *n* preparation, planning, forward planning, provision, precaution, anticipation, foresight, far-sightedness, circumspection, prudence, caution.
≠ improvidence, carelessness.

forever *adv* continually, constantly, persistently, incessantly, perpetually, endlessly, eternally, always, evermore, for all time, permanently.

foreword *n* preface, introduction, prologue.
≠ appendix, postscript, epilogue.

forfeit *n* loss, surrender, confiscation, sequestration, penalty, fine, damages.
v lose, give up, surrender, relinquish, sacrifice, forgo, renounce, abandon.

forge *v* **1** MAKE, mould, cast, shape, form, fashion, beat out, hammer out, work, create, invent. **2** *forge a document*: fake, counterfeit, falsify, copy, imitate, simulate, feign.

forgery *n* fake, counterfeit, copy, replica, reproduction, imitation, dud (*infml*), phoney (*infml*), sham, fraud.
≠ original.

forget *v* omit, fail, neglect, let slip, overlook, disregard, ignore, lose sight of, dismiss, think no more of, unlearn.
≠ remember, recall, recollect.

forgetful *adj* absent-minded, dreamy, inattentive, oblivious, negligent, lax, heedless.
≠ attentive, heedful.

forgive *v* pardon, absolve, excuse, exonerate, exculpate, acquit, remit, let off, overlook, condone.
≠ punish, censure.

forgiveness *n* pardon, absolution, exoneration, acquittal, remission, amnesty, mercy, clemency, leniency.
≠ punishment, censure, blame.

forgiving *adj* merciful, clement, lenient, tolerant, forbearing, indulgent, kind, humane, compassionate, soft-hearted, mild.
≠ merciless, censorious, harsh.

forgo *v* give up, yield, surrender, relinquish, sacrifice, forfeit, waive, renounce, abandon, resign, pass up, do without, abstain from, refrain from.
≠ claim, indulge in.

fork *v* split, divide, part, separate, diverge, branch (off).

forlorn *adj* deserted, abandoned, forsaken, forgotten, bereft, friendless, lonely, lost, homeless, destitute, desolate, hopeless, unhappy, miserable, wretched, helpless, pathetic, pitiable.
≠ cheerful.

form *v* **1** SHAPE, mould, model, fashion, make, manufacture, produce, create, found, establish, build, construct, assemble, put together, arrange, organize. **2** COMPRISE, constitute, make up, compose. **3** APPEAR, take shape, materialize, crystallize, grow, develop.
n **1** APPEARANCE, shape, mould, cast, cut, outline, silhouette, figure, build, frame, structure, format, model, pattern, design, arrangement, organization, system. **2** *a form of punishment*: type, kind, sort, order, species, variety, genre, style, manner, nature, character, description. **3** CLASS,

year, grade, stream. **4** *on top form*: health, fitness, fettle, condition, spirits. **5** ETIQUETTE, protocol, custom, convention, ritual, behaviour, manners. **6** QUESTIONNAIRE, document, paper, sheet.

formal *adj* **1** OFFICIAL, ceremonial, stately, solemn, conventional, orthodox, correct, fixed, set, regular. **2** PRIM, starchy, stiff, strict, rigid, precise, exact, punctilious, ceremonious, stilted, reserved.
≠ **2** informal, casual.

formality *n* custom, convention, ceremony, ritual, procedure, matter of form, bureaucracy, red tape, protocol, etiquette, form, correctness, propriety, decorum, politeness.
≠ informality.

formation *n* **1** STRUCTURE, construction, composition, constitution, configuration, format, organization, arrangement, grouping, pattern, design, figure. **2** CREATION, generation, production, manufacture, appearance, development, establishment.

former *adj* past, ex-, one-time, sometime, late, departed, old, old-time, ancient, bygone, earlier, prior, previous, preceding, antecedent, foregoing, above.
≠ current, present, future, following.

formerly *adv* once, previously, earlier, before, at one time, lately.
≠ currently, now, later.

formidable *adj* daunting, challenging, intimidating, threatening, frightening, terrifying, terrific, frightful, fearful, great, huge, tremendous, prodigious, impressive, awesome, overwhelming, staggering.

formula *n* recipe, prescription, proposal, blueprint, code, wording, rubric, rule, principle, form, procedure, technique, method, way.

formulate *v* create, invent, originate, found, form, devise, work out, plan, design, draw up, frame, define, express, state, specify, detail, develop, evolve.

forsake *v* desert, abandon, jilt, throw over, discard, jettison, reject, disown, leave, quit, give up, surrender, relinquish, renounce, forgo.

fort *n* fortress, castle, tower, citadel, stronghold, fortification, garrison, station, camp.

forthcoming *adj* **1** *their forthcoming wedding*: impending, imminent, approaching, coming, future, prospective, projected, expected. **2** COMMUNICATIVE, talkative, chatty, conversational, sociable, informative, expansive, open, frank, direct.
≠ **2** reticent, reserved.

forthright *adj* direct, straightforward, blunt, frank, candid, plain, open, bold, outspoken.
≠ devious, secretive.

fortify *v* **1** STRENGTHEN, reinforce, brace, shore up, buttress, garrison, defend, protect, secure. **2** INVIGORATE, sustain, support, boost, encourage, hearten, cheer, reassure.
≠ **1** weaken.

fortitude *n* courage, bravery, valour, grit, pluck, resolution, determination, perseverance, firmness, strength of mind, willpower, hardihood, endurance, stoicism.
≠ cowardice, fear.

fortuitous *adj* accidental, chance, random, arbitrary, casual, incidental, unforeseen, lucky, fortunate, providential.
≠ intentional, planned.

fortunate *adj* lucky, providential, happy, felicitous, prosperous, successful, well-off, timely, well-timed, opportune, convenient, propitious, advantageous, favourable, auspicious.
≠ unlucky, unfortunate, unhappy.

fortune *n* **1** WEALTH, riches, treasure, mint (*infml*), pile (*infml*), income, means, assets, estate, property, possessions, affluence, prosperity, success. **2** LUCK, chance, accident, providence, fate, destiny, doom, lot, portion, life, history, future.

forward *adj* **1** FIRST, head, front, fore, foremost, leading, onward, progressive, go-ahead, forward-looking, enterprising. **2** CONFIDENT, assertive, pushy, bold, audacious, brazen, brash,

barefaced, cheeky (*infml*), impudent, impertinent, fresh (*sl*), familiar, presumptuous. **3** EARLY, advance, precocious, premature, advanced, well-advanced, well-developed.
≠ **1** backward, retrograde. **2** shy, modest. **3** late, retarded.
adv forwards, ahead, on, onward, out, into view.
v advance, promote, further, foster, encourage, support, back, favour, help, assist, aid, facilitate, accelerate, speed, hurry, hasten, expedite, dispatch, send (on), post, transport, ship.
≠ impede, obstruct, hinder, slow.

foster *v* raise, rear, bring up, nurse, care for, take care of, nourish, feed, sustain, support, promote, advance, encourage, stimulate, cultivate, nurture, cherish, entertain, harbour.
≠ neglect, discourage.

foul *adj* **1** DIRTY, filthy, unclean, tainted, polluted, contaminated, rank, fetid, stinking, smelly, putrid, rotten, nauseating, offensive, repulsive, revolting, disgusting, squalid. **2** *foul language*: obscene, lewd, smutty, indecent, coarse, vulgar, gross, blasphemous, abusive. **3** NASTY, disagreeable, wicked, vicious, vile, base, abhorrent, disgraceful, shameful. **4** *foul weather*: bad, unpleasant, rainy, wet, stormy, rough.
≠ **1** clean. **4** fine.
v **1** DIRTY, soil, stain, sully, defile, taint, pollute, contaminate. **2** BLOCK, obstruct, clog, choke, foul up. **3** ENTANGLE, catch, snarl, twist, ensnare.
≠ **1** clean. **2** clear. **3** disentangle.

found *v* **1** START, originate, create, initiate, institute, inaugurate, set up, establish, endow, organize. **2** BASE, ground, bottom, rest, settle, fix, plant, raise, build, erect, construct.

foundation *n* **1** BASE, foot, bottom, ground, bedrock, substance, basis, footing. **2** SETTING UP, establishment, institution, inauguration, endowment, organization, groundwork.

founder[1] *n* originator, initiator, father, mother, benefactor, creator, author, architect, designer, inventor, maker, builder, constructor, organizer.

founder[2] *v* sink, go down, submerge, subside, collapse, break down, fall, come to grief, fail, misfire, miscarry, abort, fall through, come to nothing.

fountain *n* **1** SPRAY, jet, spout, spring, well, wellspring, reservoir, waterworks. **2** SOURCE, origin, fount, font, fountain-head, wellhead.

fracture *n* break, crack, fissure, cleft, rupture, split, rift, rent, schism, breach, gap, opening.
v break, crack, rupture, split, splinter, chip.
≠ join.

fragile *adj* brittle, breakable, frail, delicate, flimsy, dainty, fine, slight, insubstantial, weak, feeble, infirm.
≠ robust, tough, durable.

fragment *n* piece, bit, part, portion, fraction, particle, crumb, morsel, scrap, remnant, shred, chip, splinter, shiver, sliver, shard.
v break, shatter, splinter, shiver, crumble, disintegrate, come to pieces, come apart, break up, divide, split (up), disunite.
≠ hold together, join.

fragmentary *adj* bitty, piecemeal, scrappy, broken, disjointed, disconnected, separate, scattered, sketchy, partial, incomplete.
≠ whole, complete.

fragrance *n* perfume, scent, smell, odour, aroma, bouquet.

fragrant *adj* perfumed, scented, sweet-smelling, sweet, balmy, aromatic, odorous.
≠ unscented.

frail *adj* delicate, brittle, breakable, fragile, flimsy, insubstantial, slight, puny, weak, feeble, infirm, vulnerable.
≠ robust, tough, strong.

frailty *n* weakness, foible, failing, deficiency, shortcoming, fault, defect, flaw, blemish, imperfection, fallibility, susceptibility.
≠ strength, robustness, toughness.

frame *v* **1** COMPOSE, formulate, conceive, devise, contrive, concoct, cook up, plan, map out, sketch, draw

up, draft, shape, form, model, fashion, mould, forge, assemble, put together, build, construct, fabricate, make. **2** SURROUND, enclose, box in, case, mount. **3** *I've been framed*: set up, fit up (*sl*), trap.
n **1** STRUCTURE, fabric, framework, skeleton, carcase, shell, casing, chassis, construction, bodywork, body, build, form. **2** MOUNT, mounting, setting, surround, border, edge.
frame of mind state of mind, mood, humour, temper, disposition, spirit, outlook, attitude.

framework *n* structure, fabric, bare bones, skeleton, shell, frame, outline, plan, foundation, groundwork.

franchise *n* concession, licence, charter, authorization, privilege, right, suffrage, liberty, freedom, immunity, exemption.

frank *adj* honest, truthful, sincere, candid, blunt, open, free, plain, direct, forthright, straight, straightforward, downright, outspoken.
≠ insincere, evasive.

frankly *adv* to be frank, to be honest, in truth, honestly, candidly, bluntly, openly, freely, plainly, directly, straight.
≠ insincerely, evasively.

frantic *adj* agitated, overwrought, fraught, desperate, beside oneself, furious, raging, mad, wild, raving, frenzied, berserk, hectic.
≠ calm, composed.

fraternize *v* mix, mingle, socialize, consort, associate, affiliate, unite, sympathize.
≠ shun, ignore.

fraud *n* **1** DECEIT, deception, guile, cheating, swindling, double-dealing, sharp practice, fake, counterfeit, forgery, sham, hoax, trick. **2** (*infml*) CHARLATAN, impostor, pretender, phoney (*infml*), bluffer, hoaxer, cheat, swindler, double-dealer, con man (*infml*).

fraudulent *adj* dishonest, crooked (*infml*), criminal, deceitful, deceptive, false, bogus, phoney (*infml*), sham, counterfeit, swindling, double-dealing.
≠ honest, genuine.

fray *n* brawl, scuffle, dust-up (*infml*), free-for-all, set-to, clash, conflict, fight, combat, battle, quarrel, row, rumpus, disturbance, riot.

frayed *adj* ragged, tattered, worn, threadbare, unravelled.

freak *n* **1** MONSTER, mutant, monstrosity, malformation, deformity, irregularity, anomaly, abnormality, aberration, oddity, curiosity, quirk, caprice, vagary, twist, turn. **2** ENTHUSIAST, fanatic, addict, devotee, fan, buff (*infml*), fiend (*infml*), nut (*infml*).
adj abnormal, atypical, unusual, exceptional, odd, queer, bizarre, aberrant, capricious, erratic, unpredictable, unexpected, surprise, chance, fortuitous, flukey.
≠ normal, common.

free *adj* **1** AT LIBERTY, at large, loose, unattached, unrestrained, liberated, emancipated, independent, democratic, self-governing. **2** *free time*: spare, available, idle, unemployed, unoccupied, vacant, empty. **3** *free tickets*: gratis, without charge, free of charge, complimentary, on the house. **4** CLEAR, unobstructed, unimpeded, open. **5** GENEROUS, liberal, open-handed, lavish, charitable, hospitable.
≠ **1** imprisoned, confined, restricted. **2** busy, occupied.
v release, let go, loose, turn loose, set free, untie, unbind, unchain, unleash, liberate, emancipate, rescue, deliver, save, ransom, disentangle, disengage, extricate, clear, rid, relieve, unburden, exempt, absolve, acquit.
≠ imprison, confine.
free of lacking, devoid of, without, unaffected by, immune to, exempt from, safe from.

freedom *n* **1** LIBERTY, emancipation, deliverance, release, exemption, immunity, impunity. **2** INDEPENDENCE, autonomy, self-government, home rule. **3** RANGE, scope, play, leeway, latitude, licence, privilege, power, free rein, free hand, opportunity, informality.
≠ **1** captivity, confinement. **3** restriction.

freely *adv* **1** READILY, willingly, voluntarily, spontaneously, easily. **2** *give freely*: generously, liberally, lavishly, extravagantly, amply, abundantly. **3** *speak freely*: frankly, candidly, unreservedly, openly, plainly.
≠ **2** grudgingly. **3** evasively, cautiously.

freeze *v* **1** ICE OVER, ice up, glaciate, congeal, solidify, harden, stiffen. **2** DEEP-FREEZE, ice, refrigerate, chill, cool. **3** STOP, suspend, fix, immobilize, hold.
n **1** FROST, freeze-up. **2** STOPPAGE, halt, standstill, shutdown, suspension, interruption, postponement, stay, embargo, moratorium.

freezing *adj* icy, frosty, glacial, arctic, polar, Siberian, wintry, raw, bitter, biting, cutting, penetrating, numbing, cold, chilly.
≠ hot, warm.

freight *n* cargo, load, lading, pay-load, contents, goods, merchandise, consignment, shipment, transportation, conveyance, carriage, haulage.

frenzied *adj* frantic, frenetic, hectic, feverish, desperate, furious, wild, uncontrolled, mad, demented, hysterical.
≠ calm, composed.

frenzy *n* **1** TURMOIL, agitation, distraction, derangement, madness, lunacy, mania, hysteria, delirium, fever. **2** BURST, fit, spasm, paroxysm, convulsion, seizure, outburst, transport, passion, rage, fury.
≠ **1** calm, composure.

frequent *adj* **1** NUMEROUS, countless, incessant, constant, continual, persistent, repeated, recurring, regular. **2** COMMON, commonplace, everyday, familiar, usual, customary.
≠ **1** infrequent.
v visit, patronize, attend, haunt, hang out at (*infml*), associate with, hang about with (*infml*), hang out with (*infml*).

fresh *adj* **1** ADDITIONAL, supplementary, extra, more, further, other. **2** NEW, novel, innovative, original, different, unconventional, modern, up-to-date, recent, latest. **3** REFRESHING, bracing, invigorating, brisk, crisp, keen, cool, fair, bright, clear, pure. **4** *fresh fruit*: raw, natural, unprocessed, crude. **5** REFRESHED, revived, restored, renewed, rested, invigorated, energetic, vigorous, lively, alert. **6** PERT, saucy (*infml*), cheeky (*infml*), disrespectful, impudent, insolent, bold, brazen, forward, familiar, presumptuous.
≠ **2** old, hackneyed. **3** stale. **4** processed. **5** tired.

freshen *v* **1** AIR, ventilate, purify. **2** REFRESH, restore, revitalize, reinvigorate, liven, enliven, spruce up, tart up (*infml*).
≠ **2** tire.

fret *v* **1** WORRY, agonize, brood, pine. **2** VEX, irritate, nettle, bother, trouble, torment.

friction *n* **1** DISAGREEMENT, dissension, dispute, disharmony, conflict, antagonism, hostility, opposition, rivalry, animosity, ill feeling, bad blood, resentment. **2** RUBBING, chafing, irritation, abrasion, scraping, grating, rasping, erosion, wearing away, resistance.

friend *n* mate (*infml*), pal (*infml*), chum (*infml*), buddy (*infml*), crony (*infml*), intimate, confidant(e), bosom friend, soul mate, comrade, ally, partner, associate, companion, playmate, pen-friend, acquaintance, well-wisher, supporter.
≠ enemy, opponent.

friendly *adj* **1** AMIABLE, affable, genial, kind, kindly, neighbourly, helpful, sympathetic, fond, affectionate, familiar, intimate, close, matey (*infml*), pally (*infml*), chummy (*infml*), companionable, sociable, outgoing, approachable, receptive, comradely, amicable, peaceable, well-disposed, favourable. **2** *a friendly atmosphere*: convivial, congenial, cordial, welcoming, warm.
≠ **1** hostile, unsociable. **2** cold.

friendship *n* closeness, intimacy, familiarity, affinity, rapport, attachment, affection, fondness, love, harmony, concord, goodwill,

friendliness, alliance, fellowship, comradeship.
≠ enmity, animosity.

fright *n* shock, scare, alarm, consternation, dismay, dread, apprehension, trepidation, fear, terror, horror, panic.

frighten *v* alarm, daunt, unnerve, dismay, intimidate, terrorize, scare, startle, scare stiff, terrify, petrify, horrify, appal, shock.
≠ reassure, calm.

frightening *adj* alarming, daunting, formidable, fearsome, scary, terrifying, hair-raising, bloodcurdling, spine-chilling, petrifying, traumatic.

frightful *adj* unpleasant, disagreeable, awful, dreadful, fearful, terrible, appalling, shocking, harrowing, unspeakable, dire, grim, ghastly, hideous, horrible, horrid, grisly, macabre, gruesome.
≠ pleasant, agreeable.

frigid *adj* **1** UNFEELING, unresponsive, passionless, unloving, cool, aloof, passive, lifeless. **2** FROZEN, icy, frosty, glacial, arctic, cold, chill, chilly, wintry.
≠ **1** responsive. **2** hot.

frilly *adj* ruffled, crimped, gathered, frilled, trimmed, lacy, fancy, ornate.
≠ plain.

fringe *n* **1** MARGIN, periphery, outskirts, edge, perimeter, limits, borderline. **2** BORDER, edging, trimming, tassel, frill, valance.
adj unconventional, unorthodox, unofficial, alternative, avant-garde.
≠ conventional, mainstream.

frisk *v* jump, leap, skip, hop, bounce, caper, dance, gambol, frolic, romp, play, sport.

frisky *adj* lively, spirited, high-spirited, frolicsome, playful, romping, rollicking, bouncy.
≠ quiet.

fritter *v* waste, squander, dissipate, idle, misspend, blow (*sl*).

frivolity *n* fun, gaiety, flippancy, facetiousness, jest, light-heartedness, levity, triviality, superficiality, silliness, folly, nonsense.
≠ seriousness.

frivolous *adj* trifling, trivial, unimportant, shallow, superficial, light, flippant, jocular, light-hearted, juvenile, puerile, foolish, silly, idle, vain, pointless.
≠ serious, sensible.

frolic *v* gambol, caper, romp, play, lark around, rollick, make merry, frisk, prance, cavort, dance.
n fun, amusement, sport, gaiety, jollity, merriment, revel, romp, prank, lark, caper, high jinks, antics.

front *n* **1** AT THE FRONT, face, aspect, frontage, façade, outside, exterior, facing, cover, obverse, top, head, lead, vanguard, forefront, front line, foreground, forepart, bow.
2 PRETENCE, show, air, appearance, look, expression, manner, façade, cover, mask, disguise, pretext, cover-up.
≠ **1** back, rear.
adj fore, leading, foremost, head, first.
≠ back, rear, last.
in front ahead, leading, first, in advance, before, preceding.
≠ behind.

frontier *n* border, boundary, borderline, limit, edge, perimeter, confines, marches, bounds, verge.

frosty *adj* **1** ICY, frozen, freezing, frigid, wintry, cold, chilly.
2 UNFRIENDLY, unwelcoming, cool, aloof, standoffish, stiff, discouraging.
≠ warm.

froth *n* bubbles, effervescence, foam, lather, suds, head, scum.
v foam, lather, ferment, fizz, effervesce, bubble.

frown *v* scowl, glower, lour, glare, grimace.
n scowl, glower, dirty look (*infml*), glare, grimace.
frown on disapprove of, object to, dislike, discourage.
≠ approve of.

frozen *adj* iced, chilled, icy, icebound, ice-covered, arctic, ice-cold, frigid, freezing, numb, solidified, stiff, rigid, fixed.
≠ warm.

frugal *adj* thrifty, penny-wise, parsimonious, careful, provident, saving, economical, sparing, meagre.
≠ wasteful, generous.

fruit

Varieties of fruit include: apple, Bramley, Cox's Orange Pippin, Golden Delicious, Granny Smith, crab apple; pear, William, Conference; orange, Jaffa, mandarin, mineola, clementine, satsuma, tangerine, Seville; apricot, peach, plum, nectarine, cherry, sloe, damson, greengage, grape, gooseberry, goosegog (*infml*), rhubarb, tomato; banana, pineapple, olive, lemon, lime, ugli fruit, star fruit, lychee, date, fig, grapefruit, kiwi fruit, mango, avocado; melon, honeydew, cantaloupe, watermelon; strawberry, raspberry, blackberry, bilberry, loganberry, elderberry, blueberry, boysenberry, cranberry; redcurrant, blackcurrant.

fruitful *adj* **1** FERTILE, rich, teeming, plentiful, abundant, prolific, productive. **2** REWARDING, profitable, advantageous, beneficial, worthwhile, well-spent, useful, successful.
≠ **1** barren. **2** fruitless.

fruition *n* realization, fulfilment, attainment, achievement, completion, maturity, ripeness, consummation, perfection, success, enjoyment.

fruitless *adj* unsuccessful, abortive, useless, futile, pointless, vain, idle, hopeless, barren, sterile.
≠ fruitful, successful, profitable.

frustrate *v* **1** THWART, foil, balk, baffle, block, check, spike, defeat, circumvent, forestall, counter, nullify, neutralize, inhibit. **2** DISAPPOINT, discourage, dishearten, depress.
≠ **1** further, promote. **2** encourage.

fuel *n* **1** *a tax on fuel*: combustible, propellant, motive power. **2** PROVOCATION, incitement, encouragement, ammunition, material.

Fuels include: gas, calor gas®, propane, butane, methane, acetylene, electricity, coal, coke, anthracite, charcoal, oil, petrol, gasoline, diesel, derv, paraffin, kerosine, methylated spirit, wood, logs, peat, nuclear power.

v incite, inflame, fire, encourage, fan, feed, nourish, sustain, stoke up.
≠ discourage, damp down.

fugitive *n* escapee, runaway, deserter, refugee.
adj fleeting, transient, transitory, passing, short, brief, flying, temporary, ephemeral, elusive.
≠ permanent.

fulfil *v* complete, finish, conclude, consummate, perfect, realize, achieve, accomplish, perform, execute, discharge, implement, carry out, comply with, observe, keep, obey, conform to, satisfy, fill, answer.
≠ fail, break.

fulfilment *n* completion, perfection, consummation, realization, achievement, accomplishment, success, performance, execution, discharge, implementation, observance, satisfaction.
≠ failure.

full *adj* **1** FILLED, loaded, packed, crowded, crammed, stuffed, jammed. **2** ENTIRE, whole, intact, total, complete, unabridged, unexpurgated. **3** THOROUGH, comprehensive, exhaustive, all-inclusive, broad, vast, extensive, ample, generous, abundant, plentiful, copious, profuse. **4** *a full sound*: rich, resonant, loud, deep, clear, distinct. **5** *at full speed*: maximum, top, highest, greatest, utmost.
≠ **1** empty. **2** partial, incomplete. **3** superficial.

full-grown *adj* adult, grown-up, of age, mature, ripe, developed, full-blown, full-scale.
≠ young, undeveloped.

fully *adv* completely, totally, utterly, wholly, entirely, thoroughly, altogether, quite, positively, without reserve, perfectly.
≠ partly.

fumble *v* grope, feel, bungle, botch, mishandle, mismanage.

fume *v* **1** SMOKE, smoulder, boil,

steam. **2** RAGE, storm, rant, rave, seethe.

fumes *n* exhaust, smoke, gas, vapour, haze, fog, smog, pollution.

fumigate *v* deodorize, disinfect, sterilize, purify, cleanse.

fun *n* enjoyment, pleasure, amusement, entertainment, diversion, distraction, recreation, play, sport, game, foolery, tomfoolery, horseplay, skylarking, romp, merrymaking, mirth, jollity, jocularity, joking, jesting.
make fun of rag, jeer at, ridicule, laugh at, mock, taunt, tease, rib (*sl*).

function *n* **1** ROLE, part, office, duty, charge, responsibility, concern, job, task, occupation, business, activity, purpose, use. **2** RECEPTION, party, gathering, affair, do (*infml*), dinner, luncheon.
v work, operate, run, go, serve, act, perform, behave.

functional *adj* working, operational, practical, useful, utilitarian, utility, plain, hard-wearing.
≠ useless, decorative.

fund *n* pool, kitty, treasury, repository, storehouse, store, reserve, stock, hoard, cache, stack, mine, well, source, supply.
v finance, capitalize, endow, subsidize, underwrite, sponsor, back, support, promote, float.

fundamental *adj* basic, primary, first, rudimentary, elementary, underlying, integral, central, principal, cardinal, prime, main, key, essential, indispensable, vital, necessary, crucial, important.

funds *n* money, finance, backing, capital, resources, savings, wealth, cash.

funeral *n* burial, interment, entombment, cremation, obsequies, wake.

fungus

Types of fungus include: black spot, blight, botritis, brown rot, candida, downy mildew, ergot, grey mould, mushroom, orange-peel fungus, penicillium, potato blight, powdery mildew, rust, scab, smut, sooty mould, toadstool, yeast, brewer's yeast. *see also* **mushrooms and toadstools**.

funnel *v* channel, direct, convey, move, transfer, pass, pour, siphon, filter.

funny *adj* **1** HUMOROUS, amusing, entertaining, comic, comical, hilarious, witty, facetious, droll, farcical, laughable, ridiculous, absurd, silly. **2** ODD, strange, peculiar, curious, queer, weird, unusual, remarkable, puzzling, perplexing, mysterious, suspicious, dubious.
≠ **1** serious, solemn, sad. **2** normal, ordinary, usual.

furious *adj* **1** ANGRY, mad (*infml*), up in arms (*infml*), livid, enraged, infuriated, incensed, raging, fuming, boiling. **2** VIOLENT, wild, fierce, intense, vigorous, frantic, boisterous, stormy, tempestuous.
≠ **1** calm, pleased.

furnish *v* equip, fit out, decorate, rig, stock, provide, supply, afford, grant, give, offer, present.
≠ divest.

furniture *n* equipment, appliances, furnishings, fittings, fitments, household goods, movables, possessions, effects, things.

Types of furniture include: table, dining-table, gateleg table, refectory table, lowboy, side-table, coffee-table, card table; chair, easy chair, armchair, rocking-chair, recliner, dining-chair, carver, kitchen chair, stool, swivel-chair, high-chair, suite, settee, sofa, couch, studio couch, chesterfield, pouffe, footstool, bean-bag; bed, four-poster, chaise-longue, daybed, bed-settee, divan, camp-bed, bunk, water-bed, cot, cradle; desk, bureau, secretaire, bookcase, cupboard, cabinet, china cabinet, Welsh dresser, sideboard, buffet, dumb-waiter, fireplace, overmantel, fender, firescreen, hallstand, umbrella-stand, mirror, magazine rack; wardrobe, armoire, dressing-table, vanity unit, washstand, chest-of-drawers, tallboy, chiffonier, commode, ottoman, chest, coffer,

blanket box.
Styles of furniture include: Adam, Anglo-Colonial, Anglo-Indian, Art Deco, Art Nouveau, Baroque, Beidermeier, boulle, buhl, Charles II, Chippendale, Colonial, Continental Empire, Cromwellian, Dutch Colonial, Dutch Neoclassical, Edwardian, Empire, French Provincial, French Second Empire, Gainsborough, Georgian, Gothic, Hepplewhite, Louis Philippe, Louis-Quatorze, Louis-Quinze, provincial, Queen Anne, Regency, Restauration, rococo, Sheraton, Shibayama, Transitional, Vernis Martin, Victorian, William and Mary, William IV, Windsor.

furrow *n* groove, channel, trench, hollow, rut, track, line, crease, wrinkle.
v seam, flute, corrugate, groove, crease, wrinkle, draw together, knit.

further *adj* more, additional, supplementary, extra, fresh, new, other.
v advance, forward, promote, champion, push, encourage, foster, help, aid, assist, ease, facilitate, speed, hasten, accelerate, expedite.
≠ stop, frustrate.

furthermore *adv* moreover, what's more, in addition, further, besides, also, too, as well, additionally.

furthest *adj* farthest, furthermost, remotest, outermost, outmost, extreme, ultimate, utmost, uttermost.
≠ nearest.

furtive *adj* surreptitious, sly, stealthy, secretive, underhand, hidden, covert, secret.
≠ open.

fury *n* anger, rage, wrath, frenzy, madness, passion, vehemence, fierceness, ferocity, violence, wildness, turbulence, power.
≠ calm, peacefulness.

fusion *n* melting, smelting, welding, union, synthesis, blending, coalescence, amalgamation, integration, merger, federation.

fuss *n* bother, trouble, hassle (*infml*), palaver, to-do (*infml*), hoo-ha (*infml*), furore, squabble, row, commotion, stir, fluster, confusion, upset, worry, agitation, flap (*infml*), excitement, bustle, flurry, hurry.
≠ calm.
v complain, grumble, fret, worry, flap (*infml*), take pains, bother, bustle, fidget.

fussy *adj* **1** PARTICULAR, fastidious, scrupulous, finicky, pernickety, difficult, hard to please, choosy (*infml*), discriminating. **2** FANCY, elaborate, ornate, cluttered.
≠ **1** casual, uncritical. **2** plain.

futile *adj* pointless, useless, worthless, vain, idle, wasted, fruitless, profitless, unavailing, unsuccessful, abortive, unprofitable, unproductive, barren, empty, hollow, forlorn.
≠ fruitful, profitable.

futility *n* pointlessness, uselessness, worthlessness, vanity, emptiness, hollowness, aimlessness.
≠ use, purpose.

future *n* hereafter, tomorrow, outlook, prospects, expectations.
≠ past.
adj prospective, designate, to be, fated, destined, to come, forthcoming, in the offing, impending, coming, approaching, expected, planned, unborn, later, subsequent, eventual.
≠ past.

fuzzy *adj* **1** FRIZZY, fluffy, furry, woolly, fleecy, downy, velvety, napped. **2** BLURRED, unfocused, ill-defined, unclear, vague, faint, hazy, shadowy, woolly, muffled, distorted.
≠ **2** clear, distinct.

G

gadget *n* tool, appliance, device, contrivance, contraption, thing, thingumajig (*infml*), invention, novelty, gimmick.

gag[1] *v* muffle, muzzle, silence, quiet, stifle, throttle, suppress, curb, check, still.

gag[2] *n* (*infml*) joke, jest, quip, crack, wisecrack, one-liner, pun, witticism, funny (*infml*).

gaiety *n* happiness, glee, cheerfulness, joie de vivre, jollity, merriment, mirth, hilarity, fun, merrymaking, revelry, festivity, celebration, joviality, good humour, high spirits, light-heartedness, liveliness, brightness, brilliance, sparkle, colour, colourfulness, show, showiness.
≠ sadness, drabness.

gaily *adv* happily, joyfully, merrily, blithely, brightly, brilliantly, colourfully, flamboyantly.
≠ sadly, dully.

gain *v* **1** EARN, make, produce, gross, net, clear, profit, yield, bring in, reap, harvest, win, capture, secure, get, obtain, acquire, procure. **2** REACH, arrive at, come to, get to, attain, achieve, realize. **3** *gain speed*: increase, pick up, gather, collect, advance, progress, improve.
≠ **1** lose. **3** lose.
n earnings, proceeds, income, revenue, winnings, profit, return, yield, dividend, growth, increase, increment, rise, advance, progress, headway, improvement, advantage, benefit, attainment, achievement, acquisition.
≠ loss.
gain on close with, narrow the gap, approach, catch up, level with, overtake, outdistance, leave behind.

gala *n* festivity, celebration, festival, carnival, jubilee, jamboree, fête, fair, pageant, procession.

gale *n* **1** WIND, squall, storm, hurricane, tornado, typhoon, cyclone. **2** BURST, outburst, outbreak, fit, eruption, explosion, blast.

gallant *adj* chivalrous, gentlemanly, courteous, polite, gracious, courtly, noble, dashing, heroic, valiant, brave, courageous, fearless, dauntless, bold, daring.
≠ ungentlemanly, cowardly.

gallery *n* art gallery, museum, arcade, passage, walk, balcony, circle, gods (*infml*), spectators.

gallop *v* bolt, run, sprint, race, career, fly, dash, tear, speed, zoom, shoot, dart, rush, hurry, hasten.
≠ amble.

galvanize *v* electrify, shock, jolt, prod, spur, provoke, stimulate, stir, move, arouse, excite, fire, invigorate, vitalize.

gamble *v* bet, wager, have a flutter (*infml*), try one's luck, punt, play, game, stake, chance, take a chance, risk, hazard, venture, speculate, back.
n bet, wager, flutter (*infml*), punt, lottery, chance, risk, venture, speculation.

gambler *n* better, punter.

gambol *v* caper, frolic, frisk, skip, jump, bound, hop, bounce.

game[1] *n* **1** RECREATION, play, sport, pastime, diversion, distraction, entertainment, amusement, fun, frolic, romp, joke, jest.

> *Types of indoor game include*: board game, backgammon, checkers (*US*), chess, Cluedo®, draughts, halma, ludo, mah-jong, Monopoly®, nine men's morris, Scrabble®, snakes and ladders, Trivial Pursuit®; card game, baccarat, beggar-my-neighbour, bezique, blackjack, brag, bridge, canasta, chemin de fer, crib (*infml*), cribbage, faro, gin rummy, rummy, happy families, nap (*infml*),

napoleon, newmarket, old maid, patience, Pelmanism, picquet, poker, draw poker, stud poker, pontoon, vingt-et-un, snap, solitaire, twenty-one, whist, partner whist, solo whist; bagatelle, pinball, billiards, snooker, pool, bowling, ten-pin bowling, bowls, darts, dice, craps, dominoes, roulette, shove ha'penny, table tennis, ping pong.
Types of children's games include: battleships, blind man's buff, charades, Chinese whispers, consequences, fivestones, forfeits, hangman, hide-and-seek, I-spy, jacks, jackstraws, musical chairs, noughts and crosses, pass the parcel, piggy-in-the-middle, pin the tail on the donkey, postman's knock, sardines, Simon says, spillikins, spin the bottle, tiddlywinks.

2 COMPETITION, contest, match, round, tournament, event, meeting. **3** GAME BIRDS, animals, meat, flesh, prey, quarry, bag, spoils.

Types of game (killed for sport) include: antelope, badger, bear, blackcock, boar, wild boar, caribou, deer, fallow deer, red deer, roe deer, duck, elk, fox, grouse, hazel grouse, wood grouse, hare, lion, moose, mountain lion, partridge, pheasant, quail, rabbit, snipe, squirrel, stag, tiger, waterfowl.

game[2] *adj* (*infml*) **1** *game for anything*: willing, inclined, ready, prepared, eager. **2** BOLD, daring, intrepid, brave, courageous, fearless, resolute, spirited.
≠ **1** unwilling. **2** cowardly.

gamut *n* scale, series, range, sweep, scope, compass, spectrum, field, area.

gang *n* group, band, ring, pack, herd, mob, crowd, circle, clique, coterie, set, lot, team, crew, squad, shift, party.

gangster *n* mobster, desperado, hoodlum, ruffian, rough, tough, thug, heavy (*sl*), racketeer, bandit, brigand, robber, criminal, crook (*infml*).

gaol *see* **jail**.

gaoler *see* **jailer**.

gap *n* **1** SPACE, blank, void, hole, opening, crack, chink, crevice, cleft, breach, rift, divide, divergence, difference. **2** INTERRUPTION, break, recess, pause, lull, interlude, intermission, interval.

gape *v* **1** STARE, gaze, gawp (*infml*), goggle, gawk (*infml*). **2** OPEN, yawn, part, split, crack.

gaping *adj* open, yawning, broad, wide, vast, cavernous.
≠ tiny.

garage *n* lock-up, petrol station, service station.

garble *v* confuse, muddle, jumble, scramble, mix up, twist, distort, pervert, slant, misrepresent, falsify.
≠ decipher.

garden *n* yard, backyard, plot, park.

Types of garden include: allotment, alpine garden, arboretum, arbour, beer garden, border, botanical garden, bottle garden, cottage garden, fruit garden, garden of rest, hanging garden, herb garden, herbaceous border, hop garden, indoor garden, Japanese garden, kitchen garden, knot garden, lawn, market garden, ornamental garden, orchard, raised bed, rock garden, rockery, rose arbour, rose bed, rose garden, shrubbery, sink garden, sunken garden, tea garden, terrarium, vegetable plot, wall garden, water garden, window box, winter garden.

garish *adj* gaudy, lurid, loud, glaring, flashy, showy, tawdry, vulgar, tasteless.
≠ quiet, tasteful.

garland *n* wreath, festoon, decoration, flowers, laurels, honours.
v wreathe, festoon, deck, adorn, crown.

garments *n* clothes, clothing, wear, attire, gear (*infml*), togs (*infml*), outfit, get-up (*infml*), dress, costume, uniform.

garnish *v* decorate, adorn, ornament, trim, embellish, enhance, grace, set off.
≠ divest.
n decoration, ornament, trimming, embellishment, enhancement, relish.

gas

> *Types of gas include*: acetylene, ammonia, black damp, butane, carbon dioxide, carbon monoxide, chloroform, choke damp, CS gas, cyanogen, ether, ethylene, fire damp, helium, hydrogen sulphide, krypton, laughing gas, marsh gas, methane, mustard gas, natural gas, neon, nerve gas, niton, nitrous oxide, ozone, propane, radon, tear gas, town gas, xenon.

gash *v* cut, wound, slash, slit, incise, lacerate, tear, rend, split, score, gouge.
n cut, wound, slash, slit, incision, laceration, tear, rent, split, score, gouge.

gasp *v* pant, puff, blow, breathe, wheeze, choke, gulp.
n pant, puff, blow, breath, gulp, exclamation.

gate *n* barrier, door, doorway, gateway, opening, entrance, exit, access, passage.

gather *v* **1** CONGREGATE, convene, muster, rally, round up, assemble, collect, group, amass, accumulate, hoard, stockpile, heap, pile up, build. **2** INFER, deduce, conclude, surmise, assume, understand, learn, hear. **3** FOLD, pleat, tuck, pucker. **4** *gather flowers*: pick, pluck, cull, select, reap, harvest, glean.
≠ **1** scatter, dissipate.

gathering *n* assembly, convocation, convention, meeting, round-up, rally, get-together, jamboree, party, group, company, congregation, mass, crowd, throng, turnout.

gaudy *adj* bright, brilliant, glaring, garish, loud, flashy, showy, ostentatious, tinselly, glitzy (*infml*), tawdry, vulgar, tasteless.
≠ drab, plain.

gauge *v* estimate, guess, judge, assess, evaluate, value, rate, reckon, figure, calculate, compute, count, measure, weigh, determine, ascertain.
n **1** STANDARD, norm, criterion, benchmark, yardstick, rule, guideline, indicator, measure, meter, test, sample, example, model, pattern. **2** SIZE, magnitude, measure, capacity, bore, calibre, thickness, width, span, extent, scope, height, depth, degree.

gaunt *adj* **1** HAGGARD, hollow-eyed, angular, bony, thin, lean, lank, skinny, scraggy, scrawny, skeletal, emaciated, wasted. **2** BLEAK, stark, bare, desolate, forlorn, dismal, dreary, grim, harsh.
≠ **1** plump.

gawky *adj* awkward, clumsy, maladroit, gauche, inept, oafish, ungainly, gangling, unco-ordinated, graceless.
≠ graceful.

gay *adj* **1** HAPPY, joyful, jolly, merry, cheerful, blithe, sunny, carefree, debonair, fun-loving, pleasure-seeking, vivacious, lively, animated, playful, light-hearted. **2** *gay colours*: vivid, rich, bright, brilliant, sparkling, festive, colourful, gaudy, garish, flashy, showy, flamboyant. **3** HOMOSEXUAL, lesbian, queer (*sl*).
≠ **1** sad, gloomy. **3** heterosexual, straight (*sl*).
n homosexual, queer (*sl*), poof (*sl*), lesbian, dike (*sl*).
≠ heterosexual.

gaze *v* stare, contemplate, regard, watch, view, look, gape, wonder.
n stare, look.

gear *n* **1** EQUIPMENT, kit, outfit, tackle, apparatus, tools, instruments, accessories. **2** GEARWHEEL, cogwheel, cog, gearing, mechanism, machinery, works. **3** (*infml*) BELONGINGS, possessions, things, stuff, baggage, luggage, paraphernalia. **4** (*infml*) CLOTHES, clothing, garments, attire, dress, garb (*infml*), togs (*infml*), get-up (*infml*).

gel, jell *v* set, congeal, coagulate, crystallize, harden, thicken, solidify, materialize, come together, finalize, form, take shape.

gelatinous *adj* jelly-like, jellied, congealed, rubbery, glutinous, gummy, gluey, gooey (*infml*), sticky, viscous.

gem *n* gemstone, precious stone, stone, jewel, treasure, prize, masterpiece, pièce de résistance.

Gems and gemstones include: diamond, white sapphire, zircon, cubic zirconia, marcasite, rhinestone, pearl, moonstone, onyx, opal, mother-of-pearl, amber, citrine, fire opal, topaz, agate, tiger's eye, jasper, morganite, ruby, garnet, rose quartz, beryl, cornelian, coral, amethyst, sapphire, turquoise, lapis lazuli, emerald, aquamarine, bloodstone, jade, peridot, tourmaline, jet.

enealogy *n* family tree, pedigree, lineage, ancestry, descent, derivation, extraction, family, line.

eneral *adj* **1** *a general statement*: broad, sweeping, blanket, all-inclusive, comprehensive, universal, global, total, across-the-board, widespread, prevalent, extensive, overall, panoramic. **2** VAGUE, ill-defined, indefinite, imprecise, inexact, approximate, loose, unspecific. **3** USUAL, regular, normal, typical, ordinary, everyday, customary, conventional, common, public.
≠ **1** particular, limited. **2** specific. **3** rare.

enerally *adv* usually, normally, as a rule, by and large, on the whole, mostly, mainly, chiefly, broadly, commonly, universally.

enerate *v* produce, engender, whip up, arouse, cause, bring about, give rise to, create, originate, initiate, make, form, breed, propagate.
≠ prevent.

eneration *n* **1** AGE GROUP, age, era, epoch, period, time. **2** PRODUCTION, creation, origination, formation, genesis, procreation, reproduction, propagation, breeding.

enerosity *n* liberality, munificence, open-handedness, bounty, charity, magnanimity, philanthropy, kindness, big-heartedness, benevolence, goodness.
≠ meanness, selfishness.

enerous *adj* **1** LIBERAL, free, bountiful, open-handed, unstinting, unsparing, lavish. **2** MAGNANIMOUS, charitable, philanthropic, public-spirited, unselfish, kind, big-hearted, benevolent, good, high-minded, noble. **3** AMPLE, full, plentiful, abundant, copious, overflowing.
≠ **1** mean, miserly. **2** selfish. **3** meagre.

genial *adj* affable, amiable, friendly, convivial, cordial, kindly, kind, warm-hearted, warm, hearty, jovial, jolly, cheerful, happy, good-natured, easy-going (*infml*), agreeable, pleasant.
≠ cold.

genius *n* **1** VIRTUOSO, maestro, master, past master, expert, adept, egghead (*infml*), intellectual, mastermind, brain, intellect. **2** INTELLIGENCE, brightness, brilliance, ability, aptitude, gift, talent, flair, knack, bent, inclination, propensity, capacity, faculty.

gentle *adj* **1** KIND, kindly, amiable, tender, soft-hearted, compassionate, sympathetic, merciful, mild, placid, calm, tranquil. **2** *a gentle slope*: gradual, slow, easy, smooth, moderate, slight, light, imperceptible. **3** SOOTHING, peaceful, serene, quiet, soft, balmy.
≠ **1** unkind, rough, harsh, wild.

genuine *adj* real, actual, natural, pure, original, authentic, veritable, true, bona fide, legitimate, honest, sincere, frank, candid, earnest.
≠ artificial, false, insincere.

germ *n* **1** MICRO-ORGANISM, microbe, bacterium, bacillus, virus, bug (*infml*). **2** BEGINNING, start, origin, source, cause, spark, rudiment, nucleus, root, seed, embryo, bud, sprout.

germinate *v* bud, sprout, shoot, develop, grow, swell.

gesticulate *v* wave, signal, gesture, indicate, sign.

gesture *n* act, action, movement, motion, indication, sign, signal, wave, gesticulation.
v indicate, sign, motion, beckon, point, signal, wave, gesticulate.

get *v* **1** OBTAIN, acquire, procure, come by, receive, earn, gain, win, secure, achieve, realize. **2** *it's getting dark*: become, turn, go, grow. **3** *get him to help*: persuade, coax, induce, urge, influence, sway. **4** MOVE, go, come,

reach, arrive. **5** FETCH, collect, pick up, take, catch, capture, seize, grab. **6** CONTRACT, catch, pick up, develop, come down with.
≠ **1** lose. **4** leave.
get across communicate, transmit, convey, impart, put across, bring home to.
get ahead advance, progress, get on, go places (*infml*), thrive, flourish, prosper, succeed, make good, make it, get there (*infml*).
≠ fall behind, fail.
get along 1 COPE, manage, get by, survive, fare, progress, develop. **2** AGREE, harmonize, get on, hit it off.
get at 1 REACH, attain, find, discover. **2** (*infml*) BRIBE, suborn, corrupt, influence. **3** (*infml*) MEAN, intend, imply, insinuate, hint, suggest. **4** (*infml*) CRITICIZE, find fault with, pick on, attack, make fun of.
get away escape, get out, break out, break away, run away, flee, depart, leave.
get back recover, regain, recoup, repossess, retrieve.
get down 1 DEPRESS, sadden, dishearten, dispirit. **2** DESCEND, dismount, disembark, alight, get off.
≠ **1** encourage. **2** board.
get in enter, penetrate, infiltrate, arrive, come, land, embark.
get off 1 *get off a train*: alight, disembark, dismount, descend. **2** REMOVE, detach, separate, shed, get down.
≠ **1** get on. **2** put on.
get on 1 BOARD, embark, mount, ascend. **2** COPE, manage, fare, get along, make out, prosper, succeed. **3** CONTINUE, proceed, press on, advance, progress.
≠ **1** get off.
get out 1 ESCAPE, flee, break out, extricate oneself, free oneself, leave, quit, vacate, evacuate, clear out, clear off (*infml*). **2** *she got out a pen*: take out, produce.
get over 1 RECOVER FROM, shake off, survive. **2** SURMOUNT, overcome, defeat, deal with. **3** COMMUNICATE, get across, convey, put over, impart, explain.
get round 1 CIRCUMVENT, bypass, evade, avoid. **2** PERSUADE, win over, talk round, coax, prevail upon.
get together assemble, collect, gather, congregate, rally, meet, join, unite, collaborate.
get up stand (up), arise, rise, ascend, climb, mount, scale.

ghastly *adj* awful, dreadful, frightful, terrible, grim, gruesome, hideous, horrible, horrid, loathsome, repellent, shocking, appalling.
≠ delightful, attractive.

ghost *n* spectre, phantom, spook (*infml*), apparition, visitant, spirit, wraith, soul, shade, shadow.

ghostly *adj* eerie, spooky (*infml*), creepy, supernatural, unearthly, ghostlike, spectral, wraith-like, phantom, illusory.

giant *n* monster, titan, colossus, Goliath, Hercules.
adj gigantic, colossal, titanic, mammoth, jumbo (*infml*), king-size, huge, enormous, immense, vast, large.

gibe, jibe *n* jeer, sneer, mockery, ridicule, taunt, derision, scoff, dig (*infml*), crack (*infml*), poke, quip.

giddy *adj* **1** DIZZY, faint, light-headed unsteady, reeling, vertiginous. **2** SILLY flighty, wild.

gift *n* **1** PRESENT, offering, donation, contribution, bounty, largess, gratuity tip, bonus, freebie (*sl*), legacy, beques endowment. **2** TALENT, genius, flair, aptitude, bent, knack, power, faculty, attribute, ability, capability, capacity.

gifted *adj* talented, adept, skilful, expert, masterly, skilled, accomplishec able, capable, clever, intelligent, brigh brilliant.

gigantic *adj* huge, enormous, immens vast, giant, colossal, titanic, mammot gargantuan, Brobdingnagian.
≠ tiny, Lilliputian.

giggle *v, n* titter, snigger, chuckle, chortle, laugh.

gilded *adj* gilt, gold, golden, gold-plated.

gimmick *n* attraction, ploy, stratagem ruse, scheme, trick, stunt, dodge, device, contrivance, gadget.

gingerly *adv* tentatively, hesitantly, warily, cautiously, carefully, delicately.
≠ boldly, carelessly.

gipsy *see* **gypsy**.

girdle *n* belt, sash, band, waistband, corset.

girl *n* lass, young woman, girlfriend, sweetheart, daughter.

girth *n* circumference, perimeter, measure, size, bulk, strap, band.

gist *n* pith, essence, marrow, substance, matter, meaning, significance, import, sense, idea, drift, direction, point, nub, core, quintessence.

give *v* **1** PRESENT, award, confer, offer, lend, donate, contribute, provide, supply, furnish, grant, bestow, endow, gift, make over, hand over, deliver, entrust, commit, devote. **2** *give news*: communicate, transmit, impart, utter, announce, declare, pronounce, publish, set forth. **3** CONCEDE, allow, admit, yield, give way, surrender. **4** *give trouble*: cause, occasion, make, produce, do, perform. **5** SINK, yield, bend, give way, break, collapse, fall.
≠ **1** take, withhold. **5** withstand.
give away betray, inform on, expose, uncover, divulge, let slip, disclose, reveal, leak, let out.
give in surrender, capitulate, submit, yield, give way, concede, give up, quit.
≠ hold out.
give off emit, discharge, release, give out, send out, throw out, pour out, exhale, exude, produce.
give out 1 DISTRIBUTE, hand out, dole out, deal. **2** ANNOUNCE, declare, broadcast, publish, disseminate, communicate, transmit, impart, notify, advertise.
give up 1 STOP, cease, quit, resign, abandon, renounce, relinquish, waive. **2** SURRENDER, capitulate, give in.
≠ **1** start. **2** hold out.

given *adj* **1** *a given number*: specified, particular, definite. **2** INCLINED, disposed, likely, liable, prone.

glad *adj* **1** PLEASED, delighted, gratified, contented, happy, joyful, merry, cheerful, cheery, bright. **2** WILLING, eager, keen, ready, inclined, disposed.
≠ **1** sad, unhappy. **2** unwilling, reluctant.

glamorous *adj* smart, elegant, attractive, beautiful, gorgeous, enchanting, captivating, alluring, appealing, fascinating, exciting, dazzling, glossy, colourful.
≠ plain, drab, boring.

glamour *n* attraction, allure, appeal, fascination, charm, magic, beauty, elegance, glitter, prestige.

glance *v* peep, peek, glimpse, view, look, scan, skim, leaf, flip, thumb, dip, browse.
n peep, peek, glimpse, look.

glands

> *Types of gland include*: adrenal, cortex medulla, apocrine, eccrine, endocrine, exocrine, holocrine, lachrymal, lymph, lymph node, mammary, merocrine, ovary, pancreas, parathyroid, parotid, pineal, pituitary, prostate, sebaceous, testicle, thymus, thyroid.

glare *v* **1** GLOWER, look daggers, frown, scowl, stare. **2** DAZZLE, blaze, flame, flare, shine, reflect.
n **1** BLACK LOOK, dirty look (*infml*), frown, scowl, stare, look.
2 BRIGHTNESS, brilliance, blaze, flame, dazzle, spotlight.

glaring *adj* blatant, flagrant, open, conspicuous, manifest, patent, obvious, outrageous, gross.
≠ hidden, concealed, minor.

glassy *adj* **1** GLASSLIKE, smooth, slippery, icy, shiny, glossy, transparent, clear. **2** *a glassy stare*: expressionless, blank, empty, vacant, dazed, fixed, glazed, cold, lifeless, dull.

glaze *v* coat, enamel, gloss, varnish, lacquer, polish, burnish.
n coat, coating, finish, enamel, varnish, lacquer, polish, shine, lustre, gloss.

gleam *n* glint, flash, beam, ray, flicker, glimmer, shimmer, sparkle, glitter, gloss, glow.
v glint, flash, glance, flare, shine,

glisten, glimmer, glitter, sparkle, shimmer, glow.

glib *adj* fluent, easy, facile, quick, ready, talkative, plausible, insincere, smooth, slick, suave, smooth-tongued. ≠ tongue-tied, implausible.

glide *v* slide, slip, skate, skim, fly, float, drift, sail, coast, roll, run, flow.

glimmer *v* glow, shimmer, glisten, glitter, sparkle, twinkle, wink, blink, flicker, gleam, shine.
n **1** GLOW, shimmer, sparkle, twinkle, flicker, glint, gleam. **2** TRACE, hint, suggestion, grain.

glimpse *n* peep, peek, squint, glance, look, sight, sighting, view.
v spy, espy, spot, catch sight of, sight, view.

glint *v* flash, gleam, shine, reflect, glitter, sparkle, twinkle, glimmer.
n flash, gleam, shine, reflection, glitter, sparkle, twinkle, glimmer.

glisten *v* shine, gleam, glint, glitter, sparkle, twinkle, glimmer, shimmer.

glitter *v* sparkle, spangle, scintillate, twinkle, shimmer, glimmer, glisten, glint, gleam, flash, shine.
n sparkle, coruscation, scintillation, twinkle, shimmer, glimmer, glint, gleam, flash, shine, lustre, sheen, brightness, radiance, brilliance, splendour, showiness, glamour, tinsel.

gloat *v* triumph, glory, exult, rejoice, revel in, relish, crow, boast, vaunt, rub it in (*infml*).

global *adj* universal, worldwide, international, general, all-encompassing, total, thorough, exhaustive, comprehensive, all-inclusive, encylopedic, wide-ranging. ≠ parochial, limited.

globe *n* world, earth, planet, sphere, ball, orb, round.

gloom *n* **1** DEPRESSION, low spirits, despondency, dejection, sadness, unhappiness, glumness, melancholy, misery, desolation, despair. **2** DARK, darkness, shade, shadow, dusk, twilight, dimness, obscurity, cloud, cloudiness, dullness.
≠ **1** cheerfulness, happiness. **2** brightness.

gloomy *adj* **1** DEPRESSED, down, low, despondent, dejected, downcast, dispirited, down-hearted, sad, miserable, glum, morose, pessimistic, cheerless, dismal, depressing. **2** DARK, sombre, shadowy, dim, obscure, overcast, dull, dreary.
≠ **1** cheerful. **2** bright.

glorious *adj* **1** ILLUSTRIOUS, eminent distinguished, famous, renowned, noted, great, noble, splendid, magnificent, grand, majestic, triumphant. **2** FINE, bright, radiant, shining, brilliant, dazzling, beautiful, gorgeous, superb, excellent, wonderful, marvellous, delightful, heavenly.
≠ **1** unknown.

glory *n* **1** FAME, renown, celebrity, illustriousness, greatness, eminence, distinction, honour, prestige, kudos, triumph. **2** PRAISE, homage, tribute, worship, veneration, adoration, exaltation, blessing, thanksgiving, gratitude. **3** BRIGHTNESS, radiance, brilliance, beauty, splendour, resplendence, magnificence, grandeur, majesty, dignity.

gloss[1] *n* polish, varnish, lustre, sheen shine, brightness, brilliance, show, appearance, semblance, surface, front façade, veneer, window-dressing.
gloss over conceal, hide, veil, mask, disguise, camouflage, cover up, whitewash, explain away.

gloss[2] *n* annotation, note, footnote, explanation, elucidation, interpretation, translation, definition, comment, commentary.
v annotate, define, explain, elucidate interpret, construe, translate, comment.

glossy *adj* shiny, sheeny, lustrous, sleek, silky, smooth, glassy, polished, burnished, glazed, enamelled, bright, shining, brilliant.
≠ matt.

glow *n* **1** LIGHT, gleam, glimmer, radiance, luminosity, brightness, vividness, brilliance, splendour. **2** ARDOUR, fervour, intensity, warmth, passion, enthusiasm, excitement. **3** FLUSH, blush, rosiness, redness, burning.

v **1** SHINE, radiate, gleam, glimmer, burn, smoulder. **2** *their faces glowed*: flush, blush, colour, redden.

glower *v* glare, look daggers, frown, scowl.
n glare, black look, dirty look (*infml*), frown, scowl, stare, look.

glowing *adj* **1** BRIGHT, luminous, vivid, vibrant, rich, warm, flushed, red, flaming. **2** *a glowing review*: complimentary, enthusiastic, ecstatic, rhapsodic, rave (*infml*).
≠ **1** dull, colourless. **2** restrained.

glue *n* adhesive, gum, paste, size, cement.
v stick, affix, gum, paste, seal, bond, cement, fix.

glut *n* surplus, excess, superfluity, surfeit, overabundance, superabundance, saturation, overflow.
≠ scarcity, lack.

glutton *n* gourmand, gormandizer, guzzler, gorger, gobbler, pig.
≠ ascetic.

gluttony *n* gourmandise, gourmandism, greed, greediness, voracity, insatiability, piggishness.
≠ abstinence, asceticism.

gnarled *adj* gnarly, knotted, knotty, twisted, contorted, distorted, rough, rugged, weather-beaten.

gnaw *v* **1** BITE, nibble, munch, chew, eat, devour, consume, erode, wear, haunt. **2** WORRY, niggle, fret, trouble, plague, nag, prey.

go *v* **1** MOVE, pass, advance, progress, proceed, make for, travel, journey, start, begin, depart, leave, take one's leave, retreat, withdraw, disappear, vanish. **2** OPERATE, function, work, run, act, perform. **3** EXTEND, spread, stretch, reach, span, continue, unfold. **4** *time goes quickly*: pass, elapse, lapse, roll on.
≠ **2** break down, fail.
n (*infml*) **1** *have a go*: attempt, try, shot (*infml*), bash (*infml*), stab (*infml*), turn. **2** ENERGY, get-up-and-go (*infml*), vitality, life, spirit, dynamism, effort.
go about approach, begin, set about, address, tackle, attend to, undertake, engage in, perform.
go ahead begin, proceed, carry on, continue, advance, progress, move.
go away depart, leave, clear off (*infml*), withdraw, retreat, disappear, vanish.
go back return, revert, backslide, retreat.
go by **1** PASS, elapse, flow. **2** *go by the rules*: observe, follow, comply with, heed.
go down descend, sink, set, fall, drop, decrease, decline, deteriorate, degenerate, fail, founder, go under, collapse, fold (*infml*).
go for **1** (*infml*) CHOOSE, prefer, favour, like, admire, enjoy. **2** ATTACK, assail, set about, lunge at.
go in for enter, take part in, participate in, engage in, take up, embrace, adopt, undertake, practise, pursue, follow.
go into discuss, consider, review, examine, study, scrutinize, investigate, inquire into, check out, probe, delve into, analyse, dissect.
go off **1** DEPART, leave, quit, abscond, vanish, disappear. **2** EXPLODE, blow up, detonate. **3** *the milk has gone off*: deteriorate, turn, sour, go bad, rot.
go on **1** CONTINUE, carry on, proceed, persist, stay, endure, last. **2** CHATTER, rabbit (*infml*), witter (*infml*), ramble on. **3** HAPPEN, occur, take place.
go out exit, depart, leave.
go over examine, peruse, study, revise, scan, read, inspect, check, review, repeat, rehearse, list.
go through **1** SUFFER, undergo, experience, bear, tolerate, endure, withstand. **2** INVESTIGATE, check, examine, look, search, hunt, explore. **3** USE, consume, exhaust, spend, squander.
go together match, harmonize, accord, fit.
go with **1** MATCH, harmonize, co-ordinate, blend, complement, suit, fit, correspond. **2** ACCOMPANY, escort, take, usher.
≠ **1** clash.
go without abstain, forgo, do without, manage without, lack, want.

goad *v* prod, prick, spur, impel, push, drive, provoke, incite, instigate, arouse, stimulate, prompt, urge, nag, hound, harass, annoy, irritate, vex.

go-ahead *n* permission, authorization,

clearance, green light (*infml*), sanction, assent, consent, OK (*infml*), agreement.
≠ ban, veto, embargo.
adj enterprising, pioneering, progressive, ambitious, up-and-coming, dynamic, energetic.
≠ unenterprising, sluggish.

goal *n* target, mark, objective, aim, intention, object, purpose, end, ambition, aspiration.

gobble *v* bolt, guzzle, gorge, cram, stuff, devour, consume, put away (*infml*), swallow, gulp.

go-between *n* intermediary, mediator, liaison, contact, middleman, broker, dealer, agent, messenger, medium.

God *n* Supreme Being, Creator, Providence, Lord, Almighty, Holy One, Jehovah, Yahweh, Allah, Brahma, Zeus.

god, goddess *n* deity, divinity, idol, spirit, power.

god-forsaken *adj* remote, isolated, lonely, bleak, desolate, abandoned, deserted, forlorn, dismal, dreary, gloomy, miserable, wretched.

godless *adj* ungodly, atheistic, heathen, pagan, irreligious, unholy, impious, sacrilegious, profane, irreverent, bad, evil, wicked.
≠ godly, pious.

godly *adj* religious, holy, pious, devout, God-fearing, righteous, good, virtuous, pure, innocent.
≠ godless, impious.

godsend *n* blessing, boon, stroke of luck, windfall, miracle.
≠ blow, setback.

golden *adj* **1** GOLD, gilded, gilt, yellow, blond(e), fair, bright, shining, lustrous, resplendent. **2** PROSPEROUS, successful, glorious, excellent, happy, joyful, favourable, auspicious, promising, rosy.

golf clubs

> *Types of golf club include*: driver, brassie, spoon, wood, iron, driving iron, midiron, midmashie, mashie iron, mashie, spade mashie, mashie niblick, pitching niblick, niblick, putter, pitching wedge, sand wedge.

good *adj* **1** ACCEPTABLE, satisfactory, pleasant, agreeable, nice, enjoyable, pleasing, commendable, excellent, great (*infml*), super (*infml*), first-class, first-rate, superior, advantageous, beneficial, favourable, auspicious, helpful, useful, worthwhile, profitable, appropriate, suitable, fitting. **2** *good at her job*: competent, proficient, skilled, expert, accomplished, professional, skilful, clever, talented, gifted, fit, able, capable, dependable, reliable. **3** KIND, considerate, gracious, benevolent, charitable, philanthropic. **4** VIRTUOUS, exemplary, moral, upright, honest, trustworthy, worthy, righteous. **5** WELL-BEHAVED, obedient, well-mannered. **6** THOROUGH, complete, whole, substantial, considerable.
≠ **1** bad, poor. **2** incompetent. **3** unkind, inconsiderate. **4** wicked, immoral. **5** naughty, disobedient.
n **1** VIRTUE, morality, goodness, righteousness, right. **2** USE, purpose, avail, advantage, profit, gain, worth, merit, usefulness, service. **3** *for your own good*: welfare, wellbeing, interest, sake, behalf, benefit, convenience.

good-bye *n* farewell, adieu, au revoir, valediction, leave-taking, parting.

good-humoured *adj* cheerful, happy, jovial, genial, affable, amiable, friendly, congenial, pleasant, good-tempered, approachable.
≠ ill-humoured.

good-looking *adj* attractive, handsome, beautiful, fair, pretty, personable, presentable.
≠ ugly, plain.

good-natured *adj* kind, kindly, kind-hearted, sympathetic, benevolent, helpful, neighbourly, gentle, good-tempered, approachable, friendly, tolerant, patient.
≠ ill-natured.

goodness *n* virtue, uprightness, rectitude, honesty, probity, kindness, compassion, graciousness, goodwill, benevolence, unselfishness, generosity, friendliness, helpfulness.
≠ badness, wickedness.

goods *n* **1** PROPERTY, chattels, effects

possessions, belongings, paraphernalia, stuff, things, gear (*infml*).
2 MERCHANDISE, wares, commodities, stock, freight.

oodwill *n* benevolence, kindness, generosity, favour, friendliness, friendship, zeal.
≠ ill-will.

ore *v* pierce, penetrate, stab, spear, stick, impale, wound.

orge *n* canyon, ravine, gully, defile, chasm, abyss, cleft, fissure, gap, pass.
v feed, guzzle, gobble, devour, bolt, wolf, gulp, swallow, cram, stuff, fill, sate, surfeit, glut, overeat.
≠ fast.

orgeous *adj* magnificent, splendid, grand, glorious, superb, fine, rich, sumptuous, luxurious, brilliant, dazzling, showy, glamorous, attractive, beautiful, handsome, good-looking, delightful, pleasing, lovely, enjoyable, good.
≠ dull, plain.

ory *adj* bloody, sanguinary, bloodstained, blood-soaked, grisly, brutal, savage, murderous.

ossip *n* **1** IDLE TALK, prattle, chitchat, tittle-tattle, rumour, hearsay, report, scandal. **2** GOSSIP-MONGER, scandalmonger, whisperer, prattler, babbler, chatterbox, nosey parker (*infml*), busybody, talebearer, tell-tale, tattler.
v talk, chat, natter, chatter, gabble, prattle, tattle, tell tales, whisper, rumour.

ouge *v* chisel, cut, hack, incise, score, groove, scratch, claw, gash, slash, dig, scoop, hollow, extract.

ourmet *n* gastronome, epicure, epicurean, connoisseur, bon vivant.

overn *v* **1** RULE, reign, direct, manage, superintend, supervise, oversee, preside, lead, head, command, influence, guide, conduct, steer, pilot.
2 *govern one's temper*: dominate, master, control, regulate, curb, check, restrain, contain, quell, subdue, tame, discipline.

overnment *n* **1** *blame the government*: administration, executive, ministry, Establishment, authorities, powers that be, state, régime. **2** RULE, sovereignty, sway, direction, management, superintendence, supervision, surveillance, command, charge, authority, guidance, conduct, domination, dominion, control, regulation, restraint.

> *Government systems include*: absolutism, autocracy, commonwealth, communism, democracy, despotism, dictatorship, empire, federation, hierocracy, junta, kingdom, monarchy, plutocracy, puppet government, republic, theocracy, triumvirate. *see also* **parliaments and political assemblies**.

governor *n* ruler, commissioner, administrator, executive, director, manager, leader, head, chief, commander, superintendent, supervisor, overseer, controller, boss.

gown *n* robe, dress, frock, dressing-gown, habit, costume.

grab *v* seize, snatch, take, nab (*infml*), pluck, snap up, catch hold of, grasp, clutch, grip, catch, bag, capture, collar (*infml*), commandeer, appropriate, usurp, annex.

grace *n* **1** GRACEFULNESS, poise, beauty, attractiveness, loveliness, shapeliness, elegance, tastefulness, refinement, polish, breeding, manners, etiquette, decorum, decency, courtesy, charm. **2** KINDNESS, kindliness, compassion, consideration, goodness, virtue, generosity, charity, benevolence, goodwill, favour, forgiveness, indulgence, mercy, leniency, pardon, reprieve. **3** *say grace*: blessing, benediction, thanksgiving, prayer.
≠ **2** cruelty, harshness.
v favour, honour, dignify, distinguish, embellish, enhance, set off, trim, garnish, decorate, ornament, adorn.
≠ spoil, detract from.

graceful *adj* easy, flowing, smooth, supple, agile, deft, natural, slender, fine, tasteful, elegant, beautiful, charming, suave.

≠ graceless, awkward, clumsy, ungainly.

gracious *adj* elegant, refined, polite, courteous, well-mannered, considerate, sweet, obliging, accommodating, kind, compassionate, kindly, benevolent, generous, magnanimous, charitable, hospitable, forgiving, indulgent, lenient, mild, clement, merciful.
≠ ungracious.

grade *n* rank, status, standing, station, place, position, level, stage, degree, step, rung, notch, mark, brand, quality, standard, condition, size, order, group, class, category.
v sort, arrange, categorize, order, group, class, rate, size, rank, range, classify, evaluate, assess, value, mark, brand, label, pigeonhole, type.

gradient *n* slope, incline, hill, bank, rise, declivity.

gradual *adj* slow, leisurely, unhurried, easy, gentle, moderate, regular, even, measured, steady, continuous, progressive, step-by-step.
≠ sudden, precipitate.

gradually *adv* little by little, bit by bit, imperceptibly, inch by inch, step by step, progressively, by degrees, piecemeal, slowly, gently, cautiously, gingerly, moderately, evenly, steadily.

graduate *v* **1** *graduate from medical school*: pass, qualify. **2** CALIBRATE, mark off, measure out, proportion, grade, arrange, range, order, rank, sort, group, classify.

graft *n* implant, implantation, transplant, splice, bud, sprout, shoot, scion.
v engraft, implant, insert, transplant, join, splice.

grain *n* **1** BIT, piece, fragment, scrap, morsel, crumb, granule, particle, molecule, atom, jot, iota, mite, speck, modicum, trace. **2** SEED, kernel, corn, cereals. **3** TEXTURE, fibre, weave, pattern, marking, surface.

grand *adj* **1** MAJESTIC, regal, stately, splendid, magnificent, glorious, superb, sublime, fine, excellent, outstanding, first-rate, impressive, imposing, striking, monumental, large, noble, lordly, lofty, pompous, pretentious, grandiose, ambitious. **2** SUPREME, pr eminent, leading, head, chief, arch, highest, senior, great, illustrious.
≠ **1** humble, common, poor.

grandeur *n* majesty, stateliness, pom state, dignity, splendour, magnificenc nobility, greatness, illustriousness, importance.
≠ humbleness, lowliness, simplicity.

grandiose *adj* pompous, pretentious high-flown, lofty, ambitious, extravagant, ostentatious, showy, flamboyant, grand, majestic, stately, magnificent, impressive, imposing, monumental.
≠ unpretentious.

grant *v* **1** GIVE, donate, present, awa confer, bestow, impart, transmit, dispense, apportion, assign, allot, allocate, provide, supply. **2** ADMIT, acknowledge, concede, allow, permit consent to, agree to, accede to.
≠ **1** withhold. **2** deny.
n allowance, subsidy, concession, award, bursary, scholarship, gift, donation, endowment, bequest, annuity, pension, honorarium.

granular *adj* grainy, granulated, grit sandy, lumpy, rough, crumbly, friab

graph *n* diagram, chart, table, grid.

graphic *adj* vivid, descriptive, expressive, striking, telling, lively, realistic, explicit, clear, lucid, specific detailed, blow-by-blow, visual, pictorial, diagrammatic, illustrative.
≠ vague, impressionistic.

grapple *v* seize, grasp, snatch, grab, grip, clutch, clasp, hold, wrestle, tus struggle, contend, fight, combat, clas engage, encounter, face, confront, tackle, deal with, cope with.
≠ release, avoid, evade.

grasp *v* **1** HOLD, clasp, clutch, grip, grapple, seize, snatch, grab, catch. **2** *grasp a concept*: understand, comprehend, get (*infml*), follow, see realize.
n **1** GRIP, clasp, hold, embrace, clutches, possession, control, power. **2** UNDERSTANDING, comprehension

apprehension, mastery, familiarity, knowledge.

rasping *adj* avaricious, greedy, rapacious, acquisitive, mercenary, mean, selfish, miserly, close-fisted, tight-fisted, parsimonious.
≠ generous.

rass *n* turf, lawn, green, grassland, field, meadow, pasture, prairie, pampas, savanna, steppe.

> *Types of grass include*: bamboo, barley, beard grass, bent, buckwheat, cane, cocksfoot, corn, couch grass, English ryegrass, esparto, fescue, Italian ryegrass, Kentucky bluegrass, kangaroo grass, knot grass, maize, marijuana, marram grass, meadow foxtail, meadow grass, millet, oats, paddy, pampas grass, papyrus, rattan, reed, rice, rye, ryegrass, sorghum, squirrel-tail grass, sugar cane, switch grass, twitch grass, wheat, wild oat.

rate *v* **1** GRIND, shred, mince, pulverize, rub, rasp, scrape. **2** JAR, set one's teeth on edge, annoy, irritate, aggravate (*infml*), get on one's nerves, vex, irk, exasperate.

rateful *adj* thankful, appreciative, indebted, obliged, obligated, beholden.
≠ ungrateful.

ratify *v* satisfy, fulfil, indulge, pander to, humour, favour, please, gladden, delight, thrill.
≠ frustrate, thwart.

rating[1] *adj* harsh, rasping, scraping, squeaky, strident, discordant, jarring, annoying, irritating, unpleasant, disagreeable.
≠ harmonious, pleasing.

rating[2] *n* grate, grill, grid, lattice, trellis.

ratitude *n* gratefulness, thankfulness, thanks, appreciation, acknowledgement, recognition, indebtedness, obligation.
≠ ingratitude, ungratefulness.

ratuitous *adj* wanton, unnecessary, needless, superfluous, unwarranted, unjustified, groundless, undeserved, unprovoked, uncalled-for, unasked-for, unsolicited, voluntary, free, gratis, complimentary.
≠ justified, provoked.

gratuity *n* tip, bonus, perk (*infml*), gift, present, donation, reward, recompense.

grave[1] *n* burial-place, tomb, vault, crypt, sepulchre, mausoleum, pit, barrow, tumulus, cairn.

grave[2] *adj* **1** *a grave mistake*: important, significant, weighty, momentous, serious, critical, vital, crucial, urgent, acute, severe, dangerous, hazardous. **2** SOLEMN, dignified, sober, sedate, serious, thoughtful, pensive, grim, long-faced, quiet, reserved, subdued, restrained.
≠ **1** trivial, light, slight. **2** cheerful.

graveyard *n* cemetery, burial-ground, churchyard.

gravity *n* **1** IMPORTANCE, significance, seriousness, urgency, acuteness, severity, danger. **2** SOLEMNITY, dignity, sobriety, seriousness, thoughtfulness, sombreness, reserve, restraint. **3** GRAVITATION, attraction, pull, weight, heaviness.
≠ **1** triviality. **2** levity.

graze *v* scratch, scrape, skin, abrade, rub, chafe, shave, brush, skim, touch.
n scratch, scrape, abrasion.

grease *n* oil, lubrication, fat, lard, dripping, tallow.

greasy *adj* oily, fatty, lardy, buttery, smeary, slimy, slippery, smooth, waxy.

great *adj* **1** LARGE, big, huge, enormous, massive, colossal, gigantic, mammoth, immense, vast, impressive. **2** *with great care*: considerable, pronounced, extreme, excessive, inordinate. **3** FAMOUS, renowned, celebrated, illustrious, eminent, distinguished, prominent, noteworthy, notable, remarkable, outstanding, grand, glorious, fine. **4** IMPORTANT, significant, serious, major, principal, primary, main, chief, leading. **5** (*infml*) EXCELLENT, first-rate, superb, wonderful, marvellous, tremendous, terrific, fantastic, fabulous.
≠ **1** small. **2** slight. **3** unknown. **4** unimportant, insignificant.

greed *n* **1** HUNGER, ravenousness, gluttony, gourmandism, voracity, insatiability. **2** ACQUISITIVENESS, covetousness, desire, craving, longing, eagerness, avarice, selfishness.
≠ **1** abstemiousness, self-restraint.

greedy *adj* **1** HUNGRY, starving, ravenous, gluttonous, gormandizing, voracious, insatiable. **2** ACQUISITIVE, covetous, desirous, craving, eager, impatient, avaricious, grasping, selfish.
≠ **1** abstemious.

green *adj* **1** GRASSY, leafy, verdant, unripe, unseasoned, tender, fresh, budding, blooming, flourishing. **2** *green with envy*: envious, covetous, jealous, resentful. **3** IMMATURE, naïve, unsophisticated, ignorant, inexperienced, untrained, raw, new, recent, young. **4** ECOLOGICAL, environmental, eco-friendly, environmentally aware.
n common, lawn, grass, turf.

greenhouse *n* glasshouse, hothouse, conservatory, pavilion, vinery, orangery.

greet *v* hail, salute, acknowledge, address, accost, meet, receive, welcome.
≠ ignore.

greeting *n* salutation, acknowledgement, wave, hallo, the time of day, address, reception, welcome.

greetings *n* regards, respects, compliments, salutations, best wishes, good wishes, love.

gregarious *adj* sociable, outgoing, extrovert, friendly, affable, social, convivial, cordial, warm.
≠ unsociable.

grey *adj* **1** NEUTRAL, colourless, pale, ashen, leaden, dull, cloudy, overcast, dim, dark, murky. **2** GLOOMY, dismal, cheerless, depressing, dreary, bleak.

grief *n* sorrow, sadness, unhappiness, depression, dejection, desolation, distress, misery, woe, heartbreak, mourning, bereavement, heartache, anguish, agony, pain, suffering, affliction, trouble, regret, remorse.
≠ happiness, delight.

grievance *n* complaint, moan (*infml*), grumble (*infml*), resentment, objection, protest, charge, wrong, injustice, injury, damage, trouble, affliction, hardship, trial, tribulation.

grieve *v* **1** SORROW, mope, lament, mourn, wail, cry, weep. **2** SADDEN, upset, dismay, distress, afflict, pain, hurt, wound.
≠ **1** rejoice. **2** please, gladden.

grim *adj* **1** UNPLEASANT, horrible, horrid, ghastly, gruesome, grisly, sinister, frightening, fearsome, terrible, shocking. **2** STERN, severe, harsh, dour, forbidding, surly, sullen, morose gloomy, depressing, unattractive.
≠ **1** pleasant. **2** attractive.

grimace *n* frown, scowl, pout, smirk, sneer, face.
v make a face, pull a face, frown, scowl, pout, smirk, sneer.

grime *n* dirt, muck, filth, soot, dust.

grimy *adj* dirty, mucky, grubby, soiled filthy, sooty, smutty, dusty, smudgy.
≠ clean.

grind *v* crush, pound, pulverize, powder, mill, grate, scrape, gnash, rub abrade, sand, file, smooth, polish, sharpen, whet.

grip *n* hold, grasp, clasp, embrace, clutches, control, power.
v **1** HOLD, grasp, clasp, clutch, seize, grab, catch. **2** FASCINATE, thrill, enthral, spellbind, mesmerize, hypnotize, rivet, engross, absorb, involve, engage, compel.

grisly *adj* gruesome, gory, grim, macabre, horrid, horrible, ghastly, awful, frightful, terrible, dreadful, abominable, appalling, shocking.
≠ delightful.

grit *n* gravel, pebbles, shingle, sand, dust.
v clench, gnash, grate, grind.

groan *n* moan, sigh, cry, whine, wail, lament, complaint, objection, protest, outcry.
≠ cheer.
v moan, sigh, cry, whine, wail, lament, complain, object, protest.
≠ cheer.

groom *v* **1** SMARTEN, neaten, tidy, spruce up, clean, brush, curry, preen, dress. **2** *groomed for her new post*: PREPARE, train, school, educate, drill.

groove *n* furrow, rut, track, slot, channel, gutter, trench, hollow, indentation, score.
≠ ridge.

grope *v* feel, fumble, scrabble, flounder, cast about, fish, search, probe.

gross *adj* **1** *gross misconduct*: serious, grievous, blatant, flagrant, glaring, obvious, plain, sheer, utter, outright, shameful, shocking. **2** OBSCENE, lewd, improper, indecent, offensive, rude, coarse, crude, vulgar, tasteless. **3** FAT, obese, overweight, big, large, huge, colossal, hulking, bulky, heavy. **4** *gross earnings*: inclusive, all-inclusive, total, aggregate, entire, complete, whole.
≠ **3** slight. **4** net.

grotesque *adj* bizarre, odd, weird, unnatural, freakish, monstrous, hideous, ugly, unsightly, misshapen, deformed, distorted, twisted, fantastic, fanciful, extravagant, absurd, surreal, macabre.
≠ normal, graceful.

ground *n* **1** BOTTOM, foundation, surface, land, terrain, dry land, terra firma, earth, soil, clay, loam, dirt, dust. **2** *football ground*: field, pitch, stadium, arena, park.
v **1** BASE, found, establish, set, fix, settle. **2** PREPARE, introduce, initiate, familiarize with, acquaint with, inform, instruct, teach, train, drill, coach, tutor.

groundless *adj* baseless, unfounded, unsubstantiated, unsupported, empty, imaginary, false, unjustified, unwarranted, unprovoked, uncalled-for.
≠ well-founded, reasonable, justified.

grounds[1] *n* land, terrain, holding, estate, property, territory, domain, gardens, park, campus, surroundings, fields, acres.

grounds[2] *n* base, foundation, justification, excuse, vindication, reason, motive, inducement, cause, occasion, call, score, account, argument, principle, basis.

group *n* band, gang, pack, team, crew, troop, squad, detachment, party, faction, set, circle, clique, club, society, association, organization, company, gathering, congregation, crowd, collection, bunch, clump, cluster, conglomeration, constellation, batch, lot, combination, formation, grouping, class, classification, category, genus, species.
v **1** GATHER, collect, assemble, congregate, mass, cluster, clump, bunch. **2** *group them according to size*: sort, range, arrange, marshal, organize, order, class, classify, categorize, band, link, associate.

grovel *v* crawl, creep, ingratiate oneself, toady, suck up (*sl*), flatter, fawn, cringe, cower, kowtow, defer, demean oneself.

grow *v* **1** INCREASE, rise, expand, enlarge, swell, spread, extend, stretch, develop, proliferate, mushroom. **2** ORIGINATE, arise, issue, spring, germinate, shoot, sprout, bud, flower, mature, develop, progress, thrive, flourish, prosper. **3** CULTIVATE, farm, produce, propagate, breed, raise. **4** *grow cold*: become, get, go, turn.
≠ **1** decrease, shrink.

growl *v* snarl, snap, yap, rumble, roar.

grown-up *adj* adult, mature, of age, full-grown, fully-fledged.
≠ young, immature.
n adult, man, woman.
≠ child.

growth *n* **1** INCREASE, rise, extension, enlargement, expansion, spread, proliferation, development, evolution, progress, advance, improvement, success, prosperity. **2** TUMOUR, lump, swelling, protuberance, outgrowth.
≠ **1** decrease, decline, failure.

grub *v* dig, burrow, delve, probe, root, rummage, forage, ferret, hunt, search, scour, explore.
n maggot, worm, larva, pupa, caterpillar, chrysalis.

grubby *adj* dirty, soiled, unwashed,

mucky, grimy, filthy, squalid, seedy, scruffy.
≠ clean.

grudge *n* resentment, bitterness, envy, jealousy, spite, malice, enmity, antagonism, hate, dislike, animosity, ill-will, hard feelings, grievance.
≠ favour.
v begrudge, resent, envy, covet, dislike, take exception to, object to, mind.

grudging *adj* reluctant, unwilling, hesitant, half-hearted, unenthusiastic, resentful, envious, jealous.

gruelling *adj* hard, difficult, taxing, demanding, tiring, exhausting, laborious, arduous, strenuous, backbreaking, harsh, severe, tough, punishing.
≠ easy.

gruesome *adj* horrible, disgusting, repellent, repugnant, repulsive, hideous, grisly, macabre, grim, ghastly, awful, terrible, horrific, shocking, monstrous, abominable.
≠ pleasant.

gruff *adj* **1** CURT, brusque, abrupt, blunt, rude, surly, sullen, grumpy, bad-tempered. **2** *a gruff voice*: rough, harsh, rasping, guttural, throaty, husky, hoarse.
≠ **1** friendly, courteous.

grumble *v* complain, moan, whine, bleat, grouch, gripe, mutter, murmur, carp, find fault.

grumpy *adj* bad-tempered, ill-tempered, crotchety, crabbed, cantankerous, cross, irritable, surly, sullen, sulky, grouchy, discontented.
≠ contented.

guarantee *n* warranty, insurance, assurance, promise, word of honour, pledge, oath, bond, security, collateral, surety, endorsement, testimonial.
v assure, promise, pledge, swear, vouch for, answer for, warrant, certify, underwrite, endorse, secure, protect, insure, ensure, make sure, make certain.

guard *v* protect, safeguard, save, preserve, shield, screen, shelter, cover, defend, patrol, police, escort, supervise, oversee, watch, look out, mind, beware.
n **1** PROTECTOR, defender, custodian, warder, escort, bodyguard, minder (*sl*), watchman, lookout, sentry, picket, patrol, security. **2** PROTECTION, safeguard, defence, wall, barrier, screen, shield, bumper, buffer, pad.

guarded *adj* cautious, wary, careful, watchful, discreet, non-committal, reticent, reserved, secretive, cagey (*infml*).
≠ communicative, frank.

guardian *n* trustee, curator, custodian, keeper, warden, protector, preserver, defender, champion, guard, warder, escort, attendant.

guess *v* speculate, conjecture, predict, estimate, judge, reckon, work out, suppose, assume, surmise, think, believe, imagine, fancy, feel, suspect.
n prediction, estimate, speculation, conjecture, supposition, assumption, belief, fancy, idea, notion, theory, hypothesis, opinion, feeling, suspicion, intuition.

guesswork *n* speculation, conjecture, estimation, reckoning, supposition, assumption, surmise, intuition.

guest *n* visitor, caller, boarder, lodger, resident, patron, regular.

guidance *n* leadership, direction, management, control, teaching, instruction, advice, counsel, counselling, help, instructions, directions, guidelines, indications, pointers, recommendations.

guide *v* lead, conduct, direct, navigate, point, steer, pilot, manoeuvre, usher, escort, accompany, attend, control, govern, manage, oversee, supervise, superintend, advise, counsel, influence, educate, teach, instruct, train.
n **1** LEADER, courier, navigator, pilot helmsman, steersman, usher, escort, chaperon, attendant, companion, adviser, counsellor, mentor, guru, teacher, instructor. **2** MANUAL, handbook, guidebook, catalogue, directory. **3** GUIDELINE, example, model, standard, criterion, indication, pointer, signpost, sign, marker.

uilt *n* **1** *he confessed his guilt*: culpability, responsibility, blame, disgrace, dishonour. **2** *a feeling of guilt*: guilty conscience, conscience, shame, self-condemnation, self-reproach, regret, remorse, contrition.
≠ **1** innocence, righteousness. **2** shamelessness.

uilty *adj* **1** CULPABLE, responsible, blamable, blameworthy, offending, wrong, sinful, wicked, criminal, convicted. **2** CONSCIENCE-STRICKEN, ashamed, shamefaced, sheepish, sorry, regretful, remorseful, contrite, penitent, repentant.
≠ **1** innocent, guiltless, blameless. **2** shameless.

ulf *n* bay, bight, basin, gap, opening, separation, rift, split, breach, cleft, chasm, gorge, abyss, void.

ullible *adj* credulous, suggestible, impressionable, trusting, unsuspecting, foolish, naïve, green, unsophisticated, innocent.
≠ astute.

ully *n* channel, watercourse, gutter, ditch, ravine.

ulp *v* swallow, swig, swill, knock back (*infml*), bolt, wolf (*infml*), gobble, guzzle, devour, stuff.
≠ sip, nibble.
n swallow, swig, draught, mouthful.

um *n* adhesive, glue, paste, cement.
v stick, glue, paste, fix, cement, seal, clog.

un *n* firearm, handgun, pistol, revolver, shooter (*sl*), shooting iron (*sl*), rifle, shotgun, bazooka, howitzer, cannon.

gurgle *v* bubble, babble, burble, murmur, ripple, lap, splash, crow.
n babble, murmur, ripple.

gush *v* **1** FLOW, run, pour, stream, cascade, flood, rush, burst, spurt, spout, jet. **2** ENTHUSE, chatter, babble, jabber, go on (*infml*), drivel.
n flow, outflow, stream, torrent, cascade, flood, tide, rush, burst, outburst, spurt, spout, jet.

gust *n* blast, burst, rush, flurry, blow, puff, breeze, wind, gale, squall.

gusto *n* zest, relish, appreciation, enjoyment, pleasure, delight, enthusiasm, exuberance, élan, verve, zeal.
≠ distaste, apathy.

gut *v* **1** *gut fish*: disembowel, draw, clean (out). **2** STRIP, clear, empty, rifle, ransack, plunder, loot, sack, ravage.

guts *n* **1** INTESTINES, bowels, viscera, entrails, insides, innards (*infml*), belly, stomach. **2** (*infml*) COURAGE, bravery, pluck, grit, nerve, mettle.

gutter *n* drain, sluice, ditch, trench, trough, channel, duct, conduit, passage, pipe, tube.

guy (*infml*) *n* fellow, bloke (*infml*), chap (*infml*), man, boy, youth, person, individual.

gypsy, gipsy *n* Romany, traveller, wanderer, nomad, tinker.

gyrate *v* turn, revolve, rotate, twirl, pirouette, spin, whirl, wheel, circle, spiral.

H

habit *n* custom, usage, practice, routine, rule, second nature, way, manner, mode, wont, inclination, tendency, bent, mannerism, quirk, addiction, dependence, fixation, obsession, weakness.

habitat *n* home, abode, domain, element, environment, surroundings, locality, territory, terrain.

habitual *adj* **1** CUSTOMARY, traditional, wonted, routine, usual, ordinary, common, natural, normal, standard, regular, recurrent, fixed, established, familiar. **2** *habitual drinker*: confirmed, inveterate, hardened, addicted, dependent, persistent.
≠ **1** occasional, infrequent.

hack[1] *v* cut, chop, hew, notch, gash, slash, lacerate, mutilate, mangle.

hack[2] *n* scribbler, journalist, drudge, slave.

hackneyed *adj* stale, overworked, tired, worn-out, time-worn, threadbare, unoriginal, corny (*infml*), clichéed, stereotyped, stock, banal, trite, commonplace, common, pedestrian, uninspired.
≠ original, new, fresh.

hag *n* crone, witch, battle-axe (*infml*), shrew, termagant, vixen.

haggard *adj* drawn, gaunt, careworn, thin, wasted, shrunken, pinched, pale, wan, ghastly.
≠ hale.

haggle *v* bargain, negotiate, barter, wrangle, squabble, bicker, quarrel, dispute.

hail[1] *n* barrage, bombardment, volley, torrent, shower, rain, storm.
v pelt, bombard, shower, rain, batter, attack, assail.

hail[2] *v* greet, address, acknowledge, salute, wave, signal to, flag down, shout, call, acclaim, cheer, applaud, honour, welcome.

hair *n* locks, tresses, shock, mop, mar

hairdresser *n* hairstylist, stylist, barber, coiffeur, coiffeuse.

hairless *adj* bald, bald-headed, shorn, tonsured, shaven, clean-shaven, beardless.
≠ hairy, hirsute.

hair-raising *adj* frightening, scary, terrifying, horrifying, shocking, bloodcurdling, spine-chilling, eerie, alarming, startling, thrilling.

hairstyle *n* style, coiffure, hairdo (*infml*), cut, haircut, set.

> *Hairstyles include*: Afro, backcombed, bangs, beehive, bob, bouffant, braid, bun, chignon, corn rows, cowlick, crewcut, crimped, crop, curled, dreadlocks, Eton crop French pleat, fringe, frizette, marcel wave, mohican, pageboy, perm, pigtail, plait, pompadour, ponytail, pouffe, quiff, ringlets, shingle, short back and sides, sideboards, sideburns, skinhead, tonsure, topknot, undercut; hair-piece, toupee, wig.

hairy *adj* hirsute, bearded, shaggy, bushy, fuzzy, furry, woolly.
≠ bald, clean-shaven.

half *n* fifty per cent, bisection, hemisphere, semicircle, section, segment, portion, share, fraction.
adj semi-, halved, divided, fractional, part, partial, incomplete, moderate, limited.
≠ whole.
adv partly, partially, incompletely, moderately, slightly.
≠ completely.

half-hearted *adj* lukewarm, cool, weak, feeble, passive, apathetic, uninterested, indifferent, neutral.
≠ whole-hearted, enthusiastic.

halfway *adv* midway, in the middle, centrally.
adj middle, central, equidistant, mid, midway, intermediate.

hall *n* hallway, corridor, passage, passageway, entrance-hall, foyer, vestibule, lobby, concert-hall, auditorium, chamber, assembly room.

hallmark *n* stamp, mark, trademark, brand-name, sign, indication, symbol, emblem, device, badge.

hallucinate *v* dream, imagine, see things, daydream, fantasize, freak out (*sl*), trip (*sl*).

hallucination *n* illusion, mirage, vision, apparition, dream, daydream, fantasy, figment, delusion, freak-out (*sl*), trip (*sl*).

halt *v* stop, draw up, pull up, pause, wait, rest, break off, discontinue, cease, desist, quit, end, terminate, check, stem, curb, obstruct, impede.
≠ start, continue.
n stop, stoppage, arrest, interruption, break, pause, rest, standstill, end, close, termination.
≠ start, continuation.

halting *adj* hesitant, stuttering, stammering, faltering, stumbling, broken, imperfect, laboured, awkward.
≠ fluent.

halve *v* bisect, cut in half, split in two, divide, split, share, cut down, reduce, lessen.

hammer *v* hit, strike, beat, drum, bang, bash, pound, batter, knock, drive, shape, form, make.
n mallet, gavel.
hammer out settle, sort out, negotiate, thrash out, produce, bring about, accomplish, complete, finish.

hamper *v* hinder, impede, obstruct, slow down, hold up, frustrate, thwart, prevent, handicap, hamstring, shackle, cramp, restrict, curb, restrain.
≠ aid, facilitate.

hand *n* **1** FIST, palm, paw (*infml*), mitt (*sl*). **2** *give me a hand*: help, aid, assistance, support, participation, part, influence. **3** WORKER, employee, operative, workman, labourer, farm-hand, hireling.
v give, pass, offer, submit, present, yield, deliver, transmit, conduct, convey.
at hand near, close, to hand, handy, accessible, available, ready, imminent.
hand down bequeath, will, pass on, transfer, give, grant.
hand out distribute, deal out, give out, share out, dish out (*infml*), mete out, dispense.
hand over yield, relinquish, surrender, turn over, deliver, release, give, donate, present.
≠ keep, retain.

handbook *n* manual, instruction book, guide, guidebook, companion.

handful *n* few, sprinkling, scattering, smattering.
≠ a lot, many.

handicap *n* obstacle, block, barrier, impediment, stumbling-block, hindrance, drawback, disadvantage, restriction, limitation, penalty, disability, impairment, defect, shortcoming.
≠ assistance, advantage.
v impede, hinder, disadvantage, hold back, retard, hamper, burden, encumber, restrict, limit, disable.
≠ help, assist.

handicraft *n* craft, art, craftwork, handwork, handiwork.

handiwork *n* work, doing, responsibility, achievement, product, result, design, invention, creation, production, skill, workmanship, craftsmanship, artisanship.

handle *n* grip, handgrip, knob, stock, shaft, hilt.
v **1** TOUCH, finger, feel, fondle, pick up, hold, grasp. **2** *handle a situation*: tackle, treat, deal with, manage, cope with, control, supervise.

handout *n* **1** CHARITY, alms, dole, largess(e), share, issue, free sample, freebie (*sl*). **2** LEAFLET, circular, bulletin, statement, press release, literature.

hands *n* care, custody, possession, charge, authority, command, power, control, supervision.

handsome *adj* **1** GOOD-LOOKING, attractive, fair, personable, elegant. **2** GENEROUS, liberal, large, considerable, ample.
≠ **1** ugly, unattractive. **2** mean.

handwriting *n* writing, script, hand, fist (*infml*), penmanship, calligraphy.

handy *adj* **1** AVAILABLE, to hand, ready, at hand, near, accessible, convenient, practical, useful, helpful. **2** SKILFUL, proficient, expert, skilled, clever, practical.
≠ **1** inconvenient. **2** clumsy.

hang *v* **1** SUSPEND, dangle, swing, drape, drop, flop, droop, sag, trail. **2** FASTEN, attach, fix, stick. **3** *hang in the air*: float, drift, hover, linger, remain, cling.
hang about hang around, linger, loiter, dawdle, waste time, associate with, frequent, haunt.
hang back hold back, demur, hesitate, shy away, recoil.
hang on 1 WAIT, hold on, remain, hold out, endure, continue, carry on, persevere, persist. **2** GRIP, grasp, hold fast. **3** DEPEND ON, hinge on, turn on.
≠ **1** give up.

hanger-on *n* follower, minion, lackey, toady, sycophant, parasite, sponger, dependant.

hang-up *n* inhibition, difficulty, problem, obsession, preoccupation, thing (*infml*), block, mental block.

hanker for hanker after, crave, hunger for, thirst for, want, wish for, desire, covet, yearn for, long for, pine for, itch for.

hankering *n* craving, hunger, thirst, wish, desire, yearning, longing, itch, urge.

haphazard *adj* random, chance, casual, arbitrary, hit-or-miss, unsystematic, disorganized, disorderly, careless, slapdash, slipshod.
≠ methodical, orderly.

happen *v* occur, take place, arise, crop up, develop, materialize (*infml*), come about, result, ensue, follow, turn out, transpire.

happening *n* occurrence, phenomenon, event, incident, episode, occasion, adventure, experience, accident, chance, circumstance, case, affair.

happiness *n* joy, joyfulness, gladness, cheerfulness, contentment, pleasure, delight, glee, elation, bliss, ecstasy, euphoria.
≠ unhappiness, sadness.

happy *adj* **1** JOYFUL, jolly, merry, cheerful, glad, pleased, delighted, thrilled, elated, satisfied, content, contented. **2** *a happy coincidence*: lucky, fortunate, felicitous, favourable, appropriate, apt, fitting.
≠ **1** unhappy, sad, discontented. **2** unfortunate, inappropriate.

harangue *n* diatribe, tirade, lecture, speech, address.
v lecture, preach, hold forth, spout, declaim, address.

harass *v* pester, badger, harry, plague, torment, persecute, exasperate, vex, annoy, irritate, bother, disturb, hassle (*infml*), trouble, worry, stress, tire, wear out, exhaust, fatigue.

harbour *n* port, dock, quay, wharf, marina, mooring, anchorage, haven, shelter.
v **1** HIDE, conceal, protect, shelter. **2** *harbour a feeling*: hold, retain, cling to, entertain, foster, nurse, nurture, cherish, believe, imagine.

hard *adj* **1** SOLID, firm, unyielding, tough, strong, dense, impenetrable, stiff, rigid, inflexible. **2** DIFFICULT, arduous, strenuous, laborious, tiring, exhausting, backbreaking, complex, complicated, involved, knotty, baffling, puzzling, perplexing. **3** HARSH, severe, strict, callous, unfeeling, unsympathetic, cruel, pitiless, merciless, ruthless, unrelenting, distressing, painful, unpleasant.
≠ **1** soft, yielding. **2** easy, simple. **3** kind, pleasant.
adv industriously, diligently, assiduously, doggedly, steadily, laboriously, strenuously, earnestly, keenly, intently, strongly, violently, intensely, energetically, vigorously.
hard up poor, broke (*infml*), penniless, impoverished, in the red, bankrupt, bust, short, lacking.
≠ rich.

harden *v* solidify, set, freeze, bake, stiffen, strengthen, reinforce, fortify, buttress, brace, steel, nerve, toughen, season, accustom, train.
≠ soften, weaken.

hard-headed *adj* shrewd, astute, businesslike, level-headed, clear-thinking, sensible, realistic, pragmatic, practical, hard-boiled, tough, unsentimental.
≠ unrealistic.

hard-hearted *adj* callous, unfeeling, cold, hard, stony, heartless, unsympathetic, cruel, inhuman, pitiless, merciless.
≠ soft-hearted, kind, merciful.

hard-hitting *adj* condemnatory, critical, unsparing, no-holds-barred, vigorous, forceful, tough.
≠ mild.

hardly *adv* barely, scarcely, just, only just, not quite, not at all, by no means.

hardship *n* misfortune, adversity, trouble, difficulty, affliction, distress, suffering, trial, tribulation, want, need, privation, austerity, poverty, destitution, misery.
≠ ease, comfort, prosperity.

hard-wearing *adj* durable, lasting, strong, tough, sturdy, stout, rugged, resilient.
≠ delicate.

hard-working *adj* industrious, diligent, assiduous, conscientious, zealous, busy, energetic.
≠ idle, lazy.

hardy *adj* strong, tough, sturdy, robust, vigorous, fit, sound, healthy.
≠ weak, unhealthy.

harm *n* damage, loss, injury, hurt, detriment, ill, misfortune, wrong, abuse.
≠ benefit.
v damage, impair, blemish, spoil, mar, ruin, hurt, injure, wound, ill-treat, maltreat, abuse, misuse.
≠ benefit, improve.

harmful *adj* damaging, detrimental, pernicious, noxious, unhealthy, unwholesome, injurious, dangerous, hazardous, poisonous, toxic, destructive.
≠ harmless.

harmless *adj* safe, innocuous, non-toxic, inoffensive, gentle, innocent.
≠ harmful, dangerous, destructive.

harmonious *adj* **1** MELODIOUS, tuneful, musical, sweet-sounding. **2** MATCHING, co-ordinated, balanced, compatible, like-minded, agreeable, cordial, amicable, friendly, sympathetic.
≠ **1** discordant.

harmonize *v* match, co-ordinate, balance, fit in, suit, tone, blend, correspond, agree, reconcile, accommodate, adapt, arrange, compose.
≠ clash.

harmony *n* **1** TUNEFULNESS, tune, melody, euphony. **2** *live in harmony*: agreement, unanimity, accord, concord, unity, compatibility, like-mindedness, peace, goodwill, rapport, sympathy, understanding, amicability, friendliness, co-operation, co-ordination, balance, symmetry, correspondence, conformity.
≠ **1** discord. **2** conflict.

harness *n* tackle, gear, equipment, reins, straps, tack.
v control, channel, use, utilize, exploit, make use of, employ, mobilize, apply.

harrowing *adj* distressing, upsetting, heart-rending, disturbing, alarming, frightening, terrifying, nerve-racking, traumatic, agonizing, excruciating.

harry *v* badger, pester, nag, chivvy, harass, plague, torment, persecute, annoy, vex, worry, trouble, bother, hassle (*infml*), disturb, molest.

harsh *adj* **1** SEVERE, strict, Draconian, unfeeling, cruel, hard, pitiless, austere, Spartan, bleak, grim, comfortless. **2** *a harsh sound*: rough, coarse, rasping, croaking, guttural, grating, jarring, discordant, strident, raucous, sharp, shrill, unpleasant. **3** BRIGHT, dazzling, glaring, gaudy, lurid.
≠ **1** lenient. **2** soft.

harvest *n* **1** HARVEST-TIME,

ingathering, reaping, collection.
2 CROP, yield, return, produce, fruits, result, consequence.
v reap, mow, pick, gather, collect, accumulate, amass.

hash *n* mess, botch, muddle, mix-up, jumble, confusion, hotchpotch, mishmash.

haste *n* hurry, rush, hustle, bustle, speed, velocity, rapidity, swiftness, quickness, briskness, urgency, rashness, recklessness, impetuosity.
≠ slowness.

hasten *v* hurry, rush, make haste, run, sprint, dash, tear, race, fly, bolt, accelerate, speed (up), quicken, expedite, dispatch, precipitate, urge, press, advance, step up.
≠ dawdle, delay.

hasty *adj* hurried, rushed, impatient, headlong, rash, reckless, heedless, thoughtless, impetuous, impulsive, hot-headed, fast, quick, rapid, swift, speedy, brisk, prompt, short, brief, cursory.
≠ slow, careful, deliberate.

hats

Hats include: trilby, bowler, fedora, top-hat, Homburg, derby (*US*), pork-pie hat, flat-cap, beret, bonnet, Tam o'Shanter, tammy, deerstalker, hunting-cap, stovepipe hat, stetson, ten-gallon hat, boater, sunhat, panama, straw hat, picture-hat, pill-box, cloche, beanie (*US*), poke-bonnet, mob-cap, turban, fez, sombrero, sou'wester, glengarry, bearskin, busby, peaked cap, sailor-hat, baseball cap, balaclava, hood, snood, toque, helmet, mortar-board, skullcap, yarmulka, mitre, biretta.

hatch *v* **1** INCUBATE, brood, breed. **2** CONCOCT, formulate, originate, think up, dream up, conceive, devise, contrive, plot, scheme, design, plan, project.

hate *v* dislike, despise, detest, loathe, abhor, abominate, execrate.
≠ like, love.
n hatred, aversion, dislike, loathing, abhorrence, abomination.
≠ liking, love.

hatred *n* hate, aversion, dislike, detestation, loathing, repugnance, revulsion, abhorrence, abomination, execration, animosity, ill-will, antagonism, hostility, enmity, antipathy.
≠ liking, love.

haughty *adj* lofty, imperious, high and mighty, supercilious, cavalier, snooty (*infml*), contemptuous, disdainful, scornful, superior, snobbish, arrogant, proud, stuck-up (*infml*), conceited.
≠ humble, modest.

haul *v* pull, heave, tug, draw, tow, drag, trail, move, transport, convey, carry, cart, lug, hump (*infml*).
≠ push.
n LOOT, booty, plunder, swag (*sl*), spoils, takings, gain, yield, find.

haunt *v* **1** FREQUENT, patronize, visit. **2** *memories haunted her*: plague, torment, trouble, disturb, recur, prey on, beset, obsess, possess.
n resort, hangout (*infml*), stamping-ground, den, meeting-place, rendezvous.

haunting *adj* memorable, unforgettable, persistent, recurrent, evocative, nostalgic, poignant.
≠ unmemorable.

have *v* **1** OWN, possess, get, obtain, gain, acquire, procure, secure, receive, accept, keep, hold. **2** FEEL, experience, enjoy, suffer, undergo, endure, put up with. **3** CONTAIN, include, comprise, incorporate, consist of. **4** *have a baby*: give birth to, bear.
≠ **1** lack.
have to must, be forced, be compelled, be obliged, be required, ought, should.

haven *n* harbour, port, anchorage, shelter, refuge, sanctuary, asylum, retreat.

havoc *n* chaos, confusion, disorder, disruption, damage, destruction, ruin, wreck, rack and ruin, devastation, waste, desolation.

haywire (*infml*) *adj* wrong, tangled, out of control, crazy, mad, wild, chaotic, confused, disordered, disorganized, topsy-turvy.

hazard *n* risk, danger, peril, jeopardy

threat, death-trap, accident, chance.
≠ safety.
v **1** RISK, endanger, jeopardize, expose. **2** CHANCE, gamble, stake, venture, suggest, speculate.

hazardous *adj* risky, dangerous, unsafe, perilous, precarious, insecure, chancy, difficult, tricky.
≠ safe, secure.

haze *n* mist, fog, cloud, steam, vapour, film, mistiness, smokiness, dimness, obscurity.

hazy *adj* misty, foggy, smoky, clouded, cloudy, milky, fuzzy, blurred, ill-defined, veiled, obscure, dim, faint, unclear, indistinct, vague, indefinite, uncertain.
≠ clear, bright, definite.

head *n* **1** SKULL, cranium, brain, mind, mentality, brains (*infml*), intellect, intelligence, understanding, thought. **2** TOP, peak, summit, crown, tip, apex, height, climax, front, fore, lead. **3** LEADER, chief, captain, commander, boss, director, manager, superintendent, principal, head teacher, ruler.
≠ **1** foot, tail. **2** base, foot. **3** subordinate.
adj leading, front, foremost, first, chief, main, prime, principal, top, highest, supreme, premier, dominant, pre-eminent.
v lead, rule, govern, command, direct, manage, run, superintend, oversee, supervise, control, guide, steer.
head for make for, go towards, direct towards, aim for, point to, turn for, steer for.
head off forestall, intercept, intervene, interpose, deflect, divert, fend off, ward off, avert, prevent, stop.

heading *n* title, name, headline, rubric, caption, section, division, category, class.

headland *n* promontory, cape, head, point, foreland.

headlong *adj* hasty, precipitate, impetuous, impulsive, rash, reckless, dangerous, breakneck, head-first.
adv head first, hurriedly, hastily, precipitately, rashly, recklessly, heedlessly, thoughtlessly, wildly.

headquarters *n* HQ, base (camp), head office, nerve centre.

headstrong *adj* stubborn, obstinate, intractable, pigheaded, wilful, self-willed, perverse, contrary.
≠ tractable, docile.

headway *n* advance, progress, way, improvement.

heady *adj* intoxicating, strong, stimulating, exhilarating, thrilling, exciting.

heal *v* cure, remedy, mend, restore, treat, soothe, salve, settle, reconcile, patch up.

health *n* fitness, constitution, form, shape, trim, fettle, condition, tone, state, healthiness, good condition, wellbeing, welfare, soundness, robustness, strength, vigour.
≠ illness, infirmity.

healthy *adj* **1** WELL, fit, good, fine, in condition, in good shape, in fine fettle, sound, sturdy, robust, strong, vigorous, hale and hearty, blooming, flourishing, thriving. **2** *healthy food*: wholesome, nutritious, nourishing, bracing, invigorating, healthful.
≠ **1** ill, sick, infirm.

heap *n* pile, stack, mound, mountain, lot, mass, accumulation, collection, hoard, stockpile, store.
v pile, stack, mound, bank, build, amass, accumulate, collect, gather, hoard, stockpile, store, load, burden, shower, lavish.

hear *v* **1** LISTEN, catch, pick up, overhear, eavesdrop, heed, pay attention. **2** LEARN, find out, discover, ascertain, understand, gather. **3** JUDGE, try, examine, investigate.

hearing *n* **1** EARSHOT, sound, range, reach, ear, perception. **2** TRIAL, inquiry, investigation, inquest, audition, interview, audience.

hearsay *n* rumour, word of mouth, talk, gossip, tittle-tattle, report, buzz (*infml*).

heart *n* **1** SOUL, mind, character, disposition, nature, temperament, feeling, emotion, sentiment, love,

tenderness, compassion, sympathy, pity. **2** *lose heart*: courage, bravery, boldness, spirit, resolution, determination. **3** CENTRE, middle, core, kernel, nucleus, nub, crux, essence.
≠ **2** cowardice. **3** periphery.

by heart by rote, parrot-fashion, pat, off pat, word for word, verbatim.

Parts of the heart include: aortic valve, ascending aorta, bicuspid valve, carotid artery, descending thoracic aorta, inferior vena cava, left atrium, left pulmonary artery, left pulmonary veins, left ventricle, mitral valve, myocardium, papillary muscle, pulmonary valve, right atrium, right pulmonary artery, right pulmonary veins, right ventricle, superior vena cava, tricuspid valve, ventricular septum.

heartbreaking *adj* distressing, sad, tragic, harrowing, heart-rending, pitiful, agonizing, grievous, bitter, disappointing.
≠ heartwarming, heartening.

heartbroken *adj* broken-hearted, desolate, sad, miserable, dejected, despondent, downcast, crestfallen, disappointed, dispirited, grieved, crushed.
≠ delighted, elated.

hearten *v* comfort, console, reassure, cheer (up), buck up (*infml*), encourage, boost, inspire, stimulate, rouse, pep up (*infml*).
≠ dishearten, depress, dismay.

heartfelt *adj* deep, profound, sincere, honest, genuine, earnest, ardent, fervent, whole-hearted, warm.
≠ insincere, false.

heartless *adj* unfeeling, uncaring, cold, hard, hard-hearted, callous, unkind, cruel, inhuman, brutal, pitiless, merciless.
≠ kind, considerate, sympathetic, merciful.

heart-rending *adj* harrowing, heartbreaking, agonizing, pitiful, piteous, pathetic, tragic, sad, distressing, moving, affecting, poignant.

heartwarming *adj* pleasing, gratifying, satisfying, cheering, heartening, encouraging, touching, moving, affecting.
≠ heartbreaking.

hearty *adj* **1** ENTHUSIASTIC, whole-hearted, unreserved, heartfelt, sincere, genuine, warm, friendly, cordial, jovial, cheerful, ebullient, exuberant, boisterous, energetic, vigorous. **2** *a hearty breakfast*: large, sizable, substantial, filling, ample, generous.
≠ **1** half-hearted, cool, cold.

heat *n* **1** HOTNESS, warmth, sultriness, closeness, high temperature, fever. **2** ARDOUR, fervour, fieriness, passion, intensity, vehemence, fury, excitement, impetuosity, earnestness, zeal.
≠ **1** cold(ness). **2** coolness.
v warm, boil, toast, cook, bake, roast, reheat, warm up, inflame, excite, animate, rouse, stimulate, flush, glow.
≠ cool, chill.

heated *adj* angry, furious, raging, passionate, fiery, stormy, tempestuous, bitter, fierce, intense, vehement, violent, frenzied.
≠ calm.

heave *v* **1** PULL, haul, drag, tug, raise, lift, hitch, hoist, lever, rise, surge. **2** THROW, fling, hurl, cast, toss, chuck, let fly. **3** RETCH, vomit, throw up (*infml*), spew.

heaven *n* sky, firmament, next world, hereafter, after-life, paradise, utopia, ecstasy, rapture, bliss, happiness, joy.
≠ hell.

heavenly *adj* **1** BLISSFUL, wonderful, glorious, beautiful, lovely, delightful, out of this world. **2** CELESTIAL, unearthly, supernatural, spiritual, divine, godlike, angelic, immortal, sublime, blessed.
≠ **1** hellish. **2** infernal.

heavy *adj* **1** WEIGHTY, hefty, ponderous, burdensome, massive, large, bulky, solid, dense, stodgy. **2** *heavy work*: hard, difficult, tough, arduous, laborious, strenuous, demanding, taxing, harsh, severe. **3** OPPRESSIVE, intense, serious, dull, tedious.
≠ **1** light. **2** easy.

heavy-handed *adj* clumsy, awkward, unsubtle, tactless, insensitive, thoughtless, oppressive, overbearing, domineering, autocratic.

hectic *adj* busy, frantic, frenetic, chaotic, fast, feverish, excited, heated, furious, wild.
≠ leisurely.

hedge *n* hedgerow, screen, windbreak, barrier, fence, dike, boundary.
v **1** SURROUND, enclose, hem in, confine, restrict, fortify, guard, shield, protect, safeguard, cover. **2** STALL, temporize, equivocate, dodge, sidestep, evade, duck.

heed *v* listen, pay attention, mind, note, regard, observe, follow, obey.
≠ ignore, disregard.

heedless *adj* oblivious, unthinking, careless, negligent, rash, reckless, inattentive, unobservant, thoughtless, unconcerned.
≠ heedful, mindful, attentive.

hefty *adj* heavy, weighty, big, large, burly, hulking, beefy, brawny, strong, powerful, vigorous, robust, strapping, solid, substantial, massive, colossal, bulky, unwieldy.
≠ slight, small.

height *n* **1** HIGHNESS, altitude, elevation, tallness, loftiness, stature. **2** TOP, summit, peak, pinnacle, apex, crest, crown, zenith, apogee, culmination, climax, extremity, maximum, limit, ceiling.
≠ **1** depth.

heighten *v* raise, elevate, increase, add to, magnify, intensify, strengthen, sharpen, improve, enhance.
≠ lower, decrease, diminish.

hell *n* **1** *heaven and hell*: underworld, Hades, inferno, lower regions, nether world, abyss. **2** SUFFERING, anguish, agony, torment, ordeal, nightmare, misery.
≠ **1** heaven.

hellish *adj* INFERNAL, devilish, diabolical, fiendish, accursed, damnable, monstrous, abominable, atrocious, dreadful.
≠ heavenly.

helm *n* tiller, wheel, driving seat, reins, saddle, command, control, leadership, direction.

help *v* **1** AID, assist, lend a hand, serve, be of use, collaborate, co-operate, back, stand by, support. **2** IMPROVE, ameliorate, relieve, alleviate, mitigate, ease, facilitate.
≠ **1** hinder. **2** worsen.
n aid, assistance, collaboration, co-operation, support, advice, guidance, service, use, utility, avail, benefit.
≠ hindrance.

helper *n* assistant, deputy, auxiliary, subsidiary, attendant, right-hand man, PA, mate, partner, associate, colleague, collaborator, accomplice, ally, supporter, second.

helpful *adj* **1** USEFUL, practical, constructive, worthwhile, valuable, beneficial, advantageous. **2** *a helpful person*: co-operative, obliging, neighbourly, friendly, caring, considerate, kind, sympathetic, supportive.
≠ **1** useless, futile.

helping *n* serving, portion, share, ration, amount, plateful, piece, dollop (*infml*).

helpless *adj* weak, feeble, powerless, dependent, vulnerable, exposed, unprotected, defenceless, abandoned, friendless, destitute, forlorn, incapable, incompetent, infirm, disabled, paralysed.
≠ strong, independent, competent.

hem *n* edge, border, margin, fringe, trimming.
hem in surround, enclose, box in, confine, restrict.

henpecked *adj* dominated, subjugated, browbeaten, bullied, intimidated, meek, timid.
≠ dominant.

herald *n* messenger, courier, harbinger, forerunner, precursor, omen, token, signal, sign, indication.
v announce, proclaim, broadcast, advertise, publicize, trumpet, pave the way, precede, usher in, show, indicate, promise.

heraldry

Heraldic terms include: shield, crest, mantling, helmet, supporters, field, charge, compartment, motto, dexter, centre, sinister, annulet, fleur-de-lis, martlet, mullet, rampant, passant, sejant, caboched, statant, displayed, couchant, dormant, urinant, volant, chevron, pile, pall, saltire, quarter, orle, bordure, gyronny, lozenge, impale, escutcheon, antelope, camelopard, cockatrice, eagle, griffin, lion, phoenix, unicorn, wivern, addorsed, bezant, blazon, canton, cinquefoil, quatrefoil, roundel, semé, tierced, undee, urdé.

herbs and spices

Herbs and spices include: angelica, anise, basil, bay, bergamot, borage, camomile, catmint, chervil, chives, comfrey, cumin, dill, fennel, garlic, hyssop, lavender, lemon balm, lovage, marjoram, mint, oregano, parsley, rosemary, sage, savory, sorrel, tarragon, thyme; allspice, caper, caraway seeds, cardamon, cayenne pepper, chilli, cinnamon, cloves, coriander, curry, ginger, mace, mustard, nutmeg, paprika, pepper, saffron, sesame, turmeric, vanilla.

herd *n* drove, flock, swarm, pack, press, crush, mass, horde, throng, multitude, crowd, mob, the masses, rabble.
v **1** FLOCK, congregate, gather, collect, assemble, rally. **2** LEAD, guide, shepherd, round up, drive, force.

hereditary *adj* inherited, bequeathed, handed down, family, ancestral, inborn, inbred, innate, natural, congenital, genetic.

heresy *n* heterodoxy, unorthodoxy, free-thinking, apostasy, dissidence, schism, blasphemy.
≠ orthodoxy.

heretic *n* free-thinker, nonconformist, apostate, dissident, dissenter, revisionist, separatist, schismatic, sectarian, renegade.
≠ conformist.

heretical *adj* heterodox, unorthodox, free-thinking, rationalistic, schismatic, impious, irreverent, iconoclastic, blasphemous.
≠ orthodox, conventional, conformist.

heritage *n* **1** INHERITANCE, legacy, bequest, endowment, lot, portion, share, birthright, due. **2** HISTORY, past, tradition, culture.

hermit *n* recluse, solitary, monk, ascetic, anchorite.

hero *n* protagonist, lead, celebrity, star, superstar, idol, paragon, goody (*infml*), champion, conqueror.

heroic *adj* brave, courageous, fearless, dauntless, undaunted, lion-hearted, stout-hearted, valiant, bold, daring, intrepid, adventurous, gallant, chivalrous, noble, selfless.
≠ cowardly, timid.

heroism *n* bravery, courage, valour, boldness, daring, intrepidity, gallantry, prowess, selflessness.
≠ cowardice, timidity.

hesitant *adj* hesitating, reluctant, half-hearted, uncertain, unsure, indecisive, irresolute, vacillating, wavering, tentative, wary, shy, timid, halting, stammering, stuttering.
≠ decisive, resolute, confident, fluent.

hesitate *v* pause, delay, wait, be reluctant, be unwilling, think twice, hold back, shrink from, scruple, boggle, demur, vacillate, waver, be uncertain, dither, shilly-shally, falter, stumble, halt, stammer, stutter.
≠ decide.

hesitation *n* pause, delay, reluctance, unwillingness, hesitance, scruple(s), qualm(s), misgivings, doubt, second thoughts, vacillation, uncertainty, indecision, irresolution, faltering, stumbling, stammering, stuttering.
≠ eagerness, assurance.

hew *v* cut, fell, axe, lop, chop, hack, sever, split, carve, sculpt, sculpture, fashion, model, form, shape, make.

heyday *n* peak, prime, flush, bloom, flowering, golden age, boom time.

hidden *adj* **1** *a hidden door*: concealed, covered, shrouded, veiled, disguised,

camouflaged, unseen, secret. **2** OBSCURE, dark, occult, secret, covert, close, cryptic, mysterious, abstruse, mystical, latent, ulterior.
≠ **1** showing, apparent. **2** obvious.

hide[1] *v* **1** CONCEAL, cover, cloak, shroud, veil, screen, mask, disguise, camouflage, obscure, shadow, eclipse, bury, stash (*infml*), secrete, withhold, keep dark, suppress. **2** TAKE COVER, shelter, lie low, go to ground, hole up (*infml*).
≠ **1** reveal, show, display.

hide[2] *n* skin, pelt, fell, fur, leather.

hidebound *adj* set, rigid, entrenched, narrow-minded, strait-laced, conventional, ultra-conservative.
≠ liberal, progressive.

hideous *adj* ugly, repulsive, grotesque, monstrous, horrid, ghastly, awful, dreadful, frightful, terrible, grim, gruesome, macabre, terrifying, shocking, appalling, disgusting, revolting, horrible.
≠ beautiful, attractive.

hiding[1] *n* beating, flogging, whipping, caning, spanking, thrashing, walloping (*infml*).

hiding[2] *n* concealment, cover, veiling, screening, disguise, camouflage.

hiding-place *n* hide-away, hideout, lair, den, hole, hide, cover, refuge, haven, sanctuary, retreat.

hierarchy *n* pecking order, ranking, grading, scale, series, ladder, echelons, strata.

high *adj* **1** TALL, lofty, elevated, soaring, towering. **2** GREAT, strong, intense, extreme. **3** IMPORTANT, influential, powerful, eminent, distinguished, prominent, chief, leading, senior. **4** HIGH-PITCHED, soprano, treble, sharp, shrill, piercing. **5** *a high price*: expensive, dear, costly, exorbitant, excessive.
≠ **1** low, short. **3** lowly. **4** deep. **5** cheap.

high-born *adj* noble, aristocratic, blue-blooded, thoroughbred.
≠ low-born.

highbrow *n* intellectual, egghead (*infml*), scholar, academic.
adj intellectual, sophisticated, cultured, cultivated, academic, bookish, brainy (*infml*), deep, serious, classical.
≠ low-brow.

high-class *adj* upper-class, posh (*infml*), classy (*infml*), top-class, top-flight, high-quality, quality, de luxe, superior, excellent, first-rate, choice, select, exclusive.
≠ ordinary, mediocre.

high-flown *adj* florid, extravagant, exaggerated, elaborate, flamboyant, ostentatious, pretentious, high-sounding, grandiose, pompous, bombastic, turgid, artificial, stilted, affected, lofty, highfalutin, la-di-da (*infml*), supercilious.

high-handed *adj* overbearing, domineering, bossy (*infml*), imperious, dictatorial, autocratic, despotic, tyrannical, oppressive, arbitrary.

highlight *n* high point, high spot, peak, climax, best, cream.
v underline, emphasize, stress, accentuate, play up, point up, spotlight, illuminate, show up, set off, focus on, feature.

highly *adv* very, greatly, considerably, decidedly, extremely, immensely, tremendously, exceptionally, extraordinarily, enthusiastically, warmly, well.

highly-strung *adj* sensitive, neurotic, nervy, jumpy, edgy, temperamental, excitable, restless, nervous, tense.
≠ calm.

high-minded *adj* lofty, noble, moral, ethical, principled, idealistic, virtuous, upright, righteous, honourable, worthy.
≠ immoral, unscrupulous.

high-powered *adj* powerful, forceful, driving, aggressive, dynamic, go-ahead, enterprising, energetic, vigorous.

high-spirited *adj* boisterous, bouncy, exuberant, effervescent, frolicsome, ebullient, sparkling, vibrant, vivacious, lively, energetic, spirited, dashing, bold, daring.
≠ quiet, sedate.

hijack *v* commandeer, expropriate, skyjack, seize, take over.

hike *v* ramble, walk, trek, tramp, trudge, plod.
n ramble, walk, trek, tramp, march.

hilarious *adj* funny, amusing, comical, side-splitting, hysterical (*infml*), uproarious, noisy, rollicking, merry, jolly, jovial.
≠ serious, grave.

hilarity *n* mirth, laughter, fun, amusement, levity, frivolity, merriment, jollity, conviviality, high spirits, boisterousness, exuberance, exhilaration.
≠ seriousness, gravity.

hill *n* **1** HILLOCK, knoll, mound, prominence, eminence, elevation, foothill, down, fell, mountain, height. **2** *a steep hill*: slope, incline, gradient, ramp, rise, ascent, acclivity, drop, descent, declivity.

hinder *v* hamper, obstruct, impede, encumber, handicap, hamstring, hold up, delay, retard, slow down, hold back, check, curb, stop, prevent, frustrate, thwart, oppose.
≠ help, aid, assist.

hindrance *n* obstruction, impediment, handicap, encumbrance, obstacle, stumbling-block, barrier, bar, check, restraint, restriction, limitation, difficulty, drag, snag, hitch, drawback, disadvantage, inconvenience, deterrent.
≠ help, aid, assistance.

hinge *v* centre, turn, revolve, pivot, hang, depend, rest.

hint *n* **1** TIP, advice, suggestion, help, clue, inkling, suspicion, tip-off, reminder, indication, sign, pointer, mention, allusion, intimation, insinuation, implication, innuendo. **2** *a hint of garlic*: touch, trace, tinge, taste, dash, soupçon, speck.
v suggest, prompt, tip off, indicate, imply, insinuate, intimate, allude, mention.

hire *v* rent, let, lease, charter, commission, book, reserve, employ, take on, sign up, engage, appoint, retain.
≠ dismiss, fire.
n rent, rental, fee, charge, cost, price.

hiss *v* **1** WHISTLE, shrill, whizz, sizzle. **2** JEER, mock, ridicule, deride, boo, hoot.

historic *adj* momentous, consequential, important, significant, epoch-making, notable, remarkable, outstanding, extraordinary, celebrated, renowned, famed, famous.
≠ unimportant, insignificant, unknown.

historical *adj* real, actual, authentic, factual, documented, recorded, attested, verifiable.
≠ legendary, fictional.

history *n* **1** PAST, olden days, days of old, antiquity. **2** CHRONICLE, record, annals, archives, chronology, account, narrative, story, tale, saga, biography, life, autobiography, memoirs.

hit *v* **1** STRIKE, knock, tap, smack, slap, thrash, whack (*infml*), bash, thump, clout, punch, belt (*infml*), wallop (*infml*), beat, batter. **2** BUMP, collide with, bang, crash, smash, damage, harm.
n **1** STROKE, shot, blow, knock, tap, slap, smack, bash, bump, collision, impact, crash, smash. **2** SUCCESS, triumph, winner (*sl*).
≠ **2** failure.
hit back retaliate, reciprocate, counter-attack, strike back.
hit on chance on, stumble on, light on, discover, invent, realize, arrive at, guess.
hit out lash out, assail, attack, rail, denounce, condemn, criticize.

hitch *v* **1** FASTEN, attach, tie, harness, yoke, couple, connect, join, unite. **2** PULL, heave, yank (*infml*), tug, jerk, hoist, hike (up) (*infml*).
≠ **1** unhitch, unfasten.
n delay, hold-up, trouble, problem, difficulty, mishap, setback, hiccup, drawback, snag, catch, impediment, hindrance.

hoard *n* collection, accumulation, mass, heap, pile, fund, reservoir, supply, reserve, store, stockpile, cache, treasure-trove.
v collect, gather, amass, accumulate, save, put by, lay up, store, stash away

(*infml*), stockpile, keep, treasure.
≠ use, spend, squander.

hoarse *adj* husky, croaky, throaty, guttural, gravelly, gruff, growling, rough, harsh, rasping, grating, raucous, discordant.
≠ clear, smooth.

hoax *n* trick, prank, practical joke, put-on, joke, leg-pull (*infml*), spoof, fake, fraud, deception, bluff, humbug, cheat, swindle, con (*infml*).
v trick, deceive, take in, fool, dupe, gull, delude, have on (*infml*), pull someone's leg (*infml*), con (*infml*), swindle, take for a ride (*infml*), cheat, hoodwink, bamboozle (*infml*), bluff.

hobble *v* limp, stumble, falter, stagger, totter, dodder, shuffle.

hobby *n* pastime, diversion, recreation, relaxation, pursuit, sideline.

hoist *v* lift, elevate, raise, erect, jack up, winch up, heave, rear, uplift.
n jack, winch, crane, tackle, lift, elevator.

hold *v* **1** GRIP, grasp, clutch, clasp, embrace, have, own, possess, keep, retain. **2** *hold a meeting*: conduct, carry on, continue, call, summon, convene, assemble. **3** CONSIDER, regard, deem, judge, reckon, think, believe, maintain. **4** BEAR, support, sustain, carry, comprise, contain, accommodate. **5** IMPRISON, detain, stop, arrest, check, curb, restrain. **6** CLING, stick, adhere, stay.
≠ **1** drop. **5** release, free, liberate.
n **1** GRIP, grasp, clasp, embrace. **2** INFLUENCE, power, sway, mastery, dominance, authority, control, leverage.
hold back **1** CONTROL, curb, check, restrain, suppress, stifle, retain, withhold, repress, inhibit. **2** HESITATE, delay, desist, refrain, shrink, refuse.
≠ **1** release.
hold forth speak, talk, lecture, discourse, orate, preach, declaim.
hold off **1** FEND OFF, ward off, stave off, keep off, repel, rebuff. **2** PUT OFF, postpone, defer, delay, wait.
hold out **1** OFFER, give, present, extend. **2** LAST, continue, persist, endure, persevere, stand fast, hang on.
≠ **2** give in, yield.
hold up **1** SUPPORT, sustain, brace, shore up, lift, raise. **2** DELAY, detain, retard, slow, hinder, impede.
hold with agree with, go along with, approve of, countenance, support, subscribe to, accept.

holder *n* **1** *holders of British passports*: bearer, owner, possessor, proprietor, keeper, custodian, occupant, incumbent. **2** CONTAINER, receptacle, case, housing, cover, sheath, rest, stand.

hold-up *n* **1** DELAY, wait, hitch, setback, snag, difficulty, trouble, obstruction, stoppage, (traffic) jam, bottle-neck. **2** ROBBERY, heist (*sl*), stick-up (*sl*).

hole *n* aperture, opening, orifice, pore, puncture, perforation, eyelet, tear, split, vent, outlet, shaft, slot, gap, breach, break, crack, fissure, fault, defect, flaw, dent, dimple, depression, hollow, cavity, crater, pit, excavation, cavern, cave, chamber, pocket, niche, recess, burrow, nest, lair, retreat.

holiday *n* vacation, recess, leave, time off, day off, break, rest, half-term, bank-holiday, feast-day, festival, celebration, anniversary.

holiness *n* sacredness, sanctity, spirituality, divinity, piety, devoutness, godliness, saintliness, virtuousness, righteousness, purity.
≠ impiety.

hollow *adj* **1** CONCAVE, indented, depressed, sunken, deep, cavernous, empty, vacant, unfilled. **2** FALSE, artificial, deceptive, insincere, meaningless, empty, vain, futile, fruitless, worthless.
≠ **1** solid. **2** real.
n hole, pit, well, cavity, crater, excavation, cavern, cave, depression, concavity, basin, bowl, cup, dimple, dent, indentation, groove, channel, trough, valley.
v dig, excavate, burrow, tunnel, scoop, gouge, channel, groove, furrow, pit, dent, indent.

holy *adj* **1** *holy ground*: sacred,

hallowed, consecrated, sanctified, dedicated, blessed, venerated, revered, spiritual, divine, evangelical. **2** PIOUS, religious, devout, godly, God-fearing, saintly, virtuous, good, righteous, faithful, pure, perfect.
≠ **1** unsanctified. **2** impious, irreligious.

homage *n* recognition, acknowledgement, tribute, honour, praise, adulation, admiration, regard, esteem, respect, deference, reverence, adoration, awe, veneration, worship, devotion.

home *n* residence, domicile, dwelling-place, abode, base, house, pied-à-terre, hearth, fireside, birthplace, home town, home ground, territory, habitat, element.
adj domestic, household, family, internal, local, national, inland.
≠ foreign, international.
at home 1 COMFORTABLE, relaxed, at ease. **2** FAMILIAR, knowledgeable, experienced, skilled.

homeland *n* native land, native country, fatherland, motherland.

homeless *adj* itinerant, travelling, nomadic, wandering, vagrant, rootless, unsettled, displaced, dispossessed, evicted, exiled, outcast, abandoned, forsaken, destitute, down-and-out.
n travellers, vagabonds, vagrants, tramps, down-and-outs, dossers (*sl*), squatters.

homely *adj* homelike, homey, comfortable, cosy, snug, relaxed, informal, friendly, intimate, familiar, everyday, ordinary, domestic, natural, plain, simple, modest, unassuming, unpretentious, unsophisticated, folksy, homespun.
≠ grand, formal.

homicide *n* murder, manslaughter, assassination, killing, bloodshed.

homogeneous *adj* uniform, consistent, unvarying, identical, similar, alike, akin, kindred, analogous, comparable, harmonious, compatible.
≠ different.

homosexual *n* gay, queer (*sl*), poof (*sl*), lesbian, dike (*sl*).
≠ heterosexual, straight (*sl*).
adj gay, queer (*sl*), lesbian.

hone *v* sharpen, whet, point, edge, grind, file, polish.

honest *adj* **1** TRUTHFUL, sincere, frank, candid, blunt, outspoken, direct, straight, outright, forthright, straightforward, plain, simple, open, above-board, legitimate, legal, lawful, on the level (*infml*), fair, just, impartial, objective. **2** LAW-ABIDING, virtuous, upright, ethical, moral, high-minded, scrupulous, honourable, reputable, respectable, reliable, trustworthy, true, genuine, real.
≠ **1** dishonest. **2** dishonourable.

honestly *adv* truly, really, truthfully, sincerely, frankly, directly, outright, plainly, openly, legitimately, legally, lawfully, on the level, fairly, justly, objectively, honourably, in good faith.
≠ dishonestly, dishonourably.

honesty *n* **1** TRUTHFULNESS, sincerity, frankness, candour, bluntness, outspokenness, straightforwardness, plain-speaking, explicitness, openness, legitimacy, legality, equity, fairness, justness, objectivity, even-handedness. **2** VIRTUE, uprightness, honour, integrity, morality, scrupulousness, trustworthiness, genuineness, veracity.
≠ **1** dishonesty.

honorary *adj* unpaid, unofficial, titular, nominal, in name only, honorific, formal.
≠ paid.

honour *n* **1** REPUTATION, good name, repute, renown, distinction, esteem, regard, respect, credit, dignity, self-respect, pride, integrity, morality, decency, rectitude, probity. **2** AWARD, accolade, commendation, acknowledgement, recognition, tribute, privilege. **3** PRAISE, acclaim, homage, admiration, reverence, worship, adoration.
≠ **1** dishonour, disgrace.
v **1** PRAISE, acclaim, exalt, glorify, pay homage to, decorate, crown, celebrate, commemorate, remember, admire, esteem, respect, revere,

worship, prize, value. **2** *honour a promise*: keep, observe, respect, fulfil, carry out, discharge, execute, perform.
≠ **1** dishonour, disgrace.

honourable *adj* great, eminent, distinguished, renowned, respected, worthy, prestigious, trusty, reputable, respectable, virtuous, upright, upstanding, straight, honest, trustworthy, true, sincere, noble, high-minded, principled, moral, ethical, fair, just, right, proper, decent.
≠ dishonourable, unworthy, dishonest.

hoodwink *v* deceive, dupe, fool, take in, delude, bamboozle (*infml*), have on (*infml*), mislead, hoax, trick, cheat, con (*infml*), rook, gull, swindle.

hook *n* crook, sickle, peg, barb, trap, snare, catch, fastener, clasp, hasp.
v **1** BEND, crook, curve, curl. **2** CATCH, capture, bag, grab, trap, snare, ensnare, entangle. **3** FASTEN, clasp, hitch, fix, secure.

hooligan *n* ruffian, rowdy, hoodlum, mobster, bovver boy (*sl*), thug, tough, lout, yob (*sl*), vandal, delinquent.

hoop *n* ring, circle, round, loop, wheel, band, girdle, circlet.

hoot *n, v* call, cry, shout, shriek, whoop, toot, beep, whistle, boo, jeer, laugh, howl.

hop *v* jump, leap, spring, bound, vault, skip, dance, prance, frisk, limp, hobble.
n jump, leap, spring, bound, vault, bounce, step, skip, dance.

hope *n* hopefulness, optimism, ambition, aspiration, wish, desire, longing, dream, expectation, anticipation, prospect, promise, belief, confidence, assurance, conviction, faith.
≠ pessimism, despair.
v aspire, wish, desire, long, expect, await, look forward, anticipate, contemplate, foresee, believe, trust, rely, reckon on, assume.
≠ despair.

hopeful *adj* **1** OPTIMISTIC, bullish (*infml*), confident, assured, expectant, sanguine, cheerful, buoyant. **2** *a hopeful sign*: encouraging, heartening, reassuring, favourable, auspicious, promising, rosy, bright.
≠ **1** pessimistic, despairing. **2** discouraging.

hopeless *adj* **1** PESSIMISTIC, defeatist, negative, despairing, demoralized, downhearted, dejected, despondent, forlorn, wretched. **2** UNATTAINABLE, unachievable, impracticable, impossible, vain, foolish, futile, useless, pointless, worthless, poor, helpless, lost, irremediable, irreparable, incurable.
≠ **1** hopeful, optimistic. **2** curable.

horde *n* band, gang, pack, herd, drove, flock, swarm, crowd, mob, throng, multitude, host.

horizon *n* skyline, vista, prospect, compass, range, scope, perspective.

horrible *adj* unpleasant, disagreeable, nasty, unkind, horrid, disgusting, revolting, offensive, repulsive, hideous, grim, ghastly, awful, dreadful, frightful, fearful, terrible, abominable, shocking, appalling, horrific.
≠ pleasant, agreeable, lovely, attractive.

horrific *adj* horrifying, shocking, appalling, awful, dreadful, ghastly, gruesome, terrifying, frightening, scary, harrowing, bloodcurdling.

horrify *v* shock, outrage, scandalize, appal, disgust, sicken, dismay, alarm, startle, scare, frighten, terrify.
≠ please, delight.

horror *n* **1** *recoil in horror*: shock, outrage, disgust, revulsion, repugnance, abhorrence, loathing, dismay, consternation, alarm, fright, fear, terror, panic, dread, apprehension. **2** GHASTLINESS, awfulness, frightfulness, hideousness.
≠ **1** approval, delight.

horses

Breeds of horse include: Akhal-Teké, Alter-Réal, American Quarter Horse, American Saddle Horse, American Trotter, Andalusian, Anglo-Arab, Anglo-Norman, Appaloosa, Arab, Ardennias, Auxois, Barb, Bavarian Warmblood, Boulonnais, Brabançon, Breton,

British Warmblood, Brumby, Budyonny, Calabrese, Charollais Halfbred, Cleveland Bay, Clydesdale, Comtois, Criollo, Danubian, Døle Gudbrandsdal, Døle Trotter, Don, Dutch Draught, East Bulgarian, East Friesian, Einsiedler, Finnish, Frederiksborg, Freiberger, French Saddle Horse, French Trotter, Friesian, Furioso, Gelderland, German Trotter, Groningen, Hanoverian, Hispano, Holstein, Iomud, Irish Draught, Irish Hunter, Italian Heavy Draught, Jutland, Kabardin, Karabair, Karabakh, Kladruber, Knabstrup, Kustanair, Latvian Harness Horse, Limousin Halfbred, Lipizzaner, Lithuanian Heavy Draught, Lokai, Lusitano, Mangalarga, Maremmana, Masuren, Mecklenburg, Metis Trotter, Morgan, Muraköz, Murgese, Mustang, New Kirgiz, Nonius, North Swedish, Oldenburg, Orlov Trotter, Palomino, Paso Fino, Percheron, Peruvian Stepping Horse, Pinto, Pinzgauer Noriker, Plateau Persian, Poitevin, Rhineland Heavy Draught, Russian Heavy Draught, Salerno, Sardinian, Shagya Arab, Shire, Suffolk Punch, Swedish Halfbred, Tchenaran, Tennessee Walking Horse, Tersky, Thoroughbred, Toric, Trait du Nord, Trakehner, Vladimir Heavy Draught, Waler, Welsh Cob, Württemberg.
Breeds of pony include: Connemara, Dales, Dartmoor, Exmoor, Falabella, Fell, Hackney, Highland, New Forest, Przewalski's Horse, Shetland, Welsh Mountain Pony, Welsh Pony.

horseman, horsewoman *n* equestrian, rider, jockey, cavalryman, hussar.

horseplay *n* clowning, buffoonery, foolery, tomfoolery, skylarking, pranks, capers, high jinks, fun and games, rough-and-tumble.

hospitable *adj* friendly, sociable, welcoming, receptive, cordial, amicable, congenial, convivial, genial, kind, gracious, generous, liberal.
≠ inhospitable, unfriendly, hostile.

hospitality *n* friendliness, sociability, welcome, accommodation, entertainment, conviviality, warmth, cheer, generosity, open-handedness.
≠ unfriendliness.

host[1] *n* **1** COMPÈRE, master of ceremonies, presenter, announcer, anchorman, anchorwoman, linkman. **2** PUBLICAN, innkeeper, landlord, proprietor.
v present, introduce, compère.

host[2] *n* multitude, myriad, array, army, horde, crowd, throng, swarm, pack, band.

hostage *n* prisoner, captive, pawn, surety, security, pledge.

hostel *n* youth hostel, residence, dosshouse (*sl*), boarding-house, guest-house, hotel, inn.

hostile *adj* belligerent, warlike, ill-disposed, unsympathetic, unfriendly, inhospitable, inimical, antagonistic, opposed, adverse, unfavourable, contrary, opposite.
≠ friendly, welcoming, favourable.

hostilities *n* war, warfare, battle, fighting, conflict, strife, bloodshed.

hostility *n* opposition, aggression, belligerence, enmity, estrangement, antagonism, animosity, ill-will, malice, resentment, hate, hatred, dislike, aversion, abhorrence.
≠ friendliness, friendship.

hot *adj* **1** WARM, heated, fiery, burning, scalding, blistering, scorching, roasting, baking, boiling, steaming, sizzling, sweltering, sultry, torrid, tropical. **2** SPICY, peppery, piquant, sharp, pungent, strong.
≠ **1** cold, cool. **2** mild.

hotchpotch *n* mishmash, medley, miscellany, collection, mix, mixture, jumble, confusion, mess.

hotel *n* boarding-house, guest-house, pension, motel, inn, public house, pub (*infml*), hostel.

hotheaded *adj* headstrong, impetuous, impulsive, hasty, rash, reckless, fiery, volatile, hot-tempered, quick-tempered.
≠ cool, calm.

hothouse *n* greenhouse, glasshouse,

conservatory, orangery, vinery.

hound *v* chase, pursue, hunt (down), drive, goad, prod, chivvy, nag, pester, badger, harry, harass, persecute.

house *n* **1** BUILDING, dwelling, residence, home. **2** DYNASTY, family, clan, tribe.

> *Types of house include*: semi-detached, semi (*infml*), detached, terraced, town-house, council house, cottage, thatched cottage, prefab (*infml*), pied-à-terre, bungalow, chalet bungalow; flat, bedsit, apartment, studio, maisonette, penthouse, granny flat, duplex (*US*), condominium (*US*); manor, hall, lodge, grange, villa, mansion, rectory, vicarage, parsonage, manse, croft, farmhouse, homestead, ranchhouse, chalet, log cabin, shack, shanty, hut, igloo, hacienda.

v **1** LODGE, quarter, billet, board, accommodate, put up, take in, shelter, harbour. **2** HOLD, contain, protect, cover, sheathe, place, keep, store.

household *n* family, family circle, house, home, ménage, establishment, set-up.
adj domestic, home, family, ordinary, plain, everyday, common, familiar, well-known, established.

householder *n* resident, tenant, occupier, occupant, owner, landlady, freeholder, leaseholder, proprietor, landlord, home-owner, head of the household.

housing *n* **1** ACCOMMODATION, houses, homes, dwellings, habitation, shelter. **2** CASING, case, container, holder, covering, cover, sheath, protection.

hovel *n* shack, shanty, cabin, hut, shed, dump, hole (*infml*).

hover *v* **1** HANG, poise, float, drift, fly, flutter, flap. **2** *he hovered by the door*: pause, linger, hang about, hesitate, waver, fluctuate, seesaw.

however *conj* nevertheless, nonetheless, still, yet, even so, notwithstanding, though, anyhow.

howl *n, v* wail, cry, shriek, scream, shout, yell, roar, bellow, bay, yelp, hoot, moan, groan.

hub *n* centre, middle, focus, focal point, axis, pivot, linchpin, nerve centre, core, heart.

hubbub *n* noise, racket, din, clamour, commotion, disturbance, riot, uproar, hullabaloo, rumpus, confusion, disorder, tumult, hurly-burly, chaos, pandemonium.
≠ peace, quiet.

huddle *n* **1** CLUSTER, clump, knot, mass, crowd, muddle, jumble. **2** CONCLAVE, conference, meeting.
v cluster, gravitate, converge, meet, gather, congregate, crowd, flock, throng, press, cuddle, snuggle, nestle, curl up, crouch, hunch.
≠ disperse.

hue *n* colour, shade, tint, dye, tinge, nuance, tone, complexion, aspect, light.

huff *n* pique, sulks, mood, bad mood, anger, rage, passion.

hug *v* embrace, cuddle, squeeze, enfold, hold, clasp, clutch, grip, cling to, enclose.
n embrace, cuddle, squeeze, clasp, hold, clinch.

huge *adj* immense, vast, enormous, massive, colossal, titanic, giant, gigantic, mammoth, monumental, tremendous, great, big, large, bulky, unwieldy.
≠ tiny, minute.

hulking *adj* massive, heavy, unwieldy, bulky, awkward, ungainly.
≠ small, delicate.

hull *n* body, frame, framework, structure, casing, covering.

hullabaloo *n* fuss, palaver, to-do (*infml*), outcry, furore, hue and cry, uproar, pandemonium, rumpus, disturbance, commotion, hubbub.
≠ calm, peace.

hum *v* buzz, whirr, purr, drone, thrum, croon, sing, murmur, mumble, throb, pulse, vibrate.
n buzz, whirr, purring, drone, murmur, mumble, throb, pulsation, vibration.

human *adj* **1** MORTAL, fallible,

susceptible, reasonable, rational. **2** KIND, considerate, understanding, humane, compassionate.
≠ **2** inhuman.
n human being, mortal, homo sapiens, man, woman, child, person, individual, body, soul.

humane *adj* kind, compassionate, sympathetic, understanding, kind-hearted, good-natured, gentle, tender, loving, mild, lenient, merciful, forgiving, forbearing, kindly, benevolent, charitable, humanitarian, good.
≠ inhumane, cruel.

humanitarian *adj* benevolent, charitable, philanthropic, public-spirited, compassionate, humane, altruistic, unselfish.
≠ selfish, self-seeking.
n philanthropist, benefactor, good Samaritan, do-gooder, altruist.
≠ egoist, self-seeker.

humanity *n* **1** HUMAN RACE, humankind, mankind, womankind, mortality, people. **2** HUMANENESS, kindness, compassion, fellow-feeling, understanding, tenderness, benevolence, generosity, goodwill.
≠ **2** inhumanity.

humanize *v* domesticate, tame, civilize, cultivate, educate, enlighten, edify, improve, better, polish, refine.

humble *adj* **1** MEEK, submissive, unassertive, self-effacing, polite, respectful, deferential, servile, subservient, sycophantic, obsequious. **2** LOWLY, low, mean, insignificant, unimportant, common, commonplace, ordinary, plain, simple, modest, unassuming, unpretentious, unostentatious.
≠ **1** proud, assertive. **2** important, pretentious.
v bring down, lower, bring low, abase, demean, sink, discredit, disgrace, shame, humiliate, mortify, chasten, crush, deflate, subdue.
≠ exalt.

humbug *n* **1** DECEPTION, pretence, sham, fraud, swindle, trick, hoax, deceit, trickery. **2** NONSENSE, rubbish, baloney (*sl*), bunkum (*infml*), claptrap (*infml*), eye-wash (*infml*), bluff, cant, hypocrisy.

humdrum *adj* boring, tedious, monotonous, routine, dull, dreary, uninteresting, uneventful, ordinary, mundane, everyday, commonplace.
≠ lively, unusual, exceptional.

humid *adj* damp, moist, dank, clammy, sticky, muggy, sultry, steamy.
≠ dry.

humiliate *v* mortify, embarrass, confound, crush, break, deflate, chasten, shame, disgrace, discredit, degrade, demean, humble, bring low.
≠ dignify, exalt.

humiliation *n* mortification, embarrassment, shame, disgrace, dishonour, ignominy, abasement, deflation, put-down, snub, rebuff, affront.
≠ gratification, triumph.

humility *n* meekness, submissiveness, deference, self-abasement, servility, humbleness, lowliness, modesty, unpretentiousness.
≠ pride, arrogance, assertiveness.

humorist *n* wit, satirist, comedian, comic, joker, wag, jester, clown.

humorous *adj* funny, amusing, comic, entertaining, witty, satirical, jocular, facetious, playful, waggish, droll, whimsical, comical, farcical, zany (*infml*), ludicrous, absurd, hilarious, side-splitting.
≠ serious, humourless.

humour *n* **1** WIT, drollery, jokes, jesting, badinage, repartee, facetiousness, satire, comedy, farce, fun, amusement. **2** *in a bad humour*: mood, temper, frame of mind, spirits, disposition, temperament.
v go along with, comply with, accommodate, gratify, indulge, pamper, spoil, favour, please, mollify, flatter.

humourless *adj* boring, tedious, dull, dry, solemn, serious, glum, morose.
≠ humorous, witty.

hump *n* hunch, lump, knob, bump, projection, protuberance, bulge, swelling, mound, prominence.

hunch *n* premonition, presentiment, intuition, suspicion, feeling, impression, idea, guess.
v hump, bend, curve, arch, stoop, crouch, squat, huddle, draw in, curl up.

hunger *n* **1** HUNGRINESS, emptiness, starvation, malnutrition, famine, appetite, ravenousness, voracity, greed, greediness. **2** *hunger for power*: desire, craving, longing, yearning, itch, thirst.
v starve, want, wish, desire, crave, hanker, long, yearn, pine, ache, itch, thirst.

hungry *adj* **1** STARVING, underfed, undernourished, peckish (*infml*), empty, hollow, famished, ravenous, greedy. **2** *hungry for knowledge*: desirous, craving, longing, aching, thirsty, eager, avid.
≠ **1** satisfied, full.

hunk *n* chunk, lump, piece, block, slab, wedge, mass, clod.

hunt *v* **1** CHASE, pursue, hound, dog, stalk, track, trail. **2** SEEK, look for, search, scour, rummage, forage, investigate.
n chase, pursuit, search, quest, investigation.

hurdle *n* jump, fence, wall, hedge, barrier, barricade, obstacle, obstruction, stumbling-block, hindrance, impediment, handicap, problem, snag, difficulty, complication.

hurl *v* throw, toss, fling, sling, catapult, project, propel, fire, launch, send.

hurricane *n* gale, tornado, typhoon, cyclone, whirlwind, squall, storm, tempest.

hurried *adj* rushed, hectic, hasty, precipitate, speedy, quick, swift, rapid, passing, brief, short, cursory, superficial, shallow, careless, slapdash.
≠ leisurely.

hurry *v* rush, dash, fly, get a move on (*infml*), hasten, quicken, speed up, hustle, push.
≠ slow down, delay.
n rush, haste, quickness, speed, urgency, hustle, bustle, flurry, commotion.
≠ leisureliness, calm.

hurt *v* **1** *my leg hurts*: ache, pain, throb, sting. **2** INJURE, wound, maltreat, ill-treat, bruise, cut, burn, torture, maim, disable. **3** DAMAGE, impair, harm, mar, spoil. **4** UPSET, sadden, grieve, distress, afflict, offend, annoy.
n pain, soreness, discomfort, suffering, injury, wound, damage, harm, distress, sorrow.
adj **1** INJURED, wounded, bruised, grazed, cut, scarred, maimed. **2** UPSET, sad, saddened, distressed, aggrieved, annoyed, offended, affronted.

hurtful *adj* **1** UPSETTING, wounding, vicious, cruel, mean, unkind, nasty, malicious, spiteful, catty, derogatory, scathing, cutting. **2** HARMFUL, damaging, injurious, pernicious, destructive.
≠ **1** kind.

hurtle *v* dash, tear, race, fly, shoot, speed, rush, charge, plunge, dive, crash, rattle.

husband *n* spouse, partner, mate, better half, hubby (*infml*), groom, married man.

hush *v* quieten, silence, still, settle, compose, calm, soothe, subdue.
≠ disturb, rouse.
n quietness, silence, peace, stillness, repose, calm, calmness, tranquillity, serenity.
≠ noise, clamour.
interj quiet, hold your tongue, shut up, not another word.
hush up keep dark, suppress, conceal, cover up, stifle, gag.
≠ publicize.

hush-hush *adj* secret, confidential, classified, restricted, under wraps (*infml*), top-secret.
≠ open, public.

husk *n* covering, case, shell, pod, hull, rind, bran, chaff.

husky *adj* hoarse, croaky, croaking, low, throaty, guttural, gruff, rasping, rough, harsh.

hustle *v* hasten, rush, hurry, bustle, force, push, shove, thrust, bundle, elbow, jostle.

hut *n* cabin, shack, shanty, booth, shed, lean-to, shelter, den.

hybrid *n* cross, crossbreed, half-breed, mongrel, composite, combination, mixture, amalgam, compound.
adj crossbred, mongrel, composite, combined, mixed, heterogeneous, compound.
≠ pure-bred.

hygiene *n* sanitariness, sanitation, sterility, disinfection, cleanliness, purity, wholesomeness.
≠ insanitariness.

hygienic *adj* sanitary, sterile, aseptic, germ-free, disinfected, clean, pure, salubrious, healthy, wholesome.
≠ unhygienic, insanitary.

hyperbole *n* overstatement, exaggeration, magnification, extravagance.
≠ understatement.

hypnotic *adj* mesmerizing, soporific, sleep-inducing, spellbinding, fascinating, compelling, irresistible, magnetic.

hypnotism *n* hypnosis, mesmerism, suggestion.

hypnotize *v* mesmerize, spellbind, bewitch, enchant, entrance, fascinate, captivate, magnetize.

hypocrisy *n* insincerity, double-talk, double-dealing, falsity, deceit, deception, pretence.
≠ sincerity.

hypocritical *adj* insincere, two-faced, self-righteous, double-dealing, false, hollow, deceptive, spurious, deceitful, dissembling, pharisaic(al).
≠ sincere, genuine.

hypothesis *n* theory, thesis, premise, postulate, proposition, supposition, conjecture, speculation.

hypothetical *adj* theoretical, imaginary, supposed, assumed, proposed, conjectural, speculative.
≠ real, actual.

hysteria *n* agitation, frenzy, panic, hysterics, neurosis, mania, madness.
≠ calm, composure.

hysterical *adj* **1** FRANTIC, frenzied, berserk, uncontrollable, mad, raving, crazed, demented, overwrought, neurotic. **2** (*infml*) HILARIOUS, uproarious, side-splitting, priceless (*infml*), rich (*infml*).
≠ **1** calm, composed, self-possessed.

I

ice *n* frost, rime, icicle, glacier, iciness, frostiness, coldness, chill.
v freeze, refrigerate, chill, cool, frost, glaze.

icon *n* idol, portrait, image, representation, symbol.

icy *adj* **1** ICE-COLD, arctic, polar, glacial, freezing, frozen, raw, bitter, biting, cold, chill, chilly. **2** *icy roads*: frosty, slippery, glassy, frozen, icebound, frostbound. **3** HOSTILE, cold, stony, cool, indifferent, aloof, distant, formal.
≠ **1** hot. **3** friendly, warm.

idea *n* **1** THOUGHT, concept, notion, theory, hypothesis, guess, conjecture, belief, opinion, view, viewpoint, judgement, conception, vision, image, impression, perception, interpretation, understanding, inkling, suspicion, clue. **2** *a good idea*: brainwave, suggestion, proposal, proposition, recommendation, plan, scheme, design. **3** AIM, intention, purpose, reason, point, object.

ideal *n* perfection, epitome, acme, paragon, exemplar, example, model, pattern, archetype, prototype, type, image, criterion, standard.
adj **1** PERFECT, dream, utopian, best, optimum, optimal, supreme, highest, model, archetypal. **2** UNREAL, imaginary, theoretical, hypothetical, unattainable, impractical, idealistic.

idealist *n* perfectionist, romantic, visionary, dreamer, optimist.
≠ realist, pragmatist.

idealistic *adj* perfectionist, utopian, visionary, romantic, quixotic, starry-eyed, optimistic, unrealistic, impractical, impracticable.
≠ realistic, pragmatic.

idealize *v* utopianize, romanticize, glamorize, glorify, exalt, worship, idolize.
≠ caricature.

identical *adj* same, self-same, indistinguishable, interchangeable, twin, duplicate, like, alike, corresponding, matching, equal, equivalent.
≠ different.

identification *n* **1** RECOGNITION, detection, diagnosis, naming, labelling, classification. **2** EMPATHY, association, involvement, rapport, relationship, sympathy, fellow-feeling. **3** IDENTITY CARD, documents, papers, credentials.

identify *v* recognize, know, pick out, single out, distinguish, perceive, make out, discern, notice, detect, diagnose, name, label, tag, specify, pinpoint, place, catalogue, classify.
identify with empathize with, relate to, associate with, respond to, sympathize with, feel for.

identity *n* **1** INDIVIDUALITY, particularity, singularity, uniqueness, self, personality, character, existence. **2** SAMENESS, likeness.

ideology *n* philosophy, world-view, ideas, principles, tenets, doctrine(s), convictions, belief(s), faith, creed, dogma.

idiocy *n* folly, stupidity, silliness, senselessness, lunacy.
≠ wisdom, sanity.

idiom *n* phrase, expression, colloquialism, language, turn of phrase, phraseology, style, usage, jargon, vernacular.

idiosyncrasy *n* characteristic, peculiarity, singularity, oddity, eccentricity, freak, quirk, habit, mannerism, trait, feature.

idiosyncratic *adj* personal, individual, characteristic, distinctive, peculiar, singular, odd, eccentr[illegible], quirky.
≠ general, common.

idiot *n* fool, blockhead, ass (*infml*), nitwit (*infml*), dimwit, halfwit, imbecile, moron, cretin, simpleton, dunce, ignoramus.

idiotic *adj* foolish, stupid, silly, absurd, senseless, daft (*infml*), lunatic, insane, foolhardy, harebrained, halfwitted, moronic, cretinous, crazy.
≠ sensible, sane.

idle *adj* **1** INACTIVE, inoperative, unused, unoccupied, unemployed, jobless, redundant. **2** LAZY, work-shy, indolent. **3** *idle talk*: empty, trivial, casual, futile, vain, pointless, unproductive.
≠ **1** active. **2** busy.
v do nothing, laze, lounge, take it easy, kill time, potter, loiter, dawdle, fritter, waste, loaf, slack, skive (*infml*).
≠ work.

idol *n* icon, effigy, image, graven image, god, deity, fetish, favourite, darling, hero, heroine, pin-up.

idolize *v* hero-worship, lionize, exalt, glorify, worship, venerate, revere, admire, adore, love, dote on.
≠ despise.

idyllic *adj* perfect, idealized, heavenly, delightful, charming, picturesque, pastoral, rustic, unspoiled, peaceful, happy.
≠ unpleasant.

ignite *v* set fire to, set alight, catch fire, flare up, burn, conflagrate, fire, kindle, touch off, spark off.
≠ quench.

ignoble *adj* low, mean, petty, base, vulgar, wretched, contemptible, despicable, vile, heinous, infamous, disgraceful, dishonourable, shameless.
≠ noble, worthy, honourable.

ignominious *adj* humiliating, mortifying, degrading, undignified, shameful, dishonourable, disreputable, disgraceful, despicable, scandalous.
≠ triumphant, honourable.

ignorance *n* unintelligence, illiteracy, unawareness, unconsciousness, oblivion, unfamiliarity, inexperience, innocence, naïvety.
≠ knowledge, wisdom.

ignorant *adj* uneducated, illiterate, unread, untaught, untrained, inexperienced, stupid, clueless (*infml*), uninitiated, unenlightened, uninformed, ill-informed, unwitting, unaware, unconscious, oblivious.
≠ educated, knowledgeable, clever, wise.

ignore *v* disregard, take no notice of, shut one's eyes to, overlook, pass over, neglect, omit, reject, snub, cold-shoulder.
≠ notice, observe.

ill *adj* **1** SICK, poorly, unwell, indisposed, laid up, ailing, off-colour, out of sorts (*infml*), under the weather (*infml*), seedy, queasy, diseased, unhealthy, infirm, frail. **2** *an ill omen*: bad, evil, damaging, harmful, injurious, detrimental, adverse, unfavourable, inauspicious, unpromising, sinister, ominous, threatening, unlucky, unfortunate, difficult, harsh, severe, unkind, unfriendly, antagonistic.
≠ **1** well. **2** good, favourable, fortunate.

ill-advised *adj* imprudent, injudicious, unwise, foolish, ill-considered, thoughtless, hasty, rash, short-sighted, misguided, inappropriate.
≠ wise, sensible, well-advised.

ill-bred *adj* bad-mannered, ill-mannered, discourteous, impolite, rude, coarse, indelicate.
≠ well-bred, polite.

illegal *adj* unlawful, illicit, criminal, wrong, forbidden, prohibited, banned, outlawed, unauthorized, under-the-counter, black-market, unconstitutional, wrongful.
≠ legal, lawful.

illegible *adj* unreadable, indecipherable, scrawled, obscure, faint, indistinct.
≠ legible.

illegitimate *adj* **1** *an illegitimate child*: natural, bastard, born out of wedlock (*fml*). **2** ILLEGAL, unlawful, illicit, unauthorized, unwarranted, improper, incorrect, inadmissible, spurious, invalid, unsound.

≠ **1** legitimate. **2** legal.

ill-fated *adj* doomed, ill-starred, ill-omened, unfortunate, unlucky, luckless, unhappy.
≠ lucky.

illicit *adj* illegal, unlawful, criminal, wrong, illegitimate, improper, forbidden, prohibited, unauthorized, unlicensed, black-market, contraband, ill-gotten, under-the-counter, furtive, clandestine.
≠ legal, permissible.

illness *n* disease, disorder, complaint, ailment, sickness, ill health, ill-being, indisposition, infirmity, disability, affliction.

illogical *adj* irrational, unreasonable, unscientific, invalid, unsound, faulty, fallacious, specious, sophistical, inconsistent, senseless, meaningless, absurd.
≠ logical.

ill-treat *v* maltreat, abuse, injure, harm, damage, neglect, mistreat, mishandle, misuse, wrong, oppress.

illuminate *v* **1** LIGHT, light up, brighten, decorate. **2** ENLIGHTEN, edify, instruct, elucidate, illustrate, explain, clarify, clear up.
≠ **1** darken. **2** mystify.

illumination *n* light, lights, lighting, beam, ray, brightness, radiance, decoration, ornamentation.
≠ darkness.

illusion *n* apparition, mirage, hallucination, figment, fantasy, fancy, delusion, misapprehension, misconception, error, fallacy.
≠ reality, truth.

illusory *adj* illusive, deceptive, misleading, apparent, seeming, deluding, delusive, unreal, unsubstantial, sham, false, fallacious, untrue, mistaken.
≠ real.

illustrate *v* draw, sketch, depict, picture, show, exhibit, demonstrate, exemplify, explain, interpret, clarify, elucidate, illuminate, decorate, ornament, adorn.

illustration *n* **1** PICTURE, plate, half-tone, photograph, drawing, sketch, figure, representation, decoration. **2** EXAMPLE, specimen, instance, case, analogy, demonstration, explanation, interpretation.

illustrious *adj* great, noble, eminent, distinguished, celebrated, famous, famed, renowned, noted, prominent, outstanding, remarkable, notable, brilliant, excellent, splendid, magnificent, glorious, exalted.
≠ ignoble, inglorious.

ill-will *n* hostility, antagonism, bad blood, enmity, unfriendliness, malevolence, malice, spite, animosity, ill-feeling, resentment, hard feelings, grudge, dislike, aversion, hatred.
≠ goodwill, friendship.

image *n* **1** IDEA, notion, concept, impression, perception. **2** REPRESENTATION, likeness, picture, portrait, icon, effigy, figure, statue, idol, replica, reflection.

imaginable *adj* conceivable, thinkable, believable, credible, plausible, likely, possible.
≠ unimaginable.

imaginary *adj* imagined, fanciful, illusory, hallucinatory, visionary, pretend, make-believe, unreal, non-existent, fictional, fabulous, legendary, mythological, made-up, invented, fictitious, assumed, supposed, hypothetical.
≠ real.

imagination *n* imaginativeness, creativity, inventiveness, originality, inspiration, insight, ingenuity, resourcefulness, enterprise, wit, vision, mind's eye, fancy, illusion.
≠ unimaginativeness, reality.

imaginative *adj* creative, inventive, innovative, original, inspired, visionary, ingenious, clever, resourceful, enterprising, fanciful, fantastic, vivid.
≠ unimaginative.

imagine *v* **1** PICTURE, visualize, envisage, conceive, fancy, fantasize, pretend, make believe, conjure up, dream up, think up, invent, devise, create, plan, project. **2** *I imagine* *so*: think, believe, judge, suppose, guess, conjecture, assume, take it, gather.

imbalance *n* unevenness, inequality, disparity, disproportion, unfairness, partiality, bias.
≠ balance, parity.

imbecile *n* idiot, halfwit, simpleton, moron, cretin, fool, blockhead, bungler.

imbue *v* permeate, impregnate, pervade, suffuse, fill, saturate, steep, inculcate, instil, tinge, tint.

imitate *v* copy, emulate, follow, ape, mimic, impersonate, take off, caricature, parody, send up, spoof, mock, parrot, repeat, echo, mirror, duplicate, reproduce, simulate, counterfeit, forge.

imitation *n* **1** MIMICRY, impersonation, impression, take-off, caricature, parody, send-up, spoof, mockery, travesty. **2** COPY, duplicate, reproduction, replica, simulation, counterfeit, fake, forgery, sham, likeness, resemblance, reflection, dummy.
adj artificial, synthetic, man-made, ersatz, fake, phoney (*infml*), mock, pseudo, reproduction, simulated, sham, dummy.
≠ genuine.

imitative *adj* copying, mimicking, parrot-like, unoriginal, derivative, plagiarized, second-hand, simulated, mock.

imitator *n* mimic, impersonator, impressionist, parrot, copycat (*infml*), copier, emulator, follower.

immaculate *adj* perfect, unblemished, flawless, faultless, impeccable, spotless, clean, spick and span, pure, unsullied, undefiled, untainted, stainless, blameless, innocent.
≠ blemished, stained, contaminated.

immaterial *adj* irrelevant, insignificant, unimportant, minor, trivial, trifling, inconsequential.
≠ relevant, important.

immature *adj* young, under-age, adolescent, juvenile, childish, puerile, infantile, babyish, raw, crude, callow, inexperienced, green, unripe, undeveloped.
≠ mature.

immeasurable *adj* vast, immense, infinite, limitless, unlimited, boundless, unbounded, endless, bottomless, inexhaustible, incalculable, inestimable.
≠ limited.

immediate *adj* **1** INSTANT, instantaneous, direct, prompt, swift, current, present, existing, urgent, pressing. **2** NEAREST, next, adjacent, near, close, recent.
≠ **1** delayed. **2** distant.

immediately *adv* now, straight away, right away, at once, instantly, directly, forthwith, without delay, promptly, unhesitatingly.
≠ eventually, never.

immense *adj* vast, great, huge, enormous, massive, giant, gigantic, tremendous, monumental.
≠ tiny, minute.

immensity *n* magnitude, bulk, expanse, vastness, greatness, hugeness, enormousness, massiveness.
≠ minuteness.

immerse *v* plunge, submerge, submerse, sink, duck, dip, douse, bathe.

immigrant *n* incomer, settler, newcomer, alien.
≠ emigrant.

imminent *adj* impending, forthcoming, in the offing, approaching, coming, near, close, looming, menacing, threatening, brewing, in the air.
≠ remote, far-off.

immobile *adj* stationary, motionless, unmoving, still, stock-still, static, immovable, rooted, fixed, frozen, rigid, stiff.
≠ mobile, moving.

immobilize *v* stop, halt, fix, freeze, transfix, paralyse, cripple, disable.
≠ mobilize.

immodest *adj* indecent, revealing, shameless, forward, improper, immoral, obscene, lewd, coarse, risqué.

immoral *adj* unethical, wrong, bad,

sinful, evil, wicked, unscrupulous, unprincipled, dishonest, corrupt, depraved, degenerate, dissolute, lewd, indecent, pornographic, obscene, impure.
≠ moral, right, good.

immortal *adj* undying, imperishable, eternal, everlasting, perpetual, endless, ceaseless, lasting, enduring, abiding, timeless, ageless.
≠ mortal.

immortalize *v* celebrate, commemorate, memorialize, perpetuate, enshrine.

immovable *adj* fixed, rooted, immobile, stuck, fast, secure, stable, constant, firm, set, determined, resolute, adamant, unshakable, obstinate, unyielding.
≠ movable.

immune *adj* invulnerable, unsusceptible, resistant, proof, protected, safe, exempt, free, clear.
≠ susceptible.

immunity *n* resistance, protection, exemption, indemnity, impunity, exoneration, freedom, liberty, licence, franchise, privilege, right.
≠ susceptibility.

immunize *v* vaccinate, inoculate, inject, protect, safeguard.

impact *n* **1** *the impact of the reforms*: effect, consequences, repercussions, impression, power, influence, significance, meaning. **2** COLLISION, crash, smash, bang, bump, blow, knock, contact, jolt, shock, brunt.

impair *v* damage, harm, injure, hinder, mar, spoil, worsen, undermine, weaken, reduce, lessen, diminish, blunt.
≠ improve, enhance.

impale *v* pierce, puncture, perforate, run through, spear, lance, spike, skewer, spit, stick, transfix.

impart *v* tell, relate, communicate, make known, disclose, divulge, reveal, convey, pass on, give, grant, confer, offer, contribute, lend.
≠ withhold.

impartial *adj* objective, dispassionate, detached, disinterested, neutral, non-partisan, unbiased, unprejudiced, open-minded, fair, just, equitable, even-handed, equal.
≠ biased, prejudiced.

impasse *n* deadlock, stalemate, dead end, cul-de-sac, blind alley, halt, standstill.

impassive *adj* expressionless, calm, composed, unruffled, unconcerned, cool, unfeeling, unemotional, unmoved, imperturbable, unexcitable, stoical, indifferent, dispassionate.
≠ responsive, moved.

impatience *n* eagerness, keenness, restlessness, agitation, anxiety, nervousness, irritability, intolerance, shortness, brusqueness, haste, rashness.
≠ patience.

impatient *adj* eager, keen, restless, fidgety, fretful, edgy, irritable, snappy, hot-tempered, quick-tempered, intolerant, brusque, abrupt, impetuous, hasty, precipitate, headlong.
≠ patient.

impeach *v* accuse, charge, indict, arraign, denounce, impugn, disparage, criticize, censure, blame.

impeccable *adj* perfect, faultless, precise, exact, flawless, unblemished, stainless, immaculate, pure, irreproachable, blameless, innocent.
≠ faulty, flawed, corrupt.

impede *v* hinder, hamper, obstruct, block, clog, slow, retard, hold up, delay, check, curb, restrain, thwart, disrupt, stop, bar.
≠ aid, promote, further.

impediment *n* hindrance, obstacle, obstruction, barrier, bar, block, stumbling-block, snag, difficulty, handicap, check, curb, restraint, restriction.
≠ aid.

impel *v* urge, force, oblige, compel, constrain, drive, propel, push, spur, goad, prompt, stimulate, excite, instigate, motivate, inspire, move.
≠ deter, dissuade.

impending *adj* imminent, forthcoming, approaching, coming, close, near, looming, menacing, threatening.
≠ remote.

impenetrable *adj* **1** *impenetrable jungle*: solid, thick, dense, impassable. **2** UNINTELLIGIBLE, incomprehensible, unfathomable, baffling, mysterious, cryptic, enigmatic, obscure, dark, inscrutable.
≠ **2** accessible, understandable.

imperative *adj* compulsory, obligatory, essential, vital, crucial, pressing, urgent.
≠ optional, unimportant.

imperceptible *adj* inappreciable, indiscernible, inaudible, faint, slight, negligible, infinitesimal, microscopic, minute, tiny, small, fine, subtle, gradual.
≠ perceptible.

imperfect *adj* faulty, flawed, defective, damaged, broken, chipped, deficient, incomplete.
≠ perfect.

imperfection *n* fault, flaw, defect, blemish, deficiency, shortcoming, weakness, failing.
≠ perfection.

imperial *adj* sovereign, supreme, royal, regal, majestic, grand, magnificent, great, noble.

imperil *v* endanger, jeopardize, risk, hazard, expose, compromise, threaten.

imperious *adj* overbearing, domineering, autocratic, despotic, tyrannical, dictatorial, high-handed, commanding, arrogant, haughty.
≠ humble.

impersonal *adj* formal, official, businesslike, bureaucratic, faceless, aloof, remote, distant, detached, neutral, objective, dispassionate, cold, frosty, glassy.
≠ informal, friendly.

impersonate *v* imitate, mimic, take off, parody, caricature, mock, masquerade as, pose as, act, portray.

impertinence *n* rudeness, impoliteness, disrespect, insolence, impudence, cheek (*infml*), brass (*sl*), effrontery, nerve (*infml*), audacity, boldness, brazenness, forwardness, presumption.
≠ politeness, respect.

impertinent *adj* rude, impolite, ill-mannered, discourteous, disrespectful, insolent, impudent, cheeky (*infml*), saucy (*infml*), pert, bold, brazen, forward, presumptuous, fresh.
≠ polite, respectful.

imperturbable *adj* unexcitable, unflappable (*infml*), calm, tranquil, composed, collected, self-possessed, cool, unmoved, unruffled.

impervious *adj* **1** IMPERMEABLE, waterproof, damp-proof, watertight, hermetic, closed, sealed, impenetrable. **2** *impervious to criticism*: immune, invulnerable, untouched, unaffected, unmoved, resistant.
≠ **1** porous, pervious. **2** responsive, vulnerable.

impetuous *adj* impulsive, spontaneous, unplanned, unpremeditated, hasty, precipitate, rash, reckless, thoughtless, unthinking.
≠ cautious, wary, circumspect.

impetus *n* impulse, momentum, force, energy, power, drive, boost, push, spur, stimulus, incentive, motivation.

impinge *v* hit, touch (on), affect, influence, encroach, infringe, intrude, trespass, invade.

implacable *adj* inexorable, relentless, remorseless, merciless, pitiless, cruel, ruthless, intransigent, inflexible.
≠ compassionate.

implant *v* graft, engraft, embed, sow, plant, fix, root, insert, instil, inculcate.

implausible *adj* improbable, unlikely, far-fetched, dubious, suspect, unconvincing, weak, flimsy, thin, transparent.
≠ plausible, likely, reasonable.

implement *n* tool, instrument, utensil, gadget, device, apparatus, appliance.
v enforce, effect, bring about, carry out, execute, discharge, perform, do, fulfil, complete, accomplish, realize.

implicate *v* involve, embroil, entangle, incriminate, compromise, include, concern, connect, associate.
≠ exonerate.

implication *n* **1** INFERENCE, insinuation, suggestion, meaning, significance, ramification, repercusssion. **2** INVOLVEMENT, entanglement, incrimination, connection, association.

implicit *adj* **1** IMPLIED, inferred, insinuated, indirect, unsaid, unspoken, tacit, understood. **2** *implicit belief*: unquestioning, utter, total, full, complete, absolute, unqualified, unreserved, wholehearted.
≠ **1** explicit. **2** half-hearted.

imply *v* suggest, insinuate, hint, intimate, mean, signify, point to, indicate, involve, require.
≠ state.

impolite *adj* rude, discourteous, bad-mannered, ill-mannered, ill-bred, disrespectful, insolent, rough, coarse, vulgar, abrupt.
≠ polite, courteous.

importance *n* momentousness, significance, consequence, substance, matter, concern, interest, usefulness, value, worth, weight, influence, mark, prominence, eminence, distinction, esteem, prestige, status, standing.
≠ unimportance.

important *adj* **1** MOMENTOUS, noteworthy, significant, meaningful, relevant, material, salient, urgent, vital, essential, key, primary, major, substantial, valuable, seminal, weighty, serious, grave, far-reaching. **2** LEADING, foremost, high-level, high-ranking, influential, powerful, pre-eminent, prominent, outstanding, eminent, noted.
≠ **1** unimportant, insignificant, trivial.

impose *v* **1** INTRODUCE, institute, enforce, promulgate, exact, levy, set, fix, put, place, lay, inflict, burden, encumber, saddle. **2** INTRUDE, butt in, encroach, trespass, obtrude, force oneself, presume, take liberties.

imposing *adj* impressive, striking, grand, stately, majestic, dignified.
≠ unimposing, modest.

imposition *n* **1** INTRODUCTION, infliction, exaction, levying. **2** INTRUSION, encroachment, liberty, burden, constraint, charge, duty, task, punishment.

impossible *adj* hopeless, impracticable, unworkable, unattainable, unachievable, unobtainable, insoluble, unreasonable, unacceptable, inconceivable, unthinkable, preposterous, absurd, ludicrous, ridiculous.
≠ possible.

impostor *n* fraud, fake, phoney (*infml*), quack, charlatan, impersonator, pretender, con man (*infml*), swindler, cheat, rogue.

impotent *adj* powerless, helpless, unable, incapable, ineffective, incompetent, inadequate, weak, feeble, frail, infirm, disabled, incapacitated, paralysed.
≠ potent, strong.

impoverished *adj* poor, needy, impecunious, poverty-stricken, destitute, bankrupt, ruined.
≠ rich.

impracticable *adj* unworkable, unfeasible, unattainable, unachievable, impossible, unviable, useless, unserviceable, inoperable.
≠ practicable.

impractical *adj* unrealistic, idealistic, romantic, starry-eyed, impracticable, unworkable, impossible, awkward, inconvenient.
≠ practical, realistic, sensible.

imprecise *adj* inexact, inaccurate, approximate, estimated, rough, loose, indefinite, vague, woolly, hazy, ill-defined, sloppy, ambiguous, equivocal.
≠ precise, exact.

impregnable *adj* impenetrable, unconquerable, invincible, unbeatable, unassailable, indestructible, fortified, strong, solid, secure, safe, invulnerable.
≠ vulnerable.

impregnate *v* **1** SOAK, steep, saturate, fill, permeate, pervade, suffuse, imbue. **2** INSEMINATE, fertilize.

impress *v* **1** *I'm not impressed*: strike, move, touch, affect, influence, stir, inspire, excite, grab (*sl*). **2** STAMP, imprint, mark, indent, instil, inculcate.

impression *n* **1** FEELING, awareness, consciousness, sense, illusion, idea, notion, opinion, belief, conviction, suspicion, hunch, memory, recollection. **2** STAMP, mark, print, dent, outline. **3** IMPERSONATION, imitation, take-off, parody, send-up. **4** *make a good impression*: effect, impact, influence.

impressionable *adj* naïve, gullible, susceptible, vulnerable, sensitive, responsive, open, receptive.

impressive *adj* striking, imposing, grand, powerful, effective, stirring, exciting, moving, touching.
≠ unimpressive, uninspiring.

imprint *n* print, mark, stamp, impression, sign, logo.
v print, mark, brand, stamp, impress, engrave, etch.

imprison *v* jail, incarcerate, intern, detain, send down (*infml*), put away (*infml*), lock up, cage, confine, shut in.
≠ release, free.

imprisonment *n* incarceration, internment, detention, custody, confinement.
≠ freedom, liberty.

improbable *adj* uncertain, questionable, doubtful, unlikely, dubious, implausible, unconvincing, far-fetched, preposterous, unbelievable, incredible.
≠ probable, likely, convincing.

impromptu *adj* improvised, extempore, ad-lib, off the cuff, unscripted, unrehearsed, unprepared, spontaneous.
≠ rehearsed.
adv extempore, ad lib, off the cuff, off the top of one's head, spontaneously, on the spur of the moment.

improper *adj* wrong, incorrect, irregular, unsuitable, inappropriate, inopportune, incongruous, out of place, indecent, rude, vulgar, unseemly, unbecoming, shocking.
≠ proper, appropriate, decent.

improve *v* better, ameliorate, enhance, polish, touch up, mend, rectify, correct, amend, reform, upgrade, increase, rise, pick up, develop, look up, advance, progress, get better, recover, recuperate, rally, perk up, mend one's ways, turn over a new leaf.
≠ worsen, deteriorate, decline.

improvement *n* betterment, amelioration, enhancement, rectification, correction, amendment, reformation, increase, rise, upswing, gain, development, advance, progress, furtherance, recovery, rally.
≠ deterioration, decline.

improvise *v* **1** CONTRIVE, devise, concoct, invent, throw together, make do. **2** EXTEMPORIZE, ad-lib, play by ear, vamp.

imprudent *adj* unwise, ill-advised, foolish, short-sighted, rash, reckless, hasty, irresponsible, careless, heedless, impolitic, indiscreet.
≠ prudent, wise, cautious.

impudence *n* impertinence, cheek (*infml*), effrontery, nerve (*infml*), face (*infml*), boldness, insolence, rudeness, presumption.
≠ politeness.

impudent *adj* impertinent, cheeky (*infml*), saucy (*infml*), bold, forward, shameless, cocky, insolent, rude, presumptuous, fresh.
≠ polite.

impulse *n* **1** URGE, wish, desire, inclination, whim, notion, instinct, feeling, passion. **2** IMPETUS, momentum, force, pressure, drive, thrust, push, incitement, stimulus, motive.

impulsive *adj* impetuous, rash, reckless, hasty, quick, spontaneous, automatic, instinctive, intuitive.
≠ cautious, premeditated.

impure *adj* **1** UNREFINED, adulterated, diluted, contaminated, polluted, tainted, infected, corrupt, debased, unclean, dirty, foul. **2** OBSCENE, indecent, immodest.
≠ **1** pure. **2** chaste, decent.

impurity *n* adulteration, contamination, pollution, infection, corruption, dirtiness, contaminant, dirt, filth, foreign body, mark, spot.
≠ purity.

inability *n* incapability, incapacity, powerlessness, impotence, inadequacy, weakness, handicap, disability.
≠ ability.

inaccessible *adj* isolated, remote, unfrequented, unapproachable, unreachable, unget-at-able (*infml*), unattainable.
≠ accessible.

inaccuracy *n* mistake, error, miscalculation, slip, blunder, fault, defect, imprecision, inexactness, unreliability.
≠ accuracy, precision.

inaccurate *adj* incorrect, wrong, erroneous, mistaken, faulty, flawed, defective, imprecise, inexact, loose, unreliable, unfaithful, untrue.
≠ accurate, correct.

inaction *n* inactivity, immobility, inertia, rest, idleness, lethargy, torpor, stagnation.
≠ action.

inactive *adj* immobile, inert, idle, unused, inoperative, dormant, passive, sedentary, lazy, lethargic, sluggish, torpid, sleepy.
≠ active, working, busy.

inadequacy *n* **1** INSUFFICIENCY, lack, shortage, dearth, want, deficiency, scantiness, meagreness, defectiveness, ineffectiveness, inability, incompetence. **2** *the inadequacies of the system*: fault, defect, imperfection, weakness, failing, shortcoming.
≠ **1** adequacy.

inadequate *adj* **1** INSUFFICIENT, short, wanting, deficient, scanty, sparse, meagre, niggardly. **2** INCOMPETENT, incapable, unequal, unqualified, ineffective, faulty, defective, imperfect, unsatisfactory.
≠ **1** adequate. **2** satisfactory.

inadmissible *adj* unacceptable, irrelevant, immaterial, inappropriate, disallowed, prohibited.
≠ admissible.

inadvertent *adj* accidental, chance, unintentional, unintended, unplanned, unpremeditated, careless.
≠ deliberate, conscious, careful.

inadvisable *adj* unwise, imprudent, injudicious, foolish, silly, ill-advised, misguided, indiscreet.
≠ advisable, wise.

inane *adj* senseless, foolish, stupid, unintelligent, silly, idiotic, fatuous, frivolous, trifling, puerile, mindless, vapid, empty, vacuous, vain, worthless, futile.
≠ sensible.

inanimate *adj* lifeless, dead, defunct, extinct, unconscious, inactive, inert, dormant, immobile, stagnant, spiritless, dull.
≠ animate, living, alive.

inappropriate *adj* unsuitable, inapt, ill-suited, ill-fitted, irrelevant, incongruous, out of place, untimely, ill-timed, tactless, improper, unseemly, unbecoming, unfitting.
≠ appropriate, suitable.

inarticulate *adj* incoherent, unintelligible, incomprehensible, unclear, indistinct, hesitant, faltering, halting, tongue-tied, speechless, dumb, mute.
≠ articulate.

inattention *n* carelessness, negligence, disregard, absent-mindedness, forgetfulness, daydreaming, preoccupation.

inattentive *adj* distracted, dreamy, daydreaming, preoccupied, absent-minded, unmindful, heedless, regardless, careless, negligent.
≠ attentive.

inaudible *adj* silent, noiseless, imperceptible, faint, indistinct, muffled, muted, low, mumbled.
≠ audible, loud.

inaugural *adj* opening, introductory, first, initial.

inaugurate *v* institute, originate, begin, commence, start, set up, open, launch, introduce, usher in, initiate, induct, ordain, invest, install, commission, dedicate, consecrate.

inauspicious *adj* unfavourable, bad, unlucky, unfortunate, unpromising, discouraging, threatening, ominous, black.
≠ auspicious, promising.

inborn *adj* innate, inherent, natural, native, congenital, inbred, hereditary,

inherited, ingrained, instinctive, intuitive.
≠ learned.

incalculable *adj* countless, untold, inestimable, limitless, unlimited, immense, vast.
≠ limited, restricted.

incapable *adj* unable, powerless, impotent, helpless, weak, feeble, unfit, unsuited, unqualified, incompetent, inept, inadequate, ineffective.
≠ capable.

incapacitate *v* disable, cripple, paralyse, immobilize, disqualify, put out of action, lay up, scupper (*infml*).

incapacity *n* incapability, inability, disability, powerlessness, impotence, ineffectiveness, weakness, feebleness, inadequacy, incompetency.
≠ capability.

incarnation *n* personification, embodiment, manifestation, impersonation.

incautious *adj* careless, imprudent, injudicious, ill-judged, unthinking, thoughtless, inconsiderate, rash, reckless, hasty, impulsive.
≠ cautious, careful.

incense *v* anger, enrage, infuriate, madden, exasperate, irritate, rile, provoke, excite.
≠ calm.

incentive *n* bait, lure, enticement, carrot (*infml*), sweetener (*sl*), reward, encouragement, inducement, reason, motive, impetus, spur, stimulus, motivation.
≠ disincentive, discouragement, deterrent.

incessant *adj* ceaseless, unceasing, endless, never-ending, interminable, continual, persistent, constant, perpetual, eternal, everlasting, continuous, unbroken, unremitting, non-stop.
≠ intermittent, sporadic, periodic, temporary.

incidence *n* frequency, commonness, prevalence, extent, range, amount, degree, rate, occurrence.

incident *n* **1** OCCURRENCE, happening, event, episode, adventure, affair, occasion, instance. **2** CONFRONTATION, clash, fight, skirmish, commotion, disturbance, scene, upset, mishap.

incidental *adj* accidental, chance, random, minor, non-essential, secondary, subordinate, subsidiary, ancillary, supplementary, accompanying, attendant, related, contributory.
≠ important, essential.

incinerate *v* burn, cremate, reduce to ashes.

incision *n* cut, opening, slit, gash, notch.

incisive *adj* cutting, keen, sharp, acute, trenchant, piercing, penetrating, biting, caustic, acid, astute, perceptive.
≠ vague.

incite *v* prompt, instigate, rouse, foment, stir up, whip up, work up, excite, animate, provoke, stimulate, spur, goad, impel, drive, urge, encourage, egg on (*infml*).
≠ restrain.

incitement *n* prompting, instigation, agitation, provocation, spur, goad, impetus, stimulus, motivation, encouragement, inducement, incentive.
≠ discouragement.

inclement *adj* intemperate, harsh, severe, stormy, tempestuous, rough.
≠ fine.

inclination *n* **1** LIKING, fondness, taste, predilection, preference, partiality, bias, tendency, trend, disposition, propensity, leaning. **2** *an inclination of 45 degrees*: angle, slope, gradient, incline, pitch, slant, tilt, bend, bow, nod.
≠ **1** disinclination, dislike.

incline *v* **1** DISPOSE, influence, persuade, affect, bias, prejudice. **2** LEAN, slope, slant, tilt, tip, bend, bow, tend, veer.
n slope, gradient, ramp, hill, rise, ascent, acclivity, dip, descent, declivity.

inclined *adj* liable, likely, given, apt, disposed, of a mind, willing.

include *v* comprise, incorporate,

embody, comprehend, contain, enclose, embrace, encompass, cover, subsume, take in, add, allow for, take into account, involve, rope in.
≠ exclude, omit, eliminate.

inclusion *n* incorporation, involvement, addition, insertion.
≠ exclusion.

inclusive *adj* comprehensive, full, all-in, all-inclusive, all-embracing, blanket, across-the-board, general, catch-all, overall, sweeping.
≠ exclusive, narrow.

incognito *adj* in disguise, disguised, masked, veiled, unmarked, unidentified, unrecognizable, unknown.
≠ undisguised.

incoherent *adj* unintelligible, incomprehensible, inarticulate, rambling, stammering, stuttering, unconnected, disconnected, broken, garbled, scrambled, confused, muddled, jumbled, disordered.
≠ coherent, intelligible.

income *n* revenue, returns, proceeds, gains, profits, interest, takings, receipts, earnings, pay, salary, wages, means.
≠ expenditure, expenses.

incoming *adj* arriving, entering, approaching, coming, homeward, returning, ensuing, succeeding, next, new.
≠ outgoing.

incomparable *adj* matchless, unmatched, unequalled, unparalleled, unrivalled, peerless, supreme, superlative, superb, brilliant.
≠ ordinary, run-of-the-mill, poor.

incompatible *adj* irreconcilable, contradictory, conflicting, at variance, inconsistent, clashing, mismatched, unsuited.
≠ compatible.

incompetent *adj* incapable, unable, unfit, inefficient, inexpert, unskilful, bungling, stupid, useless, ineffective.
≠ competent, able.

incomplete *adj* deficient, lacking, short, unfinished, abridged, partial, part, fragmentary, broken, imperfect, defective.
≠ complete, exhaustive.

incomprehensible *adj* unintelligible, impenetrable, unfathomable, above one's head, puzzling, perplexing, baffling, mysterious, inscrutable, obscure, opaque.
≠ comprehensible, intelligible.

inconceivable *adj* unthinkable, unimaginable, mind-boggling (*infml*), staggering, unheard-of, unbelievable, incredible, implausible.
≠ conceivable.

inconclusive *adj* unsettled, undecided, open, uncertain, indecisive, ambiguous, vague, unconvincing, unsatisfying.
≠ conclusive.

incongruous *adj* inappropriate, unsuitable, out of place, out of keeping, inconsistent, conflicting, incompatible, irreconcilable, contradictory, contrary.
≠ consistent, compatible.

inconsequential *adj* minor, trivial, trifling, unimportant, insignificant, immaterial.
≠ important.

inconsiderable *adj* small, slight, negligible, trivial, petty, minor, unimportant, insignificant.
≠ considerable, large.

inconsiderate *adj* unkind, uncaring, unconcerned, selfish, self-centred, intolerant, insensitive, tactless, rude, thoughtless, unthinking, careless, heedless.
≠ considerate.

inconsistent *adj* **1** CONFLICTING, at variance, at odds, incompatible, contradictory, contrary, incongruous, discordant. **2** CHANGEABLE, variable, irregular, unpredictable, varying, unstable, unsteady, inconstant, fickle.
≠ **2** constant.

inconsolable *adj* heartbroken, brokenhearted, devastated, desolate, despairing, wretched.

inconspicuous *adj* hidden, concealed, camouflaged, plain, ordinary, unobtrusive, discreet, low-key, modest, unassuming, quiet, retiring, insignificant.
≠ conspicuous, noticeable, obtrusive.

incontrovertible *adj* indisputable, unquestionable, irrefutable, undeniable, certain, clear, self-evident.
≠ questionable, uncertain.

inconvenience *n* awkwardness, difficulty, annoyance, nuisance, hindrance, drawback, bother, trouble, fuss, upset, disturbance, disruption.
≠ convenience.
v bother, disturb, disrupt, put out, trouble, upset, irk.
≠ convenience.

inconvenient *adj* awkward, ill-timed, untimely, inopportune, unsuitable, difficult, embarrassing, annoying, troublesome, unwieldy, unmanageable.
≠ convenient.

incorporate *v* include, embody, contain, subsume, take in, absorb, assimilate, integrate, combine, unite, merge, blend, mix, fuse, coalesce, consolidate.
≠ separate.

incorrect *adj* wrong, mistaken, erroneous, inaccurate, imprecise, inexact, false, untrue, faulty, ungrammatical, improper, illegitimate, inappropriate, unsuitable.
≠ correct.

incorrigible *adj* irredeemable, incurable, inveterate, hardened, hopeless.

incorruptible *adj* honest, straight, upright, moral, honourable, trustworthy, unbribable, just.
≠ corruptible.

increase *v* raise, boost, add to, improve, enhance, advance, step up, intensify, strengthen, heighten, grow, develop, build up, wax, enlarge, extend, prolong, expand, spread, swell, magnify, multiply, proliferate, rise, mount, soar, escalate.
≠ decrease, reduce, decline.
n rise, surge, upsurge, upturn, gain, boost, addition, increment, advance, step-up, intensification, growth, development, enlargement, extension, expansion, spread, proliferation, escalation.
≠ decrease, reduction, decline.

incredible *adj* unbelievable, improbable, implausible, far-fetched, preposterous, absurd, impossible, inconceivable, unthinkable, unimaginable, extraordinary, amazing, astonishing, astounding.
≠ credible, believable.

incredulity *n* unbelief, disbelief, scepticism, doubt, distrust, mistrust.
≠ credulity.

incredulous *adj* unbelieving, disbelieving, unconvinced, sceptical, doubting, distrustful, suspicious, dubious, doubtful, uncertain.
≠ credulous.

incriminate *v* inculpate, implicate, involve, accuse, charge, impeach, indict, point the finger at, blame.
≠ exonerate.

incur *v* suffer, sustain, provoke, arouse, bring upon oneself, expose oneself to, meet with, run up, gain, earn.

incurable *adj* **1** *an incurable disease*: terminal, fatal, untreatable, inoperable, hopeless. **2** INCORRIGIBLE, inveterate, hardened, dyed-in-the-wool.
≠ **1** curable.

indebted *adj* obliged, grateful, thankful.

indecency *n* immodesty, indecorum, impurity, obscenity, pornography, lewdness, vulgarity, coarseness, crudity, foulness, grossness.
≠ decency, modesty.

indecent *adj* improper, immodest, impure, indelicate, offensive, obscene, pornographic, lewd, licentious, vulgar, coarse, crude, dirty, filthy, foul, gross, outrageous, shocking.
≠ decent, modest.

indecision *n* indecisiveness, irresolution, vacillation, wavering, hesitation, hesitancy, ambivalence, uncertainty, doubt.
≠ decisiveness, resolution.

indecisive *adj* undecided, irresolute, undetermined, vacillating, wavering, in two minds, hesitating, faltering, tentative, uncertain, unsure, doubtful, inconclusive, indefinite, indeterminate, unclear.
≠ decisive.

indeed *adv* really, actually, in fact, certainly, positively, truly, undeniably, undoubtedly, to be sure.

indefensible *adj* unjustifiable, inexcusable, unforgivable, unpardonable, insupportable, untenable, wrong, faulty.
≠ defensible, excusable.

indefinite *adj* unknown, uncertain, unsettled, unresolved, undecided, undetermined, undefined, unspecified, unlimited, ill-defined, vague, indistinct, unclear, obscure, ambiguous, imprecise, inexact, loose, general.
≠ definite, limited, clear.

indefinitely *adv* for ever, eternally, endlessly, continually, ad infinitum.

indelible *adj* lasting, enduring, permanent, fast, ineffaceable, ingrained, indestructible.
≠ erasable.

indemnity *n* compensation, reimbursement, remuneration, reparation, insurance, guarantee, security, protection, immunity, amnesty.

indentation *n* notch, nick, cut, serration, dent, groove, furrow, depression, dip, hollow, pit, dimple.

independence *n* autonomy, self-government, self-determination, self-rule, home rule, sovereignty, freedom, liberty, individualism, separation.
≠ dependence.

independent *adj* **1** AUTONOMOUS, self-governing, self-determining, sovereign, absolute, non-aligned, neutral, impartial, unbiased. **2** FREE, liberated, unconstrained, individualistic, unconventional, self-sufficient, self-supporting, self-reliant, unaided. **3** INDIVIDUAL, self-contained, separate, unconnected, unrelated.
≠ **1** dependent.

indescribable *adj* indefinable, inexpressible, unutterable, unspeakable.
≠ describable.

indestructible *adj* unbreakable, durable, tough, strong, lasting, enduring, abiding, permanent, eternal, everlasting, immortal, imperishable.
≠ breakable, mortal.

indeterminate *adj* unspecified, unstated, undefined, unfixed, imprecise, inexact, indefinite, vague, open-ended, undecided, undetermined, uncertain.
≠ known, specified, fixed.

index *n* **1** *index of names*: table, key, list, catalogue, directory, guide. **2** INDICATOR, pointer, needle, hand, sign, token, mark, indication, clue.

indicate *v* register, record, show, reveal, display, manifest, point to, designate, specify, point out, mark, signify, mean, denote, express, suggest, imply.

indication *n* mark, sign, manifestation, evidence, symptom, signal, warning, omen, intimation, suggestion, hint, clue, note, explanation.

indicator *n* pointer, needle, marker, sign, symbol, token, signal, display, dial, gauge, meter, index, guide, signpost.

indict *v* charge, accuse, arraign, impeach, summon, summons, prosecute, incriminate.
≠ exonerate.

indifference *n* apathy, unconcern, coldness, coolness, inattention, disregard, negligence, neutrality, disinterestedness.
≠ interest, concern.

indifferent *adj* **1** UNINTERESTED, unenthusiastic, unexcited, apathetic, unconcerned, unmoved, uncaring, unsympathetic, cold, cool, distant, aloof, detached, uninvolved, neutral, disinterested. **2** MEDIOCRE, average, middling, passable, moderate, fair, ordinary.
≠ **1** interested, caring. **2** excellent.

indigenous *adj* native, aboriginal, original, local, home-grown.
≠ foreign.

indignant *adj* annoyed, angry, irate, heated, fuming, livid, furious, incensed, infuriated, exasperated, outraged.
≠ pleased, delighted.

indignation *n* annoyance, anger, ire, wrath, rage, fury, exasperation, outrage, scorn, contempt.
≠ pleasure, delight.

indirect *adj* 1 ROUNDABOUT, circuitous, wandering, rambling, winding, meandering, zigzag, tortuous. 2 *an indirect effect*: secondary, incidental, unintended, subsidiary, ancillary.
≠ 1 direct. 2 primary.

indiscreet *adj* tactless, undiplomatic, impolitic, injudicious, imprudent, unwise, foolish, rash, reckless, hasty, careless, heedless, unthinking.
≠ discreet, cautious.

indiscretion *n* mistake, error, slip, boob (*infml*), faux pas, gaffe, tactlessness, rashness, recklessness, foolishness, folly.

indiscriminate *adj* general, sweeping, wholesale, random, haphazard, hit or miss, aimless, unsystematic, unmethodical, mixed, motley, miscellaneous.
≠ selective, specific, precise.

indispensable *adj* vital, essential, basic, key, crucial, imperative, required, requisite, needed, necessary.
≠ dispensable, unnecessary.

indisposed *adj* ill, sick, unwell, poorly, ailing, laid up.
≠ well.

indisputable *adj* incontrovertible, unquestionable, irrefutable, undeniable, absolute, undisputed, definite, positive, certain, sure.
≠ doubtful.

indistinct *adj* unclear, ill-defined, blurred, fuzzy, misty, hazy, shadowy, obscure, dim, faint, muffled, confused, unintelligible, vague, woolly, ambiguous, indefinite.
≠ distinct, clear.

individual *n* person, being, creature, party, body, soul, character, fellow.
adj distinctive, characteristic, idiosyncratic, peculiar, singular, unique, exclusive, special, personal, own, proper, respective, several, separate, distinct, specific, personalized, particular, single.
≠ collective, shared, general.

individuality *n* character, personality, distinctiveness, peculiarity, singularity, uniqueness, separateness, distinction.
≠ sameness.

indoctrinate *v* brainwash, teach, instruct, school, ground, train, drill.

induce *v* 1 CAUSE, effect, bring about, occasion, give rise to, lead to, incite, instigate, prompt, provoke, produce, generate. 2 COAX, prevail upon, encourage, press, persuade, talk into, move, influence, draw, tempt.
≠ 2 discourage, deter.

inducement *n* lure, bait, attraction, enticement, encouragement, incentive, reward, spur, stimulus, motive, reason.
≠ disincentive.

indulge *v* gratify, satisfy, humour, pander to, go along with, give in to, yield to, favour, pet, cosset, mollycoddle, pamper, spoil, treat, regale.

indulgence *n* extravagance, luxury, excess, immoderation, intemperance, favour, tolerance.

indulgent *adj* tolerant, easy-going (*infml*), lenient, permissive, generous, liberal, kind, fond, tender, understanding, patient.
≠ strict, harsh.

industrialist *n* manufacturer, producer, magnate, tycoon, baron, captain of industry, capitalist, financier.

industrious *adj* busy, productive, hard-working, diligent, assiduous, conscientious, zealous, active, energetic, tireless, persistent, persevering.
≠ lazy, idle.

industry *n* 1 *the steel industry*: business, trade, commerce, manufacturing, production. 2 INDUSTRIOUSNESS, diligence, application, effort, labour, toil, persistence, perseverance, determination.

inebriated *adj* drunk, intoxicated, tipsy, merry.
≠ sober.

inedible *adj* uneatable, unpalatable, indigestible, harmful, noxious, poisonous, deadly.
≠ edible.

ineffective *adj* useless, worthless, vain,

idle, futile, unavailing, fruitless, unproductive, unsuccessful, powerless, impotent, ineffectual, inadequate, weak, feeble, inept, incompetent.
≠ effective, effectual.

inefficient *adj* uneconomic, wasteful, money-wasting, time-wasting, incompetent, inexpert, unworkmanlike, slipshod, sloppy, careless, negligent.
≠ efficient.

inelegant *adj* graceless, ungraceful, clumsy, awkward, laboured, ugly, unrefined, crude, unpolished, rough, unsophisticated, uncultivated, uncouth.
≠ elegant.

ineligible *adj* disqualified, ruled out, unacceptable, undesirable, unworthy, unsuitable, unfit, unqualified, unequipped.
≠ eligible.

inept *adj* awkward, clumsy, bungling, incompetent, unskilful, inexpert, foolish, stupid.
≠ competent, skilful.

inequality *n* unequalness, difference, diversity, dissimilarity, disparity, unevenness, disproportion, bias, prejudice.
≠ equality.

inert *adj* immobile, motionless, unmoving, still, inactive, inanimate, lifeless, dead, passive, unresponsive, apathetic, dormant, idle, lazy, lethargic, sluggish, torpid, sleepy.
≠ lively, animated.

inertia *n* immobility, stillness, inactivity, passivity, unresponsiveness, apathy, idleness, laziness, lethargy, torpor.
≠ activity, liveliness.

inescapable *adj* inevitable, unavoidable, destined, fated, certain, sure, irrevocable, unalterable.
≠ escapable.

inevitable *adj* unavoidable, inescapable, necessary, definite, certain, sure, decreed, ordained, destined, fated, automatic, assured, fixed, unalterable, irrevocable, inexorable.
≠ avoidable, uncertain, alterable.

inexcusable *adj* indefensible, unforgivable, unpardonable, intolerable, unacceptable, outrageous, shameful, blameworthy, reprehensible.
≠ excusable, justifiable.

inexhaustible *adj* **1** *an inexhaustible supply*: unlimited, limitless, boundless, unbounded, infinite, endless, never-ending, abundant. **2** INDEFATIGABLE, tireless, untiring, unflagging, unwearied, unwearying.
≠ **1** limited.

inexpensive *adj* cheap, low-priced, reasonable, modest, bargain, budget, low-cost, economical.
≠ expensive, dear.

inexperience *n* inexpertness, ignorance, unfamiliarity, strangeness, newness, rawness, naïveness, innocence.
≠ experience.

inexperienced *adj* inexpert, untrained, unskilled, amateur, probationary, apprentice, unacquainted, unfamiliar, unaccustomed, new, fresh, raw, callow, young, immature, naïve, unsophisticated, innocent.
≠ experienced, mature.

inexplicable *adj* unexplainable, unaccountable, strange, mystifying, puzzling, baffling, mysterious, enigmatic, unfathomable, incomprehensible, incredible, unbelievable, miraculous.
≠ explicable.

inexpressive *adj* unexpressive, expressionless, deadpan, inscrutable, blank, vacant, empty, emotionless, impassive.
≠ expressive.

infallible *adj* accurate, unerring, unfailing, foolproof, fail-safe, sure-fire (*infml*), certain, sure, reliable, dependable, trustworthy, sound, perfect, faultless, impeccable.
≠ fallible.

infamous *adj* notorious, ill-famed, disreputable, disgraceful, shameful, shocking, outrageous, scandalous, wicked, iniquitous.
≠ illustrious, glorious.

infamy *n* notoriety, disrepute, disgrace,

shame, dishonour, discredit, ignominy, wickedness.
≠ glory.

infancy *n* **1** BABYHOOD, childhood, youth. **2** BEGINNING, start, commencement, inception, outset, birth, dawn, genesis, emergence, origins, early stages.
≠ **1** adulthood.

infant *n* baby, toddler, tot (*infml*), child, babe (*fml*), babe in arms (*fml*).
≠ adult.
adj newborn, baby, young, youthful, juvenile, immature, growing, developing, rudimentary, early, initial, new.
≠ adult, mature.

infantile *adj* babyish, childish, puerile, juvenile, young, youthful, adolescent, immature.
≠ adult, mature.

infatuated *adj* besotted, obsessed, enamoured, smitten (*infml*), crazy (*infml*), spellbound, mesmerized, captivated, fascinated, enraptured, ravished.
≠ indifferent, disenchanted.

infatuation *n* besottedness, obsession, fixation, passion, crush (*sl*), love, fondness, fascination.
≠ indifference, disenchantment.

infect *v* contaminate, pollute, defile, taint, blight, poison, corrupt, pervert, influence, affect, touch, inspire.

infection *n* illness, disease, virus, epidemic, contagion, pestilence, contamination, pollution, defilement, taint, blight, poison, corruption, influence.

infectious *adj* contagious, communicable, transmissible, infective, catching, spreading, epidemic, virulent, deadly, contaminating, polluting, defiling, corrupting.

infer *v* derive, extrapolate, deduce, conclude, assume, presume, surmise, gather, understand.

inference *n* deduction, conclusion, corollary, consequence, assumption, presumption, surmise, conjecture, extrapolation, construction, interpretation, reading.

inferior *adj* **1** LOWER, lesser, minor, secondary, junior, subordinate, subsidiary, second-class, low, humble, menial. **2** *inferior work*: substandard, second-rate, mediocre, bad, poor, unsatisfactory, slipshod, shoddy.
≠ **1** superior. **2** excellent.
n subordinate, junior, underling (*infml*), minion, vassal, menial.
≠ superior.

inferiority *n* **1** SUBORDINATION, subservience, humbleness, lowliness, meanness, insignificance. **2** MEDIOCRITY, imperfection, inadequacy, slovenliness, shoddiness.
≠ **1** superiority. **2** excellence.

infernal *adj* hellish, satanic, devilish, diabolical, fiendish, accursed, damned.
≠ heavenly.

infertile *adj* barren, sterile, childless, unproductive, unfruitful, arid, parched, dried-up.
≠ fertile, fruitful.

infest *v* swarm, teem, throng, flood, overrun, invade, infiltrate, penetrate, permeate, pervade, ravage.

infidelity *n* adultery, unfaithfulness, faithlessness, disloyalty, duplicity, treachery, betrayal, cheating, falseness.
≠ fidelity, faithfulness.

infiltrate *v* penetrate, enter, creep into, insinuate, intrude, pervade, permeate, filter, percolate.

infinite *adj* limitless, unlimited, boundless, unbounded, endless, never-ending, inexhaustible, bottomless, innumerable, numberless, uncountable, countless, untold, incalculable, inestimable, immeasurable, unfathomable, vast, immense, enormous, huge, absolute, total.
≠ finite, limited.

infinitesimal *adj* tiny, minute, microscopic, minuscule, inconsiderable, insignificant, negligible, inappreciable, imperceptible.
≠ great, large, enormous.

infinity *n* eternity, perpetuity, limitlessness, boundlessness, endlessness, inexhaustibility, countlessness, immeasurableness, vastness, immensity.
≠ finiteness, limitation.

infirm *adj* weak, feeble, frail, ill, unwell, poorly, sickly, failing, faltering, unsteady, shaky, wobbly, doddery, lame.
≠ healthy, strong.

inflame *v* anger, enrage, infuriate, incense, exasperate, madden, provoke, stimulate, excite, rouse, arouse, agitate, foment, kindle, ignite, fire, heat, fan, fuel, increase, intensify, worsen, aggravate.
≠ cool, quench.

inflamed *adj* sore, swollen, septic, infected, poisoned, red, hot, heated, fevered, feverish.

inflammable *adj* flammable, combustible, burnable.
≠ non-flammable, incombustible, flameproof.

inflammation *n* soreness, painfulness, tenderness, swelling, abscess, infection, redness, heat, rash, sore, irritation.

inflate *v* blow up, pump up, blow out, puff out, swell, distend, bloat, expand, enlarge, increase, boost, exaggerate.
≠ deflate.

inflation *n* expansion, increase, rise, escalation, hyperinflation.
≠ deflation.

inflexible *adj* rigid, stiff, hard, solid, set, fixed, fast, immovable, firm, strict, stringent, unbending, unyielding, adamant, resolute, relentless, implacable, uncompromising, stubborn, obstinate, intransigent, entrenched, dyed-in-the-wool.
≠ flexible, yielding, adaptable.

inflict *v* impose, enforce, perpetrate, wreak, administer, apply, deliver, deal, mete out, lay, burden, exact, levy.

influence *n* power, sway, rule, authority, domination, mastery, hold, control, direction, guidance, bias, prejudice, pull, pressure, effect, impact, weight, importance, prestige, standing.
v dominate, control, manipulate, direct, guide, manoeuvre, change, alter, modify, affect, impress, move, stir, arouse, rouse, sway, persuade, induce, incite, instigate, prompt, motivate, dispose, incline, bias, prejudice, predispose.

influential *adj* dominant, controlling, leading, authoritative, charismatic, persuasive, convincing, compelling, inspiring, moving, powerful, potent, effective, telling, strong, weighty, momentous, important, significant, instrumental, guiding.
≠ ineffective, unimportant.

influx *n* inflow, inrush, invasion, arrival, stream, flow, rush, flood, inundation.

inform *v* tell, advise, notify, communicate, impart, leak, tip off, acquaint, fill in (*infml*), brief, instruct, enlighten, illuminate.
inform on betray, incriminate, shop (*sl*), tell on (*infml*), squeal (*sl*), blab, grass (*sl*), denounce.

informal *adj* unofficial, unceremonious, casual, relaxed, easy, free, natural, simple, unpretentious, familiar, colloquial.
≠ formal, solemn.

information *n* facts, data, input, gen (*infml*), bumf (*sl*), intelligence, news, report, bulletin, communiqué, message, word, advice, notice, briefing, instruction, knowledge, dossier, database, databank, clues, evidence.

informative *adj* educational, instructive, edifying, enlightening, illuminating, revealing, forthcoming, communicative, chatty, gossipy, newsy, helpful, useful, constructive.
≠ uninformative.

informed *adj* **1** *we'll keep you informed*: familiar, conversant, acquainted, enlightened, briefed, primed, posted, up to date, abreast, au fait, in the know (*infml*). **2** *an informed opinion*: well-informed, authoritative, expert, versed, well-read, erudite, learned, knowledgeable, well-researched.
≠ **1** ignorant, unaware.

informer *n* informant, grass (*sl*), supergrass (*sl*), betrayer, traitor, Judas, tell-tale, sneak, spy, mole (*infml*).

infringe *v* **1** BREAK, violate, contravene, transgress, overstep, disobey, defy, flout, ignore.
2 INTRUDE, encroach, trespass, invade.

infuriate *v* anger, vex, enrage, incense, exasperate, madden, provoke, rouse, annoy, irritate, rile, antagonize.
≠ calm, pacify.

ingenious *adj* clever, shrewd, cunning, crafty, skilful, masterly, imaginative, creative, inventive, resourceful, original, innovative.
≠ unimaginative.

ingenuous *adj* artless, guileless, innocent, honest, sincere, frank, open, plain, simple, unsophisticated, naïve, trusting.
≠ artful, sly.

ingrained *adj* fixed, rooted, deep-rooted, deep-seated, entrenched, immovable, ineradicable, permanent, inbuilt, inborn, inbred.

ingratiate *v* curry favour, flatter, creep, crawl, grovel, fawn, get in with.

ingratitude *n* ungratefulness, thanklessness, unappreciativeness, ungraciousness.
≠ gratitude, thankfulness.

ingredient *n* constituent, element, factor, component, part.

inhabit *v* live, dwell, reside, occupy, possess, colonize, settle, people, populate, stay.

inhabitant *n* resident, dweller, citizen, native, occupier, occupant, inmate, tenant, lodger.

inherent *adj* inborn, inbred, innate, inherited, hereditary, native, natural, inbuilt, built-in, intrinsic, ingrained, essential, fundamental, basic.

inherit *v* succeed to, accede to, assume, come into, be left, receive.

inheritance *n* legacy, bequest, heritage, birthright, heredity, descent, succession.

inheritor *n* heir, heiress, successor, beneficiary, recipient.

inhibit *v* discourage, repress, hold back, suppress, curb, check, restrain, hinder, impede, obstruct, interfere with, frustrate, thwart, prevent, stop, stanch, stem.
≠ encourage, assist.

inhibited *adj* repressed, self-conscious, shy, reticent, withdrawn, reserved, guarded, subdued.
≠ uninhibited, open, relaxed.

inhibition *n* repression, hang-up (*sl*), self-consciousness, shyness, reticence, reserve, restraint, curb, check, hindrance, impediment, obstruction, bar.
≠ freedom.

inhuman *adj* barbaric, barbarous, animal, bestial, vicious, savage, sadistic cold-blooded, brutal, cruel, inhumane.
≠ human.

inhumane *adj* unkind, insensitive, callous, unfeeling, heartless, cold-hearted, hard-hearted, pitiless, ruthless cruel, brutal, inhuman.
≠ humane, kind, compassionate.

initial *adj* first, beginning, opening, introductory, inaugural, original, primary, early, formative.
≠ final, last.

initially *adv* at first, at the beginning, to begin with, to start with, originally, first, firstly, first of all.
≠ finally, in the end.

initiate *v* begin, start, commence, originate, pioneer, institute, set up, introduce, launch, open, inaugurate, instigate, activate, trigger, prompt, stimulate, cause.

initiation *n* admission, reception, entrance, entry, debut, introduction, enrolment, induction, investiture, installation, inauguration, inception.

initiative *n* **1** ENERGY, drive, dynamism, get-up-and-go (*infml*), ambition, enterprise, resourcefulness, inventiveness, originality, innovativeness. **2** SUGGESTION, recommendation, action, lead, first move, first step.

inject *v* **1** *inject drugs*: inoculate, vaccinate, shoot (*sl*). **2** INTRODUCE, insert, add, bring, infuse, instil.

injection *n* inoculation, vaccination, jab (*infml*), shot (*infml*), fix (*sl*), dose, insertion, introduction.

injunction *n* command, order, directive, ruling, mandate, direction, instruction, precept.

injure *v* hurt, harm, damage, impair, spoil, mar, ruin, disfigure, deface, mutilate, wound, cut, break, fracture, maim, disable, cripple, lame, ill-treat, maltreat, abuse, offend, wrong, upset, put out.

injury *n* wound, cut, lesion, fracture, trauma, hurt, mischief, ill, harm, damage, impairment, ruin, disfigurement, mutilation, ill-treatment, abuse, insult, offence, wrong, injustice.

injustice *n* unfairness, inequality, disparity, discrimination, oppression, bias, prejudice, one-sidedness, partisanship, partiality, favouritism, wrong, iniquity.
≠ justice, fairness.

inkling *n* suspicion, idea, notion, faintest (*infml*), glimmering, clue, hint, intimation, suggestion, allusion, indication, sign, pointer.

inlet *n* bay, cove, creek, fiord, opening, entrance, passage.

inn *n* public house, pub (*infml*), local (*infml*), tavern, hostelry, hotel.

innate *adj* inborn, inbred, inherent, intrinsic, native, natural, instinctive, intuitive.
≠ acquired, learnt.

inner *adj* internal, interior, inside, inward, innermost, central, middle, concealed, hidden, secret, private, personal, intimate, mental, psychological, spiritual, emotional.
≠ outer, outward.

innocence *n* **1** GUILTLESSNESS, blamelessness, honesty, virtue, righteousness, purity, chastity, virginity, incorruptibility, harmlessness, innocuousness. **2** ARTLESSNESS, guilelessness, naïveness, inexperience, ignorance, naturalness, simplicity, unsophistication, unworldliness, credulity, gullibility, trustfulness.
≠ **1** guilt. **2** experience.

innocent *adj* **1** *innocent of the crime*: guiltless, blameless, irreproachable, unimpeachable, honest, upright, virtuous, righteous, sinless, faultless, impeccable, stainless, spotless, immaculate, unsullied, untainted, uncontaminated, pure, chaste, virginal, incorrupt, inoffensive, harmless, innocuous. **2** ARTLESS, guileless, ingenuous, naïve, green, inexperienced, fresh, natural, simple, unsophisticated, unworldly, childlike, credulous, gullible, trusting.
≠ **1** guilty. **2** experienced.

innocuous *adj* harmless, safe, inoffensive, unobjectionable, innocent.
≠ harmful.

innovation *n* newness, novelty, neologism, modernization, progress, reform, change, alteration, variation, departure.

innovative *adj* new, fresh, original, creative, imaginative, inventive, resourceful, enterprising, go-ahead, progressive, reforming, bold, daring, adventurous.
≠ conservative, unimaginative.

innuendo *n* insinuation, aspersion, slur, whisper, hint, intimation, suggestion, implication.

innumerable *adj* numberless, unnumbered, countless, uncountable, untold, incalculable, infinite, numerous, many.

inoculation *n* vaccination, immunization, protection, injection, shot (*infml*), jab (*infml*).

inoffensive *adj* harmless, innocuous, innocent, peaceable, mild, unobtrusive, unassertive, quiet, retiring.
≠ offensive, harmful, provocative.

inordinate *adj* excessive, immoderate, unwarranted, undue, unreasonable, disproportionate, great.
≠ moderate, reasonable.

inquire, enquire *v* ASK, question, quiz, query, investigate, look into, probe, examine, inspect, scrutinize, search, explore.

inquiry, enquiry *n* question, query, investigation, inquest, hearing, inquisition, examination, inspection, scrutiny, study, survey, poll, search, probe, exploration.

inquisitive *adj* curious, questioning, probing, searching, prying, peeping, snooping, nosey, interfering, meddlesome, intrusive.

insane *adj* **1** MAD, crazy, mentally ill, lunatic, mental (*sl*), demented, deranged, unhinged, disturbed. **2** FOOLISH, stupid, senseless, impractical.
≠ **1** sane. **2** sensible.

insanity *n* madness, craziness, lunacy, mental illness, neurosis, psychosis, mania, dementia, derangement, folly, stupidity, senselessness, irresponsibility.
≠ sanity.

insatiable *adj* unquenchable, unsatisfiable, ravenous, voracious, immoderate, inordinate.

inscribe *v* engrave, etch, carve, cut, incise, imprint, impress, stamp, print, write, sign, autograph, dedicate.

inscription *n* engraving, epitaph, caption, legend, lettering, words, writing, signature, autograph, dedication.

inscrutable *adj* incomprehensible, unfathomable, impenetrable, deep, inexplicable, unexplainable, baffling, mysterious, enigmatic, cryptic, hidden.
≠ comprehensible, expressive.

insects

> *Insects include*: fly, gnat, midge, mosquito, tsetse-fly, locust, dragonfly, cranefly, daddy longlegs (*infml*), horsefly, mayfly, butterfly, moth, bee, bumblebee, wasp, hornet, aphid, blackfly, greenfly, whitefly, froghopper, ladybird, water boatman, lacewing; beetle, cockroach, roach (*US*), earwig, stick insect, grasshopper, cricket, cicada, flea, louse, nit, leatherjacket, termite, glowworm, woodworm, weevil, woodlouse.
> *Arachnids include*: spider, black widow, tarantula, scorpion, mite, tick.
> *Parts of an insect*: abdomen, antenna, cercus, compound eye, forewing, head, hindwing, legs, mandible, mouthpart, ocellus, ovipositor, segment, spiracle, thorax.

insecure *adj* **1** ANXIOUS, worried, nervous, uncertain, unsure, afraid. **2** UNSAFE, dangerous, hazardous, perilous, precarious, unsteady, shaky, loose, unprotected, defenceless, exposed, vulnerable.
≠ **1** confident, self-assured. **2** secure, safe.

insensible *adj* numb, anaesthetized, dead, cold, insensitive, unresponsive, blind, deaf, unconscious, unaware, oblivious, unmindful.
≠ conscious.

insensitive *adj* hardened, tough, resistant, impenetrable, impervious, immune, unsusceptible, thick-skinned, unfeeling, impassive, indifferent, unaffected, unmoved, untouched, uncaring, unconcerned, callous, thoughtless, tactless, crass.
≠ sensitive.

inseparable *adj* indivisible, indissoluble, inextricable, close, intimate, bosom, devoted.
≠ separable.

insert *v* put, place, put in, stick in, push in, introduce, implant, embed, engraft, set, inset, let in, interleave, intercalate, interpolate, interpose.
n insertion, enclosure, inset, notice, advertisement, supplement, addition.

inside *n* interior, content, contents, middle, centre, heart, core.
≠ outside.
adv within, indoors, internally, inwardly, secretly, privately.
≠ outside.
adj interior, internal, inner, innermost, inward, secret, classified, confidential, private.

insides *n* entrails, guts, intestines, bowels, innards (*infml*), organs, viscera, belly, stomach.

insidious *adj* subtle, sly, crafty, cunning, wily, deceptive, devious, stealthy, surreptitious, furtive, sneaking, treacherous.
≠ direct, straightforward.

insight *n* awareness, knowledge, comprehension, understanding, grasp, apprehension, perception, intuition, sensitivity, discernment, judgement, acumen, penetration, observation, vision, wisdom, intelligence.

insignificant *adj* unimportant, irrelevant, meaningless, inconsequential, minor, trivial, trifling, petty, paltry, small, tiny, insubstantial

inconsiderable, negligible, non-essential.
≠ significant, important.

insincere *adj* hypocritical, two-faced, double-dealing, lying, untruthful, dishonest, deceitful, devious, unfaithful, faithless, untrue, false, feigned, pretended, phoney (*infml*), hollow.
≠ sincere.

insinuate *v* imply, suggest, allude, hint, intimate, get at (*infml*), indicate.

insipid *adj* tasteless, flavourless, unsavoury, unappetizing, watery, weak, bland, wishy-washy (*infml*), colourless, drab, dull, monotonous, boring, uninteresting, tame, flat, lifeless, spiritless, characterless, trite, unimaginative, dry.
≠ tasty, spicy, piquant, appetizing.

insist *v* demand, require, urge, stress, emphasize, repeat, reiterate, dwell on, harp on, assert, maintain, claim, contend, hold, vow, swear, persist, stand firm.

insistence *n* demand, entreaty, exhortation, urging, stress, emphasis, repetition, reiteration, assertion, claim, contention, persistence, determination, resolution, firmness.

insistent *adj* demanding, importunate, emphatic, forceful, pressing, urgent, dogged, tenacious, persistent, persevering, relentless, unrelenting, unremitting, incessant.

insolent *adj* rude, abusive, insulting, disrespectful, cheeky (*infml*), impertinent, impudent, saucy (*infml*), bold, forward, fresh, presumptuous, arrogant, defiant, insubordinate.
≠ polite, respectful.

insoluble *adj* unsolvable, unexplainable, inexplicable, incomprehensible, unfathomable, impenetrable, obscure, mystifying, puzzling, perplexing, baffling.
≠ explicable.

insolvent *adj* bankrupt, bust, failed, ruined, broke (*infml*), penniless, destitute.
≠ solvent.

inspect *v* check, vet, look over, examine, search, investigate, scrutinize, study, scan, survey, superintend, supervise, oversee, visit.

inspection *n* check, check-up, examination, scrutiny, scan, study, survey, review, search, investigation, supervision, visit.

inspector *n* supervisor, superintendent, overseer, surveyor, controller, scrutineer, checker, tester, examiner, investigator, reviewer, critic.

inspiration *n* **1** CREATIVITY, imagination, genius, muse, influence, encouragement, stimulation, motivation, spur, stimulus. **2** IDEA, brainwave, insight, illumination, revelation, awakening.

inspire *v* encourage, hearten, influence, impress, animate, enliven, quicken, galvanize, fire, kindle, stir, arouse, trigger, spark off, prompt, spur, motivate, provoke, stimulate, excite, exhilarate, thrill, enthral, enthuse, imbue, infuse.

inspiring *adj* encouraging, heartening, uplifting, invigorating, stirring, rousing, stimulating, exciting, exhilarating, thrilling, enthralling, moving, affecting, memorable, impressive.
≠ uninspiring, dull.

instability *n* unsteadiness, shakiness, vacillation, wavering, irresolution, uncertainty, unpredictability, changeableness, variability, fluctuation, volatility, capriciousness, fickleness, inconstancy, unreliability, insecurity, unsafeness, unsoundness.
≠ stability.

install *v* fix, fit, lay, put, place, position, locate, site, situate, station, plant, settle, establish, set up, introduce, institute, inaugurate, invest, induct, ordain.

instalment *n* **1** *pay in instalments*: payment, repayment, portion. **2** EPISODE, chapter, part, section, division.

instant *n* flash, twinkling, trice, moment, tick (*infml*), split second, second, minute, time, occasion.

adj instantaneous, immediate, on-the-spot, direct, prompt, urgent, unhesitating, quick, fast, rapid, swift.
≠ slow.

instead *adv* alternatively, preferably, rather.
instead of in place of, in lieu of, on behalf of, in preference to, rather than.

instigate *v* initiate, set on, start, begin, cause, generate, inspire, move, influence, encourage, urge, spur, prompt, provoke, stimulate, incite, stir up, whip up, foment, rouse, excite.

instil *v* infuse, imbue, insinuate, introduce, inject, implant, inculcate, impress, din into (*infml*).

instinct *n* intuition, sixth sense, gut reaction (*infml*), impulse, urge, feeling, hunch, flair, knack, gift, talent, feel, faculty, ability, aptitude, predisposition, tendency.

instinctive *adj* natural, native, inborn, innate, inherent, intuitive, impulsive, involuntary, automatic, mechanical, reflex, spontaneous, immediate, unthinking, unpremeditated, gut (*infml*), visceral.
≠ conscious, voluntary, deliberate.

institute *v* originate, initiate, introduce, enact, begin, start, commence, create, establish, set up, organize, found, inaugurate, open, launch, appoint, install, invest, induct, ordain.
≠ cancel, discontinue, abolish.
n school, college, academy, conservatory, foundation, institution.

institution *n* **1** CUSTOM, tradition, usage, practice, ritual, convention, rule, law. **2** ORGANIZATION, association, society, guild, concern, corporation, foundation, establishment, institute, hospital, home. **3** INITIATION, introduction, enactment, inception, creation, establishment, formation, founding, foundation, installation.

instruct *v* **1** TEACH, educate, tutor, coach, train, drill, ground, school, discipline. **2** ORDER, command, direct, mandate, tell, inform, notify, advise, counsel, guide.

instruction *n* **1** *follow the instructions*: direction, recommendation, advice, guidance, information, order, command, injunction, mandate, directive, ruling. **2** EDUCATION, schooling, lesson(s), tuition, teaching, training, coaching, drilling, grounding, preparation.

instructive *adj* informative, educational, edifying, enlightening, illuminating, helpful, useful.
≠ unenlightening.

instructor *n* teacher, master, mistress, tutor, coach, trainer, demonstrator, exponent, adviser, mentor, guide, guru.

instrument *n* **1** TOOL, implement, utensil, appliance, gadget, contraption, device, contrivance, apparatus, mechanism. **2** AGENT, agency, vehicle, organ, medium, factor, channel, way, means.

instrumental *adj* active, involved, contributory, conducive, influential, useful, helpful, auxiliary, subsidiary.
≠ obstructive, unhelpful.

insufferable *adj* intolerable, unbearable, detestable, loathsome, dreadful, impossible.
≠ pleasant, tolerable.

insufficiency *n* inadequacy, shortage, deficiency, lack, scarcity, dearth, want, need, poverty.
≠ sufficiency, excess.

insufficient *adj* inadequate, short, deficient, lacking, sparse, scanty, scarce.
≠ sufficient, excessive.

insular *adj* parochial, provincial, cut off, detached, isolated, remote, withdrawn, inward-looking, blinkered, closed, narrow-minded, narrow, limited, petty.

insulate *v* cushion, pad, lag, cocoon, protect, shield, shelter, isolate, separate, cut off.

insult *v* abuse, call names, disparage, revile, libel, slander, slight, snub, injure, affront, offend, outrage.
≠ compliment, praise.
n abuse, rudeness, insolence, defamation, libel, slander, slight, snub, affront, indignity, offence, outrage.
≠ compliment, praise.

nsurance *n* cover, protection, safeguard, security, provision, assurance, indemnity, guarantee, warranty, policy, premium.

nsure *v* cover, protect, assure, underwrite, indemnify, guarantee, warrant.

nsurmountable *adj* insuperable, unconquerable, invincible, overwhelming, hopeless, impossible.
≠ surmountable.

nsurrection *n* rising, uprising, insurgence, riot, rebellion, mutiny, revolt, revolution, coup, putsch.

ntact *adj* unbroken, all in one piece, whole, complete, integral, entire, perfect, sound, undamaged, unhurt, uninjured.
≠ broken, incomplete, damaged.

ntangible *adj* insubstantial, imponderable, elusive, fleeting, airy, shadowy, vague, indefinite, abstract, unreal, invisible.
≠ tangible, real.

ntegral *adj* **1** *an integral part*: intrinsic, constituent, elemental, basic, fundamental, necessary, essential, indispensable. **2** COMPLETE, entire, full, whole, undivided.
≠ **1** extra, additional, unnecessary.

ntegrate *v* assimilate, merge, join, unite, combine, amalgamate, incorporate, coalesce, fuse, knit, mesh, mix, blend, harmonize.
≠ divide, separate.

ntegrity *n* **1** HONESTY, uprightness, probity, incorruptibility, purity, morality, principle, honour, virtue, goodness, righteousness. **2** COMPLETENESS, wholeness, unity, coherence, cohesion.
≠ **1** dishonesty. **2** incompleteness.

ntellect *n* mind, brain(s), brainpower, intelligence, genius, reason, understanding, sense, wisdom, judgement.
≠ stupidity.

ntellectual *adj* academic, scholarly, intelligent, studious, thoughtful, cerebral, mental, highbrow, cultural.
≠ low-brow.
n thinker, academic, highbrow, egghead, mastermind, genius.
≠ low-brow.

intelligence *n* **1** INTELLECT, reason, wit(s), brain(s) (*infml*), brainpower, cleverness, brightness, aptitude, quickness, alertness, discernment, perception, understanding, comprehension. **2** INFORMATION, facts, data, low-down (*sl*), knowledge, findings, news, report, warning, tip-off.
≠ **1** stupidity, foolishness.

intelligent *adj* clever, bright, smart, brainy (*infml*), quick, alert, quick-witted, sharp, acute, knowing, knowledgeable, well-informed, thinking, rational, sensible.
≠ unintelligent, stupid, foolish.

intend *v* aim, have a mind, contemplate, mean, propose, plan, project, scheme, plot, design, purpose, resolve, determine, destine, mark out, earmark, set apart.

intense *adj* great, deep, profound, strong, powerful, forceful, fierce, harsh, severe, acute, sharp, keen, eager, earnest, ardent, fervent, fervid, passionate, vehement, energetic, violent, intensive, concentrated, heightened.
≠ moderate, mild, weak.

intensify *v* increase, step up, escalate, heighten, hot up (*infml*), fire, boost, fuel, aggravate, add to, strengthen, reinforce, sharpen, whet, quicken, deepen, concentrate, emphasize, enhance.
≠ reduce, weaken.

intensive *adj* concentrated, thorough, exhaustive, comprehensive, detailed, in-depth, thoroughgoing, all-out, intense.
≠ superficial.

intent *adj* determined, resolved, resolute, set, bent, concentrated, eager, earnest, committed, steadfast, fixed, alert, attentive, concentrating, preoccupied, engrossed, wrapped up, absorbed, occupied.
≠ absent-minded, distracted.

intention *n* aim, purpose, object, end, point, target, goal, objective, idea, plan, design, view, intent, meaning.

intentional *adj* designed, wilful, conscious, planned, deliberate, prearranged, premeditated, calculated, studied, intended, meant.
≠ unintentional, accidental.

intercede *v* mediate, arbitrate, intervene, plead, entreat, beseech, speak.

intercept *v* head off, ambush, interrupt, cut off, stop, arrest, catch, take, seize, check, block, obstruct, delay, frustrate, thwart.

interchangeable *adj* reciprocal, equivalent, similar, identical, the same, synonymous, standard.
≠ different.

interest *n* **1** IMPORTANCE, significance, note, concern, care, attention, notice, curiosity, involvement, participation. **2** *leisure interests*: activity, pursuit, pastime, hobby, diversion, amusement. **3** ADVANTAGE, benefit, profit, gain.
≠ **1** boredom.
v concern, involve, touch, move, attract, appeal to, divert, amuse, occupy, engage, absorb, engross, fascinate, intrigue.
≠ bore.

interested *adj* **1** ATTENTIVE, curious, absorbed, engrossed, fascinated, enthusiastic, keen, attracted. **2** CONCERNED, involved, affected.
≠ **1** uninterested, indifferent, apathetic. **2** disinterested, unaffected.

interesting *adj* attractive, appealing, entertaining, engaging, absorbing, engrossing, fascinating, intriguing, compelling, gripping, stimulating, thought-provoking, curious, unusual.
≠ uninteresting, boring, monotonous, tedious.

interfere *v* **1** INTRUDE, poke one's nose in, pry, butt in, interrupt, intervene, meddle, tamper. **2** HINDER, hamper, obstruct, block, impede, handicap, cramp, inhibit, conflict, clash.
≠ **2** assist.

interference *n* **1** INTRUSION, prying, interruption, intervention, meddling. **2** OBSTRUCTION, opposition, conflict, clashing.
≠ **2** assistance.

interim *adj* temporary, provisional, stopgap, makeshift, improvised, stand-in, acting, caretaker.
n meantime, meanwhile, interval.

interior *adj* **1** INTERNAL, inside, inner, central, inward, mental, spiritual, private, secret, hidden. **2** HOME, domestic, inland, up-country, remote.
≠ **1** exterior, external.
n inside, centre, middle, core, heart, depths.
≠ exterior, outside.

interjection *n* exclamation, ejaculation, cry, shout, call, interpolation.

intermediary *n* mediator, go-between, middleman, broker, agent.

intermediate *adj* midway, halfway, in-between, middle, mid, median, mean, intermediary, intervening, transitional.
≠ extreme.

interminable *adj* endless, never-ending, ceaseless, perpetual, limitless, unlimited, long, long-winded, long-drawn-out, dragging, wearisome.
≠ limited, brief.

intermission *n* interval, entr'acte, interlude, break, recess, rest, respite, breather (*infml*), breathing-space, pause, lull, let-up (*infml*), remission, suspension, interruption, halt, stop, stoppage, cessation.

intermittent *adj* occasional, periodic, sporadic, spasmodic, fitful, erratic, irregular, broken.
≠ continuous, constant.

internal *adj* inside, inner, interior, inward, intimate, private, personal, domestic, in-house.
≠ external.

international *adj* global, worldwide, intercontinental, cosmopolitan, universal, general.
≠ national, local, parochial.

interplay *n* exchange, interchange, interaction, reciprocation, give-and-take.

interpose *v* insert, introduce, interject, interpolate, put in, thrust in, interrupt, intrude, interfere, come between, intervene, step in, mediate.

interpret *v* explain, expound, elucidate

clarify, throw light on, define, paraphrase, translate, render, decode, decipher, solve, make sense of, understand, construe, read, take.

interpretation *n* explanation, clarification, analysis, translation, rendering, version, performance, reading, understanding, sense, meaning.

interrogate *v* question, quiz, examine, cross-examine, grill, give the third degree, pump, debrief.

interrogation *n* questioning, cross-questioning, examination, cross-examination, grilling, third degree, inquisition, inquiry, inquest.

interrupt *v* intrude, barge in (*infml*), butt in, interject, break in, heckle, disturb, disrupt, interfere, obstruct, check, hinder, hold up, stop, halt, suspend, discontinue, cut off, disconnect, punctuate, separate, divide, cut, break.

interruption *n* intrusion, interjection, disturbance, disruption, obstruction, impediment, obstacle, hitch, pause, break, halt, stop, stoppage, suspension, discontinuance, disconnection, separation, division.

intersect *v* cross, criss-cross, cut across, bisect, divide, meet, converge.

intersection *n* junction, interchange, crossroads, crossing.

intertwine *v* entwine, interweave, interlace, interlink, twist, twine, cross, weave.

interval *n* interlude, intermission, break, rest, pause, delay, wait, interim, meantime, meanwhile, gap, opening, space, distance, period, spell, time, season.

intervene *v* **1** STEP IN, mediate, arbitrate, interfere, interrupt, intrude. **2** OCCUR, happen, elapse, pass.

intervention *n* involvement, interference, intrusion, mediation, agency, intercession.

nterview *n* audience, consultation, talk, dialogue, meeting, conference, press conference, oral examination, viva.
v question, interrogate, examine, vet.

intestines *n* bowels, guts, entrails, insides, innards (*infml*), offal, viscera, vitals.

intimacy *n* friendship, closeness, familiarity, confidence, confidentiality, privacy.
≠ distance.

intimate[1] *v* hint, insinuate, imply, suggest, indicate, communicate, impart, tell, state, declare, announce.

intimate[2] *adj* friendly, informal, familiar, cosy, warm, affectionate, dear, bosom, close, near, confidential, secret, private, personal, internal, innermost, deep, penetrating, detailed, exhaustive.
≠ unfriendly, cold, distant.
n friend, bosom friend, confidant(e), associate.
≠ stranger.

intimidate *v* daunt, cow, overawe, appal, dismay, alarm, scare, frighten, terrify, threaten, menace, terrorize, bully, browbeat, bulldoze, coerce, pressure, pressurize, lean on (*sl*).

intolerable *adj* unbearable, unendurable, insupportable, unacceptable, insufferable, impossible.
≠ tolerable.

intolerant *adj* impatient, prejudiced, bigoted, narrow-minded, small-minded, opinionated, dogmatic, illiberal, uncharitable.
≠ tolerant.

intonation *n* modulation, tone, accentuation, inflection.

intoxicated *adj* **1** DRUNK, drunken, inebriated, tipsy. **2** EXCITED, elated, exhilarated, thrilled.
≠ **1** sober.

intoxicating *adj* **1** *intoxicating liquor*: alcoholic, strong. **2** EXCITING, stimulating, heady, exhilarating, thrilling.
≠ **1** sobering.

intoxication *n* **1** DRUNKENNESS, inebriation, tipsiness. **2** EXCITEMENT, elation, exhilaration, euphoria.
≠ **1** sobriety.

intrepid *adj* bold, daring, brave, courageous, plucky, valiant, lion-hearted, fearless, dauntless, undaunted,

stout-hearted, stalwart, gallant, heroic.
≠ cowardly, timid.

intricate *adj* elaborate, fancy, ornate, rococo, complicated, complex, sophisticated, involved, convoluted, tortuous, tangled, entangled, knotty, perplexing, difficult.
≠ simple, plain, straightforward.

intrigue *n* **1** PLOT, scheme, conspiracy, collusion, machination, manoeuvre, stratagem, ruse, wile, trickery, double-dealing, sharp practice. **2** ROMANCE, liaison, affair, amour, intimacy.
v **1** FASCINATE, rivet, puzzle, tantalize, attract, charm, captivate.
2 PLOT, scheme, conspire, connive, machinate, manoeuvre.
≠ **1** bore.

introduce *v* **1** INSTITUTE, begin, start, commence, establish, found, inaugurate, launch, open, bring in, announce, present, acquaint, familiarize, initiate. **2** PUT FORWARD, advance, submit, offer, propose, suggest.
≠ **1** end, conclude. **2** remove, take away.

introduction *n* **1** INSTITUTION, beginning, start, commencement, establishment, inauguration, launch, presentation, debut, initiation.
2 FOREWORD, preface, preamble, prologue, preliminaries, overture, prelude, lead-in, opening.
≠ **1** removal, withdrawal. **2** appendix, conclusion.

introductory *adj* preliminary, preparatory, opening, inaugural, first, initial, early, elementary, basic.

introspective *adj* inward-looking, contemplative, meditative, pensive, thoughtful, brooding, introverted, self-centred, reserved, withdrawn.
≠ outward-looking.

introverted *adj* introspective, inward-looking, self-centred, withdrawn, shy, reserved, quiet.
≠ extroverted.

intrude *v* interrupt, butt in, meddle, interfere, violate, infringe, encroach, trespass.
≠ withdraw, stand back.

intruder *n* trespasser, prowler, burglar, raider, invader, infiltrator, interloper, gatecrasher.

intrusion *n* interruption, interference, violation, infringement, encroachment, trespass, invasion, incursion.
≠ withdrawal.

intuition *n* instinct, sixth sense, perception, discernment, insight, hunch, feeling, gut feeling (*infml*).
≠ reasoning.

intuitive *adj* instinctive, spontaneous, involuntary, innate, untaught.
≠ reasoned.

inundate *v* flood, deluge, swamp, engulf, submerge, immerse, drown, bury, overwhelm, overrun.

invade *v* enter, penetrate, infiltrate, burst in, descend on, attack, raid, seize, occupy, overrun, swarm over, infest, pervade, encroach, infringe, violate.
≠ withdraw, evacuate.

invalid[1] *adj* sick, ill, poorly, ailing, sickly, weak, feeble, frail, infirm, disabled, bedridden.
≠ healthy.
n patient, convalescent.

invalid[2] *adj* **1** FALSE, fallacious, unsound, ill-founded, unfounded, baseless, illogical, irrational, unscientific, wrong, incorrect.
2 ILLEGAL, null, void, worthless.
≠ **1** valid. **2** legal.

invaluable *adj* priceless, inestimable, incalculable, precious, valuable, useful
≠ worthless, cheap.

invariable *adj* fixed, set, unvarying, unchanging, unchangeable, permanent constant, steady, unwavering, uniform rigid, inflexible, habitual, regular.
≠ variable.

invariably *adv* always, without exception, without fail, unfailingly, consistently, regularly, habitually.
≠ never.

invasion *n* attack, offensive, onslaught raid, incursion, foray, breach, penetration, infiltration, intrusion, encroachment, infringement, violation
≠ withdrawal, evacuation.

invent *v* conceive, think up, design, discover, create, originate, formulate, frame, devise, contrive, improvise, fabricate, make up, concoct, cook up, trump up, imagine, dream up.

invention *n* **1** *her latest invention*: design, creation, brainchild, discovery, development, device, gadget. **2** LIE, falsehood, deceit, fabrication, fiction, tall story, fantasy, figment. **3** INVENTIVENESS, imagination, creativity, innovation, originality, ingenuity, inspiration, genius.
≠ **2** truth.

inventive *adj* imaginative, creative, innovative, original, ingenious, resourceful, fertile, inspired, gifted, clever.

inventor *n* designer, discoverer, creator, originator, author, architect, maker, scientist, engineer.

inverse *adj* inverted, upside down, transposed, reversed, opposite, contrary, reverse, converse.

invert *v* upturn, turn upside down, overturn, capsize, upset, transpose, reverse.
≠ right.

invertebrates

Invertebrates include: *sponges*: calcareous, glass, horny; *jellyfish, corals and sea anemones*: Portugese man-of-war, box jellyfish, sea wasp, dead-men's fingers, sea pansy, sea gooseberry, Venus's girdle; *echinoderms*: sea lily, feather star, starfish, crown-of-thorns, brittle star, sea urchin, sand dollar, sea cucumber; *worms*: annelid worm, arrow worm, blood fluke, bristle worm, earthworm, eelworm, flatworm, fluke, hookworm, leech, liver fluke, lugworm, peanut worm, pinworm, ragworm, ribbonworm, roundworm, sea mouse, tapeworm, threadworm; *crustaceans*: acorn barnacle, barnacle, brine shrimp, crayfish, daphnia, fairy shrimp, fiddler crab, fish louse, goose barnacle, hermit crab, krill, lobster, mantis shrimp, mussel shrimp, pill bug, prawn, sand hopper, seed shrimp, spider crab, spiny lobster, tadpole shrimp, water flea, whale louse, woodlouse; centipede, millipede, velvet worm. *see also* **butterflies and moths; insects; molluscs.**

invest *v* **1** SPEND, lay out, put in, sink. **2** PROVIDE, supply, endow, vest, empower, authorize, sanction.

investigate *v* inquire into, look into, consider, examine, study, inspect, scrutinize, analyse, go into, probe, explore, search, sift.

investigation *n* inquiry, inquest, hearing, examination, study, research, survey, review, inspection, scrutiny, analysis, probe, exploration, search.

investigator *n* examiner, researcher, detective, sleuth (*infml*), private detective, private eye (*infml*).

investment *n* asset, speculation, venture, stake, contribution, outlay, expenditure, transaction.

invigorate *v* vitalize, energize, animate, enliven, liven up, quicken, strengthen, fortify, brace, stimulate, inspire, exhilarate, perk up, refresh, freshen, revitalize, rejuvenate.
≠ tire, weary, dishearten.

invincible *adj* unbeatable, unconquerable, insuperable, unsurmountable, indomitable, unassailable, impregnable, impenetrable, invulnerable, indestructible.
≠ beatable.

invisible *adj* unseen, out of sight, hidden, concealed, disguised, inconspicuous, indiscernible, imperceptible, infinitesimal, microscopic, imaginary, non-existent.
≠ visible.

invitation *n* request, solicitation, call, summons, temptation, enticement, allurement, come-on (*infml*), encouragement, inducement, provocation, incitement, challenge.

invite *v* ask, call, summon, welcome, encourage, lead, draw, attract, tempt, entice, allure, bring on, provoke, ask for, request, solicit, seek.

inviting *adj* welcoming, appealing, attractive, tempting, seductive, enticing, alluring, pleasing, delightful,

captivating, fascinating, intriguing, tantalizing.
≠ uninviting, unappealing.

invoke *v* call upon, conjure, appeal to, petition, solicit, implore, entreat, beg, beseech, supplicate, pray.

involuntary *adj* spontaneous, unconscious, automatic, mechanical, reflex, instinctive, conditioned, impulsive, unthinking, blind, uncontrolled, unintentional.
≠ deliberate, intentional.

involve *v* **1** REQUIRE, necessitate, mean, imply, entail, include, incorporate, embrace, cover, take in, affect, concern. **2** IMPLICATE, incriminate, inculpate, draw in, mix up, embroil, associate. **3** ENGAGE, occupy, absorb, engross, preoccupy, hold, grip, rivet.
≠ **1** exclude.

involved *adj* **1** CONCERNED, implicated, mixed up, caught up, in on (*sl*), participating. **2** *an involved explanation*: complicated, complex, intricate, elaborate, tangled, knotty, tortuous, confusing.
≠ **1** uninvolved. **2** simple.

involvement *n* concern, interest, responsibility, association, connection, participation, implication, entanglement.

invulnerable *adj* safe, secure, unassailable, impenetrable, invincible, indestructible.
≠ vulnerable.

inward *adj* incoming, entering, inside, interior, internal, inner, innermost, inmost, personal, private, secret, confidential.
≠ outward, external.

iota *n* scrap, bit, mite, jot, speck, trace, hint, grain, particle, atom.

irate *adj* annoyed, irritated, indignant, up in arms, angry, enraged, mad (*infml*), furious, infuriated, incensed, worked up, fuming, livid, exasperated.
≠ calm, composed.

iron *adj* rigid, inflexible, adamant, determined, hard, steely, tough, strong.
≠ pliable, weak.
v press, smooth, flatten.

iron out resolve, settle, sort out, straighten out, clear up, put right, reconcile, deal with, get rid of, eradicate, eliminate.

ironic *adj* ironical, sarcastic, sardonic, scornful, contemptuous, derisive, sneering, scoffing, mocking, satirical, wry, paradoxical.

irony *n* sarcasm, mockery, satire, paradox, contrariness, incongruity.

irrational *adj* unreasonable, unsound, illogical, absurd, crazy, wild, foolish, silly, senseless, unwise.
≠ rational.

irreconcilable *adj* incompatible, opposed, conflicting, clashing, contradictory, inconsistent.
≠ reconcilable.

irrefutable *adj* undeniable, incontrovertible, indisputable, incontestable, unquestionable, unanswerable, certain, sure.

irregular *adj* **1** ROUGH, bumpy, uneven, crooked. **2** VARIABLE, fluctuating, wavering, erratic, fitful, intermittent, sporadic, spasmodic, occasional, random, haphazard, disorderly, unsystematic. **3** ABNORMAL, unconventional, unorthodox, improper, unusual, exceptional, anomalous.
≠ **1** smooth, level. **2** regular. **3** conventional.

irrelevant *adj* immaterial, beside the point, inapplicable, inappropriate, unrelated, unconnected, inconsequent, peripheral, tangential.
≠ relevant.

irreplaceable *adj* indispensable, essential, vital, unique, priceless, peerless, matchless, unmatched.
≠ replaceable.

irrepressible *adj* ebullient, bubbly, uninhibited, buoyant, resilient, boisterous, uncontrollable, ungovernable, unstoppable.

irreproachable *adj* irreprehensible, blameless, unimpeachable, faultless, impeccable, perfect, unblemished, immaculate, stainless, spotless, pure.
≠ blameworthy, culpable.

irresistible *adj* overwhelming,

overpowering, unavoidable, inevitable, inescapable, uncontrollable, potent, compelling, imperative, pressing, urgent, tempting, seductive, ravishing, enchanting, charming, fascinating.
≠ resistible, avoidable.

irresponsible *adj* unreliable, untrustworthy, careless, negligent, thoughtless, heedless, ill-considered, rash, reckless, wild, carefree, light-hearted, immature.
≠ responsible, cautious.

irreverent *adj* **1** IMPIOUS, godless, irreligious, profane, sacrilegious, blasphemous. **2** DISRESPECTFUL, discourteous, rude, impudent, impertinent, mocking, flippant.
≠ **1** reverent. **2** respectful.

irreversible *adj* irrevocable, unalterable, final, permanent, lasting, irreparable, irremediable, irretrievable, incurable, hopeless.
≠ reversible, remediable, curable.

irrevocable *adj* unalterable, unchangeable, changeless, invariable, immutable, final, fixed, settled, predetermined, irreversible, irretrievable.
≠ alterable, flexible, reversible.

irrigate *v* water, flood, inundate, wet, moisten, dampen.

irritable *adj* cross, bad-tempered, ill-tempered, crotchety, crusty, cantankerous, crabby, testy, short-tempered, snappish, snappy, short, impatient, touchy, edgy, thin-skinned, hypersensitive, prickly, peevish, fretful, fractious.
≠ good-tempered, cheerful.

irritate *v* **1** ANNOY, get on one's nerves, aggravate (*infml*), bother, harass, rouse, provoke, rile, anger, enrage, infuriate, incense, exasperate, peeve, put out. **2** INFLAME, chafe, rub, tickle, itch.
≠ **1** please, gratify.

irritation *n* displeasure, dissatisfaction, annoyance, aggravation, provocation, anger, vexation, indignation, fury, exasperation, irritability, crossness, testiness, snappiness, impatience.
≠ pleasure, satisfaction, delight.

isolate *v* set apart, sequester, seclude, keep apart, segregate, quarantine, insulate, cut off, detach, remove, disconnect, separate, divorce, alienate, shut out, ostracize, exclude.
≠ assimilate, incorporate.

isolated *adj* **1** REMOTE, out-of-the-way, outlying, god-forsaken, deserted, unfrequented, secluded, detached, cut off, lonely, solitary, single. **2** *an isolated occurrence*: unique, special, exceptional, atypical, unusual, freak, abnormal, anomalous.
≠ **1** populous. **2** typical.

isolation *n* quarantine, solitude, solitariness, loneliness, remoteness, seclusion, retirement, withdrawal, exile, segregation, insulation, separation, detachment, disconnection, dissociation, alienation.

issue *n* **1** MATTER, affair, concern, problem, point, subject, topic, question, debate, argument, dispute, controversy. **2** PUBLICATION, release, distribution, supply, delivery, circulation, promulgation, broadcast, announcement. **3** *last week's issue*: copy, number, instalment, edition, impression, printing.
v **1** PUBLISH, release, distribute, supply, deliver, give out, deal out, circulate, promulgate, broadcast, announce, put out, emit, produce. **2** ORIGINATE, stem, spring, rise, emerge, burst forth, gush, flow, proceed, emanate, arise.

itch *v* tickle, irritate, tingle, prickle, crawl.
n **1** ITCHINESS, tickle, irritation, prickling. **2** EAGERNESS, keenness, desire, longing, yearning, hankering, craving.

item *n* **1** OBJECT, article, thing, piece, component, ingredient, element, factor, point, detail, particular, aspect, feature, consideration, matter. **2** *an item in the local paper*: article, piece, report, account, notice, entry, paragraph.

itinerant *adj* travelling, peripatetic, roving, roaming, wandering, rambling, nomadic, migratory, rootless, unsettled.
≠ stationary, settled.

itinerary *n* route, course, journey, tour, circuit, plan, programme, schedule.

J

jab *v* poke, prod, dig, nudge, stab, push, elbow, lunge, punch, tap, thrust.

jackpot *n* prize, winnings, kitty, pool, pot, reward, award, big time (*infml*), bonanza, stakes.

jaded *adj* fatigued, exhausted, dulled, played-out, tired, tired out, weary, spent, bored, fagged (*infml*).
≠ fresh, refreshed.

jagged *adj* uneven, irregular, notched, indented, rough, serrated, saw-edged, toothed, ragged, pointed, ridged, craggy, barbed, broken.
≠ even, smooth.

jail, gaol *n* prison, jailhouse, custody, lock-up, penitentiary, guardhouse, inside (*infml*), nick (*sl*), clink (*sl*).
v imprison, incarcerate, lock up, put away, send down, confine, detain, intern, impound, immure.

jailer, gaoler *n* prison officer, warden, warder, guard, screw (*sl*), keeper, captor.

jam[1] *v* **1** CRAM, pack, wedge, squash, squeeze, press, crush, crowd, congest, ram, stuff, confine, force. **2** BLOCK, clog, obstruct, stall, stick.
n **1** CRUSH, crowd, press, congestion, pack, mob, throng, bottle-neck, traffic jam. **2** PREDICAMENT, trouble, quandary, plight, fix (*infml*).

jam[2] *n* conserve, preserve, jelly, spread, marmalade.

jangle *v* clank, clash, jar, clatter, jingle, chime, rattle, vibrate.
n clang, clash, rattle, jar, cacophony, dissonance, din, discord, racket, reverberation.
≠ euphony.

jar[1] *n* pot, container, vessel, receptacle, crock, pitcher, urn, vase, flagon, jug, mug.

jar[2] *v* **1** JOLT, agitate, rattle, shake, vibrate, jangle, rock, disturb, discompose. **2** ANNOY, irritate, grate, nettle (*infml*), offend, upset, irk. **3** BICKER, quarrel, clash, disagree.

jargon *n* **1** PARLANCE, cant, argot, vernacular, idiom. **2** NONSENSE, gobbledegook (*infml*), mumbo-jumbo (*infml*), gibberish.

jarring *adj* discordant, jangling, harsh, grating, irritating, cacophonous, rasping, strident, upsetting, disturbing, jolting.

jaundiced *adj* **1** BITTER, cynical, pessimistic, sceptical, distrustful, disbelieving, envious, jealous, hostile, jaded, suspicious, resentful. **2** DISTORTED, biased, prejudiced, preconceived.

jaunty *adj* sprightly, lively, perky, breezy, buoyant, high-spirited, self-confident, carefree, airy, cheeky, debonair, dapper, smart, showy, spruce.
≠ depressed, dowdy.

jaw (*infml*) *v* chat, chatter, gossip, natter (*infml*), talk, rabbit (on) (*infml*), gabble, babble.
n talk, gossip, chat, conversation, discussion, chinwag, natter (*infml*).

jealous *adj* **1** ENVIOUS, covetous, grudging, resentful, green (*infml*), green-eyed (*infml*). **2** SUSPICIOUS, wary, distrustful, anxious, possessive, protective.
≠ **1** contented, satisfied.

jealousy *n* **1** ENVY, covetousness, grudge, resentment, spite, ill-will. **2** SUSPICION, distrust, mistrust, possessiveness.

jeer *v* mock, scoff, taunt, jibe, ridicule, sneer, deride, make fun of, chaff, barrack, twit, knock (*infml*), heckle, banter.
n mockery, derision, ridicule, taunt, jibe, sneer, scoff, abuse, catcall, dig (*infml*), hiss, hoot.

jell *see* **gel**.

jeopardize *v* endanger, imperil, risk, hazard, venture, gamble, chance, threaten, menace, expose, stake.
≠ protect, safeguard.

jeopardy *n* danger, peril, risk, hazard, endangerment, venture, vulnerability, precariousness, insecurity, exposure, liability.
≠ safety, security.

jerk *n* jolt, tug, twitch, jar, jog, yank, wrench, pull, pluck, lurch, throw, thrust, shrug.
v jolt, tug, twitch, jog, yank, wrench, pull, jiggle, lurch, pluck, thrust, shrug, throw, bounce.

jerky *adj* fitful, twitchy, spasmodic, jumpy, jolting, convulsive, disconnected, bumpy, bouncy, shaky, rough, uncoordinated, uncontrolled, incoherent.
≠ smooth.

jest *n* joke, quip, wisecrack (*infml*), witticism, crack (*infml*), banter, fooling, gag (*infml*), prank, kidding (*infml*), leg-pull (*infml*), trick, hoax.
v joke, quip, fool, kid (*infml*), tease, mock, jeer.

jet[1] *n* gush, spurt, spout, spray, spring, sprinkler, sprayer, fountain, flow, stream, squirt.

jet[2] *adj* black, pitch-black, ebony, sable, sooty.

jetty *n* breakwater, pier, dock, groyne, quay, wharf.

jewel *n* **1** GEM, precious stone, gemstone, ornament, rock (*sl*). **2** TREASURE, find, prize, rarity, paragon, pearl.

jewellery

> *Types of jewellery include*: bangle, bracelet, charm bracelet, anklet, cufflink, tiepin, hatpin, brooch, cameo, earring, nose-ring, ring, signet-ring, solitaire ring, necklace, necklet, choker, pendant, locket, chain, beads, amulet, torque, tiara, coronet, diadem.

Jewish calendar

> *The Jewish calendar and its Gregorian equivalents*: Tishri (September-October), Hesshvan (October-November), Kislev (November-December), Tevet (December-January), Shevat (January-February), Adar (February-March), Adar Sheni (leap years only), Nisan (March-April), Iyar (April-May), Sivan (May-June), Tammuz (June-July), Av (July-August), Elul (August-September).

jibe *see* **gibe**.

jig *v* jerk, prance, caper, hop, jump, twitch, skip, bounce, bob, wiggle, shake, wobble.

jilt *v* abandon, reject, desert, discard, brush off, ditch (*infml*), drop, spurn, betray.

jingle *v* clink, tinkle, ring, chime, chink, jangle, clatter, rattle.
n **1** CLINK, tinkle, ringing, clang, rattle, clangour. **2** RHYME, verse, song, tune, ditty, doggerel, melody, poem, chant, chorus.

jingoism *n* chauvinism, flag-waving, patriotism, nationalism, imperialism, warmongering, insularity.

jinx (*infml*) *n* spell, curse, evil eye, hex, voodoo, hoodoo, black magic, gremlin (*infml*), charm, plague.
v curse, bewitch, bedevil, doom, plague.

job *n* **1** *she has a good job*: work, employment, occupation, position, post, situation, profession, career, calling, vocation, trade, métier, capacity, business, livelihood.
2 *it's a difficult job*: task, chore, duty, responsibility, charge, commission, mission, activity, affair, concern, proceeding, project, enterprise, office, pursuit, role, undertaking, venture, province, part, place, share, errand, function, contribution, stint, assignment, consignment.

jobless *adj* unemployed, out of work, laid off, on the dole, inactive, redundant.
≠ employed.

jocular *adj* joking, jesting, funny, jocose (*fml*), humorous, jovial, amusing, comical, entertaining,

facetious, droll, whimsical, teasing, witty.
≠ serious.

jog *v* **1** JOLT, jar, bump, jostle, jerk, joggle, nudge, poke, shake, prod, bounce, push, rock. **2** PROMPT, remind, stir, arouse, activate, stimulate. **3** RUN, trot.
n **1** JOLT, bump, jerk, nudge, shove, push, poke, prod, shake. **2** RUN, trot.

join *v* **1** UNITE, connect, combine, conjoin, attach, link, amalgamate, fasten, merge, marry, couple, yoke, tie, splice, knit, cement, add, adhere, annex. **2** ABUT, adjoin, border (on), verge on, touch, meet, coincide, march with. **3** ASSOCIATE, affiliate, accompany, ally, enlist, enrol, enter, sign up, team.
≠ **1** divide, separate. **3** leave.

joint *n* junction, connection, union, juncture, intersection, hinge, knot, articulation, seam.
adj combined, common, communal, joined, shared, united, collective, amalgamated, mutual, co-operative, co-ordinated, consolidated, concerted.

joke *n* **1** JEST, quip, crack (*infml*), gag (*infml*), witticism, wisecrack (*infml*), one-liner (*infml*), pun, hoot, whimsy, yarn. **2** TRICK, jape, lark, prank, spoof, fun.
v jest, quip, clown, fool, pun, wisecrack (*infml*), kid (*infml*), tease, banter, mock, laugh, frolic, gambol.

joker *n* comedian, comic, wit, humorist, jester, trickster, wag, clown, buffoon, kidder, droll, card (*infml*), character, sport.

jolly *adj* jovial, merry, cheerful, playful, hearty, happy, exuberant.
≠ sad.

jolt *v* **1** JAR, jerk, jog, bump, jostle, knock, bounce, shake, push. **2** UPSET, startle, shock, surprise, stun, discompose, disconcert, disturb.
n **1** JAR, jerk, jog, bump, blow, impact, lurch, shake. **2** SHOCK, surprise, reversal, setback, start.

jostle *v* push, shove, jog, bump, elbow, hustle, jolt, crowd, shoulder, joggle, shake, squeeze, throng.

jot down write down, take down, note, list, record, scribble, register, enter.

journal *n* newspaper, periodical, magazine, paper, publication, review, weekly, monthly, register, chronicle, diary, gazette, daybook, log, record.

journalist *n* reporter, news-writer, hack, correspondent, editor, columnist, feature-writer, commentator, broadcaster, contributor.

journey *n* voyage, trip, travel, expedition, passage, trek, tour, ramble, outing, wanderings, safari, progress.
v travel, voyage, go, trek, tour, roam, rove, proceed, wander, tramp, ramble, range, gallivant.

jovial *adj* jolly, cheery, merry, affable, cordial, genial.
≠ gloomy.

joy *n* happiness, gladness, delight, pleasure, bliss, ecstasy, elation, joyfulness, exultation, gratification, rapture.
≠ despair, grief.

joyful *adj* happy, pleased, delighted, glad, elated, ecstatic, triumphant.
≠ sorrowful.

jubilant *adj* joyful, rejoicing, overjoyed, delighted, elated, triumphant, exuberant, excited, euphoric, thrilled.

jubilee *n* celebration, commemoration, anniversary, festival, festivity, gala, fête, carnival.

judge *n* **1** JUSTICE, Law Lord, magistrate, arbiter, adjudicator, arbitrator, mediator, moderator, referee, umpire, beak (*sl*). **2** CONNOISSEUR, authority, expert, evaluator, assessor, critic.
v **1** ADJUDICATE, arbitrate, try, referee, umpire, decree, mediate, examine, sentence, review, rule, find. **2** ASCERTAIN, determine, decide, assess, appraise, evaluate, estimate, value, distinguish, discern, reckon, believe, think, consider, conclude, rate. **3** CONDEMN, criticize, doom.

judgement *n* **1** VERDICT, sentence, ruling, decree, conclusion, decision, arbitration, finding, result, mediation, order. **2** DISCERNMENT, discrimination understanding, wisdom, prudence, common sense, sense, intelligence, taste, shrewdness, penetration, enlightenment. **3** ASSESSMENT, evaluation, appraisal, estimate, opinion, view, belief, diagnosis. **4** CONVICTION, damnation, punishment, retribution, doom, fate, misfortune.

judicial *adj* legal, judiciary, magistral, forensic, official, discriminating, critical, impartial.

judicious *adj* wise, prudent, careful, cautious, astute, discerning, informed, shrewd, thoughtful, reasonable, sensible, sound, well-judged, well-advised, considered.
≠ injudicious.

jug *n* pitcher, carafe, ewer, flagon, urn, jar, vessel, container.

juggle *v* alter, change, manipulate, falsify, rearrange, rig, doctor (*infml*), cook (*infml*), disguise.

juice *n* liquid, fluid, extract, essence, sap, secretion, nectar, liquor.

juicy *adj* **1** SUCCULENT, moist, lush, watery. **2** (*infml*) INTERESTING, colourful, sensational, racy, risqué, suggestive, lurid.
≠ **1** dry.

jumble *v* disarrange, confuse, disorganize, mix (up), muddle, shuffle, tangle.
≠ order.
n disorder, disarray, confusion, mess, chaos, mix-up, muddle, clutter, mixture, hotch-potch, mishmash (*infml*), medley.

jump *v* **1** LEAP, spring, bound, vault, clear, bounce, skip, hop, prance, frolic, gambol. **2** START, flinch, jerk, recoil, jump out of one's skin (*infml*), wince, quail. **3** OMIT, leave out, miss, skip, pass over, bypass, disregard, ignore, avoid, digress. **4** RISE, increase, gain, appreciate, ascend, escalate, mount, advance, surge, spiral.
n **1** LEAP, spring, bound, vault, hop, skip, bounce, prance, frisk, frolic, pounce. **2** START, jerk, jolt, jar, lurch, shock, spasm, quiver, shiver, twitch. **3** BREAK, gap, interruption, lapse, omission, interval, breach, switch. **4** RISE, increase, escalation, boost, advance, increment, upsurge, upturn, mounting. **5** HURDLE, fence, gate, hedge, barricade, obstacle.

jumpy *adj* nervous, anxious, agitated, apprehensive, jittery, tense, edgy, fidgety, shaky.
≠ calm, composed.

junction *n* joint, join, joining, connection, juncture, union, intersection, linking, coupling, meeting-point, confluence.

junior *adj* younger, minor, lesser, lower, subordinate, secondary, subsidiary, inferior.
≠ senior.

junk *n* rubbish, refuse, trash, debris, garbage, waste, scrap, litter, clutter, oddments, rummage, dregs, wreckage.

jurisdiction *n* power, authority, control, influence, dominion, province, sovereignty, command, domination, rule, prerogative (*fml*), sway, orbit, bounds, area, field, scope, range, reach, sphere, zone.

just *adj* **1** *a just ruler*: fair, equitable, impartial, unbiased, unprejudiced, fair-minded, even-handed, objective, righteous, upright, virtuous, honourable, good, honest, irreproachable. **2** *a just punishment*: deserved, merited, fitting, well-deserved, appropriate, suitable, due, proper, reasonable, rightful, lawful, legitimate.
≠ **1** unjust. **2** undeserved.

justice *n* **1** FAIRNESS, equity, impartiality, objectivity, equitableness, justness, legitimacy, honesty, right, rightfulness, rightness, justifiableness, reasonableness, rectitude. **2** LEGALITY, law, penalty, recompense, reparation, satisfaction. **3** JUDGE, Justice of the Peace, JP, magistrate.
≠ **1** injustice, unfairness.

justifiable *adj* defensible, excusable, warranted, reasonable, justified, lawful, legitimate, acceptable, explainable, forgivable, pardonable, understandable, valid, well-founded, right, proper, explicable, fit, tenable.
≠ unjustifiable.

justification *n* defence, plea,

mitigation, apology, explanation, excuse, vindication, warrant, rationalization, reason, grounds.

justify *v* vindicate, exonerate, warrant, substantiate, defend, acquit, absolve, excuse, forgive, explain, pardon, validate, uphold, sustain, support, maintain, establish.

jut (out) *v* project, protrude, stick out, overhang, extend.
≠ recede.

juvenile *n* child, youth, minor, young person, youngster, adolescent, teenager, boy, girl, kid (*infml*), infant.
adj young, youthful, immature, childish, puerile, infantile, adolescent, babyish, unsophisticated.
≠ mature.

juxtaposition *n* contiguity, proximity, nearness, closeness, contact, vicinity, immediacy.

K

karate

> *Karate belts include*: *junior grades (Kyu)*: red belt (beginner), white belt (8th Kyu), yellow belt (7th Kyu), orange belt (6th Kyu), green belt (5th Kyu), brown belt (4th-1st Kyu), black belt (1st Dan); *senior grades (Dans)*: black belts (1st-8th Dan).

keel over 1 OVERTURN, capsize, founder, collapse, upset. **2** FAINT, pass out, swoon, fall, drop, stagger, topple over.

keen *adj* **1** EAGER, avid, fervent, enthusiastic, earnest, devoted, diligent, industrious. **2** ASTUTE, shrewd, clever, perceptive, wise, discerning, quick, deep, sensitive. **3** SHARP, piercing, penetrating, incisive, acute, pointed, intense, pungent, trenchant.
≠ **1** apathetic. **2** superficial. **3** dull.

keep *v* **1** RETAIN, hold, preserve, hold on to, hang on to, store, stock, possess, amass, accumulate, collect, stack, conserve, deposit, heap, pile, place, maintain, furnish. **2** CARRY ON, keep on, continue, persist, remain. **3** LOOK AFTER, tend, care for, have charge of, have custody of, maintain, provide for, subsidize, support, sustain, be responsible for, foster, mind, protect, shelter, guard, defend, watch (over), shield, safeguard, feed, nurture, manage. **4** DETAIN, delay, retard, check, hinder, hold (up), impede, obstruct, prevent, block, curb, interfere with, restrain, limit, inhibit, deter, hamper, keep back, control, constrain, arrest, withhold. **5** OBSERVE, comply with, respect, obey, fulfil, adhere to, recognize, keep up, keep faith with, commemorate, celebrate, hold, maintain, perform, perpetuate, mark, honour.
n **1** SUBSISTENCE, board, livelihood, living, maintenance, support, upkeep, means, food, nourishment, nurture. **2** FORT, fortress, tower, castle, citadel, stronghold, dungeon.
keep back 1 RESTRAIN, check, constrain, curb, impede, limit, prohibit, retard, stop, control, delay. **2** HOLD BACK, restrict, suppress, withhold, conceal, censor, hide, hush up, stifle, reserve, retain.
keep in 1 REPRESS, keep back, inhibit, bottle up, conceal, stifle, suppress, hide, control, restrain, quell, stop up. **2** CONFINE, detain, shut in, coop up.
≠ **1** declare. **2** release.
keep on continue, carry on, endure, persevere, persist, keep at it, last, remain, stay, stay the course, soldier on (*infml*), hold on, retain, maintain.
keep up keep pace, equal, contend, compete, vie, rival, match, emulate, continue, maintain, persevere, support, sustain, preserve.

keeper *n* guard, custodian, curator, caretaker, attendant, guardian, overseer, steward, warder, jailer, gaoler, warden, supervisor, minder (*infml*), inspector, conservator (*fml*), defender, governor, superintendent, surveyor.

keepsake *n* memento, souvenir, remembrance, relic, reminder, token, pledge, emblem.

kernel *n* core, grain, seed, nucleus, heart, nub, essence, germ, marrow, substance, nitty-gritty (*infml*), gist.

key *n* **1** CLUE, cue, indicator, pointer, explanation, sign, answer, solution, interpretation, means, secret. **2** GUIDE, glossary, translation, legend, code, table, index.
adj important, essential, vital, crucial, necessary, principal, decisive, central, chief, main, major, leading, basic, fundamental.

keynote *n* core, centre, heart, substance, theme, gist, essence, emphasis, accent, stress.

keystone *n* cornerstone, core, crux, base, basis, foundation, ground, linchpin, principle, root, mainspring, source, spring, motive.

kick *v* **1** BOOT, hit, strike, jolt. **2** (*infml*) GIVE UP, quit, stop, leave off, abandon, desist from, break.
n **1** BLOW, recoil, jolt, striking. **2** (*infml*) STIMULATION, thrill, excitement.
kick off begin, commence, start, open, get under way, open the proceedings, set the ball rolling, introduce, inaugurate, initiate.
kick out eject, evict, expel, oust, remove, chuck out (*infml*), discharge, dismiss, get rid of, sack (*infml*), throw out, reject.

kid[1] *n* child, youngster, youth, juvenile, infant, girl, boy, teenager, lad, nipper (*infml*), tot (*infml*).

kid[2] *v* tease, joke, have on (*infml*), hoax, fool, pull someone's leg (*infml*), pretend, trick, delude, dupe, con (*infml*), jest, hoodwink, humbug, bamboozle.

kidnap *v* abduct, capture, seize, hold to ransom, snatch, hijack, steal.

kill *v* **1** SLAUGHTER, murder, slay, put to death, exterminate, assassinate, do to death, do in (*infml*), bump off (*infml*), finish off, massacre, smite (*fml*), execute, eliminate (*sl*), destroy, dispatch (*infml*), do away with, butcher, annihilate, liquidate (*sl*), knock off (*infml*), rub out (*sl*).
2 STIFLE, deaden, smother, quash, quell, suppress.

killer *n* murderer, assassin, executioner, destroyer, slaughterer, exterminator, butcher (*infml*), cut-throat, gunman, hatchet man (*sl*), hit-man (*sl*).

killing *n* **1** SLAUGHTER, murder, massacre, homicide, assassination, execution, slaying, manslaughter, extermination, carnage, bloodshed, elimination, fatality, liquidation. **2** (*infml*) GAIN, fortune, windfall, profit, lucky break, coup, clean-up (*infml*), success, stroke of luck, bonanza (*infml*), hit, big hit.
adj (*infml*) **1** FUNNY, hilarious, comical, amusing, side-splitting (*infml*), ludicrous. **2** EXHAUSTING, hard, taxing, arduous.

kind *n* sort, type, class, category, set, variety, character, genus, genre, style, brand, family, breed, race, nature, persuasion, description, species, stamp, temperament, manner.
adj benevolent, kind-hearted, kindly, good-hearted, good-natured, helpful, obliging, humane, generous, compassionate, charitable, amiable, friendly, congenial, soft-hearted, thoughtful, warm, warm-hearted, considerate, courteous, sympathetic, tender-hearted, understanding, lenient, mild, hospitable, gentle, indulgent, neighbourly, tactful, giving, good, loving, gracious.
≠ cruel, inconsiderate, unhelpful.

kindle *v* **1** IGNITE, light, set alight, set on fire. **2** INFLAME, fire, stir, thrill, stimulate, rouse, arouse, awaken, excite, fan, incite, inspire, induce, provoke.

kindly *adj* benevolent, kind, compassionate, charitable, good-natured, helpful, warm, generous, cordial, favourable, giving, indulgent, pleasant, sympathetic, tender, gentle, mild, patient, polite.
≠ cruel, uncharitable.

kindness *n* **1** BENEVOLENCE, kindliness, charity, magnanimity, compassion, generosity, hospitality, humanity, loving-kindness (*fml*), courtesy, friendliness, good will, goodness, grace, indulgence, tolerance, understanding, gentleness. **2** FAVOUR, good turn, assistance, help, service.
≠ **1** cruelty, inhumanity. **2** disservice.

king *n* monarch, ruler, sovereign, majesty, emperor, chief, chieftain, prince, supremo, leading light (*infml*).

kingdom *n* monarchy, sovereignty, reign, realm, empire, dominion, commonwealth, nation, principality, state, country, domain, dynasty, province, sphere, territory, land, division.

kink *n* **1** CURL, twist, bend, dent, indentation, knot, loop, crimp, coil, tangle, wrinkle. **2** QUIRK, eccentricity, idiosyncracy, foible, perversion.

kinship *n* **1** KIN, blood, relation. **2** AFFINITY, similarity, association, alliance, connection, correspondence, relationship, tie, community, conformity.

kiosk *n* booth, stall, stand, news-stand, bookstall, cabin, box, counter.

kiss *v* **1** CARESS, peck (*infml*), smooch (*infml*), neck (*infml*), snog (*sl*). **2** TOUCH, graze, glance, brush, lick, scrape, fan.
n peck (*infml*), smack (*infml*), smacker (*sl*).

kit *n* equipment, gear, apparatus, supplies, tackle, provisions, outfit, implements, set, tools, trappings, rig, instruments, paraphernalia, utensils, effects, luggage, baggage.
kit out equip, fit out, outfit, supply, fix up, furnish, prepare, arm, deck out, dress.

kitchen utensils

Kitchen utensils include: baster, bottle opener, breadbin, breadboard, butter curler, butter dish, can-opener, cheese board, cheese slicer, chopping-board, colander, corer, corkscrew, cruet set, dough hook, egg separator, egg slicer, egg-timer, fish slice, flour dredger, fork, garlic press, grater, herb mill, ice-cream scoop, icing syringe, jelly mould, kitchen scales, knife block, lemon squeezer, mandolin, measuring jug, meat thermometer, mincer, mixing bowl, nutcracker, nutmeg grater, pasta maker, pastry board, pastry brush, pastry cutter, peeler, pepper mill, pie funnel, potato masher, pudding basin, punch bowl, rolling-pin, salad spinner, scissors, shears, sharpening steel, sieve, sifter, skewer, spatula, spice rack, stoner, storage jar, tea caddy, tea infuser, tea strainer, toast rack, tongs, tureen, vegetable brush, whisk, wine cooler, wine rack, yoghurt maker, zester; *types of knife*: boning knife, bread knife, butter-knife, carving knife, cheese knife, cleaver, cocktail knife, cook's knife, fish knife, grapefruit knife, Kitchen Devils®, palette knife, paring knife, vegetable knife; *types of spoon*: dessert spoon, draining spoon, ladle, measuring spoon, serving spoon, skimmer, straining spoon, tablespoon, teaspoon, wooden spoon.
Types of cooking utensil include: baking sheet, bun tin, cake tin, flan tin, loaf tin, muffin tin, pie plate, quiche dish; bain-marie, brochette, casserole, cocotte, deep-fat fryer, egg coddler, egg poacher, fish kettle, fondue set, frying-pan, grill pan, milk pan, preserving pan, pressure cooker, ramekin, roasting pan, saucepan, skillet, slow cooker, soufflé dish, steamer, stockpot, terrine, vegetable steamer, wok.

knack *n* flair, faculty, facility, hang (*infml*), bent, skill, talent, genius, gift, trick, propensity, ability, expertise, skilfulness, forte, capacity, handiness, dexterity, quickness, turn.

knapsack *n* bag, pack, haversack, rucksack, backpack.

knead *v* manipulate, press, massage, work, ply, squeeze, shape, rub, form, mould, knuckle.

knell *n* toll, ringing, chime, peal, knoll.

knick-knack *n* trinket, trifle, bauble, gewgaw, gimcrack, bric-à-brac, plaything.

knife *n* blade, cutter, carver, dagger, pen-knife, pocket-knife, switchblade, jack-knife, flick-knife, machete.
v cut, rip, slash, stab, pierce, wound.

knit *v* **1** JOIN, unite, secure, connect, tie, fasten, link, mend, interlace, intertwine. **2** KNOT, loop, crotchet, weave. **3** WRINKLE, furrow.

knock *v* hit, strike, rap, thump, pound, slap, smack.
n blow, box, rap, thump, cuff, clip, pounding, hammering, slap, smack.
knock about 1 WANDER, travel, roam, rove, saunter, traipse, ramble, range. **2** ASSOCIATE, go around. **3** BEAT UP,

batter, abuse, mistreat, hurt, hit, bash, damage, maltreat, manhandle, bruise, buffet.

knock down demolish, destroy, fell, floor, level, wreck, raze, pound, batter, clout, smash, wallop.

knock off 1 (*infml*) FINISH, cease, stop, pack (it) in, clock off, clock out, terminate. **2** (*infml*) STEAL, rob, pilfer, pinch (*infml*), nick (*infml*), filch. **3** DEDUCT, take away. **4** (*sl*) KILL, murder, slay, assassinate, do away with, bump off (*infml*), do in (*infml*), waste (*sl*).

knockout (*infml*) *n* success, triumph, sensation, hit, smash (*infml*), smash-hit (*infml*), winner, stunner (*infml*).
≠ flop, loser.

knot *v* tie, secure, bind, entangle, tangle, knit, entwine, ravel, weave.
n **1** TIE, bond, joint, fastening, loop, splice, hitch.

Types of knot include: bend, Blackwall hitch, blood knot, bow, bowline, running bowline, carrick bend, clove hitch, common whipping, double-overhang, Englishman's tie (or knot), figure of eight, fisherman's bend, fisherman's knot, flat knot, granny knot, half hitch, highwayman's hitch, hitch, Hunter's bend, loop knot, overhand knot or thumb knot, reef knot or square knot, rolling hitch, round turn and two half hitches, seizing, sheepshank, sheet bend or common bend or swab hitch, slipknot, spade-end knot, surgeon's knot, tie, timber hitch, Turk's head, turle knot, wall knot, weaver's knot, Windsor knot.

2 BUNCH, cluster, clump, group.

know *v* **1** *know French*: understand, comprehend, apprehend, perceive, notice, be aware, fathom, experience, realize, see, undergo. **2** *I know George*: be acquainted with, be familiar with, recognize, identify. **3** *know a good wine*: distinguish, discriminate, discern, differentiate, make out, tell.

knowledge *n* **1** LEARNING, scholarship, erudition, education, schooling, instruction, tuition, information, enlightenment, know-how. **2** ACQUAINTANCE, familiarity, awareness, cognizance, intimacy, consciousness. **3** UNDERSTANDING, comprehension, cognition, apprehension, recognition, judgement, discernment, ability, grasp, wisdom, intelligence.
≠ **1** ignorance. **2** unawareness.

knowledgeable *adj* **1** EDUCATED, scholarly, learned, well-informed, lettered, intelligent. **2** AWARE, acquainted, conscious, familiar, au fait, in the know (*infml*), conversant, experienced.
≠ **1** ignorant.

known *adj* acknowledged, recognized, well-known, noted, obvious, patent, plain, admitted, familiar, avowed, commonplace, published, confessed, celebrated, famous.

kowtow *v* defer, cringe, fawn, grovel, pander, suck up (*infml*), toady (*infml*), flatter, kneel.

L

label *n* **1** TAG, ticket, docket, mark, marker, sticker, trademark. **2** DESCRIPTION, categorization, identification, characterization, classification, badge, brand.
v **1** TAG, mark, stamp. **2** DEFINE, describe, classify, categorize, characterize, identify, class, designate, brand, call, dub, name.

laboratory apparatus

Laboratory apparatus includes: autoclave, beaker, bell jar, boiling tube, Büchner funnel, Bunsen burner, burette, centrifuge, clamp, condenser, conical flask, crucible, cylinder, desiccator, distillation apparatus, dropper, evaporating dish, filter flask, filter paper, flask, fume cupboard, funnel, glove box, Kipp's apparatus, Liebig condenser, measuring cylinder, microscope, mortar, pestle, Petri dish, pipette, retort, separating funnel, slide, spatula, stand, still, stirrer, stop clock, test tube, test tube rack, thermometer, top-pan balance, tripod, trough, U-tube, volumetric flask, Woulfe bottle.

laborious *adj* **1** HARD, arduous, difficult, strenuous, tough, backbreaking, wearisome, tiresome, uphill, onerous, heavy, toilsome. **2** HARD-WORKING, industrious, painstaking, indefatigable, diligent.
≠ **1** easy, effortless. **2** lazy.

labour *n* **1** WORK, task, job, chore, toil, effort, exertion, drudgery, grind (*infml*), slog (*infml*), sweat (*infml*). **2** WORKERS, employees, workforce, labourers. **3** CHILDBIRTH, birth, delivery, labour pains, contractions.
≠ **1** ease, leisure. **2** management.
v **1** WORK, toil, drudge, slave, strive, endeavour, struggle, grind (*infml*), sweat (*infml*), plod, travail (*fml*). **2** TOSS, pitch, roll. **3** OVERDO, overemphasize, dwell on, elaborate, overstress, strain.
≠ **1** laze, idle, lounge.

labourer *n* manual worker, blue-collar worker, navvy, hand, worker, drudge, hireling.

labyrinth *n* maze, complexity, intricacy, complication, puzzle, riddle, windings, tangle, jungle.

lace *n* **1** NETTING, mesh-work, open-work, tatting, crochet. **2** STRING, cord, thong, tie, shoelace, bootlace.
v **1** TIE, do up, fasten, thread, close, bind, attach, string, intertwine, interweave. **2** ADD TO, mix in, spike (*infml*), fortify.

lacerate *v* tear, rip, rend, cut, gash, slash, wound, claw, mangle, maim, torture, torment, distress, afflict.

lack *n* need, want, scarcity, shortage, insufficiency, dearth, deficiency, absence, scantiness, vacancy, void, privation, deprivation, destitution, emptiness.
≠ abundance, profusion.
v need, want, require, miss.

lacking *adj* needing, wanting, without, short of, missing, minus, inadequate, deficient, defective, flawed.

lacklustre *adj* drab, dull, flat, boring, leaden, lifeless, unimaginative, dim.
≠ brilliant, inspired.

laconic *adj* terse, succinct, pithy, concise, crisp, taciturn, short, curt, brief.
≠ verbose, wordy.

lad *n* boy, youth, youngster, kid (*infml*), schoolboy, chap, guy (*infml*), fellow.

ladders

Types of ladder include: accommodation ladder, companion ladder, étrier, extension ladder, folding ladder, fruit-picking ladder, gangway ladder, hook ladder, loft ladder, multipurpose ladder, platform ladder, quarter ladder, ratline, rolling ladder, roof ladder, rope ladder, scale, side ladder, stepladder, stepstool, stern ladder, stile, straight ladder, tower scaffold.

lag *v* dawdle, loiter, hang back, linger, straggle, trail, saunter, delay, shuffle, tarry, idle.
≠ hurry, lead.

lair *n* den, burrow, hole, nest, earth, form, roost, retreat, hideout, refuge, sanctuary, stronghold.

lake *n* lagoon, reservoir, loch, mere, tarn.

lame *adj* **1** DISABLED, handicapped, crippled, limping, hobbling. **2** WEAK, feeble, flimsy, inadequate, unsatisfactory, poor.
≠ **1** able-bodied. **2** convincing.

lament *v* mourn, bewail, bemoan, grieve, sorrow, weep, wail, complain, deplore, regret.
≠ rejoice, celebrate.
n lamentation, dirge, elegy, requiem, threnody (*fml*), complaint, moan, wail.

lamentable *adj* **1** DEPLORABLE, regrettable, mournful, distressing, tragic, unfortunate, sorrowful. **2** MEAGRE, low, inadequate, insufficient, mean, unsatisfactory, pitiful, miserable, poor, disappointing.

lampoon *n* satire, skit, caricature, parody, send-up (*infml*), spoof, take-off (*infml*), burlesque.
v satirize, caricature, parody, send up, take off (*infml*), spoof, make fun of, ridicule, mock, burlesque.

land *n* **1** EARTH, ground, soil, terra firma. **2** PROPERTY, grounds, estate, real estate, country, countryside, farmland, tract. **3** COUNTRY, nation, region, territory, province.
v **1** ALIGHT, disembark, dock, berth, touch down, come to rest, arrive, deposit, wind up, end up, drop, settle, turn up. **2** OBTAIN, secure, gain, get, acquire, net, capture, achieve, win.

landlord *n* owner, proprietor, host, publican, innkeeper, hotelier, restaurateur, hotel-keeper, freeholder.
≠ tenant.

landmark *n* feature, monument, signpost, turning-point, watershed, milestone, beacon, cairn.

landscape *n* scene, scenery, view, panorama, outlook, vista, prospect, countryside, aspect.

landslide *n* landslip, earthfall, rock-fall, avalanche.
adj overwhelming, decisive, emphatic, runaway.

language *n* **1** SPEECH, vocabulary, terminology, parlance. **2** TALK, conversation, discourse. **3** WORDING, style, phraseology, phrasing, expression, utterance, diction.

Language terms include: brogue, dialect, idiom, patois, tongue, pidgin, creole, lingua franca, vernacular, argot, cant, jargon, doublespeak, gobbledegook, buzzword, journalese, lingo (*infml*), patter, slang, cockney rhyming slang; etymology, lexicography, linguistics, phonetics, semantics, syntax, usage, grammar, orthography, sociolinguistics.

languages

Languages of the world include: Aborigine, Afghan, Afrikaans, Arabic, Balinese, Bantu, Basque, Bengali, Burmese, Belorussian, Catalan, Celtic, Chinese, Cornish, Czech, Danish, Dutch, English, Esperanto, Estonian, Ethiopian, Farsi, Finnish, Flemish, French, Gaelic, German, Greek, Haitian, Hawaiian, Hebrew, Hindi, Hindustani, Hottentot, Hungarian, Icelandic, Indonesian, Inuit, Irish, Iranian, Iraqi, Italian, Japanese, Kurdish, Lapp, Latin, Latvian, Lithuanian, Magyar, Malay, Maltese, Mandarin, Manx, Maori, Nahuatl, Navajo, Norwegian, Persian, Polish, Portuguese, Punjabi, Quechua, Romany, Romanian, Russian, Sanskrit, Scots, Serbo-Croat, Siamese, Sinhalese, Slavonic, Slovak, Slovenian, Somali, Spanish, Swahili, Swedish, Swiss, Tamil, Thai, Tibetan, Tupí, Turkish, Ukrainian, Urdu, Vietnamese, Volapük, Welsh, Yiddish, Zulu.

languish *v* **1** WILT, droop, fade, fail, flag, wither, waste away, weaken, sink, faint, decline, mope, waste, grieve, sorrow, sigh, sicken. **2** PINE, yearn, want, long, desire, hanker, hunger.
≠ **1** flourish.

lanky *adj* gaunt, gangling, scrawny, tall, thin, scraggy, weedy.
≠ short, squat.

lap[1] *v* drink, sip, sup, lick.

lap[2] *n* circuit, round, orbit, tour, loop, course, circle, distance.
v wrap, fold, envelop, enfold, swathe, surround, cover, swaddle, overlap.

lapse *n* **1** ERROR, slip, mistake, negligence, omission, oversight, fault, failing, indiscretion, aberration, backsliding, relapse. **2** FALL, descent, decline, drop, deterioration. **3** BREAK, gap, interval, lull, interruption, intermission, pause.
v **1** DECLINE, fall, sink, drop, deteriorate, slide, slip, fail, worsen, degenerate, backslide. **2** EXPIRE, run out, end, stop, terminate.

large *adj* **1** BIG, huge, immense, massive, vast, sizable, great, giant, gigantic, bulky, enormous, king-sized, broad, considerable, monumental, substantial. **2** FULL, extensive, generous, liberal, roomy, plentiful, spacious, grand, sweeping, grandiose.
≠ **1** small, tiny.
at large free, at liberty, on the loose, on the run, independent.

largely *adv* mainly, principally, chiefly, generally, primarily, predominantly, mostly, considerably, by and large, widely, extensively, greatly.

lark *n* escapade, antic, fling, prank, romp, skylark (*infml*), revel, mischief, frolic, caper, game.

lash[1] *n* blow, whip, stroke, swipe, hit.
v **1** WHIP, flog, beat, hit, thrash, strike, scourge. **2** ATTACK, criticize, lay into, scold.

lash[2] *v* tie, bind, fasten, secure, make fast, join, affix, rope, tether, strap.

last[1] *adj* final, ultimate, closing, latest, rearmost, terminal, furthest, concluding, remotest, utmost, extreme, conclusive, definitive.
≠ first, initial.
adv finally, ultimately, behind, after.
≠ first, firstly.
at last eventually, finally, in the end, in due course, at length.

last[2] *v* continue, endure, remain, persist, keep (on), survive, hold out, carry on, wear, stay, hold on, stand up, abide (*fml*).
≠ cease, stop, fade.

lasting *adj* enduring, unchanging, unceasing, unending, continuing, permanent, perpetual, lifelong, long-standing, long-term.
≠ brief, fleeting, short-lived.

latch *n* fastening, catch, bar, bolt, lock, hook, hasp.

late *adj* **1** OVERDUE, behind, behind-hand, slow, unpunctual, delayed, last-minute. **2** FORMER, previous, departed, dead, deceased, past, preceding, old. **3** RECENT, up-to-date, current, fresh, new.
≠ **1** early, punctual.

lately *adv* recently, of late, latterly.

latent *adj* potential, dormant, undeveloped, unrealized, lurking, unexpressed, unseen, secret, concealed, hidden, invisible, underlying, veiled.
≠ active, conspicuous.

later *adv* next, afterwards, subsequently, after, successively.
≠ earlier.

lateral *adj* sideways, side, oblique, sideward, edgeways, marginal, flanking.

lather *n* **1** FOAM, suds, soap-suds, froth, bubbles, soap, shampoo. **2** AGITATION, fluster, fuss, dither, state (*infml*), flutter, flap (*infml*), fever.
v foam, froth, soap, shampoo, whip up.

latitude *n* **1** SCOPE, range, room, space, play, clearance, breadth, width, spread, sweep, reach, span, field, extent. **2** FREEDOM, liberty, licence, leeway, indulgence.

latter *adj* last-mentioned, last, later, closing, concluding, ensuing,

succeeding, successive, second.
≠ former.

laugh *v* chuckle, giggle, guffaw, snigger, titter, chortle, split one's sides, fall about (*infml*), crease up (*infml*).
n giggle, chuckle, snigger, titter, guffaw, chortle, lark, scream (*infml*), hoot (*infml*), joke.
laugh at mock, ridicule, deride, jeer, make fun of, scoff at, scorn, taunt.

laughable *adj* **1** FUNNY, amusing, comical, humorous, hilarious, droll, farcical, diverting. **2** RIDICULOUS, absurd, ludicrous, preposterous, nonsensical, derisory, derisive.
≠ **1** serious.

laughing-stock *n* figure of fun, butt, victim, target, fair game.

laughter *n* laughing, giggling, chuckling, chortling, guffawing, tittering, hilarity, amusement, merriment, mirth, glee, convulsions.

launch *v* **1** PROPEL, dispatch, discharge, send off, project, float, set in motion, throw, fire. **2** BEGIN, commence, start, embark on, establish, found, open, initiate, inaugurate, introduce, instigate.

lavatory *n* toilet, loo (*infml*), WC, bathroom, cloakroom, washroom, water-closet, public convenience, Ladies (*infml*), Gents (*infml*), bog (*sl*), urinal, powder-room.

lavish *adj* **1** ABUNDANT, lush, luxuriant, plentiful, profuse, unlimited, prolific. **2** GENEROUS, liberal, open-handed, extravagant, thriftless, prodigal, immoderate, intemperate, unstinting.
≠ **1** scant. **2** frugal, thrifty.

law *n* **1** RULE, act, decree, edict, order, statute, regulation, command, ordinance, charter, constitution, enactment. **2** PRINCIPLE, axiom, criterion, standard, precept, formula, code, canon. **3** JURISPRUDENCE, legislation, litigation.

law-abiding *adj* obedient, upright, orderly, lawful, honest, honourable, decent, good.
≠ lawless.

lawful *adj* legal, legitimate, permissible, legalized, authorized, allowable, warranted, valid, proper, rightful.
≠ illegal, unlawful, illicit.

lawless *adj* disorderly, rebellious, anarchic(al), unruly, riotous, mutinous, unrestrained, chaotic, wild, reckless.
≠ law-abiding.

lawsuit *n* litigation, suit, action, proceedings, case, prosecution, dispute, process, trial, argument, contest, cause.

lawyer *n* solicitor, barrister, advocate, attorney, counsel, QC.

lax *adj* **1** CASUAL, careless, easy-going, slack, lenient, negligent, remiss.
2 IMPRECISE, inexact, indefinite, loose.
≠ **1** strict. **2** exact.

lay[1] *v* **1** PUT, place, deposit, set down, settle, lodge, plant, set, establish, leave. **2** ARRANGE, position, set out, locate, work out, devise, prepare, present, submit. **3** ATTRIBUTE, ascribe, assign, charge.
lay in store (up), stock up, amass, accumulate, hoard, stockpile, gather, collect, build up, glean.
lay into (*infml*) attack, assail, pitch into, set about, tear into, let fly at.
lay off 1 DISMISS, discharge, make redundant, sack (*infml*), pay off, let go. **2** (*infml*) GIVE UP, drop, stop, quit, cease, desist, leave off, leave alone, let up.
lay on provide, supply, cater, furnish, give, set up.
lay out 1 DISPLAY, set out, spread out, exhibit, arrange, plan, design. **2** (*infml*) KNOCK OUT, fell, flatten, demolish.
3 (*infml*) SPEND, pay, shell out (*infml*), fork out (*infml*), give, invest.
lay up store up, hoard, accumulate, amass, keep, save, put away.

lay[2] *adj* **1** LAIC, secular. **2** AMATEUR, non-professional, non-specialist.
≠ **1** clergy. **2** expert.

layer *n* **1** COVER, coating, coat, covering, film, blanket, mantle, sheet, lamina. **2** STRATUM, seam, thickness, tier, bed, plate, row, ply.

layman *n* **1** LAYPERSON, parishioner.
2 AMATEUR, outsider.
≠ **1** clergyman. **2** expert.

layout *n* arrangement, design, outline, plan, sketch, draft, map.

laze *v* idle, loaf (*infml*), lounge, sit around, lie around, loll.

lazy *adj* idle, slothful, slack, work-shy, inactive, lethargic.
≠ industrious.

lead *v* **1** GUIDE, conduct, escort, steer, pilot, usher. **2** RULE, govern, head, preside over, direct, supervise. **3** INFLUENCE, persuade, incline. **4** SURPASS, outdo, excel, outstrip, transcend. **5** PASS, spend, live, undergo.
≠ **1** follow.
n **1** PRIORITY, precedence, first place, start, van, vanguard, advantage, edge, margin. **2** LEADERSHIP, guidance, direction, example, model. **3** CLUE, hint, indication, guide, tip, suggestion. **4** TITLE ROLE, starring part, principal.
lead off begin, commence, open, get going, start (off), inaugurate, initiate, kick off (*infml*), start the ball rolling.
lead on entice, lure, seduce, tempt, draw on, beguile, persuade, string along, deceive, trick.
lead to cause, result in, produce, bring about, bring on, contribute to, tend towards.
lead up to prepare (the way) for, approach, introduce, make overtures, pave the way.

leader *n* head, chief, director, ruler, principal, commander, captain, boss (*infml*), superior, chieftain, ringleader, guide, conductor.
≠ follower.

leadership *n* direction, control, command, management, authority, guidance, domination, pre-eminence, premiership, administration, sway, directorship.

leading *adj* main, principal, chief, primary, first, supreme, outstanding, foremost, dominant, ruling, superior, greatest, highest, governing, pre-eminent, number one.
≠ subordinate.

leaf

Leaf parts include: auxillary bud, blade, chloroplasts, epidermis, leaf axil, leaf cells, margin, midrib, petiole, sheath, stipule, stomata, tip, vein.
Leaf shapes include: abruptly pinnate, acerose, ciliate, cordate, crenate, dentate, digitate, doubly dentate, elliptic, entire, falcate, hastate, lanceolate, linear, lobed, lyrate, obovate, orbicular, ovate, palmate, peltate, pinnate, pinnatifid, reniform, runcinate, sagittate, spathulate, subulate, ternate, trifoliate.

leaflet *n* pamphlet, booklet, brochure, circular, handout.

league *n* **1** ASSOCIATION, confederation, alliance, union, federation, confederacy, coalition, combination, band, syndicate, guild, consortium, cartel, combine, partnership, fellowship, compact. **2** CATEGORY, class, level, group.
in league allied, collaborating, conspiring.

leak *n* **1** CRACK, hole, opening, puncture, crevice, chink. **2** LEAKAGE, leaking, seepage, drip, oozing, percolation. **3** DISCLOSURE, divulgence.
v **1** SEEP, drip, ooze, escape, spill, trickle, percolate, exude, discharge. **2** DIVULGE, disclose, reveal, let slip, make known, make public, tell, give away, pass on.

leaky *adj* leaking, holey, perforated, punctured, split, cracked, porous, permeable.

lean[1] *v* **1** SLANT, slope, bend, tilt, list, tend. **2** RECLINE, prop, rest. **3** INCLINE, favour, prefer.

lean[2] *adj* **1** THIN, skinny, bony, gaunt, lank, angular, slim, scraggy, scrawny, emaciated. **2** SCANTY, inadequate, bare, barren.
≠ **1** fat.

leaning *n* tendency, inclination, propensity, partiality, liking, bent, bias, disposition, aptitude.

leap *v* **1** JUMP (OVER), bound, spring, vault, clear, skip, hop, bounce, caper, gambol. **2** SOAR, surge, increase, rocket, escalate, rise.
≠ **2** drop, fall.

n **1** JUMP, bound, spring, vault, hop, skip, caper. **2** INCREASE, upsurge, upswing, surge, rise, escalation.

learn *v* **1** GRASP, comprehend, understand, master, acquire, pick up, gather, assimilate, discern.
2 MEMORIZE, learn by heart.
3 DISCOVER, find out, ascertain, hear, detect, determine.

learned *adj* scholarly, erudite, well-informed, well-read, cultured, academic, lettered, literate, intellectual, versed.
≠ uneducated, illiterate.

learner *n* novice, beginner, student, trainee, pupil, scholar, apprentice.

learning *n* scholarship, erudition, education, schooling, knowledge, information, letters, study, wisdom, tuition, culture, edification, research.

lease *v* let, loan, rent, hire, sublet, charter.

least *adj* smallest, lowest, minimum, fewest, slightest, poorest.
≠ most.

leave[1] *v* **1** DEPART, go, go away, set out, take off, decamp, exit, move, quit, retire, withdraw, disappear, do a bunk (*infml*). **2** ABANDON, desert, forsake, give up, drop, relinquish, renounce, pull out, surrender, desist, cease. **3** ASSIGN, commit, entrust, consign, bequeath, will, hand down, leave behind, give over, transmit.
≠ **1** arrive. **3** receive.
leave off stop, cease, discontinue, desist, abstain, refrain, lay off, quit, terminate, break off, end, halt, give over.
leave out omit, exclude, overlook, ignore, except, disregard, pass over, count out, cut (out), eliminate, neglect, reject, cast aside, bar.

leave[2] *n* **1** PERMISSION, authorization, consent, allowance, sanction, concession, dispensation, indulgence, liberty, freedom. **2** HOLIDAY, time off, vacation, sabbatical, furlough.
≠ **1** refusal, rejection.

lecture *n* **1** DISCOURSE, address, lesson, speech, talk, instruction.
2 REPRIMAND, rebuke, reproof, scolding, harangue, censure, chiding, telling-off (*infml*), talking-to (*infml*), dressing-down (*infml*).
v **1** TALK, teach, hold forth, speak, expound, address. **2** REPRIMAND, reprove, scold, admonish, harangue, chide, censure, tell off (*infml*).

ledge *n* shelf, sill, mantle, ridge, projection, step.

leeway *n* space, room, latitude, elbow-room, play, scope.

left *adj* **1** LEFT-HAND, port, sinistral.
2 LEFT-WING, socialist, radical, progressive, revolutionary, liberal, communist, red (*infml*).
≠ **1** right. **2** right-wing.

left-overs *n* leavings, remainder, remains, remnants, residue, surplus, scraps, sweepings, refuse, dregs, excess.

leg *n* **1** LIMB, member, shank, pin (*infml*), stump (*infml*). **2** SUPPORT, prop, upright, brace. **3** STAGE, part, section, portion, stretch, segment, lap.

legacy *n* bequest, endowment, gift, heritage, heritance, inheritance, birthright, estate, heirloom.

legal *adj* **1** LAWFUL, legitimate, permissible, sanctioned, allowed, authorized, allowable, legalized, constitutional, valid, warranted, above-board, proper, rightful. **2** JUDICIAL, forensic. **3** judiciary.
≠ **1** illegal.

Legal terms include: *courts*: county court, courthouse, courtroom, Court of Appeal, Court of Protection, Court of Session, Crown Court, European Court of Human Rights, European Court of Justice, High Court of Justice, House of Lords, International Court of Justice, juvenile court, magistrates' court, Old Bailey, small claims court, Supreme Court (*US*); *criminal law*: acquittal, age of consent, alibi, arrest, bail, caution, charge, confession, contempt of court, dock, fine, guilty, indictment, innocent, malice aforethought, pardon, parole, plead guilty, plead not guilty, prisoner, probation, remand, reprieve, sentence; *marriage and divorce*: adultery, alimony, annulment, bigamy, decree absolute, decree nisi, divorce, maintenance, settlement; *people*: accessory, accomplice, accused, advocate, Attorney General, barrister, brief (*infml*), clerk of the court, client, commissioner for oaths, convict, coroner, criminal, defendant, Director of Public Prosecutions (DPP), executor, felon, judge, jury, justice of the peace (JP), juvenile, Law Lord, lawyer, Lord Advocate, Lord Chancellor, Lord Chief Justice, liquidator, magistrate, notary public, offender, plaintiff, procurator fiscal, receiver, Queen's Counsel (QC), sheriff, solicitor, witness, young offender; *property or ownership*: asset, conveyance, copyright, deed, easement, endowment, estate, exchange of contracts, fee simple, foreclosure, freehold, inheritance, intestacy, lease, leasehold, legacy, local search, mortgage, patent, tenancy, title, trademark, will; *miscellaneous*: act of God, Act of Parliament, adjournment, affidavit, agreement, allegation, amnesty, appeal, arbitration, bar, Bill of Rights, bench, brief, by-law, charter, civil law, claim, codicil, common law, constitution, contract, covenant, cross-examine, court case, court martial, custody, damages, defence, demand, equity, eviction, evidence, extradition, grant, hearing, hung jury, indemnity, injunction, inquest, inquiry, judgement *or* judgment, judiciary, lawsuit, legal aid, liability, mandate, misadventure, miscarriage of justice, oath, party, penalty, power of attorney, precedent, probate, proceedings, proof, proxy, public inquiry, repeal, sanction, settlement, statute, subpoena, sue, summons, testimony, trial, tribunal, verdict, waiver, ward of court, warrant, will, writ. *see also* **crime**.

legalize *v* legitimize, license, permit, sanction, allow, authorize, warrant, validate, approve.

legend *n* **1** MYTH, story, tale, folk-tale, fable, fiction, narrative. **2** INSCRIPTION, caption, key, motto.

legendary *adj* **1** MYTHICAL, fabulous, story-book, fictitious, traditional. **2** FAMOUS, celebrated, renowned, well-known, illustrious.

legible *adj* readable, intelligible, decipherable, clear, distinct, neat.
≠ illegible.

legislate *v* enact, ordain, authorize, codify, constitutionalize, prescribe, establish.

legislation *n* **1** LAW, statute, regulation, bill, act, charter, authorization, ruling, measure. **2** LAW-MAKING, enactment, codification.

legislative *adj* law-making, law-giving, judicial, parliamentary, congressional, senatorial.

legislator *n* law-maker, law-giver, member of parliament, parliamentarian.

legislature *n* assembly, chamber, house, parliament, congress, senate.

legitimate *adj* **1** LEGAL, lawful, authorized, statutory, rightful, proper, correct, real, acknowledged. **2** REASONABLE, sensible, admissible, acceptable, justifiable, warranted, well-founded, valid, true.
≠ **1** illegal. **2** invalid.

leisure *n* relaxation, rest, spare time, time off, ease, freedom, liberty, recreation, retirement, holiday, vacation.
≠ work.

leisurely *adj* unhurried, slow, relaxed, comfortable, easy, unhasty, tranquil, restful, gentle, carefree, laid-back (*infml*), lazy, loose.
≠ rushed, hectic.

lend *v* **1** LOAN, advance. **2** GIVE, grant, bestow, provide, furnish, confer, supply, impart, contribute.
≠ **1** borrow.

length *n* **1** EXTENT, distance, measure, reach, piece, portion, section, segment. **2** DURATION, period, term, stretch, space, span.

lengthen *v* stretch, extend, elongate, draw out, prolong, protract, spin out, eke (out), pad out, increase, expand, continue.
≠ reduce, shorten.

lengthy *adj* long, prolonged, protracted, extended, lengthened, overlong, long-drawn-out, long-

winded, rambling, diffuse, verbose, drawn-out, interminable.
≠ brief, concise.

lenient *adj* tolerant, forbearing, sparing, indulgent, merciful, forgiving, soft-hearted, kind, mild, gentle, compassionate.
≠ strict, severe.

lessen *v* decrease, reduce, diminish, lower, ease, abate, contract, die down, dwindle, lighten, slow down, weaken, shrink, abridge, de-escalate, erode, minimize, narrow, moderate, slack, flag, fail, deaden, impair.
≠ grow, increase.

lesser *adj* lower, secondary, inferior, smaller, subordinate, slighter, minor.
≠ greater.

lesson *n* **1** CLASS, period, instruction, lecture, tutorial, teaching, coaching. **2** ASSIGNMENT, exercise, homework, practice, task, drill. **3** EXAMPLE, model, warning, deterrent.

let *v* **1** PERMIT, allow, give leave, give permission, authorize, consent to, agree to, sanction, grant, OK, enable, tolerate. **2** LEASE, hire, rent.
≠ **1** prohibit, forbid.
let in admit, accept, receive, take in, include, incorporate, welcome.
≠ prohibit, bar, forbid.
let off **1** EXCUSE, absolve, pardon, exempt, forgive, acquit, exonerate, spare, ignore, liberate, release. **2** DISCHARGE, detonate, fire, explode, emit.
≠ **1** punish.
let out **1** FREE, release, let go, discharge, leak (*infml*). **2** REVEAL, disclose, make known, utter, betray, let slip.
≠ **1** keep in.
let up abate, subside, ease (up), moderate, slacken, diminish, decrease, stop, end, cease, halt.
≠ continue.

let-down *n* anticlimax, disappointment, disillusionment, set-back, betrayal, desertion, wash-out (*infml*).

lethal *adj* fatal, deadly, deathly, mortal, dangerous, poisonous, noxious, destructive, devastating.
≠ harmless, safe.

lethargy *n* lassitude, listlessness, sluggishness, torpor, dullness, inertia, slowness, apathy, inaction, indifference, sleepiness, drowsiness, stupor.
≠ liveliness.

letter *n* **1** NOTE, message, line, missive, epistle (*fml*), dispatch, communication, chit, acknowledgement. **2** CHARACTER, symbol, sign, grapheme.

level *adj* **1** FLAT, smooth, even, flush, horizontal, aligned, plane. **2** EQUAL, balanced, even, on a par, neck and neck, matching, uniform.
≠ **1** uneven. **2** unequal.
v **1** DEMOLISH, destroy, devastate, flatten, knock down, raze, pull down, bulldoze, tear down, lay low. **2** EVEN OUT, flush, plane, smooth, equalize. **3** DIRECT, point.
n **1** HEIGHT, elevation, altitude. **2** POSITION, rank, status, class, degree, grade, standard, standing, plane, echelon, layer, stratum, storey, stage, zone.

level-headed *adj* calm, balanced, even-tempered, sensible, steady, reasonable, composed, cool, unflappable, sane, self-possessed, dependable.

lever *n* bar, crowbar, jemmy, joy-stick, handle.
v force, prise, pry, raise, dislodge, jemmy, shift, move, heave.

levity *n* light-heartedness, frivolity, facetiousness, flippancy, irreverence, triviality, silliness.
≠ seriousness.

levy *v* tax, impose, exact, demand, charge.
n tax, toll, subscription, contribution, duty, fee, tariff, collection.

lewd *adj* obscene, smutty, indecent, bawdy, pornographic, salacious, licentious, lascivious, impure, vulgar, unchaste, lustful.
≠ decent, chaste.

liability *n* **1** ACCOUNTABILITY, duty, obligation, responsibility, onus. **2** DEBT, arrears, indebtedness. **3** DRAWBACK, disadvantage, hindrance, impediment, drag (*infml*).

liable *adj* **1** INCLINED, likely, apt,

disposed, prone, tending, susceptible. **2** RESPONSIBLE, answerable, accountable, amenable.

liaison *n* **1** CONTACT, connection, go-between, link. **2** LOVE AFFAIR, affair, romance, intrigue, amour, entanglement.

liar *n* falsifier, perjurer, deceiver, fibber (*infml*).

libel *n* defamation, slur, smear, slander, vilification, aspersion, calumny.
v defame, slur, smear, slander, vilify, malign.

libellous *adj* defamatory, vilifying, slanderous, derogatory, maligning, injurious, scurrilous, untrue.

liberal *adj* **1** BROAD-MINDED, open-minded, tolerant, lenient.
2 PROGRESSIVE, reformist, moderate.
3 GENEROUS, ample, bountiful, lavish, plentiful, handsome.
≠ **1** narrow-minded. **2** conservative.
3 mean, miserly.

liberate *v* free, emancipate, release, let loose, let go, let out, set free, deliver, unchain, discharge, rescue, ransom.
≠ imprison, enslave.

liberty *n* **1** FREEDOM, emancipation, release, independence, autonomy.
2 LICENCE, permission, sanction, right, authorization, dispensation, franchise.
3 FAMILIARITY, disrespect, overfamiliarity, presumption, impertinence, impudence.
≠ **1** imprisonment. **3** respect.
at liberty free, unconstrained, unrestricted, not confined.

licence *n* **1** PERMISSION, permit, leave, warrant, authorization, authority, certificate, charter, right, imprimatur, entitlement, privilege, dispensation, carte blanche, freedom, liberty, exemption, independence. **2** ABANDON, dissipation, excess, immoderation, indulgence, lawlessness, unruliness, anarchy, disorder, debauchery, dissoluteness, impropriety, irresponsibility.
≠ **1** prohibition, restriction.
2 decorum, moderation.

license *v* permit, allow, authorize, certify, warrant, entitle, empower, sanction, commission, accredit.
≠ ban, prohibit.

licentious *adj* debauched, dissolute, profligate, lascivious, immoral, abandoned, lewd, promiscuous, libertine, impure, lax, lustful, disorderly, wanton, unchaste.
≠ modest, chaste.

lick *v* tongue, touch, wash, lap, taste, dart, flick, flicker, play over, smear, brush.

lie[1] *v* perjure, misrepresent, fabricate, falsify, fib (*infml*), invent, equivocate, prevaricate, forswear oneself (*fml*).
n falsehood, untruth, falsification, fabrication, invention, fiction, deceit, fib (*infml*), falsity, white lie, prevarication, whopper (*infml*).
≠ truth.

lie[2] *v* be, exist, dwell, belong, extend, remain.
lie down repose, rest, recline, stretch out, lounge, couch, laze.

life *n* **1** BEING, existence, animation, breath, viability, entity, soul.
2 DURATION, course, span, career.
3 LIVELINESS, vigour, vitality, vivacity, verve, zest, energy, élan, spirit, sparkle, activity.

lifeless *adj* **1** DEAD, deceased, defunct, cold, unconscious, inanimate, insensible, stiff. **2** LETHARGIC, listless, sluggish, dull, apathetic, passive, insipid, colourless, slow. **3** BARREN, bare, empty, desolate, arid.
≠ **1** alive. **2** lively.

lifelike *adj* realistic, true-to-life, real, true, vivid, natural, authentic, faithful, exact, graphic.
≠ unrealistic, unnatural.

lifelong *adj* lifetime, long-lasting, long-standing, persistent, lasting, enduring, abiding, permanent, constant.
≠ impermanent, temporary.

lift *v* **1** *she lifted the chair*: raise, elevate, hoist, upraise. **2** *he lifted their spirits*: uplift, exalt, buoy up, boost.
3 *the ban has been lifted*: revoke, cancel, relax.
≠ **1** drop. **2** lower.

light[1] *n* **1** ILLUMINATION, brightness,

brilliance, luminescence, radiance, glow, ray, shine, glare, gleam, glint, lustre, flash, blaze.

> *Sources of light include*: *natural light*: aurora borealis, daylight, lightning, moonlight, starlight, sunlight; infrared, ultraviolet; *electric light*: Belisha beacon, brake light, chandelier, courtesy light, fairy light, flashgun, floodlight, fluorescent light, fog lamp, footlight, halogen light, headlight, indicator light, laser, light bulb, light buoy, lighthouse, navigation light, neon light, night light, pedestrian light, range light, runway light, searchlight, spotlight, standard lamp, streetlight, strip light, strobe light, sun-lamp, tail-light, torch, traffic light; *fire light*: bonfire, candlelight, fire, firework, flare, gaslight, hurricane lamp, lighter, match, oil lamp, pilot light.

2 LAMP, lantern, lighter, match, torch, candle, bulb, beacon. **3** DAY, daybreak, daylight, daytime, dawn, sunrise. **4** ENLIGHTENMENT, explanation, elucidation, understanding.
≠ **1** darkness. **3** night.
v **1** IGNITE, fire, set alight, set fire to, kindle. **2** ILLUMINATE, light up, lighten, brighten, animate, cheer, switch on, turn on, put on.
≠ **1** extinguish. **2** darken.
adj **1** ILLUMINATED, bright, brilliant, luminous, glowing, shining, well-lit, sunny. **2** PALE, pastel, fair, blond, blonde, bleached, faded, faint.
≠ **1** dark. **2** black.

light[2] *adj* **1** WEIGHTLESS, insubstantial, delicate, airy, buoyant, flimsy, feathery, slight. **2** TRIVIAL, inconsiderable, trifling, inconsequential, worthless. **3** CHEERFUL, cheery, carefree, lively, merry, blithe. **4** ENTERTAINING, amusing, funny, humorous, frivolous, witty, pleasing.
≠ **1** heavy, weighty. **2** important, serious. **3** solemn. **4** serious.

lighten[1] *v* illuminate, illumine, brighten, light up, shine.
≠ darken.

lighten[2] *v* **1** EASE, lessen, unload, lift, relieve, reduce, mitigate, alleviate. **2** BRIGHTEN, cheer, encourage, hearten, inspirit, uplift, gladden, revive, elate, buoy up, inspire.
≠ **1** burden. **2** depress.

light-headed *adj* **1** FAINT, giddy, dizzy, woozy (*infml*), delirious. **2** FLIGHTY, scatter-brained (*infml*), foolish, frivolous, silly, superficial, shallow, feather-brained (*infml*), flippant, vacuous, trifling.
≠ **2** level-headed, solemn.

light-hearted *adj* cheerful, joyful, jolly, happy-go-lucky, bright, carefree, untroubled, merry, sunny, glad, elated, jovial, playful.
≠ sad, unhappy, serious.

likable *adj* loveable, pleasing, appealing, agreeable, charming, engaging, winsome, pleasant, amiable, congenial, attractive, sympathetic.
≠ unpleasant, disagreeable.

like[1] *adj* similar, resembling, alike, same, identical, equivalent, akin, corresponding, related, relating, parallel, allied, analogous, approximating.
≠ unlike, dissimilar.

like[2] *v* **1** ENJOY, delight in, care for, admire, appreciate, love, adore, hold dear, esteem, cherish, prize, relish, revel in, approve, take (kindly) to. **2** PREFER, choose, select, feel inclined, go for (*infml*), desire, want, wish.
≠ **1** dislike. **2** reject.

likelihood *n* likeliness, probability, possibility, chance, prospect, liability.
≠ improbability, unlikeliness.

likely *adj* **1** PROBABLE, possible, anticipated, expected, liable, prone, tending, predictable, odds-on (*infml*), inclined, foreseeable. **2** CREDIBLE, believable, plausible, feasible, reasonable. **3** PROMISING, hopeful, pleasing, appropriate, proper, suitable.
≠ **1** unlikely. **3** unsuitable.
adv probably, presumably, like as not, in all probability, no doubt, doubtlessly.

liken *v* compare, equate, match, parallel, relate, juxtapose, associate, set beside.

likeness *n* **1** SIMILARITY, resemblance,

affinity, correspondence.
2 REPRESENTATION, image, copy, reproduction, replica, facsimile, effigy, picture, portrait, photograph, counterpart. **3** SEMBLANCE, guise, appearance, form.
≠ **1** dissimilarity, unlikeness.

likewise *adv* moreover, furthermore, in addition, similarly, also, further, besides, by the same token, too.

liking *n* fondness, love, affection, preference, partiality, affinity, predilection, penchant, taste, attraction, appreciation, proneness, propensity, inclination, tendency, bias, desire, weakness, fancy, soft spot.
≠ dislike, aversion, hatred.

limb *n* arm, leg, member, appendage, branch, projection, offshoot, wing, fork, extension, part, spur, extremity, bough.

limber up *v* loosen up, warm up, work out, exercise, prepare.

limelight *n* fame, celebrity, spotlight, stardom, recognition, renown, attention, prominence, publicity, public eye.

limit *n* **1** BOUNDARY, bound, border, frontier, confines, edge, brink, threshold, verge, brim, end, perimeter, rim, compass, termination, ultimate, utmost, terminus, extent. **2** CHECK, curb, restraint, restriction, limitation, ceiling, maximum, cut-off point, saturation point, deadline.
v check, curb, restrict, restrain, constrain, confine, demarcate, delimit, bound, hem in, ration, specify, hinder.

limitation *n* **1** CHECK, restriction, curb, control, constraint, restraint, delimitation, demarcation, block.
2 INADEQUACY, shortcoming, disadvantage, drawback, condition, qualification, reservation.
≠ **1** extension.

limited *adj* restricted, circumscribed, constrained, controlled, confined, checked, defined, finite, fixed, minimal, narrow, inadequate, insufficient.
≠ limitless.

limitless *adj* unlimited, unbounded, boundless, illimited, undefined, immeasurable, incalculable, infinite, countless, endless, never-ending, unending, inexhaustible, untold, vast.
≠ limited.

limp¹ *v* hobble, falter, stumble, hop, shuffle, shamble.

limp² *adj* **1** FLABBY, drooping, flaccid, floppy, loose, slack, relaxed, lax, soft, flexible, pliable, limber. **2** TIRED, weary, exhausted, spent, weak, worn out, lethargic, debilitated, enervated.
≠ **1** stiff. **2** vigorous.

line¹ *n* **1** STROKE, band, bar, stripe, mark, strip, rule, dash, strand, streak, underline, score, scratch. **2** ROW, rank, queue, file, column, sequence, series, procession, chain, trail. **3** LIMIT, boundary, border, borderline, edge, frontier, demarcation. **4** STRING, rope, cord, cable, thread, filament, wire.
5 PROFILE, contour, outline, silhouette, figure, formation, configuration.
6 CREASE, wrinkle, furrow, groove, corrugation. **7** COURSE, path, direction, track, route, axis.
8 APPROACH, avenue, course (of action), belief, ideology, policy, system, position, practice, procedure, method, scheme. **9** OCCUPATION, business, trade, profession, vocation, job, activity, interest, employment, department, calling, field, province, forte, area, pursuit, specialization, specialty, specialism, speciality. **10** ANCESTRY, family, descent, extraction, lineage, pedigree, stock, race, breed.
line up 1 ALIGN, range, straighten, marshal, order, regiment, queue up, form ranks, fall in, array, assemble. **2** ORGANIZE, lay on, arrange, prepare, produce, procure, secure, obtain.

line² *v* encase, cover, fill, pad, stuff, reinforce.

lineage *n* (*fml*) ancestry, descent, extraction, genealogy, family, line, pedigree, race, stock, birth, breed, house, heredity, ancestors, forebears, descendants, offspring, succession.

lined *adj* **1** RULED, feint. **2** WRINKLED, furrowed, wizened, worn.
≠ **1** unlined. **2** smooth.

line-up *n* array, arrangement, queue,

row, selection, cast, team, bill.

linger *v* loiter, delay, dally, tarry, wait, remain, stay, hang on, lag, procrastinate, dawdle, dilly-dally (*infml*), idle, stop, endure, hold out, last, persist, survive.
≠ leave, rush.

lining *n* inlay, interfacing, padding, backing, encasement, stiffening.

link *n* **1** CONNECTION, bond, tie, association, joint, relationship, tie-up, union, knot, liaison, attachment, communication. **2** PART, piece, element, member, constituent, component, division.
v connect, join, couple, tie, fasten, unite, bind, amalgamate, merge, associate, ally, bracket, identify, relate, yoke, attach, hook up, join forces, team up.
≠ separate, unfasten.

lip *n* edge, brim, border, brink, rim, margin, verge.

liquid *n* liquor, fluid, juice, drink, sap, solution, lotion.
adj fluid, flowing, liquefied, watery, wet, runny, melted, molten, thawed, clear, smooth.
≠ solid.

liquidate *v* **1** ANNIHILATE, terminate, do away with, dissolve, kill, murder, massacre, assassinate, destroy, dispatch, abolish, eliminate, exterminate, remove, finish off, rub out (*infml*). **2** PAY (OFF), close down, clear, discharge, wind up, sell.

liquor *n* alcohol, intoxicant, strong drink, spirits, drink, hard stuff (*infml*), booze (*infml*).

list[1] *n* catalogue, roll, inventory, register, enumeration, schedule, index, listing, record, file, directory, table, tabulation, tally, series, syllabus, invoice.
v enumerate, register, itemize, catalogue, index, tabulate, record, file, enrol, enter, note, bill, book, set down, write down.

list[2] *v* lean, incline, tilt, slope, heel (over), tip.

listen *v* hark, attend, pay attention, hear, heed, hearken, hang on (someone's) words, prick up one's ears, take notice, lend an ear, eavesdrop, overhear, give ear.

listless *adj* sluggish, lethargic, languid, torpid, enervated, spiritless, limp, lifeless, inert, inactive, impassive, indifferent, uninterested, vacant, apathetic, indolent, depressed, bored, heavy.
≠ energetic, enthusiastic.

literal *adj* **1** VERBATIM, word-for-word, strict, close, actual, precise, faithful, exact, accurate, factual, true, genuine, unexaggerated. **2** PROSAIC, unimaginative, uninspired, matter-of-fact, down-to-earth, humdrum.
≠ **1** imprecise, loose. **2** imaginative.

literary *adj* educated, well-read, bookish, learned, erudite, scholarly, lettered, literate, cultured, cultivated, refined, formal.
≠ ignorant, illiterate.

literature *n* **1** WRITINGS, letters, paper(s). **2** INFORMATION, leaflet(s), pamphlet(s), circular(s), brochure(s), hand-out(s), bumf (*infml*).

> *Types of literature include*; allegory, anti-novel, autobiography, belles-lettres (*fml*), biography, classic novel, criticism, drama, epic, epistle, essay, fiction, Gothic novel, lampoon, libretto, magnum opus, non-fiction, novel, novella, parody, pastiche, penny dreadful (*infml*), picaresque novel, poetry, polemic, postil, prose, roman novel, saga, satire, thesis, tragedy, treatise, triad, trilogy, verse. *see also* **poem**; **story**.

litigation *n* lawsuit, action, suit, case, prosecution, process, contention.

litter *n* **1** RUBBISH, debris, refuse, waste, mess, disorder, clutter, confusion, disarray, untidiness, junk (*infml*), muck, jumble, fragments, shreds. **2** OFFSPRING, young, progeny (*fml*), brood, family.
v strew, scatter, mess up, disorder, clutter.
≠ tidy.

little *adj* **1** SMALL, short, tiny, wee (*infml*), minute, teeny (*infml*), diminutive, miniature, infinitesimal, mini, microscopic, petite, pint-size(d)

(*infml*), slender. **2** SHORT-LIVED, brief, fleeting, passing, transient. **3** INSUFFICIENT, sparse, scant, meagre, paltry, skimpy. **4** INSIGNIFICANT, inconsiderable, negligible, trivial, petty, trifling, unimportant.
≠ **1** big. **2** lengthy. **3** ample. **4** considerable.
adv barely, hardly, scarcely, rarely, seldom, infrequently, not much.
≠ frequently.
n bit, dash, pinch, spot, trace, drop, dab, speck, touch, taste, particle, hint, fragment, modicum, trifle.
≠ lot.

live[1] *v* **1** BE, exist, breathe, draw breath. **2** LAST, endure, continue, remain, persist, survive. **3** DWELL, inhabit, reside, lodge, abide. **4** PASS, spend, lead.
≠ **1** die. **2** cease.

live[2] *adj* **1** ALIVE, living, existent. **2** LIVELY, vital, active, energetic, dynamic, alert, vigorous. **3** BURNING, glowing, blazing, ignited. **4** RELEVANT, current, topical, pertinent, controversial.
≠ **1** dead. **2** apathetic.

livelihood *n* occupation, employment, job, living, means, income, maintenance, work, support, subsistence, sustenance.

lively *adj* **1** ANIMATED, alert, active, energetic, spirited, vivacious, vigorous, sprightly, spry, agile, nimble, quick, keen. **2** CHEERFUL, blithe, merry, frisky, perky, breezy, chirpy (*infml*), frolicsome. **3** BUSY, bustling, brisk, crowded, eventful, exciting, buzzing. **4** VIVID, bright, colourful, stimulating, stirring, invigorating, racy, refreshing, sparkling.
≠ **1** moribund, apathetic. **3** inactive.

liven (up) enliven, vitalize, put life into, rouse, invigorate, animate, energize, brighten, stir (up), buck up (*infml*), pep up (*infml*), perk up (*infml*), hot up (*infml*).
≠ dishearten.

livery *n* uniform, costume, regalia, dress, clothes, clothing, apparel (*fml*), attire, vestments, suit, garb, habit.

livid *adj* **1** LEADEN, black-and-blue, bruised, discoloured, greyish, purple. **2** PALE, pallid, ashen, blanched, bloodless, wan, waxy, pasty. **3** (*infml*) ANGRY, furious, infuriated, irate, outraged, enraged, raging, fuming, indignant, incensed, exasperated, mad (*infml*).
≠ **3** calm.

living *adj* alive, breathing, existing, live, current, extant, operative, strong, vigorous, active, lively, vital, animated.
≠ dead, sluggish.
n **1** BEING, life, animation, existence. **2** LIVELIHOOD, maintenance, support, income, subsistence, sustenance, work, job, occupation, profession, benefice, way of life.

load *n* **1** BURDEN, onus, encumbrance, weight, pressure, oppression, millstone. **2** CARGO, consignment, shipment, goods, lading, freight.
v **1** BURDEN, weigh down, encumber, overburden, oppress, trouble, weight, saddle with. **2** PACK, pile, heap, freight, fill, stack.

loaded *adj* burdened, charged, laden, full, weighted.

loafer *n* (*infml*) idler, layabout (*infml*), shirker, skiver (*infml*), sluggard, wastrel, lounger, ne'er-do-well, lazybones (*infml*).

loan *n* advance, credit, mortgage, allowance.
v lend, advance, credit, allow.

loathe *v* hate, detest, abominate, abhor, despise, dislike.
≠ adore, love.

loathing *n* hatred, detestation, abhorrence, abomination, repugnance, revulsion, repulsion, dislike, disgust, aversion, horror.
≠ affection, love.

loathsome *adj* detestable, abhorrent, odious, repulsive, abominable, hateful, repugnant, repellent, offensive, horrible, disgusting, vile, revolting, nasty.

lobby *v* campaign for, press for, demand, persuade, call for, urge, push for, influence, solicit, pressure, promote.

n **1** VESTIBULE, foyer, porch, anteroom, hall, hallway, waiting-room, entrance hall, corridor, passage. **2** PRESSURE GROUP, campaign, ginger group.

local *adj* regional, provincial, community, district, neighbourhood, parochial, vernacular, small-town, limited, narrow, restricted, parish(-pump).
≠ national.
n **1** INHABITANT, citizen, resident, native. **2** (*infml*) PUB.

locality *n* neighbourhood, vicinity, district, area, locale, region, position, place, site, spot, scene, setting.

locate *v* **1** FIND, discover, unearth, run to earth (*infml*), track down, detect, lay one's hands on (*infml*), pin-point, identify. **2** SITUATE, settle, fix, establish, place, put, set, seat.

location *n* position, situation, place, locus, whereabouts, venue, site, locale, bearings, spot, point.

lock *n* fastening, bolt, clasp, padlock.

> *Parts of a lock include*: barrel, bolt, cylinder, cylinder hole, dead bolt, escutcheon, face plate, hasp, key, key card, keyhole, keyway, knob, latch, latch bolt, latch follower, latch lever, mortise bolt, pin, push button, rose, sash, sash bolt, spindle, spindle hole, spring, strike plate, staple.

v **1** FASTEN, secure, bolt, latch, seal, shut. **2** JOIN, unite, engage, link, mesh, entangle, entwine, clench. **3** CLASP, hug, embrace, grasp, encircle, enclose, clutch, grapple.
≠ unlock.
lock out shut out, refuse admittance to, keep out, exclude, bar, debar.
lock up imprison, jail, confine, shut in, shut up, incarcerate, secure, cage, pen, detain, close up.
≠ free.

lodge *n* hut, cabin, cottage, chalet, shelter, retreat, den, gatehouse, house, hunting-lodge, meeting-place, club, haunt.
v **1** ACCOMMODATE, put up (*infml*), quarter, board, billet, shelter. **2** LIVE, stay, reside. **3** FIX, imbed, implant, get stuck. **4** DEPOSIT, place, put, submit, register.

lodger *n* boarder, paying guest, resident, tenant, roomer, inmate, guest.

lodgings *n* accommodation, digs (*infml*), dwelling, quarters, billet, abode, boarding-house, rooms, pad (*infml*), residence.

log *n* **1** TIMBER, trunk, block, chunk. **2** RECORD, diary, journal, logbook, daybook, account, tally.
v record, register, write up, note, book, chart, tally.

logic *n* reasoning, reason, sense, deduction, rationale, argumentation.

logical *adj* reasonable, rational, reasoned, coherent, consistent, valid, sound, well-founded, clear, sensible, deducible, methodical, well-organized.
≠ illogical, irrational.

loiter *v* dawdle, hang about, idle, linger, dally, dilly-dally (*infml*), delay, mooch, lag, saunter.

lone *adj* single, sole, one, only, isolated, solitary, separate, separated, unattached, unaccompanied, unattended.
≠ accompanied.

loneliness *n* aloneness, isolation, lonesomeness, solitariness, solitude, seclusion, desolation.

lonely *adj* **1** ALONE, friendless, lonesome, solitary, abandoned, forsaken, companionless, unaccompanied, destitute. **2** ISOLATED, uninhabited, remote, out-of-the-way, unfrequented, secluded, abandoned, deserted, forsaken, desolate.
≠ **1** popular. **2** crowded, populous.

long *adj* lengthy, extensive, extended, expanded, prolonged, protracted, stretched, spread out, sustained, expansive, far-reaching, long-drawn-out, interminable, slow.
≠ brief, short, fleeting, abbreviated.
long for yearn for, crave, want, wish, desire, dream of, hanker for, pine, thirst for, lust after, covet, itch for, yen for (*infml*).

longing *n* craving, desire, yearning,

hungering, hankering, yen, thirst, wish, urge, coveting, aspiration, ambition.

long-lasting *adj* permanent, imperishable, enduring, unchanging, unfading, continuing, abiding, long-standing, prolonged, protracted.
≠ short-lived, ephemeral, transient.

long-standing *adj* established, long-established, long-lived, long-lasting, enduring, abiding, time-honoured, traditional.

long-suffering *adj* uncomplaining, forbearing, forgiving, tolerant, easy-going, patient, stoical.

long-winded *adj* lengthy, overlong, prolonged, diffuse, verbose, wordy, voluble, long-drawn-out, discursive, repetitious, rambling, tedious.
≠ brief, terse.

look *v* **1** WATCH, see, observe, view, survey, regard, gaze, study, stare, examine, inspect, scrutinize, glance, contemplate, scan, peep, gawp (*infml*). **2** SEEM, appear, show, exhibit, display.
n **1** VIEW, survey, inspection, examination, observation, sight, review, once-over (*infml*), glance, glimpse, gaze, peek. **2** APPEARANCE, aspect, manner, semblance, mien, expression, bearing, face, complexion.
look after take care of, mind, care for, attend to, take charge of, tend, keep an eye on, watch over, protect, supervise, guard.
≠ neglect.
look down on despise, scorn, sneer at, hold in contempt, disdain, look down one's nose at (*infml*), turn one's nose up at (*infml*).
≠ esteem, approve.
look forward to anticipate, await, expect, hope for, long for, envisage, envision, count on, wait for, look for.
look into investigate, probe, research, study, go into, examine, enquire about, explore, check out, inspect, scrutinize, look over, plumb, fathom.
look out pay attention, watch out, beware, be careful, keep an eye out.
look over inspect, examine, check, give a once-over (*infml*), cast an eye over, look through, scan, view.
look up 1 SEARCH FOR, research, hunt for, find, track down. **2** VISIT, call on, drop in on, look in on, pay a visit to, stop by, drop by. **3** IMPROVE, get better, pick up, progress, come on.
look up to admire, esteem, respect, revere, honour, have a high opinion of.

look-alike *n* double, replica, twin, spitting image (*infml*), living image, clone, spit (*infml*), ringer (*infml*), doppelgänger.

look-out *n* **1** GUARD, sentry, watch, watch-tower, watchman, sentinel, tower, post. **2** (*infml*) CONCERN, responsibility, worry, affair, business, problem.

loom *v* appear, emerge, take shape, menace, threaten, impend, hang over, dominate, tower, overhang, rise, soar, overshadow, overtop.

loop *n* hoop, ring, circle, noose, coil, eyelet, loophole, spiral, curve, curl, kink, twist, whorl, twirl, turn, bend.
v coil, encircle, roll, bend, circle, curve round, turn, twist, spiral, connect, join, knot, fold, braid.

loophole *n* let-out, escape, evasion, excuse, pretext, plea, pretence.

loose *adj* **1** FREE, unfastened, untied, movable, unattached, insecure, wobbly. **2** SLACK, lax, baggy, hanging. **3** IMPRECISE, vague, inexact, ill-defined, indefinite, inaccurate, indistinct.
≠ **1** firm, secure. **2** tight. **3** precise.

loosen *v* **1** EASE, relax, loose, slacken, undo, unbind, untie, unfasten. **2** FREE, set free, release, let go, let out, deliver.
≠ **1** tighten.

loot *n* spoils, booty, plunder, haul, swag (*infml*), prize.
v plunder, pillage, rob, sack, rifle, raid, maraud, ransack, ravage.

lop-sided *adj* asymmetrical, unbalanced, askew, off balance, uneven.
≠ balanced, symmetrical.

lord *n* **1** PEER, noble, earl, duke, count, baron. **2** MASTER, ruler, superior, overlord, leader, commander, governor, king.

lordly *adj* **1** NOBLE, dignified,

aristocratic. **2** PROUD, arrogant, disdainful, haughty, imperious, condescending, high-handed, domineering, overbearing.
≠ **1** low(ly). **2** humble.

lore *n* knowledge, wisdom, learning, erudition, scholarship, traditions, teaching, beliefs, sayings.

lose *v* **1** MISLAY, misplace, forget, miss, forfeit. **2** WASTE, squander, dissipate, use up, exhaust, expend, drain. **3** FAIL, fall short, suffer defeat.
≠ **1** gain. **2** make. **3** win.

loser *n* failure, also-ran, runner-up, flop (*infml*), no-hoper.
≠ winner.

loss *n* **1** DEPRIVATION, disadvantage, defeat, failure, losing, bereavement, damage, destruction, ruin, hurt. **2** WASTE, depletion, disappearance, deficiency, deficit.
≠ **1** gain.

lost *adj* **1** MISLAID, missing, vanished, disappeared, misplaced, astray. **2** CONFUSED, disoriented, bewildered, puzzled, baffled, perplexed, preoccupied. **3** WASTED, squandered, ruined, destroyed.
≠ **1** found.

lot *n* **1** COLLECTION, batch, assortment, quantity, group, set, crowd. **2** SHARE, portion, allowance, ration, quota, part, piece, parcel.

lotion *n* ointment, balm, cream, salve.

lottery *n* **1** DRAW, raffle, sweepstake. **2** SPECULATION, venture, risk, gamble.

loud *adj* **1** NOISY, deafening, booming, resounding, ear-piercing, ear-splitting, piercing, thundering, blaring, clamorous, vociferous. **2** GARISH, gaudy, glaring, flashy, brash, showy, ostentatious, tasteless.
≠ **1** quiet. **2** subdued.

lounge *v* relax, loll, idle, laze, waste time, kill time, lie about, take it easy, sprawl, recline, lie back, slump.
n sitting-room, living-room, drawing-room, day-room, parlour.

lovable *adj* adorable, endearing, winsome, captivating, charming, engaging, attractive, fetching, sweet, lovely, pleasing, delightful.
≠ detestable, hateful.

love *v* **1** *he loves his wife*: adore, cherish, dote on, treasure, hold dear, idolize, worship. **2** *I love macaroons*: like, take pleasure in, enjoy, delight in, appreciate, desire, fancy.
≠ detest, hate.
n adoration, affection, fondness, attachment, regard, liking, amorousness, ardour, devotion, adulation, passion, rapture, tenderness, warmth, inclination, infatuation, delight, enjoyment, soft spot (*infml*), weakness, taste, friendship.
≠ detestation, hate, loathing.
love affair *n* affair, romance, liaison, relationship, love, passion.

lovely *adj* beautiful, charming, delightful, attractive, enchanting, pleasing, pleasant, pretty, adorable, agreeable, enjoyable, sweet, winning, exquisite.
≠ ugly, hideous.

lover *n* beloved, admirer, boyfriend, girlfriend, sweetheart, suitor, mistress, fiancé(e), flame (*infml*).

loving *adj* amorous, affectionate, devoted, doting, fond, ardent, passionate, warm, warm-hearted, tender.

low *adj* **1** SHORT, small, squat, stunted, little, shallow, deep, depressed, sunken. **2** INADEQUATE, deficient, poor, sparse, meagre, paltry, scant, insignificant. **3** UNHAPPY, depressed, downcast, gloomy. **4** BASE, coarse, vulgar, mean, contemptible. **5** CHEAP, inexpensive, reasonable. **6** subdued, muted, soft.
≠ **1** high. **2** high. **3** cheerful. **4** honourable. **5** exorbitant. **6** loud.

lower *adj* inferior, lesser, subordinate, secondary, minor, second-class, low-level, lowly, junior.
≠ higher.
v **1** DROP, depress, sink, descend, let down. **2** REDUCE, decrease, cut, lessen, diminish.
≠ **1** raise. **2** increase.

lowly *adj* humble, low-born, obscure, poor, plebeian, plain, simple, modest, ordinary, inferior, meek, mild, mean,

submissive, subordinate.
≠ lofty, noble.

low-spirited *adj* depressed, gloomy, heavy-hearted, low, down, down-hearted, despondent, fed up (*infml*), sad, unhappy, miserable, moody.
≠ high-spirited, cheerful.

loyal *adj* true, faithful, steadfast, staunch, devoted, trustworthy, sincere, patriotic.
≠ disloyal, treacherous.

loyalty *n* allegiance, faithfulness, fidelity, devotion, steadfastness, constancy, trustworthiness, reliability, patriotism.
≠ disloyalty, treachery.

lubricate *v* oil, grease, smear, wax, lard.

luck *n* **1** CHANCE, fortune, accident, fate, fortuity (*fml*), fluke (*infml*), destiny. **2** GOOD FORTUNE, success, break (*infml*), godsend.
≠ **1** design. **2** misfortune.

luckily *adv* fortunately, happily, providentially.
≠ unfortunately.

lucky *adj* fortunate, favoured, auspicious, successful, prosperous, timely.
≠ unlucky.

lucrative *adj* profitable, well-paid, remunerative, advantageous.
≠ unprofitable.

ludicrous *adj* absurd, ridiculous, preposterous, nonsensical, laughable, farcical, silly, comical, funny, outlandish, crazy (*infml*).
≠ serious.

lug *v* pull, drag, haul, carry, tow, heave, hump.

luggage

Types of luggage include: case, suitcase, vanity-case, bag, holdall, portmanteau, valise, overnight-bag, kit-bag, flight bag, hand-luggage, travel bag, Gladstone bag, grip, rucksack, knapsack, haversack, backpack, briefcase, attaché case, portfolio, satchel, basket, hamper, trunk, chest, box.

lukewarm *adj* cool, half-hearted, apathetic, tepid, indifferent, unenthusiastic, uninterested, unresponsive, unconcerned.

lull *v* soothe, subdue, calm, hush, pacify, quieten down, quiet, quell, compose.
≠ agitate.
n calm, peace, quiet, tranquillity, stillness, let-up, pause, hush, silence.
≠ agitation.

lumber[1] *n* clutter, jumble, rubbish, bits and pieces, odds and ends, junk.

lumber[2] *v* clump, shamble, plod, shuffle, stump, trundle.

luminous *adj* glowing, illuminated, lit, lighted, radiant, shining, fluorescent, brilliant, lustrous, bright.

lump *n* **1** MASS, cluster, clump, clod, ball, bunch, piece, chunk, cake, hunk, nugget, wedge. **2** SWELLING, growth, bulge, bump, protuberance, protrusion, tumour.
v collect, mass, gather, cluster, combine, coalesce, group, consolidate, unite.

lunacy *n* madness, insanity, aberration, derangement, mania, craziness (*infml*), idiocy, imbecility, folly, absurdity, stupidity.
≠ sanity.

lunatic *n* psychotic, psychopath, madman, maniac, loony (*infml*), nutcase (*infml*), nutter (*infml*), fruitcake (*infml*).
adj mad, insane, deranged, psychotic, irrational, crazy (*infml*), bonkers (*infml*).
≠ sane.

lunge *v* thrust, jab, stab, pounce, plunge, pitch into, charge, dart, dash, dive, poke, strike (at), fall upon, grab (at), hit (at), leap.
n thrust, stab, pounce, charge, jab, pass, cut, spring.

lurch *v* roll, rock, pitch, sway, stagger, reel, list.

lure *v* tempt, entice, draw, attract, allure, seduce, ensnare, lead on.
n temptation, enticement, attraction, bait, inducement.

lurid *adj* **1** SENSATIONAL, shocking, startling, graphic, exaggerated. **2** MACABRE, gruesome, gory, ghastly, grisly. **3** BRIGHTLY COLOURED, garish, glaring, loud, vivid.

lurk *v* skulk, prowl, lie in wait, crouch, lie low, hide, snoop.

luscious *adj* delicious, juicy, succulent, appetizing, mouth-watering, sweet, tasty, savoury, desirable.

lush *adj* **1** FLOURISHING, luxuriant, abundant, prolific, overgrown, green, verdant. **2** SUMPTUOUS, opulent, ornate, plush, rich.

lust *n* **1** SENSUALITY, libido, lechery, licentiousness, lewdness. **2** CRAVING, desire, appetite, longing, passion, greed, covetousness.
lust after desire, crave, yearn for, want, need, hunger for, thirst for.

lustre *n* **1** SHINE, gloss, sheen, gleam, glow, brilliance, brightness, radiance, sparkle, resplendence, burnish, glitter, glint. **2** GLORY, honour, prestige, illustriousness.

lusty *adj* robust, strong, sturdy, vigorous, hale, hearty, healthy, gutsy (*infml*), energetic, strapping, rugged, powerful.

luxurious *adj* sumptuous, opulent, lavish, de luxe, plush, magnificent, splendid, expensive, costly, self-indulgent, pampered.
≠ austere, spartan.

luxury *n* sumptuousness, opulence, hedonism, splendour, affluence, richness, magnificence, pleasure, indulgence, gratification, comfort, extravagance, satisfaction.
≠ austerity.

lying *adj* deceitful, dishonest, false, untruthful, double-dealing, two-faced (*infml*).
≠ honest, truthful.
n dishonesty, untruthfulness, deceit, falsity, fibbing (*infml*), perjury, duplicity, fabrication, double-dealing.
≠ honesty, truthfulness.

M

macabre *adj* gruesome, grisly, grim, horrible, frightful, dreadful, ghostly, eerie.

machine *n* **1** INSTRUMENT, device, contrivance, tool, mechanism, engine, apparatus, appliance. **2** AGENCY, organization, structure, system.

machinery *n* **1** INSTRUMENTS, mechanism, tools, apparatus, equipment, tackle, gear.

> *Types of heavy machinery include*: all-terrain fork lift, bulldozer, caterpillar tractor, combine harvester, concrete mixer, concrete pump, crane, crawler crane, crawler tractor, digger, dragline excavator, dredger, dumper, dump truck, dustcart, excavator, fertilizer spreader, fire appliance, fork-lift truck, gantry crane, grader, grapple, gritter, hydraulic bale loader, hydraulic shovel, JCB®, muck spreader, pick-up loader, pile-driver, platform hoist, riding mower, road roller, road-sweeping lorry, Rotovator®, silage harvester, snowplough, straw baler, threshing machine, tower crane, tracklayer, tractor, tractor, tractor-scraper, truck crane, wheel loader.

2 ORGANIZATION, channels, structure, system, procedure.

mad *adj* **1** INSANE, lunatic, unbalanced, psychotic, deranged, demented, out of one's mind, crazy (*infml*), nuts (*infml*), barmy (*infml*), bonkers (*infml*). **2** (*infml*) ANGRY, furious, enraged, infuriated, incensed. **3** IRRATIONAL, illogical, unreasonable, absurd, preposterous, foolish. **4** FANATICAL, enthusiastic, infatuated, ardent.
≠ **1** sane. **2** calm. **3** sensible. **4** apathetic.

madden *v* anger, enrage, infuriate, incense, exasperate, provoke, annoy, irritate.
≠ calm, pacify.

madly *adv* **1** *he rolled his eyes madly*: insanely, dementedly, hysterically, wildly. **2** *madly cleaning up*: excitedly, frantically, furiously, recklessly, violently, energetically, rapidly, hastily, hurriedly. **3** *madly in love*: intensely, extremely, exceedingly, fervently, devotedly.

madman, madwoman *n* lunatic, psychotic, psychopath, maniac, loony (*infml*), nutcase (*infml*), fruitcake (*infml*).

magazine *n* **1** JOURNAL, periodical, paper, weekly, monthly, quarterly. **2** ARSENAL, storehouse, ammunition dump, depot, ordnance.

magic *n* **1** SORCERY, enchantment, occultism, black art, witchcraft, spell. **2** CONJURING, illusion, sleight of hand, trickery. **3** CHARM, fascination, glamour, allure.
adj charming, enchanting, bewitching, fascinating, spellbinding.

magician *n* sorcerer, miracle-worker, conjuror, enchanter, wizard, witch, warlock, spellbinder, wonder-worker.

magnanimous *adj* generous, liberal, open-handed, benevolent, selfless, charitable, big-hearted, kind, noble, unselfish, ungrudging.
≠ mean.

magnate *n* tycoon, captain of industry, industrialist, mogul, entrepreneur, plutocrat, baron, personage, notable.

magnetic *adj* attractive, alluring, fascinating, charming, mesmerizing, seductive, irresistible, entrancing, captivating, gripping, absorbing, charismatic.
≠ repellent, repulsive.

magnetism *n* attraction, allure,

fascination, charm, lure, appeal, drawing power, draw, pull, hypnotism, mesmerism, charisma, grip, magic, power, spell.

magnificent *adj* splendid, grand, imposing, impressive, glorious, gorgeous, brilliant, excellent, majestic, superb, sumptuous, noble, elegant, fine, rich.
≠ modest, humble, poor.

magnify *v* enlarge, amplify, increase, expand, intensify, boost, enhance, greaten, heighten, deepen, build up, exaggerate, dramatize, overemphasize, overplay, overstate, overdo, blow up (*infml*).
≠ belittle, play down.

magnitude *n* **1** SIZE, extent, measure, amount, expanse, dimensions, mass, proportions, quantity, volume, bulk, largeness, space, strength, amplitude. **2** IMPORTANCE, consequence, significance, weight, greatness, moment, intensity.

maiden *n* girl, virgin, lass, lassie, damsel (*fml*), miss.

mail *n* post, letters, correspondence, packages, parcels, delivery.
v post, send, dispatch, forward.

maim *v* mutilate, wound, incapacitate, injure, disable, hurt, impair, cripple, lame.

main *adj* principal, chief, leading, first, foremost, predominant, pre-eminent, primary, prime, supreme, paramount, central, cardinal, outstanding, essential, critical, crucial, necessary, vital.
≠ minor, unimportant, insignificant.
n pipe, duct, conduit, channel, cable, line.

mainly *adv* primarily, principally, chiefly, in the main, mostly, on the whole, for the most part, generally, in general, especially, as a rule, above all, largely, overall.

mainstay *n* support, buttress, bulwark, linchpin, prop, pillar, backbone, foundation.

maintain *v* **1** CARRY ON, continue, keep (up), sustain, retain. **2** CARE FOR, conserve, look after, take care of, preserve, support, finance, supply. **3** ASSERT, affirm, claim, contend, declare, hold, state, insist, believe, fight for.
≠ **2** neglect. **3** deny.

maintenance *n* **1** CONTINUATION, continuance, perpetuation. **2** CARE, conservation, preservation, support, repairs, protection, upkeep, running. **3** KEEP, subsistence, living, livelihood, allowance, alimony.
≠ **2** neglect.

majestic *adj* magnificent, grand, dignified, noble, royal, stately, splendid, imperial, impressive, exalted, imposing, regal, sublime, superb, lofty, monumental, pompous.
≠ lowly, unimpressive, unimposing.

majesty *n* grandeur, glory, dignity, magnificence, nobility, royalty, resplendence, splendour, stateliness, pomp, exaltedness, impressiveness, loftiness.

major *adj* greater, chief, main, larger, bigger, higher, leading, outstanding, notable, supreme, uppermost, significant, crucial, important, key, keynote, great, senior, older, superior, pre-eminent, vital, weighty.
≠ minor, unimportant, trivial.

majority *n* **1** BULK, mass, preponderance, meet, greater part. **2** ADULTHOOD, maturity, manhood, womanhood, years of discretion.
≠ **1** minority.

make *v* **1** CREATE, manufacture, fabricate, construct, build, produce, put together, originate, compose, form, shape. **2** CAUSE, bring about, effect, accomplish, occasion, give rise to, generate, render, perform. **3** COERCE, force, oblige, constrain, compel, prevail upon, pressurize, press, require. **4** APPOINT, elect, designate, nominate, ordain, install. **5** EARN, gain, net, obtain, acquire. **6** CONSTITUTE, compose, comprise, add up to, amount to.
≠ **1** dismantle. **5** spend.
n brand, sort, type, style, variety, manufacture, model, mark, kind, form, structure.

make off run off, run away, depart, bolt, leave, fly, cut and run (*infml*), beat a hasty retreat (*infml*), clear off (*infml*).
make out 1 DISCERN, perceive, decipher, distinguish, recognize, see, detect, discover, understand, work out, grasp, follow, fathom. **2** DRAW UP, complete, fill in, write out. **3** MAINTAIN, imply, claim, assert, describe, demonstrate, prove. **4** MANAGE, get on, progress, succeed, fare (*fml*).
make up 1 CREATE, invent, devise, fabricate, construct, originate, formulate, dream up, compose. **2** COMPLETE, fill, supply, meet, supplement. **3** COMPRISE, constitute, compose, form. **4** BE RECONCILED, make peace, settle differences, bury the hatchet (*infml*), forgive and forget, call it quits (*infml*).
make up for compensate for, make good, make amends for, redress, recompense, redeem, atone for.

make-believe *n* pretence, imagination, fantasy, unreality, play-acting, role-play, dream, charade.
≠ reality.

maker *n* creator, manufacturer, constructor, builder, producer, director, architect, author.

makeshift *adj* temporary, improvised, rough and ready, provisional, substitute, stop-gap, expedient, make-do.
≠ permanent.

make-up *n* **1** COSMETICS, paint, powder, maquillage, war paint (*infml*). **2** CONSTITUTION, nature, composition, character, construction, form, format, formation, arrangement, organization, style, structure, assembly.

maladjusted *adj* disturbed, unstable, confused, alienated, neurotic, estranged.
≠ well-adjusted.

male *adj* masculine, manly, virile, boyish, he-.
≠ female.

Male terms include: boy, lad, youth, man, gentleman, gent (*infml*), bachelor, chap (*infml*), bloke (*infml*), guy (*infml*), son, brother, boyfriend, beau, toy boy (*sl*), fiancé, bridegroom, husband, father, uncle, nephew, grandfather, patriarch, godfather, widower, sugar daddy (*sl*), hunk (*sl*), gigolo, homosexual, gay, rent boy, male chauvinist pig (MCP) (*sl*); bull, dog, buck, tup, cock, cockerel, stallion, billy-goat, boar, dog fox, stag, ram, tom cat, drake, gander.

malevolent *adj* malicious, malign, spiteful, vindictive, ill-natured, hostile, vicious, venomous, evil-minded.
≠ benevolent, kind.

malformation *n* irregularity, deformity, distortion, warp.

malformed *adj* misshapen, irregular, deformed, distorted, twisted, warped, crooked, bent.
≠ perfect.

malfunction *n* fault, defect, failure, breakdown.
v break down, go wrong, fail.

malice *n* malevolence, enmity, animosity, ill-will, hatred, hate, spite, vindictiveness, bitterness.
≠ love.

malicious *adj* malevolent, ill-natured, malign, spiteful, venomous, vicious, vengeful, evil-minded, bitter, resentful.
≠ kind, friendly.

malign *adj* malignant, malevolent, bad, evil, harmful, hurtful, injurious, destructive, hostile.
≠ benign.
v defame, slander, libel, disparage, abuse, run down (*infml*), harm, injure.
≠ praise.

malignant *adj* **1** MALEVOLENT, malicious, spiteful, evil, hostile, vicious, venomous, destructive, harmful, hurtful, pernicious. **2** FATAL, deadly, incurable, dangerous, cancerous, uncontrollable, virulent.
≠ **1** kind. **2** benign.

malpractice *n* misconduct, mismanagement, negligence, impropriety, dereliction of duty (*fml*), abuse, misdeed.

maltreat *v* ill-treat, mistreat, misuse, abuse, injure, harm, damage, hurt.
≠ care for.

mammals

Mammals include: aardvark, African black rhinoceros, African elephant, anteater, antelope, armadillo, baboon, Bactrian camel, badger, bat, bear, beaver, bushbaby, cat, chimpanzee, chipmunk, cow, deer, dog, dolphin, duck-billed platypus, dugong, echidna, flying lemur, fox, gerbil, gibbon, giraffe, goat, gorilla, guinea pig, hamster, hare, hedgehog, hippopotamus, horse, human being, hyena, indian elephant, kangaroo, koala, lemming, leopard, lion, manatee, marmoset, marmot, marsupial mouse, mole, mouse, opossum, orang utan, otter, pig, porcupine, porpoise, rabbit, raccoon, rat, sea cow, sea lion, seal, sheep, shrew, sloth, squirrel, tamarin, tapir, tiger, vole, wallaby, walrus, weasel, whale, wolf, zebra. *see also* **cats**; **cattle**; **dog**; **horses**; **marsupials**; **monkey**; **rodents**.

mammoth *adj* enormous, huge, vast, colossal, gigantic, giant, massive, immense, monumental, mighty.
≠ tiny, minute.

man *n* **1** MALE, gentleman, fellow, bloke (*infml*), chap (*infml*), guy (*infml*). **2** HUMAN BEING, person, individual, adult, human. **3** HUMANITY, humankind, mankind, human race, people, Homo sapiens, mortals. **4** MANSERVANT, servant, worker, employee, hand, soldier, valet, houseman, houseboy.
v staff, crew, take charge of, operate, occupy.

manacle *v* handcuff, shackle, restrain, fetter, chain, put in chains, bind, curb, check, hamper, inhibit.
≠ free, unshackle.

manage *v* **1** ACCOMPLISH, succeed, bring about, bring off, effect. **2** ADMINISTER, direct, run, command, govern, preside over, rule, superintend, supervise, oversee, conduct. **3** CONTROL, influence, deal with, handle, operate, manipulate, guide. **4** COPE, fare, survive, get by, get along, get on, make do.
≠ **1** fail. **2** mismanage.

manageable *adj* tractable, governable, controllable, amenable, submissive, docile.
≠ unmanageable.

management *n* **1** ADMINISTRATION, direction, control, government, command, running, superintendence, supervision, charge, care, handling. **2** MANAGERS, directors, directorate, executive, executives, governors, board, bosses (*infml*), supervisors.
≠ **1** mismanagement. **2** workers.

manager *n* director, executive, administrator, controller, superintendent, supervisor, overseer, governor, organizer, head, boss (*infml*).

mandate *n* order, command, decree, edict, injunction, charge, directive, warrant, authorization, authority, instruction, commission, sanction.

mandatory *adj* obligatory, compulsory, binding, required, necessary, requisite, essential.
≠ optional.

mangle *v* mutilate, disfigure, mar, maim, spoil, butcher, destroy, deform, wreck, twist, maul, distort, crush, cut, hack, tear, rend.

mangy *adj* seedy, shabby, scruffy, scabby, tatty (*infml*), shoddy, moth-eaten, dirty, mean.

manhandle *v* **1** *the porters manhandled the baggage*: haul, heave, hump, pull, push, shove, tug. **2** *the police manhandled the demonstrators*: maul, mistreat, maltreat, misuse, abuse, knock about (*infml*), rough up (*infml*).

manhood *n* **1** ADULTHOOD, maturity. **2** MASCULINITY, virility, manliness, manfulness, machismo (*infml*).

mania *n* **1** MADNESS, insanity, lunacy, psychosis, derangement, disorder, aberration, craziness (*infml*), frenzy.

Manias (by name of disorder) include: dipsomania (*alcohol*), bibliomania (*books*), ailuromania (*cats*), demomania (*crowds*), necromania (*dead bodies*), thanatomania (*death*), cynomania (*dogs*), narcomania (*drugs*), pyromania (*fire-raising*), anthomania (*flowers*), hippomania (*horses*), mythomania (*lying and exaggerating*), egomania (*oneself*), ablutomania (*personal cleanliness*), hedonomania (*pleasure*), megalomania (*power*), theomania (*religion*), nymphomania (*sex*), monomania (*single idea or thing*), kleptomania (*stealing*), tomomania (*surgery*), logomania (*talking*), ergomania (*work*). *see also* **phobia**.

2 PASSION, craze, rage, obsession, compulsion, enthusiasm, fad (*infml*), infatuation, fixation, craving.

maniac *n* **1** LUNATIC, madman, madwoman, psychotic, psychopath, loony (*infml*). **2** ENTHUSIAST, fan (*infml*), fanatic, fiend (*infml*), freak (*infml*).

manifest *adj* obvious, evident, clear, apparent, plain, open, patent, noticeable, conspicuous, unmistakable, visible, unconcealed.
≠ unclear.
v show, exhibit, display, demonstrate, reveal, set forth, expose, prove, illustrate, establish.
≠ conceal.

manifestation *n* display, exhibition, demonstration, show, revelation, exposure, disclosure, appearance, expression, sign, indication.

manifesto *n* statement, declaration, policies, platform.

manifold *adj* (*fml*) many, numerous, varied, various, diverse, multiple, kaleidoscopic, abundant, copious.

manipulate *v* **1** HANDLE, control, wield, operate, use, manoeuvre, influence, engineer, guide, direct, steer, negotiate, work. **2** FALSIFY, rig, juggle with, doctor (*infml*), cook (*infml*), fiddle (*infml*).

mankind *n* humankind, humanity, human race, man, Homo sapiens, people.

manly *adj* masculine, male, virile, manful, macho (*infml*), robust.

man-made *adj* synthetic, manufactured, simulated, imitation, artificial.
≠ natural.

manner *n* **1** WAY, method, means, fashion, style, procedure, process, form. **2** BEHAVIOUR, conduct, bearing, demeanour, air, appearance, look, character.

mannerism *n* idiosyncrasy, peculiarity, characteristic, quirk, trait, feature, foible, habit.

manners *n* behaviour, conduct, demeanour, etiquette, politeness, bearing, courtesy, formalities, social graces, p's and q's.

manoeuvre *n* move, movement, operation, action, exercise, plan, ploy, plot, ruse, strategem, machination, gambit, tactic, trick, scheme, dodge (*infml*).
v **1** MOVE, manipulate, handle, guide, pilot, steer, navigate, jockey, direct, drive, exercise. **2** CONTRIVE, engineer, plot, scheme, wangle (*infml*), pull strings (*infml*), manipulate, manage, plan, devise, negotiate.

mantle *n* cloak, cover, covering, cape, hood, blanket, shawl, veil, wrap, shroud, screen.

manual *n* handbook, guide, guidebook, instructions, Bible, vade mecum, directions.
adj hand-operated, by hand, physical, human.

manufacture *v* **1** MAKE, produce, construct, build, fabricate, create, assemble, mass-produce, turn out, process, forge, form. **2** INVENT, make up, concoct, fabricate, think up.
n production, making, construction, fabrication, mass-production, assembly, creation, formation.

manufacturer *n* maker, producer, industrialist, constructor, factory-owner, builder, creator.

manure *n* fertilizer, compost, muck, dung.

many *adj* numerous, countless, lots of (*infml*), manifold (*fml*), various, varied, sundry, diverse, umpteen (*infml*).
≠ few.

map *n* chart, plan, street plan, atlas, graph, plot.

mar *v* spoil, impair, harm, hurt, damage, deface, disfigure, mutilate, injure, maim, scar, detract from, mangle, ruin, wreck, tarnish.
≠ enhance.

marauder *n* bandit, brigand, robber, raider, plunderer, pillager, pirate, buccaneer, outlaw, ravager, predator.

march *v* walk, stride, parade, pace, file, tread, stalk.
n **1** STEP, pace, stride. **2** WALK, trek, hike, footslog (*infml*). **3** PROCESSION, parade, demonstration, demo (*infml*). **4** ADVANCE, development, progress, evolution, passage.

margin *n* **1** BORDER, edge, boundary, bound, periphery, perimeter, rim, brink, limit, confine, verge, side, skirt. **2** ALLOWANCE, play, leeway, latitude, scope, room, space, surplus, extra.

marginal *adj* borderline, peripheral, negligible, minimal, insignificant, minor, slight, doubtful, low, small.
≠ central, core.

marine *adj* sea, maritime, naval, nautical, seafaring, sea-going, ocean-going, salt-water.

mariner *n* sailor, seaman, seafarer, deckhand, navigator, tar (*infml*), sea-dog (*infml*), salt (*infml*).

marital *adj* conjugal, matrimonial, married, wedded, nuptial (*fml*), connubial (*fml*).

maritime *adj* marine, nautical, naval, seafaring, sea, seaside, oceanic, coastal.

mark *n* **1** SPOT, stain, blemish, blot, blotch, smudge, dent, impression, scar, scratch, bruise, line. **2** SYMBOL, sign, indication, emblem, brand, stamp, token, characteristic, feature, proof, evidence, badge. **3** TARGET, goal, aim, objective, purpose.
v **1** STAIN, blemish, blot, smudge, dent, scar, scratch, bruise. **2** BRAND, label, stamp, characterize, identify, distinguish. **3** EVALUATE, assess, correct, grade. **4** HEED, listen, mind, note, observe, regard, notice, take to heart.

marked *adj* **1** NOTICEABLE, obvious, conspicuous, evident, pronounced, distinct, decided, emphatic, considerable, remarkable, apparent, glaring. **2** SUSPECTED, watched, doomed.
≠ **1** unnoticeable, slight.

market *n* mart, marketplace, bazaar, fair, exchange, outlet.
v sell, retail, hawk, peddle.
≠ buy.

maroon *v* abandon, cast away, desert, put ashore, strand, leave, isolate.

marriage *n* **1** MATRIMONY, wedlock, wedding, nuptials (*fml*). **2** UNION, alliance, merger, coupling, amalgamation, link, association, confederation.
≠ **1** divorce. **2** separation.

marrow *n* essence, heart, nub, kernel, core, soul, spirit, substance, quick, stuff, gist.

marry *v* **1** WED, join in matrimony, tie the knot (*infml*), get hitched (*infml*), get spliced (*infml*). **2** UNITE, ally, join, merge, match, link, knit.
≠ **1** divorce. **2** separate.

marsh *n* marshland, bog, swamp, fen, morass, quagmire, slough.

marshal *v* **1** ARRANGE, dispose, order, line up, align, array, rank, organize, assemble, gather, muster, group, collect, draw up, deploy. **2** GUIDE, lead, escort, conduct, usher.

marsupials

Marsupials include: bandicoot, cuscus, kangaroo, rat kangaroo, tree kangaroo, wallaroo, koala, marsupial anteater, marsupial mouse, marsupial mole, marsupial rat, opossum, pademelon, phalanger, Tasmanian Devil, Tasmanian wolf, wallaby, rock wallaby, wombat.

martial *adj* warlike, military, belligerent, soldierly, militant, heroic, brave.

marvel *n* wonder, miracle, phenomenon, prodigy, spectacle, sensation, genius.
v wonder, gape, gaze, be amazed at.

marvellous *adj* **1** WONDERFUL,

excellent, splendid, superb, magnificent, terrific (*infml*), super, fantastic (*infml*). **2** EXTRAORDINARY, amazing, astonishing, astounding, miraculous, remarkable, surprising, unbelievable, incredible, glorious.
≠ **1** terrible, awful. **2** ordinary, run-of-the-mill.

masculine *adj* **1** MALE, manlike, manly, mannish, virile, macho. **2** VIGOROUS, strong, strapping, robust, powerful, muscular, red-blooded, bold, brave, gallant, resolute, stout-hearted.
≠ **1** feminine.

mash *v* crush, pulp, beat, pound, pulverize, pummel, grind, smash.

mask *n* disguise, camouflage, façade, front, concealment, cover-up, cover, guise, pretence, semblance, cloak, veil, blind, show, veneer, visor.
v disguise, camouflage, cover, conceal, cloak, veil, hide, obscure, screen, shield.
≠ expose, uncover.

masquerade *n* **1** MASQUE, masked ball, costume ball, fancy dress party. **2** DISGUISE, counterfeit, cover-up, cover, deception, front, pose, pretence, guise, cloak.
v disguise, impersonate, pose, pass oneself off, mask, play, pretend, profess, dissimulate.

mass *n* **1** HEAP, pile, load, accumulation, aggregate, collection, conglomeration, combination, entirety, whole, totality, sum, lot, group, batch, bunch. **2** QUANTITY, multitude, throng, troop, crowd, band, horde, mob. **3** MAJORITY, body, bulk. **4** SIZE, dimension, magnitude, immensity. **5** LUMP, piece, chunk, block, hunk.
adj widespread, large-scale, extensive, comprehensive, general, indiscriminate, popular, across-the-board, sweeping, wholesale, blanket.
≠ limited, small-scale.
v collect, gather, assemble, congregate, crowd, rally, cluster, muster, swarm, throng.
≠ separate.

massacre *n* slaughter, murder, extermination, carnage, butchery, holocaust, blood bath, annihilation, killing.
v slaughter, butcher, murder, mow down, wipe out, exterminate, annihilate, kill, decimate.

massage *n* manipulation, kneading, rubbing, rub-down.
v manipulate, knead, rub (down).

massive *adj* huge, immense, enormous, vast, colossal, gigantic, big, bulky, monumental, solid, substantial, heavy, large-scale, extensive.
≠ tiny, small.

master *n* **1** RULER, chief, governor, head, lord, captain, boss (*infml*), employer, commander, controller, director, manager, superintendent, overseer, principal, overlord, owner. **2** EXPERT, genius, virtuoso, past master, maestro, dab hand (*infml*), ace (*infml*), pro (*infml*). **3** TEACHER, tutor, instructor, schoolmaster, guide, guru, preceptor (*fml*).
≠ **1** servant, underling. **2** amateur. **3** learner, pupil.
adj **1** CHIEF, principal, main, leading, foremost, prime, predominant, controlling, great, grand. **2** EXPERT, masterly, skilled, skilful, proficient.
≠ **1** subordinate. **2** inept.
v **1** CONQUER, defeat, subdue, subjugate, vanquish, triumph over, overcome, quell, rule, control. **2** LEARN, grasp, acquire, get the hang of (*infml*), manage.

masterful *adj* **1** ARROGANT, authoritative, domineering, overbearing, high-handed, despotic, dictatorial, autocratic, bossy (*infml*), tyrannical, powerful. **2** EXPERT, masterly, skilful, skilled, dexterous, first-rate, professional.
≠ **1** humble. **2** inept, unskilful.

masterly *adj* expert, skilled, skilful, dexterous, adept, adroit, first-rate, ace (*infml*), excellent, superb, superior, supreme.
≠ inept, clumsy.

masterpiece *n* master-work, magnum opus, pièce de résistance, chef d'oeuvre, jewel.

mastery *n* **1** PROFICIENCY, skill,

ability, command, expertise, virtuosity, knowledge, know-how, dexterity, familiarity, grasp. **2** CONTROL, command, domination, supremacy, upper hand, dominion, authority.
≠ **1** incompetence. **2** subjugation.

match *n* **1** CONTEST, competition, bout, game, test, trial. **2** EQUAL, equivalent, peer, counterpart, fellow, mate, rival, copy, double, replica, look-alike, twin, duplicate. **3** MARRIAGE, alliance, union, partnership, affiliation.
v **1** EQUAL, compare, measure up to, rival, compete, oppose, contend, vie, pit against. **2** FIT, go with, accord, agree, suit, correspond, harmonize, tally, co-ordinate, blend, adapt, go together, relate, tone with, accompany. **3** JOIN, marry, unite, mate, link, couple, combine, ally, pair, yoke, team.
≠ **2** clash. **3** separate.

matching *adj* corresponding, comparable, equivalent, like, identical, co-ordinating, similar, duplicate, same, twin.
≠ clashing.

matchless *adj* unequalled, peerless, incomparable, unmatched, unparalleled, unsurpassed, unrivalled, inimitable, unique.

mate *n* **1** FRIEND, companion, comrade, pal (*infml*), colleague, partner, fellow-worker, co-worker, associate. **2** SPOUSE, husband, wife. **3** ASSISTANT, helper, subordinate. **4** MATCH, fellow, twin.
v **1** COUPLE, pair, breed, copulate. **2** JOIN, match, marry, wed.

material *n* **1** STUFF, substance, body, matter. **2** FABRIC, textile, cloth. **3** INFORMATION, facts, data, evidence, constituents, work, notes.
adj **1** PHYSICAL, concrete, tangible, substantial. **2** RELEVANT, significant, important, meaningful, pertinent, essential, vital, indispensable, serious.
≠ **1** abstract. **2** irrelevant.

materialize *v* appear, arise, take shape, turn up, happen, occur.
≠ disappear.

mathematics

Mathematical terms include: acute angle, addition, algebra, algorithm, analysis, angle, apex, approximate, arc, area, argument, arithmetic, arithmetic progression, asymmetrical, average, axis, axis of symmetry, bar chart, bar graph, base, bearing, binary, binomial, breadth, calculus, capacity, cardinal number, Cartesian coordinates, chance, chord, circumference, coefficient, combination, commutative operation, complement, complementary angle, complex number, concave, concentric circles, congruent, conjugate angles, constant, continuous distribution, converse, convex, coordinate, correlation, cosine, covariance, cross section, cube, cube root, curve, decimal, degree, denominator, depth, derivative, determinant, diagonal, diameter, differentiation, directed number, distribution, dividend, division, divisor, edge, equal, equation, equidistant, even number, exponent, exponential, face, factor, factorial, Fibonacci sequence, formula, fraction, function, geometric progression, geometry, gradient, graph, greater than, group, harmonic progression, height, helix, histogram, horizontal, hyperbola, hypotenuse, identity, infinity, integer, integration, irrational number, latitude, length, less than, linear, line, locus, logarithm, longitude, magic square, matrix, maximum, mean, measure, median, minimum, minus, mirror image, mirror symmetry, Möbius strip, mode, modulus, multiple, multiplication, natural logarithm, natural number, negative number, number, numerator, oblique, obtuse angle, odd number, operation, ordinal number, origin, parabola, parallel lines, parallel planes, parameter, percentage, percentile, perimeter, permutation, perpendicular, pi, pie chart, place value, plane figure, plus, point, positive number, prime number, probability, product, proportion, protractor, Pythagoras's theorem, quadrant, quadratic equation, quadrilateral, quartile, quotient, radian, radius, random sample, ratio, rational number, real numbers, reciprocal, recurring decimal, reflection, reflex angle, regression, remainder, right-angle, right-angled triangle, root, rotation, rotational symmetry, sample, scalar segment, secant, sector, set, side, simultaneous equation, sine, speed, spiral, square, square root, standard deviation, straight line, subset, subtractor, supplementary angles, symmetry, tangent, three-dimensional, total, transcendental number, triangulation, trigonometry, unit, universal set, variable, variance, vector, velocity, Venn diagram, vertex, vertical, volume, whole number, width, zero. *see also* **shape**.

matrimonial *adj* marital, nuptial, marriage, wedding, married, wedded, conjugal.

matter *n* **1** SUBJECT, issue, topic, question, affair, business, concern, event, episode, incident. **2** IMPORTANCE, significance, consequence, note. **3** TROUBLE, problem, difficulty, worry. **4** SUBSTANCE, stuff, material, body, content.
v count, be important, make a difference, mean something.

matter-of-fact *adj* emotional, prosaic, emotionless, straightforward, sober, unimaginative, flat, deadpan (*infml*).
≠ emotional.

mature *adj* **1** ADULT, grown-up, grown, full-grown, fully fledged, complete, perfect, perfected, well-thought-out. **2** RIPE, ripened, seasoned, mellow, ready.
≠ **1** childish. **2** immature.
v grow up, come of age, develop, mellow, ripen, perfect, age, bloom, fall due.

maturity *n* **1** ADULTHOOD, majority, womanhood, manhood, wisdom, experience. **2** RIPENESS, readiness, mellowness, perfection.
≠ **1** childishness. **2** immaturity.

maul *v* abuse, ill-treat, manhandle, maltreat, molest, paw, beat (up), knock about, rough up, claw, lacerate, batter.

maxim *n* saying, proverb, adage, axiom, aphorism, epigram, motto, byword, precept, rule.

maximum *adj* greatest, highest, largest, biggest, most, utmost, supreme.
≠ minimum.
n most, top (point), utmost, upper limit, peak, pinnacle, summit, height, ceiling, extremity, zenith (*fml*).
≠ mimimum.

maybe *adv* perhaps, possibly, perchance (*fml*).
≠ definitely.

maze *n* labyrinth, network, tangle, web, complex, confusion, puzzle, intricacy.

meadow *n* field, grassland, pasture, lea.

meagre *adj* **1** SCANTY, sparse, inadequate, deficient, skimpy, paltry, negligible, poor. **2** THIN, puny, insubstantial, bony, emaciated, scrawny, slight.
≠ **1** ample. **2** fat.

meal

Meals include: breakfast, wedding breakfast, elevenses (*infml*), brunch, lunch, luncheon, tea, tea-break, tea-party, tiffin, afternoon tea, cream-tea, high-tea, evening meal, dinner, TV dinner, supper, harvest supper, fork supper, banquet, feast, blow-out (*sl*), barbecue, buffet, spread, picnic, snack, take-away.

mean[1] *adj* **1** MISERLY, niggardly, parsimonious, selfish, tight (*infml*), tight-fisted, stingy (*infml*), penny-pinching (*infml*). **2** UNKIND, unpleasant, nasty, bad-tempered, cruel. **3** LOWLY, base, poor, humble, wretched.
≠ **1** generous. **2** kind. **3** splendid.

mean[2] *v* **1** SIGNIFY, represent, denote, stand for, symbolize, suggest, indicate, imply. **2** INTEND, aim, propose, design. **3** CAUSE, give rise to, involve, entail.

mean[3] *adj* average, intermediate, middle, halfway, median, normal.
≠ extreme.

n average, middle, mid-point, norm, median, compromise, middle course, middle way, happy medium, golden mean.
≠ extreme.

meander *v* **1** WIND, zigzag, turn, twist, snake, curve. **2** WANDER, stray, amble, ramble, stroll.

meaning *n* **1** SIGNIFICANCE, sense, import, implication, gist, trend, explanation, interpretation. **2** AIM, intention, purpose, object, idea. **3** VALUE, worth, point.

meaningful *adj* **1** IMPORTANT, significant, relevant, valid, useful, worthwhile, material, purposeful, serious. **2** EXPRESSIVE, speaking, suggestive, warning, pointed.
≠ **1** unimportant, worthless.

meaningless *adj* **1** SENSELESS, pointless, purposeless, useless, insignificant, aimless, futile, insubstantial, trifling, trivial. **2** EMPTY, hollow, vacuous, vain, worthless, nonsensical, absurd.
≠ **1** important, meaningful. **2** worthwhile.

means *n* **1** METHOD, mode, way, medium, course, agency, process, instrument, channel, vehicle. **2** RESOURCES, funds, money, income, wealth, riches, substance, wherewithal, fortune, affluence.

measure *n* **1** PORTION, ration, share, allocation, quota. **2** SIZE, quantity, magnitude, amount, degree, extent, range, scope, proportion. **3** RULE, gauge, scale, standard, criterion, norm, touchstone, yardstick, test, meter. **4** STEP, course, action, deed, procedure, method, act, bill, statute.
v quantify, evaluate, assess, weigh, value, gauge, judge, sound, fathom, determine, calculate, estimate, plumb, survey, compute, measure out, measure off.
measure up to equal, meet, match, compare with, touch, rival, make the grade.

measured *adj* deliberate, planned, reasoned, slow, unhurried, steady, studied, well-thought-out, calculated, careful, considered, precise.

measurement *n* **1** DIMENSION, size, extent, amount, magnitude, area, capacity, height, depth, length, width, weight, volume.

> *SI (Système Internationale d'Unités) base units include*: ampere, candela, kelvin, kilogram, metre, mole, second.
> *SI derivatives and other measurements include*: acre, angstrom, atmosphere, bar, barrel, becquerel, bushel, cable, calorie, centimetre, century, chain, coulomb, cubic centimetre, cubic foot, cubic inch, cubic metre, cubic yard, day, decade, decibel, degree, dyne, erg, farad, fathom, fluid ounce, fresnel, foot, foot-pound, furlong, gallon, gill, gram, hand, hectare, hertz, horsepower, hour, hundredweight, inch, joule, kilometre, knot, league, litre, lumen, micrometre, mile, millennium, millibar, millilitre, minute, month, nautical mile, newton, ohm, ounce, pascal, peak, pint, pound, pound per square inch, radian, rod, siemens, span, square centimetre, square foot, square inch, square kilometre, square metre, square mile, square yard, steradian, stone, therm, ton, tonne, volt, watt, week, yard, year.

2 ASSESSMENT, evaluation, estimation, computation, calculation, calibration, gauging, judgement, appraisal, appreciation, survey.

measuring instruments

> *Gauges include*: cutting gauge, drill gauge, feeler gauge, gauge glass, gauge rod, gauge wheel, marking gauge, mortise gauge, paper gauge, pressure gauge, radius gauge, rain gauge, ring gauge, snap gauge, steam gauge, strain gauge, taper gauge, tide gauge, vacuum gauge, water gauge. *Measuring instruments include*: altimeter, ammeter, anemometer, audiometer, balance, barometer, bathometer, Breathalyser®, burette, callipers, calorimeter, chronometer, clinometer, colorimeter, cyclometer, densitometer, galvanometer, Geiger counter, gravimeter, hourglass, hydrometer, hygrometer, hypsometer, manometer, measuring

cylinder, meter, micrometer, multimeter, octant, optometer, pedometer, photometer, pipette, planimeter, plumb line, protractor, psychrometer, pyranometer, pyrometer, quadrant, radiosonde, rheometer, rule, saccharometer, salinometer, seismograph, sextant, speedometer, spherometer, sphygmomanometer, steelyard, stopwatch, tachometer, tachymeter, tape measure, tensiometer, theodolite, thermometer, vinometer, voltmeter, weighbridge, Wheatstone bridge.

meat *n* **1** FLESH. **2** (*infml*) FOOD, rations, provisions, nourishment, sustenance, subsistence, eats (*infml*).

Kinds of meat include: beef, pork, lamb, mutton, ham, bacon, gammon, chicken, turkey, goose, duck, rabbit, hare, venison, pheasant, grouse, partridge, pigeon, quail; offal, liver, heart, tongue, kidney, brains, brawn, pig's knuckle, trotters, oxtail, sweetbread, tripe; steak, minced beef, sausage, rissole, faggot, beefburger, hamburger, black pudding, paté.
Cuts of meat include: shoulder, collar, hand, loin, hock, leg, chop, shin, knuckle, rib, spare-rib, breast, brisket, chine, cutlet, fillet, rump, scrag, silverside, topside, sirloin, flank, escalope, neck, saddle.

mechanical *adj* automatic, involuntary, instinctive, routine, habitual, impersonal, emotionless, cold, matter-of-fact, unfeeling, lifeless, dead, dull. ≠ conscious.

mechanism *n* **1** MACHINE, machinery, engine, appliance, instrument, tool, motor, works, workings, gadget, device, apparatus, contrivance, gears, components. **2** MEANS, method, agency, process, procedure, system, technique, medium, structure, operation, functioning, performance.

meddle *v* interfere, intervene, pry, snoop (*infml*), intrude, butt in, tamper.

meddlesome *adj* interfering, meddling, prying, intrusive, intruding, mischievous.

mediate *v* arbitrate, conciliate, intervene, referee, umpire, intercede, moderate, reconcile, negotiate, resolve, settle, step in.

mediator *n* arbitrator, referee, umpire, intermediary, negotiator, go-between, interceder, judge, moderator, intercessor, conciliator, peacemaker, Ombudsman.

medical equipment

Medical and surgical equipment includes: aspirator, audiometer, aural speculum, auriscope, autoclave, body scanner, bronchoscope, cannula, catheter, CAT scanner, clamp, curette, defibrillator, disposable enema pack, ear syringe, ECG (electrocardiograph), electroencephalograph, endoscope, first aid kit, forceps, haemodialysis unit, hypodermic needle, hypodermic syringe, incubator, inhaler, instrument table, iron lung, isolator tent, kidney dish, laparoscope, laryngoscope, microscope, nebulizer, obstetrical forceps, oesophagoscope, operating table, ophthalmoscope, oxygen cylinder, oxygen mask, rectoscope, respirator, resuscitator, retractor, rhinoscope, scales, scalpel, sliding-weight scales, specimen glass, speculum, sphygmomanometer, sterile donor-pack, sterilizer, stethoscope, stomach pump, surgical mask, surgical suture materials, swabs, syringe, thermometer, tracheostomy tube, traction apparatus, tweezers, ultrasound scanner, urethroscope, vaginal speculum, X-ray unit.

medical specialists

Medical specialists include: anaesthetist, bacteriologist, cardiologist, chiropodist, chiropractor, dentist, dermatologist, dietician, doctor, embryologist, endocrinologist, forensic pathologist, gastroenterologist, geriatrician, gerontologist, gynaecologist, haematologist, homoeopath, immunologist, microbiologist, neurologist, obstetrician, oncologist, ophthalmologist, optician (or optometrist), orthodontist, orthopaedist, orthoptist, paediatrician, pathologist, pharmacist, pharmacologist, physiotherapist, pschiatrist, psychologist, rheumatologist, toxicologist. *see also* **doctor**; **nurse**; **surgeon**.

medical terms

Medical terms include: abortion, allergy, amputation, analgesic, antibiotics, antiseptic, bandage, barium meal, biopsy, blood bank, blood count, blood donor, blood group, blood pressure, blood test, caesarean, cardiopulmonary resuscitation (CPR), case history, casualty, cauterization, cervical smear, check-up, childbirth, circulation, circumcision, clinic, complication, compress, consultant, consultation, contraception, convulsion, cure, diagnosis, dialysis, dislocate, dissection, doctor, donor, dressings, enema, examination, gene, health screening, home visit, hormone replacement therapy (HRT), hospice, hospital, immunization, implantation, incubation, infection, inflammation, injection, injury, inoculation, intensive care, labour, miscarriage, mouth-to-mouth, nurse, ointment, operation, paraplegia, post-mortem, pregnancy, prescription, prognosis, prosthesis, psychosomatic, quarantine, radiotherapy, recovery, rehabilitation, relapse, remission, respiration, resuscitation, scan, side effect, sling, smear test, specimen, splint, sterilization, steroid, surgery, suture, symptom, syndrome, therapy, tourniquet, tranquillizer, transfusion, transplant, trauma, treatment, tumour, ultrasound scanning, vaccination, vaccine, virus, X-ray. *see also* **therapy**.

medicinal *adj* therapeutic, healing, remedial, curative, restorative, medical.

medicine *n* medication, drug, cure, remedy, medicament, prescription, pharmaceutical, panacea.

Types of medicine include: tablet, capsule, pill, painkiller, lozenge, pastille, gargle, linctus, tonic, laxative, suppository, antacid, ointment, arnica, eye drops, ear drops, nasal spray, inhaler, Ventolin™, antibiotic, penicillin, emetic, gripe-water, paregoric. *see also* **drug**.
Forms of alternative medicine include: acupuncture, aromatherapy, chiropractic, herbal remedies, homeopathy, naturopathy, osteopathy, reflexology.

mediocre *adj* ordinary, average, middling, medium, indifferent, unexceptional, undistinguished, so-so (*infml*), run-of-the-mill, commonplace, insignificant, second-rate, inferior, uninspired.
≠ exceptional, extraordinary, distinctive.

mediocrity *n* **1** ORDINARINESS, unimportance, insignificance, poorness, inferiority, indifference. **2** NONENTITY, nobody.

meditate *v* **1** REFLECT, ponder, ruminate, contemplate, muse, brood, think. **2** THINK OVER, consider, deliberate, mull over, study, speculate, scheme, plan, devise, intend.

medium *adj* average, middle, median, mean, medial, intermediate, middling, midway, standard, fair.
n **1** AVERAGE, middle, mid-point, middle ground, compromise, centre, happy medium, golden mean. **2** MEANS, agency, channel, vehicle, instrument, way, mode, form, avenue, organ. **3** PSYCHIC, spiritualist, spiritist, clairvoyant.

medley *n* assortment, mixture, miscellany, pot-pourri, hotchpotch, hodge-podge, collection, jumble.

meek *adj* modest, long-suffering, forbearing, humble, docile, patient, unassuming, unpretentious, resigned, gentle, peaceful, tame, timid, submissive, spiritless.
≠ arrogant, assertive, rebellious.

meet *v* **1** ENCOUNTER, come across, run across, run into, chance on, bump into (*infml*). **2** EXPERIENCE, encounter, face, go through, undergo, endure.

3 GATHER, collect, assemble, congregate, convene. **4** FULFIL, satisfy, match, answer, measure up to, equal, discharge, perform. **5** JOIN, converge, come together, connect, cross, intersect, touch, abut, unite.
≠ **3** scatter. **5** diverge.

meeting *n* **1** ENCOUNTER, confrontation, rendezvous, engagement, assignation, introduction, tryst (*fml*). **2** ASSEMBLY, gathering, forum, conclave, session.

Types of meeting include: assembly, assignation, audience, audition, board, briefing, cabinet, committee, conference, congregation, congress, consultation, convention, council, debate, get-together (*infml*), interview, party, rally, rendezvous, reunion, seminar, service, social, soirée, symposium. *see also* **committee**.

3 CONVERGENCE, confluence, junction, intersection, union.

melancholy *adj* depressed, dejected, downcast, down, down-hearted, gloomy, low, low-spirited, heavy-hearted, sad, unhappy, despondent, dispirited, miserable, mournful, dismal, sorrowful, moody.
≠ cheerful, elated, joyful.
n depression, dejection, gloom, despondency, low spirits, blues (*infml*), sadness, unhappiness, sorrow.
≠ elation, joy.

mellow *adj* **1** MATURE, ripe, juicy, full-flavoured, sweet, tender, mild. **2** GENIAL, cordial, affable, pleasant, relaxed, placid, serene, tranquil, cheerful, happy, jolly. **3** SMOOTH, melodious, rich, rounded, soft.
≠ **1** unripe. **2** cold. **3** harsh.
v mature, ripen, improve, sweeten, soften, temper, season, perfect.

melodious *adj* tuneful, musical, melodic, harmonious, dulcet, sweet-sounding, euphonious (*fml*), silvery.
≠ discordant, grating, harsh.

melodramatic *adj* histrionic, theatrical, overdramatic, exaggerated, overemotional, sensational, hammy (*infml*).

melody *n* tune, music, song, refrain, harmony, theme, air, strain.

melt *v* liquefy, dissolve, thaw, fuse, deliquesce (*fml*).
≠ freeze, solidify.
melt away disappear, vanish, fade, evaporate, dissolve, disperse.

member *n* adherent, associate, subscriber, representative, comrade, fellow.

memento *n* souvenir, keepsake, remembrance, reminder, token, memorial, record, relic.

memoirs *n* reminiscences, recollections, autobiography, life story, diary, chronicles, annals, journals, records, confessions, experiences.

memorable *adj* unforgettable, remarkable, significant, impressive, notable, noteworthy, extraordinary, important, outstanding, momentous.
≠ forgettable, trivial, unimportant.

memorial *n* remembrance, monument, souvenir, memento, record, stone, plaque, mausoleum.
adj commemorative, celebratory.

memorize *v* learn, learn by heart, commit to memory, remember.
≠ forget.

memory *n* recall, retention, recollection, remembrance, reminiscence, commemoration.
≠ forgetfulness.

menace *v* threaten, frighten, alarm, intimidate, terrorize, loom.
n **1** INTIMIDATION, threat, terrorism, warning. **2** DANGER, peril, hazard, jeopardy, risk. **3** NUISANCE, annoyance, pest.

mend *v* **1** REPAIR, renovate, restore, refit, fix, patch, cobble, darn, heal. **2** RECOVER, get better, improve. **3** REMEDY, correct, rectify, reform, revise.
≠ **1** break. **2** deteriorate. **3** destroy.

menial *adj* low, lowly, humble, base, dull, humdrum, routine, degrading, demeaning, ignominious, unskilled, subservient, servile, slavish.
n servant, domestic, labourer, minion, attendant, drudge, slave, underling,

skivvy (*infml*), dog's-body (*infml*).

mental *adj* **1** INTELLECTUAL, abstract, conceptual, cognitive, cerebral, theoretical, rational. **2** (*infml*) MAD, insane, lunatic, crazy, unbalanced, deranged, psychotic, disturbed, loony (*infml*).
≠ **1** physical. **2** sane.

mentality *n* **1** INTELLECT, brains, understanding, faculty, rationality. **2** FRAME OF MIND, character, disposition, personality, psychology, outlook.

mention *v* refer to, speak of, allude to, touch on, name, cite, acknowledge, bring up, report, make known, impart, declare, communicate, broach, divulge, disclose, intimate, point out, reveal, state, hint at, quote.
n reference, allusion, citation, observation, recognition, remark, acknowledgement, announcement, notification, tribute, indication.

mercenary *adj* **1** GREEDY, avaricious, covetous, grasping, acquisitive, materialistic. **2** HIRED, paid, venal.

merchandise *n* goods, commodities, stock, produce, products, wares, cargo, freight, shipment.

merchant *n* trader, dealer, broker, trafficker, wholesaler, retailer, seller, shopkeeper, vendor.

merciful *adj* compassionate, forgiving, forbearing, humane, lenient, sparing, tender-hearted, pitying, gracious, humanitarian, kind, liberal, sympathetic, generous, mild.
≠ hard-hearted, merciless.

merciless *adj* pitiless, relentless, unmerciful, ruthless, hard-hearted, hard, heartless, implacable, inhumane, unforgiving, remorseless, unpitying, unsparing, severe, cruel, callous, inhuman.
≠ compassionate, merciful.

mercy *n* **1** COMPASSION, clemency, forgiveness, forbearance, leniency, pity, humanitarianism, kindness, grace. **2** BLESSING, godsend, good luck, relief.
≠ **1** cruelty, harshness.

mere *adj* sheer, plain, simple, bare, utter, pure, absolute, complete, stark, unadulterated, common, paltry, petty.

merge *v* join, unite, combine, converge, amalgamate, blend, coalesce, mix, intermix, mingle, melt into, fuse, meet, meld, incorporate, consolidate.

merger *n* amalgamation, union, fusion, combination, coalition, consolidation, confederation, incorporation.

merit *n* worth, excellence, value, quality, good, goodness, virtue, asset, credit, advantage, strong point, talent, justification, due, claim.
≠ fault.
v deserve, be worthy of, earn, justify, warrant.

merriment *n* fun, jollity, mirth, hilarity, laughter, conviviality, festivity, amusement, revelry, frolic, liveliness, joviality.
≠ gloom, seriousness.

merry *adj* jolly, light-hearted, mirthful, joyful, happy, convivial, festive, cheerful, glad.
≠ gloomy, melancholy, sober.

mesh *n* net, network, netting, lattice, web, tangle, entanglement, snare, trap.
v engage, interlock, dovetail, fit, connect, harmonize, co-ordinate, combine, come together.

mess *n* **1** CHAOS, untidiness, disorder, disarray, confusion, muddle, jumble, clutter, disorganization, mix-up, shambles (*infml*). **2** DIFFICULTY, trouble, predicament, fix (*infml*).
≠ **1** order, tidiness.
mess about mess around, fool around, play, play around, play about, muck about (*infml*), interfere, tamper, trifle.
mess up 1 DISARRANGE, jumble, muddle, tangle, dishevel, disrupt. **2** BOTCH, bungle, spoil, muck up (*infml*).

message *n* **1** COMMUNICATION, bulletin, dispatch, communiqué, report, missive (*fml*), errand, letter, memorandum, note, notice, cable. **2** MEANING, idea, point, theme, moral.

messenger *n* courier, emissary (*fml*), envoy, go-between, herald, runner, carrier, bearer, harbinger, agent, ambassador.

messy *adj* untidy, unkempt, dishevelled, disorganized, chaotic, sloppy, slovenly, confused, dirty, grubby, muddled, cluttered.
≠ neat, ordered, tidy.

metamorphosis *n* change, alteration, transformation, rebirth, regeneration, transfiguration, conversion, modification, change-over.

metaphor *n* figure of speech, allegory, analogy, symbol, picture, image.

metaphorical *adj* figurative, allegorical, symbolic.

mete out allot, apportion, deal out, dole out, hand out, measure out, share out, ration out, portion, distribute, dispense, divide out, assign, administer.

meteoric *adj* rapid, speedy, swift, sudden, overnight, instantaneous, momentary, brief, spectacular, brilliant, dazzling.

method *n* **1** WAY, approach, means, course, manner, mode, fashion, process, procedure, route, technique, style, plan, scheme, programme. **2** ORGANIZATION, order, structure, system, pattern, form, planning, regularity, routine.

methodical *adj* systematic, structured, organized, ordered, orderly, tidy, regular, planned, efficient, disciplined, businesslike, deliberate, neat, scrupulous, precise, meticulous, painstaking.
≠ chaotic, irregular, confused.

meticulous *adj* precise, scrupulous, exact, punctilious, fussy, detailed, accurate, thorough, fastidious, painstaking, strict.
≠ careless, slapdash.

metropolis *n* capital, city, municipality, megalopolis.

mettle *n* **1** CHARACTER, temperament, disposition. **2** SPIRIT, courage, vigour, nerve, boldness, daring, indomitability, pluck, resolve, valour, bravery, fortitude.

microbe *n* micro-organism, bacterium, bacillus, germ, virus, pathogen, bug (*infml*).

microscopic *adj* minute, tiny, minuscule, infinitesimal, indiscernible, imperceptible, negligible.
≠ huge, enormous.

middle *adj* central, halfway, mean, median, intermediate, inner, inside, intervening.
n centre, halfway point, midpoint, mean, heart, core, midst, inside, bull's eye.
≠ extreme, end, edge, beginning, border.

middling *adj* mediocre, medium, ordinary, moderate, average, unexceptional, unremarkable, run-of-the-mill, indifferent, modest, passable, tolerable, so-so (*infml*), OK (*infml*).

midget *n* person of resricted growth, pygmy, dwarf, Tom Thumb, gnome.
≠ giant.
adj tiny, small, miniature, little, pocket, pocket-sized.
≠ giant.

midst *n* middle, centre, mid-point, heart, hub, interior.

migrant *n* traveller, wanderer, itinerant, emigrant, immigrant, rover, nomad, globe-trotter, drifter, gypsy, tinker, vagrant.

migrate *v* move, resettle, relocate, wander, roam, rove, journey, emigrate, travel, voyage, trek, drift.

mild *adj* **1** *mild manners*: gentle, calm, peaceable, placid, tender, soft, good-natured, kind, amiable, lenient, compassionate. **2** *mild weather*: calm, temperate, warm, balmy, clement, fair, pleasant. **3** *mild coffee*: bland, mellow, smooth, subtle, soothing.
≠ **1** harsh, fierce. **2** stormy. **3** strong.

militant *adj* aggressive, belligerent, vigorous, fighting, warring.
≠ pacifist, peaceful.
n activist, combatant, fighter, struggler, warrior, aggressor, belligerent.

military *adj* martial, armed, soldierly, warlike, service.

Military terms include: about turn, absent without leave (AWOL), action, action stations, adjutant, aide-de-camp (ADC), air cover, airdrop, Airborne Warning and Control System (AWACS), allies, ambush, arm, armed forces, armistice, army, arsenal, artillery, assault course, atomic warfare, attack, attention, barracks, base, battalion, battery, battle fatigue, battle, beachhead, billet, bivouac, blockade, bomb, bombardment, brevet, bridgehead, briefing, brigade, bugle call, call up, camoflage, camp, campaign, canteen, cease-fire, charge, citation, colours, combat, command, commission, company, conquest, conscript, conscription, corps, counter-attack, court-martial, crossfire, debriefing, decamp, decoration, defeat, defence, demilitarize, demob (*infml*), demotion, depot, desertion, detachment, detail, disarmament, discharge, dispatches, division, draft, drill, duty, encampment, enemy, enlist, ensign, epaulette, evacuation, excursion, expedition, fall out, fatigues, firing line, first post, flank, fleet, flight, flotilla, foe, foray, forced march, front line, fusillade, garrison, guard, incursion, infantry, insignia, inspection, installation, insubordination, intelligence, invasion, kitbag, landing, last post, latrine, leave, left wheel, liaison, lines, logistics, manoeuvres, march, marching orders, march past, married quarters, martinet, minefield, mission, mobilize, munitions, muster, mutiny, national service, navy, Navy, Army and Air Force Institutes (NAAFI), nuclear warfare, observation post, offensive, operational command, operational fleet, operations, orders, ordnance, outpost, padre, parade, parade ground, parley, parole, patrol, pincer movement, platoon, posting, prisoner of war (POW), quartermaster, quarters, quick march, radar, range, rank, ration, rearguard, recce (*infml*), recruit, regiment, reinforcements, requisition, retreat, reveille, rifle range, roll-call, rout, route march, salute, sentry, shell, shell-shock, signal, skirmish, slow march, sniper, sortie, squad, squadron, square-bashing (*sl*), standard, stores, strategy, supplies, surrender, tactics, tank, target, task-force, tattoo, the front, training, trench, trench warfare, troop, truce, unit, vanguard, victory, wing. *see also* **armed services**; **rank**; **sailor**; **soldier**.

n army, armed forces, soldiers, forces, services.

militate against oppose, counter, counteract, count against, tell against, weigh against, contend, resist.

milk *v* drain, bleed, tap, extract, draw off, exploit, use, express, press, pump, siphon, squeeze, wring.

milky *adj* white, milk-white, chalky, opaque, clouded, cloudy.

mill *n* **1** FACTORY, plant, works, workshop, foundry. **2** GRINDER, crusher, quern, roller.
v grind, pulverize, powder, pound, crush, roll, press, grate.

mime *n* dumb show, pantomime, gesture, mimicry.
v gesture, signal, act out, represent, simulate, impersonate, mimic.

mimic *v* imitate, parody, caricature, take off (*infml*), ape, parrot, impersonate, echo, mirror, simulate, look like.
n imitator, impersonator, impressionist, caricaturist, copy-cat (*infml*), copy.

mimicry *n* imitation, imitating, impersonation, copying, parody, impression, caricature, take-off (*infml*), burlesque.

mince *v* **1** CHOP, cut, hash, dice, grind, crumble. **2** DIMINISH, suppress, play down, tone down, hold back, moderate, weaken, soften, spare.

mind *n* **1** INTELLIGENCE, intellect, brains, reason, sense, understanding, wits, mentality, thinking, thoughts, grey matter (*infml*), head, genius, concentration, attention, spirit, psyche. **2** MEMORY, remembrance, recollection. **3** OPINION, view, point of view, belief, attitude, judgement, feeling, sentiment. **4** INCLINATION, disposition, tendency, will, wish, intention, desire.
v **1** CARE, object, take offence, resent, disapprove, dislike. **2** REGARD, heed,

pay attention, pay heed to, note, obey, listen to, comply with, follow, observe, be careful, watch. **3** LOOK AFTER, take care of, watch over, guard, have charge of, keep an eye on (*infml*).
bear in mind consider, remember, note.
make up one's mind decide, choose, determine, settle, resolve.

mindful *adj* aware, conscious, alive (to), alert, attentive, careful, watchful, wary.
≠ heedless, inattentive.

mindless *adj* **1** THOUGHTLESS, senseless, illogical, irrational, stupid, foolish, gratuitous, negligent. **2** MECHANICAL, automatic, tedious.
≠ **1** thoughtful, intelligent.

mine *n* **1** PIT, colliery, coalfield, excavation, vein, seam, shaft, trench, deposit. **2** SUPPLY, source, stock, store, reserve, fund, hoard, treasury, wealth.
v excavate, dig for, dig up, delve, quarry, extract, unearth, tunnel, remove, undermine.

minerals

Minerals include: alabaster, albite, anhydrite, asbestos, aventurine, azurite, bentonite, blacklead, bloodstone, blue john, borax, cairngorm, calamine, calcite, calcspar, cassiterite, chalcedony, chlorite, chrysoberyl, cinnabar, corundum, dolomite, emery, feldspar, fluorite, fluorspar, fool's gold, French chalk, galena, graphite, gypsum, haematite, halite, haüyne, hornblende, hyacinth, idocrase, jacinth, jargoon, jet, kandite, kaolinite, lapis lazuli, lazurite, magnetite, malachite, meerschaum, mica, microcline, montmorillonite, orthoclase, plumbago, pyrites, quartz, rock salt, rutile, saltpetre, sanidine, silica, smithsonite, sodalite, spar, sphalerite, spinel, talc, uralite, uranite, vesuvianite, wurtzite, zircon.

mingle *v* **1** MIX, intermingle, intermix, combine, blend, merge, unite, alloy, coalesce, join, compound. **2** ASSOCIATE, socialize, circulate, hobnob (*infml*), rub shoulders (*infml*).

miniature *adj* tiny, small, scaled-down, minute, diminutive, baby, pocket-sized, pint-size(d) (*infml*), little, mini (*infml*).
≠ giant.

minimal *adj* least, smallest, minimum, slightest, littlest, negligible, minute, token.

minimize *v* **1** REDUCE, decrease, diminish. **2** BELITTLE, make light of, make little of, disparage, deprecate, discount, play down, underestimate, underrate.
≠ **1** maximize.

minimum *n* least, lowest point, slightest, bottom.
≠ maximum.
adj minimal, least, lowest, slightest, smallest, littlest, tiniest.
≠ maximum.

minion *n* **1** ATTENDANT, follower, underling, lackey, hireling. **2** DEPENDANT, hanger-on, favourite, darling, sycophant, yes-man (*infml*), bootlicker (*infml*).

minister *n* **1** OFFICIAL, office-holder, politician, dignitary, diplomat, ambassador, delegate, envoy, consul, cabinet minister, agent, aide, administrator, executive. **2** CLERGYMAN, churchman, cleric, parson, priest, pastor, vicar, preacher, ecclesiastic (*fml*), divine.
v attend, serve, tend, take care of, wait on, cater to, accommodate, nurse.

ministry *n* **1** GOVERNMENT, cabinet, department, office, bureau, administration. **2** THE CHURCH, holy orders, the priesthood.

minor *adj* lesser, secondary, smaller, inferior, subordinate, subsidiary, junior, younger, insignificant, inconsiderable, negligible, petty, trivial, trifling, second-class, unclassified, slight, light.
≠ major, significant, important.

mint *v* coin, stamp, strike, cast, forge, punch, make, manufacture, produce, construct, devise, fashion, invent, make up.
adj perfect, brand-new, fresh, immaculate, unblemished, excellent, first-class.

minute[1] *n* moment, second, instant, flash, jiffy (*infml*), tick (*infml*).

minute^2 *adj* **1** TINY, infinitesimal, minuscule, microscopic, miniature, inconsiderable, negligible, small. **2** DETAILED, precise, meticulous, painstaking, close, critical, exhaustive.
≠ **1** gigantic, huge. **2** cursory, superficial.

minutes *n* proceedings, record(s), notes, memorandum, transcript, transactions, details, tapes.

miracle *n* wonder, marvel, prodigy, phenomenon.

miraculous *adj* wonderful, marvellous, phenomenal, extraordinary, amazing, astounding, astonishing, unbelievable, supernatural, incredible, inexplicable, unaccountable, superhuman.
≠ natural, normal.

mirage *n* illusion, optical illusion, hallucination, fantasy, phantasm.

mirror *n* **1** GLASS, looking-glass, reflector. **2** REFLECTION, likeness, image, double, copy.
v reflect, echo, imitate, copy, represent, show, depict, mimic.

mirth *n* merriment, hilarity, gaiety, fun, laughter, jollity, jocularity, amusement, revelry, glee, cheerfulness.
≠ gloom, melancholy.

misapprehension *n* misunderstanding, misconception, misinterpretation, misreading, error, mistake, fallacy, delusion.

misappropriate *v* steal, embezzle, peculate, pocket, swindle (*infml*), misspend, misuse, misapply, abuse, pervert.

misbehave *v* offend, transgress, trespass, get up to mischief, mess about, muck about (*infml*), play up, act up (*infml*).

misbehaviour *n* misconduct, misdemeanour, impropriety, disobedience, naughtiness, insubordination.

miscalculate *v* misjudge, get wrong, slip up, blunder, boob (*infml*), miscount, overestimate, underestimate.

miscarriage *n* failure, breakdown, abortion, mishap, mismanagement, error, disappointment.
≠ success.

miscarry *v* fail, abort, come to nothing, fall through, misfire, flounder, come to grief.
≠ succeed.

miscellaneous *adj* mixed, varied, various, assorted, diverse, diversified, sundry, motley, jumbled, indiscriminate.

miscellany *n* mixture, variety, assortment, collection, anthology, medley, mixed bag, pot-pourri, hotch-potch, jumble, diversity.

mischief *n* **1** TROUBLE, harm, evil, damage, injury, disruption.
2 MISBEHAVIOUR, naughtiness, impishness, pranks.

mischievous *adj* **1** MALICIOUS, evil, spiteful, vicious, wicked, pernicious, destructive, injurious. **2** NAUGHTY, impish, rascally, roguish, playful, teasing.
≠ **1** kind. **2** well-behaved, good.

misconception *n* misapprehension, misunderstanding, misreading, error, fallacy, delusion, the wrong end of the stick (*infml*).

misconduct *n* misbehaviour, impropriety, misdemeanour, malpractice, mismanagement, wrong-doing.

miser *n* niggard, skinflint, penny-pincher (*infml*), Scrooge.
≠ spendthrift.

miserable *adj* **1** UNHAPPY, sad, dejected, despondent, downcast, heartbroken, wretched, distressed, crushed. **2** CHEERLESS, depressing, dreary, impoverished, shabby, gloomy, dismal, forlorn, joyless, squalid.
3 CONTEMPTIBLE, despicable, ignominious, detestable, disgraceful, deplorable, shameful. **4** MEAGRE, paltry, niggardly, worthless, pathetic, pitiful.
≠ **1** cheerful, happy. **2** pleasant.
4 generous.

miserly *adj* mean, niggardly, tight, stingy (*infml*), sparing, parsimonious, cheese-paring, beggarly, penny-pinching (*infml*), mingy (*infml*).
≠ generous, spendthrift.

misery *n* **1** UNHAPPINESS, sadness, suffering, distress, depression, despair, gloom, grief, wretchedness, affliction. **2** PRIVATION, hardship, deprivation, poverty, want, oppression, destitution. **3** (*infml*) SPOILSPORT, pessimist, killjoy, wet blanket (*infml*).
≠ **1** contentment. **2** comfort.

misfire *v* miscarry, go wrong, abort, fail, fall through, flop (*infml*), founder, fizzle out, come to grief.
≠ succeed.

misfit *n* individualist, nonconformist, eccentric, maverick, drop-out, loner, lone wolf.
≠ conformist.

misfortune *n* bad luck, mischance, mishap, ill-luck, setback, reverse, calamity, catastrophe, disaster, blow, accident, tragedy, trouble, hardship, trial, tribulation.
≠ luck, success.

misgiving *n* doubt, uncertainty, hesitation, qualm, reservation, apprehension, scruple, suspicion, second thoughts, niggle, anxiety, worry, fear.
≠ confidence.

misguided *adj* misled, misconceived, ill-considered, ill-advised, ill-judged, imprudent, ash, misplaced, deluded, foolish, erroneous.
≠ sensible, wise.

mishap *n* misfortune, ill-fortune, misadventure, accident, setback, calamity, disaster, adversity.

misinterpret *v* misconstrue, misread, misunderstand, mistake, distort, garble.

misjudge *v* miscalculate, mistake, misinterpret, misconstrue, misunderstand, overestimate, underestimate.

mislay *v* lose, misplace, miss, lose sight of.

mislead *v* misinform, misdirect, deceive, delude, lead astray, fool.

misleading *adj* deceptive, confusing, unreliable, ambiguous, biased, loaded, evasive, tricky (*infml*).
≠ unequivocal, authoritative, informative.

mismanage *v* mishandle, botch, bungle, make a mess of, mess up, misrule, misspend, misjudge, foul up, mar, waste.

misprint *n* mistake, error, erratum, literal, typo (*infml*).

misrepresent *v* distort, falsify, slant, pervert, twist, garble, misquote, exaggerate, minimize, misconstrue, misinterpret.

miss *v* **1** FAIL, miscarry, lose, let slip, let go, omit, overlook, pass over, slip, leave out, mistake, trip, misunderstand, err. **2** AVOID, escape, evade, dodge, forego, skip, bypass, circumvent. **3** PINE FOR, long for, yearn for, regret, grieve for, mourn, sorrow for, want, wish, need, lament.
n failure, error, blunder, mistake, omission, oversight, fault, flop (*infml*), fiasco.

misshapen *adj* deformed, distorted, twisted, malformed, warped, contorted, crooked, crippled, grotesque, ugly, monstrous.
≠ regular, shapely.

missile *n* projectile, shot, guided missile, arrow, shaft, dart, rocket, bomb, shell, flying bomb, grenade, torpedo, weapon.

missing *adj* absent, lost, lacking, gone, mislaid, unaccounted-for, wanting, disappeared, astray, strayed, misplaced.
≠ found, present.

mission *n* **1** TASK, undertaking, assignment, operation, campaign, crusade, business, errand. **2** CALLING, duty, purpose, vocation, raison d'être, aim, charge, office, job, work. **3** COMMISSION, ministry, delegation, deputation, legation, embassy.

missionary *n* evangelist, campaigner, preacher, proselytizer, apostle, crusader, propagandist, champion, promoter, emissary, envoy, ambassador.

mist *n* haze, fog, vapour, smog, cloud, condensation, film, spray, drizzle, dew, steam, veil, dimness.
mist over cloud over, fog, dim, blur, steam up, obscure, veil.
≠ clear.

mistake *n* error, inaccuracy, slip, slip-up, oversight, lapse, blunder, Ilanger (*infml*), boob (*infml*), gaffe, fault, faux pas, solecism (*fml*), indiscretion, misjudgement, miscalculation, misunderstanding, misprint, misspelling, misreading, mispronunciation, howler (*infml*).
v misunderstand, misapprehend, misconstrue, misjudge, misread, miscalculate, confound, confuse, slip up, blunder, err, boob (*infml*).

mistaken *adj* wrong, incorrect, erroneous, inaccurate, inexact, untrue, inappropriate, ill-judged, inauthentic, false, deceived, deluded, misinformed, misled, faulty.
≠ correct, right.

mistreat *v* abuse, ill-treat, ill-use, maltreat, harm, hurt, batter, injure, knock about, molest.

mistress *n* **1** LOVER, live-in lover, kept woman, concubine, courtesan, girlfriend, paramour, woman, lady-love. **2** TEACHER, governess, tutor.

mistrust *n* distrust, doubt, suspicion, wariness, misgiving, reservations, qualm, hesitancy, chariness, caution, uncertainty, scepticism, apprehension.
≠ trust.
v distrust, doubt, suspect, be wary of, beware, have reservations, fear.
≠ trust.

misty *adj* hazy, foggy, cloudy, blurred, fuzzy, murky, smoky, unclear, dim, indistinct, obscure, opaque, vague, veiled.
≠ clear.

misunderstand *v* misapprehend, misconstrue, misinterpret, misjudge, mistake, get wrong, miss the point, mishear, get hold of the wrong end of the stick (*infml*).
≠ understand.

misunderstanding *n* **1** MISTAKE, error, misapprehension, misconception, misjudgement, misinterpretation, misreading, mix-up. **2** DISAGREEMENT, argument, dispute, conflict, clash, difference, breach, quarrel, discord, rift.
≠ **1** understanding. **2** agreement.

misuse *n* mistreatment, maltreatment, abuse, harm, ill-treatment, misapplication, misappropriation, waste, perversion, corruption, exploitation.
v abuse, misapply, misemploy, ill-use, ill-treat, harm, mistreat, wrong, distort, injure, corrupt, pervert, waste, squander, misappropriate, exploit, dissipate.

mitigating *adj* extenuating, justifying, vindicating, modifying, qualifying.

mix *v* **1** COMBINE, blend, mingle, intermingle, intermix, amalgamate, compound, homogenize, synthesize, merge, join, unite, coalesce, fuse, incorporate, fold in. **2** ASSOCIATE, consort, fraternize, socialize, mingle, join, hobnob (*infml*).
≠ **1** divide, separate.
n mixture, blend, amalgam, assortment, combination, conglomerate, compound, fusion, synthesis, medley, composite, mishmash (*infml*).
mix up confuse, bewilder, muddle, perplex, puzzle, confound, mix, jumble, complicate, garble, involve, implicate, disturb, upset, snarl up.

mixed *adj* **1** *mixed race*: combined, hybrid, mingled, crossbred, mongrel, blended, composite, compound, incorporated, united, alloyed, amalgamated, fused. **2** *mixed biscuits*: assorted, varied, miscellaneous, diverse, diversified, motley. **3** *mixed feelings*: ambivalent, equivocal, conflicting, contradicting, uncertain.

mixture *n* mix, blend, combination, amalgamation, amalgam, compound, conglomeration, composite, coalescence, alloy, brew, synthesis, union, fusion, concoction, cross, hybrid, assortment, variety, miscellany, medley, mélange, mixed bag, pot-pourri, jumble, hotchpotch.

moan *n* lament, lamentation, sob, wail, howl, whimper, whine, grumble, complaint, grievance, groan.
v **1** LAMENT, wail, sob, weep, howl, groan, whimper, mourn, grieve. **2** (*infml*) COMPLAIN, grumble, whine, whinge (*infml*), gripe (*infml*), carp.
≠ **1** rejoice.

mob *n* **1** CROWD, mass, throng, multitude, horde, host, swarm, gathering, group, collection, flock, herd, pack, set, tribe, troop, company, crew, gang. **2** POPULACE, rabble, masses, hoi polloi, plebs (*infml*), riff-raff (*infml*).
v crowd, crowd round, surround, swarm round, jostle, overrun, set upon, besiege, descend on, throng, pack, pester, charge.

mobile *adj* **1** MOVING, movable, portable, peripatetic, travelling, roaming, roving, itinerant, wandering, migrant. **2** FLEXIBLE, agile, active, energetic, nimble. **3** CHANGING, changeable, ever-changing, expressive, lively.
≠ **1** immobile.

mobilize *v* assemble, marshal, rally, conscript, muster, call up, enlist, activate, galvanize, organize, prepare, ready, summon, animate.

mock *v* **1** RIDICULE, jeer, make fun of, laugh at, disparage, deride, scoff, sneer, taunt, scorn, tease. **2** IMITATE, simulate, mimic, ape, caricature, satirize.
adj imitation, counterfeit, artificial, sham, simulated, synthetic, false, fake, forged, fraudulent, bogus, phoney (*infml*), pseudo, spurious, feigned, faked, pretended, dummy.

mockery *n* **1** RIDICULE, jeering, scoffing, scorn, derision, contempt, disdain, disrespect, sarcasm. **2** PARODY, satire, sham, travesty.

mocking *adj* scornful, derisive, contemptuous, sarcastic, satirical, taunting, scoffing, sardonic, snide (*infml*), insulting, irreverent, impudent, disrespectful, disdainful, cynical.

model *n* **1** COPY, replica, representation, facsimile, imitation, mock-up. **2** EXAMPLE, exemplar, pattern, standard, ideal, mould, prototype, template. **3** DESIGN, style, type, version, mark. **4** MANNEQUIN, dummy, sitter, subject, poser.
adj exemplary, perfect, typical, ideal.
v **1** MAKE, form, fashion, mould, sculpt, carve, cast, shape, work, create, design, plan. **2** DISPLAY, wear, show off.

moderate *adj* **1** MEDIOCRE, medium, ordinary, fair, indifferent, average, middle-of-the-road. **2** REASONABLE, restrained, sensible, calm, controlled, cool, mild, well-regulated.
≠ **1** exceptional. **2** immoderate.
v control, regulate, decrease, lessen, soften, restrain, tone down, play down, diminish, ease, curb, calm, check, modulate, repress, subdue, soft-pedal, tame, subside, pacify, mitigate, allay, alleviate, abate, dwindle.

moderately *adv* somewhat, quite, rather, fairly, slightly, reasonably, passably, to some extent.
≠ extremely.

moderation *n* **1** DECREASE, reduction. **2** RESTRAINT, self-control, caution, control, composure, sobriety, abstemiousness, temperance, reasonableness.

modern *adj* current, contemporary, up-to-date, new, fresh, latest, late, novel, present, present-day, recent, up-to-the-minute, newfangled (*infml*), advanced, avant-garde, progressive, modernistic, innovative, inventive, state-of-the-art, go-ahead, fashionable, stylish, in vogue, in style, modish, trendy (*infml*).
≠ old-fashioned, old, out-of-date, antiquated.

modernize *v* renovate, refurbish, rejuvenate, regenerate, streamline, revamp, renew, update, improve, do up, redesign, reform, remake, remodel, refresh, transform, modify, progress.
≠ regress.

modest *adj* **1** UNASSUMING, humble, self-effacing, quiet, reserved, retiring, unpretentious, discreet, bashful, shy. **2** MODERATE, ordinary, unexceptional, fair, reasonable, limited, small.
≠ **1** immodest, conceited. **2** exceptional, excessive.

modesty *n* humility, humbleness, self-effacement, reticence, reserve, quietness, decency, propriety, demureness, shyness, bashfulness, coyness.
≠ immodesty, vanity, conceit.

modify *v* **1** CHANGE, alter, redesign, revise, vary, adapt, adjust, transform, reform, convert, improve, reorganize. **2** MODERATE, reduce, temper, tone down, limit, soften, qualify.

modulate *v* modify, adjust, balance, alter, soften, lower, regulate, vary, harmonize, inflect, tune.

moist *adj* damp, clammy, humid, wet, dewy, rainy, muggy, marshy, drizzly, watery, soggy.
≠ dry, arid.

moisten *v* moisturize, dampen, damp, wet, water, lick, irrigate.
≠ dry.

moisture *n* water, liquid, wetness, wateriness, damp, dampness, dankness, humidity, vapour, dew, mugginess, condensation, steam, spray.
≠ dryness.

molest *v* **1** ANNOY, disturb, bother, harass, irritate, persecute, pester, plague, tease, torment, hound, upset, worry, trouble, badger. **2** ATTACK, accost, assail, hurt, ill-treat, maltreat, mistreat, abuse, harm, injure.

molluscs

> *Molluscs include*: abalone, conch, cowrie, cuttlefish, clam, cockle, limpet, mussel, nautilus, nudibranch, octopus, oyster, periwinkle, scallop, sea slug, slug, freshwater snail, land snail, marine snail, squid, tusk shell, whelk.

moment *n* second, instant, minute, split second, trice, jiffy (*infml*), tick (*infml*).

momentary *adj* brief, short, short-lived, temporary, transient, transitory, fleeting, ephemeral, hasty, quick, passing.
≠ lasting, permanent.

momentous *adj* significant, important, critical, crucial, decisive, weighty, grave, serious, vital, fateful, historic, earth-shaking, epoch-making, eventful, major.
≠ insignificant, unimportant, trivial.

momentum *n* impetus, force, energy, impulse, drive, power, thrust, speed, velocity, impact, incentive, stimulus, urge, strength, push.

monarch *n* sovereign, crowned head, ruler, king, queen, emperor, empress, prince, princess, tsar, potentate.

monarchy *n* **1** KINGDOM, empire, principality, realm, domain, dominion. **2** ROYALISM, sovereignty, autocracy, monocracy, absolutism, despotism, tyranny.

monastery *n* friary, priory, abbey, cloister, charterhouse.

monastic *adj* reclusive, withdrawn, secluded, cloistered, austere, ascetic, celibate, contemplative.
≠ secular, worldly.

monetary *adj* financial, fiscal, pecuniary (*fml*), budgetary, economic, capital, cash.

money *n* currency, cash, legal tender, banknotes, coin, funds, capital, dough (*infml*), dosh (*infml*), riches, wealth.

mongrel *n* cross, crossbreed, hybrid, half-breed.
adj crossbred, hybrid, half-breed, bastard, mixed, ill-defined.
≠ pure-bred, pedigree.

monitor *n* **1** SCREEN, display, VDU, recorder, scanner. **2** SUPERVISOR, watchdog, overseer, invigilator, adviser, prefect.
v check, watch, keep track of, keep under surveillance, keep an eye on, follow, track, supervise, observe, note, survey, trace, scan, record, plot, detect.

monkey *n* **1** PRIMATE, simian.

> *Monkeys include*: ape, baboon, capuchin, colobus monkey, drill, guenon, guereza, howler monkey, langur, leaf monkey, macaque, mandrill, mangabey, marmoset, night monkey (or douroucouli), proboscis monkey, rhesus monkey, saki, spider monkey, squirrel monkey, tamarin, titi, toque, uakari (or cacajou), woolly monkey.

2 (*infml*) SCAMP, imp, urchin, brat, rogue, scallywag (*infml*), rascal.

monopolize *v* dominate, take over, appropriate, corner, control, hog (*infml*), engross, occupy, preoccupy, take up, tie up.
≠ share.

monotonous *adj* boring, dull, tedious, uninteresting, tiresome, wearisome, unchanging, uneventful, unvaried, uniform, toneless, flat, colourless, repetitive, routine, plodding, humdrum, soul-destroying.
≠ lively, varied, colourful.

monotony *n* tedium, dullness, boredom, sameness, tiresomeness, uneventfulness, flatness, wearisomeness, uniformity, routine, repetitiveness.
≠ liveliness, colour.

monster *n* **1** BEAST, fiend, brute, barbarian, savage, villain, giant, ogre, ogress, troll, mammoth. **2** FREAK, monstrosity, mutant.
adj huge, gigantic, giant, colossal, enormous, immense, massive, monstrous, jumbo, mammoth, vast, tremendous.
≠ tiny, minute.

monstrous *adj* **1** WICKED, evil, vicious, cruel, criminal, heinous, outrageous, scandalous, disgraceful, atrocious, abhorrent, dreadful, frightful, horrible, horrifying, terrible. **2** UNNATURAL, inhuman, freakish, grotesque, hideous, deformed, malformed, misshapen. **3** HUGE, enormous, colossal, gigantic, vast, immense, massive, mammoth.

monument *n* memorial, cenotaph, headstone, gravestone, tombstone, shrine, mausoleum, cairn, barrow, cross, marker, obelisk, pillar, statue, relic, remembrance, commemoration, testament, reminder, record, memento, evidence, token.

monumental *adj* **1** IMPRESSIVE, imposing, awe-inspiring, awesome, overwhelming, significant, important, epoch-making, historic, magnificent, majestic, memorable, notable, outstanding, abiding, immortal, lasting, classic. **2** HUGE, immense, enormous, colossal, vast, tremendous, massive, great. **3** COMMEMORATIVE, memorial.
≠ **1** insignificant, unimportant.

mood *n* **1** DISPOSITION, frame of mind, state of mind, temper, humour, spirit, tenor, whim. **2** BAD TEMPER, sulk, the sulks, pique, melancholy, depression, blues (*infml*), doldrums, dumps (*infml*).

moody *adj* changeable, temperamental, unpredictable, capricious, irritable, short-tempered, crabby (*infml*), crotchety, crusty (*infml*), testy, touchy, morose, angry, broody, mopy, sulky, sullen, gloomy, melancholy, miserable, downcast, doleful, glum, impulsive, fickle, flighty.
≠ equable, cheerful.

moon *v* idle, loaf, mooch, languish, pine, mope, brood, daydream, dream, fantasize.

moor[1] *v* fasten, secure, tie up, drop anchor, anchor, berth, dock, make fact, fix, hitch, bind.
≠ loose.

moor[2] *n* moorland, heath, fell, upland.

mop *n* head of hair, shock, mane, tangle, thatch, mass.
v swab, sponge, wipe, clean, wash, absorb, soak.

mope *v* brood, fret, sulk, pine, languish, droop, despair, grieve, idle.

moral *adj* ethical, virtuous, good, right, principled, honourable, decent, upright, upstanding, straight, righteous, high-minded, honest, incorruptible, proper, blameless, chaste, clean-living, pure, just, noble.
≠ immoral.
n lesson, message, teaching, dictum, meaning, maxim, adage, precept, saying, proverb, aphorism, epigram.

morale *n* confidence, spirits, esprit de corps, self-esteem, state of mind, heart, mood.

morality *n* ethics, morals, ideals, principles, standards, virtue, rectitude, righteousness, decency, goodness, honesty, integrity, justice, uprightness, propriety, conduct, manners.
≠ immorality.

morals *n* morality, ethics, principles, standards, ideals, integrity, scruples, behaviour, conduct, habits, manners.

morbid *adj* **1** GHOULISH, ghastly, gruesome, macabre, hideous, horrid, grim. **2** GLOOMY, pessimistic, melancholy, sombre. **3** SICK, unhealthy, unwholesome, insalubrious.

more *adj* further, extra, additional, added, new, fresh, increased, other, supplementary, repeated, alternative, spare.
≠ less.
adv further, longer, again, besides, moreover, better.
≠ less.

moreover *adv* furthermore, further, besides, in addition, as well, also, additionally, what is more.

morning *n* daybreak, daylight, dawn, sunrise, break of day, before noon.

morose *adj* ill-tempered, bad-tempered, moody, sullen, sulky, surly, gloomy, grim, gruff, sour, taciturn, glum, grouchy (*infml*), crabby (*infml*), saturnine.
≠ cheerful, communicative.

morsel *n* bit, scrap, piece, fragment, crumb, bite, mouthful, nibble, taste, soupçon, titbit, slice, fraction, modicum, grain, atom, part.

mortal *adj* **1** WORLDLY, earthly, bodily, human, perishable, temporal. **2** FATAL, lethal, deadly. **3** EXTREME, great, severe, intense, grave, awful.
≠ **1** immortal.
n human being, human, individual, person, being, body, creature.
≠ immortal, god.

mortality *n* **1** HUMANITY, death, impermanence, perishability. **2** FATALITY, death rate.
≠ **1** immortality.

mortified *adj* humiliated, shamed, ashamed, humbled, embarrassed, crushed.

mostly *adv* mainly, on the whole, principally, chiefly, generally, usually, largely, for the most part, as a rule.

mother *n* **1** PARENT, procreator (*fml*), progenitress (*fml*), dam, mamma, mum (*infml*), mummy (*infml*), matriarch, ancestor, matron, old woman (*infml*). **2** ORIGIN, source.
v **1** BEAR, produce, nurture, raise, rear, nurse, care for, cherish. **2** PAMPER, spoil, baby, indulge, overprotect, fuss over.

motherly *adj* maternal, caring, comforting, affectionate, kind, loving, protective, warm, tender, gentle, fond.
≠ neglectful, uncaring.

motif *n* theme, idea, topic, concept, pattern, design, figure, form, logo, shape, device, ornament, decoration.

motion *n* **1** MOVEMENT, action, mobility, moving, activity, locomotion, travel, transit, passage, passing, progress, change, flow, inclination. **2** GESTURE, gesticulation, signal, sign, wave, nod. **3** PROPOSAL, suggestion, recommendation, proposition.
v signal, gesture, gesticulate, sign, wave, nod, beckon, direct, usher.

motionless *adj* unmoving, still, stationary, static, immobile, at a standstill, fixed, halted, at rest, resting, standing, paralysed, inanimate, lifeless, frozen, rigid, stagnant.
≠ active, moving.

motivate *v* prompt, incite, impel, spur, provoke, stimulate, drive, lead, stir, urge, push, propel, persuade, move, inspire, encourage, cause, trigger, induce, kindle, draw, arouse, bring.
≠ deter, discourage.

motive *n* ground(s), cause, reason, purpose, motivation, object, intention, influence, rationale, thinking, incentive, impulse, stimulus, inspiration, incitement, urge, encouragement, design, desire, consideration.
≠ deterrent, disincentive.

motor vehicle

Parts of a motor vehicle include: ABS (anti-lock braking system), accelerator, airbag, air brake, air-conditioner, air inlet, antidazzle mirror, antiglare switch, anti-roll bar, antitheft device, ashtray, axle, backup light (*US*), battery, bench seat, bezel, bodywork, bonnet, boot, brake drum, brake light, brake pad, brake shoe, bumper, car radio, car phone, catalytic converter, central locking, centre console, chassis, child-safety seat, cigarette-lighter, clock, clutch, courtesy light, crankcase, cruise control, dashboard, differential gear, dimmer, disc brake, door, door-lock, drive shaft, drum brake, electric window, emergency light, engine, exhaust pipe, fender (*US*), filler cap, flasher switch, fog lamp, folding seat, four-wheel drive, fuel gauge, gas tank (*US*), gear, gearbox, gear-lever (or gear-stick), glove compartment, grill, handbrake, hazard warning light, headlight, headrest, heated rear window, heater, hood (*US*), horn, hub-cap, hydraulic brake, hydraulic suspension, ignition, ignition key, indicator, instrument panel, jack, jump lead, kingpin, license plate (*US*), lift gate (*US*), monocoque, number plate, oil gauge, overrider, parcel shelf, parking-light, petrol tank, pneumatic tyre, power brake, prop shaft, quarterlight, rack and pinion, radial-ply tyre, rear light, rear-view mirror, reclining seat, reflector, rev counter (*infml*), reversing light, roof rack, screen-washer bottle, seat belt, shaft, shock absorber, sidelight, side-impact bar, side mirror, silencer, sill, solenoid, spare tyre, speedometer, spoiler, steering-column, steering-wheel, stick shift (*US*), stoplight, sunroof, sun visor, suspension, temperature gauge, towbar, track rod, transmission, trunk (*US*), tyre, vent, wheel, wheel arch, windscreen, windscreen-washer, windscreen-wiper, windshield (*US*), wing, wing mirror. *see also* **engine**.

mottled *adj* speckled, dappled, blotchy, flecked, piebald, stippled, streaked, tabby, spotted, freckled, variegated.
≠ monochrome, uniform.

motto *n* saying, slogan, maxim, watchword, catchword, byword, precept, proverb, adage, formula, rule, golden rule, dictum.

mould[1] *n* **1** CAST, form, die, template, pattern, matrix. **2** SHAPE, form, format, pattern, structure, style, type, build, construction, cut, design, kind, model, sort, stamp, arrangement, brand, frame, character, nature, quality, line, make.
v **1** FORGE, cast, shape, stamp, make, form, create, design, construct, sculpt, model, work. **2** INFLUENCE, direct, control.

mould[2] *n* mildew, fungus, mouldiness, mustiness, blight.

mouldy *adj* mildewed, blighted, musty, decaying, corrupt, rotten, fusty, putrid, bad, spoiled, stale.
≠ fresh, wholesome.

mound *n* **1** HILL, hillock, hummock, rise, knoll, bank, dune, elevation, ridge, embankment, earthwork. **2** HEAP, pile, stack.

mount *v* **1** PRODUCE, put on, set up, prepare, stage, exhibit, display, launch. **2** INCREASE, grow, accumulate, multiply, rise, intensify, soar, swell. **3** CLIMB, ascend, get up, go up, get on, clamber up, scale, get astride.
≠ **2** decrease, descend. **3** descend, dismount, go down.
n horse, steed, support, mounting.

mountain *n* **1** HEIGHT, elevation, mount, peak, mound, alp, tor, massif. **2** HEAP, pile, stack, mass, abundance, backlog.

mountainous *adj* **1** CRAGGY, rocky, hilly, high, highland, upland, alpine, soaring, steep. **2** HUGE, towering, enormous, immense.
≠ **1** flat. **2** tiny.

mourn *v* grieve, lament, sorrow, bemoan, miss, regret, deplore, weep, wail.
≠ rejoice.

mournful *adj* sorrowful, sad, unhappy, desolate, grief-stricken, heavy-hearted, heartbroken, broken-hearted, cast-down, downcast, miserable, tragic, woeful, melancholy, sombre, depressed, dejected, gloomy, dismal.
≠ joyful.

mourning *n* bereavement, grief, grieving, lamentation, sadness, sorrow, desolation, weeping.
≠ rejoicing.

mouth *n* **1** LIPS, jaws, trap (*infml*), gob (*sl*).

Parts of the mouth include: cleft palate, gum, hard palate, hare lip, inferior dental arch, isthmus of fauces, labial commissure, lower lip, palatoglossal arch, palato-pharyngeal arch, soft palate, superior dental arch, tongue, tonsil, upper lip, uvula. *see also* **tooth**.

2 OPENING, aperture, orifice, cavity, entrance, gateway, inlet, estuary.
v enunciate, articulate, utter, pronounce, whisper, form.

movable *adj* mobile, portable, transportable, changeable, alterable, adjustable, flexible, transferable.
≠ fixed, immovable.

move *v* **1** STIR, go, advance, budge, change, proceed, progress, make strides. **2** TRANSPORT, carry, transfer. **3** DEPART, go away, leave, decamp, migrate, remove, move house, relocate. **4** PROMPT, stimulate, urge, impel, drive, propel, motivate, incite, persuade, induce, inspire. **5** AFFECT, touch, agitate, stir, impress, excite.
n **1** MOVEMENT, motion, step, manoeuvre, action, device, stratagem. **2** REMOVAL, relocation, migration, transfer.

movement *n* **1** REPOSITIONING, move, moving, relocation, activity, act, action, agitation, stirring, transfer, passage. **2** CHANGE, development, advance, evolution, current, drift, flow, shift, progress, progression, trend, tendency. **3** CAMPAIGN, crusade, drive, group, organization, party, faction.

moving *adj* **1** MOBILE, active, in motion. **2** TOUCHING, affecting, poignant, impressive, emotive, arousing, stirring, inspiring, inspirational, exciting, thrilling, persuasive, stimulating.
≠ **1** immobile. **2** unemotional.

mow *v* cut, trim, crop, clip, shear, scythe.

much *adv* greatly, considerably, a lot, frequently, often.
adj copious, plentiful, ample, considerable, a lot, abundant, great, substantial.
n plenty, a lot, lots (*infml*), loads (*infml*), heaps (*infml*), lashings (*infml*).
≠ little.

muck *n* dirt, dung, manure, mire, filth, mud, sewage, slime, gunge (*infml*), ordure, scum, sludge.
muck up ruin, wreck, spoil, mess up, make a mess of, botch, bungle, cock up (*sl*).

mud *n* clay, mire, ooze, dirt, sludge, silt.

muddle *v* **1** DISORGANIZE, disorder, mix up, mess up, jumble, scramble, tangle. **2** CONFUSE, bewilder, bemuse, perplex.
n chaos, confusion, disorder, mess, mix-up, jumble, clutter, tangle.

muddy *adj* **1** DIRTY, foul, miry, mucky, marshy, boggy, swampy, quaggy, grimy. **2** CLOUDY, indistinct, obscure, opaque, murky, hazy, blurred, fuzzy, dull.
≠ **1** clean. **2** clear.

muffle *v* **1** WRAP, envelop, cloak, swathe, cover. **2** DEADEN, dull, quieten, silence, stifle, dampen, muzzle, suppress.
≠ **2** amplify.

mug[1] *n* cup, beaker, pot, tankard.

mug[2] *v* set upon, attack, assault, waylay, steal from, rob, beat up, jump (on).

muggy *adj* humid, sticky, stuffy, sultry, close, clammy, oppressive, sweltering, moist, damp.
≠ dry.

mull over *v* reflect on, ponder, contemplate, think over, think about, ruminate, consider, weigh up, chew over, meditate, study, examine, deliberate.

multiple *adj* many, numerous, manifold, various, several, sundry, collective.

multiply *v* increase, proliferate, expand, spread, reproduce, propagate, breed, accumulate, intensify, extend, build up, augment, boost.
≠ decrease, lessen.

multitude *n* crowd, throng, horde, swarm, mob, mass, herd, congregation, host, lot, lots, legion, public, people, populace.
≠ few, scattering.

munch *v* eat, chew, crunch, masticate (*fml*).

mundane *adj* banal, ordinary, everyday, commonplace, prosaic, humdrum, workaday, routine.
≠ extraordinary.

municipal *adj* civic, city, town, urban, borough, community, public.

murder *n* homicide, killing, manslaughter, slaying, assassination, massacre, bloodshed.
v kill, slaughter, slay, assassinate, butcher, massacre.

murderer *n* killer, homicide, slayer, slaughterer, assassin, butcher, cut-throat.

murderous *adj* **1** HOMICIDAL, brutal, barbarous, bloodthirsty, bloody, cut-throat, killing, lethal, cruel, savage, ferocious, deadly. **2** (*infml*) DIFFICULT, exhausting, strenuous, unpleasant, dangerous.

murky *adj* dark, dismal, gloomy, dull, overcast, misty, foggy, dim, cloudy, obscure, veiled, grey.
≠ bright, clear.

murmur *n* mumble, muttering, whisper, undertone, humming, rumble, drone, grumble.
v mutter, mumble, whisper, buzz, hum, rumble, purr, burble.

muscular *adj* brawny, beefy (*infml*), sinewy, athletic, powerfully built, strapping, hefty, powerful, husky, robust, stalwart, vigorous, strong.
≠ puny, flabby, weak.

mushrooms and toadstools

Types of mushroom and toadstool include: *edible*: beefsteak fungus, blewits, boletus, chestnut boletus, button mushroom, cep, champignon, chanterelle, clouded agaric, common morel, cultivated mushroom, dingy agaric, fairy ring, the goat's lip, gypsy mushroom, honey fungus, horn of plenty, horse mushroom, lawyer's wig, man on horseback, march mushroom, oyster mushroom, parasol mushroom, penny bun, saffron milk cap, shaggy parasol, slippery jack, sweetbread mushroom, truffle, trumpet agaric, velvet shank, winter mushroom, wood hedgehog; *inedible/poisonous*: amanita, common ink cap, copper trumpet, death cap, destroying angel, devil's boletus, earth ball, false morel, fly agaric, mower's mushroom, panther cap, purple boletus, satan's mushroom, shaggy milk cap, stinking parasol, sulphur tuft, verdigris agaric, woolly milk cap, yellow-staining mushroom.

music

Types of music include: acid house, ballet, ballroom, bluegrass, blues, boogie-woogie, chamber, choral, classical, country-and-western, dance, disco, Dixieland, doo-wop, electronic, folk, folk rock, funk (*infml*), garage, gospel, grunge, hard rock, heavy metal, hip-hop, honky-tonk, house, incidental, instrumental, jazz, jazz-funk, jazz-pop, jazz-rock, jive, karaoke, operatic, orchestral, pop, punk rock, ragtime, rap, reggae, rhythm and blues (R & B), rock and roll, rock, sacred, ska, skiffle, soft rock, soul, swing, thrash metal (*sl*).

musical *adj* tuneful, melodious, melodic, harmonious, dulcet, sweet-sounding, lyrical.
≠ discordant, unmusical.

Musical terms include: accelerando, acciaccatura, accidental, accompaniment, acoustic, adagio, ad lib, a due, affettuoso, agitato, al fine, al segno, alla breve, alla cappella, allargando, allegretto, allegro, al segno, alto, amoroso, andante, animato, appoggiatura, arco, arpeggio, arrangement, a tempo, attacca, bar, bar line, double bar line, baritone, bass, beat, bis, breve, buffo, cadence, cantabile, cantilena, chord, chromatic, clef, alto clef, bass clef, tenor clef, treble clef, coda, col canto, con brio, concert, con fuoco, con moto, consonance, contralto, counterpoint, crescendo, crotchet, cross-fingering, cue, da capo, decrescendo, demisemiquaver, descant, diatonic, diminuendo, dissonance, dolce, doloroso, dominant, dotted note, dotted rest, downbeat, drone, duplet, triplet, quadruplet, quintuplet, sextuplet, encore, ensemble, expression, finale, fine, fingerboard, flat, double flat, forte, fortissimo, fret, glissando, grave, harmonics, harmony, hemidemisemiquaver, hold, imitation, improvisation, interval, augmented interval, diminished interval, second interval, third interval, fourth interval, fifth interval, sixth interval, seventh interval, major interval, minor interval, perfect interval, intonation, key, key signature, langsam, larghetto, largo, leading note, ledger line, legato, lento, lyric, maestoso, major, manual, marcato, mediant, medley, melody, metre, mezza voce, mezzo forte, microtone, middle C, minim, minor, moderato, mode, modulation, molto, mordent, movement, mute, natural, non troppo, note, obbligato, octave, orchestra, ostinato, part, pause, pedal point, pentatonic, perdendo, phrase, pianissimo, piano, piece, pitch, pizzicato, presto, quarter tone, quaver, rallentando, recital, refrain, resolution, rest, rhythm, rinforzando, ritenuto, root, scale, score, semibreve, semiquaver, semitone, semplice, sempre, senza, sequence, shake, sharp, double sharp, slur, smorzando, solo, soprano, sostenuto, sotto voce, spiritoso, staccato, staff, stave, subdominant, subito, submediant, sul ponticello, supertonic, swell, syncopation, tablature, tacet, tanto, tempo, tenor, tenuto, theme, tie, timbre, time signature, compound time, simple time, two-two time, three-four time, four-four time, six-eight time, tone, tonic sol-fa, transposition, treble, tremolo, triad, trill, double trill, tune, tuning, turn, tutti, upbeat, unison, vibrato, vigoroso, virtuoso, vivace.

musical compositions

Musical compositions include: arabesque, aubade, bagatelle, bourrée, canon, capriccio, cavatina, chaconne, concerto, concerto grosso, divertimento, étude, extravaganza, fanfare, fantasia, fugue, gavotte, humoresque, impromptu, intermezzo, march, minuet, nocturne, opus, overture, partita, pastorale, polonaise, prelude, requiem, rhapsody, rondo, round, scherzo, serenade, sinfonietta, sonata, sonatina, suite, symphony, toccata, voluntary. *see also* **song**.

musical instruments

Musical instruments include: balalaika, banjo, cello, double-bass, guitar, harp, hurdy-gurdy, lute, lyre, mandolin, sitar, spinet, ukulele, viola, violin, fiddle (*infml*), zither; accordion, concertina, squeeze-box (*infml*), clavichord, harmonium, harpsichord, keyboard, melodeon, organ, Wurlitzer®, piano, grand piano, Pianola®, player-piano, synthesizer, virginals; bagpipes, bassoon, bugle, clarinet, cor anglais, cornet, didgeridoo, euphonium, fife, flugelhorn, flute, French horn, harmonica, horn, kazoo, mouth-organ, oboe, Pan-pipes, piccolo, recorder, saxophone, sousaphone, trombone, trumpet, tuba; castanets, cymbal, glockenspiel, maracas, marimba, tambourine, triangle, tubular bells, xylophone; bass-drum, bongo, kettle-drum, snare-drum, tenor-drum, timpani, tom-tom.

musician

Musicians include: instrumentalist, accompanist, performer, player; bugler, busker, cellist, clarinettist, drummer, flautist, fiddler, guitarist, harpist, oboist, organist, pianist, piper, soloist, trombonist, trumpeter, violinist; singer, vocalist, balladeer, diva, prima donna; conductor, maestro; band, orchestra, group, backing group, ensemble, chamber orchestra, choir, duo, duet, trio, quartet, quintet, sextet, octet, nonet.

muster *v* assemble, convene, gather, call together, mobilize, round up, marshal, come together, congregate, collect, group, meet, rally, mass, throng, call up, summon, enrol.

musty *adj* mouldy, mildewy, stale, stuffy, fusty, dank, airless, decayed, smelly.

mutation *n* change, alteration, variation, modification, transformation, deviation, anomaly, evolution.

mute *adj* silent, dumb, voiceless, wordless, speechless, mum (*infml*), unspoken, noiseless, unexpressed, unpronounced.

≠ vocal, talkative.
v tone down, subdue, muffle, lower, moderate, dampen, deaden, soften, silence.

mutilate *v* **1** MAIM, injure, dismember, disable, disfigure, lame, mangle, cut to pieces, cut up, butcher. **2** SPOIL, mar, damage, cut, censor.

mutinous *adj* rebellious, insurgent, insubordinate, disobedient, seditious, revolutionary, riotous, subversive, bolshie (*infml*), unruly.
≠ obedient, compliant.

mutiny *n* rebellion, insurrection, revolt, revolution, rising, uprising, insubordination, disobedience, defiance, resistance, riot, strike.
v rebel, revolt, rise up, resist, protest, disobey, strike.

mutter *v* **1** MUMBLE, murmur, rumble. **2** COMPLAIN, grumble, grouse (*infml*).

mutual *adj* reciprocal, shared, common, joint, interchangeable, interchanged, exchanged, complementary.

muzzle *v* restrain, stifle, suppress, gag, mute, silence, censor, choke.

mysterious *adj* enigmatic, cryptic, mystifying, inexplicable, incomprehensible, puzzling, perplexing, obscure, strange, unfathomable, unsearchable, mystical, baffling, curious, hidden, insoluble, secret, weird, secretive, veiled, dark, furtive.
≠ straightforward, comprehensible.

mystery *n* **1** ENIGMA, puzzle, secret, riddle, conundrum, question. **2** OBSCURITY, secrecy, ambiguity.

mystical *adj* occult, arcane, mystic, esoteric, supernatural, paranormal, transcendental, metaphysical, hidden, mysterious.

mystify *v* puzzle, bewilder, baffle, perplex, confound, confuse.

myth *n* legend, fable, fairytale, allegory, parable, saga, story, fiction, tradition, fancy, fantasy, superstition.

mythical *adj* **1** MYTHOLOGICAL, legendary, fabled, fairytale.

> *Mythological creatures and spirits include*: abominable snowman (or yeti), afrit, basilisk, bunyip, Cecrops, centaur, Cerberus, Chimera, cockatrice, Cyclops, dragon, dryad, Echidna, elf, Erinyes (or Furies), Fafnir, fairy, faun, genie, Geryon, Gigantes, gnome, goblin, golem, Gorgon, griffin, Harpies, hippocampus, hippogriff, hobgoblin, imp, kelpie, kraken, lamia, leprechaun, Lilith, Loch Ness monster, mermaid, merman, Minotaur, naiad, nereid, nymph, ogre, ogress, orc, oread, Pegasus, phoenix, pixie, roc, salamander, sasquatch, satyr, sea serpent, Siren, Sphinx, sylph, troll, Typhoeus, unicorn, werewolf, wivern.

2 FICTITIOUS, imaginary, made-up, invented, make-believe, non-existent, unreal, pretended, fanciful.
≠ **1** historical. **2** actual, real.

mythology *n* legend, myths, lore, tradition(s), folklore, folk-tales, tales.

N

nag *v* scold, berate, irritate, annoy, pester, badger, plague, torment, harass, henpeck (*infml*), harry, vex, upbraid, goad.

nail *v* fasten, attach, secure, pin, tack, fix, join.
n **1** FASTENER, pin, tack, spike, skewer. **2** TALON, claw.

naïve *adj* unsophisticated, ingenuous, innocent, unaffected, artless, guileless, simple, natural, childlike, open, trusting, unsuspecting, gullible, credulous, wide-eyed.
≠ experienced, sophisticated.

naïvety *n* ingenuousness, innocence, inexperience, naturalness, simplicity, openness, frankness, gullibility, credulity.
≠ experience, sophistication.

naked *adj* **1** NUDE, bare, undressed, unclothed, uncovered, stripped, stark-naked, disrobed, denuded, in the altogether (*infml*). **2** OPEN, unadorned, undisguised, unqualified, plain, stark, overt, blatant, exposed.
≠ **1** clothed, covered. **2** concealed.

name *n* **1** TITLE, appellation (*fml*), designation, label, term, epithet, handle (*infml*). **2** REPUTATION, character, repute, renown, esteem, eminence, fame, honour, distinction, note.
v **1** CALL, christen, baptize, term, title, entitle, dub, label, style.
2 DESIGNATE, nominate, cite, choose, select, specify, classify, commission, appoint.

nameless *adj* **1** UNNAMED, anonymous, unidentified, unknown, obscure. **2** INEXPRESSIBLE, indescribable, unutterable, unspeakable, unmentionable, unheard-of.
≠ **1** named.

namely *adv* that is, ie, specifically, viz, that is to say.

nap *v* doze, sleep, snooze (*infml*), nod (off), drop off, rest, kip (*infml*).
n rest, sleep, siesta, catnap, forty winks (*infml*), kip (*infml*).

narcotic *n* drug, opiate, sedative, tranquillizer, pain-killer.
adj soporific, hypnotic, sedative, analgesic, pain-killing, numbing, dulling, calming, stupefying.

narrate *v* tell, relate, report, recount, describe, unfold, recite, state, detail.

narrative *n* story, tale, chronicle, account, history, report, detail, statement.

narrator *n* storyteller, chronicler, reporter, raconteur, commentator, writer.

narrow *adj* **1** TIGHT, confined, constricted, cramped, slim, slender, thin, fine, tapering, close. **2** LIMITED, restricted, circumscribed. **3** NARROW-MINDED, biased, bigoted, exclusive, dogmatic.
≠ **1** wide. **2** broad. **3** broad-minded, tolerant.
v constrict, limit, tighten, reduce, diminish, simplify.
≠ broaden, widen, increase.

narrow-minded *adj* illiberal, biased, bigoted, prejudiced, reactionary, small-minded, conservative, intolerant, insular, petty.
≠ broad-minded.

nasty *adj* **1** UNPLEASANT, repellent, repugnant, repulsive, objectionable, offensive, disgusting, sickening, horrible, filthy, foul, polluted, obscene. **2** MALICIOUS, mean, spiteful, vicious, malevolent.
≠ **1** agreeable, pleasant, decent. **2** benevolent, kind.

nation *n* country, people, race, state, realm, population, community, society.

national *adj* countrywide, civil, domestic, nationwide, state, internal,

general, governmental, public, widespread, social.
n citizen, native, subject, inhabitant, resident.

nationalism *n* patriotism, allegiance, loyalty, chauvinism, xenophobia, jingoism.

nationality *n* race, nation, ethnic group, birth, tribe, clan.

native *adj* **1** LOCAL, indigenous, domestic, vernacular, home, aboriginal, autochthonous (*fml*), mother, original. **2** INBORN, inherent, innate, inbred, hereditary, inherited, congenital, instinctive, natural, intrinsic, natal.
n inhabitant, resident, national, citizen, dweller, aborigine, autochthon (*fml*).
≠ foreigner, outsider, stranger.

natural *adj* **1** ORDINARY, normal, common, regular, standard, usual, typical. **2** INNATE, inborn, instinctive, intuitive, inherent, congenital, native, indigenous. **3** GENUINE, pure, authentic, unrefined, unprocessed, unmixed, real. **4** SINCERE, unaffected, genuine, artless, ingenuous, guileless, simple, unsophisticated, open, candid, spontaneous.
≠ **1** unnatural. **2** acquired. **3** artificial. **4** affected, disingenuous.

naturalistic *adj* natural, realistic, true-to-life, representational, lifelike, graphic, real-life, photographic.

naturally *adj* **1** OF COURSE, as a matter of course, simply, obviously, logically, typically, certainly, absolutely. **2** NORMALLY, genuinely, instinctively, spontaneously.

nature *n* **1** ESSENCE, quality, character, features, disposition, attributes, personality, make-up, constitution, temperament, mood, outlook, temper. **2** KIND, sort, type, description, category, variety, style, species. **3** UNIVERSE, world, creation, earth, environment. **4** COUNTRYSIDE, country, landscape, scenery, natural history.

naughty *adj* **1** BAD, badly behaved, mischievous, disobedient, wayward, exasperating, playful, roguish. **2** INDECENT, obscene, bawdy, risqué, smutty.
≠ **1** good, well-behaved. **2** decent.

nausea *n* **1** VOMITING, sickness, retching, queasiness, biliousness. **2** DISGUST, revulsion, loathing, repugnance.

nauseate *v* sicken, disgust, revolt, repel, offend, turn one's stomach (*infml*).

nautical *adj* naval, maritime, sea-going, sailing, oceanic, boating.

Nautical terms include: afloat, aft, air-sea rescue, amidships, ballast, beam, bear away, beat, bow-wave, breeches buoy, broach, capsize, cargo, cast off, chandler, circumnavigate, coastguard, compass bearing, convoy, course, cruise, current, Davy Jones's locker, dead reckoning, deadweight, disembark, dock, dockyard, dry dock, ebb tide, embark, ferry, fleet, float, flotilla, flotsam, foghorn, fore, foreshore, go about, gybe, harbour, harbour-bar, harbour dues, harbour-master, haven, heave to, head to wind, heavy swell, heel, helm, high tide, inflatable life-raft, jetsam, jetty, knot, launch, lay a course, lay up, lee, leeward, lee shore, life buoy, life-jacket, life-rocket, list, low tide, make fast, marina, marine, maroon, mayday, moor, mooring, mutiny, navigation, neap tide, on board, pitch and toss, plane, put in, put to sea, quay, reach, reef, refit, ride out, riptide, roll, row, run, run aground, run before the wind, salvage, seafaring, sea lane, sea legs, seamanship, seasick, seaworthy, set sail, sheet in, shipping, shipping lane, ship's company, ship water, shipyard, shipwreck, shore leave, sink, slip anchor, slipway, stevedore, stowaway, tack, tide, trim, voyage, wake, wash, watch, wave, weather, weigh anchor, wharf, wreck. *see also* **sail**.

navigate *v* steer, drive, direct, pilot, guide, handle, manoeuvre, cruise, sail, skipper, voyage, journey, cross, helm, plot, plan.

navigation *n* sailing, steering, cruising,

voyaging, seamanship, helmsmanship.

Navigational aids include: astro-navigation, bell buoy, channel-marker buoy, chart, chronometer, conical buoy, Decca® navigator system, depth gauge, dividers, echo-sounder, flux-gate compass, Global Positioning System (GPS), gyrocompass, lighthouse, lightship, log, loran (long-range radio navigation), magnetic compass, marker buoy, nautical table, parallel ruler, pilot, radar, sectored leading-light, sextant, VHF radio.

navy *n* fleet, ships, flotilla, armada, warships.

near *adj* **1** NEARBY, close, bordering, adjacent, adjoining, alongside, neighbouring. **2** IMMINENT, impending, forthcoming, coming, approaching. **3** DEAR, familiar, close, related, intimate, akin.
≠ **1** far. **2** distant. **3** remote.

nearby *adj* near, neighbouring, adjoining, adjacent, accessible, convenient, handy.
≠ faraway.
adv near, within reach, at close quarters, close at hand, not far away.

nearly *adv* almost, practically, virtually, closely, approximately, more or less, as good as, just about, roughly, well-nigh.
≠ completely, totally.

neat *adj* **1** TIDY, orderly, smart, spruce, trim, clean, spick-and-span (*infml*), shipshape. **2** DEFT, clever, adroit, skilful, expert. **3** UNDILUTED, unmixed, unadulterated, straight, pure.
≠ **1** untidy. **2** clumsy. **3** diluted.

nebulous *adj* vague, hazy, imprecise, indefinite, indistinct, cloudy, misty, obscure, uncertain, unclear, dim, ambiguous, confused, fuzzy, shapeless, amorphous.
≠ clear.

necessary *adj* needed, required, essential, compulsory, indispensable, vital, imperative, mandatory, obligatory, needful, unavoidable, inevitable, inescapable, inexorable, certain.
≠ unnecessary, inessential, unimportant.

necessitate *v* require, involve, entail, call for, demand, oblige, force, constrain, compel.

necessity *n* **1** REQUIREMENT, obligation, prerequisite, essential, fundamental, need, want, compulsion, demand. **2** INDISPENSABILITY, inevitability, needfulness. **3** POVERTY, destitution, hardship.

need *v* miss, lack, want, require, demand, call for, necessitate, have need of, have to, crave.
n **1** *a need for caution*: call, demand, obligation, requirement. **2** *the country's needs*: essential, necessity, requisite, prerequisite, desideratum. **3** *a need for equipment*: want, lack, insufficiency, inadequacy, neediness, shortage.

needless *adj* unnecessary, gratuitous, uncalled-for, unwanted, redundant, superfluous, useless, pointless, purposeless.
≠ necessary, essential.

needy *adj* poor, destitute, impoverished, penniless, disadvantaged, deprived, poverty-stricken, underprivileged.
≠ affluent, wealthy, well-off.

negate *v* **1** NULLIFY, annul, cancel, invalidate, undo, countermand, abrogate (*fml*), neutralize, quash, retract, reverse, revoke, rescind, wipe out, void, repeal. **2** DENY, contradict, oppose, disprove, refute, repudiate.
≠ **2** affirm.

negative *adj* **1** CONTRADICTORY, contrary, denying, opposing, invalidating, neutralizing, nullifying, annulling. **2** UNCO-OPERATIVE, cynical, pessimistic, unenthusiastic, uninterested, unwilling.
≠ **1** affirmative, positive. **2** constructive, positive.
n contradiction, denial, opposite, refusal.

neglect *v* **1** DISREGARD, ignore, leave alone, abandon, pass by, rebuff, scorn, disdain, slight, spurn. **2** FORGET, fail (in), omit, overlook, let slide, shirk, skimp.

≠ **1** cherish, appreciate. **2** remember.
n negligence, disregard, carelessness, failure, inattention, indifference, slackness, dereliction of duty, forgetfulness, heedlessness, oversight, slight, disrespect.
≠ care, attention, concern.

negligence *n* inattentiveness, carelessness, laxity, neglect, slackness, thoughtlessness, forgetfulness, indifference, omission, oversight, disregard, failure, default.
≠ attentiveness, care, regard.

negligent *adj* neglectful, inattentive, remiss, thoughtless, casual, lax, careless, indifferent, offhand, nonchalant, slack, uncaring, forgetful.
≠ attentive, careful, scrupulous.

negligible *adj* unimportant, insignificant, small, imperceptible, trifling, trivial, minor, minute.
≠ significant.

negotiate *v* **1** CONFER, deal, mediate, arbitrate, bargain, arrange, transact, work out, manage, settle, consult, contract. **2** GET ROUND, cross, surmount, traverse, pass.

negotiation *n* mediation, arbitration, debate, discussion, diplomacy, bargaining, transaction.

negotiator *n* arbitrator, go-between, mediator, intermediary, moderator, intercessor, adjudicator, broker, ambassador, diplomat.

neighbourhood *n* district, locality, vicinity, community, locale, environs, confines, surroundings, region, proximity.

neighbouring *adj* adjacent, bordering, near, nearby, adjoining, connecting, next, surrounding.
≠ distant, remote.

neighbourly *adj* sociable, friendly, amiable, kind, helpful, genial, hospitable, obliging, considerate, companionable.

nerve *n* **1** COURAGE, bravery, mettle, pluck, guts (*infml*), spunk (*infml*), spirit, vigour, intrepidity, daring, fearlessness, firmness, resolution, fortitude, steadfastness, will, determination, endurance, force. **2** (*infml*) AUDACITY, impudence, cheek (*infml*), effrontery, brazenness, boldness, chutzpah (*infml*), impertinence, insolence.
≠ **1** weakness. **2** timidity.

nerve-racking *adj* harrowing, distressing, trying, stressful, tense, maddening, worrying, difficult, frightening.

nerves *n* nervousness, tension, stress, anxiety, worry, strain, fretfulness.

nervous *adj* highly-strung, excitable, anxious, agitated, nervy (*infml*), on edge, edgy, jumpy (*infml*), jittery (*infml*), tense, fidgety, apprehensive, neurotic, shaky, uneasy, worried, flustered, fearful.
≠ calm, relaxed.

nest *n* **1** BREEDING-GROUND, den, roost, eyrie, lair. **2** RETREAT, refuge, haunt, hideaway.

nestle *v* snuggle, huddle, cuddle, curl up.

net[1] *n* mesh, web, network, netting, open-work, lattice, lace.
v catch, trap, capture, bag, ensnare, entangle, nab (*infml*).

net[2] *adj* nett, clear, after tax, final, lowest.
v bring in, clear, earn, make, realize, receive, gain, obtain, accumulate.

network *n* system, organization, arrangement, structure, interconnections, complex, grid, net, maze, mesh, labyrinth, channels, circuitry, convolution, grill, tracks.

neurosis *n* disorder, affliction, abnormality, disturbance, derangement, deviation, obsession, phobia.

neurotic *adj* disturbed, maladjusted, anxious, nervous, overwrought, unstable, unhealthy, deviant, abnormal, compulsive, obsessive.

neuter *v* castrate, emasculate, doctor, geld, spay.

neutral *adj* **1** IMPARTIAL, uncommitted, unbia(s)sed, non-aligned, disinterested, unprejudiced, undecided, non-partisan, non-committal, objective, indifferent, dispassionate, even-handed.

2 DULL, nondescript, colourless, drab, expressionless, indistinct.
≠ 1 biased, partisan. 2 colourful.

neutralize *v* counteract, counterbalance, offset, negate, cancel, nullify, invalidate, undo, frustrate.

never-ending *adj* everlasting, eternal, non-stop, perpetual, unceasing, uninterrupted, unremitting, interminable, incessant, unbroken, permanent, persistent, unchanging, relentless.
≠ fleeting, transitory.

nevertheless *adv* nonetheless, notwithstanding, still, anyway, even so, yet, however, anyhow, but, regardless.

new *adj* 1 NOVEL, original, fresh, different, unfamiliar, unusual, brand-new, mint, unknown, unused, virgin, newborn. 2 MODERN, contemporary, current, latest, recent, up-to-date, up-to-the-minute, topical, trendy (*infml*), ultra-modern, advanced, newfangled (*infml*). 3 CHANGED, altered, modernized, improved, renewed, restored, redesigned. 4 ADDED, additional, extra, more, supplementary.
≠ 1 usual. 2 outdated, out-of-date. 3 old.

newcomer *n* immigrant, alien, foreigner, incomer, colonist, settler, arrival, outsider, stranger, novice, beginner.

news *n* report, account, information, intelligence, dispatch, communiqué, bulletin, gossip, hearsay, rumour, statement, story, word, tidings, latest, release, scandal, revelation, lowdown (*infml*), exposé, disclosure, gen (*infml*), advice.

next *adj* 1 ADJACENT, adjoining, neighbouring, nearest, closest.
2 FOLLOWING, subsequent, succeeding, ensuing, later.
≠ 2 previous, preceding.
adv afterwards, subsequently, later, then.

nibble *n* bite, morsel, taste, titbit, bit, crumb, snack, piece.
v bite, eat, peck, pick at, nosh (*sl*), munch, gnaw.

nice *adj* 1 PLEASANT, agreeable, delightful, charming, likable, attractive, good, kind, friendly, well-mannered, polite, respectable. 2 SUBTLE, delicate, fine, fastidious, discriminating, scrupulous, precise, exact, accurate, careful, strict.
≠ 1 nasty, disagreeable, unpleasant. 2 careless.

nicety *n* 1 DELICACY, refinement, subtlety, distinction, nuance.
2 PRECISION, accuracy, meticulousness, scrupulousness, minuteness, finesse.

niche *n* 1 RECESS, alcove, hollow, nook, cubby-hole, corner, opening.
2 POSITION, place, vocation, calling, métier, slot.

nick *n* 1 NOTCH, indentation, chip, cut, groove, dent, scar, scratch, mark. 2 (*sl*) PRISON, jail, police station.
v 1 NOTCH, cut, dent, indent, chip, score, scratch, scar, mark, damage, snick. 2 (*sl*) STEAL, pilfer, knock off (*infml*), pinch (*infml*).

nickname *n* pet name, sobriquet, epithet, diminutive.

night *n* night-time, darkness, dark, dead of night.
≠ day, daytime.

nightfall *n* sunset, dusk, twilight, evening, gloaming.
≠ dawn, sunrise.

nightmare *n* 1 BAD DREAM, hallucination. 2 ORDEAL, horror, torment, trial.

nil *n* nothing, zero, none, nought, naught, love, duck, zilch (*sl*).

nimble *adj* agile, active, lively, sprightly, spry, smart, quick, brisk, nippy (*infml*), deft, alert, light-footed, prompt, ready, swift, quick-witted.
≠ clumsy, slow.

nip[1] *v* bite, pinch, squeeze, snip, clip, tweak, catch, grip, nibble.

nip[2] *n* dram, draught, shot, swallow, mouthful, drop, sip, taste, portion.

nobility *n* 1 NOBLENESS, dignity, grandeur, illustriousness, stateliness, majesty, magnificence, eminence, excellence, superiority, uprightness, honour, virtue, worthiness. 2

ARISTOCRACY, peerage, nobles, gentry, élite, lords, high society.
≠ **1** baseness. **2** proletariat.

Titles of the nobility include: aristocrat, baron, baroness, baronet, count, countess, dame, dowager, duchess, duke, earl, grand duke, governor, knight, lady, laird, liege, liege lord, life peer, lord, marchioness, marquess, marquis, noble, nobleman, noblewoman, peer, peeress, ruler, seigneur, squire, thane, viscount, viscountess.

noble *n* aristocrat, peer, lord, lady, nobleman, noblewoman.
≠ commoner.
adj **1** ARISTOCRATIC, high-born, titled, high-ranking, patrician, blue-blooded (*infml*). **2** MAGNIFICENT, magnanimous, splendid, stately, generous, dignified, distinguished, eminent, grand, great, honoured, honourable, imposing, impressive, majestic, virtuous, worthy, excellent, elevated, fine, gentle.
≠ **1** low-born. **2** ignoble, base, contemptible.

nobody *n* no-one, nothing, nonentity, menial, cipher.
≠ somebody.

nod *v* **1** GESTURE, indicate, sign, signal, salute, acknowledge. **2** AGREE, assent. **3** SLEEP, doze, drowse, nap.
n gesture, indication, sign, signal, salute, greeting, beck, acknowledgement.

noise *n* sound, din, racket, row, clamour, clash, clatter, commotion, outcry, hubbub, uproar, cry, blare, talk, pandemonium, tumult, babble.
≠ quiet, silence.
v report, rumour, publicize, announce, circulate.

noiseless *adj* silent, inaudible, soundless, quiet, mute, still, hushed.
≠ loud, noisy.

noisy *adj* loud, deafening, ear-splitting, clamorous, piercing, vocal, vociferous, tumultuous, boisterous, obstreperous.
≠ quiet, silent, peaceful.

nomad *n* traveller, wanderer, itinerant, rambler, roamer, rover, migrant.

nominal *adj* **1** TITULAR, supposed, purported, professed, ostensible, so-called, theoretical, self-styled, puppet, symbolic. **2** TOKEN, minimal, trifling, trivial, insignificant, small.
≠ **1** actual, genuine, real.

nominate *v* propose, choose, select, name, designate, submit, suggest, recommend, put up, present, elect, appoint, assign, commission, elevate, term.

nomination *n* proposal, choice, selection, submission, suggestion, recommendation, designation, election, appointment.

nominee *n* candidate, entrant, contestant, appointee, runner, assignee.

nonchalant *adj* unconcerned, detached, dispassionate, offhand, blasé, indifferent, casual, cool, collected, apathetic, careless, insouciant.
≠ concerned, careful.

non-committal *adj* guarded, unrevealing, cautious, wary, reserved, ambiguous, discreet, equivocal, evasive, circumspect, careful, neutral, indefinite, politic, tactful, tentative, vague.

nonconformist *n* dissenter, rebel, individualist, dissident, radical, protester, heretic, iconoclast, eccentric, maverick, secessionist.
≠ conformist.

nondescript *adj* featureless, indeterminate, undistinctive, undistinguished, unexceptional, ordinary, commonplace, plain, dull, uninspiring, uninteresting, unclassified.
≠ distinctive, remarkable.

none *pron* no-one, not any, not one, nobody, nil, zero.

nonplussed *adj* disconcerted, confounded, taken aback, stunned, bewildered, astonished, astounded, dumbfounded, perplexed, stumped, flabbergasted, flummoxed, puzzled, baffled, dismayed, embarrassed.

nonsense *n* rubbish, trash, drivel, balderdash, gibberish, gobbledygook, senselessness, stupidity, silliness, foolishness, folly, rot (*infml*), blather,

twaddle, ridiculousness, claptrap (*infml*), cobblers (*sl*).
≠ sense, wisdom.

nonsensical *adj* ridiculous, meaningless, senseless, foolish, inane, irrational, silly, incomprehensible, ludicrous, absurd, fatuous, crazy (*infml*).
≠ reasonable, sensible, logical.

non-stop *adj* never-ending, uninterrupted, continuous, incessant, constant, endless, interminable, unending, unbroken, round-the-clock, on-going.
≠ intermittent, occasional.

nook *n* recess, alcove, corner, cranny, niche, cubby-hole, hide-out, retreat, shelter, cavity.

norm *n* average, mean, standard, rule, pattern, criterion, model, yardstick, benchmark, measure, reference.

normal *adj* usual, standard, general, common, ordinary, conventional, average, regular, routine, typical, mainstream, natural, accustomed, well-adjusted, straight, rational, reasonable.
≠ abnormal, irregular, peculiar.

normality *n* usualness, commonness, ordinariness, regularity, routine, conventionality, balance, adjustment, typicality, naturalness, reason, rationality.
≠ abnormality, irregularity, peculiarity.

normally *adv* ordinarily, usually, as a rule, typically, commonly, characteristically.
≠ abnormally, exceptionally.

nosegay *n* bouquet, posy, spray, bunch.

nosey (*infml*) *adj* inquisitive, meddlesome, prying, interfering, snooping, curious, eavesdropping.

nostalgia *n* yearning, longing, regretfulness, remembrance, reminiscence, homesickness, pining.

nostalgic *adj* yearning, longing, wistful, emotional, regretful, sentimental, homesick.

notable *adj* noteworthy, remarkable, noticeable, striking, extraordinary, impressive, outstanding, marked, unusual, celebrated, distinguished, famous, eminent, well-known, notorious, renowned, rare.
≠ ordinary, commonplace, usual.
n celebrity, notability, VIP, personage, somebody, dignitary, luminary, worthy.
≠ nobody, nonentity.

notably *adv* markedly, noticeably, particularly, remarkably, strikingly, conspicuously, distinctly, especially, impressively, outstandingly, eminently.

notation *n* symbols, characters, code, signs, alphabet, system, script, noting, record, shorthand.

notch *n* cut, nick, indentation, incision, score, groove, cleft, mark, snip, degree, grade, step.
v cut, nick, score, scratch, indent, mark.

note *n* **1** COMMUNICATION, letter, message, memorandum, reminder, memo (*infml*), line, jotting, record. **2** ANNOTATION, comment, gloss, remark. **3** INDICATION, signal, token, mark, symbol. **4** EMINENCE, distinction, consequence, fame, renown, reputation. **5** HEED, attention regard, notice, observation.
v **1** NOTICE, observe, perceive, heed, detect, mark, remark, mention, see, witness. **2** RECORD, register, write down, enter.

noted *adj* famous, well-known, renowned, notable, celebrated, eminent, prominent, great, acclaimed, illustrious, distinguished, respected, recognized.
≠ obscure, unknown.

notes *n* jottings, record, impressions, report, sketch, outline, synopsis, draft.

noteworthy *adj* remarkable, significant, important, notable, memorable, exceptional, extraordinary, unusual, outstanding.
≠ commonplace, unexceptional, ordinary.

nothing *n* nought, zero, nothingness, zilch (*sl*), nullity, non-existence, emptiness, void, nobody, nonentity.
≠ something.

otice *v* note, remark, perceive, observe, mind, see, discern, distinguish, mark, detect, heed, spot.
≠ ignore, overlook.
n **1** NOTIFICATION, announcement, information, declaration, communication, intelligence, news, warning, instruction.
2 ADVERTISEMENT, poster, sign, bill.
3 REVIEW, comment, criticism.
4 ATTENTION, observation, awareness, note, regard, consideration, heed.

oticeable *adj* perceptible, observable, appreciable, unmistakable, conspicuous, evident, manifest, clear, distinct, significant, striking, plain, obvious, measurable.
≠ inconspicuous, unnoticeable.

otification *n* announcement, information, notice, declaration, advice, warning, intelligence, message, publication, statement, communication.

otify *v* inform, tell, advise, announce, declare, warn, acquaint, alert, publish, disclose, reveal.

otion *n* **1** IDEA, thought, concept, conception, belief, impression, view, opinion, understanding, apprehension.
2 INCLINATION, wish, whim, fancy, caprice.

otoriety *n* infamy, disrepute, dishonour, disgrace, scandal.

otorious *adj* infamous, disreputable, scandalous, dishonourable, disgraceful, ignominious, flagrant, well-known.

ought *n* zero, nil, zilch, naught, nothing, nothingness.

ourish *v* **1** NURTURE, feed, foster, care for, provide for, sustain, support, tend, nurse, maintain, cherish.
2 STRENGTHEN, encourage, promote, cultivate, stimulate.

ourishment *n* nutrition, food, sustenance, diet.

ovel *adj* new, original, fresh, innovative, unfamiliar, unusual, uncommon, different, imaginative, unconventional, strange.
≠ hackneyed, familiar, ordinary.
n fiction, story, tale, narrative, romance.

novelty *n* **1** NEWNESS, originality, freshness, innovation, unfamiliarity, uniqueness, difference, strangeness. **2** GIMMICK, gadget, trifle, memento, knick-knack, curiosity, souvenir, trinket, bauble, gimcrack.

novice *n* beginner, tiro, learner, pupil, trainee, probationer, apprentice, neophyte (*fml*), amateur, newcomer.
≠ expert.

now *adv* **1** IMMEDIATELY, at once, directly, instantly, straight away, promptly, next. **2** AT PRESENT, nowadays, these days.

noxious *adj* harmful, poisonous, pernicious, toxic, injurious, unhealthy, deadly, destructive, noisome, foul.
≠ innocuous, wholesome.

nuance *n* subtlety, suggestion, shade, hint, suspicion, gradation, distinction, overtone, refinement, touch, trace, tinge, degree, nicety.

nub *n* centre, heart, core, nucleus, kernel, crux, gist, pith, point, essence.

nucleus *n* centre, heart, nub, core, focus, kernel, pivot, basis, crux.

nude *adj* naked, bare, undressed, unclothed, stripped, stark-naked, uncovered, starkers (*infml*), in one's birthday suit (*infml*).
≠ clothed, dressed.

nudge *v, n* poke, prod, shove, dig, jog, prompt, push, elbow, bump.

nuisance *n* annoyance, inconvenience, bother, irritation, pest, pain (*infml*), drag (*infml*), bore, problem, trial, trouble, drawback.

null *adj* void, invalid, ineffectual, useless, vain, worthless, powerless, inoperative.
≠ valid.

nullify *v* annul, revoke, cancel, invalidate, abrogate, abolish, negate, rescind, quash, repeal, counteract.
≠ validate.

numb *adj* benumbed, insensible, unfeeling, deadened, insensitive, frozen, immobilized.
≠ sensitive.
v deaden, anaesthetize, freeze,

immobilize, paralyse, dull, stun.
≠ sensitize.

number *n* **1** FIGURE, numeral, digit, integer, unit. **2** TOTAL, sum, aggregate, collection, amount, quantity, several, many, company, crowd, multitude, throng, horde. **3** COPY, issue, edition, impression, volume, printing.
v count, calculate, enumerate, reckon, total, add, compute, include.

numerous *adj* many, abundant, several, plentiful, copious, profuse, sundry.
≠ few.

nurse *v* **1** TEND, care for, look after, treat. **2** BREAST-FEED, feed, suckle, nurture, nourish. **3** PRESERVE, sustain, support, cherish, encourage, keep, foster, promote.

Nurses include: charge nurse, children's nurse, dental nurse, district nurse, healthcare assistant, health visitor, home nurse, Iain Rennie nurse, locality manager, Macmillan nurse, matron, midwife, nanny, night nurse, night sister, nursemaid, nursery nurse, nurse tutor, occupational health nurse, psychiatric nurse, Registered General Nurse (RGN), school nurse, sister, staff nurse, State Enrolled Nurse (SEN), State Registered Nurse (SRN), theatre sister, ward sister, wet nurse.

nurture *n* **1** FOOD, nourishment. **2** REARING, upbringing, training, care, cultivation, development, education, discipline.
v **1** FEED, nourish, nurse, tend, care for, foster, support, sustain. **2** BRING UP, rear, cultivate, develop, educate, instruct, train, school, discipline.

nut

Varieties of nut include: almond, beech nut, brazil nut, cashew, chestnut, cobnut, coconut, filbert, hazelnut, macadamia, monkey nut, peanut, pecan, pistachio, walnut.

nutrition *n* food, nourishment, sustenance.

nutritious *adj* nourishing, nutritive, wholesome, healthful, health-giving, good, beneficial, strengthening, substantial, invigorating.
≠ bad, unwholesome.

O

oasis *n* **1** SPRING, watering-hole. **2** REFUGE, haven, island, sanctuary, retreat.

oath *n* **1** VOW, pledge, promise, word, affirmation, assurance, word of honour. **2** CURSE, imprecation, swear-word, profanity, expletive, blasphemy.

obedient *adj* compliant, docile, acquiescent, submissive, tractable, yielding, dutiful, law-abiding, deferential, respectful, subservient, observant.
≠ disobedient, rebellious, wilful.

obesity *n* fatness, overweight, corpulence, stoutness, grossness, plumpness, portliness, bulk.
≠ thinness, slenderness, skinniness.

obey *v* **1** COMPLY, submit, surrender, yield, be ruled by, bow to, take orders from, defer (to), give way, follow, observe, abide by, adhere to, conform, heed, keep, mind, respond. **2** CARRY OUT, discharge, execute, act upon, fulfil, perform.
≠ **1** disobey.

object[1] *n* **1** THING, entity, article, body. **2** AIM, objective, purpose, goal, target, intention, motive, end, reason, point, design. **3** TARGET, recipient, butt, victim.

object[2] *v* protest, oppose, demur, take exception, disapprove, refuse, complain, rebut, repudiate.
≠ agree, acquiesce.

objection *n* protest, dissent, disapproval, opposition, demur, complaint, challenge, scruple.
≠ agreement, assent.

objectionable *adj* unacceptable, unpleasant, offensive, obnoxious, repugnant, disagreeable, abhorrent, detestable, deplorable, despicable.
≠ acceptable.

objective *adj* impartial, unbiased, detached, unprejudiced, open-minded, equitable, dispassionate, even-handed, neutral, disinterested, just, fair.
≠ subjective.
n object, aim, goal, end, purpose, ambition, mark, target, intention, design.

obligation *n* duty, responsibility, onus, charge, commitment, liability, requirement, bond, contract, debt, burden, trust.

obligatory *adj* compulsory, mandatory, statutory, required, binding, essential, necessary, enforced.
≠ optional.

oblige *v* **1** COMPEL, constrain, coerce, require, make, necessitate, force, bind. **2** HELP, assist, accommodate, do a favour, serve, gratify, please.

obliging *adj* accommodating, co-operative, helpful, considerate, agreeable, friendly, kind, civil.
≠ unhelpful.

oblique *adj* slanting, sloping, inclined, angled, tilted.

obliterate *v* eradicate, destroy, annihilate, delete, blot out, wipe out, erase.

oblivion *n* obscurity, nothingness, unconsciousness, void, limbo.
≠ awareness.

oblivious *adj* unaware, unconscious, inattentive, careless, heedless, blind, insensible, negligent.
≠ aware.

obnoxious *adj* unpleasant, disagreeable, disgusting, loathsome, nasty, horrid, odious, repulsive, revolting, repugnant, sickening, nauseating.
≠ pleasant.

obscene *adj* indecent, improper, immoral, impure, filthy, dirty, bawdy, lewd, licentious, pornographic,

scurrilous, suggestive, disgusting, foul, shocking, shameless, offensive.
≠ decent, wholesome.

obscenity *n* **1** INDECENCY, immodesty, impurity, impropriety, lewdness, licentiousness, suggestiveness, pornography, dirtiness, filthiness, foulness, grossness, indelicacy, coarseness. **2** ATROCITY, evil, outrage, offence. **3** PROFANITY, expletive, swear-word, four-letter word.

obscure *adj* **1** UNKNOWN, unimportant, little-known, unheard-of, undistinguished, nameless, inconspicuous, humble, minor. **2** INCOMPREHENSIBLE, enigmatic, cryptic, recondite, esoteric, mysterious, deep, abstruse, confusing. **3** INDISTINCT, unclear, indefinite, shadowy, blurred, cloudy, faint, hazy, dim, misty, shady, vague, murky, gloomy, dusky.
≠ **1** famous, renowned. **2** intelligible, straightforward. **3** clear, definite.
v conceal, cloud, obfuscate, hide, cover, blur, disguise, mask, overshadow, shadow, shade, cloak, veil, shroud, darken, dim, eclipse, screen, block out.
≠ clarify, illuminate.

obsequious *adj* servile, ingratiating, grovelling, fawning, sycophantic, cringing, deferential, flattering, smarmy (*infml*), unctuous, oily, submissive, subservient, slavish.

observance *n* **1** ADHERENCE, compliance, observation, performance, obedience, fulfilment, honouring, notice, attention. **2** RITUAL, custom, ceremony, practice, celebration.

observant *adj* attentive, alert, vigilant, watchful, perceptive, eagle-eyed, wide-awake, heedful.
≠ unobservant.

observation *n* **1** ATTENTION, notice, examination, inspection, scrutiny, monitoring, study, watching, consideration, discernment. **2** REMARK, comment, utterance, thought, statement, pronouncement, reflection, opinion, finding, note.

observe *v* **1** WATCH, see, study, notice, contemplate, keep an eye on, perceive. **2** REMARK, comment, say, mention. **3** ABIDE BY, comply with, honour, keep, fulfil, celebrate, perform.
≠ **1** miss. **3** break, violate.

observer *n* watcher, spectator, viewer, witness, looker-on, onlooker, eyewitness, commentator, bystander, beholder.

obsess *v* preoccupy, dominate, rule, monopolize, haunt, grip, plague, prey on, possess.

obsession *n* preoccupation, fixation, idée fixe, ruling passion, compulsion, fetish, hang-up (*infml*), infatuation, mania, enthusiasm.

obsessive *adj* consuming, compulsive, gripping, fixed, haunting, tormenting, maddening.

obsolete *adj* outmoded, disused, out of date, old-fashioned, passé, dated, outworn, old, antiquated, antique, dead, extinct.
≠ modern, current, up-to-date.

obstacle *n* barrier, bar, obstruction, impediment, hurdle, hindrance, check, snag, stumbling-block, drawback, difficulty, hitch, catch, stop, interference, interruption.
≠ advantage, help.

obstinate *adj* stubborn, inflexible, immovable, intractable, pig-headed (*infml*), unyielding, intransigent, persistent, dogged, headstrong, bloody-minded (*sl*), strong-minded, self-willed, steadfast, firm, determined, wilful.
≠ flexible, tractable.

obstruct *v* block, impede, hinder, prevent, check, frustrate, hamper, clog, choke, bar, barricade, stop, stall, retard, restrict, thwart, inhibit, hold up, curb, arrest, slow down, interrupt, interfere with, shut off, cut off, obscure.
≠ assist, further.

obstruction *n* barrier, blockage, bar, barricade, hindrance, impediment, check, stop, stoppage, difficulty.
≠ help.

obstructive *adj* hindering, delaying, blocking, stalling, unhelpful, awkward,

difficult, restrictive, inhibiting.
≠ co-operative, helpful.

obtain *v* **1** ACQUIRE, get, gain, come by, attain, procure, secure, earn, achieve. **2** PREVAIL, exist, hold, be in force, be the case, stand, reign, rule, be prevalent.

obtrusive *adj* **1** PROMINENT, protruding, noticeable, obvious, blatant, forward. **2** INTRUSIVE, interfering, prying, meddling, nosey (*infml*), pushy (*infml*).
≠ **1** unobtrusive.

obtuse *adj* slow, stupid, thick (*infml*), dull, dense, crass, dumb (*infml*), stolid, dull-witted, thick-skinned.
≠ bright, sharp.

obvious *adj* evident, self-evident, manifest, patent, clear, plain, distinct, transparent, undeniable, unmistakable, conspicuous, glaring, apparent, open, unconcealed, visible, noticeable, perceptible, pronounced, recognizable, self-explanatory, straightforward, prominent.
≠ unclear, indistinct, obscure.

obviously *adv* plainly, clearly, evidently, manifestly, undeniably, unmistakably, without doubt, certainly, distinctly, of course.

occasion *n* **1** EVENT, occurrence, incident, time, instance, chance, case, opportunity. **2** REASON, cause, excuse, justification, ground(s). **3** CELEBRATION, function, affair, party.

occasional *adj* periodic, intermittent, irregular, sporadic, infrequent, uncommon, incidental, odd, rare, casual.
≠ frequent, regular, constant.

occasionally *adv* sometimes, on occasion, from time to time, at times, at intervals, now and then, now and again, irregularly, periodically, every so often, once in a while, off and on, infrequently.
≠ frequently, often, always.

occult *adj* mystical, magical, esoteric, mysterious, concealed, arcane, recondite, obscure, secret, hidden, veiled.

Terms associated with the occult include: amulet, astral projection, astrology, astrologer, bewitch, black cat, black magic, black mass, cabbala, charm, chiromancer, chiromancy, clairvoyance, clairvoyant, conjure, coven, crystal ball, curse, déjà vu, divination, diviner, divining-rod, dream, ectoplasm, evil eye, evil spirit, exorcism, exorcist, extrasensory perception (ESP), familiar, fetish, fortune-teller, garlic, Hallowe'en, hallucination, hoodoo, horoscope, horseshoe, hydromancer, hydromancy, illusion, incantation, jinx, juju, magic, magician, mascot, medium, necromancer, necromancy, obi, omen, oneiromancer, oneiromancy, Ouija board®, palmist, palmistry, paranormal, pentagram, planchette, poltergeist, possession, prediction, premonition, psychic, rabbit's foot, relic, rune, satanic, Satanism, Satanist, séance, second sight, shaman, shamrock, sixth sense, sorcerer, sorcery, spell, spirit, spiritualism, spiritualist, supernatural, superstition, talisman, tarot card, tarot reading, telepathist, telepathy, totem, trance, vision, voodoo, Walpurgis Night, warlock, white magic, witch, witchcraft, witch doctor, witch's broomstick, witch's sabbath.

occupant *n* occupier, holder, inhabitant, resident, householder, tenant, user, lessee, squatter, inmate.

occupation *n* **1** JOB, profession, work, vocation, employment, trade, post, calling, business, line, pursuit, craft, walk of life, activity. **2** INVASION, seizure, conquest, control, takeover. **3** OCCUPANCY, possession, holding, tenancy, tenure, residence, habitation, use.

occupy *v* **1** INHABIT, live in, possess, reside in, stay in, take possession of, own. **2** ABSORB, take up, engross, engage, hold, involve, preoccupy, amuse, busy, interest. **3** INVADE, seize, capture, overrun, take over. **4** FILL, take up, use.

occur *v* happen, come about, take place, transpire, chance, come to pass, materialize, befall, develop, crop up, arise, appear, turn up, obtain, result, exist, be present, be found.

occurrence *n* **1** INCIDENT, event, happening, affair, circumstance, episode, instance, case, development, action. **2** INCIDENCE, existence, appearance, manifestation.

odd *adj* **1** UNUSUAL, strange, uncommon, peculiar, abnormal, exceptional, curious, atypical, different, queer, bizarre, eccentric, remarkable, unconventional, weird, irregular, extraordinary, outlandish, rare. **2** OCCASIONAL, incidental, irregular, random, casual. **3** UNMATCHED, unpaired, single, spare, surplus, left-over, remaining, sundry, various, miscellaneous.
≠ **1** normal, usual. **2** regular.

oddity *n* **1** ABNORMALITY, peculiarity, rarity, eccentricity, idiosyncrasy, phenomenon, quirk. **2** CURIOSITY, character, freak, misfit.

oddment *n* bit, scrap, left-over, fragment, offcut, end, remnant, shred, snippet, patch.

odds *n* **1** LIKELIHOOD, probability, chances. **2** ADVANTAGE, edge, lead, superiority.

odious *adj* offensive, loathsome, unpleasant, obnoxious, disgusting, hateful, repulsive, revolting, repugnant, foul, execrable, detestable, abhorrent, horrible, horrid, abominable.
≠ pleasant.

odour *n* smell, scent, fragrance, aroma, perfume, redolence, stench, stink (*infml*).

off *adj* **1** ROTTEN, bad, sour, turned, rancid, mouldy, decomposed. **2** CANCELLED, postponed. **3** AWAY, absent, gone. **4** SUBSTANDARD, below par, disappointing, unsatisfactory, slack.
adv away, elsewhere, out, at a distance, apart, aside.

off-colour *adj* indisposed, off form, under the weather, unwell, sick, out of sorts, ill, poorly.

offence *n* **1** MISDEMEANOUR, transgression, violation, wrong, wrong-doing, infringement, crime, misdeed, sin, trespass. **2** AFFRONT, insult, injury. **3** RESENTMENT, indignation, pique, umbrage, outrage, hurt, hard feelings.

offend *v* **1** HURT, insult, injure, affront, wrong, wound, displease, snub, upset, annoy, outrage. **2** DISGUST, repel, sicken. **3** TRANSGRESS, sin, violate, err.
≠ **1** please.

offender *n* transgressor, wrong-doer, culprit, criminal, miscreant, guilty party, law-breaker, delinquent.

offensive *adj* **1** DISAGREEABLE, unpleasant, objectionable, displeasing, disgusting, odious, obnoxious, repellent, repugnant, revolting, loathsome, vile, nauseating, nasty, detestable, abominable. **2** INSOLENT, abusive, rude, insulting, impertinent.
≠ **1** pleasant. **2** polite.
n attack, assault, onslaught, invasion, raid, sortie.

offer *v* **1** PRESENT, make available, advance, extend, put forward, submit, suggest, hold out, provide, sell. **2** PROFFER, propose, bid, tender. **3** VOLUNTEER, come forward, show willing (*infml*).
n proposal, bid, submission, tender, suggestion, proposition, overture, approach, attempt, presentation.

offering *n* present, gift, donation, contribution, subscription.

offhand *adj* casual, unconcerned, uninterested, take-it-or-leave-it (*infml*), brusque, abrupt, perfunctory, informal, cavalier, careless.
adv impromptu, off the cuff, extempore (*fml*), off the top of one's head, immediately.
≠ calculated, planned.

office *n* **1** RESPONSIBILITY, duty, obligation, charge, commission, occupation, situation, post, employment, function, appointment, business, role, service. **2** WORKPLACE, workroom, bureau.

office equipment and furniture

Office equipment includes: acoustic hood, adhesive binder, answering machine, calculator, cash box, collating machine, comb binder, computer, copy holder, data cartridge, date-stamp, desk organizer, desk-top display calculator, Dictaphone®, dictation machine, disk storage-system, diskette mailer, duplicator, dust cover, electric typewriter, electronic organizer, electronic typewriter, facsimile machine (or fax), flip-chart easel, guillotine, hole puncher, information board, inkpad, intercom, keyboard, laminator, laptop computer, letter-folding machine, letter opener, letter scales, letter tray, message board, microcassette, microcassette recorder, microfiche reader, monitor, monitor arm, mouse, mouse mat, notice-board, overhead projector (OHP), paper-folding machine, paper punch, parcel scales, photocopier, plan file, planner, planning board, printer, printwheel, projection screen, reference book, rotary filing-system, scanner, screen, screen filter, share certificate book, shredder, slide projector, stapler, staple-remover, switchboard, tacker, telephone, telephone directory, telephone index, telex machine, terminal trolley, textphone, thermal binder, time clock, trimmer, typewriter, visitors' book, visual display unit (VDU), wages book, waste-paper bin, wire bindings, wire-binding machine, word-processor. *Office furniture includes*: boardroom table, computer desk, conference table, desk, desk lamp, display cabinet, draughtsman's chair, drawing-board, executive chair, executive desk, filing cabinet, filing cupboard, filing trolley, fire cupboard, fire-extinguisher, fire safe, lectern, partition, plan chest, printer stand, reception chair, safe, secretarial desk, stationery cupboard, stepstool, storage unit, swivel chair, typist's chair, work station, work table. *see also* **computer; stationery**.

officer *n* official, office-holder, public servant, functionary, dignitary, bureaucrat, administrator, representative, executive, agent, appointee.

official *adj* authorized, authoritative, legitimate, formal, licensed, accredited, certified, approved, authenticated, authentic, bona fide, proper.
≠ unofficial.
n office-bearer, officer, functionary, bureaucrat, executive, representative, agent.

Officials include: agent, ambassador, bailiff, bureaucrat, captain, chairman (or chairwoman or chairperson), chancellor, chief, clerk, commander, commissar, commissioner, congressman, congresswoman, consul, coroner, councillor, delegate, diplomat, director, elder, envoy, equerry, Eurocrat, executive, Euro-MP, gauleiter, governor, hakim, inspector, justice of the peace (JP), magistrate, manager, mandarin, marshal, mayor, mayoress, member of parliament (MP), minister, monitor, notary, ombudsman, overseer, prefect, president, principal, proctor, proprietor, public prosecutor, registrar, senator (*US*), sheriff, steward, superintendent, supervisor, usher.

officiate *v* preside, superintend, conduct, chair, manage, oversee, run.

officious *adj* obtrusive, dictatorial, intrusive, bossy (*infml*), interfering, meddlesome, over-zealous, self-important, pushy (*infml*), forward, bustling, importunate (*fml*).

offload *v* unburden, unload, jettison, dump, drop, deposit, get rid of, discharge.

off-putting *adj* intimidating, daunting, disconcerting, discouraging, disheartening, formidable, unnerving, unsettling, demoralizing, disturbing.

offset *v* counterbalance, compensate for, cancel out, counteract, make up for, balance out, neutralize.

offshoot *n* branch, outgrowth, limb, arm, development, spin-off, by-product, appendage.

offspring *n* child, children, young, issue, progeny (*fml*), brood, heirs, successors, descendants.
≠ parent(s).

often *adv* frequently, repeatedly, regularly, generally, again and again, time after time, time and again, much.
≠ rarely, seldom, never.

ogre *n* giant, monster, fiend, bogeyman, demon, devil, troll.

oil *v* grease, lubricate, anoint.

oily *adj* **1** GREASY, fatty. **2** UNCTUOUS, smooth, obsequious, ingratiating, smarmy (*infml*), glib, flattering.

ointment *n* salve, balm, cream, lotion, liniment, embrocation.

OK (*infml*) *adj* acceptable, all right, fine, permitted, in order, fair, satisfactory, reasonable, tolerable, passable, not bad, good, adequate, convenient, correct, accurate.
n authorization, approval, endorsement, go-ahead, permission, green light, consent, agreement.
v approve, authorize, pass, give the go-ahead to, give the green light to (*infml*), rubber-stamp, agree to.
interj all right, fine, very well, agreed, right, yes.

old *adj* **1** AGED, elderly, advanced in years, grey, senile. **2** ANCIENT, original, primitive, antiquated, mature. **3** LONG-STANDING, long-established, time-honoured, traditional. **4** OBSOLETE, old-fashioned, out of date, worn-out, decayed, decrepit. **5** FORMER, previous, earlier, one-time, ex-.
≠ **1** young. **2** new. **4** modern. **5** current.

old-fashioned *adj* outmoded, out of date, outdated, dated, unfashionable, obsolete, behind the times, antiquated, archaic, passé, obsolescent.
≠ modern, up-to-date.

omen *n* portent, sign, warning, premonition, foreboding, augury, indication.

ominous *adj* portentous, inauspicious, foreboding, menacing, sinister, fateful, unpromising, threatening.
≠ auspicious, favourable.

omission *n* exclusion, gap, oversight, failure, lack, neglect, default, avoidance.

omit *v* leave out, exclude, miss out, pass over, overlook, drop, skip, eliminate, forget, neglect, leave undone, fail, disregard, edit out.
≠ include.

once *adv* formerly, previously, in the past, at one time, long ago, in times past, once upon a time, in the old days.
at once 1 IMMEDIATELY, instantly, directly, right away, straightaway, without delay, now, promptly, forthwith. **2** SIMULTANEOUSLY, together, at the same time.

oncoming *adj* approaching, advancing, upcoming, looming, onrushing, gathering.

one *adj* **1** SINGLE, solitary, lone, individual, only. **2** UNITED, harmonious, like-minded, whole, entire, complete, equal, identical, alike.

onerous (*fml*) *adj* oppressive, burdensome, demanding, laborious, hard, taxing, difficult, troublesome, exacting, exhausting, heavy, weighty.
≠ easy, light.

one-sided *adj* **1** UNBALANCED, unequal, lopsided. **2** UNFAIR, unjust, prejudiced, biased, partial, partisan. **3** UNILATERAL, independent.
≠ **1** balanced. **2** impartial. **3** bilateral, multilateral.

ongoing *adj* **1** CONTINUING, continuous, unbroken, uninterrupted, constant. **2** DEVELOPING, evolving, progressing, growing, in progress, unfinished, unfolding.

onlooker *n* bystander, observer, spectator, looker-on, eye-witness, witness, watcher, viewer.

only *adv* just, at most, merely, simply, purely, barely, exclusively, solely.
adj sole, single, solitary, lone, unique, exclusive, individual.

onset *n* **1** BEGINNING, start, commencement, inception, outset, outbreak. **2** ASSAULT, attack, onslaught, onrush.
≠ **1** end, finish.

onslaught *n* attack, assault, offensive, charge, bombardment, blitz.

onus *n* burden, responsibility, load, obligation, duty, liability, task.

onward(s) *adv* forward, on, ahead, in front, beyond, forth.
≠ backward(s).

ooze *v* seep, exude, leak, percolate, escape, dribble, drip, drop, discharge, bleed, secrete, emit, overflow with, filter, drain.

opaque *adj* **1** CLOUDY, clouded, murky, dull, dim, hazy, muddied, muddy, turbid. **2** OBSCURE, unclear, impenetrable, incomprehensible, unintelligible, enigmatic, difficult.
≠ **1** transparent. **2** clear, obvious.

open *adj* **1** UNCLOSED, ajar, gaping, uncovered, unfastened, unlocked, unsealed, yawning, lidless. **2** UNRESTRICTED, free, unobstructed, clear, accessible, exposed, unprotected, unsheltered, vacant, wide, available. **3** OVERT, obvious, plain, evident, manifest, noticeable, flagrant, conspicuous. **4** UNDECIDED, unresolved, unsettled, debatable, problematic, moot. **5** FRANK, candid, honest, guileless, natural, ingenuous, unreserved.
≠ **1** shut. **2** restricted. **3** hidden. **4** decided. **5** reserved.
v **1** UNFASTEN, undo, unlock, uncover, unseal, unblock, uncork, clear, expose. **2** EXPLAIN, divulge, disclose, lay bare. **3** EXTEND, spread (out), unfold, separate, split. **4** BEGIN, start, commence, inaugurate, initiate, set in motion, launch.
≠ **1** close, shut. **2** hide. **4** end, finish.

open-air *adj* outdoor, alfresco.
≠ indoor.

opening *n* **1** APERTURE, breach, gap, orifice, break, chink, crack, fissure, cleft, chasm, hole, split, vent, rupture. **2** START, onset, beginning, inauguration, inception, birth, dawn, launch. **3** OPPORTUNITY, chance, occasion, break (*infml*), place, vacancy.
≠ **2** close, end.
adj beginning, commencing, starting, first, inaugural, introductory, initial, early, primary.
≠ closing.

openly *adv* overtly, frankly, candidly, blatantly, flagrantly, plainly, unashamedly, unreservedly, glaringly, in public, in full view, shamelessly.
≠ secretly, slyly.

operate *v* **1** *it operates on batteries*: function, act, perform, run, work, go. **2** *she can operate that machine*: control, handle, manage, use, utilize, manoeuvre.

operation *n* **1** FUNCTIONING, action, running, motion, movement, performance, working. **2** INFLUENCE, manipulation, handling, management, use, utilization. **3** UNDERTAKING, enterprise, affair, procedure, proceeding, process, business, deal, transaction, effort. **4** CAMPAIGN, action, task, manoeuvre, exercise.

operational *adj* working, in working order, usable, functional, going, viable, workable, ready, prepared, in service.
≠ out of order.

operative *adj* **1** OPERATIONAL, in operation, in force, functioning, active, effective, efficient, in action, workable, viable, serviceable, functional. **2** KEY, crucial, important, relevant, significant.
≠ **1** inoperative, out of service.

opinion *n* belief, judgement, view, point of view, idea, perception, stance, theory, impression, feeling, sentiment, estimation, assessment, conception, mind, notion, way of thinking, persuasion, attitute.

opinionated *adj* dogmatic, doctrinaire, dictatorial, arrogant, inflexible, obstinate, stubborn, uncompromising, single-minded, prejudiced, biased, bigoted.
≠ open-minded.

opponent *n* adversary, enemy, antagonist, foe, competitor, contestant, challenger, opposer, opposition, rival, objector, dissident.
≠ ally.

opportunity *n* chance, opening, break (*infml*), occasion, possibility, hour, moment.

oppose *v* **1** RESIST, withstand, counter, attack, combat, contest, stand up to, take a stand against, take issue with,

confront, defy, face, fight, fly in the face of, hinder, obstruct, bar, check, prevent, thwart. **2** COMPARE, contrast, match, offset, counterbalance, play off.
≠ **1** defend, support.

opposed *adj* in opposition, against, hostile, conflicting, opposing, opposite, antagonistic, clashing, contrary, incompatible, anti.
≠ in favour.

opposite *adj* **1** FACING, fronting, corresponding. **2** OPPOSED, antagonistic, conflicting, contrary, hostile, adverse, contradictory, antithetical, irreconcilable, unlike, reverse, inconsistent, different, contrasted, differing.
≠ **2** same.
n reverse, converse, contrary, antithesis, contradiction, inverse.
≠ same.

opposition *n* **1** ANTAGONISM, hostility, resistance, obstructiveness, unfriendliness, disapproval. **2** OPPONENT, antagonist, rival, foe, other side.
≠ **1** co-operation, support. **2** ally, supporter.

oppress *v* **1** BURDEN, afflict, lie heavy on, harass, depress, sadden, torment, vex. **2** SUBJUGATE, suppress, subdue, overpower, overwhelm, crush, trample, tyrannize, persecute, maltreat, abuse.

oppression *n* tyranny, subjugation, subjection, repression, despotism, suppression, injustice, cruelty, brutality, abuse, persecution, maltreatment, harshness, hardship.

oppressive *adj* **1** AIRLESS, stuffy, close, stifling, suffocating, sultry, muggy, heavy. **2** TYRANNICAL, despotic, overbearing, overwhelming, repressive, harsh, unjust, inhuman, cruel, brutal, burdensome, onerous, intolerable.
≠ **1** airy. **2** just, gentle.

oppressor *n* tyrant, bully, taskmaster, slave-driver, despot, dictator, persecutor, tormentor, intimidator, autocrat.

optical instruments

Optical instruments and devices include: astronomical telescope, binoculars, camera, compound microscope, endoscope, field-glasses, film projector, laser, magnifying glass, opera-glass, periscope, photomicroscope, reflecting telescope, refracting telescope, sextant, simple microscope, slide projector, spyglass, stereocamera, telescope, telescopic sight, theodolite. *see also* **spectacles**.

optimistic *adj* confident, assured, sanguine, hopeful, positive, cheerful, buoyant, bright, idealistic, expectant.
≠ pessimistic.

optimum *adj* best, ideal, perfect, optimal, superlative, top, choice.
≠ worst.

option *n* choice, alternative, preference, possibility, selection.

optional *adj* voluntary, discretionary, elective, free, unforced.
≠ compulsory.

oral *adj* verbal, spoken, unwritten, vocal.
≠ written.

orbit *n* **1** CIRCUIT, cycle, circle, course, path, trajectory, track, revolution, rotation. **2** RANGE, scope, domain, influence, sphere of influence, compass.
v revolve, circle, encircle, circumnavigate.

ordeal *n* trial, test, tribulation(s), affliction, trouble(s), suffering, anguish, agony, pain, persecution, torture, nightmare.

order *n* **1** COMMAND, directive, decree, injunction, instruction, direction, edict, ordinance, mandate, regulation, rule, precept, law. **2** REQUISITION, request, booking, commission, reservation, application, demand. **3** ARRANGEMENT, organization, grouping, disposition, sequence, categorization, classification, method, pattern, plan, system, array, layout, line-up, structure. **4** PEACE, quiet, calm, tranquillity, harmony, law and order, discipline. **5** ASSOCIATION, society, community, fraternity,

brotherhood, sisterhood, lodge, guild, company, organization, denomination, sect, union. **6** CLASS, kind, sort, type, rank, species, hierarchy, family.
≠ **3** confusion, disorder. **4** anarchy.
v **1** COMMAND, instruct, direct, bid, decree, require, authorize. **2** REQUEST, reserve, book, apply for, requisition. **3** ARRANGE, organize, dispose, classify, group, marshal, sort out, lay out, manage, control, catalogue.
out of order 1 BROKEN, broken down, not working, inoperative. **2** DISORDERED, disorganized, out of sequence. **3** UNSEEMLY, improper, uncalled-for, incorrect, wrong.

orderly *adj* **1** ORDERED, systematic, neat, tidy, regular, methodical, in order, well-organized, well-regulated. **2** WELL-BEHAVED, controlled, disciplined, law-abiding.
≠ **1** chaotic. **2** disorderly.

ordinary *adj* common, commonplace, regular, routine, standard, average, everyday, run-of-the-mill, usual, unexceptional, unremarkable, typical, normal, customary, common-or-garden, plain, familiar, habitual, simple, conventional, modest, mediocre, indifferent, pedestrian, prosaic, undistinguished.
≠ extraordinary, unusual.

organ *n* **1** DEVICE, instrument, implement, tool, element, process, structure, unit, member. **2** MEDIUM, agency, forum, vehicle, voice, mouthpiece, publication, newspaper, periodical, journal.

organic *adj* natural, biological, living, animate.

organization *n* **1** ASSOCIATION, institution, society, company, firm, corporation, federation, group, league, club, confederation, consortium. **2** ARRANGEMENT, system, classification, methodology, order, formation, grouping, method, plan, structure, pattern, composition, configuration, design.

organize *v* **1** STRUCTURE, co-ordinate, arrange, order, group, marshal, classify, systematize, tabulate, catalogue. **2** ESTABLISH, found, set up, develop, form, frame, construct, shape, run.
≠ **1** disorganize.

orgy *n* debauch, carousal, revelry, bout, bacchanalia, indulgence, excess, spree.

orientation *n* **1** SITUATION, bearings, location, direction, position, alignment, placement, attitude. **2** INITIATION, training, acclimatization, familiarization, adaptation, adjustment, settling in.

origin *n* **1** SOURCE, spring, fount, foundation, base, cause, derivation, provenance, roots, well-spring. **2** BEGINNING, commencement, start, inauguration, launch, dawning, creation, emergence. **3** ANCESTRY, descent, extraction, heritage, family, lineage, parentage, pedigree, birth, paternity, stock.
≠ **2** end, termination.

original *adj* **1** FIRST, early, earliest, initial, primary, archetypal, rudimentary, embryonic, starting, opening, commencing, first-hand. **2** NOVEL, innovative, new, creative, fresh, imaginative, inventive, unconventional, unusual, unique.
≠ **1** latest. **2** hackneyed, unoriginal.
n prototype, master, paradigm, model, pattern, archetype, standard, type.

originate *v* **1** RISE, arise, spring, stem, issue, flow, proceed, derive, come, evolve, emerge, be born. **2** CREATE, invent, inaugurate, introduce, give birth to, develop, discover, establish, begin, commence, start, set up, launch, pioneer, conceive, form, produce, generate.
≠ **1** end, terminate.

ornament *n* decoration, adornment, embellishment, garnish, trimming, accessory, frill, trinket, bauble, jewel.
v decorate, adorn, embellish, garnish, trim, beautify, brighten, dress up, deck, gild.

ornamental *adj* decorative, embellishing, adorning, attractive, showy.

ornate *adj* elaborate, ornamented,

fancy, decorated, baroque, rococo, florid, flowery, fussy, busy, sumptuous.
≠ plain.

orthodox *adj* conformist, conventional, accepted, official, traditional, usual, well-established, established, received, customary, conservative, recognized, authoritative.
≠ nonconformist, unorthodox.

ostensible *adj* alleged, apparent, presumed, seeming, supposed, so-called, professed, outward, pretended, superficial.
≠ real.

ostentatious *adj* showy, flashy, pretentious, vulgar, loud, garish, gaudy, flamboyant, conspicuous, extravagant.
≠ restrained.

ostracize *v* exclude, banish, exile, expel, excommunicate, reject, segregate, send to Coventry, shun, snub, boycott, avoid, cold-shoulder (*infml*), cut.
≠ accept, welcome.

other *adj* **1** DIFFERENT, dissimilar, unlike, separate, distinct, contrasting. **2** MORE, further, extra, additional, supplementary, spare, alternative.

oust *v* expel, eject, depose, displace, turn out, throw out, overthrow, evict, drive out, unseat, dispossess, disinherit, replace, topple.
≠ install, settle.

out *adj* **1** AWAY, absent, elsewhere, not at home, gone, outside, abroad. **2** REVEALED, exposed, disclosed, public, evident, manifest. **3** FORBIDDEN, unacceptable, impossible, disallowed, excluded. **4** OUT OF DATE, unfashionable, old-fashioned, dated, passé, antiquated. **5** EXTINGUISHED, finished, expired, dead, used up.
≠ **1** in. **2** concealed. **3** allowed. **4** up to date.

outbreak *n* eruption, outburst, explosion, flare-up, upsurge, flash, rash, burst, epidemic.

outburst *n* outbreak, eruption, explosion, flare-up, outpouring, burst, fit, gush, surge, storm, spasm, seizure, gale, attack, fit of temper.

outcast *n* castaway, exile, pariah, outsider, untouchable, refugee, reject, persona non grata.

outcome *n* result, consequence, upshot, conclusion, effect, end result.

outcry *n* protest, complaint, protestation, objection, dissent, indignation, uproar, cry, exclamation, clamour, row, commotion, noise, hue and cry, hullaballoo (*infml*), outburst.

outdated *adj* out of date, old-fashioned, dated, unfashionable, outmoded, behind the times, obsolete, obsolescent, antiquated, archaic.
≠ fashionable, modern.

outdo *v* surpass, exceed, beat, excel, outstrip, outshine, get the better of, overcome, outclass, outdistance.

outdoor *adj* out-of-door(s), outside, open-air.
≠ indoor.

outer *adj* **1** EXTERNAL, exterior, outside, outward, surface, superficial, peripheral. **2** OUTLYING, distant, remote, further.
≠ **1** internal. **2** inner.

outfit *n* **1** CLOTHES, costume, ensemble, get-up (*infml*), togs (*infml*), garb. **2** EQUIPMENT, gear (*infml*), kit, rig, trappings, paraphernalia. **3** (*infml*) ORGANIZATION, firm, business, corporation, company, group, team, unit, set, set-up, crew, gang, squad.

outgoing *adj* **1** SOCIABLE, friendly, unreserved, amiable, warm, approachable, expansive, open, extrovert, cordial, easy-going, communicative, demonstrative, sympathetic. **2** DEPARTING, retiring, former, last, past, ex-.
≠ **1** reserved. **2** incoming.

outing *n* excursion, expedition, jaunt, pleasure trip, trip, spin, picnic.

outlandish *adj* unconventional, unfamiliar, bizarre, strange, odd, weird, eccentric, alien, exotic, barbarous, foreign, extraordinary.
≠ familiar, ordinary.

outlaw *n* bandit, brigand, robber, desperado, highwayman, criminal, marauder, pirate, fugitive.

v ban, disallow, forbid, prohibit, exclude, embargo, bar, debar, banish, condemn.
≠ allow, legalize.

outlay *n* expenditure, expenses, outgoings, disbursement (*fml*), cost, spending.
≠ income.

outlet *n* **1** EXIT, way out, vent, egress, escape, opening, release, safety valve, channel. **2** RETAILER, shop, store, market.
≠ **1** entry, inlet.

outline *n* **1** SUMMARY, synopsis, précis, bare facts, sketch, thumbnail sketch, abstract. **2** PROFILE, form, contour, silhouette, shape.
v sketch, summarize, draft, trace, rough out.

outlook *n* **1** VIEW, viewpoint, point of view, attitude, perspective, frame of mind, angle, slant, standpoint, opinion. **2** EXPECTATIONS, future, forecast, prospect, prognosis.

outlying *adj* distant, remote, far-off, far-away, far-flung, outer, provincial.
≠ inner.

out-of-the-way *adj* remote, isolated, far-flung, far-off, far-away, distant, inaccessible, little-known, obscure, unfrequented.

output *n* production, productivity, product, yield, manufacture, achievement.

outrage *n* **1** ANGER, fury, rage, indignation, shock, affront, horror. **2** ATROCITY, offence, injury, enormity, barbarism, crime, violation, evil, scandal.
v anger, infuriate, affront, incense, enrage, madden, disgust, injure, offend, shock, scandalize.

outrageous *adj* **1** ATROCIOUS, abominable, shocking, scandalous, offensive, disgraceful, monstrous, heinous, unspeakable, horrible. **2** EXCESSIVE, exorbitant, immoderate, unreasonable, extortionate, inordinate, preposterous.
≠ **2** acceptable, reasonable.

outright *adj* total, utter, absolute, complete, downright, out-and-out, unqualified, unconditional, perfect, pure, thorough, direct, definite, categorical, straightforward.
≠ ambiguous, indefinite.
adv **1** TOTALLY, absolutely, completely, utterly, thoroughly, openly, without restraint, straightforwardly, positively, directly, explicitly. **2** *killed outright*: instantaneously, at once, there and then, instantly, immediately.

outset *n* start, beginning, opening, inception, commencement, inauguration, kick-off (*infml*).
≠ end, conclusion.

outside *adj* **1** EXTERNAL, exterior, outer, surface, superficial, outward, extraneous, outdoor, outermost, extreme. **2** *an outside chance*: remote, marginal, distant, faint, slight, slim, negligible.
≠ **1** inside.
n exterior, façade, front, surface, face, appearance, cover.
≠ inside.

outsider *n* stranger, intruder, alien, non-member, non-resident, foreigner, newcomer, visitor, intruder, interloper, misfit, odd man out.

outskirts *n* suburbs, vicinity, periphery, fringes, borders, boundary, edge, margin.
≠ centre.

outspoken *adj* candid, frank, forthright, blunt, unreserved, plain-spoken, direct, explicit.
≠ diplomatic, reserved.

outstanding *adj* **1** EXCELLENT, distinguished, eminent, pre-eminent, celebrated, exceptional, superior, remarkable, prominent, superb, great, notable, impressive, striking, superlative, important, noteworthy, memorable, special, extraordinary. **2** OWING, unpaid, due, unsettled, unresolved, uncollected, pending, payable, remaining, ongoing, leftover.
≠ **1** ordinary, unexceptional. **2** paid, settled.

outstrip *v* surpass, exceed, better, outdo, beat, top, transcend, outshine, pass, gain on, leave behind, leave standing, outrun, outdistance, overtake, eclipse.

outward *adj* external, exterior, outer, outside, surface, superficial, visible, apparent, observable, evident, supposed, professed, public, obvious, ostensible.
≠ inner, private.

outwardly *adv* apparently, externally, to all appearances, visibly, superficially, supposedly, seemingly, on the surface, at first sight.

outweigh *v* override, prevail over, overcome, take precedence over, cancel out, make up for, compensate for, predominate.

outwit *v* outsmart, outthink, get the better of, trick, better, beat, dupe, cheat, deceive, defraud, swindle.

outworn *adj* outdated, out of date, outmoded, stale, discredited, defunct, old-fashioned, hackneyed, rejected, obsolete, disused, exhausted.
≠ fresh, new.

oval *adj* egg-shaped, elliptical, ovoid, ovate.

ovation *n* applause, acclaim, acclamation, praises, plaudits (*fml*), tribute, clapping, cheering, bravos.
≠ abuse, catcalls.

over *adj* finished, ended, done with, concluded, past, gone, completed, closed, in the past, settled, up, forgotten, accomplished.
adv **1** ABOVE, beyond, overhead, on high. **2** EXTRA, remaining, surplus, superfluous, left, unclaimed, unused, unwanted, in excess, in addition.
prep **1** ABOVE, on, on top of, upon, in charge of, in command of.
2 EXCEEDING, more than, in excess of.

overact *v* overplay, exaggerate, overdo, ham (*infml*).
≠ underact, underplay.

overall *adj* total, all-inclusive, all-embracing, comprehensive, inclusive, general, universal, global, broad, blanket, complete, all-over.
≠ narrow, specific.
adv in general, on the whole, by and large, broadly, generally speaking.

overbearing *adj* imperious, domineering, arrogant, dictatorial, tyrannical, high-handed, haughty, bossy (*infml*), cavalier, autocratic, oppressive.
≠ meek, unassertive.

overcast *adj* cloudy, grey, dull, dark, sombre, sunless, hazy, lowering.
≠ bright, clear.

overcharge *v* surcharge, short-change, cheat, extort, rip off (*infml*), sting (*infml*), do (*infml*), diddle (*infml*).
≠ undercharge.

overcome *v* conquer, defeat, beat, surmount, triumph over, vanquish, rise above, master, overpower, overwhelm, overthrow, subdue.

overcrowded *adj* congested, packed (out), jam-packed, crammed full, chock-full, overpopulated, overloaded, swarming.
≠ deserted, empty.

overdo *v* exaggerate, go too far, carry to excess, go overboard (*infml*), lay it on thick (*infml*), overindulge, overstate, overact, overplay, overwork.

overdue *adj* late, behindhand, behind schedule, delayed, owing, unpunctual, slow.
≠ early.

overeat *v* gorge, binge, overindulge, guzzle, stuff oneself, make a pig of oneself, pig out (*infml*), gormandize.
≠ abstain, starve.

overflow *v* spill, overrun, run over, pour over, well over, brim over, bubble over, surge, flood, inundate, deluge, shower, submerge, soak, swamp, teem.
n overspill, spill, inundation, flood, overabundance, surplus.

overhang *v* jut, project, bulge, protrude, stick out, extend.

overhaul *v* **1** RENOVATE, repair, service, recondition, mend, examine, inspect, check, survey, re-examine, fix.
2 OVERTAKE, pull ahead of, outpace, outstrip, gain on, pass.
n reconditioning, repair, renovation, check, service, examination, inspection, going-over (*infml*).

overhead *adv* above, up above, on high, upward.
≠ below, underfoot.
adj elevated, aerial, overhanging, raised.

overjoyed *adj* delighted, elated, euphoric, ecstatic, in raptures, enraptured, thrilled, jubilant, over the moon (*infml*).
≠ sad, disappointed.

overload *v* burden, oppress, strain, tax, weigh down, overcharge, encumber.

overlook *v* **1** FRONT ON TO, face, look on to, look over, command a view of. **2** MISS, disregard, ignore, omit, neglect, pass over, let pass, let ride, slight. **3** EXCUSE, forgive, pardon, condone, wink at, turn a blind eye to.
≠ **2** notice. **3** penalize.

overpower *v* overcome, conquer, overwhelm, vanquish, defeat, beat, subdue, overthrow, quell, master, crush, immobilize, floor.

overpowering *adj* overwhelming, powerful, strong, forceful, irresistible, uncontrollable, compelling, extreme, oppressive, suffocating, unbearable, nauseating, sickening.

overrate *v* overestimate, overvalue, overpraise, magnify, blow up, make too much of.
≠ underrate.

overrule *v* overturn, override, countermand, revoke, reject, rescind, reverse, invalidate, cancel, vote down.

overrun *v* **1** INVADE, occupy, infest, overwhelm, inundate, run riot, spread over, swamp, swarm over, surge over, ravage, overgrow. **2** EXCEED, overshoot, overstep, overreach.

overseer *n* supervisor, boss (*infml*), chief, foreman, forewoman, manager, superintendent.

overshadow *v* **1** OBSCURE, cloud, darken, dim, spoil, veil. **2** OUTSHINE, eclipse, excel, surpass, dominate, dwarf, put in the shade, rise above, tower above.

oversight *n* **1** LAPSE, omission, fault, error, slip-up, mistake, blunder, carelessness, neglect. **2** SUPERVISION, responsibility, care, charge, control, custody, keeping, administration, management, direction.

overt *adj* open, manifest, plain, evident, observable, obvious, apparent, public, professed, unconcealed.
≠ covert, secret.

overtake *v* **1** PASS, catch up with, outdistance, outstrip, draw level with, pull ahead of, overhaul. **2** COME UPON, befall, happen, strike, engulf.

overthrow *v* depose, oust, bring down, topple, unseat, displace, dethrone, conquer, vanquish, beat, defeat, crush, overcome, overpower, overturn, overwhelm, subdue, master, abolish, upset.
≠ install, protect, reinstate, restore.
n ousting, unseating, defeat, deposition, dethronement, fall, rout, undoing, suppression, downfall, end, humiliation, destruction, ruin.

overtone *n* suggestion, intimation, nuance, hint, undercurrent, insinuation, connotation, association, feeling, implication, sense, flavour.

overture *n* **1** APPROACH, advance, offer, invitation, proposal, proposition, suggestion, signal, move, motion. **2** PRELUDE, opening, introduction, opening move, (opening) gambit.

overturn *v* **1** CAPSIZE, upset, upturn, tip over, topple, overbalance, keel over, knock over, spill. **2** OVERTHROW, repeal, rescind, reverse, annul, abolish, destroy, quash, set aside.

overwhelm *v* **1** OVERCOME, overpower, destroy, defeat, crush, rout, devastate. **2** OVERRUN, inundate, snow under, submerge, swamp, engulf. **3** CONFUSE, bowl over, stagger, floor.

overwork *v* overstrain, overload, exploit, exhaust, overuse, overtax, strain, wear out, oppress, burden, weary.

overwrought *adj* tense, agitated, keyed up, on edge, worked up, wound up, frantic, overcharged, overexcited, excited, beside oneself, uptight (*infml*).
≠ calm.

owing *adj* unpaid, due, owed, in arrears, outstanding, payable, unsettled, overdue.
owing to because of, as a result of, on account of, thanks to.

own *adj* personal, individual, private, particular, idiosyncratic.
v possess, have, hold, retain, keep, enjoy.
own up admit, confess, come clean (*infml*), tell the truth, acknowledge.

owner *n* possessor, holder, landlord, landlady, proprietor, proprietress, master, mistress, freeholder.

P

pace *n* step, stride, walk, gait, tread, movement, motion, progress, rate, speed, velocity, celerity, quickness, rapidity, tempo, measure.
v step, stride, walk, march, tramp, pound, patrol, mark out, measure.

pacifist *n* peace-lover, pacificist, conscientious objector, peacemaker, peace-monger, dove.
≠ warmonger, hawk.

pacify *v* appease, conciliate, placate, mollify, calm, compose, soothe, assuage, allay, moderate, soften, lull, still, quiet, silence, quell, crush, put down, tame, subdue.
≠ anger.

pack *n* **1** PACKET, box, carton, parcel, package, bundle, burden, load, backpack, rucksack, haversack, knapsack, kitbag. **2** GROUP, company, troop, herd, flock, band, crowd, gang, mob.
v **1** WRAP, parcel, package, bundle, stow, store. **2** FILL, load, charge, cram, stuff, crowd, throng, press, ram, wedge, compact, compress.

package *n* parcel, pack, packet, box, carton, bale, consignment.
v parcel (up), wrap (up), pack (up), box, batch.

packed *adj* filled, full, jam-packed, chock-a-block, crammed, crowded, congested.
≠ empty, deserted.

packet *n* pack, carton, box, bag, package, parcel, case, container, wrapper, wrapping, packing.

pact *n* treaty, convention, covenant, bond, alliance, cartel, contract, deal, bargain, compact, agreement, arrangement, understanding.
≠ disagreement, quarrel.

pad *n* **1** CUSHION, pillow, wad, buffer, padding, protection. **2** WRITING-PAD, note-pad, jotter, block.
v fill, stuff, wad, pack, wrap, line, cushion, protect.
pad out expand, inflate, fill out, augment, amplify, elaborate, flesh out, lengthen, stretch, protract, spin out.

padding *n* **1** FILLING, stuffing, wadding, packing, protection. **2** VERBIAGE, verbosity, wordiness, waffle (*infml*), bombast, hot air.

paddle[1] *n* oar, scull.
v row, oar, scull, propel, steer.

paddle[2] *v* wade, splash, slop, dabble.

pagan *n* heathen, atheist, unbeliever, infidel, idolater.
≠ believer.
adj heathen, irreligious, atheistic, godless, infidel, idolatrous.

page[1] *n* LEAF, sheet, folio, side.

page[2] *n* page-boy, attendant, messenger, bell-boy, footman, servant.
v call, send for, summon, bid, announce.

pageant *n* procession, parade, show, display, tableau, scene, play, spectacle, extravaganza.

pageantry *n* pomp, ceremony, grandeur, magnificence, splendour, glamour, glitter, spectacle, parade, display, show, extravagance, theatricality, drama, melodrama.

pain *n* **1** HURT, ache, throb, cramp, spasm, twinge, pang, stab, sting, smart, soreness, tenderness, discomfort, distress, suffering, affliction, trouble, anguish, agony, torment, torture. **2** (*infml*) NUISANCE, bother, bore (*infml*), annoyance, vexation, burden, headache (*infml*).
v hurt, afflict, torment, torture, agonize, distress, upset, sadden, grieve.
≠ please, delight, gratify.

pained *adj* hurt, injured, wounded, stung, offended, aggrieved, reproachful, distressed, upset, saddened, grieved.
≠ pleased, gratified.

painful *adj* **1** SORE, tender, aching, throbbing, smarting, stabbing, agonizing, excruciating. **2** *a painful experience*: unpleasant, disagreeable, distressing, upsetting, saddening, harrowing, traumatic. **3** HARD, difficult, laborious, tedious.
≠ **1** painless, soothing. **2** pleasant, agreeable. **3** easy.

pain-killer *n* analgesic, anodyne, anaesthetic, palliative, sedative, drug, remedy.

painless *adj* pain-free, trouble-free, effortless, easy, simple, undemanding.
≠ painful, difficult.

pains *n* trouble, bother, effort, labour, care, diligence.

painstaking *adj* careful, meticulous, scrupulous, thorough, conscientious, diligent, assiduous, industrious, hardworking, dedicated, devoted, persevering.
≠ careless, negligent.

paint *n* colour, colouring, pigment, dye, tint, stain.

Paints include: acrylic paint, colourwash, distemper, eggshell, emulsion, enamel, gloss paint, gouache, glaze, lacquer, masonry paint, matt paint, oil paint, oils, pastel, poster paint, primer, undercoat, varnish, watercolour, whitewash.

v **1** COLOUR, dye, tint, stain, lacquer, varnish, glaze, apply, daub, coat, cover, decorate. **2** PORTRAY, depict, describe, recount, picture, represent.

painting *n* oil painting, oil, watercolour, picture, portrait, landscape, still life, miniature, illustration, fresco, mural.

Painting terms include: abstract, alla prima, aquarelle, aquatint, art gallery, bleeding, bloom, brush, filbert brush, flat brush, round brush, rigger, sable brush, brush strokes, canvas, canvas board, capriccio, cartoon, charcoal, chiaroscuro, collage, composition, craquelure, diptych, easel, encaustic, facture, fête champêtre, fête galante, figurative, foreshortening, fresco, frieze, frottage, gallery, genre painting, gesso, gouache, grisaille, grotesque, hard edge, illustration, icon, impasto, landscape, mahlstick, miniature, monochrome, montage, mural, oil painting, paint, palette, palette knife, pastels, pastoral, paysage, pencil sketch, pentimento, perspective, picture, pietà, pigment, pochade box, pointillism, portrait, primer, scumble, secco, sfumato, sgraffito, silhouette, sketch, still life, stipple, tempera, thinners, tint, tondo, tone, triptych, trompe l'oeil, turpentine, underpainting, vignette, wash, watercolour. *see also* **art**; **paint**; **picture**.

pair *n* couple, brace, twosome, duo, twins, two of a kind.
v match (up), twin, team, mate, marry, wed, splice, join, couple, link, bracket, put together.
≠ separate, part.

palace *n* castle, château, mansion, stately home, basilica, dome.

palatable *adj* tasty, appetizing, eatable, edible, acceptable, satisfactory, pleasant, agreeable, enjoyable, attractive.
≠ unpalatable, unacceptable, unpleasant, disagreeable.

palate *n* taste, appreciation, liking, relish, enjoyment, appetite, stomach, heart.

palatial *adj* grand, magnificent, splendid, majestic, regal, stately, grandiose, imposing, luxurious, de luxe, sumptuous, opulent, plush, spacious.

pale *adj* **1** PALLID, livid, ashen, ashy, white, chalky, pasty, pasty-faced, waxen, waxy, wan, sallow, anaemic. **2** *pale blue*: light, pastel, faded, washed-out, bleached, colourless, insipid, vapid, weak, feeble, faint, dim.
≠ **1** ruddy. **2** dark.
v whiten, blanch, bleach, fade, dim.
≠ colour, blush.

pall[1] *n* shroud, veil, mantle, cloak, cloud, shadow, gloom, damper.

pall[2] *v* tire, weary, jade, sate, satiate, cloy, sicken.

palm *n* hand, paw (*infml*), mitt (*sl*).
v take, grab, snatch, appropriate.
palm off foist, impose, fob off, offload, unload, pass off.

palpable *adj* solid, substantial, material, real, touchable, tangible, visible, apparent, clear, plain, obvious, evident, manifest, conspicuous, blatant, unmistakable.
≠ impalpable, imperceptible, intangible, elusive.

palpitate *v* flutter, quiver, tremble, shiver, vibrate, beat, pulsate, pound, thump, throb.

paltry *adj* meagre, derisory, contemptible, mean, low, miserable, wretched, poor, sorry, small, slight, trifling, inconsiderable, negligible, trivial, minor, petty, unimportant, insignificant, worthless.
≠ substantial, significant, valuable.

pamper *v* cosset, coddle, mollycoddle, humour, gratify, indulge, overindulge, spoil, pet, fondle.
≠ neglect, ill-treat.

pamphlet *n* leaflet, brochure, booklet, folder, circular, handout, notice.

pan *n* saucepan, frying-pan, pot, casserole, container, vessel.

panache *n* flourish, flamboyance, ostentation, style, flair, élan, dash, spirit, enthusiasm, zest, energy, vigour, verve.

pandemonium *n* chaos, disorder, confusion, commotion, rumpus, turmoil, turbulence, tumult, uproar, din, bedlam, hubbub, hullaballoo, hue and cry, to-do (*infml*).
≠ order, calm, peace.

pander to humour, indulge, pamper, please, gratify, satisfy, fulfil, provide, cater to.

panel *n* board, committee, jury, team.

pang *n* pain, ache, twinge, stab, sting, prick, stitch, gripe, spasm, throe, agony, anguish, discomfort, distress.

panic *n* agitation, flap (*infml*), alarm, dismay, consternation, fright, fear, horror, terror, frenzy, hysteria.
≠ calmness, confidence.
v lose one's nerve, lose one's head, go to pieces, flap (*infml*), overreact.
≠ relax.

panic-stricken *adj* alarmed, frightened, horrified, terrified, petrified, scared stiff, in a cold sweat, panicky, frantic, frenzied, hysterical.
≠ relaxed, confident.

panorama *n* view, vista, prospect, scenery, landscape, scene, spectacle, perspective, overview, survey.

panoramic *adj* scenic, wide, sweeping, extensive, far-reaching, widespread, overall, general, universal.
≠ narrow, restricted, limited.

pant *v* puff, blow, gasp, wheeze, breathe, sigh, heave, throb, palpitate.

pants *n* **1** UNDERPANTS, drawers, panties, briefs, knickers (*infml*), Y-fronts, boxer shorts, trunks, shorts. **2** TROUSERS, slacks, jeans.

paper *n* **1** NEWSPAPER, daily, broadsheet, tabloid, rag (*sl*), journal, organ. **2** DOCUMENT, credential, authorization, identification, certificate, deed. **3** *a paper on alternative medicine*: essay, composition, dissertation, thesis, treatise, article, report.

> *Types of paper include*: art paper, bank, blotting paper, bond, carbon paper, cartridge paper, crêpe paper, greaseproof paper, graph paper, manila, notepaper, parchment, rice paper, silver paper, sugar paper, tissue paper, toilet paper, tracing paper, vellum, wallpaper, wrapping paper, writing-paper; card, cardboard, pasteboard; A4, foolscap, quarto, atlas, crown.

parable *n* fable, allegory, lesson, moral tale, story.

parade *n* procession, cavalcade, motorcade, march, column, file, train, review, ceremony, spectacle, pageant, show, display, exhibition.
v **1** MARCH, process, file past. **2** SHOW, display, exhibit, show off, vaunt, flaunt, brandish.

paradise *n* heaven, Utopia, Shangri-La, Elysium, Eden, bliss, delight.
≠ hell, Hades.

paradox *n* contradiction, inconsistency, incongruity, absurdity, oddity, anomaly, mystery, enigma, riddle, puzzle.

paradoxical *adj* self-contradictory, contradictory, conflicting, inconsistent, incongruous, absurd, illogical, improbable, impossible, mysterious, enigmatic, puzzling, baffling.

paragon *n* ideal, exemplar, epitome, quintessence, model, pattern, archetype, prototype, standard, criterion.

paragraph *n* passage, section, part, portion, subsection, subdivision, clause, item.

parallel *adj* equidistant, aligned, coextensive, alongside, analogous, equivalent, corresponding, matching, like, similar, resembling.
≠ divergent, different.
n **1** MATCH, equal, twin, duplicate, analogue, equivalent, counterpart. **2** SIMILARITY, resemblance, likeness, correspondence, correlation, equivalence, analogy, comparison.
v match, echo, conform, agree, correspond, correlate, compare, liken.
≠ diverge, differ.

paralyse *v* cripple, lame, disable, incapacitate, immobilize, anaesthetize, numb, deaden, freeze, transfix, halt, stop.

paralysed *adj* paralytic, paraplegic, quadriplegic, crippled, lame, disabled, incapacitated, immobilized, numb.
≠ able-bodied.

paralysis *n* paraplegia, quadriplegia, palsy, numbness, deadness, immobility, halt, standstill, stoppage, shutdown.

parameter *n* variable, guideline, indication, criterion, specification, limitation, restriction, limit, boundary.

paramount *adj* supreme, highest, topmost, predominant, pre-eminent, prime, principal, main, chief, cardinal, primary, first, foremost.
≠ lowest, last.

paraphernalia *n* equipment, gear, tackle, apparatus, accessories, trappings, bits and pieces, odds and ends, belongings, effects, stuff, things, baggage.

paraphrase *n* rewording, rephrasing, restatement, version, interpretation, rendering, translation.
v reword, rephrase, restate, interpret, render, translate.

parasite *n* sponger, scrounger, cadger, hanger-on, leech, bloodsucker.

parcel *n* package, packet, pack, box, carton, bundle.
v package, pack, wrap, bundle, tie up.
parcel out divide, carve up, apportion, allocate, allot, share out, distribute, dispense, dole out, deal out, mete out.

parch *v* dry (up), desiccate, dehydrate, bake, burn, scorch, sear, blister, wither, shrivel.

parched *adj* **1** ARID, waterless, dry, dried up, dehydrated, scorched, withered, shrivelled. **2** (*infml*) THIRSTY, gasping (*infml*).

pardon *v* forgive, condone, overlook, excuse, vindicate, acquit, absolve, remit, let off, reprieve, free, liberate, release.
≠ punish, discipline.
n forgiveness, mercy, clemency, indulgence, amnesty, excuse, acquittal, absolution, reprieve, release, discharge.
≠ punishment, condemnation.

pardonable *adj* forgivable, excusable, justifiable, warrantable, understandable, allowable, permissible, minor, venial.
≠ inexcusable.

pare *v* peel, skin, shear, clip, trim, crop, cut, dock, lop, prune, cut back, reduce, decrease.

parent *n* father, mother, dam, sire, progenitor, begetter, procreator, guardian.

parish *n* district, community, parishioners, church, churchgoers, congregation, flock, fold.

park *n* grounds, gardens, woodland.

> *Types of park include*: amusement park, arboretum, botanical garden, estate, game reserve, municipal park,

national park, parkland, pleasance, pleasure garden, pleasure ground, recreation ground, reserve, theme park, wildlife park.

v put, position, deposit, leave.

parliament *n* legislature, senate, congress, house, assembly, convocation, council, diet.

parliaments and political assemblies

Names of parliaments and political assemblies include: House of Representatives, Senate (*Australia*); Nationalrat, Bundesrat (*Austria*); Narodno Sobraniye (*Bulgaria*); House of Commons, Senate (*Canada*); National People's Congress (*China*); Folketing (*Denmark*); People's Assembly (*Egypt*); Eduskunta (*Finland*); National Assembly, Senate (*France*); Bundesrat, Bundestag, Landtag (*Germany*); Althing (*Iceland*); Lok Sabha, Rajya Sabha (*India*); Majlis (*Iran*); Dáil, Seanad (*Ireland*); Knesset (*Israel*); Camera del Deputati, Senato (*Italy*); Diet (*Japan*); Staten-Generaal (*Netherlands*); House of Representatives (*New Zealand*); Storting (*Norway*); Sejm (*Poland*); Cortes (*Portugal*); Congress of People's Deputies, Supreme Soviet (*Russia*); House of Assembly (*South Africa*); Cortes (*Spain*); Riksdag (*Sweden*); Nationalrat, Ständerat, Bundesrat (*Switzerland*); Porte (*Turkey*); House of Commons, House of Lords (*UK*); House of Representatives, Senate (*US*); National Assembly (*Vietnam*).

parliamentary *adj* governmental, senatorial, congressional, legislative, law-making.

parochial *adj* insular, provincial, parish-pump, petty, small-minded, narrow-minded, inward-looking, blinkered, limited, restricted, confined.
≠ national, international.

parody *n* caricature, lampoon, burlesque, satire, send-up, spoof, skit, mimicry, imitation, take-off, travesty, distortion.

v caricature, lampoon, burlesque, satirize, send up, spoof, mimic, imitate, ape, take off.

paroxysm *n* fit, seizure, spasm, convulsion, attack, outbreak, outburst, explosion.

parry *v* ward off, fend off, repel, repulse, field, deflect, block, avert, avoid, evade, duck, dodge, sidestep, shun.

parson *n* vicar, rector, priest, minister, pastor, preacher, clergyman, reverend, cleric, churchman.

part *n* **1** COMPONENT, constituent, element, factor, piece, bit, particle, fragment, scrap, segment, fraction, portion, share, section, division, department, branch, sector, district, region, territory. **2** ROLE, character, duty, task, responsibility, office, function, capacity.
≠ **1** whole, totality.

v separate, detach, disconnect, sever, split, tear, break, break up, take apart, dismantle, come apart, split up, divide, disunite, part company, disband, disperse, scatter, leave, depart, withdraw, go away.

part with relinquish, let go of, give up, yield, surrender, renounce, forgo, abandon, discard, jettison.

partial *adj* **1** *a partial victory*: incomplete, limited, restricted, imperfect, fragmentary, unfinished. **2** BIASED, prejudiced, partisan, one-sided, discriminatory, unfair, unjust, predisposed, coloured, affected.
≠ **1** complete, total. **2** impartial, disinterested, unbiased, fair.

partial to fond of, keen on, crazy about (*infml*), mad about (*infml*).

partiality *n* liking, fondness, predilection (*fml*), proclivity, inclination, preference, predisposition.

participant *n* entrant, contributor, participator, member, party, co-operator, helper, worker.

participate *v* take part, join in, contribute, engage, be involved, enter, share, partake, co-operate, help, assist.

participation *n* involvement, sharing,

partnership, co-operation, contribution, assistance.

particle *n* bit, piece, fragment, scrap, shred, sliver, speck, morsel, crumb, iota, whit, jot, tittle, atom, grain, drop.

particular *adj* **1** *on that particular day*: specific, precise, exact, distinct, special, peculiar. **2** EXCEPTIONAL, remarkable, notable, marked, thorough, unusual, uncommon. **3** FUSSY, discriminating, choosy (*infml*), finicky, fastidious.
≠ **1** general.
n detail, specific, point, feature, item, fact, circumstance.

particularly *adv* especially, exceptionally, remarkably, notably, extraordinarily, unusually, uncommonly, surprisingly, in particular, specifically, explicitly, distinctly.

parting *n* **1** DEPARTURE, going, leave-taking, farewell, goodbye, adieu. **2** DIVERGENCE, separation, division, partition, rift, split, rupture, breaking.
≠ **1** meeting. **2** convergence.
adj departing, farewell, last, dying, final, closing, concluding.
≠ first.

partisan *n* devotee, adherent, follower, disciple, backer, supporter, champion, stalwart, guerrilla, irregular.
adj biased, prejudiced, partial, predisposed, discriminatory, one-sided, factional, sectarian.
≠ impartial.

partition *n* **1** DIVIDER, barrier, wall, panel, screen, room-divider. **2** DIVISION, break-up, splitting, separation, parting, severance.
v **1** SEPARATE, divide, subdivide, wall off, fence off, screen. **2** SHARE, divide, split up, parcel out.

partly *adv* somewhat, to some extent, to a certain extent, up to a point, slightly, fractionally, moderately, relatively, in part, partially, incompletely.
≠ completely, totally.

partner *n* associate, ally, confederate, colleague, team-mate, collaborator, accomplice, helper, mate, sidekick (*infml*), oppo (*infml*), companion, comrade, consort, spouse, husband, wife.

partnership *n* **1** ALLIANCE, confederation, affiliation, combination, union, syndicate, co-operative, association, society, corporation, company, firm, fellowship, fraternity, brotherhood. **2** COLLABORATION, co-operation, participation, sharing.

party *n* **1** CELEBRATION, festivity, knees-up (*sl*), get-together, gathering, reunion, function, reception, at-home.

> *Kinds of party include*: acid-house party, barbecue, bash (*sl*), beanfeast (*infml*), beano (*infml*), birthday party, bunfight (*infml*), ceilidh, dinner party, disco, discotheque, do (*infml*), flatwarming, garden party, gathering of the clan (*infml*), Hallowe'en party, hen party, hooley, hootnanny (*US infml*), housewarming, orgy, picnic, pyjama party, rave, rave-up (*sl*), social, soirée, stag party, stag night, supper party, tea party, thrash (*infml*), welcoming party.

2 *a search party*: team, squad, crew, gang, band, group, company, detachment. **3** *a political party*: faction, side, league, cabal, alliance, association, grouping, combination. **4** PERSON, individual, litigant, plaintiff, defendant.

pass[1] *v* **1** SURPASS, exceed, go beyond, outdo, outstrip, overtake, leave behind. **2** *pass time*: spend, while away, fill, occupy. **3** GO PAST, go by, elapse, lapse, proceed, roll, flow, run, move, go, disappear, vanish. **4** GIVE, hand, transfer, transmit. **5** ENACT, ratify, validate, adopt, authorize, sanction, approve. **6** *pass an exam*: succeed, get through, qualify, graduate.
n **1** THROW, kick, move, lunge, swing. **2** PERMIT, passport, identification, ticket, licence, authorization, warrant, permission.
pass away die, pass on, expire, decease, give up the ghost.
pass off **1** FEIGN, counterfeit, fake, palm off. **2** HAPPEN, occur, take place, go off.
pass out **1** FAINT, lose consciousness, black out, collapse, flake out, keel over

(*infml*), drop. **2** GIVE OUT, hand out, dole out, distribute, deal out, share out.
pass over disregard, ignore, overlook, miss, omit, leave, neglect.

pass[2] *n* col, defile, gorge, ravine, canyon, gap, passage.

passable *adj* **1** SATISFACTORY, acceptable, allowable, tolerable, average, ordinary, unexceptional, moderate, fair, adequate, all right, OK (*infml*), mediocre. **2** CLEAR, unobstructed, unblocked, open, navigable.
≠ **1** unacceptable, excellent. **2** obstructed, blocked, impassable.

passage *n* **1** PASSAGEWAY, aisle, corridor, hall, hallway, lobby, vestibule, doorway, opening, entrance, exit. **2** THOROUGHFARE, way, route, road, avenue, path, lane, alley. **3** EXTRACT, excerpt, quotation, text, paragraph, section, piece, clause, verse. **4** JOURNEY, voyage, trip, crossing.

passenger *n* traveller, voyager, commuter, rider, fare, hitch-hiker.

passer-by *n* bystander, witness, looker-on, onlooker, spectator.

passing *adj* ephemeral, transient, short-lived, temporary, momentary, fleeting, brief, short, cursory, hasty, quick, slight, superficial, shallow, casual, incidental.
≠ lasting, permanent.

passion *n* feeling, emotion, love, adoration, infatuation, fondness, affection, lust, itch, desire, craving, fancy, mania, obsession, craze, eagerness, keenness, avidity, enthusiasm, zest, fanaticism, zeal, ardour, fervour, warmth, heat, fire, spirit, intensity, vehemence, anger, indignation, wrath, fury, rage, outburst.
≠ coolness, indifference, self-possession.

passionate *adj* **1** ARDENT, fervent, eager, keen, avid, enthusiastic, fanatical, zealous, warm, hot, fiery, inflamed, aroused, excited, impassioned, intense, strong, fierce, vehement, violent, stormy, tempestuous, wild, frenzied. **2** EMOTIONAL, excitable, hot-headed, impetuous, impulsive, quick-tempered, irritable. **3** LOVING, affectionate, lustful, erotic, sexy, sensual, sultry.
≠ **1** phlegmatic, laid back (*infml*). **3** frigid.

passive *adj* receptive, unassertive, submissive, docile, unresisting, non-violent, patient, resigned, long-suffering, indifferent, apathetic, lifeless, inert, inactive, non-participating.
≠ active, lively, responsive, involved.

past *adj* **1** OVER, ended, finished, completed, done, over and done with. **2** FORMER, previous, preceding, foregoing, late, recent. **3** ANCIENT, bygone, olden, early, gone, no more, extinct, defunct, forgotten.
≠ **2** future.
n **1** *in the past*: history, former times, olden days, antiquity. **2** LIFE, background, experience, track record.
≠ **1** future.

pasta

Forms and shapes of pasta include: agnolotti, anelli, angel's hair, bombolotti, bucatini, cannelloni, capelletti, casarecci, conchiglie, crescioni, ditali, elbow macaroni, farfalline, fedelini, fettuccine, fiochetti, fusilli, gnocchi, lasagne, lasagne verde, linguini, lumache, macaroni, mafalde, manicotti, maruzze, mezzani, noodles, noodle farfel, penne, pennine, ravioli, rigatoni, ruoti, spaghetti, spaghetti bolognese, stelline, tagliatelle, tortellini, trofie, vermicelli, ziti.

paste *n* adhesive, glue, gum, mastic, putty, cement.
v stick, glue, gum, cement, fix.

pastel *adj* delicate, soft, soft-hued, light, pale, subdued, faint.

pastime *n* hobby, activity, game, sport, recreation, play, fun, amusement, entertainment, diversion, distraction, relaxation.
≠ work, employment.

pastoral *adj* **1** RURAL, country, rustic, bucolic, agricultural, agrarian, idyllic. **2** ECCLESIASTICAL, clerical, priestly, ministerial.
≠ **1** urban.

pastry

Types of pastry include: American crust, biscuit-crumb, cheese pastry, choux, Danish, filo, flaky, flan pastry, hot-water crust, one-stage pastry, pâte à savarin, pâte brisée, pâte frolle, pâte sablée, pâte sucrée, plain pastry, pork-pie pastry, puff, rich shortcrust, rough-puff, short, shortcrust, suetcrust, sweet pastry.

pasture *n* grass, grassland, meadow, field, paddock, pasturage, grazing.

pasty *adj* pale, pallid, wan, anaemic, pasty-faced, sickly, unhealthy.
≠ ruddy, healthy.

pat *v* tap, dab, slap, touch, stroke, caress, fondle, pet.
n tap, dab, slap, touch, stroke, caress.
adv precisely, exactly, perfectly, flawlessly, faultlessly, fluently.
≠ imprecisely, inaccurately, wrongly.
adj glib, fluent, smooth, slick, ready, easy, facile, simplistic.

patch *n* piece, bit, scrap, spot, area, stretch, tract, plot, lot, parcel.
v mend, repair, fix, cover, reinforce.

patchy *adj* uneven, irregular, inconsistent, variable, random, fitful, erratic, sketchy, bitty, spotty, blotchy.
≠ even, uniform, regular, consistent.

patent *adj* obvious, evident, conspicuous, manifest, clear, transparent, apparent, visible, palpable, unequivocal, open, overt, blatant, flagrant, glaring.
≠ hidden, opaque.

path *n* route, course, direction, way, passage, road, avenue, lane, footpath, bridleway, trail, track, walk.

pathetic *adj* **1** PITIABLE, poor, sorry, lamentable, miserable, sad, distressing, moving, touching, poignant, plaintive, heart-rending, heartbreaking. **2** (*infml*) CONTEMPTIBLE, derisory, deplorable, useless, worthless, inadequate, meagre, feeble.
≠ **1** cheerful. **2** admirable, excellent, valuable.

patience *n* calmness, composure, self-control, restraint, tolerance, forbearance, endurance, fortitude, long-suffering, submission, resignation, stoicism, persistence, perseverance, diligence.
≠ impatience, intolerance, exasperation.

patient *adj* calm, composed, self-possessed, self-controlled, restrained, even-tempered, mild, lenient, indulgent, understanding, forgiving, tolerant, accommodating, forbearing, long-suffering, uncomplaining, submissive, resigned, philosophical, stoical, persistent, persevering.
≠ impatient, restless, intolerant, exasperated.
n invalid, sufferer, case, client.

patriotic *adj* nationalistic, chauvinistic, jingoistic, loyal, flag-waving.

patrol *n* **1** GUARD, sentry, sentinel, watchman. **2** *on patrol*: watch, surveillance, policing, protection, defence.
v police, guard, protect, defend, go the rounds, tour, inspect.

patron *n* **1** BENEFACTOR, philanthropist, sponsor, backer, supporter, sympathizer, advocate, champion, defender, protector, guardian, helper. **2** CUSTOMER, client, frequenter, regular, shopper, buyer, purchaser, subscriber.

patronage *n* custom, business, trade, sponsorship, backing, support.

patronize *v* **1** SPONSOR, fund, back, support, maintain, help, assist, promote, foster, encourage. **2** FREQUENT, shop at, buy from, deal with.

patronizing *adj* condescending, stooping, overbearing, high-handed, haughty, superior, snobbish, supercilious, disdainful.
≠ humble, lowly.

patter *v* tap, pat, pitter-patter, beat, pelt, scuttle, scurry.
n **1** PATTERING, tapping, pitter-patter, beating. **2** *a salesman's patter*: chatter, gabble, jabber, line, pitch, spiel (*sl*), jargon, lingo (*infml*).

pattern *n* **1** SYSTEM, method, order, plan. **2** DECORATION, ornamentation, ornament, figure, motif, design, style.

3 MODEL, template, stencil, guide, original, prototype, standard, norm.

patterned *adj* decorated, ornamented, figured, printed.
≠ plain.

paunch *n* abdomen, belly, pot-belly, beer-belly, corporation (*infml*).

pause *v* halt, stop, cease, discontinue, break off, interrupt, take a break, rest, wait, delay, hesitate.
n halt, stoppage, interruption, break, rest, breather (*infml*), lull, let-up (*infml*), respite, gap, interval, interlude, intermission, wait, delay, hesitation.

pave *v* flag, tile, floor, surface, cover, asphalt, tarmac, concrete.

paw *v* maul, manhandle, mishandle, molest.
n foot, pad, forefoot, hand.

pawn[1] *n* dupe, puppet, tool, instrument, toy, plaything.

pawn[2] *v* deposit, pledge, stake, mortgage, hock (*sl*), pop (*sl*).

pay *v* **1** REMIT, settle, discharge, reward, remunerate, recompense, reimburse, repay, refund, spend, pay out. **2** BENEFIT, profit, pay off, bring in, yield, return. **3** ATONE, make amends, compensate, answer, suffer.
n remuneration, wages, salary, earnings, income, fee, stipend, honorarium, emoluments, payment, reward, recompense, compensation, reimbursement.
pay back 1 REPAY, refund, reimburse, recompense, settle, square.
2 RETALIATE, get one's own back, take revenge, get even with, reciprocate, counter-attack.
pay off 1 DISCHARGE, settle, square, clear. **2** DISMISS, fire, sack (*infml*), lay off. **3** *the preparations paid off*: succeed, work.
pay out spend, disburse, hand over, fork out (*infml*), shell out (*infml*), lay out.

payable *adj* owed, owing, unpaid, outstanding, in arrears, due, mature.

payment *n* remittance, settlement, discharge, premium, outlay, advance, deposit, instalment, contribution, donation, allowance, reward, remuneration, pay, fee, hire, fare, toll.

peace *n* **1** SILENCE, quiet, hush, stillness, rest, relaxation, tranquillity, calm, calmness, composure, contentment. **2** ARMISTICE, truce, cease-fire, conciliation, concord, harmony, agreement, treaty.
≠ **1** noise, disturbance. **2** war, disagreement.

peaceable *adj* pacific, peace-loving, unwarlike, non-violent, conciliatory, friendly, amicable, inoffensive, gentle, placid, easy-going (*infml*), mild.
≠ belligerent, aggressive.

peaceful *adj* quiet, still, restful, relaxing, tranquil, serene, calm, placid, unruffled, undisturbed, untroubled, friendly, amicable, peaceable, pacific, gentle.
≠ noisy, disturbed, troubled, violent.

peacemaker *n* appeaser, conciliator, mediator, arbitrator, intercessor, peace-monger, pacifist.

peak *n* top, summit, pinnacle, crest, crown, zenith, height, maximum, climax, culmination, apex, tip, point.
≠ nadir, trough.
v climax, culminate, come to a head.

peal *n* chime, carillon, toll, knell, ring, clang, ringing, reverberation, rumble, roar, crash, clap.
v chime, toll, ring, clang, resonate, reverberate, resound, rumble, roll, roar, crash.

peasant *n* rustic, provincial, yokel, bumpkin, oaf, boor, lout.

peculiar *adj* **1** *a peculiar sound*: strange, odd, curious, funny, weird, bizarre, extraordinary, unusual, abnormal, exceptional, unconventional, offbeat, eccentric, way-out (*sl*), outlandish, exotic. **2** CHARACTERISTIC, distinctive, specific, particular, special, individual, personal, idiosyncratic, unique, singular.
≠ **1** ordinary, normal. **2** general.

peculiarity *n* oddity, bizarreness, abnormality, exception, eccentricity, quirk, mannerism, feature, trait, mark, quality, attribute, characteristic, distinctiveness, particularity, idiosyncrasy.

pedantic *adj* stilted, fussy, particular, precise, exact, punctilious, hair-splitting, nit-picking, finical, academic, bookish, erudite.
≠ imprecise, informal, casual.

peddle *v* sell, vend, flog (*infml*), hawk, tout, push, trade, traffic, market.

pedestal *n* plinth, stand, support, mounting, foot, base, foundation, platform, podium.

pedestrian *n* walker, foot-traveller.
adj dull, boring, flat, uninspired, banal, mundane, run-of-the-mill, commonplace, ordinary, mediocre, indifferent, prosaic, stodgy, plodding.
≠ exciting, imaginative.

pedigree *n* genealogy, family tree, lineage, ancestry, descent, line, family, parentage, derivation, extraction, race, breed, stock, blood.

peel *v* pare, skin, strip, scale, flake (off).
n skin, rind, zest, peeling.

peep *v* look, peek, glimpse, spy, squint, peer, emerge, issue, appear.
n look, peek, glimpse, glance, squint.

peephole *n* spyhole, keyhole, pinhole, hole, opening, aperture, slit, chink, crack, fissure, cleft, crevice.

peer[1] *v* look, gaze, scan, scrutinize, examine, inspect, spy, snoop, peep, squint.

peer[2] *n* **1** ARISTOCRAT, noble, nobleman, lord, duke, marquess, marquis, earl, count, viscount, baron. **2** EQUAL, counterpart, equivalent, match, fellow.

peerage *n* aristocracy, nobility, upper crust.

peeress *n* aristocrat, noble, noblewoman, lady, dame, duchess, marchioness, countess, viscountess, baroness.

peevish *adj* petulant, querulous, fractious, fretful, touchy, irritable, cross, grumpy, ratty (*infml*), crotchety, ill-tempered, crabbed, cantankerous, crusty, snappy, short-tempered, surly, sullen, sulky.
≠ good-tempered.

peg *v* **1** FASTEN, secure, fix, attach, join, mark. **2** *peg prices*: control, stabilize, limit, freeze, fix, set.
n pin, dowel, hook, knob, marker, post, stake.

pejorative *adj* derogatory, disparaging, belittling, slighting, unflattering, uncomplimentary, unpleasant, bad, negative.
≠ complimentary.

pelt *v* **1** THROW, hurl, bombard, shower, assail, batter, beat, hit, strike. **2** POUR, teem, rain cats and dogs (*infml*). **3** RUSH, hurry, charge, belt (*infml*), tear, dash, speed, career.

pen[1] *n* fountain-pen, ballpoint, Biro®, felt-tip pen.
v write, compose, draft, scribble, jot down.

pen[2] *n* enclosure, fold, stall, sty, coop, cage, hutch.
v enclose, fence, hedge, hem in, confine, cage, coop, shut up.

penalize *v* punish, discipline, correct, fine, handicap.
≠ reward.

penalty *n* punishment, retribution, fine, forfeit, handicap, disadvantage.
≠ reward.

penance *n* atonement, reparation, punishment, penalty, mortification.

pendant *n* medallion, locket, necklace.

pending *adj* impending, in the offing, forthcoming, imminent, undecided, in the balance.
≠ finished, settled.

penetrate *v* pierce, stab, prick, puncture, probe, sink, bore, enter, infiltrate, permeate, seep, pervade, suffuse.

penetrating *adj* piercing, stinging, biting, incisive, sharp, keen, acute, shrewd, discerning, perceptive, observant, profound, deep, searching, probing.
≠ blunt.

penitence *n* repentance, contrition, remorse, regret, shame, self-reproach.

penitent *adj* repentant, contrite, sorry, apologetic, remorseful, regretful, conscience-stricken, shamefaced, humble.
≠ unrepentant, hard-hearted, callous.

penniless *adj* poor, poverty-stricken, impoverished, destitute, bankrupt, ruined, bust, broke (*infml*), stony-broke (*sl*).
≠ rich, wealthy, affluent.

pension *n* annuity, superannuation, allowance, benefit.

pensive *adj* thoughtful, reflective, contemplative, meditative, ruminative, absorbed, preoccupied, absent-minded, wistful, solemn, serious, sober.
≠ carefree.

pent-up *adj* repressed, inhibited, restrained, bottled-up, suppressed, stifled.

people *n* persons, individuals, humans, human beings, mankind, humanity, folk, public, general public, populace, rank and file, population, inhabitants, citizens, community, society, race, nation.
v populate, inhabit, occupy, settle, colonize.

pep (*infml*) *n* energy, vigour, verve, spirit, vitality, liveliness, get-up-and-go (*infml*), exuberance, high spirits.
pep up (*infml*) invigorate, vitalize, liven up, quicken, stimulate, excite, exhilarate, inspire.
≠ tone down.

perceive *v* **1** SEE, discern, make out, detect, discover, spot, catch sight of, notice, observe, view, remark, note, distinguish, recognize. **2** SENSE, feel, apprehend, learn, realize, appreciate, be aware of, know, grasp, understand, gather, deduce, conclude.

perceptible *adj* perceivable, discernible, detectable, appreciable, distinguishable, observable, noticeable, obvious, evident, conspicuous, clear, plain, apparent, visible.
≠ imperceptible, inconspicuous.

perception *n* sense, feeling, impression, idea, conception, apprehension, awareness, consciousness, observation, recognition, grasp, understanding, insight, discernment, taste.

perceptive *adj* discerning, observant, sensitive, responsive, aware, alert, quick, sharp, astute, shrewd.
≠ unobservant.

perch *v* land, alight, settle, sit, roost, balance, rest.

percolate *v* filter, strain, seep, ooze, leak, drip, penetrate, permeate, pervade.

peremptory *adj* imperious, commanding, dictatorial, autocratic, authoritative, assertive, high-handed, overbearing, domineering, bossy (*infml*), abrupt, curt, summary, arbitrary.

perennial *adj* lasting, enduring, everlasting, eternal, immortal, undying, imperishable, unceasing, incessant, never-ending, constant, continual, uninterrupted, perpetual, persistent, unfailing.

perfect *adj* **1** FAULTLESS, impeccable, flawless, immaculate, spotless, blameless, pure, superb, excellent, matchless, incomparable. **2** EXACT, precise, accurate, right, correct, true. **3** IDEAL, model, exemplary, ultimate, consummate, expert, accomplished, experienced, skilful. **4** *perfect strangers*: utter, absolute, sheer, complete, entire, total.
≠ **1** imperfect, flawed, blemished. **2** inaccurate, wrong. **3** inexperienced, unskilled.
v fulfil, consummate, complete, finish, polish, refine, elaborate.
≠ spoil, mar.

perfection *n* faultlessness, flawlessness, excellence, superiority, ideal, model, paragon, crown, pinnacle, acme, consummation, completion.
≠ imperfection, flaw.

perfectionist *n* idealist, purist, pedant, stickler.

perfectly *adv* **1** UTTERLY, absolutely, quite, thoroughly, completely, entirely, wholly, totally, fully. **2** FAULTLESSLY, flawlessly, impeccably, ideally, exactly, correctly.
≠ **1** partially. **2** imperfectly, badly.

perforate *v* hole, punch, drill, bore, pierce, prick, stab, puncture, penetrate.

perforation *n* hole, bore, prick, puncture, dotted line.

perform *v* **1** DO, carry out, execute,

discharge, fulfil, satisfy, complete, achieve, accomplish, bring off, pull off, effect, bring about. **2** *perform a play*: stage, put on, present, enact, represent, act, play, appear as. **3** FUNCTION, work, operate, behave, produce.

performance *n* **1** appearance, gig (*sl*), presentation, interpretation, representation, portrayal, acting.

> *Types of performance include*: act, audition, benefit, box-office hit, bomb (*US infml*), charity concert, command performance, concert, début, dress rehearsal, dry run, encore, entertainment, exhibition, farewell performance, first house, first night, flop (*infml*), full house, gala night, gig, last night, last night at the Proms, matinée, one-night stand, opening night, play, pop concert, première, preview, production, readthrough, recital, rehearsal, rendition, runthrough, second house, sell-out, short run, show, sketch, smash hit (*infml*), sneak preview, theatre, turn. *see also* **theatrical**.

2 ACTION, deed, doing, carrying out, execution, implementation, discharge, fulfilment, completion, achievement, accomplishment. **3** FUNCTIONING, operation, behaviour, conduct.

performer *n* actor, actress, player, artiste, entertainer.

perfume *n* scent, fragrance, smell, odour, aroma, bouquet, sweetness, balm, essence, cologne, toilet water, incense.

perhaps *adv* maybe, possibly, conceivably, feasibly.

peril *n* danger, hazard, risk, jeopardy, uncertainty, insecurity, threat, menace.
≠ safety, security.

perilous *adj* dangerous, unsafe, hazardous, risky, chancy, precarious, insecure, unsure, vulnerable, exposed, menacing, threatening, dire.
≠ safe, secure.

perimeter *n* circumference, edge, border, boundary, frontier, limit, bounds, confines, fringe, margin, periphery.
≠ middle, centre, heart.

period *n* era, epoch, age, generation, date, years, time, term, season, stage, phase, stretch, turn, session, interval, space, span, spell, cycle.

periodic *adj* occasional, infrequent, sporadic, intermittent, recurrent, repeated, regular, periodical, seasonal.

periodical *n* magazine, journal, publication, weekly, monthly, quarterly.

peripheral *adj* **1** MINOR, secondary, incidental, unimportant, irrelevant, unnecessary, marginal, borderline, surface, superficial. **2** OUTLYING, outer, outermost.
≠ **1** major, crucial. **2** central.

perish *v* rot, decay, decompose, disintegrate, crumble, collapse, fall, die, expire, pass away.

perishable *adj* destructible, biodegradable, decomposable, short-lived.
≠ imperishable, durable.

perk (*infml*) *n* perquisite, fringe benefit, benefit, bonus, dividend, gratuity, tip, extra, plus (*infml*).
perk up (*infml*) brighten, cheer up, buck up (*infml*), revive, liven up, pep up (*infml*), rally, recover, improve, look up.

permanence *n* fixedness, stability, imperishability, perpetuity, constancy, endurance, durability.
≠ impermanence, transience.

permanent *adj* fixed, stable, unchanging, imperishable, indestructible, unfading, eternal, everlasting, lifelong, perpetual, constant, steadfast, perennial, long-lasting, lasting, enduring, durable.
≠ temporary, ephemeral, fleeting.

permeable *adj* porous, absorbent, absorptive, penetrable.
≠ impermeable, watertight.

permeate *v* pass through, soak through, filter through, seep through, penetrate, infiltrate, pervade, imbue, saturate, impregnate, fill.

permissible *adj* permitted, allowable, allowed, admissible, all right, acceptable, proper, authorized,

sanctioned, lawful, legal, legitimate.
≠ prohibited, banned, forbidden.

permission *n* consent, assent, agreement, approval, go-ahead, green light (*infml*), authorization, sanction, leave, warrant, permit, licence, dispensation, freedom, liberty.
≠ prohibition.

permissive *adj* liberal, broad-minded, tolerant, forbearing, lenient, easy-going (*infml*), indulgent, overindulgent, lax, free.
≠ strict, rigid.

permit *v* allow, let, consent, agree, admit, grant, authorize, sanction, warrant, license.
≠ prohibit, forbid.
n pass, passport, visa, licence, warrant, authorization, sanction, permission.
≠ prohibition.

perpendicular *adj* vertical, upright, erect, straight, sheer, plumb.
≠ horizontal.

perpetrate *v* commit, carry out, execute, do, perform, inflict, wreak.

perpetual *adj* eternal, everlasting, infinite, endless, unending, never-ending, interminable, ceaseless, unceasing, incessant, continuous, uninterrupted, constant, persistent, continual, repeated, recurrent, perennial, permanent, lasting, enduring, abiding, unchanging.
≠ intermittent, temporary, ephemeral, transient.

perpetuate *v* continue, keep up, maintain, preserve, keep alive, immortalize, commemorate.

perplex *v* puzzle, baffle, mystify, stump, confuse, muddle, confound, bewilder, dumbfound.

persecute *v* hound, pursue, hunt, bother, worry, annoy, pester, harass, molest, abuse, ill-treat, maltreat, oppress, tyrannize, victimize, martyr, distress, afflict, torment, torture, crucify.
≠ pamper, spoil.

persecution *n* harassment, molestation, abuse, maltreatment, discrimination, oppression, subjugation, suppression, tyranny, punishment, torture, martyrdom.

perseverance *n* persistence, determination, resolution, doggedness, tenacity, diligence, assiduity, dedication, commitment, constancy, steadfastness, stamina, endurance, indefatigability.

persevere *v* continue, carry on, stick at it (*infml*), keep going, soldier on, persist, plug away (*infml*), remain, stand firm, stand fast, hold on, hang on.
≠ give up, stop, discontinue.

persist *v* remain, linger, last, endure, abide, continue, carry on, keep at it, persevere, insist.
≠ desist, stop.

persistent *adj* **1** INCESSANT, endless, never-ending, interminable, continuous, unrelenting, relentless, unremitting, constant, steady, continual, repeated, perpetual, lasting, enduring.
2 *persistent effort*: persevering, determined, resolute, dogged, tenacious, stubborn, obstinate, steadfast, zealous, tireless, unflagging, indefatigable.

person *n* individual, being, human being, human, man, woman, body, soul, character, type.

personal *adj* own, private, confidential, intimate, special, particular, individual, exclusive, idiosyncratic, distinctive.
≠ public, general, universal.

personality *n* **1** CHARACTER, nature, disposition, temperament, individuality, psyche, traits, make-up, charm, charisma, magnetism.
2 CELEBRITY, notable, personage, public figure, VIP (*infml*), star.

personify *v* embody, epitomize, typify, exemplify, symbolize, represent, mirror.

personnel *n* staff, workforce, workers, employees, crew, human resources, manpower, people, members.

perspective *n* aspect, angle, slant, attitude, standpoint, viewpoint, point of view, view, vista, scene, prospect, outlook, proportion, relation.

perspiration *n* sweat, secretion, moisture, wetness.

perspire *v* sweat, exude, secrete, swelter, drip.

persuade *v* coax, prevail upon, lean on, cajole, wheedle, inveigle, talk into, induce, bring round, win over, convince, convert, sway, influence, lead on, incite, prompt, urge.
≠ dissuade, deter, discourage.

persuasion *n* **1** COAXING, cajolery, wheedling, inducement, enticement, pull, power, influence, conviction, conversion. **2** OPINION, school (of thought), party, faction, side, conviction, faith, belief, denomination, sect.

persuasive *adj* convincing, plausible, cogent, sound, valid, influential, forceful, weighty, effective, telling, potent, compelling, moving, touching.
≠ unconvincing.

pertinent *adj* appropriate, suitable, fitting, apt, apposite, relevant, to the point, material, applicable.
≠ inappropriate, unsuitable, irrelevant.

perturb *v* disturb, bother, trouble, upset, worry, alarm, disconcert, unsettle, discompose, ruffle, fluster, agitate, vex.
≠ reassure, compose.

peruse *v* study, pore over, read, browse, look through, scan, scrutinize, examine, inspect, check.

pervade *v* affect, penetrate, permeate, percolate, charge, fill, imbue, infuse, suffuse, saturate, impregnate.

pervasive *adj* prevalent, common, extensive, widespread, general, universal, inescapable, omnipresent, ubiquitous.

perverse *adj* contrary, wayward, wrong-headed, wilful, headstrong, stubborn, obstinate, unyielding, intransigent, disobedient, rebellious, troublesome, unmanageable, ill-tempered, cantankerous, unreasonable, incorrect, improper.
≠ obliging, co-operative, reasonable.

perversion *n* **1** CORRUPTION, depravity, debauchery, immorality, vice, wickedness, deviance, kinkiness (*infml*), abnormality. **2** TWISTING, distortion, misrepresentation, travesty, misinterpretation, aberration, deviation, misuse, misapplication.

pervert *v* **1** *pervert the truth*: twist, warp, distort, misrepresent, falsify, garble, misinterpret. **2** CORRUPT, lead astray, deprave, debauch, debase, degrade, abuse, misuse, misapply.
n deviant, debauchee, degenerate, weirdo (*infml*).

perverted *adj* twisted, warped, distorted, deviant, kinky (*infml*), unnatural, abnormal, unhealthy, corrupt, depraved, debauched, debased, immoral, evil, wicked.
≠ natural, normal.

pessimistic *adj* negative, cynical, fatalistic, defeatist, resigned, hopeless, despairing, despondent, dejected, downhearted, glum, morose, melancholy, depressed, dismal, gloomy, bleak.
≠ optimistic.

pest *n* nuisance, bother, annoyance, irritation, vexation, trial, curse, scourge, bane, blight, bug.

pester *v* nag, badger, hound, hassle (*infml*), harass, plague, torment, provoke, worry, bother, disturb, annoy, irritate, pick on, get at (*infml*).

pet *n* favourite, darling, idol, treasure, jewel.
adj favourite, favoured, preferred, dearest, cherished, special, particular, personal.
v stroke, caress, fondle, cuddle, kiss, neck (*sl*), snog (*sl*).

peter out dwindle, taper off, fade, wane, ebb, fail, cease, stop.

petition *n* appeal, round robin, application, request, solicitation, plea, entreaty, prayer, supplication, invocation.
v appeal, call upon, ask, crave, solicit, bid, urge, press, implore, beg, plead, entreat, beseech, supplicate, pray.

petrify *v* terrify, horrify, appal, paralyse, numb, stun, dumbfound.

petty *adj* **1** MINOR, unimportant, insignificant, trivial, secondary, lesser, small, little, slight, trifling, paltry, inconsiderable, negligible. **2** SMALL-MINDED, mean, ungenerous, grudging, spiteful.
≠ **1** important, significant. **2** generous.

petulant *adj* fretful, peevish, cross, irritable, snappish, bad-tempered, ill-humoured, moody, sullen, sulky, sour, ungracious.

phantom *n* ghost, spectre, spirit, apparition, vision, hallucination, illusion, figment.

phase *n* stage, step, time, period, spell, season, chapter, position, point, aspect, state, condition.
phase out wind down, run down, ease off, taper off, eliminate, dispose of, get rid of, remove, withdraw, close, terminate.

phenomenal *adj* marvellous, sensational, stupendous, amazing, remarkable, extraordinary, exceptional, unusual, unbelievable, incredible.

phenomenon *n* **1** OCCURRENCE, happening, event, incident, episode, fact, appearance, sight. **2** WONDER, marvel, miracle, prodigy, rarity, curiosity, spectacle, sensation.

philanthropic *adj* humanitarian, public-spirited, altruistic, unselfish, benevolent, kind, charitable, alms-giving, generous, liberal, open-handed.
≠ misanthropic.

philanthropist *n* humanitarian, benefactor, patron, sponsor, giver, donor, contributor, altruist.
≠ misanthrope.

philanthropy *n* humanitarianism, public-spiritedness, altruism, unselfishness, benevolence, kind-heartedness, charity, alms-giving, patronage, generosity, liberality, open-handedness.
≠ misanthropy.

philosophical *adj* **1** *a philosophical discussion*: metaphysical, abstract, theoretical, analytical, rational, logical, erudite, learned, wise, thoughtful. **2** RESIGNED, patient, stoical, unruffled, calm, composed.

philosophy *n* reason, thought, thinking, wisdom, knowledge, ideology, world-view, doctrine, beliefs, convictions, values, principles, attitude, viewpoint.

> *Philosophical terms include*: absolutism, aesthetics, agnosticism, altruism, antinomianism, a posteriori, a priori, ascetism, atheism, atomism, behaviourism, deduction, deism, deontology, determinism, dialectical materialism, dogmatism, dualism, egoism, empiricism, entailment, Epicureanism, epistemology, ethics, existentialism, fatalism, hedonism, historicism, humanism, idealism, identity, induction, instrumentalism, interactionism, intuition, jurisprudence, libertarianism, logic, logical positivism, materialism, metaphysics, monism, naturalism, nihilism, nominalism, objectivism, ontology, pantheism, phenomenalism, phenomenology, positivism, pragmatism, prescriptivism, rationalism, realism, reductionism, relativism, scepticism, scholasticism, sensationalism, sense data, solipsism, stoicism, structuralism, subjectivism, substance, syllogism, teleology, theism, transcendentalism, utilitarianism.

phlegmatic *adj* placid, stolid, impassive, unemotional, unconcerned, indifferent, matter-of-fact, stoical.
≠ emotional, passionate.

phobia *n* fear, terror, dread, anxiety, neurosis, obsession, hang-up (*infml*), thing (*infml*), aversion, dislike, hatred, horror, loathing, revulsion, repulsion.
≠ love, liking.

> *Phobias (by name of fear) include*: zoophobia (*animals*), apiphobia (*bees*), ailurophobia (*cats*), necrophobia (*corpses*), scotophobia (*darkness*), cynophobia (*dogs*), claustrophobia (*enclosed places*), panphobia (*everything*), pyrophobia (*fire*), xenophobia (*foreigners*), phasmophobia (*ghosts*), acrophobia (*high places*), hippophobia (*horses*), entomophobia (*insects*), astraphobia

(*lightning*), autophobia (*loneliness*), agoraphobia (*open spaces*), toxiphobia (*poison*), herpetophobia (*reptiles*), tachophobia (*speed*), ophiophobia (*snakes*), arachnophobia (*spiders*), triskaidekaphobia (*thirteen*), brontophobia (*thunder*), hydrophobia (*water*).

phone *v* telephone, ring (up), call (up), dial, contact, get in touch, give a buzz (*infml*), give a tinkle (*infml*).

phoney (*infml*) *adj* fake, counterfeit, forged, bogus, trick, false, spurious, assumed, affected, put-on, sham, pseudo, imitation.
≠ real, genuine.

photocopy *v* copy, duplicate, Photostat®, Xerox®, print, run off.
n copy, duplicate, Photostat®, Xerox®.

photograph *n* photo, snap, snapshot, print, shot, slide, transparency, picture, image, likeness.
v snap, take, film, shoot, video, record.

photography

Photographic equipment includes: camera, stand, tripod, flash umbrella, boom arm; developer bath, developing tank, dry mounting press, easel, enlarger, enlarger timer, film-drying cabinet, fixing bath, focus magnifier, light-box, negative carrier, print washer, contact printer, print-drying rack, paper drier, safelight, stop bath, Vertoscope®, viewer; slide viewer, slide projector, film projector, screen.
Photographic accessories include: air-shutter release, battery, cable release, camera bag, eye-cup, eyepiece magnifier, film, cartridge film, cassette film, disc film, film pack, filter, colour filter, heat filter, polarizing filter, skylight filter, flashbulb, flashcube, flashgun, flash unit, hot shoe, lens, afocal lens, auxiliary lens, close-up lens, fish-eye lens, macro lens, supplementary lens, telephoto lens, teleconverter, wide-angle lens, zoom lens, lens cap, lens hood, lens shield, light meter, exposure meter, spot meter, diffuser, barn doors, honeycomb diffuser, parabolic reflector, snoot, slide mount, viewfinder, right-angle finder; camcorder battery discharger/charger/tester, cassette adaptor, remote control, tele-cine converter, video editor, video light, video mixer. *see also* **camera**.

phrase *n* construction, clause, idiom, expression, saying, utterance, remark.
v word, formulate, frame, couch, present, put, express, say, utter, pronounce.

physical *adj* bodily, corporeal, fleshy, incarnate, mortal, earthly, material, concrete, solid, substantial, tangible, visible, real, actual.
≠ mental, spiritual.

physician *n* doctor, medical practitioner, medic (*infml*), general practitioner, GP, houseman, intern, registrar, consultant, specialist, healer.

physics

Terms used in physics include: absolute zero, acceleration, acoustics, alpha particles, analogue signal, applied physics, Archimedes principle, area, atom, beta particles, Big Bang theory, boiling point, bubble-chamber, capillary action, centre of gravity, centre of mass, centrifugal force, chain reaction, charge, charged particle, circuit, circuit-breaker, couple, critical mass, cryogenics, density, diffraction, digital, dynamics, efficiency, elasticity, electric current, electric discharge, electricity, electrodynamics, electromagnetic spectrum, electromagnetic waves, electron, energy, engine, entropy, equation, equilibrium, evaporation, field, flash point, force, formula, freezing point, frequency, friction, fundamental constant, gamma ray, gas, gate, grand united theory (GUT), gravity, half-life, heat, heavy water, hydraulics, hydrodynamics, hydrostatics, incandescence, indeterminacy principle, inertia, infrared, interference, ion, kinetic energy, kinetic theory, Kelvin effect, laser (light amplification by stimulated emission of radiation), latent heat, law, laws of motion, laws of reflection, laws of refraction, laws of thermodynamics, lens, lever, light, light emission, light intensity, light source, liquid, longitudinal wave, luminescence, Mach number, magnetic field, magnetism, mass, mechanics, microwaves, mirror, Mohs scale, molecule, moment, momentum, motion, neutron, nuclear, nuclear fission, nuclear fusion, nuclear physics, nucleus, optical centre, optics, oscillation, parallel motion, particle, periodic law, perpetual motion, phonon, photon, photosensitivity, polarity, potential energy, power, pressure, principle, process, proton, quantum chromodynamics (QCD), quantum electrodynamics (QED), quantum mechanics, quantum theory, quark, radiation, radioactive element, radioactivity, radioisotope, radio wave, ratio, reflection, refraction, relativity, resistance, resonance, rule, semiconductor, sensitivity, separation, SI unit, sound, sound wave, specific gravity, specific heat capacity, spectroscopy, spectrum, speed, states of matter, statics, substance, superstring theory, supersymmetry, surface tension, temperature, tension, theory, theory of relativity, thermodynamics, Thomson effect, transverse wave, ultrasound, ultraviolet, uncertainty principle, velocity, visible spectrum, viscosity, volume, wave, wave property, weight, white heat, work, X-ray. *see also* **atom**; **electricity**.

physique *n* body, figure, shape, form, build, frame, structure, constitution, make-up.

pick *v* **1** SELECT, choose, opt for, decide on, settle on, single out. **2** GATHER, collect, pluck, harvest, cull.
n **1** CHOICE, selection, option, decision, preference. **2** BEST, cream, flower, élite, elect.
pick on bully, torment, persecute, nag, get at (*infml*), needle (*infml*), bait.
pick out spot, notice, perceive, recognize, distinguish, tell apart, separate, single out, hand-pick, choose, select.
pick up 1 LIFT, raise, hoist. **2** *I'll pick you up at eight*: call for, fetch, collect. **3** LEARN, master, grasp, gather. **4** IMPROVE, rally, recover, perk up (*infml*). **5** BUY, purchase. **6** OBTAIN, acquire, gain. **7** *pick up an infection*: catch, contract, get.

picket *n* picketer, protester, demonstrator, striker.
v protest, demonstrate, boycott, blockade, enclose, surround.

pickle *v* preserve, conserve, souse, marinade, steep, cure, salt.

pictorial *adj* graphic, diagrammatic, schematic, representational, vivid, striking, expressive, illustrated, picturesque, scenic.

picture
1 DEPICTION, portrayal, description, account, report, impression.

Kinds of picture include: abstract, cameo, caricature, cartoon, collage, design, doodle, drawing, effigy, engraving, etching, fresco, graffiti, graphics, icon, identikit, illustration, image, kakemono, landscape, likeness, miniature, montage, mosaic, mugshot (*infml*), mural, negative, oil-painting, old master, painting, passport photo, Photofit®, photograph, photogravure, pin-up, plate, portrait, print, representation, reproduction, self-portrait, silhouette, sketch, slide, snap (*infml*), snapshot, still life, tableau, tapestry, tracing, transfer, transparency, triptych, trompe l'oeil, vignette, watercolour.

2 *the picture of health*: embodiment, personification, epitome, archetype, essence. **3** FILM, movie (*infml*), motion picture.
v **1** IMAGINE, envisage, envision, conceive, visualize, see. **2** DEPICT, describe, represent, show, portray, draw, sketch, paint, photograph, illustrate.

picturesque *adj* **1** ATTRACTIVE, beautiful, pretty, charming, quaint, idyllic, scenic. **2** DESCRIPTIVE, graphic, vivid, colourful, striking.
≠ **1** unattractive. **2** dull.

piece *n* **1** FRAGMENT, bit, scrap,

morsel, mouthful, bite, lump, chunk, slice, sliver, snippet, shred, offcut, sample, component, constituent, element, part, segment, section, division, fraction, share, portion, quantity. **2** ARTICLE, item, study, work, composition, creation, specimen, example.

pier *n* **1** JETTY, breakwater, landing-stage, quay, wharf. **2** SUPPORT, upright, pillar, post.

pierce *v* penetrate, enter, stick into, puncture, drill, bore, probe, perforate, punch, prick, stab, lance, bayonet, run through, spear, skewer, spike, impale, transfix.

piercing *adj* **1** *a piercing cry*: shrill, high-pitched, loud, ear-splitting, sharp. **2** PENETRATING, probing, searching. **3** COLD, bitter, raw, biting, keen, fierce, severe, wintry, frosty, freezing. **4** PAINFUL, agonizing, excruciating, stabbing, lacerating.

piety *n* piousness, devoutness, godliness, saintliness, holiness, sanctity, religion, faith, devotion, reverence. ≠ impiety, irreligion.

pig *n* swine, hog, sow, boar, animal, beast, brute, glutton, gourmand.

pigeonhole *n* compartment, niche, slot, cubby-hole, cubicle, locker, box, place, section, class, category, classification.
v compartmentalize, label, classify, sort, file, catalogue, alphabetize, shelve, defer.

pigment *n* colour, hue, tint, dye, stain, paint, colouring, tincture.

pile¹ *n* stack, heap, mound, mountain, mass, accumulation, collection, assortment, hoard, stockpile.
v stack, heap, mass, amass, accumulate, build up, gather, assemble, collect, hoard, stockpile, store, load, pack, jam, crush, crowd, flock, flood, stream, rush, charge.

pile² *n* post, column, upright, support, bar, beam, foundation.

pile³ *n* nap, shag, plush, fur, hair, fuzz, down.

pilfer *v* steal, pinch (*infml*), nick (*infml*), knock off (*sl*), filch, lift, shoplift, rob, thieve.

pilgrim *n* crusader, traveller, wanderer.

pilgrimage *n* crusade, mission, expedition, journey, trip, tour.

pill *n* tablet, capsule, pellet.

pillar *n* column, shaft, post, mast, pier, upright, pile, support, prop, mainstay, bastion, tower of strength.

pilot *n* **1** FLYER, aviator, airman. **2** NAVIGATOR, steersman, helmsman, coxswain, captain, leader, director, guide.
v fly, drive, steer, direct, control, handle, manage, operate, run, conduct, lead, guide, navigate.
adj experimental, trial, test, model.

pimple *n* spot, zit (*sl*), blackhead, boil, swelling.

pin *v* tack, nail, fix, affix, attach, join, staple, clip, fasten, secure, hold down, restrain, immobilize.
n tack, nail, screw, spike, rivet, bolt, peg, fastener, clip, staple, brooch.
pin down 1 PINPOINT, identify, determine, specify. **2** FORCE, make, press, pressurize.

pinch *v* **1** SQUEEZE, compress, crush, press, tweak, nip, hurt, grip, grasp. **2** (*infml*) STEAL, nick, pilfer, filch, snatch.
n **1** SQUEEZE, tweak, nip. **2** DASH, soupçon, taste, bit, speck, jot, mite. **3** EMERGENCY, crisis, predicament, difficulty, hardship, pressure, stress.

pine *v* long, yearn, ache, sigh, grieve, mourn, wish, desire, crave, hanker, hunger, thirst.

pinnacle *n* **1** PEAK, summit, top, cap, crown, crest, apex, vertex, acme, zenith, height, eminence. **2** SPIRE, steeple, turret, pyramid, cone, obelisk, needle.

pinpoint *v* identify, spot, distinguish, locate, place, home in on, zero in on (*infml*), pin down, determine, specify, define.

pioneer *n* colonist, settler, frontiersman, frontierswoman, explorer, developer, pathfinder, trail-blazer, leader, innovator, inventor,

discoverer, founder.
v invent, discover, originate, create, initiate, instigate, begin, start, launch, institute, found, establish, set up, develop, open up.

pious *adj* **1** DEVOUT, godly, saintly, holy, spiritual, religious, reverent, good, virtuous, righteous, moral. **2** SANCTIMONIOUS, holier-than-thou, self-righteous, goody-goody (*infml*), hypocritical.
≠ **1** impious, irreligious, irreverent.

pipe *n* tube, hose, piping, tubing, pipeline, line, main, flue, duct, conduit, channel, passage, conveyor.
v **1** CHANNEL, funnel, siphon, carry, convey, conduct, transmit, supply, deliver. **2** WHISTLE, chirp, tweet, cheep, peep, twitter, sing, warble, trill, play, sound.

piquant *adj* **1** *piquant sauce*: spicy, tangy, savoury, salty, peppery, pungent, sharp, biting, stinging. **2** LIVELY, spirited, stimulating, provocative, interesting, sparkling.
≠ **1** bland, insipid. **2** dull, banal.

pique *n* annoyance, irritation, vexation, displeasure, offence, huff (*infml*), resentment, grudge.

piqued *adj* annoyed, irritated, vexed, riled, angry, displeased, offended, miffed (*infml*), peeved (*infml*), put out, resentful.

pit *n* mine, coalmine, excavation, trench, ditch, hollow, depression, indentation, dent, hole, cavity, crater, pothole, gulf, chasm, abyss.

pitch *v* **1** THROW, fling, toss, chuck (*infml*), lob, bowl, hurl, heave, sling, fire, launch, aim, direct. **2** PLUNGE, dive, plummet, drop, fall headlong, tumble, lurch, roll, wallow. **3** *pitch camp*: erect, put up, set up, place, station, settle, plant, fix.
n **1** *cricket pitch*: ground, field, playing-field, arena, stadium. **2** SOUND, tone, timbre, modulation, frequency, level. **3** GRADIENT, incline, slope, tilt, angle, degree, steepness.

piteous *adj* poignant, moving, touching, distressing, heart-rending, plaintive, mournful, sad, sorrowful, woeful, wretched, pitiful, pitiable, pathetic.

pitfall *n* danger, peril, hazard, trap, snare, stumbling-block, catch, snag, drawback, difficulty.

pith *n* importance, significance, moment, weight, value, consequence, substance, matter, marrow, meat, gist, essence, crux, nub, heart, core, kernel.

pithy *adj* succinct, concise, compact, terse, short, brief, pointed, trenchant, forceful, cogent, telling.
≠ wordy, verbose.

pitiful *adj* **1** CONTEMPTIBLE, despicable, low, mean, vile, shabby, deplorable, lamentable, woeful, inadequate, hopeless, pathetic (*infml*), insignificant, paltry, worthless. **2** PITEOUS, doleful, mournful, distressing, heart-rending, pathetic, pitiable, sad, miserable, wretched, poor, sorry.

pitiless *adj* merciless, cold-hearted, unsympathetic, unfeeling, uncaring, hard-hearted, callous, cruel, inhuman, brutal, cold-blooded, ruthless, relentless, unremitting, inexorable, harsh.
≠ merciful, compassionate, kind, gentle.

pittance *n* modicum, crumb, drop (in the ocean), chicken-feed (*infml*), peanuts (*sl*), trifle.

pitted *adj* dented, holey, potholed, pockmarked, blemished, scarred, marked, notched, indented, rough.

pity *n* **1** SYMPATHY, commiseration, regret, understanding, fellow-feeling, compassion, kindness, tenderness, mercy, forbearance. **2** *what a pity!*: shame, misfortune, bad luck.
≠ **1** cruelty, anger, scorn.
v feel sorry for, feel for, sympathize with, commiserate with, grieve for, weep for.

pivot *n* axis, hinge, axle, spindle, kingpin, linchpin, swivel, hub, focal point, centre, heart.
v **1** SWIVEL, turn, spin, revolve, rotate, swing. **2** DEPEND, rely, hinge, hang, lie.

placard *n* poster, bill, notice, sign, advertisement.

placate *v* appease, pacify, conciliate, mollify, calm, assuage, soothe, lull, quiet.
≠ anger, enrage, incense, infuriate.

place *n* **1** SITE, locale, venue, location, situation, spot, point, position, seat, space, room. **2** CITY, town, village, locality, neighbourhood, district, area, region. **3** BUILDING, property, dwelling, residence, house, flat, apartment, home.
v put, set, plant, fix, position, locate, situate, rest, settle, lay, stand, deposit, leave.
in place of instead of, in lieu of, as a replacement for, as a substitute for, as an alternative to.
out of place inappropriate, unsuitable, unfitting, unbecoming, unseemly.
take place happen, occur, come about.

placid *adj* calm, composed, unruffled, untroubled, cool, self-possessed, level-headed, imperturbable, mild, gentle, equable, even-tempered, serene, tranquil, still, quiet, peaceful, restful.
≠ excitable, agitated, disturbed.

plagiarize *v* crib, copy, reproduce, imitate, counterfeit, pirate, infringe copyright, poach, steal, lift, appropriate, borrow.

plague *n* **1** PESTILENCE, epidemic, disease, infection, contagion, infestation. **2** NUISANCE, annoyance, curse, scourge, trial, affliction, torment, calamity.
v annoy, vex, bother, disturb, trouble, distress, upset, pester, harass, hound, haunt, bedevil, afflict, torment, torture, persecute.

plain *adj* **1** *plain cookery*: ordinary, basic, simple, unpretentious, modest, unadorned, unelaborate, restrained. **2** OBVIOUS, evident, patent, clear, understandable, apparent, visible, unmistakable. **3** FRANK, candid, blunt, outspoken, direct, forthright, straightforward, unambiguous, plain-spoken, open, honest, truthful. **4** UNATTRACTIVE, ugly, unprepossessing, unlovely. **5** *plain fabric*: unpatterned, unvariegated, uncoloured, self-coloured.
≠ **1** fancy, elaborate. **2** unclear, obscure. **3** devious, deceitful. **4** attractive, good-looking. **5** patterned.
n grassland, prairie, steppe, lowland, flat, plateau, tableland.

plaintive *adj* doleful, mournful, melancholy, wistful, sad, sorrowful, grief-stricken, piteous, heart-rending, high-pitched.

plan *n* **1** BLUEPRINT, layout, diagram, chart, map, drawing, sketch, representation, design. **2** IDEA, suggestion, proposal, proposition, project, scheme, plot, system, method, procedure, strategy, programme, schedule, scenario.
v **1** PLOT, scheme, design, invent, devise, contrive, formulate, frame, draft, outline, prepare, organize, arrange. **2** AIM, intend, propose, contemplate, envisage, foresee.

planet

> *Planets within the Earth's solar system (nearest the sun shown first) are*: Mercury, Venus, Earth, Mars, Jupiter, Saturn, Uranus, Neptune, Pluto.

plant

> *Plants include*: annual, biennial, perennial, herbaceous plant, evergreen, succulent, cultivar, hybrid, house plant, pot plant; flower, herb, shrub, bush, tree, vegetable, grass, vine, weed, cereal, wild flower, air-plant, water-plant, cactus, fern, moss, algae, lichen, fungus; bulb, corm, seedling, sapling, bush, climber. *see also* **algae and lichen**; **bulbs and corms**; **flower**; **grass**; **leaf**; **poisonous**; **shrubs**; **weeds**; **wild flowers**.

n factory, works, foundry, mill, shop, yard, workshop, machinery, apparatus, equipment, gear.
v **1** SOW, seed, bury, transplant. **2** INSERT, put, place, set, fix, lodge, root, settle, found, establish.

plaster *n* sticking-plaster, dressing,

bandage, plaster of Paris, mortar, stucco.
v daub, smear, coat, cover, spread.

plastic *adj* soft, pliable, flexible, supple, malleable, mouldable, ductile, receptive, impressionable, manageable.
≠ rigid, inflexible.

Types of plastic include: Bakelite®, Biopol®, celluloid®, epoxy resin, Perspex®, phenolic resin, plexiglass, polyester, polyethylene, polymethyl methacrylate, polynorbornene, polypropylene, polystyrene, polythene, polyurethane, PTFE (polytetrafluoroethylene), PVC (polyvinyl chloride), uPVC (unplasticized polyvinyl chloride), silicone, Teflon®, transpolyisoprene, urea formaldehyde, vinyl.

plate *n* **1** DISH, platter, salver, helping, serving, portion. **2** ILLUSTRATION, picture, print, lithograph.
v coat, cover, overlay, veneer, laminate, electroplate, anodize, galvanize, platinize, gild, silver, tin.

platform *n* **1** STAGE, podium, dais, rostrum, stand. **2** POLICY, party line, principles, tenets, manifesto, programme, objectives.

platitude *n* banality, commonplace, truism, cliché, chestnut.

plausible *adj* credible, believable, reasonable, logical, likely, possible, probable, convincing, persuasive, smooth-talking, glib.
≠ implausible, unlikely, improbable.

play *v* **1** AMUSE ONESELF, have fun, enjoy oneself, revel, sport, romp, frolic, caper. **2** PARTICIPATE, take part, join in, compete. **3** *France played Italy*: oppose, vie with, challenge, take on. **4** ACT, perform, portray, represent, impersonate.
≠ **1** work.
n **1** FUN, amusement, entertainment, diversion, recreation, sport, game, hobby, pastime. **2** DRAMA, tragedy, comedy, farce, show, performance. **3** MOVEMENT, action, flexibility, give, leeway, latitude, margin, scope, range, room, space.
≠ **1** work.
play down minimize, make light of, gloss over, underplay, understate, undervalue, underestimate.
≠ exaggerate.
play on exploit, take advantage of, turn to account, profit by, trade on, capitalize on.
play up 1 EXAGGERATE, highlight, spotlight, accentuate, emphasize, stress. **2** MISBEHAVE, malfunction, trouble, bother, annoy, hurt.

playboy *n* philanderer, womanizer, ladies' man, rake, libertine.

player *n* **1** CONTESTANT, competitor, participant, sportsman, sportswoman. **2** PERFORMER, entertainer, artiste, actor, actress, musician, instrumentalist.

playful *adj* sportive, frolicsome, lively, spirited, mischievous, roguish, impish, puckish, kittenish, good-natured, jesting, teasing, humorous, tongue-in-cheek.
≠ serious.

playwright *n* dramatist, scriptwriter, screenwriter.

plea *n* **1** APPEAL, petition, request, entreaty, supplication, prayer, invocation. **2** DEFENCE, justification, excuse, explanation, claim.

plead *v* **1** BEG, implore, beseech, entreat, appeal, petition, ask, request. **2** *plead ignorance*: assert, maintain, claim, allege.

pleasant *adj* agreeable, nice, fine, lovely, delightful, charming, likable, amiable, friendly, affable, good-humoured, cheerful, congenial, enjoyable, amusing, pleasing, gratifying, satisfying, acceptable, welcome, refreshing.
≠ unpleasant, nasty, unfriendly.

please *v* **1** DELIGHT, charm, captivate, entertain, amuse, cheer, gladden, humour, indulge, gratify, satisfy, content, suit. **2** WANT, will, wish, desire, like, prefer, choose, think fit.
≠ **1** displease, annoy, anger, sadden.

pleased *adj* contented, satisfied, gratified, glad, happy, delighted, thrilled, euphoric.
≠ displeased, annoyed.

pleasing *adj* gratifying, satisfying, acceptable, good, pleasant, agreeable, nice, delightful, charming, attractive, engaging, winning.
≠ unpleasant, disagreeable.

pleasure *n* amusement, entertainment, recreation, fun, enjoyment, gratification, satisfaction, contentment, happiness, joy, delight, comfort, solace.
≠ sorrow, pain, trouble, displeasure.

pleat *v* tuck, fold, crease, flute, crimp, gather, pucker.

pledge *n* **1** PROMISE, vow, word of honour, oath, bond, covenant, guarantee, warrant, assurance, undertaking. **2** DEPOSIT, security, surety, bail.
v promise, vow, swear, contract, engage, undertake, vouch, guarantee, secure.

plentiful *adj* ample, abundant, profuse, copious, overflowing, lavish, generous, liberal, bountiful, fruitful, productive.
≠ scarce, scanty, rare.

plenty *n* abundance, profusion, plethora, lots (*infml*), loads (*infml*), masses (*infml*), heaps (*infml*), piles (*infml*), stacks (*infml*), enough, sufficiency, quantity, mass, volume, fund, mine, store.
≠ scarcity, lack, want, need.

pliable *adj* pliant, flexible, bendable, bendy (*infml*), supple, lithe, malleable, plastic, yielding, adaptable, accommodating, manageable, tractable, docile, compliant, biddable, persuadable, responsive, receptive, impressionable, susceptible.
≠ rigid, inflexible, headstrong.

plight *n* predicament, quandary, dilemma, extremity, trouble, difficulty, straits, state, condition, situation, circumstances, case.

plod *v* **1** TRUDGE, tramp, stump, lumber, plough through. **2** DRUDGE, labour, toil, grind, slog, persevere, soldier on.

plot *n* **1** CONSPIRACY, intrigue, machination, scheme, plan, stratagem. **2** STORY, narrative, subject, theme, storyline, thread, outline, scenario. **3** *plot of land*: patch, tract, area, allotment, lot, parcel.
v **1** CONSPIRE, intrigue, machinate, scheme, hatch, lay, cook up, devise, contrive, plan, project, design, draft. **2** CHART, map, mark, locate, draw, calculate.

plotter *n* conspirator, intriguer, machinator, schemer.

ploy *n* manoeuvre, strategem, tactic, move, device, contrivance, scheme, game, trick, artifice, dodge, wile, ruse, subterfuge.

pluck *n* courage, bravery, spirit, mettle, nerve (*infml*), guts (*infml*), grit, backbone, fortitude, resolution, determination.
≠ cowardice.
v **1** PULL, draw, tug, snatch, pull off, remove, pick, collect, gather, harvest. **2** *pluck a guitar*: pick, twang, strum.

plucky *adj* brave, courageous, bold, daring, intrepid, heroic, valiant, spirited.
≠ cowardly, weak, feeble.

plug *n* **1** STOPPER, bung, cork, spigot. **2** (*infml*) ADVERTISEMENT, publicity, mention, puff.
v **1** STOP (UP), bung, cork, block, choke, close, seal, fill, pack, stuff. **2** (*infml*) ADVERTISE, publicize, promote, push, mention.

plumb *adv* **1** VERTICALLY, perpendicularly. **2** PRECISELY, exactly, dead, slap (*infml*), bang (*infml*).
v sound, fathom, measure, gauge, penetrate, probe, search, explore.

plumbing

Plumbing materials and equipment include: auger, back boiler, ball valve, ballcock, basin, basin spanner, bath, bend, bidet, blowtorch, boiler, bowl, ceiling joint, cistern, compression fitting, copper pipe, copper tube, coupler, cylinder, draincock, elbow joint, electric water heater, expansion (or header) tank, faucet (*US*), flare joint, float, flux, gas water heater, gasket, gate valve, geyser, hose, immersion heater, joint, jointing compound, lavatory, lavatory chain, lever tap, lockshield valve, mains pipe, mixer tap, monkey wrench, motorized zone valve, nipple, nipple key, overflow bend, pan, pedestal, pipe, pipe clip, pipe coupling, pipe wrench, plug, plunger, programmer, P-trap, pump, radiator, septic tank, shower, shower attachment, shower head, sink, siphon washer, soil vent, solder, stopcock, Stillson wrench®, sump pump, tank, tap, tee, thermostat, thermostatic valve, toilet, trap, tube cutter, tube flaring tool, U-bend, union, urinal, washer, waste disposal unit, waste pipe, water closet, WC, Y-branch.

plummet *v* plunge, dive, nose-dive, descend, drop, fall, tumble.
≠ soar.

plump *adj* fat, obese, dumpy, tubby, stout, round, rotund, portly, chubby, podgy, fleshy, full, ample, buxom.
≠ thin, skinny.

plump for opt for, choose, select, favour, back, support.

plunder *v* loot, pillage, ravage, devastate, sack, raid, ransack, rifle, steal, rob, strip.
n loot, pillage, booty, swag (*sl*), spoils, pickings, ill-gotten gains, prize.

plunge *v* **1** DIVE, jump, nose-dive, swoop, dive-bomb, plummet, descend, go down, sink, drop, fall, pitch, tumble, hurtle, career, charge, dash, rush, tear. **2** IMMERSE, submerge, dip.
n dive, jump, swoop, descent, drop, fall, tumble, immersion, submersion.

ply *n* layer, fold, thickness, strand, sheet, leaf.

poach *v* steal, pilfer, appropriate, trespass, encroach, infringe.

pocket *n* pouch, bag, envelope, receptacle, compartment, hollow, cavity.
adj small, little, mini (*infml*), concise, compact, portable, miniature.
v take, appropriate, help oneself to, lift, pilfer, filch, steal, nick (*infml*), pinch (*infml*).

pod *n* shell, husk, case, hull.

poem

Types of poem include: ballad, elegy, epic, haiku, idyll, lay, limerick, lyric, madrigal, nursery-rhyme, ode, pastoral, roundelay, sonnet, tanka.

poet *n* versifier, rhymer, rhymester, lyricist, bard, minstrel.

poetic *adj* poetical, lyrical, moving, artistic, graceful, flowing, metrical, rhythmical, rhyming.
≠ prosaic.

poignant *adj* moving, touching, affecting, tender, distressing, upsetting, heartbreaking, heart-rending, piteous, pathetic, sad, painful, agonizing.

point *n* **1** FEATURE, attribute, aspect, facet, detail, particular, item, subject, topic. **2** *what's the point?*: use, purpose, motive, reason, object, intention, aim, end, goal, objective. **3** ESSENCE, crux, core, pith, gist, thrust, meaning, drift, burden. **4** PLACE, position, situation, location, site, spot. **5** MOMENT, instant, juncture, stage, time, period. **6** DOT, spot, mark, speck, full stop.
v **1** *point a gun*: aim, direct, train, level. **2** INDICATE, signal, show, signify, denote, designate.
point of view opinion, view, belief, judgement, attitude, position, standpoint, viewpoint, outlook, perspective, approach, angle, slant.
point out show, indicate, draw attention to, point to, reveal, identify, specify, mention, bring up, allude to, remind.

point-blank *adj* direct, forthright, straightforward, plain, explicit, open, unreserved, blunt, frank, candid.
adv directly, forthrightly, straightforwardly, plainly, explicitly, openly, bluntly, frankly, candidly.

pointed *adj* sharp, keen, edged, barbed, cutting, incisive, trenchant, biting, penetrating, telling.

pointer *n* **1** ARROW, indicator, needle, hand. **2** TIP, recommendation, suggestion, hint, guide, indication, advice, warning, caution.

pointless *adj* useless, futile, vain, fruitless, unproductive, unprofitable, worthless, senseless, absurd, meaningless, aimless.
≠ useful, profitable, meaningful.

poise *n* calmness, composure, self-possession, presence of mind, coolness, equanimity, aplomb, assurance, dignity, elegance, grace, balance, equilibrium.
v balance, position, hover, hang, suspend.

poised *adj* **1** DIGNIFIED, graceful, calm, composed, unruffled, collected, self-possessed, cool, self-confident, assured. **2** *poised for action*: prepared, ready, set, waiting, expectant.

poison *n* toxin, venom, bane, blight, cancer, malignancy, contagion, contamination, corruption.
v infect, contaminate, pollute, taint, adulterate, corrupt, deprave, pervert, warp.

poisonous *adj* toxic, venomous, lethal, deadly, fatal, mortal, noxious, pernicious, malicious.

> *Poisonous plants include*: aconite, amanita, anemone, banewort, belladonna, black nightshade, castor oil plant, common nightshade, cowbane, cuckoo pint, deadly nightshade, digitalis, dwale, foxglove, giant hockweed, helmet flower, hemlock, hemlock water dropwort, Jimsonweed, laburnum, lantana, lords-and-ladies, meadow saffron, monkshood, naked boys, naked lady, oleander, poison ivy, stinkweed, stramonium, thorn apple, wake-robin, wild arum, windflower, wolfsbane. *see also* **mushrooms and toadstools**.

poke *v* prod, stab, jab, stick, thrust, push, shove, nudge, elbow, dig, butt, hit, punch.
n prod, jab, thrust, shove, nudge, dig, butt, punch.

pole[1] *n* bar, rod, stick, shaft, spar, upright, post, stake, mast, staff.

pole[2] *n* antipode, extremity, extreme, limit.
poles apart irreconcilable, worlds apart, incompatible, like chalk and cheese.

police *n* police force, constabulary, the Law (*infml*), the Bill (*sl*), the fuzz (*sl*).
v check, control, regulate, monitor, watch, observe, supervise, oversee, patrol, guard, protect, defend, keep the peace.

policeman, policewoman *n* officer, constable, PC, cop (*sl*), copper (*infml*), bobby (*infml*).

policy *n* **1** CODE OF PRACTICE, rules, guidelines, procedure, method, practice, custom, protocol. **2** COURSE OF ACTION, line, course, plan, programme, scheme, stance, position.

polish *v* **1** SHINE, brighten, smooth, rub, buff, burnish, clean, wax. **2** IMPROVE, enhance, brush up, touch up, finish, perfect, refine, cultivate.
≠ **1** tarnish, dull.
n **1** *a tin of polish*: wax, varnish. **2** SHINE, gloss, sheen, lustre, brightness, brilliance, sparkle, smoothness, finish, glaze, veneer. **3** REFINEMENT, cultivation, class, breeding, sophistication, finesse, style, elegance, grace, poise.
≠ **2** dullness. **3** clumsiness.

polished *adj* **1** SHINING, shiny, glossy, lustrous, gleaming, burnished, smooth, glassy, slippery. **2** FAULTLESS, flawless, impeccable, perfect, outstanding, superlative, masterly, expert, professional, skilful, accomplished, perfected. **3** REFINED, cultivated, genteel, well-bred, polite, sophisticated, urbane, suave, elegant, graceful.
≠ **1** tarnished. **2** inexpert. **3** gauche.

polite *adj* courteous, well-mannered, respectful, civil, well-bred, refined, cultured, gentlemanly, ladylike, gracious, obliging, thoughtful, considerate, tactful, diplomatic.
≠ impolite, discourteous, rude.

political ideologies

> *Political ideologies include*: absolutism, anarchism, authoritarianism, Bolshevism, Christian democracy, collectivism, communism, conservatism, democracy, egalitarianism, fascism, federalism, holism, imperialism, individualism, liberalism, Maoism, Marxism, nationalism, Nazism, neocolonialism, neo-fascism, neo-nazism, pluralism, republicanism, social democracy, socialism, syndicalism, Thatcherism, theocracy,

totalitarianism, unilateralism, Trotskyism, Whiggism.

politics *n* public affairs, civics, affairs of state, statecraft, government, diplomacy, statesmanship, political science.

Terms used in politics include: alliance, apartheid, ballot, bill, blockade, cabinet, campaign, civil service, coalition, constitution, council, coup d'état, détente, election, electoral register, ethnic cleansing, general election, glasnost, go to the country, government, green paper, Hansard, judiciary, left wing, lobby, local government, majority, mandate, manifesto, nationalization, parliament, party, party line, perestroika, prime minister's question time, privatization, propaganda, proportional representation, rainbow coalition, referendum, right wing, sanction, shadow cabinet, sovereignty, state, summit, summit conference, term of office, trade union, veto, vote, welfare state, whip, three-line whip, white paper. *People in politics include*: activist, ambassador, Black Rod, capitalist, Communist, commie (*infml*), comrade, Conservative, Democrat, Deputy Speaker, dictator, dissident, dry (*infml*), extremist, Green, high commissioner, independent, lefty (*infml*), legislator, Liberal, Liberal Democrat, loyalist, Marxist, Marxist-Leminist, member of parliament, minister, moderate, MP, party chairman, party member, party worker, pinko (*infml*), politician, premier, president, prime minister, radical, red (*infml*), Republican, revolutionary, secretary of state, Social Democrat, Socialist, speaker, statesman, stateswoman, Tory, Trotskyite, true-blue, wet (*infml*), Whig. *Political parties include*: Alliance, Co-operative, Communist, Conservative and Unionist, Democratic, Democratic Left, Democratic Unionist, Fianna Fáil, Fine Gael, Green, Labour, Liberal, Liberal Democratic, Militant Labour, National Front, Parliamentary, Parliamentary Labour, Plaid Cymru, Progressive Democrats, Republican, Scottish Conservative and Unionist, Scottish Liberal Democratic, Scottish National, Sinn Féin, Social and Liberal Democratic, Social Democratic and Labour, Ulster Democratic Unionist, Ulster Popular Unionist, Ulster Unionist, Welsh Liberal Democratic. *see also* **government systems**; **parliaments and assemblies**; **political ideologies**.

poll *n* ballot, vote, voting, plebiscite, referendum, straw-poll, sampling, canvass, opinion poll, survey, census, count, tally.

pollute *v* contaminate, infect, poison, taint, adulterate, debase, corrupt, dirty, foul, soil, defile, sully, stain, mar, spoil.

pollution *n* impurity, contamination, infection, taint, adulteration, corruption, dirtiness, foulness, defilement.
≠ purification, purity, cleanness.

pomp *n* ceremony, ceremonial, ritual, solemnity, formality, ceremoniousness, state, grandeur, splendour, magnificence, pageantry, show, display, parade, ostentation, flourish.
≠ austerity, simplicity.

pompous *adj* self-important, arrogant, grandiose, supercilious, overbearing, imperious, magisterial, bombastic, high-flown, overblown, windy, affected, pretentious, ostentatious.
≠ unassuming, modest, simple, unaffected.

pool[1] *n* puddle, pond, lake, mere, tarn, watering-hole, paddling-pool, swimming-pool.

pool[2] *n* **1** FUND, reserve, accumulation, bank, kitty, purse, pot, jackpot.
2 SYNDICATE, cartel, ring, combine, consortium, collective, group, team.
v contribute, chip in (*infml*), combine, amalgamate, merge, share, muck in (*infml*).

poor *adj* **1** IMPOVERISHED, poverty-stricken, badly off, hard-up, broke (*infml*), stony-broke (*sl*), skint (*sl*), bankrupt, penniless, destitute, miserable, wretched, distressed,

straitened, needy, lacking, deficient, insufficient, scanty, skimpy, meagre, sparse, depleted, exhausted. **2** BAD, substandard, unsatisfactory, inferior, mediocre, below par, low-grade, second-rate, third-rate, shoddy, imperfect, faulty, weak, feeble, pathetic (*infml*), sorry, worthless, fruitless. **3** UNFORTUNATE, unlucky, luckless, ill-fated, unhappy, miserable, pathetic, pitiable, pitiful.
≠ **1** rich, wealthy, affluent. **2** superior, impressive. **3** fortunate, lucky.

poorly *adj* ill, sick, unwell, indisposed, ailing, sickly, off colour, below par, out of sorts (*infml*), under the weather (*infml*), seedy, groggy, rotten (*infml*).
≠ well, healthy.

pop *v* burst, explode, go off, bang, crack, snap.
n bang, crack, snap, burst, explosion.

popular *adj* well-liked, favourite, liked, favoured, approved, in demand, sought-after, fashionable, modish, trendy (*infml*), prevailing, current, accepted, conventional, standard, stock, common, prevalent, widespread, universal, general, household, famous, well-known, celebrated, idolized.
≠ unpopular.

popularise *v* spread, propagate, universalize, democratize, simplify.

popularly *adv* commonly, widely, universally, generally, usually, customarily, conventionally, traditionally.

populate *v* people, occupy, settle, colonize, inhabit, live in, overrun.

population *n* inhabitants, natives, residents, citizens, occupants, community, society, people, folk.

populous *n* crowded, packed, swarming, teeming, crawling, overpopulated.
≠ deserted.

porcelain

Types of porcelain include: biscuit, bisque, blue and white, bone china, Canton, Capodimonte, chinoiserie, Compagnie des Indes, copper red, eggshell, faience, famille-rose, famille-verte, First Period Worcester, hard paste, Imari, Kakiemon, Kraak, nankeen, Parian, saltglazed, soapstone paste, soft paste, Yingqing. *Famous makes of porcelain include*: Arita, Belleek, Bow, Bristol, Caughley, Chantilly, Chelsea, Coalport, Copeland, Derby, Dresden, Limoges, Meissen, Ming, Minton, Nanking, Rockingham, Royal Doulton, Royal Worcester, Satsuma, Sèvres, Vienna, Wedgwood, Worcester.

pornographic *adj* obscene, indecent, dirty, filthy, blue, risqué, bawdy, coarse, gross, lewd, erotic, titillating.

porous *adj* permeable, pervious, penetrable, absorbent, spongy, honeycombed, pitted.
≠ impermeable, impervious.

portable *adj* movable, transportable, compact, lightweight, manageable, handy, convenient.
≠ fixed, immovable.

porter[1] *n* bearer, carrier, baggage-attendant, baggage-handler.

porter[2] *n* doorman, commissionaire, door-keeper, gatekeeper, janitor, caretaker, concierge.

portion *n* share, allocation, allotment, parcel, allowance, ration, quota, measure, part, section, division, fraction, percentage, bit, fragment, morsel, piece, segment, slice, serving, helping.

portly *adj* stout, corpulent, rotund, round, fat, plump, obese, overweight, heavy, large.
≠ slim, thin, slight.

portrait *n* picture, painting, drawing, sketch, caricature, miniature, icon, photograph, likeness, image, representation, vignette, profile, characterization, description, depiction, portrayal.

portray *v* draw, sketch, paint, illustrate, picture, represent, depict, describe, evoke, play, impersonate, characterize, personify.

portrayal *n* representation, characterization, depiction, description, evocation, presentation, performance, interpretation, rendering.

pose *v* **1** MODEL, sit, position. **2** PRETEND, feign, affect, put on an act, masquerade, pass oneself off, impersonate. **3** *pose a question*: set, put forward, submit, present.
n **1** POSITION, stance, air, bearing, posture, attitude. **2** PRETENCE, sham, affectation, façade, front, masquerade, role, act.

poser[1] *n* puzzle, riddle, conundrum, brain-teaser, mystery, enigma, problem, vexed question.

poser[2] *n* poseur, poseuse, posturer, attitudinizer, exhibitionist, show-off, pseud (*infml*), phoney (*infml*).

posh (*infml*) *adj* smart, stylish, fashionable, high-class, upper-class, la-di-da (*sl*), grand, luxurious, lavish, swanky (*infml*), luxury, deluxe, up-market, exclusive, select, classy (*infml*), swish (*infml*).
≠ inferior, cheap.

position *n* **1** PLACE, situation, location, site, spot, point. **2** POSTURE, stance, pose, arrangement, disposition. **3** JOB, post, occupation, employment, office, duty, function, role. **4** RANK, grade, level, status, standing. **5** OPINION, point of view, belief, view, outlook, viewpoint, standpoint, stand.
v put, place, set, fix, stand, arrange, dispose, lay out, deploy, station, locate, situate, site.

positive *adj* **1** SURE, certain, convinced, confident, assured. **2** *positive criticism*: helpful, constructive, practical, useful, optimistic, hopeful, promising. **3** DEFINITE, decisive, conclusive, clear, unmistakable, explicit, unequivocal, express, firm, emphatic, categorical, undeniable, irrefutable, indisputable, incontrovertible. **4** ABSOLUTE, utter, sheer, complete, perfect.
≠ **1** uncertain. **2** negative. **3** indefinite, vague.

possess *v* **1** OWN, have, hold, enjoy, be endowed with. **2** SEIZE, take, obtain, acquire, take over, occupy, control, dominate, bewitch, haunt.

possession *n* ownership, title, tenure, occupation, custody, control, hold, grip.

possessions *n* belongings, property, things, paraphernalia, effects, goods, chattels, movables, assets, estate, wealth, riches.

possessive *adj* selfish, clinging, overprotective, domineering, dominating, jealous, covetous, acquisitive, grasping.
≠ unselfish, sharing.

possibility *n* likelihood, probability, odds, chance, risk, danger, hope, prospect, potentiality, conceivability, practicability, feasibility.
≠ impossibility, impracticability.

possible *adj* potential, promising, likely, probable, imaginable, conceivable, practicable, feasible, viable, tenable, workable, achievable, attainable, accomplishable, realizable.
≠ impossible, unthinkable, impracticable, unattainable.

possibly *adv* perhaps, maybe, hopefully (*infml*), by any means, at all, by any chance.

post[1] *n* pole, stake, picket, pale, pillar, column, shaft, support, baluster, upright, stanchion, strut, leg.
v display, stick up, pin up, advertise, publicize, announce, make known, report, publish.

post[2] *n* office, job, employment, position, situation, place, vacancy, appointment, assignment, station, beat.
v station, locate, situate, position, place, put, appoint, assign, second, transfer, move, send.

post[3] *n* mail, letters, dispatch, collection, delivery.
v mail, send, dispatch, transmit.

poster *n* notice, bill, sign, placard, sticker, advertisement, announcement.

posterity *n* descendants, successors, progeny, issue, offspring, children.

postpone *v* put off, defer, put back, hold over, delay, adjourn, suspend, shelve, pigeonhole, freeze, put on ice.
≠ advance, forward.

postscript *n* PS (*infml*), addition, supplement, afterthought, addendum, codicil, appendix, afterword, epilogue.
≠ introduction, prologue.

postulate *v* theorize, hypothesize, suppose, assume, propose, advance, lay down, stipulate.

posture *n* position, stance, pose, attitude, disposition, bearing, carriage, deportment.

posy *n* bouquet, spray, buttonhole, corsage.

pot *n* receptacle, vessel, teapot, coffee pot, urn, jar, vase, bowl, basin, pan, cauldron, crucible.

potent *adj* powerful, mighty, strong, intoxicating, pungent, effective, impressive, cogent, convincing, persuasive, compelling, forceful, dynamic, vigorous, authoritative, commanding, dominant, influential, overpowering.
≠ impotent, weak.

potential *adj* possible, likely, probable, prospective, future, aspiring, would-be, promising, budding, embryonic, undeveloped, dormant, latent, hidden, concealed, unrealized.
n possibility, ability, capability, capacity, aptitude, talent, powers, resources.

potion *n* mixture, concoction, brew, beverage, drink, draught, dose, medicine, tonic, elixir.

potpourri *n* medley, mixture, jumble, hotchpotch, miscellany, collection.

potter *v* tinker, fiddle, mess about (*infml*), dabble, loiter, fritter.

pottery *n* ceramics, crockery, china.

> *Terms used in pottery include*: armorial, art pottery, basalt, blanc-de-chine, bronzing, celadon, ceramic, china clay, cloisonné, crackleware, crazing, creamware, delft, earthenware, enamel, faience, fairing, figure, firing, flambé, flatback, glaze, grotesque, ground, ironstone, jasper, kiln, lustre, maiolica, majolica, maker's mark, mandarin palette, model, monogram, overglaze, porcelain, sagger, scratch blue, sgraffito, slip, slip-cast, spongeware, Staffordshire, stoneware, terracotta, tin-glazed earthenware, transfer printing, underglaze, Willow pattern. *see also* **porcelain**.

pounce *v* fall on, dive on, swoop, drop, attack, strike, ambush, spring, jump, leap, snatch, grab.

pound[1] *v* **1** STRIKE, thump, beat, drum, pelt, hammer, batter, bang, bash, smash. **2** PULVERIZE, powder, grind, mash, crush. **3** *his heart was pounding*: throb, pulsate, palpitate, thump, thud.

pound[2] *n* enclosure, compound, corral, yard, pen, fold.

pour *v* **1** *pour a drink*: serve, decant, tip. **2** SPILL, issue, discharge, flow, stream, run, rush, spout, spew, gush, cascade, crowd, throng, swarm.

pout *v* scowl, glower, grimace, pull a face, sulk, mope.
≠ grin, smile.
n scowl, glower, grimace, long face.
≠ grin, smile.

poverty *n* poorness, impoverishment, insolvency, bankruptcy, pennilessness, penury, destitution, distress, hardship, privation, need, necessity, want, lack, deficiency, shortage, inadequacy, insufficiency, depletion, scarcity, meagreness, paucity, dearth.
≠ wealth, richness, affluence, plenty.

powdery *adj* dusty, sandy, grainy, granular, powdered, pulverized, ground, fine, loose, dry, crumbly, friable, chalky.

power *n* **1** COMMAND, authority, sovereignty, rule, dominion, control, influence. **2** RIGHT, privilege, prerogative, authorization, warrant. **3** POTENCY, strength, intensity, force, vigour, energy. **4** ABILITY, capability, capacity, potential, faculty, competence.
≠ **1** subjection. **3** weakness. **4** inability.

powerful *adj* dominant, prevailing, leading, influential, high-powered, authoritative, commanding, potent, effective, strong, mighty, robust, muscular, energetic, forceful, telling, impressive, convincing, persuasive, compelling, winning, overwhelming.
≠ impotent, ineffective, weak.

powerless *adj* impotent, incapable, ineffective, weak, feeble, frail, infirm, incapacitated, disabled, paralysed,

helpless, vulnerable, defenceless, unarmed.
≠ powerful, potent, able.

practicable *adj* possible, feasible, performable, achievable, attainable, viable, workable, practical, realistic.
≠ impracticable.

practical *adj* **1** REALISTIC, sensible, commonsense, practicable, workable, feasible, down-to-earth, matter-of-fact, pragmatic, hardnosed (*infml*), hard-headed, businesslike, experienced, trained, qualified, skilled, accomplished, proficient, hands on, applied. **2** USEFUL, handy, serviceable, utilitarian, functional, working, everyday, ordinary.
≠ **1** impractical, unskilled, theoretical.

practically *adv* **1** ALMOST, nearly, well-nigh, virtually, pretty well, all but, just about, in principle, in effect, essentially, fundamentally, to all intents and purposes. **2** REALISTICALLY, sensibly, reasonably, rationally, pragmatically.

practice *n* **1** CUSTOM, tradition, convention, usage, habit, routine, way, method, system, procedure, policy. **2** REHEARSAL, run-through, dry run, dummy run, try-out, training, drill, exercise, work-out, study, experience. **3** *in practice*: effect, reality, actuality, action, operation, performance, use, application.
≠ **3** theory, principle.

practise *v* **1** DO, perform, execute, implement, carry out, apply, put into practice, follow, pursue, engage in, undertake. **2** REHEARSE, run through, repeat, drill, exercise, train, study, perfect.

practised *adj* experienced, seasoned, veteran, trained, qualified, accomplished, skilled, versed, knowledgeable, able, proficient, expert, masterly, consummate, finished.
≠ unpractised, inexperienced, inexpert.

pragmatic *adj* practical, realistic, sensible, matter-of-fact, businesslike, efficient, hard-headed, hardnosed (*infml*), unsentimental.
≠ unrealistic, idealistic, romantic.

praise *n* approval, admiration, commendation, congratulation, compliment, flattery, adulation, eulogy, applause, ovation, cheering, acclaim, recognition, testimonial, tribute, accolade, homage, honour, glory, worship, adoration, devotion, thanksgiving.
≠ criticism, revilement.
v commend, congratulate, admire, compliment, flatter, eulogize, wax lyrical, rave over (*infml*), extol, promote, applaud, cheer, acclaim, hail, recognize, acknowledge, pay tribute to, honour, laud, glorify, magnify, exalt, worship, adore, bless.
≠ criticize, revile.

praiseworthy *adj* commendable, fine, excellent, admirable, worthy, deserving, honourable, reputable, estimable, sterling.
≠ blameworthy, dishonourable, ignoble.

prank *n* trick, practical joke, joke, stunt, caper, frolic, lark, antic, escapade.

pray *v* invoke, call on, supplicate, entreat, implore, plead, beg, beseech, petition, ask, request, crave, solicit.

prayer *n* collect, litany, devotion, communion, invocation, supplication, entreaty, plea, appeal, petition, request.

preach *v* address, lecture, harangue, pontificate, sermonize, evangelize, moralize, exhort, urge, advocate.

precarious *adj* unsafe, dangerous, treacherous, risky, hazardous, chancy, uncertain, unsure, dubious, doubtful, unpredictable, unreliable, unsteady, unstable, shaky, wobbly, insecure, vulnerable.
≠ safe, certain, stable, secure.

precaution *n* safeguard, security, protection, insurance, providence, forethought, caution, prudence, foresight, anticipation, preparation, provision.

precautionary *adj* safety, protective, preventive, provident, cautious, prudent, judicious, preparatory, preliminary.

precede *v* come before, lead, come

first, go before, take precedence, introduce, herald, usher in.
≠ follow, succeed.

precedence *n* priority, preference, pride of place, superiority, supremacy, pre-eminence, lead, first place, seniority, rank.

precedent *n* example, instance, pattern, model, standard, criterion.

precinct *n* **1** ZONE, area, district, quarter, sector, division, section. **2** BOUNDARY, limit, bound, confine.

precious *adj* **1** VALUED, treasured, prized, cherished, beloved, dearest, darling, favourite, loved, adored, idolized. **2** VALUABLE, expensive, costly, dear, priceless, inestimable, rare, choice, fine.

precipitate *v* hasten, hurry, speed, accelerate, quicken, expedite, advance, further, bring on, induce, trigger, cause, occasion.
adj sudden, unexpected, abrupt, quick, swift, rapid, brief, hasty, hurried, headlong, breakneck, frantic, violent, impatient, hot-headed, impetuous, impulsive, rash, reckless, heedless, indiscreet.
≠ cautious, careful.

precipitation

> *Types of precipitation include*: dew, downpour, drizzle, fog, hail, mist, rain, rainfall, rainstorm, shower, sleet, snow, snowfall, snowflake.

precipitous *adj* steep, sheer, perpendicular, vertical, high.
≠ gradual.

precise *adj* exact, accurate, right, punctilious, correct, factual, faithful, authentic, literal, word-for-word, express, definite, explicit, unequivocal, unambiguous, clear-cut, distinct, detailed, blow-by-blow, minute, nice, particular, specific, fixed, rigid, strict, careful, meticulous, scrupulous, fastidious.
≠ imprecise, inexact, ambiguous, careless.

precisely *adv* exactly, absolutely, just so, accurately, correctly, literally, verbatim, word for word, strictly, minutely, clearly, distinctly.

precision *n* exactness, accuracy, correctness, faithfulness, explicitness, distinctness, detail, particularity, rigour, care, meticulousness, scrupulousness, neatness.
≠ imprecision, inaccuracy.

precocious *adj* forward, ahead, advanced, early, premature, mature, developed, gifted, clever, bright, smart, quick, fast.
≠ backward.

preconceive *v* presuppose, presume, assume, anticipate, project, imagine, conceive, envisage, expect, visualize, picture.

preconception *n* presupposition, presumption, assumption, conjecture, anticipation, expectation, prejudgement, bias, prejudice.

precondition *n* condition, stipulation, requirement, prerequisite, essential, necessity, must.

precursor *n* antecedent, forerunner, sign, indication, herald, harbinger, messenger, usher, pioneer, trail-blazer.
≠ follower, successor.

predecessor *n* ancestor, forefather, forebear, antecedent, forerunner, precursor.
≠ successor, descendant.

predestination *n* destiny, fate, lot, doom, predetermination, foreordination.

predetermined *adj* **1** PREDESTINED, destined, fated, doomed, ordained, foreordained. **2** PREARRANGED, arranged, agreed, fixed, set.

predicament *n* situation, plight, trouble, mess, fix, spot (*infml*), quandary, dilemma, impasse, crisis, emergency.

predict *v* foretell, prophesy, foresee, forecast, prognosticate, project.

predictable *adj* foreseeable, expected, anticipated, likely, probable, imaginable, foreseen, foregone, certain, sure, reliable, dependable.
≠ unpredictable, uncertain.

prediction *n* prophecy, forecast, prognosis, augury, divination, fortune-telling, soothsaying.

predispose *v* dispose, incline, prompt, induce, make, sway, influence, affect, bias, prejudice.

predominant *adj* dominant, prevailing, preponderant, chief, main, principal, primary, capital, paramount, supreme, sovereign, ruling, controlling, leading, powerful, potent, prime, important, influential, forceful, strong.
≠ minor, lesser, weak.

pre-eminent *adj* supreme, unsurpassed, unrivalled, unequalled, unmatched, matchless, incomparable, inimitable, chief, foremost, leading, eminent, distinguished, renowned, famous, prominent, outstanding, exceptional, excellent, superlative, transcendent, superior.
≠ inferior, unknown.

preface *n* foreword, introduction, preamble, prologue, prelude, preliminaries.
≠ epilogue, postscript.
v precede, prefix, lead up to, introduce, launch, open, begin, start.
≠ end, finish, complete.

prefer *v* favour, like better, would rather, would sooner, want, wish, desire, choose, select, pick, opt for, go for, plump for, single out, advocate, recommend, back, support, fancy, elect, adopt.
≠ reject.

preferable *adj* better, superior, nicer, preferred, favoured, chosen, desirable, advantageous, advisable, recommended.
≠ inferior, undesirable.

preference *n* **1** FAVOURITE, first choice, choice, pick, selection, option, wish, desire. **2** LIKING, fancy, inclination, predilection, partiality, favouritism, preferential treatment.

preferential *adj* better, superior, favoured, privileged, special, favourable, advantageous.
≠ equal.

pregnant *adj* **1** *a pregnant woman*: expectant, expecting, with child (*fml*). **2** *a pregnant pause*: meaningful, significant, eloquent, expressive, suggestive, charged, loaded, full.

prejudice *n* **1** BIAS, partiality, partisanship, discrimination, unfairness, injustice, intolerance, narrow-mindedness, bigotry, chauvinism, racism, sexism. **2** HARM, damage, impairment, hurt, injury, detriment, disadvantage, loss, ruin.
≠ **1** fairness, tolerance. **2** benefit, advantage.
v **1** BIAS, predispose, incline, sway, influence, condition, colour, slant, distort, load, weight. **2** HARM, damage, impair, hinder, undermine, hurt, injure, mar, spoil, ruin, wreck.
≠ **2** benefit, help, advance.

prejudiced *adj* biased, partial, predisposed, subjective, partisan, one-sided, discriminatory, unfair, unjust, loaded, weighted, intolerant, narrow-minded, bigoted, chauvinist, racist, sexist, jaundiced, distorted, warped, influenced, conditioned.
≠ impartial, fair, tolerant.

prejudicial *adj* harmful, damaging, hurtful, injurious, detrimental, disadvantageous, unfavourable, inimical.
≠ beneficial, advantageous.

preliminaries *n* preparation, groundwork, foundations, basics, rudiments, formalities, introduction, preface, prelude, opening, beginning, start.

preliminary *adj* preparatory, prior, advance, exploratory, experimental, trial, test, pilot, early, earliest, first, initial, primary, qualifying, inaugural, introductory, opening.
≠ final, closing.

prelude *n* overture, introduction, preface, foreword, preamble, prologue, opening, opener, preliminary, preparation, beginning, start, commencement, precursor, curtain raiser.
≠ finale, epilogue.

premature *adj* early, immature, green, unripe, embryonic, half-formed, incomplete, undeveloped, abortive, hasty, ill-considered, rash, untimely, inopportune, ill-timed.
≠ late, tardy.

premeditated *adj* planned, intended, intentional, deliberate, wilful, conscious, cold-blooded, calculated, considered, contrived, preplanned, prearranged, predetermined.
≠ unpremeditated, spontaneous.

première *n* first performance, opening, opening night, first night, début.

premise *n* proposition, statement, assertion, postulate, thesis, argument, basis, supposition, hypothesis, presupposition, assumption.

premises *n* building, property, establishment, office, grounds, estate, site, place.

premonition *n* presentiment, feeling, intuition, hunch, idea, suspicion, foreboding, misgiving, fear, apprehension, anxiety, worry, warning, omen, sign.

preoccupation *n* **1** OBSESSION, fixation, hang-up (*infml*), concern, interest, enthusiasm, hobby-horse. **2** DISTRACTION, absent-mindedness, reverie, obliviousness, oblivion.

preoccupied *adj* **1** OBSESSED, intent, immersed, engrossed, engaged, taken up, wrapped up, involved. **2** DISTRACTED, abstracted, absent-minded, daydreaming, absorbed, faraway, heedless, oblivious, pensive.

preparation *n* **1** READINESS, provision, precaution, safeguard, foundation, groundwork, spadework, basics, rudiments, preliminaries, plans, arrangements. **2** MIXTURE, compound, concoction, potion, medicine, lotion, application.

preparatory *adj* preliminary, introductory, opening, initial, primary, basic, fundamental, rudimentary, elementary.

prepare *v* **1** GET READY, warm up, train, coach, study, make ready, adapt, adjust, plan, organize, arrange, pave the way. **2** *prepare a meal*: make, produce, construct, assemble, concoct, contrive, devise, draft, draw up, compose. **3** PROVIDE, supply, equip, fit out, rig out.
prepare oneself brace oneself, steel oneself, gird oneself, fortify oneself.

prepared *adj* ready, waiting, set, fit, inclined, disposed, willing, planned, organized, arranged.
≠ unprepared, unready.

preponderant *adj* greater, larger, superior, predominant, prevailing, overriding, overruling, controlling, foremost, important, significant.

preposterous *adj* incredible, unbelievable, absurd, ridiculous, ludicrous, foolish, crazy, nonsensical, unreasonable, monstrous, shocking, outrageous, intolerable, unthinkable, impossible.
≠ sensible, reasonable, acceptable.

prerequisite *n* precondition, condition, proviso, qualification, requisite, requirement, imperative, necessity, essential, must.
≠ extra.

prescribe *v* ordain, decree, dictate, rule, command, order, require, direct, assign, specify, stipulate, lay down, set, appoint, impose, fix, define, limit.

prescription *n* **1** INSTRUCTION, direction, formula. **2** MEDICINE, drug, preparation, mixture, remedy, treatment.

presence *n* **1** ATTENDANCE, company, occupancy, residence, existence. **2** AURA, air, demeanour, bearing, carriage, appearance, poise, self-assurance, personality, charisma. **3** NEARNESS, closeness, proximity, vicinity.
≠ **1** absence. **3** remoteness.

present[1] *adj* **1** ATTENDING, here, there, near, at hand, to hand, available, ready. **2** *at the present time*: current, contemporary, present-day, immediate, instant, existent, existing.
≠ **1** absent. **2** past, out-of-date.

present[2] *v* **1** SHOW, display, exhibit, demonstrate, mount, stage, put on, introduce, announce. **2** AWARD, confer, bestow, grant, give, donate, hand over, entrust, extend, hold out, offer, tender, submit.

present[3] *n* gift, prezzie (*infml*), offering, donation, grant, endowment, benefaction, bounty, largess, gratuity, tip, favour.

presentable *adj* neat, tidy, clean, respectable, decent, proper, suitable, acceptable, satisfactory, tolerable.
≠ unpresentable, untidy, shabby.

presentation *n* **1** SHOW, performance, production, staging, representation, display, exhibition, demonstration, talk, delivery, appearance, arrangement. **2** AWARD, conferral, bestowal, investiture.

present-day *adj* current, present, existing, living, contemporary, modern, up-to-date, fashionable.
≠ past, future.

presently *adv* **1** SOON, shortly, in a minute, before long, by and by.
2 CURRENTLY, at present, now.

preserve *v* **1** PROTECT, safeguard, guard, defend, shield, shelter, care for, maintain, uphold, sustain, continue, perpetuate, keep, retain, conserve, save, store. **2** *preserve food*: bottle, tin, can, pickle, salt, cure, dry.
≠ **1** destroy, ruin.
n **1** *home-made preserves*: conserve, jam, marmalade, jelly, pickle.
2 DOMAIN, realm, sphere, area, field, speciality. **3** RESERVATION, sanctuary, game reserve, safari park.

preside *v* chair, officiate, conduct, direct, manage, administer, control, run, head, lead, govern, rule.

press *v* **1** CRUSH, squash, squeeze, compress, stuff, cram, crowd, push, depress. **2** *press clothes*: iron, smooth, flatten. **3** HUG, embrace, clasp, squeeze. **4** URGE, plead, petition, campaign, demand, insist on, compel, constrain, force, pressure, pressurize, harass.
n **1** CROWD, throng, multitude, mob, horde, swarm, pack, crush, push.
2 JOURNALISTS, reporters, correspondents, the media, newspapers, papers, Fleet Street, fourth estate.

pressing *adj* urgent, high-priority, burning, crucial, vital, essential, imperative, serious, important.
≠ unimportant, trivial.

pressure *n* **1** FORCE, power, load, burden, weight, heaviness, compression, squeezing, stress, strain.
2 DIFFICULTY, problem, demand, constraint, obligation, urgency.

pressurize *v* force, compel, constrain, oblige, drive, bulldoze, coerce, press, pressure, lean on (*infml*), browbeat, bully.

prestige *n* status, reputation, standing, stature, eminence, distinction, esteem, regard, importance, authority, influence, fame, renown, kudos, credit, honour.
≠ humbleness, unimportance.

prestigious *adj* esteemed, respected, reputable, important, influential, great, eminent, prominent, illustrious, renowned, celebrated, exalted, imposing, impressive, up-market.
≠ humble, modest.

presume *v* **1** ASSUME, take it, think, believe, suppose, surmise, infer, presuppose, take for granted, count on, rely on, depend on, bank on, trust.
2 *presume to criticize*: dare, make so bold, go so far, venture, undertake.

presumption *n* **1** ASSUMPTION, belief, opinion, hypothesis, presupposition, supposition, surmise, conjecture, guess, likelihood, probability.
2 PRESUMPTUOUSNESS, boldness, audacity, impertinence, cheek (*infml*), nerve (*infml*), impudence, insolence, forwardness, assurance.
≠ **2** humility.

presumptuous *adj* bold, audacious, impertinent, impudent, insolent, over-familiar, forward, pushy, arrogant, over-confident, conceited.
≠ humble, modest.

pretence *n* show, display, appearance, cover, front, façade, veneer, cloak, veil, mask, guise, sham, feigning, faking, simulation, deception, trickery, wile, ruse, excuse, pretext, bluff, falsehood, deceit, fabrication, invention, make-believe, charade, acting, play-acting, posturing, posing, affectation, pretension, pretentiousness.
≠ honesty, openness.

pretend *v* **1** AFFECT, put on, assume, feign, sham, counterfeit, fake, simulate, bluff, impersonate, pass oneself off, act, play-act, mime, go through the motions. **2** CLAIM, allege, profess, purport. **3** IMAGINE, make believe, suppose.

pretender *n* claimant, aspirant, candidate.

pretension *n* **1** PRETENTIOUSNESS, pomposity, self-importance, airs, conceit, vanity, snobbishness, affectation, pretence, show, showiness, ostentation. **2** CLAIM, profession, demand, aspiration, ambition.
≠ **1** modesty, humility, simplicity.

pretentious *adj* pompous, self-important, conceited, immodest, snobbish, affected, mannered, showy, ostentatious, extravagant, over-the-top, exaggerated, magniloquent, high-sounding, inflated, grandiose, ambitious, overambitious.
≠ modest, humble, simple, straightforward.

pretext *n* excuse, ploy, ruse, cover, cloak, mask, guise, semblance, appearance, pretence, show.

pretty *adj* attractive, good-looking, beautiful, fair, lovely, bonny, cute, winsome, appending, charming, dainty, graceful, elegant, fine, delicate, nice.
≠ plain, unattractive, ugly.
adv fairly, somewhat, rather, quite, reasonably, moderately, tolerably.

prevail *v* **1** PREDOMINATE, preponderate, abound. **2** WIN, triumph, succeed, overcome, overrule, reign, rule.
≠ **2** lose.
prevail upon persuade, talk into, prompt, induce, incline, sway, influence, convince, win over.

prevailing *adj* predominant, preponderant, main, principal, dominant, controlling, powerful, compelling, influential, reigning, ruling, current, fashionable, popular, mainstream, accepted, established, set, usual, customary, common, prevalent, widespread.
≠ minor, subordinate.

prevalent *adj* widespread, cxtensive, rampant, rife, frequent, general, customary, usual, universal, ubiquitous, common, everyday, popular, current, prevailing.
≠ uncommon, rare.

prevaricate *v* hedge, equivocate, quibble, cavil, dodge, evade, shift, shuffle, lie, deceive.

prevent *v* stop, avert, avoid, head off, ward off, stave off, intercept, forestall, anticipate, frustrate, thwart, check, restrain, inhibit, hinder, hamper, impede, obstruct, block, bar.
≠ cause, help, foster, encourage, allow.

prevention *n* avoidance, frustration, check, hindrance, impediment, obstruction, obstacle, bar, elimination, precaution, safeguard, deterrence.
≠ cause, help.

preventive *adj* preventative, anticipatory, pre-emptive, inhibitory, obstructive, precautionary, protective, counteractive, deterrent.
≠ causative.

previous *adj* preceding, foregoing, earlier, prior, past, former, ex-, one-time, sometime, erstwhile.
≠ following, subsequent, later.

previously *adv* formerly, once, earlier, before, beforehand.
≠ later.

prey *n* quarry, victim, game, kill.
prey on **1** HUNT, kill, devour, feed on, live off, exploit. **2** *prey on one's mind*: haunt, trouble, distress, worry, burden, weigh down, oppress.

price *n* value, worth, cost, expense, outlay, expenditure, fee, charge, levy, toll, rate, bill, assessment, valuation, estimate, quotation, figure, amount, sum, payment, reward, penalty, forfeit, sacrifice, consequences.
v value, rate, cost, evaluate, assess, estimate.

priceless *adj* **1** INVALUABLE, inestimable, incalculable, expensive, costly, dear, precious, valuable, prized, treasured, irreplaceable. **2** (*infml*) FUNNY, amusing, comic, hilarious, riotous, side-splitting, killing (*infml*), rich (*infml*).
≠ **1** cheap, run-of-the-mill.

prick *v* pierce, puncture, perforate,

punch, jab, stab, sting, bite, prickle, itch, tingle.
n puncture, perforation, pinhole, stab, pang, twinge, sting, bite.

prickle *n* thorn, spine, barb, spur, point, spike, needle.
v tingle, itch, smart, sting, prick.

prickly *adj* **1** THORNY, brambly, spiny, barbed, spiky, bristly, rough, scratchy. **2** IRRITABLE, edgy, touchy, grumpy, short-tempered.
≠ **1** smooth. **2** relaxed, easy-going (*infml*).

pride *n* **1** CONCEIT, vanity, egotism, bigheadedness, boastfulness, smugness, arrogance, self-importance, presumption, haughtiness, superciliousness, snobbery, pretentiousness. **2** DIGNITY, self-respect, self-esteem, honour. **3** SATISFACTION, gratification, pleasure, delight.
≠ **1** humility, modesty. **2** shame.

priest *n* minister, vicar, padre, father, man of God, man of the cloth, clergyman, churchman.

priggish *adj* smug, self-righteous, goody-goody (*infml*), sanctimonious, holier-than-thou, puritanical, prim, prudish, narrow-minded.
≠ broadminded.

prim *adj* prudish, strait-laced, formal, demure, proper, priggish, prissy, fussy, particular, precise, fastidious.
≠ informed, relaxed, easy-going (*infml*).

primarily *adv* chiefly, principally, mainly, mostly, basically, fundamentally, especially, particularly, essentially.

primary *adj* **1** FIRST, earliest, original, initial, introductory, beginning, basic, fundamental, essential, radical, rudimentary, elementary, simple. **2** CHIEF, principal, main, dominant, leading, foremost, supreme, cardinal, capital, paramount, greatest, highest, ultimate.
≠ **2** secondary, subsidiary, minor.

prime *adj* best, choice, select, quality, first-class, first-rate, excellent, top, supreme, pre-eminent, superior, senior, leading, ruling, chief, principal, main, predominant, primary.
≠ second-rate, secondary.
n height, peak, zenith, heyday, flower, bloom, maturity, perfection.

primeval *adj* earliest, first, original, primordial, early, old, ancient, prehistoric, primitive, instinctive.
≠ modern.

primitive *adj* **1** CRUDE, rough, unsophisticated, uncivilized, barbarian, savage. **2** EARLY, elementary, rudimentary, primary, first, original, earliest.
≠ **1** advanced, sophisticated, civilized.

princely *adj* **1** SOVEREIGN, imperial, royal, regal, majestic, stately, grand, noble. **2** *princely sum*: generous, liberal, lavish, sumptuous, magnificent, handsome.

principal *adj* main, chief, key, essential, cardinal, primary, first, foremost, leading, dominant, prime, paramount, pre-eminent, supreme, highest.
≠ minor, subsidiary, lesser, least.
n head, head teacher, headmaster, headmistress, chief, leader, boss, director, manager, superintendent.

principally *adv* mainly, mostly, chiefly, primarily, predominantly, above all, particularly, especially.

principle *n* **1** RULE, formula, law, canon, axiom, dictum, precept, maxim, truth, tenet, doctrine, creed, dogma, code, standard, criterion, proposition, fundamental, essential. **2** *a man of principle*: HONOUR, integrity, rectitude, uprightness, virtue, decency, morality, morals, ethics, standards, scruples, conscience.

print *v* mark, stamp, imprint, impress, engrave, copy, reproduce, run off, publish, issue.
n **1** LETTERS, characters, lettering, type, typescript, typeface, fount. **2** MARK, impression, fingerprint, footprint. **3** COPY, reproduction, picture, engraving, lithograph, photograph, photo.

Printing methods include: bubble-jet printing, collotype, colour-process

printing, copper engraving, die-stamping, duplicating, electrostatic printing, engraving, etching, flexography, gravure, ink- jet printing, intaglio, laser printing, letterpress, lino blocking, litho, lithography, offset lithography, offset printing, photoengraving, rotary press, screen printing, silk-screen printing, stencilling, thermography, twin-etching, xerography.
Printing terms include: anodized plate, author's proof, back margin, backing-up, bad break, base alignment, batter, bi-directional printing, black printer, blanket-to-blanket press, bold face, bromide, camera-ready copy, carding, caret, cast-off, catchword, centre, character set, chase, cliché, cold composition, collograph, colour control bar, colour separation, column inch/centimetre, compose, composing room, composition size, compositor, condensed, copy, cylinder press, dampers, dot-etching, dot gain, drum printer, electrotype, em, en, end even, expanded type, feathering, finishing, first proof, flat-bed press, flong, forme, font, galley, gutter, hard hyphen, hot-metal typesetting, image printing, imposition, impression, indent, initial caps, inking roller, Intertype®, italic, justification, keep standing, kern, kiss impression, large print, leaders, leading, letterset, line printer, Linotype®, literal, logotype, lower-case, machine composition, machine proof, mackle, makeready, manuscript, margin, matrix, misprint, moiré, Monophoto®, Monotype®, mottling, newsprint, non-image area, non-impact printing, offprint, orphan, overprint, Ozalid®, perfecting, phototypesetting, planographic, printing press, progressive proofs, proof, quoin, ragged right/left, registration, relief printing, reprint, roman, run-around, running head, running text, sans serif, see-through, signature, small capitals, soft hyphen, specimen page, spoilage, stereotype, stet, strike-on, strip in, take in, take over, text, thermal printer, tint, trim marks, type, type scale, type spec, typeface, typescript, typesetting, typo, typographer (*US*), upper-case, web-fed, web offset, widow, woodcut, wood engraving, zinco.

prior *adj* earlier, preceding, foregoing, previous, former.
≠ later.
prior to before, preceding, earlier than.
≠ after, following.

priority *n* right of way, precedence, seniority, rank, superiority, pre-eminence, supremacy, the lead, first place, urgency.
≠ inferiority.

prison *n* jail, nick (*sl*), clink (*sl*), cooler (*sl*), penitentiary, cell, lock-up, cage, dungeon, imprisonment, confinement, detention, custody.

prisoner *n* captive, hostage, convict, jail-bird (*infml*), inmate, internee, detainee.

privacy *n* secrecy, confidentiality, independence, solitude, isolation, seclusion, concealment, retirement, retreat.

private *adj* secret, classified, hush-hush (*infml*), off the record, unofficial, confidential, intimate, personal, individual, own, exclusive, particular, special, separate, independent, solitary, isolated, secluded, hidden, concealed, reserved, withdrawn.
≠ public, open.
in private privately, in confidence, secretly, in secret, behind closed doors, in camera.
≠ publicly, openly.

privilege *n* advantage, benefit, concession, birthright, title, due, right, prerogative, entitlement, freedom, liberty, franchise, licence, sanction, authority, immunity, exemption.
≠ disadvantage.

privileged *adj* advantaged, favoured, special, sanctioned, authorized, immune, exempt, élite, honoured, ruling, powerful.
≠ disadvantaged, under-privileged.

prize *n* reward, trophy, medal, award, winnings, jackpot, purse, premium, stake(s), honour, accolade.
adj best, top, first-rate, excellent, outstanding, champion, winning, prize-winning, award-winning.
≠ second-rate.
v treasure, value, appreciate, esteem, revere, cherish, hold dear.
≠ despise.

probability *n* likelihood, odds, chances, expectation, prospect, chance, possibility.
≠ improbability.

probable *adj* likely, odds-on, expected, credible, believable, plausible, feasible, possible, apparent, seeming.
≠ improbable, unlikely.

probation *n* apprenticeship, trial period, trial, test.

probe *v* prod, poke, pierce, penetrate, sound, plumb, explore, examine, scrutinize, investigate, go into, look into, search, sift, test.
n **1** BORE, drill. **2** INQUIRY, inquest, investigation, exploration, examination, test, scrutiny, study, research.

problem *n* **1** TROUBLE, worry, predicament, quandary, dilemma, difficulty, complication, snag. **2** QUESTION, poser, puzzle, brain-teaser, conundrum, riddle, enigma.
adj difficult, unmanageable, uncontrollable, unruly, delinquent.
≠ well-behaved, manageable.

procedure *n* routine, process, method, system, technique, custom, practice, policy, formula, course, scheme, strategy, plan of action, move, step, action, conduct, operation, performance.

proceed *v* **1** *the permission to proceed*: advance, go ahead, move on, progress, continue, carry on, press on. **2** ORIGINATE, derive, flow, start, stem, spring, arise, issue, result, ensue, follow, come.
≠ **1** stop, retreat.

proceedings *n* **1** MATTERS, affairs, business, dealings, transactions, report, account, minutes, records, archives, annals. **2** EVENTS, happenings, deeds, doings, moves, steps, measures, action, course of action.

proceeds *n* revenue, income, returns, receipts, takings, earnings, gain, profit, yield, produce.
≠ expenditure, outlay.

process *n* **1** PROCEDURE, operation, practice, method, system, technique, means, manner, mode, way, stage, step. **2** COURSE, progression, advance, progress, development, evolution, formation, growth, movement, action, proceeding.
v deal with, handle, treat, prepare, refine, transform, convert, change, alter.

procession *n* march, parade, cavalcade, motorcade, cortège, file, column, train, succession, series, sequence, course, run.

proclaim *v* announce, declare, pronounce, affirm, give out, publish, advertise, make known, profess, testify, show, indicate.

proclamation *n* announcement, declaration, pronouncement, affirmation, publication, promulgation, notice, notification, manifesto, decree, edict.

procrastinate *v* defer, put off, postpone, delay, retard, stall, temporize, play for time, dally, dilly-dally (*infml*), drag one's feet, prolong, protract.
≠ advance, proceed.

procure *v* acquire, buy, purchase, get, obtain, find, come by, pick up, lay hands on, earn, gain, win, secure, appropriate, requisition.
≠ lose.

prod *v* poke, jab, dig, elbow, nudge, push, shove, goad, spur, urge, egg on (*infml*), prompt, stimulate, motivate.
n poke, jab, dig, elbow, nudge, push, shove, prompt, reminder, stimulus, motivation.

prodigy *n* genius, virtuoso, wonder, marvel, miracle, phenomenon, sensation, freak, curiosity, rarity, child genius, wonder child, whizz kid (*infml*).

produce *v* **1** CAUSE, occasion, give rise to, provoke, bring about, result in, effect, create, originate, invent, make, manufacture, fabricate, construct, compose, generate, yield, bear, deliver. **2** ADVANCE, put forward, present, offer, give, supply, provide, furnish, bring out, bring forth, show, exhibit, demonstrate. **3** *produce a play*: direct, stage, mount, put on.
n crop, harvest, yield, output, product.

product *n* **1** COMMODITY, merchandise, goods, end-product, artefact, work, creation, invention, production, output, yield, produce, fruit, return. **2** RESULT, consequence, outcome, issue, upshot, offshoot, spin-off, by-product, legacy.
≠ **2** cause.

production *n* **1** MAKING, manufacture, fabrication, construction, assembly, creation, origination, preparation, formation. **2** *an amateur production*: staging, presentation, direction, management.
≠ **1** consumption.

productive *adj* fruitful, profitable, rewarding, valuable, worthwhile, useful, constructive, creative, inventive, fertile, rich, teeming, busy, energetic, vigorous, efficient, effective.
≠ unproductive, fruitless, useless.

productivity *n* productiveness, yield, output, work rate, efficiency.

profane *adj* secular, temporal, lay, unconsecrated, unhallowed, unsanctified, unholy, irreligious, impious, sacrilegious, blasphemous, ungodly, irreverent, disrespectful, abusive, crude, coarse, foul, filthy, unclean.
≠ sacred, religious, respectful.
v desecrate, pollute, contaminate, defile, debase, pervert, abuse, misuse.
≠ revere, honour.

profess *v* admit, confess, acknowledge, own, confirm, certify, declare, announce, proclaim, state, assert, affirm, maintain, claim, allege, make out, pretend.

profession *n* **1** CAREER, job, occupation, employment, business, line (of work), trade, vocation, calling, métier, craft, office, position. **2** ADMISSION, confession, acknowledgement, declaration, announcement, statement, testimony, assertion, affirmation, claim.

professional *adj* qualified, licensed, trained, experienced, practised, skilled, expert, masterly, proficient, competent, businesslike, efficient.
≠ amateur, unprofessional.
n expert, authority, specialist, pro (*infml*), master, virtuoso, dab hand (*infml*).
≠ amateur.

proficiency *n* skill, skilfulness, expertise, mastery, talent, knack, dexterity, finesse, aptitude, ability, competence.
≠ incompetence.

proficient *adj* able, capable, skilled, qualified, trained, experienced, accomplished, expert, masterly, gifted, talented, clever, skilful, competent, efficient.
≠ unskilled, incompetent.

profile *n* **1** SIDE VIEW, outline, contour, silhouette, shape, form, figure, sketch, drawing, diagram, chart, graph. **2** BIOGRAPHY, curriculum vitae, thumbnail sketch, vignette, portrait, study, analysis, examination, survey, review.

profit *n* gain, surplus, excess, bottom line, revenue, return, yield, proceeds, receipts, takings, earnings, winnings, interest, advantage, benefit, use, avail, value, worth.
≠ loss.
v gain, make money, pay, serve, avail, benefit.
≠ lose.
profit by, profit from exploit, take advantage of, use, utilize, turn to advantage, capitalize on, cash in on, reap the benefit of.

profitable *adj* cost-effective, economic, commercial, money-making, lucrative, remunerative, paying, rewarding, successful, fruitful, productive, advantageous, beneficial, useful,

valuable, worthwhile.
≠ unprofitable, loss-making, non-profit-making.

profound *adj* **1** DEEP, great, intense, extreme, heartfelt, marked, far-reaching, extensive, exhaustive. **2** *a profound remark*: serious, weighty, penetrating, thoughtful, philosophical, wise, learned, erudite, abstruse.
≠ **1** shallow, slight, mild.

profuse *adj* ample, abundant, plentiful, copious, generous, liberal, lavish, rich, luxuriant, excessive, immoderate, extravagant, overabundant, superabundant, overflowing.
≠ inadequate, sparse.

profusion *n* abundance, plenty, wealth, multitude, plethora, glut, excess, surplus, superfluity, extravagance.
≠ inadequacy, scarcity.

programme *n* **1** SCHEDULE, timetable, agenda, calendar, order of events, listing, line-up, plan, scheme, project, syllabus, curriculum. **2** *radio programme*: broadcast, transmission, show, performance, production, presentation.

progress *n* movement, progression, passage, journey, way, advance, headway, step forward, breakthrough, development, evolution, growth, increase, improvement, betterment, promotion.
≠ recession, deterioration, decline.
v proceed, advance, go forward, forge ahead, make progress, make headway, come on, develop, grow, mature, blossom, improve, better, prosper, increase.
≠ deteriorate, decline.

progression *n* cycle, chain, string, succession, series, sequence, order, course, advance, headway, progress, development.

progressive *adj* **1** MODERN, avant-garde, advanced, forward-looking, enlightened, liberal, radical, revolutionary, reformist, dynamic, enterprising, go-ahead, up-and-coming. **2** ADVANCING, continuing, developing, growing, increasing, intensifying.
≠ **1** regressive.

prohibit *v* forbid, ban, bar, veto, proscribe, outlaw, rule out, preclude, prevent, stop, hinder, hamper, impede, obstruct, restrict.
≠ permit, allow, authorize.

project *n* assignment, contract, task, job, work, occupation, activity, enterprise, undertaking, venture, plan, scheme, programme, design, proposal, idea, conception.
v **1** PREDICT, forecast, extrapolate, estimate, reckon, calculate. **2** THROW, fling, hurl, launch, propel. **3** PROTRUDE, stick out, bulge, jut out, overhang.

projection *n* **1** PROTUBERANCE, bulge, overhang, ledge, sill, shelf, ridge. **2** PREDICTION, forecast, extrapolation, estimate, reckoning, calculation, computation.

proliferate *v* multiply, reproduce, breed, increase, build up, intensify, escalate, mushroom, snowball, spread, expand, flourish, thrive.
≠ dwindle.

prolific *adj* productive, fruitful, fertile, profuse, copious, abundant.
≠ unproductive.

prolong *v* lengthen, extend, stretch, protract, draw out, spin out, drag out, delay, continue, perpetuate.
≠ shorten.

prominence *n* **1** FAME, celebrity, renown, eminence, distinction, greatness, importance, reputation, name, standing, rank, prestige. **2** BULGE, protuberance, bump, hump, lump, mound, rise, elevation, projection, process, headland, promontory, cliff, crag.
≠ **1** unimportance, insignificance.

prominent *adj* **1** NOTICEABLE, conspicuous, obvious, unmistakable, striking, eye-catching. **2** BULGING, protuberant, projecting, jutting, protruding, obtrusive. **3** *a prominent writer*: famous, well-known, celebrated, renowned, noted, eminent, distinguished, respected, leading, foremost, chief, main, important, popular, outstanding.
≠ **1** inconspicuous. **3** unknown, unimportant, insignificant.

promiscuity *n* looseness, laxity, permissiveness, wantonness, immorality, licentiousness, debauchery, depravity.
≠ chastity, morality.

promiscuous *adj* loose, immoral, licentious, dissolute, casual, random, haphazard, indiscriminate.
≠ chaste, moral.

promise *v* **1** VOW, pledge, swear, take an oath, contract, undertake, give one's word, vouch, warrant, guarantee, assure. **2** AUGUR, presage, indicate, suggest, hint at.
n **1** VOW, pledge, oath, word of honour, bond, compact, covenant, guarantee, assurance, undertaking, engagement, commitment.
2 POTENTIAL, ability, capability, aptitude, talent.

promising *adj* auspicious, propitious, favourable, rosy, bright, encouraging, hopeful, talented, gifted, budding, up-and-coming.
≠ unpromising, inauspicious, discouraging.

promote *v* **1** ADVERTISE, plug (*infml*), publicize, hype (*sl*), popularize, market, sell, push, recommend, advocate, champion, endorse, sponsor, support, back, help, aid, assist, foster, nurture, further, forward, encourage, boost, stimulate, urge. **2** UPGRADE, advance, move up, raise, elevate, exalt, honour.
≠ **1** disparage, hinder. **2** demote.

promotion *n* **1** ADVANCEMENT, upgrading, rise, preferment, elevation, exaltation. **2** ADVERTISING, plugging (*infml*), publicity, hype (*sl*), campaign, progaganda, marketing, pushing, support, backing, furtherance, development, encouragement, boosting.
≠ **1** demotion. **2** disparagement, obstruction.

prompt¹ *adj* punctual, on time, immediate, instantaneous, instant, direct, quick, swift, rapid, speedy, unhesitating, willing, ready, alert, responsive, timely, early.
≠ slow, hesitant, late.
adv promptly, punctually, exactly, on the dot, to the minute, sharp.

prompt² *v* cause, give rise to, result in, occasion, produce, instigate, call forth, elicit, provoke, incite, urge, encourage, inspire, move, stimulate, motivate, spur, prod, remind.
≠ deter, dissuade.
n reminder, cue, hint, help, jolt, prod, spur, stimulus.

prone *adj* **1** LIKELY, given, inclined, disposed, predisposed, bent, apt, liable, subject, susceptible, vulnerable. **2** *she lay prone*: face down, prostrate, flat, horizontal, full-length, stretched, recumbent.
≠ **1** unlikely, immune. **2** upright, supine.

pronounce *v* **1** SAY, utter, speak, express, voice, vocalize, sound, enunciate, articulate, stress.
2 DECLARE, announce, proclaim, decree, judge, affirm, assert.

pronounced *adj* clear, distinct, definite, positive, decided, marked, noticeable, conspicuous, evident, obvious, striking, unmistakable, strong, broad.
≠ faint, vague.

pronunciation *n* speech, diction, elocution, enunciation, articulation, delivery, accent, stress, inflection, intonation, modulation.

proof *n* evidence, documentation, demonstration, verification, confirmation, corroboration, substantiation.

prop *v* **1** SUPPORT, sustain, uphold, maintain, shore, stay, buttress, bolster, underpin, set. **2** *propped against the wall*: lean, rest, stand.
n support, stay, mainstay, strut, buttress, brace, truss.

propaganda *n* advertising, publicity, hype (*sl*), indoctrination, brainwashing, disinformation.

propagate *v* **1** SPREAD, transmit, broadcast, diffuse, disseminate, circulate, publish, promulgate, publicize, promote. **2** INCREASE, multiply, proliferate, generate, produce, breed, beget, spawn, procreate, reproduce.

propel *v* move, drive, impel, force, thrust, push, shove, launch, shoot, send.
≠ stop.

proper *adj* **1** RIGHT, correct, accurate, exact, precise, true, genuine, real, actual. **2** ACCEPTED, correct, suitable, appropriate, fitting, decent, respectable, polite, formal.
≠ **1** wrong. **2** improper, indecent.

property *n* **1** ESTATE, land, real estate, acres, premises, buildings, house(s), wealth, riches, resources, means, capital, assets, holding(s), belongings, possessions, effects, goods, chattels. **2** FEATURE, trait, quality, attribute, characteristic, idiosyncrasy, peculiarity, mark.

prophecy *n* prediction, augury, forecast, prognosis.

prophesy *v* predict, foresee, augur, foretell, forewarn, forecast.

prophet *n* seer, soothsayer, foreteller, forecaster, oracle, clairvoyant, fortune-teller.

proportion *n* **1** PERCENTAGE, fraction, part, division, share, quota, amount. **2** RATIO, relationship, correspondence, symmetry, balance, distribution.
≠ **2** disproportion, imbalance.

proportional *adj* proportionate, relative, commensurate, consistent, corresponding, analogous, comparable, equitable, even.
≠ disproportionate.

proportions *n* dimensions, measurements, size, magnitude, volume, capacity.

proposal *n* proposition, suggestion, recommendation, motion, plan, scheme, project, design, programme, manifesto, presentation, bid, offer, tender, terms.

propose *v* **1** SUGGEST, recommend, move, advance, put forward, introduce, bring up, table, submit, present, offer, tender. **2** INTEND, mean, aim, purpose, plan, design. **3** NOMINATE, put up.
≠ **1** withdraw.

proprietor, proprietress *n* landlord, landlady, title-holder, freeholder, leaseholder, landowner, owner, possessor.

prosecute *v* accuse, indict, sue, prefer charges, take to court, litigate, summon, put on trial, try.
≠ defend.

prosody

Forms of prosody include: abstract verse, Alcaic verse, alexandrine, alliteration, amphibrach, amphimacer, Anacreontic verse, anacrusis, analysed rhyme, anapaest, antibacchius, antispast, Archilochian verse, asclepiad, assonance, asynartete, ballade, blank verse, broken rhyme, bouts rimés, caesura, canto, catalexis, choliamb, choree, choriamb, cinquain, couplet, dactyl, decastich, dipody, dispondee, distich, ditrochee, dizain, dochmius, elision, enjambment, envoy, epitrite, epode, eye rhyme, false quantity, feminine caesura, feminine ending, feminine rhyme, foot, free verse, galliambic, glyconic, heptameter, heptapody, heroic couplet, hexameter, hexastich, hypermetrical, iamb, ictus, Ionic, kyrielle, laisse, Leonine rhyme, linked verse, long-measure, macaronic, masculine ending, masculine rhyme, metre, miurus, monometer, monorhyme, paeon, pantoum, pentameter, pentastich, Petrarchan sonnet, Pherecratean, Pindaric, poulters' measure, pyrrhic, Pythian verse, quatorzain, quatrain, reported verses, rhopalic, rhyme royal, rime riche, rime suffisante, rondeau, rondel, rove-over, Sapphic, senarius, septenarius, sonnet, Spencerian stanza, spondee, sprung rhythm, strophe, substitution, synaphea, tetrameter, tetrapody, tetrastich, tribrach, trimeter, triolet, tripody, triseme, trochee, villanelle, virelay.

prospect *n* chance, odds, probability, likelihood, possibility, hope, expectation, anticipation, outlook, future.
≠ unlikelihood.

prospective *adj* future, -to-be, intended, designate, destined,

forthcoming, approaching, coming, imminent, awaited, expected, anticipated, likely, possible, probable, potential, aspiring, would-be.
≠ current.

prospectus *n* plan, scheme, programme, syllabus, manifesto, outline, synopsis, pamphlet, leaflet, brochure, catalogue, list.

prosper *v* boom, thrive, flourish, flower, bloom, succeed, get on, advance, progress, grow rich.
≠ fail.

prosperity *n* boom, plenty, affluence, wealth, riches, fortune, well-being, luxury, the good life, success, good fortune.
≠ adversity, poverty.

prosperous *adj* booming, thriving, flourishing, blooming, successful, fortunate, lucky, rich, wealthy, affluent, well-off, well-to-do.
≠ unfortunate, poor.

prostrate *adj* flat, horizontal, prone, fallen, overcome, overwhelmed, crushed, paralysed, powerless, helpless, defenceless.
≠ triumphant.
v lay low, overcome, overwhelm, crush, overthrow, tire, wear out, fatigue, exhaust, drain, ruin.
≠ strengthen.
prostrate oneself bow down, kneel, kowtow, submit, grovel, cringe, abase oneself.

protagonist *n* hero, heroine, lead, principal, leader, prime mover, champion, advocate, supporter, proponent, exponent.

protect *v* safeguard, defend, guard, escort, cover, screen, shield, secure, watch over, look after, care for, support, shelter, harbour, keep, conserve, preserve, save.
≠ attack, neglect.

protection *n* **1** *protection of the environment*: care, custody, charge, guardianship, safekeeping, conservation, preservation, safety, safeguard. **2** BARRIER, buffer, bulwark, defence, guard, shield, armour, screen, cover, shelter, refuge, security, insurance.
≠ **1** neglect, attack.

protective *adj* **1** POSSESSIVE, defensive, motherly, maternal, fatherly, paternal, watchful, vigilant, careful. **2** *protective clothing*: waterproof, fireproof, insulating.
≠ **1** aggressive, threatening.

protest *n* objection, disapproval, opposition, dissent, complaint, protestation, outcry, appeal, demonstration.
≠ acceptance.
v **1** OBJECT, take exception, complain, appeal, demonstrate, oppose, disapprove, disagree, argue. **2** *protest one's innocence*: assert, maintain, contend, insist, profess.
≠ **1** accept.

protester *n* demonstrator, agitator, rebel, dissident, dissenter.

protocol *n* procedure, formalities, convention, custom, etiquette, manners, good form, propriety.

protracted *adj* long, lengthy, prolonged, extended, drawn-out, long-drawn-out, overlong, interminable.
≠ brief, shortened.

protrude *v* stick out, poke out, come through, bulge, jut out, project, extend, stand out, obtrude.

proud *adj* **1** CONCEITED, vain, egotistical, bigheaded, boastful, smug, complacent, arrogant, self-important, cocky, presumptuous, haughty, high and mighty, overbearing, supercilious, snooty (*infml*), snobbish, toffee-nosed (*infml*), stuck-up (*infml*). **2** SATISFIED, contented, gratified, pleased, delighted, honoured. **3** DIGNIFIED, noble, honourable, worthy, self-respecting.
≠ **1** humble, modest, unassuming. **2** ashamed. **3** deferential, ignoble.

prove *v* show, demonstrate, attest, verify, confirm, corroborate, substantiate, bear out, document, certify, authenticate, validate, justify, establish, determine, ascertain, try, test, check, examine, analyse.
≠ disprove, discredit, falsify.

proverb *n* saying, adage, aphorism, maxim, byword, dictum, precept.

proverbial *adj* axiomatic, accepted, conventional, traditional, customary, time-honoured, famous, well-known, legendary, notorious, typical, archetypal.

provide *v* **1** SUPPLY, furnish, stock, equip, outfit, prepare for, cater, serve, present, give, contribute, yield, lend, add, bring. **2** PLAN FOR, allow, make provision, accommodate, arrange for, take precautions. **3** STATE, specify, stipulate, lay down, require.
≠ **1** take, remove.

providence *n* **1** FATE, destiny, divine intervention, God's will, fortune, luck. **2** PRUDENCE, far-sightedness, foresight, caution, care, thrift.
≠ **2** improvidence.

provident *adj* prudent, far-sighted, judicious, cautious, careful, thrifty, economical, frugal.
≠ improvident.

providential *adj* timely, opportune, convenient, fortunate, lucky, happy, welcome, heaven-sent.
≠ untimely.

providing *conj* provided, with the proviso, given, as long as, on condition, on the understanding.

province *n* **1** REGION, area, district, zone, county, shire, department, territory, colony, dependency. **2** RESPONSIBILITY, concern, duty, office, role, function, field, sphere, domain, department, line.

provincial *adj* regional, local, rural, rustic, country, home-grown, small-town, parish-pump, parochial, insular, inward-looking, limited, narrow, narrow-minded, small-minded.
≠ national, cosmopolitan, urban, sophisticated.

provision *n* **1** PLAN, arrangement, preparation, measure, precaution. **2** STIPULATION, specification, proviso, condition, term, requirement.

provisional *adj* temporary, interim, transitional, stopgap, makeshift, conditional, tentative.
≠ permanent, fixed, definite.

provisions *n* food, foodstuff, groceries, eatables (*infml*), sustenance, rations, supplies, stocks, stores.

proviso *n* condition, term, requirement, stipulation, qualification, reservation, restriction, limitation, provision, clause, rider.

provocation *n* cause, grounds, justification, reason, motive, stimulus, motivation, incitement, instigation, annoyance, aggravation (*infml*), vexation, grievance, offence, insult, affront, injury, taunt, challenge, dare.

provocative *adj* **1** ANNOYING, aggravating (*infml*), galling, outrageous, offensive, insulting, abusive. **2** STIMULATING, exciting, challenging. **3** EROTIC, titillating, arousing, sexy, seductive, alluring, tempting, inviting, tantalizing, teasing, suggestive.
≠ **1** conciliatory.

provoke *v* **1** ANNOY, irritate, rile, aggravate (*infml*), offend, insult, anger, enrage, infuriate, incense, madden, exasperate, tease, taunt. **2** CAUSE, occasion, give rise to, produce, generate, induce, elicit, evoke, excite, inspire, move, stir, prompt, stimulate, motivate, incite, instigate.
≠ **1** please, pacify. **2** result.

prowess *n* accomplishment, attainment, ability, aptitude, skill, expertise, mastery, command, talent, genius.

proximity *n* closeness, nearness, vicinity, neighbourhood, adjacency, juxtaposition.
≠ remoteness.

proxy *n* agent, factor, deputy, stand-in, substitute, representative, delegate, attorney.

prudent *adj* wise, sensible, politic, judicious, shrewd, discerning, careful, cautious, wary, vigilant, circumspect, discreet, provident, far-sighted, thrifty.
≠ imprudent, unwise, careless, rash.

pry *v* meddle, interfere, poke one's nose in, intrude, peep, peer, snoop, nose, ferret, dig, delve.
≠ mind one's own business.

pseudonym *n* false name, assumed

name, alias, incognito, pen name, nom de plume, stage name.

psychic *adj* spiritual, supernatural, occult, mystic(al), clairvoyant, extrasensory, telepathic, mental, psychological, intellectual, cognitive.

psychological *adj* mental, cerebral, intellectual, cognitive, emotional, subjective, subconscious, unconscious, psychosomatic, irrational, unreal.
≠ physical, real.

puberty *n* pubescence, adolescence, teens, youth, growing up, maturity.
≠ childhood, immaturity, old age.

public *adj* **1** *public buildings*: state, national, civil, community, social, collective, communal, common, general, universal, open, unrestricted. **2** KNOWN, well-known, recognized, acknowledged, overt, open, exposed, published.
≠ **1** private, personal. **2** secret.
n people, nation, country, population, populace, masses, citizens, society, community, voters, electorate, followers, supporters, fans, audience, patrons, clientèle, customers, buyers, consumers.
public house pub (*infml*), local (*infml*), bar, saloon, inn, tavern.

publication *n* **1** BOOK, newspaper, magazine, periodical, booklet, leaflet, pamphlet, handbill. **2** ANNOUNCEMENT, declaration, notification, disclosure, release, issue, printing, publishing.

publicity *n* advertising, plug (*infml*), hype (*sl*), promotion, build-up, boost, attention, limelight, splash.

publicize *v* advertise, plug (*infml*), hype (*sl*), promote, push, spotlight, broadcast, make known, blaze.

publish *v* **1** ANNOUNCE, declare, communicate, make known, divulge, disclose, reveal, release, publicize, advertise. **2** *publish a book*: produce, print, issue, bring out, distribute, circulate, spread, diffuse.

pucker *v* gather, ruffle, wrinkle, shrivel, crinkle, crumple, crease, furrow, purse, screw up, contract, compress.

puerile *adj* childish, babyish, infantile, juvenile, immature, irresponsible, silly, foolish, inane, trivial.
≠ mature.

puff *n* **1** BREATH, waft, whiff, draught, flurry, gust, blast. **2** *a puff on a cigarette*: pull, drag.
v **1** BREATHE, pant, gasp, gulp, wheeze, blow, waft, inflate, expand, swell. **2** *puff a cigarette*: smoke, pull, drag, draw, suck.

puffy *adj* puffed up, inflated, swollen, bloated, distended, enlarged.

pugnacious *adj* hostile, aggressive, belligerent, contentious, disputatious, argumentative, quarrelsome, hot-tempered.
≠ peaceable.

pull *v* **1** TOW, drag, haul, draw, tug, jerk, yank (*infml*). **2** REMOVE, take out, extract, pull out, pluck, uproot, pull up, rip, tear. **3** ATTRACT, draw, lure, allure, entice, tempt, magnetize. **4** DISLOCATE, sprain, wrench, strain.
≠ **1** push, press. **3** repel, deter, discourage.
n **1** TOW, drag, tug, jerk, yank (*infml*). **2** ATTRACTION, lure, allurement, drawing power, magnetism, influence, weight.
pull apart separate, part, dismember, dismantle, take to pieces.
≠ join.
pull down destroy, demolish, knock down, bulldoze.
≠ build, erect, put up.
pull off 1 ACCOMPLISH, achieve, bring off, succeed, manage, carry out. **2** DETACH, remove.
≠ **1** fail. **2** attach.
pull out retreat, withdraw, leave, depart, quit, move out, evacuate, desert, abandon.
≠ join, arrive.
pull through recover, rally, recuperate, survive, weather.
pull together co-operate, work together, collaborate, team up.
≠ fight.
pull up 1 STOP, halt, park, draw up, pull in, pull over, brake. **2** REPRIMAND, tell off (*infml*), tick off (*infml*), take to task, rebuke, criticize.

pulp *n* flesh, marrow, paste, purée, mash, mush, pap.
v crush, squash, pulverize, mash, purée, liquidize.

pulsate *v* pulse, beat, throb, pound, hammer, drum, thud, thump, vibrate, oscillate, quiver.

pulse *n* beat, stroke, rhythm, throb, pulsation, beating, pounding, drumming, vibration, oscillation.

pulverize *v* **1** CRUSH, pound, grind, mill, powder. **2** DEFEAT, destroy, demolish, annihilate.

pump *v* push, drive, force, inject, siphon, draw, drain.
pump up blow up, inflate, puff up, fill.

pun *n* play on words, double entendre, witticism, quip.

punch[1] *v* hit, strike, pummel, jab, bash, clout, cuff, box, thump, sock (*sl*), wallop (*infml*).
n **1** BLOW, jab, bash, clout, thump, wallop (*infml*). **2** FORCE, impact, effectiveness, drive, vigour, verve, panache.

punch[2] *v* perforate, pierce, puncture, prick, bore, drill, stamp, cut.

punctilious *adj* scrupulous, conscientious, meticulous, careful, exact, precise, strict, formal, proper, particular, finicky, fussy.
≠ lax, informal.

punctual *adj* prompt, on time, on the dot, exact, precise, early, in good time.
≠ unpunctual, late.

punctuation

Punctuation marks include: comma, full stop, period, colon, semicolon, brackets, parentheses, square brackets, inverted commas, speech marks, quotation marks, quotes (*infml*), exclamation mark, question mark, apostrophe, asterisk, star, hyphen, dash, oblique stroke, solidus, backslash.

puncture *n* **1** FLAT TYRE, flat (*infml*), blow-out. **2** LEAK, hole, perforation, cut, nick.
v prick, pierce, penetrate, perforate, hole, cut, nick, burst, rupture, flatten, deflate.

pungent *adj* strong, hot, peppery, spicy, aromatic, tangy, piquant, sharp, keen, acute, sour, bitter, acrid, caustic, stinging, biting, cutting, incisive, pointed, piercing, penetrating, sarcastic, scathing.
≠ mild, bland, tasteless.

punish *v* penalize, discipline, correct, chastise, castigate, scold, beat, flog, lash, cane, spank, fine, imprison.
≠ reward.

punishment *n* discipline, correction, chastisement, penalty, sentence, deserts, retribution, revenge.
≠ reward.

Forms of punishment include: banging up (*sl*), banishment, beating, belting, the birch, borstal, the cane, capital punishment, cashiering, chain gang, confinement, confiscation, corporal punishment, defrocking, demotion, deportation, detention, dressing-down, excommunication, execution, exile, expulsion, fine, flaying, flogging, gaol, gating, grounding, hiding (*infml*), hitting, horsewhipping, house arrest, imprisonment, incarceration, internment, jail, jankers, keelhauling, larruping (*infml*), lashing, leathering, lines, penal colony, prison, probation, being put away (*infml*), the rack, rap across the knuckles, scourging, being sent down (*infml*), being sent to Coventry, sequestration, slapping, the slipper, smacking, spanking, the stocks, suspension, tanning someone's hide (*infml*), tarring and feathering, torturing, thrashing, transportation, unfrocking, walking the plank, walloping, whipping. *see also* **execution**.

punitive *adj* penal, disciplinary, retributive, retaliatory, vindictive, punishing.

puny *adj* weak, feeble, frail, sickly, undeveloped, underdeveloped, stunted, undersized, diminutive, little, tiny, insignificant.
≠ strong, sturdy, large, important.

pupil *n* student, scholar, schoolboy, schoolgirl, learner, apprentice,

beginner, novice, disciple, protégé(e).
≠ teacher.

purchase *v* buy, pay for, invest in (*infml*), procure, acquire, obtain, get, secure, gain, earn, win.
≠ sell.
n acquisition, buy (*infml*), investment, asset, possession, property.
≠ sale.

purchaser *n* buyer, consumer, shopper, customer, client.
≠ seller, vendor.

pure *adj* **1** *pure gold*: unadulterated, unalloyed, unmixed, undiluted, neat, solid, simple, natural, real, authentic, genuine, true. **2** STERILE, uncontaminated, unpolluted, germ-free, aseptic, antiseptic, disinfected, sterilized, hygienic, sanitary, clean, immaculate, spotless, clear. **3** SHEER, utter, complete, total, thorough, absolute, perfect, unqualified. **4** CHASTE, virginal, undefiled, unsullied, moral, upright, virtuous, blameless, innocent. **5** *pure mathematics*: theoretical, abstract, conjectural, speculative, academic.
≠ **1** impure, adulterated. **2** contaminated, polluted. **4** immoral. **5** applied.

purely *adv* **1** UTTERLY, completely, totally, entirely, wholly, thoroughly, absolutely. **2** ONLY, simply, merely, just, solely, exclusively.

purge *v* **1** PURIFY, cleanse, clean out, scour, clear, absolve. **2** OUST, remove, get rid of, eject, expel, root out, eradicate, exterminate, wipe out, kill.
n removal, ejection, expulsion, witch hunt, eradication, extermination.

purify *v* refine, filter, clarify, clean, cleanse, decontaminate, sanitize, disinfect, sterilize, fumigate, deodorize.
≠ contaminate, pollute, defile.

purist *n* pedant, literalist, formalist, stickler, quibbler, nit-picker.

puritanical *adj* puritan, moralistic, disciplinarian, ascetic, abstemious, austere, severe, stern, strict, strait-laced, prim, proper, prudish, disapproving, stuffy, stiff, rigid, narrow-minded, bigoted, fanatical, zealous.
≠ hedonistic, liberal, indulgent, broad-minded.

purity *n* **1** CLEARNESS, clarity, cleanness, cleanliness, untaintedness, wholesomeness. **2** SIMPLICITY, authenticity, genuineness, truth. **3** CHASTITY, decency, morality, integrity, rectitude, uprightness, virtue, innocence, blamelessness.
≠ **1** impurity. **3** immorality.

purpose *n* **1** INTENTION, aim, objective, end, goal, target, plan, design, vision, idea, point, object, reason, motive, rationale, principle, result, outcome. **2** DETERMINATION, resolve, resolution, drive, single-mindedness, dedication, devotion, constancy, steadfastness, persistence, tenacity, zeal. **3** USE, function, application, good, advantage, benefit, value.
on purpose purposely, deliberately, intentionally, consciously, knowingly, wittingly, wilfully.
≠ accidentally, impulsively, spontaneously.

purposeful *adj* determined, decided, resolved, resolute, single-minded, constant, steadfast, persistent, persevering, tenacious, strong-willed, positive, firm, deliberate.
≠ purposeless, aimless.

purse *n* **1** MONEY-BAG, wallet, pouch. **2** MONEY, means, resources, finances, funds, coffers, treasury, exchequer. **3** REWARD, award, prize.
v pucker, wrinkle, draw together, close, tighten, contract, compress.

pursue *v* **1** *pursue an activity*: perform, engage in, practise, conduct, carry on, continue, keep on, keep up, maintain, persevere in, persist in, hold to, aspire to, aim for, strive for, try for. **2** CHASE, go after, follow, track, trail, shadow, tail, dog, harass, harry, hound, hunt, seek, search for, investigate, inquire into.

pursuit *n* **1** CHASE, hue and cry, tracking, stalking, trail, hunt, quest, search, investigation. **2** ACTIVITY, interest, hobby, pastime, occupation, trade, craft, line, speciality, vocation.

push *v* **1** PROPEL, thrust, ram, shove, jostle, elbow, prod, poke, press, depress, squeeze, squash, drive, force, constrain. **2** PROMOTE, advertise, publicize, boost, encourage, urge, egg on (*infml*), incite, spur, influence, persuade, pressurize, bully.
≠ **1** pull. **2** discourage, dissuade.
n **1** KNOCK, shove, nudge, jolt, prod, poke, thrust. **2** ENERGY, vigour, vitality, go (*infml*), drive, effort, dynamism, enterprise, initiative, ambition, determination.

pushy *adj* assertive, self-assertive, ambitious, forceful, aggressive, over-confident, forward, bold, brash, arrogant, presumptuous, assuming, bossy (*infml*).
≠ unassertive, unassuming.

put *v* **1** PLACE, lay, deposit, plonk (*infml*), set, fix, settle, establish, stand, position, dispose, situate, station, post. **2** APPLY, impose, inflict, levy, assign, subject. **3** WORD, phrase, formulate, frame, couch, express, voice, utter, state. **4** *put a suggestion*: submit, present, offer, suggest, propose.
put across put over, communicate, convey, express, explain, spell out, bring home to, get through to.
put aside put by, set aside, keep, retain, save, reserve, store, stow, stockpile, stash (*infml*), hoard, salt away.
put away (*infml*) **1** CONSUME, devour, eat, drink. **2** IMPRISON, jail, lock up, commit, certify.
put back 1 DELAY, defer, postpone, reschedule. **2** REPLACE, return.
≠ **1** bring forward.
put down 1 WRITE DOWN, transcribe, enter, log, register, record, note. **2** CRUSH, quash, suppress, defeat, quell, silence, snub, slight, squash, deflate, humble, take down a peg, shame, humiliate, mortify. **3** *put down a sick dog*: kill, put to sleep. **4** ASCRIBE, attribute, blame, charge.
put forward advance, suggest, recommend, nominate, propose, move, table, introduce, present, submit, offer, tender.
put in insert, enter, input, submit, install, fit.
put off 1 DELAY, defer, postpone, reschedule. **2** DETER, dissuade, discourage, dishearten, demoralize, daunt, dismay, intimidate, disconcert, confuse, distract.
≠ **2** encourage.
put on 1 ATTACH, affix, apply, place, add, impose. **2** PRETEND, feign, sham, fake, simulate, affect, assume. **3** STAGE, mount, produce, present, do, perform.
put out 1 PUBLISH, announce, broadcast, circulate. **2** EXTINGUISH, quench, douse, smother, switch off, turn off. **3** INCONVENIENCE, impose on, bother, disturb, trouble, upset, hurt, offend, annoy, irritate, irk, anger, exasperate.
≠ **2** light.
put through accomplish, achieve, complete, conclude, finalize, execute, manage, bring off.
put up 1 ERECT, build, construct, assemble. **2** ACCOMMODATE, house, lodge, shelter. **3** *put up prices*: raise, increase. **4** PAY, invest, give, advance, float, provide, supply, pledge, offer.
put up to prompt, incite, encourage, egg on (*infml*), urge, goad.
≠ discourage, dissuade.
put up with stand, bear, abide, stomach, endure, suffer, tolerate, allow, accept, stand for, take, take lying down.
≠ object to, reject.

putrid *adj* rotten, decayed, decomposed, mouldy, off, bad, rancid, addled, corrupt, contaminated, tainted, polluted, foul, rank, fetid, stinking.
≠ fresh, wholesome.

put-upon *adj* imposed on, taken advantage of, exploited, used, abused, maltreated, persecuted.

puzzle *v* **1** BAFFLE, mystify, perplex, confound, stump (*infml*), floor (*infml*), confuse, bewilder, flummox (*infml*). **2** THINK, ponder, meditate, consider, mull over, deliberate, figure, rack one's brains.
n question, poser, brain-teaser, mind-bender, crossword, rebus, anagram, riddle, conundrum, mystery, enigma, paradox.

puzzle out solve, work out, figure out, decipher, decode, crack, unravel, untangle, sort out, resolve, clear up.

puzzled *adj* baffled, mystified, perplexed, confounded, at a loss, beaten, stumped (*infml*), confused, bewildered, nonplussed, lost, at sea, flummoxed (*infml*).
≠ clear.

pyromaniac *n* arsonist, incendiary, fire-raiser, firebug (*infml*).

Q

quagmire *n* bog, marsh, quag, fen, swamp, morass, mire, quicksand.

quail *v* recoil, back away, shy away, shrink, flinch, cringe, cower, tremble, quake, shudder, falter.

quaint *adj* picturesque, charming, twee (*infml*), old-fashioned, antiquated, old-world, olde-worlde (*infml*), unusual, strange, odd, curious, bizarre, fanciful, whimsical.
≠ modern.

quake *v* shake, tremble, shudder, quiver, shiver, quail, vibrate, wobble, rock, sway, move, convulse, heave.

qualification *n* **1** CERTIFICATE, diploma, training, skill, competence, ability, capability, capacity, aptitude, suitability, fitness, eligibility.
2 RESTRICTION, limitation, reservation, exception, exemption, condition, caveat, provision, proviso, stipulation, modification.

qualified *adj* **1** CERTIFIED, chartered, licensed, professional, trained, experienced, practised, skilled, accomplished, expert, knowledgeable, skilful, talented, proficient, competent, efficient, able, capable, fit, eligible.
2 *qualified praise*: reserved, guarded, cautious, restricted, limited, bounded, contingent, conditional, provisional, equivocal.
≠ **1** unqualified. **2** unconditional, whole-hearted.

qualify *v* **1** TRAIN, prepare, equip, fit, pass, graduate, certify, empower, entitle, authorize, sanction, permit.
2 MODERATE, reduce, lessen, diminish, temper, soften, weaken, mitigate, ease, adjust, modify, restrain, restrict, limit, delimit, define, classify.
≠ **1** disqualify.

quality *n* **1** PROPERTY, characteristic, peculiarity, attribute, aspect, feature, trait, mark. **2** *of poor quality*: standard, grade, class, kind, sort, nature, character, calibre, status, rank, value, worth, merit, condition. **3** EXCELLENCE, superiority, pre-eminence, distinction, refinement.

qualm *n* misgiving, apprehension, fear, anxiety, worry, disquiet, uneasiness, scruple, hesitation, reluctance, uncertainty, doubt.

quandary *n* dilemma, predicament, impasse, perplexity, bewilderment, confusion, mess, fix, hole (*infml*), problem, difficulty.

quantity *n* amount, number, sum, total, aggregate, mass, lot, share, portion, quota, allotment, measure, dose, proportion, part, content, capacity, volume, weight, bulk, size, magnitude, expanse, extent, length, breadth.

quarrel *n* row, argument, slanging match (*infml*), wrangle, squabble, tiff, misunderstanding, disagreement, dispute, dissension, controversy, difference, conflict, clash, contention, strife, fight, scrap, brawl, feud, vendetta, schism.
≠ agreement, harmony.
v row, argue, bicker, squabble, wrangle, be at loggerheads, fall out, disagree, dispute, dissent, differ, be at variance, clash, contend, fight, scrap, feud.
≠ agree.

quarrelsome *adj* argumentative, disputatious, contentious, belligerent, ill-tempered, irritable.
≠ peaceable, placid.

quarry *n* prey, victim, object, goal, target, game, kill, prize.

quarter *n* district, sector, zone, neighbourhood, locality, vicinity, area, region, province, territory, division, section, part, place, spot, point, direction, side.

v station, post, billet, accommodate, put up, lodge, board, house, shelter.

quarters *n* accommodation, lodgings, billet, digs (*infml*), residence, dwelling, habitation, domicile, rooms, barracks, station, post.

quash *v* annul, revoke, rescind, overrule, cancel, nullify, void, invalidate, reverse, set aside, squash, crush, quell, suppress, subdue, defeat, overthrow.
≠ confirm, vindicate, reinstate.

quaver *v* shake, tremble, quake, shudder, quiver, vibrate, pulsate, oscillate, flutter, flicker, trill, warble.

quay *n* wharf, pier, jetty, dock, harbour.

queasy *adj* sick, ill, unwell, queer, groggy, green, nauseated, sickened, bilious, squeamish, faint, dizzy, giddy.

queen *n* **1** monarch, sovereign, ruler, majesty, princess, empress, consort. **2** beauty, belle.

queer *adj* **1** ODD, mysterious, strange, unusual, uncommon, weird, unnatural, bizarre, eccentric, peculiar, funny, puzzling, curious, remarkable. **2** *I feel queer*: unwell, ill, sick, queasy, light-headed, faint, giddy, dizzy. **3** SUSPECT, suspicious, shifty, dubious, shady (*infml*). **4** (*sl*) HOMOSEXUAL, gay, lesbian.
≠ **1** ordinary, usual, common. **2** well.

quell *v* subdue, quash, crush, squash, suppress, put down, overcome, conquer, defeat, overpower, moderate, mitigate, allay, alleviate, soothe, calm, pacify, hush, quiet, silence, stifle, extinguish.

quench *v* **1** *quench one's thirst*: slake, satisfy, sate, cool. **2** EXTINGUISH, douse, put out, snuff out.

querulous *adj* peevish, fretful, fractious, cantankerous, cross, irritable, complaining, grumbling, discontented, dissatisfied, critical, carping, captious, fault-finding, fussy.
≠ placid, uncomplaining, contented.

query *v* ask, inquire, question, challenge, dispute, quarrel with, doubt, suspect, distrust, mistrust, disbelieve.
≠ accept.
n question, inquiry, problem, uncertainty, doubt, suspicion, scepticism, reservation, hesitation.

quest *n* search, hunt, pursuit, investigation, inquiry, mission, crusade, enterprise, undertaking, venture, journey, voyage, expedition, exploration, adventure.

question *v* interrogate, quiz, grill, pump, interview, examine, cross-examine, debrief, ask, inquire, investigate, probe, query, challenge, dispute, doubt, disbelieve.
n **1** QUERY, inquiry, poser, problem, difficulty. **2** ISSUE, matter, subject, topic, point, proposal, proposition, motion, debate, dispute, controversy.

questionable *adj* debatable, disputable, unsettled, undetermined, unproven, uncertain, arguable, controversial, vexed, doubtful, dubious, suspicious, suspect, shady (*infml*), fishy (*infml*), iffy (*sl*).
≠ unquestionable, indisputable, certain.

questionnaire *n* quiz, test, survey, opinion poll.

queue *n* line, tailback, file, crocodile, procession, train, string, succession, series, sequence, order.

quibble *v* carp, cavil, split hairs, nit-pick, equivocate, prevaricate.
n complaint, objection, criticism, query.

quick *adj* **1** FAST, swift, rapid, speedy, express, hurried, hasty, cursory, fleeting, brief, prompt, ready, immediate, instant, instantaneous, sudden, brisk, nimble, sprightly, agile. **2** CLEVER, intelligent, quick-witted, smart, sharp, keen, shrewd, astute, discerning, perceptive, responsive, receptive.
≠ **1** slow, sluggish, lethargic. **2** unintelligent, dull.

quicken *v* **1** ACCELERATE, speed, hurry, hasten, precipitate, expedite, dispatch, advance. **2** ANIMATE, enliven, invigorate, energize, galvanize, activate, rouse, arouse, stimulate, excite, inspire, revive,

refresh, reinvigorate, reactivate.
≠ **1** slow, retard. **2** dull.

quiet *adj* **1** SILENT, noiseless, inaudible, hushed, soft, low. **2** PEACEFUL, still, tranquil, serene, calm, composed, undisturbed, untroubled, placid. **3** SHY, reserved, reticent, uncommunicative, taciturn, unforthcoming, retiring, withdrawn, thoughtful, subdued, meek. **4** *a quiet spot*: isolated, unfrequented, lonely, secluded, private.
≠ **1** noisy, loud. **2** excitable. **3** extrovert.
n quietness, silence, hush, peace, lull, stillness, tranquillity, serenity, calm, rest, repose.
≠ noise, loudness, disturbance, bustle.

quieten *v* **1** SILENCE, hush, mute, soften, lower, diminish, reduce, stifle, muffle, deaden, dull. **2** SUBDUE, pacify, quell, quiet, still, smooth, calm, soothe, compose, sober.
≠ **2** disturb, agitate.

quilt *n* bedcover, coverlet, bedspread, counterpane, eiderdown, duvet.

quip *n* joke, jest, crack, gag (*infml*), witticism, riposte, retort, gibe.

quirk *n* freak, eccentricity, curiosity, oddity, peculiarity, idiosyncrasy, mannerism, habit, trait, foible, whim, caprice, turn, twist.

quit *v* **1** LEAVE, depart, go, exit, decamp, desert, forsake, abandon, renounce, relinquish, surrender, give up, resign, retire, withdraw. **2** *quit smoking*: stop, cease, end, discontinue, desist, drop, give up, pack in (*sl*).

quite *adv* **1** MODERATELY, rather, somewhat, fairly, relatively, comparatively. **2** UTTERLY, absolutely, totally, completely, entirely, wholly, fully, perfectly, exactly, precisely.

quiver *v* shake, tremble, shudder, shiver, quake, quaver, vibrate, palpitate, flutter, flicker, oscillate, wobble.
n shake, tremble, shudder, shiver, tremor, vibration, palpitation, flutter, flicker, oscillation, wobble.

quiz *n* questionnaire, test, examination, competition.
v question, interrogate, grill, pump, examine, cross-examine.

quizzical *adj* questioning, inquiring, curious, amused, humorous, teasing, mocking, satirical, sardonic, sceptical.

quota *n* ration, allowance, allocation, assignment, share, portion, part, slice, cut (*infml*), percentage, proportion.

quotation *n* **1** CITATION, quote (*infml*), extract, excerpt, passage, piece, cutting, reference. **2** ESTIMATE, quote (*infml*), tender, figure, price, cost, charge, rate.

quote *v* cite, refer to, mention, name, reproduce, echo, repeat, recite, recall, recollect.

R

rabble *n* crowd, throng, horde, herd, mob, masses, populace, riff-raff.

rabble-rouser *n* agitator, troublemaker, incendiary, demagogue, ringleader.

race[1] *n* competition, contest, contention, rivalry, chase, pursuit, quest.

> *Types of race and famous races include*: cycle race, cyclo-cross, road race, time trial, Milk Race, Tour de France; greyhound race, Greyhound Derby; horse race, Cheltenham Gold Cup, the Classics (Derby, Oaks, One Thousand Guineas, St. Leger, Two Thousand Guineas), Grand National, Kentucky Derby, Melbourne Cup, Prix de l'Arc de Triomphe, steeplechase, trotting race, harness race (*US*); motorcycle race, motocross, scramble, speedway, Isle of Man Tourist Trophy (TT); motor-race, Grand Prix, Indianapolis 500, Le Mans, Monte Carlo rally, RAC Rally, stock car race; rowing, regatta, Boat Race; running, cross-country, dash (*US*), hurdles, marathon, London Marathon, relay, sprint, steeplechase, track event; ski race, downhill, slalom; swimming race; walking race, walkathon; yacht race, Admiral's Cup, America's Cup; egg-and-spoon race, pancake race, sack race, wheelbarrow race.

v run, sprint, dash, tear, fly, gallop, speed, career, dart, zoom, rush, hurry, hasten.

race[2] *n* nation, people, tribe, clan, house, dynasty, family, kindred, ancestry, line, blood, stock, genus, species, breed.

race-course *n* racetrack, course, track, circuit, lap, turf, speedway.

racial *adj* national, tribal, ethnic, folk, genealogical, ancestral, inherited, genetic.

racism *n* racialism, xenophobia, chauvinism, jingoism, discrimination, prejudice, bias.

rack *n* shelf, stand, support, structure, frame, framework.

racket *n* **1** NOISE, din, uproar, row, fuss, outcry, clamour, commotion, disturbance, pandemonium, hurly-burly, hubbub. **2** SWINDLE, con (*infml*), fraud, fiddle, deception, trick, dodge, scheme, business, game.

racy *adj* **1** RIBALD, bawdy, risqué, naughty, indecent, indelicate, suggestive. **2** LIVELY, animated, spirited, energetic, dynamic, buoyant, boisterous.

radiance *n* light, luminosity, incandescence, radiation, brightness, brilliance, shine, lustre, gleam, glow, glitter, resplendence, splendour, happiness, joy, pleasure, delight, rapture.

radiant *adj* bright, luminous, shining, gleaming, glowing, beaming, glittering, sparkling, brilliant, resplendent, splendid, glorious, happy, joyful, delighted, ecstatic.
≠ dull, miserable.

radiate *v* shine, gleam, glow, beam, shed, pour, give off, emit, emanate, diffuse, issue, disseminate, scatter, spread (out), diverge, branch.

radical *adj* **1** BASIC, fundamental, primary, essential, natural, native, innate, intrinsic, deep-seated, profound. **2** *radical changes*: drastic, comprehensive, thorough, sweeping, far-reaching, thoroughgoing, complete, total, entire. **3** FANATICAL, militant, extreme, extremist, revolutionary.
≠ **1** superficial. **3** moderate.
n fanatic, militant, extremist,

revolutionary, reformer, reformist, fundamentalist.

raffle *n* draw, lottery, sweepstake, sweep, tombola.

rage *n* **1** ANGER, wrath, fury, frenzy, tantrum, temper. **2** (*infml*) *all the rage*: craze, fad, thing (*infml*), fashion, vogue, style, passion, enthusiasm, obsession.
v fume, seethe, rant, rave, storm, thunder, explode, rampage.

ragged *adj* **1** *ragged clothes*: frayed, torn, ripped, tattered, worn-out, threadbare, tatty, shabby, scruffy, unkempt, down-at-heel. **2** JAGGED, serrated, indented, notched, rough, uneven, irregular, fragmented, erratic, disorganized.

raid *n* attack, onset, onslaught, invasion, inroad, incursion, foray, sortie, strike, blitz, swoop, bust (*sl*), robbery, break-in, hold-up.
v loot, pillage, plunder, ransack, rifle, maraud, attack, descend on, invade, storm.

raider *n* attacker, invader, looter, plunderer, ransacker, marauder, robber, thief, brigand, pirate.

railing *n* fence, paling, barrier, parapet, rail, balustrade.

railway *n* track, line, rails.

> *Types of railway include*: branch line, broad gauge, cable railway, cutting, electric railway, elevated railway, feeder line, funicular railway, garden railway, high-speed line, InterCity®, light railway, main line, marshalling yard, metro, model railway, monorail, mountain railway, narrow gauge, rack railway, rack-and-pinion railway, railroad (*US*), rapid transit system, siding, standard gauge, subway (*US*), tramway, trunk line, tube, underground.

rain *n* rainfall, precipitation, raindrops, drizzle, shower, cloudburst, downpour, deluge, torrent, storm, thunderstorm, squall.
v spit, drizzle, shower, pour, teem, pelt, bucket (*infml*), deluge.

rainy *adj* wet, damp, showery, drizzly.
≠ dry.

raise *v* **1** LIFT, elevate, hoist, jack up, erect, build, construct. **2** INCREASE, augment, escalate, magnify, heighten, strengthen, intensify, amplify, boost, enhance. **3** *raise funds*: get, obtain, collect, gather, assemble, rally, muster, recruit. **4** BRING UP, rear, breed, propagate, grow, cultivate, develop. **5** *raise a subject*: bring up, broach, introduce, present, put forward, moot, suggest.
≠ **1** lower. **2** decrease, reduce. **5** suppress.

rake *v* hoe, scratch, scrape, graze, comb, scour, search, hunt, ransack, gather, collect, amass, accumulate.

rally *v* **1** GATHER, collect, assemble, congregate, convene, muster, summon, round up, unite, marshal, organize, mobilize, reassemble, regroup, reorganize. **2** RECOVER, recuperate, revive, improve, pick up.
n **1** GATHERING, assembly, convention, convocation, conference, meeting, jamboree, reunion, march, demonstration. **2** RECOVERY, recuperation, revival, comeback, improvement, resurgence, renewal.

ram *v* **1** HIT, strike, butt, hammer, pound, drum, crash, smash, slam. **2** FORCE, drive, thrust, cram, stuff, pack, crowd, jam, wedge.

ramble *v* **1** WALK, hike, trek, tramp, traipse, stroll, amble, saunter, straggle, wander, roam, rove, meander, wind, zigzag. **2** CHATTER, babble, rabbit (on) (*infml*), witter (on) (*infml*), expatiate, digress, drift.
n walk, hike, trek, tramp, stroll, saunter, tour, trip, excursion.

rambler *n* hiker, walker, stroller, rover, roamer, wanderer, wayfarer.

rambling *adj* **1** SPREADING, sprawling, straggling, trailing. **2** CIRCUITOUS, roundabout, digressive, wordy, long-winded, long-drawn-out, disconnected, incoherent.
≠ **2** direct.

ramification *n* branch, offshoot,

development, complication, result, consequence, upshot, implication.

ramp *n* slope, incline, gradient, rise.

rampage *v* run wild, run amok, run riot, rush, tear, storm, rage, rant, rave.
n rage, fury, frenzy, storm, uproar, violence, destruction.
on the rampage wild, amok, berserk, violent, out of control.

rampant *adj* unrestrained, uncontrolled, unbridled, unchecked, wanton, excessive, fierce, violent, raging, wild, riotous, rank, profuse, rife, widespread, prevalent.

ramshackle *adj* dilapidated, tumbledown, broken-down, crumbling, ruined, derelict, jerry-built, unsafe, rickety, shaky, unsteady, tottering, decrepit.
≠ solid, stable.

rancid *adj* sour, off, bad, musty, stale, rank, foul, fetid, putrid, rotten.
≠ sweet.

random *adj* arbitrary, chance, fortuitous, casual, incidental, haphazard, irregular, unsystematic, unplanned, accidental, aimless, purposeless, indiscriminate, stray.
≠ systematic, deliberate.

range *n* **1** SCOPE, compass, scale, gamut, spectrum, sweep, spread, extent, distance, reach, span, limits, bounds, parameters, area, field, domain, province, sphere, orbit. **2** *a range of fittings*: variety, diversity, assortment, selection, sort, kind, class, order, series, string, chain.
v **1** EXTEND, stretch, reach, spread, vary, fluctuate. **2** ALIGN, arrange, order, rank, classify, catalogue.

rank[1] *n* **1** GRADE, degree, class, caste, status, standing, position, station, condition, estate, echelon, level, stratum, tier, classification, sort, type, group, division. **2** ROW, line, range, column, file, series, order, formation.

Ranks in the armed services include: *air force*: aircraftman, aircraftwoman, corporal, sergeant, warrant officer, pilot officer, flying officer, flight lieutenant, squadron-leader, wing commander, group-captain, air-commodore, air-vice-marshal, air-marshal, air-chief-marshal, marshal of the Royal Air Force; *army*: private, lance-corporal, corporal, sergeant, warrant officer, lieutenant, captain, major, lieutenant-colonel, colonel, brigadier, major general, lieutenant-general, general, field marshal; *navy*: able seaman, rating, petty officer, chief petty officer, sublieutenant, lieutenant, lieutenant-commander, commander, captain, commodore, rear admiral, vice-admiral, admiral, admiral of the fleet. *see also* **soldier**.

v grade, class, rate, place, position, range, sort, classify, categorize, order, arrange, organize, marshal.

rank[2] *adj* **1** UTTER, total, complete, absolute, unmitigated, thorough, sheer, downright, out-and-out, arrant, gross, flagrant, glaring, outrageous. **2** FOUL, repulsive, disgusting, revolting, stinking, putrid, rancid, stale.

rankle *v* annoy, irritate, rile, nettle, gall, irk, anger.

ransack *v* search, scour, comb, rummage, rifle, raid, sack, strip, despoil, ravage, loot, plunder, pillage.

ransom *n* price, money, payment, pay-off, redemption, deliverance, rescue, liberation, release.
v buy off, redeem, deliver, rescue, liberate, free, release.

rant *v* shout, cry, yell, roar, bellow, declaim, bluster, rave.

rap *v* **1** KNOCK, hit, strike, tap, thump. **2** (*sl*) REPROVE, reprimand, criticize, censure.
n **1** KNOCK, blow, tap, thump. **2** (*sl*) REBUKE, reprimand, censure, blame, punishment.

rape *n* violation, assault, abuse, maltreatment.
v violate, assault, abuse, maltreat.

rapid *adj* swift, speedy, quick, fast, express, lightning, prompt, brisk, hurried, hasty, precipitate, headlong.
≠ slow, leisurely, sluggish.

rapport *n* bond, link, affinity, relationship, empathy, sympathy, understanding, harmony.

rapt *adj* engrossed, absorbed, preoccupied, intent, gripped, spellbound, enthralled, captivated, fascinated, entranced, charmed, enchanted, delighted, ravished, enraptured, transported.

rapture *n* delight, happiness, joy, bliss, ecstasy, euphoria, exaltation.

rare *adj* **1** UNCOMMON, unusual, scarce, sparse, sporadic, infrequent. **2** EXQUISITE, superb, excellent, superlative, incomparable, exceptional, remarkable, precious.
≠ **1** common, abundant, frequent.

rarefied *adj* exclusive, select, private, esoteric, refined, high, noble, sublime.

rarely *adv* seldom, hardly ever, infrequently, little.
≠ often, frequently.

raring *adj* eager, keen, enthusiastic, ready, willing, impatient, longing, itching, desperate.

rarity *n* **1** CURIOSITY, curio, gem, pearl, treasure, find. **2** UNCOMMONNESS, unusualness, strangeness, scarcity, shortage, sparseness, infrequency.
≠ **2** commonness, frequency.

rascal *n* rogue, scoundrel, scamp, scallywag, imp, devil, villain, good-for-nothing, wastrel.

rash[1] *adj* reckless, ill-considered, foolhardy, ill-advised, madcap, hare-brained, hot-headed, headstrong, impulsive, impetuous, hasty, headlong, unguarded, unwary, indiscreet, imprudent, careless, heedless, unthinking.
≠ cautious, wary, careful.

rash[2] *n* eruption, outbreak, epidemic, plague.

rasp *n* grating, scrape, grinding, scratch, harshness, hoarseness, croak.
v grate, scrape, grind, file, sand, scour, abrade, rub.

rate *n* **1** SPEED, velocity, tempo, time, ratio, proportion, relation, degree, grade, rank, rating, standard, basis, measure, scale. **2** CHARGE, fee, hire, toll, tariff, price, cost, value, worth, tax, duty, amount, figure, percentage.
v **1** JUDGE, regard, consider, deem, count, reckon, figure, estimate, evaluate, assess, weigh, measure, grade, rank, class, classify. **2** ADMIRE, respect, esteem, value, prize. **3** DESERVE, merit.

rather *adv* **1** MODERATELY, relatively, slightly, a bit, somewhat, fairly, quite, pretty, noticeably, significantly, very. **2** PREFERABLY, sooner, instead.

ratify *v* approve, uphold, endorse, sign, legalize, sanction, authorize, establish, affirm, confirm, certify, validate, authenticate.
≠ repudiate, reject.

rating *n* class, rank, degree, status, standing, position, placing, order, grade, mark, evaluation, assessment, classification, category.

ratio *n* percentage, fraction, proportion, relation, relationship, correspondence, correlation.

ration *n* quota, allowance, allocation, allotment, share, portion, helping, part, measure, amount.
v apportion, allot, allocate, share, deal out, distribute, dole out, dispense, supply, issue, control, restrict, limit, conserve, save.

rational *adj* logical, reasonable, sound, well-founded, realistic, sensible, clear-headed, judicious, wise, sane, normal, balanced, lucid, reasoning, thinking, intelligent, enlightened.
≠ irrational, illogical, insane, crazy.

rationale *n* logic, reasoning, philosophy, principle, basis, grounds, explanation, reason, motive, motivation, theory.

rationalize *v* **1** JUSTIFY, excuse, vindicate, explain, account for. **2** REORGANIZE, streamline.

rations *n* food, provisions, supplies, stores.

rattle *v* clatter, jingle, jangle, clank, shake, vibrate, jolt, jar, bounce, bump.
rattle off reel off, list, run through, recite, repeat.

raucous *adj* harsh, rough, hoarse, husky, rasping, grating, jarring, strident, noisy, loud.

ravage *v* destroy, devastate, lay waste, demolish, raze, wreck, ruin, spoil, damage, loot, pillage, plunder, sack, despoil.
n destruction, devastation, havoc, damage, ruin, desolation, wreckage, pillage, plunder.

rave *v* rage, storm, thunder, roar, rant, ramble, babble, splutter.
adj (*infml*) enthusiastic, rapturous, favourable, excellent, wonderful.

ravenous *adj* hungry, starving, starved, famished, greedy, voracious, insatiable.

ravine *n* canyon, gorge, gully, pass.

raving *adj* mad, insane, crazy, hysterical, delirious, wild, frenzied, furious, berserk.

ravish *v* enrapture, delight, overjoy, enchant, charm, captivate, entrance, fascinate, spellbind.

ravishing *adj* delightful, enchanting, charming, lovely, beautiful, gorgeous, stunning, radiant, dazzling, alluring, seductive.

raw *adj* **1** *raw vegetables*: uncooked, fresh. **2** UNPROCESSED, unrefined, untreated, crude, natural. **3** PLAIN, bare, naked, basic, harsh, brutal, realistic. **4** SCRATCHED, grazed, scraped, open, bloody, sore, tender, sensitive. **5** COLD, chilly, bitter, biting, piercing, freezing, bleak. **6** *a raw recruit*: new, green, immature, callow, inexperienced, untrained, unskilled.
≠ **1** cooked, done. **2** processed, refined. **5** warm. **6** experienced, skilled.

ray *n* beam, shaft, flash, gleam, flicker, glimmer, glint, spark, trace, hint, indication.

raze *v* demolish, pull down, tear down, bulldoze, flatten, level, destroy.

razor

Types of razor include: battery shaver, cut-throat, disposable razor, double-edged razor, electric razor, Ladyshave®, rechargeable razor, safety razor, shaver, wet razor, wet-and-dry shaver.

re *prep* about, concerning, regarding, with regard to, with reference to.

reach *v* arrive at, get to, attain, achieve, make, amount to, hit, strike, touch, contact, stretch, extend, grasp.
n range, scope, compass, distance, spread, extent, stretch, grasp, jurisdiction, command, power, influence.

react *v* respond, retaliate, reciprocate, reply, answer, acknowledge, act, behave.

reaction *n* response, effect, reply, answer, acknowledgement, feedback, counteraction, reflex, recoil, reciprocation, retaliation.

reactionary *adj* conservative, right-wing, rightist, die-hard, counter-revolutionary.
≠ progressive, revolutionary.
n conservative, right-winger, rightist, die-hard, counter-revolutionary.
≠ progressive, revolutionary.

read *v* **1** STUDY, peruse, pore over, scan, skim, decipher, decode, interpret, construe, understand, comprehend. **2** RECITE, declaim, deliver, speak, utter. **3** *the gauge read zero*: indicate, show, display, register, record.

readable *adj* **1** LEGIBLE, decipherable, intelligible, clear, understandable, comprehensible. **2** INTERESTING, enjoyable, entertaining, gripping, unputdownable (*infml*).
≠ **1** illegible. **2** unreadable.

readily *adv* willingly, unhesitatingly, gladly, eagerly, promptly, quickly, freely, smoothly, easily, effortlessly.
≠ unwillingly, reluctantly.

reading *n* **1** STUDY, perusal, scrutiny, examination, inspection, interpretation, understanding, rendering, version, rendition, recital. **2** *a reading from the Bible*: passage, lesson.

ready *adj* **1** *ready to go*: prepared, waiting, set, fit, arranged, organized, completed, finished. **2** WILLING, inclined, disposed, happy, game (*infml*), eager, keen. **3** AVAILABLE, to hand, present, near, accessible, convenient, handy. **4** PROMPT,

immediate, quick, sharp, astute, perceptive, alert.
≠ **1** unprepared. **2** unwilling, reluctant, disinclined. **3** unavailable, inaccessible. **4** slow.

real *adj* actual, existing, physical, material, substantial, tangible, genuine, authentic, bona fide, official, rightful, legitimate, valid, true, factual, certain, sure, positive, veritable, honest, sincere, heartfelt, unfeigned, unaffected.
≠ unreal, imaginary, false.

realistic *adj* **1** PRACTICAL, down-to-earth, commonsense, sensible, level-headed, clear-sighted, businesslike, hard-headed, pragmatic, matter-of-fact, rational, logical, objective, detached, unsentimental, unromantic. **2** LIFELIKE, faithful, truthful, true, genuine, authentic, natural, real, real-life, graphic, representational.
≠ **1** unrealistic, impractical, irrational, idealistic.

reality *n* truth, fact, certainty, realism, actuality, existence, materiality, tangibility, genuineness, authenticity, validity.

realize *v* **1** UNDERSTAND, comprehend, grasp, catch on, cotton on (*infml*), recognize, accept, appreciate. **2** ACHIEVE, accomplish, fulfil, complete, implement, perform. **3** SELL FOR, fetch, make, earn, produce, net, clear.

really *adv* actually, truly, honestly, sincerely, genuinely, positively, certainly, absolutely, categorically, very, indeed.

realm *n* kingdom, monarchy, principality, empire, country, state, land, territory, area, region, province, domain, sphere, orbit, field, department.

rear *n* back, stern, end, tail, rump, buttocks, posterior, behind, bottom, backside (*infml*).
≠ front.
adj back, hind, hindmost, rearmost, last.
≠ front.
v **1** *rear a child*: bring up, raise, breed, grow, cultivate, foster, nurse, nurture, train, educate. **2** RISE, tower, soar, raise, lift.

reason *n* **1** CAUSE, motive, incentive, rationale, explanation, excuse, justification, defence, warrant, ground, basis, case, argument, aim, intention, purpose, object, end, goal. **2** SENSE, logic, reasoning, rationality, sanity, mind, wit, brain, intellect, understanding, wisdom, judgement, common sense, gumption.
v work out, solve, resolve, conclude, deduce, infer, think.
reason with urge, persuade, move, remonstrate with, argue with, debate with, discuss with.

reasonable *adj* **1** SENSIBLE, wise, well-advised, sane, intelligent, rational, logical, practical, sound, reasoned, well-thought-out, plausible, credible, possible, viable. **2** *a reasonable price*: acceptable, satisfactory, tolerable, moderate, average, fair, just, modest, inexpensive.
≠ **1** irrational. **2** exorbitant.

reasoning *n* logic, thinking, thought, analysis, interpretation, deduction, supposition, hypothesis, argument, case, proof.

reassure *v* comfort, cheer, encourage, hearten, inspirit, brace, bolster.
≠ alarm.

rebate *n* refund, repayment, reduction, discount, deduction, allowance.

rebel *v* revolt, mutiny, rise up, run riot, dissent, disobey, defy, resist, recoil, shrink.
≠ conform.
n revolutionary, insurrectionary, mutineer, dissenter, nonconformist, schismatic, heretic.

rebellion *n* revolt, revolution, rising, uprising, insurrection, insurgence, mutiny, resistance, opposition, defiance, disobedience, insubordination, dissent, heresy.

rebellious *adj* revolutionary, insurrectionary, insurgent, seditious, mutinous, resistant, defiant, disobedient, insubordinate, unruly,

disorderly, ungovernable, unmanageable, intractable, obstinate.
≠ obedient, submissive.

rebirth *n* reincarnation, resurrection, renaissance, regeneration, renewal, restoration, revival, revitalization, rejuvenation.

rebound *v* recoil, backfire, return, bounce, ricochet, boomerang.

rebuff *v* spurn, reject, refuse, decline, turn down, repulse, discourage, snub, slight, cut, cold-shoulder.
n rejection, refusal, repulse, check, discouragement, snub, brush-off (*infml*), slight, put-down, cold shoulder.

rebuke *v* reprove, castigate, chide, scold, tell off (*infml*), admonish, tick off (*infml*), reprimand, upbraid, rate, censure, blame, reproach.
≠ praise, compliment.
n reproach, reproof, reprimand, lecture, dressing-down (*infml*), telling-off (*infml*), ticking-off (*infml*), admonition, censure, blame.
≠ praise, commendation.

recall *v* remember, recollect, cast one's mind back, evoke, bring back.

recapitulate *v* recap, summarize, review, repeat, reiterate, restate, recount.

recede *v* go back, return, retire, withdraw, retreat, ebb, wane, sink, decline, diminish, dwindle, decrease, lessen, shrink, slacken, subside, abate.
≠ advance.

receipt *n* **1** VOUCHER, ticket, slip, counterfoil, stub, acknowledgement. **2** RECEIVING, reception, acceptance, delivery.

receipts *n* takings, income, proceeds, profits, gains, return.

receive *v* **1** TAKE, accept, get, obtain, derive, acquire, pick up, collect, inherit. **2** *receive guests*: admit, let in, greet, welcome, entertain, accommodate. **3** EXPERIENCE, undergo, suffer, sustain, meet with, encounter. **4** REACT TO, respond to, hear, perceive, apprehend.
≠ **1** give, donate.

recent *adj* late, latest, current, present-day, contemporary, modern, up-to-date, new, novel, fresh, young.
≠ old, out-of-date.

recently *adv* lately, newly, freshly.

receptacle *n* container, vessel, holder.

reception *n* **1** ACCEPTANCE, admission, greeting, recognition, welcome, treatment, response, reaction, acknowledgement, receipt. **2** PARTY, function, do (*infml*), entertainment.

receptive *adj* open-minded, amenable, accommodating, suggestible, susceptible, sensitive, responsive, open, accessible, approachable, friendly, hospitable, welcoming, sympathetic, favourable, interested.
≠ narrow-minded, resistant, unresponsive.

recess *n* **1** BREAK, interval, intermission, rest, respite, holiday, vacation. **2** ALCOVE, niche, nook, corner, bay, cavity, hollow, depression, indentation.

recession *n* slump, depression, downturn, decline.
≠ boom, upturn.

recipe *n* formula, prescription, ingredients, instructions, directions, method, system, procedure, technique.

reciprocal *adj* mutual, joint, shared, give-and-take, complementary, alternating, corresponding, equivalent, interchangeable.

reciprocate *v* respond, reply, requite, return, exchange, swap, trade, match, equal, correspond, interchange, alternate.

recital *n* performance, concert, recitation, reading, narration, account, rendition, interpretation, repetition.

recitation *n* passage, piece, party piece, poem, monologue, narration, story, tale, recital, telling.

recite *v* repeat, tell, narrate, relate, recount, speak, deliver, articulate, declaim, perform, reel off, itemize, enumerate.

reckless *adj* heedless, thoughtless, mindless, careless, negligent, irresponsible, imprudent, ill-advised,

indiscreet, rash, hasty, foolhardy, daredevil, wild.
≠ cautious, wary, careful, prudent.

reckon *v* **1** CALCULATE, compute, figure out, work out, add up, total, tally, count, number, enumerate. **2** DEEM, regard, consider, esteem, value, rate, judge, evaluate, assess, estimate, gauge. **3** THINK, believe, imagine, fancy, suppose, surmise, assume, guess, conjecture.
reckon on rely on, depend on, bank on, count on, trust in, hope for, expect, anticipate, foresee, plan for, bargain for, figure on, take into account, face.

reckoning *n* **1** *by my reckoning*: calculation, computation, estimate. **2** BILL, account, charge, due, score, settlement. **3** JUDGEMENT, retribution, doom.

reclaim *v* recover, regain, recapture, retrieve, salvage, rescue, redeem, restore, reinstate, regenerate.

recline *v* rest, repose, lean back, lie, lounge, loll, sprawl, stretch out.

recognition *n* **1** IDENTIFICATION, detection, discovery, recollection, recall, remembrance, awareness, perception, realization, understanding. **2** CONFESSION, admission, acceptance, acknowledgement, gratitude, appreciation, honour, respect, greeting, salute.

recognize *v* **1** IDENTIFY, know, remember, recollect, recall, place, see, notice, spot, perceive. **2** CONFESS, own, acknowledge, accept, admit, grant, concede, allow, appreciate, understand, realize.

recollect *v* recall, remember, cast one's mind back, reminisce.

recollection *n* recall, remembrance, memory, souvenir, reminiscence, impression.

recommend *v* advocate, urge, exhort, advise, counsel, suggest, propose, put forward, advance, praise, commend, plug (*infml*), endorse, approve, vouch for.
≠ disapprove.

recommendation *n* advice, counsel, suggestion, proposal, advocacy, endorsement, approval, sanction, blessing, praise, commendation, plug (*infml*), reference, testimonial.
≠ disapproval.

recompense *n* compensation, indemnification, damages, reparation, restitution, amends, requital, repayment, reward, payment, remuneration, pay, wages.

reconcile *v* reunite, conciliate, pacify, appease, placate, propitiate, accord, harmonize, accommodate, adjust, resolve, settle, square.
≠ estrange, alienate.

reconciliation *n* reunion, conciliation, pacification, appeasement, propitiation, rapprochement, détente, settlement, agreement, harmony, accommodation, adjustment, compromise.
≠ estrangement, separation.

reconnoitre *v* explore, survey, scan, spy out, recce (*sl*), inspect, examine, scrutinize, investigate, patrol.

reconstruct *v* remake, rebuild, reassemble, re-establish, refashion, remodel, reform, reorganize, recreate, restore, renovate, regenerate.

record *n* **1** REGISTER, log, report, account, minutes, memorandum, note, entry, document, file, dossier, diary, journal, memoir, history, annals, archives, documentation, evidence, testimony, trace. **2** RECORDING, disc, single, CD, compact disc, album, release, LP. **3** *break the record*: fastest time, best performance, personal best, world record. **4** BACKGROUND, track record, curriculum vitae, career.
v **1** NOTE, enter, inscribe, write down, transcribe, register, log, put down, enrol, report, minute, chronicle, document, keep, preserve. **2** TAPE-RECORD, tape, videotape, video, cut.

recording *n* release, performance.

> *Types of recording include*: album, audiotape, cassette, CD, compact disc, digital recording, disc, EP (extended play), 45, gramophone record, long-playing record, LP, magnetic tape, mono recording, record, 78, single, stereo recording,

tape, tape-recording, tele-recording, video, videocassette, video disc, videotape, vinyl (*infml*).

recount *v* tell, relate, impart, communicate, report, narrate, describe, depict, portray, detail, repeat, rehearse, recite.

recoup *v* recover, retrieve, regain, get back, make good, repay, refund, reimburse, compensate.

recover *v* **1** *recover from illness*: get better, improve, pick up, rally, mend, heal, pull through, get over, recuperate, revive, convalesce, come round. **2** REGAIN, get back, recoup, retrieve, retake, recapture, repossess, reclaim, restore.
≠ **1** worsen. **2** lose, forfeit.

recovery *n* **1** RECUPERATION, convalescence, rehabilitation, mending, healing, improvement, upturn, rally, revival, restoration. **2** RETRIEVAL, salvage, reclamation, repossession, recapture.
≠ **1** worsening. **2** loss, forfeit.

recreation *n* fun, enjoyment, pleasure, amusement, diversion, distraction, entertainment, hobby, pastime, game, sport, play, leisure, relaxation, refreshment.

recrimination *n* countercharge, accusation, counter-attack, retaliation, reprisal, retort, quarrel, bickering.

recruit *v* enlist, draft, conscript, enrol, sign up, engage, take on, mobilize, raise, gather, obtain, procure.
n beginner, novice, initiate, learner, trainee, apprentice, conscript, convert.

rectify *v* correct, put right, right, remedy, cure, repair, fix, mend, improve, amend, adjust, reform.

recuperate *v* recover, get better, improve, pick up, rally, revive, mend, convalesce.
≠ worsen.

recur *v* repeat, persist, return, reappear.

recurrent *adj* recurring, chronic, persistent, repeated, repetitive, regular, periodic, frequent, intermittent.

recycle *v* reuse, reprocess, reclaim, recover, salvage, save.

red *adj* **1** SCARLET, vermilion, cherry, ruby, crimson, maroon, pink, reddish, bloodshot, inflamed. **2** RUDDY, florid, glowing, rosy, flushed, blushing, embarrassed, shamefaced. **3** *red hair*: ginger, carroty, auburn, chestnut, Titian.

redden *v* blush, flush, colour, go red, crimson.

redeem *v* **1** BUY BACK, repurchase, cash (in), exchange, change, trade, ransom, reclaim, regain, repossess, recoup, recover, recuperate, retrieve, salvage. **2** COMPENSATE FOR, make up for, offset, outweigh, atone for, expiate, absolve, acquit, discharge, release, liberate, emancipate, free, deliver, rescue, save.

reduce *v* **1** LESSEN, decrease, contract, shrink, slim, shorten, curtail, trim, cut, slash, discount, rebate, lower, moderate, weaken, diminish, impair. **2** DRIVE, force, degrade, downgrade, demote, humble, humiliate, impoverish, subdue, overpower, master, vanquish.
≠ **1** increase, raise, boost.

reduction *n* decrease, drop, fall, decline, lessening, moderation, weakening, diminution, contraction, compression, shrinkage, narrowing, shortening, curtailment, restriction, limitation, cutback, cut, discount, rebate, devaluation, depreciation, deduction, subtraction, loss.
≠ increase, rise, enlargement.

redundant *adj* **1** UNEMPLOYED, out of work, laid off, dismissed. **2** SUPERFLUOUS, surplus, excess, extra, supernumerary, unneeded, unnecessary, unwanted. **3** WORDY, verbose, repetitious, tautological.
≠ **2** necessary, essential. **3** concise.

reel *v* stagger, totter, wobble, rock, sway, waver, falter, stumble, lurch, pitch, roll, revolve, gyrate, spin, wheel, twirl, whirl, swirl.

refer *v* **1** SEND, direct, point, guide, pass on, transfer, commit, deliver. **2** *refer to a catalogue*: consult, look up, turn to, resort to. **3** ALLUDE, mention, touch on, speak of, bring up, recommend, cite, quote. **4** APPLY, concern, relate, belong, pertain.

referee *n* umpire, judge, adjudicator, arbitrator, mediator, ref (*infml*).
v umpire, judge, adjudicate, arbitrate.

reference *n* **1** ALLUSION, remark, mention, citation, quotation, illustration, instance, note. **2** TESTIMONIAL, recommendation, endorsement, character. **3** RELATION, regard, respect, connection, bearing.

refine *v* process, treat, purify, clarify, filter, distil, polish, hone, improve, perfect, elevate, exalt.

refined *adj* civilized, cultured, cultivated, polished, sophisticated, urbane, genteel, gentlemanly, ladylike, well-bred, well-mannered, polite, civil, elegant, fine, delicate, subtle, precise, exact, sensitive, discriminating.
≠ coarse, vulgar, rude.

refinement *n* **1** MODIFICATION, alteration, amendment, improvement. **2** CULTIVATION, sophistication, urbanity, gentility, breeding, style, elegance, taste, discrimination, subtlety, finesse.
≠ **1** deterioration. **2** coarseness, vulgarity.

reflect *v* **1** MIRROR, echo, imitate, reproduce, portray, depict, show, reveal, display, exhibit, manifest, demonstrate, indicate, express, communicate. **2** THINK, ponder, consider, mull (over), deliberate, contemplate, meditate, muse.

reflection *n* **1** IMAGE, likeness, echo, impression, indication, manifestation, observation, view, opinion. **2** THINKING, thought, study, consideration, deliberation, contemplation, meditation, musing.

reform *v* change, amend, improve, ameliorate, better, rectify, correct, mend, repair, rehabilitate, rebuild, reconstruct, remodel, revamp, renovate, restore, regenerate, reconstitute, reorganize, shake up (*infml*), revolutionize, purge.
n change, amendment, improvement, rectification, correction, rehabilitation, renovation, reorganization, shake-up (*infml*), purge.

refrain *v* stop, cease, quit, leave off, renounce, desist, abstain, forbear, avoid.

refresh *v* **1** COOL, freshen, enliven, invigorate, fortify, revive, restore, renew, rejuvenate, revitalize, reinvigorate. **2** *refresh one's memory*: jog, stimulate, prompt, prod.
≠ **1** tire, exhaust.

refreshing *adj* cool, thirst-quenching, bracing, invigorating, energizing, stimulating, inspiring, fresh, new, novel, original.

refreshment *n* sustenance, food, drink, snack, revival, restoration, renewal, reanimation, reinvigoration, revitalization.

refuge *n* sanctuary, asylum, shelter, protection, security, retreat, hideout, hide-away, resort, harbour, haven.

refugee *n* exile, émigré, displaced person, fugitive, runaway, escapee.

refund *v* repay, reimburse, rebate, return, restore.
n repayment, reimbursement, rebate, return.

refusal *n* rejection, no, rebuff, repudiation, denial, negation.
≠ acceptance.

refuse[1] *v* reject, turn down, decline, spurn, repudiate, rebuff, repel, deny, withhold.
≠ accept, allow, permit.

refuse[2] *n* rubbish, waste, trash, garbage, junk, litter.

refute *v* disprove, rebut, confute, give the lie to, discredit, counter, negate.

regain *v* recover, get back, recoup, reclaim, repossess, retake, recapture, retrieve, return to.

regal *adj* majestic, kingly, queenly, princely, imperial, royal, sovereign, stately, magnificent, noble, lordly.

regard *v* consider, deem, judge, rate, value, think, believe, suppose, imagine, look upon, view, observe, watch.
n care, concern, consideration,

attention, notice, heed, respect, deference, honour, esteem, admiration, affection, love, sympathy.
≠ disregard, contempt.

regarding *prep* with regard to, as regards, concerning, with reference to, re, about, as to.

regardless *adj* disregarding, heedless, unmindful, neglectful, inattentive, unconcerned, indifferent.
≠ heedful, mindful, attentive.
adv anyway, nevertheless, nonetheless, despite everything, come what may.

regime *n* government, rule, administration, management, leadership, command, control, establishment, system.

regimented *adj* strict, disciplined, controlled, regulated, standardized, ordered, methodical, systematic, organized.
≠ free, lax, disorganized.

region *n* land, terrain, sector, neighbourhood, range, scope, expanse, sphere, field, division, section, part, place.

Types of geographical region and community include: antarctic, arctic, area, bailiwick, banana republic, basin, belt, Black Country, borough, built-up area, burgh, capital city, catchment area, city, coast, colony, commune, continent, country, countryside, county, county town, desert, development area, diocese, district, dockland, domain, dominion, duchy, East End, emirate, empire, estate, The Fens, forest, free state, ghetto, ghost town, grassland, green belt, hamlet, health resort, heartland, heath, hemisphere, home-town, hundred, industrial park, inner city, interior, jungle, kibbutz, kingdom, lowlands, manor, market town, marshland, metropolis, The Midlands, mission, municipality, nation, new town, no-man's land, old country, orient, outback, outpost, outskirts, pampas, parish, plain, port, postal district, prairie, principality, protectorate, province, quarter, realm, red-light district, region, republic, reservation, resort, riding, riviera, rural district, satellite town, savannah, scrubland, seaside, settlement, shanty town, shire, spa, state, steppe, subcontinent, suburb, territory, Third World, time zone, town, township, tract, tropics, tundra, urban district, veld, village, wasteland, West Country, West End, wilderness, woodland, zone. *see also* **park**.

register *n* roll, roster, list, index, catalogue, directory, log, record, chronicle, annals, archives, file, ledger, schedule, diary, almanac.
v **1** RECORD, note, log, enter, inscribe, mark, list, catalogue, chronicle, enrol, enlist, sign on, check in. **2** SHOW, reveal, betray, display, exhibit, manifest, express, say, read, indicate.

regret *v* rue, repent, lament, mourn, grieve, deplore.
n remorse, contrition, compunction, self-reproach, shame, sorrow, grief, disappointment, bitterness.

regretful *adj* remorseful, rueful, repentant, contrite, penitent, conscience-stricken, ashamed, sorry, apologetic, sad, sorrowful, disappointed.
≠ impenitent, unashamed.

regrettable *adj* unfortunate, unlucky, unhappy, sad, disappointing, upsetting, distressing, lamentable, deplorable, shameful, wrong, ill-advised.
≠ fortunate, happy.

regular *adj* **1** ROUTINE, habitual, typical, usual, customary, time-honoured, conventional, orthodox, correct, official, standard, normal, ordinary, common, commonplace, everyday. **2** PERIODIC, rhythmic, steady, constant, fixed, set, unvarying, uniform, even, level, smooth, balanced, symmetrical, orderly, systematic, methodical.
≠ **1** unusual, unconventional. **2** irregular.

regulate *v* control, direct, guide, govern, rule, administer, manage, handle, conduct, run, organize, order, arrange, settle, square, monitor, set, adjust, tune, moderate, balance.

regulation *n* rule, statute, law, ordinance, edict, decree, order, commandment, precept, dictate, requirement, prodecure.
adj standard, official, statutory, prescribed, required, orthodox, accepted, customary, usual, normal.

rehearsal *n* practice, drill, exercise, dry run, run-through, preparation, reading, recital, narration, account, enumeration, list.

rehearse *v* practise, drill, train, go over, prepare, try out, repeat, recite, recount, relate.

reign *n* rule, sway, monarchy, empire, sovereignty, supremacy, power, command, dominion, control, influence.
v rule, govern, command, prevail, predominate, influence.

reimburse *v* refund, repay, return, restore, recompense, compensate, indemnify, remunerate.

reinforce *v* strengthen, fortify, toughen, harden, stiffen, steel, brace, support, buttress, shore, prop, stay, supplement, augment, increase, emphasize, stress, underline.
≠ weaken, undermine.

reinforcements *n* auxiliaries, reserves, back-up, support, help.

reinstate *v* restore, return, replace, recall, reappoint, reinstall, re-establish.

reject *v* refuse, deny, decline, turn down, veto, disallow, condemn, despise, spurn, rebuff, jilt, exclude, repudiate, repel, renounce, eliminate, scrap, discard, jettison, cast off.
≠ accept, choose, select.
n failure, second, discard, cast-off.

rejection *n* refusal, denial, veto, dismissal, rebuff, brush-off, exclusion, repudiation, renunciation, elimination.
≠ acceptance, choice, selection.

rejoice *v* celebrate, revel, delight, glory, exult, triumph.

rejoicing *n* celebration, revelry, merrymaking, festivity, happiness, gladness, joy, delight, elation, jubilation, exultation, triumph.

relapse *v* worsen, deteriorate, degenerate, weaken, sink, fail, lapse, revert, regress, backslide.
n worsening, deterioration, setback, recurrence, weakening, lapse, reversion, regression, backsliding.

relate *v* **1** LINK, connect, join, couple, ally, associate, correlate. **2** REFER, apply, concern, pertain, appertain. **3** *relate an anecdote*: tell, recount, narrate, report, describe, recite. **4** IDENTIFY, sympathize, empathize, understand, feel for.

related *adj* kindred, akin, affiliated, allied, associated, connected, linked, interrelated, interconnected, accompanying, concomitant, joint, mutual.
≠ unrelated, unconnected.

relation *n* **1** LINK, connection, bond, relationship, correlation, comparison, similarity, affiliation, interrelation, interconnection, interdependence, regard, reference. **2** RELATIVE, family, kin, kindred.

relations *n* **1** RELATIVES, family, kin, kindred. **2** RELATIONSHIP, terms, rapport, liaison, intercourse, affairs, dealings, interaction, communications, contact, associations, connections.

relationship *n* bond, link, connection, association, liaison, rapport, affinity, closeness, similarity, parallel, correlation, ratio, proportion.

relative *adj* comparative, proportional, proportionate, commensurate, corresponding, respective, appropriate, relevant, applicable, related, connected, interrelated, reciprocal, dependent.
n relation, family, kin.

relax *v* slacken, loosen, lessen, reduce, diminish, weaken, lower, soften, moderate, abate, remit, relieve, ease, rest, unwind, calm, tranquillize, sedate.
≠ tighten, intensify.

relaxation *n* **1** REST, repose, refreshment, leisure, recreation, fun, amusement, entertainment, enjoyment, pleasure. **2** SLACKENING, lessening, reduction, moderation, abatement, let-up (*infml*), détente, easing.
≠ **2** tension, intensification.

relaxed *adj* informal, casual, laid-back

(*infml*), easy-going (*infml*), carefree, happy-go-lucky, cool, calm, composed, collected, unhurried, leisurely.
≠ tense, nervous, formal.

relay *n* **1** BROADCAST, transmission, programme, communication, message, dispatch. **2** *work in relays*: shift, turn.
v broadcast, transmit, communicate, send, spread, carry, supply.

release *v* loose, unloose, unleash, unfasten, extricate, free, liberate, deliver, emancipate, acquit, absolve, exonerate, excuse, exempt, discharge, issue, publish, circulate, distribute, present, launch, unveil.
≠ imprison, detain, check.
n freedom, liberty, liberation, deliverance, emancipation, acquittal, absolution, exoneration, exemption, discharge, issue, publication, announcement, proclamation.
≠ imprisonment, detention.

relent *v* give in, give way, yield, capitulate, unbend, relax, slacken, soften, weaken.

relentless *adj* unrelenting, unremitting, incessant, persistent, unflagging, ruthless, remorseless, implacable, merciless, pitiless, unforgiving, cruel, harsh, fierce, grim, hard, punishing, uncompromising, inflexible, unyielding, inexorable.
≠ merciful, yielding.

relevant *adj* pertinent, material, significant, germane, related, applicable, apposite, apt, appropriate, suitable, fitting, proper, admissible.
≠ irrelevant, inapplicable, inappropriate, unsuitable.

reliable *adj* unfailing, certain, sure, dependable, responsible, trusty, trustworthy, honest, true, faithful, constant, staunch, solid, safe, sound, stable, predictable, regular.
≠ unreliable, doubtful, untrustworthy.

reliance *n* dependence, trust, faith, belief, credit, confidence, assurance.

relic *n* memento, souvenir, keepsake, token, survival, remains, remnant, scrap, fragment, vestige, trace.

relief *n* reassurance, consolation, comfort, ease, alleviation, cure, remedy, release, deliverance, help, aid, assistance, support, sustenance, refreshment, diversion, relaxation, rest, respite, break, breather (*infml*), remission, let-up (*infml*), abatement.

relieve *v* reassure, console, comfort, ease, soothe, alleviate, mitigate, cure, release, deliver, free, unburden, lighten, soften, slacken, relax, calm, help, aid, assist, support, sustain.
≠ aggravate, intensify.

religion

> *Religions include*: Christianity, Church of England (C of E), Church of Scotland, Baptists, Catholicism, Methodism, Protestantism, Presbyterianism, Anglicanism, Congregationalism, Calvinism, evangelicalism, Free Church, Jehovah's Witnesses, Mormonism, Quakerism, Amish; Baha'ism, Buddhism, Confucianism, Hinduism, Islam, Jainism, Judaism, Sikhism, Taoism, Shintoism, Zen, Zoroastrianism, voodoo, druidism.

religious *adj* **1** SACRED, holy, divine, spiritual, devotional, scriptural, theological, doctrinal. **2** *a religious person*: devout, godly, pious, God-fearing, church-going, reverent, righteous.
≠ **1** secular. **2** irreligious, ungodly.

religious officer

> *Religious officers include*: abbess, abbot, archbishop, archdeacon, bishop, canon, cardinal, chancellor, chaplain, clergy, clergyman, clergywoman, curate, deacon, deaconess, dean, elder, father, friar, minister, monk, Monsignor, mother superior, nun, padre, parson, pastor, pope, prelate, priest, prior, proctor, rector, vicar; ayatollah, Dalai Lama, guru, imam, rabbi.

relinquish *n* let go, release, hand over, surrender, yield, cede, give up, resign, renounce, repudiate, waive, forgo, abandon, desert, forsake, drop, discard.
≠ keep, retain.

relish *v* like, enjoy, savour, appreciate, revel in.

n **1** SEASONING, condiment, sauce, pickle, spice, piquancy, tang. **2** ENJOYMENT, pleasure, delight, gusto, zest.

reluctant *adj* unwilling, disinclined, indisposed, hesitant, slow, backward, loth, averse, unenthusiastic, grudging.
≠ willing, ready, eager.

rely *v* depend, lean, count, bank, reckon, trust, swear by.

remain *v* stay, rest, stand, dwell, abide, last, endure, survive, prevail, persist, continue, linger, wait.
≠ go, leave, depart.

remainder *n* rest, balance, surplus, excess, remnant, remains.

remaining *adj* left, unused, unspent, unfinished, residual, outstanding, surviving, persisting, lingering, lasting, abiding.

remains *n* rest, remainder, residue, dregs, leavings, leftovers, scraps, crumbs, fragments, remnants, oddments, traces, vestiges, relics, body, corpse, carcase, ashes, debris.

remark *v* comment, observe, note, mention, say, state, declare.
n comment, observation, opinion, reflection, mention, utterance, statement, assertion, declaration.

remarkable *adj* striking, impressive, noteworthy, surprising, amazing, strange, odd, unusual, uncommon, extraordinary, phenomenal, exceptional, outstanding, notable, conspicuous, prominent, distinguished.
≠ average, ordinary, commonplace, usual.

remedy *n* cure, antidote, countermeasure, corrective, restorative, medicine, treatment, therapy, relief, solution, answer, panacea.
v correct, rectify, put right, redress, counteract, cure, heal, restore, treat, help, relieve, soothe, ease, mitigate, mend, repair, fix, solve.

remember *v* **1** RECALL, recollect, summon up, think back, reminisce, recognize, place. **2** MEMORIZE, learn, retain.
≠ **1** forget.

remind *v* prompt, nudge, hint, jog one's memory, refresh one's memory, bring to mind, call to mind, call up.

reminder *n* prompt, nudge, hint, suggestion, memorandum, memo, souvenir, memento.

reminiscence *n* memory, remembrance, memoir, anecdote, recollection, recall, retrospection, review, reflection.

reminiscent *adj* suggestive, evocative, nostalgic.

remit *v* send, transmit, dispatch, post, mail, forward, pay, settle.
n brief, orders, instructions, guidelines, terms of reference, scope, authorization, responsibility.

remittance *n* sending, dispatch, payment, fee, allowance, consideration.

remnant *n* scrap, piece, bit, fragment, end, off cut, leftover, remainder, balance, residue, shred, trace, vestige.

remorse *n* regret, compunction, ruefulness, repentance, penitence, contrition, self-reproach, shame, guilt, bad conscience, sorrow, grief.

remote *adj* **1** DISTANT, far, faraway, far-off, outlying, out-of-the-way, inaccessible, god-forsaken, isolated, secluded, lonely. **2** DETACHED, aloof, standoffish, uninvolved, reserved, withdrawn. **3** *a remote possibility*: slight, small, slim, slender, faint, negligible, unlikely, improbable.
≠ **1** close, nearby, accessible. **2** friendly.

remove *v* detach, pull off, amputate, cut off, extract, pull out, withdraw, take away, take off, strip, shed, doff, expunge, efface, erase, delete, strike out, get rid of, abolish, purge, eliminate, dismiss, discharge, eject, throw out, oust, depose, displace, dislodge, shift, move, transport, transfer, relocate.

remuneration *n* pay, wages, salary, emolument, stipend, fee, retainer, earnings, income, profit, reward, recompense, payment, remittance, repayment, reimbursement, compensation, indemnity.

render *v* **1** *they rendered it harmless*: make, cause to be, leave. **2** GIVE, provide, supply, tender, present, submit, hand over, deliver. **3** TRANSLATE, transcribe, interpret, explain, clarify, represent, perform, play, sing.

renew *v* **1** RENOVATE, modernize, refurbish, refit, recondition, mend, repair, overhaul, remodel, reform, transform, recreate, reconstitute, re-establish, regenerate, revive, resuscitate, refresh, rejuvenate, reinvigorate, revitalize, restore, replace, replenish, restock. **2** REPEAT, restate, reaffirm, extend, prolong, continue, recommence, restart, resume.

renounce *v* abandon, forsake, give up, resign, relinquish, surrender, discard, reject, spurn, disown, repudiate, disclaim, deny, recant, abjure.

renovate *v* restore, renew, recondition, repair, overhaul, modernize, refurbish, refit, redecorate, do up, remodel, reform, revamp, improve.

renown *n* fame, celebrity, stardom, acclaim, glory, eminence, illustriousness, distinction, note, mark, esteem, reputation, honour.
≠ obscurity, anonymity.

renowned *adj* famous, well-known, celebrated, acclaimed, famed, noted, eminent, distinguished, illustrious, notable.
≠ unknown, obscure.

rent *n* rental, lease, hire, payment, fee.
v let, sublet, lease, hire, charter.

repair *v* mend, fix, patch up, overhaul, service, rectify, redress, restore, renovate, renew.
n mend, patch, darn, overhaul, service, maintenance, restoration, adjustment, improvement.

repartee *n* banter, badinage, jesting, wit, riposte, retort.

repay *v* refund, reimburse, compensate, recompense, reward, remunerate, pay, settle, square, get even with, retaliate, reciprocate, revenge, avenge.

repeal *v* revoke, rescind, abrogate, quash, annul, nullify, void, invalidate, cancel, countermand, reverse, abolish.
≠ enact.

repeat *v* restate, reiterate, recapitulate, echo, quote, recite, relate, retell, reproduce, duplicate, renew, rebroadcast, reshow, replay, rerun, redo.
n repetition, echo, reproduction, duplicate, rebroadcast, reshowing, replay, rerun.

repeatedly *adv* time after time, time and (time) again, again and again, over and over, frequently, often.

repel *v* **1** DRIVE BACK, repulse, check, hold off, ward off, parry, resist, oppose, fight, refuse, decline, reject, rebuff. **2** DISGUST, revolt, nauseate, sicken, offend.
≠ **1** attract. **2** delight.

repent *n* regret, rue, sorrow, lament, deplore, atone.

repentance *n* penitence, contrition, remorse, compunction, regret, sorrow, grief, guilt, shame.

repentant *adj* penitent, contrite, sorry, apologetic, remorseful, regretful, rueful, chastened, ashamed.
≠ unrepentant.

repercussion *n* result, consequence, backlash, reverberation, echo, rebound, recoil.

repetition *n* restatement, reiteration, recapitulation, echo, return, reappearance, recurrence, duplication, tautology.

repetitive *adj* recurrent, monotonous, tedious, boring, dull, mechanical, unchanging, unvaried.

replace *v* **1** *replace the lid*: put back, return, restore, make good, reinstate, re-establish. **2** SUPERSEDE, succeed, follow, supplant, oust, deputize, substitute.

replacement *n* substitute, stand-in, understudy, fill-in, supply, proxy, surrogate, successor.

replenish *v* refill, restock, reload, recharge, replace, restore, renew, supply, provide, furnish, stock, fill, top up.

replica *n* model, imitation,

reproduction, facsimile, copy, duplicate, clone.

reply *v* answer, respond, retort, rejoin, react, acknowledge, return, echo, reciprocate, counter, retaliate.
n answer, response, retort, rejoinder, riposte, repartee, reaction, comeback, acknowledgement, return, echo, retaliation.

report *n* article, piece, write-up, record, account, relation, narrative, description, story, tale, gossip, hearsay, rumour, talk, statement, communiqué, declaration, announcement, communication, information, news, word, message, note.
v state, announce, declare, proclaim, air, broadcast, relay, publish, circulate, communicate, notify, tell, recount, relate, narrate, describe, detail, cover, document, record, note.

reporter *n* journalist, correspondent, columnist, newspaperman, newspaperwoman, hack, newscaster, commentator, announcer.

represent *v* stand for, symbolize, designate, denote, mean, express, evoke, depict, portray, describe, picture, draw, sketch, illustrate, exemplify, typify, epitomize, embody, personify, appear as, act as, enact, perform, show, exhibit, be, amount to, constitute.

representation *n* **1** LIKENESS, image, icon, picture, portrait, illustration, sketch, model, statue, bust, depiction, portrayal, description, account, explanation. **2** PERFORMANCE, production, play, show, spectacle.

representative *n* delegate, deputy, proxy, stand-in, spokesperson, spokesman, spokeswoman, ambassador, commissioner, agent, salesman, saleswoman, rep (*infml*), traveller.
adj typical, illustrative, exemplary, archetypal, characteristic, usual, normal, symbolic.
≠ unrepresentative, atypical.

repress *v* inhibit, check, control, curb, restrain, suppress, bottle up, hold back, stifle, smother, muffle, silence, quell, crush, quash, subdue, overpower, overcome, master, subjugate, oppress.

repression *n* inhibition, restraint, suppression, suffocation, gagging, censorship, authoritarianism, despotism, tyranny, oppression, domination, control, constraint, coercion.

repressive *adj* oppressive, authoritarian, despotic, tyrannical, dictatorial, autocratic, totalitarian, absolute, harsh, severe, tough, coercive.

reprieve *v* pardon, let off, spare, rescue, redeem, relieve, respite.
n pardon, amnesty, suspension, abeyance, postponement, deferment, remission, respite, relief, let-up (*infml*), abatement.

reprimand *n* rebuke, reproof, reproach, admonition, telling-off (*infml*), ticking-off (*infml*), lecture, talking-to (*infml*), dressing-down (*infml*), censure, blame.
v rebuke, reprove, reproach, admonish, scold, chide, tell off (*infml*), tick off (*infml*), lecture, criticize, slate (*infml*), censure, blame.

reprisal *n* retaliation, counter-attack, retribution, requital, revenge, vengeance.

reproach *v* rebuke, reprove, reprimand, upbraid, scold, chide, reprehend, blame, censure, condemn, criticize, disparage, defame.
n rebuke, reproof, reprimand, scolding, blame, censure, condemnation, criticism, disapproval, scorn, contempt, shame, disgrace.

reproachful *adj* reproving, upbraiding, scolding, censorious, critical, fault-finding, disapproving, scornful.
≠ complimentary.

reproduce *v* **1** COPY, transcribe, print, duplicate, mirror, echo, repeat, imitate, emulate, match, simulate, recreate, reconstruct. **2** BREED, spawn, procreate, generate, propagate, multiply.

reproduction *n* **1** COPY, print, picture, duplicate, facsimile, replica, clone,

imitation. **2** BREEDING, procreation, generation, propagation, multiplication.
≠ **1** original.

reproductive *adj* procreative, generative, sexual, sex, genital.

reproof *n* rebuke, reproach, reprimand, admonition, upbraiding, dressing-down (*infml*), scolding, telling-off (*infml*), ticking-off (*infml*), censure, condemnation, criticism.
≠ praise.

reprove *v* rebuke, reproach, reprimand, upbraid, scold, chide, tell off (*infml*), reprehend, admonish, censure, condemn, criticize.
≠ praise.

reptiles

> *Reptiles include*: adder, puff adder, grass snake, tree snake, asp, viper, rattlesnake, sidewinder, anaconda, boa constrictor, cobra, king cobra, mamba, python; lizard, frilled lizard, chameleon, gecko, iguana, skink, slow-worm; turtle, green turtle, hawksbill turtle, terrapin, tortoise, giant tortoise; alligator, crocodile. *see also* **dinosaurs**.

repugnance *n* reluctance, distaste, dislike, aversion, hatred, loathing, abhorrence, horror, repulsion, revulsion, disgust.
≠ liking, pleasure, delight.

repulsive *adj* repellent, repugnant, revolting, disgusting, nauseating, sickening, offensive, distasteful, objectionable, obnoxious, foul, vile, loathsome, abominable, abhorrent, hateful, horrid, unpleasant, disagreeable, ugly, hideous, forbidding.
≠ attractive, pleasant, delightful.

reputable *adj* respectable, reliable, dependable, trustworthy, upright, honourable, creditable, worthy, good, excellent, irreproachable.
≠ disreputable, infamous.

reputation *n* honour, character, standing, stature, esteem, opinion, credit, repute, fame, renown, celebrity, distinction, name, good name, bad name, infamy, notoriety.

reputed *adj* alleged, supposed, said, rumoured, believed, thought, considered, regarded, estimated, reckoned, held, seeming, apparent, ostensible.
≠ actual, true.

request *v* ask for, solicit, demand, require, seek, desire, beg, entreat, supplicate, petition, appeal.
n appeal, call, demand, requisition, desire, application, solicitation, suit, petition, entreaty, supplication, prayer.

require *v* **1** NEED, want, wish, desire, lack, miss. **2** *you are required to attend*: oblige, force, compel, constrain, make, ask, request, instruct, direct, order, demand, necessitate, take, involve.

requirement *n* need, necessity, essential, must, requisite, prerequisite, demand, stipulation, condition, term, specification, proviso, qualification, provision.

requisite *adj* required, needed, necessary, essential, obligatory, compulsory, set, prescribed.

requisition *v* request, put in for, demand, commandeer, appropriate, take, confiscate, seize, occupy.

rescue *v* save, recover, salvage, deliver, free, liberate, release, redeem, ransom.
≠ capture, imprison.
n saving, recovery, salvage, deliverance, liberation, release, redemption, salvation.
≠ capture.

research *n* investigation, inquiry, fact-finding, groundwork, examination, analysis, scrutiny, study, search, probe, exploration, experimentation.
v investigate, examine, analyse, scrutinize, study, search, probe, explore, experiment.

resemblance *n* likeness, similarity, sameness, parity, conformity, closeness, affinity, parallel, comparison, analogy, correspondence, image, facsimile.
≠ dissimilarity.

resemble *v* be like, look like, take after, favour, mirror, echo, duplicate, parallel, approach.
≠ differ from.

resent *v* grudge, begrudge, envy, take offence at, take umbrage at, take amiss, object to, grumble at, take exception to, dislike.
≠ accept, like.

resentful *adj* grudging, envious, jealous, bitter, embittered, hurt, wounded, offended, aggrieved, put out, miffed (*infml*), peeved (*infml*), indignant, angry, vindictive.
≠ satisfied, contented.

resentment *n* grudge, envy, jealousy, bitterness, spite, malice, ill-will, ill-feeling, animosity, hurt, umbrage, pique, displeasure, irritation, indignation, vexation, anger, vindictiveness.
≠ contentment, happiness.

reservation *n* **1** DOUBT, scepticism, misgiving, qualm, scruple, hesitation, second thought. **2** PROVISO, stipulation, qualification. **3** RESERVE, preserve, park, sanctuary, homeland, enclave. **4** BOOKING, engagement, appointment.

reserve *v* **1** SET APART, earmark, keep, retain, hold back, save, store, stockpile. **2** *reserve a seat*: book, engage, order, secure.
≠ **1** use up.
n **1** STORE, stock, supply, fund, stockpile, cache, hoard, savings.
2 SHYNESS, reticence, secretiveness, coolness, aloofness, modesty, restraint.
3 RESERVATION, preserve, park, sanctuary. **4** REPLACEMENT, substitute, stand-in.
≠ **2** friendliness, openness.

reserved *adj* **1** BOOKED, engaged, taken, spoken for, set aside, earmarked, meant, intended, designated, destined, saved, held, kept, retained. **2** SHY, retiring, reticent, unforthcoming, uncommunicative, secretive, silent, taciturn, unsociable, cool, aloof, standoffish, unapproachable, modest, restrained, cautious.
≠ **1** unreserved, free, available.
2 friendly, open.

reside *v* live, inhabit, dwell, lodge, stay, sojourn, settle, remain.

residence *n* dwelling, habitation, domicile, abode, seat, place, home, house, lodgings, quarters, hall, manor, mansion, palace, villa, country-house, country-seat.

resident *n* inhabitant, citizen, local, householder, occupier, tenant, lodger, guest.
≠ non-resident.

residual *adj* remaining, leftover, unused, unconsumed, net.

resign *v* stand down, leave, quit, abdicate, vacate, renounce, relinquish, forgo, waive, surrender, yield, abandon, forsake.
≠ join.
resign oneself reconcile oneself, accept, bow, submit, yield, comply, acquiesce.
≠ resist.

resignation *n* **1** STANDING-DOWN, abdication, retirement, departure, notice, renunciation, relinquishment, surrender. **2** ACCEPTANCE, acquiescence, submission, non-resistance, passivity, patience, stoicism, defeatism.
≠ **2** resistance.

resigned *adj* reconciled, philosophical, stoical, patient, unprotesting, unresisting, submissive, defeatist.
≠ resistant.

resilient *adj* **1** *resilient material*: flexible, pliable, supple, plastic, elastic, springy, bouncy. **2** STRONG, tough, hardy, adaptable, buoyant.
≠ **1** rigid, brittle.

resist *v* oppose, defy, confront, fight, combat, weather, withstand, repel, counteract, check, avoid, refuse.
≠ submit, accept.

resistant *adj* **1** OPPOSED, antagonistic, defiant, unyielding, intransigent, unwilling. **2** PROOF, impervious, immune, invulnerable, tough, strong.
≠ **1** compliant, yielding.

resolute *adj* determined, resolved, set, fixed, unwavering, staunch, firm, steadfast, relentless, single-minded, persevering, dogged, tenacious, stubborn, obstinate, strong-willed, undaunted, unflinching, bold.
≠ irresolute, weak-willed, half-hearted.

resolution *n* 1 DETERMINATION, resolve, willpower, commitment, dedication, devotion, firmness, steadfastness, persistence, perseverance, doggedness, tenacity, zeal, courage, boldness. 2 DECISION, judgement, finding, declaration, proposition, motion.
≠ 1 half-heartedness, uncertainty, indecision.

resolve *v* decide, make up one's mind, determine, fix, settle, conclude, sort out, work out, solve.

resort *v* go, visit, frequent, patronize, haunt.
n recourse, refuge, course (of action), alternative, option, chance, possibility.
resort to turn to, use, utilize, employ, exercise.

resound *v* resonate, reverberate, echo, re-echo, ring, boom, thunder.

resounding *adj* 1 RESONANT, reverberating, echoing, ringing, sonorous, booming, thunderous, full, rich, vibrant. 2 *a resounding victory*: decisive, conclusive, crushing, thorough.
≠ 1 faint.

resource *n* 1 SUPPLY, reserve, stockpile, source, expedient, contrivance, device.
2 RESOURCEFULNESS, initiative, ingenuity, inventiveness, talent, ability, capability.

resourceful *adj* ingenious, imaginative, creative, inventive, innovative, original, clever, bright, sharp, quick-witted, able, capable, talented.

resources *n* materials, supplies, reserves, holdings, funds, money, wealth, riches, capital, assets, property, means.

respect *n* 1 ADMIRATION, esteem, appreciation, recognition, honour, deference, reverence, veneration, politeness, courtesy. 2 *in every respect*: point, aspect, facet, feature, characteristic, particular, detail, sense, way, regard, reference, relation, connection.
≠ 1 disrespect.
v 1 ADMIRE, esteem, regard, appreciate, value. 2 OBEY, observe, heed, follow, honour, fulfil.
≠ 1 despise, scorn. 2 ignore, disobey.

respectable *adj* 1 HONOURABLE, worthy, respected, dignified, upright, honest, decent, clean-living. 2 ACCEPTABLE, tolerable, passable, adequate, fair, reasonable, appreciable, considerable.
≠ 1 dishonourable, disreputable.
2 inadequate, paltry.

respectful *adj* deferential, reverential, humble, polite, well-mannered, courteous, civil.
≠ disrespectful.

respective *adj* corresponding, relevant, various, several, separate, individual, personal, own, particular, special.

respond *v* answer, reply, retort, acknowledge, react, return, reciprocate.

response *n* answer, reply, retort, comeback, acknowledgement, reaction, feedback.
≠ query.

responsibility *n* fault, blame, guilt, culpability, answerability, accountability, duty, obligation, burden, onus, charge, care, trust, authority, power.

responsible *adj* 1 GUILTY, culpable, at fault, to blame, liable, answerable, accountable. 2 *a responsible citizen*: dependable, reliable, conscientious, trustworthy, honest, sound, steady, sober, mature, sensible, rational.
3 IMPORTANT, authoritative, executive, decision-making.
≠ 2 irresponsible, unreliable, untrustworthy.

rest[1] *n* 1 LEISURE, relaxation, repose, lie-down, sleep, snooze, nap, siesta, idleness, inactivity, motionlessness, standstill, stillness, tranquillity, calm.
2 BREAK, pause, breathing-space, breather (*infml*), intermission, interlude, interval, recess, holiday, vacation, halt, cessation, lull, respite.
3 SUPPORT, prop, stand, base.
≠ 1 action, activity. 2 work.
v 1 PAUSE, halt, stop, cease. 2 RELAX,

repose, sit, recline, lounge, laze, lie down, sleep, snooze, doze. **3** DEPEND, rely, hinge, hang, lie. **4** LEAN, prop, support, stand.
≠ **1** continue. **2** work.

rest[2] *n* remainder, others, balance, surplus, excess, residue, remains, leftovers, remnants.

restaurant

Types of restaurant include: bistro, brasserie, buffet, burger bar, café, cafeteria, canteen, carvery, chippy (*infml*), coffee bar, diner (*US*), dining-car, dining-room, eating-house, fish-and-chip shop, greasy spoon (*sl*), grill, grill room, health food restaurant, ice-cream parlour, luncheonette (*US*), McDonald's®, mess room, milk bar, motorway café, NAAFI (Navy, Army and Air Force Institutes), pizzeria, pull-in, refectory, sandwich bar, self-service restaurant, snack-bar, steakhouse, tea room, tea shop, teahouse, transport café, trattoria.

restful *adj* relaxing, soothing, calm, tranquil, serene, peaceful, quiet, undisturbed, relaxed, comfortable, leisurely, unhurried.
≠ tiring, restless.

restless *adj* fidgety, unsettled, disturbed, troubled, agitated, nervous, anxious, worried, uneasy, fretful, edgy, jumpy, restive, unruly, turbulent, sleepless.
≠ calm, relaxed, comfortable.

restore *v* **1** REPLACE, return, reinstate, rehabilitate, re-establish, reintroduce, re-enforce. **2** *restore a building*: renovate, renew, rebuild, reconstruct, refurbish, retouch, recondition, repair, mend, fix. **3** REVIVE, refresh, rejuvenate, revitalize, strengthen.
≠ **1** remove. **2** damage. **3** weaken.

restrain *v* hold back, keep back, suppress, subdue, repress, inhibit, check, curb, bridle, stop, arrest, prevent, bind, tie, chain, fetter, manacle, imprison, jail, confine, restrict, regulate, control, govern.
≠ encourage, liberate.

restrained *adj* moderate, temperate, mild, subdued, muted, quiet, soft, low-key, unobtrusive, discreet, tasteful, calm, controlled, steady, self-controlled.
≠ unrestrained.

restraint *n* moderation, inhibition, self-control, self-discipline, hold, grip, check, curb, rein, bridle, suppression, bondage, captivity, confinement, imprisonment, bonds, chains, fetters, straitjacket, restriction, control, constraint, limitation, tie, hindrance, prevention.
≠ liberty.

restrict *v* limit, bound, demarcate, control, regulate, confine, contain, cramp, constrain, impede, hinder, hamper, handicap, tie, restrain, curtail.
≠ broaden, free.

restriction *n* limit, bound, confine, limitation, constraint, handicap, check, curb, restraint, ban, embargo, control, regulation, rule, stipulation, condition, proviso.
≠ freedom.

result *n* effect, consequence, sequel, repercussion, reaction, outcome, upshot, issue, end-product, fruit, score, answer, verdict, judgement, decision, conclusion.
≠ cause.
v follow, ensue, happen, occur, issue, emerge, arise, spring, derive, stem, flow, proceed, develop, end, finish, terminate, culminate.
≠ cause.

resume *v* restart, recommence, reopen, reconvene, continue, carry on, go on, proceed.
≠ cease.

resumption *n* restart, recommencement, reopening, renewal, resurgence, continuation.
≠ cessation.

resurrect *v* restore, revive, resuscitate, reactivate, bring back, reintroduce, renew.
≠ kill, bury.

resurrection *n* restoration, revival, resuscitation, renaissance, rebirth, renewal, resurgence, reappearance, return, comeback.

resuscitate *v* revive, resurrect, save, rescue, reanimate, quicken, reinvigorate, revitalize, restore, renew.

retain *v* **1** KEEP, hold, reserve, hold back, save, preserve. **2** *retain information*: remember, memorize. **3** EMPLOY, engage, hire, commission.
≠ **1** release. **2** forget. **3** dismiss.

retaliate *v* reciprocate, counter-attack, hit back, strike back, fight back, get one's own back, get even with, take revenge.

retaliation *n* reprisal, counter-attack, revenge, vengeance, retribution.

reticent *adj* reserved, shy, uncommunicative, unforthcoming, tight-lipped, secretive, taciturn, silent, quiet.
≠ communicative, forward, frank.

retire *v* leave, depart, withdraw, retreat, recede.
≠ join, enter, advance.

retirement *n* withdrawal, retreat, solitude, loneliness, seclusion, privacy, obscurity.

retiring *adj* shy, bashful, timid, shrinking, quiet, reticent, reserved, self-effacing, unassertive, modest, unassuming, humble.
≠ bold, forward, assertive.

retort *v* answer, reply, respond, rejoin, return, counter, retaliate.
n answer, reply, response, rejoinder, riposte, repartee, quip.

retract *v* take back, withdraw, recant, reverse, revoke, rescind, cancel, repeal, repudiate, disown, disclaim, deny.
≠ assert, maintain.

retreat *v* draw back, recoil, shrink, turn tail (*infml*), withdraw, retire, leave, depart, quit.
≠ advance.
n **1** WITHDRAWAL, departure, evacuation, flight. **2** SECLUSION, privacy, hideaway, den, refuge, asylum, sanctuary, shelter, haven.
≠ **1** advance, charge.

retrieve *v* fetch, bring back, regain, get back, recapture, repossess, recoup, recover, salvage, save, rescue, redeem, restore, return.
≠ lose.

retrograde *adj* retrogressive, backward, reverse, negative, downward, declining, deteriorating.
≠ progressive.

retrospect *n* hindsight, afterthought, re-examination, review, recollection, remembrance.
≠ prospect.

return *v* **1** COME BACK, reappear, recur, go back, backtrack, regress, revert. **2** GIVE BACK, hand back, send back, deliver, put back, replace, restore. **3** *return a favour*: reciprocate, requite, repay, refund, reimburse, recompense.
≠ **1** leave, depart. **2** take.
n **1** REAPPEARANCE, recurrence, comeback, home-coming. **2** REPAYMENT, recompense, replacement, restoration, reinstatement, reciprocation. **3** REVENUE, income, proceeds, takings, yield, gain, profit, reward, advantage, benefit.
≠ **1** departure, disappearance. **2** removal. **3** payment, expense, loss.

reveal *v* expose, uncover, unveil, unmask, show, display, exhibit, manifest, disclose, divulge, betray, leak, tell, impart, communicate, broadcast, publish, announce, proclaim.
≠ hide, conceal, mask.

revel in enjoy, relish, savour, delight in, thrive on, bask in, glory in, lap up, indulge in, wallow in, luxuriate in.

revelation *n* uncovering, unveiling, exposure, unmasking, show, display, exhibition, manifestation, disclosure, confession, admission, betrayed, giveaway, leak, news, information, communication, broadcasting, publication, announcement, proclamation.

revelry *n* celebration, festivity, party, merrymaking, jollity, fun, carousal, debauchery.
≠ sobriety.

revenge *n* vengeance, satisfaction, reprisal, retaliation, requital, retribution.
v avenge, repay, retaliate, get one's own back.

revenue *n* income, return, yield, interest, profit, gain, proceeds, receipts, takings.
≠ expenditure.

reverberate *v* echo, re-echo, resound, resonate, ring, boom, vibrate.

revere *v* respect, esteem, honour, pay homage to, venerate, worship, adore, exalt.
≠ despise, scorn.

reverence *n* respect, deference, honour, homage, admiration, awe, veneration, worship, adoration, devotion.
≠ contempt, scorn.

reverent *adj* reverential, respectful, deferential, humble, dutiful, awed, solemn, pious, devout, adoring, loving.
≠ irreverent, disrespectful.

reversal *n* negation, cancellation, annulment, nullification, countermanding, revocation, rescinding, repeal, reverse, turnabout, turnaround, U-turn, volte-face, upset.
≠ advancement, progress.

reverse *v* **1** BACK, retreat, backtrack, undo, negate, cancel, annul, invalidate, countermand, overrule, revoke, rescind, repeal, retract, quash, overthrow. **2** TRANSPOSE, turn round, invert, up-end, overturn, upset, change, alter.
≠ **1** advance, enforce.
n **1** UNDERSIDE, back, rear, inverse, converse, contrary, opposite, antithesis. **2** MISFORTUNE, mishap, misadventure, adversity, affliction, hardship, trial, blow, disappointment, setback, check, delay, problem, difficulty, failure, defeat.
adj opposite, contrary, converse, inverse, inverted, backward, back, rear.

revert *v* return, go back, resume, lapse, relapse, regress.

review *v* **1** CRITICIZE, assess, evaluate, judge, weigh, discuss, examine, inspect, scrutinize, study, survey, recapitulate. **2** *review the situation*: reassess, re-evaluate, re-examine, reconsider, rethink, revise.
n **1** CRITICISM, critique, assessment, evaluation, judgement, report, commentary, examination, scrutiny, analysis, study, survey, recapitulation, reassessment, re-evaluation, re-examination, revision. **2** MAGAZINE, periodical, journal.

revise *v* **1** *revise one's opinion*: change, alter, modify, amend, correct, update, edit, rewrite, reword, recast, revamp, reconsider, re-examine, review. **2** STUDY, learn, swot up (*infml*), cram (*infml*).

revival *n* resuscitation, revitalization, restoration, renewal, renaissance, rebirth, reawakening, resurgence, upsurge.

revive *v* resuscitate, reanimate, revitalize, restore, renew, refresh, animate, invigorate, quicken, rouse, awaken, recover, rally, reawaken, rekindle, reactivate.
≠ weary.

revoke *v* repeal, rescind, quash, abrogate, annul, nullify, invalidate, negate, cancel, countermand, reverse, retract, withdraw.
≠ enforce.

revolt *n* revolution, rebellion, mutiny, rising, uprising, insurrection, putsch, coup (d'état), secession, defection.
v **1** REBEL, mutiny, rise, riot, resist, dissent, defect. **2** DISGUST, sicken, nauseate, repel, offend, shock, outrage, scandalize.
≠ **1** submit. **2** please, delight.

revolting *adj* disgusting, sickening, nauseating, repulsive, repellent, obnoxious, nasty, horrible, foul, loathsome, abhorrent, distasteful, offensive, shocking, appalling.
≠ pleasant, delightful, attractive, palatable.

revolution *n* **1** REVOLT, rebellion, mutiny, rising, uprising, insurrection, putsch, coup (d'état), reformation, change, transformation, innovation, upheaval, cataclysm. **2** ROTATION, turn, spin, cycle, circuit, round, circle, orbit, gyration.

revolutionary *n* rebel, mutineer, insurgent, anarchist, revolutionist.
adj **1** REBEL, rebellious, mutinous, insurgent, subversive, seditious,

anarchistic. **2** *revolutionary ideas*: new, innovative, avant-garde, different, drastic, radical, thoroughgoing.
≠ **1** conservative.

revolve *v* rotate, turn, pivot, swivel, spin, wheel, whirl, gyrate, circle, orbit.

revulsion *n* repugnance, disgust, distaste, dislike, aversion, hatred, loathing, abhorrence, abomination.
≠ delight, pleasure, approval.

reward *n* prize, honour, medal, decoration, bounty, pay-off, bonus, premium, payment, remuneration, recompense, repayment, requital, compensation, gain, profit, return, benefit, merit, desert, retribution.
≠ punishment.
v pay, remunerate, recompense, repay, requite, compensate, honour, decorate.
≠ punish.

rewarding *adj* profitable, remunerative, lucrative, productive, fruitful, worthwhile, valuable, advantageous, beneficial, satisfying, gratifying, pleasing, fulfilling, enriching.
≠ unrewarding.

rhetoric *n* eloquence, oratory, grandiloquence, magniloquence, bombast, pomposity, hyperbole, verbosity, wordiness.

rhetorical *adj* oratorical, grandiloquent, magniloquent, bombastic, declamatory, pompous, high-sounding, grand, high-flown, flowery, florid, flamboyant, showy, pretentious, artificial, insincere.
≠ simple.

Rhetorical devices include: abscission, alliteration, amplification, anacoluthon, anadiplosis, anaphora, anastrophe, anticlimax, antimetabole, antimetathesis, antiphrasis, antithesis, antonomasia, aporia, apostrophe, asyndeton, auxesis, bathos, catachresis, chiasmus, climax, diallage, diegesis, dissimile, double entendre, dramatic irony, dysphemism, ellipsis, enantiosis, enumeration, epanadiplosis, epanalepsis, epanaphora, epanodos, epanorthosis, epigram, epiphonema, epistrophe, epizeuxis, erotema, erotetic, euphemism, figure of speech, hendiadys, hypallage, hyperbole, hypostrophe, hypotyposis, hysteron-proteron, increment, innuendo, irony, litotes, meiosis, metalepsis, metaphor, mixed metaphor, metonymy, onomatopoeia, oxymoron, parabole, paradox, paraleipsis, parenthesis, pathetic fallacy, personification, prolepsis, pun, rhetorical question, simile, syllepsis, symploce, synchoresis, synchysis, synecdoche, synoeciosis, tautology, transferred epithet, trope, vicious circle, zeugma.

rhyme *n* poetry, verse, poem, ode, limerick, jingle, song, ditty.

rhythm *n* beat, pulse, time, tempo, metre, measure, movement, flow, lilt, swing, accent, cadence, pattern.

rhythmic *adj* rhythmical, metric, metrical, pulsating, throbbing, flowing, lilting, periodic, regular, steady.

rich *adj* **1** WEALTHY, affluent, moneyed, prosperous, well-to-do, well-off, loaded (*sl*). **2** PLENTIFUL, abundant, copious, profuse, prolific, ample, full. **3** FERTILE, fruitful, productive, lush. **4** *rich food*: creamy, fatty, full-bodied, heavy, full-flavoured, strong, spicy, savoury, tasty, delicious, luscious, juicy, sweet. **5** *rich colours*: deep, intense, vivid, bright, vibrant, warm. **6** EXPENSIVE, precious, valuable, lavish, sumptuous, opulent, luxurious, splendid, gorgeous, fine, elaborate, ornate.
≠ **1** poor, impoverished. **3** barren. **4** plain, bland. **5** dull, soft. **6** plain.

riches *n* wealth, affluence, money, gold, treasure, fortune, assets, property, substance, resources, means.
≠ poverty.

rickety *adj* unsteady, wobbly, shaky, unstable, insecure, flimsy, jerry-built, decrepit, ramshackle, broken-down, dilapidated, derelict.
≠ stable, strong.

rid *v* clear, purge, free, deliver, relieve, unburden.

riddle[1] *n* enigma, mystery, conundrum, brain-teaser, puzzle, poser, problem.

riddle[2] *v* **1** PERFORATE, pierce, puncture, pepper, fill, permeate, pervade, infest. **2** SIFT, sieve, strain, filter, mar, winnow.

ride *v* sit, move, progress, travel, journey, gallop, trot, pedal, drive, steer, control, handle, manage.
n journey, trip, outing, jaunt, spin, drive, lift.

ridicule *n* satire, irony, sarcasm, mockery, jeering, scorn, derision, taunting, teasing, chaff, banter, badinage, laughter.
≠ praise.
v satirize, send up, caricature, lampoon, burlesque, parody, mock, make fun of, jeer, scoff, deride, sneer, tease, rib (*infml*), humiliate, taunt.
≠ praise.

ridiculous *adj* ludicrous, absurd, nonsensical, silly, foolish, stupid, contemptible, derisory, laughable, farcical, comical, funny, hilarious, outrageous, preposterous, incredible, unbelievable.
≠ sensible.

rife *adj* abundant, rampant, teeming, raging, epidemic, prevalent, widespread, general, common, frequent.
≠ scarce.

rift *n* **1** SPLIT, breach, break, fracture, crack, fault, chink, cleft, cranny, crevice, gap, space, opening. **2** DISAGREEMENT, difference, separation, division, schism, alienation.
≠ **2** unity.

rig *n* equipment, kit, outfit, gear, tackle, apparatus, machinery, fittings, fixtures.
rig out equip, kit out, outfit, fit (out), supply, furnish, clothe, dress (up).

right *adj* **1** *the right answer*: correct, accurate, exact, precise, true, factual, actual, real. **2** PROPER, fitting, seemly, becoming, appropriate, suitable, fit, admissible, satisfactory, reasonable, desirable, favourable, advantageous. **3** FAIR, just, equitable, lawful, honest, upright, good, virtuous, righteous, moral, ethical, honourable. **4** RIGHT-WING, conservative, Tory.
≠ **1** wrong, incorrect. **2** improper, unsuitable. **3** unfair, wrong. **4** left-wing.
adv **1** CORRECTLY, accurately, exactly, precisely, factually, properly, satisfactorily, well, fairly. **2** *right to the bottom*: straight, directly, completely, utterly.
≠ **1** wrongly, incorrectly, unfairly.
n **1** PRIVILEGE, prerogative, due, claim, business, authority, power. **2** JUSTICE, legality, good, virtue, righteousness, morality, honour, integrity, uprightness.
≠ **2** wrong.
v rectify, correct, put right, fix, repair, redress, vindicate, avenge, settle, straighten, stand up.
right away straight away, immediately, at once, now, instantly, directly, forthwith, without delay, promptly.
≠ later, eventually.

rightful *adj* legitimate, lawful, legal, just, bona fide, true, real, genuine, valid, authorized, correct, proper, suitable, due.
≠ wrongful, unlawful.

rigid *adj* stiff, inflexible, unbending, cast-iron, hard, firm, set, fixed, unalterable, invariable, austere, harsh, severe, unrelenting, strict, rigorous, stringent, stern, uncompromising, unyielding.
≠ flexible, elastic.

rigorous *adj* strict, stringent, rigid, firm, exact, precise, accurate, meticulous, painstaking, scrupulous, conscientious, thorough.
≠ lax, superficial.

rile *v* annoy, irritate, nettle, pique, peeve (*infml*), put out, upset, irk, vex, anger, exasperate.
≠ calm, soothe.

rim *n* lip, edge, brim, brink, verge, margin, border, circumference.
≠ centre, middle.

rind *n* peel, skin, husk, crust.

ring[1] *n* **1** CIRCLE, round, loop, hoop, halo, band, girdle, collar, circuit, arena, enclosure. **2** GROUP, cartel, syndicate, association, organization,

gang, crew, mob, band, cell, clique, coterie.
v surround, encircle, gird, circumscribe, encompass, enclose.

ring[2] *v* **1** CHIME, peal, toll, tinkle, clink, jingle, clang, sound, resound, resonate, reverberate, buzz. **2** TELEPHONE, phone, call, ring up.
n **1** CHIME, peal, toll, tinkle, clink, jingle, clang. **2** PHONE CALL, call, buzz (*infml*), tinkle (*infml*).

rinse *v* swill, bathe, wash, clean, cleanse, flush, wet, dip.

riot *n* insurrection, rising, uprising, revolt, rebellion, anarchy, lawlessness, affray, disturbance, turbulence, disorder, confusion, commotion, tumult, turmoil, uproar, row, quarrel, strife.
≠ order, calm.
v revolt, rebel, rise up, run riot, run wild, rampage.

rip *v* tear, rend, split, separate, rupture, burst, cut, slit, slash, gash, lacerate, hack.
n tear, rent, split, cleavage, rupture, cut, slit, slash, gash, hole.
rip off (*sl*) overcharge, swindle, defraud, cheat, diddle, do (*infml*), fleece, sting (*sl*), con (*infml*), trick, dupe, exploit.

ripe *adj* **1** RIPENED, mature, mellow, seasoned, grown, developed, complete, finished, perfect. **2** READY, suitable, right, favourable, auspicious, propitious, timely, opportune.
≠ **2** untimely, inopportune.

ripen *v* develop, mature, mellow, season, age.

rise *v* **1** GO UP, ascend, climb, mount, slope (up), soar, tower, grow, increase, escalate, intensify. **2** STAND UP, get up, arise, jump up, spring up. **3** ADVANCE, progress, improve, prosper. **4** ORIGINATE, spring, flow, issue, emerge, appear.
≠ **1** fall, descend. **2** sit down. **3** declare.
n **1** ASCENT, climb, slope, incline, hill, elevation. **2** INCREASE, increment, upsurge, upturn, advance, progress, improvement, advancement, promotion.
≠ **1** descent, valley. **2** fall.

risk *n* danger, peril, jeopardy, hazard, chance, possibility, uncertainty, gamble, speculation, venture, adventure.
≠ safety, certainty.
v endanger, imperil, jeopardize, hazard, chance, gamble, venture, dare.

risky *adj* dangerous, unsafe, perilous, hazardous, chancy, uncertain, touch-and-go, dicey (*infml*), tricky, precarious.
≠ safe.

risqué *adj* indecent, improper, indelicate, suggestive, coarse, crude, earthy, bawdy, racy, naughty, blue.
≠ decent, proper.

ritual *n* custom, tradition, convention, usage, practice, habit, wont, routine, procedure, ordinance, prescription, form, formality, ceremony, ceremonial, solemnity, rite, sacrament, service, liturgy, observance, act.
adj customary, traditional, conventional, habitual, routine, procedural, prescribed, set, formal, ceremonial.
≠ informal.

rival *n* competitor, contestant, contender, challenger, opponent, adversary, antagonist, match, equal, peer.
≠ colleague, associate.
adj competitive, competing, opposed, opposing, conflicting.
≠ associate.
v compete with, contend with, vie with, oppose, emulate, match, equal.
≠ co-operate.

rivalry *n* competitiveness, competition, contest, contention, conflict, struggle, strife, opposition, antagonism.
≠ co-operation.

river *n* waterway, watercourse.

Forms of river or watercourse include: beck, billabong, bourn, brook, burn, canal, channel, confluence, creek, cut, delta, estuary, inlet, mountain stream, mouth, rill, rillet, rivulet, runnel, source, stream, tributary, wadi, waterway.

roads

> *Types of road include*: A-road, alley, autobahn, arterial road, avenue, B-road, boulevard, bridle path, bridle way, bypass, byroad, byway, carriageway, cart-track, cartway, causeway, clearway, close, course, crescent, cul-de-sac, dead end, dirt-road, dirt-track, drive, driveway, dual carriageway, expressway (*US*), flyover, freeway (*US*), highway (*US*), lane, main road, motorway, one-way street, overpass (*US*), path, pathway, primary route, ring road, roadway, route, service road, side road, side street, single-track road, slip road, street, thoroughfare, toll road, towpath, track, trail, trunk road, turnpike (*US*), unadopted road, underpass, way.

roam *v* wander, rove, range, travel, walk, ramble, stroll, amble, prowl, drift, stray.
≠ stay.

roar *v, n* bellow, yell, shout, cry, bawl, howl, hoot, guffaw, thunder, crash, blare, rumble.
≠ whisper.

rob *v* steal from, hold up, raid, burgle, loot, pillage, plunder, sack, rifle, ransack, swindle, rip off (*sl*), do (*infml*), cheat, defraud, deprive.

robbery *n* theft, stealing, larceny, hold-up, stick-up (*sl*), heist (*sl*), raid, burglary, pillage, plunder, fraud, embezzlement, swindle, rip-off (*sl*).

robot *n* automaton, machine, android, zombie.

robust *adj* strong, sturdy, tough, hardy, vigorous, powerful, muscular, athletic, fit, healthy, well.
≠ weak, feeble, unhealthy.

rock[1] *n* boulder, stone, pebble, crag, outcrop.

> *Rocks include*: basalt, breccia, chalk, coal, conglomerate, flint, gabbro, gneiss, granite, gravel, lava, limestone, marble, marl, obsidian, ore, porphyry, pumice stone, sandstone, schist, serpentine, shale, slate.

rock[2] *v* **1** SWAY, swing, tilt, tip, shake, wobble, roll, pitch, toss, lurch, reel, stagger, totter. **2** *news that rocked the nation*: shock, stun, daze, dumbfound, astound, astonish, surprise, startle.

rocky[1] *adj* stony, pebbly, craggy, rugged, rough, hard, flinty.
≠ smooth, soft.

rocky[2] *adj* unsteady, shaky, wobbly, staggering, tottering, unstable, unreliable, uncertain, weak.
≠ steady, stable, dependable, strong.

rod *n* bar, shaft, strut, pole, stick, baton, wand, cane, switch, staff, mace, sceptre.

rodents

> *Kinds of rodent include*: agouti, bandicoot, beaver, black rat, brown rat, cane rat, capybara, cavy, chinchilla, chipmunk, cony, coypu, dormouse, fieldmouse, ferret, gerbil, gopher, grey squirrel, groundhog, guinea pig, hamster, hare, harvest mouse, hedgehog, jerboa, kangaroo rat, lemming, marmot, meerkat, mouse, muskrat, musquash, pika, porcupine, prairie dog, rabbit, rat, red squirrel, sewer-rat, squirrel, vole, water rat, water vole, woodchuck.

rogue *n* scoundrel, rascal, scamp, villain, miscreant, crook (*infml*), swindler, fraud, cheat, con man (*infml*), reprobate, wastrel, ne'er-do-well.

role *n* part, character, representation, portrayal, impersonation, function, capacity, task, duty, job, post, position.

roll *v* **1** ROTATE, revolve, turn, spin, wheel, twirl, whirl, gyrate, move, run, pass. **2** WIND, coil, furl, twist, curl, wrap, envelop, enfold, bind. **3** *the ship rolled*: rock, sway, swing, pitch, toss, lurch, reel, wallow, undulate. **4** PRESS, flatten, smooth, level. **5** RUMBLE, roar, thunder, boom, resound, reverberate.
n **1** ROLLER, cylinder, drum, reel, spool, bobbin, scroll. **2** REGISTER, roster, census, list, inventory, index, catalogue, directory, schedule, record, chronicle, annals. **3** ROTATION, revolution, cycle, turn, spin, wheel,

twirl, whirl, gyration, undulation.
4 RUMBLE, roar, thunder, boom, resonance, reverberation.
roll up (*infml*) arrive, assemble, gather, congregate, convene.
≠ leave.

romance *n* **1** LOVE AFFAIR, affair, relationship, liaison, intrigue, passion. **2** LOVE STORY, novel, story, tale, fairytale, legend, idyll, fiction, fantasy. **3** ADVENTURE, excitement, melodrama, mystery, charm, fascination, glamour, sentiment.
v lie, fantasize, exaggerate, overstate.

romantic *adj* **1** IMAGINARY, fictitious, fanciful, fantastic, legendary, fairy-tale, idyllic, utopian, idealistic, quixotic, visionary, starry-eyed, dreamy, unrealistic, impractical, improbable, wild, extravagant, exciting, fascinating. **2** SENTIMENTAL, loving, amorous, passionate, tender, fond, lovey-dovey (*infml*), soppy, mushy, sloppy.
≠ **1** real, practical. **2** unromantic, unsentimental.
n sentimentalist, dreamer, visionary, idealist, utopian.
≠ realist.

roofs

Types of roof include: bell roof, conical broach roof, cupola, dome, flat roof, French roof, gable roof, gable-and-valley roof, gambrel roof, geodesic dome, helm roof, hip roof, imbricated roof, imperial roof, lean-to roof, mansard roof, monitor roof, ogee roof, onion dome, pavilion roof, pendentive dome, pitched roof, saddle roof, saucer dome, sawtooth roof, sloped turret, span roof, thatched roof.

room *n* space, volume, capacity, headroom, legroom, elbow-room, scope, range, extent, leeway, latitude, margin, allowance, chance, opportunity.

Types of room include: attic, loft, box-room, bedroom, boudoir, spare room, dressing-room, guest room, nursery, playroom, sitting-room, lounge, front room, living-room, drawing-room, salon, reception room, chamber, lounge-diner, dining-room, study, den (*infml*), library, kitchen, kitchen-diner, kitchenette, breakfast room, larder, pantry, scullery, bathroom, en suite bathroom, toilet, lavatory, WC, loo (*infml*), cloakroom, laundry, utility room, porch, hall, landing, conservatory, sun lounge, cellar, basement; classroom, music-room, laboratory, office, sick-room, dormitory, workroom, studio, workshop, storeroom, waiting-room, anteroom, foyer, mezzanine, family room, games room.

roomy *adj* spacious, capacious, large, sizable, broad, wide, extensive, ample, generous.
≠ cramped, small, tiny.

root[1] *n* **1** TUBER, rhizome, stem. **2** ORIGIN, source, derivation, cause, starting point, fount, fountainhead, seed, germ, nucleus, heart, core, nub, essence, seat, base, bottom, basis, foundation.
v anchor, moor, fasten, fix, set, stick, implant, embed, entrench, establish, ground, base.
root out unearth, dig out, uncover, discover, uproot, eradicate, extirpate, eliminate, exterminate, destroy, abolish, clear away, remove.

root[2] *v* dig, delve, burrow, forage, hunt, rummage, ferret, poke, pry, nose.

roots *n* beginning(s), origins, family, heritage, background, birthplace, home.

rope

Kinds of rope include: bobstay, bowline, brace, bridle, buntline, cable, clew-line, cord, cordage, cringle, dragline, dragrope, gantline, guy, guy-rope, hackamore, halyard, halter, hawser, head rope, hobble, lanyard, lariat, lashing, lasso, line, marline, noose, painter, ratline, stay, strand, string, tack, tackle, tether, towrope, vang, warp, widdy.

v tie, bind, lash, fasten, hitch, moor, tether.
rope in enlist, engage, involve, persuade, inveigle.

roster *n* rota, schedule, register, roll, list.

rostrum *n* platform, stage, dais, podium.

rot *v* decay, decompose, putrefy, fester, perish, corrode, spoil, go bad, go off, degenerate, deteriorate, crumble, disintegrate, taint, corrupt.
n **1** DECAY, decomposition, putrefaction, corrosion, rust, mould. **2** (*infml*) NONSENSE, rubbish, poppycock (*infml*), drivel, claptrap.

rotary *adj* rotating, revolving, turning, spinning, whirling, gyrating.
≠ fixed.

rotate *v* revolve, turn, spin, gyrate, pivot, swivel, roll.

rotation *n* revolution, turn, spin, gyration, orbit, cycle, sequence, succession, turning, spinning.

rotten *adj* **1** DECAYED, decomposed, putrid, addled, bad, off, mouldy, fetid, stinking, rank, foul, rotting, decaying, disintegrating. **2** INFERIOR, bad, poor, inadequate, low-grade, lousy, crummy (*sl*), ropy (*sl*), mean, nasty, beastly, dirty, despicable, contemptible, dishonourable, wicked. **3** (*infml*) ILL, sick, unwell, poorly, grotty (*sl*), rough (*infml*).
≠ **1** fresh. **2** good. **3** well.

rough *adj* **1** UNEVEN, bumpy, lumpy, rugged, craggy, jagged, irregular, coarse, bristly, scratchy. **2** HARSH, severe, tough, hard, cruel, brutal, drastic, extreme, brusque, curt, sharp. **3** APPROXIMATE, estimated, imprecise, inexact, vague, general, cursory, hasty, incomplete, unfinished, crude, rudimentary. **4** *rough sea*: choppy, agitated, turbulent, stormy, tempestuous, violent, wild. **5** (*infml*) ILL, sick, unwell, poorly, off colour, rotten (*infml*).
≠ **1** smooth. **2** mild. **3** accurate. **4** calm. **5** well.

round *adj* **1** SPHERICAL, globular, ball-shaped, circular, ring-shaped, disc-shaped, cylindrical, rounded, curved. **2** ROTUND, plump, stout, portly.
n **1** CIRCLE, ring, band, disc, sphere, ball, orb. **2** CYCLE, series, sequence, succession, period, bout, session. **3** BEAT, circuit, lap, course, routine.
v circle, skirt, flank, bypass.
round off finish (off), complete, end, close, conclude, cap, crown.
≠ begin.
round on turn on, attack, lay into, abuse.
round up herd, marshal, assemble, gather, rally, collect, group.
≠ disperse, scatter.

roundabout *adj* circuitous, tortuous, twisting, winding, indirect, oblique, devious, evasive.
≠ straight, direct.

rouse *v* wake (up), awaken, arouse, call, stir, move, start, disturb, agitate, anger, provoke, stimulate, instigate, incite, inflame, excite, galvanize, whip up.
≠ calm.

rout *n* defeat, conquest, overthrow, beating, thrashing, flight, stampede.
≠ win.
v defeat, conquer, overthrow, crush, beat, hammer (*infml*), thrash, lick, put to flight, chase, dispel, scatter.

route *n* course, run, path, road, avenue, way, direction, itinerary, journey, passage, circuit, round, beat.

routine *n* **1** PROCEDURE, way, method, system, order, pattern, formula, practice, usage, custom, habit. **2** *comedy routine*: act, piece, programme, performance.
adj customary, habitual, usual, typical, ordinary, run-of-the-mill, normal, standard, conventional, unoriginal, predictable, familiar, everyday, banal, humdrum, dull, boring, monotonous, tedious.
≠ unusual, different, exciting.

row[1] *n* line, tier, bank, rank, range, column, file, queue, string, series, sequence.

row[2] *n* **1** ARGUMENT, quarrel, dispute, controversy, squabble, tiff, slanging match (*infml*), fight, brawl. **2** NOISE, racket, din, uproar, commotion, disturbance, rumpus, fracas.
≠ **2** calm.
v argue, quarrel, wrangle, bicker, squabble, fight, scrap.

rowdy *adj* noisy, loud, rough,

boisterous, disorderly, unruly, riotous, wild.
≠ quiet, peaceful.

royal *adj* regal, majestic, kingly, queenly, princely, imperial, monarchical, sovereign, august, grand, stately, magnificent, splendid, superb.

rub *v* apply, spread, smear, stroke, caress, massage, knead, chafe, grate, scrape, abrade, scour, scrub, clean, wipe, smooth, polish, buff, shine.
rub out erase, efface, obliterate, delete, cancel.

rubbish *n* **1** REFUSE, garbage, trash, junk, litter, waste, dross, debris, flotsam and jetsam. **2** NONSENSE, drivel, claptrap, twaddle, gibberish, gobbledegook, balderdash, poppycock (*infml*), rot (*infml*), cobblers (*sl*).
≠ **2** sense.

ruddy *adj* red, scarlet, crimson, blushing, flushed, rosy, glowing, healthy, blooming, florid, sunburnt.
≠ pale.

rude *adj* **1** IMPOLITE, discourteous, disrespectful, impertinent, impudent, cheeky (*infml*), insolent, offensive, insulting, abusive, ill-mannered, ill-bred, uncouth, uncivilized, unrefined, unpolished, uneducated, untutored, uncivil, curt, brusque, abrupt, sharp, short. **2** *a rude joke*: obscene, vulgar, coarse, dirty, naughty, gross.
≠ **1** polite, courteous, civil. **2** clean, decent.

rudimentary *adj* primary, initial, introductory, elementary, basic, fundamental, primitive, undeveloped, embryonic.
≠ advanced, developed.

rudiments *n* basics, fundamentals, essentials, principles, elements, ABC, beginnings, foundations.

rugged *adj* **1** ROUGH, bumpy, uneven, irregular, jagged, rocky, craggy, stark. **2** STRONG, robust, hardy, tough, muscular, weather-beaten.
≠ **1** smooth.

ruin *n* destruction, devastation, wreckage, havoc, damage, disrepair, decay, disintegration, breakdown, collapse, fall, downfall, failure, defeat, overthrow, ruination, undoing, insolvency, bankruptcy, crash.
≠ development, reconstruction.
v spoil, mar, botch, mess up (*infml*), damage, break, smash, shatter, wreck, destroy, demolish, raze, devastate, overwhelm, overthrow, defeat, crush, impoverish, bankrupt.
≠ develop, restore.

rule *n* **1** REGULATION, law, statute, ordinance, decree, order, direction, guide, precept, tenet, canon, maxim, axiom, principle, formula, guideline, standard, criterion. **2** REIGN, sovereignty, supremacy, dominion, mastery, power, authority, command, control, influence, regime, government, leadership. **3** CUSTOM, convention, practice, routine, habit, wont.
v **1** *rule a country*: reign, govern, command, lead, administer, manage, direct, guide, control, regulate, prevail, dominate. **2** JUDGE, adjudicate, decide, find, determine, resolve, establish, decree, pronounce.
as a rule usually, normally, ordinarily, generally.
rule out exclude, eliminate, reject, dismiss, preclude, prevent, ban, prohibit, forbid, disallow.

ruler

Titles of rulers include: Aga, begum, caesar, caliph, consul, duce, emir, emperor, empress, Führer, governor, governor-general, head of state, kaiser, khan, king, maharajah, maharani, mikado, monarch, nawab, nizam, pharoah, president, prince, princess, queen, rajah, rani, regent, shah, sheikh, shogun, sovereign, sultan, sultana, suzerain, tsar, viceroy.

ruling *n* judgement, adjudication, verdict, decision, finding, resolution, decree, pronouncement.
adj reigning, sovereign, supreme, governing, commanding, leading, main, chief, principal, dominant, predominant, controlling.

rumour *n* hearsay, gossip, talk,

whisper, word, news, report, story, grapevine, bush telegraph.

run *v* **1** SPRINT, jog, race, career, tear, dash, hurry, rush, speed, bolt, dart, scoot, scuttle. **2** GO, pass, move, proceed, issue. **3** FUNCTION, work, operate, perform. **4** *run a company*: head, lead, administer, direct, manage, superintend, supervise, oversee, control, regulate. **5** COMPETE, contend, stand, challenge. **6** LAST, continue, extend, reach, stretch, spread, range. **7** FLOW, stream, pour, gush.
n **1** JOG, gallop, race, sprint, spurt, dash, rush. **2** DRIVE, ride, spin, jaunt, excursion, outing, trip, journey. **3** SEQUENCE, series, string, chain, course.
run after chase, pursue, follow, tail.
≠ flee.
run away escape, flee, abscond, bolt, scarper (*sl*), beat it (*infml*), run off, make off, clear off (*infml*).
≠ stay.
run down 1 CRITICIZE, belittle, disparage, denigrate, defame. **2** RUN OVER, knock over, hit, strike. **3** TIRE, weary, exhaust, weaken. **4** *run down production*: reduce, decrease, drop, cut, trim, curtail.
≠ **1** praise. **4** increase.
run into meet, encounter, run across, bump into, hit, strike, collide with.
≠ miss.
run out expire, terminate, end, cease, close, finish, dry up, fail.

runaway *n* escaper, escapee, fugitive, absconder, deserter, refugee.
adj escaped, fugitive, loose, uncontrolled.

rundown *n* **1** REDUCTION, decrease, decline, drop, cut. **2** SUMMARY, résumé, synopsis, outline, review, recap, run-through.

runner *n* jogger, sprinter, athlete, competitor, participant, courier, messenger.

running *adj* successive, consecutive, unbroken, uninterrupted, continuous, constant, perpetual, incessant, unceasing, moving, flowing.
≠ broken, occasional.
n **1** ADMINISTRATION, direction, management, organization, co-ordination, superintendency, supervision, leadership, charge, control, regulation, functioning, working, operation, performance, conduct. **2** *out of the running*: contention, contest, competition.

runny *adj* flowing, fluid, liquid, liquefied, melted, molten, watery, diluted.
≠ solid.

run-of-the-mill *adj* ordinary, common, everyday, average, unexceptional, unremarkable, undistinguished, unimpressive, mediocre.
≠ exceptional.

rupture *n* split, tear, burst, puncture, break, breach, fracture, crack, separation, division, estrangement, schism, rift, disagreement, quarrel, falling-out, bust-up (*infml*).
v split, tear, burst, puncture, break, fracture, crack, sever, separate, divide.

rural *adj* country, rustic, pastoral, agricultural, agrarian.
≠ urban.

rush *v* hurry, hasten, quicken, accelerate, speed (up), press, push, dispatch, bolt, dart, shoot, fly, tear, career, dash, race, run, sprint, scramble, stampede, charge.
n hurry, haste, urgency, speed, swiftness, dash, race, scramble, stampede, charge, flow, surge.

rust *n* corrosion, oxidation.
v corrode, decay, rot, oxidize, tarnish, deteriorate, decline.

rustic *adj* **1** PASTORAL, sylvan, bucolic, countrified, country, rural. **2** PLAIN, simple, rough, crude, coarse, rude, clumsy, awkward, artless, unsophisticated, unrefined, uncultured, provincial, uncouth, boorish, oafish.
≠ **1** urban. **2** urbane, sophisticated, cultivated, polished.

rustle *v, n* crackle, whoosh, swish, whisper.

rusty *adj* **1** CORRODED, rusted, rust-covered, oxidized, tarnished, discoloured, dull. **2** UNPRACTISED, weak, poor, deficient, dated, old-fashioned, outmoded, antiquated, stale, stiff, creaking.

ruthless *adj* merciless, pitiless, hard-hearted, hard, heartless, unfeeling, callous, cruel, inhuman, brutal, savage, cut-throat, fierce, ferocious, relentless, unrelenting, inexorable, implacable, harsh, severe.
≠ merciful, compassionate.

S

sabotage *v* damage, spoil, mar, disrupt, vandalize, wreck, destroy, thwart, scupper, cripple, incapacitate, disable, undermine, weaken.
n vandalism, damage, impairment, disruption, wrecking, destruction.

sack (*infml*) *v* dismiss, fire, discharge, axe (*infml*), lay off, make redundant.
n dismissal, discharge, one's cards, notice, the boot (*infml*), the push (*infml*), the elbow (*infml*), the axe (*infml*), the chop (*infml*).

sacred *adj* holy, divine, heavenly, blessed, hallowed, sanctified, consecrated, dedicated, religious, devotional, ecclesiastical, priestly, saintly, godly, venerable, revered, sacrosanct, inviolable.
≠ temporal, profane.

sacred writings

> *Sacred writings include*: Holy Bible, the Gospel, Old Testament, New Testament, Epistle, Torah, Pentateuch, Talmud, Koran, Bhagavad-Gita, Veda, Granth, Zend-Avesta.

sacrifice *v* surrender, forfeit, relinquish, let go, abandon, renounce, give up, forgo, offer, slaughter.
n offering, immolation, slaughter, destruction, surrender, renunciation, loss.

sacrilege *n* blasphemy, profanity, heresy, desecration, profanation, violation, outrage, irreverence, disrespect, mockery.
≠ piety, reverence, respect.

sacrosanct *adj* sacred, hallowed, untouchable, inviolable, impregnable, protected, secure.

sad *adj* **1** UNHAPPY, sorrowful, tearful, grief-stricken, heavy-hearted, upset, distressed, miserable, low-spirited, downcast, glum, long-faced, crestfallen, dejected, down-hearted, despondent, melancholy, depressed, low, gloomy, dismal. **2** *sad news*: upsetting, distressing, painful, depressing, touching, poignant, heart-rending, tragic, grievous, lamentable, regrettable, sorry, unfortunate, serious, grave, disastrous.
≠ **1** happy, cheerful. **2** fortunate, lucky.

sadden *v* upset, distress, grieve, depress, dismay, discourage, dishearten.
≠ cheer, please, gratify, delight.

saddle *v* burden, encumber, lumber, impose, tax, charge, load.

sadistic *adj* cruel, inhuman, brutal, savage, vicious, merciless, pitiless, barbarous, bestial, unnatural, perverted.

safe *adj* **1** HARMLESS, innocuous, non-toxic, non-poisonous, uncontaminated. **2** UNHARMED, undamaged, unscathed, uninjured, unhurt, intact, secure, protected, guarded, impregnable, invulnerable, immune. **3** UNADVENTUROUS, cautious, prudent, conservative, sure, proven, tried, tested, sound, dependable, reliable, trustworthy.
≠ **1** dangerous, harmful. **2** vulnerable, exposed. **3** risky.

safeguard *v* protect, preserve, defend, guard, shield, screen, shelter, secure.
≠ endanger, jeopardize.
n protection, defence, shield, security, surety, guarantee, assurance, insurance, cover, precaution.

safe-keeping *n* protection, care, custody, keeping, charge, trust, guardianship, surveillance, supervision.

safety *n* protection, refuge, sanctuary, shelter, cover, security, safeguard, immunity, impregnability, safeness, harmlessness, reliability, dependability.

≠ danger, jeopardy, risk.

sag *v* bend, give, bag, droop, hang, fall, drop, sink, dip, decline, slump, flop, fail, flag, weaken, wilt.
≠ bulge, rise.

sail *v* **1** *sail for France*: embark, set sail, weigh anchor, put to sea, cruise, voyage. **2** CAPTAIN, skipper, pilot, navigate, steer. **3** GLIDE, plane, sweep, float, skim, scud, fly.

Types of sail include: Bermuda rig, canvas, course, foreroyal, foresail, forestaysail, foretop, fore-topgallant, fore-topsail, gaff sail, genoa, headsail, jib, jigger, kite, lateen sail, lugsail, main course, mainsail, maintopsail, mizzen, moonraker, rig, fore-and-aft rig, jury rig, royal, skysail, spanker, spinnaker, spritsail, square sail, staysail, studdingsail, topgallant, topsail, trysail.

sailor *n* seafarer, mariner, seaman.

Types of sailor include: able-bodied seaman *or* able seaman (AB), bargee, boatman, boatswain, bosun, buccaneer, cabin boy, captain, cox, coxswain, crewman, deck hand, fisherman, galiogee, gob (*US*), hearty, helmsman, Jack tar, lascar, leatherneck, limey (*US sl*), marine, master, mate, matelot (*sl*), navigator, oarsman, pilot, pirate, purser, rating, rower, salt, sculler, sea dog, skipper, tar (*infml*), tarry-breeks, water rat, Wren, yachtsman, yachtswoman.

saintly *adj* godly, pious, devout, God-fearing, holy, religious, blessed, angelic, pure, spotless, innocent, blameless, sinless, virtuous, upright, worthy, righteous.
≠ godless, unholy, wicked.

sake *n* benefit, advantage, good, welfare, wellbeing, gain, profit, behalf, interest, account, regard, respect, cause, reason.

salary *n* pay, remuneration, emolument, stipend, wages, earnings, income.

sale *n* selling, marketing, vending, disposal, trade, traffic, transaction, deal.

Types of sale include: auction, autumn sale, bargain offer, bazaar, bazumble, boot-sale, bring-and-buy, car-boot sale, charity sale, church bazaar, clearance sale, closing-down sale, cold-call, end-of-line sale, end-of-season sale, exhibition, exposition, fair, fleamarket, forced sale, garage sale, grand opening sale, introductory offer, January sale, jumble sale, mail order, market, mid-season sale, on-promotion, open market, private sale, public sale, pyramid selling, remainder sale, rummage sale, sale of bankrupt stock, sale of the century, sale of work, second-hand sale, special offer, spring sale, stocktaking sale, summer sale, tabletop sale, telesales, trade show, trash and treasure sale, winter sale.

salesperson *n* salesman, saleswoman, sales assistant, shop assistant, shop-boy, shop-girl, shopkeeper, representative, rep (*infml*).

salient *adj* important, significant, chief, main, principal, striking, conspicuous, noticeable, obvious, prominent, outstanding, remarkable.

sallow *adj* yellowish, pale, pallid, wan, pasty, sickly, unhealthy, anaemic, colourless.
≠ rosy, healthy.

salt *n* seasoning, taste, flavour, savour, relish, piquancy.

salty *adj* salt, salted, saline, briny, brackish, savoury, spicy, piquant, tangy.
≠ fresh, sweet.

salubrious *adj* sanitary, hygienic, health-giving, healthy, wholesome, pleasant.

salutary *adj* good, beneficial, advantageous, profitable, valuable, helpful, useful, practical, timely.

salute *v* greet, acknowledge, recognize, wave, hail, address, nod, bow, honour.
n greeting, acknowledgement, recognition, wave, gesture, hail, address, handshake, nod, bow, tribute, reverence.

salvage *v* save, preserve, conserve,

rescue, recover, recuperate, retrieve, reclaim, redeem, repair, restore.
≠ waste, abandon.

salvation *n* deliverance, liberation, rescue, saving, preservation, redemption, reclamation.
≠ loss, damnation.

salve *n* ointment, lotion, cream, balm, liniment, embrocation, medication, preparation, application.

same *adj* identical, twin, duplicate, indistinguishable, equal, selfsame, very, alike, like, similar, comparable, equivalent, matching, corresponding, mutual, reciprocal, interchangeable, substitutable, synonymous, consistent, uniform, unvarying, changeless, unchanged.
≠ different, inconsistent, variable, changeable.

sample *n* specimen, example, cross-section, model, pattern, swatch, piece, demonstration, illustration, instance, sign, indication, foretaste.
v try, test, taste, sip, inspect, experience.
adj representative, specimen, demonstration, illustrative, dummy, trial, test, pilot.

sanctify *v* hallow, consecrate, bless, anoint, dedicate, cleanse, purify, exalt, canonize.
≠ desecrate, defile.

sanctimonious *adj* self-righteous, holier-than-thou, pious, moralizing, smug, superior, hypocritical, pharisaical.
≠ humble.

sanction *n* authorization, permission, agreement, OK (*infml*), approval, go-ahead, ratification, confirmation, support, backing, endorsement, licence, authority.
≠ veto, disapproval.
v authorize, allow, permit, approve, ratify, confirm, support, back, endorse, underwrite, accredit, license, warrant.
≠ veto, forbid, disapprove.

sanctions *n* restrictions, boycott, embargo, ban, prohibition, penalty.

sanctity *n* holiness, sacredness, inviolability, piety, godliness, religiousness, devotion, grace, spirituality, purity, goodness, righteousness.
≠ unholiness, secularity, worldliness, godlessness, impurity.

sanctuary *n* **1** CHURCH, temple, tabernacle, shrine, altar. **2** ASYLUM, refuge, protection, shelter, haven, retreat.

sand *n* beach, shore, strand, sands, grit.

sane *adj* normal, rational, right-minded, all there (*infml*), balanced, stable, sound, sober, level-headed, sensible, judicious, reasonable, moderate.
≠ insane, mad, crazy, foolish.

sanitary *adj* clean, pure, uncontaminated, unpolluted, aseptic, germ-free, disinfected, hygienic, salubrious, healthy, wholesome.
≠ insanitary, unwholesome.

sanity *n* normality, rationality, reason, sense, common sense, balance of mind, stability, soundness, level-headedness, judiciousness.
≠ insanity, madness.

sap *v* bleed, drain, exhaust, weaken, undermine, deplete, reduce, diminish, impair.
≠ strengthen, build up, increase.

sarcasm *n* irony, satire, mockery, sneering, derision, scorn, contempt, cynicism, bitterness.

sarcastic *adj* ironical, satirical, mocking, taunting, sneering, derisive, scathing, disparaging, cynical, incisive, cutting, biting, caustic.

sardonic *adj* mocking, jeering, sneering, derisive, scornful, sarcastic, biting, cruel, heartless, malicious, cynical, bitter.

sash *n* belt, girdle, cummerbund, waistband.

satanic *adj* satanical, diabolical, devilish, demonic, fiendish, hellish, infernal, inhuman, malevolent, wicked, evil, black.
≠ holy, divine, godly, saintly, benevolent.

satire *n* ridicule, irony, sarcasm,

burlesque, skit, send-up, spoof, take-off, parody, caricature, travesty.

satirical *adj* ironical, sarcastic, mocking, irreverent, taunting, derisive, sardonic, incisive, cutting, biting, caustic, cynical, bitter.

satirize *v* ridicule, mock, make fun of, burlesque, lampoon, send up, take off, parody, caricature, criticize, deride.
≠ acclaim, honour.

satisfaction *n* **1** GRATIFICATION, contentment, happiness, pleasure, enjoyment, comfort, ease, well-being, fulfilment, self-satisfaction, pride. **2** SETTLEMENT, compensation, reimbursement, indemnification, damages, reparation, amends, redress, recompense, requital, vindication.
≠ **1** dissatisfaction, displeasure.

satisfactory *adj* acceptable, passable, up to the mark, all right, OK (*infml*), fair, average, competent, adequate, sufficient, suitable, proper.
≠ unsatisfactory, unacceptable, inadequate.

satisfy *v* **1** GRATIFY, indulge, content, please, delight, quench, slake, sate, satiate, surfeit. **2** *satisfy requirements*: meet, fulfil, discharge, settle, answer, fill, suffice, serve, qualify. **3** ASSURE, convince, persuade.
≠ **1** dissatisfy. **2** fail.

saturate *v* soak, steep, souse, drench, waterlog, impregnate, permeate, imbue, suffuse, fill.

saucy (*infml*) *adj* cheeky (*infml*), impertinent, impudent, insolent, disrespectful, pert, forward, presumptuous, flippant.
≠ polite, respectful.

saunter *v* stroll, amble, mosey (*infml*), mooch (*infml*), wander, ramble, meander.
n stroll, walk, constitutional, ramble.

savage *adj* wild, untamed, undomesticated, uncivilized, primitive, [illegible]baric, barbarous, fierce, ferocious, [illegible]us, beastly, cruel, inhuman, brutal, [illegible] bloodthirsty, bloody, [illegible]us, pitiless, merciless, ruthless, [illegible]
[illegible]lized, humane, mild.
n brute, beast, barbarian.
v attack, bite, claw, tear, maul, mangle.

save *v* **1** ECONOMIZE, cut back, conserve, preserve, keep, retain, hold, reserve, store, lay up, set aside, put by, hoard, stash (*infml*), collect, gather. **2** RESCUE, deliver, liberate, free, salvage, recover, reclaim. **3** PROTECT, guard, screen, shield, safeguard, spare, prevent, hinder.
≠ **1** spend, squander, waste, discard.

savings *n* capital, investments, nest egg, fund, store, reserves, resources.
n economy, thrift, discount, reduction, bargain, cut, conservation, preservation.
≠ expense, waste, loss.

saviour *n* rescuer, deliverer, redeemer, liberator, emancipator, guardian, protector, defender, champion.
≠ destroyer.

savour *n* taste, flavour, smack, smell, tang, piquancy, salt, spice, relish, zest.
v relish, enjoy, delight in, revel in, like, appreciate.
≠ shrink from.

savoury *adj* **1** TASTY, appetizing, delicious, mouthwatering, luscious, palatable. **2** *savoury pancakes*: salty, spicy, aromatic, piquant, tangy.
≠ **1** unappetizing, tasteless, insipid. **2** sweet.

saws

Kinds of saw include: band-saw, bench saw, chainsaw, circular saw, compass saw, coping-saw, crosscut saw, fretsaw, hacksaw, handsaw, jigsaw, panel saw, power-driven saw, pruning-saw, rabbet saw, radial-arm saw, ripsaw, scroll-saw, tenon saw.

say

Other words for say include: accuse, acknowledge, add, admit, admonish, advise, affirm, agree, allege, announce, answer, argue, ask, assert, assume, babble, banter, bark, bawl, beg, begin, bellow, blare, blaspheme, blurt, boast, brag, call, chant, chatter, claim, coax, command, comment, complain, conclude, confide, continue, contradict, correct, counter, croak, cry, curse, declare, demand, deny, describe, detail, disclose, dispute, divulge, echo, elaborate, elucidate, emphasize, enjoin, enquire, estimate, exclaim, expostulate, express, falter, finish, flounder, gasp, greet, groan, growl, grumble, grunt, guess, hint, howl, imagine, implore, imply, indicate, infer, inform, insinuate, instruct, interrogate, interrupt, intervene, intimate, jeer, jest, joke, laugh, lecture, lie, mention, mimic, moan, mock, mouth, mumble, murmur, mutter, nag, observe, offer, orate, order, persist, persuade, phrase, pipe, plead, point out, predict, press, presume, proclaim, profess, proffer, prompt, pronounce, propose, protest, query, question, quote, rage, rail, rant, read, reassure, rebuke, recite, reckon, recommend, rehearse, reiterate, rejoice, relate, remark, remonstrate, renounce, repeat, reply, report, request, resolve, respond, retaliate, retort, retract, reveal, roar, scoff, scold, scream, screech, shout, shriek, snap, snarl, speak, specify, squeak, stammer, state, storm, stutter, submit, suggest, surmise, swear, sympathize, taunt, tease, tell, testify, thunder, urge, utter, venture, voice, volunteer, vow, whine, whisper, wonder, yell.

saying *n* adage, proverb, dictum, precept, axiom, aphorism, maxim, motto, slogan, phrase, expression, quotation, statement, remark.

scale[1] *n* ratio, proportion, measure, degree, extent, spread, reach, range, scope, compass, spectrum, gamut, sequence, series, progression, order, hierarchy, ranking, ladder, steps, gradation, graduation, calibration, register.
v climb, ascend, mount, clamber, scramble, shin up, conquer, surmount.

scale[2] *n* encrustation, deposit, crust, layer, film, lamina, plate, flake, scurf.

scamp *n* rogue, rascal, scallywag, monkey, imp, devil.

scamper *v* scuttle, scurry, scoot, dart, dash, run, sprint, rush, hurry, hasten, fly, romp, frolic, gambol.

scan *v* **1** EXAMINE, scrutinize, study, search, survey, sweep, investigate, check. **2** SKIM, glance at, flick through, thumb through.
n screening, examination, scrutiny, search, probe, check, investigation, survey, review.

scandal *n* outrage, offence, outcry, uproar, furore, gossip, rumours, smear, dirt, discredit, dishonour, disgrace, shame, embarrassment, ignominy.

scandalize *v* shock, horrify, appal, dismay, disgust, repel, revolt, offend, affront, outrage.

scandalous *adj* shocking, appalling, atrocious, abominable, monstrous, unspeakable, outrageous, disgraceful, shameful, disreputable, infamous, improper, unseemly, defamatory, scurrilous, slanderous, libellous, untrue.

scanty *adj* deficient, short, inadequate, insufficient, scant, little, limited, restricted, narrow, poor, meagre, insubstantial, thin, skimpy, sparse, bare.
≠ adequate, sufficient, ample, plentiful, substantial.

scar *n* mark, lesion, wound, injury, blemish, stigma.
v mark, disfigure, spoil, damage, brand, stigmatize.

scarce *adj* few, rare, infrequent, uncommon, unusual, sparse, scanty, insufficient, deficient, lacking.
≠ plentiful, common.

scarcely *adv* hardly, barely, only just.

scarcity *n* lack, shortage, dearth, deficiency, insufficiency, paucity, rareness, rarity, infrequency, uncommonness, sparseness, scantiness.
≠ glut, plenty, abundance, sufficiency, enough.

scare *v* frighten, startle, alarm, dismay, daunt, intimidate, unnerve, threaten, menace, terrorize, shock, appal, panic, terrify.
≠ reassure, calm.
n fright, start, shock, alarm, panic, hysteria, terror.
≠ reassurance, comfort.

scared *adj* frightened, fearful, nervous, anxious, worried, startled, shaken, panic-stricken, terrified.
≠ confident, reassured.

scary *adj* frightening, alarming, daunting, intimidating, disturbing, shocking, horrifying, terrifying, hair-raising, bloodcurdling, spine-chilling, chilling, creepy, eerie, spooky (*infml*).

scathing *adj* sarcastic, scornful, critical, trenchant, cutting, biting, caustic, acid, vitriolic, bitter, harsh, brutal, savage, unsparing.
≠ complimentary.

scatter *v* disperse, dispel, dissipate, disband, disunite, separate, divide, break up, disintegrate, diffuse, broadcast, disseminate, spread, sprinkle, sow, strew, fling, shower.
≠ gather, collect.

scatterbrained *adj* forgetful, absent-minded, empty-headed, feather-brained, scatty (*infml*), careless, inattentive, thoughtless, unreliable, irresponsible, frivolous.
≠ sensible, sober, efficient, careful.

scattering *n* sprinkling, few, handful, smattering.
≠ mass, abundance.

scavenge *v* forage, rummage, rake, search, scrounge.

scenario *n* outline, synopsis, summary, résumé, storyline, plot, scheme, plan, programme, projection, sequence, situation, scene.

scene *n* **1** PLACE, area, spot, locale, site, situation, position, whereabouts, location, locality, environment, milieu, setting, context, background, backdrop, set, stage. **2** LANDSCAPE, panorama, view, vista, prospect, sight, spectacle, picture, tableau, pageant. **3** EPISODE, incident, part, division, act, clip. **4** *don't make a scene*: fuss, commotion, to-do (*infml*), ...rmance, drama, exhibition, ...v, show.

... landscape, terrain, ... view, vista, outlook, scene, ... setting, surroundings,

scenic *adj* panoramic, picturesque, attractive, pretty, beautiful, grand, striking, impressive, spectacular, breathtaking, awe-inspiring.
≠ dull, dreary.

scent *n* **1** PERFUME, fragrance, aroma, bouquet, smell, odour. **2** *follow the scent*: track, trail.
≠ **1** stink.
v smell, sniff (out), nose (out), sense, perceive, detect, discern, recognize.

scented *adj* perfumed, fragrant, sweet-smelling, aromatic.
≠ malodorous, stinking.

sceptic *n* doubter, unbeliever, disbeliever, agnostic, atheist, rationalist, questioner, scoffer, cynic.
≠ believer.

sceptical *adj* doubting, doubtful, unconvinced, unbelieving, disbelieving, questioning, distrustful, mistrustful, hesitating, dubious, suspicious, scoffing, cynical, pessimistic.
≠ convinced, confident, trusting.

scepticism *n* doubt, unbelief, disbelief, agnosticism, atheism, rationalism, distrust, suspicion, cynicism, pessimism.
≠ belief, faith.

schedule *n* timetable, programme, agenda, diary, calendar, itinerary, plan, scheme, list, inventory, catalogue, table, form.
v timetable, time, table, programme, plan, organize, arrange, appoint, assign, book, list.

schematic *adj* diagrammatic, representational, symbolic, illustrative, graphic.

scheme *n* **1** PROGRAMME, schedule, plan, project, idea, proposal, proposition, suggestion, draft, outline, blueprint, schema, diagram, chart, layout, pattern, design, shape, configuration, arrangement. **2** INTRIGUE, plot, conspiracy, device, stratagem, ruse, ploy, shift, manoeuvre, tactic(s), strategy, procedure, system, method.
v plot, conspire, connive, collude, intrigue, machinate, manoeuvre, manipulate, pull strings, mastermind,

plan, project, contrive, devise, frame, work out.

schism *n* **1** DIVISION, split, rift, rupture, break, breach, disunion, separation, severance, estrangement, discord. **2** SPLINTER GROUP, faction, sect.

scholar *n* pupil, student, academic, intellectual, egghead (*infml*), authority, expert.
≠ dunce, ignoramus.

scholarly *adj* learned, erudite, lettered, academic, scholastic, school, intellectual, highbrow, bookish, studious, knowledgeable, well-read, analytical, scientific.
≠ uneducated, illiterate.

scholarship *n* **1** ERUDITION, learnedness, learning, knowledge, wisdom, education, schooling. **2** *a scholarship to a public school*: grant, award, bursary, endowment, fellowship, exhibition.

school *n* college, academy, institute, institution, seminary, faculty, department, discipline, class, group, pupils, students.
v educate, teach, instruct, tutor, coach, train, discipline, drill, verse, prime, prepare, indoctrinate.

schooling *n* education, book-learning, teaching, instruction, tuition, coaching, training, drill, preparation, grounding, guidance, indoctrination.

science *n* technology, discipline, specialization, knowledge, skill, proficiency, technique, art.

> *Sciences include*: acoustics, aerodynamics, aeronautics, agricultural science, anatomy, anthropology, archaeology, astronomy, astrophysics, behavioural science, biochemistry, biology, biophysics, botany, chemistry, chemurgy, climatology, computer science, cybernetics, diagnostics, dietetics, domestic science, dynamics, earth science, ecology, economics, electrodynamics, electronics, engineering, entomology, environmental science, food science, genetics, geochemistry, geographical science, geology, geophysics, graphology, hydraulics, information technology, inorganic chemistry, life science, linguistics, macrobiotics, materials science, mathematics, mechanical engineering, mechanics, medical science, metallurgy, meteorology, microbiology, mineralogy, morphology, natural science, nuclear physics, organic chemistry, ornithology, pathology, pharmacology, physics, physiology, political science, psychology, radiochemistry, robotics, sociology, space technology, telecommunications, thermodynamics, toxicology, ultrasonics, veterinary science, zoology.

scientific *adj* methodical, systematic, controlled, regulated, analytical, mathematical, exact, precise, accurate, scholarly, thorough.

scientific instruments

> *Types of scientific instrument include*: absorptiometer, barostat, cathode ray oscilloscope, centrifuge, chronograph, coherer, collimator, cryostat, decoherer, dephlegmator, dipleidoscope, electromyograph, electrosonde, eudiometer, fluoroscope, Fresnel lens, Geissler tube, heliograph, heliostat, hodoscope, humidistat, hydrophone, hydroscope, hydrostat, hygrograph, hygrostat, iconoscope, image converter, image tube, interferometer, microtome, nephograph, optical character reader, oscillograph, oscilloscope, pantograph, parametric amplifier, phonendoscope, radarscope, radiosonde, rheocord, rheostat, slide-rule, spectroscope, stactometer, stauroscope, strobe, stroboscope, tachistoscope, tachograph, teinoscope, telemeter, telethermoscope, tesla coil, thermostat, thyratron, torsion-balance, transformer, transponder, tunnel diode, vernier, zymoscope.
> *see also* **laboratory apparatus**; **measuring instruments**; **medical equipment**.

scintillating *adj* sparkling, glittering, flashing, bright, shining, brilliant,

dazzling, exciting, stimulating, lively, animated, vivacious, ebullient, witty.
≠ dull.

scoff[1] *v* mock, ridicule, poke fun, taunt, tease, rib (*sl*), jeer, sneer, pooh-pooh, scorn, despise, revile, deride, belittle, disparage, knock (*infml*).
≠ praise, compliment, flatter.

scoff[2] *v* eat, consume, devour, put away (*infml*), gobble, guzzle, wolf (*infml*), bolt, gulp.
≠ fast, abstain.

scold *v* chide, tell off (*infml*), tick off (*infml*), reprimand, reprove, rebuke, take to task, admonish, upbraid, reproach, blame, censure, lecture, nag.
≠ praise, commend.

scolding *n* castigation, telling-off, ticking-off (*infml*), dressing-down, reprimand, reproof, rebuke, lecture, talking-to, earful (*infml*).
≠ praise, commendation.

scoop *n* **1** LADLE, spoon, dipper, bailer, bucket, shovel. **2** EXCLUSIVE, coup, inside story, revelation, exposé, sensation, latest (*infml*).
v gouge, scrape, hollow, empty, excavate, dig, shovel, ladle, spoon, dip, bail.

scope *n* **1** RANGE, compass, field, area, sphere, ambit, terms of reference, confines, reach, extent, span, breadth, coverage. **2** *scope for improvement*: room, space, capacity, elbow-room, latitude, leeway, freedom, liberty, opportunity.

scorch *v* burn, singe, char, blacken, scald, roast, sear, parch, shrivel, wither.

scorching *adj* burning, boiling, baking, roasting, sizzling, blistering, sweltering, torrid, tropical, searing, red-hot.

score *n* **1** RESULT, total, sum, tally, points, marks. **2** SCRATCH, line, groove, mark, nick, notch.
v **1** RECORD, register, chalk up, notch up, count, total, make, earn, gain, achieve, attain, win, have the advantage, have the edge, be one up. **2** SCRATCH, scrape, graze, mark, groove, gouge, cut, incise, engrave, indent, nick, slash.

scorn *n* contempt, scornfulness, disdain, sneering, derision, mockery, ridicule, sarcasm, disparagement, disgust.
≠ admiration, respect.
v despise, look down on, disdain, sneer at, scoff at, deride, mock, laugh at, slight, spurn, refuse, reject, dismiss.
≠ admire, respect.

scornful *adj* contemptuous, disdainful, supercilious, haughty, arrogant, sneering, scoffing, derisive, mocking, jeering, sarcastic, scathing, disparaging, insulting, slighting, dismissive.
≠ admiring, respectful.

scour[1] *v* scrape, abrade, rub, polish, burnish, scrub, clean, wash, cleanse, purge, flush.

scour[2] *v* search, hunt, comb, drag, ransack, rummage, forage, rake.

scourge *n* **1** AFFLICTION, misfortune, torment, terror, bane, evil, curse, plague, penalty, punishment. **2** WHIP, lash.
≠ **1** blessing, godsend, boon.
v **1** AFFLICT, torment, curse, plague, devastate, punish, chastise, discipline. **2** WHIP, flog, beat, lash, cane, flail, thrash.

scout *v* spy out, reconnoitre, explore, investigate, check out, survey, case (*sl*), spy, snoop, search, seek, hunt, probe, look, watch, observe.
n spy, reconnoitre, vanguard, outrider, escort, lookout, recruiter, spotter.

scowl *v, n* frown, glower, glare, grimace, pout.
≠ smile, grin, beam.

scraggy *adj* scrawny, skinny, thin, lean, lanky, bony, angular, gaunt, undernourished, emaciated, wasted.
≠ plump, sleek.

scramble *v* **1** CLIMB, scale, clamber, crawl, shuffle, scrabble, grope. **2** RUSH, hurry, hasten, run, push, jostle, struggle, strive, vie, contend.
n rush, hurry, race, dash, hustle, bustle, commotion, confusion, muddle, struggle, free-for-all, mêlée.

scrap[1] *n* bit, piece, fragment, part, fraction, crumb, morsel, bite,

mouthful, sliver, shred, snippet, atom, iota, grain, particle, mite, trace, vestige, remnant, leftover, waste, junk.
v discard, throw away, jettison, shed, abandon, drop, dump, ditch (*sl*), cancel, axe, demolish, break up, write off.
≠ recover, restore.

scrap² *n* fight, scuffle, brawl, dust-up (*infml*), quarrel, row, argument, squabble, wrangle, dispute, disagreement.
≠ peace, agreement.
v fight, brawl, quarrel, argue, fall out, squabble, bicker, wrangle, disagree.
≠ agree.

scrape *v* grate, grind, rasp, file, abrade, scour, rub, clean, remove, erase, scrabble, claw, scratch, graze, skin, bark, scuff.

scrappy *adj* bitty, disjointed, piecemeal, fragmentary, incomplete, sketchy, superficial, slapdash, slipshod.
≠ complete, finished.

scratch *v* claw, gouge, score, mark, cut, incise, etch, engrave, scrape, rub, scuff, graze, gash, lacerate.
n mark, line, scrape, scuff, abrasion, graze, gash, laceration.

scrawny *adj* scraggy, skinny, thin, lean, lanky, angular, bony, underfed, undernourished, emaciated.
≠ fat, plump.

scream *v, n* shriek, screech, cry, shout, yell, bawl, roar, howl, wail, squeal, yelp.

screen *v* **1** *screen a film*: show, present, broadcast. **2** SHIELD, protect, safeguard, defend, guard, cover, mask, veil, cloak, shroud, hide, conceal, shelter, shade. **3** SORT, grade, sift, sieve, filter, process, evaluate, gauge, examine, scan, vet.
≠ **2** uncover, expose.
n partition, divider, shield, guard, cover, mask, veil, cloak, shroud, concealment, shelter, shade, awning, canopy, net, mesh.

screw *v* fasten, adjust, tighten, contract, compress, squeeze, extract, extort, force, constrain, pressurize, turn, wind, twist, wring, distort, wrinkle.

scribble *v* write, pen, jot, dash off, scrawl, doodle.

scribe *n* writer, copyist, amanuensis, secretary, clerk.

script *n* **1** *a film script*: text, lines, words, dialogue, screenplay, libretto, book. **2** WRITING, handwriting, hand, longhand, calligraphy, letters, manuscript, copy.

scrounge *v* cadge, beg, sponge.

scrounger *n* cadger, sponger, parasite.

scrub *v* **1** *scrub the floor*: rub, brush, clean, wash, cleanse, scour. **2** (*infml*) ABOLISH, cancel, delete, abandon, give up, drop, discontinue.

scruffy *adj* untidy, messy, unkempt, dishevelled, bedraggled, run-down, tattered, shabby, disreputable, worn-out, ragged, seedy, squalid, slovenly.
≠ tidy, well-dressed.

scruple *n* reluctance, hesitation, doubt, qualm, misgiving, uneasiness, difficulty, perplexity.
v hesitate, think twice, hold back, shrink.

scruples *n* standards, principles, morals, ethics.

scrupulous *adj* **1** PAINSTAKING, meticulous, conscientious, careful, rigorous, strict, exact, precise, minute, nice. **2** PRINCIPLED, moral, ethical, honourable, upright.
≠ **1** superficial, careless, reckless. **2** unscrupulous, unprincipled.

scrutinize *v* examine, inspect, study, scan, analyse, sift, investigate, probe, search, explore.

scrutiny *n* examination, inspection, study, analysis, investigation, inquiry, search, exploration.

scuff *v* scrape, scratch, graze, abrade, rub, brush, drag.

scuffle *v* fight, scrap, tussle, brawl, grapple, struggle, contend, clash.
n fight, scrap, tussle, brawl, fray, set-to, rumpus, commotion, disturbance, affray.

sculpt *v* sculpture, carve, chisel, hew, cut, model, mould, cast, form, shape, fashion.

sculpture

> *Types of sculpture include*: bas-relief, bronze, bust, carving, caryatid, cast, effigy, figure, figurine, group, head, herm, maquette, marble, moulding, plaster cast, relief, statue, statuette, telamon, waxwork.

scum *n* froth, foam, film, impurities, dross, dregs, rubbish, trash.

scurrilous *adj* rude, vulgar, coarse, foul, obscene, indecent, salacious, offensive, abusive, insulting, disparaging, defamatory, slanderous, libellous, scandalous.
≠ polite, courteous, complimentary.

scurry *v* dash, rush, hurry, hasten, bustle, scramble, scuttle, scamper, scoot, dart, run, sprint, trot, race, fly, skim, scud.

sea *n* **1** OCEAN, main, deep, briny (*infml*). **2** *a sea of faces*: multitude, abundance, profusion, mass.
adj marine, maritime, ocean, oceanic, salt, saltwater, aquatic, seafaring.
≠ land, air.
at sea adrift, lost, confused, bewildered, baffled, puzzled, perplexed, mystified.

seafaring *adj* sea-going, ocean-going, sailing, nautical, naval, marine, maritime.

seal *v* **1** *seal a jar*: close, shut, stop, plug, cork, stopper, waterproof, fasten, secure. **2** SETTLE, conclude, finalize, stamp.
≠ **1** unseal.
n stamp, signet, insignia, imprimatur, authentication, assurance, attestation, confirmation, ratification.
seal off block up, close off, shut off, fence off, cut off, segregate, isolate, quarantine.
≠ open up.

seam *n* **1** JOIN, joint, weld, closure, line. **2** *coal seam*: layer, stratum, vein, lode.

seamy *adj* disreputable, sleazy, sordid, squalid, unsavoury, rough, dark, low, nasty, unpleasant.
≠ respectable, wholesome, pleasant.

sear *v* burn, scorch, brown, fry, sizzle, seal, cauterize, brand, parch, shrivel, wither.

search *v* seek, look, hunt, rummage, rifle, ransack, scour, comb, sift, probe, explore, frisk (*sl*), examine, scrutinize, inspect, check, investigate, inquire, pry.
n hunt, quest, pursuit, rummage, probe, exploration, examination, scrutiny, inspection, investigation, inquiry, research, survey.

searching *adj* penetrating, piercing, keen, sharp, close, intent, probing, thorough, minute.
≠ vague, superficial.

seaside *n* coast, shore, beach, sands.

season *n* period, spell, phase, term, time, span, interval.
v **1** *season food*: flavour, spice, salt. **2** AGE, mature, ripen, harden, toughen, train, prepare, condition, treat, temper.

seasonable *adj* timely, well-timed, welcome, opportune, convenient, suitable, appropriate, fitting.
≠ unseasonable, inopportune.

seasoned *adj* mature, experienced, practised, well-versed, veteran, old, hardened, toughened, conditioned, acclimatized, weathered.
≠ inexperienced, novice.

seasoning *n* flavouring, spice, condiment, salt, pepper, relish, sauce, dressing.

seat *n* **1** CHAIR, bench, pew, stool, throne. **2** *country seat*: residence, abode, house, mansion. **3** PLACE, site, situation, location, headquarters, centre, heart, hub, axis, source, cause, bottom, base, foundation, footing, ground.
v sit, place, set, locate, install, fit, fix, settle, accommodate, hold, contain, take.

seating *n* seats, chairs, places, room, accommodation.

secluded *adj* private, cloistered, sequestered, shut away, cut off, isolated, lonely, solitary, remote, out-of-the-way, sheltered, hidden, concealed.
≠ public, accessible.

seclusion *n* privacy, retirement, retreat, isolation, solitude, remoteness, shelter, hiding, concealment.

second[1] *adj* duplicate, twin, double, repeated, additional, further, extra, supplementary, alternative, other, alternate, next, following, subsequent, succeeding, secondary, subordinate, lower, inferior, lesser, supporting.
n helper, assistant, backer, supporter.
v approve, agree with, endorse, back, support, help, assist, aid, further, advance, forward, promote, encourage.

second[2] *n* minute, tick (*infml*), moment, instant, flash, jiffy (*infml*).

secondary *adj* subsidiary, subordinate, lower, inferior, lesser, minor, unimportant, ancillary, auxiliary, supporting, relief, back-up, reserve, spare, extra, second, alternative, indirect, derived, resulting.
≠ primary, main, major.

second-hand *adj* used, old, worn, hand-me-down, borrowed, derivative, secondary, indirect, vicarious.
≠ new.

second-rate *adj* inferior, substandard, second-class, second-best, poor, low-grade, shoddy, cheap, tawdry, mediocre, undistinguished, uninspired, uninspiring.
≠ first-rate.

secrecy *n* privacy, seclusion, confidentiality, confidence, covertness, concealment, disguise, camouflage, furtiveness, surreptitiousness, stealthiness, stealth, mystery.
≠ openness.

secret *adj* **1** PRIVATE, discreet, covert, hidden, concealed, unseen, shrouded, covered, disguised, camouflaged, undercover, furtive, surreptitious, stealthy, sly, underhand, under-the-counter, hole-and-corner, cloak-and-dagger, clandestine, underground, backstairs, back-door. **2** CLASSIFIED, restricted, confidential, hush-hush (*infml*), unpublished, undisclosed, unrevealed, unknown. **3** CRYPTIC, mysterious, occult, arcane, recondite, deep. **4** SECRETIVE, close, retired, secluded, out-of-the-way.
≠ **1** public, open. **2** well-known.
n confidence, mystery, enigma, code, key, formula, recipe.

secretary *n* personal assistant, PA, typist, stenographer, clerk.

secrete[1] *v* hide, conceal, stash away (*infml*), bury, cover, screen, shroud, veil, disguise, take, appropriate.
≠ uncover, reveal, disclose.

secrete[2] *v* exude, discharge, release, give off, emit, emanate, produce.

secretion *n* exudation, discharge, release, emission.

secretive *adj* tight-lipped, close, cagey (*infml*), uncommunicative, unforthcoming, reticent, reserved, withdrawn, quiet, deep, cryptic, enigmatic.
≠ open, communicative, forthcoming.

sect *n* denomination, cult, division, subdivision, group, splinter group, faction, camp, wing, party, school.

sectarian *adj* factional, partisan, cliquish, exclusive, narrow, limited, parochial, insular, narrow-minded, bigoted, fanatical, doctrinaire, dogmatic, rigid.
≠ non-sectarian, cosmopolitan, broad-minded.

section *n* division, subdivision, chapter, paragraph, passage, instalment, part, component, fraction, fragment, bit, piece, slice, portion, segment, sector, zone, district, area, region, department, branch, wing.
≠ whole.

sector *n* zone, district, quarter, area, region, section, division, subdivision, part.
≠ whole.

secular *adj* lay, temporal, worldly, earthly, civil, state, non-religious, profane.
≠ religious.

secure *adj* **1** SAFE, unharmed, undamaged, protected, sheltered, shielded, immune, impregnable, fortified, fast, tight, fastened, lock[ed], fixed, immovable, stable, stea[dy], firm, well-founded, reliabl[e], dependable, steadfast

conclusive, definite. **2** CONFIDENT, assured, reassured.
≠ **1** insecure, vulnerable. **2** uneasy, ill at ease.
v **1** OBTAIN, acquire, gain, get. **2** FASTEN, attach, fix, make fast, tie, moor, lash, chain, lock (up), padlock, bolt, batten down, nail, rivet.
≠ **1** lose. **2** unfasten.

security *n* **1** SAFETY, immunity, asylum, sanctuary, refuge, cover, protection, defence, surveillance, safe-keeping, preservation, care, custody. **2** *security for a loan*: collateral, surety, pledge, guarantee, warranty, assurance, insurance, precautions, safeguards. **3** CONFIDENCE, conviction, certainty, positiveness.
≠ **1** insecurity.

sedate *adj* staid, dignified, solemn, grave, serious, sober, decorous, proper, seemly, demure, composed, unruffled, serene, tranquil, calm, quiet, cool, collected, imperturbable, unflappable (*infml*), deliberate, slow-moving.
≠ undignified, lively, agitated.

sedative *adj* calming, soothing, anodyne, lenitive, tranquillizing, relaxing, soporific, depressant.
≠ rousing.
n tranquillizer, sleeping-pill, narcotic, barbiturate.

sedentary *adj* sitting, seated, desk-bound, inactive, still, stationary, immobile, unmoving.
≠ active.

sediment *n* deposit, residue, grounds, lees, dregs.

sedition *n* agitation, rabble-rousing, subversion, disloyalty, treachery, treason, insubordination, mutiny, rebellion, revolt.
≠ calm, lo[illegible]y.

sed[illegible] lure, allure, attract, [illegible]guile, ensnare, lead [illegible]eceive, corrupt, [illegible]nt, lure, [illegible] come-on [illegible]n. [illegible]lluring,

attractive, tempting, tantalizing, inviting, come-hither (*infml*), flirtatious, sexy, provocative, beguiling, captivating, bewitching, irresistible.
≠ unattractive, repulsive.

see *v* **1** PERCEIVE, glimpse, discern, spot, make out, distinguish, identify, sight, notice, observe, watch, view, look at, mark, note. **2** IMAGINE, picture, visualize, envisage, foresee, anticipate. **3** *I see your point*: understand, comprehend, grasp, fathom, follow, realize, recognize, appreciate, regard, consider, deem. **4** DISCOVER, find out, learn, ascertain, determine, decide. **5** LEAD, usher, accompany, escort, court, go out with, date. **6** VISIT, consult, interview, meet.
see to attend to, deal with, take care of, look after, arrange, organize, manage, do, fix, repair, sort out.

seed *n* pip, stone, kernel, nucleus, grain, germ, sperm, ovum, egg, ovule, spawn, embryo, source, start, beginning.

seedy *adj* **1** SHABBY, scruffy, tatty, mangy, sleazy, squalid, grotty (*infml*), crummy (*sl*), run-down, dilapidated, decaying. **2** UNWELL, ill, sick, poorly, ailing, off-colour.
≠ **2** well.

seek *v* look for, search for, hunt, pursue, follow, inquire, ask, invite, request, solicit, petition, entreat, want, desire, aim, aspire, try, attempt, endeavour, strive.

seem *v* appear, look, feel, sound, pretend to be.

seeming *adj* apparent, ostensible, outward, superficial, surface, quasi-, pseudo, specious.
≠ real.

seep *v* ooze, leak, exude, well, trickle, dribble, percolate, permeate, soak.

seethe *v* **1** BOIL, simmer, bubble, effervesce, fizz, foam, froth, ferment, rise, swell, surge, teem, swarm. **2** RAGE, fume, smoulder, storm.

see-through *adj* transparent, translucent, sheer, filmy, gauzy, gossamer(y), flimsy.
≠ opaque.

segment *n* section, division, compartment, part, bit, piece, slice, portion, wedge.
≠ whole.

segregate *v* separate, keep apart, cut off, isolate, quarantine, set apart, exclude.
≠ unite, join.

segregation *n* separation, isolation, quarantine, apartheid, discrimination.
≠ unification.

seize *v* grab, snatch, grasp, clutch, grip, hold, take, confiscate, impound, appropriate, commandeer, hijack, annex, abduct, catch, capture, arrest, apprehend, nab (*infml*), collar (*infml*).
≠ let go, release, hand back.

seizure *n* **1** FIT, attack, convulsion, paroxysm, spasm. **2** TAKING, confiscation, appropriation, hijack, annexation, abduction, capture, arrest, apprehension.
≠ **2** release, liberation.

seldom *adv* rarely, infrequently, occasionally, hardly ever.
≠ often, usually.

select *v* choose, pick, single out, decide on, appoint, elect, prefer, opt for.
adj selected, choice, top, prime, first-class, first-rate, hand-picked, élite, exclusive, limited, privileged, special, excellent, superior, posh (*infml*).
≠ second-rate, ordinary, general.

selection *n* choice, pick, option, preference, assortment, variety, range, line-up, miscellany, medley, potpourri, collection, anthology.

selective *adj* particular, choosy (*infml*), careful, discerning, discriminating.
≠ indiscriminate.

self *n* ego, personality, identity, person.

self-centred *adj* selfish, self-seeking, self-serving, self-interested, egotistic(al), narcissistic, self-absorbed, egocentric.
≠ altruistic.

self-confident *adj* confident, self-reliant, self-assured, assured, self-possessed, cool, fearless.
≠ unsure, self-conscious.

self-conscious *adj* uncomfortable, ill at ease, awkward, embarrassed, shamefaced, sheepish, shy, bashful, coy, retiring, shrinking, self-effacing, nervous, insecure.
≠ natural, unaffected, confident.

self-control *n* calmness, composure, cool, patience, self-restraint, restraint, self-denial, temperance, self-discipline, self-mastery, will-power.

self-denial *n* moderation, temperance, abstemiousness, asceticism, self-sacrifice, unselfishness, selflessness.
≠ self-indulgence.

self-evident *adj* obvious, manifest, clear, undeniable, axiomatic, unquestionable, incontrovertible, inescapable.

self-government *n* autonomy, independence, home rule, democracy.
≠ subjection.

self-indulgent *adj* hedonistic, dissolute, dissipated, profligate, extravagant, intemperate, immoderate.
≠ abstemious.

selfish *adj* self-interested, self-seeking, self-serving, mean, miserly, mercenary, greedy, covetous, self-centred, egocentric, egotistic(al).
≠ unselfish, selfless, generous, considerate.

selfless *adj* unselfish, altruistic, self-denying, self-sacrificing, generous, philanthropic.
≠ selfish, self-centred.

self-respect *n* pride, dignity, self-esteem, self-assurance, self-confidence.

self-righteous *adj* smug, complacent, superior, goody-goody (*infml*), pious, sanctimonious, holier-than-thou, pietistic, hypocritical, pharisaical.

self-sacrifice *n* self-denial, self-renunciation, selflessness, altruism, unselfishness, generosity.
≠ selfishness.

self-satisfied *adj* smug, complacer self-congratulatory, self-righteou
≠ humble.

self-styled *adj* self-appoint professed, so-called, woul

self-supporting *adj* se financing, independe
≠ dependent.

sell *v* barter, exchange, trade, auction, vend, retail, stock, handle, deal in, trade in, traffic in, merchandise, hawk, peddle, push, advertise, promote, market.
≠ buy.

seller *n* vendor, merchant, trader, supplier, stockist.
≠ buyer, purchaser.

> *Types of seller include*: agent, auctioneer, bagman, barrow-boy, broker, cold caller, colporteur, commercial traveller, costermonger, dealer, demonstrator, door-to-door salesman/saleswoman, estate agent, factor, hawker, huckster, jobber, knight of the road, market trader, merchandizer, milkman, milklady, pedlar, peddler (*US*), rep (*infml*), representative, retailer, saleslady, salesman, saleswoman, shop assistant, shopkeeper, storekeeper, street trader, tallyman, telephone sales-person, ticket agent, tout, tradesman, tradeswoman, traveller, wholesaler. *see also* **shops**.

semblance *n* appearance, air, show, pretence, guise, mask, front, façade, veneer, apparition, image, resemblance, likeness, similarity.

send *v* **1** POST, mail, dispatch, consign, remit, forward, convey, deliver.
2 TRANSMIT, broadcast, communicate.
3 PROPEL, drive, move, throw, fling, hurl, launch, fire, shoot, discharge, emit, direct.
send for summon, call for, request, order, command.
≠ dismiss.
send up satirize, mock, ridicule, parody, take off, mimic, imitate.

send-off *n* farewell, leave-taking, …parture, start, goodbye.

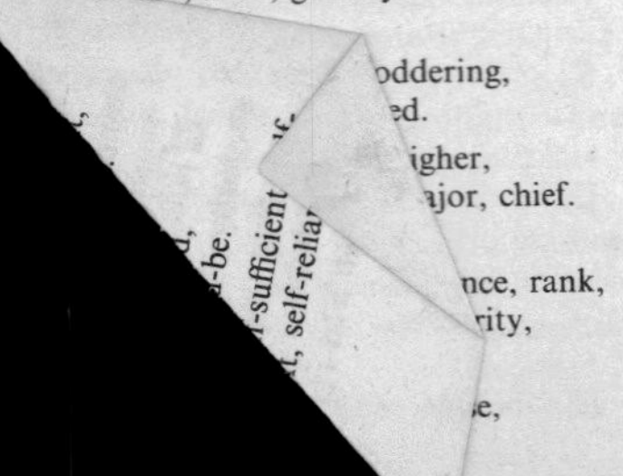

impression, perception, awareness, consciousness, emotion. **2** *the report caused a sensation*: commotion, stir, agitation, excitement, thrill, furore, outrage, scandal.

sensational *adj* **1** EXCITING, thrilling, electrifying, breathtaking, startling, amazing, astounding, staggering, dramatic, spectacular, impressive, exceptional, excellent, wonderful, marvellous, smashing (*infml*).
2 SCANDALOUS, shocking, horrifying, revealing, melodramatic, lurid.
≠ **1** ordinary, run-of-the-mill.

sense *n* **1** FEELING, sensation, impression, perception, awareness, consciousness, appreciation, faculty. **2** REASON, logic, mind, brain(s), wit(s), wisdom, intelligence, cleverness, understanding, discernment, judgement, intuition. **3** MEANING, significance, definition, interpretation, implication, point, purpose, substance.
≠ **2** foolishness. **3** nonsense.
v feel, suspect, intuit, perceive, detect, notice, observe, realize, appreciate, understand, comprehend, grasp.

senseless *adj* **1** FOOLISH, stupid, unwise, silly, idiotic, mad, crazy, daft (*infml*), ridiculous, ludicrous, absurd, meaningless, nonsensical, fatuous, irrational, illogical, unreasonable, pointless, purposeless, futile.
2 UNCONSCIOUS, out, stunned, anaesthetized, deadened, numb, unfeeling.
≠ **1** sensible, meaningful. **2** conscious.

sensible *adj* wise, prudent, judicious, well-advised, shrewd, far-sighted, intelligent, level-headed, down-to-earth, commonsense, sober, sane, rational, logical, reasonable, realistic, practical, functional, sound.
≠ senseless, foolish, unwise.

sensitive *adj* **1** SUSCEPTIBLE, vulnerable, impressionable, tender, emotional, thin-skinned, temperamental, touchy, irritable, sensitized, responsive, aware, perceptive, discerning, appreciative.
2 DELICATE, fine, exact, precise.
≠ **1** insensitive, thick-skinned.
2 imprecise, approximate.

sensual *adj* self-indulgent, voluptuous, worldly, physical, animal, carnal, fleshly, bodily, sexual, erotic, sexy, lustful, randy (*infml*), lecherous, lewd, licentious.
≠ ascetic.

sensuous *adj* pleasurable, gratifying, voluptuous, rich, lush, luxurious, sumptuous.
≠ ascetic, plain, simple.

sentence *n* judgement, decision, verdict, condemnation, pronouncement, ruling, decree, order.
v judge, pass judgement on, condemn, doom, punish, penalize.

sentiment *n* **1** THOUGHT, idea, feeling, opinion, view, judgement, belief, persuasion, attitude. **2** EMOTION, sensibility, tenderness, soft-heartedness, romanticism, sentimentality, mawkishness.

sentimental *adj* tender, soft-hearted, emotional, gushing, touching, pathetic, tear-jerking, weepy (*infml*), maudlin, mawkish, nostalgic, romantic, lovey-dovey (*infml*), slushy, mushy, sloppy, schmaltzy, soppy, corny (*infml*).
≠ unsentimental, realistic, cynical.

sentry *n* sentinel, guard, picket, watchman, watch, look-out.

separable *adj* divisible, detachable, removable, distinguishable, distinct.
≠ inseparable.

separate *v* divide, sever, part, split (up), divorce, part company, diverge, disconnect, uncouple, disunite, disaffiliate, disentangle, segregate, isolate, cut off, abstract, remove, detach, withdraw, secede.
≠ join, unite, combine.
adj single, individual, particular, independent, alone, solitary, segregated, isolated, apart, divorced, divided, disunited, disconnected, disjointed, detached, unattached, unconnected, unrelated, different, disparate, distinct, discrete, several, sundry.
≠ together, attached.

separation *n* division, severance, parting, leave-taking, farewell, split-up, break-up, divorce, split, rift, gap, divergence, disconnection, disengagement, dissociation, estrangement, segregation, isolation, detachment.
≠ unification.

septic *adj* infected, poisoned, festering, putrefying, putrid.

sequel *n* follow-up, continuation, development, result, consequence, outcome, issue, upshot, pay-off, end, conclusion.

sequence *n* succession, series, run, progression, chain, string, train, line, procession, order, arrangement, course, track, cycle, set.

serene *adj* calm, tranquil, cool, composed, placid, untroubled, undisturbed, still, quiet, peaceful.
≠ troubled, disturbed.

series *n* set, cycle, succession, sequence, run, progression, chain, string, line, train, order, arrangement, course.

serious *adj* **1** IMPORTANT, significant, weighty, momentous, crucial, critical, urgent, pressing, acute, grave, worrying, difficult, dangerous, grim, severe, deep, far-reaching. **2** UNSMILING, long-faced, humourless, solemn, sober, stern, thoughtful, pensive, earnest, sincere.
≠ **1** trivial, slight. **2** smiling, facetious, frivolous.

sermon *n* address, discourse, lecture, harangue, homily, talking-to (*infml*).

serrated *adj* toothed, notched, indented, jagged.
≠ smooth.

servant *n* attendant, retainer, hireling, menial, help, helper, assistant, ancillary.
≠ master, mistress.

Kinds of servant include: au pair, barmaid, barman, batman, bell-hop (*US*), boots, butler, care assistant, carer, chambermaid, char (*infml*), charlady, chauffeur, chauffeuse, chef, cleaner, coachman, commissionaire, cook, daily (*infml*), dogsbody (*infml*), domestic, errand boy, factotum, fag, flunkey, footman, governess, groom, home help, house boy, housekeeper, housemaid, kitchen-maid, lackey, lady-in-waiting, lady's maid, maid, manservant, nanny, ostler, page, parlour-maid, scullery maid, scullion, seneschal, skivvy (*infml*), slave, steward, stewardess, tweeny (*infml*), valet, waiter, waitress, wet nurse.

serve *v* **1** WAIT ON, attend, minister to, work for, help, aid, assist, benefit, further. **2** *serve a purpose*: fulfil, complete, answer, satisfy, discharge, perform, act, function. **3** DISTRIBUTE, dole out, present, deliver, provide, supply.

service *n* **1** EMPLOYMENT, work, labour, business, duty, function, performance. **2** USE, usefulness, utility, advantage, benefit, help, assistance. **3** SERVICING, maintenance, overhaul, check. **4** *church service*: worship, observance, ceremony, rite.
v maintain, overhaul, check, repair, recondition, tune.

serviceable *adj* usable, useful, helpful, profitable, advantageous, beneficial, utilitarian, simple, plain, unadorned, strong, tough, durable, hard-wearing, dependable, efficient, functional, practical, convenient.
≠ unserviceable, unusable.

servile *adj* obsequious, sycophantic, toadying, cringing, fawning, grovelling, bootlicking, slavish, subservient, subject, submissive, humble, abject, low, mean, base, menial.
≠ assertive, aggressive.

session *n* sitting, hearing, meeting, assembly, conference, discussion, period, time, term, semester, year.

set *v* **1** PUT, place, locate, situate, position, arrange, prepare, lodge, fix, stick, park, deposit. **2** SCHEDULE, appoint, designate, specify, name, prescribe, ordain, assign, allocate, impose, fix, establish, determine, decide, conclude, settle, resolve. **3** ADJUST, regulate, synchronize, co-ordinate. **4** *the sun sets*: go down, sink, dip, subside, disappear, vanish. **5** CONGEAL, thicken, gel, stiffen, solidify, harden, crystallize.
≠ **4** rise.
n batch, series, sequence, kit, outfit, compendium, assortment, collection, class, category, group, band, gang, crowd, circle, clique, faction.
adj scheduled, appointed, arranged, prepared, prearranged, fixed, established, definite, decided, agreed, settled, firm, strict, rigid, inflexible, prescribed, formal, conventional, traditional, customary, usual, routine, regular, standard, stock, stereotyped, hackneyed.
≠ movable, free, spontaneous, undecided.
set about begin, start, embark on, undertake, tackle, attack.
set aside 1 PUT ASIDE, lay aside, keep (back), save, reserve, set apart, separate, select, earmark. **2** ANNUL, abrogate, cancel, revoke, reverse, overturn, overrule, reject, discard.
set back delay, hold up, slow, retard, hinder, impede.
set off 1 LEAVE, depart, set out, start (out), begin. **2** DETONATE, light, ignite, touch off, trigger off, explode. **3** DISPLAY, show off, enhance, contrast.
set on set upon, attack, turn on, go for, fall upon, lay into, beat up (*infml*).
set out 1 LEAVE, depart, set off, start (out), begin. **2** LAY OUT, arrange, display, exhibit, present, describe, explain.
set up raise, elevate, erect, build, construct, assemble, compose, form, create, establish, institute, found, inaugurate, initiate, begin, start, introduce, organize, arrange, prepare.

setback *n* delay, hold-up, problem, snag, hitch, hiccup, reverse, misfortune, upset, disappointment, defeat.
≠ boost, advance, help, advantage.

setting *n* mounting, frame, surroundings, milieu, environment, background, context, perspective, period, position, location, locale, site, scene, scenery.

settle *v* **1** ARRANGE, order, adjust, reconcile, resolve, complete, conclude. **2** SINK, subside, drop, fall, descend, land, alight. **3** CHOOSE, appoint, fix, establish, determine, decide, agree, confirm. **4** COLONIZE, occupy, populate, people, inhabit, live, reside. **5** *settle a bill*: pay, clear, discharge.

settlement *n* **1** RESOLUTION, agreement, arrangement, decision, conclusion, termination, satisfaction. **2** PAYMENT, clearance, clearing, discharge. **3** COLONY, outpost, community, kibbutz, camp, encampment, hamlet, village.

settler *n* colonist, colonizer, pioneer, frontiersman, frontierswoman, planter, immigrant, incomer, newcomer, squatter.
≠ native.

set-up *n* system, structure, organization, arrangement, business, conditions, circumstances.

sever *v* cut, cleave, split, rend, part, separate, divide, cut off, amputate, detach, disconnect, disjoin, disunite, dissociate, estrange, alienate, break off, dissolve, end, terminate.
≠ join, unite, combine, attach.

several *adj* some, many, various, assorted, sundry, diverse, different, distinct, separate, particular, individual.

severe *adj* **1** STERN, disapproving, sober, strait-laced, strict, rigid, unbending, harsh, tough, hard, difficult, demanding, arduous, punishing, rigorous, grim, forbidding, cruel, biting, cutting, scathing, pitiless, merciless, oppressive, relentless, inexorable, acute, bitter, intense, extreme, fierce, violent, distressing, serious, grave, critical, dangerous. **2** PLAIN, simple, unadorned, unembellished, functional, restrained, austere, ascetic.
≠ **1** kind, compassionate, sympathetic, lenient, mild. **2** decorated, ornate.

sew *v* stitch, tack, baste, hem, darn, embroider.

sex *n* **1** GENDER, sexuality. **2** SEXUAL INTERCOURSE, intercourse, sexual relations, copulation, coitus, lovemaking, fornication, reproduction, union, intimacy.

sexual *adj* sex, reproductive, procreative, genital, coital, venereal, carnal, sensual, erotic.

sexuality

> *Sexual orientations include*: bisexual, AC/DC (*sl*), hermaphrodite, unisexual, heterosexual, homosexual, gay, queer (*sl*), cissy (*sl*), pretty boy (*sl*), nancy (*sl*), nancy boy (*sl*), pansy (*sl*), faggot (*US sl*), rent boy, lesbian, lez (*sl*), dyke (*sl*), butch (*sl*), transsexual, transvestite, cross-dresser.

sexy *adj* sensual, voluptuous, nubile, beddable (*infml*), seductive, inviting, flirtatious, arousing, provoking, provocative, titillating, pornographic, erotic, salacious, suggestive.
≠ sexless.

shabby *adj* **1** RAGGED, tattered, frayed, worn, worn-out, mangy, moth-eaten, scruffy, tatty, disreputable, dilapidated, run-down, seedy, dirty, dingy, poky. **2** *a shabby trick*: contemptible, despicable, rotten, mean, low, cheap, shoddy, shameful, dishonourable.
≠ **1** smart. **2** honourable, fair.

shack *n* hut, cabin, shanty, hovel, shed, lean-to.

shade *n* **1** SHADINESS, shadow, darkness, obscurity, semi-darkness, dimness, gloom, gloominess, twilight, dusk, gloaming. **2** AWNING, canopy, cover, shelter, screen, blind, curtain, shield, visor, umbrella, parasol. **3** COLOUR, hue, tint, tone, tinge. **4** TRACE, dash, hint, suggestion, suspicion, nuance, gradation, degree, amount, variety. **5** GHOST, spectre, phantom, spirit, apparition, semblance.
v shield, screen, protect, cover, shroud, veil, hide, conceal, obscure, cloud, dim, darken, shadow, overshadow.

shadow *n* **1** SHADE, darkness, obscurity, semi-darkness, dimness, gloom, twilight, dusk, gloaming, cloud, cover, protection. **2** SILHOUETTE, shape, image, representation. **3** TRACE, hint, suggestion, suspicion, vestige, remnant.

v **1** OVERSHADOW, overhang, shade, shield, screen, obscure, darken. **2** FOLLOW, tail, dog, stalk, trail, watch.

shadowy *adj* dark, gloomy, murky, obscure, dim, faint, indistinct, ill-defined, vague, hazy, nebulous, intangible, unsubstantial, ghostly, spectral, illusory, dreamlike, imaginary, unreal.

shady *adj* **1** SHADED, shadowy, dim, dark, cool, leafy. **2** (*infml*) DUBIOUS, questionable, suspect, suspicious, fishy (*infml*), dishonest, crooked, unreliable, untrustworthy, disreputable, unscrupulous, unethical, underhand.
≠ **1** sunny, sunlit, bright. **2** honest, trustworthy, honourable.

shaft *n* handle, shank, stem, upright, pillar, pole, rod, bar, stick, arrow, dart, beam, ray, duct, passage.

shaggy *adj* hairy, long-haired, hirsute, bushy, woolly, unshorn, dishevelled, unkempt.
≠ bald, shorn, close-cropped.

shake *v* **1** WAVE, flourish, brandish, wag, waggle, agitate, rattle, joggle, jolt, jerk, twitch, convulse, heave, throb, vibrate, oscillate, fluctuate, waver, wobble, totter, sway, rock, tremble, quiver, quake, shiver, shudder. **2** *the news shook her*: upset, distress, shock, frighten, unnerve, intimidate, disturb, discompose, unsettle, agitate, stir, rouse.
shake off get rid of, dislodge, lose, elude, give the slip, leave behind, outdistance, outstrip.

shake-up (*infml*) *n* reorganization, rearrangement, reshuffle, disturbance, upheaval.

shaky *adj* **1** TREMBLING, quivering, faltering, tentative, uncertain. **2** UNSTABLE, unsteady, insecure, precarious, wobbly, rocky, tottery, rickety, weak. **3** DUBIOUS, questionable, suspect, unreliable, unsound, unsupported.
≠ **2** firm, strong.

shallow *adj* superficial, surface, skin-deep, slight, flimsy, trivial, frivolous, foolish, idle, empty, meaningless, unscholarly, ignorant, simple.
≠ deep, profound.

sham *n* pretence, fraud, counterfeit, forgery, fake, imitation, simulation, hoax, humbug.
adj false, fake, counterfeit, spurious, bogus, phoney (*infml*), pretended, feigned, put-on, simulated, artificial, mock, imitation, synthetic.
≠ genuine, authentic, real.
v pretend, feign, affect, put on, simulate, imitate, fake, counterfeit.

shame *n* disgrace, dishonour, discredit, stain, stigma, disrepute, infamy, scandal, ignominy, humiliation, degradation, shamefacedness, remorse, guilt, embarrassment, mortification.
≠ honour, credit, distinction, pride.
v embarrass, mortify, abash, confound, humiliate, ridicule, humble, put to shame, show up, disgrace, dishonour, discredit, debase, degrade, sully, taint, stain.

shamefaced *adj* ashamed, conscience-stricken, remorseful, contrite, apologetic, sorry, sheepish, red-faced, blushing, embarrassed, mortified, abashed, humiliated, uncomfortable.
≠ unashamed, proud.

shameful *adj* **1** *a shameful waste of money*: disgraceful, outrageous, scandalous, indecent, abominable, atrocious, wicked, mean, low, vile, reprehensible, contemptible, unworthy, ignoble. **2** EMBARRASSING, mortifying, humiliating, ignominious.
≠ **1** honourable, creditable, worthy.

shameless *adj* **1** UNASHAMED, unabashed, unrepentant, impenitent, barefaced, flagrant, blatant, brazen, brash, audacious, insolent, defiant, hardened, incorrigible. **2** IMMODEST, indecent, improper, unprincipled, wanton, dissolute, corrupt, depraved.
≠ **1** ashamed, shamefaced, contrite. **2** modest.

shape *n* **1** FORM, outline, silhouette, profile, model, mould, pattern, cut, lines, contours, figure, physique, build, frame, format, configuration. **2** APPEARANCE, guise, likeness, semblance. **3** *in good shape*: condition, state, form, health, trim, fettle.

Geometrical shapes include: polygon, circle, semicircle, quadrant, oval, ellipse, crescent, triangle, equilateral triangle, isosceles triangle, scalene triangle, quadrilateral, square, rectangle, oblong, rhombus, diamond, kite, trapezium, parallelogram, pentagon, hexagon, heptagon, octagon, nonagon, decagon; polyhedron, cube, cuboid, prism, pyramid, tetrahedron, pentahedron, octahedron, cylinder, cone, sphere, hemisphere.

v form, fashion, model, mould, cast, forge, sculpt, carve, whittle, make, produce, construct, create, devise, frame, plan, prepare, adapt, adjust, regulate, accommodate, modify, remodel.

shapeless *adj* formless, amorphous, unformed, nebulous, unstructured, irregular, misshapen, deformed, dumpy.

share *v* divide, split, go halves, partake, participate, share out, distribute, dole out, give out, deal out, apportion, allot, allocate, assign.
n portion, ration, quota, allowance, allocation, allotment, lot, part, division, proportion, percentage, cut (*infml*), dividend, due, contribution, whack (*infml*).

sharks

Types of shark include: basking, blue, dogfish, fox, ghost, goblin, Greenland, grey reef, hammerhead, leopard, mackerel, mako, man-eating, nurse, porbeagle, requiem, saw, thresher, tiger, whale.

sharp *adj* **1** *a sharp needle*: pointed, keen, edged, knife-edged, razor-sharp, cutting, serrated, jagged, barbed, spiky. **2** CLEAR, clear-cut, well-defined, distinct, marked, crisp. **3** QUICK-WITTED, alert, shrewd, astute, perceptive, observant, discerning, penetrating, clever, crafty, cunning, artful, sly. **4** SUDDEN, abrupt, violent, fierce, intense, extreme, severe, acute, piercing, stabbing. **5** PUNGENT, piquant, sour, tart, vinegary, bitter, acerbic, acid. **6** TRENCHANT, incisive, cutting, biting, caustic, sarcastic, sardonic, scathing, vitriolic, acrimonious.
≠ **1** blunt. **2** blurred. **3** slow, stupid. **4** gentle. **5** bland. **6** mild.
adv punctually, promptly, on the dot, exactly, precisely, abruptly, suddenly, unexpectedly.
≠ approximately, roughly.

sharpen *v* edge, whet, hone, grind, file.
≠ blunt.

shatter *v* break, smash, splinter, shiver, crack, split, burst, explode, blast, crush, demolish, destroy, devastate, wreck, ruin, overturn, upset.

sheath *n* **1** SCABBARD, case, sleeve, envelope, shell, casing, covering. **2** CONDOM, rubber (*sl*), French letter (*sl*).

shed[1] *v* cast (off), moult, slough, discard, drop, spill, pour, shower, scatter, diffuse, emit, radiate, shine, throw.

shed[2] *n* outhouse, lean-to, hut, shack.

sheen *n* lustre, gloss, shine, shimmer, brightness, brilliance, shininess, polish, burnish.
≠ dullness, tarnish.

sheepish *adj* ashamed, shamefaced, embarrassed, mortified, chastened, abashed, uncomfortable, self-conscious, silly, foolish.
≠ unabashed, brazen, bold.

sheer *adj* **1** UTTER, complete, total, absolute, thorough, mere, pure, unadulterated, downright, out-and-out, rank, thoroughgoing, unqualified, unmitigated. **2** *a sheer drop*: vertical, perpendicular, precipitous, abrupt, steep. **3** THIN, fine, flimsy, gauzy, gossamer, translucent, transparent, see-through.
≠ **2** gentle, gradual. **3** thick, heavy.

sheet *n* cover, blanket, covering, coating, coat, film, layer, stratum, skin, membrane, lamina, veneer, overlay, plate, leaf, page, folio, piece, panel, slab, pane, expanse, surface.

shelf *n* ledge, mantelpiece, sill, step, bench, counter, bar, bank, sandbank, reef, terrace.

shell *n* covering, hull, husk, pod, rind, crust, case, casing, body, chassis, frame, framework, structure, skeleton.
v **1** *shell nuts*: hull, husk, pod. **2** BOMB, bombard, barrage, blitz, attack.

shelter *v* cover, shroud, screen, shade, shadow, protect, safeguard, defend, guard, shield, harbour, hide, accommodate, put up.
≠ expose.
n cover, roof, shade, shadow, protection, defence, guard, security, safety, sanctuary, asylum, haven, refuge, retreat, accommodation, lodging.
≠ exposure.

sheltered *adj* covered, shaded, shielded, protected, cosy, snug, warm, quiet, secluded, isolated, retired, withdrawn, reclusive, cloistered, unworldly.
≠ exposed.

shelve *v* postpone, defer, put off, suspend, halt, put aside, pigeonhole, put on ice, mothball.
≠ expedite, implement.

shield *n* buckler, escutcheon, defence, bulwark, rampart, screen, guard, cover, shelter, protection, safeguard.
v defend, guard, protect, safeguard, screen, shade, shadow, cover, shelter.
≠ expose.

shift *v* change, vary, fluctuate, alter, adjust, move, budge, remove, dislodge, displace, relocate, reposition, rearrange, transpose, transfer, switch, swerve, veer.
n change, fluctuation, alteration, modification, move, removal, displacement, rearrangement, transposition, transfer, switch.

shifty *adj* untrustworthy, dishonest, deceitful, scheming, contriving, tricky, wily, crafty, cunning, devious, evasive, slippery, furtive, underhand, dubious, shady (*infml*).
≠ dependable, honest, open.

shimmer *v* glisten, gleam, glimmer, glitter, scintillate, twinkle.
n lustre, gleam, glimmer, glitter, glow.

shine *v* **1** BEAM, radiate, glow, flash, glare, gleam, glint, glitter, sparkle, twinkle, shimmer, glisten, glimmer. **2** POLISH, burnish, buff, brush, rub. **3** *shine at athletics*: excel, stand out.
n **1** LIGHT, radiance, glow, brightness, glare, gleam, sparkle, shimmer. **2** GLOSS, polish, burnish, sheen, lustre, glaze.

shining *adj* **1** BRIGHT, radiant, glowing, beaming, flashing, gleaming, glittering, glistening, shimmering, twinkling, sparkling, brilliant, resplendent, splendid, glorious. **2** *a shining example*: conspicuous, outstanding, leading, eminent, celebrated, distinguished, illustrious.
≠ **1** dark.

shiny *adj* polished, burnished, sheeny, lustrous, glossy, sleek, bright, gleaming, glistening.
≠ dull, matt.

ship *n* vessel, craft, liner, steamer, tanker, trawler, ferry, boat, yacht.

> *Parts of a ship include*: anchor, berth, bilge, boiler room, bollard, bridge, brig, bulkhead, bulwarks, bunk, cabin, capstan, chain locker, chart room, cleat, companion ladder, companion way, crow's nest, davit, deck, after deck, boat deck, flight deck, gun deck, lower deck, main deck, poop deck, promenade deck, quarter deck, top deck, engine room, figurehead, forecastle (fo'c'sle), funnel, galley, gangplank, gangway, gunwale (gunnel), hammock, hatch, hatchway, hawser, head, hold, keel, landing, mast, oar, paddle wheel, pilot house, Plimsoll line, port, porthole, prow, quarter, radio room, rigger, rowlock, rudder, sail, stabilizer, stanchion, starboard, stateroom, stern, superstructure, tiller, transom, wardroom, waterline, wheel, winch. *see also* **sail**.

shirk *v* dodge, evade, avoid, duck (*infml*), shun, slack, skive (*infml*).

shiver *v* shudder, tremble, quiver, quake, shake, vibrate, palpitate, flutter.
n shudder, quiver, shake, tremor, twitch, start, vibration, flutter.

shock *v* disgust, revolt, sicken, offend, appal, outrage, scandalize, horrify, astound, stagger, stun, stupefy, numb,

paralyse, traumatize, jolt, jar, shake, agitate, unsettle, disquiet, unnerve, confound, dismay.
≠ delight, please, gratify, reassure.
n fright, start, jolt, impact, collision, surprise, bombshell, thunderbolt, blow, trauma, upset, distress, dismay, consternation, disgust, outrage.
≠ delight, pleasure, reassurance.

shocking *adj* appalling, outrageous, scandalous, horrifying, disgraceful, deplorable, intolerable, unbearable, atrocious, abominable, monstrous, unspeakable, detestable, abhorrent, dreadful, awful, terrible, frightful, ghastly, hideous, horrible, disgusting, revolting, repulsive, sickening, nauseating, offensive, distressing.
≠ acceptable, satisfactory, pleasant, delightful.

shoddy *adj* inferior, second-rate, cheap, tawdry, tatty, trashy, rubbishy, poor, careless, slipshod, slapdash.
≠ superior, well-made.

shoot *v* **1** FIRE, discharge, launch, propel, hurl, fling, project. **2** DART, bolt, dash, tear, rush, race, sprint, speed, charge, hurtle. **3** HIT, kill, blast, bombard, gun down, snipe at, pick off.
n sprout, bud, offshoot, branch, twig, sprig, slip, scion.

shops

> *Types of shop include*: bazaar, market, indoor market, mini-market, corner shop, shopping mall, department store, supermarket, superstore, hypermarket, cash-and-carry; butcher, baker, grocer, greengrocer, fishmonger, dairy, delicatessen, health-food shop, farm shop, fish and chip shop, take-away, off-licence, tobacconist, sweet shop, confectioner, tuck shop; bookshop, newsagent, stationer, chemist, pharmacy, tailor, outfitter, dress shop, boutique, milliner, shoe shop, haberdasher, draper, florist, jeweller, toy shop, hardware shop, ironmonger, saddler, radio and TV shop, video shop; launderette, hairdresser, barber, betting shop, bookmaker, bookie (*infml*), pawnbroker, post office.

shore[1] *n* seashore, beach, sand(s), shingle, strand, waterfront, front, promenade, coast, seaboard, lakeside, bank.

shore[2] *v* support, hold, prop, stay, underpin, buttress, brace, strengthen, reinforce.

short *adj* **1** BRIEF, cursory, fleeting, momentary, transitory, ephemeral, concise, succinct, terse, pithy, compact, compressed, shortened, curtailed, abbreviated, abridged, summarized. **2** BRUSQUE, curt, gruff, snappy, sharp, abrupt, blunt, direct, rude, impolite, discourteous, uncivil. **3** SMALL, little, low, petite, diminutive, squat, dumpy. **4** INADEQUATE, insufficient, deficient, lacking, wanting, low, poor, meagre, scant, sparse.
≠ **1** long, lasting. **2** polite. **3** tall. **4** adequate, ample.

shortage *n* inadequacy, insufficiency, deficiency, shortfall, deficit, lack, want, need, scarcity, paucity, poverty, dearth, absence.
≠ sufficiency, abundance, surplus.

shortcoming *n* defect, imperfection, fault, flaw, drawback, failing, weakness, foible.

shorten *v* cut, trim, prune, crop, dock, curtail, truncate, abbreviate, abridge, reduce, lessen, decrease, diminish, take up.
≠ lengthen, enlarge, amplify.

shortly *adv* soon, before long, presently, by and by.

short-sighted *adj* **1** MYOPIC, near-sighted. **2** IMPROVIDENT, imprudent, injudicious, unwise, impolitic, ill-advised, careless, hasty, ill-considered.
≠ **1** long-sighted, far-sighted.

shot *n* **1** BULLET, missile, projectile, ball, pellet, slug (*infml*), discharge, blast. **2** (*infml*) ATTEMPT, try, effort, endeavour, go (*infml*), bash (*infml*), crack (*infml*), stab (*infml*), guess, turn.

shoulder *v* **1** PUSH, shove, jostle, thrust, press. **2** ACCEPT, assume, take on, bear, carry, sustain.

shout *n, v* call, cry, scream, shriek, yell, roar, bellow, bawl, howl, bay, cheer.

shove *v* push, thrust, drive, propel, force, barge, jostle, elbow, shoulder, press, crowd.

shovel *n* spade, scoop, bucket. *v* dig, scoop, dredge, clear, move, shift, heap.

show *v* **1** REVEAL, expose, uncover, disclose, divulge, present, offer, exhibit, manifest, display, indicate, register, demonstrate, prove, illustrate, exemplify, explain, instruct, teach, clarify, elucidate. **2** *show him out*: lead, guide, conduct, usher, escort, accompany, attend.
≠ **1** hide, cover.
n **1** OSTENTATION, parade, display, flamboyance, panache, pizzazz (*infml*), showiness, exhibitionism, affectation, pose, pretence, illusion, semblance, façade, impression, appearance, air. **2** DEMONSTRATION, presentation, exhibition, exposition, fair, display, parade, pageant, extravaganza, spectacle, entertainment, performance, production, staging, showing, representation.
show off parade, strut, swagger, brag, boast, swank (*infml*), flaunt, brandish, display, exhibit, demonstrate, advertise, set off, enhance.
show up 1 (*infml*) ARRIVE, come, turn up, appear, materialize (*infml*). **2** HUMILIATE, embarrass, mortify, shame, disgrace, let down. **3** REVEAL, show, expose, unmask, lay bare, highlight, pinpoint.

showdown *n* confrontation, clash, crisis, climax, culmination.

shower *n* rain, stream, torrent, deluge, hail, volley, barrage.
v spray, sprinkle, rain, pour, deluge, inundate, overwhelm, load, heap, lavish.

show-off *n* swaggerer, braggart, boaster, swanker (*infml*), exhibitionist, peacock, poser, poseur, egotist.

showy *adj* flashy, flamboyant, ostentatious, gaudy, garish, loud, tawdry, fancy, ornate, pretentious, pompous, swanky (*infml*), flash (*infml*).
≠ quiet, restrained.

shred *n* ribbon, tatter, rag, scrap, snippet, sliver, bit, piece, fragment, jot, iota, atom, grain, mite, whit, trace.

shrewd *adj* astute, judicious, well-advised, calculated, far-sighted, smart, clever, intelligent, sharp, keen, acute, alert, perceptive, observant, discerning, discriminating, knowing, calculating, cunning, crafty, artful, sly.
≠ unwise, obtuse, naïve, unsophisticated.

shriek *v, n* scream, screech, squawk, squeal, cry, shout, yell, wail, howl.

shrill *adj* high, high-pitched, treble, sharp, acute, piercing, penetrating, screaming, screeching, strident, ear-splitting.
≠ deep, low, soft, gentle.

shrink *v* **1** CONTRACT, shorten, narrow, decrease, lessen, diminish, dwindle, shrivel, wrinkle, wither. **2** RECOIL, back away, shy away, withdraw, retire, balk, quail, cower, cringe, wince, flinch, shun.
≠ **1** expand, stretch. **2** accept, embrace.

shrivel *v* wrinkle, pucker, wither, wilt, shrink, dwindle, parch, dehydrate, desiccate, scorch, sear, burn, frizzle.

shroud *v* wrap, envelop, swathe, cloak, veil, screen, hide, conceal, blanket, cover.
≠ uncover, expose.
n winding-sheet, pall, mantle, cloak, veil, screen, blanket, covering.

shrubs

> *Shrubs include*: azalea, berberis, broom, buddleia, camellia, clematis, cotoneaster, daphne, dogwood, euonymus, firethorn, flowering currant, forsythia, fuchsia, heather, hebe, holly, honeysuckle, hydrangea, ivy, japonica, jasmine, laburnum, laurel, lavender, lilac, magnolia, mallow, mimosa, mock orange, peony, privet, musk rose, rhododendron, rose, spiraea, viburnum, weigela, witch hazel, wistaria. *see also* **flower**; **plant**.

shudder *v* shiver, shake, tremble, quiver, quake, heave, convulse.
n shiver, quiver, tremor, spasm, convulsion.

shuffle *v* **1** MIX (UP), intermix, jumble, confuse, disorder, rearrange, reorganize, shift around, switch. **2** *shuffle across the room*: shamble, scuffle, scrape, drag, limp, hobble.

shun *v* avoid, evade, elude, steer clear of, shy away from, spurn, ignore, cold-shoulder, ostracize.
≠ accept, embrace.

shut *v* close, slam, seal, fasten, secure, lock, latch, bolt, bar.
≠ open.
shut down close, stop, cease, terminate, halt, discontinue, suspend, switch off, inactivate.
shut in enclose, box in, hem in, fence in, immure, confine, imprison, cage.
shut off seclude, isolate, cut off, separate, segregate.
shut out 1 EXCLUDE, bar, debar, lock out, ostracize, banish. **2** HIDE, conceal, cover, mask, screen, veil.
shut up 1 SILENCE, gag, quiet, hush up, pipe down (*infml*), hold one's tongue, clam up (*infml*). **2** CONFINE, coop up, imprison, incarcerate, jail, intern.

shy *adj* timid, bashful, reticent, reserved, retiring, diffident, coy, self-conscious, inhibited, modest, self-effacing, shrinking, hesitant, cautious, chary, suspicious, nervous.
≠ bold, assertive, confident.

sick *adj* **1** ILL, unwell, indisposed, laid up, poorly, ailing, sickly, under the weather, weak, feeble. **2** VOMITING, queasy, bilious, seasick, airsick. **3** *sick of waiting*: bored, fed up (*infml*), tired, weary, disgusted, nauseated.
≠ **1** well, healthy.

sicken *v* nauseate, revolt, disgust, repel, put off, turn off (*sl*).
≠ delight, attract.

sickening *adj* nauseating, revolting, disgusting, offensive, distasteful, foul, vile, loathsome, repulsive.
≠ delightful, pleasing, attractive.

sickly *adj* **1** UNHEALTHY, infirm, delicate, weak, feeble, frail, wan, pallid, ailing, indisposed, sick, bilious, faint, languid. **2** NAUSEATING, revolting, sweet, syrupy, cloying, mawkish.
≠ **1** healthy, robust, sturdy, strong.

sickness *n* **1** ILLNESS, disease, malady, ailment, complaint, affliction, ill-health, indisposition, infirmity. **2** VOMITING, nausea, queasiness, biliousness.
≠ **1** health.

side *n* **1** EDGE, margin, fringe, periphery, border, boundary, limit, verge, brink, bank, shore, quarter, region, flank, hand, face, facet, surface. **2** STANDPOINT, viewpoint, view, aspect, angle, slant. **3** TEAM, party, faction, camp, cause, interest.
adj lateral, flanking, marginal, secondary, subsidiary, subordinate, lesser, minor, incidental, indirect, oblique.
side with agree with, team up with, support, vote for, favour, prefer.

sidestep *v* avoid, dodge, duck, evade, elude, skirt, bypass.
≠ tackle, deal with.

sidetrack *v* deflect, head off, divert, distract.

sideways *adv* sidewards, edgeways, laterally, obliquely.
adj sideward, side, lateral, slanted, oblique, indirect, sidelong.

sidle *v* slink, edge, inch, creep, sneak.

sieve *v* sift, strain, separate, remove.
n colander, strainer, sifter, riddle, screen.

sift *v* **1** SIEVE, strain, filter, riddle screen, winnow, separate, sort. **2** EXAMINE, scrutinize, investigate, analyse, probe, review.

sigh *v* breathe, exhale, moan, complain, lament, grieve.

sight *n* **1** VISION, eyesight, seeing, observation, perception. **2** VIEW, look, glance, glimpse, range, field of vision, visibility. **3** APPEARANCE, spectacle, show, display, exhibition, scene, eyesore, monstrosity, fright (*infml*).
v see, observe, spot, glimpse, perceive, discern, distinguish, make out.

sightseer *n* tourist, visitor, holidaymaker, tripper, excursionist.

sign *n* **1** SYMBOL, token, character, figure, representation, emblem, badge, insignia, logo. **2** INDICATION, mark,

signal, gesture, evidence, manifestation, clue, pointer, hint, suggestion, trace.
3 NOTICE, poster, board, placard.
4 PORTENT, omen, forewarning, foreboding.
v autograph, initial, endorse, write.
sign up enlist, enrol, join (up), volunteer, register, sign on, recruit, take on, hire, engage, employ.

signal *n* sign, indication, mark, gesture, light, alert, warning, tip-off.

> *Kinds of signal and warning include*: alarm, burglar alarm, car alarm, fire alarm, personal alarm, security alarm, alarm-bell, alarm clock, amber light, beacon, Belisha beacon, lighthouse beacon, bell, bicycle bell, curfew bell, bleeper, buoy, buzzer, cue, distress signal, drumbeat, final warning, fire, flag, flare, flashing light, foghorn, gale warning, go-ahead, gong, green light, hand signal, heliograph, honk, hooter, horn, car horn, hurricane warning, indicator, klaxon, knell, larum, larum-bell, Lutine bell, mayday, Morse code, pager, password, red alert, red flag, red light, reveille, rocket, semaphore signal, a shot across the bows, shout, signal box, signal letters, siren, smoke signal, SOS, starter's gun, storm cone, storm signal, storm warning, tattoo, time signal (pips), tocsin, toot, trafficator, traffic lights, Very light, vigia, warning light, whistle, police whistle, winker, written warning, yellow card, yellow flag.

v wave, gesticulate, gesture, beckon, motion, nod, sign, indicate, communicate.

signature *n* autograph, initials, mark, endorsement, inscription.

significance *n* importance, relevance, consequence, matter, interest, consideration, weight, force, meaning, implication, sense, point, message.
≠ insignificance, unimportance, pettiness.

significant *adj* **1** IMPORTANT, relevant, consequential, momentous, weighty, serious, noteworthy, critical, vital, marked, considerable, appreciable.
2 MEANINGFUL, symbolic, expressive, suggestive, indicative, symptomatic.
≠ **1** insignificant, unimportant, trivial.
2 meaningless.

signify *v* **1** MEAN, denote, symbolize, represent, stand for, indicate, show, express, convey, transmit, communicate, intimate, imply, suggest.
2 MATTER, count.

silence *n* quiet, quietness, hush, peace, stillness, calm, lull, noiselessness, soundlessness, muteness, dumbness, speechlessness, taciturnity, uncommunicativeness, reticence, reserve.
≠ noise, sound, din, uproar.
v quiet, quieten, hush, mute, deaden, muffle, stifle, gag, muzzle, suppress, subdue, quell, still, dumbfound.

silent *adj* inaudible, noiseless, soundless, quiet, peaceful, still, hushed, muted, mute, dumb, speechless, tongue-tied, taciturn, mum, reticent, reserved, tacit, unspoken, unexpressed, understood, voiceless, wordless.
≠ noisy, loud, talkative.

silhouette *n* outline, contour, delineation, shape, form, configuration, profile, shadow.

silky *adj* silken, fine, sleek, lustrous, glossy, satiny, smooth, soft, velvety.

silly *adj* foolish, stupid, imprudent, senseless, pointless, idiotic, daft (*infml*), ridiculous, ludicrous, preposterous, absurd, meaningless, irrational, illogical, childish, puerile, immature, irresponsible, scatterbrained.
≠ wise, sensible, sane, mature, clever, intelligent.

silt *n* sediment, deposit, alluvium, sludge, mud, ooze.
silt up block, clog, choke.

similar *adj* like, alike, close, related, akin, corresponding, equivalent, analogous, comparable, uniform, homogeneous.
≠ dissimilar, different.

similarity *n* likeness, resemblance, similitude, closeness, relation, correspondence, congruence, equivalence, analogy, comparability, compatibility, agreement, affinity,

homogeneity, uniformity.
≠ dissimilarity, difference.

simmer *v* boil, bubble, seethe, stew, burn, smoulder, fume, rage.
simmer down calm down, cool down, control oneself, collect oneself.

simple *adj* **1** *a simple question*: easy, elementary, straightforward, uncomplicated, uninvolved, clear, lucid, plain, understandable, comprehensible. **2** UNSOPHISTICATED, natural, innocent, artless, guileless, ingenuous, naïve, green, foolish, stupid, silly, idiotic, half-witted, simple-minded, feeble-minded, backward.
≠ **1** difficult, hard, complicated, intricate. **2** sophisticated, worldly, artful, clever.

simplicity *n* simpleness, ease, straightforwardness, uncomplicatedness, clarity, purity, plainness, restraint, naturalness, innocence, artlessness, candour, openness, sincerity, directness.
≠ difficulty, complexity, intricacy, sophistication.

simplify *v* disentangle, untangle, decipher, clarify, paraphrase, abridge, reduce, streamline.
≠ complicate, elaborate.

simplistic *adj* oversimplified, superficial, shallow, sweeping, facile, simple, naïve.
≠ analytical, detailed.

simply *adv* **1** MERELY, just, only, solely, purely, utterly, completely, totally, wholly, absolutely, quite, really, undeniably, unquestionably, clearly, plainly, obviously. **2** EASILY, straightforwardly, directly, intelligibly.

simulate *v* pretend, affect, assume, put on, act, feign, sham, fake, counterfeit, reproduce, duplicate, copy, imitate, mimic, parrot, echo, reflect.

simultaneous *adj* synchronous, synchronic, concurrent, contemporaneous, coinciding, parallel.
≠ asynchronous.

sin *n* wrong, offence, transgression, trespass, misdeed, lapse, fault, error, crime, wrongdoing, sinfulness, wickedness, iniquity, evil, impiety, ungodliness, unrighteousness, guilt.
v offend, transgress, trespass, lapse, err, misbehave, stray, go astray, fall, fall from grace.

sincere *adj* honest, truthful, candid, frank, open, direct, straightforward, plain-spoken, serious, earnest, heartfelt, wholehearted, real, true, genuine, pure, unadulterated, unmixed, natural, unaffected, artless, guileless, simple.
≠ insincere, hypocritical, affected.

sincerity *n* honour, integrity, probity, uprightness, honesty, truthfulness, candour, frankness, openness, directness, straightforwardness, seriousness, earnestness, wholeheartedness, genuineness.
≠ insincerity.

sinewy *adj* muscular, brawny, strong, sturdy, robust, vigorous, athletic, wiry, stringy.

sinful *adj* wrong, wrongful, criminal, bad, wicked, iniquitous, erring, fallen, immoral, corrupt, depraved, impious, ungodly, unholy, irreligious, guilty.
≠ sinless, righteous, godly.

sing *v* chant, intone, vocalize, croon, serenade, yodel, trill, warble, chirp, pipe, whistle, hum.

singe *v* scorch, char, blacken, burn, sear.

singers

> *Singers include*: balladeer, minstrel, troubadour, opera singer, diva, prima donna, soloist, precentor, choirboy, choirgirl, chorister, chorus, folk-singer, pop star, crooner, carol-singer; soprano, coloratura soprano, castrato, tenor, treble, contralto, alto, baritone, bass; songster, vocalist.

single *adj* one, unique, singular, individual, particular, exclusive, sole, only, lone, solitary, separate, distinct, free, unattached, unmarried, celibate, unshared, undivided, unbroken, simple, one-to-one, man-to-man.
≠ multiple.
single out choose, select, pick, hand-

pick, distinguish, identify, separate, set apart, isolate, highlight, pinpoint.

single-handed *adj, adv* solo, alone, unaccompanied, unaided, unassisted, independent(ly).

single-minded *adj* determined, resolute, dogged, persevering, tireless, unwavering, fixed, unswerving, undeviating, steadfast, dedicated, devoted.

sinister *adj* ominous, menacing, threatening, disturbing, disquieting, unlucky, inauspicious, malevolent, evil.
≠ auspicious, harmless, innocent.

sink *v* **1** DESCEND, slip, fall, drop, slump, lower, stoop, succumb, lapse, droop, sag, dip, set, disappear, vanish. **2** DECREASE, lessen, subside, abate, dwindle, diminish, ebb, fade, flag, weaken, fail, decline, worsen, degenerate, degrade, decay, collapse. **3** FOUNDER, dive, plunge, plummet, submerge, immerse, engulf, drown. **4** *sink a well*: bore, drill, penetrate, dig, excavate, lay, conceal.
≠ **1** rise. **2** increase. **3** float.

sinner *n* wrong-doer, miscreant, offender, transgressor, trespasser, backslider, reprobate, evil-doer, malefactor.

sinuous *adj* lithe, slinky, curved, wavy, undulating, tortuous, twisting, winding, meandering, serpentine, coiling.
≠ straight.

sip *v* taste, sample, drink, sup.
n taste, drop, spoonful, mouthful.

sit *v* **1** SETTLE, rest, perch, roost, brood, pose. **2** SEAT, accommodate, hold, contain. **3** MEET, assemble, gather, convene, deliberate.

site *n* location, place, spot, position, situation, station, setting, scene, plot, lot, ground, area.
v locate, place, position, situate, station, set, install.

sitting *n* session, period, spell, meeting, assembly, hearing, consultation.

situation *n* **1** SITE, location, position, place, spot, seat, locality, locale, setting, scenario. **2** STATE OF AFFAIRS, case, circumstances, predicament, state, condition, status, rank, station, post, office, job, employment.

sizable *adj* large, substantial, considerable, respectable, goodly, largish, biggish, decent, generous.
≠ small, tiny.

size *n* magnitude, measurement(s), dimensions, proportions, volume, bulk, mass, height, length, extent, range, scale, amount, greatness, largeness, bigness, vastness, immensity.
size up gauge, assess, evaluate, weigh up, measure.

sizzle *v* hiss, crackle, spit, sputter, fry, frizzle.

skeleton *n* bones, frame, structure, framework, bare bones, outline, draft, sketch.

sketch *v* draw, depict, portray, represent, pencil, paint, outline, delineate, draft, rough out, block out.
n drawing, vignette, design, plan, diagram, outline, delineation, skeleton, draft.

sketchy *adj* rough, vague, incomplete, unfinished, scrappy, bitty, imperfect, inadequate, insufficient, slight, superficial, cursory, hasty.
≠ full, complete.

skilful *adj* able, capable, adept, competent, proficient, deft, adroit, handy, expert, masterly, accomplished, skilled, practised, experienced, professional, clever, tactical, cunning.
≠ inept, clumsy, awkward.

skill *n* skilfulness, ability, aptitude, facility, handiness, talent, knack, art, technique, training, experience, expertise, expertness, mastery, proficiency, competence, accomplishment, cleverness, intelligence.

skilled *adj* trained, schooled, qualified, professional, experienced, practised, accomplished, expert, masterly, proficient, able, skilful.
≠ unskilled, inexperienced.

skim *v* **1** BRUSH, touch, skate, plane, float, sail, glide, fly. **2** SCAN, look through, skip. **3** CREAM, separate.

skimp *v* economize, scrimp, pinch, cut corners, stint, withhold.
≠ squander, waste.

skin *n* hide, pelt, membrane, film, coating, surface, outside, peel, rind, husk, casing, crust.
v flay, fleece, strip, peel, scrape, graze.

skinny *adj* thin, lean, scrawny, scraggy, skeletal, skin-and-bone, emaciated, underfed, undernourished.
≠ fat, plump.

skip *v* **1** HOP, jump, leap, dance, gambol, frisk, caper, prance. **2** *skip a page*: miss, omit, leave out, cut.

skirmish *n* fight, combat, battle, engagement, encounter, conflict, clash, brush, scrap, tussle, set-to, dust-up (*infml*).

skirt *v* circle, circumnavigate, border, edge, flank, bypass, avoid, evade, circumvent.

skit *n* satire, parody, caricature, spoof, take-off, sketch.

skulk *v* lurk, hide, prowl, sneak, creep, slink.

sky *n* space, atmosphere, air, heavens, blue.

slab *n* piece, block, lump, chunk, hunk, wodge (*infml*), wedge, slice, portion.

slack *adj* **1** LOOSE, limp, sagging, baggy. **2** LAZY, sluggish, slow, quiet, idle, inactive. **3** NEGLECTFUL, negligent, careless, inattentive, remiss, permissive, lax, relaxed, easy-going (*infml*).
≠ **1** tight, taut, stiff, rigid. **2** busy. **3** diligent.
n looseness, give, play, room, leeway, excess.
v idle, shirk, skive (*infml*), neglect.

slacken off loosen, release, relax, ease, moderate, reduce, lessen, decrease, diminish, abate, slow (down).
≠ tighten, increase, intensify, quicken.

slacker *n* idler, shirker, skiver (*infml*), dawdler, clock-watcher, good-for-nothing, layabout.

slam *v* **1** BANG, crash, dash, smash, throw, hurl, fling. **2** (*infml*) CRITICIZE, slate (*infml*), pan (*infml*).

slander *n* defamation, calumny, misrepresentation, libel, scandal, smear, slur, aspersion, backbiting.
v defame, vilify, malign, denigrate, disparage, libel, smear, slur, backbite.
≠ praise, compliment.

slanderous *adj* defamatory, false, untrue, libellous, damaging, malicious, abusive, insulting.

slant *v* **1** TILT, slope, incline, lean, list, skew, angle. **2** DISTORT, twist, warp, bend, weight, bias, colour.
n **1** SLOPE, incline, gradient, ramp, camber, pitch, tilt, angle, diagonal. **2** BIAS, emphasis, attitude, viewpoint.

slanting *adj* sloping, tilted, oblique, diagonal.

slap *n* smack, spank, cuff, blow, bang, clap.
v **1** SMACK, spank, hit, strike, cuff, clout, bang, clap. **2** DAUB, plaster, spread, apply.

slash *v* cut, slit, gash, lacerate, rip, tear, rend.
n cut, incision, slit, gash, laceration, rip, tear, rent.

slate *v* scold, rebuke, reprimand, berate, censure, blame, criticize, slam (*infml*).
≠ praise.

slaughter *n* killing, murder, massacre, extermination, butchery, carnage, blood-bath, bloodshed.
v kill, slay, murder, massacre, exterminate, liquidate, butcher.

slave *n* servant, drudge, vassal, serf, villein, captive.
v toil, labour, drudge, sweat, grind, slog.

slaver *v* dribble, drivel, slobber, drool, salivate.

slavery *n* servitude, bondage, captivity, enslavement, serfdom, thraldom, subjugation.
≠ freedom, liberty.

slavish *adj* **1** UNORIGINAL, imitative, unimaginative, uninspired, literal, strict. **2** SERVILE, abject, submissive, sycophantic, grovelling, cringing, fawning, menial, low, mean.
≠ **1** original, imaginative.

2 independent, assertive.

sleek *adj* shiny, glossy, lustrous, smooth, silky, well-groomed.
≠ rough, unkempt.

sleep *v* doze, snooze, slumber, kip (*sl*), doss (down) (*sl*), hibernate, drop off, nod off, rest, repose.
n doze, snooze, nap, forty winks, shut-eye (*infml*), kip (*sl*), slumber, hibernation, rest, repose, siesta.

sleepless *adj* unsleeping, awake, wide-awake, alert, vigilant, watchful, wakeful, restless, disturbed, insomniac.

sleepy *adj* drowsy, somnolent, tired, weary, heavy, slow, sluggish, torpid, lethargic, inactive, quiet, dull, soporific, hypnotic.
≠ awake, alert, wakeful, restless.

slender *adj* **1** SLIM, thin, lean, slight, svelte, graceful. **2** *a slender chance*: faint, remote, slight, inconsiderable, tenuous, flimsy, feeble, inadequate, insufficient, meagre, scanty.
≠ **1** fat. **2** appreciable, considerable, ample.

slice *n* piece, sliver, wafer, rasher, tranche, slab, wedge, segment, section, share, portion, helping, cut (*infml*), whack (*infml*).
v carve, cut, chop, divide, segment.

slick *adj* **1** GLIB, plausible, deft, adroit, dexterous, skilful, professional. **2** SMOOTH, sleek, glossy, shiny, polished.

slide *v* slip, slither, skid, skate, ski, toboggan, glide, plane, coast, skim.

slight *adj* **1** MINOR, unimportant, insignificant, negligible, trivial, paltry, modest, small, little, inconsiderable, insubstantial. **2** SLENDER, slim, diminutive, petite, delicate.
≠ **1** major, significant, noticeable, considerable. **2** large, muscular.
v scorn, despise, disdain, disparage, insult, affront, offend, snub, cut, cold-shoulder, ignore, disregard, neglect.
≠ respect, praise, compliment, flatter.
n insult, affront, slur, snub, rebuff, rudeness, discourtesy, disrespect, contempt, disdain, indifference, disregard, neglect.

slim *adj* **1** SLENDER, thin, lean, svelte, trim. **2** SLIGHT, remote, faint, poor.
≠ **1** fat, chubby. **2** strong, considerable.
v lose weight, diet, reduce.

slimy *adj* **1** MUDDY, miry, mucous, viscous, oily, greasy, slippery. **2** SERVILE, obsequious, sycophantic, toadying, smarmy, oily, unctuous.

sling *v* **1** THROW, hurl, fling, catapult, heave, pitch, lob, toss, chuck (*infml*). **2** HANG, suspend, dangle, swing.

slink *v* sneak, steal, creep, sidle, slip, prowl, skulk.

slinky *adj* close-fitting, figure-hugging, clinging, skin-tight, sleek, sinuous.

slip[1] *v* slide, glide, skate, skid, stumble, trip, fall, slither, slink, sneak, steal, creep.
n mistake, error, slip-up (*infml*), bloomer (*infml*), blunder, fault, indiscretion, boob (*infml*), omission, oversight, failure.

slip[2] *n* piece, strip, voucher, chit, coupon, certificate.

slippery *adj* **1** SLIPPY, icy, greasy, glassy, smooth, dangerous, treacherous, perilous. **2** *a slippery character*: dishonest, untrustworthy, false, duplicitous, two-faced, crafty, cunning, devious, evasive, smooth, smarmy.
≠ **1** rough. **2** trustworthy, reliable.

slipshod *adj* careless, slap-dash, sloppy, slovenly, untidy, negligent, lax, casual.
≠ careful, fastidious, neat, tidy.

slit *v* cut, gash, slash, slice, split, rip, tear.
n opening, aperture, vent, cut, incision, gash, slash, split, tear, rent.

slither *v* slide, slip, glide, slink, creep, snake, worm.

sliver *n* flake, shaving, paring, slice, wafer, shred, fragment, chip, splinter, shiver, shard.

slobber *v* dribble, drivel, slaver, drool, salivate.

slogan *n* jingle, motto, catch-phrase, catchword, watchword, battle-cry, war cry.

slop *v* spill, overflow, slosh, splash, splatter, spatter.

slopes

Ways of describing slopes include: up: acclivity, ascent, climb, incline, rise, uphill, upward; *down*: decline, declivity, descent, dip, downgrade, downhill, downward, drop, fall; *up or down*: bajada, brae, cant, escalator, escarp, glacis, gradient, ramp, scarp, staircase, stairs, stairway, steps, tilt, versant.

sloppy *adj* **1** WATERY, wet, liquid, runny, mushy, slushy. **2** *sloppy work*: careless, hit-or-miss, slap-dash, slipshod, slovenly, untidy, messy, clumsy, amateurish. **3** SOPPY, sentimental, schmaltzy, slushy, mushy.
≠ **1** solid. **2** careful, exact, precise.

slot *n* hole, opening, aperture, slit, vent, groove, channel, gap, space, time, vacancy, place, spot, position, niche.
v insert, fit, place, position, assign, pigeonhole.

slouch *v* stoop, hunch, droop, slump, lounge, loll, shuffle, shamble.

slovenly *adj* sloppy, careless, slipshod, untidy, scruffy, slatternly, sluttish.
≠ neat, smart.

slow *adj* **1** LEISURELY, unhurried, lingering, loitering, dawdling, lazy, sluggish, slow-moving, creeping, gradual, deliberate, measured, plodding, delayed, late, unpunctual. **2** STUPID, slow-witted, dim, thick (*infml*). **3** PROLONGED, protracted, long-drawn-out, tedious, boring, dull, uninteresting, uneventful.
≠ **1** quick, fast, swift, rapid, speedy. **2** clever, intelligent. **3** brisk, lively, exciting.
v brake, decelerate, delay, hold up, retard, handicap, check, curb, restrict.
≠ speed, accelerate.

sluggish *adj* lethargic, listless, torpid, heavy, dull, slow, slow-moving, slothful, lazy, idle, inactive, lifeless, unresponsive.
≠ brisk, vigorous, lively, dynamic.

slump *v* **1** COLLAPSE, fall, drop, plunge, plummet, sink, decline, deteriorate, worsen, crash, fail. **2** DROOP, sag, bend, stoop, slouch, loll, lounge, flop.
n recession, depression, stagnation, downturn, low, trough, decline, deterioration, worsening, fall, drop, collapse, crash, failure.
≠ boom.

sly *adj* wily, foxy, crafty, cunning, artful, guileful, clever, canny, shrewd, astute, knowing, subtle, devious, shifty, tricky, furtive, stealthy, surreptitious, underhand, covert, secretive, scheming, conniving, mischievous, roguish.
≠ honest, frank, candid, open.

smack *v* hit, strike, slap, spank, whack (*infml*), thwack (*infml*), clap, box, cuff, pat, tap.
n blow, slap, spank, whack (*infml*), thwack (*infml*), box, cuff, pat, tap.
adv bang, slap-bang, right, plumb, straight, directly, exactly, precisely.

small *adj* **1** LITTLE, tiny, minute, minuscule, short, slight, puny, petite, diminutive, pint-size(d) (*infml*), miniature, mini, pocket, pocket-sized, young. **2** PETTY, trifling, trivial, unimportant, insignificant, minor, inconsiderable, negligible.
3 INADEQUATE, insufficient, scanty, meagre, paltry, mean, limited.
≠ **1** large, big, huge. **2** great, considerable. **3** ample.

small-minded *adj* petty, mean, ungenerous, illiberal, intolerant, bigoted, narrow-minded, parochial, insular, rigid, hidebound.
≠ liberal, tolerant, broad-minded.

smarmy *adj* smooth, oily, unctuous, servile, obsequious, sycophantic, toadying, ingratiating, crawling, fawning.

smart *adj* **1** *smart clothes*: elegant, stylish, chic, fashionable, modish, neat, tidy, spruce, trim, well-groomed.
2 CLEVER, intelligent, bright, sharp, acute, shrewd, astute.
≠ **1** dowdy, unfashionable, untidy, scruffy. **2** stupid, slow.
v sting, hurt, prick, burn, tingle, twinge, throb.

smarten *v* neaten, tidy, spruce up,

groom, clean, polish, beautify.

smash *v* **1** *smash a window*: break, shatter, shiver, ruin, wreck, demolish, destroy, defeat, crush. **2** CRASH, collide, strike, bang, bash, thump.
n accident, crash, collision, pile-up.

smattering *n* bit, modicum, dash, sprinkling, basics, rudiments, elements.

smear *v* **1** DAUB, plaster, spread, cover, coat, rub, smudge, streak. **2** DEFAME, malign, vilify, blacken, sully, stain, tarnish.
n **1** STREAK, smudge, blot, blotch, splodge, daub. **2** DEFAMATION, slander, libel, mudslinging, muck-raking.

smells

> *Ways of describing smells include*: *pleasant*: aroma, bouquet, fragrance, incense, nose, odour, pot pourri, perfume, redolence, scent; *unpleasant*: b.o. (body odour), fetor, funk (*US*), hum, malodour, mephitis, miasma, niff (*sl*), pong (*infml*), pungency, reek, sniff, stench, stink, whiff.

smelly *adj* malodorous, pongy (*infml*), stinking, reeking, foul, bad, off, fetid, putrid, high, strong.

smile *n, v* grin, beam, simper, smirk, leer, laugh.

smoke *n* fumes, exhaust, gas, vapour, mist, fog, smog.
v fume, smoulder, cure, dry.

smoky *adj* sooty, black, grey, grimy, murky, cloudy, hazy, foggy.

smooth *adj* **1** LEVEL, plane, even, flat, horizontal, flush. **2** STEADY, unbroken, flowing, regular, uniform, rhythmic, easy, effortless. **3** SHINY, polished, glossy, silky, glassy, calm, undisturbed, serene, tranquil, peaceful. **4** SUAVE, agreeable, smooth-talking, glib, plausible, persuasive, slick, smarmy, unctuous, ingratiating.
≠ **1** rough, lumpy. **2** irregular, erratic, unsteady. **3** rough, choppy.
v **1** IRON, press, roll, flatten, level, plane, file, sand, polish. **2** EASE, alleviate, assuage, allay, mitigate, calm, mollify.
≠ **1** roughen, wrinkle, crease.

smother *v* suffocate, asphyxiate, strangle, throttle, choke, stifle, extinguish, snuff, muffle, suppress, repress, hide, conceal, cover, shroud, envelop, wrap.

smoulder *v* burn, smoke, fume, rage, seethe, simmer.

smudge *v* blur, smear, daub, mark, spot, stain, dirty, soil.
n blot, stain, spot, blemish, blur, smear, streak.

smug *adj* complacent, self-satisfied, superior, holier-than-thou, self-righteous, priggish, conceited.
≠ humble, modest.

snack *n* refreshment(s), bite, nibble, titbit, elevenses (*infml*).

snag *n* disadvantage, inconvenience, drawback, catch, problem, difficulty, complication, setback, hitch, obstacle, stumbling-block.
v catch, rip, tear, hole, ladder.

snap *v* **1** *the twig snapped*: break, crack, split, separate. **2** BITE, nip, bark, growl, snarl, retort, crackle, pop. **3** SNATCH, seize, catch, grasp, grip.
n break, crack, bite, nip, flick, fillip, crackle, pop.
adj immediate, instant, on-the-spot, abrupt, sudden.

snappy *adj* **1** SMART, stylish, chic, fashionable, modish, trendy (*infml*). **2** QUICK, hasty, brisk, lively, energetic. **3** CROSS, irritable, edgy, touchy, brusque, quick-tempered, ill-natured, crabbed, testy.
≠ **1** dowdy. **2** slow.

snare *v* trap, ensnare, entrap, catch, net.
n trap, wire, net, noose, catch, pitfall.

snarl[1] *v* growl, grumble, complain.

snarl[2] *v* tangle, knot, ravel, entangle, enmesh, embroil, confuse, muddle, complicate.

snatch *v* grab, seize, kidnap, take, nab (*infml*), pluck, pull, wrench, wrest, gain, win, clutch, grasp, grip.

sneak *v* **1** CREEP, steal, slip, slink, sidle, skulk, lurk, prowl, smuggle, spirit. **2** TELL TALES, split (*sl*), inform on, grass on (*sl*).
n tell-tale, informer, grass (*sl*).

sneaking *adj* private, secret, furtive, surreptitious, hidden, lurking, suppressed, grudging, nagging, niggling, persistent, worrying, uncomfortable, intuitive.

sneer *v* scorn, disdain, look down on, deride, scoff, jeer, mock, ridicule, gibe, laugh, snigger.
n scorn, disdain, derision, jeer, mockery, ridicule, gibe, snigger.

snide *adj* derogatory, disparaging, sarcastic, cynical, scornful, sneering, hurtful, unkind, nasty, mean, spiteful, malicious, ill-natured.
≠ complimentary.

sniff *v* breathe, inhale, snuff, snuffle, smell, nose, scent.

snigger *v, n* laugh, giggle, titter, chuckle, sneer.

snip *v* cut, clip, trim, crop, dock, slit, nick, notch.

snippet *n* piece, scrap, cutting, clipping, fragment, particle, shred, snatch, part, portion, segment, section.

snobbery *n* snobbishness, superciliousness, snootiness (*infml*), airs, loftiness, arrogance, pride, pretension, condescension.

snobbish *adj* supercilious, disdainful, snooty (*infml*), stuck-up (*infml*), toffee-nosed (*infml*), superior, lofty, high and mighty, arrogant, pretentious, affected, condescending, patronizing.

snoop *v* spy, sneak, pry, nose, interfere, meddle.

snooze *v* nap, doze, sleep, kip (*sl*).
n nap, catnap, forty winks, doze, siesta, sleep, kip (*sl*).

snub *v* rebuff, brush off, cut, cold-shoulder, slight, rebuke, put down, squash, humble, shame, humiliate, mortify.
n rebuff, brush-off, slight, affront, insult, rebuke, put-down, humiliation.

snug *adj* cosy, warm, comfortable, homely, friendly, intimate, sheltered, secure, tight, close-fitting.

soak *v* wet, drench, saturate, penetrate, permeate, infuse, bathe, marinate, souse, steep, submerge, immerse.

soaking *adj* soaked, drenched, sodden, waterlogged, saturated, sopping, wringing, dripping, streaming.
≠ dry.

soar *v* fly, wing, glide, plane, tower, rise, ascend, climb, mount, escalate, rocket.
≠ fall, plummet.

sob *v* cry, weep, bawl, howl, blubber, snivel.

sober *adj* **1** TEETOTAL, temperate, moderate, abstinent, abstemious. **2** SOLEMN, dignified, serious, staid, steady, sedate, quiet, serene, calm, composed, unruffled, unexcited, cool, dispassionate, level-headed, practical, realistic, reasonable, rational, clear-headed. **3** *sober dress*: sombre, drab, dull, plain, subdued, restrained.
≠ **1** drunk, intemperate. **2** frivolous, excited, unrealistic, irrational. **3** flashy, garish.

so-called *adj* alleged, supposed, purported, ostensible, nominal, self-styled, professed, would-be, pretended.

sociable *adj* outgoing, gregarious, friendly, affable, companionable, genial, convivial, cordial, warm, hospitable, neighbourly, approachable, accessible, familiar.
≠ unsociable, withdrawn, unfriendly, hostile.

social *adj* communal, public, community, common, general, collective, group, organized.
n party, do (*infml*), get-together, gathering.

socialize *v* mix, mingle, fraternize, get together, go out, entertain.

society *n* **1** COMMUNITY, population, culture, civilization, nation, people, mankind, humanity. **2** CLUB, circle, group, association, organization, company, corporation, league, union, guild, fellowship, fraternity, brotherhood, sisterhood, sorority. **3** FRIENDSHIP, companionship, camaraderie, fellowship, company. **4** UPPER CLASSES, aristocracy, gentry, nobility, elite.

soft *adj* **1** YIELDING, pliable, flexible, elastic, plastic, malleable, spongy,

squashy, pulpy. **2** *soft colours*: pale, light, pastel, delicate, subdued, muted, quiet, low, dim, faint, diffuse, mild, bland, gentle, soothing, sweet, mellow, melodious, dulcet, pleasant. **3** FURRY, downy, velvety, silky, smooth. **4** LENIENT, lax, permissive, indulgent, tolerant, easy-going (*infml*), kind, generous, gentle, merciful, soft-hearted, tender, sensitive, weak, spineless.
≠ **1** hard. **2** harsh. **3** rough. **4** strict, severe.

soften *v* **1** MODERATE, temper, mitigate, lessen, diminish, abate, alleviate, ease, soothe, palliate, quell, assuage, subdue, mollify, appease, calm, still, relax. **2** MELT, liquefy, dissolve, reduce. **3** CUSHION, pad, muffle, quicken, lower, lighten.

soft-hearted *adj* sympathetic, compassionate, kind, benevolent, charitable, generous, warm-hearted, tender, sentimental.
≠ hard-hearted, callous.

soggy *adj* wet, damp, moist, soaked, drenched, sodden, waterlogged, saturated, sopping, dripping, heavy, boggy, spongy, pulpy.

soil[1] *n* earth, clay, loam, humus, dirt, dust, ground, land, region, country.

soil[2] *v* dirty, begrime, stain, spot, smudge, smear, foul, muddy, pollute, defile, besmirch, sully, tarnish.

solace *n* comfort, consolation, relief, alleviation, support, cheer.

soldiers

> *Types of soldier include*: cadet, private, sapper, NCO, orderly, officer, gunner, infantryman, trooper, fusilier, rifleman, paratrooper, sentry, guardsman, marine, commando, tommy, dragoon, cavalryman, lancer, hussar, conscript, recruit, regular, Territorial, GI (*US*), warrior, mercenary, legionnaire, guerrilla, partisan, centurion; troops; serviceman, servicewoman, fighter. *see also* **rank[1]**.

sole *adj* only, unique, exclusive, individual, single, singular, one, lone, solitary, alone.
≠ shared, multiple.

solemn *adj* **1** *a solemn expression*: serious, grave, sober, sedate, sombre, glum, thoughtful, earnest, awed, reverential. **2** GRAND, stately, majestic, ceremonial, ritual, formal, ceremonious, pompous, dignified, august, venerable, awe-inspiring, impressive, imposing, momentous.
≠ **1** light-hearted. **2** frivolous.

solicit *v* ask, request, seek, crave, beg, beseech, entreat, implore, pray, supplicate, sue, petition, canvass, importune.

solicitor *n* lawyer, advocate, attorney, barrister, QC.

solicitous *adj* caring, attentive, considerate, concerned, anxious, worried.

solid *adj* **1** HARD, firm, dense, compact, strong, sturdy, substantial, sound, unshakable. **2** *a solid white line*: unbroken, continuous, uninterrupted. **3** RELIABLE, dependable, trusty, worthy, decent, upright, sensible, level-headed, stable, serious, sober. **4** REAL, genuine, pure, concrete, tangible.
≠ **1** liquid, gaseous, hollow. **2** broken, dotted. **3** unreliable, unstable. **4** unreal.

solidarity *n* unity, agreement, accord, unanimity, consensus, harmony, concord, cohesion, like-mindedness, camaraderie, team spirit, soundness, stability.
≠ discord, division, schism.

solidify *v* harden, set, jell, congeal, coagulate, clot, cake, crystallize.
≠ soften, liquefy, dissolve.

solitary *adj* sole, single, lone, alone, lonely, lonesome, friendless, unsociable, reclusive, withdrawn, retired, sequestered, cloistered, secluded, separate, isolated, remote, out-of-the-way, inaccessible, unfrequented, unvisited, untrodden.
≠ accompanied, gregarious, busy.

solitude *n* aloneness, loneliness, reclusiveness, retirement, privacy, seclusion, isolation, remoteness.
≠ companionship.

solution *n* **1** ANSWER, result, explanation, resolution, key, remedy. **2** MIXTURE, blend, compound, suspension, emulsion, liquid.

solve *v* work out, figure out, puzzle out, decipher, crack, disentangle, unravel, answer, resolve, settle, clear up, clarify, explain, interpret.

sombre *adj* dark, funereal, drab, dull, dim, obscure, shady, shadowy, gloomy, dismal, melancholy, mournful, sad, joyless, sober, serious, grave.
≠ bright, cheerful, happy.

someday *adv* sometime, one day, eventually, ultimately.
≠ never.

sometimes *adv* occasionally, now and again, now and then, once in a while, from time to time.
≠ always, never.

song *n* tune, melody, lyric, number.

> *Types of song include*: air, anthem, aria, ballad, barcarole, bird call, bird song, blues, calypso, cantata, canticle, cantilena, canzone, canzonet, carol, chanson, chansonette, chant, chorus, descant, dirge, ditty, elegy, epinikion, epithalamium, folk-song, gospel song, hymn, jingle, love-song, lied, lilt, lullaby, madrigal, nursery rhyme, ode, plainchant, plainsong, pop song, psalm, recitative, requiem, rock and roll, roundelay, serenade, shanty, spiritual, Negro spiritual, war song, wassail, yodel.

soon *adv* shortly, presently, in a minute, before long, in the near future.

soothe *v* alleviate, relieve, ease, salve, comfort, allay, calm, compose, tranquillize, settle, still, quiet, hush, lull, pacify, appease, mollify, assuage, mitigate, soften.
≠ aggravate, irritate, annoy, vex.

sophisticated *adj* **1** URBANE, cosmopolitan, worldly, worldly-wise, cultured, cultivated, refined, polished. **2** *sophisticated technology*: advanced, highly-developed, complicated, complex, intricate, elaborate, delicate, subtle.
≠ **1** unsophisticated, naïve. **2** primitive, simple.

soporific *adj* sleep-inducing, hypnotic, sedative, tranquillizing, sleepy, somnolent.
≠ stimulating, invigorating.

soppy *adj* sentimental, lovey-dovey (*infml*), weepy (*infml*), sloppy, slushy, mushy, corny (*infml*), mawkish, cloying, soft, silly, daft (*infml*).

sorcery *n* magic, black magic, witchcraft, wizardry, necromancy, voodoo, spell, incantation, charm, enchantment.

sordid *adj* dirty, filthy, unclean, foul, vile, squalid, sleazy, seamy, seedy, disreputable, shabby, tawdry, corrupt, degraded, degenerate, debauched, low, base, despicable, shameful, wretched, mean, miserly, niggardly, grasping, mercenary, selfish, self-seeking.
≠ pure, honourable, upright.

sore *adj* **1** PAINFUL, hurting, aching, smarting, stinging, tender, sensitive, inflamed, red, raw. **2** ANNOYED, irritated, vexed, angry, upset, hurt, wounded, afflicted, aggrieved, resentful.
≠ **2** pleased, happy.
n wound, lesion, swelling, inflammation, boil, abscess, ulcer.

sorrow *n* sadness, unhappiness, grief, mourning, misery, woe, distress, affliction, anguish, heartache, heartbreak, misfortune, hardship, trouble, worry, trial, tribulation, regret, remorse.
≠ happiness, joy.

sorry *adj* **1** APOLOGETIC, regretful, remorseful, contrite, penitent, repentant, conscience-stricken, guilt-ridden, shamefaced. **2** *in a sorry state*: pathetic, pitiful, poor, wretched, miserable, sad, unhappy, dismal. **3** SYMPATHETIC, compassionate, understanding, pitying, concerned, moved.
≠ **1** impenitent, unashamed. **2** happy, cheerful. **3** uncaring.

sort *n* kind, type, genre, ilk, family, race, breed, species, genus, variety, order, class, category, group, denomination, style, make, brand, stamp, quality, nature, character, description.

v class, group, categorize, distribute, divide, separate, segregate, sift, screen, grade, rank, order, classify, catalogue, arrange, organize, systematize.
sort out resolve, clear up, clarify, tidy up, neaten, choose, select.

soul *n* **1** SPIRIT, psyche, mind, reason, intellect, character, inner being, essence, life, vital force.
2 INDIVIDUAL, person, man, woman, creature.

sound[1] *n* noise, din, report, resonance, reverberation, tone, timbre, tenor, description.

> *Sounds include*: bang, blare, blast, bleep, boom, buzz, chime, chink, chug, clack, clang, clank, clap, clash, clatter, click, clink, crack, crackle, crash, creak, crunch, cry, drone, echo, explosion, fizz, grate, grizzle, groan, gurgle, hiccup, hiss, honk, hoot, hum, jangle, jingle, knock, moan, murmur, patter, peal, ping, pip, plop, pop, rattle, report, reverberation, ring, rumble, rustle, scream, sigh, sizzle, skirl, slam, slurp, smack, snap, sniff, snore, snort, sob, splutter, squeal, squelch, swish, tap, throb, thud, thump, thunder, tick, ting, tinkle, toot, twang, wail, whimper, whine, whirr, whistle, whoop, yell.
> *Animal sounds include*: bark, bay, bellow, bleat, bray, cackle, caw, chirp, chirrup, cluck, coo, croak, crow, gobble, growl, grunt, hiss, hoot, howl, low, mew, miaow, moo, neigh, purr, quack, roar, screech, snarl, squawk, squeak, tweet, twitter, warble, whinny, woof, yap, yelp, yowl.

v **1** RING, toll, chime, peal, resound, resonate, reverberate, echo.
2 ARTICULATE, enunciate, pronounce, voice, express, utter, say, declare, announce.

sound[2] *adj* **1** FIT, well, healthy, vigorous, robust, sturdy, firm, solid, whole, complete, intact, perfect, unbroken, undamaged, unimpaired, unhurt, uninjured. **2** VALID, well-founded, reasonable, rational, logical, orthodox, right, true, proven, reliable, trustworthy, secure, substantial, thorough, good.
≠ **1** unfit, ill, shaky. **2** unsound, unreliable, poor.

sound[3] *v* measure, plumb, fathom, probe, examine, test, inspect, investigate.

sour *adj* **1** TART, sharp, acid, pungent, vinegary, bitter, rancid.
2 EMBITTERED, acrimonious, ill-tempered, peevish, crabbed, crusty, disagreeable.
≠ **1** sweet, sugary. **2** good-natured, generous.

source *n* origin, derivation, beginning, start, commencement, cause, root, rise, spring, fountainhead, wellhead, supply, mine, originator, authority, informant.

souvenir *n* memento, reminder, remembrance, keepsake, relic, token.

sovereign *n* ruler, monarch, king, queen, emperor, empress, potentate, chief.
adj ruling, royal, imperial, absolute, unlimited, supreme, paramount, predominant, principal, chief, dominant, independent, autonomous.

sow *v* plant, seed, scatter, strew, spread, disseminate, lodge, implant.

space *n* **1** ROOM, place, seat, accommodation, capacity, volume, extent, expansion, scope, range, play, elbow-room, leeway, margin. **2** BLANK, omission, gap, opening, lacuna, interval, intermission, chasm.

spacious *adj* roomy, capacious, ample, big, large, sizable, broad, wide, huge, vast, extensive, open, uncrowded.
≠ small, narrow, cramped, confined.

span *n* spread, stretch, reach, range, scope, compass, extent, length, distance, duration, term, period, spell.
v arch, vault, bridge, link, cross, traverse, extend, cover.

spank *v* smack, slap, wallop (*infml*), whack (*infml*), thrash, slipper, cane.

spare *adj* reserve, emergency, extra, additional, leftover, remaining, unused, over, surplus, superfluous, supernumerary, unwanted, free, unoccupied.
≠ necessary, vital, used.
v **1** PARDON, let off, reprieve, release,

free. **2** GRANT, allow, afford, part with.

sparing *adj* economical, thrifty, careful, prudent, frugal, meagre, miserly.
≠ unsparing, liberal, lavish.

spark *n* flash, flare, gleam, glint, flicker, hint, trace, vestige, scrap, atom, jot.
v kindle, set off, trigger, start, cause, occasion, prompt, provoke, stimulate, stir, excite, inspire.

sparkle *v* **1** TWINKLE, glitter, scintillate, flash, gleam, glint, glisten, shimmer, coruscate, shine, beam. **2** EFFERVESCE, fizz, bubble.
n twinkle, glitter, flash, gleam, glint, flicker, spark, radiance, brilliance, dazzle, spirit, vitality, life, animation.

sparse *adj* scarce, scanty, meagre, scattered, infrequent, sporadic.
≠ plentiful, thick, dense.

spartan *adj* austere, harsh, severe, rigorous, strict, disciplined, ascetic, abstemious, temperate, frugal, plain, simple, bleak, joyless.
≠ luxurious, self-indulgent.

spasm *n* burst, eruption, outburst, frenzy, fit, convulsion, seizure, attack, contraction, jerk, twitch, tic.

spasmodic *adj* sporadic, occasional, intermittent, erratic, irregular, fitful, jerky.
≠ continuous, uninterrupted.

spate *n* flood, deluge, torrent, rush, outpouring, flow.

speak *v* talk, converse, say, state, declare, express, utter, voice, articulate, enunciate, pronounce, tell, communicate, address, lecture, harangue, hold forth, declaim, argue, discuss.

speaker *n* lecturer, orator, spokesperson, spokesman, spokeswoman.

special *adj* **1** *a special occasion*: important, significant, momentous, major, noteworthy, distinguished, memorable, remarkable, extraordinary, exceptional. **2** DIFFERENT, distinctive, characteristic, peculiar, singular, individual, unique, exclusive, select, choice, particular, specific, unusual, precise, detailed.
≠ **1** normal, ordinary, usual. **2** general, common.

specialist *n* consultant, authority, expert, master, professional, connoisseur.

speciality *n* strength, forte, talent, field, specialty, pièce de résistance.

specific *adj* precise, exact, fixed, limited, particular, special, definite, unequivocal, clear-cut, explicit, express, unambiguous.
≠ vague, approximate.

specification *n* requirement, condition, qualification, description, listing, item, particular, detail.

specify *v* stipulate, spell out, define, particularize, detail, itemize, enumerate, list, mention, cite, name, designate, indicate, describe, delineate.

specimen *n* sample, example, instance, illustration, model, pattern, paradigm, exemplar, representative, copy, exhibit.

spectacle *n* show, performance, display, exhibition, parade, pageant, extravaganza, scene, sight, curiosity, wonder, marvel, phenomenon.

spectacles

Types of spectacles include: bifocals, contact lens, eyeglass, diving mask, goggles, half-glasses, lorgnette, monocle, pince-nez, Polaroid® glasses, quizzing glass, reading glasses, safety glasses, shooting glasses, sports spex, sunglasses, trifocals, varifocals.

spectacular *adj* grand, splendid, magnificent, sensational, impressive, striking, stunning, staggering, amazing, remarkable, dramatic, daring, breathtaking, dazzling, eye-catching, colourful.
≠ unimpressive, ordinary.

spectator *n* watcher, viewer, onlooker, looker-on, bystander, passer-by, witness, eye-witness, observer.
≠ player, participant.

spectre *n* ghost, phantom, spirit, wraith, apparition, vision, presence.

speculate *v* wonder, contemplate, meditate, muse, reflect, consider, deliberate, theorize, suppose, guess, conjecture, surmise, gamble, risk, hazard, venture.

speculative *adj* conjectural, hypothetical, theoretical, notional, abstract, academic, tentative, risky, hazardous, uncertain, unpredictable.

speech *n* **1** DICTION, articulation, enunciation, elocution, delivery, utterance, voice, language, tongue, parlance, dialect, jargon. **2** *make a speech*: oration, address, discourse, talk, lecture, harangue, spiel (*sl*), conversation, dialogue, monologue, soliloquy.

speechless *adj* dumbfounded, thunderstruck, amazed, aghast, tongue-tied, inarticulate, mute, dumb, silent, mum.
≠ talkative.

speed *n* velocity, rate, pace, tempo, quickness, swiftness, rapidity, celerity, alacrity, haste, hurry, dispatch, rush, acceleration.
≠ slowness, delay.
v race, tear, belt (*infml*), zoom, career, bowl along, sprint, gallop, hurry, rush, hasten, accelerate, quicken, put one's foot down (*infml*), step on it (*infml*).
≠ slow, delay.

speedy *adj* fast, quick, swift, rapid, nimble, express, prompt, immediate, hurried, hasty, precipitate, cursory.
≠ slow, leisurely.

spell[1] *n* period, time, bout, session, term, season, interval, stretch, patch, turn, stint.

spell[2] *n* charm, incantation, magic, sorcery, witchery, bewitchment, enchantment, fascination, glamour.

spellbound *adj* transfixed, hypnotized, mesmerized, fascinated, enthralled, gripped, entranced, captivated, bewitched, enchanted, charmed.

spend *v* **1** *spend money*: disburse, pay out, fork out (*infml*), shell out (*infml*), invest, lay out, splash out (*infml*), waste, squander, fritter, expend, consume, use up, exhaust. **2** PASS, fill, occupy, use, employ, apply, devote.
≠ **1** save, hoard.

spendthrift *n* squanderer, prodigal, profligate, wastrel.
≠ miser.
adj improvident, extravagant, prodigal, wasteful.

sphere *n* **1** BALL, globe, orb, round. **2** DOMAIN, realm, province, department, territory, field, range, scope, compass, rank, function, capacity.

spherical *adj* round, rotund, ball-shaped, globe-shaped.

spicy *adj* **1** PIQUANT, hot, pungent, tangy, seasoned, aromatic, fragrant. **2** RACY, risqué, ribald, suggestive, indelicate, improper, indecorous, unseemly, scandalous, sensational.
≠ **1** bland, insipid. **2** decent.

spike *n* point, prong, tine, spine, barb, nail, stake.
v impale, stick, spear, skewer, spit.

spill *v* overturn, upset, slop, overflow, disgorge, pour, tip, discharge, shed, scatter.

spin *v* turn, revolve, rotate, twist, gyrate, twirl, pirouette, wheel, whirl, swirl, reel.
n **1** TURN, revolution, twist, gyration, twirl, pirouette, whirl, swirl. **2** COMMOTION, agitation, panic, flap (*infml*), state (*infml*), tizzy (*infml*). **3** DRIVE, ride, run.
spin out prolong, protract, extend, lengthen, amplify, pad out.

spindle *n* axis, pivot, pin, rod, axle.

spine *n* **1** BACKBONE, spinal column, vertebral column, vertebrae. **2** THORN, barb, prickle, bristle, quill.

spineless *adj* weak, feeble, irresolute, ineffective, cowardly, faint-hearted, lily-livered, yellow (*sl*), soft, wet, submissive, weak-kneed.
≠ strong, brave.

spiral *adj* winding, coiled, corkscrew, helical, whorled, scrolled, circular.
n coil, helix, corkscrew, screw, whorl, convolution.

spire *n* steeple, pinnacle, peak, summit, top, tip, point, spike.

spirit *n* **1** SOUL, psyche, mind, breath,

life. **2** GHOST, spectre, phantom, apparition, angel, demon, fairy, sprite. **3** LIVELINESS, vivacity, animation, sparkle, vigour, energy, zest, fire, ardour, motivation, enthusiasm, zeal, enterprise, resolution, willpower, courage, backbone, mettle. **4** *the spirit of the law*: meaning, sense, substance, essence, gist, tenor, character, quality. **5** MOOD, humour, temper, disposition, temperament, feeling, morale, attitude, outlook.

spirited *adj* lively, vivacious, animated, sparkling, high-spirited, vigorous, energetic, active, ardent, zealous, bold, courageous, mettlesome, plucky.
≠ spiritless, lethargic, cowardly.

spiritual *adj* unworldly, incorporeal, immaterial, otherwordly, heavenly, divine, holy, sacred, religious, ecclesiastical.
≠ physical, material.

spit *v* expectorate, eject, discharge, splutter, hiss.
n spittle, saliva, slaver, drool, dribble, sputum, phlegm, expectoration.

spite *n* spitefulness, malice, venom, gall, bitterness, rancour, animosity, ill feeling, grudge, malevolence, malignity, ill nature, hate, hatred.
≠ goodwill, compassion, affection.
v annoy, irritate, irk, vex, provoke, gall, hurt, injure, offend, put out.

spiteful *adj* malicious, venomous, catty, bitchy, snide, barbed, cruel, vindictive, vengeful, malevolent, malignant, ill-natured, ill-disposed, nasty.
≠ charitable, affectionate.

splash *v* **1** BATHE, wallow, paddle, wade, dabble, plunge, wet, wash, shower, spray, squirt, sprinkle, spatter, splatter, splodge, spread, daub, plaster, slop, slosh, plop, surge, break, dash, strike, buffet, smack. **2** PUBLICIZE, flaunt, blazon, trumpet.
n **1** SPOT, patch, splatter, splodge, burst, touch, dash. **2** PUBLICITY, display, ostentation, effect, impact, stir, excitement, sensation.

splendid *adj* brilliant, dazzling, glittering, lustrous, bright, radiant, glowing, glorious, magnificent, gorgeous, resplendent, sumptuous, luxurious, lavish, rich, fine, grand, stately, imposing, impressive, great, outstanding, remarkable, exceptional, sublime, supreme, superb, excellent, first-class, wonderful, marvellous, admirable.
≠ drab, ordinary, run-of-the-mill.

splendour *n* brightness, radiance, brilliance, dazzle, lustre, glory, resplendence, magnificence, richness, grandeur, majesty, solemnity, pomp, ceremony, display, show, spectacle.
≠ drabness, squalor.

splice *v* join, unite, wed, marry, bind, tie, plait, braid, interweave, interlace, intertwine, entwine, mesh, knit, graft.

splinter *n* sliver, shiver, chip, shard, fragment, flake, shaving, paring.
v split, fracture, smash, shatter, shiver, fragment, disintegrate.

split *v* divide, separate, partition, part, disunite, disband, open, gape, fork, diverge, break, splinter, shiver, snap, crack, burst, rupture, tear, rend, rip, slit, slash, cleave, halve, slice up, share, distribute, parcel out.
n **1** DIVISION, separation, partition, break, breach, gap, cleft, crevice, crack, fissure, rupture, tear, rent, rip, rift, slit, slash. **2** SCHISM, disunion, dissension, discord, difference, divergence, break-up.
adj divided, cleft, cloven, bisected, dual, twofold, broken, fractured, cracked, ruptured.
split up part, part company, disband, break up, separate, divorce.

spoil *v* **1** MAR, upset, wreck, ruin, destroy, damage, impair, harm, hurt, injure, deface, disfigure, blemish. **2** *spoil a child*: indulge, pamper, cosset, coddle, mollycoddle, baby, spoon-feed. **3** DETERIORATE, go bad, go off, sour, turn, curdle, decay, decompose.

spoils *n* plunder, loot, booty, haul, swag (*sl*), pickings, gain, acquisitions, prizes, winnings.

sponge *v* **1** WIPE, mop, clean, wash. **2** CADGE, scrounge.

sponger *n* cadger, scrounger, parasite, hanger-on.

spongy *adj* soft, cushioned, yielding, elastic, springy, porous, absorbent, light.

sponsor *n* patron, backer, angel (*infml*), promoter, underwriter, guarantor, surety.
v finance, fund, bankroll, subsidize, patronize, back, promote, underwrite, guarantee.

spontaneous *adj* natural, unforced, untaught, instinctive, impulsive, unpremeditated, free, willing, unhesitating, voluntary, unprompted, impromptu, extempore.
≠ forced, studied, planned, deliberate.

sporadic *adj* occasional, intermittent, infrequent, isolated, spasmodic, erratic, irregular, uneven, random, scattered.
≠ frequent, regular.

sport *n* **1** GAME, exercise, activity, pastime, amusement, entertainment, diversion, recreation, play. **2** FUN, mirth, humour, joking, jesting, banter, teasing, mockery, ridicule.

Sports include: badminton, fives, lacrosse, squash, table-tennis, ping-pong (*infml*), tennis; American football, baseball, basketball, billiards, boules, bowls, cricket, croquet, football, golf, handball, hockey, netball, pétanque, pitch and putt, polo, pool, putting, rounders, Rugby, snooker, soccer, tenpin bowling, volleyball; athletics, cross-country, decathlon, discus, high-jump, hurdling, javelin, long-jump, marathon, pentathlon, pole vault, running, shot put, triple-jump; angling, canoeing, diving, fishing, rowing, sailing, skin-diving, surfing, swimming, synchronized swimming, water polo, water-skiing, windsurfing, yachting; bobsleigh, curling, ice-hockey, ice-skating, skiing, speed skating, tobogganing (luging); aerobics, fencing, gymnastics, jogging, keep-fit, roller-skating, trampolining; archery, darts, quoits; boxing, judo, jujitsu, karate, tae kwon do, weightlifting, wrestling; climbing, mountaineering, rock-climbing, walking, orienteering, pot-holing; cycle racing, drag-racing, go-karting, motor racing, speedway racing, stock-car racing, greyhound-racing, horse-racing, show-jumping, trotting, hunting, shooting, clay-pigeon shooting; gliding, sky-diving.

v wear, display, exhibit, show off.

sporting *adj* sportsmanlike, gentlemanly, decent, considerate, fair.
≠ unsporting, ungentlemanly, unfair.

sports equipment

Kinds of sports equipment include: ball, basketball, boule, bowl, jack, wood, football, netball, rugby ball, tenpin bowling ball, volleyball; fishing-rod, fly rod, spinning rod, fishing-line, paternoster, reel, fly reel, hook, gaff, gang-hook, jig, trace, lure, bait, fly, float, net, keep-net, priest, disgorger; bow, arrow, crossbow, bolt; badminton racket, shuttlecock, net; baseball bat, baseball, mitt, catcher's glove; boxing glove, gum shield, punch-bag, punch-ball; cricket bat, cricket ball, wicket, stump, bail, nets; épée, foil, sabre, face-guard, mask; discus, hammer, javelin, shot; golf club, golfball, tee, golfing glove; asymmetrical bars, horizontal bar, isometric bar, parallel-bars, beam, balance-beam, mat, pommel horse, vaulting horse, rings, rope, springboard, trampoline; hockey stick, hockey ball, ice-hockey stick, puck, hockey skate; curling stone; ice-skate, roller-skate, rollerblade, roller boot, speed skate, skateboard; ski, ski stick, snow board, toboggan; snooker ball, billiard ball, cue ball, table, cue, rest, bridge, rack, chalk; squash racket, squash ball; table-tennis bat, table-tennis ball, net; tennis racket, tennis ball, net, racket press; oar, aqualung, snorkel, water-ski, sailboard, surfboard. *see also* **golf clubs**.

sporty *adj* **1** ATHLETIC, fit, energetic, outdoor. **2** STYLISH, trendy (*infml*), jaunty, natty (*infml*), snazzy (*infml*), showy, loud, flashy, casual, informal.

spot *n* **1** DOT, speckle, fleck, mark, speck, blotch, blot, smudge, daub, splash, stain, discoloration, blemish,

flaw, pimple. **2** PLACE, point, position, situation, location, site, scene, locality. **3** (*infml*) PLIGHT, predicament, quandary, difficulty, trouble, mess.
v see, notice, observe, detect, discern, identify, recognize.

spotless *adj* immaculate, clean, white, gleaming, spick and span, unmarked, unstained, unblemished, unsullied, pure, chaste, virgin, untouched, innocent, blameless, faultless, irreproachable.
≠ dirty, impure.

spotted *adj* dotted, speckled, flecked, mottled, dappled, pied.

spotty *adj* pimply, pimpled, blotchy, spotted.

spouse *n* husband, wife, partner, mate, better half (*infml*).

spout *v* jet, spurt, squirt, spray, shoot, gush, stream, surge, erupt, emit, discharge.
n jet, fountain, geyser, gargoyle, outlet, nozzle, rose, spray.

sprawl *v* spread, straggle, trail, ramble, flop, slump, slouch, loll, lounge, recline, repose.

spray[1] *v* shower, spatter, sprinkle, scatter, diffuse, wet, drench.
n **1** MOISTURE, drizzle, mist, foam, froth. **2** AEROSOL, atomizer, sprinkler.

spray[2] *n* sprig, branch, corsage, posy, bouquet, garland, wreath.

spread *v* **1** STRETCH, extend, sprawl, broaden, widen, dilate, expand, swell, mushroom, proliferate, escalate, open, unroll, unfurl, unfold, fan out, cover, lay out, arrange. **2** SCATTER, strew, diffuse, radiate, disseminate, broadcast, transmit, communicate, promulgate, propagate, publicize, advertise, publish, circulate, distribute.
≠ **1** close, fold. **2** suppress.
n **1** STRETCH, reach, span, extent, expanse, sweep, compass. **2** *the spread of disease*: advance, development, expansion, increase, proliferation, escalation, diffusion, dissemination, dispersion.

spree *n* bout, fling, binge, splurge, orgy, revel.

sprightly *adj* agile, nimble, spry, active, energetic, lively, spirited, vivacious, hearty, brisk, jaunty, cheerful, blithe, airy.
≠ doddering, inactive, lifeless.

spring[1] *v* **1** JUMP, leap, vault, bound, hop, bounce, rebound, recoil. **2** ORIGINATE, derive, come, stem, arise, start, proceed, issue, emerge, emanate, appear, sprout, grow, develop.
n **1** JUMP, leap, vault, bound, bounce. **2** SPRINGINESS, resilience, give, flexibility, elasticity, buoyancy.

spring[2] *n* source, origin, beginning, cause, root, fountainhead, wellhead, wellspring, well, geyser, spa.

springy *adj* bouncy, resilient, flexible, elastic, stretchy, rubbery, spongy, buoyant.
≠ hard, stiff.

sprinkle *v* shower, spray, spatter, scatter, strew, dot, pepper, dust, powder.

sprint *v* run, race, dash, tear, belt (*infml*), dart, shoot.

sprout *v* shoot, bud, germinate, grow, develop, come up, spring up.

spruce *adj* smart, elegant, neat, trim, dapper, well-dressed, well-turned-out, well-groomed, sleek.
≠ scruffy, untidy.
spruce up neaten, tidy, smarten up, groom.

spur *v* goad, prod, poke, prick, stimulate, prompt, incite, drive, propel, impel, urge, encourage, motivate.
≠ curb, discourage.
n incentive, encouragement, inducement, motive, stimulus, incitement, impetus, fillip.
≠ curb, disincentive.

spurious *adj* false, fake, counterfeit, forged, bogus, phoney (*infml*), mock, sham, feigned, pretended, simulated, imitation, artificial.
≠ genuine, authentic, real.

spurn *v* reject, turn down, scorn, despise, disdain, rebuff, repulse, slight, snub, cold-shoulder, ignore, disregard.
≠ accept, embrace.

spurt *v* gush, squirt, jet, shoot, burst, erupt, surge.
n burst, rush, surge, spate, fit, access.

spy *n* secret agent, undercover agent, double agent, mole (*infml*), fifth columnist, scout, snooper.
v spot, glimpse, notice, observe, discover.

squabble *v* bicker, wrangle, quarrel, row, argue, dispute, clash, brawl, scrap, fight.

squad *n* crew, team, gang, band, group, company, brigade, troop, force, outfit.

squalid *adj* dirty, filthy, unclean, foul, disgusting, repulsive, sordid, seedy, dingy, untidy, slovenly, unkempt, broken-down, run-down, neglected, uncared-for, low, mean, nasty.
≠ clean, pleasant, attractive.

squander *v* waste, misspend, misuse, lavish, blow (*sl*), fritter away, throw away, dissipate, scatter, spend, expend, consume.

square *v* settle, reconcile, tally, agree, accord, harmonize, correspond, match, balance, straighten, level, align, adjust, regulate, adapt, tailor, fit, suit.
adj **1** QUADRILATERAL, rectangular, right-angled, perpendicular, straight, true, even, level. **2** FAIR, equitable, just, ethical, honourable, honest, genuine, above-board, on the level (*infml*).

squash *v* **1** CRUSH, flatten, press, squeeze, compress, crowd, trample, stamp, pound, pulp, smash, distort. **2** SUPPRESS, silence, quell, quash, annihilate, put down, snub, humiliate.
≠ **1** stretch, expand.

squat *adj* short, stocky, thickset, dumpy, chunky, stubby.
≠ slim, lanky.
v crouch, stoop, bend, sit.

squawk *v, n* screech, shriek, cry, croak, cackle, crow, hoot.

squeak *v, n* squeal, whine, creak, peep, cheep.

squeal *v, n* cry, shout, yell, yelp, wail, scream, screech, shriek, squawk.

squeamish *adj* queasy, nauseated, sick, delicate, fastidious, particular, prudish.

squeeze *v* **1** PRESS, squash, crush, pinch, nip, compress, grip, clasp, clutch, hug, embrace, enfold, cuddle. **2** *squeeze into a corner*: cram, stuff, pack, crowd, wedge, jam, force, ram, push, thrust, shove, jostle. **3** WRING, wrest, extort, milk, bleed, force, lean on (*infml*).
n **1** PRESS, squash, crush, crowd, congestion, jam. **2** HUG, embrace, hold, grasp, clasp.

squirt *v* spray, spurt, jet, shoot, spout, gush, ejaculate, discharge, emit, eject, expel.
n spray, spurt, jet.

stab *v* pierce, puncture, cut, wound, injure, gore, knife, spear, stick, jab, thrust.
n **1** ACHE, pang, twinge, prick, puncture, cut, incision, gash, wound, jab. **2** (*infml*) TRY, attempt, endeavour, bash (*infml*).

stability *n* steadiness, firmness, soundness, constancy, steadfastness, strength, sturdiness, solidity, durability, permanence.
≠ instability, unsteadiness, insecurity, weakness.

stable *adj* steady, firm, secure, fast, sound, sure, constant, steadfast, reliable, established, well-founded, deep-rooted, strong, sturdy, durable, lasting, enduring, abiding, permanent, unchangeable, unalterable, invariable, immutable, fixed, static, balanced.
≠ unstable, wobbly, shaky, weak.

stack *n* heap, pile, mound, mass, load, accumulation, hoard, stockpile.
v heap, pile, load, amass, accumulate, assemble, gather, save, hoard, stockpile.

staff *n* **1** *member of staff*: personnel, workforce, employees, workers, crew, team, teachers, officers. **2** STICK, cane, rod, baton, wand, pole, prop.

stage *n* point, juncture, step, phase, period, division, lap, leg, length, level, floor.
v mount, put on, present, produce, give, do, perform, arrange, organize,

stage-manage, orchestrate, engineer.

tagger *v* **1** LURCH, totter, teeter, wobble, sway, rock, reel, falter, hesitate, waver. **2** SURPRISE, amaze, astound, astonish, stun, stupefy, dumbfound, flabbergast (*infml*), shake, shock, confound, overwhelm.

tagnant *adj* still, motionless, standing, brackish, stale, sluggish, torpid, lethargic.
≠ fresh, moving.

tagnate *v* vegetate, idle, languish, decline, deteriorate, degenerate, decay, rot, rust.

taid *adj* sedate, calm, composed, sober, demure, solemn, serious, grave, quiet, steady.
≠ jaunty, debonair, frivolous, adventurous.

tain *v* **1** MARK, spot, blemish, blot, smudge, discolour, dirty, soil, taint, contaminate, sully, tarnish, blacken, disgrace. **2** DYE, tint, tinge, colour, paint, varnish.
n mark, spot, blemish, blot, smudge, discoloration, smear, slur, disgrace, shame, dishonour.

take[1] *n* post, pole, standard, picket, pale, paling, spike, stick.

take[2] *n* bet, wager, pledge, interest, concern, involvement, share, investment, claim.
v gamble, bet, wager, pledge, risk, chance, hazard, venture.

tale *adj* **1** *stale bread*: dry, hard, old, musty, fusty, flat, insipid, tasteless. **2** OVERUSED, hackneyed, clichéed, stereotyped, jaded, worn-out, unoriginal, trite, banal, commonplace.
≠ **1** crisp. **2** new.

talemate *n* draw, tie, deadlock, impasse, standstill, halt.
≠ progress.

talk[1] *v* track, trail, hunt, follow, pursue, shadow, tail, haunt.

talk[2] *n* stem, twig, branch, trunk.

tall *v* temporize, play for time, delay, hedge, equivocate, obstruct, stonewall.

talwart *adj* strong, sturdy, robust, rugged, stout, strapping, muscular, athletic, vigorous, valiant, daring, intrepid, indomitable, determined, resolute, staunch, steadfast, reliable, dependable.
≠ weak, feeble, timid.

stamina *n* energy, vigour, strength, power, force, grit, resilience, resistance, endurance, indefatigability, staying power.
≠ weakness.

stammer *v* stutter, stumble, falter, hesitate, splutter.

stamp *v* **1** TRAMPLE, crush, beat, pound. **2** IMPRINT, impress, print, inscribe, engrave, emboss, mark, brand, label, categorize, identify, characterize.
n print, imprint, impression, seal, signature, authorization, mark, hallmark, attestation, brand, cast, mould, cut, form, fashion, sort, kind, type, breed, character, description.

stampede *n* charge, rush, dash, sprint, flight, rout.
v charge, rush, dash, tear, run, sprint, gallop, shoot, fly, flee, scatter.

stance *n* posture, deportment, carriage, bearing, position, standpoint, viewpoint, angle, point of view, attitude.

stand *v* **1** PUT, place, set, erect, up-end, position, station. **2** *I can't stand it*: bear, tolerate, abide, endure, suffer, experience, undergo, withstand, weather. **3** RISE, get up, stand up.
n base, pedestal, support, frame, rack, table, stage, platform, place, stall, booth.
stand by support, back, champion, defend, stick up for, uphold, adhere to, hold to, stick by.
≠ let down.
stand down step down, resign, abdicate, quit, give up, retire, withdraw.
≠ join.
stand for represent, symbolize, mean, signify, denote, indicate.
stand in for deputize for, cover for, understudy, replace, substitute for.
stand out show, catch the eye, stick out, jut out, project.
stand up for defend, stick up for, side with, fight for, support, protect,

champion, uphold.
≠ attack.
stand up to defy, oppose, resist, withstand, endure, face, confront, brave.
≠ give in to.

standard *n* **1** NORM, average, type, model, pattern, example, sample, guideline, benchmark, touchstone, yardstick, rule, measure, gauge, level, criterion, requirement, specification, grade, quality. **2** FLAG, ensign, pennant, pennon, colours, banner.
adj normal, average, typical, stock, classic, basic, staple, usual, customary, popular, prevailing, regular, approved, accepted, recognized, official, orthodox, set, established, definitive.
≠ abnormal, unusual, irregular.

standardize *v* normalize, equalize, homogenize, stereotype, mass-produce.
≠ differentiate.

standards *n* principles, ideals, morals, ethics.

standoffish *adj* aloof, remote, distant, unapproachable, unsociable, uncommunicative, reserved, cold.
≠ friendly.

standpoint *n* position, station, vantagepoint, stance, viewpoint, angle, point of view.

standstill *n* stop, halt, pause, lull, rest, stoppage, jam, log-jam, hold-up, impasse, deadlock, stalemate.
≠ advance, progress.

staple *adj* basic, fundamental, primary, key, main, chief, major, principal, essential, necessary, standard.
≠ minor.

star *n* celebrity, personage, luminary, idol, lead, leading man, leading lady, superstar.

Types of star include: nova, supernova, pulsar, falling-star, shooting-star, meteor, comet, Halley's comet, red giant, supergiant, white dwarf, red dwarf, brown dwarf, neutron star, Pole Star, Polaris, North Star.

stare *v* gaze, look, watch, gape, gawp, gawk, goggle, glare.
n gaze, look, glare.

stark *adj* **1** *stark landscape*: bare, barren, bleak, bald, plain, simple, austere, harsh, severe, grim, dreary, gloomy, depressing. **2** UTTER, unmitigated, total, consummate, absolute, sheer, downright, out-and-out, flagrant, arrant.

start *v* **1** BEGIN, commence, originate initiate, introduce, pioneer, create, found, establish, set up, institute, inaugurate, launch, open, kick off (*infml*), instigate, activate, trigger, se off, set out, leave, depart, appear, arise, issue. **2** JUMP, jerk, twitch, flinch, recoil.
≠ **1** stop, finish, end.
n **1** BEGINNING, commencement, outset, inception, dawn, birth, break, outburst, onset, origin, initiation, introduction, foundation, inauguratic launch, opening, kick-off (*infml*). **2** JUMP, jerk, twitch, spasm, convulsio fit.
≠ **1** stop, finish, end.

startle *v* surprise, amaze, astonish, astound, shock, scare, frighten, alarn agitate, upset, disturb.
≠ calm.

starvation *n* hunger, undernourishment, malnutrition, famine.
≠ plenty, excess.

starve *v* hunger, fast, diet, deprive, refuse, deny, die, perish.
≠ feed, gorge.

starving *adj* hungry, underfed, undernourished, ravenous, famished.

state *v* say, declare, announce, report communicate, assert, aver, affirm, specify, present, express, put, formulate, articulate, voice.
n **1** CONDITION, shape, situation, position, circumstances, case.
2 NATION, country, land, territory, kingdom, republic, government.
3 (*infml*) PANIC, flap (*infml*), tizzy (*infml*), bother, plight, predicament.
4 POMP, ceremony, dignity, majesty, grandeur, glory, splendour.
adj national, governmental, public, official, formal, ceremonial, pompous stately.

stately *adj* grand, imposing, impressive, elegant, majestic, regal, royal, imperial, noble, august, lofty, pompous, dignified, measured, deliberate, solemn, ceremonious.
≠ informal, unimpressive.

statement *n* account, report, bulletin, communiqué, announcement, declaration, proclamation, communication, utterance, testimony.

static *adj* stationary, motionless, immobile, unmoving, still, inert, resting, fixed, constant, changeless, unvarying, stable.
≠ dynamic, mobile, varying.

station *n* place, location, position, post, headquarters, base, depot.
v locate, set, establish, install, garrison, post, send, appoint, assign.

stationary *adj* motionless, immobile, unmoving, still, static, inert, standing, resting, parked, moored, fixed.
≠ mobile, moving, active.

stationery

Items of stationery include: account book, address book, adhesive tape, blotter, bulldog clip, calendar, carbon paper, card index, cartridge ribbon, cash book, clipboard, computer disk, copying paper, correcting paper, correction fluid, correction ribbon, desk-diary, diary, divider, document folder, document wallet, drawing pin, dry-transfer lettering, elastic band, envelope, brown manila envelope, reply-paid envelope, self-seal envelope, window envelope, eraser, expanding file, file, file tab, filing tray, Filofax®, flip chart, floppy disk, folder, graph paper, headed notepaper, index card, ink, Jiffy bag®, label, lever arch file, marker, memo pad, notepaper, paper clip, paper fastener, paper knife, pen, pencil, pencil-sharpener, personal organizer, pin, pocket calculator, pocket folder, Post-it note®, printer label, printer paper, printer ribbon, reinforcement ring, ring binder, rubber, rubber band, rubber stamp, ruler, scissors, Sellotape®, shorthand notebook, spiral notebook, stamp pad, staple, suspension file, tape dispenser, Tipp-Ex®, toner, treasury tag, typewriter ribbon, wall chart, writing paper. *see also* **paper**.

statue *n* figure, head, bust, effigy, idol, statuette, carving, bronze.

status *n* rank, grade, degree, level, class, station, standing, position, state, condition, prestige, eminence, distinction, importance, consequence, weight.
≠ unimportance, insignificance.

staunch *adj* loyal, faithful, hearty, strong, stout, firm, sound, sure, true, trusty, reliable, dependable, steadfast.
≠ unfaithful, weak, unreliable.

stay *v* **1** LAST, continue, endure, abide, remain, linger, persist. **2** RESIDE, dwell, live, settle, sojourn, stop, halt, pause, wait.
≠ **1** go, leave.
n visit, holiday, stopover, sojourn.

steady *adj* stable, balanced, poised, fixed, immovable, firm, settled, still, calm, imperturbable, equable, even, uniform, consistent, unvarying, unchanging, constant, persistent, unremitting, incessant, uninterrupted, unbroken, regular, rhythmic, steadfast, unwavering.
≠ unsteady, unstable, variable, wavering.
v balance, stabilize, fix, secure, brace, support.

steal *v* **1** *steal a car*: thieve, pilfer, filch, pinch (*infml*), nick (*infml*), take, appropriate, snatch, swipe, shoplift, poach, embezzle, lift, plagiarize.
2 CREEP, tiptoe, slip, slink, sneak.
≠ **1** return, give back.

stealthy *adj* surreptitious, clandestine, covert, secret, unobtrusive, secretive, quiet, furtive, sly, cunning, sneaky, underhand.
≠ open.

steam *n* vapour, mist, haze, condensation, moisture, dampness.

steep *adj* **1** *a steep slope*: sheer, precipitous, headlong, abrupt, sudden, sharp. **2** (*infml*) EXCESSIVE, extreme, stiff, unreasonable, high, exorbitant, extortionate, overpriced.

≠ 1 gentle, gradual. 2 moderate, low.

steer *v* pilot, guide, direct, control, govern, conduct.

stem[1] *n* stalk, shoot, stock, branch, trunk.

stem[2] *v* stop, halt, arrest, stanch, staunch, block, dam, check, curb, restrain, contain, resist, oppose.
≠ encourage.

stench *n* stink, reek, pong (*infml*), smell, odour.

step *n* **1** PACE, stride, footstep, tread, footprint, print, trace, track. **2** MOVE, act, action, deed, measure, procedure, process, proceeding, progression, movement, stage, phase, degree. **3** RUNG, stair, level, rank, point.
v pace, stride, tread, stamp, walk, move.
step down stand down, resign, abdicate, quit, leave, retire, withdraw.
≠ join.
step up increase, raise, augment, boost, build up, intensify, escalate, accelerate, speed up.
≠ decrease.

stereotype *n* formula, convention, mould, pattern, model.
v categorize, pigeonhole, typecast, standardize, formalize, conventionalize, mass-produce.
≠ differentiate.

sterile *adj* **1** GERM-FREE, aseptic, sterilized, disinfected, antiseptic, uncontaminated. **2** INFERTILE, barren, arid, bare, unproductive, fruitless, pointless, useless, abortive.
≠ **1** septic. **2** fertile, fruitful.

sterilize *v* disinfect, fumigate, purify, clean, cleanse.
≠ contaminate, infect.

stern *adj* strict, severe, authoritarian, rigid, inflexible, unyielding, hard, tough, rigorous, stringent, harsh, cruel, unsparing, relentless, unrelenting, grim, forbidding, stark, austere.
≠ kind, gentle, mild, lenient.

stew *v* boil, simmer, braise, casserole.

stick[1] *v* **1** THRUST, poke, stab, jab, pierce, penetrate, puncture, spear, transfix. **2** GLUE, gum, paste, cement, bond, fuse, weld, solder, adhere, cling, hold. **3** ATTACH, affix, fasten, secure, fix, pin, join, bind. **4** put, place, position, set, install, deposit, drop.
stick at persevere, plug away (*infml*), persist, continue.
≠ give up.
stick out protrude, jut out, project, extend.
stick up for stand up for, speak up fo[r], defend, champion, support, uphold.
≠ attack.

stick[2] *n* branch, twig.

Types of stick include: alpenstock, baton, birch, bludgeon, cane, club, crutch, cudgel, hockey stick, lathi, lug, pike, pole, rod, sceptre, shillelagh, staff, stake, tripod stick, waddy, walking-frame, walking stick, wand, whip, Zimmer frame®.

sticky *adj* **1** ADHESIVE, gummed, tacky, gluey, gummy, viscous, glutinous, gooey (*infml*). **2** (*infml*) *a sticky situation*: difficult, tricky, thorny, unpleasant, awkward, embarrassing, delicate. **3** HUMID, clammy, muggy, close, oppressive, sultry.
≠ **1** dry. **2** easy. **3** fresh, cool.

stiff *adj* **1** RIGID, inflexible, unbending, unyielding, hard, solid, hardened, solidified, firm, tight, taut, tense. **2** FORMAL, ceremonious, pompous, stand-offish, cold, prim, priggish, austere, strict, severe, harsh. **3** DIFFICULT, hard, tough, arduous, laborious, awkward, exacting, rigorous.
≠ **1** flexible. **2** informal. **3** easy.

stiffen *v* harden, solidify, tighten, tense, brace, reinforce, starch, thicken, congeal, coagulate, jell, set.

stifle *v* smother, suffocate, asphyxiate, strangle, choke, extinguish, muffle, dampen, deaden, silence, hush, suppress, quell, check, curb, restrain, repress.
≠ encourage.

stigma *n* brand, mark, stain, blot, spot, blemish, disgrace, shame, dishonour.
≠ credit, honour.

still *adj* stationary, motionless, lifeless,

stagnant, smooth, undisturbed, unruffled, calm, tranquil, serene, restful, peaceful, hushed, quiet, silent, noiseless.
≠ active, disturbed, agitated, noisy.
v calm, soothe, allay, tranquillize, subdue, restrain, hush, quieten, silence, pacify, settle, smooth.
≠ agitate, stir up.
adv yet, even so, nevertheless, nonetheless, notwithstanding, however.

tilted *adj* artificial, unnatural, stiff, wooden, forced, constrained.
≠ fluent, flowing.

timulate *v* rouse, arouse, animate, quicken, fire, inflame, inspire, motivate, encourage, induce, urge, impel, spur, prompt, goad, provoke, incite, instigate, trigger off.
≠ discourage, hinder, prevent.

timulus *n* incentive, encouragement, inducement, spur, goad, provocation, incitement.
≠ discouragement.

ting *v* **1** *bees sting*: bite, prick, hurt, injure, wound. **2** SMART, tingle, burn, pain.
n bite, nip, prick, smart, tingle.

tingy *adj* mean, miserly, niggardly, tight-fisted (*infml*), parsimonious, penny-pinching.
≠ generous, liberal.

tink *v* smell, reek, pong (*infml*), hum (*sl*).
n smell, odour, stench, pong (*infml*), niff (*sl*).

tint *n* spell, stretch, period, time, shift, turn, bit, share, quota.

tipulate *v* specify, lay down, require, demand, insist on.

tipulation *n* specification, requirement, demand, condition, proviso.

tir *v* **1** MOVE, budge, touch, affect, inspire, excite, thrill, disturb, agitate, shake, tremble, quiver, flutter, rustle. **2** MIX, blend, beat.
n activity, movement, bustle, flurry, commotion, ado, fuss, to-do (*infml*), uproar, tumult, disturbance, disorder, agitation, excitement, ferment.
≠ calm.
stir up rouse, arouse, awaken, animate, quicken, kindle, fire, inflame, stimulate, spur, prompt, provoke, incite, instigate, agitate.
≠ calm, discourage.

stock *n* **1** GOODS, merchandise, wares, commodities, capital, assets, inventory, repertoire, range, variety, assortment, source, supply, fund, reservoir, store, reserve, stockpile, hoard.
2 PARENTAGE, ancestry, descent, extraction, family, line, lineage, pedigree, race, breed, species, blood.
3 LIVESTOCK, animals, cattle, horses, sheep, herds, flocks.
adj standard, basic, regular, routine, ordinary, run-of-the-mill, usual, customary, traditional, conventional, set, stereotyped, hackneyed, overused, banal, trite.
≠ original, unusual.
v keep, carry, sell, trade in, deal in, handle, supply, provide.
stock up gather, accumulate, amass, lay in, provision, fill, replenish, store (up), save, hoard, pile up.

stocky *adj* sturdy, solid, thickset, chunky, short, squat, dumpy, stubby.
≠ tall, skinny.

stoical *adj* patient, long-suffering, uncomplaining, resigned, philosophical, indifferent, impassive, unemotional, phlegmatic, dispassionate, cool, calm, imperturbable.
≠ excitable, anxious.

stolid *adj* slow, heavy, dull, bovine, wooden, blockish, lumpish, impassive, phlegmatic, unemotional.
≠ lively, interested.

stomach *n* tummy (*infml*), gut, inside(s), belly, abdomen, paunch, pot.
v tolerate, bear, stand, abide, endure, suffer, submit to, take.

stony *adj* **1** BLANK, expressionless, hard, cold, frigid, icy, indifferent, unfeeling, heartless, callous, merciless, pitiless, inexorable, hostile. **2** *stony beach*: pebbly, shingly, rocky.
≠ **1** warm, soft-hearted, friendly.

stoop *v* **1** HUNCH, bow, bend, incline, lean, duck, squat, crouch, kneel.

2 *stoop to blackmail*: descend, sink, lower oneself, resort, go so far as, condescend, deign.

stop *v* **1** HALT, cease, end, finish, conclude, terminate, discontinue, suspend, interrupt, pause, quit, refrain, desist, pack in (*sl*). **2** PREVENT, bar, frustrate, thwart, intercept, hinder, impede, check, restrain. **3** SEAL, close, plug, block, obstruct, arrest, stem, stanch.
≠ **1** start, continue.
n **1** STATION, terminus, destination. **2** REST, break, pause, stage. **3** HALT, standstill, stoppage, cessation, end, finish, conclusion, termination, discontinuation.
≠ **3** start, beginning, continuation.

stoppage *n* stop, halt, standstill, arrest, blockage, obstruction, check, hindrance, interruption, shutdown, closure, strike, walk-out, sit-in.
≠ start, continuation.

stopper *n* cork, bung, plug.

store *v* save, keep, put aside, lay by, reserve, stock, lay in, deposit, lay down, lay up, accumulate, hoard, salt away, stockpile, stash (*infml*).
≠ use.
n **1** STOCK, supply, provision, fund, reserve, mine, reservoir, hoard, cache, stockpile, accumulation, quantity, abundance, plenty, lot. **2** STOREROOM, storehouse, warehouse, repository, depository.
≠ **1** scarcity.

storey *n* floor, level, stage, tier, flight, deck.

storm *n* outburst, uproar, furore, outcry, row, rumpus, commotion, disturbance, tumult, turmoil, stir, agitation, rage, outbreak, attack, assault.
≠ calm.

Kinds of storm include: blizzard, buran, cloudburst, cyclone, downpour, dust-devil, dust-storm, electrical storm, gale, haboob, hailstorm, hurricane, monsoon, rainstorm, sand storm, snow storm, squall, tempest, thunderstorm, tornado, typhoon, whirlwind. *see also* **wind**.

v charge, rush, attack, assault, assail, roar, thunder, rage, rant, rave, fume.

stormy *adj* tempestuous, squally, rough, choppy, turbulent, wild, raging, windy, gusty, blustery, foul.
≠ calm.

story *n* **1** TALE, novel, fiction, yarn, anecdote, episode, plot, narrative, history, chronicle, record, account, relation, recital, report, article, feature

Types of story include: adventure story, bedtime story, blockbuster (*infml*), children's story, comedy, black comedy, crime story, detective story, fable, fairy-tale, fantasy, folk tale, ghost story, historical novel, horror story, legend, love story, Mills & Boon®, mystery, myth, parable, romance, saga, science fiction, sci-fi (*infml*), short story, spiel, spine-chiller, spy story, supernatural tale, tall story, thriller, western, whodunit (*infml*).

2 LIE, falsehood, untruth.

stout *adj* **1** FAT, plump, fleshy, portly, corpulent, overweight, heavy, bulky, big, brawny, beefy, hulking, burly, muscular, athletic. **2** *stout packaging*: strong, tough, durable, thick, sturdy, robust, hardy, vigorous. **3** BRAVE, courageous, valiant, plucky, fearless, bold, intrepid, dauntless, resolute, stalwart.
≠ **1** thin, lean, slim. **2** weak. **3** cowardly, timid.

stow *v* put away, store, load, pack, cram, stuff, stash (*infml*).
≠ unload.

straight *adj* **1** *a straight line*: level, even, flat, horizontal, upright, vertical, aligned, direct, undeviating, unswerving, true, right. **2** TIDY, neat, orderly, shipshape, organized. **3** HONOURABLE, honest, law-abiding, respectable, upright, trustworthy, reliable, straightforward, fair, just. **4** FRANK, candid, blunt, forthright, direct. **5** *straight whisky*: undiluted, neat, unadulterated, unmixed.
≠ **1** bent, crooked. **2** untidy. **3** dishonest. **4** evasive. **5** diluted.
adv directly, point-blank, honestly,

frankly, candidly.
straight away at once, immediately, instantly, right away, directly, now, there and then.
≠ later, eventually.

raighten *v* unbend, align, tidy, neaten, order, arrange.
≠ bend, twist.
straighten out clear up, sort out, settle, resolve, correct, rectify, disentangle, regularize.
≠ confuse, muddle.

raightforward *adj* **1** EASY, simple, uncomplicated, clear, elementary. **2** HONEST, truthful, sincere, genuine, open, frank, candid, direct, forthright.
≠ **1** complicated. **2** evasive, devious.

rain[1] *v* **1** PULL, wrench, twist, sprain, tear, stretch, extend, tighten, tauten. **2** SIEVE, sift, screen, separate, filter, purify, drain, wring, squeeze, compress, express. **3** WEAKEN, tire, tax, overtax, overwork, labour, try, endeavour, struggle, strive, exert, force, drive.
n stress, anxiety, burden, pressure, tension, tautness, pull, sprain, wrench, injury, exertion, effort, struggle, force.
≠ relaxation.

train[2] *n* **1** STOCK, ancestry, descent, extraction, family, lineage, pedigree, blood, variety, type. **2** TRAIT, streak, vein, tendency, trace, suggestion, suspicion.

trained *adj* forced, constrained, laboured, false, artificial, unnatural, stiff, tense, unrelaxed, uneasy, uncomfortable, awkward, embarrassed, self-conscious.
≠ natural, relaxed.

trait-laced *adj* prudish, stuffy, starchy, prim, proper, strict, narrow, narrow-minded, puritanical, moralistic.
≠ broad-minded.

trand *n* fibre, filament, wire, thread, string, piece, length.

tranded *adj* marooned, high and dry, abandoned, forsaken, in the lurch, helpless, aground, grounded, beached, shipwrecked, wrecked.

trange *adj* **1** ODD, peculiar, funny (*infml*), curious, queer, weird, bizarre, eccentric, abnormal, irregular, uncommon, unusual, exceptional, remarkable, extraordinary, mystifying, perplexing, unexplained. **2** NEW, novel, untried, unknown, unheard-of, unfamiliar, unacquainted, foreign, alien, exotic.
≠ **1** ordinary, common. **2** well-known, familiar.

stranger *n* newcomer, visitor, guest, non-member, outsider, foreigner, alien.
≠ local, native.

strangle *v* throttle, choke, asphyxiate, suffocate, stifle, smother, suppress, gag, repress, inhibit.

strap *n* thong, tie, band, belt, leash.
v **1** BEAT, lash, whip, flog, belt. **2** FASTEN, secure, tie, bind.

stratagem *n* plan, scheme, plot, intrigue, ruse, ploy, trick, dodge, manoeuvre, device, artifice, wile, subterfuge.

strategic *adj* important, key, critical, decisive, crucial, vital, tactical, planned, calculated, deliberate, politic, diplomatic.
≠ unimportant.

strategy *n* tactics, planning, policy, approach, procedure, plan, programme, design, scheme.

stray *v* wander (off), get lost, err, ramble, roam, rove, range, meander, straggle, drift, diverge, deviate, digress.
adj **1** LOST, abandoned, homeless, wandering, roaming. **2** RANDOM, chance, accidental, freak, odd, erratic.

streak *n* line, stroke, smear, band, stripe, strip, layer, vein, trace, dash, touch, element, strain.
v **1** BAND, stripe, fleck, striate, smear, daub. **2** SPEED, tear, hurtle, sprint, gallop, fly, dart, flash, whistle, zoom, whizz, sweep.

stream *n* **1** RIVER, creek, brook, beck, burn, rivulet, tributary. **2** CURRENT, drift, flow, run, gush, flood, deluge, cascade, torrent.
v issue, well, surge, run, flow, course, pour, spout, gush, flood, cascade.

streamer *n* ribbon, banner, pennant, pennon, flag, ensign, standard.

streamlined *adj* aerodynamic, smooth, sleek, graceful, efficient, well-run, smooth-running, rationalized, time-saving, organized, slick.
≠ clumsy, inefficient.

strength *n* toughness, robustness, sturdiness, lustiness, brawn, muscle, sinew, power, might, force, vigour, energy, stamina, health, fitness, courage, fortitude, spirit, resolution, firmness, effectiveness, potency, concentration, intensity, vehemence.
≠ weakness, feebleness, impotence.

strengthen *v* reinforce, brace, steel, fortify, buttress, bolster, support, toughen, harden, stiffen, consolidate, substantiate, corroborate, confirm, encourage, hearten, refresh, restore, invigorate, nourish, increase, heighten, intensify.
≠ weaken, undermine.

strenuous *adj* **1** *strenuous work*: hard, tough, demanding, gruelling, taxing, laborious, uphill, arduous, tiring, exhausting. **2** ACTIVE, energetic, vigorous, eager, earnest, determined, resolute, spirited, tireless, indefatigable.
≠ **1** easy, effortless.

stress *n* **1** PRESSURE, strain, tension, worry, anxiety, weight, burden, trauma, hassle (*infml*). **2** EMPHASIS, accent, accentuation, beat, force, weight, importance, significance.
≠ **1** relaxation.
v emphasize, accentuate, highlight, underline, underscore, repeat.
≠ understate, downplay.

stretch *n* **1** EXPANSE, spread, sweep, reach, extent, distance, space, area, tract. **2** PERIOD, time, term, spell, stint, run.
v pull, tighten, tauten, strain, tax, extend, lengthen, elongate, expand, spread, unfold, unroll, inflate, swell, reach.
≠ compress.
stretch out extend, relax, hold out, put out, lie down, reach.
≠ draw back.

strict *adj* **1** *a strict teacher*: stern, authoritarian, no-nonsense, firm, rigid, inflexible, stringent, rigorous, harsh, severe, austere. **2** EXACT, precise, accurate, literal, faithful, true, absolute, utter, total, complete, thoroughgoing, meticulous, scrupul[ous], particular, religious.
≠ **1** easy-going (*infml*), flexible. **2** loose.

strident *adj* loud, clamorous, vociferous, harsh, raucous, grating, rasping, shrill, screeching, unmusica[l], discordant, clashing, jarring, janglin[g].
≠ quiet, soft.

strife *n* conflict, discord, dissension, controversy, animosity, friction, rivalry, contention, quarrel, row, wrangling, struggle, fighting, comba[t], battle, warfare.
≠ peace.

strike *n* **1** INDUSTRIAL ACTION, wo[rk-]to-rule, go-slow, stoppage, sit-in, w[alk-]out, mutiny, revolt. **2** HIT, blow, stroke, raid, attack.
v **1** STOP WORK, down tools, work[-to-]rule, walk out, protest, mutiny, rev[olt]. **2** HIT, knock, collide with, slap, smack, cuff, clout, thump, wallop (*infml*), beat, pound, hammer, buff[et], raid, attack, afflict. **3** IMPRESS, affe[ct], touch, register. **4** FIND, discover, unearth, uncover, encounter, reach.
strike out cross out, delete, strike through, cancel, strike off, remove.
≠ add.

striking *adj* noticeable, conspicuous salient, outstanding, remarkable, extraordinary, memorable, impressi[ve], dazzling, arresting, astonishing, stunning.
≠ unimpressive.

string *n* **1** *a piece of string*: twine, cord, rope, cable, line, strand, fibre. **2** SERIES, succession, sequence, chai[n], line, row, file, queue, procession, tr[ain].
v thread, link, connect, tie up, han[g], suspend, festoon, loop.

stringent *adj* binding, strict, severe, rigorous, tough, rigid, inflexible, tig[ht].
≠ lax, flexible.

strip[1] *v* peel, skin, flay, denude, divest[,] deprive, undress, disrobe, unclothe, uncover, expose, lay bare, bare, empt[y], clear, gut, ransack, pillage, plunder, l[oot]

≠ dress, clothe, cover.

strip[2] *n* ribbon, thong, strap, belt, sash, band, stripe, lath, slat, piece, bit, slip, shred.

stripe *n* band, line, bar, chevron, flash, streak, fleck, strip, belt.

strive *v* try, attempt, endeavour, struggle, strain, work, toil, labour, fight, contend, compete.

stroke *n* **1** CARESS, pat, rub. **2** BLOW, hit, knock, swipe. **3** SWEEP, flourish, movement, action, move, line.
v caress, fondle, pet, touch, pat, rub, massage.

stroll *v* saunter, amble, dawdle, ramble, wander.
n saunter, amble, walk, constitutional, turn, ramble.

strong *adj* **1** TOUGH, resilient, durable, hard-wearing, heavy-duty, robust, sturdy, firm, sound, lusty, strapping, stout, burly, well-built, beefy, brawny, muscular, sinewy, athletic, fit, healthy, hardy, powerful, mighty, potent.
2 INTENSE, deep, vivid, fierce, violent, vehement, keen, eager, zealous, fervent, ardent, dedicated, staunch, stalwart, determined, resolute, tenacious, strong-minded, strong-willed, self-assertive.
3 HIGHLY-FLAVOURED, piquant, hot, spicy, highly-seasoned, sharp, pungent, undiluted, concentrated. **4** *strong argument*: convincing, persuasive, cogent, effective, telling, forceful, weighty, compelling, urgent.
≠ **1** weak, feeble. **2** indecisive. **3** mild, bland. **4** unconvincing.

stronghold *n* citadel, bastion, fort, fortress, castle, keep, refuge.

structure *n* construction, erection, building, edifice, fabric, framework, form, shape, design, configuration, conformation, make-up, formation, arrangement, organization, set-up.
v construct, assemble, build, form, shape, design, arrange, organize.

struggle *v* strive, work, toil, labour, strain, agonize, fight, battle, wrestle, grapple, contend, compete, vie.
≠ yield, give in.
n difficulty, problem, effort, exertion, pains, agony, work, labour, toil, clash, conflict, strife, fight, battle, skirmish, encounter, combat, hostilities, contest.
≠ ease, submission, co-operation.

stub *n* end, stump, remnant, fag-end (*infml*), dog-end (*infml*), butt, counterfoil.

stubborn *adj* obstinate, stiff-necked, mulish, pig-headed, obdurate, intransigent, rigid, inflexible, unbending, unyielding, dogged, persistent, tenacious, headstrong, self-willed, wilful, refractory, difficult, unmanageable.
≠ compliant, flexible, yielding.

stuck *adj* **1** FAST, jammed, firm, fixed, fastened, joined, glued, cemented.
2 BEATEN, stumped (*infml*), baffled.
≠ **1** loose.

stuck-up (*infml*) *adj* snobbish, toffee-nosed (*infml*), supercilious, snooty (*infml*), haughty, high and mighty, condescending, proud, arrogant, conceited, bigheaded (*infml*).
≠ humble, modest.

student *n* undergraduate, postgraduate, scholar, schoolboy, schoolgirl, pupil, disciple, learner, trainee, apprentice.

studied *adj* deliberate, conscious, wilful, intentional, premeditated, planned, calculated, contrived, forced, unnatural, over-elaborate.
≠ unplanned, impulsive, natural.

studio *n* workshop, workroom.

studious *adj* scholarly, academic, intellectual, bookish, serious, thoughtful, reflective, diligent, hard-working, industrious, assiduous, careful, attentive, earnest, eager.
≠ lazy, idle, negligent.

study *v* read, learn, revise, cram, swot (*infml*), mug up (*infml*), read up, research, investigate, analyse, survey, scan, examine, scrutinize, peruse, pore over, contemplate, meditate, ponder, consider, deliberate.
n **1** READING, homework, preparation, learning, revision, cramming, swotting (*infml*), research, investigation, inquiry, analysis, examination, scrutiny, inspection, contemplation, consideration, attention.

Subjects of study include: accountancy, agriculture, anatomy, anthropology, archaeology, architecture, art, astrology, astronomy, biology, botany, building studies, business studies, calligraphy, chemistry, CDT (craft, design and technology), civil engineering, the Classics, commerce, computer studies, cosmology, craft, dance, design, domestic science, drama, dressmaking, driving, ecology, economics, education, electronics, engineering, environmental studies, ethnology, eugenics, fashion, fitness, food technology, forensics, genetics, geography, geology, heraldry, history, home economics, horticulture, information technology (IT), journalism, languages, law, leisure studies, lexicography, linguistics, literature, logistics, management studies, marketing, mathematics, mechanics, media studies, medicine, metallurgy, metaphysics, meteorology, music, mythology, natural history, oceanography, ornithology, pathology, penology, personal and social education (PSE); personal, health and social education (PHSE), pharmacology, philosophy, photography, physics, physiology, politics, pottery, psychology, religious studies, science, shorthand, social sciences, sociology, sport, statistics, surveying, technology, theology, typewriting, visual arts, word processing, writing, zoology.

2 REPORT, essay, thesis, paper, monograph, survey, review, critique. **3** OFFICE, den (*infml*).

stuff *v* **1** PACK, stow, load, fill, cram, crowd, force, push, shove, ram, wedge, jam, squeeze, compress. **2** GORGE, gormandise, overindulge, guzzle, gobble, sate, satiate.
≠ **1** unload, empty. **2** nibble.
n **1** MATERIAL, fabric, matter, substance, essence. **2** (*infml*) BELONGINGS, possessions, things, objects, articles, goods, luggage, paraphernalia, gear (*infml*), clobber (*infml*), kit, tackle, equipment, materials.

stuffing *n* padding, wadding, quilting, filling, force-meat.

stuffy *adj* **1** *a stuffy room*: musty, stale, airless, unventilated, suffocating, stifling, oppressive, heavy, close, muggy, sultry. **2** STAID, strait-laced, prim, conventional, old-fashioned, pompous, dull, dreary, uninteresting, stodgy.
≠ **1** airy, well-ventilated. **2** informal, modern, lively.

stumble *v* **1** TRIP, slip, fall, lurch, reel, stagger, flounder, blunder. **2** STAMMER, stutter, hesitate, falter.
stumble on come across, chance upon, happen upon, find, discover, encounter.

stumbling-block *n* obstacle, hurdle, barrier, bar, obstruction, hindrance, impediment, difficulty, snag.

stump *n* end, remnant, trunk, stub.
v (*infml*) defeat, outwit, confound, perplex, puzzle, baffle, mystify, confuse, bewilder, flummox (*infml*), bamboozle (*infml*), dumbfound.
≠ assist.
stump up (*infml*) pay, hand over, fork out (*infml*), shell out (*infml*), donate, contribute, cough up (*infml*).
≠ receive.

stun *v* amaze, astonish, astound, stagger, shock, daze, stupefy, dumbfound, flabbergast (*infml*), overcome, confound, confuse, bewilder.

stunning (*infml*) *adj* beautiful, lovely, gorgeous, ravishing, dazzling, brilliant, striking, impressive, spectacular, remarkable, wonderful, marvellous, great, sensational.
≠ ugly, awful.

stunt[1] *n* feat, exploit, act, deed, enterprise, trick, turn, performance.

stunt[2] *v* stop, arrest, check, restrict, slow, retard, hinder, impede, dwarf.
≠ promote, encourage.

stupefy *v* daze, stun, numb, dumbfound, shock, stagger, amaze, astound.

stupendous *adj* huge, enormous, gigantic, colossal, vast, prodigious, phenomenal, tremendous,

breathtaking, overwhelming, staggering, stunning, amazing, astounding, fabulous, fantastic, superb, wonderful, marvellous.
≠ ordinary, unimpressive.

stupid *adj* **1** SILLY, foolish, irresponsible, ill-advised, indiscreet, foolhardy, rash, senseless, mad, lunatic, brainless, half-witted, idiotic, imbecilic, moronic, feeble-minded, simple-minded, slow, dim, dull, dense, thick, dumb, dopey, crass, inane, puerile, mindless, futile, pointless, meaningless, nonsensical, absurd, ludicrous, ridiculous, laughable.
2 DAZED, groggy, stupefied, stunned, sluggish, semiconscious.
≠ **1** sensible, wise, clever, intelligent. **2** alert.

stupor *n* daze, stupefaction, torpor, lethargy, inertia, trance, coma, numbness, insensibility, unconsciousness.
≠ alertness, consciousness.

sturdy *adj* strong, robust, durable, well-made, stout, substantial, solid, well-built, powerful, muscular, athletic, hardy, vigorous, flourishing, hearty, staunch, stalwart, steadfast, firm, resolute, determined.
≠ weak, flimsy, puny.

stutter *v* stammer, hesitate, falter, stumble, mumble.

style *n* **1** APPEARANCE, cut, design, pattern, shape, form, sort, type, kind, genre, variety, category. **2** ELEGANCE, smartness, chic, flair, panache, stylishness, taste, polish, refinement, sophistication, urbanity, fashion, vogue, trend, mode, dressiness, flamboyance, affluence, luxury, grandeur. **3** *style of working*: technique, approach, method, manner, mode, fashion, way, custom.
4 WORDING, phrasing, expression, tone, tenor.
≠ **2** inelegance, tastelessness.
v **1** DESIGN, cut, tailor, fashion, shape, adapt. **2** DESIGNATE, term, name, call, address, title, dub, label.

stylish *adj* chic, fashionable, á la mode, modish, in vogue, voguish, trendy (*infml*), snappy, natty (*infml*), snazzy (*infml*), dressy, smart, elegant, classy (*infml*), polished, refined, sophisticated, urbane.
≠ old-fashioned, shabby.

suave *adj* polite, courteous, charming, agreeable, affable, soft-spoken, smooth, unctuous, sophisticated, urbane, worldly.
≠ rude, unsophisticated.

subconscious *adj* subliminal, unconscious, intuitive, inner, innermost, hidden, latent, repressed, suppressed.
≠ conscious.

subdue *v* overcome, quell, suppress, repress, overpower, crush, defeat, conquer, vanquish, overrun, subject, subjugate, humble, break, tame, master, discipline, control, check, moderate, reduce, soften, quieten, damp, mellow.
≠ arouse, awaken.

subdued *adj* **1** SAD, downcast, dejected, crestfallen, quiet, serious, grave, solemn. **2** QUIET, muted, hushed, soft, dim, shaded, sombre, sober, restrained, unobtrusive, low-key, subtle.
≠ **1** lively, excited. **2** striking, obtrusive.

subject *n* **1** TOPIC, theme, matter, issue, question, point, case, affair, business, discipline, field. **2** NATIONAL, citizen, participant, client, patient, victim.
≠ **2** monarch, ruler, master.
adj **1** LIABLE, disposed, prone, susceptible, vulnerable, open, exposed.
2 SUBJUGATED, captive, bound, obedient, answerable, subordinate, inferior, subservient, submissive.
3 DEPENDENT, contingent, conditional.
≠ **1** invulnerable. **2** free, superior. **3** unconditional.
v expose, lay open, submit, subjugate, subdue.

subjection *n* subjugation, defeat, captivity, bondage, chains, shackles, slavery, enslavement, oppression, domination, mastery.

subjective *adj* biased, prejudiced,

personal, individual, idiosyncratic, emotional, intuitive, instinctive.
≠ objective, unbiased, impartial.

sublime *adj* exalted, elevated, high, lofty, noble, majestic, great, grand, imposing, magnificent, glorious, transcendent, spiritual.
≠ lowly, base.

submerge *v* submerse, immerse, plunge, duck, dip, sink, drown, engulf, overwhelm, swamp, flood, inundate, deluge.
≠ surface.

submerged *adj* submersed, immersed, underwater, sunk, sunken, drowned, swamped, inundated, hidden, concealed, unseen.

submission *n* **1** SURRENDER, capitulation, resignation, acquiescence, assent, compliance, obedience, deference, submissiveness, meekness, passivity. **2** PRESENTATION, offering, contribution, entry, suggestion, proposal.
≠ **1** intransigence, intractability.

submissive *adj* yielding, unresisting, resigned, patient, uncomplaining, accommodating, biddable, obedient, deferential, ingratiating, subservient, humble, meek, docile, subdued, passive.
≠ intransigent, intractable.

submit *v* **1** YIELD, give in, surrender, capitulate, knuckle under, bow, bend, stoop, succumb, agree, comply. **2** PRESENT, tender, offer, put forward, suggest, propose, table, state, claim, argue.
≠ **1** resist. **2** withdraw.

subordinate *adj* secondary, auxiliary, ancillary, subsidiary, dependent, inferior, lower, junior, minor, lesser.
≠ superior, senior.
n inferior, junior, assistant, attendant, second, aide, dependant, underling (*infml*).
≠ superior, boss.

subscribe *v* **1** *subscribe to a theory*: support, endorse, back, advocate, approve, agree. **2** GIVE, donate, contribute.

subscription *n* membership fee, dues, payment, donation, contribution, offering, gift.

subsequent *adj* following, later, future, next, succeeding, consequent, resulting, ensuing.
≠ previous, earlier.

subside *v* sink, collapse, settle, descend, fall, drop, lower, decrease, lessen, diminish, dwindle, decline, wane, ebb, recede, moderate, abate, die down, quieten, slacken, ease.
≠ rise, increase.

subsidiary *adj* auxiliary, supplementary, additional, ancillary, assistant, supporting, contributory, secondary, subordinate, lesser, minor.
≠ primary, chief, major.
n branch, offshoot, division, section, part.

subsidize *v* support, back, underwrite, sponsor, finance, fund, aid, promote.

subsidy *n* grant, allowance, assistance, help, aid, contribution, sponsorship, finance, support, backing.

subsistence *n* living, survival, existence, livelihood, maintenance, support, keep, sustenance, nourishment, food, provisions, rations.

substance *n* **1** MATTER, material, stuff, fabric, essence, pith, entity, body, solidity, concreteness, reality, actuality, ground, foundation. **2** SUBJECT, subject-matter, theme, gist, meaning, significance, force.

substandard *adj* second-rate, inferior, imperfect, damaged, shoddy, poor, inadequate, unacceptable.
≠ first-rate, superior, perfect.

substantial *adj* large, big, sizable, ample, generous, great, considerable, significant, important, worthwhile, massive, bulky, hefty, well-built, stout, sturdy, strong, sound, durable.
≠ small, insignificant, weak.

substantiate *v* prove, verify, confirm, support, corroborate, authenticate, validate.
≠ disprove, refute.

substitute *v* **1** CHANGE, exchange, swap, switch, interchange, replace. **2** STAND IN, fill in (*infml*), cover,

deputize, understudy, relieve.
n reserve, stand-by, temp (*infml*), supply, locum, understudy, stand-in, replacement, relief, surrogate, proxy, agent, deputy, makeshift, stopgap.
adj reserve, temporary, acting, surrogate, proxy, replacement, alternative.

subterfuge *n* trick, stratagem, scheme, ploy, ruse, dodge, manoeuvre, machination, deviousness, evasion, deception, artifice, pretence, excuse.
≠ openness, honesty.

subtle *adj* **1** DELICATE, understated, implied, indirect, slight, tenuous, faint, mild, fine, nice, refined, sophisticated, deep, profound. **2** ARTFUL, cunning, crafty, sly, devious, shrewd, astute.
≠ **1** blatant, obvious. **2** artless, open.

subtract *v* deduct, take away, remove, withdraw, debit, detract, diminish.
≠ add.

suburbs *n* suburbia, commuter belt, residential area, outskirts.
≠ centre, heart.

subversive *adj* seditious, treasonous, treacherous, traitorous, inflammatory, incendiary, disruptive, riotous, weakening, undermining, destructive.
≠ loyal.
n seditionist, terrorist, freedom fighter, dissident, traitor, quisling, fifth columnist.

succeed *v* **1** TRIUMPH, make it, get on, thrive, flourish, prosper, make good, manage, work. **2** *winter succeeds autumn*: follow, replace, result, ensue.
≠ **1** fail. **2** precede.

succeeding *adj* following, next, subsequent, ensuing, coming, to come, later, successive.
≠ previous, earlier.

success *n* **1** TRIUMPH, victory, luck, fortune, prosperity, fame, eminence, happiness. **2** CELEBRITY, star, somebody, winner, bestseller, hit, sensation.
≠ **1** failure, disaster.

successful *adj* **1** VICTORIOUS, winning, lucky, fortunate, prosperous, wealthy, thriving, flourishing, booming, moneymaking, lucrative, profitable, rewarding, satisfying, fruitful, productive. **2** *a successful writer*: famous, well-known, popular, leading, bestselling, top, unbeaten.
≠ **1** unsuccessful, unprofitable, fruitless. **2** unknown.

succession *n* sequence, series, order, progression, run, chain, string, cycle, continuation, flow, course, line, train, procession.

successive *adj* consecutive, sequential, following, succeeding.

succinct *adj* short, brief, terse, pithy, concise, compact, condensed, summary.
≠ long, lengthy, wordy, verbose.

succulent *adj* fleshy, juicy, moist, luscious, mouthwatering, lush, rich, mellow.
≠ dry.

succumb *v* give way, yield, give in, submit, knuckle under, surrender, capitulate, collapse, fall.
≠ overcome, master.

suck *v* draw in, imbibe, absorb, soak up, extract, drain.

sudden *adj* unexpected, unforeseen, surprising, startling, abrupt, sharp, quick, swift, rapid, prompt, hurried, hasty, rash, impetuous, impulsive, snap (*infml*).
≠ expected, predictable, gradual, slow.

sue *v* prosecute, charge, indict, summon, solicit, appeal.

suffer *v* **1** HURT, ache, agonize, grieve, sorrow. **2** BEAR, support, tolerate, endure, sustain, experience, undergo, go through, feel.

suffering *n* pain, discomfort, agony, anguish, affliction, distress, misery, hardship, ordeal, torment, torture.
≠ ease, comfort.

sufficient *adj* enough, adequate, satisfactory, effective.
≠ insufficient, inadequate.

suffocate *v* asphyxiate, smother, stifle, choke, strangle, throttle.

sugar

Kinds of sugar include: beet sugar, brown sugar, cane sugar, caster sugar, crystallized sugar, demerara, dextrose, fructose, glucose, golden syrup, granulated sugar, icing sugar, invert sugar, jaggery, lactose, maltose, maple syrup, molasses, powdered sugar, refined sugar, sucrose, sugar loaf, sugar lump, sweets, candy (*US*), sugar candy (*US*), syrup, treacle, unrefined sugar. *Artificial sweeteners include*: acesulfame K, aspartame, Canderel®, cyclamate, Hermesetas®, NutraSweet®, saccharin, sorbitol, Sweetex®. *see also* **sweets**.

suggest *v* **1** PROPOSE, put forward, advocate, recommend, advise, counsel. **2** IMPLY, insinuate, hint, intimate, evoke, indicate.

suggestion *n* **1** PROPOSAL, proposition, motion, recommendation, idea, plan. **2** IMPLICATION, insinuation, innuendo, hint, intimation, suspicion, trace, indication.

suggestive *adj* **1** EVOCATIVE, reminiscent, expressive, meaning, indicative. **2** *a suggestive remark*: indecent, immodest, improper, indelicate, off-colour, risqué, bawdy, dirty, smutty, provocative.
≠ **1** inexpressive. **2** decent, clean.

suit *v* **1** SATISFY, gratify, please, answer, match, tally, agree, correspond, harmonize. **2** FIT, befit, become, tailor, adapt, adjust, accommodate, modify.
≠ **1** displease, clash.
n outfit, costume, dress, clothing.

suitable *adj* appropriate, fitting, convenient, opportune, suited, due, apt, apposite, relevant, applicable, fit, adequate, satisfactory, acceptable, befitting, becoming, seemly, proper, right.
≠ unsuitable, inappropriate.

sulk *v* mope, brood, pout.

sulky *adj* brooding, moody, morose, resentful, grudging, disgruntled, put out, cross, bad-tempered, sullen, aloof, unsociable.
≠ cheerful, good-tempered, sociable.

sullen *adj* **1** SULKY, moody, morose, glum, gloomy, silent, surly, sour, perverse, obstinate, stubborn. **2** DARK, gloomy, sombre, dismal, cheerless, dull, leaden, heavy.
≠ **1** cheerful, happy. **2** fine, clear.

sully *v* dirty, soil, defile, pollute, contaminate, taint, spoil, mar, spot, blemish, besmirch, stain, tarnish, disgrace, dishonour.
≠ cleanse, honour.

sultry *adj* hot, sweltering, stifling, stuffy, oppressive, close, humid, muggy, sticky.
≠ cool, cold.

sum *n* total, sum total, aggregate, whole, entirety, number, quantity, amount, tally, reckoning, score, result.
sum up summarize, review, recapitulate conclude, close.

summarize *v* outline, précis, condense abridge, abbreviate, shorten, sum up, encapsulate, review.
≠ expand (on).

summary *n* synopsis, résumé, outline, abstract, précis, condensation, digest, compendium, abridgement, summing-up, review, recapitulation.
adj short, succinct, brief, cursory, hasty, prompt, direct, unceremonious, arbitrary.
≠ lengthy, careful.

summit *n* top, peak, pinnacle, apex, point, crown, head, zenith, acme, culmination, height.
≠ bottom, foot, nadir.

summon *v* call, send for, invite, bid, beckon, gather, assemble, convene, rally, muster, mobilize, rouse, arouse.
≠ dismiss.

sumptuous *adj* luxurious, plush, lavish, extravagant, opulent, rich, costly, expensive, dear, splendid, magnificent, gorgeous, superb, grand.
≠ plain, poor.

sunbathe *v* sun, bask, tan, brown, bake.

sunburnt *adj* brown, tanned, bronzed, weather-beaten, burnt, red, blistered, peeling.
≠ pale.

sundry *adj* various, diverse,

miscellaneous, assorted, varied, different, several, some, a few.

sunken *adj* submerged, buried, recessed, lower, depressed, concave, hollow, haggard, drawn.

sunny *adj* **1** FINE, cloudless, clear, summery, sunshiny, sunlit, bright, brilliant. **2** CHEERFUL, happy, joyful, smiling, beaming, radiant, light-hearted, buoyant, optimistic, pleasant.
≠ **1** sunless, dull. **2** gloomy.

sunrise *n* dawn, crack of dawn, daybreak, daylight.

sunset *n* sundown, dusk, twilight, gloaming, evening, nightfall.

superb *adj* excellent, first-rate, first-class, superior, choice, fine, exquisite, gorgeous, magnificent, splendid, grand, wonderful, marvellous, admirable, impressive, breathtaking.
≠ bad, poor, inferior.

superficial *adj* surface, external, exterior, outward, apparent, seeming, cosmetic, skin-deep, shallow, slight, trivial, lightweight, frivolous, casual, cursory, sketchy, hasty, hurried, passing.
≠ internal, deep, thorough.

superfluous *adj* extra, spare, excess, surplus, remaining, redundant, supernumerary, unnecessary, needless, unwanted, uncalled-for, excessive.
≠ necessary, needed, wanted.

superintend *v* supervise, oversee, overlook, inspect, run, manage, administer, direct, control, handle.

superior *adj* **1** EXCELLENT, first-class, first-rate, top-notch (*infml*), top-flight (*infml*), high-class, exclusive, choice, select, fine, de luxe, admirable, distinguished, exceptional, unrivalled, par excellence. **2** BETTER, preferred, greater, higher, senior. **3** HAUGHTY, lordly, pretentious, snobbish, snooty (*infml*), supercilious, disdainful, condescending, patronizing.
≠ **1** inferior, average. **2** worse, lower. **3** humble.
n senior, elder, better, boss, chief, principal, director, manager, foreman, supervisor.
≠ inferior, junior, assistant.

superiority *n* advantage, lead, edge, supremacy, ascendancy, pre-eminence, predominance.
≠ inferiority.

superlative *adj* best, greatest, highest, supreme, transcendent, unbeatable, unrivalled, unparalleled, matchless, peerless, unsurpassed, unbeaten, consummate, excellent, outstanding.
≠ poor, average.

supernatural *adj* paranormal, unnatural, abnormal, metaphysical, spiritual, psychic, mystic, occult, hidden, mysterious, miraculous, magical, phantom, ghostly.
≠ natural, normal.

supersede *v* succeed, replace, supplant, usurp, oust, displace, remove.

superstition *n* myth, old wives' tale, fallacy, delusion, illusion.

superstitious *adj* mythical, false, fallacious, irrational, groundless, delusive, illusory.
≠ rational, logical.

supervise *v* oversee, watch over, look after, superintend, run, manage, administer, direct, conduct, preside over, control, handle.

supervision *n* surveillance, care, charge, superintendence, oversight, running, management, administration, direction, control, guidance, instruction.

supervisor *n* overseer, inspector, superintendent, boss, chief, director, administrator, manager, foreman, forewoman.

supplant *v* replace, supersede, usurp, oust, displace, remove, overthrow, topple, unseat.

supple *adj* flexible, bending, pliant, pliable, plastic, lithe, graceful, loose-limbed, double-jointed, elastic.
≠ stiff, rigid, inflexible.

supplement *n* addition, extra, insert, pull-out, addendum, appendix, codicil, postscript, sequel.
v add to, augment, boost, reinforce, fill up, top up, complement, extend, eke out.
≠ deplete, use up.

supplementary *adj* additional, extra, auxiliary, secondary, complementary, accompanying.

supplier *n* dealer, seller, vendor, wholesaler, retailer.

supplies *n* stores, provisions, food, equipment, materials, necessities.

supply *v* provide, furnish, equip, outfit, stock, fill, replenish, give, donate, grant, endow, contribute, yield, produce, sell.
≠ take, receive.
n source, amount, quantity, stock, fund, reservoir, store, reserve, stockpile, hoard, cache.
≠ lack.

support *v* **1** BACK, second, defend, champion, advocate, promote, foster, help, aid, assist, rally round, finance, fund, subsidize, underwrite. **2** HOLD UP, bear, carry, sustain, brace, reinforce, strengthen, prop, buttress, bolster. **3** MAINTAIN, keep, provide for, feed, nourish. **4** *support a statement*: endorse, confirm, verify, authenticate, corroborate, substantiate, document.
≠ **1** oppose. **3** live off. **4** contradict.
n **1** BACKING, allegiance, loyalty, defence, protection, patronage, sponsorship, approval, encouragement, comfort, relief, help, aid, assistance. **2** PROP, stay, post, pillar, brace, crutch, foundation, underpinning.
≠ **1** opposition, hostility.

supporter *n* fan, follower, adherent, advocate, champion, defender, seconder, patron, sponsor, helper, ally, friend.
≠ opponent.

supportive *adj* helpful, caring, attentive, sympathetic, understanding, comforting, reassuring, encouraging.
≠ discouraging.

suppose *v* assume, presume, expect, infer, conclude, guess, conjecture, surmise, believe, think, consider, judge, imagine, conceive, fancy, pretend, postulate, hypothesize.
≠ know.

supposed *adj* alleged, reported, rumoured, assumed, presumed, reputed, putative, imagined, hypothetical.
≠ known, certain.
supposed to meant to, intended to, expected to, required to, obliged to.

supposition *n* assumption, presumption, guess, conjecture, speculation, theory, hypothesis, idea, notion.
≠ knowledge.

suppress *v* crush, stamp out, quash, quell, subdue, stop, silence, censor, stifle, smother, strangle, conceal, withhold, hold back, contain, restrain, check, repress, inhibit.
≠ encourage, incite.

supreme *adj* best, greatest, highest, top, crowning, culminating, first, leading, foremost, chief, principal, head, sovereign, pre-eminent, predominant, prevailing, world-beating, unsurpassed, second-to-none, incomparable, matchless, consummate, transcendent, superlative, prime, ultimate, extreme, final.
≠ lowly, poor.

sure *adj* **1** CERTAIN, convinced, assured, confident, decided, positive, definite, unmistakable, clear, accurate, precise, unquestionable, indisputable, undoubted, undeniable, irrevocable, inevitable, bound. **2** SAFE, secure, fast, solid, firm, steady, stable, guaranteed, reliable, dependable, trustworthy, steadfast, unwavering, unerring, unfailing, infallible, effective.
≠ **1** unsure, uncertain, doubtful. **2** unsafe, insecure.

surface *n* outside, exterior, façade, veneer, covering, skin, top, side, face, plane.
≠ inside, interior.
v rise, arise, come up, emerge, appear, materialize, come to light.
≠ sink, disappear, vanish.

surgeon

Types of surgeon include: brain surgeon, cosmetic surgeon, dental surgeon, eye surgeon, general surgeon, heart surgeon, house surgeon, neurosurgeon, oral surgeon, plastic surgeon, veterinary surgeon.

surly *adj* gruff, brusque, churlish,

ungracious, bad-tempered, cross, crabbed, grouchy, crusty, sullen, sulky, morose.
≠ friendly, polite.

surpass *v* beat, outdo, exceed, outstrip, better, excel, transcend, outshine, eclipse.

surplus *n* excess, residue, remainder, balance, superfluity, glut, surfeit.
≠ lack, shortage.
adj excess, superfluous, redundant, extra, spare, remaining, unused.

surprise *v* startle, amaze, astonish, astound, stagger, flabbergast (*infml*), bewilder, confuse, nonplus, disconcert, dismay.
n amazement, astonishment, incredulity, wonder, bewilderment, dismay, shock, start, bombshell, revelation.
≠ composure.

surprised *adj* startled, amazed, astonished, astounded, staggered, flabbergasted (*infml*), thunderstruck, dumbfounded, speechless, shocked, nonplussed.
≠ unsurprised, composed.

surprising *adj* amazing, astonishing, astounding, staggering, stunning, incredible, extraordinary, remarkable, startling, unexpected, unforeseen.
≠ unsurprising, expected.

surrender *v* capitulate, submit, resign, concede, yield, give in, cede, give up, quit, relinquish, abandon, renounce, forgo, waive.
n capitulation, resignation, submission, yielding, relinquishment, renunciation.

surreptitious *adj* furtive, stealthy, sly, covert, veiled, hidden, secret, clandestine, underhand, unauthorized.
≠ open, obvious.

surround *v* encircle, ring, girdle, encompass, envelop, encase, enclose, hem in, besiege.

surrounding *adj* encircling, bordering, adjacent, adjoining, neighbouring, nearby.

surroundings *n* neighbourhood, vicinity, locality, setting, environment, background, milieu, ambience.

survey *v* view, contemplate, observe, supervise, scan, scrutinize, examine, inspect, study, research, review, consider, estimate, evaluate, assess, measure, plot, plan, map, chart, reconnoitre.
n review, overview, scrutiny, examination, inspection, study, poll, appraisal, assessment, measurement.

survive *v* outlive, outlast, endure, last, stay, remain, live, exist, withstand, weather.
≠ succumb, die.

susceptible *adj* liable, prone, inclined, disposed, given, subject, receptive, responsive, impressionable, suggestible, weak, vulnerable, open, sensitive, tender.
≠ resistant, immune.

suspect *v* **1** DOUBT, distrust, mistrust, call into question. **2** *I suspect you're right*: believe, fancy, feel, guess, conjecture, speculate, surmise, suppose, consider, conclude, infer.
adj suspicious, doubtful, dubious, questionable, debatable, unreliable, iffy (*sl*), dodgy (*infml*), fishy (*infml*).
≠ acceptable, reliable.

suspend *v* **1** HANG, dangle, swing. **2** ADJOURN, interrupt, discontinue, cease, delay, defer, postpone, put off, shelve. **3** EXPEL, dismiss, exclude, debar.
≠ **2** continue. **3** restore, reinstate.

suspense *n* uncertainty, insecurity, anxiety, tension, apprehension, anticipation, expectation, expectancy, excitement.
≠ certainty, knowledge.

suspension *n* adjournment, interruption, break, intermission, respite, remission, stay, moratorium, delay, deferral, postponement, abeyance.
≠ continuation.

suspicion *n* **1** DOUBT, scepticism, distrust, mistrust, wariness, caution, misgiving, apprehension. **2** TRACE, hint, suggestion, soupçon, touch, tinge, shade, glimmer, shadow. **3** IDEA, notion, hunch.
≠ **1** trust.

suspicious *adj* **1** DOUBTFUL, sceptical, unbelieving, suspecting, distrustful, mistrustful, wary, chary, apprehensive, uneasy. **2** DUBIOUS, questionable, suspect, irregular, shifty, shady (*infml*), dodgy (*infml*), fishy (*infml*).
≠ **1** trustful, confident. **2** trustworthy, innocent.

sustain *v* **1** NOURISH, provide for, nurture, foster, help, aid, assist, comfort, relieve, support, uphold, endorse, bear, carry. **2** MAINTAIN, keep going, keep up, continue, prolong, hold.

sustained *adj* prolonged, protracted, long-drawn-out, steady, continuous, constant, perpetual, unremitting.
≠ broken, interrupted, intermittent, spasmodic.

sustenance *n* nourishment, food, provisions, fare, maintenance, subsistence, livelihood.

swagger *v* bluster, boast, crow, brag, swank (*infml*), parade, strut.
n bluster, show, ostentation, arrogance.

swallow *v* **1** CONSUME, devour, eat, gobble up, guzzle, drink, quaff, knock back (*infml*), gulp, down (*infml*). **2** ENGULF, enfold, envelop, swallow up, absorb, assimilate, accept, believe.

swamp *n* bog, marsh, fen, slough, quagmire, quicksand, mire, mud.
v flood, inundate, deluge, engulf, submerge, sink, drench, saturate, waterlog, overload, overwhelm, besiege, beset.

swap, swop *v* exchange, transpose, switch, interchange, barter, trade, traffic.

swarm *n* crowd, throng, mob, mass, multitude, myriad, host, army, horde, herd, flock, drove, shoal.
v **1** flock, flood, stream, mass, congregate, crowd, throng. **2** *swarming with tourists*: teem, crawl, bristle, abound.

swarthy *adj* dark, dark-skinned, dark-complexioned, dusky, black, brown, tanned.
≠ fair, pale.

sway *v* **1** ROCK, roll, lurch, swing, wave, oscillate, fluctuate, bend, incline, lean, divert, veer, swerve. **2** INFLUENCE, affect, persuade, induce, convince, convert, overrule, dominate, govern.

swear *v* **1** VOW, promise, pledge, avow, attest, asseverate, testify, affirm, assert, declare, insist. **2** CURSE, blaspheme.

swear-word *n* expletive, four-letter word, curse, oath, imprecation, obscenity, profanity, blasphemy, swearing, bad language.

sweat *n* **1** PERSPIRATION, moisture, stickiness. **2** ANXIETY, worry, agitation, panic. **3** TOIL, labour, drudgery, chore.
v perspire, swelter, exude.

sweaty *adj* damp, moist, clammy, sticky, sweating, perspiring.
≠ dry, cool.

sweep *v* **1** *sweep the floor*: brush, dust, clean, clear, remove. **2** PASS, sail, fly, glide, scud, skim, glance, whisk, tear, hurtle.
n arc, curve, bend, swing, stroke, movement, gesture, compass, scope, range, extent, span, stretch, expanse, vista.

sweeping *adj* general, global, all-inclusive, all-embracing, blanket, across-the-board, broad, wide-ranging, extensive, far-reaching, comprehensive, thoroughgoing, radical, wholesale, indiscriminate, oversimplified, simplistic.
≠ specific, narrow.

sweet *adj* **1** SUGARY, syrupy, sweetened, honeyed, saccharine, luscious, delicious. **2** PLEASANT, delightful, lovely, attractive, beautiful, pretty, winsome, cute, appealing, lovable, charming, agreeable, amiable, affectionate, tender, kind, treasured, precious, dear, darling. **3** FRESH, clean, wholesome, pure, clear, perfumed, fragrant, aromatic, balmy. **4** *sweet music*: melodious, tuneful, harmonious, euphonious, musical, dulcet, soft, mellow.
≠ **1** savoury, salty, sour, bitter.

2 unpleasant, nasty, ugly. **3** foul. **4** discordant.
n dessert, pudding, afters (*infml*).

sweets

Sweets include: barley sugar, bull's eye, butterscotch, caramel, chewing-gum, chocolate, fondant, fruit pastille, fudge, gobstopper, gumdrop, humbug, jelly, jelly bean, liquorice, liquorice allsort, lollipop, Mars®, marshmallow, marzipan, nougat, peppermint, praline, rock, Edinburgh rock, toffee, toffee apple, truffle, Turkish delight.

sweeten *v* sugar, honey, mellow, soften, soothe, appease, temper, cushion.
≠ sour, embitter.

swell *v* expand, dilate, inflate, blow up, puff up, bloat, distend, fatten, bulge, balloon, billow, surge, rise, mount, increase, enlarge, extend, grow, augment, heighten, intensify.
≠ shrink, contract, decrease, dwindle.
n billow, wave, undulation, surge, rise, increase, enlargement.

swelling *n* lump, tumour, bump, bruise, blister, boil, inflammation, bulge, protuberance, puffiness, distension, enlargement.

sweltering *adj* hot, tropical, baking, scorching, stifling, suffocating, airless, oppressive, sultry, steamy, sticky, humid.
≠ cold, cool, fresh, breezy, airy.

swerve *v* turn, bend, incline, veer, swing, shift, deviate, stray, wander, diverge, deflect, sheer.

swift *adj* fast, quick, rapid, speedy, express, flying, hurried, hasty, short, brief, sudden, prompt, ready, agile, nimble, nippy (*infml*).
≠ slow, sluggish, unhurried.

swimsuit *n* swimming costume, bathing-costume, bathing-suit, bikini, trunks.

swindle *v* cheat, defraud, diddle, do (*infml*), overcharge, fleece, rip off (*sl*), trick, deceive, dupe, con (*infml*), bamboozle (*infml*).
n fraud, fiddle, racket, sharp practice, double-dealing, trickery, deception, con (*infml*), rip-off (*sl*).

swindler *n* cheat, fraud, impostor, con man (*infml*), trickster, shark, rogue, rascal.

swing *v* hang, suspend, dangle, wave, brandish, sway, rock, oscillate, vibrate, fluctuate, vary, veer, swerve, turn, whirl, twirl, spin, rotate.
n sway, rock, oscillation, vibration, fluctuation, variation, change, shift, movement, motion, rhythm.

swingeing *adj* harsh, severe, stringent, drastic, punishing, devastating, excessive, extortionate, oppressive, heavy.
≠ mild.

swipe *v* **1** HIT, strike, lunge, lash out, slap, whack (*infml*), wallop (*infml*), sock (*sl*). **2** (*infml*) STEAL, pilfer, lift, pinch (*infml*).
n stroke, blow, slap, smack, clout, whack (*infml*), wallop (*infml*).

swirl *v* churn, agitate, spin, twirl, whirl, wheel, eddy, twist, curl.

switch *v* change, exchange, swap, trade, interchange, transpose, substitute, replace, shift, rearrange, turn, veer, deviate, divert, deflect.
n change, alteration, shift, exchange, swap, interchange, substitution, replacement.

swivel *v* pivot, spin, rotate, revolve, turn, twirl, pirouette, gyrate, wheel.

swollen *adj* bloated, distended, inflated, tumid, puffed up, puffy, inflamed, enlarged, bulbous, bulging.
≠ shrunken, shrivelled.

swoop *v* dive, plunge, drop, fall, descend, stoop, pounce, lunge, rush.
n dive, plunge, drop, descent, pounce, lunge, rush, attack, onslaught.

swop *see* **swap**.

sword *n* blade, foil, rapier, sabre, scimitar.

swot (*infml*) *v* study, work, learn, memorize, revise, cram, mug up (*infml*), bone up (*sl*).

syllabus *n* curriculum, course, programme, schedule, plan.

symbol *n* sign, token, representation, mark, emblem, badge, logo, character, ideograph, figure, image.

> *Symbols include*: badge, brand, cipher, coat of arms, crest, emblem, hieroglyph, icon, ideogram, insignia, logo, logogram, monogram, motif, pictograph, swastika, token, totem, trademark; ampersand, asterisk, caret, dagger, double-dagger, obelus.

symbolic *adj* symbolical, representative, emblematic, token, figurative, metaphorical, allegorical, meaningful, significant.

symbolize *v* represent, stand for, denote, mean, signify, typify, exemplify, epitomize, personify.

symmetrical *adj* balanced, even, regular, parallel, corresponding, proportional.
≠ asymmetrical, irregular.

symmetry *n* balance, evenness, regularity, parallelism, correspondence, proportion, harmony, agreement.
≠ asymmetry, irregularity.

sympathetic *adj* understanding, appreciative, supportive, comforting, consoling, commiserating, pitying, interested, concerned, solicitous, caring, compassionate, tender, kind, warm-hearted, well-disposed, affectionate, agreeable, friendly, congenial, like-minded, compatible.
≠ unsympathetic, indifferent, callous, antipathetic.

sympathize *v* understand, comfort, commiserate, pity, feel for, empathize, identify with, respond to.
≠ ignore, disregard.

sympathy *n* **1** UNDERSTANDING, comfort, consolation, condolences, commiseration, pity, compassion, tenderness, kindness, warmth, thoughtfulness, empathy, fellow-feeling, affinity, rapport. **2** AGREEMENT, accord, correspondence, harmony.
≠ **1** indifference, insensitivity, callousness. **2** disagreement.

symptom *n* sign, indication, evidence, manifestation, expression, feature, characteristic, mark, token, warning.

symptomatic *adj* indicative, typical, characteristic, associated, suggestive.

synonymous *adj* interchangeable, substitutable, the same, identical, similar, comparable, tantamount, equivalent, corresponding.
≠ antonymous, opposite.

synopsis *n* outline, abstract, summary, résumé, précis, condensation, digest, abridgement, review, recapitulation.

synthesize *v* unite, combine, amalgamate, integrate, merge, blend, compound, alloy, fuse, weld, coalesce, unify.
≠ separate, analyse, resolve.

synthetic *adj* manufactured, man-made, simulated, artificial, ersatz, imitation, fake, bogus, mock, sham, pseudo.
≠ genuine, real, natural.

system *n* **1** METHOD, mode, technique, procedure, process, routine, practice, usage, rule. **2** ORGANIZATION, structure, set-up, systematization, co-ordination, orderliness, methodology, logic, classification, arrangement, order, plan, scheme.

systematic *adj* methodical, logical, ordered, well-ordered, planned, well-planned, organized, well-organized, structured, systematized, standardized, orderly, businesslike, efficient.
≠ unsystematic, arbitrary, disorderly, inefficient.

T

tab *n* flap, tag, marker, label, sticker, ticket.

table *n* **1** BOARD, slab, counter, worktop, desk, bench, stand. **2** DIAGRAM, chart, graph, timetable, schedule, programme, list, inventory, catalogue, index, register, record.
v propose, suggest, submit, put forward.

taboo *adj* forbidden, prohibited, banned, proscribed, unacceptable, unmentionable, unthinkable.
≠ permitted, acceptable.
n ban, interdiction, prohibition, restriction, anathema, curse.

tacit *adj* unspoken, unexpressed, unvoiced, silent, understood, implicit, implied, inferred.
≠ express, explicit.

taciturn *adj* silent, quiet, uncommunicative, unforthcoming, reticent, reserved, withdrawn, aloof, distant, cold.
≠ talkative, communicative, forthcoming.

tack *n* **1** NAIL, pin, drawing-pin, staple. **2** COURSE, path, bearing, heading, direction, line, approach, method, way, technique, procedure, plan, tactic, attack.
v add, append, attach, affix, fasten, fix, nail, pin, staple, stitch, baste.

tackle *n* **1** *a rugby tackle*: attack, challenge, interception, intervention, block. **2** EQUIPMENT, tools, implements, apparatus, rig, outfit, gear, trappings, paraphernalia.
v **1** BEGIN, embark on, set about, try, attempt, undertake, take on, challenge, confront, encounter, face up to, grapple with, deal with, attend to, handle, grab, seize, grasp. **2** INTERCEPT, block, halt, stop.
≠ **1** avoid, sidestep.

tact *n* tactfulness, diplomacy, discretion, prudence, delicacy, sensitivity, perception, discernment, judgement, understanding, thoughtfulness, consideration, skill, adroitness, finesse.
≠ tactlessness, indiscretion.

tactful *adj* diplomatic, discreet, politic, judicious, prudent, careful, delicate, subtle, sensitive, perceptive, discerning, understanding, thoughtful, considerate, polite, skilful, adroit.
≠ tactless, indiscreet, thoughtless, rude.

tactic *n* approach, course, way, means, method, procedure, plan, stratagem, scheme, ruse, ploy, subterfuge, trick, device, shift, move, manoeuvre.

tactical *adj* strategic, planned, calculated, artful, cunning, shrewd, skilful, clever, smart, prudent, politic, judicious.

tactics *n* strategy, campaign, plan, policy, approach, line of attack, moves, manoeuvres.

tactless *adj* undiplomatic, indiscreet, indelicate, inappropriate, impolitic, imprudent, careless, clumsy, blundering, insensitive, unfeeling, hurtful, unkind, thoughtless, inconsiderate, rude, impolite, discourteous.
≠ tactful, diplomatic, discreet.

tag *n* label, sticker, tab, ticket, mark, identification, note, slip, docket.
v **1** LABEL, mark, identify, designate, term, call, name, christen, nickname, style, dub. **2** ADD, append, annex, adjoin, affix, fasten.
tag along follow, shadow, tail, trail, accompany.

tail *n* end, extremity, rear, rear end, rump, behind (*infml*), posterior (*infml*), appendage.
v follow, pursue, shadow, dog, stalk, track, trail.
tail off decrease, decline, drop, fall away,

fade, wane, dwindle, taper off, peter out, die (out).
≠ increase, grow.

tailor *n* outfitter, dressmaker.
v fit, suit, cut, trim, style, fashion, shape, mould, alter, modify, adapt, adjust, accommodate.

tailor-made *adj* made-to-measure, custom-built, ideal, perfect, right, suited, fitted.
≠ unsuitable.

taint *v* contaminate, infect, pollute, adulterate, corrupt, deprave, stain, blemish, blot, smear, tarnish, blacken, dirty, soil, muddy, defile, sully, harm, damage, blight, spoil, ruin, shame, disgrace, dishonour.
n contamination, infection, pollution, corruption, stain, blemish, fault, flaw, defect, spot, blot, smear, stigma, shame, disgrace, dishonour.

take *v* **1** SEIZE, grab, snatch, grasp, hold, catch, capture, get, obtain, acquire, secure, gain, win, derive, adopt, assume, pick, choose, select, accept, receive. **2** REMOVE, eliminate, take away, subtract, deduct, steal, filch, purloin, nick (*infml*), pinch (*infml*), appropriate, abduct, carry off. **3** NEED, necessitate, require, demand, call for. **4** *take me home*: convey, carry, bring, transport, ferry, accompany, escort, lead, guide, conduct, usher. **5** BEAR, tolerate, stand, stomach, abide, endure, suffer, undergo, withstand.
≠ **1** leave, refuse. **2** replace, put back.
take aback surprise, astonish, astound, stagger, stun, startle, disconcert, bewilder, dismay, upset.
take apart take to pieces, dismantle, disassemble, analyse.
take back reclaim, repossess, withdraw, retract, recant, repudiate, deny, eat one's words.
take down 1 DISMANTLE, disassemble, demolish, raze, level, lower. **2** NOTE, record, write down, put down, set down, transcribe.
take in 1 ABSORB, assimilate, digest, realize, appreciate, understand, comprehend, grasp, admit, receive, shelter, accommodate, contain, include, comprise, incorporate, embrace, encompass, cover. **2** DECEIVE, fool, dupe, con (*infml*), mislead, trick, hoodwink, bamboozle (*infml*), cheat, swindle.
take off 1 REMOVE, doff, divest, shed, discard, drop. **2** LEAVE, depart, go, decamp, disappear. **3** IMITATE, mimic, parody, caricature, satirize, mock, send up.
take on 1 ACCEPT, assume, acquire, undertake, tackle, face, contend with, fight, oppose. **2** *take on staff*: employ, hire, enlist, recruit, engage, retain.
take up 1 OCCUPY, fill, engage, engross, absorb, monopolize, use up. **2** *take up a hobby*: start, begin, embark on, pursue, carry on, continue. **3** RAISE, lift. **4** ACCEPT, adopt, assume.

take-off *n* imitation, mimicry, impersonation, parody, caricature, spoof, send-up, travesty.

takeover *n* merger, amalgamation, combination, incorporation, coup.

takings *n* receipts, gate, proceeds, profits, gain, returns, revenue, yield, income, earnings, pickings.

tale *n* story, yarn, anecdote, spiel (*sl*), narrative, account, report, rumour, tall story, old wives' tale, superstition, fable, myth, legend, saga, lie, fib, falsehood, untruth, fabrication.

talent *n* gift, endowment, genius, flair, feel, knack, bent, aptitude, faculty, skill, ability, capacity, power, strength, forte.
≠ inability, weakness.

talented *adj* gifted, brilliant, well-endowed, versatile, accomplished, able, capable, proficient, adept, adroit, deft, clever, skilful.
≠ inept.

talk *v* speak, utter, articulate, say, communicate, converse, chat, gossip, natter (*infml*), chatter, discuss, confer, negotiate.
n **1** CONVERSATION, dialogue, discussion, conference, meeting, consultation, negotiation, chat, chatter, natter (*infml*), gossip, hearsay, rumour, tittle-tattle. **2** *give a talk*: lecture, seminar, symposium, speech, address,

discourse, sermon, spiel (*sl*).
3 LANGUAGE, dialect, slang, jargon, speech, utterance, words.
talk into encourage, coax, sway, persuade, convince, bring round, win over.
≠ dissuade.
talk out of discourage, deter, put off, dissuade.
≠ persuade, convince.

talkative *adj* garrulous, voluble, vocal, communicative, forthcoming, unreserved, expansive, chatty, gossipy, verbose, wordy.
≠ taciturn, quiet, reserved.

talking-to (*infml*) *n* lecture, dressing-down (*infml*), telling-off (*infml*), ticking-off (*infml*), scolding, reprimand, rebuke, reproof, reproach, criticism.
≠ praise, commendation.

tall *adj* high, lofty, elevated, soaring, towering, big, great, giant, gigantic.
≠ short, low, small.

tally *v* **1** AGREE, concur, tie in, square, accord, harmonize, coincide, correspond, match, conform, suit, fit. **2** ADD (UP), total, count, reckon, figure.
≠ **1** disagree, differ.
n record, count, total, score, reckoning, account.

tame *adj* **1** *a tame rabbit*: domesticated, broken in, trained, disciplined, manageable, tractable, amenable, gentle, docile, meek, submissive, unresisting, obedient, biddable. **2** DULL, boring, tedious, uninteresting, humdrum, flat, bland, insipid, weak, feeble, uninspired, unadventurous, unenterprising, lifeless, spiritless.
≠ **1** wild, unmanageable, rebellious. **2** exciting.
v domesticate, house-train, break in, train, discipline, master, subjugate, conquer, bridle, curb, repress, suppress, quell, subdue, temper, soften, mellow, calm, pacify, humble.

tamper *v* interfere, meddle, mess (*infml*), tinker, fiddle, fix, rig, manipulate, juggle, alter, damage.

tang *n* sharpness, bite, piquancy, pungency, taste, flavour, savour, smack, smell, aroma, scent, whiff, tinge, touch, trace, hint, suggestion, overtone.

tangible *adj* touchable, tactile, palpable, solid, concrete, material, substantial, physical, real, actual, perceptible, discernible, evident, manifest, definite, positive.
≠ intangible, abstract, unreal.

tangle *n* knot, snarl-up, twist, coil, convolution, mesh, web, maze, labyrinth, mess, muddle, jumble, mix-up, confusion, entanglement, embroilment, complication.
v entangle, knot, snarl, ravel, twist, coil, interweave, interlace, intertwine, catch, ensnare, entrap, enmesh, embroil, implicate, involve, muddle, confuse.
≠ disentangle.

tangled *adj* knotty, snarled, matted, tousled, dishevelled, messy, muddled, jumbled, confused, twisted, convoluted, tortuous, involved, complicated, complex, intricate.

tangy *adj* sharp, biting, acid, tart, spicy, piquant, pungent, strong, fresh.
≠ tasteless, insipid.

tank *n* container, reservoir, cistern, aquarium, vat, basin.

tantalize *v* tease, taunt, torment, torture, provoke, lead on, titillate, tempt, entice, bait, balk, frustrate, thwart.
≠ gratify, satisfy, fulfil.

tantamount *adj* as good as, equivalent, commensurate, equal, synonymous, the same as.

tantrum *n* temper, rage, fury, storm, outburst, fit, scene, paddy (*infml*).

tap[1] *v* hit, strike, knock, rap, beat, drum, pat, touch.
n knock, rap, beat, pat, touch.

tap[2] *n* **1** STOPCOCK, valve, faucet, spigot, spout. **2** STOPPER, plug, bung.
v use, utilize, exploit, mine, quarry, siphon, bleed, milk, drain.

tape *n* band, strip, binding, ribbon, video, cassette.
v record, video, bind, secure, stick, seal.

taper *v* narrow, attenuate, thin, slim, decrease, reduce, lessen, dwindle, fade, wane, peter out, tail off, die away.
≠ widen, flare, swell, increase.
n spill, candle, wick.

target *n* aim, object, end, purpose, intention, ambition, goal, destination, objective, butt, mark, victim, prey, quarry.

tariff *n* price list, schedule, charges, rate, toll, tax, levy, customs, excise, duty.

tarnish *v* discolour, corrode, rust, dull, dim, darken, blacken, sully, taint, stain, blemish, spot, blot, mar, spoil.
≠ polish, brighten.

tart[1] *n* pie, flan, pastry, tartlet, patty.

tart[2] *adj* sharp, acid, sour, bitter, vinegary, tangy, piquant, pungent, biting, cutting, trenchant, incisive, caustic, astringent, acerbic, scathing, sardonic.
≠ bland, sweet.

task *n* job, chore, duty, charge, imposition, assignment, exercise, mission, errand, undertaking, enterprise, business, occupation, activity, employment, work, labour, toil, burden.

taste *n* **1** FLAVOUR, savour, relish, smack, tang.

> *Ways of describing taste include*: acid, acrid, appetizing, bitter, bittersweet, citrus, creamy, delicious, flavoursome, fruity, hot, meaty, moreish, peppery, piquant, pungent, sapid, salty, savoury, scrumptious (*infml*), sharp, sour, spicy, sugary, sweet, tangy, tart, tasty, yummy (*infml*).

2 SAMPLE, bit, piece, morsel, titbit, bite, nibble, mouthful, sip, drop, dash, soupçon. **3** *a taste for adventure*: liking, fondness, partiality, preference, inclination, leaning, desire, appetite.
4 DISCRIMINATION, discernment, judgement, perception, appreciation, sensitivity, refinement, polish, culture, cultivation, breeding, decorum, finesse, style, elegance, tastefulness.
≠ **1** blandness. **3** distaste.
4 tastelessness.
v savour, relish, sample, nibble, sip, try, test, differentiate, distinguish, discern, perceive, experience, undergo, feel, encounter, meet, know.

tasteful *adj* refined, polished, cultured, cultivated, elegant, smart, stylish, aesthetic, artistic, harmonious, beautiful, exquisite, delicate, graceful, restrained, well-judged, judicious, correct, fastidious, discriminating.
≠ tasteless, garish, tawdry.

tasteless *adj* **1** FLAVOURLESS, insipid, bland, mild, weak, watery, flat, stale, dull, boring, uninteresting, vapid.
2 INELEGANT, graceless, unseemly, improper, indiscreet, crass, rude, crude, vulgar, kitsch, naff (*sl*), cheap, tawdry, flashy, gaudy, garish, loud.
≠ **1** tasty. **2** tasteful, elegant.

tasty *adj* luscious, palatable, appetizing, mouthwatering, delicious, flavoursome, succulent, scrumptious (*infml*), yummy (*sl*), tangy, piquant, savoury, sweet.
≠ tasteless, insipid.

tattered *adj* ragged, frayed, threadbare, ripped, torn, tatty, shabby, scruffy.
≠ smart, neat.

tatters *n* rags, shreds, ribbons, pieces.

taunt *v* tease, torment, provoke, bait, goad, jeer, mock, ridicule, gibe, rib (*sl*), deride, sneer, insult, revile, reproach.
n jeer, catcall, gibe, dig, sneer, insult, reproach, taunting, teasing, provocation, ridicule, sarcasm, derision, censure.

taut *adj* tight, stretched, contracted, strained, tense, unrelaxed, stiff, rigid.
≠ slack, loose, relaxed.

tautological *adj* repetitive, superfluous, redundant, pleonastic, verbose, wordy.
≠ succinct, economical.

tautology *n* repetition, duplication, superfluity, redundancy, pleonasm.

tawdry *adj* cheap, vulgar, tasteless, fancy, showy, flashy, gaudy, garish, tinselly, glittering.
≠ fine, tasteful.

tax *n* levy, charge, rate, tariff, customs, contribution, imposition, burden, load.

Taxes include: airport tax, capital gains tax, capital transfer tax, community charge, corporation tax, council tax, customs, death duty, estate duty, excise, income tax, inheritance tax, PAYE, poll tax, property tax, rates, surtax, tithe, toll, value added tax (VAT).

v levy, charge, demand, exact, assess, impose, burden, load, strain, stretch, try, tire, weary, exhaust, drain, sap, weaken.

teach *v* instruct, train, coach, tutor, lecture, drill, ground, verse, discipline, school, educate, enlighten, edify, inform, impart, inculcate, advise, counsel, guide, direct, show, demonstrate.
≠ learn.

teacher *n* schoolteacher, educator, guide.
≠ pupil.

Kinds of teacher include: adviser, coach, college lecturer, counsellor, crammer, dean, demonstrator, deputy head, doctor, don, duenna, form teacher, governess, guru, head of department, head of year, headmaster, headmistress, headteacher, housemaster, housemistress, instructor, lecturer, maharishi, master, mentor, middle school teacher, mistress, nursery school teacher, pastoral head, pedagogue, pedant, preceptor, preceptress, primary school teacher, principal, private tutor, professor, pundit, reception teacher, school-ma'am, schoolmaster, schoolmistress, schoolteacher, secondary school teacher, senior lecturer, student teacher, subject co-ordinator, supply teacher, trainer, tutor, university lecturer, upper school teacher.

teaching *n* **1** INSTRUCTION, tuition, education, pedagogy.

Methods of teaching include: apprenticeship, briefing, coaching, computer-aided learning, correspondence course, counselling, demonstration, distance learning, drilling, familiarization, grounding, guidance, hands-on training, home-learning, indoctrination, induction training, in-service training, instruction, job training, lecturing, lesson, master-class, on-the-job training, practical, preaching, private tuition, rote learning, schooling, seminar, shadowing, special tuition, theory, training, tuition, tutelage, tutorial, vocational training, work experience.

2 DOGMA, doctrine, tenet, precept, principle.

team *n* side, line-up, squad, shift, crew, gang, band, group, company, stable.
team up join, unite, couple, combine, band together, co-operate, collaborate, work together.

tear *v* **1** RIP, rend, divide, rupture, sever, shred, scratch, claw, gash, lacerate, mutilate, mangle. **2** PULL, snatch, grab, seize, wrest. **3** *tear down the street*: dash, rush, hurry, speed, race, run, sprint, fly, shoot, dart, bolt, belt (*infml*), career, charge.
n rip, rent, slit, hole, split, rupture, scratch, gash, laceration.

tearful *adj* crying, weeping, sobbing, whimpering, blubbering, sad, sorrowful, upset, distressed, emotional, weepy (*infml*).
≠ happy, smiling, laughing.

tears *n* crying, weeping, sobbing, wailing, whimpering, blubbering, sorrow, distress.

tease *v* taunt, provoke, bait, annoy, irritate, aggravate (*infml*), needle (*infml*), badger, worry, pester, plague, torment, tantalize, mock, ridicule, gibe, banter, rag (*sl*), rib (*sl*).

technical *adj* mechanical, scientific, technological, electronic, computerized, specialized, expert, professional.

technique *n* method, system, procedure, manner, fashion, style, mode, way, means, approach, course, performance, execution, delivery, artistry, craftsmanship, skill, facility, proficiency, expertise, know-how (*infml*), art, craft, knack, touch.

tedious *adj* boring, monotonous, uninteresting, unexciting, dull, dreary,

drab, banal, humdrum, tiresome, wearisome, tiring, laborious, long-winded, long-drawn-out.
≠ lively, interesting, exciting.

teeming *adj* swarming, crawling, alive, bristling, seething, full, packed, brimming, overflowing, bursting, replete, abundant, fruitful, thick.
≠ lacking, sparse, rare.

teenage *adj* teenaged, adolescent, young, youthful, juvenile, immature.

teenager *n* adolescent, youth, boy, girl, minor, juvenile.

teetotal *adj* temperate, abstinent, abstemious, sober, on the wagon (*sl*).

telepathy *n* mind-reading, thought transference, sixth sense, ESP, clairvoyance.

telephone *n* phone, handset, receiver, blower (*infml*).

> *Types of telephone include*: Ansaphone®, answering machine, caller display phone, car phone, cardphone, cashphone, cellphone, corded phone, cordless phone, fax, fax-phone, hazardous area phone, Minicom®, mobile phone, pager, payphone, push-button telephone, system phone, textphone, tone-dialling phone, Touchtone®, Uniphone®, videophone, weather resistant phone.

v phone, ring (up), call (up), dial, buzz (*infml*), contact, get in touch.

telescope *v* contract, shrink, compress, condense, abridge, squash, crush, shorten, curtail, truncate, abbreviate, reduce, cut, trim.

television *n* TV, receiver, set, telly (*infml*), the box (*infml*), goggle-box (*infml*), idiot box (*infml*), small screen.

tell *v* **1** INFORM, notify, let know, acquaint, impart, communicate, speak, utter, say, state, confess, divulge, disclose, reveal. **2** *tell a story*: narrate, recount, relate, report, announce, describe, portray, mention. **3** ORDER, command, direct, instruct, authorize. **4** DIFFERENTIATE, distinguish, discriminate, discern, recognize, identify, discover, see, understand, comprehend.
tell off (*infml*) scold, chide, tick off (*infml*), upbraid, reprimand, rebuke, reprove, lecture, berate, dress down (*infml*), reproach, censure.

temerity *n* impudence, impertinence, cheek (*infml*), gall, nerve (*infml*), audacity, boldness, daring, rashness, recklessness, impulsiveness.
≠ caution, prudence.

temper *n* **1** MOOD, humour, nature, temperament, character, disposition, constitution. **2** ANGER, rage, fury, passion, tantrum, paddy (*infml*), annoyance, irritability, ill-humour. **3** CALM, composure, self-control, cool (*sl*).
≠ **2** calmness, self-control. **3** anger, rage.
v **1** MODERATE, lessen, reduce, calm, soothe, allay, assuage, palliate, mitigate, modify, soften. **2** HARDEN, toughen, strengthen.

temperament *n* nature, character, personality, disposition, tendency, bent, constitution, make-up, soul, spirit, mood, humour, temper, state of mind, attitude, outlook.

temperamental *adj* **1** MOODY, emotional, neurotic, highly-strung, sensitive, touchy, irritable, impatient, passionate, fiery, excitable, explosive, volatile, mercurial, capricious, unpredictable, unreliable. **2** NATURAL, inborn, innate, inherent, constitutional, ingrained.
≠ **1** calm, level-headed, steady.

temperance *n* teetotalism, prohibition, abstinence, abstemiousness, sobriety, continence, moderation, restraint, self-restraint, self-control, self-discipline, self-denial.
≠ intemperance, excess.

temperate *adj* **1** *temperate climate*: mild, clement, balmy, fair, equable, balanced, stable, gentle, pleasant, agreeable. **2** TEETOTAL, abstinent, abstemious, sober, continent, moderate, restrained, controlled, even-tempered, calm, composed, reasonable, sensible.
≠ **2** intemperate, extreme, excessive.

tempestuous *adj* stormy, windy, gusty, blustery, squally, turbulent, tumultuous, rough, wild, violent, furious, raging, heated, passionate, intense.
≠ calm.

temple *n* shrine, sanctuary, church, tabernacle, mosque, pagoda.

tempo *n* time, rhythm, metre, beat, pulse, speed, velocity, rate, pace.

temporal *adj* secular, profane, worldly, earthly, terrestrial, material, carnal, fleshly, mortal.
≠ spiritual.

temporary *adj* impermanent, provisional, interim, makeshift, stopgap, temporal, transient, transitory, passing, ephemeral, evanescent, fleeting, brief, short-lived, momentary.
≠ permanent, everlasting.

tempt *v* entice, coax, persuade, woo, bait, lure, allure, attract, draw, seduce, invite, tantalize, provoke, incite.
≠ discourage, dissuade, repel.

temptation *n* enticement, inducement, coaxing, persuasion, bait, lure, allure, appeal, attraction, draw, pull, seduction, invitation.

tenable *adj* credible, defensible, justifiable, reasonable, rational, sound, arguable, believable, defendable, plausible, viable, feasible.
≠ untenable, indefensible, unjustifiable.

tenant *n* renter, lessee, leaseholder, occupier, occupant, resident, inhabitant.

tend[1] *v* incline, lean, bend, bear, head, aim, lead, go, move, gravitate.

tend[2] *v* look after, care for, cultivate, keep, maintain, manage, handle, guard, protect, watch, mind, nurture, nurse, minister to, serve, attend.
≠ neglect, ignore.

tendency *n* trend, drift, movement, course, direction, bearing, heading, bias, partiality, predisposition, propensity, readiness, liability, susceptibility, proneness, inclination, leaning, bent, disposition.

tender[1] *adj* **1** KIND, gentle, caring, humane, considerate, compassionate, sympathetic, warm, fond, affectionate, loving, amorous, romantic, sentimental, emotional, sensitive, tender-hearted, soft-hearted. **2** YOUNG, youthful, immature, green, raw, new, inexperienced, impressionable, vulnerable. **3** SOFT, succulent, fleshy, dainty, delicate, fragile, frail, weak, feeble. **4** SORE, painful, aching, smarting, bruised, inflamed, raw.
≠ **1** hard-hearted, callous. **2** mature. **3** tough, hard.

tender[2] *v* offer, proffer, extend, give, present, submit, propose, suggest, advance, volunteer.
n **1** *legal tender*: currency, money. **2** OFFER, bid, estimate, quotation, proposal, proposition, suggestion, submission.

tense *adj* **1** TIGHT, taut, stretched, strained, stiff, rigid. **2** NERVOUS, anxious, worried, jittery, uneasy, apprehensive, edgy, fidgety, restless, jumpy, overwrought, keyed up. **3** STRESSFUL, exciting, worrying, fraught.
≠ **1** loose, slack. **2** calm, relaxed.
v tighten, contract, brace, stretch, strain.
≠ loosen, relax.

tension *n* **1** TIGHTNESS, tautness, stiffness, strain, stress, pressure. **2** NERVOUSNESS, anxiety, worry, uneasiness, apprehension, edginess, restlessness, suspense.
≠ **1** looseness. **2** calm(ness), relaxation.

tents

Types of tent include: barrel-vaulted tent, bell tent, big top, bivvy, black tent, box tent, canopy, canvas, conical tent, crossover pole tent, dome tent, double-A pole mountain tent, frame tent, hooped bivvy, kata, lodge, marquee, mat tent, ridge tent, single hoop tent, sloping ridge tent, sloping wedge tent, tabernacle, tepee, touring tent, trailer tent, tunnel tent, tupik, wigwam, yaranga.

tentative *adj* experimental,

exploratory, speculative, hesitant, faltering, cautious, unsure, uncertain, doubtful, undecided, provisional, indefinite, unconfirmed.
≠ definite, decisive, conclusive, final.

tenuous *adj* thin, slim, slender, fine, slight, insubstantial, flimsy, fragile, delicate, weak, shaky, doubtful, dubious, questionable.
≠ strong, substantial.

tepid *adj* lukewarm, cool, half-hearted, unenthusiastic, apathetic.
≠ cold, hot, passionate.

term *n* **1** WORD, name, designation, appellation, title, epithet, phrase, expression. **2** TIME, period, course, duration, spell, span, stretch, interval, space, semester, session, season.
v call, name, dub, style, designate, label, tag, title, entitle.

terminal *adj* **1** LAST, final, concluding, ultimate, extreme, utmost. **2** *terminal illness*: FATAL, deadly, lethal, mortal, incurable.
≠ **1** initial.

terminate *v* finish, complete, conclude, cease, end, stop, close, discontinue, wind up, cut off, abort, lapse, expire.
≠ begin, start, initiate.

terminology *n* language, jargon, phraseology, vocabulary, words, terms, nomenclature.

terminus *n* end, close, termination, extremity, limit, boundary, destination, goal, target, depot, station, garage, terminal.

terms *n* **1** *on good terms*: relations, relationship, footing, standing, position. **2** CONDITIONS, specifications, stipulations, provisos, provisions, qualifications, particulars. **3** RATES, charges, fees, prices, tariff.

terrain *n* land, ground, territory, country, countryside, landscape, topography.

terrestrial *adj* earthly, worldly, global, mundane.
≠ cosmic, heavenly.

terrible *adj* bad, awful, frightful, dreadful, shocking, appalling, outrageous, disgusting, revolting, repulsive, offensive, abhorrent, hateful, horrid, horrible, unpleasant, obnoxious, foul, vile, hideous, gruesome, horrific, harrowing, distressing, grave, serious, severe, extreme, desperate.
≠ excellent, wonderful, superb.

terribly (*infml*) *adv* very, much, greatly, extremely, exceedingly, awfully, frightfully, decidedly, seriously.

terrific (*infml*) *adj* **1** EXCELLENT, wonderful, marvellous, super, smashing (*infml*), outstanding, brilliant, magnificent, superb, fabulous (*infml*), fantastic (*infml*), sensational, amazing, stupendous, breathtaking. **2** HUGE, enormous, gigantic, tremendous, great, intense, extreme, excessive.
≠ **1** awful, terrible, appalling.

terrify *v* petrify, horrify, appal, shock, terrorize, intimidate, frighten, scare, alarm, dismay.

territory *n* country, land, state, dependency, province, domain, preserve, jurisdiction, sector, region, area, district, zone, tract, terrain.

terror *n* fear, panic, dread, trepidation, horror, shock, fright, alarm, dismay, consternation, terrorism, intimidation.

terrorize *v* threaten, menace, intimidate, oppress, coerce, bully, browbeat, frighten, scare, alarm, terrify, petrify, horrify, shock.

terse *adj* short, brief, succinct, concise, compact, condensed, epigrammatic, pithy, incisive, snappy, curt, brusque, abrupt, laconic.
≠ long-winded, verbose.

test *v* try, experiment, examine, assess, evaluate, check, investigate, analyse, screen, prove, verify.
n trial, try-out, experiment, examination, assessment, evaluation, check, investigation, analysis, proof, probation, ordeal.

testify *v* give evidence, depose, state, declare, assert, swear, avow, attest, vouch, certify, corroborate, affirm, show, bear witness.

testimonial *n* reference, character,

credential, certificate, recommendation, endorsement, commendation, tribute.

testimony *n* evidence, statement, affidavit, submission, deposition, declaration, profession, attestation, affirmation, support, proof, verification, confirmation, witness, demonstration, manifestation, indication.

tether *n* chain, rope, cord, line, lead, leash, bond, fetter, shackle, restraint, fastening.
v tie, fasten, secure, restrain, chain, rope, leash, bind, lash, fetter, shackle, manacle.

text *n* words, wording, content, matter, body, subject, topic, theme, reading, passage, paragraph, sentence, book, textbook, source.

texture *n* consistency, feel, surface, grain, weave, tissue, fabric, structure, composition, constitution, character, quality.

thank *v* say thank you, be grateful, appreciate, acknowledge, recognize, credit.

thankful *adj* grateful, appreciative, obliged, indebted, pleased, contented, relieved.
≠ ungrateful, unappreciative.

thankless *adj* unrecognized, unappreciated, unrequited, unrewarding, unprofitable, fruitless.
≠ rewarding, worthwhile.

thanks *n* gratitude, gratefulness, appreciation, acknowledgement, recognition, credit, thanksgiving, thank-offering.
thanks to because of, owing to, due to, on account of, as a result of, through.

thaw *v* melt, defrost, defreeze, de-ice, soften, liquefy, dissolve, warm, heat up.
≠ freeze.

theatre

Parts of a theatre include: apron, auditorium, backstage, balcony, border, box, bridge, catwalk, circle, coulisse, cut drop, cyclorama, downstage, flat, flies, forestage, fourth wall, gallery, the gods (*infml*), green room, grid, leg drop, loge, loggia, mezzanine, open stage, opposite prompt, orchestra pit, picture-frame stage, pit, prompt side, proscenium, proscenium arch, revolving stage, rostrum, safety curtain, scruto, set, stage, stalls, tormentor, trapdoor, upper circle, upstage, wings.

theatrical *adj* **1** DRAMATIC, thespian.

Theatrical forms include: ballet, burlesque, cabaret, circus, comedy, black comedy, comedy of humours, comedy of manners, comedy of menace, commedia dell'arte, duologue, farce, fringe theatre, Grand Guignol, kabuki, Kensington gore, Kitchen-Sink, legitimate drama, masque, melodrama, mime, miracle play, monologue, morality play, mummery, music hall, musical, musical comedy, mystery play, Noh, opera, operetta, pageant, pantomime, play, Punch and Judy, puppet theatre, revue, street theatre, tableau, theatre-in-the-round, Theatre of the Absurd, Theatre of Cruelty, tragedy. *see also* **performance**.

2 MELODRAMATIC, histrionic, mannered, affected, artificial, pompous, ostentatious, showy, extravagant, exaggerated, overdone.

theft *n* robbery, thieving, stealing, pilfering, larceny, shop-lifting, kleptomania, fraud, embezzlement.

theme *n* subject, topic, thread, motif, keynote, idea, gist, essence, burden, argument, thesis, dissertation, composition, essay, text, matter.

theorem *n* formula, principle, rule, statement, deduction, proposition, hypothesis.

theoretical *adj* hypothetical, conjectural, speculative, abstract, academic, doctrinaire, pure, ideal.
≠ practical, applied, concrete.

theorize *v* hypothesize, suppose, guess, conjecture, speculate, postulate, propound, formulate.

theory *n* hypothesis, supposition,

assumption, presumption, surmise, guess, conjecture, speculation, idea, notion, abstraction, philosophy, thesis, plan, proposal, scheme, system.
≠ certainty, practice.

therapeutic *adj* remedial, curative, healing, restorative, tonic, medicinal, corrective, good, beneficial.
≠ harmful, detrimental.

therapy *n* treatment, remedy, cure, healing, tonic.

Types of therapy include: acupressure, acupuncture, Alexander technique, aromatherapy, art therapy, aversion therapy, behaviour therapy, biofeedback, chemotherapy, chiropractic, dramatherapy, electro-convulsive therapy, faith healing, group therapy, heat treatment, herbalism, homeopathy, hydrotherapy, hypnotherapy, irradiation, moxibustion, naturopathy, occupational therapy, osteopathy, phototherapy, physiotherapy, primal therapy, psychotherapy, radiotherapy, reflexology, Rolfing, shiatsu, speech therapy, ultrasound, zone therapy.

therefore *adv* so, then, consequently, as a result.

thesis *n* **1** *doctoral thesis*: dissertation, essay, composition, treatise, paper, monograph. **2** SUBJECT, topic, theme, idea, opinion, view, theory, hypothesis, proposal, proposition, premise, statement, argument, contention.

thick *adj* **1** WIDE, broad, fat, heavy, solid, dense, impenetrable, close, compact, concentrated, condensed, viscous, coagulated, clotted. **2** FULL, packed, crowded, chock-a-block, swarming, teeming, bristling, brimming, bursting, numerous, abundant. **3** (*infml*) STUPID, foolish, slow, dull, dim-witted, brainless, simple.
≠ **1** thin, slim, slender, slight. **2** sparse. **3** clever, brainy (*infml*).

thicken *v* condense, stiffen, congeal, coagulate, clot, cake, gel, jell, set.
≠ thin.

thicket *n* wood, copse, coppice, grove, spinney.

thickness *n* **1** WIDTH, breadth, diameter, density, viscosity, bulk, body. **2** LAYER, stratum, ply, sheet, coat.
≠ **1** thinness.

thick-skinned *adj* insensitive, unfeeling, callous, tough, hardened, hard-boiled.
≠ thin-skinned, sensitive.

thief *n* robber, bandit, mugger, pickpocket, shop-lifter, burglar, house-breaker, plunderer, poacher, stealer, pilferer, filcher, kleptomaniac, swindler, embezzler.

thin *adj* **1** LEAN, slim, slender, narrow, attenuated, slight, skinny, bony, skeletal, scraggy, scrawny, lanky, gaunt, spare, underweight, undernourished, emaciated. **2** *thin fabric*: fine, delicate, light, flimsy, filmy, gossamer, sheer, see-through, transparent, translucent. **3** SPARSE, scarce, scattered, scant, meagre, poor, inadequate, deficient, scanty, skimpy. **4** WEAK, feeble, runny, watery, diluted.
≠ **1** fat, broad. **2** thick, dense, solid. **3** plentiful, abundant. **4** strong.
v **1** NARROW, attenuate, diminish, reduce, trim, weed out. **2** WEAKEN, dilute, water down, rarefy, refine.

thing *n* **1** ARTICLE, object, entity, creature, body, substance, item, detail, particular, feature, factor, element, point, fact, concept, thought. **2** DEVICE, contrivance, gadget, tool, implement, instrument, apparatus, machine, mechanism. **3** ACT, deed, feat, action, task, responsibility, problem. **4** CIRCUMSTANCE, eventuality, happening, occurrence, event, incident, phenomenon, affair, proceeding. **5** (*infml*) OBSESSION, preoccupation, fixation, fetish, phobia, hang-up (*infml*).

things *n* belongings, possessions, effects, paraphernalia, stuff (*infml*), goods, luggage, baggage, equipment, gear (*infml*), clobber (*infml*), odds and ends, bits and pieces.

think *v* **1** BELIEVE, hold, consider, regard, esteem, deem, judge, estimate, reckon, calculate, determine, conclude,

reason. **2** CONCEIVE, imagine, suppose, presume, surmise, expect, foresee, envisage, anticipate. **3** *think it over*: ponder, mull over, chew over, ruminate, meditate, contemplate, muse, cogitate, reflect, deliberate, weigh up, recall, recollect, remember.
think up devise, contrive, dream up, imagine, conceive, visualize, invent, design, create, concoct.

thinker *n* philosopher, theorist, ideologist, brain, intellect, mastermind.

thinking *n* reasoning, philosophy, thoughts, conclusions, theory, idea, opinion, view, outlook, position, judgement, assessment.
adj reasoning, rational, intellectual, intelligent, cultured, sophisticated, philosophical, analytical, reflective, contemplative, thoughtful.

third-rate *adj* low-grade, poor, bad, inferior, mediocre, indifferent, shoddy, cheap and nasty.
≠ first-rate.

thirst *n* **1** THIRSTINESS, dryness, drought. **2** DESIRE, longing, yearning, hankering, craving, hunger, appetite, lust, passion, eagerness, keenness.

thirsty *adj* **1** DRY, parched (*infml*), gasping (*infml*), dehydrated, arid. **2** *thirsty for knowledge*: desirous, longing, yearning, hankering, craving, hungry, burning, itching, dying, eager, avid, greedy.

thorn *n* spike, point, barb, prickle, spine, bristle, needle.

thorough *adj* full, complete, total, entire, utter, absolute, perfect, pure, sheer, unqualified, unmitigated, out-and-out, downright, sweeping, all-embracing, comprehensive, all-inclusive, exhaustive, thoroughgoing, intensive, in-depth, conscientious, efficient, painstaking, scrupulous, meticulous, careful.
≠ partial, superficial, careless.

though *conj* although, even if, notwithstanding, while, allowing, granted.
adv however, nevertheless, nonetheless, yet, still, even so, all the same, for all that.

thought *n* **1** THINKING, attention, heed, regard, consideration, study, scrutiny, introspection, meditation, contemplation, cogitation, reflection, deliberation. **2** IDEA, notion, concept, conception, belief, conviction, opinion, view, judgement, assessment, conclusion, plan, design, intention, purpose, aim, hope, dream, expectation, anticipation.
3 THOUGHTFULNESS, consideration, kindness, care, concern, compassion, sympathy, gesture, touch.

thoughtful *adj* **1** PENSIVE, wistful, dreamy, abstracted, reflective, contemplative, introspective, thinking, absorbed, studious, serious, solemn.
2 CONSIDERATE, kind, unselfish, helpful, caring, attentive, heedful, mindful, careful, prudent, cautious, wary.
≠ **2** thoughtless, insensitive, selfish.

thoughtless *adj* **1** INCONSIDERATE, unthinking, insensitive, unfeeling, tactless, undiplomatic, unkind, selfish, uncaring. **2** absent-minded, inattentive, heedless, mindless, foolish, stupid, silly, rash, reckless, ill-considered, imprudent, careless, negligent, remiss.
≠ **1** thoughtful, considerate. **2** careful.

thrash *v* **1** PUNISH, beat, whip, lash, flog, scourge, cane, belt, spank, clobber, wallop (*infml*), lay into.
2 DEFEAT, beat, trounce, hammer (*infml*), slaughter (*infml*), crush, overwhelm, rout. **3** THRESH, flail, toss, jerk.
thrash out discuss, debate, negotiate, settle, resolve.

thread *n* **1** yarn, strand, fibre, filament, string, line.

> *Types of thread include*: button thread, cotton, coton à broder, mercerized cotton, pearl cotton, machine twist, quick-match, stranded cotton, embroidery thread, machine embroidery thread, embroidery silk, embroidery wool, floss, metallic thread, polyester, purl, silk, wool, knitting wool, 2-ply, 3-ply, 4-ply, baby wool, chunky wool, double-knitting, tapestry wool, crewel wool, Persian wool.

2 COURSE, direction, drift, tenor, theme, motif, plot, storyline.

threadbare *adj* **1** *threadbare clothes*: worn, frayed, ragged, moth-eaten, scruffy, shabby. **2** HACKNEYED, overused, old, stale, tired, trite, commonplace, stock, stereotyped.
≠ **1** new. **2** fresh.

threat *n* menace, warning, omen, portent, presage, foreboding, danger, risk, hazard, peril.

threaten *v* menace, intimidate, browbeat, pressurize, bully, terrorize, warn, portend, presage, forebode, foreshadow, endanger, jeopardize, imperil.

threatening *adj* menacing, intimidatory, warning, cautionary, ominous, inauspicious, sinister, grim, looming, impending.

threshold *n* doorstep, sill, doorway, door, entrance, brink, verge, starting-point, dawn, beginning, start, outset, opening.

thrift *n* economy, husbandry, saving, conservation, frugality, prudence, carefulness.
≠ extravagance, waste.

thrifty *adj* economical, saving, frugal, sparing, prudent, careful.
≠ extravagant, profligate, prodigal, wasteful.

thrill *n* excitement, adventure, pleasure, stimulation, charge, kick, buzz (*sl*), sensation, glow, tingle, throb, shudder, quiver, tremor.
v excite, electrify, galvanize, exhilarate, rouse, arouse, move, stir, stimulate, flush, glow, tingle, throb, shudder, tremble, quiver, shake.
≠ bore.

thrive *v* flourish, prosper, boom, grow, increase, advance, develop, bloom, blossom, gain, profit, succeed.
≠ languish, stagnate, fail, die.

throb *v* pulse, pulsate, beat, palpitate, vibrate, pound, thump.
n pulse, pulsation, beat, palpitation, vibration, pounding, thumping.

throttle *v* strangle, choke, asphyxiate, suffocate, smother, stifle, gag, silence, suppress, inhibit.

through *prep* **1** BETWEEN, by, via, by way of, by means of, using. **2** *all through the night*: throughout, during, in. **3** BECAUSE OF, as a result of, thanks to.
adj **1** FINISHED, ended, completed, done. **2** *through train*: direct, express, non-stop.

throw *v* **1** HURL, heave, lob, pitch, chuck (*infml*), sling, cast, fling, toss, launch, propel, send. **2** *throw light*: shed, cast, project, direct. **3** BRING DOWN, floor, upset, overturn, dislodge, unseat, unsaddle, unhorse. **4** (*infml*) PERPLEX, baffle, confound, confuse, disconcert, astonish, dumbfound.
n heave, lob, pitch, sling, fling, toss, cast.
throw away 1 DISCARD, jettison, dump, ditch (*sl*), scrap, dispose of, throw out. **2** WASTE, squander, fritter away, blow (*sl*).
≠ **1** keep, preserve, salvage, rescue.
throw off shed, cast off, drop, abandon, shake off, get rid of, elude.
throw out 1 EVICT, turn out, expel, turf out (*infml*), eject, emit, radiate, give off. **2** REJECT, discard, dismiss, turn down, jettison, dump, ditch (*sl*), throw away, scrap.
throw up 1 (*infml*) VOMIT, spew, regurgitate, disgorge, retch, heave. **2** abandon, renounce, relinquish, resign, quit, leave. **3** GIVE UP.

thrust *v* push, shove, butt, ram, jam, wedge, stick, poke, prod, jab, lunge, pierce, stab, plunge, press, force, impel, drive, propel.
n push, shove, poke, prod, lunge, stab, drive, impetus, momentum.

thud *n, v* thump, clump, knock, clunk, smack, wallop (*infml*), crash, bang, thunder.

thug *n* ruffian, tough, robber, bandit, mugger, killer, murderer, assassin, gangster, hooligan.

thump *n* knock, blow, punch, clout, box, cuff, smack, whack (*infml*), wallop (*infml*), crash, bang, thud, beat, throb.
v hit, strike, knock, punch, clout, box, cuff, smack, thrash, whack (*infml*), wallop (*infml*), crash, bang,

thud, batter, pound, hammer, beat, throb.

thunder *n* boom, reverberation, crash, bang, crack, clap, peal, rumble, roll, roar, blast, explosion.
v boom, resound, reverberate, crash, bang, crack, clap, peal, rumble, roll, roar, blast.

thunderous *adj* booming, resounding, reverberating, roaring, loud, noisy, deafening, ear-splitting.

thus *adv* so, hence, therefore, consequently, then, accordingly, like this, in this way, as follows.

thwart *v* frustrate, foil, stymie, defeat, hinder, impede, obstruct, block, check, baffle, stop, prevent, oppose.
≠ help, assist, aid.

tick *n* **1** CLICK, tap, stroke, tick-tock. **2** (*infml*) *wait a tick*: moment, instant, flash, jiffy (*infml*), second, minute.
v **1** MARK, indicate, choose, select. **2** CLICK, tap, beat.
tick off (*infml*) scold, chide, reprimand, rebuke, reproach, reprove, upbraid, tell off (*infml*).
≠ praise, compliment.

ticket *n* pass, card, certificate, token, voucher, coupon, docket, slip, label, tag, sticker.

tickle *v* excite, thrill, delight, please, gratify, amuse, entertain, divert.

ticklish *adj* sensitive, touchy, delicate, thorny, awkward, difficult, tricky, critical, risky, hazardous, dodgy (*infml*).
≠ easy, simple.

tide *n* current, ebb, flow, stream, flux, movement, course, direction, drift, trend, tendency.

tidy *adj* **1** NEAT, orderly, methodical, systematic, organized, clean, spick-and-span, shipshape, smart, spruce, trim, well-kept, ordered, uncluttered. **2** (*infml*) *a tidy sum*: large, substantial, sizable, considerable, good, generous, ample.
≠ **1** untidy, messy, disorganized. **2** small, insignificant.
v neaten, straighten, order, arrange, clean, smarten, spruce up, groom.

tie *v* knot, fasten, secure, moor, tether, attach, join, connect, link, unite, rope, lash, strap, bind, restrain, restrict, confine, limit, hamper, hinder.
n **1** KNOT, fastening, joint, connection, link, liaison, relationship, bond, affiliation, obligation, commitment, duty, restraint, restriction, limitation, hindrance. **2** DRAW, dead heat, stalemate, deadlock.
tie up 1 MOOR, tether, attach, secure, rope, lash, bind, truss, wrap up, restrain. **2** CONCLUDE, terminate, wind up, settle. **3** OCCUPY, engage, engross.

tier *n* floor, storey, level, stage, stratum, layer, belt, zone, band, echelon, rank, row, line.

tight *adj* **1** TAUT, stretched, tense, rigid, stiff, firm, fixed, fast, secure, close, cramped, constricted, compact, snug, close-fitting. **2** SEALED, hermetic, -proof, impervious, airtight, watertight. **3** (*infml*) MEAN, stingy, miserly, niggardly, parsimonious, tight-fisted (*infml*). **4** *tight security*: strict, severe, stringent, rigorous.
≠ **1** loose, slack. **2** open. **3** generous. **4** lax.

tighten *v* tauten, stretch, tense, stiffen, fix, fasten, secure, narrow, close, cramp, constrict, crush, squeeze.
≠ loosen, relax.

tight-fisted (*infml*) *adj* mean, stingy, miserly, mingy (*infml*), niggardly, penny-pinching, sparing, parsimonious, tight (*infml*), grasping.
≠ generous, charitable.

till *v* cultivate, work, plough, dig, farm.

tilt *v* slope, incline, slant, pitch, list, tip, lean.
n slope, incline, angle, inclination, slant, pitch, list.

timber *n* wood, trees, forest, beam, lath, plank, board, log.

time *n* **1** SPELL, stretch, period, term, season, session, span, duration, interval, space, while. **2** TEMPO, beat, rhythm, metre, measure. **3** point, juncture, stage, instance, occasion, date. **4** life, generation, heyday, peak.

> *Periods of time include*: eternity, eon, era, age, generation, epoch, millennium, chiliad, century, lifetime, decade, decennium, quinquennium, year, light-year, yesteryear, quarter, month, fortnight, week, midweek, weekend, long weekend, day, today, tonight, yesterday, tomorrow, morrow, weekday, hour, minute, second, moment, instant, millisecond, microsecond, nanosecond; dawn, sunrise, sun-up, the early hours, wee small hours (*infml*), morning, morn, a.m., daytime, midday, noon, high noon, p.m., afternoon, tea-time, evening, twilight, dusk, sunset, nightfall, bedtime, night, night-time; season, spring, summer, midsummer, autumn, fall (US), winter.

v clock, measure, meter, regulate, control, set, schedule, timetable.

timeless *adj* ageless, immortal, everlasting, eternal, endless, permanent, changeless, unchanging.

timely *adj* well-timed, seasonable, suitable, appropriate, convenient, opportune, propitious, prompt, punctual.
≠ ill-timed, unsuitable, inappropriate.

timetable *n* schedule, programme, agenda, calendar, diary, rota, roster, list, listing, curriculum.

timid *adj* shy, bashful, modest, shrinking, retiring, nervous, apprehensive, afraid, timorous, fearful, cowardly, faint-hearted, spineless, irresolute.
≠ brave, bold, audacious.

tinge *n* tint, dye, colour, shade, touch, trace, suggestion, hint, smack, flavour, pinch, drop, dash, bit, sprinkling, smattering.
v tint, dye, stain, colour, shade, suffuse, imbue.

tingle *v* sting, prickle, tickle, itch, thrill, throb, quiver, vibrate.
n stinging, prickling, pins and needles, tickle, tickling, itch, itching, thrill, throb, quiver, shiver, gooseflesh, goose-pimples.

tinker *v* fiddle, play, toy, trifle, potter, dabble, meddle, tamper.

tint *n* dye, stain, rinse, wash, colour, hue, shade, tincture, tinge, tone, cast, streak, trace, touch.
v dye, colour, tinge, streak, stain, taint, affect.

tiny *adj* minute, microscopic, infinitesimal, teeny (*infml*), small, little, slight, negligible, insignificant, diminutive, petite, dwarfish, pint-sized (*infml*), pocket, miniature, mini (*infml*).
≠ huge, enormous, immense.

tip[1] *n* end, extremity, point, nib, apex, peak, pinnacle, summit, acme, top, cap, crown, head.
v cap, crown, top, surmount.

tip[2] *v* lean, incline, slant, list, tilt, topple over, capsize, upset, overturn, spill, pour out, empty, unload, dump.
n dump, rubbish-heap, refuse-heap.

tip[3] *n* **1** CLUE, pointer, hint, suggestion, advice, warning, tip-off, information, inside information, forecast.
2 GRATUITY, gift, perquisite.
v **1** ADVISE, suggest, warn, caution, forewarn, tip off, inform, tell. **2** *tip the driver*: reward, remunerate.

tire *v* weary, fatigue, wear out, exhaust, drain, enervate.
≠ enliven, invigorate, refresh.

tired *adj* **1** WEARY, drowsy, sleepy, flagging, fatigued, worn out, exhausted, dog-tired, drained, jaded, fagged (*sl*), bushed (*infml*), whacked (*infml*), shattered (*infml*), beat (*infml*), dead-beat (*infml*), all in (*infml*), knackered (*infml*). **2** *tired of waiting*: fed up, bored, sick.
≠ **1** lively, energetic, rested, refreshed. **3** new.

tireless *adj* untiring, unwearied, unflagging, indefatigable, energetic, vigorous, diligent, industrious, resolute, determined.
≠ tired, lazy.

tiresome *adj* troublesome, trying, annoying, irritating, exasperating, wearisome, dull, boring, tedious, monotonous, uninteresting, tiring, fatiguing, laborious.
≠ interesting, stimulating, easy.

tiring *adj* wearying, fatiguing,

exhausting, draining, demanding, exacting, taxing, arduous, strenuous, laborious.

tissue *n* substance, matter, material, fabric, stuff, gauze, web, mesh, network, structure, texture.

titbit *n* morsel, scrap, appetizer, snack, delicacy, dainty, treat.

titillate *v* stimulate, arouse, turn on (*sl*), excite, thrill, tickle, provoke, tease, tantalize, intrigue, interest.

title *n* **1** NAME, appellation, denomination, term, designation, label, epithet, nickname, pseudonym, rank, status, office, position. **2** HEADING, headline, caption, legend, inscription. **3** RIGHT, prerogative, privilege, claim, entitlement, ownership, deeds.
v entitle, name, call, dub, style, term, designate, label.

titter *v* laugh, chortle, chuckle, giggle, snigger, mock.

titular *adj* honorary, formal, official, so-called, nominal, token.

toast *v* grill, brown, roast, heat, warm.
n drink, pledge, tribute, salute, compliment, health.

tobacco

Forms of tobacco include: baccy (*infml*), cheroot, chewing tobacco, cigar, Havana cigar, cigarette, cork-tipped cigarette, filter-tip cigarette, king-size cigarette, menthol cigarette, Russian cigarette, ciggie (*infml*), coffin nail (*sl*), fag (*infml*), cigarette end, cigarette butt, dog-end (*sl*), fag end (*sl*), cigarillo, corona, high-tar, low-tar, panatella, plug, snuff, flake tobacco, pipe tobacco, shag tobacco, Turkish tobacco, Virginia tobacco, the weed (*infml*).
Tobacco accessories include: ashtray, cigar box, cigar case, cigar cutter, cigar-holder, cigarette box, cigarette case, cigarette-holder, cigarette lighter, gas lighter, petrol lighter, cigarette machine, cigarette paper, cigarette roller, humidor, match, matchbook, box of matches, match striker, pipe, chibouk, churchwarden, clay pipe, hookah, meerschaum, narghile, peace pipe (pipe of peace), tobacco pipe, pipe-cleaner, pipe-rack, pipe-rest, smoker's companion, snuffbox, tobacco-pouch, vesta.

together *adv* jointly, in concert, side by side, shoulder to shoulder, in unison, as one, simultaneously, at the same time, all at once, collectively, en masse, closely, continuously, consecutively, successively, in succession, in a row, hand in hand.
≠ separately, individually, alone.

toil *n* labour, hard work, donkey-work, drudgery, sweat, graft (*infml*), industry, application, effort, exertion, elbow grease.
v labour, work, slave, drudge, sweat, grind, slog, graft (*infml*), plug away (*infml*), persevere, strive, struggle.

toilet *n* lavatory, WC, loo (*infml*), bog (*sl*), bathroom, cloakroom, washroom, rest room, public convenience, Ladies (*infml*), Gents (*infml*), urinal, convenience, powder room.

token *n* **1** SYMBOL, emblem, representation, mark, sign, indication, manifestation, demonstration, expression, evidence, proof, clue, warning, reminder, memorial, memento, souvenir, keepsake. **2** *gift token*: voucher, coupon, counter, disc.
adj symbolic, emblematic, nominal, minimal, perfunctory, superficial, cosmetic, hollow, insincere.

tolerable *adj* bearable, endurable, sufferable, acceptable, passable, adequate, reasonable, fair, average, all right, OK (*infml*), not bad, mediocre, indifferent, so-so (*infml*), unexceptional, ordinary, run-of-the-mill.
≠ intolerable, unbearable, insufferable.

tolerance *n* **1** TOLERATION, patience, forbearance, open-mindedness, broad-mindedness, magnanimity, sympathy, understanding, lenity, indulgence, permissiveness. **2** VARIATION, fluctuation, play, allowance, clearance. **3** RESISTANCE, resilience, toughness, endurance, stamina.
≠ **1** intolerance, prejudice, bigotry, narrow-mindedness.

tolerant *adj* patient, forbearing, long-

suffering, open-minded, fair, unprejudiced, broad-minded, liberal, charitable, kind-hearted, sympathetic, understanding, forgiving, lenient, indulgent, easy-going (*infml*), permissive, lax, soft.
≠ intolerant, biased, prejudiced, bigoted, unsympathetic.

tolerate *v* endure, suffer, put up with, bear, stand, abide, stomach, swallow, take, receive, accept, admit, allow, permit, condone, countenance, indulge.

toll[1] *v* ring, peal, chime, knell, sound, strike, announce, call.

toll[2] *n* charge, fee, payment, levy, tax, duty, tariff, rate, cost, penalty, demand, loss.

tomb *n* grave, burial-place, vault, crypt, sepulchre, catacomb, mausoleum, cenotaph.

tone *n* **1** *tone of voice*: note, timbre, pitch, volume, intonation, modulation, inflection, accent, stress, emphasis, force, strength. **2** TINT, tinge, colour, hue, shade, cast, tonality. **3** AIR, manner, attitude, mood, spirit, humour, temper, character, quality, feel, style, effect, vein, tenor, drift.
v match, co-ordinate, blend, harmonize.
tone down moderate, temper, subdue, restrain, soften, dim, dampen, play down, reduce, alleviate, assuage, mitigate.

tongue *n* language, speech, discourse, talk, utterance, articulation, parlance, vernacular, idiom, dialect, patois.

tongue-tied *adj* speechless, dumbstruck, inarticulate, silent, mute, dumb, voiceless.
≠ talkative, garrulous, voluble.

tonic *n* cordial, pick-me-up, restorative, refresher, bracer, stimulant, shot in the arm (*infml*), boost, fillip.

too *adv* **1** ALSO, as well, in addition, besides, moreover, likewise. **2** EXCESSIVELY, inordinately, unduly, over, overly, unreasonably, ridiculously, extremely, very.

tool *n* **1** IMPLEMENT, instrument, utensil, gadget, device, contrivance, contraption, apparatus, appliance, machine, means, vehicle, medium, agency, agent, intermediary. **2** PUPPET, pawn, dupe, stooge, minion, hireling.

> *Types of tool include*: bolster, caulking-iron, crowbar, hod, jackhammer, jointer, mattock, pick, pick-axe, plumb-line, sledgehammer; chaser, clamp, dividers, dolly, drill, hacksaw, jack, pincers, pliers, protractor, punch, rule, sander, scriber, snips, socket-wrench, soldering-iron, spraygun, tommy bar, vice; auger, awl, brace and bit, bradawl, chisel, file, fretsaw, hammer, handsaw, jack-plane, jigsaw, level, mallet, plane, rasp, saw, screwdriver, set-square, spirit level, tenon-saw, T-square; billhook, chainsaw, chopper, dibber, fork, grass-rake, hay fork, hoe, pitchfork, plough, pruning-knife, pruning-shears, rake, scythe, secateurs, shears, shovel, sickle, spade, thresher, trowel; needle, scissors, pinking-shears, bodkin, crochet hook, forceps, scalpel, tweezers, tongs, cleaver, steel, gimlet, mace, mortar, pestle, paper-cutter, paper-knife, stapler, pocket-knife, penknife.

tooth

> *Types of tooth include*: baby tooth, back tooth, bicuspid, bucktooth, canine, carnassial, dog-tooth, eye tooth, false tooth, cap, crown, fang, first tooth, gold tooth, grinder, incisor, central incisor, lateral incisor, milk tooth, molar, first molar, second molar, third molar, premolar, first premolar, second premolar, snaggletooth, tush, tusk, wisdom tooth; false teeth, bridge, denture, dentures, plate.

top *n* **1** HEAD, tip, vertex, apex, crest, crown, peak, pinnacle, summit, acme, zenith, culmination, height. **2** LID, cap, cover, cork, stopper.
≠ **1** bottom, base, nadir.
adj highest, topmost, upmost, uppermost, upper, superior, head, chief, leading, first, foremost, principal, sovereign, ruling, pre-eminent, dominant, prime, paramount, greatest,

maximum, best, finest, supreme, crowning, culminating.
≠ bottom, lowest, inferior.
v **1** TIP, cap, crown, cover, finish (off), decorate, garnish. **2** BEAT, exceed, outstrip, better, excel, best, surpass, eclipse, outshine, outdo, surmount, transcend. **3** HEAD, lead, rule, command.

topic *n* subject, theme, issue, question, matter, point, thesis, text.

topical *adj* current, contemporary, up-to-date, up-to-the-minute, recent, newsworthy, relevant, popular, familiar.

topple *v* totter, overbalance, tumble, fall, collapse, upset, overturn, capsize, overthrow, oust.

torment *v* tease, provoke, annoy, vex, trouble, worry, harass, hound, pester, bother, bedevil, plague, afflict, distress, harrow, pain, torture, persecute.
n provocation, annoyance, vexation, bane, scourge, trouble, bother, nuisance, harassment, worry, anguish, distress, misery, affliction, suffering, pain, agony, ordeal, torture, persecution.

torrent *n* stream, volley, outburst, gush, rush, flood, spate, deluge, cascade, downpour.
≠ trickle.

tortuous *adj* twisting, winding, meandering, serpentine, zigzag, circuitous, roundabout, indirect, convoluted, complicated, involved.
≠ straight, straightforward.

torture *v* pain, agonize, excruciate, crucify, rack, martyr, persecute, torment, afflict, distress.
n pain, agony, suffering, affliction, distress, misery, anguish, torment, martyrdom, persecution.

toss *v* **1** FLIP, cast, fling, throw, chuck (*infml*), sling, hurl, lob. **2** ROLL, heave, pitch, lurch, jolt, shake, agitate, rock, thrash, squirm, wriggle.
n flip, cast, fling, throw, pitch.

total *n* sum, whole, entirety, totality, all, lot, mass, aggregate, amount.
adj full, complete, entire, whole, integral, all-out, utter, absolute, unconditional, unqualified, outright, undisputed, perfect, consummate, thoroughgoing, sheer, downright, thorough.
≠ partial, limited, restricted.
v add (up), sum (up), tot (up), count (up), reckon, amount to, come to, reach.

totter *v* stagger, reel, lurch, stumble, falter, waver, teeter, sway, rock, shake, quiver, tremble.

touch *n* **1** FEEL, texture, brush, stroke, caress, pat, tap, contact. **2** *a touch of garlic*: trace, spot, dash, pinch, soupçon, suspicion, hint, suggestion, speck, jot, tinge, smack. **3** SKILL, art, knack, flair, style, method, manner, technique, approach.
v **1** FEEL, handle, finger, brush, graze, stroke, caress, fondle, pat, tap, hit, strike, contact, meet, abut, adjoin, border. **2** MOVE, stir, upset, disturb, impress, inspire, influence, affect, concern, regard. **3** REACH, attain, equal, match, rival, better.
touch on mention, broach, speak of, remark on, refer to, allude to, cover, deal with.

touched *adj* **1** MOVED, stirred, affected, disturbed, impressed. **2** MAD, crazy, deranged, disturbed, eccentric, dotty (*infml*), daft (*infml*), barmy (*infml*).

touching *adj* moving, stirring, affecting, poignant, pitiable, pitiful, pathetic, sad, emotional, tender.

touchy *adj* irritable, irascible, quick-tempered, bad-tempered, grumpy, grouchy, crabbed, cross, peevish, captious, edgy, over-sensitive.
≠ calm, imperturbable.

tough *adj* **1** STRONG, durable, resilient, resistant, hardy, sturdy, solid, rigid, stiff, inflexible, hard, leathery. **2** *tough criminal*: rough, violent, vicious, callous, hardened, obstinate. **3** HARSH, severe, strict, stern, firm, resolute, determined, tenacious. **4** ARDUOUS, laborious, exacting, hard, difficult, puzzling, perplexing, baffling, knotty, thorny, troublesome.
≠ **1** fragile, delicate, weak, tender. **2** gentle, soft. **3** gentle. **4** easy, simple.

n brute, thug, bully, ruffian, hooligan, lout, yob (*sl*).

tour *n* circuit, round, visit, expedition, journey, trip, outing, excursion, drive, ride, course.
v visit, go round, sightsee, explore, travel, journey, drive, ride.

tourist *n* holidaymaker, visitor, sightseer, tripper, excursionist, traveller, voyager, globetrotter.

tournament *n* championship, series, competition, contest, match, event, meeting.

tow *v* pull, tug, draw, trail, drag, lug, haul, transport.

towards *prep* **1** TO, approaching, nearing, close to, nearly, almost. **2** *his feelings towards her*: regarding, with regard to, with respect to, concerning, about, for.

towers

> *Types of tower and famous towers include*: barbican, bastille, bastion, belfry, bell tower, belvedere, campanile, castle, church tower, citadel, column, demi-bastion, donjon, Eiffel Tower, fort, fortification, fortress, gate-tower, high-rise building, hill-fort, keep, lookout tower, martello tower, minar, minaret, mirador, pagoda, peel-tower, scaffold tower, skyscraper, smock mill, spire, steeple, tower block, tower mill, Tower of London, Tower of Pisa, turret, watchtower, water tower.

v rise, rear, ascend, mount, soar, loom, overlook, dominate, surpass, transcend, exceed, top.

towering *adj* soaring, tall, high, lofty, elevated, monumental, colossal, gigantic, great, magnificent, imposing, impressive, sublime, supreme, surpassing, overpowering, extreme, inordinate.
≠ small, tiny, minor, trivial.

toxic *adj* poisonous, harmful, noxious, unhealthy, dangerous, deadly, lethal.
≠ harmless, safe.

toy *n* plaything, knick-knack.

> *Kinds of toy include*: Action Man®, activity centre, aeroplane, baby-bouncer, baby-walker, ball, balloon, bicycle, bike (*infml*), mountain bike, blackboard and easel, boxing-gloves, building-block, building-brick, catapult, climbing-frame, computer game, crayon, doll, Barbie doll®, kewpie doll, rag-doll, Sindy doll®, Tiny-Tears doll®, doll's buggy, doll's cot, doll's house, doll's pram, drum set, electronic game, executive toy, farm, fivestones, football, fort, frisbee, game, garage, glove puppet, go-kart, golliwog, guitar, gun, cap-gun, pop-gun, gyroscope, hobby-horse, hula-hoop, jack-in-the-box, jigsaw puzzle, kaleidoscope, kite, box-kite, Lego®, marble, Matchbox®, Meccano®, model car, model kit, model railway, modelling clay, musical box, ocarina, paddling-pool, paints, pantograph, pedal-car, peashooter, Plasticene®, Play-Doh®, playhouse, pogo stick, puzzle, rattle, rocker, rocking-horse, Rubik's Cube®, sandpit, Scalextric®, scooter, seesaw, sewing machine, shape-sorter, skateboard, skipping-rope, slide, soft toy, spacehopper, Space Invaders®, spinning top, Subbuteo®, swing, swingball, teaset, teddy-bear, toy soldier, train set, trampoline, tricycle, trike (*infml*), Turtles®, typewriter, video game, Game Boy®, Nintendo®, Sega®, Super Mario®, walkie-talkie (*infml*), water pistol, Wendy house, yo-yo.
> *see also* **game**.

v play, tinker, fiddle, sport, trifle, dally.

trace *n* trail, track, spoor, footprint, footmark, mark, token, sign, indication, evidence, record, relic, remains, remnant, vestige, shadow, hint, suggestion, suspicion, soupçon, dash, drop, spot, bit, jot, touch, tinge, smack.
v **1** COPY, draw, sketch, outline, delineate, depict, mark, record, map, chart. **2** FIND, discover, detect, unearth, track (down), trail, stalk, hunt, seek, follow, pursue, shadow.

track *n* footstep, footprint, footmark, scent, spoor, trail, wake, mark, trace, slot, groove, rail, path, way, route,

orbit, line, course, drift, sequence.
v stalk, trail, hunt, trace, follow, pursue, chase, dog, tail, shadow.
track down find, discover, trace, hunt down, run to earth, sniff out, ferret out, dig up, unearth, expose, catch, capture.

tract *n* stretch, extent, expanse, plot, lot, territory, area, region, zone, district, quarter.

trade *n* **1** COMMERCE, traffic, business, dealing, buying, selling, shopkeeping, barter, exchange, transactions, custom. **2** OCCUPATION, job, business, profession, calling, craft, skill.
v traffic, peddle, do business, deal, transact, buy, sell, barter, exchange, swap, switch, bargain.

trademark *n* brand, label, name, sign, symbol, logo, insignia, crest, emblem, badge, hallmark.

trader *n* merchant, tradesman, broker, dealer, buyer, seller, vendor, supplier, wholesaler, retailer, shopkeeper, trafficker, peddler.

tradition *n* convention, custom, usage, way, habit, routine, ritual, institution, folklore.

traditional *adj* conventional, customary, habitual, usual, accustomed, established, fixed, long-established, time-honoured, old, historic, folk, oral, unwritten.
≠ unconventional, innovative, new, modern, contemporary.

traffic *n* **1** VEHICLES, shipping, transport, transportation, freight, passengers. **2** TRADE, commerce, business, dealing, trafficking, barter, exchange. **3** COMMUNICATION, dealings, relations.
v peddle, buy, sell, trade, do business, deal, bargain, barter, exchange.

tragedy *n* adversity, misfortune, unhappiness, affliction, blow, calamity, disaster, catastrophe.

tragic *adj* sad, sorrowful, miserable, unhappy, unfortunate, unlucky, ill-fated, pitiable, pathetic, heartbreaking, shocking, appalling, dreadful, awful, dire, calamitous, disastrous, catastrophic, deadly, fatal.
≠ happy, comic, successful.

trail *v* **1** DRAG, pull, tow, droop, dangle, extend, stream, straggle, dawdle, lag, loiter, linger. **2** TRACK, stalk, hunt, follow, pursue, chase, shadow, tail.
n track, footprints, footmarks, scent, trace, path, footpath, road, route, way.

train *v* **1** TEACH, instruct, coach, tutor, educate, improve, school, discipline, prepare, drill, exercise, work out, practise, rehearse. **2** POINT, direct, aim, level.
n **1** *train of events*: sequence, succession, series, progression, order, string, chain, line, file, procession, convoy, cortège, caravan. **2** RETINUE, entourage, attendants, court, household, staff, followers, following.

trainer *n* teacher, instructor, coach, tutor, handler.

training *n* teaching, instruction, coaching, tuition, education, schooling, discipline, preparation, grounding, drill, exercise, working-out, practice, learning, apprenticeship.

trait *n* feature, attribute, quality, characteristic, idiosyncrasy, peculiarity, quirk.

traitor *n* betrayer, informer, deceiver, double-crosser, turncoat, renegade, deserter, defector, quisling, collaborator.
≠ loyalist, supporter, defender.

tramp *v* walk, march, tread, stamp, stomp, stump, plod, trudge, traipse, trail, trek, hike, ramble, roam, rove.
n vagrant, vagabond, hobo, down-and-out, dosser (*sl*).

trample *v* tread, stamp, crush, squash, flatten.

trance *n* dream, reverie, daze, stupor, unconsciousness, spell, ecstasy, rapture.

tranquil *adj* calm, composed, cool, imperturbable, unexcited, placid, sedate, relaxed, laid-back (*infml*), serene, peaceful, restful, still, undisturbed, untroubled, quiet, hushed, silent.
≠ agitated, disturbed, troubled, noisy.

tranquillizer *n* sedative, opiate, narcotic, barbiturate.

transaction *n* deal, bargain, agreement, arrangement, negotiation, business, affair, matter, proceeding, enterprise, undertaking, deed, action, execution, discharge.

transcend *v* surpass, excel, outshine, eclipse, outdo, outstrip, beat, surmount, exceed, overstep.

transcribe *v* write out, copy, reproduce, rewrite, transliterate, translate, render, take down, note, record.

transcript *n* transcription, copy, reproduction, duplicate, transliteration, translation, version, note, record, manuscript.

transfer *v* change, transpose, move, shift, remove, relocate, transplant, transport, carry, convey, transmit, consign, grant, hand over.
n change, changeover, transposition, move, shift, removal, relocation, displacement, transmission, handover, transference.

transfix *v* **1** FASCINATE, spellbind, mesmerize, hypnotize, paralyse. **2** IMPALE, spear, skewer, spike, stick.

transform *v* change, alter, adapt, convert, remodel, reconstruct, transfigure, revolutionize.
≠ preserve, maintain.

transformation *n* change, alteration, mutation, conversion, metamorphosis, transfiguration, revolution.
≠ preservation, conservation.

transient *adj* transitory, passing, flying, fleeting, brief, short, momentary, ephemeral, short-lived, temporary, short-term.
≠ lasting, permanent.

transit *n* passage, journey, travel, movement, transfer, transportation, conveyance, carriage, haulage, shipment.

transition *n* passage, passing, progress, progression, development, evolution, flux, change, alteration, conversion, transformation, shift.

transitional *adj* provisional, temporary, passing, intermediate, developmental, changing, fluid, unsettled.
≠ initial, final.

translate *v* interpret, render, paraphrase, simplify, decode, decipher, transliterate, transcribe, change, alter, convert, transform, improve.

translation *n* rendering, version, interpretation, gloss, crib, rewording, rephrasing, paraphrase, simplification, transliteration, transcription, change, alteration, conversion, transformation.

transmission *n* **1** BROADCASTING, diffusion, spread, communication, conveyance, carriage, transport, shipment, sending, dispatch, relaying, transfer. **2** *a live transmission*: broadcast, programme, show, signal.
≠ **1** reception.

transmit *v* communicate, impart, convey, carry, bear, transport, send, dispatch, forward, relay, transfer, broadcast, radio, disseminate, network, diffuse, spread.
≠ receive.

transparency *n* slide, photograph, picture.

transparent *adj* **1** *transparent plastic*: clear, see-through, translucent, sheer. **2** PLAIN, distinct, clear, lucid, explicit, unambiguous, unequivocal, apparent, visible, obvious, evident, manifest, patent, undisguised, open, candid, straightforward.
≠ **1** opaque. **2** unclear, ambiguous.

transplant *v* move, shift, displace, remove, uproot, transfer, relocate, resettle, repot.
≠ leave.

transport *v* convey, carry, bear, take, fetch, bring, move, shift, transfer, ship, haul, remove, deport.
n conveyance, carriage, transfer, transportation, shipment, shipping, haulage, removal.

transpose *v* swap, exchange, switch, interchange, transfer, shift, rearrange, reorder, change, alter, move, substitute.

transverse *adj* cross, crosswise, transversal, diagonal, oblique.

trap *n* snare, net, noose, springe, gin, booby-trap, pitfall, danger, hazard,

ambush, trick, wile, ruse, strategem, device, trickery, artifice, deception.
v snare, net, entrap, ensnare, enmesh, catch, take, ambush, corner, trick, deceive, dupe.

trash *n* rubbish, garbage, refuse, junk, waste, litter, sweepings, offscourings, scum, dregs.

trauma *n* injury, wound, hurt, damage, pain, suffering, anguish, agony, torture, ordeal, shock, jolt, upset, disturbance, upheaval, strain, stress.
≠ healing.

traumatic *adj* painful, hurtful, injurious, wounding, shocking, upsetting, distressing, disturbing, unpleasant, frightening, stressful.
≠ healing, relaxing.

travel *v* journey, voyage, go, wend, move, proceed, progress, wander, ramble, roam, rove, tour, cross, traverse.
≠ stay, remain.

> *Methods of travel include*: fly, aviate, pilot, shuttle, sail, cruise, punt, paddle, row, steam, ride, cycle, bike (*infml*), freewheel, drive, motor, bus, walk, hike, march, ramble, trek, orienteer, hitch-hike, commute.

n travelling, touring, tourism, globetrotting.

> *Forms of travel include*: flight, cruise, sail, voyage, ride, drive, march, walk, hike, ramble, excursion, holiday, jaunt, outing, tour, trip, visit, expedition, safari, trek, circumnavigation, exploration, journey, migration, mission, pilgrimage.

traveller *n* **1** TOURIST, explorer, voyager, globetrotter, holidaymaker, tripper (*infml*), excursionist, passenger, commuter, wanderer, rambler, hiker, wayfarer, migrant, nomad, gypsy, itinerant, tinker, vagrant. **2** SALESMAN, saleswoman, representative, rep (*infml*), agent.

travelling *adj* touring, wandering, roaming, roving, wayfaring, migrant, migratory, nomadic, itinerant, peripatetic, mobile, moving, vagrant, homeless.
≠ fixed.

travels *n* voyage, expedition, passage, journey, trip, excursion, tour, wanderings.

travesty *n* mockery, parody, take-off, send-up, farce, caricature, distortion, sham, apology.

treacherous *adj* **1** TRAITOROUS, disloyal, unfaithful, faithless, unreliable, untrustworthy, false, untrue, deceitful, double-crossing. **2** *treacherous roads*: dangerous, hazardous, risky, perilous, precarious, icy, slippery.
≠ **1** loyal, faithful, dependable. **2** safe, stable.

treachery *n* treason, betrayal, disloyalty, infidelity, falseness, duplicity, double-dealing.
≠ loyalty, dependability.

tread *v* walk, step, pace, stride, march, tramp, trudge, plod, stamp, trample, walk on, press, crush, squash.
n walk, footfall, footstep, step, pace, stride.

treason *n* treachery, perfidy, disloyalty, duplicity, subversion, sedition, mutiny, rebellion.
≠ loyalty.

treasonable *adj* traitorous, perfidious, disloyal, false, subversive, seditious, mutinous.
≠ loyal.

treasure *n* fortune, wealth, riches, money, cash, gold, jewels, hoard, cache.
v prize, value, esteem, revere, worship, love, adore, idolize, cherish, preserve, guard.
≠ disparage, belittle.

treat *n* indulgence, gratification, pleasure, delight, enjoyment, fun, entertainment, excursion, outing, party, celebration, feast, banquet, gift, surprise, thrill.
v **1** DEAL WITH, manage, handle, use, regard, consider, discuss, cover. **2** TEND, nurse, minister to, attend to, care for, heal, cure. **3** PAY FOR, buy, stand, give, provide, entertain, regale, feast.

treatise *n* essay, dissertation, thesis, monograph, paper, pamphlet, tract, study, exposition.

treatment *n* **1** HEALING, cure, remedy, medication, therapy, surgery, care, nursing. **2** MANAGEMENT, handling, use, usage, conduct, discussion, coverage.

treaty *n* pact, convention, agreement, covenant, compact, negotiation, contract, bond, alliance.

tree *n* bush, shrub, evergreen, conifer.

> *Trees include*: acacia, acer, alder, almond, apple, ash, aspen, balsa, bay, beech, birch, blackthorn, blue gum, box, cedar, cherry, chestnut, coconut palm, cottonwood, cypress, date palm, dogwood, Dutch elm, ebony, elder, elm, eucalyptus, fig, fir, gum, hawthorn, hazel, hickory, hornbeam, horse chestnut, Japanese maple, larch, laurel, lime, linden, mahogany, maple, monkey puzzle, mountain ash, oak, palm, pear, pine, plane, plum, poplar, prunus, pussy willow, redwood, rowan, rubber tree, sandalwood, sapele, sequoia, silver birch, silver maple, spruce, sycamore, teak, walnut, weeping willow, whitebeam, willow, witch hazel, yew, yucca; bonsai, conifer, deciduous, evergreen, fruit, hardwood, ornamental, palm, softwood.

trek *n* hike, walk, march, tramp, journey, expedition, safari.
v hike, walk, march, tramp, trudge, plod, journey, rove, roam.

tremble *v* shake, vibrate, quake, shiver, shudder, quiver, wobble, rock.
n shake, vibration, quake, shiver, shudder, quiver, tremor, wobble.
≠ steadiness.

tremendous *adj* wonderful, marvellous, stupendous, sensational, spectacular, extraordinary, amazing, incredible, terrific, impressive, huge, immense, vast, colossal, gigantic, towering, formidable.
≠ ordinary, unimpressive.

tremor *n* shake, quiver, tremble, shiver, quake, quaver, wobble, vibration, agitation, thrill, shock, earthquake.
≠ steadiness.

trend *n* course, flow, drift, tendency, inclination, leaning, craze, rage (*infml*), fashion, vogue, mode, style, look.

trespass *v* invade, intrude, encroach, poach, infringe, violate, offend, wrong.
≠ obey, keep to.
n invasion, intrusion, encroachment, poaching, infringement, violation, contravention, offence, misdemeanour.

trespasser *n* intruder, poacher, offender, criminal.

trial *n* **1** LITIGATION, lawsuit, hearing, inquiry, tribunal. **2** EXPERIMENT, test, examination, check, dry run, dummy run, practice, rehearsal, audition, contest. **3** AFFLICTION, suffering, grief, misery, distress, adversity, hardship, ordeal, trouble, nuisance, vexation, tribulation.
≠ **3** relief, happiness.
adj experimental, test, pilot, exploratory, provisional, probationary.

tribe *n* race, nation, people, clan, family, house, dynasty, blood, stock, group, caste, class, division, branch.

tribute *n* **1** PRAISE, commendation, compliment, accolade, homage, respect, honour, credit, acknowledgement, recognition, gratitude. **2** PAYMENT, levy, charge, tax, duty, gift, offering, contribution.

trick *n* fraud, swindle, deception, deceit, artifice, illusion, hoax, practical joke, joke, leg-pull (*infml*), prank, antic, caper, frolic, feat, stunt, ruse, wile, dodge, subterfuge, trap, device, knack, technique, secret.
adj false, mock, artificial, imitation, ersatz, fake, forged, counterfeit, feigned, sham, bogus.
≠ real, genuine.
v deceive, delude, dupe, fool, hoodwink, beguile, mislead, bluff, hoax, pull someone's leg (*infml*), cheat, swindle, diddle, defraud, con (*infml*), trap, outwit.

trickery *n* deception, illusion, sleight-of-hand, pretence, artifice, guile, deceit, dishonesty, cheating, swindling, fraud, imposture, double-dealing, monkey

business, funny business (*sl*), chicanery, skulduggery, hocus-pocus.
≠ straightforwardness, honesty.

trickle *v* dribble, run, leak, seep, ooze, exude, drip, drop, filter, percolate.
≠ stream, gush.
n dribble, drip, drop, leak, seepage.
≠ stream, gush.

tricky *adj* **1** *a tricky problem*: difficult, awkward, problematic, complicated, knotty, thorny, delicate, ticklish.
2 CRAFTY, artful, cunning, sly, wily, foxy, subtle, devious, slippery, scheming, deceitful.
≠ **1** easy, simple. **2** honest.

trifle *n* **1** LITTLE, bit, spot, drop, dash, touch, trace. **2** TOY, plaything, trinket, bauble, knick-knack, triviality, nothing.
v toy, play, sport, flirt, dally, dabble, fiddle, meddle, fool.

trifling *adj* small, paltry, slight, negligible, inconsiderable, unimportant, insignificant, minor, trivial, petty, silly, frivolous, idle, empty, worthless.
≠ important, significant, serious.

trigger *v* cause, start, initiate, activate, set off, spark off, provoke, prompt, elicit, generate, produce.
n lever, catch, switch, spur, stimulus.

trim *adj* **1** NEAT, tidy, orderly, shipshape, spick-and-span, spruce, smart, dapper. **2** SLIM, slender, streamlined, compact.
≠ **1** untidy, scruffy.
v **1** CUT, clip, crop, dock, prune, pare, shave. **2** DECORATE, ornament, embellish, garnish, dress, array, adjust, arrange, order, neaten, tidy.
n condition, state, order, form, shape, fitness, health.

trimmings *n* **1** GARNISH, decorations, ornaments, frills, extras, accessories.
2 CUTTINGS, clippings, parings, ends.

trinket *n* bauble, jewel, ornament, knick-knack.

trio *n* threesome, triad, triumvirate, trinity, triplet, trilogy.

trip *n* outing, excursion, tour, jaunt, ride, drive, spin, journey, voyage, expedition, foray.
v stumble, slip, fall, tumble, stagger, totter, blunder.

triple *adj* treble, triplicate, threefold, three-ply, three-way.
v treble, triplicate.

trite *adj* banal, commonplace, ordinary, run-of-the-mill, stale, tired, worn, threadbare, unoriginal, hackneyed, overused, stock, stereotyped, clichéed, corny (*infml*).
≠ original, new, fresh.

triumph *n* **1** WIN, victory, conquest, walk-over, success, achievement, accomplishment, feat, coup, masterstroke, hit, sensation.
2 EXULTATION, jubilation, rejoicing, celebration, elation, joy, happiness.
≠ **1** failure.
v win, succeed, prosper, conquer, vanquish, overcome, overwhelm, prevail, dominate, celebrate, rejoice, glory, gloat.
≠ lose, fail.

triumphant *adj* winning, victorious, conquering, successful, exultant, jubilant, rejoicing, celebratory, glorious, elated, joyful, proud, boastful, gloating, swaggering.
≠ defeated, humble.

trivial *adj* unimportant, insignificant, inconsequential, incidental, minor, petty, paltry, trifling, small, little, inconsiderable, negligible, worthless, meaningless, frivolous, banal, trite, commonplace, everyday.
≠ important, significant, profound.

triviality *n* unimportance, insignificance, pettiness, smallness, worthlessness, meaninglessness, frivolity, trifle, detail, technicality.
≠ importance, essential.

troop *n* contingent, squadron, unit, division, company, squad, team, crew, gang, band, bunch, group, body, pack, herd, flock, horde, crowd, throng, multitude.
v go, march, parade, stream, flock, swarm, throng.

troops *n* army, military, soldiers, servicemen, servicewomen.

trophy *n* cup, prize, award, souvenir, memento.

tropical *adj* hot, torrid, sultry, sweltering, stifling, steamy, humid.
≠ arctic, cold, cool, temperate.

trot *v* jog, run, scamper, scuttle, scurry.

trouble *n* **1** PROBLEM, difficulty, struggle, annoyance, irritation, bother, nuisance, inconvenience, misfortune, adversity, trial, tribulation, pain, suffering, affliction, distress, grief, woe, heartache, concern, uneasiness, worry, anxiety, agitation. **2** UNREST, strife, tumult, commotion, disturbance, disorder, upheaval. **3** *back trouble*: disorder, complaint, ailment, illness, disease, disability, defect. **4** EFFORT, exertion, pains, care, attention, thought.
≠ **1** relief, calm. **2** order. **3** health.
v annoy, vex, harass, torment, bother, inconvenience, disturb, upset, distress, sadden, pain, afflict, burden, worry, agitate, disconcert, perplex.
≠ reassure, help.

troublemaker *n* agitator, rabble-rouser, incendiary, instigator, ringleader, stirrer, mischief-maker.
≠ peacemaker.

troublesome *adj* **1** ANNOYING, irritating, vexatious, irksome, bothersome, inconvenient, difficult, hard, tricky, thorny, taxing, demanding, laborious, tiresome, wearisome. **2** UNRULY, rowdy, turbulent, trying, unco-operative, insubordinate, rebellious.
≠ **1** easy, simple. **2** helpful.

trough *n* gutter, conduit, trench, ditch, gully, channel, groove, furrow, hollow, depression.

trousers *n* pants, slacks, jeans, denims, Levis®, flannels, bags (*infml*), dungarees, breeches, shorts.

truancy *n* absence, absenteeism, shirking, skiving (*infml*).
≠ attendance.

truant *n* absentee, deserter, runaway, idler, shirker, skiver (*infml*), dodger.
adj absent, missing, runaway.

truce *n* cease-fire, peace, armistice, cessation, moratorium, suspension, stay, respite, let-up (*infml*), lull, rest, break, interval, intermission.
≠ war, hostilities.

truck *n* lorry, van, wagon, trailer, float, cart, barrow.

trudge *v* tramp, plod, clump, stump, lumber, traipse, slog, labour, trek, hike, walk, march.
n tramp, traipse, slog, haul, trek, hike, walk, march.

true *adj* **1** REAL, genuine, authentic, actual, veritable, exact, precise, accurate, correct, right, factual, truthful, veracious, sincere, honest, legitimate, valid, rightful, proper. **2** FAITHFUL, loyal, constant, steadfast, staunch, firm, trustworthy, trusty, honourable, dedicated, devoted.
≠ **1** false, wrong, incorrect, inaccurate. **2** unfaithful, faithless.

truism *n* truth, platitude, commonplace, cliché.

truly *adv* very, greatly, extremely, really, genuinely, sincerely, honestly, truthfully, undeniably, indubitably, indeed, in fact, in reality, exactly, precisely, correctly, rightly, properly.
≠ slightly, falsely, incorrectly.

trumpet *n* bugle, horn, clarion, blare, blast, roar, bellow, cry, call.
v blare, blast, roar, bellow, shout, proclaim, announce, broadcast, advertise.

truncate *v* shorten, abbreviate, curtail, cut, lop, dock, prune, pare, clip, trim, crop.
≠ lengthen, extend.

trunk *n* **1** CASE, suitcase, chest, coffer, box, crate. **2** TORSO, body, frame, shaft, stock, stem, stalk.

truss *v* tie, strap, bind, pinion, fasten, secure, bundle, pack.
≠ untie, loosen.
n binding, bandage, support, brace, prop, stay, shore, strut, joist.

trust *n* **1** FAITH, belief, credence, credit, hope, expectation, reliance, confidence, assurance, conviction, certainty. **2** CARE, charge, custody, safekeeping, guardianship, protection, responsibility, duty.
≠ **1** distrust, mistrust, scepticism, doubt.

v **1** BELIEVE, imagine, assume, presume, suppose, surmise, hope, expect, rely on, depend on, count on, bank on, swear by. **2** ENTRUST, commit, consign, confide, give, assign, delegate.
≠ **1** distrust, mistrust, doubt, disbelieve.

trusting *adj* trustful, credulous, gullible, naïve, innocent, unquestioning, unsuspecting, unguarded, unwary.
≠ distrustful, suspicious, cautious.

trustworthy *adj* honest, upright, honourable, principled, dependable, reliable, steadfast, true, responsible, sensible.
≠ untrustworthy, dishonest, unreliable, irresponsible.

truth *n* **1** TRUTHFULNESS, veracity, candour, frankness, honesty, sincerity, genuineness, authenticity, realism, exactness, precision, accuracy, validity, legitimacy, honour, integrity, uprightness, faithfulness, fidelity, loyalty, constancy. **2** *tell the truth*: facts, reality, actuality, fact, axiom, maxim, principle, truism.
≠ **1** deceit, dishonesty, falseness. **2** lie, falsehood.

truthful *adj* veracious, frank, candid, straight, honest, sincere, true, veritable, exact, precise, accurate, correct, realistic, faithful, trustworthy, reliable.
≠ untruthful, deceitful, false, untrue.

try *v* **1** ATTEMPT, endeavour, venture, undertake, seek, strive. **2** HEAR, judge. **3** EXPERIMENT, test, sample, taste, inspect, examine, investigate, evaluate, appraise.
n **1** ATTEMPT, endeavour, effort, go (*infml*), bash (*infml*), crack (*infml*), shot (*infml*), stab (*infml*).
2 EXPERIMENT, test, trial, ample, taste.

trying *adj* annoying, irritating, aggravating (*infml*), vexatious, exasperating, troublesome, tiresome, wearisome, difficult, hard, tough, arduous, taxing, demanding, testing.
≠ easy.

tub *n* bath, basin, vat, tun, butt, cask, barrel, keg.

tube *n* hose, pipe, cylinder, duct, conduit, spout, channel.

tuck *v* **1** INSERT, push, thrust, stuff, cram. **2** FOLD, pleat, gather, crease.
n fold, pleat, gather, pucker, crease.

tuft *n* crest, beard, tassel, knot, clump, cluster, bunch.

tug *v* pull, draw, tow, haul, drag, lug, heave, wrench, jerk, pluck.
n pull, tow, haul, heave, wrench, jerk, pluck.

tuition *n* teaching, instruction, coaching, training, lessons, schooling, education.

tumble *v* fall, stumble, trip, topple, overthrow, drop, flop, collapse, plummet, pitch, roll, toss.
n fall, stumble, trip, drop, plunge, roll, toss.

tumult *n* commotion, turmoil, disturbance, upheaval, stir, agitation, unrest, disorder, chaos, pandemonium, noise, clamour, din, racket, hubbub, hullabaloo, row, rumpus, uproar, riot, fracas, brawl, affray, strife.
≠ peace, calm, composure.

tumultuous *adj* turbulent, stormy, raging, fierce, violent, wild, hectic, boisterous, rowdy, noisy, disorderly, unruly, riotous, restless, agitated, troubled, disturbed, excited.
≠ calm, peaceful, quiet.

tune *n* melody, theme, motif, song, air, strain.
v pitch, harmonize, set, regulate, adjust, adapt, temper, attune, synchronize.

tuneful *adj* melodious, melodic, catchy, musical, euphonious, harmonious, pleasant, mellow, sonorous.
≠ tuneless, discordant.

tunnel *n* passage, passageway, gallery, subway, underpass, burrow, hole, mine, shaft, chimney.
v burrow, dig, excavate, mine, bore, penetrate, undermine, sap.

turbulent *adj* rough, choppy, stormy, blustery, tempestuous, raging, furious, violent, wild, tumultuous, unbridled, boisterous, rowdy, disorderly, unruly, undisciplined, obstreperous, rebellious,

mutinous, riotous, agitated, unsettled, unstable, confused, disordered.
≠ calm, composed.

turmoil *n* confusion, disorder, tumult, commotion, disturbance, trouble, disquiet, agitation, turbulence, stir, ferment, flurry, bustle, chaos, pandemonium, bedlam, noise, din, hubbub, row, uproar.
≠ calm, peace, quiet.

turn *v* **1** REVOLVE, circle, spin, twirl, whirl, twist, gyrate, pivot, hinge, swivel, rotate, roll, move, shift, invert, reverse, bend, veer, swerve, divert. **2** MAKE, transform, change, alter, modify, convert, adapt, adjust, fit, mould, shape, form, fashion, remodel. **3** *turn cold*: go, become, grow. **4** RESORT, have recourse, apply, appeal. **5** SOUR, curdle, spoil, go off, go bad.
n **1** REVOLUTION, cycle, round, circle, rotation, spin, twirl, twist, gyration, bend, curve, loop, reversal. **2** CHANGE, alteration, shift, deviation. **3** *it's your turn*: go, chance, opportunity, occasion, stint, period, spell. **4** ACT, performance, performer.
turn away reject, avert, deflect, deviate, depart.
≠ accept, receive.
turn down 1 *turn down an offer*: reject, decline, refuse, spurn, rebuff, repudiate. **2** LOWER, lessen, quieten, soften, mute, muffle.
≠ **1** accept. **2** turn up.
turn in 1 GO TO BED, retire. **2** HAND OVER, give up, surrender, deliver, hand in, tender, submit, return, give back.
≠ **1** get up. **2** keep.
turn off 1 BRANCH OFF, leave, quit, depart from, deviate, divert. **2** SWITCH OFF, turn out, stop, shut down, unplug, disconnect. **3** (*sl*) REPEL, sicken, nauseate, disgust, offend, displease, disenchant, alienate, bore, discourage, put off.
≠ **1** join. **2** turn on. **3** turn on (*sl*).
turn on 1 SWITCH ON, start (up), activate, connect. **2** (*sl*) AROUSE, stimulate, excite, thrill, please, attract. **3** HINGE ON, depend on, rest on. **4** ATTACK, round on, fall on.
≠ **1** turn off. **2** turn off (*sl*).
turn out 1 HAPPEN, come about, transpire, ensue, result, end up, become, develop, emerge. **2** SWITCH OFF, turn off, unplug, disconnect. **3** APPEAR, present, dress, clothe. **4** PRODUCE, make, manufacture, fabricate, assemble. **5** EVICT, throw out, expel, deport, banish, dismiss, discharge, drum out, kick out, sack (*infml*). **6** *turn out the attic*: empty, clear, clean out.
≠ **2** turn on. **5** admit. **6** fill.
turn over 1 THINK OVER, think about, mull over, ponder, deliberate, reflect on, contemplate, consider, examine. **2** HAND OVER, surrender, deliver, transfer. **3** OVERTURN, upset, upend, invert, capsize, keel over.
turn up 1 ATTEND, come, arrive, appear, show up (*infml*). **2** AMPLIFY, intensify, raise, increase. **3** DISCOVER, find, unearth, dig up, expose, disclose, reveal, show.
≠ **1** stay away. **2** turn down.

turning *n* turn-off, junction, crossroads, fork, bend, curve, turn.

turning-point *n* crossroads, watershed, crux, crisis.

turnout *n* **1** ATTENDANCE, audience, gate, crowd, assembly, congregation. **2** APPEARANCE, outfit, dress, clothes.

tutor *n* teacher, instructor, coach, educator, lecturer, supervisor, guide, mentor, guru, guardian.
v teach, instruct, train, drill, coach, educate, school, lecture, supervise, direct, guide.

tweak *v, n* twist, pinch, squeeze, nip, pull, tug, jerk, twitch.

twee (*infml*) *adj* sweet, cute, pretty, dainty, quaint, sentimental, affected, precious.

twiddle *v* turn, twirl, swivel, twist, wiggle, adjust, fiddle, finger.

twilight *n* dusk, half-light, gloaming, gloom, dimness, sunset, evening.

twin *n* double, look-alike, likeness, duplicate, clone, match, counterpart, corollary, fellow, mate.
adj identical, matching, corresponding, symmetrical, parallel, matched, paired, double, dual,

duplicate, twofold.
v match, pair, couple, link, join.

twine *n* string, cord, thread, yarn.
v wind, coil, spiral, loop, curl, bend, twist, wreathe, wrap, surround, encircle, entwine, plait, braid, knit, weave.

twinge *n* pain, pang, throb, spasm, throe, stab, stitch, pinch, prick.

twinkle *v* sparkle, glitter, shimmer, glisten, glimmer, flicker, wink, flash, glint, gleam, shine.
n sparkle, scintillation, glitter, shimmer, glisten, glimmer, flicker, wink, flash, glint, gleam, light.

twirl *v* spin, whirl, pirouette, wheel, rotate, revolve, swivel, pivot, turn, twist, gyrate, wind, coil.
n spin, whirl, pirouette, rotation, revolution, turn, twist, gyration, convlution, spiral, coil.

twist *v* **1** TURN, screw, wring, spin, swivel, wind, zigzag, bend, coil, spiral, curl, wreathe, twine, entwine, intertwine, weave, entangle, wriggle, squirm, writhe. **2** *twist one's ankle*: wrench, rick, sprain, strain. **3** CHANGE, alter, garble, misquote, misrepresent, distort, contort, warp, pervert.
n **1** TURN, screw, spin, roll, bend, curve, arc, curl, loop, zigzag, coil, spiral, convolution, squiggle, tangle. **2** CHANGE, variation, break. **3** PERVERSION, distortion, contortion. **4** SURPRISE, quirk, oddity, peculiarity.

twisted *adj* warped, perverted, deviant, unnatural.
≠ straight.

twitch *v* jerk, jump, start, blink, tremble, shake, pull, tug, tweak, snatch, pluck.
n spasm, convulsion, tic, tremor, jerk, jump, start.

twitter *v* chirp, chirrup, tweet, cheep, sing, warble, whistle, chatter.

two-faced *adj* hypocritical, insincere, false, lying, deceitful, treacherous, double-dealing, devious, untrustworthy.
≠ honest, candid, frank.

tycoon *n* industrialist, entrepreneur, captain of industry, magnate, mogul, baron, supremo, capitalist, financier.

type *n* **1** SORT, kind, form, genre, variety, strain, species, breed, group, class, category, subdivision, classification, description, designation, stamp, mark, order, standard. **2** ARCHETYPE, embodiment, prototype, original, model, pattern, specimen, example. **3** PRINT, printing, characters, letters, lettering, face, fount, font.

typhoon *n* whirlwind, cyclone, tornado, twister (*infml*), hurricane, tempest, storm, squall.

typical *adj* standard, normal, usual, average, conventional, orthodox, stock, model, representative, illustrative, indicative, characteristic, distinctive.
≠ atypical, unusual.

typify *v* embody, epitomize, encapsulate, personify, characterize, exemplify, symbolize, represent, illustrate.

tyrannical *adj* dictatorial, despotic, autocratic, absolute, arbitrary, authoritarian, domineering, overbearing, high-handed, imperious, magisterial, ruthless, harsh, severe, oppressive, overpowering, unjust, unreasonable.
≠ liberal, tolerant.

tyranny *n* dictatorship, despotism, autocracy, absolutism, authoritarianism, imperiousness, ruthlessness, harshness, severity, oppression, injustice.
≠ democracy, freedom.

tyrant *n* dictator, despot, autocrat, absolutist, authoritarian, bully, oppressor, slave-driver, taskmaster.

U

ubiquitous *adj* omnipresent, ever-present, everywhere, universal, global, pervasive, common, frequent.
≠ rare, scarce.

ugly *adj* **1** UNATTRACTIVE, unsightly, plain, unprepossessing, ill-favoured, hideous, monstrous, misshapen, deformed. **2** UNPLEASANT, disagreeable, nasty, horrid, objectionable, offensive, disgusting, revolting, repulsive, vile, frightful, terrible.
≠ **1** attractive, beautiful, handsome, pretty. **2** pleasant.

ulterior *adj* secondary, hidden, concealed, undisclosed, unexpressed, covert, secret, private, personal, selfish.
≠ overt.

ultimate *adj* final, last, closing, concluding, eventual, terminal, furthest, remotest, extreme, utmost, greatest, highest, supreme, superlative, perfect, radical, fundamental, primary.

ultimately *adv* finally, eventually, at last, in the end, after all.

umpire *n* referee, linesman, judge, adjudicator, arbiter, arbitrator, mediator, moderator.
v referee, judge, adjudicate, arbitrate, mediate, moderate, control.

umpteen (*infml*) *adj* a good many, numerous, plenty, millions, countless, innumerable.
≠ few.

unabashed *adj* unashamed, unembarrassed, brazen, blatant, bold, confident, undaunted, unconcerned, undismayed.
≠ abashed, sheepish.

unable *adj* incapable, powerless, impotent, unequipped, unqualified, unfit, incompetent, inadequate.
≠ able, capable.

unacceptable *adj* intolerable, inadmissible, unsatisfactory, undesirable, unwelcome, objectionable, offensive, unpleasant.
≠ acceptable, satisfactory.

unaccompanied *adj* alone, unescorted, unattended, lone, solo, single-handed.
≠ accompanied.

unaccountable *adj* inexplicable, unexplainable, unfathomable, impenetrable, incomprehensible, baffling, puzzling, mysterious, astonishing, extraordinary, strange, odd, peculiar, singular, unusual, uncommon, unheard-of.
≠ explicable, explainable.

unaccustomed *adj* **1** *unaccustomed to such luxury*: unused, unacquainted, unfamiliar, unpractised, inexperienced. **2** STRANGE, unusual, uncommon, different, new, unexpected, surprising, uncharacteristic, unprecedented.
≠ **1** accustomed, familiar. **2** customary.

unaffected *adj* **1** UNMOVED, unconcerned, indifferent, impervious, untouched, unchanged, unaltered. **2** UNSOPHISTICATED, artless, naïve, ingenuous, unspoilt, plain, simple, straightforward, unpretentious, unassuming, sincere, honest, genuine.
≠ **1** moved, influenced. **2** affected, pretentious, insincere.

unalterable *adj* unchangeable, invariable, unchanging, immutable, final, inflexible, unyielding, rigid, fixed, permanent.
≠ alterable, flexible.

unanimity *n* consensus, unity, agreement, concurrence, accord, like-mindedness, concord, harmony, unison, concert.
≠ disagreement, disunity.

unanimous *adj* united, concerted, joint, common, as one, in agreement,

in accord, harmonious.
≠ disunited, divided.

unapproachable *adj* inaccessible, remote, distant, aloof, standoffish, withdrawn, reserved, unsociable, unfriendly, forbidding.
≠ approachable, friendly.

unarmed *adj* defenceless, unprotected, exposed, open, vulnerable, weak, helpless.
≠ armed, protected.

unashamed *adj* shameless, unabashed, impenitent, unrepentant, unconcealed, undisguised, open, blatant.

unasked *adj* uninvited, unbidden, unrequested, unsought, unsolicited, unwanted, voluntary, spontaneous.
≠ invited, wanted.

unassuming *adj* unassertive, self-effacing, retiring, modest, humble, meek, unobtrusive, unpretentious, simple, restrained.
≠ presumptuous, assertive, pretentious.

unattached *adj* unmarried, single, free, available, footloose, fancy-free, independent, unaffiliated.
≠ engaged, committed.

unattended *adj* ignored, disregarded, unguarded, unwatched, unsupervised, unaccompanied, unescorted, alone.
≠ attended, escorted.

unauthorized *adj* unofficial, unlawful, illegal, illicit, illegitimate, irregular, unsanctioned.
≠ authorized, legal.

unavoidable *adj* inevitable, inescapable, inexorable, certain, sure, fated, destined, obligatory, compulsory, mandatory, necessary.
≠ avoidable.

unaware *adj* oblivious, unconscious, ignorant, uninformed, unknowing, unsuspecting, unmindful, heedless, blind, deaf.
≠ aware, conscious.

unbalanced *adj* **1** INSANE, mad, crazy, lunatic, deranged, disturbed, demented, irrational, unsound. **2** *an unbalanced report*: biased, prejudiced, one-sided, partisan, unfair, unjust, unequal, uneven, asymmetrical, lopsided, unsteady, unstable.
≠ **1** sane. **2** unbiased.

unbearable *adj* intolerable, unacceptable, insupportable, insufferable, unendurable, excruciating.
≠ bearable, acceptable.

unbeatable *adj* invincible, unconquerable, unstoppable, unsurpassable, matchless, supreme, excellent.

unbecoming *adj* unseemly, improper, unsuitable, inappropriate, unbefitting, ungentlemanly, unladylike, unattractive, unsightly.
≠ suitable, attractive.

unbelief *n* atheism, agnosticism, scepticism, doubt, incredulity, disbelief.
≠ belief, faith.

unbelievable *adj* incredible, inconceivable, unthinkable, unimaginable, astonishing, staggering, extraordinary, impossible, improbable, unlikely, implausible, unconvincing, far-fetched, preposterous.
≠ believable, credible.

unborn *adj* embryonic, expected, awaited, coming, future.

unbounded *adj* boundless, limitless, unlimited, unrestricted, unrestrained, unchecked, unbridled, infinite, endless, immeasurable, vast.
≠ limited, restrained.

unbreakable *adj* indestructible, shatterproof, toughened, resistant, proof, durable, strong, tough, rugged, solid.
≠ breakable, fragile.

unbridled *adj* immoderate, excessive, uncontrolled, unrestrained, unchecked.

unbroken *adj* **1** INTACT, whole, entire, complete, solid, undivided. **2** UNINTERRUPTED, continuous, endless, ceaseless, incessant, unceasing, constant, perpetual, progressive, successive. **3** *unbroken record*: unbeaten, unsurpassed, unequalled, unmatched.
≠ **1** broken. **2** intermittent, fitful.

uncalled-for *adj* gratuitous, unprovoked, unjustified, unwarranted,

undeserved, unnecessary, needless.
≠ timely.

uncanny *adj* weird, strange, queer, bizarre, mysterious, unaccountable, incredible, remarkable, extraordinary, fantastic, unnatural, unearthly, supernatural, eerie, creepy, spooky (*infml*).

uncaring *adj* unconcerned, unmoved, unsympathetic, inconsiderate, unfeeling, cold, callous, indifferent, uninterested.
≠ caring, concerned.

unceasing *adj* ceaseless, incessant, unending, endless, never-ending, non-stop, continuous, unbroken, constant, perpetual, continual, persistent, relentless, unrelenting, unremitting.
≠ intermittent, spasmodic.

uncertain *adj* **1** UNSURE, unconvinced, doubtful, dubious, undecided, ambivalent, hesitant, wavering, vacillating. **2** INCONSTANT, changeable, variable, erratic, irregular, shaky, unsteady, unreliable. **3** UNPREDICTABLE, unforeseeable, undetermined, unsettled, unresolved, unconfirmed, indefinite, vague, insecure, risky, iffy (*sl*).
≠ **1** certain, sure. **2** steady. **3** predictable.

uncertainty *n* doubt, scepticism, irresolution, dilemma, hesitation, misgiving, confusion, bewilderment, perplexity, puzzlement, unreliability, unpredictability, insecurity.
≠ certainty.

unchanging *adj* unvarying, changeless, steady, steadfast, constant, perpetual, lasting, enduring, abiding, eternal, permanent.
≠ changing, changeable.

uncharitable *adj* unkind, cruel, hard-hearted, callous, unfeeling, insensitive, unsympathetic, unfriendly, mean, ungenerous.
≠ kind, sensitive, charitable, generous.

uncharted *adj* unexplored, undiscovered, unplumbed, foreign, alien, strange, unfamiliar, new, virgin.
≠ familiar.

uncivilized *adj* primitive, barbaric, savage, wild, untamed, uncultured, unsophisticated, unenlightened, uneducated, illiterate, uncouth, antisocial.
≠ civilized, cultured.

unclean *adj* dirty, soiled, filthy, foul, polluted, contaminated, tainted, impure, unhygienic, unwholesome, corrupt, defiled, sullied.
≠ clean, hygienic.

unclear *adj* indistinct, hazy, dim, obscure, vague, indefinite, ambiguous, equivocal, uncertain, unsure, doubtful, dubious.
≠ clear, evident.

uncomfortable *adj* **1** CRAMPED, hard, cold, ill-fitting, irritating, painful, disagreeable. **2** AWKWARD, embarrassed, self-conscious, uneasy, troubled, worried, disturbed, distressed, disquieted, conscience-stricken.
≠ **1** comfortable. **2** relaxed.

uncommon *adj* rare, scarce, infrequent, unusual, abnormal, atypical, unfamiliar, strange, odd, curious, bizarre, extraordinary, remarkable, notable, outstanding, exceptional, distinctive, special.
≠ common, usual, normal.

uncommunicative *adj* silent, taciturn, tight-lipped, close, secretive, unforthcoming, unresponsive, curt, brief, reticent, reserved, shy, retiring, withdrawn, unsociable.
≠ communicative, forthcoming.

uncompromising *adj* unyielding, unbending, inflexible, unaccommodating, rigid, firm, strict, tough, hard-line, inexorable, intransigent, stubborn, obstinate, die-hard.
≠ flexible.

unconcealed *adj* open, patent, obvious, evident, manifest, blatant, conspicuous, noticeable, visible, apparent.
≠ hidden, secret.

unconcerned *adj* indifferent, apathetic, uninterested, nonchalant, carefree, relaxed, complacent, cool, composed, untroubled, unworried,

unruffled, unmoved, uncaring, unsympathetic, callous, aloof, remote, distant, detached, dispassionate, uninvolved, oblivious.
≠ concerned, worried, interested.

unconditional *adj* unqualified, unreserved, unrestricted, unlimited, absolute, utter, full, total, complete, entire, whole-hearted, thoroughgoing, downright, outright, positive, categorical, unequivocal.
≠ conditional, qualified, limited.

unconnected *adj* **1** IRRELEVANT, unrelated, unattached, detached, separate, independent.
2 DISCONNECTED, incoherent, irrational, illogical.
≠ **1** connected, relevant.

unconscious *adj* **1** STUNNED, knocked out, out, out cold, out for the count, concussed, comatose, senseless, insensible. **2** UNAWARE, oblivious, blind, deaf, heedless, unmindful, ignorant. **3** *an unconscious reaction*: involuntary, automatic, reflex, instinctive, impulsive, innate, subconscious, subliminal, repressed, suppressed, latent, unwitting, inadvertent, accidental, unintentional.
≠ **1** conscious. **2** aware. **3** intentional.

uncontrollable *adj* ungovernable, unmanageable, unruly, wild, mad, furious, violent, strong, irrepressible.
≠ controllable, manageable.

uncontrolled *adj* unrestrained, unbridled, unchecked, rampant, wild, unruly, undisciplined.
≠ controlled, restrained.

unconventional *adj* unorthodox, alternative, different, offbeat, eccentric, idiosyncratic, individual, original, odd, unusual, irregular, abnormal, bizarre, way-out (*sl*).
≠ conventional, orthodox.

unconvincing *adj* implausible, unlikely, improbable, questionable, doubtful, dubious, suspect, weak, feeble, flimsy, lame.
≠ convincing, plausible.

unco-ordinated *adj* clumsy, awkward, ungainly, ungraceful, inept, disjointed.
≠ graceful.

uncouth *adj* coarse, crude, vulgar, rude, ill-mannered, unseemly, improper, clumsy, awkward, gauche, graceless, unrefined, uncultivated, uncultured, uncivilized, rough.
≠ polite, refined, urbane.

uncover *v* unveil, unmask, unwrap, strip, bare, open, expose, reveal, show, disclose, divulge, leak, unearth, exhume, discover, detect.
≠ cover, conceal, suppress.

uncritical *adj* undiscerning, undiscriminating, unselective, unquestioning, credulous, accepting, trusting, gullible, naive.
≠ discerning, discriminating, sceptical.

uncultivated *adj* fallow, wild, rough, natural.
≠ cultivated.

uncultured *adj* unsophisticated, unrefined, uncultivated, uncivilized, rough, uncouth, boorish, rustic, coarse, crude, ill-bred.
≠ cultured, sophisticated.

undaunted *adj* undeterred, undiscouraged, undismayed, unbowed, resolute, steadfast, brave, courageous, fearless, bold, intrepid, dauntless, indomitable.
≠ discouraged, timorous.

undecided *adj* uncertain, unsure, in two minds, ambivalent, doubtful, hesitant, wavering, irresolute, uncommitted, indefinite, vague, dubious, debatable, moot, unsettled, open.
≠ decided, certain, definite.

undemonstrative *adj* aloof, distant, remote, withdrawn, reserved, reticent, uncommunicative, stiff, formal, cool, cold, unemotional, restrained, impassive, phlegmatic.
≠ demonstrative, communicative.

undeniable *adj* irrefutable, unquestionable, incontrovertible, sure, certain, undoubted, proven, clear, obvious, patent, evident, manifest, unmistakable.
≠ questionable.

under *prep* below, underneath, beneath, lower than, less than, inferior to, subordinate to.

≠ over, above.
under way moving, in motion, going, in operation, started, begun, in progress, afoot.

undercover *adj* secret, hush-hush (*infml*), private, confidential, spy, intelligence, underground, clandestine, surreptitious, furtive, covert, hidden, concealed.
≠ open, unconcealed.

undercurrent *n* undertone, overtone, hint, suggestion, tinge, flavour, aura, atmosphere, feeling, sense, movement, tendency, trend, drift.

underestimate *v* underrate, undervalue, misjudge, miscalculate, minimize, belittle, disparage, dismiss.
≠ overestimate, exaggerate.

undergo *v* experience, suffer, sustain, submit to, bear, stand, endure, weather, withstand.

underground *adj* **1** *an underground passage*: subterranean, buried, sunken, covered, hidden, concealed. **2** SECRET, covert, undercover, revolutionary, subversive, radical, experimental, avant-garde, alternative, unorthodox, unofficial.

undergrowth *n* brush, scrub, vegetation, ground cover, bracken, bushes, brambles, briars.

underhand *adj* unscrupulous, unethical, immoral, improper, sly, crafty, sneaky, stealthy, surreptitious, furtive, clandestine, devious, dishonest, deceitful, deceptive, fraudulent, crooked (*infml*), shady (*infml*).
≠ honest, open, above board.

underline *v* mark, underscore, stress, emphasize, accentuate, italicize, highlight, point up.
≠ play down, soft-pedal.

underlying *adj* basic, fundamental, essential, primary, elementary, root, intrinsic, latent, hidden, lurking, veiled.

undermine *v* mine, tunnel, excavate, erode, wear away, weaken, sap, sabotage, subvert, vitiate, mar, impair.
≠ strengthen, fortify.

underprivileged *adj* disadvantaged, deprived, poor, needy, impoverished, destitute, oppressed.
≠ privileged, fortunate, affluent.

underrate *v* underestimate, undervalue, belittle, disparage, depreciate, dismiss.
≠ overrate, exaggerate.

undersized *adj* small, tiny, minute, miniature, pygmy, dwarf, stunted, underdeveloped, underweight, puny.
≠ oversized, big, overweight.

understand *v* **1** *I don't understand*: grasp, comprehend, take in, follow, get (*infml*), cotton on (*infml*), fathom, penetrate, make out, discern, perceive, see, realize, recognize, appreciate, accept. **2** SYMPATHIZE, empathize, commiserate. **3** BELIEVE, think, know, hear, learn, gather, assume, presume, suppose, conclude.
≠ **1** misunderstand.

understanding *n* **1** GRASP, comprehension, knowledge, wisdom, intelligence, intellect, sense, judgement, discernment, insight, appreciation, awareness, impression, perception, belief, idea, notion, opinion, interpretation. **2** AGREEMENT, arrangement, pact, accord, harmony. **3** SYMPATHY, empathy.
adj sympathetic, compassionate, kind, considerate, sensitive, tender, loving, patient, tolerant, forbearing, forgiving.
≠ unsympathetic, insensitive, impatient, intolerant.

understate *v* underplay, play down, soft-pedal, minimize, make light of, belittle, dismiss.
≠ exaggerate.

understood *adj* accepted, assumed, presumed, implied, implicit, inferred, tacit, unstated, unspoken, unwritten.

understudy *n* stand-in, double, substitute, replacement, reserve, deputy.

undertake *v* **1** PLEDGE, promise, guarantee, agree, contract, covenant. **2** BEGIN, commence, embark on, tackle, try, attempt, endeavour, take on, accept, assume.

undertaking *n* **1** ENTERPRISE, venture, business, affair, task, project, operation, attempt, endeavour, effort. **2** PLEDGE, commitment, promise, vow, word, assurance.

undertone *n* hint, suggestion, whisper, murmur, trace, tinge, touch, flavour, feeling, atmosphere, undercurrent.

undervalue *v* underrate, underestimate, misjudge, minimize, depreciate, disparage, dismiss.
≠ overrate, exaggerate.

underwater *adj* subaquatic, undersea, submarine, submerged, sunken.

underwear *n* underclothes, undergarments, lingerie, undies (*infml*), smalls (*infml*).

underweight *adj* thin, undersized, underfed, undernourished, half-starved.
≠ overweight.

underwrite *v* endorse, authorize, sanction, approve, back, guarantee, insure, sponsor, fund, finance, subsidize, subscribe, sign, initial, countersign.

undesirable *adj* unwanted, unwelcome, unacceptable, unsuitable, unpleasant, disagreeable, distasteful, repugnant, offensive, objectionable, obnoxious.
≠ desirable, pleasant.

undignified *adj* inelegant, ungainly, clumsy, foolish, unseemly, improper, unsuitable, inappropriate.
≠ dignified, elegant.

undisguised *adj* unconcealed, open, overt, explicit, frank, genuine, apparent, patent, obvious, evident, manifest, blatant, naked, unadorned, stark, utter, outright, thoroughgoing.
≠ secret, concealed, hidden.

undisputed *adj* uncontested, unchallenged, unquestioned, undoubted, indisputable, incontrovertible, undeniable, irrefutable, accepted, acknowledged, recognized, sure, certain, conclusive.
≠ debatable, uncertain.

undistinguished *adj* unexceptional, unremarkable, unimpressive, ordinary, run-of-the-mill, everyday, banal, indifferent, mediocre, inferior.
≠ distinguished, exceptional.

undivided *adj* solid, unbroken, intact, whole, entire, full, complete, combined, united, unanimous, concentrated, exclusive, whole-hearted.

undo *v* **1** UNFASTEN, untie, unbuckle, unbutton, unzip, unlock, unwrap, unwind, open, loose, loosen, separate. **2** ANNUL, nullify, invalidate, cancel, offset, neutralize, reverse, overturn, upset, quash, defeat, undermine, subvert, mar, spoil, ruin, wreck, shatter, destroy.
≠ **1** fasten, do up.

undoing *n* downfall, ruin, ruination, collapse, destruction, defeat, overthrow, reversal, weakness, shame, disgrace.

undone *adj* **1** UNACCOMPLISHED, unfulfilled, unfinished, uncompleted, incomplete, outstanding, left, omitted, neglected, forgotten. **2** UNFASTENED, untied, unlaced, unbuttoned, unlocked, open, loose.
≠ **1** done, accomplished, complete. **2** fastened.

undoubted *adj* unchallenged, undisputed, acknowledged, unquestionable, indisputable, incontrovertible, undesirable, indubitable, sure, certain, definite, obvious, patent.

undress *v* strip, peel off (*infml*), disrobe, take off, divest, remove, shed.

undressed *adj* unclothed, disrobed, stripped, naked, stark naked, nude.
≠ clothed.

undue *adj* unnecessary, needless, uncalled-for, unwarranted, undeserved, unreasonable, disproportionate, excessive, immoderate, inordinate, extreme, extravagant, improper.
≠ reasonable, moderate, proper.

unduly *adv* too, over, excessively, immoderately, inordinately, disproportionately, unreasonably, unjustifiably, unnecessarily.
≠ moderately, reasonably.

unearth *v* dig up, exhume, disinter, excavate, uncover, expose, reveal, find, discover, detect.
≠ bury.

unearthly *adj* **1** SUPERNATURAL, ghostly, eerie, uncanny, weird, strange, spine-chilling. **2** *at this unearthly hour*: unreasonable, outrageous, ungodly.
≠ **2** reasonable.

uneasy *adj* uncomfortable, anxious, worried, apprehensive, tense, strained, nervous, agitated, shaky, jittery, edgy, upset, troubled, disturbed, unsettled, restless, impatient, unsure, insecure.
≠ calm, composed.

uneducated *adj* unschooled, untaught, unread, ignorant, illiterate, uncultivated, uncultured, philistine, benighted.
≠ educated.

unemotional *adj* cool, cold, unfeeling, impassive, indifferent, apathetic, unresponsive, undemonstrative, unexcitable, phlegmatic, objective, dispassionate.
≠ emotional, excitable.

unemployed *adj* jobless, out of work, laid off, redundant, unwaged, on the dole (*infml*), idle, unoccupied.
≠ employed, occupied.

unending *adj* endless, never-ending, unceasing, ceaseless, incessant, interminable, constant, continual, perpetual, everlasting, eternal, undying.
≠ transient, intermittent.

unenviable *adj* undesirable, unpleasant, disagreeable, uncongenial, uncomfortable, thankless, difficult.
≠ enviable, desirable.

unequal *adj* different, varying, dissimilar, unlike, unmatched, uneven, unbalanced, disproportionate, asymmetrical, irregular, unfair, unjust, biased, discriminatory.
≠ equal.

unequivocal *adj* unambiguous, explicit, clear, plain, evident, distinct, unmistakable, express, direct, straight, definite, positive, categorical, incontrovertible, absolute, unqualified, unreserved.
≠ ambiguous, vague, qualified.

unethical *adj* unprofessional, immoral, improper, wrong, unscrupulous, unprincipled, dishonourable, disreputable, illegal, illicit, dishonest, underhand, shady (*infml*).
≠ ethical.

uneven *adj* **1** *uneven ground*: rough, bumpy. **2** ODD, unequal, inequitable, unfair, unbalanced, one-sided, asymmetrical, lopsided, crooked. **3** IRREGULAR, intermittent, spasmodic, fitful, jerky, unsteady, variable, changeable, fluctuating, erratic, inconsistent, patchy.
≠ **1** flat, level. **2** even, equal. **3** regular.

uneventful *adj* uninteresting, unexciting, quiet, unvaried, boring, monotonous, tedious, dull, routine, humdrum, ordinary, commonplace, unremarkable, unexceptional, unmemorable.
≠ eventful, memorable.

unexceptional *adj* unremarkable, unmemorable, typical, average, normal, usual, ordinary, indifferent, mediocre, unimpressive.
≠ exceptional, impressive.

unexpected *adj* unforeseen, unanticipated, unpredictable, chance, accidental, fortuitous, sudden, abrupt, surprising, startling, amazing, astonishing, unusual.
≠ expected, predictable.

unfair *adj* unjust, inequitable, partial, biased, prejudiced, bigoted, discriminatory, unbalance, one-sided, partisan, arbitrary, undeserved, unmerited, unwarranted, uncalled-for, unethical, unscrupulous, unprincipled, wrongful, dishonest.
≠ fair, just, unbiased, deserved.

unfaithful *adj* disloyal, treacherous, false, untrue, deceitful, dishonest, untrustworthy, unreliable, fickle, inconstant, adulterous, two-timing, duplicitous, double-dealing, faithless, unbelieving, godless.
≠ faithful, loyal, reliable.

unfamiliar *adj* strange, unusual, uncommon, curious, alien, foreign, uncharted, unexplored, unknown, different, new, novel, unaccustomed, unacquainted, inexperienced, unpractised, unskilled, unversed.
≠ familiar, customary, conversant.

unfashionable *adj* outmoded, dated, out of date, out, passé, old-fashioned, antiquated, obsolete.
≠ fashionable.

unfasten *v* undo, untie, loosen, unlock, open, uncouple, disconnect, separate, detach.
≠ fasten.

unfavourable *adj* inauspicious, unpromising, ominous, threatening, discouraging, inopportune, untimely, unseasonable, ill-suited, unfortunate, unlucky, disadvantageous, bad, poor, adverse, contrary, negative, hostile, unfriendly, uncomplimentary.
≠ favourable, auspicious, promising.

unfeeling *adj* insensitive, cold, hard, stony, callous, heartless, hard-hearted, cruel, inhuman, pitiless, uncaring, unsympathetic, apathetic.
≠ sensitive, sympathetic.

unfinished *adj* incomplete, uncompleted, half-done, sketchy, rough, crude, imperfect, lacking, wanting, deficient, undone, unaccomplished, unfulfilled.
≠ finished, perfect.

unfit *adj* **1** UNSUITABLE, inappropriate, unsuited, ill-equipped, unqualified, ineligible, untrained, unprepared, unequal, incapable, incompetent, inadequate, ineffective, useless. **2** UNHEALTHY, out of condition, flabby, feeble, decrepit.
≠ **1** fit, suitable, competent. **2** healthy.

unfold *v* **1** DEVELOP, evolve. **2** REVEAL, disclose, show, present, describe, explain, clarify, elaborate. **3** *unfold a map*: open, spread, flatten, straighten, stretch out, undo, unfurl, unroll, uncoil, unwrap, uncover.
≠ **2** withhold, suppress. **3** fold, wrap.

unforeseen *adj* unpredicted, unexpected, unanticipated, surprising, startling, sudden, unavoidable.
≠ expected, predictable.

unforgettable *adj* memorable, momentous, historic, noteworthy, notable, impressive, remarkable, exceptional, extraordinary.
≠ unmemorable, unexceptional.

unforgivable *adj* unpardonable, inexcusable, unjustifiable, indefensible, reprehensible, shameful, disgraceful, deplorable.
≠ forgivable, venial.

unfortunate *adj* **1** UNLUCKY, luckless, hapless, unsuccessful, poor, wretched, unhappy, doomed, ill-fated, hopeless, calamitous, disastrous, ruinous. **2** REGRETTABLE, lamentable, deplorable, adverse, unfavourable, unsuitable, inappropriate, inopportune, untimely, ill-timed.
≠ **1** fortunate, happy. **2** favourable, appropriate.

unfounded *adj* baseless, groundless, unsupported, unsubstantiated, unproven, unjustified, idle, false, spurious, trumped-up, fabricated.
≠ substantiated, justified.

unfriendly *adj* unsociable, standoffish, aloof, distant, unapproachable, inhospitable, uncongenial, unneighbourly, unwelcoming, cold, chilly, hostile, aggressive, quarrelsome, inimical, antagonistic, ill-disposed, disagreeable, surly, sour.
≠ friendly, amiable, agreeable.

ungainly *adj* clumsy, awkward, gauche, inelegant, gawky, uncoordinated, lumbering, unwieldy.
≠ graceful, elegant.

ungodly *adj* **1** UNREASONABLE, outrageous, intolerable, unearthly, unsocial. **2** IMPIOUS, irreligious, godless, blasphemous, profane, immoral, corrupt, depraved, sinful, wicked.

ungrateful *adj* unthankful, unappreciative, ill-mannered, ungracious, selfish, heedless.
≠ grateful, thankful.

unguarded *adj* **1** *in an unguarded moment*: unwary, careless, incautious, imprudent, impolitic, indiscreet, undiplomatic, thoughtless, unthinking, heedless, foolish, foolhardy, rash, ill-considered. **2** UNDEFENDED, unprotected, exposed, vulnerable, defenceless.
≠ **1** guarded, cautious. **2** defended, protected.

unhappy *adj* **1** SAD, sorrowful,

miserable, melancholy, depressed, dispirited, despondent, dejected, downcast, crestfallen, long-faced, gloomy. **2** UNFORTUNATE, unlucky, ill-fated, unsuitable, inappropriate, inapt, ill-chosen, tactless, awkward, clumsy.
≠ **1** happy. **2** fortunate, suitable.

unharmed *adj* undamaged, unhurt, uninjured, unscathed, whole, intact, safe, sound.
≠ harmed, damaged.

unhealthy *adj* **1** UNWELL, sick, ill, poorly, ailing, sickly, infirm, invalid, weak, feeble, frail, unsound. **2** UNWHOLESOME, insanitary, unhygienic, harmful, detrimental, morbid, unnatural.
≠ **1** healthy, fit. **2** wholesome, hygienic, natural.

unheard-of *adj* **1** UNTHINKABLE, inconceivable, unimaginable, undreamed-of, unprecedented, unacceptable, offensive, shocking, outrageous, preposterous. **2** UNKNOWN, unfamiliar, new, unusual, obscure.
≠ **1** normal, acceptable. **2** famous.

unheeded *adj* ignored, disregarded, disobeyed, unnoticed, unobserved, unremarked, overlooked, neglected, forgotten.
≠ noted, observed.

unhesitating *adj* immediate, instant, instantaneous, prompt, ready, automatic, spontaneous, unquestioning, unwavering, unfaltering, whole-hearted, implicit.
≠ hesitant, tentative.

unholy *adj* **1** IMPIOUS, irreligious, sinful, iniquitous, immoral, corrupt, depraved, wicked, evil. **2** (*infml*) *an unholy mess*: unreasonable, shocking, outrageous, ungodly, unearthly.
≠ **1** holy, pious, godly. **2** reasonable.

unhurried *adj* slow, leisurely, deliberate, easy, relaxed, calm, easy-going (*infml*), laid-back (*sl*).
≠ hurried, hasty, rushed.

unidentified *adj* unknown, unrecognized, unmarked, unnamed, nameless, anonymous, incognito, unfamiliar, strange, mysterious.
≠ identified, known, named.

uniform *n* outfit, costume, livery, insignia, regalia, robes, dress, suit.
adj same, identical, like, alike, similar, homogeneous, consistent, regular, equal, smooth, even, flat, monotonous, unvarying, unchanging, constant, unbroken.
≠ different, varied, changing.

unify *v* unite, join, bind, combine, integrate, merge, amalgamate, consolidate, coalesce, fuse, weld.
≠ separate, divide, split.

unimaginable *adj* inconceivable, mind-boggling (*infml*), unbelievable, incredible, impossible, fantastic, undreamed-of, unthinkable, unheard-of.

unimaginative *adj* uninspired, unoriginal, predictable, hackneyed, banal, ordinary, dull, boring, routine, matter-of-fact, dry, barren, lifeless, unexciting, tame.
≠ imaginative, creative, original.

unimportant *adj* insignificant, inconsequential, irrelevant, immaterial, minor, trivial, trifling, petty, slight, negligible, worthless.
≠ important, significant, relevant, vital.

unimpressive *adj* unspectacular, undistinguished, unexceptional, unremarkable, uninteresting, dull, average, commonplace, indifferent, mediocre.
≠ impressive, memorable, notable.

uninhabited *adj* unoccupied, vacant, empty, deserted, abandoned, unpeopled, unpopulated.

uninhibited *adj* unconstrained, unreserved, unselfconscious, liberated, free, unrestricted, uncontrolled, unrestrained, abandoned, natural, spontaneous, frank, candid, open, relaxed, informal.
≠ inhibited, repressed, constrained, restrained.

unintelligible *adj* incomprehensible, incoherent, inarticulate, double Dutch, garbled, scrambled, jumbled, muddled, indecipherable, illegible.
≠ intelligible, comprehensible, clear.

unintentional *adj* unintended, accidental, fortuitous, inadvertent, unplanned, unpremeditated, involuntary, unconscious, unwitting.
≠ intentional, deliberate.

uninterested *adj* indifferent, unconcerned, uninvolved, bored, listless, apathetic, unenthusiastic, blasé, impassive, unresponsive.
≠ interested, concerned, enthusiastic, responsive.

uninteresting *adj* boring, tedious, monotonous, humdrum, dull, drab, dreary, dry, flat, tame, uneventful, unexciting, uninspiring, unimpressive.
≠ interesting, exciting.

uninterrupted *adj* unbroken, continuous, non-stop, unending, constant, continual, steady, sustained, undisturbed, peaceful.
≠ broken, intermittent.

uninvited *adj* unasked, unsought, unsolicited, unwanted, unwelcome.
≠ invited.

union *n* alliance, coalition, league, association, federation, confederation, confederacy, merger, combination, amalgamation, blend, mixture, synthesis, fusion, unification, unity.
≠ separation, alienation, estrangement.

unique *adj* single, one-off, sole, only, lone, solitary, unmatched, matchless, peerless, unequalled, unparalleled, unrivalled, incomparable, inimitable.
≠ common.

unison *n* concert, co-operation, unanimity, unity.

unit *n* item, part, element, constituent, piece, component, module, section, segment, portion, entity, whole, one, system, assembly.

unite *v* join, link, couple, marry, ally, co-operate, band, associate, federate, confederate, combine, pool, amalgamate, merge, blend, unify, consolidate, coalesce, fuse.
≠ separate, sever.

united *adj* allied, affiliated, corporate, unified, combined, pooled, collective, concerted, one, unanimous, agreed, in agreement, in accord, like-minded.
≠ disunited.

unity *n* agreement, accord, concord, harmony, peace, consensus, unanimity, solidarity, integrity, oneness, wholeness, union, unification.
≠ disunity, disagreement, discord, strife.

universal *adj* worldwide, global, all-embracing, all-inclusive, general, common, across-the-board, total, whole, entire, all-round, unlimited.

unjust *adj* unfair, inequitable, wrong, partial, biased, prejudiced, one-sided, partisan, unreasonable, unjustified, undeserved.
≠ just, fair, reasonable.

unjustifiable *adj* indefensible, inexcusable, unforgivable, unreasonable, unwarranted, immoderate, excessive, unacceptable, outrageous.
≠ justifiable, acceptable.

unkempt *adj* dishevelled, tousled, rumpled, uncombed, ungroomed, untidy, messy, scruffy, shabby, slovenly.
≠ well-groomed, tidy.

unkind *adj* cruel, inhuman, inhumane, callous, hard-hearted, unfeeling, insensitive, thoughtless, inconsiderate, uncharitable, nasty, malicious, spiteful, mean, malevolent, unfriendly, uncaring, unsympathetic.
≠ kind, considerate.

unknown *adj* unfamiliar, unheard-of, strange, alien, foreign, mysterious, dark, obscure, hidden, concealed, undisclosed, secret, untold, new, uncharted, unexplored, undiscovered, unidentified, unnamed, nameless, anonymous, incognito.
≠ known, familiar.

unlawful *adj* illegal, criminal, illicit, illegitimate, unconstitutional, outlawed, banned, prohibited, forbidden, unauthorized.
≠ lawful, legal.

unlikely *adj* **1** IMPROBABLE, implausible, far-fetched, unconvincing, unbelievable, incredible, unimaginable, unexpected, doubtful, dubious, questionable, suspect, suspicious.

2 SLIGHT, faint, remote, distant.
≠ 1 likely, plausible.

unlimited *adj* limitless, unrestricted, unbounded, boundless, infinite, endless, countless, incalculable, immeasurable, vast, immense, extensive, great, indefinite, absolute, unconditional, unqualified, all-encompassing, total, complete, full, unconstrained, unhampered.
≠ limited.

unload *v* unpack, empty, discharge, dump, offload, unburden, relieve.
≠ load.

unlock *v* unbolt, unlatch, unfasten, undo, open, free, release.
≠ lock, fasten.

unloved *adj* unpopular, disliked, hated, detested, unwanted, rejected, spurned, loveless, uncared-for, neglected.
≠ loved.

unlucky *adj* unfortunate, luckless, unhappy, miserable, wretched, ill-fated, ill-starred, jinxed, doomed, cursed, unfavourable, inauspicious, ominous, unsuccessful, disastrous.
≠ lucky.

unmanageable *adj* 1 UNWIELDY, bulky, cumbersome, awkward, inconvenient, unhandy.
2 UNCONTROLLABLE, wild, unruly, disorderly, difficult.
≠ 1 manageable. 2 controllable.

unmarried *adj* single, unwed, celibate, unattached, available.
≠ married.

unmask *v* unveil, uncloak, uncover, bare, expose, reveal, show, disclose, discover, detect.
≠ mask, conceal.

unmentionable *adj* unspeakable, unutterable, taboo, immodest, indecent, shocking, scandalous, shameful, disgraceful, abominable.

unmistakable *adj* clear, plain, distinct, pronounced, obvious, evident, manifest, patent, glaring, explicit, unambiguous, unequivocal, positive, definite, sure, certain, unquestionable, indisputable, undeniable.
≠ unclear, ambiguous.

unmoved *adj* unaffected, untouched, unshaken, dry-eyed, unfeeling, cold, dispassionate, indifferent, impassive, unresponsive, unimpressed, firm, adamant, inflexible, unbending, undeviating, unwavering, steady, unchanged, resolute, resolved, determined.
≠ moved, affected, shaken.

unnatural *adj* 1 ABNORMAL, anomalous, freakish, irregular, unusual, strange, odd, peculiar, queer, bizarre, extraordinary, uncanny, supernatural, inhuman, perverted.
2 AFFECTED, feigned, artificial, false, insincere, unspontaneous, contrived, laboured, stilted, forced, strained, self-conscious, stiff.
≠ 1 natural, normal. 2 sincere, fluent.

unnecessary *adj* unneeded, needless, uncalled-for, unwanted, non-essential, dispensable, expendable, superfluous, redundant, tautological.
≠ necessary, essential, indispensable.

unnerve *adj* daunt, intimidate, frighten, scare, discourage, demoralize, dismay, disconcert, upset, worry, shake, rattle (*infml*), confound, fluster.
≠ nerve, brace, steel.

unnoticed *adj* unobserved, unremarked, unseen, unrecognized, undiscovered, overlooked, ignored, disregarded, neglected, unheeded.
≠ noticed, noted.

unobtrusive *adj* inconspicuous, unnoticeable, unassertive, self-effacing, humble, modest, unostentatious, unpretentious, restrained, low-key, subdued, quiet, retiring.
≠ obtrusive, ostentatious.

unoccupied *adj* uninhabited, vacant, empty, free, idle, inactive, workless, jobless, unemployed.
≠ occupied, busy.

unofficial *adj* unauthorized, illegal, informal, off-the-record, personal, private, confidential, undeclared, unconfirmed.
≠ official.

unorthodox *adj* unconventional, nonconformist, heterodox, alternative,

fringe, irregular, abnormal, unusual.
≠ orthodox, conventional.

unpaid *adj* **1** *unpaid bills*: outstanding, overdue, unsettled, owing, due, payable. **2** *unpaid work*: voluntary, honorary, unsalaried, unwaged, unremunerative, free.
≠ **1** paid.

unpalatable *adj* **1** UNAPPETIZING, distasteful, insipid, bitter, uneatable, inedible. **2** UNPLEASANT, disagreeable, unattractive, offensive, repugnant.
≠ **1** palatable. **2** pleasant.

unparalleled *adj* unequalled, unmatched, matchless, peerless, incomparable, unrivalled, unsurpassed, supreme, superlative, rare, exceptional, unprecedented.

unpleasant *adj* disagreeable, ill-natured, nasty, objectionable, offensive, distasteful, unpalatable, unattractive, repulsive, bad, troublesome.
≠ pleasant, agreeable, nice.

unpopular *adj* disliked, hated, detested, unloved, unsought-after, unfashionable, undesirable, unwelcome, unwanted, rejected, shunned, avoided, neglected.
≠ popular, fashionable.

unprecedented *adj* new, original, revolutionary, unknown, unheard-of, exceptional, remarkable, extraordinary, abnormal, unusual, freakish, unparalleled, unrivalled.
≠ usual.

unpredictable *adj* unforeseeable, unexpected, changeable, variable, inconstant, unreliable, fickle, unstable, erratic, random, chance.
≠ predictable, foreseeable, constant.

unprepared *adj* unready, surprised, unsuspecting, ill-equipped, unfinished, incomplete, half-baked, unplanned, unrehearsed, spontaneous, improvised, ad-lib, off-the-cuff.
≠ prepared, ready.

unpretentious *adj* unaffected, natural, plain, simple, unobtrusive, honest, straightforward, humble, modest, unassuming, unostentatious.
≠ pretentious.

unproductive *adj* infertile, sterile, barren, dry, arid, unfruitful, fruitless, futile, vain, idle, useless, ineffective, unprofitable, unremunerative, unrewarding.
≠ productive, fertile.

unprofessional *adj* amateurish, inexpert, unskilled, sloppy, incompetent, inefficient, casual, negligent, lax, unethical, unprincipled, improper, unseemly, unacceptable, inadmissible.
≠ professional, skilful.

unprotected *adj* unguarded, unattended, undefended, unfortified, unarmed, unshielded, unsheltered, uncovered, exposed, open, naked, vulnerable, defenceless, helpless.
≠ protected, safe, immune.

unqualified *adj* **1** UNTRAINED, inexperienced, amateur, ineligible, unfit, incompetent, incapable, unprepared, ill-equipped. **2** ABSOLUTE, categorical, utter, total, complete, thorough, consummate, downright, unmitigated, unreserved, whole-hearted, outright, unconditional, unrestricted.
≠ **1** qualified, professional. **2** conditional, tentative.

unravel *v* unwind, undo, untangle, disentangle, free, extricate, separate, resolve, sort out, solve, work out, figure out, puzzle out, penetrate, interpret, explain.
≠ tangle, complicate.

unreal *adj* false, artificial, synthetic, mock, fake, sham, imaginary, visionary, fanciful, make-believe, pretend (*infml*), fictitious, made-up, fairy-tale, legendary, mythical, fantastic, illusory, immaterial, insubstantial, hypothetical.
≠ real, genuine.

unrealistic *adj* impractical, idealistic, romantic, quixotic, impracticable, unworkable, unreasonable, impossible.
≠ realistic, pragmatic.

unreasonable *adj* **1** UNFAIR, unjust, biased, unjustifiable, unjustified, unwarranted, undue, uncalled-for. **2** IRRATIONAL, illogical, inconsistent,

arbitrary, absurd, nonsensical, far-fetched, preposterous, mad, senseless, silly, foolish, stupid, headstrong, opinionated, perverse. **3** *unreasonable prices*: excessive, immoderate, extravagant, exorbitant, extortionate.
≠ **1** reasonable, fair. **2** rational, sensible. **3** moderate.

unrecognizable *adj* unidentifiable, disguised, incognito, changed, altered.

unrefined *adj* raw, untreated, unprocessed, unfinished, unpolished, crude, coarse, vulgar, unsophisticated, uncultivated, uncultured.
≠ refined, finished.

unrelated *adj* unconnected, unassociated, irrelevant, extraneous, different, dissimilar, unlike, disparate, distinct, separate, independent.
≠ related, similar.

unrelenting *adj* relentless, unremitting, uncompromising, inexorable, incessant, unceasing, ceaseless, endless, unbroken, continuous, constant, continual, perpetual, steady, unabated, remorseless, unmerciful, merciless, pitiless, unsparing.
≠ spasmodic, intermittent.

unreliable *adj* unsound, fallible, deceptive, false, mistaken, erroneous, inaccurate, unconvincing, implausible, uncertain, undependable, untrustworthy, unstable, fickle, irresponsible.
≠ reliable, dependable, trustworthy.

unrepentant *adj* impenitent, unapologetic, unabashed, unashamed, shameless, incorrigible, confirmed, hardened, obdurate.
≠ repentant, penitent, ashamed.

unrest *n* protest, rebellion, turmoil, agitation, restlessness, dissatisfaction, dissension, disaffection, worry.
≠ peace, calm.

unrestricted *adj* unlimited, unbounded, unopposed, unhindered, unimpeded, unobstructed, clear, free, open, public, unconditional, absolute.
≠ restricted, limited.

unripe *adj* unripened, green, immature, undeveloped, unready.
≠ ripe, mature.

unrivalled *adj* unequalled, unparalleled, unmatched, matchless, peerless, incomparable, inimitable, unsurpassed, supreme, superlative.

unruffled *adj* undisturbed, untroubled, imperturbable, collected, composed, cool, calm, tranquil, serene, peaceful, smooth, level, even.
≠ troubled, anxious.

unruly *adj* uncontrollable, unmanageable, ungovernable, intractable, disorderly, wild, rowdy, riotous, rebellious, mutinous, lawless, insubordinate, disobedient, wayward, wilful, headstrong, obstreperous.
≠ manageable, orderly.

unsafe *adj* dangerous, perilous, risky, hazardous, treacherous, unreliable, uncertain, unsound, unstable, precarious, insecure, vulnerable, exposed.
≠ safe, secure.

unsatisfactory *adj* unacceptable, imperfect, defective, faulty, inferior, poor, weak, inadequate, insufficient, deficient, unsuitable, displeasing, dissatisfying, unsatisfying, frustrating, disappointing.
≠ satisfactory, pleasing.

unscathed *adj* unhurt, uninjured, unharmed, undamaged, untouched, whole, intact, safe, sound.
≠ hurt, injured.

unscrupulous *adj* unprincipled, ruthless, shameless, dishonourable, dishonest, crooked (*infml*), corrupt, immoral, unethical, improper.
≠ scrupulous, ethical, proper.

unseemly *adj* improper, indelicate, indecorous, unbecoming, undignified, unrefined, disreputable, discreditable, undue, inappropriate, unsuitable.
≠ seemly, decorous.

unseen *adj* unnoticed, unobserved, undetected, invisible, hidden, concealed, veiled, obscure.
≠ visible.

unselfish *adj* selfless, altruistic, self-denying, self-sacrificing, disinterested, noble, magnanimous, generous, liberal, charitable, philanthropic, public-spirited, humanitarian, kind.

≠ selfish.

unsentimental *adj* realistic, practical, pragmatic, hard-headed, tough, unromantic, level-headed.
≠ sentimental, idealistic.

unsettle *v* disturb, upset, trouble, bother, discompose, ruffle, fluster, unbalance, shake, agitate, rattle (*infml*), disconcert, confuse, throw.

unsettled *adj* **1** DISTURBED, upset, troubled, agitated, anxious, uneasy, tense, edgy, flustered, shaken, unnerved, disoriented, confused. **2** UNRESOLVED, undetermined, undecided, open, uncertain, doubtful. **3** *unsettled weather*: changeable, variable, unpredictable, inconstant, unstable, insecure, unsteady, shaky. **4** UNPAID, outstanding, owing, payable, overdue.
≠ **1** composed. **2** certain. **3** settled. **4** paid.

unshakable *adj* firm, well-founded, fixed, stable, immovable, unassailable, unwavering, constant, steadfast, staunch, sure, resolute, determined.
≠ insecure.

unsightly *adj* ugly, unattractive, unprepossessing, hideous, repulsive, repugnant, off-putting, unpleasant, disagreeable.
≠ attractive.

unskilled *adj* untrained, unqualified, inexperienced, unpractised, inexpert, unprofessional, amateurish, incompetent.
≠ skilled.

unsociable *adj* unfriendly, aloof, distant, standoffish, withdrawn, introverted, reclusive, retiring, reserved, taciturn, unforthcoming, uncommunicative, cold, chilly, uncongenial, unneighbourly, inhospitable, hostile.
≠ sociable, friendly.

unsolicited *adj* unrequested, unsought, uninvited, unasked, unwanted, unwelcome, uncalled-for, gratuitous, voluntary, spontaneous.
≠ requested, invited.

unsophisticated *adj* artless, guileless, innocent, ingenuous, naïve, inexperienced, unworldly, childlike, natural, unaffected, unpretentious, unrefined, plain, simple, straightforward, uncomplicated, uninvolved.
≠ sophisticated, worldly, complex.

unsound *adj* **1** *unsound reasoning*: faulty, flawed, defective, ill-founded, fallacious, false, erroneous, invalid, illogical. **2** UNHEALTHY, unwell, ill, diseased, weak, frail, unbalanced, deranged, unhinged. **3** UNSTABLE, unsteady, wobbly, shaky, insecure, unsafe.
≠ **1** sound. **2** well. **3** stable.

unspeakable *adj* unutterable, inexpressible, indescribable, awful, dreadful, frightful, terrible, horrible, shocking, appalling, monstrous, inconceivable, unbelievable.

unspoilt *adj* preserved, unchanged, untouched, natural, unaffected, unsophisticated, unharmed, undamaged, unimpaired, unblemished, perfect.
≠ spoilt, affected.

unspoken *adj* unstated, undeclared, unuttered, unexpressed, unsaid, voiceless, wordless, silent, tacit, implicit, implied, inferred, understood, assumed.
≠ stated, explicit.

unstable *adj* **1** CHANGEABLE, variable, fluctuating, vacillating, wavering, fitful, erratic, inconsistent, volatile, capricious, inconstant, unpredictable, unreliable, untrustworthy. **2** UNSTEADY, wobbly, shaky, rickety, insecure, unsafe, risky, precarious, tottering, unbalanced.
≠ **1** stable. **2** steady.

unsteady *adj* unstable, wobbly, shaky, rickety, insecure, unsafe, treacherous, precarious, tottering, unreliable, inconstant, irregular, flickering.
≠ steady, firm.

unsuccessful *adj* failed, abortive, vain, futile, useless, ineffective, unavailing, fruitless, unproductive, sterile, luckless, unlucky, unfortunate, losing, beaten, defeated, frustrated, thwarted.

≠ successful, effective, fortunate, winning.

unsuitable *adj* inappropriate, inapt, unsuited, unfit, unacceptable, improper, unseemly, unbecoming, incompatible, incongruous.
≠ suitable, appropriate.

unsung *adj* unhonoured, unpraised, unacknowledged, unrecognized, overlooked, disregarded, neglected, forgotten, unknown, obscure.
≠ honoured, famous, renowned.

unsure *adj* uncertain, doubtful, dubious, suspicious, sceptical, unconvinced, unpersuaded, undecided, hesitant, tentative.
≠ sure, certain, confident.

unsurpassed *adj* surpassing, supreme, transcendent, unbeaten, unexcelled, unequalled, unparalleled, unrivalled, incomparable, matchless, superlative, exceptional.

unsuspecting *adj* unwary, unaware, unconscious, trusting, trustful, unsuspicious, credulous, gullible, ingenuous, naïve, innocent.
≠ suspicious, knowing.

unsympathetic *adj* unpitying, unconcerned, unmoved, unresponsive, indifferent, insensitive, unfeeling, cold, heartless, soulless, hard-hearted, callous, cruel, inhuman, unkind, hard, stony, hostile, antagonistic.
≠ sympathetic, compassionate.

untangle *v* disentangle, extricate, unravel, undo, resolve, solve.
≠ tangle, complicate.

unthinkable *adj* inconceivable, unimaginable, unheard-of, unbelievable, incredible, impossible, improbable, unlikely, implausible, unreasonable, illogical, absurd, preposterous, outrageous, shocking.

unthinking *adj* thoughtless, inconsiderate, insensitive, tactless, indiscreet, rude, heedless, careless, negligent, rash, impulsive, instinctive, unconscious, automatic, mechanical.
≠ considerate, conscious.

untidy *adj* messy, cluttered, disorderly, muddled, jumbled, unsystematic, chaotic, topsy-turvy, scruffy, dishevelled, unkempt, slovenly, sloppy, slipshod.
≠ tidy, neat.

untie *v* undo, unfasten, unknot, unbind, free, release, loose, loosen.
≠ tie, fasten.

untimely *adj* early, premature, unseasonable, ill-timed, inopportune, inconvenient, awkward, unsuitable, inappropriate, unfortunate, inauspicious.
≠ timely, opportune.

untiring *adj* unflagging, tireless, indefatigable, dogged, persevering, persistent, tenacious, determined, resolute, devoted, dedicated, constant, incessant, unremitting, steady, staunch, unfailing.
≠ inconstant, wavering.

untold *adj* uncounted, unnumbered, unreckoned, incalculable, innumerable, uncountable, countless, infinite, measureless, boundless, inexhaustible, undreamed-of, unimaginable.

untouched *adj* unharmed, undamaged, unimpaired, unhurt, uninjured, unscathed, safe, intact, unchanged, unaltered, unaffected.
≠ damaged, affected.

untrained *adj* unskilled, untaught, unschooled, uneducated, inexperienced, unqualified, amateur, unprofessional, inexpert.
≠ trained, expert.

untried *adj* untested, unproved, experimental, exploratory, new, novel, innovative, innovatory.
≠ tried, tested, proven.

untrue *adj* **1** FALSE, fallacious, deceptive, misleading, wrong, incorrect, inaccurate, mistaken, erroneous.
2 UNFAITHFUL, disloyal, untrustworthy, dishonest, deceitful, untruthful.
≠ **1** true, correct. **2** faithful, honest.

untrustworthy *adj* dishonest, deceitful, untruthful, disloyal, unfaithful, faithless, treacherous, false, untrue, capricious, fickle, fly-by-night, unreliable, untrusty.
≠ trustworthy, reliable.

untruth *n* lie, fib, whopper (*infml*), story, tale, fiction, invention, fabrication, falsehood, lying, untruthfulness, deceit, perjury.
≠ truth.

untruthful *adj* lying, deceitful, dishonest, crooked (*infml*), hypocritical, two-faced, insincere, false, untrue.
≠ truthful, honest.

unused *adj* leftover, remaining, surplus, extra, spare, available, new, fresh, blank, clean, untouched, unexploited, unemployed, idle.
≠ used.

unusual *adj* uncommon, rare, unfamiliar, strange, odd, curious, queer, bizarre, unconventional, irregular, abnormal, extraordinary, remarkable, exceptional, different, surprising, unexpected.
≠ usual, normal, ordinary.

unveil *v* uncover, expose, bare, reveal, disclose, divulge, discover.
≠ cover, hide.

unwanted *adj* undesired, unsolicited, uninvited, unwelcome, outcast, rejected, unrequired, unneeded, unnecessary, surplus, extra, superfluous, redundant.
≠ wanted, needed, necessary.

unwarranted *adj* unjustified, undeserved, unprovoked, uncalled-for, groundless, unreasonable, unjust, wrong.
≠ warranted, justifiable, deserved.

unwary *adj* unguarded, incautious, careless, imprudent, indiscreet, thoughtless, unthinking, heedless, reckless, rash, hasty.
≠ wary, cautious.

unwelcome *adj* **1** UNWANTED, undesirable, unpopular, uninvited, excluded, rejected. **2** *unwelcome news*: unpleasant, disagreeable, upsetting, worrying, distasteful, unpalatable, unacceptable.
≠ **1** welcome, desirable. **2** pleasant.

unwell *adj* ill, sick, poorly, indisposed, off-colour, ailing, sickly, unhealthy.
≠ well, healthy.

unwieldy *adj* unmanageable, inconvenient, awkward, clumsy, ungainly, bulky, massive, hefty, weighty, ponderous, cumbersome.
≠ handy, dainty.

unwilling *adj* reluctant, disinclined, indisposed, resistant, opposed, averse, loath, slow, unenthusiastic, grudging.
≠ willing, enthusiastic.

unwind *v* **1** UNROLL, unreel, unwrap, undo, uncoil, untwist, unravel, disentangle. **2** (*infml*) RELAX, wind down, calm down.
≠ **1** wind, roll.

unwitting *adj* unaware, unknowing, unsuspecting, unthinking, unconscious, involuntary, accidental, chance, inadvertent, unintentional, unintended, unplanned.
≠ knowing, conscious, deliberate.

unworldly *adj* spiritual, transcendental, metaphysical, otherworldly, visionary, idealistic, impractical, unsophisticated, inexperienced, innocent, naïve.
≠ worldly, materialistic, sophisticated.

unworthy *adj* undeserving, inferior, ineligible, unsuitable, inappropriate, unfitting, unbecoming, unseemly, improper, unprofessional, shameful, disgraceful, dishonourable, discreditable, ignoble, base, contemptible, despicable.
≠ worthy, commendable.

unwritten *adj* verbal, oral, word-of-mouth, unrecorded, tacit, implicit, understood, accepted, recognized, traditional, customary, conventional.
≠ written, recorded.

upbraid *v* reprimand, admonish, rebuke, reprove, reproach, scold, chide, castigate, berate, criticize, censure.
≠ praise, commend.

upbringing *n* bringing-up, raising, rearing, breeding, parenting, care, nurture, cultivation, education, training, instruction, teaching.

update *v* modernize, revise, amend, correct, renew, renovate, revamp.

upgrade *v* promote, advance, elevate, raise, improve, enhance.

≠ downgrade, demote.

upheaval *n* disruption, disturbance, upset, chaos, confusion, disorder, turmoil, shake-up (*infml*), revolution, overthrow.

uphill *adj* hard, difficult, arduous, tough, taxing, strenuous, laborious, tiring, wearisome, exhausting, gruelling, punishing.
≠ easy.

uphold *v* support, maintain, hold to, stand by, defend, champion, advocate, promote, back, endorse, sustain, fortify, strengthen, justify, vindicate.
≠ abandon, reject.

upkeep *n* maintenance, preservation, conservation, care, running, repair, support, sustenance, subsistence, keep.
≠ neglect.

upper *adj* higher, loftier, superior, senior, top, topmost, uppermost, high, elevated, exalted, eminent, important.
≠ lower, inferior, junior.

uppermost *adj* highest, loftiest, top, topmost, greatest, supreme, first, primary, foremost, leading, principal, main, chief, dominant, predominant, paramount, pre-eminent.
≠ lowest.

upright *adj* **1** VERTICAL, perpendicular, erect, straight. **2** RIGHTEOUS, good, virtuous, upstanding, noble, honourable, ethical, principled, incorruptible, honest, trustworthy.
≠ **1** horizontal, flat. **2** dishonest.

uprising *n* rebellion, revolt, mutiny, rising, insurgence, insurrection, revolution.

uproar *n* noise, din, racket, hubbub, hullabaloo, pandemonium, tumult, turmoil, turbulence, commotion, confusion, disorder, clamour, outcry, furore, riot, rumpus.

uproot *v* pull up, rip up, root out, weed out, remove, displace, eradicate, destroy, wipe out.

upset *v* **1** DISTRESS, grieve, dismay, trouble, worry, agitate, disturb, bother, fluster, ruffle, discompose, shake, unnerve, disconcert, confuse, disorganize. **2** TIP, spill, overturn, capsize, topple, overthrow, destabilize, unsteady.
n **1** TROUBLE, worry, agitation, disturbance, bother, disruption, upheaval, shake-up (*infml*), reverse, surprise, shock. **2** *stomach upset*: disorder, complaint, bug (*infml*), illness, sickness.
adj distressed, grieved, hurt, annoyed, dismayed, troubled, worried, agitated, disturbed, bothered, shaken, disconcerted, confused.

upshot *n* result, consequence, outcome, issue, end, conclusion, finish, culmination.

upside down inverted, upturned, wrong way up, upset, overturned, disordered, muddled, jumbled, confused, topsy-turvy, chaotic.

up-to-date *adj* current, contemporary, modern, fashionable, trendy (*infml*), latest, recent, new.
≠ out-of-date, old-fashioned.

upturn *n* revival, recovery, upsurge, upswing, rise, increase, boost, improvement.
≠ downturn, drop.

urban *adj* town, city, inner-city, metropolitan, municipal, civic, built-up.
≠ country, rural.

urge *v* advise, counsel, recommend, advocate, encourage, exhort, implore, beg, beseech, entreat, plead, press, constrain, compel, force, push, drive, impel, goad, spur, hasten, induce, incite, instigate.
≠ discourage, dissuade, deter, hinder.
n desire, wish, inclination, fancy, longing, yearning, itch, impulse, compulsion, impetus, drive, eagerness.
≠ disinclination.

urgency *n* hurry, haste, pressure, stress, importance, seriousness, gravity, imperativeness, need, necessity.

urgent *adj* immediate, instant, top-priority, important, critical, crucial, imperative, exigent, pressing, compelling, persuasive, earnest, eager, insistent, persistent.
≠ unimportant.

usable *adj* working, operational, serviceable, functional, practical, exploitable, available, current, valid.
≠ unusable, useless.

usage *n* **1** TREATMENT, handling, management, control, running, operation, employment, application, use. **2** TRADITION, custom, practice, habit, convention, etiquette, rule, regulation, form, routine, procedure, method.

use *v* utilize, employ, exercise, practise, operate, work, apply, wield, handle, treat, manipulate, exploit, enjoy, consume, exhaust, expend, spend.
n utility, usefulness, value, worth, profit, advantage, benefit, good, avail, help, service, point, object, end, purpose, reason, cause, occasion, need, necessity, usage, application, employment, operation, exercise.
use up finish, exhaust, drain, sap, deplete, consume, devour, absorb, waste, squander, fritter.

used *adj* second-hand, cast-off, hand-me-down, nearly new, worn, dog-eared, soiled.
≠ unused, new, fresh.

useful *adj* handy, convenient, all-purpose, practical, effective, productive, fruitful, profitable, valuable, worthwhile, advantageous, beneficial, helpful.
≠ useless, ineffective, worthless.

useless *adj* futile, fruitless, unproductive, vain, idle, unavailing, hopeless, pointless, worthless, unusable, broken-down, clapped-out (*sl*), unworkable, impractical, ineffective, inefficient, incompetent, weak.
≠ useful, helpful, effective.

usher *n* usherette, doorkeeper, attendant, escort, guide.
v escort, accompany, conduct, lead, direct, guide, show, pilot, steer.

usual *adj* normal, typical, stock, standard, regular, routine, habitual, customary, conventional, accepted, recognized, accustomed, familiar, common, everyday, general, ordinary, unexceptional, expected, predictable.
≠ unusual, strange, rare.

usually *adv* normally, generally, as a rule, ordinarily, typically, traditionally, regularly, commonly, by and large, on the whole, mainly, chiefly, mostly.
≠ exceptionally.

usurp *v* take over, assume, arrogate, seize, take, annex, appropriate, commandeer, steal.

utensil *n* tool, implement, instrument, device, contrivance, gadget, apparatus, appliance.

utility *n* usefulness, use, value, profit, advantage, benefit, avail, service, convenience, practicality, efficacy, efficiency, fitness, serviceableness.

utmost *adj* **1** *with the utmost care*: extreme, maximum, greatest, highest, supreme, paramount. **2** FARTHEST, furthermost, remotest, outermost, ultimate, final, last.
n best, hardest, most, maximum.

utter[1] *adj* absolute, complete, total, entire, thoroughgoing, out-and-out, downright, sheer, stark, arrant, unmitigated, unqualified, perfect, consummate.

utter[2] *v* speak, say, voice, vocalize, verbalize, express, articulate, enunciate, sound, pronounce, deliver, state, declare, announce, proclaim, tell, reveal, divulge.

utterance *n* statement, remark, comment, expression, articulation, delivery, speech, declaration, announcement, proclamation, pronouncement.

utterly *adv* absolutely, completely, totally, fully, entirely, wholly, thoroughly, downright, perfectly.

U-turn *n* about-turn, volte-face, reversal, backtrack.

V

vacancy *n* opportunity, opening, position, post, job, place, room, situation.

vacant *adj* **1** EMPTY, unoccupied, unfilled, free, available, void, not in use, unused, uninhabited. **2** BLANK, expressionless, vacuous, inane, inattentive, absent, absent-minded, unthinking, dreamy.
≠ **1** occupied, engaged.

vacate *v* leave, depart, evacuate, abandon, withdraw, quit.

vacuum *n* emptiness, void, nothingness, vacuity, space, chasm, gap.

vague *adj* **1** ILL-DEFINED, blurred, indistinct, hazy, dim, shadowy, misty, fuzzy, nebulous, obscure. **2** INDEFINITE, imprecise, unclear, uncertain, undefined, undetermined, unspecific, generalized, inexact, ambiguous, evasive, loose, woolly.
≠ **1** clear. **2** definite.

vain *adj* **1** *a vain attempt*: useless, worthless, futile, abortive, fruitless, pointless, unproductive, unprofitable, unavailing, hollow, groundless, empty, trivial, unimportant. **2** CONCEITED, proud, self-satisfied, arrogant, self-important, egotistical, bigheaded (*infml*), swollen-headed (*infml*), stuck-up (*infml*), affected, pretentious, ostentatious, swaggering.
≠ **1** fruitful, successful. **2** modest, self-effacing.

valiant *adj* brave, courageous, gallant, fearless, intrepid, bold, dauntless, heroic, plucky, indomitable, staunch.
≠ cowardly, fearful.

valid *adj* **1** LOGICAL, well-founded, well-grounded, sound, good, cogent, convincing, telling, conclusive, reliable, substantial, weighty, powerful, just. **2** OFFICIAL, legal, lawful, legitimate, authentic, bona fide, genuine, binding, proper.
≠ **1** false, weak. **2** unofficial, invalid.

valley *n* dale, vale, dell, glen, hollow, cwm, depression, gulch.

valuable *adj* **1** *valuable necklace*: precious, prized, valued, costly, expensive, dear, high-priced, treasured, cherished, estimable. **2** *valuable suggestions*: helpful, worthwhile, useful, beneficial, invaluable, constructive, fruitful, profitable, important, serviceable, worthy, handy.
≠ **1** worthless. **2** useless.

value *n* **1** COST, price, rate, worth. **2** WORTH, use, usefulness, utility, merit, importance, desirability, benefit, advantage, significance, good, profit.
v **1** PRIZE, appreciate, treasure, esteem, hold dear, respect, cherish. **2** EVALUATE, assess, estimate, price, appraise, survey, rate.
≠ **1** disregard, neglect. **2** undervalue.

vanish *v* disappear, fade, dissolve, evaporate, disperse, melt, die out, depart, exit, fizzle out, peter out.
≠ appear, materialize.

vanity *n* **1** CONCEIT, conceitedness, pride, arrogance, self-conceit, self-love, self-satisfaction, narcissism, egotism, pretension, ostentation, affectation, airs, bigheadedness (*infml*), swollen-headedness (*infml*). **2** WORTHLESSNESS, uselessness, emptiness, futility, pointlessness, unreality, hollowness, fruitlessness, triviality.
≠ **1** modesty, worth.

vapour *n* steam, mist, fog, smoke, breath, fumes, haze, damp, dampness, exhalation.

variable *adj* changeable, inconstant, varying, shifting, mutable, unpredictable, fluctuating, fitful, unstable, unsteady, wavering, vacillating, temperamental, fickle, flexible.
≠ fixed, invariable, stable.

variance *n* **1** VARIATION, difference, discrepancy, divergence, inconsistency, disagreement. **2** DISAGREEMENT, disharmony, conflict, discord, division, dissent, dissension, quarrelling, strife.
≠ **1** agreement. **2** harmony.

variation *n* diversity, variety, deviation, discrepancy, diversification, alteration, change, difference, departure, modification, modulation, inflection, novelty, innovation.
≠ monotony, uniformity.

varied *adj* assorted, diverse, miscellaneous, mixed, various, sundry, heterogeneous (*fml*), different, wide-ranging.
≠ standardized, uniform.

variegated *adj* multicoloured, many-coloured, parti-coloured, varicoloured, speckled, mottled, dappled, pied, streaked, motley.
≠ monochrome, plain.

variety *n* **1** ASSORTMENT, miscellany, mixture, collection, medley, pot-pourri, range. **2** DIFFERENCE, diversity, dissimilarity, discrepancy, variation, multiplicity. **3** SORT, kind, class, category, species, type, breed, brand, make, strain.
≠ **2** uniformity, similitude.

various *adj* different, differing, diverse, varied, varying, assorted, miscellaneous, heterogeneous (*fml*), distinct, diversified, mixed, many, several.

varnish *n* lacquer, glaze, resin, polish, gloss, coating.

vary *v* **1** CHANGE, alter, modify, modulate, diversify, reorder, transform, alternate, inflect, permutate. **2** DIVERGE, differ, disagree, depart, fluctuate.

vast *adj* huge, immense, massive, gigantic, enormous, great, colossal, extensive, tremendous, sweeping, unlimited, fathomless, immeasurable, never-ending, monumental, monstrous, far-flung.

vault[1] *v* leap, spring, bound, clear, jump, hurdle, leap-frog.

vault[2] *n* **1** CELLAR, crypt, strongroom, repository, cavern, depository, wine-cellar, tomb, mausoleum. **2** ARCH, roof, span, concave.

vaunt (*fml*) *v* boast, brag, exult in, flaunt, show off, parade, trumpet, crow.
≠ belittle, minimize.

veer *v* swerve, swing, change, shift, diverge, deviate, wheel, turn, sheer, tack.

vegetable

Vegetables include: artichoke, aubergine, bean, beetroot, broad bean, broccoli, Brussels sprout, butter bean, cabbage, calabrese, capsicum, carrot, cauliflower, celeriac, celery, chicory, courgette, cress, cucumber, eggplant (*US*), endive, fennel, French bean, garlic, kale, leek, lentil, lettuce, mange tout, marrow, mushroom, okra, onion, parsnip, pea, pepper, petit pois, potato, spud (*infml*), pumpkin, radish, runner bean, shallot, soya bean, spinach, spring onion, swede, sweetcorn, sweet potato, turnip, watercress, yam, zucchini (*US*). *Vegetable dishes include*: aubergine roll, baba ganoush, bhaji, onion bhaji, bubble and squeak, cauliflower cheese, champ, chillada, colcannon, coleslaw, couscous, crudités, dal, dolma, duchesse potatoes, fasolia, felafel, fondue, gado-gado, gnocchi, guacamole, gumbo, hummus, imam bayildi, latke, macaroni cheese, macedoine, mushy peas, nut cutlet, paella, pakora, pease pudding, peperonata, pilau, pissaladière, polenta, ratatouille, raita, risotto, rösti, salad, caesar salad, green salad, hot salad, mixed salad, salade niçoise, Waldorf salad, winter salad, sauerkraut, stovies, stuffed marrow, stuffed mushroom, succotash, tabbouleh, tahina, tsatsiki, vegetable chilli, vegetable curry, vegetable soup, vegetarian goulash, vichyssoise.

vegetate *v* stagnate, degenerate, deteriorate, rusticate, go to seed, idle, rust, languish.

vehement *adj* impassioned, passionate,

ardent, fervent, intense, forceful, emphatic, heated, strong, powerful, urgent, enthusiastic, animated, eager, earnest, forcible, fierce, violent, zealous.
≠ apathetic, indifferent.

vehicle *n* **1** CONVEYANCE, transport. **2** MEANS, agency, channel, medium, mechanism, organ.

Vehicles include: plane, boat, ship, car, taxi, hackney-carriage, bicycle, bike (*infml*), cycle, tandem, tricycle, boneshaker (*infml*), penny-farthing, motor-cycle, motor-bike, scooter, bus, omnibus, minibus, double-decker (*infml*), coach, charabanc, caravan, caravanette, camper, train, Pullman, sleeper, wagon-lit, tube, tram, monorail, maglev, trolleybus; van, Transit®, lorry, truck, juggernaut, pantechnicon, trailer, tractor, fork-lift truck, steam-roller, tank, wagon; bobsleigh, sled, sledge, sleigh, toboggan, troika; barouche, brougham, dog-cart, dray, four-in-hand, gig, hansom, landau, phaeton, post-chaise, stagecoach, sulky, surrey, trap; rickshaw, sedan-chair, litter. *see also* **aircraft**; **boats and ships**; **car**.

veil *v* screen, cloak, cover, mask, shadow, shield, obscure, conceal, hide, disguise, shade.
≠ expose, uncover.
n cover, cloak, curtain, mask, screen, disguise, film, blind, shade, shroud.

vein *n* **1** STREAK, stripe, stratum, seam, lode, blood vessel.

Veins and arteries include: aorta, axillary, brachial, carotid, femoral, frontal, gastric, hepatic, iliac, jugular, portal, pulmonary, radial, renal, saphena, subclavian, superior, temporal, tibial.

2 MOOD, tendency, bent, strain, temper, tenor, tone, frame of mind, mode, style.

vendetta *n* feud, blood-feud, enmity, rivalry, quarrel, bad blood, bitterness.

veneer *n* front, façade, appearance, coating, surface, show, mask, gloss, pretence, guise, finish.

venerable *adj* respected, revered, esteemed, honoured, venerated, dignified, grave, wise, august, aged, worshipped.

venerate *v* revere, respect, honour, esteem, worship, hallow (*fml*), adore.
≠ despise, anathematize.

vengeance *n* retribution, revenge, retaliation, reprisal, requital, tit for tat.
≠ forgiveness.

venom *n* **1** POISON, toxin. **2** RANCOUR, ill-will, malice, malevolence, spite, bitterness, acrimony, hate, virulence.

venomous *adj* **1** POISONOUS, toxic, virulent, harmful, noxious.
2 MALICIOUS, spiteful, vicious, vindictive, baleful, hostile, malignant, rancorous, baneful.
≠ **1** harmless.

vent *n* opening, hole, aperture, outlet, passage, orifice, duct.
v air, express, voice, utter, release, discharge, emit.

ventilate *v* **1** *ventilate a room*: air, aerate, freshen. **2** *ventilate one's feelings*: air, broadcast, debate, discuss.

venture *v* **1** DARE, advance, make bold, put forward, presume, suggest, volunteer. **2** RISK, hazard, endanger, imperil, jeopardize, speculate, wager, stake.
n risk, chance, hazard, speculation, gamble, undertaking, project, adventure, endeavour, enterprise, operation, fling.

verbal *adj* spoken, oral, verbatim, unwritten, word-of-mouth.

verbatim *adv* word for word, exactly, literally, to the letter, precisely.

verbose *adj* long-winded, wordy, prolix, loquacious, diffuse, circumlocutory.
≠ succinct, brief.

verdict *n* decision, judgement, conclusion, finding, adjudication, assessment, opinion, sentence.

verge *n* border, edge, margin, limit, rim, brim, brink, boundary, threshold, extreme, edging.
verge on approach, border on, come close to, near.

verify *v* confirm, corroborate, substantiate, authenticate, bear out, prove, support, validate, testify, attest.
≠ invalidate, discredit.

vernacular *adj* indigenous, local, native, popular, vulgar, informal, colloquial, common.
n language, speech, tongue, parlance, dialect, idiom, jargon.

versatile *adj* adaptable, flexible, all-round, multipurpose, multifaceted, adjustable, many-sided, general-purpose, functional, resourceful, handy, variable.
≠ inflexible.

verse *n* poetry, rhyme, stanza, metre, doggerel, jingle.

versed *adj* skilled, proficient, practised, experienced, familiar, acquainted, learned, knowledgeable, conversant, seasoned, qualified, competent, accomplished.

version *n* **1** RENDERING, reading, interpretation, account, translation, paraphrase, adaptation, portrayal. **2** TYPE, kind, variant, form, model, style, design.

vertical *adj* upright, perpendicular, upstanding, erect, on end.
≠ horizontal.

vertigo *n* dizziness, giddiness, light-headedness.

verve *n* vitality, vivacity, animation, energy, dash, élan, liveliness, sparkle, vigour, enthusiasm, gusto, life, relish, spirit, force.
≠ apathy, lethargy.

very *adv* extremely, greatly, highly, deeply, truly, terribly (*infml*), remarkably, excessively, exceeding(ly), acutely, particularly, really, absolutely, noticeably, unusually.
≠ slightly, scarcely.
adj actual, real, same, selfsame, identical, true, genuine, simple, utter, sheer, pure, perfect, plain, mere, bare, exact, appropriate.

vestige *n* trace, suspicion, indication, sign, hint, evidence, whiff, inkling, glimmer, token, scrap, remains, remainder, remnant, residue.

vet *v* investigate, examine, check, scrutinize, scan, inspect, survey, review, appraise, audit.

veteran *n* master, pastmaster, old hand, old stager, old-timer, pro (*infml*), war-horse.
≠ novice, recruit.
adj experienced, practised, seasoned, long-serving, expert, adept, proficient, old.
≠ inexperienced.

veto *v* reject, turn down, forbid, disallow, ban, prohibit, rule out, block.
≠ approve, sanction.
n rejection, ban, embargo, prohibition, thumbs down (*infml*).
≠ approval, assent.

vex *v* irritate, annoy, provoke, pester, trouble, upset, worry, bother, put out (*infml*), harass, hassle (*infml*), aggravate (*infml*), needle (*infml*), disturb, distress, agitate, exasperate, torment, fret.
≠ calm, soothe.

vexed *adj* **1** IRRITATED, annoyed, provoked, upset, troubled, worried, nettled, put out, exasperated, bothered, confused, perplexed, aggravated (*infml*), harassed, hassled (*infml*), ruffled, riled, disturbed, distressed, displeased, agitated. **2** *a vexed question*: difficult, controversial, contested, disputed.

viable *adj* feasible, practicable, possible, workable, usable, operable, achievable, sustainable.
≠ impossible, unworkable.

vibrant *adj* **1** ANIMATED, vivacious, vivid, bright, brilliant, colourful, lively, responsive, sparkling, spirited, sensitive. **2** THRILLING, dynamic, electrifying, electric.

vibrate *v* quiver, pulsate, shudder, shiver, resonate, reverberate, throb, oscillate, tremble, undulate, sway, swing, shake.

vice *n* **1** EVIL, evil-doing, depravity, immorality, wickedness, sin, corruption, iniquity (*fml*), profligacy (*fml*), degeneracy. **2** FAULT, failing, defect, shortcoming, weakness, imperfection, blemish, bad habit, besetting sin.
≠ **1** virtue, morality.

vicinity *n* neighbourhood, area, locality, district, precincts, environs, proximity.

vicious *adj* **1** WICKED, bad, wrong, immoral, depraved, unprincipled, diabolical, corrupt, debased, perverted, profligate (*fml*), vile, heinous. **2** MALICIOUS, spiteful, vindictive, virulent, cruel, mean, nasty, slanderous, venomous, defamatory. **3** SAVAGE, wild, violent, barbarous, brutal, dangerous.
≠ **1** virtuous. **2** kind.

victim *n* sufferer, casualty, prey, scapegoat, martyr, sacrifice, fatality.
≠ offender, attacker.

victimize *v* **1** OPPRESS, persecute, discriminate against, pick on, prey on, bully, exploit. **2** CHEAT, deceive, defraud, swindle (*infml*), dupe, hoodwink, fool.

victorious *adj* conquering, champion, triumphant, winning, unbeaten, successful, prize-winning, top, first.
≠ defeated, unsuccessful.

victory *n* conquest, win, triumph, success, superiority, mastery, vanquishment, subjugation, overcoming.
≠ defeat, loss.

vie *v* strive, compete, contend, struggle, contest, fight, rival.

view *n* **1** OPINION, attitude, belief, judgement, estimation, feeling, sentiment, impression, notion. **2** SIGHT, scene, vision, vista, outlook, prospect, perspective, panorama, landscape. **3** SURVEY, inspection, examination, observation, scrutiny, scan. **4** GLIMPSE, look, sight, perception.
v **1** CONSIDER, regard, contemplate, judge, think about, speculate. **2** OBSERVE, watch, see, examine, inspect, look at, scan, survey, witness, perceive.

viewer *n* spectator, watcher, observer, onlooker.

viewpoint *n* attitude, position, perspective, slant, standpoint, stance, opinion, angle, feeling.

vigilant *adj* watchful, alert, attentive, observant, on one's guard, on the lookout, cautious, wide-awake, sleepless, unsleeping.
≠ careless.

vigorous *adj* energetic, active, lively, healthy, strong, strenuous, robust, lusty, sound, vital, brisk, dynamic, forceful, forcible, powerful, stout, spirited, full-blooded, effective, efficient, enterprising, flourishing, intense.
≠ weak, feeble.

vigour *n* energy, vitality, liveliness, health, robustness, stamina, strength, resilience, soundness, spirit, verve, gusto, activity, animation, power, potency, force, forcefulness, might, dash, dynamism.
≠ weakness.

vile *adj* **1** *a vile sinner*: base, contemptible, debased, depraved, degenerate, bad, wicked, wretched, worthless, sinful, miserable, mean, evil, impure, corrupt, despicable, disgraceful, degrading, vicious, appalling. **2** *a vile meal*: disgusting, foul, nauseating, sickening, repulsive, repugnant, revolting, noxious, offensive, nasty, loathsome, horrid.
≠ **1** pure, worthy. **2** pleasant, lovely.

villain *n* evil-doer, miscreant (*fml*), scoundrel, rogue, malefactor (*fml*), criminal, reprobate, rascal.

villainous *adj* wicked, bad, criminal, evil, sinful, vicious, notorious, cruel, inhuman, vile, depraved, disgraceful, terrible.
≠ good.

vindicate (*fml*) *v* **1** CLEAR, acquit, excuse, exonerate, absolve, rehabilitate. **2** JUSTIFY, uphold, support, maintain, defend, establish, advocate, assert, verify.

vindictive *adj* spiteful, unforgiving, implacable, vengeful, relentless, unrelenting, revengeful, resentful, punitive, venomous, malevolent, malicious.
≠ forgiving.

vintage *n* year, period, era, epoch, generation, origin, harvest, crop.

adj choice, best, fine, prime, select, superior, rare, mature, old, ripe, classic, venerable, veteran.

violate *v* **1** CONTRAVENE, disobey, disregard, transgress, break, flout, infringe. **2** OUTRAGE, debauch, defile, rape, ravish, dishonour, desecrate, profane, invade.
≠ **1** observe.

violence *n* **1** FORCE, strength, power, vehemence, might, intensity, ferocity, fierceness, severity, tumult, turbulence, wildness. **2** BRUTALITY, destructiveness, cruelty, bloodshed, murderousness, savagery, passion, fighting, frenzy, fury, hostilities.

violent *adj* **1** INTENSE, strong, severe, sharp, acute, extreme, harmful, destructive, devastating, injurious, powerful, painful, agonizing, forceful, forcible, harsh, ruinous, rough, vehement, tumultuous, turbulent. **2** CRUEL, brutal, aggressive, bloodthirsty, impetuous, hot-headed, headstrong, murderous, savage, wild, vicious, unrestrained, uncontrollable, ungovernable, passionate, furious, intemperate, maddened, outrageous, riotous, fiery.
≠ **1** calm, moderate. **2** peaceful, gentle.

virgin *n* girl, maiden, celibate, vestal.
adj virginal, chaste, intact, immaculate, maidenly, pure, modest, new, fresh, spotless, stainless, undefiled, untouched, unsullied.

virile *adj* man-like, masculine, male, manly, macho (*infml*), robust, vigorous, potent, lusty, red-blooded, forceful, strong, rugged.
≠ effeminate, impotent.

virtual *adj* effective, essential, practical, implied, implicit, potential.

virtually *adv* practically, in effect, almost, nearly, as good as, in essence.

virtue *n* **1** GOODNESS, morality, rectitude, uprightness, worthiness, righteousness, probity (*fml*), integrity, honour, incorruptibility, justice, high-mindedness, excellence. **2** QUALITY, worth, merit, advantage, asset, credit, strength.
≠ **1** vice.

virtuoso *n* expert, master, maestro, prodigy, genius.

virtuous *adj* good, moral, righteous, upright, worthy, honourable, irreproachable, incorruptible, exemplary, unimpeachable, high-principled, blameless, clean-living, excellent, innocent.
≠ immoral, vicious.

virulent *adj* **1** POISONOUS, toxic, venomous, deadly, lethal, malignant, injurious, pernicious, intense. **2** HOSTILE, resentful, spiteful, acrimonious, bitter, vicious, vindictive, malevolent, malicious.
≠ **1** harmless.

visible *adj* perceptible, discernible, detectable, apparent, noticeable, observable, distinguishable, discoverable, evident, unconcealed, undisguised, unmistakable, conspicuous, clear, obvious, manifest, open, palpable, plain, patent.
≠ invisible, indiscernible, hidden.

vision *n* **1** APPARITION, hallucination, illusion, delusion, mirage, phantom, ghost, chimera, spectre, wraith. **2** IDEA, ideal, conception, insight, view, picture, image, fantasy, dream, daydream. **3** SIGHT, seeing, eyesight, perception, discernment, far-sightedness, foresight, penetration.

visionary *adj* idealistic, impractical, romantic, dreamy, unrealistic, utopian, unreal, fanciful, prophetic, speculative, unworkable, illusory, imaginary.
n idealist, romantic, dreamer, daydreamer, fantasist, prophet, mystic, seer, utopian, rainbow-chaser, theorist.
≠ pragmatist.

visit *v* call on, call in, stay with, stay at, drop in on (*infml*), stop by (*infml*), look in, look up, pop in (*infml*), see.
n call, stay, stop, excursion, sojourn (*fml*).

visitor *n* caller, guest, company, tourist, holidaymaker.

vista *n* view, prospect, panorama, perspective, outlook, scene.

visualize *v* picture, envisage, imagine, conceive.

vital *adj* **1** CRITICAL, crucial, important, imperative, key, significant, basic, fundamental, essential, necessary, requisite, indispensable, urgent, life-or-death, decisive, forceful. **2** LIVING, alive, lively, life-giving, invigorating, spirited, vivacious, vibrant, vigorous, dynamic, animated, energetic, quickening (*fml*).
≠ **1** inessential, peripheral. **2** dead.

vitality *n* life, liveliness, animation, vigour, energy, vivacity, spirit, sparkle, exuberance, go (*infml*), strength, stamina.

vitamin

Vitamins include: retinol, aneurin (thiamine), riboflavin, pantothenic acid, nicotinic acid (niacin), pyridoxine (adermin), cyanocobalamin, folic acid, pteroic acid, ascorbic acid, calciferol, cholecalciferol, ergocalciferol, toçopherol, linoleic acid, linolenic acid, biotin, phylloquinone, menadione, bioflavonoid/citrin.

vitriolic *adj* bitter, abusive, virulent, vicious, venomous, malicious, caustic, biting, sardonic, scathing, destructive.

vivacious *adj* lively, animated, spirited, high-spirited, effervescent, ebullient, cheerful, sparkling, bubbly, light-hearted.

vivid *adj* **1** BRIGHT, colourful, intense, strong, rich, vibrant, brilliant, glowing, dazzling, vigorous, expressive, dramatic, flamboyant, animated, lively, lifelike, spirited. **2** MEMORABLE, powerful, graphic, clear, distinct, striking, sharp, realistic.
≠ **1** colourless, dull. **2** vague.

vocabulary *n* language, words, glossary, lexicon, dictionary, word-book, thesaurus, idiom.

vocal *adj* **1** SPOKEN, said, oral, uttered, voiced. **2** ARTICULATE, eloquent, expressive, noisy, clamorous, shrill, strident, outspoken, frank, forthright, plain-spoken.
≠ **1** unspoken. **2** inarticulate.

vocation *n* calling, pursuit, career, métier, mission, profession, trade, employment, work, role, post, job, business, office.

vociferous *adj* noisy, vocal, clamorous, loud, obstreperous, strident, vehement, thundering, shouting.
≠ quiet.

vogue *n* fashion, mode, style, craze, popularity, trend, prevalence, acceptance, custom, fad (*infml*), the latest (*infml*), the rage (*infml*), the thing (*infml*).

voice *n* **1** SPEECH, utterance, articulation, language, words, sound, tone, intonation, inflection, expression, mouthpiece, medium, instrument, organ. **2** SAY, vote, opinion, view, decision, option, will.
v express, say, utter, air, articulate, speak of, verbalize, assert, convey, disclose, divulge, declare, enunciate.

void *adj* **1** EMPTY, emptied, free, unfilled, unoccupied, vacant, clear, bare, blank, drained. **2** ANNULLED, inoperative, invalid, cancelled, ineffective, futile, useless, vain, worthless.
≠ **1** full. **2** valid.
n emptiness, vacuity, vacuum, chasm, blank, blankness, space, lack, want, cavity, gap, hollow, opening.

volatile *adj* changeable, inconstant, unstable, variable, erratic, temperamental, unsteady, unsettled, fickle, mercurial, unpredictable, capricious, restless, giddy, flighty, up and down (*infml*), lively.
≠ constant, steady.

volley *n* barrage, bombardment, hail, shower, burst, blast, discharge, explosion.

voluble *adj* fluent, glib, articulate, loquacious (*fml*), talkative, forthcoming, garrulous.

volume *n* **1** BULK, size, capacity, dimensions, amount, mass, quantity, aggregate, amplitude, body. **2** BOOK, tome, publication.

voluminous *adj* roomy, capacious, ample, spacious, billowing, vast, bulky, huge, large.

voluntary *adj* **1** FREE, gratuitous, optional, spontaneous, unforced, willing, unpaid, honorary. **2** CONSCIOUS, deliberate, purposeful, intended, intentional, wilful.
≠ **1** compulsory. **2** involuntary.

volunteer *v* offer, propose, put forward, present, suggest, step forward, advance.

voluptuous *adj* **1** SENSUAL, licentious, luxurious. **2** EROTIC, shapely, sexy (*infml*), seductive, provocative, enticing.

vomit *v* be sick, bring up, heave, retch, throw up (*infml*), puke (*infml*).

vote *n* ballot, poll, election, franchise, referendum.
v elect, ballot, choose, opt, plump for, declare, return.

vouch for guarantee, support, back, endorse, confirm, certify, affirm, assert, attest to, speak for, swear to, uphold.

vow *v* promise, pledge, swear, dedicate, devote, profess, consecrate, affirm.
n promise, oath, pledge.

voyage *n* journey, trip, passage, expedition, crossing.

vulgar *adj* **1** TASTELESS, flashy, gaudy, tawdry, cheap and nasty (*infml*). **2** UNREFINED, uncouth, coarse, common, crude, ill-bred, impolite, indecorous. **3** INDECENT, suggestive, risqué, rude, indelicate. **4** ORDINARY, general, popular, vernacular.
≠ **1** tasteful. **2** correct. **3** decent.

vulnerable *adj* unprotected, exposed, defenceless, susceptible, weak, sensitive, wide open.
≠ protected, strong.

W

wad *n* chunk, plug, roll, ball, wodge (*infml*), lump, hunk, mass, block.

waddle *v* toddle, totter, wobble, sway, rock, shuffle.

waffle *v* jabber, prattle, blather, rabbit on (*infml*), witter on (*infml*).
n blather, prattle, wordiness, padding, nonsense, gobbledegook (*infml*), hot air (*infml*).

waft *v* drift, float, blow, transport, transmit.
n breath, puff, draught, current, breeze, scent, whiff.

wag *v* shake, waggle, wave, sway, swing, bob, nod, wiggle, oscillate, flutter, vibrate, quiver, rock.

wage *n* pay, fee, earnings, salary, wage-packet, payment, stipend, remuneration, emolument (*fml*), allowance, reward, hire, compensation, recompense.
v carry on, conduct, engage in, undertake, practise, pursue.

waif *n* orphan, stray, foundling.

wail *v* moan, cry, howl, lament, weep, complain, yowl (*infml*).
n moan, cry, howl, lament, complaint, weeping.

wait *v* delay, linger, hold back, hesitate, pause, hang around, hang fire, remain, rest, stay.
≠ proceed, go ahead.
n hold-up, hesitation, delay, interval, pause, halt.

waive *v* renounce, relinquish, forgo, resign, surrender, yield.

wake[1] *v* **1** RISE, get up, arise, rouse, came to, bring round. **2** STIMULATE, stir, activate, arouse, animate, excite, fire, galvanize.
≠ **1** sleep.
n funeral, death-watch, vigil, watch.

wake[2] *n* trail, track, path, aftermath, backwash, wash, rear, train, waves.

walk

Ways to describe walking include: amble, crawl, creep, dodder, hike, hobble, limp, lope, lurch, march, mince, mooch (*infml*), pace, pad, paddle, parade, patter, perambulate, plod, potter, promenade, prowl, ramble, saunter, scuttle, shamble, shuffle, slink, stagger, stalk, steal, step, stride, stroll, strut, stumble, swagger, tiptoe, toddle (*infml*), totter, tramp, trample, traipse, tread, trek, trip, troop, trot, trudge, trundle, waddle, wade, wander.

n **1** *he has an odd walk*: carriage, gait, step, pace, stride. **2** *go for a walk*: stroll, amble, ramble, saunter, march, hike, tramp, trek, traipse, trudge, trail. **3** *a tree-lined walk*: footpath, path, walkway, avenue, pathway, promenade, alley, esplanade, lane, pavement, sidewalk.
walk of life field, area, sphere, line, activity, arena, course, pursuit, calling, métier, career, vocation, profession, trade.

walker *n* pedestrian, rambler, hiker.

walk-out *n* strike, stoppage, industrial action, protest, rebellion, revolt.

walk-over *n* pushover (*infml*), doddle (*infml*), child's play, piece of cake (*infml*), cinch (*infml*).

walls

Types of wall and famous walls include: abutment, bailey, barricade, barrier, breeze-block wall, brick wall, bulkhead, bulwark, buttress, cavity wall, curtain wall, dam, dike, divider, embankment, enclosure wall, fence, flying buttress, fortification, garden wall, Great Wall of China, Hadrian's Wall, hedge, inner wall, load-bearing wall, obstacle, outer bailey, paling, palisade, parapet, partition, party wall, retaining wall, screen, sea-wall, shield wall, stockade, stud partition, wall of death.

wallow *v* **1** *wallow in mud*: loll, lie, roll, wade, welter, lurch, flounder, splash. **2** *wallow in nostalgia*: indulge, luxuriate, relish, revel, bask, enjoy, glory, delight.

wand *n* rod, baton, staff, stick, sprig, mace, sceptre, twig.

wander *v* **1** ROAM, rove, ramble, meander, saunter, stroll, prowl, drift, range, stray, straggle. **2** DIGRESS, diverge, deviate, depart, go astray, swerve, veer, err. **3** RAMBLE, rave, babble, gibber.
n excursion, ramble, stroll, saunter, meander, prowl, cruise.

wanderer *n* itinerant, traveller, voyager, drifter, rover, rambler, stroller, stray, straggler, ranger, nomad, gypsy, vagrant, vagabond, rolling stone (*infml*).

wane *v* diminish, decrease, decline, weaken, subside, fade, dwindle, ebb, lessen, abate, sink, drop, taper off, dim, droop, contract, shrink, fail, wither.
≠ increase, wax.

wangle (*infml*) *v* manipulate, arrange, contrive, engineer, fix, scheme, manoeuvre, work, pull off, manage, fiddle (*infml*).

want *v* **1** DESIRE, wish, crave, covet, fancy, long for, pine for, yearn for, hunger for, thirst for.
2 NEED, require, demand, lack, miss, call for.
n **1** DESIRE, demand, longing, requirement, wish, need, appetite.
2 LACK, dearth, insufficiency, deficiency, shortage, inadequacy.
3 POVERTY, privation, destitution.

wanting *adj* **1** ABSENT, missing, lacking, short, insufficient.
2 INADEQUATE, imperfect, faulty, defective, substandard, poor, deficient, unsatisfactory.
≠ **1** sufficient. **2** adequate.

wanton *adj* malicious, immoral, shameless, arbitrary, unprovoked, unjustifiable, unrestrained, rash, reckless, wild.

war *n* warfare, hostilities, fighting, battle, combat, conflict, strife, struggle, bloodshed, contest, contention, enmity.
≠ peace, cease-fire.

Types of war include: ambush, armed conflict, assault, attack, battle, biological warfare, blitz, blitzkrieg, bombardment, chemical warfare, civil war, cold war, counter-attack, engagement, germ warfare, guerrilla warfare, holy war, hot war, invasion, jihad, jungle warfare, limited war, manoeuvres, nuclear war, private war, resistance, skirmish, state of siege, struggle, total war, trade war, war of attrition, war of nerves, world war.
Famous wars include: American Civil War (Second American Revolution), American Revolution (War of Independence), Boer War, Crimean War, Crusades, English Civil War, Falklands War, Franco-Prussian War, Gulf War, Hundred Years' War, Indian Wars, Iran-Iraq War, Korean War, Mexican War, Napoleonic War, Peasants' War, Russo-Finnish War (Winter War), Russo-Japanese War, Russo-Turkish Wars, Seven Years' War, Six-Day War, Spanish-American War, Spanish-American Wars of Independence, Spanish Civil War, Suez Crisis, Thirty Years' War, Vietnam War, War of 1812, War of the Pacific, Wars of the Roses, World War I (the Great War), World War II.

v wage war, fight, take up arms, battle, clash, combat, strive, skirmish, struggle, contest, contend.

ward *n* **1** ROOM, apartment, unit. **2** DIVISION, area, district, quarter, precinct, zone. **3** CHARGE, dependant, protégé(e), minor.
ward off avert, fend off, deflect, parry, repel, stave off, thwart, beat off, forestall, evade, turn away, block, avoid.

warden *n* keeper, custodian, guardian, warder, caretaker, curator, ranger, steward, watchman, superintendent, administrator, janitor.

warder *n* jailer, keeper, prison officer, guard, wardress, custodian.

wardrobe *n* **1** CUPBOARD, closet. **2** CLOTHES, outfit, attire.

warehouse *n* store, storehouse, depot, depository, repository, stockroom, entrepot.

wares *n* goods, merchandise, commodities, stock, products, produce, stuff.

warfare *n* war, fighting, hostilities, battle, arms, combat, strife, struggle, passage of arms, contest, conflict, contention, discord, blows.
≠ peace.

warlike *adj* belligerent, aggressive, bellicose, pugnacious, combative, bloodthirsty, war-mongering, militaristic, hostile, antagonistic, unfriendly.
≠ friendly, peaceable.

warm *adj* **1** HEATED, tepid, lukewarm. **2** ARDENT, passionate, fervent, vehement, earnest, zealous. **3** *warm colours*: rich, intense, mellow, cheerful. **4** FRIENDLY, amiable, cordial, affable, kindly, genial, hearty, hospitable, sympathetic, affectionate, tender. **5** FINE, sunny, balmy, temperate, close.
≠ **1** cool. **2** indifferent. **3** cold. **4** unfriendly. **5** cool.
v **1** HEAT (UP), reheat, melt, thaw. **2** ANIMATE, interest, please, delight, stimulate, stir, rouse, excite.
≠ **1** cool.

warmth *n* **1** WARMNESS, heat. **2** FRIENDLINESS, affection, cordiality, tenderness. **3** ARDOUR, enthusiasm, passion, fervour, zeal, eagerness.
≠ **1** coldness. **2** unfriendliness. **3** indifference.

warn *v* caution, alert, admonish, advise, notify, counsel, put on one's guard, inform, tip off (*infml*).

warning *n* **1** CAUTION, alert, admonition, advice, notification, notice, advance notice, counsel, hint, lesson, alarm, threat, tip-off (*infml*). **2** OMEN, augury, premonition, presage, sign, signal, portent.

warp *v* twist, bend, contort, deform, distort, kink, misshape, pervert, corrupt, deviate.
≠ straighten.
n twist, bend, contortion, deformation, distortion, bias, kink, irregularity, turn, bent, defect, deviation, quirk, perversion.

warrant *n* authorization, authority, sanction, permit, permission, licence, guarantee, warranty, security, pledge, commission, voucher.
v **1** GUARANTEE, pledge, certify, assure, declare, affirm, vouch for, answer for, underwrite, uphold, endorse. **2** AUTHORIZE, entitle, empower, sanction, permit, allow, license, justify, excuse, approve, call for, commission, necessitate, require.

wary *adj* cautious, guarded, careful, chary, on one's guard, on the lookout, prudent, distrustful, suspicious, heedful, attentive, alert, watchful, vigilant, wide-awake.
≠ unwary, careless, heedless.

wash *v* **1** CLEAN, cleanse, launder, scrub, swab down, rinse, swill. **2** BATHE, bath, shower, douche, shampoo.
n **1** CLEANING, cleansing, bath, bathe, laundry, laundering, scrub, shower, shampoo, washing, rinse. **2** FLOW, sweep, wave, swell.

wash-out (*infml*) *n* failure, disaster, disappointment, fiasco, flop (*infml*), debacle.
≠ success, triumph.

waste *v* **1** SQUANDER, misspend, misuse, fritter away, dissipate, lavish, spend, throw away, blow (*infml*). **2** CONSUME, erode, exhaust, drain, destroy, spoil.
≠ **1** economize. **2** preserve.
n **1** SQUANDERING, dissipation, prodigality, wastefulness, extravagance, loss. **2** MISAPPLICATION, misuse, abuse, neglect. **3** RUBBISH, refuse, trash, garbage, leftovers, debris, dregs, effluent, litter, scrap, slops, offscouring(s), dross.
adj **1** USELESS, worthless, unwanted, unused, left-over, superfluous, supernumerary, extra. **2** BARREN, desolate, empty, uninhabited, bare, devastated, uncultivated, unprofitable, wild, dismal, dreary.

wasted *adj* **1** UNNECESSARY, needless,

useless. **2** EMACIATED, withered, shrivelled, shrunken, gaunt, washed-out, spent.
≠ **1** necessary. **2** robust.

wasteful *adj* extravagant, spendthrift, prodigal, profligate, uneconomical, thriftless, unthrifty, ruinous, lavish, improvident.
≠ economical, thrifty.

wasteland *n* wilderness, desert, barrenness, waste, wild(s), void.

watch *v* **1** OBSERVE, see, look at, regard, note, notice, mark, stare at, peer at, gaze at, view. **2** GUARD, look after, keep an eye on, mind, protect, superintend, take care of, keep. **3** PAY ATTENTION, be careful, take heed, look out.
n **1** TIMEPIECE, wristwatch, clock, chronometer. **2** VIGILANCE, watchfulness, vigil, observation, surveillance, notice, lookout, attention, heed, alertness, inspection, supervision.
watch out notice, be vigilant, look out, keep one's eyes open.
watch over guard, protect, stand guard over, keep an eye on, look after, mind, shield, defend, shelter, preserve.

watchdog *n* **1** GUARD DOG, house-dog. **2** MONITOR, inspector, scrutineer, vigilante, ombudsman, guardian, custodian, protector.

watcher *n* spectator, observer, onlooker, looker-on, viewer, lookout, spy, witness.

watchful *adj* vigilant, attentive, heedful, observant, alert, guarded, on one's guard, wide awake, suspicious, wary, chary, cautious.
≠ unobservant, inattentive.

watchman *n* guard, security guard, caretaker, custodian.

water *n* rain, sea, ocean, lake, river, stream.
v wet, moisten, dampen, soak, spray, sprinkle, irrigate, drench, flood, hose.
≠ dry out, parch.
water down dilute, thin, water, weaken, adulterate, mix, tone down, soften, qualify.

waterfall *n* fall, cascade, chute, cataract, torrent.

watertight *adj* **1** WATERPROOF, sound, hermetic. **2** IMPREGNABLE, unassailable, airtight, flawless, foolproof, firm, incontrovertible.
≠ **1** leaky.

watery *adj* **1** LIQUID, fluid, moist, wet, damp. **2** WEAK, watered-down, diluted, insipid, tasteless, thin, runny, soggy, flavourless, washy, wishy-washy (*infml*).
≠ **1** dry.

wave *v* **1** BECKON, gesture, gesticulate, indicate, sign, signal, direct. **2** BRANDISH, flourish, flap, flutter, shake, sway, swing, waft, quiver, ripple.
n **1** BREAKER, roller, billow, ripple, tidal wave, wavelet, undulation, white horse (*infml*). **2** SURGE, sweep, swell, upsurge, ground swell, current, drift, movement, rush, tendency, trend, stream, flood, outbreak, rash.

waver *v* **1** VACILLATE, falter, hesitate, dither, fluctuate, vary, seesaw. **2** OSCILLATE, shake, sway, wobble, tremble, totter, rock.
≠ **1** decide.

wavy *adj* undulating, rippled, curly, curvy, ridged, sinuous, winding, zigzag.

wax *v* grow, increase, rise, swell, develop, enlarge, expand, magnify, mount, fill out, become.
≠ decrease, wane.

way *n* **1** METHOD, approach, manner, technique, procedure, means, mode, system, fashion. **2** CUSTOM, practice, habit, usage, characteristic, idiosyncrasy, trait, style, conduct, nature. **3** DIRECTION, course, route, path, road, channel, access, avenue, track, passage, highway, street, thoroughfare, lane.
by the way incidentally, in passing.

wayward *adj* wilful, capricious, perverse, contrary, changeable, fickle, unpredictable, stubborn, self-willed, unmanageable, headstrong, obstinate, disobedient, rebellious, insubordinate, intractable, unruly, incorrigible.
≠ tractable, good-natured.

weak *adj* **1** FEEBLE, frail, infirm,

unhealthy, sickly, delicate, debilitated, exhausted, fragile, flimsy. **2** VULNERABLE, unprotected, unguarded, defenceless, exposed. **3** POWERLESS, impotent, spineless, cowardly, indecisive, ineffectual, irresolute, poor, lacking, lame, inadequate, defective, deficient, inconclusive, unconvincing, untenable. **4** FAINT, slight, low, soft, muffled, dull, imperceptible. **5** INSIPID, tasteless, watery, thin, diluted, runny.
≠ **1** strong. **2** secure. **3** powerful. **4** strong. **5** strong.

weaken *v* **1** ENFEEBLE, exhaust, debilitate, sap, undermine, dilute, diminish, lower, lessen, reduce, moderate, mitigate, temper, soften (up), thin, water down. **2** TIRE, flag, fail, give way, droop, fade, abate, ease up, dwindle.
≠ **1** strengthen.

weakness *n* **1** FEEBLENESS, debility, infirmity, impotence, frailty, powerlessness, vulnerability. **2** FAULT, failing, flaw, shortcoming, blemish, defect, deficiency, foible. **3** LIKING, inclination, fondness, penchant, passion, soft spot (*infml*).
≠ **1** strength. **2** strength. **3** dislike.

wealth *n* **1** MONEY, cash, riches, assets, affluence, prosperity, funds, mammon, fortune, capital, opulence, means, substance, resources, goods, possessions, property, estate. **2** ABUNDANCE, plenty, bounty, fullness, profusion, store.
≠ **1** poverty.

wealthy *adj* rich, prosperous, affluent, well-off, moneyed, opulent, comfortable, well-heeled, well-to-do, flush (*infml*), loaded (*sl*), rolling in it (*infml*).
≠ poor, impoverished.

weapon

Weapons include: gun, airgun, pistol, revolver, automatic, Colt®, Luger®, magnum, Mauser, six-gun, six-shooter, rifle, air rifle, Winchester® rifle, carbine, shotgun, blunderbuss, musket, elephant gun, machine-gun, kalashnikov, submachine-gun, Uzi, tommy-gun, sten gun, Bren gun, cannon, field gun, gatling-gun, howitzer, mortar, turret-gun; knife, bowie knife, flick-knife, stiletto, dagger, dirk, poniard, sword, épée, foil, rapier, sabre, scimitar, bayonet, broadsword, claymore, lance, spear, pike, machete; bomb, atom bomb, H-bomb, cluster-bomb, depth-charge, incendiary bomb, Mills bomb, mine, land-mine, napalm bomb, time-bomb; bow and arrow, longbow, crossbow, blowpipe, catapult, boomerang, sling, harpoon, bolas, rocket, bazooka, ballistic missile, Cruise missile, Exocet®, Scud (*infml*), torpedo, hand grenade, flame-thrower; battleaxe, pole-axe, halberd, tomahawk, cosh, cudgel, knuckleduster, shillelagh, truncheon; gas, CS gas, mustard gas, tear-gas.

wear *v* **1** DRESS IN, have on, put on, don, sport, carry, bear, display, show. **2** DETERIORATE, erode, corrode, consume, fray, rub, abrade, waste, grind.
n **1** CLOTHES, clothing, dress, garments, outfit, costume, attire. **2** DETERIORATION, erosion, corrosion, wear and tear, friction, abrasion.
wear off decrease, abate, dwindle, diminish, subside, wane, weaken, fade, lessen, ebb, peter out, disappear.
≠ increase.
wear out 1 EXHAUST, fatigue, tire (out), enervate, sap. **2** DETERIORATE, wear through, erode, impair, consume, fray.

wearing *adj* exhausting, fatiguing, tiresome, tiring, wearisome, trying, taxing, oppressive, irksome, exasperating.
≠ refreshing.

weary *adj* tired, exhausted, fatigued, sleepy, worn out, drained, drowsy, jaded, all in (*infml*), done in (*infml*), fagged out (*infml*), knackered (*infml*), dead beat (*infml*), dog-tired (*infml*), whacked (*infml*).
≠ refreshed.

wearying *adj* tiring, fatiguing, exhausting, wearisome, wearing, taxing, trying.
≠ refreshing.

weather *n* climate, conditions, temperature.

Types of weather include: breeze, wind, squall, gale, hurricane, tornado, typhoon, monsoon, cyclone, whirlwind, chinook, mistral, cloud, mist, dew, fog, smog, rain, drizzle, shower, deluge, downpour, rainbow, sunshine, heatwave, haze, drought, storm, tempest, thunder, lightning, frost, hoar frost, hail, sleet, snow, snowstorm, ice, black ice, thaw, slush. *see also* **precipitation**; **wind**.

v **1** ENDURE, survive, live through, come through, ride out, rise above, stick out, withstand, surmount, stand, brave, overcome, resist, pull through, suffer. **2** EXPOSE, toughen, season, harden.
≠ **1** succumb.

weave *v* **1** INTERLACE, lace, plait, braid, intertwine, spin, knit, entwine, intercross, fuse, merge, unite. **2** CREATE, compose, construct, contrive, put together, fabricate. **3** WIND, twist, zigzag, criss-cross.

web *n* network, net, netting, lattice, mesh, webbing, interlacing, weft, snare, tangle, trap.

wedding *n* marriage, matrimony, nuptials (*fml*), wedlock, bridal.
≠ divorce.

wedge *n* lump, block, chunk, wodge, chock.
v jam, cram, pack, ram, squeeze, stuff, push, lodge, block, thrust, crowd, force.

weeds

Weeds include: annual nettle, bindweed, birdsfoot trefoil, bracken, broad-leaved dock, burnet saxifrage, Canadian pondweed, chickweed, cinquefoil, coltsfoot, common burdock, common chickweed, common persicaria, common plantain, common reed, couch grass, creeping buttercup, creeping thistle, creeping yellow cress, curled dock, daisy, dandelion, deadnettle, dock, duckweed, fat hen, field wood rush, greater or rat-tailed plantain, ground elder, ground ivy, groundsel, hairy bittercress, horsetail, Japanese knotgrass, knapweed, knotgrass, large bindweed, lesser celandine, lesser yellow trefoil, liverwort, meadow grass, mind your own business, moss, mouse-ear chickweed, oxalis, pearlwort, perennial nettle, perennial oat-grass, petty spurge, pineapple weed, ragweed, ribwort, rough hawkbit, salad burnet, self-heal, shepherd's purse, sheep's sorrel, small bindweed, snakeweed, sow thistle, speedwell, spurge, stemless thistle, sun spurge, thale cress, vetch, white clover, yarrow. *see also* **wild flowers**.

weedy (*infml*) *adj* thin, skinny, puny, scrawny, undersized, weak, feeble, frail, weak-kneed, insipid, wet (*infml*), wimpish (*infml*).
≠ strong.

weep *v* cry, sob, moan, lament, wail, mourn, grieve, bawl, blubber, snivel, whimper, blub (*infml*).
≠ rejoice.

weigh *v* **1** BEAR DOWN, oppress. **2** CONSIDER, contemplate, evaluate, meditate on, mull over, ponder, think over, examine, reflect on, deliberate.
weigh down oppress, overload, load, burden, bear down, weigh upon, press down, get down (*infml*), depress, afflict, trouble, worry.
≠ lighten, hearten.
weigh up assess, examine, size up, balance, consider, contemplate, deliberate, mull over, ponder, think over, discuss, chew over (*infml*).

weight *n* **1** HEAVINESS, gravity, burden, load, pressure, mass, force, ballast, tonnage, poundage. **2** IMPORTANCE, significance, substance, consequence, impact, moment, influence, value, authority, clout (*infml*), power, preponderance, consideration.
≠ **1** lightness.
v **1** LOAD, weigh down, oppress, handicap. **2** BIAS, unbalance, slant, prejudice.

weighty *adj* **1** HEAVY, burdensome, substantial, bulky. **2** IMPORTANT,

significant, consequential, crucial, critical, momentous, serious, grave, solemn. **3** DEMANDING, difficult, exacting, taxing.
≠ **1** light. **2** unimportant.

weird *adj* strange, uncanny, bizarre, eerie, creepy, supernatural, unnatural, ghostly, freakish, mysterious, queer, grotesque, spooky (*infml*), far-out (*infml*), way-out (*infml*).
≠ normal, usual.

welcome *adj* acceptable, desirable, pleasing, pleasant, agreeable, gratifying, appreciated, delightful, refreshing.
≠ unwelcome.
n reception, greeting, salutation (*infml*), acceptance, hospitality, red carpet (*infml*).
v greet, hail, receive, salute, meet, accept, approve of, embrace.
≠ reject, snub.

weld *v* fuse, unite, bond, join, solder, bind, connect, seal, link, cement.
≠ separate.

welfare *n* well-being, health, prosperity, happiness, benefit, good, advantage, interest, profit, success.

well[1] *n* spring, well-spring, fountain, fount, source, reservoir, well-head.

> *Types of well include*: artesian well, borehole, draw-well, gas well, geyser, gusher, hot spring, inkwell, lift-shaft, mineral spring, oil-well, pump-well, stairwell, thermal spring, waterhole, wishing-well.

v flow, spring, surge, gush, stream, brim over, jet, spout, spurt, swell, pour, flood, ooze, run, trickle, rise, seep.

well[2] *adv* rightly, correctly, properly, skilfully, ably, expertly, successfully, adequately, sufficiently, suitably, easily, satisfactorily, thoroughly, greatly, fully, considerably, completely, agreeably, pleasantly, happily, kindly, favourably, splendidly, substantially, comfortably, readily, carefully, clearly, highly, deeply, justly.
≠ badly, inadequately, incompetently, wrongly.
adj **1** HEALTHY, in good health, fit, able-bodied, sound, robust, strong, thriving, flourishing. **2** SATISFACTORY, right, all right, good, pleasing, proper, agreeable, fine, lucky, fortunate.
≠ **1** ill. **2** bad.

well-balanced *adj* **1** RATIONAL, reasonable, level-headed, well-adjusted, stable, sensible, sane, sound, sober, together (*sl*). **2** SYMMETRICAL, even, harmonious.
≠ **1** unbalanced. **2** asymmetrical.

well-being *n* welfare, happiness, comfort, good.

well-bred *adj* well-mannered, polite, well-brought-up, mannerly, courteous, civil, refined, cultivated, cultured, genteel.
≠ ill-bred.

well-dressed *adj* smart, well-groomed, elegant, fashionable, chic, stylish, neat, trim, spruce, tidy.
≠ badly dressed, scruffy.

well-known *adj* famous, renowned, celebrated, famed, eminent, notable, noted, illustrious, familiar.
≠ unknown.

well-off *adj* rich, wealthy, affluent, prosperous, well-to-do, moneyed, thriving, successful, comfortable, fortunate.
≠ poor, badly-off.

well-thought-of *adj* respected, highly regarded, esteemed, admired, honoured, revered.
≠ despised.

well-worn *adj* timeworn, stale, tired, trite, overused, unoriginal, hackneyed, commonplace, stereotyped, threadbare, corny (*infml*).
≠ original.

wet *adj* **1** DAMP, moist, soaked, soaking, sodden, saturated, soggy, sopping, watery, waterlogged, drenched, dripping, spongy, dank, clammy. **2** RAINING, rainy, showery, teeming, pouring, drizzling, humid. **3** (*infml*) WEAK, feeble, weedy, wimpish (*infml*), spineless, soft, ineffectual, namby-pamby, irresolute, timorous.
≠ **1** dry. **2** dry. **3** strong.
n wetness, moisture, damp, dampness,

liquid, water, clamminess, condensation, humidity, rain, drizzle.
≠ dryness.
v moisten, damp, dampen, soak, saturate, drench, steep, water, irrigate, spray, splash, sprinkle, imbue, dip.
≠ dry.

whack *v* hit, strike, smack, thrash, slap, beat, bash (*infml*), bang, cuff, thump, box, buffet, rap, wallop (*infml*), belt (*infml*), clobber (*infml*), clout (*infml*), sock (*infml*).
n smack, slap, blow, hit, rap, stroke, thump, cuff, box, bang, clout (*infml*), bash (*infml*), wallop (*infml*).

wharf *n* dock, quay, quayside, jetty, landing-stage, dockyard, marina, pier.

wheedle *v* cajole, coax, persuade, inveigle, charm, flatter, entice, court, draw.
≠ force.

wheel *n* turn, revolution, circle, rotation, gyration, pivot, roll, spin, twirl, whirl.

> *Types of wheel include*: balance-wheel, big wheel, buff-wheel, cartwheel, castor, Catherine wheel, charka, cogwheel, crown-wheel, drive-wheel, escape wheel, Ferris wheel, flywheel, gearwheel, idle wheel, mill wheel, paddle wheel, potter's wheel, prayer wheel, ratchet-wheel, roulette wheel, spinning-jenny, spinning-wheel, sprocket, spur gear, steering-wheel, wagon wheel, water-wheel, wheel of fortune, worm wheel.

v turn, rotate, circle, gyrate, orbit, spin, twirl, whirl, swing, roll, revolve, swivel.

wheeze *v* pant, gasp, cough, hiss, rasp, whistle.

whereabouts *n* location, position, place, situation, site, vicinity.

whet *v* **1** SHARPEN, hone, file, grind. **2** STIMULATE, stir, rouse, arouse, provoke, kindle, quicken, incite, awaken, increase.
≠ **1** blunt. **2** dampen.

whiff *n* breath, puff, hint, trace, blast, draught, odour, smell, aroma, sniff, scent, reek, stink, stench.

whim *n* fancy, caprice, notion, quirk, freak, humour, conceit, fad, vagary, urge.

whimper *v* cry, sob, weep, snivel, whine, grizzle, mewl, moan, whinge (*infml*).
n sob, snivel, whine, moan.

whimsical *adj* fanciful, capricious, playful, impulsive, eccentric, funny, droll, curious, queer, unusual, weird, odd, peculiar, quaint, dotty (*infml*).

whine *n* **1** CRY, sob, whimper, moan, wail. **2** COMPLAINT, grumble, grouse, gripe (*infml*), grouch (*infml*).
v **1** CRY, sob, whimper, grizzle, moan, wail. **2** COMPLAIN, carp, grumble, whinge (*infml*), gripe (*infml*), grouch (*infml*).

whip *v* **1** BEAT, flog, lash, flagellate, scourge, birch, cane, strap, thrash, punish, chastise, discipline, castigate (*fml*). **2** PULL, jerk, snatch, whisk, dash, dart, rush, tear, flit, flash, fly. **3** GOAD, drive, spur, push, urge, stir, rouse, agitate, incite, provoke, instigate.
n lash, scourge, switch, birch, cane, horsewhip, riding-crop, cat-o'-nine-tails.

whirl *v* swirl, spin, turn, twist, twirl, pivot, pirouette, swivel, wheel, rotate, revolve, reel, roll, gyrate, circle.
n **1** SPIN, twirl, twist, gyration, revolution, pirouette, swirl, turn, wheel, rotation, circle, reel, roll. **2** CONFUSION, daze, flurry, commotion, agitation, bustle, hubbub, hurly-burly, giddiness, tumult, uproar.

whirlwind *n* tornado, cyclone, vortex.
adj hasty, impulsive, quick, rapid, speedy, swift, lightning, headlong, impetuous, rash.
≠ deliberate, slow.

whisk *v* **1** WHIP, beat. **2** DART, dash, rush, hurry, speed, hasten, race. **3** BRUSH, sweep, flick, wipe, twitch.

whisper *v* **1** MURMUR, mutter, mumble, breathe, hiss, rustle, sigh. **2** HINT, intimate, insinuate, gossip, divulge.
≠ **1** shout.

n **1** MURMUR, undertone, sigh, hiss, rustle. **2** HINT, suggestion, suspicion, breath, whiff, rumour, report, innuendo, insinuation, trace, tinge, soupçon, buzz.

white *adj* **1** PALE, pallid, wan, ashen, colourless, anaemic, pasty. **2** LIGHT, snowy, milky, creamy, ivory, hoary, silver, grey. **3** PURE, immaculate, spotless, stainless, undefiled.
≠ **1** ruddy. **2** dark. **3** defiled.

whiten *v* bleach, blanch, whitewash, pale, fade.
≠ blacken, darken.

whittle *v* **1** CARVE, cut, scrape, shave, trim, pare, hew, shape. **2** ERODE, eat away, wear away, diminish, consume, reduce, undermine.

whole *adj* **1** COMPLETE, entire, integral, full, total, unabridged, uncut, undivided, unedited. **2** INTACT, unharmed, undamaged, unbroken, inviolate, perfect, in one piece, mint, unhurt. **3** WELL, healthy, fit, sound, strong.
≠ **1** partial. **2** damaged. **3** ill.
n total, aggregate, sum total, entirety, all, fullness, totality, ensemble, entity, unit, lot, piece, everything.
≠ part.
on the whole generally, mostly, in general, generally speaking, as a rule, for the most part, all in all, all things considered, by and large.

whole-hearted *adj* unreserved, unstinting, unqualified, passionate, enthusiastic, earnest, committed, dedicated, devoted, heartfelt, emphatic, warm, sincere, unfeigned, genuine, complete, true, real, zealous.
≠ half-hearted.

wholesale *adj* comprehensive, far-reaching, extensive, sweeping, wide-ranging, mass, broad, outright, total, massive, indiscriminate.
≠ partial.

wholesome *adj* **1** *wholesome food*: healthy, hygienic, salubrious, sanitary, nutritious, nourishing, beneficial, salutary, invigorating, bracing. **2** *wholesome entertainment*: moral, decent, clean, proper, improving, edifying, uplifting, pure, virtuous, righteous, honourable, respectable.
≠ **1** unhealthy. **2** unwholesome.

wholly *adv* completely, entirely, fully, purely, absolutely, totally, utterly, comprehensively, altogether, perfectly, thoroughly, all, exclusively, only.
≠ partly.

wicked *adj* **1** EVIL, sinful, immoral, depraved, corrupt, vicious, unprincipled, iniquitous, heinous, debased, abominable, ungodly, unrighteous, shameful. **2** BAD, unpleasant, harmful, offensive, vile, worthless, difficult, dreadful, distressing, awful, atrocious, severe, intense, nasty, injurious, troublesome, terrible, foul, fierce. **3** NAUGHTY, mischievous, roguish.
≠ **1** good, upright. **2** harmless.

wide *adj* **1** BROAD, roomy, spacious, vast, immense. **2** DILATED, expanded, full. **3** EXTENSIVE, wide-ranging, comprehensive, far-reaching, general. **4** LOOSE, baggy. **5** OFF-TARGET, distant, remote.
≠ **1** narrow. **3** restricted. **5** near.
adv **1** ASTRAY, off course, off target, off the mark. **2** FULLY, completely, all the way.
≠ **1** on target.

widen *v* distend, dilate, expand, extend, spread, stretch, enlarge, broaden.
≠ narrow.

widespread *adj* extensive, prevalent, rife, general, sweeping, universal, wholesale, far-reaching, unlimited, broad, common, pervasive, far-flung.
≠ limited.

width *n* breadth, diameter, wideness, compass, thickness, span, scope, range, measure, girth, beam, amplitude, extent, reach.

wield *v* **1** *wield a weapon*: brandish, flourish, swing, wave, handle, ply, manage, manipulate. **2** *wield power*: have, hold, possess, employ, exert, exercise, use, utilize, maintain, command.

wife *n* partner, spouse, mate, better half, bride.

wild *adj* **1** UNTAMED, undomesticated,

feral, savage, barbarous, primitive, uncivilized, natural, ferocious, fierce. **2** UNCULTIVATED, desolate, waste, uninhabited. **3** unrestrained, unruly, unmanageable, violent, turbulent, rowdy, lawless, disorderly, riotous, boisterous. **4** STORMY, tempestuous, rough, blustery, choppy. **5** UNTIDY, unkempt, messy, dishevelled, tousled. **6** RECKLESS, rash, imprudent, foolish, foolhardy, impracticable, irrational, outrageous, preposterous, wayward, extravagant. **7** MAD, crazy (*infml*), frenzied, distraught, demented.
≠ **1** civilized, tame. **2** cultivated. **3** restrained. **4** calm. **5** tidy. **6** sensible. **7** sane.

wilderness *n* desert, wasteland, waste, wilds, jungle.

wild flowers

Wild flowers include: Aaron's rod, ale hoof, bird's foot trefoil, birthwort, bistort, black-eyed susan, bladder campion, bluebell, broomrape, butter-and-eggs, buttercup, campion, celandine, clary, clustered bellflower, clover, columbine, comfrey, common evening-primrose, common mallow, common toadflax, cowslip, crane's bill, crowfoot, cuckoo flower, daisy, edelweiss, field cow-wheat, foxglove, goatsbeard, goldcup, goldenrod, great mullein, harebell, heartsease, heather, horsetail, lady's slipper, lady's smock, lungwort, marguerite, masterwort, moneywort, multiflora rose, New England aster, oxeye daisy, oxslip, pennyroyal, poppy, primrose, ragged robin, rock rose, rough-fruited cinquefoil, self-heal, shepherd's club, solomon's seal, stiff-haired sunflower, stonecrop, teasel, toadflax, violet, water lily, white campion, wild chicory, wild endive, wild gladiolus, wild iris, wild orchid, wild pansy, wood anemone, yarrow, yellow rocket. *see also* **weed**.

wiles *n* trick, stratagem, ruse, ploy, device, contrivance, guile, manoeuvre, subterfuge, cunning, dodge (*infml*), deceit, cheating, trickery, fraud, craftiness, chicanery.
≠ guilelessness.

wilful *adj* **1** DELIBERATE, conscious, intentional, voluntary, premeditated. **2** SELF-WILLED, obstinate, stubborn, pig-headed, obdurate, intransigent, inflexible, perverse, wayward, contrary.
≠ **1** unintentional. **2** good-natured.

will *n* **1** VOLITION, choice, option, preference, decision, discretion. **2** WISH, desire, inclination, feeling, fancy, disposition, mind. **3** PURPOSE, resolve, resolution, determination, will-power, aim, intention, command.
v **1** WANT, desire, choose, compel, command, decree, order, ordain. **2** BEQUEATH, leave, hand down, pass on, transfer, confer, dispose of.

willing *adj* disposed, inclined, agreeable, compliant, ready, prepared, consenting, content, amenable, biddable, pleased, well-disposed, favourable, happy, eager, enthusiastic.
≠ unwilling, disinclined, reluctant.

wilt *v* droop, sag, wither, shrivel, flop, flag, dwindle, weaken, diminish, fail, fade, languish, ebb, sink, wane.
≠ perk up.

wily *adj* shrewd, cunning, scheming, artful, crafty, foxy, intriguing, tricky, underhand, shifty, deceitful, deceptive, astute, sly, guileful, designing, crooked, fly (*infml*).
≠ guileless.

win *v* **1** BE VICTORIOUS, triumph, succeed, prevail, overcome, conquer, come first, carry off, finish first. **2** GAIN, acquire, achieve, attain, accomplish, receive, procure, secure, obtain, get, earn, catch, net.
≠ **1** fail, lose.
n victory, triumph, conquest, success, mastery.
≠ defeat.
win over persuade, prevail upon, convince, influence, convert, sway, talk round, charm, allure, attract.

wind[1] *n* air, breeze, draught, gust, puff, breath, air-current, blast, current, bluster, gale, hurricane, tornado.

Types of wind include: anticyclone, austral wind, berg wind, bise, bora, Cape doctor, chinook, cyclone, doctor, east wind, El Niño, etesian, Favonian wind, föhn, gregale, harmattan, helm wind, khamsin, levant, libeccio, meltemi, mistral, monsoon, north wind, nor'wester, pampero, prevailing wind, samiel, simoom, sirocco, snow eater, southerly, southerly buster, trade wind, tramontana, westerly, wet chinook, williwaw, willy-willy, zephyr, zonda.

wind[2] *v* coil, twist, turn, curl, curve, bend, loop, spiral, zigzag, twine, encircle, furl, deviate, meander, ramble, wreath, roll, reel.

wind down 1 SLOW (DOWN), slacken off, lessen, reduce, subside, diminish, dwindle, decline. **2** RELAX, unwind, quieten down, ease up, calm down.
≠ **1** increase.

wind up 1 CLOSE (DOWN), end, conclude, terminate, finalize, finish, liquidate. **2** END UP, finish up, find oneself, settle. **3** (*infml*) ANNOY, irritate, disconcert, fool, trick, kid (*infml*).
≠ **1** begin.

windfall *n* bonanza, godsend, jackpot, treasure-trove, stroke of luck, find.

window *n* pane, light, opening.

Types of window include: bay, bow, bull's eye, casement, Catherine wheel, compass, decorated, dormer, double-glazed, double-glazing, early English, fanlight, French, lancet, louvre window, lucarne, mullioned window, Norman, oeil-de-boeuf, oriel, patio door, perpendicular, porthole, quarterlight, rose window, sash, secondary-glazed, shop window, skylight, sliding window, stained glass window, ticket window, windscreen, windowpane.

windy *adj* breezy, blowy, blustery, squally, windswept, stormy, tempestuous, gusty.
≠ calm.

wine

Types of wine include: alcohol-free, dry, brut, sec, demi-sec, sweet, sparkling, table wine, house wine, red wine, house red (*infml*), white wine, house white (*infml*), rosé, blush wine, fortified wine, mulled wine, tonic wine, vintage wine, plonk (*infml*); sherry, dry sherry, fino, medium sherry, amontillado, sweet sherry, oloroso; port, ruby, tawny, white port, vintage port. *Varieties of wine include*: Alsace, Asti, Auslese, Beaujolais, Beaujolais Nouveau, Beaune, Bordeaux, Burgundy, cabernet sauvignon, Chablis, Chambertin, champagne, Chardonnay, Chianti, claret, Côtes du Rhône, Dao, Douro, Frascati, Graves, hock, Lambrusco, Liebfraumilch, Mâcon, Madeira, Malaga, Marsala, Mateus Rosé, Médoc, Merlot, moselle, Muscadet, muscatel, Niersteiner, retsina, Riesling, Rioja, Sauterne, Sekt, Soave, Spätlese, Tarragona, Valpolicella, vinho verde.

wine-bottle sizes

Sizes of wine-bottles include: magnum, flagon, jeroboam, methuselah, rehoboam, salmanazar, balthazar, nebuchadnezzar.

wing *n* branch, arm, section, faction, group, grouping, flank, circle, coterie, set, segment, side, annexe, adjunct, extension.

wink *v* blink, flutter, glimmer, glint, twinkle, gleam, sparkle, flicker, flash.
n **1** BLINK, flutter, sparkle, twinkle, glimmering, gleam, glint. **2** INSTANT, second, split second, flash.

winner *n* champion, victor, prizewinner, medallist, title-holder, world-beater, conqueror.
≠ loser.

winning *adj* **1** CONQUERING, triumphant, unbeaten, undefeated, victorious, successful. **2** WINSOME, charming, attractive, captivating, engaging, fetching, enchanting, endearing, delightful, amiable, alluring, lovely, pleasing, sweet.
≠ **1** losing. **2** unappealing.

winnow *v* sift, separate, screen, divide, cull, select, part, fan.

wintry *adj* cold, chilly, bleak, cheerless, desolate, dismal, harsh, snowy, frosty, freezing, frozen, icy.

wipe *v* **1** RUB, clean, dry, dust, brush, mop, swab, sponge, clear. **2** REMOVE, erase, take away, take off.
wipe out eradicate, obliterate, destroy, massacre, exterminate, annihilate, erase, expunge, raze, abolish, blot out, efface.

wiry *adj* muscular, sinewy, lean, tough, strong.
≠ puny.

wisdom *n* discernment, penetration, sagacity, reason, sense, astuteness, comprehension, enlightenment, judgement, judiciousness, understanding, knowledge, learning, intelligence, erudition, foresight, prudence.
≠ folly, stupidity.

wise *adj* **1** DISCERNING, sagacious, perceptive, rational, informed, well-informed, understanding, erudite, enlightened, knowing, intelligent, clever, aware, experienced. **2** WELL-ADVISED, judicious, prudent, reasonable, sensible, sound, long-sighted, shrewd.
≠ **1** foolish, stupid. **2** ill-advised.

wish *v* **1** DESIRE, want, yearn, long, hanker, covet, crave, aspire, hope, hunger, thirst, prefer, need. **2** ASK, bid, require, order, instruct, direct, command.
n **1** DESIRE, want, hankering, aspiration, inclination, hunger, thirst, liking, preference, yearning, urge, whim, hope. **2** REQUEST, bidding, order, command, will.

wisp *n* shred, strand, thread, twist, piece, lock.

wispy *adj* thin, straggly, frail, fine, attenuated, insubstantial, light, flimsy, fragile, delicate, ethereal, gossamer, faint.
≠ substantial.

wistful *adj* **1** THOUGHTFUL, pensive, musing, reflective, wishful, contemplative, dreamy, dreaming, meditative. **2** MELANCHOLY, sad, forlorn, disconsolate, longing, mournful.

wit *n* **1** HUMOUR, repartee, facetiousness, drollery, banter, jocularity, levity. **2** INTELLIGENCE, cleverness, brains, sense, reason, common sense, wisdom, understanding, judgement, insight, intellect. **3** HUMORIST, comedian, comic, satirist, joker, wag.
≠ **1** seriousness. **2** stupidity.

witch *n* sorceress, enchantress, occultist, magician, hag.

witchcraft *n* sorcery, magic, wizardry, occultism, the occult, the black art, black magic, enchantment, necromancy, voodoo, spell, incantation, divination, conjuration.

withdraw *v* **1** RECOIL, shrink back, draw back, pull back. **2** RECANT, disclaim, take back, revoke, rescind, retract, cancel, abjure, recall, take away. **3** DEPART, go (away), absent oneself, retire, remove, leave, back out, fall back, drop out, retreat, secede. **4** DRAW OUT, extract, pull out.

withdrawal *n* **1** REPUDIATION, recantation, disclaimer, disavowal, revocation, recall, secession, abjuration. **2** DEPARTURE, exit, exodus, retirement, retreat. **3** EXTRACTION, removal.

withdrawn *adj* **1** RESERVED, unsociable, shy, introvert, quiet, retiring, aloof, detached, shrinking, uncommunicative, unforthcoming, taciturn, silent. **2** REMOTE, isolated, distant, secluded, out-of-the-way, private, hidden, solitary.
≠ **1** extrovert, outgoing.

wither *v* shrink, shrivel, dry, wilt, droop, decay, disintegrate, wane, perish, fade, languish, decline, waste.
≠ flourish, thrive.

withering *adj* **1** DESTRUCTIVE, deadly, death-dealing, devastating. **2** SCORNFUL, contemptuous, scathing, snubbing, humiliating, mortifying, wounding.
≠ **2** encouraging, supportive.

withhold *v* keep back, retain, hold back, suppress, restrain, repress, control, check, reserve, deduct, refuse, hide, conceal.
≠ give, accord.

withstand *v* resist, oppose, stand fast,

stand one's ground, stand, stand up to, confront, brave, face, cope with, take on, thwart, defy, hold one's ground, hold out, last out, hold off, endure, bear, tolerate, put up with, survive, weather.
≠ give in, yield.

witness *n* **1** TESTIFIER, attestant, deponent (*fml*). **2** ONLOOKER, eye-witness, looker-on, observer, spectator, viewer, watcher, bystander.
v **1** SEE, observe, notice, note, view, watch, look on, mark, perceive.
2 TESTIFY, attest, bear witness, depose (*fml*), confirm, bear out, corroborate.
3 ENDORSE, sign, countersign.

witty *adj* humorous, amusing, comic, sharp-witted, droll, whimsical, original, brilliant, clever, ingenious, lively, sparkling, funny, facetious, fanciful, jocular.
≠ dull, unamusing.

wizard *n* **1** SORCERER, magician, warlock, enchanter, necromancer, occultist, witch, conjurer. **2** (*infml*) EXPERT, adept, virtuoso, ace, master, maestro, prodigy, genius, star (*infml*), whiz (*infml*), hotshot (*infml*).

wizened *adj* shrivelled, shrunken, dried up, withered, wrinkled, gnarled, thin, worn, lined.

wobble *v* shake, oscillate, tremble, quake, sway, teeter, totter, rock, seesaw, vibrate, waver, dodder, fluctuate, hesitate, dither, vacillate, shilly-shally.

wobbly *adj* unstable, shaky, rickety, unsteady, wonky (*infml*), teetering, tottering, doddering, doddery, uneven, unbalanced, unsafe.
≠ stable, steady.

woman *n* female, lady, girl, matriarch, maiden, maid.

womanly *adj* feminine, female, ladylike, womanish.

wonder *n* **1** MARVEL, phenomenon, miracle, prodigy, sight, spectacle, rarity, curiosity. **2** AWE, amazement, astonishment, admiration, wonderment, fascination, surprise, bewilderment.
v **1** MEDITATE, speculate, ponder, ask oneself, question, conjecture, puzzle, enquire, query, doubt, think. **2** MARVEL, gape, be amazed, be surprised.

wonderful *adj* **1** MARVELLOUS, magnificent, oustanding, excellent, superb, admirable, delightful, phenomenal, sensational, stupendous, tremendous, super (*infml*), terrific (*infml*), brilliant (*infml*), great (*infml*), fabulous (*infml*), fantastic (*infml*).
2 AMAZING, astonishing, astounding, startling, surprising, extraordinary, incredible, remarkable, staggering, strange.
≠ **1** appalling, dreadful. **2** ordinary.

woo *v* **1** (*fml*) *woo a lover*: court, chase, pursue. **2** *woo custom*: encourage, cultivate, attract, look for, seek.

wood *n* **1** TIMBER, lumber, planks.

> *Types of wood include*: timber, lumber (*US*), hardwood, softwood, heartwood, sapwood, seasoned wood, green wood, bitterwood, brushwood, cordwood, firewood, kindling, matchwood, plywood, pulpwood, whitewood, chipboard, hardboard, wood veneer; afrormosia, ash, balsa, beech, cedar, cherry, chestnut, cottonwood, deal, ebony, elm, mahogany, African mahogany, maple, oak, pine, redwood, rosewood, sandalwood, sapele, satinwood, teak, walnut, willow. *see also* **tree**.

2 FOREST, woods, woodland, trees, plantation, thicket, grove, coppice, copse, spinney.

wooded *adj* forested, timbered, woody, tree-covered, sylvan (*fml*).

wooden *adj* **1** TIMBER, woody.
2 EMOTIONLESS, expressionless, awkward, clumsy, stilted, lifeless, spiritless, unemotional, stiff, rigid, leaden, deadpan, blank, empty, slow.
≠ **2** lively.

wool *n* fleece, down, yarn.

woolly *adj* **1** WOOLLEN, fleecy, woolly-haired, downy, shaggy, fuzzy, frizzy.
2 UNCLEAR, ill-defined, hazy, blurred, confused, muddled, vague, indefinite, nebulous.

≠ **2** clear, distinct.
n jumper, sweater, jersey, pullover, cardigan.

word *n* **1** NAME, term, expression, designation, utterance, vocable (*fml*). **2** CONVERSATION, chat, talk, discussion, consultation. **3** INFORMATION, news, report, communication, notice, message, bulletin, communiqué, statement, dispatch, declaration, comment, assertion, account, remark, advice, warning. **4** PROMISE, pledge, oath, assurance, vow, guarantee. **5** COMMAND, order, decree, commandment, go-ahead (*infml*), green light (*infml*).
v phrase, express, couch, put, say, explain, write.

words *n* **1** ARGUMENT, dispute, quarrel, disagreement, altercation, bickering, row, squabble. **2** LYRICS, libretto, text, book.

wordy *adj* verbose, long-winded, loquacious (*fml*), garrulous, prolix, rambling, diffuse, discursive.
≠ concise.

work *n* **1** OCCUPATION, job, employment, profession, trade, business, career, calling, vocation, line, métier, livelihood, craft, skill. **2** TASK, assignment, undertaking, job, chore, responsibility, duty, commission. **3** TOIL, labour, drudgery, effort, exertion, industry, slog (*infml*), graft (*infml*), elbow grease (*infml*). **4** CREATION, production, achievement, composition, opus.
≠ **1** play, rest, hobby.
v **1** BE EMPLOYED, have a job, earn one's living. **2** LABOUR, toil, drudge, slave. **3** FUNCTION, go, operate, perform, run, handle, manage, use, control. **4** BRING ABOUT, accomplish, achieve, create, cause, pull off (*infml*). **5** CULTIVATE, farm, dig, till. **6** MANIPULATE, knead, mould, shape, form, fashion, make, process.
≠ **1** be unemployed. **2** play, rest. **3** fail.
work out **1** SOLVE, resolve, calculate, figure out, puzzle out, sort out, understand, clear up. **2** DEVELOP, evolve, go well, succeed, prosper, turn out, pan out (*infml*). **3** PLAN, devise, arrange, contrive, invent, construct, put together. **4** ADD UP TO, amount to, total, come out.
work up incite, stir up, rouse, arouse, animate, excite, move, stimulate, inflame, spur, instigate, agitate, generate.

worker *n* employee, labourer, working man, working woman, artisan, craftsman, tradesman, hand, operative, wage-earner, breadwinner, proletarian.

workforce *n* workers, employees, personnel, labour force, staff, labour, work-people, shop-floor.

working *n* functioning, operation, running, routine, manner, method, action.
adj **1** FUNCTIONING, operational, running, operative, going. **2** EMPLOYED, active.
≠ **1** inoperative. **2** idle.

workmanship *n* skill, craft, craftsmanship, expertise, art, handicraft, handiwork, technique, execution, manufacture, work, finish.

works *n* **1** FACTORY, plant, workshop, mill, foundry, shop. **2** ACTIONS, acts, doings. **3** PRODUCTIONS, output, oeuvre, writings, books. **4** MACHINERY, mechanism, workings, action, movement, parts, installations.

workshop *n* **1** WORKS, workroom, atelier, studio, factory, plant, mill, shop. **2** STUDY GROUP, seminar, symposium, discussion group, class.

world *n* **1** EARTH, globe, planet, star, universe, cosmos, creation, nature. **2** EVERYBODY, everyone, people, human race, humankind, humanity. **3** SPHERE, realm, field, area, domain, division, system, society, province, kingdom. **4** TIMES, epoch, era, period, age, days, life.

worldly *adj* **1** TEMPORAL, earthly, mundane, terrestrial, physical, secular, unspiritual, profane. **2** WORLDLY-WISE, sophisticated, urbane, cosmopolitan, experienced, knowing, streetwise (*infml*). **3** MATERIALISTIC, selfish, ambitious, grasping, greedy, covetous, avaricious.

≠ **1** spiritual, eternal.
2 unsophisticated.

worn *adj* **1** SHABBY, threadbare, worn-out, tatty, tattered, frayed, ragged. **2** EXHAUSTED, tired, weary, spent, fatigued, careworn, drawn, haggard, jaded.
≠ **1** new, unused. **2** fresh.
worn out 1 SHABBY, threadbare, useless, used, tatty, tattered, on its last legs, ragged, moth-eaten, frayed, decrepit. **2** TIRED OUT, exhausted, weary, done in (*infml*), all in (*infml*), dog-tired (*infml*), knackered (*infml*).
≠ **1** new, unused. **2** fresh.

worried *adj* anxious, troubled, uneasy, ill at ease, apprehensive, concerned, bothered, upset, fearful, afraid, frightened, on edge, overwrought, tense, strained, nervous, disturbed, distraught, distracted, fretful, distressed, agonized.
≠ calm, unworried, unconcerned.

worry *v* **1** BE ANXIOUS, be troubled, be distressed, agonize, fret. **2** IRRITATE, plague, pester, torment, upset, unsettle, annoy, bother, disturb, vex, tease, nag, harass, harry, perturb, hassle (*infml*). **3** ATTACK, go for, savage.
≠ **1** be unconcerned. **2** comfort.
n **1** PROBLEM, trouble, responsibility, burden, concern, care, trial, annoyance, irritation, vexation. **2** ANXIETY, apprehension, unease, misgiving, fear, disturbance, agitation, torment, misery, perplexity.
≠ **2** comfort, reassurance.

worsen *v* **1** EXACERBATE, aggravate, intensify, heighten. **2** GET WORSE, weaken, deteriorate, degenerate, decline, sink, go downhill (*infml*).
≠ improve.

worship *v* venerate, revere, reverence, adore, exalt, glorify, honour, praise, idolize, adulate, love, respect, pray to, deify.
≠ despise, hate.
n veneration, reverence, adoration, devotion(s), homage, honour, glory, glorification, exaltation, praise, prayer(s), respect, regard, love, adulation, deification, idolatory.

worth *n* worthiness, merit, value, benefit, advantage, importance, significance, use, usefulness, utility, quality, good, virtue, excellence, credit, desert(s), cost, rate, price, help, assistance, avail.
≠ worthlessness.

worthless *adj* **1** VALUELESS, useless, pointless, meaningless, futile, unavailing, unimportant, insignificant, trivial, unusable, cheap, poor, rubbishy, trashy, trifling, paltry. **2** CONTEMPTIBLE, despicable, good-for-nothing, vile.
≠ **1** valuable. **2** worthy.

worthwhile *adj* profitable, useful, valuable, worthy, good, helpful, beneficial, constructive, gainful, justifiable, productive.
≠ worthless.

worthy *adj* praiseworthy, laudable, creditable, commendable, valuable, worthwhile, admirable, fit, deserving, appropriate, respectable, reputable, good, honest, honourable, excellent, decent, upright, righteous.
≠ unworthy, disreputable.

wound *n* **1** INJURY, trauma, hurt, cut, gash, lesion, laceration, scar. **2** HURT, distress, trauma, torment, heartbreak, harm, damage, anguish, grief, shock.
v **1** DAMAGE, harm, hurt, injure, hit, cut, gash, lacerate, slash, pierce. **2** DISTRESS, offend, insult, pain, mortify, upset, slight, grieve.

wrangle *n* argument, quarrel, dispute, controversy, squabble, tiff, row (*infml*), bickering, disagreement, clash, altercation, contest, slanging match (*infml*), set-to (*infml*).
≠ agreement.
v argue, quarrel, disagree, dispute, bicker, altercate, contend, fall out (*infml*), row (*infml*), squabble, scrap, fight, spar.
≠ agree.

wrap *v* envelop, fold, enclose, cover, pack, shroud, wind, surround, package, muffle, cocoon, cloak, roll up, bind, bundle up, immerse.
≠ unwrap.
wrap up 1 WRAP, pack up, package, parcel. **2** (*infml*) CONCLUDE, finish off,

end, bring to a close, terminate, wind up, complete, round off.

wrapper *n* wrapping, packaging, envelope, cover, jacket, dust jacket, sheath, sleeve, paper.

wreak *v* inflict, exercise, create, cause, bring about, perpetrate, vent, unleash, express, execute, carry out, bestow.

wreath *n* garland, coronet, chaplet, festoon, crown, band, ring.

wreck *v* destroy, ruin, demolish, devastate, shatter, smash, break, spoil, play havoc with, ravage, write off.
≠ conserve, repair.
n ruin, destruction, devastation, mess, demolition, ruination, write-off, disaster, loss, disruption.

wreckage *n* debris, remains, rubble, ruin, fragments, flotsam, pieces.

wrench *v* yank, wrest, jerk, pull, tug, force, sprain, strain, rick, tear, twist, wring, rip, distort.

wrestle *v* struggle, strive, fight, scuffle, grapple, tussle, combat, contend, contest, vie, battle.

wretch *n* scoundrel, rogue, villain, good-for-nothing, ruffian, rascal, vagabond, miscreant, outcast.

wretched *adj* **1** ATROCIOUS, awful, deplorable, appalling. **2** UNHAPPY, sad, miserable, melancholy, depressed, dejected, disconsolate, downcast, forlorn, gloomy, doleful, distressed, broken-hearted, crestfallen. **3** PATHETIC, pitiable, pitiful, unfortunate, sorry, hopeless, poor. **4** CONTEMPTIBLE, despicable, vile, worthless, shameful, inferior, low, mean, paltry.
≠ **1** excellent. **2** happy. **3** enviable. **4** worthy.

wriggle *v* squirm, writhe, wiggle, worm, twist, snake, slink, crawl, edge, sidle, manoeuvre, squiggle, dodge, extricate, zigzag, waggle, turn.
n wiggle, twist, squirm, jiggle, jerk, turn, twitch.

wring *v* **1** SQUEEZE, twist, wrench, wrest, extract, mangle, screw. **2** EXACT, extort, coerce, force. **3** DISTRESS, pain, hurt, rack, rend, pierce, torture, wound, stab, tear.

wrinkle *n* furrow, crease, corrugation, line, fold, gather, pucker, crumple.
v crease, corrugate, furrow, fold, crinkle, crumple, shrivel, gather, pucker.

write *v* pen, inscribe, record, jot down, set down, take down, transcribe, scribble, scrawl, correspond, communicate, draft, draw up, copy, compose, create.
write off 1 DELETE, cancel, cross out, disregard. **2** WRECK, destroy, crash, smash up.

writer

> *Writers include*: annalist, author, autobiographer, bard, biographer, calligraphist, chronicler, clerk, columnist, contributor, copyist, copywriter, correspondent, court reporter, diarist, dramatist, editor, essayist, fabler, fiction writer, ghost writer, hack, historian, journalist, leader-writer, lexicographer, librettist, lyricist, novelist, pen-friend, penman, pen-pal, penpusher (*infml*), penwoman, playwright, poet, poet laureate, reporter, rhymer, satirist, scribbler, scribe, scriptwriter, short-story writer, sonneteer, stenographer.

writhe *v* squirm, wriggle, thresh, thrash, twist, wiggle, toss, coil, contort, struggle.

writing *n* **1** HANDWRITING, calligraphy, script, penmanship, scrawl, scribble, hand, print. **2** DOCUMENT, composition, work, publication.

> *Types of writing include*: account, advertising copy, annals, article, autobiography, biography, book, chronicle, commentary, confessions, copywriting, correspondence, criticism, critique, curriculum vitae, diary, discourse, dissertation, documentary, drama, editorial, epistle, essay, feature, history, journal, legal document, letter, life story, literature, lyric, memoir, monograph, narrative, news, newspaper column, paper, parable, poem, profile, propaganda, record, report, review, satire, scientific writing, script, sketch, sonnet,

statement, story, study, tale, thesis, travelogue, treatise, yearbook. *see also* **book**; **literature**; **poem**; **story**; **sacred writings**.

writing instruments

Types of writing instrument include: pen, ballpoint, Biro®, calligraphy pen, cartridge pen, dip pen, eraser pen, felt-tip pen, fountain pen, rollerball pen, writing brush, pencil, chinagraph pencil, coloured pencil, crayon, ink pencil, lead-pencil, propelling pencil, marker pen, board marker, laundry marker, permanent marker, highlighter; cane pen, quill, reed, Roman metal pen, steel pen, stylus; brailler, typewriter, word-processor.

wrong *adj* **1** INACCURATE, incorrect, mistaken, erroneous, false, fallacious, in error, imprecise. **2** INAPPROPRIATE, unsuitable, unseemly, improper, indecorous, unconventional, unfitting, incongruous, inapt. **3** UNJUST, unethical, unfair, unlawful, immoral, illegal, illicit, dishonest, criminal, crooked (*infml*), reprehensible, blameworthy, guilty, to blame, bad, wicked, sinful, iniquitous, evil. **4** DEFECTIVE, faulty, out of order, amiss, awry.
≠ **1** correct, right. **2** suitable, right. **3** good, moral.
adv amiss, astray, awry, inaccurately, incorrectly, wrongly, mistakenly, faultily, badly, erroneously, improperly.
≠ right.
n sin, misdeed, offence, crime, immorality, sinfulness, transgression, wickedness, wrong-doing, trespass (*fml*), injury, grievance, abuse, injustice, iniquity, inequity, infringement, unfairness, error.
≠ right.
v abuse, ill-treat, mistreat, maltreat, injure, ill-use, hurt, harm, discredit, dishonour, misrepresent, malign, oppress, cheat.

wrongdoer *n* offender, law-breaker, transgressor, criminal, delinquent, felon, miscreant, evil-doer, sinner, trespasser, culprit.

wrongful *adj* immoral, improper, unfair, unethical, unjust, unlawful, illegal, illegitimate, illicit, dishonest, criminal, blameworthy, dishonourable, wrong, reprehensible, wicked, evil.
≠ rightful.

wry *adj* **1** *wry humour*: ironic, sardonic, dry, sarcastic, mocking, droll. **2** TWISTED, distorted, deformed, contorted, warped, uneven, crooked.
≠ **2** straight.

Y

yank *v, n* jerk, tug, pull, wrench, snatch, haul, heave.

yap *v* **1** BARK, yelp. **2** (*infml*) CHATTER, jabber, babble, prattle, yatter, jaw (*infml*).

yardstick *n* measure, gauge, criterion, standard, benchmark, touchstone, comparison.

yarn *n* **1** THREAD, fibre, strand. **2** STORY, tale, anecdote, fable, fabrication, tall story, cock-and-bull story (*infml*).

yawning *adj* gaping, wide, wide-open, huge, vast, cavernous.

yearly *adj* annual, per year, per annum, perennial.
adv annually, every year, once a year, perennially.

yearn for long for, pine for, desire, want, wish for, crave, covet, hunger for, hanker for, ache for, languish for, itch for.

yell *v* shout, scream, bellow, roar, bawl, shriek, squeal, howl, holler (*infml*), screech, squall, yelp, yowl, whoop.
≠ whisper.
n shout, scream, cry, roar, bellow, shriek, howl, screech, squall, whoop.
≠ whisper.

yelp *v* yap, bark, squeal, cry, yell, yowl, bay.
n yap, bark, yip, squeal, cry, yell, yowl.

yield *v* **1** SURRENDER, relinquish, abandon, abdicate, cede, part with, relinquish. **2** GIVE WAY, capitulate, concede, submit, succumb, give (in), admit defeat, bow, cave in, knuckle under, resign oneself, go along with, permit, allow, acquiesce, accede, agree, comply, consent. **3** PRODUCE, bear, supply, provide, generate, bring in, bring forth, furnish, return, earn, pay.
≠ **1** hold. **2** resist, withstand.
n return, product, earnings, harvest, crop, produce, output, profit, revenue, takings, proceeds, income.

yoke *n* **1** HARNESS, bond, link. **2** BURDEN, bondage, enslavement, slavery, oppression, subjugation, servility.
v couple, link, join, tie, harness, hitch, bracket, connect, unite.

young *adj* **1** YOUTHFUL, juvenile, baby, infant, junior, adolescent. **2** IMMATURE, early, new, recent, green, growing, fledgling, unfledged, inexperienced.
≠ **1** adult, old. **2** mature, old.
n offspring, babies, issue, litter, progeny, brood, children, family.

youngster *n* child, boy, girl, toddler, youth, teenager, kid (*infml*).

youth *n* **1** ADOLESCENT, youngster, juvenile, teenager, kid (*infml*), boy, young man. **2** YOUNG PEOPLE, the young, younger generation. **3** ADOLESCENCE, childhood, immaturity, boyhood, girlhood.
≠ **3** adulthood.

youthful *adj* young, boyish, girlish, childish, immature, juvenile, inexperienced, fresh, active, lively, well-preserved.
≠ aged.

Z

zany (*infml*) *adj* comical, funny, amusing, eccentric, droll, crazy (*infml*), clownish, loony (*infml*), wacky (*infml*).
≠ serious.

zeal *n* ardour, fervour, passion, warmth, fire, enthusiasm, devotion, spirit, keenness, zest, eagerness, earnestness, dedication, fanaticism, gusto, verve.
≠ apathy, indifference.

zealot *n* fanatic, extremist, bigot, militant, partisan.

zealous *adj* ardent, fervent, impassioned, passionate, devoted, burning, enthusiastic, intense, fanatical, militant, keen, eager, earnest, spirited.
≠ apathetic, indifferent.

zenith *n* summit, peak, height, pinnacle, apex, high point, top, optimum, climax, culmination, acme, meridian, vertex.
≠ nadir.

zero *n* nothing, nought, nil, nadir, bottom, cipher, zilch (*infml*), duck, love.

zest *n* **1** GUSTO, appetite, enthusiasm, enjoyment, keenness, zeal, exuberance, interest. **2** FLAVOUR, taste, relish, savour, spice, tang, piquancy.
≠ **1** apathy.

zigzag *v* meander, snake, wind, twist, curve.
adj meandering, crooked, serpentine, sinuous, twisting, winding.
≠ straight.

zodiac

> *The signs of the zodiac (with their symbols) are*: Aries (Ram), Taurus (Bull), Gemini (Twins), Cancer (Crab), Leo (Lion), Virgo (Virgin), Libra (Balance), Scorpio (Scorpion), Sagittarius (Archer), Capricorn (Goat), Aquarius (Water-bearer), Pisces (Fishes).

zone *n* region, area, district, territory, section, sector, belt, sphere, tract, stratum.

zoom *v* race, rush, tear, dash, speed, fly, hurtle, streak, flash, shoot, whirl, dive, buzz, zip.